REGNUM HANDBOOKS

International Handbook on Creation Care and Eco-Diakonia

REGNUM HANDBOOKS

Series Preface

These reference books are the result of collaborative efforts between a huge number of scholars from across the world. Working together with a distinguished team of editors, each volume brings together the latest contextual thinking on its subject, presenting landmark works which will stand the test of time. Spanning denominations, continents, cultures and churches, these will continue to serve the church for years to come.

For more in the series see the final page of this volume.

REGNUM HANDBOOKS

International Handbook on Creation Care and Eco-Diakonia

Concepts and Theological Perspectives of Churches
from the Global South

Editors:
Daniel Beros, Eale Bosela, Lesmore Ezekiel, Kambale Kahongya,
Ruomin Liu, Grace Moon, Marisa Strizzi, Dietrich Werner (lead editor)

First published 2022 by Regnum Books International

Regnum is an imprint of the Oxford Centre for Mission Studies
St. Philip and St. James Church
Woodstock Road
Oxford OX2 6HR, UK
www.regnumbooks.net

09 08 07 06 05 04 03 8 7 6 5 4 3 2 1

Produced in partnership with Bread for the World, AACC, CCA, UEM and REET

British Library Cataloguing in Publication Data
A catalogue record for this book is available from the British Library

ISBN: 978-1-5064-9758-7

Typeset by Words by Design Ltd
www.wordsbydesign.co.uk

Cover design by Lucy D'Souza-Krone

Distributed by Fortress Press in the US, Canada, India, and Brazil

Contents

Section II
Concepts and Profiles of Creation Care and Eco-Diakonia in Different Regions and Denominational Traditions

Africa and Middle East

Asia and Pacific

WORDS OF GREETING

Prof. Jürgen Moltmann

We are at the beginning of what is called the 'Great Transformation'. The transformation of industries is already under way: renewable energies, models of circular economy, e-cars etc. Social and ecological justice must accompany this transformation, otherwise there can be no peace on earth and with the earth. Only peace with nature on earth secures the survival of humankind, which is so much threatened today. For this we need a new understanding of nature, a new understanding of the human being, a new lifestyle and a cosmic spirituality, in short: a new experience of God in the creation-community.

This unique *International Handbook on Creation Care and Eco Diakonia* is bringing together major 'voices of the global South'. The peoples and nations in Asia, Pacific, Africa and Latin America have been victims of western imperial powers and industrialized modernity. Those who in former centuries had been colonized and exploited by slavery in Africa, Asia or Latin America now raise their voices in this volume. The 'cry of the earth' and the 'cry of the poor' inseparably belong together. Social and ecological justice are intimately bound together and should never be separated.

Praise and gratitude should be expressed to those organizations and the group of editors which stood together to compile this massive volume, particularly the regional ecumenical organizations and church conferences in Asia, Pacific, Africa, Caribbean and in Latin America. Half of the contributions are from women. Those who know how difficult the drafting and editing processes towards so many contributions are, will welcome this opus magnum with respect. The relevance of these 'voices of the global South' for the Great Transformation in which humanity is participating currently, cannot be overestimated.

The concepts of 'eco-Diakonia' are of particular interest for me as I feel reminded of the third beatitude of Jesus which reads, "Blessed are the gentle: for the earth will be their heritage" (Matthew 5:5).

Those who are gentle and meek are those who carry on the discipleship of Jesus who is inviting everybody: "Take my yoke upon you, and learn from me, for I am gentle and lowly in heart, and you will find rest for your souls. For my yoke is easy, and my burden is light" (Matthew 11:28). It is not the mighty and powerful, but those who are "gentle and lowly in heart" which will own the earth. To deal with the earth gently, i.e. to treat plants and trees in a spirit of gentleness and humility, implies to recognize the intrinsic value of them and not just to calculate their utilization value for human beings. Treating animals gently implies to recognize them as co-creatures and as part of the creation community and in reverse also to see human beings as co-creatures of animals. Being gentle implies having empathy, attention, mindfulness, patience, sensitivity and respect for life in all what lives on earth, establishing and reaffirming a living community and organic interaction and co-working with nature instead of exercising the rule of power and exploitation.

'(Scientific) Knowledge is power' used to be the slogan of modernity, the era of western civilization. Gentleness instead prefers the close intersection of knowledge and wisdom.

Prof. Dr. D. h.c. mult. Jürgen Moltmann. Protestant Theological Faculty of the University of Tübingen, Germany; author of *God in Creation: an ecological doctrine of creation (1985)*

Dr. Fidon Mwombeki, All African Conference of Churches

The issues of creation care and eco-diaconia are pivotal at this time. One needs to be of special character and disposition to doubt the reality of the risk the world is facing due to our disregard to the integrity of creation. Africa, in spite of all its other challenges, faces unprecedented calamities more frequently, which are spread across the continent. We are no longer oblivious to the fact that the world is ONE. We are all interlinked like a chain, and each and every link is crucial for the proper functioning of the chain. This is more so true with climate change and its concomitant disasters.

It is for that reason I find this volume a monumental contribution to the world. While we continue to deal with more locally limited impacts of climate change, we are reminded through this volume that the whole world shares the responsibility for our global life together. Granted that Africa does not, comparatively, contribute much of the toxic agents devastating the world, it still has a significant role to play according to its situation. People of Africa are not only victims of climate change, but they do have some contribution to it as well. Therefore, the churches in Africa are also called to contribute to the global theological discourse on creation care and eco-diaconia. And many are doing exactly that in this volume. Africa's voices are heard.

I welcome this volume. I commend the authors, who represent the different voices and contexts in our ONE world. We see the different ways we study and understand the scriptures and formulate appropriate theology. I am particularly impressed by the presentation of models and methods for training, which are very crucial for AACC as we embark of a full-fledged program focusing on climate justice.

I therefore, without any hesitation, recommend this volume for use by our member churches, church related programs and agencies, and broader communities in Africa for use as a study and training resource.

Rev. Dr. Fidon Mwombeki, General Secretary of the All Africa Conference Of Churches (AACC)

Dr. Iyad Abumoghli

Simply put, this is an incredible, magnificent, and colossal work that has ever been done in such a comprehensive and inclusive manner. The *International Handbook on Creation Care and Eco-Diakonia* should be recognized as the 'Encyclopedia of Christian Perspectives on Sustainable Development'. A handbook of handbooks that addresses all the right checks on the list of sustainability.

This amazing resource collection addresses almost all contemporary global environmental challenges facing our world today and that are expected to continue challenging future generations, if no serious and tangible actions are taken today. From issues related to agriculture, climate change, ecosystems restoration, wildlife, forests, biodiversity, and food systems, to issues related to economy, migration, gender, and youth, this handbook represents a true Christian global agenda to achieve the sustainable development goals. Moreover, the handbook addresses the often-forgotten elements of sustainability including justice, ethics, stewardship, citizenship, environmental rights, and cultural values.

While it is argued, in some secular spheres, that religions have chosen to stay distant, or in some cases, were made distant from global affairs, this handbook is a demonstration that this argument is false and that religions are intrinsically related to issues of sustainable development, including social, economic, and profoundly here, environmental. The care for creation, as indicated in the handbook, is not about saving animals or planting trees, it is about the divine relationship that connects the web of life on this earth.

I am forever grateful for the editorial group, the supporting organizations, and the ecumenical advisory group for gifting humanity with this resource that is based on the spiritual and moral teachings of Christianity. It is only hoped, as it has been iterated by the editorial group, that this publication becomes an inspiration for a global multi-faith work that brings more voices from different religions and spiritual beliefs.

Voices anywhere and everywhere are important to be heard, especially those based on faith values demonstrating our moral responsibility to care for the creation. Being written by scholars and professionals from the Global South representing all continents is, by itself, a unique contribution to environmental sciences. The cry of the South is as important as the cry of the poor and the cry of the planet. Very often, global publications address the global South as a target, but never before such an inclusive effort has been made to collect voices from the South to serve voices everywhere.

As the founder and director of the Faith for Earth Initiative of the United Nations Environment Programme, the highest global authority on environmental policy, I am eager to use this handbook in many of our capacity-building and knowledge-sharing activities that we hope will lead into developing environmental policies that are ethically based and spiritually enriched.

I have repeatedly agreed with the notion that the multiple challenges we are facing today are crises of ethics and lack of moral responsibility. 'Anthropocene' is in fact a term that should reflect greed, selfishness, materialism, and human superiority over God's creation. What we face today cannot be tackled by technology alone. If there is a shortage in water supply, we cannot simply burn more fossil fuel to desalinate sea water. We need to use water sensibly and sustainably, having in mind those who lack water access and resources to obtain water. This principle applies to all natural resource elements necessary for a dignified living by all humans, while conserving these resources for future generations. This requires a deep ethical approach to equality and human rights.

Greening religions is a concept highlighted in the handbook and is a matter that will definitely bear fruit. What we need is to model religious approaches by adopting such approaches in our churches, mosques, and temples, for ourselves, faith actors and faith-based organizations. The handbook basically is calling to practice what we preach. The massive financial resources and assets that are owned by the church, and other religious institutions, should use integrated greening principles and become minarets to guide us all.

I applaud the authors, editors and all those who have contributed to such rich handbook and hope for its deployment not only to educational institutions, but also to politicians, scientists, civil society organizations and the public.

Dr. Iyad Abumoghli, Founder and Director of Faith for Earth Initiative,
United Nations Environment Programme, Nairobi

President Dr. Dagmar Pruin

Creation Care and Eco-Diakonia, i.e. diaconal work on behalf of those who are increasingly victimized and made the most vulnerable by the impacts of progressing climate change and biodiversity destruction, is part of the essence of what it means to be the church today. The horizon in which the Gospel is to be communicated is the '*whole world*', the 'oicoumene' (Matthew 24:14). 'All creation' will receive his judgement and righteousness (Psalm 96:13). In Christ, God is reconciling *the whole world* to himself (2 Cor:5,19). Christ's ministry is to reconcile to himself *all things, whether on earth or in heaven* (Colossians 1:20). The suffering and *groaning of creation* is not alien to God, but is known by God and by his believers (Romans 8:22). The recent global ecumenical debate on the understanding of mission therefore has underlined the interconnection of the work of the Holy Spirit and the flourishing of creation: "Humanity cannot be saved alone while the rest of the created world perishes. Eco-justice cannot be separated from salvation, and salvation cannot come without a new humility that respects the needs of all life on earth."[1]

[1] Jooseop Keum (ed.): *Together towards Life. Mission and Evangelism in Changing Landscapes*, WCC Publications 2013, No 19ff, here page 11

This is why the ecumenical movement since long has emphasized a concern for eco-theology and the ethics of sustainability since its early decades. Already in 1974 the WCC was a pioneer to have articulated an ambitious and reflected concept of 'sustainability', almost 20 years prior to the Rio UN conference on environment and development.[2] In 1991 the most advanced theological concept of understanding the creation as part of the Trinitarian mission and the work of the Holy Spirit taking place in the healing and renewing of suffering creation was unfolded during the WCC assembly in Canberra.[3] This is why this publication can be seen as a proper continuation, deepening and substantial advancement of this line of thinking within ecumenical diakonia and ecumenical social ethics.

Brot für die Welt, in its new strategy from 2021 onwards, had indicated and shared with its partners a strategic interest "to reflect about the challenges of climate change politically as well as ethically and theologically, in order to become critical actors for eco-social transformation processes in developmental policies." This masterpiece of broad ecumenical-ecological scholarship is exactly answering this need and priority.

We are very grateful for this joint initiative between All African Conference of Churches (AACC), Christian Conference of Asia (CCA), Cooperation Platform for Ecumenical Theological Education in Latin America (REET Argentina), United Evangelical Mission (UEM) and several other partner organizations to have jointly produced this outstanding volume under the able leadership of Prof. Dr. Dietrich Werner and his team for ecumenical-theological and conceptual work of Brot für die Welt. This is a valuable resource collection on different approaches to Creation Care and Eco-Diaconia in many different regions of the global South and from a great variety of denominational traditions.

This publication underlines the enormous contributions, potentials and new perspectives from churches and church-related agencies in the global South, which need to be regarded as vital partners for regional and global networking in the area of witness and service for creation care, protection of biodiversity, climate justice and ethics for sustainability. The churches are giants of commitment and alternative orientations, which are urgently needed as basis for ethical and ecological transformation in this world. This *International Handbook on Creation Care and Eco-Diakonia* is a visible expression of mutual South-South learning and sharing of perspectives between churches, agencies and Christian social initiatives on how to give witness to the ongoing presence of God in his creation and the work of the Holy Spirit to contribute for healing and more sustainability in this world. We do hope that this handbook will find many interested readers and will enhance competence building and training for providing new leadership for creation care, eco-diakonia, sustainable development, as well as political advocacy and lobbying work for climate justice both in churches and in ecumenical agencies globally which is as urgently needed as never before.

Rev. Dr. Dagmar Pruin, President of Brot für die Welt, Chief Executive,
Evangelisches Werk für Diakonie und Entwicklung
(EWDE, Protestant Agency for Diaconia and Development), Berlin, Germany

Dr. Mathews George Chunakara

Diakonia focuses on all aspects of God's creation and it cares for all who are in need, by carrying out God's vision in word and action. While Diakonia begins in unconditional service to neighbours in need, it bears witness to God's presence amidst us. In this broken world where sin and injustice abound, God in Christ

[2] Dietrich Werner: 'Eco-Theology – Elements of the Learning Journey in the Ecumenical Movement', in *Kairos for Creation*, Wuppertal 2019, p. 45ff

[3] Come Holy Spirit, renew your whole creation! Was the prayer theme of the Canberra assembly which in its sections I-IV formulated the most advanced teachings on eco-theology heard of until then: http://wcc2006.info/en/about-the-assembly/previous-assemblies/canberra.html.

through the power of the Holy Spirit shapes us as a gathered community to become the agents of grace for the healing and transformation of the world. Diakonia is not merely a mission of the strong serving the weak or carrying a branded label of 'charity'. In a global context where power is controlled and regulated by wealth and resources, only a few privileged ones can avail and use or misuse resources. In such situations, participating in God's mission of care for creation is the need of the hour.

When Diakonia is expected to reach out to all God's creation, we are called to be prepared to work together in God's mission towards renewal, reconciliation and restoration of creation. The human position in the created world needs to be better understood, as humans share a common identity with the rest of the creatures and their fate is bound to the fate of creation. A question that is pertinent in our contemporary world is: what does it mean to be human, or what is the position of humanity in the created world? Are human beings a part of nature or the 'crown of creation', or both? The Bible tells about humans who are exceptional among creation, and are made in the image of God with authority given for dominion over the natural world, as well as distinct from all other creatures (Gen. 1:26-27). With regard to the unique position of humans, the Psalmist amplifies the Genesis narrative as follows:

> What is man that you are mindful of him, the son of man that you care for him? You made him a little lower than the heavenly beings and crowned him with glory and honor. You made him ruler over the works of your hands; you put everything under his feet: all flocks and herds, and the beasts of the field, and the birds of the air, and the fish of the sea, all that swim the paths of the seas. (Ps. 8:4-8, NIV, 1984).

The human position in the created world should be identified as the particular role humans play between God and creation. A conceptual linkage between 'the image of God' and 'dominion over creation' denotes that caring for creation was the noble first task which was bestowed on humans as a way of representing God. In other words, humans were expected to reflect God's love and justice by taking care of creation (Gen. 2:15). It is not implied or understood in this context that 'dominion over creation' is a reason for exploitation by humans of the created world for selfish purposes. We are often reminded that the first covenant that God made with Adam and Eve included creation order and human responsibility for the created world. As a result of sin, however, the overall creation order was disrupted and the human relationship with the created world was marred. God's mission is broad enough to include human responsibility for the care of creation, both synchronically and diachronically. God, who designs the redemptive plan includes God's ultimate aim of restoration of the original creation. God's plan embraces all creation and witnesses to the cosmic dimension of salvation, while calling for a stewardship commitment to sustain and care for God's creation.

It is gratifying that the Christian Conference of Asia has been able to be a prime partner in this joint effort to produce a special volume together with various regional and international ecumenical organizations such as All Africa Conference of Churches (AACC), REET Argentina, and UEM Germany through the timely initiative of the Brot für die Welt (BfdW), Germany. The implementation of this project, meticulously planned and coordinated under the leadership of Prof. Dr. Dietrich Werner of the BfdW, my friend and former colleague in WCC, who needs to be specially recognized and commended. It is our hope that this volume will be of great help to churches around the world. I am sure the Asian churches and the Asian ecumenical organizations who are engaged in a ministry of creation care will also benefit richly from this valuable and insightful resource on 'Creation Care and Eco-Diakonia'.

Dr. Mathews George Chunakara, Ph.D., General Secretary, Christian Conference of Asia

Dr. Jochen Motte

The United Evangelical Mission welcomes the rich contributions published in this *International Handbook on Creation Care and Eco-Diaconia*. UEM, as a communion of 39 churches and institutions in Africa, Asia and Germany, is extremely grateful that this project with the special objective to offer insights in creation care, sustainability, eco-church and diaconia with perspectives from the global south could be realised by Bread for the World in a joint project with the AACC, the CCA, REET, the Sino Theological network, and UEM.

In 2008, the General Assembly of UEM declared climate change and environmental protection a priority theme and programmatic focus of UEM. At that time, an exhibition had been launched in Germany exposing the live threatening consequences of climate change in countries in the Global South especially for vulnerable and marginalised communities (see poster left). The exhibition had been presented in various congregations, public institutions and at the German 'Kirchentag' in Munich in 2010. Along with the exhibition, UEM introduced in its annual human rights campaign the global threat of climate change as an issue of global justice.

From 2008 on, UEM established two positions of climate and environmental consultants in Africa and Asia with experts from Tanzania and Indonesia, who built regional networks on climate and environmental protection, and who assisted churches in developing and implementing projects in the field of sustainability and climate protection especially for vulnerable people.

Already at that time, UEM observed that there is a lack of available materials, theological reflections, spiritual and contextual perspectives, songs and poems from the Global South with regard to climate and sustainability. In a two years project, UEM therefor started to collect such contributions from among its members in Africa and Asia and published them in 2014 under the title, *Climate Spirituality – Peace with the Earth*.[4]

Over many years UEM has taken part in various church and secular networks, including e.g. the World Council of Churches working Group on Climate and the German Klima Allianz. In order to strengthen global advocacy for climate protection at COPs, as well as on national levels in the Global North, it always emphasized the need for theological reflection, networking and ecumenical co-operation to respond ecumenically as faith-based community to the global threat of climate change, environmental destruction, and the extinction of species form this planet.

One of the main causes of this development has been and still is the unsustainable economic order which contributes to a widening gap between rich and poor and the marginalization of millions of people, especially in the Global South.

In 2019, UEM together with the World Council of Churches, the Protestant Church in Germany, Bread for the World, and the Association of Protestant Churches and Missions in Germany conducted an international consultation with 52 participants from 22 countries in order give a message to the ecumenical movement that there is an urgent need for churches to act now before it is too late. The message, 'Wuppertal Call', together with the contributions from the participants have been published under the title, *Kairos for Creation. Confessing Hope for the Earth*.[5] In the message, participants of the Wuppertal conference call

[4] See: https://www.vemission.org/climate_spirituality.

[5] See: https://www.vemission.org/kairos-for-creation.

upon the ecumenical movement and the World Council of Churches to "declare a Decade for the Healing of Creation."

The publication of this handbook with rich resources on creation care and eco-diaconia representing so many voices from the global South is a long time needed, inspiring complementary and unique steps underlining the urgency of church witness and deeds for immediate action towards a fundamental ecological and economic transformation, by presenting simultaneously practical perspectives which give hope to the earth.

UEM congratulates all who have been part of this project and expresses its sincere thanks especially to the authors as well the editorial team.

Rev. Dr. Jochen Motte, Executive Secretary and Deputy General Secretary of the UEM and head of the Department for Justice, Peace and the Integrity of Creation

Archbishop Panti Filibus Musa

It is an honour to commend this *International Handbook on Creation Care and Eco-Diakonia*. The volume brings together contemporary voices that are unique theological perspectives and contextual practices from the Global South. The conversation recorded in this handbook is an example of the way that faith-based organizations and church world communions continue to translate our faithful vocation to care for creation into earth-conscious action and advocacy.

In harmony with many of the traditions represented in this volume, Lutherans understand earth-keeping as part of, and expression of, our love for God and our neighbour. The Lutheran World Federation and its member churches are committed to advocate for climate justice, and care for creation. The LWF promotes a faithful, ecological sense of being human, and spirituality that is creation-oriented, that shapes the way we live out our Lutheran tradition through loving service for the well-being of all creation.

The LWF 12th Assembly in Windhoek, Namibia in 2017, passed resolutions encouraging member churches to become more theologically grounded in their teaching on the inherent dignity of all creatures, our identity as creatures, and our proper relationship to creation. This volume contributes to this goal. The resolution also affirmed that climate change, resulting from our unjust misuse of the earth, harms the wellbeing of humans and all creatures. Engaging in acts of eco-diakonia that safeguard creation are key to sustaining healthy ecosystems and societies. This book presents many such practices.

The Bible in Psalm 24:1 reminds us, "the earth is the Lord's, and everything in it, the world, and all who live in it." It is good, and the good news of abundant life extends to all creation. Lutherans profess that the message of grace liberates us to love and serve the creator and all creatures. Caring for the wellbeing of creation is a profound way to fulfil our human vocation to till and keep the earth, and to proclaim the good news to all creation in words and in deeds.

While this vocation applies to people of many faiths and good will around the world, there are unique perspectives to be learned from the ways this call is lived out social and bioregions. From my own perspective in Nigeria, the earth is life, and care for human life is inseparable from care for creation. It is becoming clearer that care for creation is an issue for every human being that is already getting beyond measure.

By highlighting contextual perspectives from the global south, this volume uniquely contributes to the global conversation. However, the particularity of these perspectives is universally significant. Each author contributes to our collective wisdom and knowledge. They instruct and inspire the global Christian family to interrogate their own local traditions, cultures, and ecologies. In doing so, they help us continue to discern the diverse ways that we can faithfully join in the ecumenical and interdisciplinary ministry to care for the whole inhabited earth.

This volume is one of the most diverse, contextual, yet globally relevant theological reflections I have seen on the ecumenical and interdisciplinary approach to care for the earth. Therefore, I append my commendation for the publication as reference material for our joint ecumenical diaconal response to care for creation.

Most Rev. Panti Filibus Musa, Ph.D., Archbishop of the Lutheran Church of Christ in Nigeria and President, Lutheran World Federation.

Pastor Sonia Skupch

From the Lutheran World Federation we are pleased to present the *International Handbook on Creation Care and Eco-Diakonia*. We congratulate the editing team and all the organizations that have supported this work for their effort, dedication and for making this publication possible. This handbook is in itself a testimony and a declaration that another better world, fairer and with decent conditions for all, is really possible.

For decades the earth, the rivers, the seas, the air, animals and human beings, everything that lives and inhabits this world, groans and cries out for liberation (Romans 8), liberation from the yoke of exploitation that leads to death. We human beings have transformed the God-created world in which we live into an object of commerce, and in doing so we have begun our own self-destruction. This sin, which translates into excessive greed, the desire to possess and consume without limits, scandalous inequality and a short-term vision, has led us as humanity to a turning point, a unique moment in which we can either continue as we are and, in a short time, convert our planet into an uninhabitable space (at least for a large part of the population), or we can take this momentum as an opportunity to make changes, to transform ourselves and by doing so, also transform our surroundings and our relationship with the creation of which we are a part.

It is in this context just mentioned, that churches, faith-based organizations and ecumenical bodies have a prophetic word to say and an important role to play. Our biblical foundation reminds us over and over again through different texts that this world was created from the breath of God who, seeing everything created, said that it was good (Genesis 1). On the other hand, the biblical texts also draw our attention again and again to the responsibility we have as human beings, called to repentance, conversion and transformation.

In this sense, the *International Handbook on Creation Care and Eco-Diakonia* demonstrates the responsibility taken by religious institutions in their call for public advocacy and in the transformation process that humanity needs.

I want to highlight three aspects of the handbook that, being linked to each other, are a unique contribution:

- It deepens the close link between the prevailing economic model and our current climate and environmental emergency. It is not possible to separate one element from another. In this sense, a deep transformation can only take place if there is also an ethical reflection and a transformation in the values that guide and lead our insertion in this world and how we interact with God's Creation.
- It reflects the diversity and multiplicity of religious and non-religious institutions that yearn, dream and seek for a better world. The networking of the different actors involved is fundamental in the realization of concrete steps towards a fairer world.
- It is oriented to the work of our churches. It seeks to be a tool in the work of the congregations, in the different leadership spaces of our communities and in our diaconic institutions and works of service. In that sense, I highlight this publication as a useful and necessary tool.

On the occasion of the 500th anniversary of the Reformation in 2017, The Lutheran World Federation published *Creation – Not for Sale*. In this book, one of the authors, Rev. Cibele Kuss, wrote:

> Creation is not for sale and our theological consciences even less so. Our greatest challenge is to read the signs of the times. To struggle for life is to struggle for the whole of creation, for people's freedom and for the right to diversity, the right to be different, the right for the well-being of the earth and for the song of the birds. This means reaffirming the God of history, who is still insistently calling us into the future, so that we can continue to be involved in the struggles of the poor for change.[6]

May the *International Handbook on Creation Care and Eco-Diakonia*, which is part of this recently expressed vision, be a tool to materialize the call to take concrete steps towards justice with God's creation. On that path, our faith and our hope are our strength.

Pastor Sonia Skupch, Regional Secretary for Latin America and the Caribbean and North America Lutheran World Federation

Dr. Darío Barolin

From the Alliance of Presbyterian and Reformed Churches of Latin America (AIPRAL), we greet and are extremely happy for the international effort in the production of this material on the care of creation and eco-diakonia. We believe that this intersection is vital in the mission and witness of the church in Latin America and the Caribbean.

From our alliance we have been promoting awareness, knowledge and critical theological thinking on these issues, seeking a concrete diaconic practice, a spirituality of sufficiency as well as advocacy actions at different levels. In 2011, our assembly in Guatemala was organized around the 'rights of water' and the one in 2016 in Brazil on the climate crisis with the affirmation, 'we are on time'. Today it continues to be one of the main lines of work of our alliance, and especially in the search for a missiological understanding of the church in the face of the climate crisis in our 'Miradas' project.[7]

In this sense, a publication like this one is not only in tune with our path, but it will also allow us to delve into the theme, incorporating new voices from other confessional traditions, as well as from other parts of the globe.

We believe that the insistence on connecting the current climate crisis with the extractivist capitalist model, whether in its neoliberal model or as 'state capitalism', is correct. A theology, an ethics, are necessary, and ones that place us in a perspective of care rather than exploitation. In this sense, John Calvin's comment on Genesis 2:15 takes on a more than relevant value when read from the crisis that unlimited human production brings to God's creation.

> Moses adds, that the custody of the garden was given in charge to Adam, to show that we possess the things which God has committed to our hands, on the condition, that being content with a frugal and moderate use of them, we should take care of what shall remain. Let him who possesses a field, so partake of its yearly fruits, that he may not suffer the ground to be injured by his negligence; but let him endeavour to hand it down to posterity as he received it, or even better cultivated. Let him so feed on its fruits that he neither dissipates it by luxury, nor permits to be marred or ruined by neglect. Moreover, that this economy, and this diligence, with respect to those good things which God has given us to enjoy, may flourish among us; let every one regard himself as the steward

---

[6] Cibele Kuss, "Creation is not for sale, but what about our Theological Conscience?," in *Creation – Not for Sale,* ed. Anna Burghardt (Geneva: The Lutheran World Federation, 2016), 52-53, accessed on March 7, 2022, https://2017.lutheranworld.org/content/reformation-booklets-creation-%E2%80%93-not-sale-131.

[7] See "MIRADAS teológicas y diaconales en tiempos de pandemia," AiPRAL, accessed March 7, 2022, https://aipral.net/miradas.

> of God in all things which he possesses. Then he will neither conduct himself dissolutely, nor corrupt by abuse those things which God requires to be preserved.[8]

On the other hand, as the Accra Confession of 2004 points out, "We believe that the integrity of our faith is at stake if we remain silent or refuse to act in the face of the current system of neoliberal economic globalization."[9]

Therefore, the climate crisis, the diakonic requirements regarding this issue are not secondary or optional matters to our faith. Silence in the face of it not only makes us accomplices but also means in concrete terms the denial of faith in the God preached by Jesus Christ.

That is why we express our gratitude for this publication and encourage our communities in Latin America to read and study it so that we can be living testimonies of God's covenant with Noah and all of creation: "As long as the earth endures, seedtime and harvest, cold and heat, summer and winter, day and night, shall not cease" (Genesis 8:22).

Rev. Dr. Darío Barolin General Secretary of the Alliance of Presbyterian and Reformed Churches of Latin America (AIPRAL)

Rev Professor Dr Ioan Sauca

I warmly welcome this new International Handbook on Creation Care and Eco-Diakonia. In recognising our ecological responsibilities as stewards of God's earth, Christians are called to work actively to halt and reverse the damage done to the environment in recent decades. As a global fellowship, the World Council of Churches has been actively involved in this work since the WCC's 6th Assembly held in Vancouver in 1983, the conciliar process on Justice, Peace and Integrity of Creation and the subsequent World Convocation in Seoul in 1990. This comprehensive volume represents key voices of Christian leadership from the Global South. It is an important resource for the wider and global ecumenical movement.

The WCC has been present at all COP summits of the United Nations Framework Convention on Climate Change (UNFCCC) since their creation and has always brought the voices of faith to negotiations and demanding Climate Justice. The WCC's Pilgrimage of Justice and Peace has accompanied churches and has encouraged good practice concerning the witness, advocacy and lobbying work of churches concerning the issues of creation care, protection of biodiversity and climate justice. Addressing the UN Sustainable Development Goals and the Paris Agreement on Climate Change are of increasingly urgent, even existential, importance – irrespective of other competing political and economic priorities. The emerging concept of Eco-Diakonia is a welcome and important development in addressing the diaconal challenges that humanity is already experiencing through climate change, not least in the increasing scarcity of drinking water whilst simultaneously sea levels are rising, extremes of hot weather are deleterious to human health and the sustainability of agriculture is adversely affected.

This new *International Handbook on Creation Care and Eco-Diakonia*, brought into being by key representatives from regional ecumenical organizations under the able leadership of former WCC staff colleague Rev. Prof. Dr. Dietrich Werner, is like a collection of team visits and situational reports from a vast variety of settings in Africa, Latin America, Asia, the Middle East and the Pacific region. It sheds light on the specificity of contextual challenges, of creative responses and innovative reflections of churches in the Global South in their contributions for climate justice, protection of biodiversity and Eco-Diakonia. It

---

[8] John Calvin, *Commentary on Genesis,* Vol. 1, trans. John King (Calvin Translation Society, 1847), accessed on christian.net on March 7, 2022, https://christian.net/pub/resources/text/m.sion/cvgn1-05.htm.

[9] World Alliance of Reformed Churches, *The Accra Confession* (2004), #16, accessed on March 7, 2022, http://wcrc.ch/accra/the-accra-confession.

is a timely contribution to and resource for the 11th Assembly of the WCC in Karlsruhe, Germany, 31st August – 8th September 2022, with its theme 'Christ's love moves the world to reconciliation and unity'.

I thank all involved in the collaborative effort to produce this book, particularly for the support given by Brot fuer die Welt in Berlin. I hope that the messages contained in this unique publication are given the serious engagement they deserve.

Rev Professor Dr Ioan Sauca, Acting General Secretary, World Council of Churches

Editorial: Creation Care in the Context of a Global Pandemic, Rising Economic Inequality and Worsening Ecological Crisis

The global COVID19 pandemic which unfolded since the start of 2020 has not solved the climate and environmental crisis. Instead, the pandemic has aggravated its effects, as well as existing deep inequalities within our current social and economic systems.[1] The pandemic has underlined the vulnerability of humankind and its dependency on functioning systems of ecological balances, the protection of rainforests and the relation between human civilization and wildlife which has been disturbed by the accelerated spread of industrialized agriculture, of extractivist industries and rapid urbanization. We are reminded once again, that humanity is a biological species in the midst of a biological world. Humanity is not above nature, but rather interconnected with it and intertwined with a myriad of bacteriological and virological species in the organic world. If carefully maintained balances between human civilization and natural habitats of other species are disturbed and destabilized by aggressive intrusion of human civilization into wildlife, the result can be seen in major pandemics like COVID 19 which most likely is caused by zoonosis (an infectious disease which is caused by a pathogen that has jumped from an animal to a human species). We seem to be at the beginning only of a pandemic era, where COVID19 is just one of several serious warnings that humanity with its capitalist civilization, under the unrestrained impulse of its economic powers, has transgressed the planetary boundaries within which human and animal life can be sustained on earth. We are forced to fully grasp again: when humankind is living against nature, then nature fights back and turns its own dynamics against humankind. Therefore, creation care – or, the protection of natural resources and ecological balances which are essential for sustaining life on earth – is high on the international agenda for the twenty-first century and a global imperative without alternative.

While many national governments and international organizations are still absorbed coping with the immediate effects of the COVID19 pandemic and the focus of many discourses is on vaccination and vaccination equity issues, faith-based organizations, churches and ecumenical networks have a unique role to articulate the deeper questions: they have to raise their public voice on the unsolved systemic issues concerning the environmental crisis, climate change and destruction of biodiversity and species which belong to the underlying long-term causes for the health related threats humankind is experiencing at present. The years following the outbreak of the Corona pandemic in 2020/2021 should have been crucial years for increased international political measures against global warming and for the protection of biodiversity, in order to still reach some of the key goals of the UN sustainable development agenda and with it also improved 'one health' approaches, which are vital for protecting humanity over against pandemics of this scale. The publication of this *International Handbook on Creation Care and Eco-Diakonia* in 2022 marks the 50th anniversary, both of the publication of the 'Limits to Growth Report'[2] from the Club of Rome in 1972 (which had argued that without substantial changes in resource consumption, the most probable result might be an uncontrollable decline in both population and industrial capacity for the whole world still in the twenty-first century), but also the first UN conference on environment and

---

[1] See Oxfam's January 2022 report. 'Inequity Kills', which documents that since the onset of the pandemic, the wealth of the ten richest people on the planet doubled, while the incomes of 99% of humanity declined sharply. The report argues that, "widening economic, gender, and racial inequalities – as well as the inequality that exists between countries – are tearing our world apart. This is not by chance, but choice: 'economic violence' is perpetrated when structural policy choices are made for the richest and most powerful people.", see: https://www.oxfam.org/en/research/inequality-kills; summary in: https://oxfamilibrary.openrepository.com/bitstream/handle/10546/621341/bp-inequality-kills-170122-summ-en.pdf?sequence=2; already in 2021 Oxfam published the study, 'The Inequality Virus', see: https://oxfamilibrary.openrepository.com/bitstream/handle/10546/621149/bp-the-inequality-virus-250121-en.pdf.

[2] See https://www.clubofrome.org/publication/the-limits-to-growth/.

development in Stockholm in 1972 (which, for the first time in human history, placed environmental issues at the forefront of global political concerns at UN levels and marked the start of a dialogue between industrialized and developing countries on the link between economic growth, the pollution of the air, water, and oceans and the well-being of people around the world).[3] The intersectionality of climate justice, global nutrition policy and food issues, as well as the global health crisis since then, has also been amply indicated by important recent UN conferences such as the Kunmin conference in China (October 2021) on the protection of biodiversity (COP 15 to the Convention on Biological Diversity (CBD)), the Glasgow Conference of Parties to the UN Climate Change Conference in October 2021 (COP 26), as well as the Global Health Summit in Berlin (October 2021) and others. However, implementation efforts of measures to curb climate warming and biodiversity destruction are still lacking behind. And after the tragedy of rising East-West tensions due to the war in the Ukraine since 24 February 2022, and the new spirit of polarization between Western and Asian countries, trends for the doubling of military expenditure are emerging exceeding by far financial commitments for investments for climate change mitigation and biodiversity restoration. After millions of USD or Euros have been readily invested by western countries into COVID recovery measures and now again millions are offered and set aside to boost military expenditure and deterrence, the 100 billion US$ per year which rich countries had pledged as funding support for climate change activities to developing countries back in 2009 at the Copenhagen climate summit, still are not met.[4]

It holds true, however, that time for changing the course of humanity in terms of green-house gas emissions is running short, as the recent IPCC Sixth Assessment Report from August 2021,[5] or the IPCC Report from 2022,[6] have clearly shown. The IPCC has strongly pointed to the fact that regions like Africa, but also many other regions, will be experiencing drastic consequences of a possibly unavoidable 2 degree C raising of global temperatures, with increases in drought and dangerous fire weather causing heavy impacts on agriculture, forestry, health and ecosystems, particularly in Southern Africa.[7]

Regional Voices for Care of Creation and Eco-Diakonia in Churches of the Global South

Several regional ecumenical organizations (REOs), National Councils of Churches and members of both World Council of Churches (WCC) and Action of Churches Together (ACT Alliance) have taken a pioneering role in keeping imperatives related to climate resilience, environmental stewardship and ecological consciousness on the international agenda. Churches, faiths actors and civil society organizations more strongly than ever are stating that there are limits to the commercialization, financialization and exploitation of nature, natural resources and indigenous people. There is growing recognition that continued destruction of natural habitats will definitely destroy the sensitive interactive systems between plants, animals, fungi and fishes on earth. Ecumenical agencies like ACT Alliance in collaboration with its members (like Bread for the World) have spearheaded many advocacy efforts for issues of climate justice, protection of biodiversity and the needed 'great transformation' which is demanded for in the core goals of the sustainable development agenda (SDG) since 2015. However, so far little is shared, made visible and published internationally in terms of the vast contextual theological work, advocacy efforts and practical as well as educational projects of **churches from the global South** in the area of eco-theologies, creation care, climate justice and ethics of sustainability, although at the core of their contribution there is a far-reaching

---

[3] See: https://www.un.org/en/conferences/environment/stockholm1972.

[4] Instead, some 11 million US$ per minute (or US$5.9 trillion per year) are paid globally as the total subsidies in 2020 for producing and burning oil, natural gas and coal. See: https://www.boell.de/en/2021/10/26/broken-promises-developed-countries-fail-keep-their-100-billion-dollar-climate-pledge.

[5] See: https://www.ipcc.ch/report/ar6/wg1/.

[6] See: IPCC Report Climate Change 2022: Impacts, Adaptation and Vulnerability, in: https://www.ipcc.ch/report/ar6/wg2/.

[7] https://africatimes.com/2021/08/09/ipcc-report-details-projected-climate-impacts-for-africa/.

re-definition of the whole paradigm of development going on which is of relevance for all. This provided motivation for this project to be prepared, in collaboration with several regional ecumenical organizations which for several years have increased their work in the area of creation care, climate justice and eco-diakonia – efforts on which the contributions of this volume are built upon:

In **Asia** the Christian Conference of Asia (CCA) had planned for the Asian Ecumenical Institute (AEI)[8] which took place in November 2020, and invited prominent speakers to address future leaders of Christian churches throughout Asian Christianity to deal with issues around the theme, 'We are Called to be Stewards for Renewal and Restoration of God's Creation'.[9] Care for creation and commitment for climate justice have become a core programmatic thrust in CCA which is defined as 'Ecumenical Solidarity for Accompaniment and Diakonia in Asia' (ESADA). CCA is also planning to hold its next 15th General Assembly probably in early 2023 and to unfold the significance of churches' involvement for creation care etc. under the theme 'God renew us in your spirit and restore our creation'.

In the **Pacific** context the Pacific Conference of Churches (PCC) has become a strong advocate for a new vision of a nuclear-free Pacific ('The Pacific we want') and in February 2021 hosted the fourth edition of the World Council of Churches (WCC) 'Eco-School on Water, Food and Climate Justice'[10] in their region. In five countries (Fiji, Tonga, Vanuatu, Tuvalu & Solomon Islands) PCC has contributed significantly to a new conceptual discourse on an Ecological Framework of Development, which is bringing together traditional Pacific values with modern insights and challenges for rethinking the ways in which we measure growth and define the goals of human development.[11]

On the continent of **Africa**, the All Africa Conference of Christian Churches (AACC) has for many years engaged in issues of climate justice, food security and water scarcity (Maputo Assembly in 2009) and recommended to its member churches ten crucial steps of witness for climate justice in 2019 (AACC 10 Action Points For Climate Action).[12] In 2021, the AACC held a continent-wide African consultation with faiths actors on issues related to environmental care, climate justice and protection of biodiversity in Addis Abeba.[13] A common voice of AACC member churches on burning issues like deforestation, environmental degradation, and protection of biodiversity was articulated, which also served the interest to build a stronger network of faith actors on eco-diakonia, in collaboration with the existing African climate advocacy network and other ecumenical networks on eco-theological concerns.

For several decades churches in **Latin America** have been struggling against the devastating impacts of the extractive industries, the destruction of the rainforests and the monocultural orientation of large agrobusiness, demanding a fundamental shift in agricultural policies of export-centred mono-culture orientation, including the violation of basis human rights for indigenous people. Plans are there to intensify education and learning in higher theological education (programs such as REET in Buenos Aires in Argentina) to advance training on environmental care, climate justice and alternative ways of agro-ecology which can be of benefit both for indigenous populations, as well as for the environmental situation as such.

Churches in Germany, with international partners (United Evangelical Mission), mission agencies, as well as Bread for the World as a leading Protestant developmental agency, have been engaged in bringing

---

[8] https://www.cca.org.hk/news-and-events/asian-ecumenical-institute-aei-2020-set-to-begin/.

[9] https://www.cca.org.hk/news-and-events/second-week-of-aei-2020-focuses-on-interrelatedness-of-earth-sciences-and-theology-to-restore-the-creation/.

[10] https://www.oikoumene.org/sites/default/files/2020-10/WCC%20Eco%20School%202020%20Brochure_Final.pdf.

[11] Reweaving the Ecological Mat Framework: Towards an Ecological Framework for Development, Pacific Theological College Fiji, August 2020, in: https://drive.google.com/file/d/1f1kamvePGZjv_gtl116lsFlhOncyAEdv/view.

[12] http://www.aacc-ceta.org/en/news/165-aacc-10-action-points-for-climate-action.

[13] http://aacc-ceta.org/en/news/302-african-faith-leaders-fully-committed-to-battling-climate-change; https://www.aciafrica.org/news/3507/cop26-church-leaders-in-africa-confident-climate-policies-will-be-friendly-to-continent.

together partners and faith-based organisations on issues of climate justice, environmental protection and issues of ethics of sustainability since long.[14] Bread for the World sees climate change, creation care and engagement for climate justice as one of five key thematic areas in its new overall strategy 2021+, where it is stated:

> BfdW is supporting churches and church-related networks in the global South and in Germany directly and indirectly in activities which enhance efforts to shape their own infrastructure and activities in climate sensitive ways and to reflect about the challenges of climate change politically as well as ethically and theologically, in order to become critical actors for eco-social transformation processes in developmental policies.

The volume presented here is also answering this strategic interest "to reflect about the challenges of climate change politically as well as ethically and theologically."

Preparing for the WCC Assembly in 2022

The key incentive and occasion for this volume to be produced was the WCC assembly in Karlsruhe in September 2022. The WCC has been engaged in issues of care for creation and climate change since the 1970s and has done advocacy in all crucial COP parties conferences at the level of UN negotiations.[15] The call and Manifesto for an Ecological Reformation of Christianity (The Volos Call)[16] was strongly articulated in ecumenical circles and in resonance with the initiatives of the Ecumenical Patriarchate back in 2017.[17] The WCC study document on 'Called to Transformative Action: Ecumenical Diakonia' from 2019 (updated and enlarged from 2022) in chapter 10 talks about the environmental crisis and the need to advance the churches involvement in the field of **Eco-Diakonia**. New WCC mission study texts, like the study document 'Together towards life: Mission and Evangelism in Changing Landscapes' from 2013, talk about the imperatives for an *ecological* mission towards a 'flourishing of creation'.[18] In 2020 the WCC published the 'Roadmap for Congregations, Communities and Churches for an Economy of Life and Ecological Justice', which highlighted crucial areas of learning and practical engagement for more sustainable lifestyles.[19]

The forthcoming WCC Assembly, which due to the pandemic was postponed to September 2022 in Karlsruhe (Germany), presents a unique chance to put issues of environmental protection, climate justice and accessibility of water high on the international ecumenical agenda. It also provides the opportunity to listen to voices particularly from churches in the Global South and to make their contributions more visible. Several of the planned Ecumenical Conversations during the assembly, as well as in the Ecumenical Encounter program, will be related to Creation Care and Eco-Diakonia.[20] The heart of what inspires the

---

[14] See: Kairos for Creation – Confessing Hope for the Earth 2019: https://www.vemission.org/kairos-for-creation

[15] https://www.oikoumene.org/what-we-do/care-for-creation-and-climate-justice; Douglas John Hall, 'Art Creation', in *Dictionary of the Ecumenical Movement* (Geneva: WCC, 2002), 274ff.

[16] https://www.oikoumene.org/resources/documents/manifesto-on-an-ecological-reformation-of-all-christian-traditions;
https://repository.globethics.net/bitstream/handle/20.500.12424/236754/Manifesto_ecological_reformation_Christian_traditions_final.pdf?sequence=1&isAllowed=y.

[17] https://www.oikoumene.org/news/conference-calls-for-ecological-reformation-of-christianity.

[18] No 19ff in the study on 'Together towards life', in:
https://www.oikoumene.org/sites/default/files/File/Together%20towards%20Life_Mission%20and%20Evangelism.pdf.

[19] https://www.oikoumene.org/resources/documents/roadmap-for-congregations-communities-and-churches-for-an-economy-of-life-and-ecological-justice.

[20] See: Ecumenical Conversation 7,8 and 9 in the tentative plans for the assembly which will highlight issues of "Creation Justice Now! Climate Action and Water for Life", "Health Ministries – Promoting the churches' role in

Christian attitude towards creation is well described in the meditation on the theme of the Karlsruhe assembly: "The first and foremost attitude of God towards the world is love, for every child, woman and man who has ever become part of human history, and, indeed, for the whole of creation."[21]

The Project: An International Handbook on Creation Care and Eco-Diakonia

Thus, the occasion of a global assembly of the ecumenical movement presented a stimulus and occasion to plan for this *International Handbook on Creation Care and Eco-Diakonia.* This volume underlines the unique role of churches from the Global South to address both major changes in mentalities, values and ethical attitudes related to climate change, protection of biodiversity and environmental protection ('Care for Creation'), as well as best practise models and learning programs on ethics of sustainability and climate change mitigation by which churches, as major providers of educational programs, practically contribute to changes at grassroots levels as well as in their advocacy and lobbying work ('Eco-Diakonia'). The contributions within this volume therefore have both conceptual and foundational, as well as educational and praxis related dimensions, as both are needed to contribute to the advancement of formal and informal training and ecumenical awareness building on issues of environmental care, climate justice and eco-diakonia.

The volume has intended to stay open and flexible with regard to working with different terminologies which are used in different denominational settings and regional contexts ('Christian services for creation care'; 'ecological mission'; 'Christian witness for environment and climate justice'; 'advocacy for sustainability ethics and protection of biodiversity'); therefore no forcefully unifying monolineare terminology was imposed on the individual contributions. However, recognizing that the notion of 'Eco-Diakonia' has become a new umbrella term in the international discourses and documents of the ecumenical movement,[22] this term was frequently referred to in several articles. The term 'ecological Christian social services' or 'Eco-Diakonia' denotes the integrated whole of prophetic witness, social Christian (or interfaith) witness for creation care and joint ecumenical action and services of advocacy and lobbying work to tackle root causes of the global environmental crisis, of biodiversity destruction, and of climate change, as well as related health threats on both local, regional and global levels.

How This Volume Came About: Goals, Structure and Contents

Based on long years of collaboration between the Ecumenical-Theological Desk in Bread for the World and the theological and educational desks in regional ecumenical organisations, some initial brainstorming between Bread for the World and organizations like Christian Conference of Asia (CCA), All African Conference of Churches (AACC), and networks of ecumenical theological education and research in Latin America (REET Argentina) took place in late 2020. Early in 2021, it was agreed to embark on an ambitious and short-term working process in the years of 2021 and 2022 to produce a joint international resources collection (working title *International Handbook on Creation Care and Eco-Diakonia*) which would be

---

healing and wholeness" and issues of "Economy of Life in a time of inequality, persistent hunger, climate change and the 4th industrial revolution".

[21] Quoted in: Christ's Love Moves the World to Reconciliation and Unity. A reflection on the theme of the 11th Assembly of the World Council of Churches, Karlsruhe 2022, page 15, in: https://www.oikoumene.org/sites/default/files/2021-01/ENG_WCC_2022Assembly_Booklet_PAGESH.pdf; Originally this statement of faith is part of a Faith and Order Paper: The Church: Towards a Common Vision, Faith and Order Paper
214, §58 (Geneva: WCC Publications, 2013), https://archive.org/details/wccfops2.221/page/32/mode/2up.

[22] The term „Eco-Diakonia" is prominently used in the new framework study document of the WCC on ecumenical diakonia from 2020, see chapter 10.11 on "The Environmental Crisis and Eco-diakonia"

presented both as a tangible and printed resource book from churches of the Global South, as well as a digital resources collection to the forthcoming WCC assembly. Other regional ecumenical organizations joined at a later stage of the working process by providing advice and content, but not as members of the editor's board (such as the Pacific Conference of Churches, Caribbean Conference of Churches, Middle East Council of Churches).

In February 2021 an international editorial group was brought together which then worked out general project outlines and guidelines for authors etc. From March/April 2021 onwards invitation letters were sent out via the regional ecumenical organizations to more than one hundred suggested specialist and authors from the regions. From October 2021 onwards, manuscripts submitted were reviewed and edited in cooperation with regional teams in Nairobi, Buenos Aires, Bangkok and Hamburg. From February 2022 onwards, the edited papers were processed and copy-edited at the Oxford-based office of Regnum Books in OCMS and its working partner, Words by Design. Simultaneously, a complex process started in Latin America to edit the Spanish and Portuguese texts submitted and to have them translated into English.

The handbook is designed to provide a basic and ecumenically-oriented resource collection for training future church leaders, students and practitioners in the areas of education for sustainability, eco-diakonia and ecological transformation in churches and (mainly Christian) faith-based organizations around the world. The aim is to allow for more South-South (and North-South) exchange in terms of Creation Care and to encourage mutual learning between churches, ecumenical agencies and networks of ecologically sensitive players in different cultural, political and geographical contexts in this area of church witness and service. While the common intention of the project was to make available one solid international version of this handbook in English language, it was part of the project plans from the very beginning as well to encourage regional versions of the resource collection in Spanish (and if feasible, in Portuguese or later other languages), in order to allow for maximum benefit in the different language realms of Global Christianity. At the same time, while being sound in the quality of its contributions, the handbook was planned not as a purely academic resource collection only to be used in universities and colleges, but to be readable and accessible also for practitioners in environmental work, in FBOs/NGOs, in churches, for church leaders, as well as for secular experts who would wish to learn about the churches' engagement with these concerns.

Instructions and guidelines for authors were developed which identified different formats and lengths of contributions, so as to make a difference between a longer foundational essay, an introductory survey article or a shorter presentation of a best practise model. The responses received from authors were quite overwhelming and encouraging, and the editors could not accept all the contributions simply for quantitative reasons. As a result, this innovative handbook presents the most comprehensive global survey volume on issues of climate change, protection of biodiversity, food-security, and ethics of sustainability from the perspective of the churches in the Global South to date. Great efforts have been devoted to include essays, survey articles and best practise reports from different denominational, political and regional backgrounds, and to present a multi-faceted picture from the immense variety of theological reflections and action-oriented learning models on creation care and eco-diakonia, ranging from Orthodox, Protestant, Roman-Catholic, Evangelical to Charismatic and Independent church backgrounds from all over the world.

The volume mainly focuses on contributions coming from the ecumenical fellowship of churches and from Christian authors. A fully inclusive interfaith volume with equal representation and visibility of all faith traditions (Islam, Buddhism, Daoism, Judaism etc), though this would be desirable, was beyond the feasibility and the mandate of this project. However, a good visibility has also been given to contributions from multi-faith ownership and underline the interfaith solidarity and collaboration between Christian, secular and other faith actors with regard to issues of climate change and sustainability. Articles contributed represent the opinions and theological positions of the individual authors, not necessarily the position of the editorial group or the funding partners in every detail. The editors did not impose any rigid principle of coherence – therefore quite a variety of theological and ethical positions is expressed, representing the pluriverse of ethical and theological positions within eco-theological reflections amongst the different regions. While the editors did not apply a rigorous academic double-blind academic peer review process, in order to be inclusive for contributions which did not come from a purely academic background, an intensive and rigorous editorial process has maintained core standards of quality, coherence and language, whilst respecting difference in style and expression.

The content structure of this unique volume was determined by the editor's group as follows:

a. **Section I**: Biblical and Theological Foundations for Creation Care and Eco-Diakonia (biblical-theological-ethical section).
b. **Section II**: Concepts and Profiles of Creation Care and Eco-Diakonia in Different Regions and Denominational Traditions (regional and denominational survey section).
c. **Section III**: Trends, Key Issues and Best Practise Models for Creation Care and Eco-Diakonia Trends, Crucial Concerns and Best Practise Models for Eco-Diakonia (theme oriented and practical approaches section).
d. **Section IV**: Models and Methods for Training and Competency Building in Creation Care and Eco-Diakonia (educational and training related section).

Each section includes some 25 to 30 articles organized in regional sub-sections – Africa/Middle East, Asia (plus China and Pacific), Latin America (and Caribbean) – and try to properly respect criteria of denominational, gender, geographical and cultural diversity balances.

Core Editorial Group

The key to the success of this volume was a small but determined editorial group of some eight people who were the driving force and decision-making group behind this one-and-a-half year intensive working process (January 2021 until July 2022). Organizationally the process was related to Bread for the World, Ecumenical-Theological Department, which contributed expertise in producing larger resource volumes for theological resource, development cooperation, religion and development competence training and theological education from earlier years.[23]

Persons which served in the Core Editorial group included the following:

a. Africa (AACC): Rev. Dr. Lesmore Gibson Ezechiel (Director of Programs); Dr. Bosela Eale (Executive Staff for Theology and Interfaith) (assisted by Joan Mwayo as intern);
b. Asia (CCA): Rev. Jun Eun Grace Moon (Executive staff) (assisted by Rosiana Indah Purnomo as intern and Chalvin Tehuayou);
c. Latin-America (REET): Rev. Prof. Dr. Daniel Beros, and Prof. Dr. Marisa Strizzi (Theological Seminary Buenos Aires), Argentina, in collaboration with Dr. Kathleen Griffin for Spanish-English translations;
d. Sino-Theological Network in Germany: Rev. Prof. Dr. Ruomin Liu, Missionsacademy Hamburg/Nanjing (assisted by Isabel Friemann, Chinese Christianity Liaison Desk Hamburg);
e. United Evangelical Mission (UEM): Rev. Prof. Dr. Kambale Kahongya, Executive Staff for Africa Region United Evangelical Mission, Dar Es Salaam, Tanzania;
f. Bread for the World: Rev. Prof. Dr. Dr. h.c. Dietrich Werner (Senior Theological Advisor; Head of Ecumenical Theology Unit; Berlin).

Ecumenical Advisory Group

There were also a number of additional experts which had been asked in certain stages to give advice to this project as a whole or on individual themes and contributions and therefore served on an occasional

[23] https://www.ocms.ac.uk/handbook-free-downloads/

basis in an international ecumenical advisory group for this project. People asked for advice included amongst others: Rev. Dr. Andar Parlindungan (UEM; Indonesia); Rev. Dr. Chad Rimmer (LWF, USA); Rev. Godwin Ampony, Tanzania; Rev. Prof. Dennis Solon, Philippines; Rev. Prof. Drea Fröchtling (passed away in Dec 2021); Dr. Dinesh Suna (WCC): Rev. Dr. Anton Knuth (Missionsacademy Hamburg); Caroline Sonnabend (Bread for the World, Churches helping Churches); Father Antoine Al Ahmar from Middle East Council of Churches (MECC Lebanon); Rev. Dr. James Bhagwan from Pacific Conference of Churches, Rev. Dr. Gerard Granado, Conference of Caribbean Churches (CCC).

Key Learnings and Practical Relevance of This Volume

The finalized volume, with all its unique contributions from various contexts of the churches in the Global South, is a strong indication that the 'greening of religions'[24] has taken place to a large extent in major parts of Global Christianity in the South, while there is still an urgent need for a broadening of this movement in all its various layers. Religion plays an enormous role in reversing climate change, states the UN.[25] This collection of significant voices from Africa, Asia, Latin America and elsewhere underlines several key convictions which emerged and were reinforced during the working process for this volume:

a. Churches in the Global South are giants with an enormous potential for mobilization and value change with regard to ecological as well as ethical resources needed for the 'great transformation'

There is a significant potential for identifying unique contributions of church and faith actors in the Global South and thus contributing to mutual South-South as well as South-North as well as East-West learning on best practise models for climate justice, protection of biodiversity and environmental care. For the ongoing dialogue on religion and development, the intersection of sustainability and religion is the most crucial thematic avenue for future research and international strategic dialogue which currently is realized only by a certain minority of international think-tanks and research programs.[26] Churches are indispensable partners for joint action and collaboration with public actors on both local, regional, national and global levels. The voices of churches in the Global South need to be heard more, made visible and commonly reflected about, as it is in their region that the effects of rapid climate change and loss of biodiversity are having the largest impact on the livelihoods and living conditions of vulnerable majority populations. There is an immense unrealized potential of faith actors for ecological transformation, both globally and regionally. We need an expansion of partnerships between faith actors and public sectors, secular stakeholders and UN agencies in the era of biodiversity protection and climate justice. Therefore 'waking the giant'[27] is a good motto for enhancing and widening a global ecumenical ecological initiative aiming to strengthen churches' capacity to effectively contribute to the achievement of the 2030 Agenda for Sustainable Development, together with several ecumenical actors (such as National Christian Councils (NCCs), Christian aid agencies and regional ecumenical organizations etc.). 'Delay means death'[28] – this applies not only to scaling up initiatives and drastic action for relevant measures for creation care and

[24] Jonathan Chaplin, 'The global greening of religion', in *Palgrave Communications* 2 (1) July 2016; in https://www.researchgate.net/publication/305272778_The_global_greening_of_religion.

[25] https://www.euronews.com/green/2020/10/06/religion-plays-an-enormous-role-in-reversing-climate-change-says-un.

[26] https://in-rcsd.org/en/about-us; see also Yale Forum on Religion and Ecology: https://fore.yale.edu/. See also the article from Juliane Stork and others in IV on the international research program at Humboldt University Berlin on 'The South African-German Research Hub on Religion and Sustainability (SAGRaS)'.

[27] https://wakingthegiant.lutheranworld.org/.

[28] https://www.reuters.com/business/cop/delay-means-death-un-climate-report-urges-immediate-drastic-action-2022-02-28/.

climate justice, but also for the deliberate inclusion and mobilization of faiths actors which articulate not only a significant moral voice in this world, but also can mobilize millions for more responsible life styles.

b. The ecological reformation of Christianity is in full swing

The blunt accusation that Christianity or the Jewish-Christian tradition as such are the major cause of the ecological destruction of this earth (which has been made by Lynn White[29]) reflects neither the historical realities in mission history, which demand a more differentiated view, nor the contemporary realities in the majority of churches in the Global South as an intense awareness building process has been developing in many of the churches of the Global South. Ecological sensibilization and reformation of Christianity, the 'earthing of Christian faith'[30] and the 'greening of churches'[31] which has frequently been demanded for,[32] has irrevocably started and is in full swing (although with huge differences in speed and broadness) – this is shown in several contributions to this volume. This, however, does not mean that nothing remains to be done. There are huge differences in the eco-theological sensitivity and engagement of ethics of sustainability, both within certain denominations, between certain denominations, as well as between the regions. This underlines the significance of this volume to serve more exchange, both between the regions, as well as between the different Christian denominations. As most of the authors have met only in this volume on paper, not in reality, using this collection of a vast spectrum of ecologically engaged voices for a series of regional or global training seminars or even interfaith academies on ethics of sustainability, in collaboration with regional networks of theological schools, with Faith for Earth or Religions for Peace, might well prove a strategic outcome and proper utilization of this volume.

It has often been argued by experts that the urgency of the global ecological challenges demands the creation of an International Academy of Religions on Sustainability and Peace, which could serve as an institutional tool for bringing together leading think tanks, representatives from religious communities, as well as politics, business, natural sciences and civil society in order to advance synergies and public engagement in these vital issues.

c. Intersection between ecological sensitization and transformed concepts of masculinity and gender justice

About half of the contributions of this volume come from female authors. Several authors have underlined that there is an intersection between the roles and attitudes with which women are seen and treated, and the role and attitudes by which nature is treated in certain cultures. The wounds and scars which are inflicted on women are closely interconnected to wounds and injuries imposed on nature as a whole. The struggle for gender justice and the struggles concerning ecological transformation are therefore mutually interrelated and cannot be separated. There are several articles in this volume which point to the intersection between eco-theologies, theologies of the body, theology of the fertile soil, agro-ecology and the theology of the table fellowship, in which men and women, the young and elderly are equally involved. Major studies in the past, as well as the current global strategy of ACT Alliance, underline the interrelatedness of gender

[29] https://www.cmu.ca/faculty/gmatties/lynnwhiterootsofcrisis.pdf.

[30] See Ernst Conradie and Pan Chiu Lai (eds), *An Earthed Faith: Telling the Story amid the 'Anthropocene'. Taking a Deep Breath for the Story to Begin* (Cape Town: OASIS, 2021).

[31] See for instance: https://www.euronews.com/green/2021/07/10/how-churches-are-empowering-communities-to-beat-the-effects-of-climate-change-in-zimbabwe.

[32] https://www.oikoumene.org/resources/documents/manifesto-on-an-ecological-reformation-of-all-christian-traditions.

justice and climate justice.[33] “Somebody fighting for gender justice cannot leave climate justice to others. It’s so interconnected.”[34]

d. Answering the cries of the earth and the cries of the poor together

The contributions also show that there is no principal contradiction between approaches trying to address the cries of the poor and those trying to answer the cries of suffering creation. As Pope Francis has stated repeatedly, answering the cries of the poor and the cries of nature belong together. [35] Churches are marked by combining a specific triangular sensitivity to justice, to the vulnerable and to living creatures in creation. As the Pope stated in *Laudato Si*, “a true ecological approach always becomes a social approach; it must integrate questions of justice in debates on the environment, so as to hear both cry of the earth and the cry of the poor.”[36] The cry of the earth continues to ring loudly in the multiple manifestations of the contemporary ecological crisis: droughts, floods and hurricanes, destruction of life-sustaining ecosystems and unprecedented levels of biodiversity loss, pollution of the land, atmosphere and water bodies, water scarcity, deforestation, and a thousand other ways that expose the travail and agony of mother earth. At the same time, the poor and vulnerable communities around the world are currently the first and most disproportionately affected victims of ecological degradation. “Both everyday experience and scientific research show that the gravest effects of all attacks on the environment are suffered by the poorest”.[37] Listening to both of these cries in their distinctive forms might motivate and compel churches to intensify their listening to a third cry, often forgotten during the COVID19 pandemic, the cries of the children. “What kind of world do we want to leave to those who come after us, to children who are now growing up?” was one of the questions asked in Laudato Si (No. 160). The demographic compositions of the majority of the churches in the Global South is quite different from the aging populations of those in the North. Recent years have seen masses of children and young people taking to the streets around the world, in large and growing numbers, expressing their frustrations about apathy and inaction of political leadership. There are several younger authors amongst the contributors of this volume – listening to the voices of the younger generations, who are reversing the question back to us and telling us clearly that we have no right to steal their future, can re-energize the intergenerational dialogue within churches and societies about climate justice and ecological transformation.

e. Unequal accessibility of resources for eco-theological education and research on climate change and biodiversity losses

Both the working process for the volume, carried out together with staff from CCA, AACC, REET and several other regional ecumenical actors such as REET and other theological institutions, as well as the final volume available here, have enhanced mutual connectivity and deeper knowledge about what churches and faith actors have developed in this regard and will continue to motivate mutual learning, thus increasing South-South cooperation on issues of climate justice, protection of biodiversity and ethics of sustainability. The accessibility of ethical, theological and strategic resources, training and practical materials, however, still is quite unequal and particularly low in countries of the Global South. Therefore this volume can also

[33] Geraldine Terry: Gender Justice and Climate Change, Oxfam 2016: https://oxfamilibrary.openrepository.com/bitstream/handle/10546/115359/bk-climate-change-gender-justice-091109-en.pdf?sequence=5

[34] Ruth Manorama, a dalit activist from India representing the Asia Dalit Rights Forum (ADRF), quoted in the new ACT Alliance strategy 2019: https://actalliance.org/act-news/climate-justice-and-gender-justice-go-hand-in-hand/

[35] https://ofm.org/wp-content/uploads/2016/07/CuraCreato-EN.pdf

[36] Laudato Si’, 49

[37] Laudato Si’, 48

be seen as another passionate plea for more resources for theological scholarship,[38] for focussed international and inter-contextual research programs on issues of ecology, climate change and care for creation (some of which indicated in section IV), and for targeted ecumenical scholarship programs for younger generations trying to build up their competence and expertise in areas of eco-theology, climate justice and ethics of sustainability. Otherwise, the huge needs for further expertise and research hubs for the giant global transition needs in terms of ecological transformation cannot be answered and related competences cannot be properly built up. Therefore this volume can be seen as a strategic contribution towards scaling up collaboration between FBOS and public actors and policy makers on sustainability education, and to launch a broad-based movement for supporting education and research for ecological conversion.

Therefore, this volume is handed over and shared with the World Council of Churches and its member churches,[39] with ACT Alliance, the umbrella organization of Christian development actors,[40] with the Partnership on Religion and Development (PaRD), particularly with its WECARE working stream[41] and with the Faith4Earth network[42] of UN Environment with the deliberate wish and vision that it may contribute to more environmental and sustainability education and policy making on all levels.

Acknowledgements

The editors want to acknowledge with deep gratitude the contribution of several colleagues and institutions which assisted greatly in the organizational, financial and administrative processes around this demanding project:

- Prof. Dr. Kathleen Griffin, Buenos Aires for meticulous and very committed work on translation of Spanish and Portuguese texts into English versions;
- Rev. Leonardo Schindler, Church President of the IERP and Lic. Nicholas Rosenthal from IERP Diakonia Foundation for assisting in administrative aspects of the project in Latin America;
- Joan Mwayo (AACC) and Rosina Purnomo (CCA) for handling part of the correspondence work with the authors and their invitation letters;
- Martina Grassmel, Daniel Kinigopoulos, Janna Lang and Arne Marburg for handling different kinds of administrative, financial and organizational aspects of the whole editorial processes;
- Different program units of Bread for the World to provide advice and also financial support for the project (international program unit; churches helping churches; small projects fund);
- Rev. Nada Zheng from Liushi Christian Church from Wenzhou City/China for generous support for the overall project on behalf of his church;
- Dr. Tony Gray from Words by Design, Oxford and Dr. Paul Bendor-Samuel from Oxford Centre for Mission Studies, Oxford, for their enthusiastic support and meticulous copyediting work on this large volume.
- Masterprint Graphics Ltd from Nairobi, Kenya; Ediciones 'La Aurora' from Buenos Aires; and Wanida Printing from Chang Mai in Thailand, who worked tirelessly to produce the regional print runs and regional editions of this volume in their continents.

---

[38] See earlier initiatives from WCC/ETE and Bossey Ecumenical Institute: in: https://www.oikoumene.org/news/global-survey-documents-trends-in-theological-education; also in: https://archived.oikoumene.org/en/press-centre/news/green-reformation-consultation-renews-commitment-to-care-for-creation.

[39] https://www.oikoumene.org/what-we-do/care-for-creation-and-climate-justice.

[40] https://actalliance.org/climate-justice/.

[41] https://www.partner-religion-development.org/work-streams/water-environment-and-climate-action-work-stream-wecare.

[42] https://www.unep.org/about-un-environment/faith-earth-initiative.

The hope which has inspired us in bringing this monumental work together and facing all the obstacles and difficulties involved with such a demanding project – as well as with raising one's voices for creation care and climate justice in today's world – is well articulated by Brazilian theologian Rubem Alves (1933-2014) who once stated:

> Let's plant dates even if those who plant them will never eat them.
> We must live for the love of what we shall never see. This is the secret discipline.
> It allows us to avoid weakening the creative power by just limiting it to the momentary experience.
> And it means an abiding commitment to the future of our own grandchildren.
> It is love trained in this way that gave power to prophets, revolutionaries and saints to die for the future they saw before them.
>
> Ruben Alves

We commend this volume to the glory of God and the many witnesses and servants of God who continue to work with passion, steadfastness and dedication to give justice to those who suffer and listen to the cries both of the poor as well as in creation and are ambassadors for creation care and eco-diakonia around the world.

The Editors

Daniel Beros

Eale Bosela

Lesmore Ezechiel

Kambale Kahongya

Ruomin Liu

Grace Moon

Marisa Strizzi

Dietrich Werner (lead editor)

Explanation and Meditation on the Cover Design and Similar Paintings on Creation: The Role of Christian Art for Strengthening Creation Care – The Example of the Art Work of the Indian School of Art for Peace

Lucy Krone-D'Souza[1] and Andreas Krone[2]

A picture says more than thousand words. This is all the more true in our time, when we are flooded by pictures in print, TV, the Internet and social media. In recent years we have been shocked again and again by burning forests, melting ice glaciers and other calamities which we observe more with fear than with wonder. These images are deeply imprinted in our collective memory – pictures on how our planet earth is becoming ruined.

In this situation, art can and should play a prophetic role in visualizing the mostly invisible or ignored dangers, to make people aware of the wider context of the catastrophe we are heading towards, and finally to strengthen people by a hope, which is even stronger than destruction. To strengthen hope for the healing of creation, to empower churches and people for environmental stewardship and to deepen the understanding for God's continued presence and work within his suffering creation, is the goal of this *International Handbook on Creation Care and Eco-Diakonia*. Therefore, we are glad to have been invited to contribute a piece of Christian art to the cover of this volume. The ecological crisis is also a crisis of the images which we have from our world. Our visual cultures on the internet and social media are dominated by images which put emphasis on commodification, functionality and utilization by human beings. Encountering both the beauty of creation and the immensity of suffering which is going on within it demands another dimension of empathy and sensitivity to the visual imagery which comes out of the encounter with God's creation and its beauty. This implies that we also need to talk about the role of Christian art, where terms such as 'creator', 'creation', 'hope', 'humans as the image of God', 'stewardship of the earth and all creatures' are essential.

Artists from the Indian School of Art for Peace, located in southern India near Bangalore, have long been working in this field. This applies to the founder, the Christian artist Jyoti Sahi in Silvepura Village in Karnataka, India.[3] This also applies to his disciple, Lucy D'Souza-Krone, who for several years has lived both in Germany and in India. We have chosen the cover picture and some other paintings by her to exemplify several aspects where Christian art could strengthen commitment to creation care.

---

[1] Lucy D'Souza-Krone, born in Goa/India, worked first as a teacher, became a painter, painted the hunger veil in 1990, 'Biblical women, guides towards the kingdom of God' for Misereor – this was used in many countries in the world. Since her marriage in 1996 she has lived in Germany. Her artwork was shown in several countries in four continents, and she is engaged in themes like women, ecology and climate justice. See https://lucy-art.de/.

[2] Andreas Krone is a (retired) ordained pastor of the church in Hessen-Nassau, husband to Lucy D'Souza-Krone. He was trained in ecumenical theology in India and for decades has engaged in ecology and environment ethics issues in dialogue with churches in Asia and Africa. Andreas Krone lived for four years in India and published several articles in the area of environmental care and eco-theology, for example, 'Celebrating the harvest of renewable energy'. See further information on this on the following website: https://lucy-art.de/eerntedank.htm.

[3] See: https://artandtheology.org/tag/jyoti-sahi/.

God's Eye Watches over the Earth Protecting the Continuity of Its Live-Giving Rhythms

The key painting which has been chosen as a cover picture for this international volume is about the fidelity of God as the creator to his beloved creation. The presence of God in his creation maintains the life-giving rhythms, which guarantee the very functioning of life in its growth and de-growth, in its flourishing and its withering. Already in the Old Testament, the wellbeing of people, animals and the whole earth is seen in connection with the ethical attitudes of people: "If you shall faithfully obey my commandments … I will give your land rain in season, autumn rain and spring, so that you may harvest your corn, your wine, your oil. I shall provide grass in the fields for your cattle, and you will eat and have all you want." (Deuteronomy 11:13-15)

The eye of God in the center watches over the seasons: winter, spring, summer and autumn. The blue colors stand for the cold season, grey for the snow (below right), the warm colors stand for the summer (top left) and autumn (top right). When God's eye watches over the earth, as he has promised in the Noachian covenant, which includes both humans and all animals and created life together, everything goes well for humans and all living beings. In some world regions there are four seasons, although in other world regions there are two main seasons, the monsoon and the dry season. However, basically it remains the continued rhythm of natural patterns of weather – with rain and dryness, and hot and cold seasons which guarantee the fertility, continuity and life-giving functions and balances within creation. Thus, this is a painting of hope – despite all the ongoing destruction, God is still present in his created world. He/She is still at work within the whole of creation!

It is the grace and fidelity of God that nature is not in a state of pure chaos but there are blissful rhythms in nature: day and night, winter and summer, patterns of rain and so on. However, today anthropocentric induced climate change alters even the essential and most fundamental rhythms of life on earth, i.e. the weather cycle, and so threatens agricultural cycles. The question is raised: does humanity change the life-giving created order to an extend that we endanger the future of life on earth? Is humankind able to challenge and even threaten God's goodness at work in his creation?

The painting wants to raise our awareness to preserve the beneficial rhythms at work within creation and thus to maintain and respect the ecological balance in nature – so that we do not destroy this wonderful earth. It is a major task of Christian art to make people aware about the importance of these rhythms inbuilt in creation. That is why the Bible says, "And God saw it was good."

Invitation for meditation: You can think where in your environment nature is threatening to get out of control and to create awareness that we cannot live against the God-given rhythms of creation.

There are a number of additional paintings which continue to invoke the issue of environmental destruction and healing of creation:

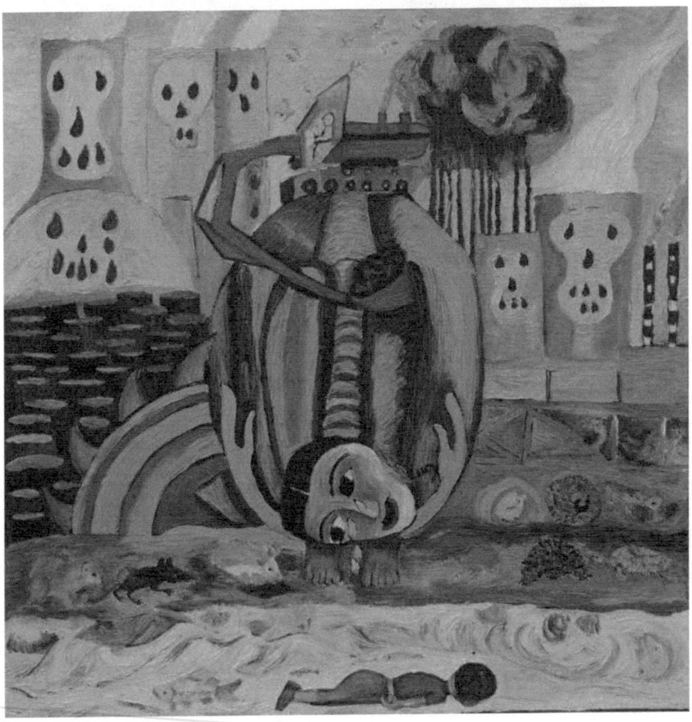

Groaning Mother Earth – Mother Earth Weeps about Death and Annihilation on Earth

This painting is meant to shock and awaken the viewers. It was inspired by the Encyclical *Laudato Si* of Pope Francis. Polluted air, deforestation, atomic and coal power plants – all this burdens our environment. People suffer from this, become sick and weep about their destiny. Animals, insects and birds are exterminated. Artists are called to visualize the drama.

In the year 2015, a small Syrian boy, Aylan, drowned while fleeing across the sea. Mother Earth looks at Aylan and weeps. How can the global community come together to care for one another and for the planet – especially for the poor and needy?

Invitation for meditation: Observe your own surrounding and you will find issues to express the dramatic circumstances in which we find ourselves.

The Tree of Curse and Blessing – in the Future Ahead of Us: Curse or Blessing

"If only you obey the voice of Yahweh your God … blessed will be the produce of your soil." (Deuteronomy 28:2&4, see also Leviticus 26). Then there will be water and blue sky, wine, oil and bread to strengthen us and to delight our hearts. But if we do not listen to the voice of God and the signs of the times, "the earth will become a desert by reason of its inhabitants, in return for what they have done." (Micah 7:13, see also Jeremiah 9:11-13).

In the painting both possibilities are made visible by the fertile and the withering side of the tree. Our attitude today determines curse and blessing on this planet. When this painting was shown for the first time, a scientist from the famous Potsdam Institute for Climate Impact Research said: "The left side of the tree depicts exactly what he had referred on his speech the evening before – large parts of Africa will warm up as if they are being grilled."

Invitation for meditation: You can consider how the possibilities could be presented for what the earth could look like in the future due to human influence.

Water plays an essential role in life; this can be visualized as follows:

Clap Your Hands, You Rivers – the Rivers Are the Veins of Life

Like the blood circulates in our body, so rivers are essential for the wellbeing on earth. "Let the streams rush with jubilation" says Psalm 98. But how can they, when there is no more life in streams and rivers, but instead lots of plastic, waste and chemicals?! We need clean rivers – let us keep the veins of life clean so that the rivers can rejoice!

Invitation for meditation: You can think how to depict essential services of nature in your context to express the divine wisdom and glory in nature and to be a river keeper!

Art should open up new perspectives and motivate people to make use of what God gives to us.

The Sun as Engine of Life – Energy in Abundance and Fullness

The sun in the center drives all the flows of energy on earth. By the heat of the sun the water of the ocean evaporates, wind arises, which can be harvested by wind turbines. The clouds rain down, fill rivers, energy can be harvested from the flowing water, too. Sun and water let grow the vegetation on earth, biomass emerges by this. We can make use of the sun for cooking with solar cookers and with solar panels which form the outer circle. With the sun God provides us energy in abundance. It is time to harvest energy from sun, wind and other renewables, to make use of them and to give thanks by celebrating the harvest of renewable energy.

Invitation for meditation: This you can also celebrate in your local community by widening the understanding of harvest thanksgiving.

With the last image, we already touch on the third aspect to strengthen people by pointing to a hope and to a source from which we can draw strength for our actions.

Tree of Compassion, Justice and Love – for a Life of All Worth Its Future

A tree as person bearing fruits for others – trust (yellow), hope in God (blue) and all compassionate love (red). With our eyes we see the misery of others – our hands and hearts reach out to stand by them. I painted eyes in the green hands, because it makes sense in these days to see and to reach out your hands to the others. As images of God we are called to act for our fellow human beings and the whole planet, our MOTHER EARTH.

Invitation for meditation: You also can think how to express care for others and for the creation.

Ecological Angel

The heavenly being protects the tree and takes care of it. The tree is a habitat for countless creatures. For the environment they are all very precious, for us and further generations. This is indicated by the two saplings growing next to the great tree.

Invitation for meditation: Can you imagine being like the angel who cares for the tree and our precious environment?

River of Life – Drawing Strength from the Current of Life

This painting gives us a perspective and hope which goes beyond our personal actions.

Out of the heart of the holy person springs the river and in her presence everything thrives. Along the river, on either bank, 24 trees bring forth all kind of fruits all year through and their leaves serve for medicine (see Ezekiel 47:1-12, Revelation 22:1-2). The fishing nets are a sign that fish will be 'plentiful' (v.10) because the water is wholesome.

In total you see 153 fish in the painting, as mentioned in the gospel – in ancient times this was a number for fullness, which can be understood nowadays as also a symbol for biodiversity. The river has its origin in God and is comparable to a heart full of love, that the people grow in the stream of life and brings healing to them.

The sun and the moon stand for day and night. May the river of life also flow in you at all times and help you to preserve the blue planet with plants, animals and humans – as a place for life!

Invitation for meditation: You can think how to combine the prophetic vision of the Bible with Eco-Diakonia and find suitable expressions.

The Tree of Life

This is the middle part of a painting with five sections, 'The Feminine Aspect of God'. Do we see a person hanging on that tree or is the tree the person? A dying person and a dying tree still bearing fruit. It stands for mother earth, which is in the process of collapsing due to environmental damages.

Lucy writes:

> While meditating on this motif as the central panel in my painting of the feminine aspect of God, I was bearing in mind a certain women's movement: the Chipko-movement. It originated 300 years ago in the province of Rajasthan. About 300 women risked their lives in order to prevent the cutting down of khejri trees that were

> sacred to them. They embraced the trees and clung to them in such a way that many of them were killed as the trees were cut down. This group of 300 people was led by a woman called Amrita Devi. The Chipko-movement has its origin in that event. Finally, the maharaja who had ordered the holy grove to be cut down was so much impressed that he ordered that no tree may be felled any more if a woman embraced it and called it her brother. Up to the present day, the women of the Chipko-movement regard trees as their brothers and treat them with deep respect. Since in our days the forests in India are again in danger, the Chipko-movement has been revived in recent years.

The trees were the basis of life for these people – they hold the earth and water, give shade, fruit and firewood – the trees are the insurance against desertification.

In the Bible, the life of human beings is often compared to that of trees (Psalm 1:3; Job 29:19; Proverbs 3:18; Jeremiah 17:8; Ezekiel 19:10-12; Revelation 22:2). Many times, the fruitfulness and healing power of trees are emphasised. Nowadays this is rediscovered in the movement of Shinrin-yoku from Japan. It has a positive impact on one's health: "Go to a Forest. Walk slowly. Breathe. Open all your senses. This is the healing way of Shinrin-yoku Forest Therapy, the medicine of simply being in the forest."

The tree of life is standing central to this painting. Lucy concludes:

> While painting it, I had the feeling that the four elements depicted in the four surrounding paintings come together in the care and sorrow for the tree of life that suffers and is in danger of being cut down. Each of the persons depicted under the tree represents one of the four elements. The earth clothed in red is clinging to the tree. Water in blue is at the foot of the tree and fire in yellow clothes express deep pain. Brother wind, likewise in blue dress, embraces the tree. All are present and help to revive the tree. They are one with the tree that symbolises life, the whole cosmos of living beings.

As the four elements are one with the tree of life, so we are destined to become united with all of creation and to be spiritually one with God and the life of Christ. So, the tree of life will start flowering and we shall experience God's gentle breath of blessing.

Herbal Mandala

> The eye of divine wisdom looks at the earth,
> which nourishes and heals us with its herbs.

With this encouraging picture we would like to come to an end as it gives us a perspective for our work and hope on earth, rooted in the Bible:

> The Lord looked to the earth and filled it with his goods. (Sirach 16:29)

The eye in the middle is followed by plants of the Bible: wheat, grapes, barley, olives, figs, dates and pomegranates. Then follow Ayurvedic medicinal herbs: Amla, Bharmi, Haritakj, Licorice. These are followed by many other herbs and vegetables.

This mandala visualizes our call to keep the earth green, like a fruitful garden which is entrusted by God to humanity – as the Middle Ages saint, Hildegard von Bingen, wrote, "There is a power from eternity and this power is green."

> **Invitation for meditation:** Think and find ways how to preserve the diversity of plants together with bees, insects, butterflies, birds and all the others. Everything grows on earth to nourish and heal people and animals. Biblical wisdom invites us to live in harmony with creation.

The paintings above may encourage readers of this volume and others to perform art that motivates and inspires others, that leaves traces in the consciousness to strengthen the engagement for creation care, so that we act and live according to God's plan – to be Gods good stewards on earth.

Suggestions for Further Reading

Anand Amaladass SJ and Gudrun Löwner: *Christian Themes in Indian Art*, New Delhi 2012, 268-281.
Gudrun Löwner: *Intercultural Dialogue in Art and Religion*, New Delhi 2018, 115-124.
Lucy D'Souza-Krone: *Unterwegs mit Gottvertrauen, mein Leben, meine Bilder*, Altenstadt 2020[4].
Hanna Strack, Pinnow/Schwerin: VIRIDITAS bei Hildegard von Bingen, https://www.hanna-strack.de/user_files/test_1303107939_1778.pdf.

LIST OF CONTRIBUTORS AND EDITORS

Abednego, Nkamuhabwa Keshomshahara, Bishop PhD (Tanzania)
Bishop of the Evangelical Lutheran Church in Tanzania (ELCT), Northwestern Diocese (NWD) along Lake Victoria in Bukoba, Tanzania since 2015. He worked as a lecturer at Tumaini University Makumira, Josiah Kibira University College (2012 -2015), as Vice Principal of the Bukoba Teachers College and as Principal of the Theological College and Bible School at Ruhija (2000-2003).
Contact: abednegokeshomshahara@gmail.com

Agrawal, Sushant, PhD (India)
Director of CASA and Former Moderator of Act Alliance. Contact: sushant@casa-india.org

Amanze, James Prof., PhD (Botswana)
Canon of the Anglican Church of Botswana, former Professor for Systematic Theology at the University of Botswana, currently teaching at St. Augustine Theological School, Gaborone, Botswana. Contact: amanzejames@gmail.com or amanzejn@ub.ac.bw

Anim, Emmanuel, Rev. PhD Prof. (Ghana)
He holds the dual responsibility as the acting Pro-Vice Chancellor and the Director of School of Theology, Ministry, and Leadership at of the Pentecost University in Ghana. He is from the Church of Pentecost in Ghana. Contact: emmanuelanim@yahoo.co.uk

Appiah-Kubi, Seth, PhD (Ghana)
The National Director of A Rocha Ghana. Seth holds a PhD in finance and is a Chartered Management Accountant, a member of Chartered Institute of Management Accountant (CIMA), UK. He has been involved in conservation and the security of natural resources for the past 12 years and has been a key part in formulating the conservation models used by A Rocha Ghana, involving community-based conservation, conservation education and conservation research. Contact: seth.appiah-kubi@arocha.org

Arakawa, Osamu (Japan)
Associate Director of ARI cum Farm Manager. He has been working at ARI since 2001. Contact: osamu@ari-edu.org

Arakawa, Tomoko (Japan)
Director of Asian Rural Institute. She has been working at ARI since 1995 and has served as Director since 2015. Contact: tomoko_arakawa@ari-edu.org

Arriola, Martha (Argentina)
An argentinian, a popular educator, with a degree in Natural Sciences. She is a social psychologist and a student of the Master's Degree in Latin American Theology at the Central American University 'José Simeón Cañas'. She has experience in public policies for community participation in the prevention of violence and youth. Referent of the National Movement of Caregivers of the Common Home. Member of the National Justice and Peace Commission of the Argentine Episcopal Conference. Contact: mmarriola@yahoo.com.ar

Asamoah-Gyadu, J. Kwabena Rev., Prof., PhD, FGA (Ghana)
President and Baeta-Grau Professor of Contemporary African Christianity and Pentecostalism at Trinity Theological Seminary in Legon, Ghana. He has been Senior Research Fellow at the Center for the Study of World Religions, Harvard University (2004) and Schiotz Visiting Professor of African Christianity at the

Luther Seminary, St. Paul, Minnesota, USA (2007). He also served as Senior Scholar in Residence at the Overseas Ministries Study Center, New Haven, USA 2012. Asamoah-Gyadu is an adjunct faculty at the Akrofi-Christaller Institute of Theology, Mission and Culture in Ghana.
Contact: kwabena.asamoahgyadu@gmail.com

Astudillo, Neddy, Prof. PhD (Venezuela/USA)
Pastor of the Presbyterian Church (U. S. A.), an eco-theologian and coordinator for Latin America of the organization: GreenFaith. Contact: neddy@greenfaith.org

Awudi, Emmanuel, Rev. (Ghana)
Adjunct Lecturer at the Pentecost University and a District Pastor with the Church of Pentecost in Ghana. He is a PhD candidate at the Akrofi-Christaller Institute of Theology, Missions and Culture, Akropong, Ghana. Contact: awudi_e@yahoo.com

Bencke, Romi Marcia, Rev. (Brazil)
Pastor of the Evangelical Church of the Lutheran Confession in Brazil (IECLB), general secretary of the National Council of Christian Churches of Brazil and a member of the coordination of the Ecumenical Forum ACT Brazil. Contact: romibencke@gmail.com

Benedict, Barde Cham Rev. (Nigeria)
An ordained Pastor with Lutheran Church of Christ in Nigeria he is a lecturer in the Biblical Theology Department, Bronnum Lutheran Seminary Yola, Nigeria and a PhD student in the Theological College of Northern Nigeria Jos, Nigeria. Contact: barde.benedict@gmail.com

Beros, Daniel Carlos, Prof. PhD (Argentina)
Professor and General Coordinator of the Ecumenical Network of Theological Education (REET, for its initials in Spanish) and Head of its Department of Systematic Theology and Ethics.
Contact: danielberos@gmail.com

Blasi, Márcia, Prof. PhD (Brazil)
Professor in the Faculdades EST; Coordinator of the Program of Gender and Religion. She also leads the Nucleus of Gender Investigation. Contact: retalhos13@hotmail.com

Bookless, Dave, PhD (England/India)
Director of Theology for A Rocha International and co-lead of the global Lausanne / World Evangelical Alliance Creation Care Network. He is also on the Church of England's Environment Working Group and the global Season of Creation Steering Committee. He was born and raised in India and has a deep appreciation for Indian culture and Indian Christianity.

Bosu, Daryl E. (Ghana)
Deputy National Director of A Rocha Ghana. Daryl holds an LLB and postgraduate certificate in Conservation Finance and Green Business Modelling and Finance; advanced certificate in Terrestrial Carbon Accounting and a first degree in Natural Resource Management. He is an Environmental Sustainability and Natural Resource Management Professional. Contact: daryl.bosu@arocha.org

Brown, Edward R., Rev. (USA/Tanzania)
The Lausanne catalyst for creation care. He is also the director and CEO of Care of Creation, guiding its work in the US, Kenya, and Tanzania. Contact: ed@careofcreation.org

Carino, Theresa, PhD (China/Philippines)
Senior Research Consultant and Adviser to the Amity Foundation Nanjing (China) in its international relations. Contact: tccarino@yahoo.com

Chan, Keith Ka-fu, PhD (China)
Professor at the Center for Judaic and Inter-religious Studies, School of Philosophy and Social Development, Shandong University, China. Former work at the Institute of Sino-Christian Studies and Hong Kong Baptist University. Contact: keithchan@sdu.edu.cn

Chris Naylor (Lebanon) †
He was the Executive Director of A Rocha International (2016-2019). He joined A Rocha in 1997 working until 2009 as Lebanon Director, where he cofounded the work. He tragically died in South Africa 2019 due to a car accident

Chunakara, Mathews George, PhD (India/Thailand)
General Secretary of the Christian Conference of Asia (CCA). He was Director of the Commission of the Churches on International Affairs of the World Council of Churches CCIA / WCC) in Switzerland. Contact: mathews@cca.org.hk

Cirigliano-Heffel, Deborah (Argentina)
She is a Graduate in Psychology and co-coordinator of the Pastoral Ministry for the Promotion of Creation Care (PPCC) at Hora de Obrar and a member of the Evangelical Church of River Plate (IERP), living in Paraná, Entre Ríos, Argentina. Contact: deborahciriglianoheffel@hotmail.com

Conradie, Ernst, M., Prof. PhD (South Africa)
Senior Professor in the Department of Religion and Theology at the University of the Western Cape in South Africa. Contact: econradie@uwc.ac.za

Conradie, Sas Rev. Dr. (South Africa, UK)
Tearfund Theology and Networking Manager (Africa). He is a minister in the Dutch Reformed Church in South Africa, focussing on church and community development in Africa, church based economic development, ecology and theological education. Contact: sas.conradie@tearfund.org

Das, David Anirudha, Rev. (Bangladesh)
General Secretary of the National Council of Churches in Bangladesh Dhaka, Bangladesh.
Contact: nccb.gs@gmail.com; www.ncc-b.org fb.com/nccbfanpage

Dohmann, Romario (Argentina)
He is a member of the coordination team of the Pastoral for the Promotion of Creation Care of the Iglesia Evangélica del Río de la Plata (IERP)/ Evangelical Church of the River Plate and is responsible for the Crece Selva Misionera program, developed by the Protestant Diaconia Foundation Hora de Obrar. He also performs the function of general coordinator of the youth of the IERP. He is currently finishing his studies in Forestry Engineering at the National University of Misiones, Argentine Republic.
Contact: romario.dohmann@horadeobrar.org.ar

DU, Qiying, Rev. (China)
Vice Provost of the Academic Affairs Office of Fujian Theological Seminary, He is now studying for a doctorate in the school of philosophy of Renmin University of China. Contact: yueqh3@hotmail.com

Eale, Bosela, Rev., Prof. PhD (Kenya, DRC)
Director for Theology, Interfaith Relations and Ecclesial Leadership Development at the All Africa Conference of Churches (AACC) in Nairobi, Kenya. He is also serving as a co-chair member of African Union (AU) Interfaith Dialogue Forum Steering Committee for Central Africa Region. He served as Vice-Chancellor at International Leadership University in Burundi. He is Associate Professor of Theological Ethics. Contact: boselaeale@aacc-ceta.org

Effungani, Salli Ndombo, Rev., PhD (Kenya, Cameroon)
Programme officer for the programme for Christian-Muslim relations in Africa (PROCMURA) and Lecturer in religious studies (Christian-Muslim relations), also Adjunct lecturer St Paul University, Limuru Kenya. She is an Ordained minister of the Presbyterian Church in Cameroon (PCC) and Member of the Circle of Concerned African Women Theologians.
Contact: ndombosalli@yahoo.com; programmeofficer@procmura.org

El Azzi, Desiree, Prof. PhD (Lebanon)
Associate Professor at the Holy Spirit University of Kaslik. Ph.D. in Hydrology, Hydrochemistry, Soil and Environment. Agricultural Engineer with a specialization in Environmental Quality and Resource Management. Master's degree in Ecosystem Functioning and Anthropization.
Contact: desireeelazzi@usek.edu.lb

Ezekiel, Lesmore Gibson, Rev., PhD, FCAI (Nigeria/Kenya)
Director of Programmes at the AACC / CETA, Nairobi, Kenya. He is an ordained minister of the Lutheran Church of Christ in Nigeria. Fellow, Institute of Corporate Administration. Member, Board of Directors, CORAT-Africa. Contact: lesmore-ger@aacc-ceta.org

Florio, Lucio, Rev. Prof. PhD (Argentina)
Catholic priest serving in parishes of the City of La Plata, Buenos Aires, Argentina. Researcher and teacher at the Faculty of Philosophy and Letters and at the Faculty of Theology of the UCA. He chairs the Foundation "Dialogue between Science and Religion" (DECyR) and the journal Quaerentibus. Theology and Science (www.quaerentibus.org). Contact: lflorio.18@gmail.com

Fonseca, Abiud, Prof. MS. (Ecuador)
Professor of Systematic Theology and Old Testament at the Seminario Sudamericano Semisud. He is a theologian and anthropologist with research on Latin American Pentecostalism and an ordained pastor of the Church of God in Ecuador. Contact: afonseca@semisud.edu.ec

Frouisou, Samuel, Rev. Prof. (Cameroon)
General Secretary and Director of Doctoral School and Head of the Department of History and Religious Sciences of the Faculty of Protestant Theology and Religious Sciences of the Protestant University of Central Africa in Yaoundé-Cameroon. Contact: sfrouisou@gmail.com

Gasparis, Francesca de (South Africa)
Executive Director of the Southern African Faith Communities' Environment Institute (SAFCEI) in Johannesburg. SAFCEI is a multi-faith environmental organization committed to supporting faith leaders and their communities in Southern Africa to increase awareness, understanding and action on eco-justice, sustainable living, and climate change. Contact: francesca@safcei.org.za

Gabaitse, Rosinah Mmannana, Prof. PhD (Botswana)
Senior Lecturer at the UB · Department of Theology and Religious Studies at the University of Botswana in Gaborone- Contact: Gabaitser@UB.AC.BW

Getor, Junita, Rev. (Indonesia)
Ordained Pastor in the Toraja Church, South Sulawesi, in Indonesia. Contact: junitam7@gmail.com

Gichimu, John Njeru, Rev. MA (Kenya)
Archdeacon in the African Independent Pentecostal Church of Africa (AIPCA) which was founded in 1920s in Kenya during the Gikuyu nationalist movements. He has worked at the organization of African Instituted Churches (OAIC) in Nairobi since 1995 as a Facilitator for Theological Education by Extension (TEE) and currently is the Director Programme for Theology and Ministerial Formation. Contact: gichimu@oaic.org

Gobena, Abate, Fr. (Ethiopia)
Lecturer at Sankt Ignatios College (Stockholm School of Theology), PhD Candidate at University College Stockholm, and serving priest of the Ethiopian Orthodox Tewahido Church in UK & Sweden. He worked as a Coordinator of Integrated Rural Development Projects (IRDPs) at EOC-DICAC in Ethiopia; Rural Policy Intern at campaign to Protect Rural England (CPRE) in London, UK.
Contact: abate.gobena@sanktignatios.org

González-Ortega, Dan, Prof. PhD (Mexico)
Doctor of Theology (PhD), pastor of the Mexican Communion of Reformed and Presbyterian Churches (CMIRP) and Professor of Bible and Biblical Hermeneutics at the Latin American Faculty of Reformed Theology (FLATER). He is also rector of the Theological Community of Mexico (CTdeM), Executive Secretary of the Community of Ecumenical Theological Education of Latin America and the Caribbean (CETELA). Contact: rectoria@comunidadteologica.org.mx

Ham, Carlos, Rev, Prof. PhD (Cuba)
Pastor of the Presbyterian-Reformed Church in Cuba for more than forty years. Former Executive Staff of the World Council of Churches' (WCC) for Diakonia & Latin America-Caribbean. Currently Rector and Professor of Mission and Diakonia at the Matanzas Evangelical Seminary of Theology in Cuba. Contact: cehams@gmail.com

Han, Kyeong Ho, Rev. (South Korea)
An ordained pastor active in the ecological movement of Korean churches and a key representative of the 'Korea Christian Life-giving Agriculture Forum'. He is an editor of the theological journal of 'Rural Society and Ministry'. Contact: jagafocus@yonsei.ac.kr

Hanna-Wakim, Lara, Prof., PhD (Lebanon)
National Coordinator of the "Faith for Earth Initiative" at the United Nations for Environment Program (UNEP). Professor of Sustainable Food Systems and Global Food Security at the Holy Spirit University of Kaslik, Ph.D. in Food Process Engineering, Diploma in Agricultural Engineering, Master's Degree in Food Quality Assurance and Management. Contact: larahanna@usek.edu.lb.

Hutcherson, Caleb (Lebanon)
Lecturer in historical theology at the Arab Baptist Theological Seminary in Beirut, Lebanon, PhD candidate researching the practice of theological reflection in the MENA region.
Contact: chutcherson@abtslebanon.org.

Immanuel, Jimmy Marcos, Rev. (Indonesia)
Pastor of the Protestant Church in Western Indonesia. He currently works as an Executive Secretary of Communion of Churches in Indonesia (CCI) who is responsible for Witness and Integrity of Creation desk. He is active in interfaith dialogues and as co-founder of some interfaith and ecological platforms in Indonesia. Contact: jimmysormin@gmail.com

Isaak, Paul John, Prof. PhD (Namibia)
Retired Professor at the University of Namibia; Periods as Visiting Professor at *Kirchliche Hochschule* in Wuppertal, Germany, at the Wartburg Theological Seminary in Dubuque, Iowa, USA and at Makumira University College, Arusha, Tanzania. He also was Professor of Missiology at the Ecumenical Institute Bossey, Geneva, Switzerland, affiliated to the University of Geneva. He was the Chief Electoral Officer and Director of Elections at the Electoral Commission of Namibia from 2013-2018. Since 2019 he is the Rector of the United Lutheran Theological Seminary-Paulinum in Windhoek.
Contact: profisaak@yahoo.com

Ishola-Esan, Helen, Rev., Prof. PhD (Nigeria)
Associate Professor in the Department of Christian Education and has served as the Head of Department as well as the Dean of the Faculty of Education in the Nigerian Baptist Theological Seminary, Ogbomoso, Nigeria. She is currently the President of Baptist Theological Seminary, Eku, Nigeria. She is a member of Council for Association of Christian Theological Education in Africa (ACTEA) and also a member of some professional bodies such as African Association for the Study of Religions (AASR); Society Professors in Christian Education (SPCE); International Professional Managers Association (IPMA) and a Certified International Professional Manager (CIPM). Contact: helenisholaesan@gmail.com

Jianrong, Wu, Dr. (China)
Director-General of YMCA of Shanghai and Director-General of National Councils of YMCAs of China.
Contact: jianrw@hotmail.com

Kadiva, Ernest William, Rev., Dr. (Tanzania)
The United Evangelical Mission (UEM) Deputy Executive Secretary for the Africa region and ordained pastor of the Evangelical Lutheran Church in Tanzania Eastern and Coastal Diocese since August 2002. In 2014 he was a member of Tanzania special parliament assembly for constitutional review. Rev. Kadiva is conducting missional leadership training programs for clergy and lay ministers.
Contact: revkadiva@hotmail.com; kadiva-e@vemission.org

Kahongya, Bwiruka Kambale J.-B., Rev., Prof. Dr. (Dem. Rep. Congo)
Ordained pastor of the Baptist Church in Central Africa (CBCA), PhD in Intercultural Theology and Missiology at the Kirchliche Hochschule Wuppertal/Bethel in Germany. Professor in Universities and UEM-Advocacy Officer for Africa Region.
Contact: Kahongya-K@vemission.org; Kahongyabwiruka1@gmail.com

Kalimba, Jered, Rt Rvd. Dr. (Rwanda)
Bishop of Shyogwe Diocese since June 1997 up to now and Dean of Bishops since 2018 in Anglican Church of Rwanda. He is also Lecturer of Contextual Ethics in Protestant Institute of Arts and Sciences (PIASS) at Huye and the Anglican College at Kigali named: East African Christian College (EACC). He is a Member of Protestant Council of Rwanda (CPR) and President of RDIS (Rural and Development Inter-Diocesan Service). Contact: kalimbaj60@yahoo.fr

Kamaara, Eunice, Prof. PhD (Kenya)
Professor of African Christian Ethics at Moi University, Eldoret, Kenya. She is an ethicist with over thirty-year experience in holistic health development participatory research and practice. She has consulted for the All Africa Conference of Churches (AACC), World Council of Churches (WCC), the World Bank, United States Agency for International Development (USAID), the United Nations Population Fund (UNFPA), Templeton World Charity Foundation Inc. (TWCF), and Institute of Development Studies/Partnership for African Social Governance Research (PASGR). Eunice is Presbyterian by birth, Roman Catholic by marriage and Catholic by choice. Contact: ekamaara@gmail.com

Khai, Ciin Sian Dr. theol. (Myanmar)
Is Academic Dean, Zomi Theological Seminary, Kalaymyo, Myanmar; Pastor Suang Khen Pau is the Assistant Pastor of Emmanuel Baptist Church in Kalaymyo. He earned a Master of Sacred Theology from Dallas Theological Seminary

Kivatsi, Kavusa Jonathan, Prof. PhD (DRC Congo)
He is an Alexander von Humboldt Research Fellow at *Humboldt Universität zu Berlin.* Kivatsi is also Research Associate in the Department of Old Testament and Hebrew Scriptures at the Faculty of Theology and Religion of the University of Pretoria. He teaches Old Testament at the Faculty of Theology of the *Université Libre des Pays des Grands Lacs*. Contact: jokakiv@yahoo.fr

Kondemo, Marthe Maleke, Rev., Dr. (DRC Congo)
An ordained pastor of the United Evangelical Churches of Lulonga (CADELU), DRC she completed her PhD at the university of Pretoria, South Africa. Contact: marthemaleke@yahoo.fr

Kureethadam, Joshtrom Isaac, PhD Fr. (India/Italy)
Co-ordinator of the "Ecology and Creation" Sector in the Vatican Dicastery for Promoting Integral Human Development. He is also Chair of Philosophy of Science and Director of the Institute of Social and Political Sciences in the Faculty of Philosophy at the Salesian Pontifical University in Rome.
Contact: j.kureethadam@humandevelopment.va

LAI, Pan-chiu (LAI Pinchao 賴品超), Prof. PhD (China)
Professor in the Department of Cultural and Religious Studies, The Chinese University of Hong Kong.

LI, Xinnong (China) is an assistant editor of *Nanjing Theological Review* and lecturer in Old Testament field, Nanjing Theological Seminary. Contact: 1649788140@qq.com

Liu, Ruomin Rev. PhD. (China/Germany)
Head of Studies at Missionsakademie of University Hamburg and Professor of Systematic Theology at Nanjing Theological Seminary, China.
Contact: ruomin.liu@missionsakademie.de, ruomin.liu@foxmail.com;

Lu, Ms. Yifan (China)
An Ordained Pastor in Chuzhou in China she is now a doctoral candidate at Missionsakademie of University of Hamburg, Germany

Madi, Hauwa Eve Abadi (Nigeria, USA)
Lecturer in the Department of Biblical Studies, Theological College of Northern Nigeria (TCNN) Jos, Plateau State Nigeria; Doctoral student at Luther Seminary, Saint Paul, Minesota, MN, USA.
Contact: evehauwa4bornagain@yahoo.com

Magezi, El hajj Abdel Nasser (Uganda)
Co-chair of the African Interfaith Youth Network (AIYN) of Religion for Peace together with Agathe Mossane Sagne (2016 – 2021). Working with Uganda Interfaith Youth Network (UIYN).

Mapangdol, Gloria Lita, Rev. Dr. (Philippines)
President and Dean of St. Andrew's Theological Seminary (SATS), Quezon City, Philippines. She is also an ordained priest of the Episcopal Church in the Philippines and teaching New Testament courses at SATS.
Contact: gloriamapangdol@yahoo.com

Maseno, Loreen, PhD (South Africa)
Senior Lecturer Department of Religion, Theology and Philosophy and Research Fellow, Department of Ancient and Biblical studies, UNISA. Contact: loreenmas@gmail.com

Mash, Rachel, Rev. Dr. (South Africa)
Environmental Coordinator of the Anglican Church of Southern Africa (South Africa, Eswatini, Lesotho, Namibia, Mozambique and Angola). Contact: rmash@mweb.co.za

Matshobane, Mangaliso, Rev. (South Africa)
The founder and an ordained Apostle of an Independent Pentecostal Church, named Community Church, based in South Africa. A board member of a professional body for clergy in South Africa called an Association for Christian Religious Practitioners (ACRP, acrpafrica.co.za). He also is a PhD graduate in Practical Theology at the University of Pretoria in South Africa, PhD research on Pastoral Succession in Independent Pentecostal Churches. Contact: matshobane@gmail.com

Michelin Salomon, Álvaro Rev., Prof. PhD (Uruguay/Argentina)
A Waldensian Pastor, Doctor of Theology from the University Institute – ISEDET (Buenos Aires) and Professor of Practical Theology at the Ecumenical Network of Theological Education (REET). He studied at the Protestant Faculty of Theology at the University of Tübingen, Germany.
Contact: alvaro.michelin.salomon@gmail.com

Míguez, Néstor, Rev., Prof. PhD (Argentina)
Pastor and Emeritus Professor of Biblical Hermeneutics and Systematic Theology from ISEDET, Buenos Aires. He has been president of the Argentine Federation of Evangelical Churches

Miselis Solano, Jocabed (Panamá)
The author belongs to the Gunadule nation of Panama. She was born in the time of medicinal plants, she is the director of Memoria Indígena and completed a master's degree in interdisciplinary theology at the Community of Interdisciplinary Theological Studies (CETI) and at Carey Theological College of Canada. Contact: playerjrsm@gmail.com

Mok, Bryan K. M., Prof. PhD (China)
Research Associate in the Centre for the Study of Religious Ethics and Chinese Culture, the Chinese University of Hong Kong (CUHK) and a Part-Time Lecturer in the Divinity School of Chung Chi College, CUHK. Contact: kiemanbryanmok@cuhk.edu.hk

Moon, Jung Eun Grace, Rev. (South Korea)
Program coordinator of the Christian Conference of Asia and an ordained pastor of the Presbyterian Church of Korea. Grace Moon works to empower youth and women in CCA constituencies through theological education and leadership development initiatives and strengthen an active network of ecumenical theologians and theological educators in Asia. Contact: gracemoon@cca.org.hk

Mpofu, Buhle Rev. PhD (South Africa, Zimbabwe)
Lecturer of Religion and Mission studies within the Faculty of Theology and Religion at the University of Pretoria in South Africa. Mpofu did his Post-Doctoral Fellowship with the University of KwaZulu-Natal, School of Religion, Classics and Philosophy and is also an ordained minister with the Uniting Presbyterian Church in Southern Africa (UPCSA). He served as the General Secretary of the African Communion of Reformed Churches (ACRC). Contact: buhle.mpofu@up.ac.za

Naibaho, Jhon Kristo, Rev. (Indonesia)
An ordained pastor of HKBP (Protestant Christian Batak Church). Having completed his doctoral studies at STFT Jakarta (Jakarta Theological Seminary) in the field of ethics he serves as Head of Research and Development Agency of the HKBP. Contact: jhonkristo@gmail.com

Nassif, Bassam, Fr., Prof. PhD (Lebanon)
Associate Professor of Pastoral Theology and Marriage Counseling at the Saint John of Damascus Institute of Theology, University of Balamand. Contact: bnassif@balamand.edu.lb

Nduye, Gabriel Ezekia, Rev. PhD (Tanzania)
He works with the Evangelical Lutheran Church in Tanzania (ELCT) Southern Diocese (SD) in different capacities such as an ordained Minister and Director for the Centre for Agricultural Development (CAD) and Lecturer at Amani College of Management and Technology (ACMT) in Njombe region of Tanzania. Contact: gabriel.nduye2@gmail.com

Newman, Las, PhD (Jamaica)
Lausanne Global Associate Director for Regions and Regional Director for the Caribbean. He organized and hosted the first Lausanne Global Consultation on Creation Care and the Gospel in Jamaica in 2012. He used to serve also as president of the Caribbean Graduate School of Theology.

Norval, María Esther (Argentina)
María Esther Norval retired from the National Highway Administration of the Argentine Republic, Río Negro Regional, where she served for 33 years as Executive Secretary of the Presidency. She has a degree in Social Work, a member of the Evangelical Church of the Río de la Plata. Secretary of the Board of Directors of the Protestant Diakonia Foundation *Hora de Obrar*. Contact: maria_norval@hotmail.com

Nuriadin, Ade (Indonesia)
Lecturer, independent filmmaker, and founder of the Tana Sanggamu Institute, focusing on economic, social, cultural, and environmental issues after the disasters that occurred in Palu, Sigi and Donggala in Indonesia

Orevillo-Montenegro, Muriel, PhD (Philippines)
The first female Dean of Silliman University Divinity School's Faculty. She also is a lay feminist theologian, teacher-learner, and gardener. She was the coordinator of Silliman's Justice and Peace Center. She is a member of the Association of Women in Theology in the Philippines and the Asian Women's Resource Centre. She co-founded the Philippine Ecumenical Peace Platform (PEPP) that pioneered in calling the Government of the Republic of the Philippines and the National Democratic Front of the Philippines to resume the peace. Contact: muriel.orevillomontenegro@gmail.com

Ortiz Roca, Humberto (Perú)
Assistant to the President of the Peruvian Episcopal Conference, member of the team "Nuevas Economías y Buen Vivir" of the Secretariat for Latin America and the Caribbean of Caritas (SELACC).
Contact: apresidente@iglesiacatolica.org.pe

Oviedo, Lorena Prof. (Argentina)
Professor of Theology and Pastoral Care with a lay orientation from the Catholic Institute of Teachers of Córdoba. She teaches at the General Paz Military Lyceum, and at the Ntra. Sra. Del Valle School. She is treasurer of the "Dialogue between Science and Religion (DeCyR) Foundation and secretary of the magazine Quaerentibus-Theology and Sciences (www.quaerentibus.org), also a member of the "Permanent

Seminary of Theology, Philosophy, Science and Technology" of the Faculty of Theology of the UCA, Contact: lvoviedo12@gmail.com

PAE, Chong-hun, Rev. Dr. Prof. (South Korea)
An Ordained Pastor of the Presbyterian Church of Korea and Old Testament Scholar with a Ph.D, from Graduate Theological Union, USA. He was former faculty member at Daejeon Theological University, Korea, and presently is teaching Old Testament at the Presbyterian University & Theological Seminary, Korea. Contact: chpae25@puts.ac.kr

Park, Seong Won, Prof. PhD (South Korea)
Professor of Youngnam Theological College and Seminary in Gyeongsan, Korea. Also since 2017 he is president of Gyeongan Graduate University in Andong, which is the capital of Korean Spiritual Culture and Neo-Confuzian tradition. He also was a Central Committee member of World Council of Churches. He is a prominent theologian, and ecumenical activist and pioneer for ecumenical formation for theology of life and social transformation. Park also serves at the Ecumenical Committee of the Presbyterian Church of Korea and in CCA. Contact: parkswon@gmail.com

Pérez Vela, Rolando (Perú)
Rolando Pérez-Vela is a sociologist and social communicator, researcher in the field of media and religion, associate professor at the Pontifical Catholic University of Peru (PUCP), director of the Peace and Hope Institute. Contact: rperez@pucp.edu.pe

Perkins, Anna Prof. PhD (Jamaika)
As a Jamaican Roman Catholic theologian she is adjunct faculty at St Michael's Theological College and Seminary, and senior programme officer in the Quality Assurance Unit at The University of the West Indies, Regional Headquarters, Jamaica. Contact: anna.perkins@uwimona.edu.jm

Pesha, Modest, Rev. (Tanzania)
National Coordinator of Action of Churches Together (ACT Alliance), National Tanzania Forum.
Contact: modestpesha@yahoo.com

Pioli, Javier (Uruguay)
Graduated in Theology from the University Institute – ISEDET and in history (secondary school teacher) from the Instituto de Profesores Artigas. He currently works as the theological secretary at the *Centro Emmanuel* (Colonia Valdense, Uruguay) and teaches in secondary and technical-professional education. He is a member of the Evangelical Waldensian Church of the River Plate.
Contact: teologia@centroemmanuel.org

Purba, Jenny, Rev. PhD (Indonesia)
An ordained Pastor of the Simalungun Protestant Christian Church (GKPS) in North Sumatera, Indonesia. A Doctor of Diaconic Science from Institute of Diakonic Management Bethel, Germany.
Contact: purbajenny@yahoo.co.id

Qian, Tiezheng (China)
Staff of the Research Department of YMCA and YWCA of Shanghai. His main research interests include religious sociology, religious policy and social participation of religious groups.
Contact: bridgestoneq@hotmail.com

Quispe, Sofía Nicolasa Chipana (Bolivia)
Sofía Chipana Quispe is Aymara from Bolivia. She is a Member of the Community of Wise Women and Indigenous Theologians of Abya Yala, and of the Andean Theology and Pastoral Community of Peru, Bolivia and Argentina. Contact: warmi_pacha@hotmail.com

Rao, Vasantha Chilkuri, Rev. Prof. PhD (India)
Professor in the Department of Biblical Studies (Old Testament) and Principal of the United Theological College, Bengaluru, India. He is an ordained Presbyter of the Church of South India and member of the Society of Biblical Literature, Atlanta, USA. Contact: utcvasantharao@gmail.com

Ribeiro, Claudio de Olivera Prof. PhD (Brazil)
Methodist pastor and professor of Religious Sciences at the Federal University of Juiz de Fora (Brazil). Contact: cdeoliveiraribeiro@gmail.com

Rojas Salazar, Marilú, Prof. PhD (México)
Doctor in Systematic Theology from the Catholic University of Louvain, Belgium. She is a Feminist theologian and Professor at the Ibero-American University of Mexico City and the Department of Religious Sciences. She is also a professor at the Theological Community of Mexico. Contact: saroma24@gmail.com

Sagne, Agathe Mossane (Senegal)
The Youth Representative in African Council of Religious Leaders-Religions for Peace. She is a Senegalese by nationality who comes from a strong Catholic family. Her career started with the young catholic students (YCS) where she also joined the YCS National Team of Senegal in 2007. From being Secretary in charge of Information, communication and documentation, she ended up being responsible for projects and programs after being in charge of training at national Level. She also worked with YCS at the university level and currently serves as regional coordinator of IYCS Africa. Contact: agathasagne@gmail.com

Salazar-Sanzana, Elizabeth, Prof. PhD (Chile)
A Chilean theologian and pedagogue. PhD, Methodist University of Sao Paulo, she is a member of ASETT, FTL and the Christian Unity Commission of the Pentecostal World Fellowship. Professor of Theology at the Evangelical Theological Community of Chile, and at other Latin American institutions.
Contact: draelizabethsalazar@gmail.com

Satigi, Irna, Rev. (Indonesia)
Ordained pastor in the Central Sulawesi church (GKST) and a lecturer in UKDW (Duta Wacana Christian University) in Yogyakarta, Java in Indonesia. Contact: irnawati_satigi@yahoo.com

Schwittay, Ruth (Argentina)
Secondary level teacher, former catechist, translator, retired, member of the Evangelical Church of the River Plate (IERP), living in CABA, Argentina. Contact: ruthsch@gmail.com

Setume, Senzokuhle Doreen, PhD (Botswana)
Lecturer in the Department of Theology and Religious Studies at the University of Botswana. She teaches courses such as African Indigenous Religions, Religions of Botswana, Religion and Science, Research methodology. Contact: okuhlessd@gmail.com, setumesd@ub.ac.bw

Similox Salazar, Vitalino, Prof. PhD (Guatemala)
Maya kaqchikel. Presbyterian Pastor. Protestant theologian. Ph.D. in Sociology. Collaborator in the organization of the Mayan universities in Guatemala. First Rector of the Maya Ixil University and current Rector of the Maya Kaqchikel University, Chimaltenango, Guatemala. Contact: vsimilox@yahoo.com

Simon, Benita (Guatemala)
An indigenous woman from the Maya Kaqchikel people of Guatemala, specialized in care, restoration and environmental education issues. She is currently the coordinator of the Environment Program of the Fundación Centro Esdras. In addition she coordinates local advocacy projects in her hometown with the Rujotay organization. Contact: benita@centroesdras.org

Strizzi, Marisa, Prof. PhD (Argentina)
Professor in the Ecumenical Network for Theological Education (REET), where she coordinates the Department of Theology and Interdisciplinary Studies. Contact: strizzimarisa@gmail.com

Su, Tong (China)
Project Coordinator of Amity Foundation Hong Kong. She began to work for Amity in 1992 and has accumulated extensive knowledge, skills and network in the field of social development work.
Contact: tongsu@amityfoundation.org

Sugito, Petrus, Rev (Indonesia)
An ordained pastor of GKJTU or Javanese Protestant Church from North Central Java. Currently working in United Evangelical Mission as Deputy Executive Secretary for Asia. Contact: Sugito-P@vemission.org

Takure, Sostina (Zimbabwe)
An experienced development practitioner with many years of working in the non-profit organization management industry and in strategic planning and program development, currently serving as the ACT Zimbabwe Coordinator.

Tayviah, Margaret Makafui, PhD. (Ghana)
Lecturer in the Department of Religious Studies at the Kwame Nkrumah University of Science and Technology (KNUST), Kumasi-Ghana. She is a member and currently the Area Advisor of the Ghana Committee as well as the Anglophone West Africa coordinator of the Programme for Christian-Muslim Relations in Africa (PROCMURA), which has its Central Office in Nairobi-Kenya.
Contact: makafui2007jub@yahoo.com

Thorat, Joycia, PhD (India)
Project Officer and National Gender Focal Point of CASA in India
Contact: joycia@casa-india.org

Togarasei, Lovemore, PhD (Zimbabwe/Botswana)
Professor and Programme Leader at Zimbabwe Open University in the Department of Religious Studies and Philosophy, teaching courses in Biblical Studies. Contact: ltogarasei@gmail.com

Turkson, Emmanuel (Ghana)
Creation Care Officer at A Rocha Ghana. B.Sc. in Entomology and Wildlife from the University of Cape Coast. Bachelor's Degree in Biblical Studies from the American Bible University (Ghana Campus). Facilitated interfaith dialogues to promote environmental action, climate change and biodiversity conservation. Contact: emmanuel.turkson@arocha.org

Umuziranenge, Gloriose, PhD (Rwanda)
Head of Department of Natural Resources and Environmental Management at Protestant Institute of Arts and Social Sciences (PIASS) in Rwanda. Contact: u.gloriose@gmail.com

Vaai, Upolu Luma, PhD (Samoa)
Principal and Professor of Theology & Ethics at the Pacific Theological College, Suva, Fiji, the first and only tertiary regional ecumenical institution of the Pasifika churches since 1965. Contact: ulvaai@ptc.ac.fj

Valério G. Schaper, Prof. PhD (Brazil)
Professor in the Faculdades EST; Coordinator of the Institute of Sustainability for Latin America and the Caribbean. He also leads the Nucleus of Investigation on Human Rights and the Nucleus of Studies on Contemporary Ethics. Contact: valerio@est.edu.br

Valverde Campos, Juan Carlos, Prof. PhD (Costa Rica)
Professor of the Ecumenical School of Religious Sciences of the National University of Costa Rica. He obtained a Bachelor of Theology and a Master of Biblical Theology from the Catholic Institute of Paris and a doctorate in Philosophy of Religion from the University of Strasbourg, France.
Contact: juancavalcam@hotmail.com; juan.valverde.campos@una.cr

van Andel, Arianne Rev. MS. (Holland/Chile)
A Dutch eco-theologian from the reformed tradition, Coordinator of Training in the organization Otros Cruces (Other Crossings) and of the Interreligious and Spiritual Alliance for the Climate (AIEC) in Chile. Organizational Coach. Fellow of GreenFaith. Teacher of Theology in the "Comunidad Teológica Evangélica" (CTE) and the Methodist Seminary in Santiago de Chile and activist in the Civil Society for Climate Action network (SCAC) and the "Mesa Ciudadana sobre Cambio Climático".
Contact: ariannevanandel@gmail.com

van Saane, Wilbert (Lebanon)
Assistant professor of systematic theology and mission at the Near East School of Theology and lecturer in religion at Haigazian University. Contact: wilbert.vansaane@haigazian.edu.lb

Vargas, Laura (Perú)
Laura Vargas is Executive Secretary of the Interreligious Council of Peru-Religions for Peace and Coordinator of the Interfaith Rainforest Initiative, IRI-Peru.
Contact: laurav1948@gmail.com; laura.vargas@interfaithrainforest.org

Varkey, Mothy, Rev. Dr (India)
Ordained priest of the Malankara Mar Thoma Church, India. He is Professor of New Testament at the Mar Thoma Theological Seminary, Kerala, India. He is also a visiting fellow at the Murdoch University, Perth, Australia. Contact: mothy1234@yahoo.com

Weiler, Birgit, Prof. PhD (Perú/Germany)
A member of the Congregation of Medical Missionary Sisters, of German nationality, and has lived in Peru since 1988. She is a theologian and professor in the Department of Theology at the Pontifical Catholic University of Peru (PUCP). She is also a member of the team of theologians of the Episcopal Council of Latin America (CELAM) and of the Ecumenical Dialogue Team of the Pan-Amazonian Ecclesial Network (REPAM). Contact: weiler.mms@gmail.com

Weishein, Jorge Rev. (Argentina)
A theologian and social worker, pastor of the Evangelical Church of the River Plate (IERP), member of the coordination team of the Pastoral for the Promotion of Creation Care (PPCC) and of the team of the Protestant Foundation of Diakonia *Hora de Obrar*. Contact: jorge.weishein@horadeobrar.org.ar

Werner, Dietrich, Rev. Prof. PhD Dr. h.c. (Germany)
Head of Theology and Ecumenism Desk at Bread for the World, Berlin. An Ordained pastor of Evangelical-Lutheran Church in Northern Germany. Former Director of Ecumenical Theological Education Program (ETE) at WCC Geneva and Director of Studies in Missionsacademy at the University of Hamburg, Chair of Religion and Development Working Group (CoPRD) at ACT Alliance. Guest Researcher at Humboldt University Berlin; Research Program on Religious Communities and Sustainable Development.
Contact: dietrich.werner@brot-fuer-die-welt.de; dietrich.werner@hu-berlin.de

Yue, Rebecca (China)
Director of student Affairs in Fujian Theological Seminary. She is now studying for a master's degree at the Hong Kong Lutheran Theological Seminary.

Zachariah, George, PhD (New Zealand)
He serves the Trinity Methodist Theological College, Auckland, Aotearoa New Zealand as Wesley Lecturer in Theological Studies. He has also served at the Gurukul Lutheran Theological College and Research Institute, Chennai, India and the United Theological College, Bengaluru, India.
Contact: gzachariahk@gmail.com

Section I

Biblical and Theological Foundations For Creation Care and Eco-Diakonia

PART I: AFRICA AND THE MIDDLE EAST

1. CHRISTIAN STEWARDSHIP AND CREATION: AFRICAN PERSPECTIVES ON ENVIRONMENT AND DEVELOPMENT

J. Kwabena Asamoah-Gyadu[1]

Preamble

The evangelical Christianity community, through its scholarship, has become quite concerned about creation care over the last three decades.[2] The current distress of the earth and the human awakening to it is now becoming an important theological theme. At Harvard University, between 1996 and 1998, a series of conferences on "religions of the world and ecology" were hosted by the University's Center for the Study of World Religions. The proceedings relating to Christianity and Ecology were published in a huge volume of more than six hundred pages. Elizabeth A. Johnson in the first article of the volume makes certain observations; I suggest that these lay the foundation of any discussion relating the issues of creation and earth care from Christian perspectives:

> The Christian scriptures, while focused on life in Christ, bear rich themes that are implicitly earth-affirming: incarnation, where the Word becomes flesh and so enters into the living matter of this world; resurrection of the body, signifying an eternal worth to the flesh; eucharistic sharing, in which bread and wine made from grain and grape usher the assembled people into communion with the Divine; and hope, that the future will bring on a cosmic scale the gracious redemption that has already occurred in Christ, the firstborn of all creation.[3]

In this article, we examine the Christian theology of stewardship as it relates to creation. In his book *Divine Action: Examining God's Role in an Open and Emergent Universe,* Keith Ward writes that "God creates the universe with the structure it has for a purpose – because that structure will have the best chance of achieving the particular set of unique goods [God] has in mind."[4] Ward continues to note that there is constraint on Divine action, as far as creation is concerned because the Divine, as he puts it, "must normally operate within the possibilities inherent in the structure God has created."[5] A former head of the Methodist

---

[1] J. Kwabena Asamoah-Gyadu, PhD, FGA, is President and Baeta-Grau Professor of Contemporary African Christianity and Pentecostalism at Trinity Theological Seminary in Legon, Ghana. Professor Asamoah-Gyadu studied at the Trinity Theological Seminary, Ghana; the University of Ghana, Legon; and the University of Birmingham, UK (PhD, Theology, 2000). He has been Senior Research Fellow at the Center for the Study of World Religions, Harvard University (2004) and Schiotz Visiting Professor of African Christianity at the Luther Seminary, St. Paul, Minnesota, USA (2007). In 2012, he served as Senior Scholar in Residence at the Overseas Ministries Study Center, New Haven, USA. Prof. Asamoah-Gyadu is also an adjunct faculty at the Akrofi-Christaller Institute of Theology, Mission and Culture in Ghana. Contact: kwabena.asamoahgyadu@gmail.com.

[2] See the following articles: Dana L. Robert, "Historical Trends in Missions and Earth Care"; M.L. Daneel, "Christian Mission and Earth-Care: An African Case Study"; Charles Sorley, "Christ, Creation Stewardship, and Missions: How Discipleship into a Biblical Worldview on Environmental Stewardship Can Transform People and their Land." *International Bulletin of Missionary Research,* Vol. 35, 3 (July 2011), 123-128; 130-136; 137-140.

[3] Elizabeth A. Johnson, "Losing and Finding Creation in the Christian Tradition," in Dieter T. Hessel and Rosemary Radford Reuther (eds), *Christianity and Ecology: Seeking the Wellbeing of Earth and Humans* (Cambridge, MA: Harvard University Press, 2000), 5.

[4] Keith Ward, *Divine Action: Examining God's Role in an Open and Emergent Universe* (Philadelphia and London: Templeton Foundation Press, 1990, 2007), 119.

[5] Ward, *Divine Action,* 119.

Church Ghana, advising local parishes on the judicious utilisation of land in putting up church structures admonished that "God is not creating more land."[6] In other words, God is constrained by the fact that he has already created the land he wants to create and therefore the church must apply Divine wisdom in the utilisation of what is already there.

Already, by the end of the twentieth century, both the Catholic and historic Protestant mission and Orthodox churches had had adopted a theology of justice, peace, and integrity of creation as critical to "the nature of Christian witness" through the ministry of the World Council of Churches.[7] At the heart of the intersection between creation and care is the issue of stewardship of the earth, a theological issue that ought to have as its primary motivation God's agenda of flourishing for all of humanity. This much is clear from the dominion mandate that God gave to humanity at creation:

> Be fruitful and multiply, and fill the earth and subdue it; and have dominion over the fish of the sea and over the birds of the air and over every living thing that moves upon the earth (Genesis 1:28).

Our discussion on the stewardship of creation is warranted precisely because of the misapplication of this dominion mandate by which the earth has been exploited in self-centred ways turning that which God saw as good into a monster that is now hunting humanity through hurricanes, flash floods, mudslides, and the outbreak of pandemics such as COVID-19.

The Earth is the Lord's

The evolutionary view of creation normally explains its existence without reference to the existence of God. This has implications for Christian stewardship and environmental care. In the biblical view of stewardship and creation care, the position is that for humanity to be able to enjoy the blessing of God's creation for sustainable development, there must be conscious recognition of the Divine ownership of creation. The "history of agricultural missions" according to Dana L. Robert, is replete with stories of missionaries increasing local capacities for food production through modern farming methods and the planting drought-resistant seed varieties. Robert articulates the contribution of agricultural missions to environment care and stewardship as follows:

> Agricultural missionaries introduced crop rotation, contour ridges, and reforestation projects, even as their efforts enabled missions to be self-sustaining in food production. They typically saw their work as integral to the missionary message of abundant life through conversion to Jesus Christ.[8]

Despite this sensitivity to environmental conservation as part of a theology of the ownership of the earth as Divine, there is the other side of the equation in which the demonisation of traditional beliefs by missionaries undermined natural reverence for creation. One of the issues raised in this presentation is the historical importance of traditional African beliefs in the environment as delivered to humanity by a Supreme Being with various earth-bound deities as its custodians. The environment had a divine presence and the exploitation of forests and rivers was governed and protected by various taboos. Christian missions working in non-Western contexts disregarded traditional beliefs that contributed immensely to creation care from a primal religious viewpoint, without substituting it with a Christian alternative.

---

[6] The late Most Rev. Dr. Samuel Asante-Antwi was President of the Trinity Theological Seminary (1985-1990) and Presiding Bishop of the Methodist Church Ghana (1999-2005). He made this statement several times as head of the Methodist Church Ghana.

[7] Robert, "Historical Trends in Mission and Earth Care," 123.

[8] Robert, "Historical Trends in Missions and Earth Care," 125.

If stewardship of the earth is carried out with the consciousness that the earth is the Lord's, there will be concerted efforts to take care of the environment. The thesis of these reflections is that creation – defined as the natural order and all that is in it including humanity – is both the gift and handiwork of God. The implication of this theological position is that Christian stewardship ought to include environmental care for development and flourishing because, as Robert rightly points out, a theology of prosperity and God's blessing can become an excuse for personal greed that undermines the sanctity of creation.[9]

Africa, the Bible, and Environmental Care

In Africa, as in other non-Western contexts, environmental degradation has contributed consistently and immensely to endemic poverty; poverty, in turn, has had a dehumanising effect on people.[10] A major criticism often levelled against Christianity in Africa is its inability to translate spirituality into ways that impact everyday lives in practical ways. Environmental stewardship does not feature in Christian theological education, Bible studies, and preaching in any meaningful way. Where it exists, the environment and creation would at best be listed as a subject in theology or religion and development. However, with climate change and discussions of the need for environmental preservation, African theologians are now beginning to come to terms with this lacuna. In recent years, some efforts have also been made to reflect on the intersections between the Bible and theology on one side and stewardship of the environment as part of Christian education on the other.[11]

The disconnection between our theology of stewardship and environmental care is outlined by African biblical scholar, Benjamin A. Ntreh as follows:

> To a very large extent Christians have compartmentalised their lives. They read the Bible in church and sometimes in their homes, but they live their lives separate from what is read in the Bible… This is the reason for my call to make our voices accessible to the church so that we can influence the lifestyles of the members of the church about the relationship with the land.[12]

It is ironic that although conservative evangelical Christians generally reject the theories of evolution as accounting for the origins of the universe, our belief in God as creator has not necessarily translated into the stewardship of creation. In view of the severity of the situation, Jürgen Moltmann goes as far as to call for the prosecution of crimes against the natural environment, suggesting that "these possibilities can be actualised if we want a globalisation of human responsibility, and not only an extension of the human power to dominate."[13] In my thinking, the problem is with the reduction of a Divine mandate to exercise dominion into a human right of access to nature in an aggressive and selfish manner. The commercialisation of the natural order and the desire to exploit it to serve the entertainment needs of humanity are part of the problem.

Western scholars who are so inclined, struggle to make the point that the agenda of environmental care could be pushed drastically forward if the world took on an ontological view of, and approach to, nature. This is understandable given the enlightenment worldview of the West in which things that cannot be

---

[9] Robert, "Historical Trends in Missions and Earth Care," 127.

[10] Nyambura J. Njoroge, "The Struggle for Full Humanity in Poverty-Stricken Kenya", in Peter J. Paris (eds), *Religion and Poverty: Pan-African Perspectives* (Durham, NC: Duke University Press, 2009), 166-190.

[11] See for example: Benjamin Abotchie Ntreh, Mark S. Aidoo, and Daniel Nii Aboagye-Aryeh (eds), *Essays on the Land, Ecotheology, and Traditions in Africa* (Eugene, OR: Wipf and Stock, 2019).

[12] Benjamin Abotchie Ntreh, "The Bible and Caring for the Land," in Benjamin Abotchie Ntreh, Mark S. Aidoo, and Daniel Nii Aboagye-Aryeh (eds), *Essays on the Land, Ecotheology, and Traditions in Africa* (Eugene, OR: Wipf and Stock, 2019), 3.

[13] Jürgen Moltmann, "The Destruction and Healing of the Earth: Ecology and Theology," in Max L. Stackhouse with Don S. Browning (eds), *God and Globalization,* Vol. 2, *The Spirit and the Modern Authorities* (NY: Trinity Press International, 2001), 167.

proven by rationality and science may be deemed not to exist. One ecofeminist Rosemary Radford Ruether speaks in tones that can be identified in African eco-philosophical thought when she posits that humanity's destiny and calling is of and for this earth and that we "need to use our capacities to contemplate and understand these processes so that we may harmonize our lives with the life of the whole earth community."[14] In African thought this "whole earth community" that Ruether refers to include the physical earth which is gendered feminine and her custodial or allodial owners, the ancestors whose mortal remains lie in the belly of the earth as their souls keep watch over its inhabitants. This proposal for an ontological approach to nature may be alien to the West, but in Africa, it is taken for granted. In traditional Africa, we argue, the earth has always been considered sacred, and thus, there are ontological principles governing the use of its resources in the service of humanity. It is the demystification of creation through a certain type of Christian monotheism, Western scientific and evolutionary thought that then set in motion environmental degradation in the world and in Africa.

The destruction of the environment, most environmentally concerned activists agree, has been caused in part by the global economic system. As Moltmann notes, globalisation in modern industrial societies has thrown the equilibrium of the organism of the earth out of balance. These ecological catastrophes, he notes, have intensified the already precarious socio-economic problems of poorer non-Western countries. Contrary to popular scientific perceptions, non-Western cultures, Moltmann argues, were anything but "primitive" and "underdeveloped", at least not as far as the equilibrium of the environment was concerned. Contrary to those perceptions, premodern civilisations were "highly complicated systems of equilibrium which ordered the relation of people to nature and to the gods."[15] Western-styled development, including a monotheism that treated God as being so transcendent as not to be concerned with earthly matters, stripped nature of its mystical awe leading to the disrespectful breaches of the sacred taboos that Africans have always known to govern nature and the environment.

Christian theology takes for granted the fact that creation is God's gift to humanity. This theological position is based on the sentence constituting the main title of this article: "In the beginning God created heaven and earth" (Genesis 1:1). Alister McGrath virtually recommends to his Western readers what has always been part of the primal imagination in non-Western contexts like traditional Africa:

> An ontology is clearly demanded, setting out what the world *is,* so that our response is determined by the external constraints of reality, not simply an internal decision to view matters in certain, potentially arbitrary manners.[16]

Nature and Ontological Reality

This Christian position coheres with certain underlying assumptions on the intersection between creation and evolution in the African traditional cultural context. These assumptions are that:

1. There is purposefulness in creation because it is ordained by God, that is, at least in African Christian theology, nature is not simply a socially constructed reality;
2. Human life is sacred because we are created in the image of God;
3. The created order is enchanted with the presence of divinity;
4. Purposefulness in creation must be understood against the backdrop of stewardship;
5. In the African Christian context in particular, the inseparable relationship between "sacred/secular", "heaven/earth" realities have implications for how nature is handled and therefore, also for environmental stewardship.

---

[14] Rosemary Radford Ruether, "Ecofeminism: The Challenge to Theology," in Dieter Hessel and Rosemary Radford Ruether, *Christianity and Ecology: Seeking the Well-Being of Earth and Humans* Cambridge: MA Harvard University Press, 2000), 104.

[15] Moltmann, "Destruction and Healing of the Earth," 171.

[16] McGrath, *Nature,* 116.

What these underlying assumptions mean is that from a non-Western perspective, we cannot explain creation just in theoretical evolutionary terms. Creation must always be explained in terms of Divine interest, purposefulness, and stewardship. Humanity has been given custody of creation as its steward. Christian stewardship of the environment must therefore lead to sustainable development that is defined in terms of "development that meets the needs of the present without compromising the ability of future generations to meet their own needs."[17]

These reflections on creation, Christian stewardship and our common humanity flourishing seek to make the point that the Christian church would need to fall on its biblical and theological resources to help with the recovery process of environmental degradation as part of its mission. Nyambura J. Njoroge speaking to the same issue from an East African context noted as follows:

> [Both] religious scholars and the church in Kenya must play a critical role in transforming the political, cultural, spiritual, material, and psychological structures so that they might produce in the citizenry the type of social conscience needed to realise the fullness of humanity in a poverty-stricken society [...] The poor and the oppressed alone cannot transform this dehumanising reality. Thus, the church, its leadership, and scholars must participate in achieving this social change.[18]

The situation of endemic poverty in Africa, for example, is related directly to the unscientific and irresponsible exploitation and treatment of the environment because of the Western distinction made between "sacred" and "secular" realities as far as creation is concerned. Studies have shown that, in non-Western contexts, the inseparability between sacred and secular realities means environmental conservation efforts are unlikely to succeed if the people's sense of the universe as enchanted is not taken into consideration.[19]

Kwame Bediako, following Harold W. Turner, cites "a sense of kinship with nature, in which animals and plants, no less than human beings, had 'their own spiritual existence and place in the universe' as interdependent parts of a whole" as a key feature of the African primal imagination. According to Bediako, who wrote with reference to Turner,

> [Any] object of the natural environment may enter into a totemic spiritual relationship with human beings or become tutelary and guardian spirits whilst the environment itself is used realistically and unsentimentally but with profound respect and reverence and without exploitation. This 'ecological aspect' of primal religions, [Turner] considered to be 'a profoundly religious attitude to man's natural setting in the world'.[20]

Kwame Bediako discussed Turner's six-feature analysis of the nature of the primal world in the light of how indigenous Christian religious functionaries embraced that world and carried on a certain type of Christian ministry that was sympathetic to African cosmological ideas.

The understanding of God since the Renaissance in Western Europe has been one-sided, Moltmann argues, because in the Western tradition God was reshuffled into the transcendent sphere, with the world understood in a purely immanent and this-worldly sense. With God thought of as outwith the world, the

---

[17] Brundtland Report, quoted in C.K. Brown, "Sustainable Development and the Environment: Definitions and Goals", in Ghana Academy of Arts and Sciences Proceedings, *Sustainable Development and the Environment* (Accra: GAAS, 1992), 8.

[18] Njoroge, "Full Humanity", 167.

[19] Joseph Kofi Antwi, *Akan Religio-Cultural Thought and Environmental Management: The Case of the Atiwa District, Ghana.* Unpublished PhD Thesis, Department of Religious Studies, Kwame Nkrumah University of Science and Technology, Kumasi, Ghana (2018), 4-5, 162.

[20] Kwame Bediako, "The Primal Imagination and the Opportunity for a New Theological Idiom," in Kwame Bediako, *Jesus in Africa: The Christian Gospel in African History and Experience* (Akropong, Akuapem: Regnum Africa, 2000), 87.

world then loses "the divine mystery of its creation" leading to the secularisation of the world and nature that makes it possible for its exploitation without blinking.[21] The traditional non-Western affinity with nature means indigenous societies held a natural reverence for the environment, seeing it as enchanted or inhabited by supernatural powers that reacted to the irresponsible uses of this heritage. The church, on account of its allegiance to Jesus Christ, may hold some reservations concerning the enchanted nature of the African natural environment, but must see it as part of her mission to articulate a response to the menace of degradation as part of theological education. Africa cannot develop until the continent is able to approach her environment as a God-given heritage with the expectation that humanity has a responsibility of stewardship towards the earth.

Charismatic Theology and Creation Care

Care for the environment has become imperative especially with the massive growth of Christianity on the continent. At least one stream of Christianity, the Pentecostal/charismatic versions of the faith, has developed a new dominion theology that suggests that God wants human beings to prosper although such prosperity has not yet been linked to environmental conservation. This theology is partly a response to the old Western missionary paradigm that virtually glorified material poverty as a sign of spirituality. Kossi A. Ayedze notes that, throughout its history, the church has tended to exhort believers to despise wealth.[22] African Christians were not left out. During the missionary period, Africans were introduced to a type of Christianity that glorified poverty to the point where it looked like African converts loathed profit. This "poverty gospel", Ayedze notes, is unfortunately still prevalent in Africa, especially among mainline churches. In contrast to the negative attitude towards wealth obviously based on a certain eschatological mindset, a new version of Christianity that glorifies wealth and prosperity is now burgeoning throughout Africa.[23]

One study suggests that, in comparison with secular non-governmental organisations that are often the recipients of large grants for development in Africa, Pentecostal churches emerge as the more effective agents of change.[24] In the theology of the new prosperity preachers, God wants to bless his people spiritually, physically, and materially. Renewal Christians, Katherine Attanasi points out, "believe that God's ongoing work include granting believer's prosperity and health" in this world.[25] Contemporary Pentecostalism holds a theology of dominion in which God gives believers the power to make wealth through dominating social and economic systems. The prosperity theology has empowered many upwardly mobile youths to seek education, invest extra resources and cultivate stable family lives. In the process, some of these young people have been helped to escape the cycles of poverty that have become synonymous with African domestic economies.

However, as Christine Schliesser notes, the popularity of the prosperity gospel in contemporary Africa must not be divorced from the major economic crisis that hit the continent in the 1980s and 1990s. It was in this period that the prosperity preaching churches "radically redefined their view on worldly things so that instead of the continued perception of poverty as spiritual virtue, material riches now become the

---

[21] Moltmann, "Destruction and Healing of the Earth," 172.
[22] Kossi A. Ayeddze, "Poverty Among African People and the Ambiguous Role of Christian Thought," in Peter Paris (ed), *Religion and Poverty: Pan African Perspectives* (Durham, NC: Duke University Press, 2009), 197.
[23] Ayeddze, "Poverty Among African People and the Ambiguous Role of Christian Thought," 197.
[24] Christine Schliesser, "On a Long Neglected Player: The Religious Factor in Poverty Alleviation: The Example of the So-Called 'Prosperity Gospel in Africa'", *Exchange* 43 (2014), 339-359.
[25] Katherine Attanasi, "Introduction: The Plurality of Prosperity Theologies and Pentecostalism", in Katherine Attanasi and Amos Yong (eds), *Pentecostalism and Prosperity: The Socio-Economics of the Global Charismatic Movement* (NY: Palgrave Macmillan, 2012), 3.

hallmark of God's blessings."[26] Although Pentecostalism has motivated young people to do something about their future through the prosperity theology of dominion, the lack of attention to the fundamental issue of care for the environment could render such aspirations a mirage.

Contrary to aspects of prosperity preaching that dwell on a principle of "naming and claiming", we cannot, for example, command restoration back into degraded farmlands and river bodies. God is not creating fresh land, as we noted at the beginning of these reflections. Theological education in contemporary Africa would therefore need to challenge the churches – both historic mission denominations and Pentecostal/charismatic communities – to mainstream environmental studies in their curriculum. This would not just be to bridge the gaps between academic theology and contextual experiences, but also to find ways to engage with governance systems and thereby bring Christian influence to bear on society through Christian stewardship. In addition to our conventional disciplines of biblical studies, Christian doctrine, church history and mission, Christian ethics and practical theology, theological education may need to pay some attention to environmental studies due to the potential that religion in general and Christianity in particular holds for making a difference in Africa. This could occur through the teaching and study of a theology of the environment in systematic theology or even as part of African traditional ethics.

Religion, the Environment and Stewardship

What is the situation on the ground as far as the African physical environment and the care for it is concerned? The following is an observation from a Ghana Catholic Bishops Conference communiqué issued more than two decades ago:

> Grave socio-economic problems exist which affect especially our rural communities and have disastrous consequences on the environment. Many rural communities lack the basic places of convenience and the squalor in some parts of our cities is an eyesore. The serious lack of water supply in many rural communities, worsened sometimes by reckless exploitation of the environment, can be alarming. Many rivers and rivulets, which are the only sources of drinking water for people, are being polluted with frightening rapidity. In many places, large sections of our population are still exposed to waterborne diseases such as cholera, bilharzia, dysentery, guinea worm and river blindness. We cannot but repeat our insistent appeals to Ghanaians to safeguard the sanctity of our arable land and forests which are being destroyed in the quest for precious minerals and timber, to the detriment and impoverishment of many rural communities. The short-term economic advantage of these activities can never be compared with the catastrophic consequences that await us in the future because of our heartless desecration of our environment.[27]

What is said of Ghana here on the consequences of environmental degradation, is sadly true of the whole of Africa and beyond. The sad situation is that, although these observations were made with a particular African country in mind, the truth is that these sentiments are equally true of virtually all other countries in sub-Saharan Africa. From a Christian theological viewpoint, the corrective to these episcopal lamentations on the human destruction of the environment is proper environmental stewardship.

Destructive environmental activities have implications for our survival on planet earth beyond present generations. Conferences have been held, including some at the international level, to sensitise individuals and governments, highlighting the need to take good care of the environment because the survival of humanity depends on a good environment. Without proper environmental ethics, sustainable development is simply not possible. Science cannot help humankind without using natural resources. At the level of the globalised world, discussions on this matter have mostly been conducted with appeals to scientific

[26] Schliesser, "Religious Factor in Poverty Alleviation," 346.

[27] *Ghana Bishops Speak: A Collection of Communiques, Memoranda and Pastoral Letters of the Ghana Catholic Bishops' Conference* (Accra: Ghana Catholic Secretariat, 1999), 222-223.

environmental theories. The specific biblical call to exercise dominion over creation is to care for the environment in a way that allows it to sustain the life that God grants humanity and that guarantees sustenance for the future.

The bottom line is that humanity has become a poor steward of creation, especially of the environment. This problem, as I have argued, is due in part to the de-ontologised approach that science and technology have taken to development and the desperation to eke out a living in the face of environmental disasters. Deforestation and the pollution of water bodies occur mainly through human activity in the search for economic survival. In the case of African countries generally, the use of firewood for example, continues to be the main source of energy supply for cooking. The overreliance on firewood as the main source of fuel is a sign of poverty and underdevelopment. Recent news reports in Africa have shown how encroachment on forest reserves to poach engendered animal species, and human settlements along the banks of rivers that serve as sources of water supply have put natural assets in grave danger of depletion and pollution. The sources of drinking water for many communities have been polluted through small-scale mining activities that also affect the forest cover.

Globalisation may have benefitted people by promoting of democratic governance, human rights, and the protection of biodiversity. In several non-Western countries, unfortunately, these benefits are often negated by ecological devastation, deforestation, depletion of fish stocks and the spread of infectious diseases due to such morally depraving practices as sexual tourism. Most of the world that operates within the religion of globalisation Dwight Hopkins notes, "experiences a theological anthropology of exclusion from the earth's resources, victimisation at the hands of extreme social polarisation, and a truncated humanity."[28] The lack of effective laws to protect the environment and the poor planning and execution of infrastructural projects mean that stewardship has been neglected and the Christian church has a responsibility to respond to this trend.

There is hope for the future. In the foreword of a book resulting from a collaborative conference between the World Bank and faith communities in Africa, George Carey, a former Anglican Archbishop of Canterbury, noted that there was an important common ground between faith and development. In most developing countries, he observed, religious leaders are close to the poor and among their most trusted representatives. Faith communities offer health services, education, and shelter the vulnerable and disadvantaged.[29] I use the expression "development" in this context to refer to a quality of life and existence that affirms the sacred nature of human life and the dignity of the human person as created in the image of God. To all intents and purposes, then, God's will for humanity as outlined in the Christian scriptures is to enjoy the fullness of life made available in Jesus Christ the Lord. In the words of Jesus himself, he came that we might have life and do so in abundance (John 10:10). I interpret this abundance of life generally as having to do with the spiritual and physical well-being of God's creation and humanity.

God's Blessing and Africa's Story

The story of Africa indicates that this abundant life, which comes partly through eking out our living from the earth, has not been realised. This goes directly to the heart of the mission of the church and her responsibility in the execution of God's *shalom* – holistic wellbeing – for humanity. We have spoken about the ontological worldview of the Bible and how Africa shares in that worldview as far as creation is concerned. Humanity, having been created in the image of God, was given the responsibility to take charge

---

[28] Dwight Hopkins, "The Religion of Globalization," in Dwight N. Hopkins, Lois Ann Lorentzen, Eduardo Mendieta, & David Batstone (eds), *Religions/Globalizations: Theories and Cases* (Durham, NC: Duke University Press, 2001), 13.

[29] Deryke Belshaw, Robert Calderisi, and Chris Sugden (eds), *Faith in Development: Partnership Between the World Bank and the Churches of Africa* (Oxford: Regnum International, 2001), vii.

of the world and its resources – represented here by the environment – and to work for its survival. The biblical passage that best describes this responsibility is Genesis 1:28-30. The critical words in that text include the expressions "be fruitful", "multiply", "fill the earth", "subdue the earth" and have "dominion."

In the passage, as was noted at the beginning of this article, God gives the human being power to reproduce their kind and to exercise dominion over the earth. The human person, made in the image of God, is given the responsibility to share in the task of being stewards of the earth (Psalm 8:6-8). The point is that the palpable absence of what may be considered God's blessings in terms of holistic living and human dignity has led many to speak of Africa in terms of a continent under a curse. The creation story and the instructions given to humanity in the Bible concerning the environment and our responsibility within it means we are dealing here with a sacred order.

We learnt at the beginning of this article that the sacred worldview underpinning creation is not alien to African cultures as rivers, mountains, forests and even the sea are associated with transcendent realities. Crucial to indigenous thought in Africa, according to Ogbu U. Kalu, "is a religious cosmology complete with an awareness of the integral relationship of symbolic and material life."[30] By sacralising nature, he notes, indigenous worldviews purvey an ideology that is co-extensive, eco-musical, and devoid of the harsh flutes of those who see nature as a challenge to be conquered.[31] The over-sacralisation of nature in Africa means that there is often a lack of an ideology of preservation, conservation and replacement. The gods take the blame when resources get depleted and then as Kalu notes, environmentally degrading practices diminish biodiversity and wipe out sustainability.[32] For those who explain creation in evolutionary terms, stringent environmental laws and legal regimes help environmental sustainability.

In non-Western contexts, natural resources serve as hierophantic entities accounting for the many taboos associated with mountains, hills, rivers, and trees; because of which such resources have been preserved for generations. As we lose the sense of supernatural in relation to the created order, the environment is also exploited selfishly to our own peril and that of generations after us. In the Western context where the sense of the supernatural has been diminished because of evolution theory, science and development, respect has been developed for nature through the enactment of strict legislation to deal with irresponsible exploitation of our common heritage. In Africa, the interest of the gods and deities in the environment explain why exploitation sometimes demands the performance of appropriate rituals to gain access to what may otherwise be the abode or property of a deity.

This situation is typified by the relationship between fishermen and the seas as Emmanuel Akyeampong illustrates with the case of the Anlo of South-Eastern Ghana:

> For the Anlo, sea fishing represented harvesting where one had not sown. An important feature of sea fishing in Anlo is the performance of the *agbodedefu* (sending a ram into the sea) ritual, annually observed to promote bountiful fishing. For the Anlo, the sea is a natural and supernatural realm populated by fish and deities. The sea yields its largesse when a proper and harmonious relationship is struck with it. The result of the sea on the Anlo shoreline, after a previous century of coastal accretion, seemed to signal some irreparable damage in the human relationship with the supernatural.[33]

We have talked about the sacred nature of the earth in African philosophical thought. In African contexts, Mother Earth is for example animated by a divine principle; because of this, the earth is not to be polluted by the shedding of innocent blood or by defiling her sacredness through sexual intercourse on the bare

---

[30] Ogbu U. Kalu, *Clio in a Sacred Garb: Essays on Christian Presence and African Responses: 1900-2000* (Trenton, NJ: Africa World Press, 2008), 24.
[31] Kalu, *Clio in a Sacred Garb*, 24.
[32] Kalu, *Clio in a Sacred Garb,* 25.
[33] Emmanuel Kweku Acheampong, *Between the Sea and the Lagoon: An Eco-Social History of the Anlo of Southeastern Ghana c. 1850 to Recent Times* (Athens: Ohio University Press/Oxford: James Currey, 2001), 18-19.

ground. Indeed, the ancestors are the custodians of land in African traditional thought and that is why, in principle, land in traditional Africa is not sold. It is the property of the ancestors and must be preserved as such. A similar thought is present in Jewish thought as found in the book of Leviticus. In Leviticus 25:23-24, we read as follows:

> The land must not be sold permanently, because the land is mine and you are but aliens and my tenants. Throughout the country that you hold as a possession, you must provide for the redemption of the land.

The people of Israel, therefore, had access to the land only by the will and favour of the Lord. They were just agents of God. As the Akan say, *se wo hwe obi ade yie a, eye wo de* [if you take good care of another's property in your custody, ownership eventually reverts to you]. It was when Christian theology started decoupling the almighty Creator from his creation that nature was stripped of its divine mystery and therefore became a victim of desacralisation through secularisation. In order to reverse this trend, Moltmann calls to rediscover the Creator's immanence in creation in order that the whole of the created order may be included in our reverence for the Creator.[34]

Creation and Humankind's Stewardship

For religions like Christianity which believe in a Creator-God, creation came into being through the activity of God. It did not evolve naturally nor is it due to any big bang eons ago. From the Christian point of view, there is an inseparable relationship between faith and the preservation of the environment. A key biblical reference here is Psalm 24:1-2 where God is presented as the owner of the environment, suggesting that humankind is only a custodian of what belongs to God:

> The earth is the Lord's, and everything in it, the world, and all who live in it;
> For he founded it upon the seas and established it upon the waters.

A good grasp of the biblical concept of creation is germane to the Christian understanding of nature. From a Christological perspective, Colossians 1:15-16 where Jesus is identified as "the image of the invisible God" and as "the firstborn of all creation" has been identified as constituting a legitimate basis for laying a biblical foundation of stewardship and care of the created order.[35] This biblical account challenges the pantheistic view that sees creation as an extension of the essence of God. That God is the creator of the universe and therefore nature and the environment also challenge the gnostic worldview that matter was utterly and irretrievably evil. Contrary to these views, we are told that, "God saw everything he has made and behold it was very good." From a Christian theological standpoint therefore, the divine ownership of creation places a moral obligation on humankind, as God's agents in the created order.

It is noteworthy that in the exploitation of edible fruits, human custodians of the earth are told specifically to eat "seed-bearing plant" and that seems to suggest the earth must be reforested with the seeds that are found in the seed-bearing plants. In other words, humanity's relationship with the created order, from the biblical account, is expected to be a responsible dominion that finds expression through tender care and respect for nature. Emmanuel Asante puts the position succinctly in the following words:

> Humanity is charged "to till the garden and to keep it" (vs. 15). The expression *tilling* implies that humanity is to serve the created order by applying itself to improving or developing creation's productive capacity. The other

[34] Moltmann, "Destruction and Healing of the Earth," 176.
[35] Sorley, "Christ, Creation and Stewardship," 139.

expression defining the human's dominion over nature is *keeping,* which implies that humanity preserve, maintain, and ensure the safe keeping of the created order.[36]

The stewardship of humanity over creation is also seen in the privilege to name the items of creation, a privilege that implies not just a given authority over nature, but also a respect for nature as an entity that is related to humanity in a special way.[37] The raw material for the creation of humanity was obtained from nature: the human being was formed from the dust of the ground and the breath of God brought the organised mud to life. Kalu writes of, how at birth, the outdoor ceremony not only provided the opportunity to declare who has returned to the family, it covenants the individual to the land and the community:

> Eight days earlier, the child's umbilical cord would have been put in a calabash and sprinkled with herbs and after some pronouncements, buried under a tree at the back of the house. The child is rooted in the land with which it shares an everlasting bond.[38]

In the case of Israel, the Israelites' continued stay and enjoyment of the benefits of the land depended on their acknowledging its sacred nature and honouring the Lord by taking good care of it. The Old Testament is thus full of warnings against misuse and over-exploitation of the land (Jeremiah 2:7; 3:2) and this includes not polluting the land through the spilling of innocent blood (Numbers 35:33-34):

> Do not pollute the land where you are. Bloodshed pollutes the land, and atonement cannot be made for the land on which blood has been shed, except by the blood of the one who shed it. Do not defile the land where you live and where I dwell, for I, the Lord, dwell among the Israelites.

All this is to make the point that we need to pay due regard to the very serious peril we are in by neglecting the care which, by divine appointment, we ought to have been taking of the wonderful creation in which God has placed us. Christian G. Baëta, in a speech on "God's Creation and Responsible Development" noted that: "Whatever had a beginning also has an end and our study impresses upon us that, owing to our failure to maintain the sustainability of our earth as far as possible, we are necessarily hastening its catastrophic demise."[39]

Conclusion: Religion, Environment, and Stewardship

From the Christian point of view then, as from the traditional African position, there is an unquestioning relationship between allegiance to God and the gods and preservation of the environment. Preserving the environment for posterity is part of our total response to God's initiative in Christ. A major implication of the Christian theology of creation is that God loves his creation. Creation is the wonder of God's hands and, as people created in his image, we must love creation and take care of it. The way to take stewardship seriously is to value whatever has been placed in your charge. That is what we find the Psalmist suggest in Psalm 8:

> O Lord, our Lord, how majestic is your name in all the earth! [...] When I consider your heavens, the work of your fingers, the moon and the stars, which you have set in place, what is man that you are mindful of him? [...]

---

36 Emmanuel Asante, 'Ecological Crisis: A Christian Answer', *Trinity Journal of Church and Theology,* vol. 4, 2 (1994/5), 14.
37 Asante, 'Ecological Crisis', 14.
38 Kalu, *Clio in a Sacred Garb,* 34.
39 Christian G. Baëta, "God's Creation and Responsible Development," *Sustainable Development and the Environment,* Ghana Academy of Arts and Sciences Proceedings (1992), 7.

> You have made him ruler over the works of your hands; and put everything under his feet: all flocks and herds, and the beasts of the field, the birds of the air, and the fish of the sea, all that swim the paths of the seas.

In our own day in Africa, we may recall the senseless murder of the Nigerian Ogoni activist, Ken Sarowiwa who died in November 1994 at the hands of Sani Abacha for spearheading agitations for the preservation of the 'ancestral lands' of the Ogoni people. Commenting on the events leading to Sarowiwa's execution, the Nigerian Nobel laureate for literature, Wole Soyinka explains as follows:

> The purpose of Abacha's bloody provocations was straightforward: to make it impossible for the victims of oil exploration to present a united front in their demands for reparations for their polluted land, a fair share in the resources of their land, and a voice in the control of their own development.[40]

In traditional Africa, people protect ancestral and God-given resources with their blood. The example of the continuing skirmishes between Nigeria and Cameroon over the oil-rich Bakassi Peninsular serves as another apt example in this direction. The battle rages on even after the International Court of Justice ruled in favour of Cameroon's ownership. Richard Young in his book, *Healing the Earth,* has pointed out that the injunction to till the earth and manage it implies the need for a manager to help keep order and harmony in creation. "The service is to be rendered to God, not to ourselves."[41]

The theory of evolution as means of explaining the origins of creation is unlikely to go away in the world that has come to depend increasingly on science and technology for development. However, when it comes to creation and care, there is no point creating a dichotomy between science and faith because both can be explained in terms of the wisdom of God and the empowerment of humanity. From the perspective of African-initiated Christianity, it is revealing that environmental care has assumed sacramental proportions with Zimbabwean members confessing their "ecological sins" as part of earth-keeping worship services.[42] An ontological approach to creation helps to establish an important sense of being custodians or stewards and that mindset would help current generations to investigate the future in terms of preservation and responsibility for natural resources. If our lives depend on the environment, then it means we cannot even explain salvation without creation care.

The ultimate example in this process of salvation is in the Incarnation – during which the Creator became part of his own creation to redeem it. If the environment is not handled rightly as a God-given asset, what should be exploited for the common good could then turn around and consume us because pollution causes illness, disabilities, and death. Consequently, struggles and ethnic conflicts over limited resources increase, as do pressures on governments and agitations for more salaries to cater for rising medical bills. The relationship between the environment and development is a direct one and we all have a responsibility to preserve this invaluable asset not just for ourselves but also for posterity because it is the best legacy that current generations can bequeath to the next generation. Herein lies the relationship between creation and humanity and Christian stewardship and development in our world today.

Suggestions for Further Reading

Asamoah-Gyadu, Kwabena J. "God's Laws of Productivity: Creation in African Pentecostal Hermeneutics", in Amos Yong, Ed. *The Spirit Renews the Face of the Earth: Pentecostal Forays in Science and Theology of Creation.* Eugene, OR: Pickwick Publications, 2009: 175-190.

---

[40] Wole Soyinka, *The Open Sore of a Continent: A Personal Narrative of the Nigerian Crisis* (Oxford: Oxford University Press, 1996), 151.

[41] Richard A. Young, *Healing the Earth: A Theocentric Perspective on Environmental Problems and their Solutions* (Nashville, Tennessee: Broadman and Holman Publishers, 1994), 163.

[42] Daneel, "Christian Mission and Earth Care," 131.

Asamoah-Gyadu, Kwabena J. "Spirit and Empowerment: The African Initiated Church Movement and Development", in Philipp Öhlmann, Wilhelm Gräb and Marie-Luise Frost, Eds. *African Initiated Christianity and the Decolonisation of Development: Sustainable Development in Pentecostal and Independent Churches.* London and New York: Routledge, 2020: 33-50.

Daneel, Marthinus L. "Earthkeeping Churches at the Grassroots," in Dieter T. Hessel, and Rosemary Radford Ruether, Eds. *Christianity and Ecology: Seeking the Wellbeing of Earth and Humans.* Cambridge, MA: Harvard University Press, 2000: 531-552.

Daneel, M.L. "Christian Mission and Earth-Care: An African Case Study." *International Bulletin of Missionary Research.* 35(3), (July 2011), 130-136.

Greene, Sandra E. *Sacred Sites and the Colonial Encounter: A History of Meaning and Memory in Ghana.* Bloomington and Indianapolis, IN: Indiana University Press, 2002.

Hessel, Dieter T and Rosemary Radford Ruether, Eds. *Christianity and Ecology: Seeking the Wellbeing of Earth and Humans.* Cambridge, MA: Harvard University Press, 2000.

Ntreh, Benjamin Abotchie, Mark S. Aidoo, and Daniel Nii Aboagye Aryeh, Eds. *Essays on the Land, Ecotheology, and Traditions in Africa.* Eugene, OR: Resource Publications, 2019.

Öhlmann, Philipp, Wilhelm Gräb and Marie-Luise Frost, Eds. *African Initiated Christianity and the Decolonisation of Development: Sustainable Development in Pentecostal and Independent Churches.* London and New York: Routledge, 2020.

Ossom-Batsa, George, Nicoletta Gatti and Rabiatu Deinyo Ammah, Eds. *Religion and Sustainable Development: Ghanaian Perspectives.* Rome: Urbaniana University Press, 2018.

Robert, Dana L. "Historical Trends in Missions and Earth Care." *International Bulletin of Missionary Research.* 35(3), (July 2011), 123-128.

Sorley, Charles. "Christ, Creation Stewardship, and Missions: How Discipleship into a Biblical Worldview on Environmental Stewardship Can Transform People and their Land." *International Bulletin of Missionary Research,* 35(3), (July 2011), 137-140.

Yong, Amos, Ed. *The Spirit Renews the Face of the Earth: Pentecostal Forays in Science and Theology of Creation.* Eugene, OR: Pickwick Publications, 2009.

2. Care for Creation: An Ecotheological Reading of Genesis 2

Marthe Maleke Kondemo[1]

Introduction

Today, questions of ecology are at the forefront of theologians' concerns as they seek to respond to the detrimental impact that human activity is having on the environment. These ecological issues have led to a new breed of activist theologian who call themselves ecotheologians, green theologians amongst other names. It also led to the birth of the eco-feminist movement, which offers a framework both for reconsideration of feminist theory and for developing an ecological ethic that takes seriously the links between the rule of men over women and the abuse of nature.[2] Out of the struggle to bring healing and sustainable vitality to our living planet, theologians have been re-examining Scripture, Christian doctrines, and ethical principles to see what wisdom divine revelation and historic Christian faith have for us in this struggle.[3] Conradie defines eco-theology as, "an attempt to retrieve the ecological wisdom in Christianity as a response to environmental threats and injustices. At the same time, it is an attempt to reinvestigate, rediscover and renew the Christian tradition in the light of the challenges posed by the environmental crisis".[4] Ecotheology offers a Christian critique of the cultural habits underlying ecological destruction. As Conradie further explains, "ecological theology is not only concerned with how Christianity can respond to environment concerns; it also offers Christianity an opportunity for renewal and reformation".[5]

The environmental crisis being experienced today threatens humanity with its possible extinction. Jingcheng and Meifang writes,

> the Earth, our Mother Nature, has seen devastating changes, and the ecosystem in a vicious circle has been suffering myriads of ecological disasters, natural or human, manufacturing pollution, global warming, expanding population, acid rain, deforestation, desertification, irregular earthquakes and eruption of volcanoes, ozone layer depletion and melting of polar glaciers, under which circumstance the human beings' dwelling on earth and all creatures at large thus have been in danger and under hazards as well.[6]

Rajotte and Breuilly[7] view these factors as cumulatively affecting the entire earth and constituting an ecological crisis threatening the survival of whole ecosystems and vulnerable human communities. Hence, the environmental crisis calls for urgent reflection on the relationship between humanity and nature, or more precisely, on the place of humanity within the earth community.[8] Although the environment crisis affects natural eco-systems more directly, it is not primarily a crisis pertaining to nature but to the dominant and increasingly global economic system and the consumerist culture values supporting it. As Rasmussen

---

[1] Rev Dr. Marthe Maleke Kondemo, is an ordained pastor of the united evangelical churches of Lulonga (CADELU), DRC; she completed her PhD at the University of Pretoria, South Africa.

[2] K.J. Warren, "The Power and the Promise of Ecological Feminism", in M.H. Mackinnon & M. McIntyre (eds), *Reading in Ecology and Feminist Theology*. (Kansas City, KS: Sheed &Ward, 1995), 172-195: 172.

[3] Alan Padgett, *Ecotheology: Developing New Perspective*. https://biologos.org/articles/ecotheology-developing-new-perspective. [Last accessed 20th October 2021], 1.

[4] Ernst M. Conradie, *An Ecological Christian Anthropology. At home on Earth?* (Burlington, VT.: Ashgate, 2005), 1.

[5] Conradie, *An Ecological Christian Anthropology*, 2.

[6] Jingcheng Xu and Meifang Nan Gong, "A Study of the Social Ecological Wisdom in H.W. Longfellow's Poetry," TPLS 2/1 (2012): 6.

[7] Rajotte and Breuilly, "What is the Crisis?", in Elizabeth Breuilly and Martin Palmer (eds), *Christianity and Ecology*. (London: Cassell, 1992): 1-3.

[8] Conradie, *An Ecological Christian Anthropology*, 2.

observes, "earth's distress is a crisis of culture."[9] This is "a pathological sign of cultural failure and bankruptcy which requires a new vision and discernment of the place, status, role and responsibility of human beings in the community of life".[10]

Both the Bible and Christian tradition as a whole have some vital and profound insights for the care of creation. The Bible provides us with several beautiful, theologically rich accounts of creation stories which mainly are to be found in Genesis 1 and 2. While Genesis 1 focuses more on the ordered structure, meaning, and purpose of creation, Genesis 2 emphasises the intended harmony of the proper relationships we should have with God, the natural world, and with each other. Genesis 2 tells the story of the creation of humanity and a garden somewhere "in the East" (v.8 NRSV). This chapter is packed with theological truths, yet we unfortunately often miss them as many parts of this chapter are often viewed merely as a setup for Genesis 1. Whatever might be the historical transmission of these accounts, they now stand together as a single witness to the creation of the world.

One of the theological concerns that Genesis 2 addresses is the relationship between humanity and creation, and how protecting creation is a sacred duty. If Genesis 2 is approached from an ecotheological point of view, what might we learn from it? Reading Genesis 2 from an ecotheological perspective should help us to understand our role and responsibility as intended by God. It could be of value to add this to the possible solutions to the impending ecological crisis.[11] Approaching environmental issues through Christian lenses offers valuable ethical and spiritual dimensions that may contribute to environmental work both within and outside the church.[12]

Genesis 2: Till, Keep and Eat!

The Genesis 2 creation account is not only about the creation of human beings but of all living beings and all elements of creation. It establishes an important relationship between humans and the earth characterised by intrinsic value, interconnection and interrelation that becomes an important foundation for the development of an ecological consciousness.[13] It gives the origin and basic principles of existence, sustenance; the purpose of humanity on the landed earth amid the plants and animals is the focus of attention, based on the larger surrounding cosmic environment having already been established in Genesis 1.[14] Genesis 2 opens with a story of a garden into which the man, Adam, immediately after being formed, is placed: *"The LORD God took the man and put him in the garden of Eden to till it and keep it. And the LORD God commanded the man, You may freely eat of every tree of the garden"* (vv.15-16 NRSV). "Tilling" refers to cultivating, ploughing, or working, while 'keeping' means caring, protecting, overseeing, and preserving."[15] The first man is placed in the garden not just to inhabit it with other creatures, but also with a God-given purpose "to work and keep it". Working and keeping the garden is part of the mission of

[9] Larry L Rasmussen, *Earth Community. Earth Ethics*. (Maryknoll, NY: Orbis Books,1996), 7.
[10] Conradie, *An Ecological Christian Anthropology*, 2.
[11] Gale A Yee, Hugh R. Page Jr and Matthew J.M. Coomber (eds), *The Pentateuch: Fortress Commentary on the Bible Study Edition.* (Minneapolis, MN: Fortress, 2016), 94.
[12] David Pickering, Alan Werritty and Richard Murray, *Idea for Action 3 Theology and the Environment*, Eco-Congregation Scotland, 2012, [Available at: http://www.ecocongregationscotland.org/wp-content/uploads/2013/06/Theology-and-the-environment.pdf].
[13] Stephen Grosse, "Building a Relationship with the Earth: Humans and Ecology in Genesis 1-3." Denison Journal of Religion (2005), 5, Article 4, [Available at: http://digitalcommons.denison.edu/religion/vol5/iss1/], [Last accessed: 18th October 2021].
[14] Richard Averbeck, "A literature day, inter-textual, and contextual reading of Genesis 1-2" in J. Daryl Charles (ed), *Reading Genesis 1-2. An evangelical conversation.* (Massachusetts: Hendrickson Publication), 7-34: 32.
[15] Fr Reese, "Humans Must Care for Creation and Share Its Fruits – On Care, Sabbath, Relationship, Life, & the Common Good". *Laudato Si'*, [Available at: https://catholicclimatemovement.global/laudato-si-ch-2-commentary-by-fr-reese/], [Last accessed: 18th October 2021].

humankind. God inherently gave humankind the responsibility to cultivate, multiply, care before eating from it, while obtaining food from it. In other words, if we want creation to sustain and feed us, we need to care for it. It is only by being responsible that we can profit from the earth: "Each community can take from the bounty of the earth whatever it needs for subsistence, but it also has the duty to protect the earth and to ensure its fruitfulness for coming generations."[16] Humankind is privileged to use God's Garden but to do so in a responsible way.

According to Matthew Henry, "[t]he place appointed for Adam's residence was a garden not an ivory house nor a palace overlaid with gold, but a garden, furnished and adorned by nature, not by art. The heaven was the roof of Adam's house, and the earth was his floor. The situation of this garden was extremely sweet. It was in Eden, which signifies delight and pleasure."[17] Thus, Adam was placed in a most delightful garden to inhabit it as the head of a household, and thus did God surround him with riches and delights on all sides. Indeed, having created the world out of nothing, God could have made it to be fully self-sustaining. We read that the earth did not bring forth its fruits by itself, but purely by the almighty power of God (v.9). God himself planted a garden in Eden and, out of the ground, God made every tree grow. Rain also is the gift of God; God takes care to water the plants that are of his own planting. God could have created human beings to simply live and enjoy the luxury of God's creation without ever having to contribute anything. Indeed, the garden story provides another perspective on the relationship that humanity is called to have with nature. It reminds us that humans are both a part of nature and that they have a particular responsibility for it.

Many contemporary readers with anthropocentric interests have placed an emphasis on a human-centred creation. Actually, humans are only a small part of a much larger picture. Emerging from the text is a complex description of creation that is defined by the formation of interconnected relationships between God, earth, and all entities of creation. We are created out of the dust of the earth as the Hebrew word for human *adam* comes from *adamah,* the word for dust. As Pope Francis observes, "We have forgotten that we ourselves are dust of the earth (cf.v.7); our very bodies are made up of her elements, we breathe her air, and we receive life and refreshment from her waters".[18] From beginning to end, this story of creation insists on the deep connection between human beings and the world in which we live. Human beings are made to be at one with the garden, to tend it and preserve it as a beautiful and abundant paradise in which all living things can thrive. Our future depends on the connection and relation we entertain with the rest of the creation.

In Genesis 2: 19, we are told that after forming every animal of the field and every bird of the air, God brought them to the man to be named. By allowing Adam to name the animals, God did not allow him to have control and power over these creatures. Naming here is about a relational identity, a question of recognition, not of power. Naming is not a sign of domination but rather reflective of how the human earthling establishes relationships with other creatures. It expresses the bond between humans and animals, not a divinely ordained domination of animals by humans.[19] Humans are viewed as the heart of God's creation and the on-going link between God and nonhuman beings. They are appointed not only to reproduce like other species (Gen. 1:22), but to exercise jurisdiction or guardianship over other living beings that cohabit with them.[20] The divine purpose for humankind in Genesis 2 is to be found in verse 15. It is

---

[16] Fr Reese, "Humans Must Care for Creation", 1.

[17] Matthew Henry, *Matthew Henry's Commentary in One Volume* (Grand Rapids, MI: Wm B. Eerdmans, 1960), 1-6.

[18] Fr Reese, "Humans Must Care for Creation", 2.

[19] Anne M. Clifford, "When being human becomes truly earthly: An ecofeminist proposal for solidarity" in Ann O'Hara Graff (ed), *In the Embrace of God: Feminist approaches to theological anthropology* (Maryknoll, NY: Orbis Books,1995), 173-189: 181.

[20] Samuel Dean McBride, "Divine Protocol: Genesis 1:1-2:3 as Prologue to the Pentateuch", in William P. Brown and Samuel Dean McBride (eds), *God who Creates: Essays in Honour of W Sibley Towner* (Grand Rapids/Cambridge: Eerdmans), 3-41: 15.

expressed with the word šāmar (keep), "protect".[21] This gives responsibility to the human being, not simply for the maintenance and preservation, but for intra-creational development, bringing the world along toward its fullest possible potential. Adam is then commanded to work, serve, watch, preserve and to guard the garden. The verb "guard" or "keep" functions together with the verb "to serve" indicating the kind of labour which humans are to put into the earth. "The human is not asked to be like the lumber barons who destroyed whole ecosystems to retrieve one type of tree, but like a shepherd who tends and cares for sheep while also working (or serving) as a shepherd".[22] One agrees with Neil that our reading of Genesis 2 should banish from our minds any idea that creation care is somehow "secular" work for a Christian, or that it is otherwise not our responsibility.

To keep the garden was the first task given to humanity, an act of serving and worshiping God by cultivating and protecting the natural world. Lynn White deplores that "Christianity bears a huge burden of guilt" for having established a dualism between humans and nature. For him, much of historical Christianity insisted that it is God's will for humans to exploit and rule over nature for their benefit, and thereby made possible the active modern technological conquest of nature that caused the ecological crisis.[23] Human actions should carry out the true reflection of God's nature. This role involves not only simply maintenance or preservation, but a part of the creative process itself through multiplication. The nature is not something which one should interfere with; it is a source of joy, wonder, praise, and gratitude for the gift of life. Every creature in the world is a mirror of God's presence and is therefore worthy of being treated with respect.[24] Human dominion consists of caring for the nonhuman beings with compassion and justice for the glory of God.

Care for Creation: Dominion or Stewardship?

The power that the humans of Genesis 1 have to implement over creation is meant to be "servanthood", as a brother or a sister may rule over others in the family. Consequently, "the human dominion over other living beings is not domination of superiors over inferiors but the responsibility of some creatures for their brothers and sisters' creatures".[25] Our being created in God's image and given dominion over the earth does not justify an absolute domination over other creatures. Indeed, we should see in the image of God, as Steck affirms, "the 'central position' that humans occupy in the priestly creation as God's stewards for promoting life of all beings".[26] Therefore, the entire creation takes its posture from humanity, and it is oriented toward God who is seen as the "provider" of order in God's Creation. As human beings are created in the image of God, humans are made to be stewards and accountable to God for their fellow creatures.

Taken together, Genesis 1 and 2 have led to the development of the stewardship model based primarily on Genesis 2:15 where humans are given the task by Yahweh to act as gardeners in the mythical Garden of Eden, that is, to "till" and "to guard" it. This approach assumes that Genesis 1:26-28 should be read in light of Genesis 2:15 where the role of humans is to "till and keep the garden." Viewed as being in the image of God and the climax of the creation, humans stand in the place of God in order to serve as a lynchpin that

[21] Neil M. Alexander, *The New Interpreter's Bible: A commentary in twelve volumes.* Volume I (Nashville: Abingdon Press, 1994), 349.
[22] John L. Thompson, *Reformation Commentary on Scripture. Old Testament I. Genesis I-II* (Downers Grove, IL: InterVarsity Press, 2012), 86.
[23] Lynn White, "The Historical Roots of Our Ecological Crisis". *Science* 155 (1967): 1207.
[24] Conradie, *An Ecological Christian Anthropology*, 34.
[25] Jonathan K. Kavusa, "Humans and Ecosystems in the Priestly Creation Account: an ecological reading of Genesis 1:1-2:4". MArt diss., University of South Africa, Pretoria, 2012: 59.
[26] Odil Hannes Steck, *World and Environment* (Eugene, OR: Wipf and Stock, 2008).

holds creation together.[27] Humans are viewed as the heart of God's creation, and the on-going link between God and nonhuman beings. Humans are set upon the earth as stewards to carry out God's sovereign rule over other creatures in Genesis 1. Stewardship means that we are morally accountable to God for keeping his creation in the care and well-being that brings honour to Him and best serves His kingdom.[28] Stewardship is a responsibility to care for something that does not belong to you. It may be perceived as a model that allows the concepts of both "dominion" and "subduing" to be held together. The stewardship model retains the relationship between humanity, the earth and God. Writing from an African perspective, Marthinus Daneel notes, "the land is the people, the animals, the plants, the entire earth community – unborn, living, dead. In other word, the land is the totality of known and unknown existence."[29] Human well-being consists in keeping in harmony with the cosmic totality so that the vital force of each human life is in intimate rapport with other forces.[30] For Emmanuel Asante, "the whole of nature must be understood as sacred because it derives its being from the supreme Being who is the Creator-Animator of the universe."[31] Humankind is therefore accountable to the one who vested him this responsibility.

The stewardship concept[32] however has also received many critics among contemporary ecological scholars. One of them is Palmer[33] who considers the political message encoded in stewardship as one of power and oppression. In criticising the anthropocentric view of Genesis 1:26-28, he maintains, the stewardship model falls into an implicit form of anthropocentrism. He further observes that, "Stewardship of the natural world, whether Christian or otherwise, then, remains profoundly anthropocentric and un-ecological, legitimating and encouraging increased human use of the natural world".[34] Stewardship tends to be viewed as human-orientated, a temptation to place human concerns at the centre, "indicating that nature is somehow deficient in maintaining itself and that a healthy ecosystem could only be maintained through constant human interference."[35] It assumes human supremacy above the other species. Though contemporary ecology has demonstrated that nature does not need constant interference and is naturally self-sustaining, the stewardship emphasis still is more on responsibility instead of domination. Therefore, proper stewardship has one eye tending the earth for today and one eye toward tending the earth for future generations. All depend on what the human does with what God presents.

If God's intention is for humans to act as caretakers, then they are called to follow instructions from God, the owner of the whole creation. If dominion is responsibility to care for creation, then stewardship

---

[27] M.M. Wilfong, "Human Creation in Canonical Context: Genesis 1:26-31 and beyond", in W.P. Brown and S.D. McBride (eds), *God Who Creates: Essays in Honour of W Sibley Towner*. (Grand Rapids, MI: Eerdmans, 2000), 42-52: 46-47.

[28] Thomas D. Watts, *Environmental Stewardship in the Judeo-Christian Tradition: Jewish, Catholic, and Protestant Wisdom on the Environment by the Acton Institute for the Study of Religion and Liberty*. (Grand Rapids, MI: Acton Institute, 2006), 70.

[29] M.L. Daneel, "African Christian Theology and the Challenge of Earth Keeping", In J. Mouton and B.C. Lategan, *The Relevance of Theology for the 1990s*. (Pretoria: Human Sciences Research Council, 1998), 435-476,

[30] John Vernon Taylor, *The Primal Vision: Christian Presence Amid African Religion*. (Nairobi: Acton Publishers, 2001), 45-48.

[31] E. Asante, "Ecology: untapped resource of pan-vitalism in Africa". *AFER: African Ecclesial Review* 27 (1995): 289-293: 290-292.

[32] The criticism on the stewardship model has led to new concepts such as "partnership" (cf Rasmussen, *Earth Community, Earth Ethics*; Felix L. Chingota, "Bible Study Notes on Creation," in Martin Ott and Fulata L. Moyo, *Christianity and the Environment*. (Blantyre, Malawi: Christian Literature Association in Malawi, 2002); "created co-creators" (cf. Philip Hefner, The Human Factor: Evolution, Culture, and Religion. (Minneapolis, MN: Fortress, 1993).

[33] C. Palmer, "Stewardship: A Case Study in Environmental Ethics", in I. Ball, M. Goodall, C. Palmer and J. Reader (eds), *The Earth Beneath: A Critical Guide to Green Theology*. (London: SPCK, 1992), 67-86: 76.

[34] Palmer, *Stewardship: A Case Study in Environmental Ethics*, 77-78, 84.

[35] Peet J. van Dyk, "'Responsible Stewardship' – The Root of All Evil in Eco-Theology?" *OTE* 28 (2015) 2523-35: 2523.

describes how we exercise this dominion. We govern creation for the good of humanity and other parts of creation, not in a domineering, selfish and exploitive manner, but by nurturing creation, preserving it, and helping it to function as God intended.[36] Field, in an article entitled "Stewards of Shalom", identifies various strengths of the stewardship concept as he writes:

> (1) It emphasises that the earth belongs to God and not to human beings and thus human beings do not have the right to use and abuse the earth as they please. (2) It emphasises that human beings are responsible for the way in which they use the earth and its inhabitants. (3) It emphasises that humanity is commissioned to protect, care for, and promote the flourishing of nonhuman creation. (4) It emphasises the dignity and value of human persons as representatives of God in creation. The symbol has thus been particularly attractive to those who are disempowered and oppressed by the dominant political and economic order. (5) The model for the steward is the self-sacrifice on behalf of both fellow human beings and the nonhuman creation.[37]

Therefore, good stewardship requires attention as to how creation was designed to work. As Barr affirms, "biblical traditions of creation are not about the exploitation of the earth but its protection and preservation".[38] In the priestly creation story, there is no motif of caring for others, but about the co-responsibility of all. The life of the universe depends on how each individual creature implements its distinctive role allotted to him by the Creator.[39] By electing human beings to till and work in the garden, God has not granted them an absolute power to alter and exploit the creation for their own use. Humans do not replace God, the designer, and the redeemer of the created world. God did not retreat from the creation area, but rather, he continues to sustain his creation so that each creature executes its particular role to maintain the ecological balance.[40] God has shaped the created order in such a way that the creator and the creatures share overlapping spheres of interdependence and creative responsibility.[41] As the earth provides for human welfare and needs, humans are also commanded to care for the earth and all its creatures.

Care for Our Common Home, God's Household

Human beings are inhabitants of God's household and they live together with other creatures by God's grace. We are to respond to God's grace in a grateful and responsible way. "Caring for creation is a relational act, an act of love from us towards God. We love and serve God by being good stewards of God's creation – a very practical way to love God and neighbour".[42] The Scriptures are clear that all of creation exists to bring glory to God. Everything is expected to acknowledge and appreciate God's power, majesty,

---

36 Jared Hyneman and Christopher Shore, "Why Are We Stewards of Creation? World Vision's Biblical Understanding of How We Relate to Creation", *World Vision International* (Uxbridge, UK: World Vision International, 2013). [Available at: https://www.wvi.org/sites/default/files/World%20Vision%E2%80%99s%20Biblical%20Understanding%20of%20How%20we%20Relate%20to%20Creation_Full.pdf], [Last accessed: 12 October 2021].

37 D.N. Field, "Stewards of Shalom: Toward a trinitarian ecological ethic", *Quarterly Review* 22(4), (2002), 383-396: 383-384.

38 James Barr, "Man and Nature. The Ecological Controversy and Old Testament", *BJRL* 55 (1972): 30.

39 Kavusa, "Humans and Ecosystems", 61-62.

40 Kavusa, "Humans and Ecosystems", 65.

41 Neil M. Alexander, in: The New Interpreter's Bible (in twelve volumes), vol. 1: Genesis to Leviticus. Volume I. (Nashville, TN: Abingdon Press, 1994), 355.; see also: https://www.logos.com/product/8803/new-interpreters-bible-a-commentary-in-twelve-volumes.

42 Jeremaia Waqainabete, "Christian Environmentalism: An Ecotheological Approach to Earth Keeping" *WWF-Pacific* (Suva, Fiji: WWF-Pacific, World Wide Fund for Nature, 2018). [Available online at: https://wwfasia.awsassets.panda.org/downloads/theological_mindset_english_2018_sep.pdf], [Last accessed: 14th January 2022].

holiness, wisdom, and love.[43] God reveals Himself through His Creation. Human beings are embedded in a community not only with other human beings, but also with all other beings. "The whole cosmos was created out of God's love, a God who remains the continuing source of life and goal of the world's existence. Such a theocentric vision may indeed help us to understand our place within the earth community and the wider cosmos."[44] Writing about human finitude, Conradie opines that the

> [...] human species is indeed unique, but that every other species is unique too. We do have dignity in God's eyes and should therefore treat other human beings with dignity too. However, such dignity does not necessarily entitle us to a special place, a position of privilege in God's household. We have a special position of responsibility, but that is primarily a function of human power and the devastating impact of human presence on the earth's ecosystems. In exercising this responsibility, we have to realise our dependence on other forms of life and on the planet's ecosystems as a whole.[45]

As we work and care for creation, let us resist the urge to merely think about creation as something to serve our individual needs. Pope Paul VI stress that, "We are the heirs of earlier generations, and we reap benefits from the efforts of our contemporaries; we are under obligation to all men. Therefore, we cannot disregard the welfare of those who will come after us to increase the human family. The reality of human solidarity brings us not only benefits but also obligations."[46] Creation care is action for the well-being of the planet and action against climate change and environmental degradation. Ecotheology must lead to action. In turn, action must inform ecotheology. Ideally, ecotheologies lead to radical actions against environmental degradation and climate change. These actions should facilitate eco-justice and eco-ethics. Preferably, these actions lead to innovative eco-technologies and result in social systems that nurture and protect the environment.[47] No matter how small our actions can be, they make a difference if we all contribute. Let us acknowledge the dignity of all living things and treat them in a manner that is worthy of God the Creator. Care of creation should consist of environmental justice to care for nature and for all those suffering, especially the poor. Having a responsibility to care implies not only saving the environment from destruction, but also saving the human future and this is inseparable from the future of all living things.

Conclusion

As we grow in the conviction regarding our roles as stewards of God's creation, our view of how we interact with our surroundings should change. Our minds and hearts should increasingly see life through God's lens, which should begin to shape our daily choices. If we take the ecological message evident as a primary theme in the first chapters of Genesis seriously, then it is necessary for humans to interact with the earth in a way that is vitally concerned with the well-being of all entities of creation. This new reality calls for a voice to rise from within the world community that no longer ignores the natural world but instead addresses the ecological crisis. By living this new reality, humans can work together in harmony for the protection and sustainability of life on our planet for thousands of years to come.[48]

---

[43] Thompson, *Reformation Commentary on Scripture*, 87.
[44] Conradie, *An Ecological Christian Anthropology*, 131.
[45] Conradie, *An Ecological Christian Anthropology*, 135.
[46] Blessed Pope Paul VI's encyclical: *Populorum Progressio* (The Development of Peoples) – 50 years. The Newsletter of the Catholic Commission for Social Justice Issue 24, June 2017.
[47] Graham Hill, *Global Church: Reshaping our conversations, renewing our mission, revitalizing our churches* (Downers Grove, IL: InterVarsity Press, 2016), 176.
[48] Lausanne Global Consultation on Creation Care and the Gospel, "Consultation Statement", St. Ann, Jamaica, November 2012, [Available online at: www.lausanne.org/content/statement/creation-care-call-to-action], [Last accessed: 14th January 2022].

Suggestions for Further Reading

Asante, E. 1995. 'Ecology: Untapped Resource of Pan-vitalism in Africa'. *AFER: African Ecclesial Review* 27 (1995), 289-293.

Averbeck, Richard E. "A literature day, inter-textual, and contextual reading of Genesis 1-2", in Daryl J. Charles, Ed. *Reading Genesis 1-2. An Evangelical Conversation*. Peabody, MA: Hendrickson.

Barr, James. "Man and Nature. The Ecological Controversy and Old Testament," *BJRL* 55 (1972), 9-32.

Chingota, Felix L. "Bible Study Notes on Creation", in F. Moyo and M. Ott, Eds. *Christianity and the Environment*. Kachere text No.13. Blantyre, Malawi: Christian Literature Association in Malawi, 2002.

Clifford, Anne M. "When being human becomes truly earthly: An ecofeminist proposal for solidarity", in Ann O'Hara Graff, Ed. *In the Embrace of God: Feminist Approaches to Theological Anthropology*. Maryknoll, NY: Orbis Books, 1995: 173-189.

Conradie, Ernst M. *An Ecological Christian Anthropology: At Home on Earth?* Burlington, VT: Ashgate, 2005.

Daneel, M.L. "African Christian theology and the challenge of earth keeping", in J. Mouton and B.C. Lategan, Eds. *The Relevance of Theology for the 1990s*. Pretoria: Human Sciences Research Council, 1998: 435-476.

van Dyk, Peet J. "'Responsible Stewardship' – The Root of All Evil in Eco-Theology?" *OTE* 28(2), (2015): 523-535.

Field, D.N. "Stewards of Shalom: Toward a Trinitarian Ecological Ethic", *Quarterly Review* 22(4), (2002), 383-396.

Gale A Yee, Hugh R Page Jr and Matthew J.M. Coomber, Eds. *The Pentateuch: Fortress Commentary on the Bible Study Edition*. Minneapolis, MN: Fortress, 2016.

Grosse, Stephen. "Building a Relationship with the Earth: Humans and Ecology in Genesis 1-3." *Denison Journal of Religion* 5 (2005), Article 4, [Available at: http://digitalcommons.denison.edu/religion/vol5/iss1/], [Last accessed: 14th January 2022].

Hallman, David G. *A Place in Creation: Ecological visions in science, religion, and economics*. Geneva: world council of churches, 1992.

Hefner, Philip. *The Human Factor: Evolution, Culture, and Religion*. Minneapolis, MN: Fortress, 1993.

Hill, Graham. Global Church: Reshaping our conversations, renewing our mission, revitalizing our churches. Downers Grove, IL: InterVarsity Press, 2016.

Jingcheng, Xu and Meifang Nan Gong, "A Study of the Social Ecological Wisdom in H.W. Longfellow's Poetry," *TPLS* 2(1), (2012): 24-30.

Kavusa, Jonathan K. "Humans and ecosystems in the priestly creation account: an ecological reading of genesis 1:1-2:4". MArt diss., University of South Africa, Pretoria, 2012.

Lausanne Global Consultation on Creation Care and the Gospel, "Consultation Statement", St. Ann, Jamaica, November 2012, [Available at: www.lausanne.org/content/statement/creation-care-call-to-action], [Last accessed: 18 October 2021].

Henry, Matthew. *Matthew Henry's Commentary in One Volume*. Grand Rapids, MI: Wm B Eerdmans, 1960.

McBride, Samuel Dean. "Divine Protocol: Genesis 1:1-2:3 as Prologue to the Pentateuch", in W.P. Brown and S.D. McBride, Eds. *God who Creates: Essays in Honour of W Sibley Towner*. Grand Rapids/Cambridge: Eerdmans, 2000: 3-41.

Neil M Alexander. *The New Interpreter's Bible: A Commentary in Twelve Volumes*. Volume I. Nashville, TN: Abingdon Press, 1994.

Padgett Alan. "Ecotheology: Developing New Perspective". *Biologos* 29th March 2021, [Available at: https://biologos.org/articles/ecotheology-developing-new-perspective], [Last accessed: 14th January 2022].

Palmer, C. "Stewardship: A Case Study in Environmental Ethics", in I. Ball, M. Goodall, C. Palmer and J. Reader, Eds. *The Earth Beneath: A Critical Guide to Green Theology*. London: SPCK, 1992: 67-86.

Rajotte, Freda. "What is the Crisis?", in Elizabeth Breuilly and Martin Palmer, Eds. *Christianity and Ecology*. London: Cassell, 1992: 1-18.

Rasmussen, Larry L. *Earth Community: Earth Ethics*. Maryknoll, NY: Orbis Books, 1996.

Fr Reese, "Humans Must Care for Creation and Share Its Fruits – On Care, Sabbath, Relationship, Life, & the Common Good". *Laudato Si'*, [Available at: https://catholicclimatemovement.global/laudato-si-ch-2-commentary-by-fr-reese/], [Last accessed: 18th October 2021].

Steck, Odil Hannes. *World and Environment*. Nashville, TN: Abingdon, 1980.

Taylor, John Vernon. *Christian Presence Amid African Religion.* Nairobi: Acton, 2001.

Thompson, John L. *Reformation Commentary on Scripture. Old Testament I. Genesis I-II*. Downers Grove, IL: InterVarsity Press, 2012.

Waqainabete, Jeremaia. *Christian Environmentalism: An Ecotheological Approach to Earth Keeping*. Suva, Fiji: WWF-Pacific, World Wide Fund for Nature, 2018. [Available at: https://wwfasia.awsassets.panda.org/downloads/theological_mindset_english_2018_sep.pdf], [Last accessed: 20 October 2021].

Warren, K. J. "The Power and the Promise of Ecological Feminism", in M.H. Mackinnon and M. McIntyre, Eds. *Reading in Ecology and Feminist Theology.* Kansas City, KS: Sheed & Ward, 1995: 172-195.

Watts, Thomas D. *Environmental Stewardship in the Judeo-Christian Tradition: Jewish, Catholic, and Protestant Wisdom on the Environment by the Acton Institute for the Study of Religion and Liberty*. Grand Rapids, MI: Acton Institute, 2006.

Wilfong, M.M. "Human Creation in Canonical Context: Genesis 1:26-31 and Beyond", in W.P. Brown and S.D. McBride, Eds. *God Who Creates: Essays in Honour of W Sibley Towner*. Grand Rapids, MI: Eerdmans, 2000: 42-52.

3. The Ecclesial Mandate of Eco-Diakonia in the Mission of God: An African Lutheran Perspective

Abednego Nkamuhabwa Keshomshahara[1]

Introduction

Eco-diakonia is a word which has been formed by combining two words: "Eco" for ecology, which deals with the relations of organisms to one another and to their physical surroundings; and "Diakonia", taken to mean a commission to render social services to the needy on behalf of God while at the same time advocating for vulnerable people by negating the causes of miseries in the world. Eco-diakonia is, therefore, a manifestation of faith in action while touching various aspects of caring for God's creation including human beings and also protecting nature against any harm.

Taking care of God's creation includes the protection of environment against its degradation; it addresses climate change; and it strives for human rights and wealth creation without destroying the environment. As such, eco-diakonia deals with protection, care, cure and advocating against any harm coming to God's creation. It is prevention in as much as preventive measures are taken to avoid more damage to the environment and, at the same time, involves curing or healing the victims of environmental degradation as an ecclesial mandate. Hence, eco-diakonia is a very important aspect of our Christian faith and discipleship as it expresses love to our neighbours and God's creation at large.

Alfred Jaeger observes that, unlike non-governmental organisations (NGOs) which also offer social services, diakonia offers social services with eschatological dimensions that emphasise God's presence in human history while liberating people from their sufferings and death (Rev. 21:4).[2] At the same time, God urges people to help and protect others bearing in mind that, during the judgment day, they will be rewarded or punished eternally based on how they responded to the needs of the poor, prisoners, the hungry and the naked (Mt. 25:40).[3]

The environmental crisis needs a quick response from the church in view of eco-diakonia. Samson K Gitau, in his book entitled *The Environmental Crisis: A Challenge for Christianity*, argues that the church has remained behind in the struggle to protect the environment. He adds that if Christians could treat the environment as they treat holy communion, with faith and awe, the church would have made a big contribution in mitigating the effects of global warming.[4] As J.N.K. Mugambi puts it: unless there is a quick intervention with conscious effort to reverse the challenge of environmental degradation, there will not be any habitat to be talked about at the end of 21st century given the reckless plundering of the environment in the name of human development.[5]

---

[1] Bishop Dr Abednego Nkamuhabwa Keshomshahara is a Bishop of the Evangelical Lutheran Church in Tanzania (ELCT), Northwestern Diocese (NWD) along Lake Victoria in Bukoba, Tanzania since 2015. He holds a PhD in Theology from Germany at Kirchliche Hochschule Wuppertal/Bethel (2008). He has published books and several articles on church and society. Before his consecration as a Bishop, he worked as a lecturer at Tumaini University Makumira, Josiah Kibira University College (2012-2015). He also worked as Vice Principal of the Bukoba Teachers College, Principal of the Theological College and Bible School at Ruhija (2000-2003), and Parish Pastor at the ELCT NWD Cathedral (1998).

[2] Alfred Jaeger, *Diakonie als Christilisches Unternehmen: Theologische Wirtschaftsethik im Kontext diakonischer Unternehmenspolitik* (Guethersloh: Guethersloher Verlagshaus Gerd Mohn, 1986), 67.

[3] Jaeger, *Diakonie als Christilisches Unternehmen*, 67.

[4] Samson K. Gitau, *The Environmental Crisis: A Challenge for African Christianity* (Nairobi: Acton, 2000), 3.

[5] Mugambi, "Forword" in Gitau, *The Environmental Crisis*, i-ii.

It seems absurd to note that the victims of global warming are found in the developing nations where the majority of world's population is found while their nations do not contribute much to global warming unlike the industrialised nations. The industrialised nations form a small portion of the world population who benefit from the world's resources at the expense of the environment and the poor. This situation demands for an increased commitment to a prophetic diakonia that answers the need for advocacy of the vulnerable. This prophetic diakonia goes beyond helping them with basic needs as it must include combating the causes of their miseries.

This article is based on the African Traditional Religious perspectives, the bible, church history that enlightens us on Lutheran background of diakonia and the current situation of eco-diakonia. As Reinhard Boettcher puts it very clearly, the basis for diakonia includes the bible, church history and contexts where the people live.[6] This article will cover: Eco-Diakonia from the perspectives of African Traditional Religion; the Biblical Basis for Eco-Diakonia; Eco-Diakonia in Church History; and the Current Situation of Eco-Diakonia in Africa.

Eco-Diakonia from the African Traditional Religious Perspectives

Scholars admit that primal religions have had a big contribution to the conservation of nature worldwide. Samson K. Gitau says that present generations miss the primal traditions and religions, which are very important in protecting the environment and the entire realm of God's creation. He observes that the problem is caused by some scholars of religion who view those primal religions as primitive and only dealing with manipulation of spirits, thus failing to see their relevance for the conservation of nature.[7] In a similar way, J.N.K. Mugambi urges people to learn from the cultures who have resisted utilitarianism in the exploitation of the environment as these primal religions regard nature as part and parcel of God's creation. He contends that the Western civilisations have assumed that humans are separate from nature and are above it, however, contrary to this perspective, the African, Native American and Asian civilisations venerate nature and God as ontological categories together with humans without putting humans above other creatures.[8]

Wilson Niwagila, in his article "Our Struggle for Justice, Peace and Integrity of Creation", contends that the platonic philosophy that separates nature from the spirit has led to disregarding nature and, subsequently, nature's destruction. He further argues that Christianity is embedded with a predominant mode of thinking which tends to have interests in heaven and saving souls without sufficient concern for planet earth.[9] For him, African Traditional Religion has something to contribute to the conservation of nature given its philosophy of holism whereby all things have interconnectedness – a connection between the spiritual and material aspects of life.[10] This is the reference point and basis for this section, since eco-diakonia ought to be pursued and practiced in the context where the believers are found.

The Concept of God in Relationship with Humanity and Nature

The African traditional religions perceive God as being in a relationship with nature and humanity. Thus, the Africans understood God as creator, omniscient, omnipresent, eternal, sustainer, helper, and the one

---

[6] Reinhard Boettcher, "Toward Lutheran Theological Understandings of the Diaconal Ministry" in Reinhard Boettcher (ed), *The Diaconal Ministry in the Mission of the Church* (Geneva: LWF, 2006).
[7] Gitau, *The Environmental Crisis*, 135.
[8] Mugambi, "Foreword" in Gitau, *The Environmental Crisis*, ii.
[9] Wilson B. Niwagila, "Our Struggle for Justice, Peace and Integrity of Creation: A Quest for a Theology of Reconstruction in Africa" in J.N.K. Mugambi (ed), *The Church and Reconstruction of Africa: Theological Considerations* (Nairobi: All Africa Conference of Churches, 1997), 176-179.
[10] Niwagila, "Our Struggle for Justice", 172-179.

with eyes like a basket.[11] As Gustaf Aulen argues on the basis of Romans 1:18-20, God revealed himself to the Gentiles as long as God revealed himself to them via nature.[12] As a creator of all things, which are visible and invisible, God is connected with his entire creation including human beings. This understanding makes the Africans see nature as sacred. Hence, nature is respected and sometimes feared. It is because of such a worldview that Africans could not simply cut forests down without permission from the religious and political leaders, both of whom were mandated by God to lead and guide people for their prosperity in material and spiritual dimensions.

As has been stated earlier, the coming of western civilisations and Christianity to Africa as a whole disregarded the African worldviews and led to the destruction of nature in the name of development. Wilson Niwagila shares an exciting example of the tension between western civilisation and African traditional religion by describing a case in the 1960s when the traditional prophet challenged the politicians who were mobilising people to clear forests for crop production in the Kagera region, Tanzania. He further argues that the traditional prophet condemned the Christians who had ordered the African Christians to cut all big trees. The Haya ethnic groups used to worship under those trees. The traditional prophecy foresaw that bad things would happen to Bugabo County following the deforestation and uprooting of the big trees. Niwagila further explains that, after a few years, the Bugabo County started to suffer from ecological crisis in the form of a long draught period. Wild animals including monkeys, that used to feed on forest fruits, instead invaded people's plantations and ate everything that they had planted. Also, worms were forced to migrate from forests to banana plantations to survive; as a result, banana trees in Bugabo fell down and the whole society suffered from famine resulting from the deforestation.[13]

However, it ought to be noted that the African traditional religion also prohibited Africans from developing and utilising their resources in modern ways in view of increased population and needs. At the same time, the western culture was also extreme in over-utilising the resources to the extent of causing environmental degradation. In this case, what is needed is moderation in everything – both overutilisation and underutilisation of nature is not good. Humans have to use nature to meet their needs but should not allow human greed to dominate as this is dangerous to God's creation.

The African traditional prayer is of cardinal importance in showing the relationship between God, humans and nature. Niwagila explores this: the one who prays asks the ruling spirit (who is below God in the hierarchy) to give people health until they bend in old age, they ask for guidance and protection from all dangers and diseases, they ask for protection of their children and grandchildren and their welfare, they ask for protection of their spouse, properties and livestock. They further also pray for the wellbeing of the snakes, rats, lizards and spiders.[14] When this prayer was shared in German, some Germans could not imagine how people could pray for snakes and lizards. The African religion was categorised as animism since the Africans were seen as worshippers of nature.[15]

Where God is viewed as the one who knows everything, as omniscient, omnipresent or the one who has eyes like a basket, this results in the protection of the environment and humans by guaranteeing morality in the society. In the African traditional religion, people feared to harm others or nature since God and the spirits had the ability to be everywhere and to see everything. As such, people respected nature, including other humans, lest they encounter punishment for evil deeds. Africans feared to burn bushes, to engage in deforestation, to kill humans, to exploit and oppress others since they knew that God and the ancestors forbade such deeds. Instead, their traditional religion encouraged people to protect nature, including other humans. Orphans and widows were supported by their relatives and all their neighbours since failure to

---

[11] Abednego Keshomshahara, "The Lutheran Doctrine of the Holy Spirit and the Challenge of the Traditional Spirit Beliefs among the Haya People" (M.Th. Thesis, Tumaini University Makumira, 2000), 9.
[12] Keshomshahara, "The Lutheran Doctrine", 9.
[13] Niwagila, "Our Struggle for Justice", 174.
[14] Niwagila, "Our Struggle for Justice", 172-175.
[15] Niwagila, "Our Struggle for Justice", 173.

support and help such people would result in punishment by God via ancestral spirits. Already we see the glimpse of a culture of eco-diakonia in the African traditional religions, especially where it concerns taking care of nature and rendering services to humans without harming the environment.

Community Life and Hospitality in African Traditional Religion as a Basis for Eco-Diaconal Services in Africa

A community is defined as a group of people with shared characteristics and also who share a space or have certain attitudes and interests in common. The African traditional religion shaped the African communities. They were characterised by hierarchical order which started with God under whom there are ancestral spirits (the living dead), and then humans, animals, insects and inanimate things. God and ancestral spirits were regarded as important members of the community. The ancestral spirits were regarded as the pioneers of community life. They were respected as the ones who instituted the morals that guaranteed law and order and protected nature, including humans. Those who went astray were punished by God and spirits. Punishments included periods of bad luck, extra-ordinary deaths and fines by clan or community elders or traditional priests.

As a result of the moral traditions that were founded by the ancestors, sharing of resources was emphasised so that no one would lack basic needs in the community. Greed and individualism were discouraged and were hated attributes. Orphans, widows, old people, sick people and the disabled were taken care of by communities, clan members and families. This created a society based on love, compassion, empathy, security and justice. Samson Gitau says that "sharing of resources with the unfortunate members of a given family implied that starvation would be minimised. When people had the basic necessities for life, it meant less strain on the environment. Secondly, the African sense of community, based on clan systems ensured security, justice, and social welfare to all members of the society".[16]

However, traditional African community life, by encouraging community social rights, also tended towards suppressing individual rights. Individual initiatives and freedoms were not emphasised.[17] Also, it created dependence on others whereby some capable people could depend on their relatives for help unnecessarily.[18] This shows that, sometimes, African community life can be abused. Other leaders corruptly favoured people of their own ethnic groups or their own families by using public funds to protect their political positions and interests.[19] Rebecca Ganusah argues that African community life has led to political instability in Africa since people have not been trained to think beyond their families, clans and ethnic boundaries to encompass the whole national or continental development.[20]

Also, despite the good elements of community life, social changes and modernity have shaken African values, although many people are still influenced by traditional ways of participating in community life.[21] Jean Marc Ela advised Africans not to revive or romanticise the past traditions of community life although he appreciates the traditional concept of holism.[22] That is why African community life should be adjusted

---

[16] Gitau, *The Environmental Crisis*, 54.
[17] Keshomshahara, *A Theology of Poverty Reduction*, 38-39.
[18] Klaus Nürnberger, "Gottes Mission in der Praxis: Der Kampf um Befreiung, Würde und Gerechtigkeit in Afrikanischen Gesellschaften", in *Mission Dei Heute: Zur Aktualität eines missionstheologischen Schlüsselbegriffs* (Hamburg: Evangelisches Missionswerk in Deutschland, 2003), 66-67.
[19] Nuernberger, "Gottes Mission", 67-67.
[20] Rebecca Ganusah, "Social Integration and Development in Contemporary Africa" in Mugambi (ed), *Democracy*, 123-125; Keshomshahara, *A Theology of Poverty Reduction*, 39.
[21] John Mbiti, *African Religions and Philosophy* (London: Heinemann,1969), 262-267. Also Abednego Keshomshahara, *A Theology of Poverty Reduction in Tanzania: A Quest for Christian-Socio-Economic and Political Vision* (Dodoma: Central Tanganyika Press, 2008), 36-38.
[22] Valentine Dedji, *Reconstruction and Renewal in African Christian Theology* (Nairobi: Acton, 2003), 226. Also Keshomshahara, *A Theology of Poverty Reduction*, 36.

to modern changes through national policies for the protection of the whole nation.[23] This can be exemplified by augmenting community life through policies in the form of saving and Credit Cooperative Societies (SACCOS) and Community Health Insurances (CHF) by which people support each other in a modern way, in a formal and official way.[24]

However, as has been mentioned earlier, traditional community life is still visible in rural areas of Africa. This means that the church can carry out eco-diakonia by using both models of African traditional community life and modernised community life. Churches in the rural areas still encourage Christians to take care of their relatives in their respective clans and families. At the same time, diakonia is undertaken in formal ways within church institutions, for example, church health facilities and facilities for the blind, deaf, mentally challenged people, elderly people, epileptic, and others who have need.

The Ecclesial Mandate for Eco-Diakonia from Biblical Perspectives

Eco-Diakonia in the Old Testament

The creation story in Genesis 1:2-4a is a priestly account that shows that human beings were the last to be created after plants and animals. Humans were created with a significant difference since they were created in the image of God, both female and males (Gen. 1:27). This sets them apart from the rest of creation. Having been created in the image of God, humans are charged with a responsibility towards other creatures and God's creation as God has a responsibility towards humans in the order that can be expressed as "God-humans-nature".[25]

Another creation story from Genesis 2:4b-3:24 depicts God creating a human being from the earth. God puts him in the Garden of Eden far away from the wild animals. The garden has good trees and a pleasant atmosphere. According to Yahwist tradition, the human beings are dominant over the rest of nature.[26] However, as Mugambi observes, dominion over nature does not imply ruling over nature as that would lead to abuse and misuse of it, rather it implies stewardship that enhances responsible management of environment that was given to humans by God to take care and use it for their benefits and sustenance of lives.[27] Humans are given responsibility to till and keep the garden (Gen.2:15).

Humans are considered superior to nature because they are created in the image of God and also as Adam was given the privilege of naming the rest of the creatures. However, Niwagila does not accept the assumed superiority of humans based on their status of giving names to creatures. Rather, the duty of naming creatures implies a close relationship between humans and other creatures. Thus, he adds, humans become ambassadors of God in recognising nature as a partner, as an interdependent relationship. Hence, he concludes that destruction of God's creation is also destruction of humanity.[28]

It is very important to note that there was a grade of beauty in the process of creation. When God had created the universe and everything in it, he made a pronunciation that it was "good". After creating human beings, God pronounced the totality of all He had created to be "very good" (Gen. 1:26-31). God's marking of creation as "very good", gives value and respect to his creation. Also, the human being, as a co-creator, is expected to improve creation: "Adam and Eve to make good earth, which God has created even better",[29] not worsen it Animals and humans are given almost the same food: humans are ordered to eat seeds and

[23] Keshomshahara, *A Theology of Poverty Reduction*, 37.
[24] Keshomshahara, *A Theology of Poverty Reduction*, 37.
[25] Gitau, *The Environmental Crisis*, 60-61. Creation of humans in the image of God falls under the priestly account of creation which is younger than the Yahwist account of creation. Gitau, *The Environmental Crisis*, 60-62.
[26] Gitau, *The Environmental Crisis*, 65.
[27] Mugambi, "The Ecological Crisis", 160.
[28] Niwagila, "Our Struggle for Justice", 175-179.
[29] Gitau, *The Environmental Crisis*, 65.

fruits while animals are ordered to eat leaves and stems. Humans are not allowed to kill animals. Humans are caretakers of God's creation and not owners of it. They are stewards of God; they dominate the earth for the sake of God. Although they are allowed to eat fruits and seeds, they are given limits not to eat from the tree of knowledge of good and evil (Gen. 2:16-17). Tempted into selfishness, Adam and Eve tried to take everything for themselves; they were not satisfied with what they were given. As a result, humans are punished for violating the law of God; even nature is punished (Gen. 3:17-19).

Disharmony emerges as Adam and Eve are sent away from paradise, from happiness and a mutual relationship with the creator. Humans begin to experience conflict, suspicion and distrust. The story of Cain and Abel portrays lack of care and love. Cain kills Abel and does not like to be asked about Abel's whereabouts. But God still loves the sinners shown when he protects Cain from being killed. The same applies to Adam and Eve who were clothed by God after breaking God's command.[30] In the same way, God protects nature whereby Noah and the other creatures are protected from floods. At the end, God makes a covenant promising not to destroy nature again.

The Old Testament uncovers hope after the fall of man. It hopes for a "Messiah" – the anointed one who is the expected redeemer of God's people. The Messiah is expected to bring about a new harmony between humans and nature whereby peace and joy will prevail. Prophet Isaiah (11:6-9) and prophet Micah (4:5) are propagators of a messianic hope that will change the world from one of suffering to one of redemption, harmony, love and peace among people and nature at large.[31]

As far as the diaconal spirit is concerned, the Old Testament has many texts that encourage and challenge people to sympathise with the needy while also stretching out their hands to help them. In the Book of Isaiah 58:5-7, the prophet challenges people to avoid showing people that they have fasted as a measure of their righteousness. Instead, he tells them that good and meaningful fasting is that of sharing with the poor, breaking the yokes around others and repenting sins.

Eco-Diakonia from the New Testament Perspective

Samson Gitau calls Jesus Christ an environmentalist due his life of simplicity whereby Jesus desired only the minimum necessary goods. He adds that Jesus had both interior and exterior detachment from material goods. This attitude did not strain the environment.[32] Jesus was concerned with others. He stressed sharing resources and assisting the needy. He challenged the rich not only to share resources with others but also to make sure that their wealth is obtained justifiably. Zacchaeus had to repent his corruption, theft and failure to help the poor when he met Jesus (Luke 19).[33] Already, the message of Jesus Christ has a basis for an environmentally friendly life while challenging his disciples to have the diaconal spirit of love for the neighbour in need.

Jesus taught that human beings represent God on earth to maintain creation of God and be accountable to God as stewards; this widens the responsibility of taking care of nature. The same applies to those parables that encourage people to use their talents fruitfully while knowing that God is the invisible and absent landlord who eventually will hold people accountable regarding how they used and took care of the environment and resources entrusted to them.[34]

The epistles also contain foundations for the conservation of nature and caring for others in the world in the form of eco-diakonia. Apostle Paul says that Jesus Christ came to restore the respect of God's creation because he is superior to all created things as he has visible likeness to the invisible God, through whom everything was created, and he has union with the whole creation of God (Col. 1:16-17). For Paul, nature

---

[30] Gitau, *The Environmental Crisis,* 64-67.
[31] Gitau, *The Environmental Crisis,* 70-71.
[32] Gitau, *The Environmental Crisis*, 72-74.
[33] Gitau, *The Environmental Crisis*, 72.
[34] Gitau, *The Environmental Crisis*, 73.

is also an object of salvation, it is not only human beings who are in need of salvation but also the entire creation is waiting eagerly for salvation (Rom. 8:19-23). Hence, redemption history that began with the creation of heaven and earth (Gen. 1:1) will be consummated in making of the new heaven and new earth (Deut. 21:1-5). This again shows that both humans and nature need redemption and a new harmony as was the case before the first humans fell into sin and thus broke their relationship with God. This does not only refer to spiritual aspects of life but also to material conditions of life.

The epistles also challenge believers to address the needs of the poor. James 1:27 reminds believers that religion accepted by God includes looking after orphans and widows in their distress and keeping oneself from being polluted by the world. Paul asks believers to carry each other's burdens so as to fulfil Christ's law (Gal. 6:2). Paul insists that believers to do good acts to others by using different words and emphases. In Galatians 6:9, he tells people not to get tired of doing good things since, at a proper time, they will harvest their rewards. In Hebrews 13:16, he says "do not forget to do good, for God is pleased by such sacrifices". In 2 Thessalonians 3:13, Paul urges the Christians not to give up doing good, rather they should continue to do what is right without weakening on that resolve. Such good deeds to help the needy or for the entirety of God's creation should not be perceived as a way of attaining salvation or the favour of God, rather, it should be viewed as necessary fruits of faith (Gal. 5:22-23). Such fruits of faith include love, joy, peace, patience, goodness, faithfulness and self-control. These attributes are part and parcel of taking care of God's creation, including other humans.

The Ecclesial Mandate to Address the Current Ecological Crisis as God's Mission in View of Eco-Diakonia in Africa and Worldwide

The Current Environmental Crisis

As time goes on, if we don't take sufficient measures to protect the environment, the environmental crisis worsens. As Karen Bloomquist observes, climate change – also known as global warming – is caused by humans disrupting the global weather and climate systems, especially due to emissions of greenhouse gases by burning fossil fuels. In her introduction to *God, Creation and Climate Change: Spiritual and Ethical Perspectives*, she summarises the current environmental crisis as so:

> These gases trap solar radiation entering the atmosphere, thus warming the atmosphere, land oceans and increasing the frequency and intensity of storms, floods, and drought. Sea levels rise and the coastal lands that are home and provide a livelihood for many millions of people throughout the world, not to mention all the other creatures that depend on such natural habitats, are destroyed. Climate change is not only an environmental matter but also correlated with more severe food shortages, loss of livelihood, conflicts over land and water, increasing impoverishment and the forced migration of peoples, along with other economic and political crises.[35]

The book, as a whole, also explores other effects of climate change, such as unpredictability of weather and seasons, the eruption of diseases like malaria due to increasing temperatures that favour breeding of mosquitoes, deterioration of air quality, especially in the industrial countries, and heat-related deaths.[36]

Other elements of the environmental crisis, as discussed by Colette Bouka Coula, include deforestation, soil degradation which reduces soil fertility (and the related problem of increased soil salinity), loss of biodiversity, and excessive use of land that leads to firewood shortages.[37] J.N.K Mugambi investigates other

---

[35] Karen L. Bloomquist, "Introduction", in Karen L. Bloomquist (ed), *God, Creation and Climate Change: Spiritual and Ethical Perspectives* (Geneva: LWF, 2009), 5.

[36] Bloomquist, "Introduction", 13.

[37] Colette Bouka Coula, "Addressing Realities on the Ground", in Bloomquist (ed), *God, Creation and Climate Change*, 29.

causes of environmental crisis: overfishing, overhunting, population growth and the introduction of non-native species. He observes that human-caused disruption of nature and global climate may imply unintended "ecological suicide" or "eco-suicide".[38] Wilson Niwagila makes a similarly observation saying that which humans call development or civilisation through subduing and conquering nature is, in reality, movement towards our own deaths and destruction as a species. He adds that this trend of jeopardising our own habitat is a deadly progress which Eugen Drewermann names "der tödliche Fortschritt" in German.[39]

An Eco-Diakonal Response to the Environmental Crisis

Conservation of the Environment in Africa and Worldwide

Although churches and Christians in general have not yet engaged fully in the issues of environment conservation in the same way as they deal with other ecclesial activities,[40] some efforts have been made to combat environmental degradation in Africa and worldwide. Such activities include tree planting in various parishes to help protect the environment and, at the same time, increase wealth for the parishes and church institutions. Christians are urged to plant native trees that can increase habitat rather than monocultures for resource use. Churches are also campaigning for the use of solar energy, especially in Africa where there is a surplus of sunshine. Being renewable, the use of solar power avoids using other forms of energy, especially fossil fuels, that are damaging the environment.[41]

Awareness is rising among the Christians and community members as far as the causes and mitigations of ecological crisis are concerned. Such awareness-raising projects are taking place through seminars to the congregants; however, these are not yet done in all congregations systematically. Other activities include campaigns for switching people to energy-saving stoves and environmentally friendly alternative sources of energy.

Response of Eco-Diakonia to Human Needs caused by Environmental and Non-Environmental Crisis

Eco-diakonia has many tasks to undertake. Besides the initiatives trying to prevent ecological challenges through addressing the causes of the crisis, there are also obligations to address people's needs when the crisis makes them more vulnerable. As has been mentioned earlier, churches respond to those who lack basic needs like food, shelter and clothes. The same applies to their need for health services and education. The environmental crisis leads to drought, floods, crop diseases, human diseases, and dangerous winds. Such natural calamities create masses of poor people who require assistance. It is in such contexts that churches and individual Christians are challenged to be good Samaritans and stewards who protect lives by providing people with necessary basic human needs.

Besides those human challenges which are directly caused by environmental crisis, there are also other human needs unrelated to environmental degradation. These needs also need to be addressed in the spirit of eco-diakonia. For example, the North-Western Diocese (NWD) of the Evangelical Lutheran Church in Tanzania (ELCT) has put in place an institution that takes care of people with mental disabilities, elderly people who have no relatives to take care of them and those suffering from epilepsy. The diocese has a special school for blind and deaf children who are given chance to learn like other children. The diocese also has a centre for taking care of street children who were previously abused by their parents and/or other

---

[38] Mugambi, "Ecological Crisis", 147.
[39] Niwagila, "Our Struggle for Justice", 165.
[40] Gitau, *The Environmental Crisis*, 3.
[41] Jonas Lutamingwa, Rev. C. Mbuga and Lilian Lwakatare, "Community Economic Empowerment in the North Western Diocese: Initiatives and Challenges" in *ELCT/NWD Partnership in Mission: Collection of Papers presented on Evangelism, Education, Diaconal Services and Community Economic Empowerment* (Bukoba: North Western Diocese Evangelical Lutheran Church In Tanzania, 2015), 7.

guardians. Besides taking care of them, the centre gives them the opportunity to go to school and reunites the children with their families after counselling their families to avoid more problems. Also, the church takes care of children whose mothers die during childbirth or whose mothers give them up being unable to take care of them due to financial difficulties. Such children are taken care of in the church orphanage.[42]

Churches have established health facilities to make sure that people are able to access medical services. Churches in Tanzania offer forty percent of health services in the country in the form of hospitals, health centres and dispensaries. Patients pay money for medical services to enable the church health facilities to run.[43] They are regarded as non-profit facilities. In the North-Western Diocese, those who are not able to pay for their medical services are assisted by a project known as the Poor Patient Fund which has support from German partners, although the funds are not enough to meet the demands of all the needy. Other poor patients are helped by individual Christians or parishes in the diocese.

Eco-Prophetic Diakonia against the Causes of Environmental Crisis and Other Miseries

Eco-diakonia is more than just the conservation of the environment and assisting the victims of environmental crises. It is more than merely addressing the needs of the poor. It also must include speaking out – using the prophetic voice – against the structures that cause miseries. Such structures include local and national governments which make policies in favour of economic players and, as such, do not take environmental concerns seriously. Some governments fail to regulate businesses and those who pursue their economic interests at the expense of nature and other people. Eco-prophetic diakonia criticises companies, insisting that they take better care of nature while pursuing their interests for sustainability, lest temporary gains lead to long-term destruction of nature and people. This aspect of eco-diakonia forces people to go beyond their personal temporal interests to consider future generations.

Conclusion and Recommendations

This paper has argued that there is already an environmental crisis both in Africa and in the wider world. The effects of environmental degradation include floods, drought, famine, excessive heat, destructive winds, diseases, conflicts over resources, etc which all have repercussions. Humans are the major cause of this environmental crisis. While the developing nations are contributing to the environmental crisis, the developed industrial nations are the major cause of environmental crisis due to their much higher emissions of greenhouse gases.

Evidence points to the fact that it is still possible to mitigate the ecological crisis by using the insights from the primal religions and cultures that respect nature and avoid the overutilisation of nature that leads to ecological chaos. At the same time, the primal cultures and religions uphold communal aspects of life which aim at supporting one another without leaving anybody behind – this has many similarities with the diaconal spirit. This can be of great help to the victims of environmental crisis such as the most vulnerable including orphans, widows and people with disabilities.

The Bible has numerous texts to mobilise congregations that urge people to take care of nature including their fellow people and fight greed, corruption, and exploitation of others. For example, one could talk about Jesus' lifestyle choices; he had an internal and external detachment to material goods, an attitude that does not strain the environment. Jesus stressed sharing resources and assisting the needy. He challenged the rich

---

[42] "Diaconal Services in the North Western Diocese" in "ELCT/NWD Partnership in Mission: Collection of Papers presented on Evangelism, Education, Diaconal Services and Community Economic Empowerment" (Bukoba, North Western Diocese Evangelical Lutheran Church In Tanzania, 2015).

[43] Payment for medical services in the government facilities are relatively lower compared to church health facilities. Those who go to church health facilities are partly attracted by quality services and spiritual aspects.

not only to share resources with others but also to make sure that their wealth is obtained justifiably. This means that the Bible is not only concerned with taking care of the victims of environmental degradation, but also negates the causes of such miseries.

Government intervention, through environmental policies, could make sure that the pursuit of individual interests does not lead to destruction of nature and people at large. Moreover, the international community ought to adhere to their agreements to reduce the emission of greenhouses gases that cause the climate crisis. This should go hand in hand with compensation for loss and damage affecting people already, because those already suffering are the poor whose contribution to the ecological crisis is minor. Prevention can be attempting through tree planting and other drawdown techniques, but at the same time, we need to work on adaptation to the ecological crisis, continued awareness-raising, and mitigation to help those whose lives and livelihoods suffer.

Suggestions for Further Reading

Bloomquist, Karen L. Ed. *God, Creation and Climate Change: Spiritual and Ethical Perspectives*. Geneva: LWF, 2009. [Especially Karen L. Bloomquist, "Introduction" and Colette Bouka Coula, "Addressing Realities on the Ground"].

Boettcher, Reinhard, Ed. *The Diaconal Ministry in the Mission of the Church*. Geneva: LWF, 2006. [Especially Reinhard Boettcher. "Toward Lutheran Theological Understandings of the Diaconal Ministry"].

Dedji, Valentine. *Reconstruction and Renewal in African Christian Theology*. Nairobi: Acton, 2003.

Ganusah, Rebecca. "Social Integration and Development in Contemporary Africa" in J.N.K. Mugambi, Ed. *Democracy and Development in Africa: the role of churches.* Nairobi: All Africa Conference of Churches, 1997.

Gitau, Samson K. *The Environmental Crisis: A Challenge for African Christianity*. Nairobi: Acton Publishers, 2000.

Jaeger, Alfred. *Diakonie als Christliches Unternehmen: Theologische Wirtschaftsethik im Kontext diakonischer Unternehmenspolitik*. Güthersloh: Gütherslober Verlagshaus Gerd Mohn, 1993.

Keshomshahara, Abednego. *A Theology of Poverty Reduction in Tanzania: Quest for Christian Socio-Political and Economic Vision.* Dodoma: CTP, 2008.

—— "The Lutheran Doctrine of the Holy Spirit and the Challenge of the Traditional Spirit Beliefs among the Haya People". M.Th. Thesis, Tumaini University, Makumira, 2000.

Lutamingwa, Jonas Mbuga, C and Lwakatare, Lilian. "Community Economic Empowerment in the North-Western Diocese: Initiatives and Challenges" in *ELCT/NWD Partnership in Mission: Collection of Papers presented on Evangelism, Education, Diaconal Services and Community Economic Empowerment.* Bukoba: North Western Diocese Evangelical Lutheran Church In Tanzania, 2015.

Mbiti, John. *African Religions and Philosophy*. London: Heinemann, 1969.

Mugambi, J.N.K., Ed. *The Church and Reconstruction of Africa: Theological Considerations.* Nairobi: All Africa Conference of Churches, 1997. [Especially Wilson B. Niwagila. "Our Struggle for Justice, Peace and Integrity of Creation: A Quest for a Theology of Reconstruction in Africa".

Nuernberger, Klaus. "Gottes Mission in der Praxis: Der Kampf um Befreiung, Wuerde und Gerechtigkeit in Afrikanischen Gesellschaten" in *Mission Dei Heute: Zur Aktualitaet eines Missionstheologischen Schluesselbegriffs*. Hamburg: Evangelisches Missionswerk in Deutschland, 2003.

4. God's Mission, God's Economy or God's Joy as the Deepest Source of Resilience amidst Forces of Death and Destruction?

Ernst M. Conradie[1]

Why Should Christians be Engaged in Earthkeeping?[2]

Christians may well take an answer to this question for granted. Is it not obvious why there is a need for Christians to be engaged in earthkeeping? Upon further reflection, it emerges that there are different possible answers to this question – and that these may well be in conflict with each other. Consider the following:

A first option would be to point to the gravity of ecological destruction, for example with reference to global concerns regarding climate change, ocean acidification, ozone depletion, deforestation, overfishing, toxic pollution and the rapid loss of biodiversity. One may of course also refer to more specific local issues. If so, there is a duty on all human beings, especially those who have contributed most to such destruction, to engage in earthkeeping. A related option, which makes good sense in the African context, would be to point to the resources available in Christianity in terms of trusted leadership, moral codes, regular gatherings and loyal membership to suggest that mustering such resources may make a significant difference. We need all the help we can get!

Another option may be to refer to the accusation from environmental activists and Indigenous religions alike that Christianity is deeply complicit in the root causes of such ecological destruction. From the outside that seems plausible if only because those countries with high historic carbon emissions were predominantly Christian by the advent of the industrial revolution.[3] This is despite the subsequent shift in the geographic centre of gravity in Christianity. If Christianity is indeed to be associated with the root causes of the problem, getting its own house in order may also prove to be crucial in addressing the problem.[4] The alternative would be to abandon not only Christendom but Christianity itself as hopelessly entangled in the web of slavery, colonialism and domination.

Would this suffice to inspire Christians to engage in earthkeeping, especially amid death and destruction where resilience is needed in order to cope with an escalating crisis? That seems doubtful. Instead, in order to maintain such resilience, an ecological praxis, ethos, and spirituality needs to be deeply rooted in the Christian tradition, in the crux of the gospel and in the Trinitarian pulse of the Christian faith. It is the indicative of God's grace that needs to sustain the imperative of Christian earthkeeping.

To reflect theologically on the interplay between such an ecological praxis, ethos and spirituality is one way of describing the task of Christian ecotheology. At first, in the 1970s and 1980s, the focus was on revisiting the doctrine of creation and more specifically the place of humanity in God's creation for the sake of an environmental ethics. This yielded an anthropology where *Adam* became better rooted in *adamah*, humans in humus, in all humility. Nevertheless, human responsibility was described by some in terms of metaphors such as stewardship, priesthood, being co-creators, partnership, friendship and so forth –

---

[1] Ernst M. Conradie is Senior Professor in the Department of Religion and Theology at the University of the Western Cape in South Africa. His email address is econradie@uwc.ac.za.

[2] In *Christianity and Earthkeeping: In Search of an Inspiring Vision* (Stellenbosch: Sun Press, 2011), I offered a survey of 18 conflicting theological rationales for Christian earthkeeping, each with biblical references!

[3] This insight provided the hermeneutical key for structuring the *T&T Clark Handbook of Christian Theology and Climate Change*, edited by Ernst M. Conradie and Hilda P. Koster (London: T&T Clark, 2019).

[4] See the document produced by the South African Council of Churches, *Climate Change – A Challenge to the Churches in South Africa* (Braamfontein: SACC, 2009).

metaphors fiercely contested by others. Such a narrow anthropological, often apologetic rationale for earthkeeping was never going to be sufficient, despite the legitimate emphasis on present responsibility.

Two other key options subsequently emerged. One focused on creation as a sacred gift from God where humans become the guardians or fellow trustees of the land.[5] Such a sense of the sacred could draw on an understanding of God's holiness, on the role of the liturgy and especially the sacraments. It could also find common ground with Indigenous ecological wisdom, especially but not only, in Africa. This approach elicited considerable energy but it may be fair to state that it typically does not offer the required resilience in the face of capitalist modes of production and of consumerist culture and aspirations. A sense of the sacred may slow down destruction but can scarcely resist the onslaught, even if tied to prophetic critique.

The second option is to retrieve an eschatological vision for the future as a source of inspiration, the coming of God's reign, on earth as it is heaven.[6] Such a vision could be sustained by the promises of God and the symbols of exodus and resurrection. In the long run, such a moral vision, perhaps one of "Justice, Peace and the Integrity of Creation" can outlive the power of Empire and prophetically challenge prevailing forms of destruction. However, Christian eschatology is often interpreted by its own adherents in an escapist way. If not, the emphasis on social transformation can be in tension with one on stability and sustainability.

In the rest of this contribution, I will explore two further avenues to root Christian earthkeeping more deeply in the core convictions of the Christian faith, namely in terms of the well-known ecumenical themes of God's mission and God's economy. I will then propose another avenue, namely in terms of God's profound joy in creatures.

Missio Dei and Earthkeeping

There is no need here to revisit the shifts and turns in ecumenical discourse on the notion of *missio Dei* since the Willingen conference of the International Missionary Council in 1952. That may fill volumes. Suffice it to highlight two observations:

First, the focus on God's mission to the world helped to resist an ecclesiocentric orientation in mission, as if the church is an aim in itself. Instead, the church is there as a sign, an instrument, an icon, a symbol of the coming reign of God, situated in the tension between the *already* of God's reign inaugurated by Jesus Christ and the *not yet* of that reign, especially given prevailing injustice, oppression, conflict and destruction. The church's missions depend first and foremost on the Triune God's own activity.

Second, the notion of God's mission was radicalised in some circles to suggest that mission takes place primarily in the world, outside the boundaries of the institutional church. The Spirit is also present where the church is not, preparing the way for God's work of salvation. Moreover, some have added, the church is not even the primary agent of God's mission. The Holy Spirit may make use of other instruments – as demonstrated by the role of King Cyrus in the return from Babylonian exile. Such a radical decentralisation of the church at first seemed attractive in the context of secularisation, where the influence of the institutional church was waning. However, the notion of God's mission itself subsequently became secularised – harbouring the danger of self-secularisation. If God's mission is evident primarily in the course of (secular) history and, even broader, in the history of biological evolution or in cosmic history, then it is no longer clear what difference it makes to say that such developments may be understood in terms of God's mission. God's mission is then just a decorative way of speaking about human agendas that can also be accounted for in purely secular terms. If so, a theological reading of history contributes little if

[5] See the typology offered by Rosemary Radford Ruether in her "Conclusion: Eco-justice at the Center of the Church's Mission" in Dieter T. Hessel and Rosemary Radford Ruether (eds), *Christianity and Ecology: Seeking the Well-being of Earth and Humans* (Cambridge, MA: Harvard University Press, 2000), 603-614.

[6] Such as eschatological approach to Christian earthkeeping may draw inspiration from diverse sources, including Alfred North Whitehead, Teilhard de Chardin and Jürgen Moltmann. For a discussion, see my *Hope for the Earth: Vistas on a New Century* (Eugene, OR: Wipf & Stock, 2005).

anything to understand the direction of history. One may still suggest that using the symbols of the Christian tradition could serve as a source of inspiration for Christians to be involved in processes of social transformation, but this is then understood in pragmatic terms, that is, wherever the role of churches in civil society to deal with social problems is still recognised. Accordingly, the church is one role player in civil society, alongside other religious traditions and civil organisations that may contribute to the common good. The universal claims embedded in the notion of God's mission are clearly lost.

Where the focus shifts away too quickly from the indicative of God's grace to the ethical imperative of an ecological reformation of Christianity and a transformation of the global economy from reliance on fossil fuels to sustainable alternatives, this will have disastrous consequences. Then environmental activists would need to "save the planet" themselves. Given overwhelming ecological destruction, this would breed a climate of despondency. How then can the focus on God's work of salvation be maintained in the face of ecological destruction? Is it indeed plausible to witness to what God is doing? Is God doing anything at all? Or is the Father's only response one of not intervening, even when his only Son is being crucified? Is this God's way of allowing us to see how careless we have become? Is the church then after all left to do God's work as God's instruments due to an embarrassing inability to account for God's work? Or does God perhaps make use of other agents far beyond the institutional church?

These observations and questions suggest the need to clarify the content of any notion of *missio Dei*. In South African missiology, this was done with reference to the multi-dimensional nature of mission. Participants at a conference held at the University of the Western Cape in 1986 formulated this accordingly:

> The church's mission (*missio ecclesiae*) flows from the realisation that mission is first and foremost God's mission (*missio Dei*) and that the churches' calling to a holistic witness (*marturia*) should include the following dimensions: proclaiming the Word (*kerugma*), acts/services of love (*diakonia*), the forming of a new community of love and unity (*koinonia*), the zeal for a just society (*dikaioma*) and worship (*leitourgia*) (see Van der Watt, 2010: 165-166).[7]

Such a multi-dimensional notion of mission was already expressed in David Bosch's *Witness to the World* (1981) where he used the "creative tension" between "ecumenical" and "evangelical" notions of mission from the 1970s to identify *kerygma*, *diakonia* and *koinonia* as three core dimensions of mission.[8] In *Transforming Mission* (1991), he developed this further to identify fourteen dimensions of an emerging "ecumenical paradigm" in mission.[9] What remained unclear is how these aspects are related to God's work of redemption. Is the priority assigned merely based on the context? How does liberation relate to reconciliation and reconstruction? What is the place of *diakonia* and *dikaioma* in God's mission?

Another southern African publication (in collaboration with some Australian colleagues) related such an understanding of mission explicitly to earthkeeping. In *The Church in God's Household,* five dimensions of Christian witnessing were explored, namely in terms of liturgy (*leitourgia*, including *laitreia*: learning to see the world in the light of the Light of the World); proclamation (*kerygma*: speaking truth to power, preaching, lament, proverbs, ecclesial resolutions); service (*diakonia*: a wide variety of earthkeeping projects), fellowship (*koinonia*: the role of eco-congregations in establishing sustainable communities) and witness (*marturia*) itself. In each case, both an ecological critique of current forms of witnessing and a

---

[7] See Gideon van der Watt, "Recent Developments and Challenges in Understanding the Dutch Reformed Family of Churches' Missional Identity and Calling", *Ned Geref Teologiese Tydskrif* 51:3&4 (2010), 164-176: 165-166.

[8] David J. Bosch, *Witness to the World: The Christian Mission in Theological Perspective* (Atlanta, GA: John Knox, 1980).

[9] David J. Bosch, *Transforming Mission: Paradigm Shifts in Theology of Mission* (Maryknoll, NY: Orbis Books, 1991).

retrieval of its potential were offered.[10] The volume also recognised the connection between God's mission and God's economy (see below).

God's Economy and Earthkeeping

One may situate God's mission in the even wider perspective of God's economy. This is based on the Greek notion of the *oikonomia tou Theou*, that is, the whole work of the Triune God to create, sustain, guide, reconcile, redeem, and fulfil God's intentions in and for God's household.[11] One may say that the whole work of God includes at least seven "chapters", namely: 1) creation in the beginning; 2) ongoing creation throughout the history of the universe and the evolution of life on earth; 3) the emergence of humanity as one brief episode in this much larger story, in all its cultural grandeur but also all its misery (the legacy of sin); 4) God's providential care despite the impact of sin; 5) the history of election and salvation as witnessed by the children of Abraham; 6) the formation of the church, its governance, ministries, and missions; and 7) the expected consummation and final fulfilment of God's work.[12]

The Greek term *oikonomia* refers to a house (*oikia*) or household (*oikos*), here understood as the whole household of God – which is larger than the church and is indeed cosmic in scope. As is often noted in ecumenical discourse, the Greek root is also found in English terms such as "economy", "ecology", and "ecumenical". The "economy" describes the rules (*nomoi*) according to which the household is managed. "Ecology" refers to the underlying logic (*logos*) or principles according to which the household is structured. Originally, the term *oikoumene* referred to the whole inhabited world. "Ecumenicity" may therefore be understood as the inhabitation of the household, by human beings and by other forms of life.[13] Accordingly, the world in which the church is situated may be re-described as God's household, while God's economy, God's acts of house-holding (or housekeeping), then includes the full spectrum of God's work (economy).[14] The root metaphor of "the whole household of God" thus holds together ecclesiology, ecology and economy.

Four comments may be offered on situating Christian earthkeeping in God's economy in this way:[15]

First, compared with the use of the term "God's mission", it allows for a more differentiated way of speaking about God's work, one that includes salvation but is not restricted to that. It retains the dynamism of God's mission but places this mission in a larger orbit between creation and eschatological consummation.

Second, the place of the church's mission is indicated in this way. The mission of the church is only one aspect of one "chapter" of God's economy. It is decentralised given that human history is such a small episode in cosmic history. The history of the church over 2000 years pales into insignificance, given the 4.6 billion years of the earth's existence and the 13.7 billion years of the history of the universe. Yet the witness of the church could become re-centred if this is the place where the deepest mystery of cosmic history (i.e. knowledge of the Triune God) is treasured. However, given the ecologically destructive legacy

---

[10] See Clive W. Ayre and Ernst M. Conradie (eds), *The Church in God's Household: Protestant Perspectives on Ecclesiology and Ecology* (Pietermaritzburg: Cluster Publications, 2016).

[11] See Steve de Gruchy, "Agency, Sin and Grace: Protestant Reflections on Mission and Creation", in Lukas Vischer (ed), *Witnessing in the Midst of a Suffering Creation: A Challenge for the Mission of the Church* (Geneva: World Council of Churches, 2007), 97-114.

[12] See, especially, my *The Earth in God's Economy: Creation, Salvation and Consummation in Ecological Perspective* (Berlin: LIT Verlag, 2015); also Ernst M. Conradie, Sigurd Bergmann, Celia Deane-Drummond and Denis Edwards (eds), *Christian Faith and the Earth: Current Paths and Emerging Horizons in Ecotheology* (London: T. & T. Clark, 2014).

[13] See the essays in Ernst M. Conradie (ed), *South African Perspectives on Notions and Forms of Ecumenicity* (Stellenbosch: Sun Press, 2013).

[14] See Conradie, *The Earth in God's Economy.*

[15] This discussion draws from Ayre and Conradie, *The Church in God's Household*, 109-113.

of Christianity, any such a claim for re-centring the significance of the church should not be made too quickly. It may merely demonstrate an anthropocentric and androcentric arrogance that can only banalise such a sense of mystery.

Third, the household of God cannot be restricted to the institutional church. The ecological significance of the term "God's economy" should not be underestimated. One may say that the earth itself is situated in God's house-holding.

Fourth, the polemic thrust of the term "God's economy" should be recognised. To speak of *God's* economy is to say that the current global economic order belongs to God. It is situated within God's salvific presence in and embrace of an evolving world. Given Christian witness to the identity and character of the Triune God (characterised by mercy, justice and loyalty), this necessarily implies a critique of economic injustices and the gross economic inequalities that are so characteristic of the current global economic order. This is crucial for (prophetic) witness regarding ecological destruction since the roots of ecological destruction are clearly related to economic modes of production and cultural patterns of consumption. Christians do not believe in just any god. The specific identity and character of God matters.

God's Joy and Earthkeeping

The inner secret of Christian earthkeeping lies with the identity and character of the Triune God, that is with the immanent Trinity. This is not the place to explore God's identity in any detail. Christian discourse on the Trinity fills volumes and all too often results in far-reaching inner-Trinitarian speculation. Naming God as Triune is also open to a gendered critique. Calvin already suggested that the language of Father, Son and Holy Spirit can be explained in terms of Source, Wisdom and Power.[16] Suffice it to say that only a thoroughly Trinitarian praxis, ethos, spirituality and theology will do, but that is far easier to confess than to maintain, especially if a short-cut is taken that avoids a focus on the work of God (the economic Trinity).[17] In fact, the history of Christianity provides ample evidence of the difficulties in holding together the work of the Father and Christ (creation and redemption), the work of Christ and the Spirit (the *filioque* controversy[18]), and the work of the Father and the Spirit (dialogue with other living faiths).

The aim of speaking of God's identity is to express God's character but that should not be reduced to the divine characteristics that have long plagued Christianity, following its engagement with Greek philosophy. Accordingly, the omnipotence, omnipresence and omniscience of God were highlighted. This yielded an imperial God that cannot do justice to the core message of Jesus that God is more like a loving parent than a far-away fierce and fearsome emperor. It cannot do justice to the passionate God of the Bible and the mystery of a crucified God. The contrast between God's omnibenevolence and omnipotence – and the prevailing oppression, injustice and suffering of God's creatures – yielded the perplexing theodicy problem that often leads to further abstractions.

How, then, should God's character be understood? Let me briefly mention two contributions in this regard from within the Reformed tradition and then explore a third in more detail.

In his one volume systematic theology entitled *Christian Faith* (1985), Hendrikus Berkhof seeks to move away from these omni-characteristics by describing God's character ambiguously as "holy love,"

---

[16] See Calvin's *Institutes* I.13.18.

[17] See my argument in "Only a Fully Trinitarian Theology Will Do, But Where Can That Be Found?", *Ned Geref Teologiese Tydskrif* 54:1&2 (2013), 1-9, building on a famous essay by Arnold van Ruler, entitled "The Necessity of a Trinitarian Theology", in John Bolt (ed),*Calvinist Trinitarianism and Theocentric Politics: Essays towards a Public Theology* (Lampeter: Edwin Mellen Press, 1989), 1-26.

[18] This not only divides Eastern and Western traditions of Christianity but also those who emphasise that the Spirit works through Christ (the body of Christ, the offices instituted by Christ, the biblical witnesses to Christ) and those who emphasise the relative independence of the Spirit. In the African context, this is a divide between so-called mainline churches and a variety of Pentecostal and indigenous churches.

"defenceless superior power," and "changeable faithfulness."[19] This does better justice to the biblical witnesses than the characteristics derived from Greek philosophy.

In *God the Spirit* (1994), Michael Welker suggests that the core message of the Old Testament, affirmed in the ministry of Jesus of Nazareth and in the early church, may be captured in three themes, namely mercy, justice and the knowledge of God. Knowing God means knowing God's compassion for the weak and vulnerable, for homeless nomads, runaway slaves, marginalised people, the poor and the oppressed.[20] God's justice is a function of God's compassion, namely to address the root causes of suffering in terms of injustices. God's compassion even includes perpetrators (also found among the marginalised) but then requires justice to be done. God's justice and God's compassion therefore also require long-lasting loyalty.

One may say that the three Pauline virtues of faith, hope and love correspond to aspects of God's character. It is because of God's loyalty (or faithfulness) that we may have faith in God. God's faithfulness is to God's promise to make all things new – the source of our hope. It is because God loves the world so much that we can abide in that love.

The Dutch reformed theologian Arnold van Ruler often joked that Paul should have added joy as a fourth virtue.[21] He added that, upon further reflection, the apostle would surely agree that joy is even higher than love. Joy is a central theme in Van Ruler's theology and this was also the source of inspiration for Jürgen Moltmann's *Theology of Joy*.[22] Van Ruler would say that joy is the real reason why God created the world. It was not necessary for God to create. God did not need the world because God was lonely, for instance. It was willed by God. God finds pleasure in this world and regards it as "very good". It was not created out of anything, not even out of nothingness (*creatio ex nihilo*). Creation should not be understood as emanation out of God, which would suggest the need for the world to return to God in neo-Platonist terms. Our earthly reality is therefore not somehow divine. It exists alongside God, allowing for interaction between God and the world. God has pleasure in creation so that creatures may reciprocally have pleasure in God. He repeatedly states that "God granted us the pleasure of being."[23] This subsequent interaction between God and the world is described by Van Ruler in terms of categories such as play, dance and even erotic lust.[24] He lyrically describes the joy and pleasure that God derives from the world in all its otherness. *Homo ludens* [humans as playful] is possible on the basis of *Deus ludens* [God as playful]. Such mutuality would be thwarted if the distinction between Creator and creature was absolved. The world, he says, is God's joke played on us, but it is a good joke.[25]

Such joy is best expressed in the unencumbered playfulness of children instead of the "barbaric seriousness" of theologians. Joy is perhaps the most basic Christian attitude towards life, precisely because it indicates that creation was the outcome of God's will and the object of God's desire.[26] The analogy with the joy of human parents over their wanted children is obvious. Moreover, humans may enjoy God long

---

[19] See Hendrikus Berkhof, *Christian Faith: An Introduction to the Study of the Faith* (Grand Rapids, MI: Eerdmans, 1986), 119-154.

[20] Welker, *God the Spirit* (Minneapolis, MN: Fortress Press, 1994), 108-124.

[21] The theme of joy recurs throughout Van Ruler's voluminous writings. Few of these have been translated into English however. See especially his *Verzameld Werk Deel II: God, Schepping, Mens, Zonde*, edited by Dirk van Keulen (Zoetermeer: Boekencentrum, 2009). See, e.g. 102-110, 115-129, 104-124, 430-443. For a discussion in English, see my *Saving the Earth? The Legacy of Reformed views on "Re-creation"* (Berlin: LIT Verlag, 2013), 217-276. I am drawing here on my earlier discussion.

[22] Moltmann, *Theology of Joy* (London: SCM, 1973).

[23] E.g. Van Ruler, *Verzameld Werk III*, 410.

[24] On God asking us for a dance, see Van Ruler, *Verzameld Werk III,* 105, 170.

[25] See e.g. Van Ruler, *Verzameld Werk III,* 104, 163, 332, 410, 426, 440, 496.

[26] See Van Ruler's essay "De Vreugde as Wezenlijk Christelijk Levensgevoel" ("Joy as Quintessential Christian Attitude to Life", 1966) in *Verzameld Werk III*, 439-443.

before they may be able to contemplate God.[27] The meaning of our existence is not merely that we live from God's grace, but that we can find joy in God and God in us.

Van Ruler insists that the material world is willed by God (as much as spirit) and is the object of God's joy. However, a proper appreciation of materiality is not possible merely by looking at matter without seeing it as God's creation. This would be reductionist or inversely elicits the divinisation of matter. The problem is not only that one loses sight of God and grace in the process, but that matter itself is lost! Van Ruler comments: "Then the world is nothing but the world. The body is a mere thing, an instrument. Sexuality is a momentary expression of lust. Everything has lost its taste. The end can be nothing more than endless boredom, a disgust that engulfs everything, a radical despair."[28] Van Ruler thus calls for a true appreciation of matter on the basis of the distinction between Creator and creature – which would ensure that our existence is infused with music. He repeatedly criticises Augustine's distinction between *uti* and *frui*, arguing that we cannot enjoy the Creator without finding joy in the creature (which is what God does).[29] Van Ruler concludes that to appreciate matter as God does, namely as something worth dying for, may well be the article upon which the entire Christian faith stands or falls.[30] In short, "matter is holy"![31]

For Van Ruler himself, such a theology of joy was certainly no cheap form of hedonism, given his personal inclination towards depression.[32] Joy cannot be reduced to the good life, human flourishing, being entertained or "having fun". An "Ode to Joy" cannot merely offer an escape from injustice and suffering.[33] It is a joy despite – and in the face of – the anxieties, suffering and injustices that also characterise life on earth. Building on Van Ruler, one may say that God's joy may be deepened in two ways:

The first is related to suffering derived from natural sources, excluding the impact of human sin. God's creatures are finite beings and far from the perfections of omnipotence, omniscience and omnipresence. There is deformity, inequality (in intelligence, power, agility and beauty) transience, anxiety, pain, suffering, sickness and death in God's good creation. Van Ruler did not elaborate much on this but acknowledged that by asking rhetorically whether the leaves fell from the trees in the garden of Eden? If so, there is at least seasonal dying and death. Does this imply counter-evidence for such joy? How could God be joyful given such suffering? Does this not turn God into a sadist? This need not be the case, not if God is best understood as a loving parent as portrayed in the New Testament. Consider the pain and anguish of a parent over a less talented child, perhaps one with some serious disability or prone to illness, dying from leukaemia. Is such pain not mixed with joy in having such a child? Does such pain not deepen the sense of joy? Is this not epitomised by the joy that a Down-syndrome child brings to a family? Indeed, true religion is not the opium of the people constructed to ease the pain but the infectious ability to find joy amidst suffering, to weep tears of joy. Indeed, with Pascal, "Joy, joy, joy, tears of joy."[34]

The second is related to suffering induced by sin, injustice, violence, oppression, by radical evil. The real needs of the world are not addressed if the demonic impact of sin is eschewed. The cross is the Christian symbol of pain, suffering and cruel death. Does this not provoke God's anger rather than God's joy? Is love not able to deal with the impact of sin better than joy? How could one laugh and rejoice if there are so many tears to be wiped from one's eyes? The biblical witnesses, captured in the doctrine of justification, clearly

[27] Van Ruler, *Verzameld Werk III*, 440.
[28] Van Ruler, *Verzameld Werk III*, 121 (my translation).
[29] See Van Ruler, *Verzameld Werk III*, 121-122. The argument appears in numerous other places in his oeuvre.
[30] See Van Ruler, *Verzameld Werk III*, 122.
[31] Van Ruler, *Verzameld Werk III*, 121.
[32] See especially Dirk van Keulen's essay, "We zijn een Grap van God: Van Ruler over de Vreugde"" ("We are God's Joke") in Dirk J. van Keulen, George Harinck and Gijsbert van den Brink (eds), *Men moet Telkens Opnieuw de Reuzenzwaai aan de Rekstok Maken: Verder met Van Ruler* (Zoetermeer: Boekencentrum, 2009), 69-79.
[33] See Jürgen Moltmann, "Christianity: A Religion of Joy", in Miroslav Volf and Justin E. Crisp (eds), *Joy and Human Flourishing: Essays on Theology, Culture, and the Good Life* (Minneapolis, MN: Fortress, 2015), 1-15: 12.
[34] See also Moltmann, "Christianity: A Religion of Joy", 4.

suggest that God's love is not conditional, that it extends to the marginalised victims of history and even to perpetrators. Through God's eyes, the beggar is recognised as a brother, the prostitute as a sister, the rapist as an uncle. God's love transforms us. God does not love us because we are lovely; we become lovely because God loves us. Whereas God's joy may be "because of", God's love is "despite of", even though we are still sinners.

All this may be true but still misses the depth of God's joy. God's love is arguably motivated by God's joy. God does not love creatures because or insofar as they bring joy to God. God is able to see something attractive in every creature – and finds joy in that, despite everything else. In the words of Zephaniah 3:17, the joyous and singing God "will take great delight in you; in his love he will no longer rebuke you, but will rejoice over you with singing." Cultivating joy is then an act of resistance against despair and its forces.[35] Joy is a form of resilient protest that injustice cannot have the last word. One may conclude that because God's creative intent was thwarted by sin, God's acts of salvation became necessary – but then precisely in order to once again find joy in being. The world was created for the sake of joy. Finding joy in fellow creatures is therefore a gift before it becomes a command. A child's joy over such a gift may be the inner source of inspiration for any form of earthkeeping. Such joy involves all the human senses.

Conclusion

Earthkeeping does require considerable resilience given the many obstacles faced, the despondency that may well set in given so much destruction, the challenges that lie ahead and the temptations along the way. Such resilience is a virtue, best understood in terms of the classic virtue of courage. Where does such resilience come from? How can it be fostered? The discussion above suggests that, for Christians, there may be many sources of such resilience. Christians may drink from the abundance (*pleroma*) of each of these sources. There is no need to merely reiterate the stern imperative towards earthkeeping – as if that will by itself make the difference.

Each of the three sources discussed here – God's mission, God's economy and God's joy – roots the imperative of earthkeeping in the indicative of grace. There may well be a Trinitarian logic at play here (perhaps the sending of the Comforter, the role of the Messiah, the motherly heart of the Father) so that the one source may infuse and reinforce the other. Without the one, the others may run dry. The apostle Paul thought that love is "higher" than faith or hope and perhaps that is appropriately playful. If so, one may well claim that the river of joy runs "deeper" than either God's mission or God's economy.

Suggestions for Further Reading

Andrianos, Louk, Ed. *Kairos for Creation: Confessing Hope for the Earth.* Solingen: Foedus-Verlag, 2019.

Ayre, Clive W. and Ernst M. Conradie, Eds. *The Church in God's Household: Protestant Perspectives on Ecclesiology and Ecology.* Pietermaritzburg: Cluster Publications, 2016.

Bergmann, Sigurd, Ernst M. Conradie, Celia Deane-Drummond and Denis Edwards, Eds. *Christian Faith and the Earth: Current Paths and Emerging Horizons in Ecotheology.* London: T. & T. Clark, 2014.

Bosch, David J. *Transforming Mission: Paradigm Shifts in Theology of Mission.* Maryknoll, NY: Orbis Books, 1991.

Conradie, Ernst M. *The Earth in God's Economy: Creation, Salvation and Consummation in Ecological Perspective.* LIT Verlag, Berlin, 2015.

_____. *Christianity and Earthkeeping: In Search of an Inspiring Vision.* Stellenbosch: Sun Press, 2011.

Hessel, Dieter T. and Rosemary Radford Ruether, Eds. *Christianity and Ecology: Seeking the Well-being*

[35] See the conversation with Willie Jennings on "Theology and Joy", [Available at: https://www.youtube.com/watch?v=1fKD4Msh3rE], [Last accessed: 15th June 2021].

of Earth and Humans. Cambridge, MA: Harvard University Press, 2000.
Moltmann, Jürgen. *Theology of Joy.* London: SCM, 1973.
Van Ruler, Arnold A. *Calvinist Trinitarianism and Theocentric Politics: Essays towards a Public Theology,* edited by John Bolt. Lampeter: Edwin Mellen Press, 1989.
Vischer, Lukas, Ed. *Witnessing in the Midst of a Suffering Creation: A Challenge for the Mission of the Church.* Geneva: World Council of Churches, 2007.

5. Ecological Stewardship from African Indigenous Thoughts in Dialogue with Christian Traditions: Resisting Ecological Violence in Africa

Jonathan Kivatsi Kavusa[1]

Introduction

Martinez Cobo report defines indigenous communities as "those which, having a historical continuity with pre-invasion and pre-colonial societies […] consider themselves distinct from other sectors of the society."[2] Contrary to America and Australia, this definition does not fit with Africa where all peoples think of themselves as native and any attempt to name one group as indigenous but not another, provokes confusion. The majority of Africans still live in rural areas, attached to the land of their ancestors.

However, many of the ongoing transformations that prepare the future of the African continent for good or for worse are played out in rural areas, such as forest clearing, large-scale land commodification, cultural disruptions and population migration. These changes offer, at best, hope for the future and possibilities of growth, but they also alienate the individual.[3] The locals view these changes as being deprived of ancestors (as land means ancestors' abode), and also the land becomes an object of all sort of manipulations. Exploitation of the natural world is driven forward by a neo-liberalism mentality, which "transforms everything and everyone into a commodity for sale at a price."[4]

Thus, since 2015, Africa has been categorised as having a "bio-capacity deficit" where the footprint is greater than the capacity of ecosystems to produce useful biological materials and absorb human waste.[5] Hence, research towards the ecological sustainability of Africa should be of great interest for the coming decades to avoid escalation. Churches cannot be left out the process. Dietrich Werner showed how African Independent Churches (AICs) have the potential to offer sustainable solutions to African ecological dilemmas in Africa as they incorporate traditional worldviews in their worship.[6] This way of doing needs to be extended to other Christian bodies.

The Central Committee of the World Council of Churches meeting in Geneva, Switzerland, 26th August-2nd September 2009, urged member churches to:

> Learn from the leadership of Indigenous Peoples, women, peasant and forest communities who point to alternative ways of thinking and living within creation, especially as these societies often emphasise the value of

[1] Dr. Kavusa is an Alexander von Humboldt Research Fellow at *Humboldt Universität zu Berlin.* Kavusa is also Research Associate in the Department of Old Testament and Hebrew Scriptures at the Faculty of Theology and Religion of the University of Pretoria. He teaches Old Testament at the Faculty of Theology of the *Université Libre des Pays des Grands Lacs*. jokakiv@yahoo.fr.

[2] Martinez Cobo, "Study of the Problem of Discrimination against Indigenous Populations," 1986, para. 376, E/CN.4/sub.2/1986/7/paragraph 376.

[3] John Mbiti, *African Religions and Philosophy* (London: Heinemann, 1985), 219.

[4] World Council of Churches, *Alternative Globalization: Addressing Peoples and Earth* (Geneva: WCC Publications, 2005), 3.

[5] World Wild Fund, "African Ecological Futures 2015" (Nairobi, 2015), 18, https://wwfint.awsassets.panda.org/downloads/african_ecological_futures_report_english.pdf.

[6] Dietrich Werner, "The Challenge of Environment and Climate Justice: Imperatives of an Eco-Theological Reformation of Christianity in African Contexts," in Philipp Öhlmann, Wilhelm Gräb, and Marie-Louise Frost (eds), *African Initiated Churches and the Decolonization of Development: Sustainable Development in Pentecotal and Independent Churhes* (New York, 2020), 51-72: 53.

> relationships, of caring and sharing, as well as practice traditional, ecologically respectful forms of production and consumption.[7]

Indigenous traditions are deemed as having the potential to foster ecological stewardship. The question is to what extent indigenous knowledge can foster Christian ecological stewardship in Africa. African traditional societies were built upon a threefold worldview, namely *the moral or spiritual dimension of nature; the pre-eminence of the community over individual interests*; and *the cosmological dimension of the chieftaincy*. With a proper reconfiguration, this trilogy can be transformed into a highly effective vehicle of Christian ecological stewardship in Africa.

We will first look at existing ecological hermeneutics before articulating how necessary an African ecological hermeneutics would be to inaugurate in our churches.

Existing Ecological Christian Hermeneutics

A detailed analysis of prevailing ecological hermeneutics can be found in my article, which was published in 2019.[8] I am providing here the key insights of the major existing trends of ecotheology in which scholars operate now, including a section on earlier attempts by African theologians in the area of ecotheology.

Apologetic reading or reading of recovery

This ecological hermeneutics is also called a "strategy of recovery",[9] trying to demonstrate the green side of the Bible. It was a reaction against Lynn White's allegations that Christianity and its anthropocentric traditions bear a huge burden for the current ecological crisis for preaching that it is God's will that human beings exploit nature for their proper ends.[10] In reaction, apologetic readers tried to rescue the Bible from these allegations. They put forth the notion that the Bible is not itself the problem, but the problem came through the acts of later interpreters, who obscured the original meaning of the text.[11] The Green Bible project is an illustration of this approach. It printed in green ink those biblical texts which support creation care and *green discipleship*.[12]

The Earth Bible project

This is a completely opposite reading advocating for a radical resistance against and rejection of the so-called "grey texts", texts deemed ecologically harmful (ex. Gen 1:26-28). The interpreter reads the text not as steward over creation, but as kin, a relative and member within the earth community, sharing with it benefits and problems.[13] Alongside its hermeneutics of suspicion, identification and retrieval, the Earth

---

[7] World Council of Churches, "Statement on Eco-Justice and Ecological Debt," 2009, [Available at: https://www.oikoumene.org/en/resources/documents/central-committee/2009/report-on-public-issues/statement-on-eco-justice-and-ecological-debt].

[8] Kivatsi Jonathan Kavusa, "Ecological Hermeneutics and the Interpretation of Biblical Texts Yesterday, Today and Onwards: Critical Reflection and Assessment," *Old Testament Essays* 32, no. 1 (2019), 229-255, https://doi.org/10.17159/2312-3621/2019/v32n1a13.

[9] F. Watson, "Strategies of Recovery and Resistance: Hermeneutical Reflection on Genesis 1-3 and Its Pauline Reception," *Journal for the Study of the New Testament* 45 (1992), 79-103: 81.

[10] Lynn White, "The Historical Roots of Our Ecological Crisis," *Science* 155, no. 3767 (1967), 1203-1207: 1205.

[11] D.G. Horrell, C. Hunt, and C. Southgate, "Appeal to the Bible in Ecotheology and Environmental Ethics: A Typology of Hermeneutical Stances," *Studies in Christian Ethics* 21, no. 2 (2008), 221.

[12] D.G. Horrell, "The Green Bible: A Timely Idea Deeply Flawed," *ExpT* 121, no. 4 (2010), 180-186.

[13] The Earth Bible Team, "Guiding Ecojustice Principles," in Norman C. Habel (ed), *Reading From the Perspective of Earth* (Sheffield: Sheffield Academic Press, 2000), 38-53: 39.

Bible Project developed six eco-justice principles,[14] acting as an *ecological canon* by which biblical texts are measured. The insights of the six eco-justice principles are in line with African worldviews.

Eco-feminist approach

Ecological feminism is a kind of convergence of ecology and feminism into a new social theory and political movement.[15] Françoise d'Eaubonne coined the word eco-feminism to offer an ethical framework, which takes seriously links between the rule of men over women and the oppression of nature.[16] Its supporters argue that women and nature are both victim of the patriarchal conception of the world.[17] The liberation of women and nature can only be attained by a radical deconstruction of patriarchal traditions of the Bible.[18]

Resisting ecological readings of the Bible

The fundamentalist scholar Cumbey[19] alleged that the words such as friends of Earth, stewardship or planetary awareness belong to the New Age movement, which is itself a mask of satanic influence. In this way, the American Southern Baptist Church (SBC) affirmed that stewardship might drive Christians from the worship of the Creator towards neo-pagan nature worship (Rom. 1:25)[20] as well as diverting Christians from the "Great commission"[21] of making disciples (Mt. 28:16-20). The 2006 Convention of SBC clearly declared:

> Some in our culture have completely rejected God the Father in favour of deifying "Mother Earth," made environmentalism into a neo-pagan religion, and elevated animal and plant life to the place of equal – or greater – value with human life.[22]

In commenting on these distorted conceptualisations of environmental concerns by fundamentalist Christians, Ernst Conradie remarked that, in many parts of the world and especially in Africa, "Christians are not environmental activists and environmental activists are not Christians."[23] There is, thus, the need to reinforce the idea that creation care is an expression of Christian concern for mission and *not* as a distraction from it. Christian paradigms of evangelism therefore need to shift the focus from "people salvation" to a more holistic message of "creation salvation" according to Romans 8:18-23.

Existing African Ecotheological Initiatives

African scholars adopted either a reading of recovery or a resisting tendency of the Earth Bible project. In their over-eagerness to find something positive in the Bible about nature, many African ecotheologians

---

[14] The Earth Bible Team, "Guiding Ecojustice Principles", 38-53.
[15] V. Plumwood, *Feminism and the Mastery of Nature* (New York: Routledge, 1993), 39.
[16] Karen P. Waren, "The Power and the Promise of Ecological Feminism," in M. Mackinnon and M. McIntyre (eds), *In Reading in Ecology and Feminist Theology* (Kansas City, KS: Sheed & Ward, 1995), 172-195: 172.
[17] Robert B. Fowler, *The Greening of Protestant Thought* (London: University of North Carolina Press, 1995), 124.
[18] Rosemary Radford Ruether, *Gaia and God: An Ecofeminist Theology of Earth Healing* (New York: HarperCollins, 1992), 115.
[19] C. Cumbey, *The Hidden Dangers of the Rainbow: The New Age Movement and Our Coming Age of Barbarism* (Lafayette: Huntington House, 1983), 167.
[20] Bernard D. Zaleha and Andrew Szasz, "Why Conservative Christians Don't Believe in Climate Change," *Bulletin of the Atomic Scientists* 71, no. 5 (2015), 19-30: 20, https://doi.org/10.1177/0096340215599789.
[21] Southern Baptist Convention, "On Environmentalism and Evangelicals," 2006, [Available at: https://www.sbc.net/resource-library/resolutions/on-environmentalism-and-evangelicals/].
[22] Southern Baptist Convention, "On Environmentalism and Evangelicals.
[23] Ernst M. Conradie, "The Church and the Environment: Seven Stations Towards the Sanctification of the Whole Earth," *Scriptura* 107(0), (2011), 156-170: 158, [Available at: https://doi.org/10.7833/107-0-133].

resorted to cherry picking.[24] Ademiluka, for instance, said that the Leviticus traditions of a distinction between being clean and unclean anticipate some aspects of African environmental sanitation issues to prevent outbreaks of communicable diseases.[25] Meyer criticised his fellow African of trying to find "things in the text that we want (and need) to see, but things which are not really there."[26]

Recently, Maluleke pledged a sustainable theology of the environment in Africa. In his analysis of the *theological impotence* of African Christianity, Maluleke showed how Missions played a role in facilitating the alienation of people and nature in Africa. The Bible, the land (nature) and Africans (people and their culture) were all robbed of their true essence.[27] The Bible was only a tool of colonisation in some areas. Nature was reduced to a lifeless *thing*, which can be owned, manipulated and exploited at all cost.[28] For him, we need not to antagonise our traditions and the Bible in order to discern the liberating message of Christianity in Africa.

Hence, informed by her northern Sotho culture, Masenya inaugurated an African eco-feminist approach called "eco-bosadi" (eco-motherhood or womanwood, sadi=wife). As opposed to Western eco-feminist approaches, Masenya reads Psalm 127:3-5 and explains how African Mothers and Mother Earth suffer common abuse from the male drive for reproduction.[29] Masenya investigates whether the Israelite and African worldviews about procreation can be empowering for African women.

Masenya's approach tried to exploit the horizons (cosmology) of the text and that of African readers. This article aligns with her way of interacting with the text. Interacting with an ancient text implies the fusion of two horizons[30] or cosmologies: that of the Bible and that of African readers.

Traditional Cosmologies as a Vehicle of Ecological Christian Stewardship

The word "cosmology" can be understood as the totality of community's shared beliefs and worldview. Cosmology is the hermeneutical framework through which people make sense of reality. The word cosmology is therefore synonymous with the word "worldview" (*Weltanschauung* in German) and refers to a cultural construct expressing people's beliefs of how the cosmos originated, how it is structured and how it functions.

Thus, a cosmology consists of a set of assumptions that guide the thoughts and attitudes of a certain community and makes it difficult for them to think adequately outwith this framework. African traditional societies believed in 1) *the sacredness of all life* (*the moral dimension of nature*); 2) *the pre-eminence of the community over individual interests* and 3) *the cosmological dimension of chieftaincy* (Governance). The value of this framework is that it lines with "de-growth" ideals advocating for a type of development

[24] P. Van-Dyk, "Eco-Theology: In and out of the Wilderness," *Old Testament Essays* 30(3), (2017), 835-851: 835, [https://doi.org/10.17159/2312-3621/2017/v30n3a17].
[25] Solomon Olusola Ademiluka, "An Ecological Interpretation of Leviticus 11-15 in an African (Nigerian) Context," *Old Testament Essays* 22(3), (2009), 525-534: 529.
[26] Esias E. Meyer, "Respect for Animal Life in the Book of Leviticus: How Green Were the Priestly Authors?", *Old Testament Essays* 24(1), (2011), 142-158: 144.
[27] T. Maluleke, "Black and African Theologies in Search of Contemporary Environmental Justice," *Journal of Theology for Southern Africa* 167 (2020), 5-19: 14.
[28] H. Sindima, "Community of Life: Ecological Theology in African Continent," in C. Birch, W. Eaken, and J. McDaniel (eds), *Liberating Life: Contemporary Approaches to Ecological Theology* (New York: Orbis Books, 1990), 137-147: 139.
[29] Madipoane J. Masenya, "An Ecobosadi Reading of Psalm 127:3-5," in Norman C. Habel (ed), *The Earth Story in the Psalms and the Prophets* (Sheffield: Sheffield Academic Press, 2001), 109-122: 122.
[30] Joshua Foa Dienstag, "Hans-Georg Gadamer, Truth and Method," in Jacob T. Levy (ed), *The Oxford Handbook of Classics in Contemporary Political Theory* (Oxford: Oxford University Press, 2016), 1-14: 6, [Available at: https://doi.org/10.1093/oxfordhb/9780198717133.013.20].

that includes ethical, spiritual, cultural and ecological sustainability in the process.[31] In this way, this section wants to show how the threefold African traditional cosmology can serve as a vehicle for ecological Christian hermeneutics.

Regaining the Sense of Sacredness for All Life

The first creation story of the Bible (Genesis 1:1-2:4a) concludes with the Sabbath. With Sabbath as the climax of creation, the Bible presents the whole creation as a *sacred arena*, a *cosmic temple*.[32] By including the earth, water, flora and fauna in the perspective of Sabbath, Genesis 1 rejects utilitarian views that would consider these entities as mere objects/things. In this sense, every seventh year, all agrarian activity stopped in order to enable the land to observe the Sabbath for YHWH (Lev. 25:1-7). The Bible also warns that the land could vomit the defilers of the land (Lev. 24-25). The land therefore could not be sold in perpetuity, as it was seen not as a *commodity* but as God's property (Lev. 25:23). People are only tenants, not owners.

Just as in the Bible, traditional Africa did not know the dichotomy between sacred and natural (physical) or the designation *subjects* and *object*. John Mbiti explains this vision of nature as follows:

> Nature in the broadest sense of the word is not an empty impersonal object or phenomenon; it is filled with religious significance [...] This is one of the most fundamental heritages of the African peoples [...] The physical and spiritual are but two dimensions of one and the same universe. These dimensions intertwined into each other to the extent that at times and in places one is apparently more real than, but not exclusive of, the other. To African peoples this religious universe is not an academic proposition: it is an empirical experience [...][33]

Unfortunately, this was simply termed by missionaries as "nature worship" or animism. Their insistence on the salvation of *only* the soul was very crucial to detach humans from the rest, treating everything nonhuman as only lifeless *objects* that can be exploited, not feared. Some missionaries might have not preached this for the sake of alienating the people; however, the accent on individual salvation detached people from their "holistic" cosmology, which viewed people and other beings as members of the same community.

In the process, locals stopped believing that flora, fauna, rivers, places and mountains were living subjects belonging to their family. The converted locals and their converters were then ready to multiply, fill and subdue the earth together, having dominion over every living that moves upon the earth (Gen. 1:28). This trivialised the whole traditional mode of life and its cosmological framework.[34]

Nothing explains this tragedy better than the statement of Emmanuel Anim as he recounted:

> The village in the North of Ghana where I grew up was located close to a forest and a river. In the forest from ancient times onwards the ancestors live, therefore it was sacred. In the river there lived the spirit of the water, therefore it was sacred as well. Then people of my village became Christians. Now, according to the new Christian worldview, there were no ancestors any more in the forest and also there were no spirits any more in the river. The taboos were disintegrating and disappearing. Instead, the people started to make use and exploit

[31] Bengi Akbulut et al., "Who Promotes Sustainability? Five Theses on the Relationships between the Degrowth and the Environmental Justice Movements," *Ecological Economics* 165 (June 2019), 1-9: 2, [Available at: https://doi.org/10.1016/j.ecolecon.2019.106418].

[32] W.P. Brown, *The Seven Pillars of Creation: The Bible, Science, and the Ecology of Wonder* (Oxford: Oxford University Press, 2010), 40.

[33] Mbiti, *African Religions and Philosophy*, 73-74.

[34] V.Y. Mudimbe, *The Invention of Africa* (Bloomington, IN: Indiana University Press, 1988), 17.

both the forest and the water of the river for their own purposes. Today next to this village there is no forest left anymore and the river is now a cesspool. Who has done a major mistake here? And for what reason?[35]

The key question raised in this narrative certainly is the moral factor of the crisis. In fact, "What people do about their ecology depends on what they think about themselves in relation to things around them."[36] Pope John Paul II continued that "people must be told that the environmental crisis is a moral crisis."[37] This does not preclude promoting religious solutions to ecological problems, but suggests that moral re-education or religion is an important social mechanism to influence people's behaviours.

In the Encyclical *Laudato Si*, Pope Francis notes that authentic human development should have a moral character.[38] This may help us to understand why anthropogenic climate change points in the direction of not merely a physical crisis but towards a deeper cultural, moral, ethical and spiritual failure. In other words, the problem has to be addressed through moral *re-education* of the society and not merely by providing further *scientific* evidence of the crisis. Solutions to ecological crisis are not simply an issue of agreeing with a certain statement issued by a Summit either.[39]

Therefore, as far as moral re-imagination of human-nature relationships is concerned, the ecological Reformation of African Christianity[40] is crucial. Insights from African worldviews and those from Christianity would be not only promising for the ecological healing of Africa, but also foster homemade sustainable solutions for the continent.

Today, some African cultural systems have, as yet, resisted secularisation. For example, a 100-year old tree, close to the Kibilizi Hospital in Rwanda, has been named by the locals as the "tree of healing" (*igiti cy'umukiza*), because of experiences of sick people sitting under the tree being healed.[41] In this way, doctors, although Christians, have kept and maintained the tree close to the hospital. Such trees in traditional Rwanda were believed to be *places where a person can encounter the invisible*.

African scholars, theologians and pastors should seek a meaningful way to integrate this wisdom in the ecological witness of the Church in Africa.

Community versus Individuality

Psalm 148 presents creation as a cosmic community. The Psalmist summons all creatures, calling them "all his hosts" (v.2), echoing Genesis 1:31 where this expression is used to name of the created beings as having the same fate. The enlisted beings (sun, moon, stars and skies, waters, etc.) are 22, the equivalent of the Hebrew alphabet, giving an impression of fullness. In a sense, the believer (the humans) is "a choir leader",

[35] Werner, "The Challenge of Environment and Climate Justice," 52.
[36] White, "The Historical Roots of Our Ecological Crisis," 1207.
[37] Pope John Paul II, "God Made Man the Steward of Creation," General Audience Address, 2001, 2, [Available at: http://www.vatican.va/content/john-paul-ii/en/audiences/2001/documents/hf_jp-ii_aud_20010117.pdf].
[38] Pope Francis, *Laudato Si : On Care for Our Common Home (Encyclical Letter)* (Vatican: Vatican Press, 2015), 20, [Available at: http://www.vatican.va/content/dam/francesco/pdf/encyclicals/documents/papa-francesco_20150524_enciclica-laudato-si_en.pdf].
[39] South African Council of Churches, *Climate Change – A Challenge to the Churches in South Africa* (Marshalltown: South African Council of Churches, 2009), 39.
[40] Ernst Conradie, Dietrich Werner, and Ekaterini Tsalampouni, "Manifesto for an Ecological Reformation of Christianity: The Volos Call March 2016," 2016, [Available at: https://www.oikoumene.org/resources/documents/manifesto-on-an-ecological-reformation-of-all-christian-traditions].
[41] Ernest Nsanzimana, "Gisagara : Inkomoko y'.Igiti Cy'Umukiza Kitavugwaho Rumwe," UKWEZI, 2020, [Available at: http://www.ukwezi.rw/mu-rwanda/Umuco/article/Gisagara-Inkomoko-y-Igiti-cy-Umukiza-kitavugwaho-rumwe].

leading all the cosmic community towards God, inviting all the created beings to sing an "alleluia" of praise for the Creator.[42]

African community comprises of the livings, the unborn, the departed, ancestors' spirits, totems (animal or tree) and God. In this way, it was a taboo to number people or livestock because numbering separate the individual from the rest.[43] The Rwandan philosopher Alexis Kagame defined African indigenous ontology in terms of four interrelated existences: *Muntu* (human being), *Kintu* (nonhuman being); *Hantu* (place, time) and *Kuntu* (means).[44] The presence of *Ntu* in all existences means humans and nonhumans have the same essence.

Therefore, the relationships that Africans established with natural domains (flora or fauna) and phenomena (wind, storms) were identical to those they establish between themselves.[45] In this way, many African languages use the verb "to be" when stating land ownership. The Banyarwanda say *Ndi n'ubuthaka* while the Batswana say *50hris le lefatshe* to mean "I am with the land". This view implies that humans and nature (the land) stand "side by side in a relationship of interdependence from and equality with one another."[46] Just as in Leviticus 25:23, the land in Africa could never be sold in perpetuity, as it was not perceived as a commodity.

By losing the sense of nature's spirit, people engage in unethical behaviours, which seriously endanger the life of people and other earth-members. Instead of being the choir leader of Psalm 148, Africans have set themselves as "mercenaries" unconnected to the land, fellow Africans and future generations. When asked about this, the Langham scholar Eraston Kighoma compared "mercenary attitudes in Africa" with "defecating in the river of the village", saying:

> In my Nande culture, it was a taboo to defaecate in water or at the river spring: this protected rivers, springs, and waters against microbiological contamination and, thus, human and animals are protected against cholera and measles (orally collected, May 2021).

Many African groups raise this taboo to discourage actions that threaten the survival of the community as a whole. They believe that rivers are the abode of the keepers of the community (the ancestors) and the basis of life for the village. In fact, many issues of the community were resolved either under a tree or around the river. The river was also a space for the public. It was the place where members of the community would meet after farming activities.

By learning from the spirit of community, Africa would have attained better sustainable growth in many sectors. The question would be on what is community in our contemporary times and how should the word "community" be re-imagined, re-created and re-constructed in a meaningful way. The East African Community is a clear example of how African community spirit can be re-imagined to facilitate sustainable economic, social, political and cultural integration of the continent.[47] A Kinyarwanda proverb says "*umugabo umwe agerwa kuri nyina*" (a sole person, can only do what their mother can help them to do).

Cosmological Function of Chieftaincy (Good Governance)

Africans viewed chieftaincy within the context of human relationships with the forces of nature. African cosmology was thought of as comprising the world of the livings (the world of harmony) and that of the

[42] John Paul II, "God Made Man the Steward of Creation," 1.
[43] Mbiti, *African Religions and Philosophy*, 56.
[44] Alexis Kagame, *Sprache Und Sein: Die Ontologie Des Bantu Des Zentralafrikas* (Heidelberg: P.Kivouvou Verlag/Editions Bantoues, 1985), 106.
[45] Tatsopa, interviewed April 2021
[46] Maluleke, "Black and African Theologies in Search of Contemporary Environmental Justice," 19.
[47] https://www.eac.int/ [Last accessed 18th May 2021].

bush (the world of chaos). The chief was the primary mediator between the two worlds since the fertility of the land, that of people and animals all depended on the strict regulation of the relationship between the two worlds. With judicial and political power, the traditional chiefs helped regulate social relations among his subjects and prevent actions that violate communal value and thus disrupt the homestead. In an interview, the Cameroonian theologian Louis Epiemembong Ebong observed:

> Whenever there was a crisis (epidemics, deaths, drought or flooding), which disturbed harmonious bio-cultural diversity existence, the chief called the traditional council for a meeting and most often sacrifices or appeasements are made to the ancestors. Of course such a decision is arrived at with the consultation of diviners (Ebong, interviewed April 2021).

In this way, 1 Timothy 2:1-2 recommends petitions and prayers, intercession and thanksgiving for the rulers "so that we may lead tranquil and quiet lives in all godliness and dignity." Prayers must express a concern for the whole society and for those in power to influence life. In the context of the book of 1 Timothy, praying for or doing ministry in favour of emperors like Nero, proconsuls like Gallio, governors like Pilate, kings like Herod was a great challenge for the church. However, Paul insists that the church should minister political leaders because of the cosmological implications of their decisions, which may advance or impede sustainable living.

The reason is that the blooming or waning of the land is directly bound with a waxing or failing chieftaincy. In this way, Deuteronomy 17:14 recommends ample wisdom in the appointment or election of leaders: they must be God-chosen and brothers (not foreigners) in order for them to be accountable vis-à-vis their brothers. The problem of Africa is the illegitimacy of many political leaders, who got power either by putsch or by biased democratic elections. Thus, most of them do not see themselves as accountable and subsequently act as mercenaries. In traditional Africa and in Deuteronomy 17:16-20, legitimate leaders are expected to abide by the cosmological rules of the community and insure its sustainability.

The question is how modern governments could fit together monetary economy with traditions. An African proverb states, "A man who does not know where he is coming from does not know where he is going to."[48] Despite of many challenges facing Africa, African leaders must avoid inviting growth plans that decimate future possibilities for the continent. They should find a way to learn from African wisdom of the cosmological role of the leader in conjunction with modern development theories.

Conclusions

This article shows the relevance of using the threefold African cosmology as a vehicle for ecological stewardship in Africa and African churches. The sacredness or moral dimension of nature, the holistic sense of community and the cosmological role of governance can be reformulated in a meaningful way to act as a vehicle of ecological stewardship in Africa and African churches.

African theological seminaries should think on elaborating modules on "ecological Christian stewardship" based on the Bible and insights from African traditional cosmologies. What is required is not a wholesale rejection of the modern scientific view on nature, but rather a rejection of the idea that we can accumulate enough knowledge to subdue nature limitlessly.

[48] Elvis Acheampong, "The Role of Ghanaian Culture and Tradition in Environmental Sustainability," *Modern Africa*, 28th November 2010, [Available at: https://www.modernghana.com/news/306123/1/the-role-of-ghanaian-culture-and-tradition-in-envi.html].

Suggestions for Further Reading

Bauckham, Richard J. *The Bible and Ecology: Rediscovering the Community of Creation*. Waco, TX: Baylor University Press, 2010.

Fowler, Robert B. *The Greening of Protestant Thought.* London: University of North Carolina Press, 1995.

Kavusa, Kivatsi Jonathan. "Ecological Hermeneutics and the Interpretation of Biblical Texts Yesterday, Today and Onwards: Critical Reflection and Assessment." *Old Testament Essays* 32(1), (2019): 229-55. [Available at: https://doi.org/10.17159/2312-3621/2019/v32n1a13].

Maluleke, T. "Black and African Theologies in Search of Contemporary Environmental Justice." *Journal of Theology for Southern Africa* 167 (2020): 5-19.

Sindima, H. "Community of Life: Ecological Theology in African Continent." In C. Birch, W. Eaken, and J. McDaniel, Eds. *Liberating Life: Contemporary Approaches to Ecological Theology*. New York: Orbis Books, 1990. 137-47.

South African Council of Churches. *Climate Change – A Challenge to the Churches in South Africa*. Marshalltown: South African Council of Churches, 2009.

Werner, Dietrich. "The Challenge of Environment and Climate Justice: Imperatives of an Eco-Theological Reformation of Christianity in African Contexts." In Philipp Öhlmann, Wilhelm Gräb, and Marie-Louise Frost, Eds. *African Initiated Churches and the Decolonization of Development: Sustainable Development in Pentecostal and Independent Churches.* New York: Taylor & Francis, 2020. 51-72.

6. A MISSIO-AFRICAN DISCOURSE ON ECO-DIAKONIA

John Paul Isaak[1]

Introduction

This article addresses the topic of a Missio-African Discourse on Eco-Diakonia. The author is greatly influenced on the understanding of *Missio Dei* and how it should be applied in theological and missiological research and studies by the South African theologian David Bosch.

In 1991, David Bosch wrote the influential book, *Transforming Mission*,[2] where he recognised that the 20th century world changed profoundly. Thus, only one option remains for any meaningful studies, research, and doing missiology at the start of the 21st century and especially for the people like us in the Global South. They cannot continue doing mission as it was done by missionaries from the Global North since 14th century.

Therefore, Bosch argues in favour of a paradigm shift of *Missio Dei* as follows: if mission was to engage with the pluralistic character of the post-modern, post-colonial, and post-apartheid world, it must be inclusive and multidimensional. This means that nothing less than holistic or integral mission would be an adequate model, because that approach seeks to hold together the different dimensions of mission and argues that we need to see people as whole people in their whole contexts.

Mission is about word *and* deed and should adhere to the age-old message of *ora et labora* (pray and struggle for justice). The nature of the Church from a biblical understanding is the Church as People of God, the Church as the Body of Christ, the Church as Temple of the Holy Spirit, and the Church as Koinonia/Communion/Diakonia, to which we add from African Christian insights the Church as Ubuntu.

Now I am throwing down the gauntlet. I am in agreement with Bosch for the following reason: today by contextualisation or by studying and doing theology and missiology we must do such studies and teaching at all our seminaries, universities, and colleges in the context of post-colonial and post-apartheid era or in the context at the start of 21st century where Africa is free from such evils of colonialism and apartheid.

Today, Africa is one of the major growth areas of Christianity. In 1893, 80% of those who professed the Christian faith lived in Europe and North America, while at the end of the 20th century, almost 60% lived in Africa, Asia, Latin America and the Pacific. "Christianity began in the twentieth century as a Western religion, and indeed *the* Western religion; it ended the century as a non-Western religion, on track to become progressively more so".[3]

---

[1] Paul John Isaak is a Namibian. He studied in the United States of America and obtained two Master's degrees. His PhD degree was on The Status of Anthropology and Ethics in the Theology of Karl Barth: An African Lutheran Perspective. He has held various positions as one of the leading academics in Namibia: Professor at the University of Namibia; Visiting Professor at *Kirchliche Hochschule* in Wuppertal, Germany; Visiting Professor at two occasions at the Wartburg Theological Seminary in Dubuque, Iowa, USA; Visiting Professor at Makumira University College, Arusha, Tanzania, and Professor of Missiology at Ecumenical Institute Bossey, Geneva, Switzerland, affiliated to the University of Geneva. He was the Chief Electoral Officer and Director of Elections at the Electoral Commission of Namibia from 2013-2018. Since 2019, he is the Rector of the United Lutheran Theological Seminary – Paulinum in Windhoek. He is married to Mina Isaak and they have three daughters: Katrina, Thandi, and Aisha. His email address is profisaak@yahoo.com.

[2] David Bosch, *Transforming Mission: Paradigm Shifts in Theology of Mission* (Maryknoll, NY: Orbis Books, 1991).

[3] Paul John Isaak, *The Influences of Missionary Work in Namibia: A Theological Commentary* (Windhoek: Macmillan Namibia, 2007): 8.

This demographic shift in Christianity means that the time has passed when Africa, Asia, Latin America and the Pacific sat at the feet of Europe and North America in order to learn, study, research and do any field of theological studies.

We study and do such theology and missiology or any other branch of religious field, to borrow from Bosch in bold humility, "not as judges or lawyers, but as witnesses; not as soldiers, but as envoys of peace; not as high-pressure salespersons, but as ambassadors of the Servant Jesus".[4] Faithfulness to the Servant Jesus and crucified Christ come as expressions of our faith here, along with the conviction of *simul iustus et peccator* as the foundation for such Christian humility and witness.

This article consists of two parts: the first addresses *Missio Dei* as a Missio-African discourse on eco-diakonia with particular emphasis on Christianity and ecology. I shall focus on the key issue of the roots of ecology in the Bible with special references to Genesis 1:26 and Genesis 2:15 where God took Adam and Eve and put them in the Garden of Eden to *abad* in Hebrew, that means to "cultivate" or to "serve" or being in the service of co-humanity while being engaged in the processes of cultivating mother earth. In short, from a Christian ecological perspective we shall maintain that God has made us stewards on this mother earth to cultivate it and to ensure climate justice.

The second part addresses the theological-social issue of diakonia. The word, diakonia, taken from the Greek verb, means to serve humanity and being in service relationship with co-humanity or better expressed in an African word, *Ubuntu*. The entire African religion and morality are rooted upon *Ubuntu* – or humaneness.

In this *Ubuntu* culture and ethos, we say, "A person is a person through other persons". It is not one of "I think, therefore I am". Instead it says, "My humanity is caught up, is inextricably bound up, in yours". In other words, a person with *Ubuntu* is open and available to others and to empower them or provide humanitarian or health services, affirming of others as God's children, and does not see the other as an enemy, but as a brother, a sister, a comrade.

To put it differently, love of God and love of neighbour cannot be separated. In *The Freedom of a Christian*, Luther speaks of being "a Christ" to one's neighbour. That is, in serving one's neighbour, the Christian is not serving God: on the contrary, they are being united with God by faith, and is participating in the work of God.[5] In short, the African Christian confessional tradition and African religious and ethical inheritance of Ubuntu is similar to Luther's understanding of being a Christ to one's neighbour.

Therefore, no matter how brutal colonialism was in Africa and apartheid in Southern Africa, even to the degree of causing the first 20th Century genocide in Namibia and African anthropological poverty, the colonisers and white rulers from South Africa could not touch the soul of African spirituality and Ubuntu. In short, from an African Christian perspective being one's neighbour means sharing Ubuntu. In serving one's neighbour, we are directly involved in mission as eco-diakonia.

Christianity and Ecology

Let me first express my appreciation to Saint Francis of Assisi. On 29th November 1979, Pope John Paul II issued a papal bull that declared St Francis of Assisi the patron of ecology. In the bull, John Paul II wrote, "Among the holy and admirable men who have revered nature as a wonderful gift of God to the human race, St Francis of Assisi deserves special consideration." Naming Francis of Assisi as the patron Saint of Ecology came at the end of the 1970s, a decade that witnessed the birth of the modern environmental movement and began with the celebration of the first Earth Day.[6]

---

[4] Bosch, *Transforming Mission*, 489.

[5] Martin Luther, *Luther's Works*, *Volume* 3. (Philadelphia, PA: Fortress, 1955-1986): 364-367.

[6] See Brian Roewe, "Why is Francis of Assisi the patron saint of ecology?", 2nd October 2020, NCR, [Available at: https://www.ncronline.org/news/earthbeat/why-francis-assisi-patron-saint-ecology], [Last accessed: 6th April 2022].

Saint Francis saw all creation as being loved by God and as loving God. To contextualise. we can say in Namibian that this country in its beauty is enclosed by two deserts: in the west by the Namib and in the east by the Kalahari and on the western side the blue Atlantic Ocean. While being enclosed by the desert and ocean, the country has one of the world's biggest deposits of gemstone diamonds, with large quantities of copper, zinc, uranium and salt, not to mention the vast tracts of land ideal for cattle, sheep and goat farming, and sea waters abundant with fish.

If Saint Francis shall see Namibia, he would be absolutely glad to see all the deserts, ocean, diamonds, cattle, sheep, goats, the sky while praising God, its creator. For Saint Francis, God was not the stern Father as taught in our churches. God was the creator Mother who gave birth to all and cared, lovingly, for all. So, when he called the earth, Mother Earth, he saw her as being a part of God. When he spoke of the cattle, goats, sheep, birds and animals as being his sisters and brothers, he meant that they were part of the same great extended family under God.[7]

Saint Francis' theology of ecology inspired me to do more research on two biblical texts that deal with creation, namely Genesis 1:26 and 28: "Then God said, "Let us make humankind in our image, according to our likeness; and let them have dominion over the fish of the sea, and over the birds of the air, and over the cattle, and over every creeping thing that creeps on the earth [...] And God blessed them. And God said to them, "Be fruitful and multiply and fill the earth and subdue it. Be masters over the fish of the sea and over the birds of the heavens and over every living thing that moves on the earth." In this text, we shall pay special attention to the two phrases, "dominion" and "masters over."

Genesis 1:26 must be read together with Genesis 2:15 where God took Adam and Eve and put them in the Garden of Eden to "*abad*". In Hebrew, that means to cultivate or to serve or being in the service and in the process of cultivating mother earth.

These two texts deal with the issues of dominion and mastery over in Genesis 1:26 and 28 and cultivation of earth in Genesis 2:15. The basic issue here, in light of our topic eco-diakonia, is what the rightful attitude of us as humans ought to be to the earth or entire creation. Today there is a growing concern for the environment and the human effect upon it and the word, dominion, ought to be closely interrogated.

In this context, we ought to take words of Dom Helder Camara seriously to contemplate the consequences of "dominion" and how it is interpreted. He has denounced as "blasphemous" humanity's usurpation of mother earth as "the power to liquidate life on our planet" as well as enforcement of power "over the poor, the landless, and indeed over the bounty of nature itself"[8] and, in the process of being "masters over" God's creation and God's people, the powerful of this world entrusted themselves with such powers to exploit creation or mother earth and oppressed people.

For us from the Global South, the connotation of "dominion" and "masters over" is closely linked to European colonialism, the Euro-American transatlantic slave trade, and South African Apartheid. The oppressors gave themselves unlimited power and licence to oppress other people who were not white and to exploit nature for their own use.

For example, the richness of Namibia with its diamonds, grazing and farming land, and fish made the country too valuable an asset to let be. For such reasons, Germany and South Africa considered Namibia suitable for extensive settlement by Europeans and thereby colonialised it and imposed apartheid upon it. Consequently, such policies made the settlers richer and richer and left the indigenous people poor. Under these conditions, any challenge to colonial rule was tantamount to disparaging national honour and grandeur. Take the historical case on the first genocide of the 20th century.

As the process of colonialism was unacceptable to the Namibians, they demonstrated democratically and as responsible people of the land against the colonial rule from above. This justified action from below, namely to be engaged in "*iure bellare*" (a just war) by launching the anti-colonial liberation struggle, was

[7] Elizabeth Breuilly and Martin Palmer (eds), *Christianity and Ecology* (London: Cassel, 1992): 79-80.
[8] Pamela Smith, *Environmental Ethics*? (New York: Paulist Press, 1997): 57.

vigorously opposed by the colonial rulers. Consequently, the first genocide of the 20th century took place[9] when the German colonial regime brutally killed almost 80% of the Herero people, 50% of the Nama and many Damara and San between 1903 to 1908.

At the same time, it should be noted that the German authorities always gave an exact number of casualties in the case of German soldiers, officers, and settlers as well as the date, place, and probable cause of such deaths. For example, during the period January 1904 to March 1907, the total German losses amounted to 2,348. The breakdown of losses was 676 dead, 76 missing, 907 wounded, and 689 having succumbed to disease. African losses cannot be determined from various sources with such precision, but most of the cases are given in round numbers or merely as estimations.[10]

Consequently, this first genocide of the 20th century was executed on 2nd October 1904, when the German commander General Lothar von Trotha, issued the following extermination proclamation (*Vernichtungsbefehl*): "I, the great General of the German soldiers, send this letter to the Herero nation. The Hereros are no longer German subjects. They have murdered and robbed, they have cut off the ears and the noses and private parts of the wounded soldiers and they are now too cowardly to fight […] The Herero nation must now leave the country. If the people do it not, I will compel them with the big tube [artillery]. Within the German frontiers, with or without rifle, with or without cattle [all the Hereros] will be shot. I will not take over any more women or children; I will either drive them back to your people or have them fired on. These are my words to the nation of the Hereros. The great General of the Mighty Emperor. Von Trotha."[11]

The general was true to his word. The Herero and Nama and later Damara and San were machine-gunned and their wells poisoned. Finally, they were either driven into the desert to die or taken to the concentration camps such as Shark Island as prisoners of war. This was how colonisation and even mission work by German missionaries began in what is today Namibia.

Sadly, the issue of genocide history has not yet been satisfactory answered especially to the Herero and Nama people – the main groups directly affected by the genocide. The key fundamental perspective from the side of Namibia is a strategy based on three pillars: that Germany unconditionally accept they committed genocide in Namibia, they apologise, and they pay reparations. These pillars are still under negotiations between the German and Namibian governments while facing major protest from the affected communities that they are not included at the round tables of negotiations.

In Genesis 2:15, the human being is seen to be in service of the earth, upon which we are called upon to be in diakonia because such diakonia services provide food, water, medicine, housing, education, jobs or welfare for all the people. Therefore, we ought to stress Genesis 2:15 for the following reason: We humans are viewed as God's representatives in creation (see Genesis 1:27 where humankind is created in God's image and according to God's likeness). In short, according to this interpretation of being God's representatives, this refers to the sanctity and innate worth of *all* human being and presumes that all persons be treated with equal dignity.

---

[9] The international legal definition of *genocide* is found in Article II of the 1948 Convention on the Prevention and Punishment of Genocide: "Article II: In the present Convention, *genocide* means any of the following acts committed with intent to destroy, in whole or in part, a national, ethnic, racial or religious group, as such: (a) Killing members of the group; (b) Causing serious bodily or mental harm to members of the group; (c) Deliberately inflicting on the group conditions of life calculated to bring about its physical destruction in whole or in part; (d) Imposing measures intended to prevent births within the group; (e) Forcibly transferring children of the group to another group".

[10] Jon Bridgman, *The Revolt of the Hereros* (Berkeley, CA: University of California Press, 1981): 108, 164. See also Nils Ole Oermann, *Mission, Church and State relations in South West Africa under German rule 1884-1915* (Stuttgart: Franz Steiner Verlag, 1999): 102.

[11] Carl-J. Hellberg, *Mission, Colonialism, and Liberation: The Lutheran Church in Namibia 1840-1966* (Windhoek: New Namibian Books, 1997): 113-114.

In summary, as Bevans and Schroeder say, such cultivation or mission as eco-diakonia is "a dance" in which God invites us to be partners with God as God "moves through the world, inviting the world – material creation, human beings – to join in the dance."[12] Human beings and the creation need such a dance in light of Genesis 2:15 today to overcome the war against the poorest of this world or the cutting death-deals of the rich in their pursuit to exercise "dominion" on ecology, war against the creation, and war against the welfare of the people by the rulers and powerful for satisfy their own excessive consumerism.

Finally, if there is one environmental, ethical and diaconal principle on which world's religions seem to agree with near unanimity, it is that human beings ought to regard conduct conducive to the "sustainability" of the Earth as a moral and eco-diakonial imperative, particularly by emphasising respect for the community of living beings and preservation of earth, life, air, water and soil.[13]

When such a dance is happening, African Christianity will be ready to join worship services in an atmosphere that is thoroughly-embodied, deeply-musical, highly-choreographed sacred drama – with hands clapping, feet tapping, elders humming, choirs swaying, ushers marching, preachers sweating, and congregants shouting, all for the glorification of God, the edification of the human spirit and the transformation of a troubled world so that everywhere and anywhere we shall celebrate mission as eco-diakonia.

The Theological-Social Issue of Diakonia

The word, diakonia, taken from the Greek verb, means to serve humanity and being in service relationship with co-humanity or Ubuntu. To put it differently, love of God and love of neighbour cannot be separated. In serving one's neighbour, the Christian is not serving God alone: on the contrary, they are being united with God by faith, and are participating in the work of God, namely in mission as eco-diakonia. In short, diakonia means the responsibility service of the gospel by deeds and by words performed by Christians and people of other faith traditions to the needs of people.

Let us clearly state that in Christianity the greatest commandment is expressed and articulated in Mark 12:30-31: "Love the Lord your God with all your heart and with all your soul and with all your mind and with all your strength. The second is this: Love your neighbour as yourself." In short, as Christians and citizens of this world, we are called upon to pray and to work simultaneously by linking *orthodoxy* (correct teachings and doctrines of the Church as contained in the Holy Scriptures and Church tradition), *orthokardia* (right-heartedness or spirituality towards God and neighbours), and *orthopraxis* (transformative social action and involvement in the affairs of this world or to participate in mission as eco-diakonia).

Differently expressed, in Matthew 25:31-46, Jesus comes to us in those who are hungry, homeless, sick and imprisoned. Basic human needs are listed here: food, clothing, shelter, health care and, by implication, the basic political need for human dignity and integrity. Put plainly, a Christian's zeal to cultivate the soil so that those without food be empowered by having access to food and water is illustrated here. God's honour and dignity must show itself in corresponding action that is directed toward the neighbours. Such an understanding of Christian ministry and eco-diakonia means that God breaks into our world and invites us to be involved in the creative and liberating dynamics of God's love in history. Moreover, while human efforts cannot remove sin from the world, God's creativity involves us in these dynamics, so that we engage in cultivating partial, provisional and relative victories and this is the *Missio Dei* as eco-diakonia in which the African missional church is participating today.

---

[12] Stephen Bevans and Roger Schroeder, *Constants in Context: A Theology of Mission for Today* (Maryknoll, NY: Orbis, 2011): 10.

[13] Pamela Smith, *What Are They Saying About Environmental Ethics?* 67.

Such direct and intimate linking insists that spirituality and faith inspired by God's Word must express itself in social action. In other words, God must not be de-emphasised, faith not neglected, and praxis not avoided. These are the primarily pillars upon which mission as eco-diakonia is constructed.

Unfortunately, diakonia was misunderstood in the history of Protestant Churches with the ordinary health and social services of the State. Especially, in the Protestant Churches, there has been a tendency to hand over diakonia, clinics, hospitals, and schools to the state. But it should not be this way. For example, the aim of diakonia is to help people to be in service, or diakonial relationships, with co-humanity. The care for the entire human being means to care for the spiritual or *orthokardia* dimensions as well as psychological and social needs or *orthopraxis*.

Thus, schools, hospitals and diakonia ministries are essential services required from the church as well as from the society. In short, such critical services are regarded as part and parcel of the social responsibilities of faith-based organisations and the State. It is beautifully expressed in the Namibian Constitution, Article 95 on the Promotion of the Welfare of the People. Such welfare of the people in relation to eco-diakonia means practically:

- enacting legislation to ensure equality of opportunity for women, to enable them to participate fully in all spheres of Namibian society; in particular, the Government shall ensure the implementation of the principle of non-discrimination in remuneration of men and women; further, the Government shall seek, through appropriate legislation, to provide maternity and related benefits for women;
- enacting legislation to ensure that the health and strength of the workers, men and women, and the tender age of children are not abused and that citizens are not forced by economic necessity to enter vocations unsuited to their age and strength;
- ensuring that senior citizens are entitled to and do receive a regular pension adequate for the maintenance of a decent standard of living and the enjoyment of social and cultural opportunities;
- enacting legislation to ensure that the unemployed, the incapacitated, the indigent and the disadvantaged are accorded such social benefits and amenities as are determined by Parliament to be just and affordable with due regard to the resources of the State;
- ensuring that workers are paid a living wage adequate for the maintenance of a decent standard of living and the enjoyment of social and cultural opportunities; [*and most importantly as related to our topic in ecological issues and care for the entire creation or as mission and Eco-Diakonia*]
- maintaining ecosystems, essential ecological processes and the biological diversity of Namibia and utilisation of living natural resources on a sustainable basis for the benefit of all Namibians, both present and future; in particular, the Government shall provide measures against the dumping or recycling of foreign nuclear and toxic waste on Namibian territory.[14]

Conclusion

What can we say about mission as eco-diakonia as the church grapples with contemporary issues today? From an African Christian perspective, let us not hesitate to connect theology, diakonia, ecological and ethics of environmental sustainability, and economics. To quote David Bosch, when Christians proclaim the Gospel, it links the "word" with the "deed". The "deed" or action without the "word" or prayer is dumb; the word/prayer without the deed/action is empty.[15]

Thus, today we have to enable the Church to tell the gospel truth in bold humility and be directly engaged in mission as eco-diakonia. Truth-telling, struggling for justice, and working towards reconciliation and nation-building: this is the ongoing mission activity of the Church in the society in which it participates.

[14] *The Constitution of the Republic of Namibia* (Windhoek: The Ministry of Information and Communication Technology, 1998): 50-51.
[15] David Bosch, *Transforming Mission,* 420.

These processes imply that churches must endeavour to create safe and hospitable spaces where truth can be spoken and heard and where healing and health of the body take place or, as expressed in Matthew 25, where we empower people to have daily food, jobs, water, housing, and medicine.

In order to achieve this noble task, the churches are always called upon to execute on praxis or in their own contexts the serious questions concerning the original meaning and contemporary validity of mission as eco-diakonia. It is the *Missio Dei* where Christians and churches are called upon to respond to welfare of the people and ethics of environmental sustainability. It is the thrust to play on the title of Ulrich Duchrow's *Christenheit und Weltverantwortung*,[16] it is the responsibility of Christians to the world or the mission as eco-diakonia.

Suggestions for Further Reading

Bevans, Stephen and Roger Schroeder. *Constants in Context: A Theology of Mission for Today*. Maryknoll, NY: Orbis, 2011.

Bosch, David. *Transforming Mission: Paradigm Shifts in Theology of Mission*. Maryknoll, NY: Orbis, 1991.

Breuilly, Elizabeth and Martin Palmer, Eds. *Christianity and Ecology*. London: Cassel, 1992.

Hellberg, Carl-J. *Mission, Colonialism, and Liberation: The Lutheran Church in Namibia 1840-1966*. Windhoek: New Namibian Books, 1997.

Isaak, Paul John. *The Influences of Missionary Work in Namibia: A Theological Commentary*. Windhoek: Macmillan Namibia, 2007.

Smith, Pamela. *What Are They Saying About Environmental Ethics*? New York: Paulist Press, 1997.

[16] Ulrich Duchrow, *Christenheit und Weltverantwortung. Traditionsgeschichte und systematische Struktur der Zweireichelehre* (Stuttgart: Klett-Cotta, 1970).

7. Water, Bringer of Life for People and Wildlife – Perspectives from Lebanon[1]

Chris Naylor[2]

(God) makes springs pour water into the ravines;
it flows between the mountains.
They give water to all the beasts of the field;
the wild donkeys quench their thirst.
The birds of the sky nest by the waters;
they sing among the branches.
He waters the mountains from his upper chambers;
the land is satisfied by the fruit of his work.
He makes grass grow for the cattle,
and plants for people to cultivate—
bringing forth food from the earth:
wine that gladdens human hearts,
oil to make their faces shine,
and bread that sustains their hearts.
The trees of the Lord are well watered,
the cedars of Lebanon that he planted.
(Psalm 104, 10-16)

Water for Wildlife and People

This Psalm, from the Bible, is a wonderful ancient song of praise, drawing inspiration from the habitats of Mount Lebanon to praise God. Perhaps the most obvious thing we notice is that there is a clear link between God's blessing and water; God makes the springs pour water, and it is from this water that consequential blessings flow. But the question I would like to consider briefly is – who is the water for?

The Psalm speaks of God as provider. Throughout this Psalm, God gives: he makes springs pour water; he gives water; he waters the mountains; he makes grass grow; he gives plants and so on. But who is it all for? In the second section of the Psalm, the answer is for mankind. Plants are for people to cultivate; oil is to make the face shine. But the first answer, and the answer in the passage above is that God gives, God provides for the beasts of the field: the donkeys so they can quench their thirst; the birds of the air. In other words, this Psalm has a very integrated understanding of God's provision. Using water as a picture, the passage speaks of God providing for mankind certainly, but for wildlife too.

We may think we know the Bible's stories well. We tend to think they are all about what God has to say to us and about us. We often overlook wider creation when we zoom in on what we think is the only narrative in the Bible – that is the one that is all about people – all about us.

I will give you another example of what I mean, again using water. This time water is not the provider of life, it is the great destroyer. Let's look at Noah, the ark and the flood. God sends a cataclysmic flood

---

[1] This text was first published in Wilbert van Saane (ed), *The Symbolism of Water in Religion: Proceedings of an interreligious conference on water and religion held at Haigazian University on March 2, 2018* (Beirut: Haigazian University Press, 2019), 99-104. It has been included in this volume with permission by Haigazian University Press.
[2] Chris Naylor (1961-2019) was the Executive Director of A Rocha International. He joined A Rocha in 1997 working, until 2009, as Lebanon Director, where he cofounded the work.

wiping out all life on earth except the life preserved in the ark – Noah, his family and the animals. In the book of Genesis, after the flood, when God gave the rainbow as a sign, who did he make the covenant with? The covenant that he would never again destroy the earth? Was it with Noah? Noah and his family? The whole human race? The answer is perhaps a surprise – the covenant was between God and the Earth. "I have set my rainbow in the clouds, and it will be the sign of the covenant between me and the earth." (Gen. 9:13) Now, I am sure humanity is included and so explicitly is "every living creature." But scripture actually says the covenant is between God and the Earth. God cares about the Earth – the Bible message is not all about humanity – it is not all about us.

Christian Responses to the Ecological Crisis

Although it is true to say that through much of modern church history "Care for Creation" has been lost as part of the gospel message, today the church is again waking up to this more integrated, holistic – more authentically biblical – faith. As an example, the Anglican Communion set out, in what it sees as the role of the church, one of the five marks of mission as: "to strive to safeguard the integrity of creation, and sustain and renew the life of the earth."

As the environmental crisis deepens so Christian responses gain momentum. Many groups are involved in practical action. While theological enquiry is informing the pulpit, deeply held materialist attitudes in many Christian communities are slowly changing. Certainly, the environmental crisis is deepening. Scientists now describe the present time as the Anthropocene. That is, the current geological age is viewed as the period during which human activity is the dominant influence on climate and the environment.

Currently, all environmental statistics are frightening. The WWF & ZSL (Living Planet Report 2014) catalogue a 52% decline in wildlife populations since 1970. That is a halving of life on earth in less than 50 years! But for freshwater wildlife populations the decline reaches a staggering 76% decline since 1970.

The Case of the Aammiq Wetland

It seems water is an early casualty in a landscape in crisis. That is certainly what I discovered when I lived in the Bekaa in the early 1990s, when the Aammiq conservation project was born. Much of the water that sustains the Aammiq wetland in the West Bekaa starts as snow on the Barouk Mountain Ridge. The snow melts through the season to recharge the aquifer and then at the spring line bursts out of the ground to form the pools that drain into the wetland and eventually into the Litani River. As the water makes its way to the river, it creates habitats: open water, reedbed, flooded pasture, riverine, avenues of trees, and rich farmland. Historically, the wetland covered a huge area all the way to Zahle but, by the end of the Lebanese civil war, only a remnant patch work of seasonal pools remained, close to obliteration.

The Christian Conservation Organization A Rocha Lebanon, together with the landowners, local municipality, tenant farmers, the Ministry of Environment and the neighbouring Al Shouf Cedar Reserve, worked to restore and protect the wetland for people and wildlife. Among the wildlife that depends on the Aammiq wetlands are huge numbers of migrating birds such as storks. The Aammiq wetland is particularly important as a roosting stopover for migrating birds on their pan-continental journey. But other species also benefit from the wetland: reptiles, amphibians, mammals, fish, and many other birds. The natural flow of the river into the wetland profits people as well, especially by: creating grazing areas for cattle; acting as a sponge for water for crops; creating a microclimate; improving soil health and maintenance of aquifers. Among the problems that had to be faced by the project were: hunting, pollution, over-extraction of water, over-grazing, and habitat loss. Through years of hard work, A Rocha and its partners achieved a wetland that is no longer dried up during the summer months, but contained water all year long.

The Role of Faith-Based NGOs

What do faith-based NGOs bring to the water conservation story? I have thought long and hard about this question. One key component badly lacking in the world of conservation is hope. Faith brings hope and, as faith-based conservation NGOs, we need to bring it to the party. If you go to Aammiq, you can join in that party and celebrate at Tawlet Aammiq. This eco-restaurant was born out of the A Rocha conservation project. Designed to provide an eco-tourist entry to the wetland and Shouf Cedar Reserve, employment opportunities for the different sectarian communities of the West Bekaa, and cash for the conservation of the precious habitats of marsh and mountain, it is a place to celebrate, have hope and a great meal.

Returning to Psalm 104, there are five species of animal mentioned by name that were breeding in Lebanon at the time the Psalm was written. Today, three are extinct in Lebanon, one still migrates through but no longer breeds and one still breeds. But there is hope! The lion is extinct and is unlikely to be reintroduced. The wild donkey is extinct and the Bekaa plains are now too populated for it to be reintroduced. The wild goat or ibex still lives in Jordan and there are plans to reintroduce it as a wild animal to the Shouf Cedar Reserve. The white stork now regularly summers in Aammiq and, if hunting remains under control, there is no reason why it should not breed. The rock hyrax or coney is still found as a breeding mammal on the mountains of the Shouf.

Suggestions for Further Reading

Website Arocha Lebanon: https://lebanon.arocha.org/

The Ecological Importance of Aammiq wetland: https://natalyhaddad.wordpress.com/ and https://natalyhaddad.wordpress.com/2017/10/06/aammiq-wetland-a-nature-reserve/

Lebanon's National Biodiversity and Strategy Action Plan 2016: https://www.cbd.int/doc/world/lb/lb-nbsap-v2-en.pdf

8. The Protection of the Common Good and the Integrity of the Natural Environment as a Common Responsibility of all Inhabitants of the Earth – Message for World Day of Creation

Ecumenical Patriarch Bartholomew I[1]

Dearest brother Hierarchs and beloved children in the Lord,

It is a shared conviction that, in our time, the natural environment is threatened like never before in the history of humankind. The magnitude of this threat becomes manifest in the fact that what is at stake is not anymore the quality, but the preservation of life on our planet. For the first time in history, man is capable of destroying the conditions of life on earth. Nuclear weapons are the symbol of man's Promethean titanism, the tangible expression of the "complex of omnipotence" of the contemporary "man-god."

In using the power that stems from science and technology, what is revealed today is the ambivalence of man's freedom. Science serves life; it contributes to progress, to confronting illnesses and many conditions that were hitherto considered "fateful"; it creates new positive perspectives for the future. However, at the same time, it provides man with all-powerful means, whose misuse can be turned destructive. We are experiencing the unfolding destruction of the natural environment, of biodiversity, of flora and fauna, of the pollution of aquatic resources and the atmosphere, the progressing collapse of climate balance, as well as other excesses of boundaries and measures in many dimensions of life. The Holy and Great Council of the Orthodox Church (Crete, 2016) rightly and splendidly decreed that "scientific knowledge does not mobilise the moral will of man, who knows the dangers but continues to act as if he did not know" (*Encyclical*, § 11).

It is apparent that the protection of the common good, of the integrity of the natural environment, is the common responsibility of all inhabitants of the earth. The contemporary categorical imperative for humankind is that we live without destroying the environment. However, while on a personal level and on the level of many communities, groups, movements and organisations, there is a demonstration of great sensitivity and ecological responsibility, nations and economic agents are unable – in the name of geopolitical ambitions and the "autonomy of the economy" – to adopt the correct decisions for the protection of creation and instead cultivate the illusion that the pretended "global ecological destruction" is an ideological fabrication of ecological movements and that the natural environment has the power of renewing itself. Yet the crucial question remains: how much longer will nature endure the fruitless discussions and consultations, as well as any further delay in assuming decisive actions for its protection?

[1] The Ecumenical Patriarch, the Archbishop of Constantinople-New Rome and Ecumenical Patriarch To All the Plenitude of the Church, for many years has been a strong voice pleading for the ecological responsibility of humanity and World Christianity, not only in the Middle East but far beyond, now recognised globally as one of the foremost spiritual leaders on climate and environmental issues. In an encyclical from 1989, he had invited all Orthodox and other Christian faithful "to lift up prayers of thanksgiving to the Creator of all for "the great gift of Creation" along with petitions for its preservation". Since then, the Season of Creation is celebrated globally each year starting on 1st September (https://seasonofcreation.org/about/). That is why The Ecumenical Patriarch also has been called the "Green Patriarch". As one example of his passionate engagement for ecological renewal his message for the world day of prayer for creation from 2020 is quoted here: https://www.vaticannews.va/en/church/news/2020-09/bartholomew-i-message-for-world-day-of-creation-full-text.html; See a similar message for 2021: https://seasonofcreation.org/2021/09/03/ecumenical-patriarch-bartholomews-message-for-2021-world-day-of-prayer-for-the-care-of-creation/; see also: John Chryssavgis, *On Earth as in Heaven: Ecological Vision and Initiatives of Ecumenical Patriarch Bartholomew*, Fordham University Press, 2011. John Chryssavgis, *Cosmic Grace – Humble Prayer: The Ecological Vision of the Green Patriarch Bartholomew I* (Grand Rapids, MI: Eerdmans, 2008).

The fact that, during the period of the pandemic of the novel coronavirus COVID-19, with the mandatory restrictions of movement, the shutdown of factories, and the diminishment in industrial activity and production, we observed a reduction of pollution and encumbrance of the atmosphere, has proved the anthropogenic nature of the contemporary ecological crisis. It became once again clear that industry, the contemporary means of transportation, the automobile and the airplane, the non-negotiable priority of economic indicators and the like, negatively impact the environmental balance and that a change of direction toward an ecological economy constitutes an unwavering necessity. There is no genuine progress that is founded on the destruction of the natural environment. It is inconceivable that we adopt economic decisions without also taking into account their ecological consequences. Economic development cannot remain a nightmare for ecology. We are certain that there is an alternative way of economic structure and development besides the economism and the orientation of economic activity toward the maximisation of profiteering. The future of humanity is not the *homo œconomicus*.

The Ecumenical Patriarchate, which in recent decades has pioneered in the field of the protection of the creation, will continue its ecological initiatives, the organisation of ecological conferences, the mobilisation of its faithful and especially the youth, the promotion of the environment's protection as a fundamental subject for interreligious dialogue and the common initiatives of religions, the contacts with political leaders and institutions, the co-operation with environmental organisations and ecological movements. It is evident that the collaboration for the protection of the environment creates additional avenues of communication and possibilities for new common actions.

We repeat that the environmental activities of the Ecumenical Patriarchate are an extension of its ecclesiological self-consciousness and do not comprise a simple circumstantial reaction to a new phenomenon. The very life of the Church is an applied ecology. The sacraments of the Church, its entire life of worship, its asceticism and communal life, the daily life of its faithful, express and generate the deepest respect for creation. The ecological sensitivity of Orthodoxy was not created by but emerged from the contemporary environmental crisis. The struggle for the protection of creation is a central dimension of our faith. Respect for the environment is an act of doxology of God's name, while the destruction of creation is an offense against the Creator, entirely irreconcilable with the basic tenets of Christian theology.

Most honourable brothers and dearly beloved children,

The eco-friendly values of the Orthodox tradition, the precious legacy of the Fathers, constitute an embankment against the culture, whose axiological foundation is the domination of man over nature. Faith in Christ inspires and strengthens the human endeavour even before the immense challenges. From the perspective of faith, we are able to discover and assess not only the problematic dimensions, but also the positive possibilities and prospects of contemporary civilisation. We call upon Orthodox young men and women to realise the significance of living as faithful Christians and contemporary people. Faith in the eternal destiny of man strengthens our witness in the world.

In this spirit, from the Phanar, we wish all of you a propitious and all-blessed new ecclesiastical year, fruitful in Christ-like deeds, for the benefit of all creation and to the glory of the all-wise Creator of all. And we invoke upon you, through the intercessions of the All-Holy Theotokos, the *Pammakaristos*, the grace and mercy of the God of wonders.

1st September 2020

+Bartholomew of Constantinople

Part II: Asia and Pacific

9. 'Eco-Diakonia': Echoing the 'Green God' in the Age of the Pandemic

Mothy Varkey[1]

> "Nature sustains us. It's where we originated. The lesson for humanity from this pandemic is not to be afraid of nature, but rather to restore it, embrace it, and understand how to live with and benefit from it. [...] The wise way forward is to invest in conservation and science, and to embrace nature and the glorious variety of life with which we share this planet. A healthy future for humanity and a healthy biodiverse planet goes hand in hand."
>
> Thomas E. Lovejoy

Introduction

Emergent pandemic diseases are anthropogenic diseases – that is, they are caused by human activities and not natural disasters. As Vandana Shiva rightly puts it, "Human greed, with no respect for the rights of other species or even for our fellow human beings, is at the root of this pandemic and future pandemics."[2] The COVID-19 pandemic has reminded us in a devastating way of the interconnected nature of the economy, environment, and human health; "everything on our planet is interconnected – and we are part of the equation."[3] The well-known Brazilian liberation theologian Leonardo Boff strongly argues that the coronavirus pandemic demands "a different relationship with nature and the Earth. If after the crisis has passed, we don't make the necessary changes, the next time may be the last, since we will have become staunch enemies of the Earth. And she may no longer want us here."[4]

We cannot continue to have this dangerous illusion of mastery of nature and become the reason for the next pandemic, and finally, to extinction. American author Eileen Crist argues that the techno-managerial "portfolio – which would include such initiatives as climate geoengineering, desalination, de-extinction, and off-planet colonisation – is in keeping with the social rubric of human distinction."[5] The pandemic will not only change human life but also raise some important questions about the emergence of a new human being in the post-COVID world, argues the Moroccan politician Ilyas El Omari.[6] This calls for a post-

---

[1] Rev Dr Mothy Varkey is Professor of New Testament at the Mar Thoma Theological Seminary, Kottayam, Kerala. He is also the visiting fellow at the Murdoch University, Perth, Australia. Among his many and influential works in English are *Concept of Power in Matthew: A Postcolonial Reading* (CSS, 2010), *Salvation in Continuity: Reconsidering Matthew's Soteriology* (Fortress, 2017), *Inheritance and Resistance: Reclaiming Bible, Body and Power* (CWI, 2020), and *Church and Diakonia in the Age of COVID-19* (ISPCK, 2020).

[2] Vandana Shiva, "A virus, humanity, and the earth," 5th April 2020. [Available at: https://www.deccanherald.com/specials/sunday-spotlight/a-virus-humanity-and-the-earth-821527.html].

[3] World Wide Fund For Nature, "Everything on our planet is interconnected – and we are part of the equation," 22nd May 2020. [Available at: https://updates.panda.org/interconnected].

[4] Mada Jurado, 26th March 2020. [Available at: https://leonardoboff.org/2020/05/08/what-may-come-after-the-coronavirus/].

[5] Eileen Crist, "Reimagining Human," *Science* 14th December 2018. Vol 362, Issue 6420, 1242-1244. [Available at: https://science.sciencemag.org/content/362/6420/1242].

[6] Ilyas El Omari, "A new human being will emerge in the post-Covid-19 world," *Observer Researcher Foundation* 8th April 2020. [Available at: https://www.orfonline.org/expert-speak/a-new-human-being-will-emege-in-the-post-covid-19-world-64275/].

pandemic reimagination of the human being, which will be and have to be different from the pre-pandemic generation.

As the "earth is in the throes of a mass extinction event and climate change upheaval,"[7] any attempt to signify justice, ekklēsia and diakonia in the context of COVID-19 must take as its vantage point planetary shifts, the stark reminders of ecological predicament and the possible environmental measures to be taken to avert the next pandemic. Like all other fatal emergencies in the past, COVID has also undeniably proved human beings' Promethean impulse, to be masters of nature and manipulate, exploit and control other species as objects for profit. Human beings are not separate from nature. "The Earth will continue to evolve, with or without us."[8] This compels the faith community (church) in the post-pandemic matrix to reimagine a human that no longer identifies with speciesism.

COVID-19 is a persuasive proof of how closely the planet's health and pandemics are linked. The World Economic Forum states, "Just as carbon is not the cause of climate change, it is human activity – not nature – that causes many pandemics."[9] Any attempt therefore to find solutions to convalesce from the crisis must take the ecology of the pandemic as its method and basis: "COVID-19 and nature are linked. So should be the recovery."[10] The recent Seychelles' marine-protection initiative offers us hope that if every country does its part, the planet can be safer and healthier. In other words, the decisions we make on how to respond to the coronavirus pandemic will impact the future health of people and the planet, and a poor response would be detrimental to the survival of the human species itself; "nature is our best antiviral." But strategies to mitigate COVID-19 have also led to another ecological crisis due to the increased use of single-use disposable face masks and latex gloves around the world.

Radical environmentalist philosopher Derrick Jensen, in his impassionate polemic *The Myth of Human Supremacy*, debunks one of culture's most pernicious and nature-devouring myths, that of human supremacy. In this much-necessary and provocative book, Jensen dissects suicidal impulses that constitute the human craving for dominance and the fatal belief in progress that triggers ecocide. To problematise the paralysis of conventional science and technology, he explores the complexities, intelligence and sentience of all other beings than human. Only by destroying the sociopathy of our consciousness as the "anointed species" will we be able to save ourselves and our planet. The world as an interconnected web of beings calls for demythologising the "hegemonic human being." Boff makes it categorical: "There is no escape. Either we recognise ourselves as humans – co-equal in the same Common Home – or we will all sink."[11]

Green God, Earth Ethics and Eco-Diakonia

Lynn White's article entitled "The Historical Roots of our Ecologic Crisis" (1967), perhaps the most cited piece in the whole ecotheological debate, is still considered in academic circles not only as a watershed in religious thought regarding the environment, but also as a definitive indictment of Christianity for crimes against nature.[12] It has stimulated examination of the relationship between religion, particularly Christianity, and attitudes toward nature across the globe. White maintained that because modern science and technology are products of western culture, and because western culture has at its roots in Christian attitudes and principles, then Christianity "bears a huge burden of guilt" for our current ecological crisis.

---

[7] Crist, "Reimagining Human".

[8] Shiva, "A virus, humanity, and the earth".

[9] Marie Quinney, "COVID-19 and nature are linked. So should be the recovery," *World Economic Forum* 14th April 2020. [Available at: https://www.weforum.org/agenda/2020/04/covid-19-nature-deforestation-recovery/]

[10] Marie Quinney, "COVID-19 and nature are linked. So should be the recovery".

[11] Leonardo Boff, "Indignación, fatalismo, fe, esperanza y aprendizaje: Covid-19," [Available at: http://www.redescristianas.net/?s=boff]M

[12] Lynn White Jr., "The Historical Roots of Our Ecologic Crisis", *Science* 155(3767), (March 1967): 1203-1207.

In his analysis, White noted that the human capacity to wreak damage and destruction upon the environment grows out of western technological and scientific advances which occurred in a social context informed by the Judaeo-Christian tradition. The overemphasis on anthropocentrism gives humans an unbridled permission to exploit *nature* and transform it into *culture*. White argued that within Christian theology, "nature has no reason for existence [...] [but exists] to serve [humans]".

At the end of Genesis 1, the writer concludes, "God saw everything that had been made and indeed, it was very good" (Gen. 1:31). This scripture also describes a special relationship that God has with humans through the *imago dei*, which asserts that human beings are created in the image and likeness of God. Following Jewish tradition, it is argued that being made in the *imago dei* does not mean that God possesses human-like features, but rather that the statement is figurative language for God bestowing special honour unto humankind, which he did not confer unto the rest of creation.[13] The human person in the image of God (Gen. 1:26-28; 5:1-3; 9:6), like the image of a sovereign on a coin, is a representative and a regent who represent the sovereign in the midst of all other subjects where the sovereign is not directly and personally present. Thus, the human person is entrusted with "dominion" (Gen. 1:28; Ps. 8:5-8).[14] According to this world view, White suggests, everything that exists in the natural world was "planned" by God "explicitly for man's benefit and rule; no item in the physical creation had any purpose [...] [but] serve man's purpose".

Genesis could be interpreted as providing a justification for exploitation of nature, without regard for the consequences of that exploitation. In Genesis, when God considers the creation of humans, God says, "Let us make humankind in our image, according to our likeness; and let them have dominion over the fish of the sea, and over the birds of the air, and over the cattle, and over all the wild animals of the earth, and over every creeping thing that creeps upon the earth" (Gen. 1:26). White points explicitly to this "monarchy" of humanity over the rest of creation as the culprit for a Christian attitude that denigrates the importance of nature. For Boff, anthropocentrism is "the imperial and anti-ecological anthropology". Such an 'anthropocentric anthropology' creates, as Sallie McFague rightly argues, a "hegemonic human being". This human monarchy over the rest of creation seems implied in the Christian doctrine of the *imago dei*, humans created in the image of God.

Needless to say, White's thesis touched off a firestorm of controversy. While White has had his defenders, many Christians – including the former US Vice President Al Gore in his book, *Earth in the Balance: Ecology and Human Spirit* (1992) – have argued that White has missed the theological point contained in the creation stories of Genesis, where nature is depicted positively.[15] Yet, for many other Christians, White's thesis clearly struck an important chord. The gradual evolution of an ecological consciousness within the Church caused many to begin questioning traditional anthropocentric interpretations of scripture. Today, the nature of God, God's relationship to the world, humanity's place in the earth's complex and fragile life system, and the notion of the salvation of the world and not just of humans are a few of the issues open for re-examination and reinterpretation. This calls for "green reading" of the *imago dei* in Genesis.

---

[13] Mothy Varkey, "Earth as a Collective Inheritance: Towards a Green Image of God," *NCCR* CXXVI/11 (December 2016): 673-678.

[14] "God blessed them, and God said to them, "Be fruitful and multiply, and fill the earth and subdue it; and have *dominion* over the fish of the sea and over the birds of the air and over every living thing that moves upon the earth." (Gen. 1:28 NRSV); "Yet you have made them a little lower than God, and crowned them with glory and honour. You have given them *dominion* over the works of your hands; you have put all things under their feet, all sheep and oxen, and also the beasts of the field, the birds of the air, and the fish of the sea, whatever passes along the paths of the seas (Ps. 8:5-9 NRSV).

[15] *Earth in Balance* explains the world's ecological predicament and describes a range of policies to deal with the most pressing problems. It includes a proposed Global Marshall Plan to address current ecological issues.

According to Walter Brueggemann, the Old Testament does not portray human beings as autonomous.[16] Brueggemann said that being made in God's image meant that humans were created to rule over creation "in the way that God ruled over creation". Creatively using power to invite, evoke, and permit was what made *Homo sapiens* special and a reflection of God, because this is the way that God exercised God's power. God ruled as a servant-king, but not as a dictator-tyrant; so should act the species made in God's image.[17] He contends that the Old Testament human persons are understood as situated in the same transactional processes with the holiness of Yahweh as in Israel, so that in a very general way the character and destiny of human persons replicates and reiterates the character and destiny of Israel ("covenantal notions of personhood"). This transactional process causes a "biblical understanding" of human persons to stand at a critical distance and as a critical protest against all modern notions of humanness that move in the direction of autonomy.

The human family, created in the "image of God" (Gen. 1:27), is integrally connected to God-creation continuum. The phrase *imago dei* basically refers to those characteristics of human beings that make communication with God possible and enable them to take up the God-given responsibilities outlined in Genesis 1:28. Process theologian Marjorie Suchocki asserted that being made in God's image meant that humans were created in interrelationship with all living things, just as God exists in relationship with all that is. Being consciously in relationship with all life on earth – human and nonhuman – was what made *Homo sapiens* special and a reflection of God, because God intentionally and intimately relates to all that God has made. God exists in loving relationship with all living things in the creation; so should the species made in God's image.[18]

In no place is God separated from the creation because in whom "we live and have our being" (Col. 1:15-20), any more than "you" are separate from your body, although God is certainly more than the creation as a whole. For Jürgen Moltmann, the relationship between God and the creation is analogous to the relation of human body and mind.[19] The defence for such an understanding however does not compromise the ontological transcendence of God. The belief that the creation exists only through God's concurrence is also endorsed here. It means that God did create the universe, not *outside* of God's self, but organically related to himself/herself.

It democratises an ancient Near Eastern royal usage of image language; all human beings are created in the image of God, not just kings.[20] The result is that all interhuman hierarchical understandings are set aside; all human beings of whatever station in life stand together as images of God. It rejects all essentialist notions of human personhood; thus, the human person is to be understood in relational and not essentialist ways. For Mark Brett, the democratising tendency in Genesis 1:26-38 can be seen as anti-monarchic.[21]

Moreover, the idea that humanity is made in the image of God is actually not as dominant in the Old Testament as one would think. It is found primarily in the opening chapters of Genesis (Gen. 1:26-27; 5:3; cf. Wisd 2:23). The other place in the Old Testament where a similar idea is expressed, linked with a strong statement about humanity's dominion over the earth, is Psalms 8:5-6 ("Thou hast made him a little lower than God, And dost crown him with glory and majesty! Thou dost make him to rule over the works of Thy hands; Thou hast put all things under his feet"). Keith Carley, also writing in the Earth Bible series, argues that this Psalm represents "an apology for human domination" which does not conform to the ecojustice principles.

---

[16] Walter Brueggemann, *Genesis* (Atlanta: John Knox Press, 1982), 32.
[17] Brueggemann, *Genesis*, 32.
[18] Marjorie Suchocki, Public Lecture, Franklin College, Franklin, Indiana (May, 1989).
[19] Jürgen Moltmann, *God in Creation: An Ecological Doctrine of Creation* (London: SCM, 1985).
[20] Walter Brueggemann, Bruce C. Birch et.al. *A Theological Introduction to the Old Testament* (Nashville, TN: Abingdon, 1999), 50.
[21] Mark Brett, *Genesis: Procreation and Politics of Identity* (London and NY: Routledge, 2000), 28.

The "Image of God" is not self-contained, self-sufficient and static as if God is an asocial reality. In the triune Godhead, the divine flows into the other without subjugating and without being subjugated. It implies that the fullness of humanity is shared, participatory and reciprocal. One might identify the two directions of the notion of participation (*metousia*): vertical and horizontal. The vertical participation is between the human beings and the uncreated creator. On the other hand, the horizontal participation is found on each level of the created order.

In a homily on Beatitudes, the Cappadocian Father Gregory of Nyssa said: "image of God means participation in the very characteristics of God to be the perfection of all good, all beauty, all love, all wisdom and all power". It means humanity is ordained to participate in the divine and to be co-creators and co-workers on earth. All the mysteries of the created order are not meant to be known, unravelled and understood. This dialectics of continuity and discontinuity between the creation and the creator explains why humanity is an intrinsic part of the created order, and not made at par with the creator.

According to Paulos Mar Gregorios, the discontinuity between God and the creation (*diastema*) is the ground of God's ontological transcendence and incomprehensibility. While the creator is self-emanant and thus is not dependent on the creation (Ps. 90:1-5), the creation is no being in itself. The creation emanates from God, subsists only by the will of God, and cannot exist by itself. The forbidden fruit in Genesis is the symbolic representation of this discontinuity (diastemic existence) and continuity (created existence) between the creator and the creation. In no way does this prohibition diminish the glory of humanity, instead it takes the entire created order in due respect.

Unlike the first creation story (Gen. 1:1-2:4a), the second creation story (Gen. 2:4b-25) provides a somewhat green image of God. Genesis 2-3 provides two images of God: *potter*, and *farmer/gardener*. God as a *potter* (Gen. 2:7) does a "hands on" craft on the subject. It has often noted that the verb *form* (*ysr*) as it pertains to creation is not by dictum, but by actual engagement with the raw stuff out of which the object is formed.[22] It underscores human dependence *on* the rest of the creation and not human domination *over* the earth.[23]

According to George Zachariah, Genesis 2-3 would have emerged from an agrarian community. Zachariah argues that "the vision of humanity that emerged from a farming community – a community of ecological and social relations of solidarity and communion which is antithetical to the logical of an imperial exploitative system – is that of a dependent and responsible member of the ecosystem with the vocation to farmers".[24] This green image of a God with his hands in the dirt is remarkable; this no naïve theology, but a statement about the depths to which God has entered into the life of the creation. God's very life is then breathed into human; something of God's own self becomes an integral part of human identity, enabling life to move from God out into the larger world.

God is also imaged a *farmer/gardener*, placing two trees in this garden; they are associated with the life and death and human choices related thereto (Deut. 30:15-20). Yahweh as *gardener* is often the subject of the verb *plant*. In Isaiah 5:1-2 in particular, the gardener-vinedresser is involved with the founding of the garden, and uses are, attentiveness, and extravagance in creating the best possible vineyard ("Let me sing for my beloved my love-song concerning his vineyard: My beloved had a vineyard on a very fertile hill. He dug it and cleared it of stones, and planted it with choice vines; he built a watchtower in the midst of it, and hewed out a wine vat in it; he expected it to yield grapes, but it yielded wild grapes" – Isa. 5:1-2 NRSV).

God created human beings to "till and keep" the creation (Gen. 2:15). It means that God created humanity in such a way that they would take care of the creation, as the creator would do. Humanity is made creator and hence they have not replaced the creator nor do they act on behalf of the creator, rather they are co-

---

[22] Brueggemann, *Genesis*, 32.

[23] Brueggemann et.al. *A Theological Introduction to the Old Testament*, 51-52.

[24] George Zachariah, *Gospel in a Groaning World: Climate Justice and Public Witness* (NCCI/CSS: Thiruvalla, 2012), 66. See also Claus Westermann, *Creation* (translated by John J. Scullion; London: SPCK, 1971), 81-82.

workers with the creator. However, they do reflect the *goodness* (image) of God and participate in the creative activity of God. The understanding of human family as the participants in God's plan for the creation does not dishonour the sovereignty of God nor exalt the human family above the ordained limits. Hence, the primary responsibility of human beings created in the "green-image of God" is ecological.[25]

As with Zachariah, Mark Brett also persuasively stresses how the concerns of the words "dominion" and "rule" in Genesis 1:28 ("Be fruitful and multiply, and fill the earth, and *subdue* it; and *rule over* the fish of the sea and *over* the birds of the sky, and over every living thing that moves on the earth") reflect the ancient agrarian setting. According to Brett, possessing the land and domesticating animals can be seen as essential aspects of sustaining human life in such a setting, and the "dominion" over the animals may be seen primarily as related to real threats posed by wild animals and the desire to control or remove such threats to human wellbeing.[26]

Conclusions

After closing down at the onset of the coronavirus pandemic, Barcelona's Gran Teatre del Liceu opera house reopened on 22nd June 2020 with its first concert to an atypical audience of 2,292 potted plants filling the seats. This unique concert was organised a day after Spain lifted its coronavirus lockdown. The event was the work of conceptual artist Eugenio Ampudia to examine our relationship with nature and the impact the lockdown has had on public spaces. The UceLi Quartet performed Puccini's 1890 movement Crisantemi ("Chrysanthemums"). After the concert, all the plants were to be donated to healthcare professionals working on the frontlines against the virus. The famed opera house said in a statement that following this "strange, painful period," organisers wanted to "offer us a different perspective for our return to activity, a perspective that brings us closer to something as essential as our relationship with nature." This challenges people and faith communities not only to curb COVID-19 in an eco-friendly manner but also to reimagine a post-COVID world and its "ecosystem services."

A radical ecological conversion challenges the conventional anthropocentric understanding of ekklēsia and diakonia, which is rooted in human being's supremacy and self-referentiality. The word ekklēsia literally means "called out"; here the question is called *from* what and called *to* what. Is God's calling an ontological human prerogative? What about all creation other than human beings? God has created all species with an intention or purpose. The purpose of creation is not something to which a species arrives at a later stage. Purpose and creation cannot be separated in terms of chronology. If so, God's purpose of creation is God's calling. This inherent vocation of all species de-privileges human beings.[27]

All created species are interconnected and thus participate in the calling/purpose and the principles of the shared breath of life. If God's calling is not different from the purpose of creation, then *klesis* (calling) should not be taken as separated in a privileged/ontological/biological sense. As opposed to *creatio ex nihilo*, which assumes that evil is disorder and not unjust order, Catherine Keller proposes *creatio ex profundis*. Keller's *tehomopholic* non-anthropocentric idea of creation suggests the agency of all species. "Calling" means "to be" in the web of life and thus experience fullness of life in this relationship. This calls for a new way of being a faith community (*ekklēsia*) in relation to the earth (eco-metanoia) and its bio-history – *ecoklesia/bioklesia*.

Not just ekklēsia alone but practising diakonia ecologically is also vital in the face of COVID-19. By unsettling the rhizomatic layers of planetary interdependence and colonising the commons, we subvert God's creation and its biorhythm. An unsparing autopsy of the coronavirus would expose the truth that it is the abuse of wild animals and the systemic and consistent disdain for environmental protocols that caused

[25] Mothy Varkey, *Inheritance and Resistance: Reclaiming Bible, Body, and Power* (Delhi: CWI, 2021), 1-11.
[26] Brett, *Genesis*, 28-29.
[27] See Mothy Varkey, Church and Diakonia in the Age of COVID-19 (Delhi: ISPCK, 2021), 1-21.

the outbreak. The coronavirus pandemic is a zoonotic disease. Hence, diakonia in the age of the pandemic means participating in the mutual web of life wherein different organisms of life sustain each other – ecodiakonia; in Keller's words, ecodiakonia means "creative collaboration with nature."[28] This co-participation with nature as green ethical beings may be realised through compassion, coexistence and cooperation. It implies de-privileging and decolonising human agency. Such a befitting non-anthropocentric faith response to the pandemic could be achieved by being an "ally of ecojustice struggles" and through "inter-faith collisions." In pursuing the latter, ecodiakonia/biodiakonia can draw on Buddhist traditions and notions of ecodharma, and other evolving ecological paradigms such as 'agroecology.'

Preamble, A People's Manifesto for Ecological Democracy[29]

Our planet is not a lump of inanimate matter circling the sun every year, providing humans free lodging, boarding and endless resources to exploit recklessly. She is a living, breathing, sentient Being, to be treated with love, care and deep respect. Revered in all ancient cultures around the world as Pachamama, Gaia, Bhumi or Mother Earth – She gives us generously but her respect needs to be earned too.

Humans, even though they pretend to dominate it, are not masters of the planet. We are not mysteriously destined to rule over all other species – whether plants, animals or microbes. Humans, like every other living organism, are the children of Mother Earth and just one out of millions of other forms of life. And it is the ability to coexist peacefully amidst immense diversity, that makes all life itself possible.

The quest for endless and ruthless domination of everything around us is the root cause of our historical downfall, because we do unto others within our species, what we do unto members of other species. Much before the exploitation of humans by humans, came the exploitation of Nature by humans. The idea of colonisation of Mother Earth has to be defeated in order to truly end the colonial domination of race, caste, gender and wealth within human societies.

The source of all spirituality, over the millennia, has been the awe-inspiring beauty and compassion of our planet as well as the deeply humbling realisation of the ephemeral and transient nature of human life. There is a need today to recover our lost spirituality by connecting back with Mother Earth and all its life forms, not just for the sake of the planet but for our own survival and salvation.

Are human beings at all redeemable? Yes, of course they are. Humans are the only creatures on the planet, who look after, not just their young, but also their elderly, sick and disabled members. Humans are in other words, at their finest, when they fight against injustice or show solidarity and empathy towards each other, especially the weakest in their midst. It is these noble qualities, of an otherwise flawed species, that need to be preserved and nurtured at all costs, in all that we do. They are the only source of hope for our future.

Suggestions for Further Reading

Bauckham, Richard. *The Bible and Ecology: Rediscovering the Community of Creation.* Waco, TX: Baylor University Press, 2010.

Hiers, Richard H. "Ecology, biblical theology, and methodology: biblical perspectives on the environment". *Zygon* 19/1 (1984): 43-59.

Joerstad, Mari. *The Hebrew Bible and Environmental Ethics*. Cambridge: Cambridge University Press, 2021.

---

[28] Catherine Keller, "A Letter from Catherine Keller," *Medium* 2nd April 2020. [Available at: https://medium.com/@dostlund_42808/a-letter-from-catherine-keller-1930029c4914].

[29] "Preamble, A People's Manifesto for Ecological Democracy," *Counter Currents* 15th April 2020. [Available at: https://countercurrents.org/2020/08/a-peoples-manifesto-for-ecological-democracy/?fbclid=IwAR2QW3-YmSj9ryfVQNINiG2sz23rBvgog6QvzFjcDo232CatQrPwVw5BHqQ].

Kiel, Micah D. *Apocalyptic Ecology: The Book of Revelation, the Earth, and the Future*. Collegeville, MN: Michael Glazier, 2017.
Myers, Ched. "Prophetic Visions of Redemption as Rehydration: A Call to Watershed Discipleship". *Anglican Theological Review* 100/1 (2018): 61-77.
Trible, Phyllis. "Ecology and The Bible: The Dilemma of Dominion". *Canon & Culture* 6/2 (2012): 5-19.
Uval, Beth. "Ecology in the Bible". *Jewish Bible Quarterly* 28/4 (2000): 260-263.
Zachariah, George. *Gospel in a Groaning World: Climate Justice and Public Witness*. Thiruvalla: NCCI/CSS, 2012.

10. First Commission for Creation Care: Interpreting "To Have Dominion" Biblical Reflections from an Indian Context

Chilkuri Vasantha Rao[1]

The Interpretation of the Verb "To Have Dominion" in Genesis 1:26-28

"In the history of biblical interpretation and dogmatic speculation, Gen. 1:26-28 have proved remarkably fecund as a source of exegetical and theological reflection".[2] One strand of interpretation makes this biblical passage the foundation for the exploitation of the earth and its resources. For instance, Ian McHarg, in his book *Design with Nature,* says: "the biblical creation story of the first chapter of Genesis [...] in its insistence upon dominion and subjugation of nature encourages the most exploitative and destructive instincts in man [...] there could be no better injunction than this text."[3]

Thus, Lynn White, whose article is cited in almost every theological writing on ecology, notes that, on the basis of the creation story in Genesis, Christianity insisted that it is God's will that human beings exploit nature for their proper ends.[4]

The creation story of Genesis 1:1-2:4 as a whole and Genesis 1:26-28 in particular and the terms *Radah* ("to have dominion"; "to rule") and *Kabash* ("to subdue") specifically are blamed as being a basis for the present exploitation of creation. Certainly, such an interpretation is a misreading of the texts, and Walter Houston says that such interpretations are found frequently in writers who are not Old Testament scholars.[5]

So, then, the task at hand must be to re-investigate these terms *Radah* and *Kabash* but due to the limitations of space, here, we will restrict our study to the first: *Radah* "to have dominion".

The Nature and Function of "To Have Dominion" in Biblical Texts

The Hebrew verb *Radah* is used all over the Old Testament. Looking into a few instances would help us to understand how God expects dominion to be exercised over creation.

Radah in Leviticus 25:43, 46, 53 indicates the rule of a master over a hired servant. The verb also refers to the rule of chief officers over labourers in 1 Kings. 5:30, 9:23; and in 2 Chronicles 8:10. When the nature of the relationship of master towards the servants is specified, the stress is on humane treatment; the master is charged that the hired servants be not ruled "with harshness" (Lev. 25:43, 46, 53). The implication could be the same as far as the officers in charge of the labourers are concerned (1 Kgs. 5:30, 9:23; and 2 Chr. 8:10).

There are other texts where *Radah* indicates the rule of one nation over another nation (Lev. 26:17; Num. 24:19; Isa. 14:2, 6; Ezek. 29:15; Neh. 9:28). There is also the dominion of a king over people (1 Kgs. 4:24;

---

[1] Rev. Dr. Chilkuri Vasantha Rao is Professor in the Department of Biblical Studies (Old Testament) and Principal of the United Theological College, Bengaluru, India. He is an ordained Presbyter of the Church of South India. He is a member of the Society of Biblical Literature, Atlanta, USA. He has published widely in the area of Ecology and Bible. You can contact him at utcvasantharao@gmail.com.

[2] Phyllis A. Bird, "'Male and Female He Created Them' Gen. 1:27b in the Context of the Priestly Account of Creation," *Harvard Theological Review* 74, no. 2 (1981): 149.

[3] Ian L. McHarg, *Design with Nature.* (Garden City: The Natural History Press, 1969), 26.

[4] Lynn White Jr., "The Historical Roots of Our Ecological Crisis," *Science* 155, no. 3767 (1967): 1205.

[5] Walter Houston, *'And Let Them Have Dominion ... '. Biblical Views of Man in Relation to the Environmental Crisis and Related Themes.* (Journal for the Study of Old Testament Supp. Series 11. Sheffield: JSOT Press (1979), 167, nt. 25.

Ezek. 34:4; Ps. 72:8; Ps. 110:2). Only in Genesis 1:26 and 28 does the verb indicate rule over an object other than human beings, and that is to have dominion over the creation.

Most of the occurrences of *Radah* cited above are in political contexts, to do with the rule of a king or the rule of one nation over another which would be exercised through a king. Two types of ruling are evident from the above-mentioned texts. One is of positive rule which perpetuates peace, and the other is the negation of the hostile rule that does not perpetuate peace.

Radah in Psalms 68:28 (Hebrew Bible) is referring to not more than a leader.[6] In the context of 1 Kings 5:4 (Hebrew Bible), it is not necessarily a strong verb to express Solomon's dominion – a peaceful rule over the west Euphrates territory. James Barr[7] commends the New English Bible at 1 Kings. 4:24 as "he was paramount [*Radah*] over all the land".

The Rule of the King Including Social Care and Care for Creation

In Psalms 72, which was probably used as part of the coronation liturgy for a new king, the wish is expressed that he would "have dominion" (*Radah*) from sea to sea (72:8). The Psalm invoking God's blessings upon the king, furnishes a kind of charter for his administration in a prayer form, stressing the marks which ought to characterise the rule of the king over his people. The prayer asks that his rule be accompanied by prosperity (3) and that righteousness and peace (7) abound. The king is to have special concern for the poor and needy and disadvantaged (2-4 and 12-14).

The important thing to note is that the Israelite king is expected to exercise responsible care over the whole domain of his rule.

At this juncture, Deuteronomy 17:18-20 needs to be noticed, where it is stated clearly that the king is to read and follow diligently the Deuteronomic law – a law code which is full of concerns. For instance, the slaves who escape are not to be returned to their masters (Dt. 23:15); interest on loans is not to be charged to fellow Israelites (Dt. 23:19); neighbours are not to be withheld from eating from one's orchards and standing grains (Dt. 23:24-25); in view of the sojourners, widows, and orphans might find food, one's crop is not to be harvested completely (Dt. 24:19-22). Concern for creation such as: care for trees (Dt. 20:19-20),[8] birds (Dt. 22:6-7)[9] and animals (Dt.25:4)[10] is part of his rule. This is the nature of rule to be exercised by the king with care for the whole creation.

Critique of Exploitative and Violent Forms of Rule: Rule with Force and Harshness

When kings began to exploit their subjects for their selfish interests, such as taking the wife and destroying the life of a soldier (David- 2 Sam. 11); taking the property of a poor man (Ahab- 1 Kgs. 21) or refurbishing the royal palace in Cedar, while exploiting labour and neglecting the needs of the poor (Jehoiakim- Jer. 22:13), prophets appear to accuse the kings with failure to measure up to the standards expected of a king in Israel. We note that, for the kings "to have dominion" does not mean to play the role of the arrogant despot, exploiting and destroying the people and creation that they rule. On the contrary, "to have dominion" means to exercise responsible care for all the subjects.

---

[6] Klaus Koch, *"Gestaltet die Erde, doch heget das Leben! Einige Klarstellungen Zum Dominum terrace in Genesis* 1," in *Wenn Nicht Jetzt, Wann dann? Festschrift, Hans Joachim Kraus.* (Neukirchen, Vluyu: Neukirchener Verlag, 1983): 33.

[7] James Barr, "Man and Nature – The Ecological Controversy and the Old Testament," *Bulletin of the John Rylands Library* 55, no.1 (1972): 22.

[8] Chilkuri Vasantha Rao, *Let the Mother Bird Go: Preservation Motif in Pentateuch* (Delhi: ISPCK, 2007), 11-36.

[9] Rao, "Let the Mother Bird Go," 37-62.

[10] Chilkuri Vasantha Rao, *Animal Rights and Animal Laws in the Bible: The Daily Practice of Reverence for Life.* (New York, Ontario, Wales: The Edwin Mellen Press, 2013), 169-221.

Ezekiel living in the period of the exile utters indictments against the kings of Israel whom he refers to as shepherds. And *Radah* "to rule" here is qualified in a negative sense by the attributes "with force and harshness": "You have not strengthened the weak, you have not healed the sick, you have not bound up the injured, you have not brought back the strayed, you have not sought the lost, but with force and harshness you have ruled them." (Ez. 34:4. NRSV).

Here is a picture of how kings ought not to rule. To rule with "force and harshness" i.e., to exploit rather than to care for, is to misrule! And such rule was contrary to divine intentions. So *Radah* is not necessarily arbitrary or despotic rule, for wherever the function of rule is indicated in the Old Testament, a further predicate is often used, as also in the case of slaves (Lev. 25:43, 46, 53.) The predicate is also present in Isaiah 14:6 which reads, "rule in anger": "that is to say a harsh rule is contrary to the nature and will of a liberating God who cares for the marginalised of society".[11]

The Shepherd Image for the Proper Rule of the King

It is easy to relate the Ezekiel passage with Psalm 23 where the shepherd motif can be more clearly seen – God as shepherd, leading the sheep by the still waters, restoring the sheep, protecting them from evil and providing comfort. In Isaiah 40:11, the prophet says that God shall feed "the flock like a shepherd".[12]

Walter Brueggemann rightly observes that the "dominance is that of a shepherd who cares for, tends, and feeds the animals… if transferred to the political arena, the image is that of a shepherd king".[13] So also Norbert Lohfink says that such a metaphor of shepherd king is consistent with the ancient west Asian shepherd figure which served as a symbol of the ruler; and suggests that the sense "to rule" is guiding and leading; and thereby the real root meaning of *Radah* may be "to lead about".[14] Thus, James Barr is truthful when he sees the role given to human beings in Genesis 1:26 and 28 as one of leadership rather than exploitation.[15]

In the apocalyptic literature such as in Daniel, the irresponsible rulers whose function was the organised exploitation of the world are represented as the figures of beasts. Daniel 7 is the classic text. The same is also found in Revelations 13. Bad rulers are represented as beasts, since beasts have no dominion and are not required to act responsibly.[16] In Daniel 4, where Nebuchadnezzer fails to exercise dominion responsibly, he loses the power to rule. It is said, "Let his mind be changed from that of a human, and let the mind of an animal be given to him…" (4:16 NRSV).

The groaning of creation in travail in Romans 8:22 then is not because human beings have lost their dominion, but because of the tyrannical perversion of human dominion extended far beyond anything the biblical writers could have imagined;[17] leading to the destruction of the land, pollution of the air and waters, mass extinction of species of fish, birds, animals and trees ultimately turning the creation into chaos. The problem lies in human beings' relationship to the world, their fellow creatures, and their Creator, and in their refusal to accept limitations on their creative power.[18]

---

[11] V. Steven Parrish, "From Domination to Eco-Justice Rereading Selected Creation Texts in the Hebrew Bible," *Memphis Theological Seminary Journal* 29 (1991): 57.

[12] Nancy Regensburger, "Shepherding God's Creatures," *The Bible Today* 26 (1988): 140.

[13] Walter Brueggemann, *Genesis: Interpretation A Bible Commentary for Teaching and Preaching.* (Atlanta: John Knox Press, 1982), 32.

[14] Norbert Lohfink, "Growth: The Priestly Document and the Limits of Growth," in his book *Great Themes from the Old Testament*, translated by Ronald Walls. (Edinburgh: T&T Clark Ltd., 1982), 178-179.

[15] Barr, "Man and Nature," 9-32.

[16] Houston, "And Let Them Have Dominion," 170.

[17] Houston, "And Let Them Have Dominion," 170.

[18] G.W. Coats, "The God of Death: Power and Obedience in the Primeval History," *Interpretation* 29, no.3 (1975): 232.

To return to the Genesis text 1:26-28 and to the occurrences of the verb *Radah,* human beings are charged "to rule" or "to have dominion" over the creation. There are two things to be considered: first, as Wildberger notes, the verb *Radah* echoes the ancient west Asian royal ideology (as in Ps. 110:2; 72:8; Isa. 14:6; Ez. 34:4), and the use of the verb in Genesis 1 is said to be a clear indication of the perseverance of an old element of the royal ideology,[19] which has a positive connotation of peaceful rule, in the image of a shepherd and servant.

Second, with the *Radah* expression, human beings are called to play the role of a king over the rest of the creation. The biblical image of kingship stresses the aspect of responsible care for over which dominion is exercised (Ps. 72) and specifically, Ezekiel 34, rejects the notion of the king as a rapacious despot. This means that human beings are charged with the task of caring for the creation; fish of the sea, the birds of the heavens, the cattle and the beasts of the earth and for all the creeping things that move upon the earth.[20]

God's First Commission to the Human Beings

God's first commission to the human beings in Genesis 1:26-28 is thus a clarion call for the care of the creation. This can be summarised in the words of Philo, who writes in his commentary on Genesis 1:28, "So the creator made man […] and charged him with the care of animals and plants, like a kind of *Uparxos* to the chief and great king".[21]

This is well illustrated when God spoke to Noah and his family and gave them the responsibility for the animals, "to lead" them into the ark, "to preserve" them (Gen. 6:19, 20; 7:3) and "to bring" them out of the ark (8:17), that the animals may realise the blessing of being fruitful and multiplying. Noah as the exemplary preserver of animals makes clear, that having dominion over the animals means:[22] "to rescue them, to nurture them and finally to set them free upon the earth"[23] irrespective of whether they are domesticated ones from human settlements or wild beasts. In fact, Noah had to "preserve" all the animal species (Gen. 7:14) in the pre-flood era when human beings had no utilitarian value in them, since vegetarian diet was prescribed to them (Gen. 1:29, 30). Thus, their preservation was intended for their welfare for God's sake, which is an idea reminiscent of the peaceable kingdom of the eleventh chapter of Isaiah, focusing the vision into an ideal future and presenting Genesis 1 as an ideal past. The human dominion over the animals in these contexts is very much unconditional, in a non-literal pattern as the Sun rules over the day and the Moon over the night,[24] causing day and night and seasons, thus sustaining the whole creation and preserving all life.

God also made a covenant with the animals (Gen. 9:8-17). The sign of the covenant is the bow in the clouds (13), which is a pledge by God for the perpetuation of creation without destruction. The perpetual existence of the created order until the end of time stands on the gracious nature of God[25] and the divine commitment to preservation.

---

[19] Hans Wildberger, *"Das Abbild Gottes" Theologische Zeitschrift* 21 (1965): 259.

[20] James Limburg, "What Does it Mean to Have Dominion Over the Earth"? *Dialogue* 10, no.3 (1971): 223.

[21] Cited by David Jobling, "'And Have Dominion …' The Interpretation of Genesis 1:28 in Philo Judaeus," *Journal for the Study of Judaism* 8, no.1 (1977): 57.

[22] R.J. Clifford, "Genesis 1-3: Permission to Exploit Nature?" *The Bible Today* 26 (1988): 135.

[23] James Limburg, "The Responsibility of Royalty: Genesis 1-11 and the Care of the Earth," *Word & World* 9, no. 2 (1991): 126.

[24] Claus Westermann, *Genesis 1-11: A Commentary*, translated by John J. Scullion. (Minneapolis, MN: Augsburg Publishing House, 1984), 159.

[25] W. J. Dumbrell, *Covenant and Creation.* (London: Paternost Press, 1984), 26-27.

On the one hand, the Noachian covenant proclaims the good news that God's creation covenant is not to be jeopardised by human cruelty and harshness.[26] On the other hand, human beings are given the responsibility to respond to God in the name of other creatures since they cannot respond themselves.[27]

Responses of Church and State

The Spirit of God which brooded over the chaotic waters and caused this beautiful creation is also now brooding over humanity in general and the Church in particular to respond to today's ecological crisis. The World Council of Churches (WCC) in 1983, in its Vancouver Assembly introduced the theme of "Justice Peace and Integrity of Creation" (JPIC). In the 1990 WCC's world convocation on JPIC in Seoul, South Korea, the church's response to the ecological crisis was concrete. In 1991, in its Canberra Assembly the theme "Come Holy Spirit – Renew the Whole Creation" was adopted and the first sub-theme was "Giver of Life – Sustain your Creation". The concern for the care for creation has continued ever since. The Member Churches of the WCC pursue this responsibility in their respective geographical locations. In India, the Church of South India (CSI) through its Department of Ecological Concerns[28] has been educating the values of sustainability through Eco-Ministry, Campaigns for Climate Justice Ministries, Green Protocol and a Green School Program. Eco-conservation is in its constitution and in the mission statement of the church. Since 1992, the church seeks to create awareness among all people for environmental and ecological concerns and thereby to care for God's creation. The CSI encourages parishes to incorporate ecological concerns in their order of worship and include both advocacy and direct action for social justice and the integrity of creation in missional activities.

The Indian nation is engaged with multiple initiatives to protect the environment.[29] The Indian church's commitment to the care of creation in the COVID-19 pandemic[30] is commendable. This is the hope for creation in the process of its redemption.

> God bless the creation and preserve the creation:
> God make God's face to shine upon all creatures,
> and be gracious to all beings:
> God lift up God's countenance
> upon the whole creation and give peace.[31]

Suggestions for Further Reading

Books

Brueggemann, Walter. *Genesis: Interpretation A Bible Commentary for Teaching and Preaching.* Atlanta, GA: John Knox Press, 1982.

Dumbrell, W.J. *Covenant and Creation.* London: Paternoster Press, 1984.

McHarg, Ian L. *Design with Nature.* Garden City: The Natural History Press, 1969.

---

[26] M.D. Ambrose, "Cosmic Experience of God According to Genesis II; The Noachian Covenant," *Indian Theological Studies* 28, no. 2 (1991): 161.

[27] Gerhard von Rad, *Genesis: A Commentary*. 3rd Rev. ed. (London: SCM Press, 1972), 131-133.

[28] The Church of South India Department of Ecological Concerns, "Digital Bulletin Eco Activities 2021," https://csi-synod.s3.ap-south-1.amazonaws.com/s3/1638450471229EcoBullettin-November2021-Final-WEB1638450470396.pdf.

[29] See Chilkuri Vasantha Rao, "Living in the Here and Now," in Chilkuri Vasantha Rao & David Reichardt (eds), *Cross-cultural Eco-theology in an Indian Ocean-Context* (Delhi: ISPCK, 2018): 160-180.

[30] See Chilkuri Vasantha Rao, "Corona Call to Heal Our Sick Mother Earth," in Francis Gonsalves & Vinod Victor (eds), *Corona of Thorns? Or Corona of Life? Changing Church in the Covid Context (*Delhi: ISPCK, 2020): 102-107.

[31] An ecological version of the Aaronic blessing in Numbers 6:24-26 rendered by the present author.

Rao, Chilkuri Vasantha. *Animal Rights and Animal Laws in the Bible: The Daily Practice of Reverence for Life*. New York, Ontario, Wales: The Edwin Mellen Press, 2013.
— *Let the Mother Bird Go: Preservation Motif in Pentateuch*, Delhi: ISPCK, 2007.
von Rad, Gerhard. *Genesis: A Commentary.* 3rd rev. ed. *London: SCM Press.* 1972.
Westermann, Claus. *Genesis 1-11: A Commentary,* translated by John J. Scullion. Minneapolis, MN: Augsburg Publishing House, 1984.

Chapters in Edited Books

Houston, Walter. "'And Let Them Have Dominion…' Biblical Views of Man in Relation to the Environmental Crisis." In E.A. Livingstone, Ed. *Studies Biblica 1978: I Papers on Old Testament and Related Themes.* Journal for the Study of Old Testament Supp. Series 11. Sheffield: JSOT Press, 1979. 161-184.
Koch, Klaus. "Gestaltet die Erde, doch heget das Leben! Einige Klarstellungen Zum Dominum terrace in Genesis 1." In Hans-Georg Geyer, Ed. *Wenn Nicht Jetzt, Wann dann? Festschrift, Hans Joachim Kraus.* Neukirchen,Vluyu: Neukirchener Verlag, 1983. 23-36.
Lohfink, Norbert "Growth: The Priestly Document and the Limits of Growth." In Norbert Lohfink, Ed. *Great Themes from the Old Testament.* translated by Ronald Walls. Edinburgh: T&T Clark, 1982. 167-182.
Rao, Chilkuri Vasantha. "Living in the Here and Now." In Chilkuri Vasantha Rao & David Reichardt, Eds. *Cross-cultural Eco-theology in an Indian Ocean-Context*. Delhi: ISPCK, 2018. 160-180.
Rao, Chilkuri Vasantha. "Corona Call to Heal Our Sick Mother Earth." in Francis Gonsalves & Vinod Victor, Eds. *Corona of Thorns? Or Corona of Life? Changing Church in the Covid Context*. Delhi: ISPCK, 2020. 102-107.

Journal Articles

Ambrose, M. Devadass. "Cosmic Experience of God According to Genesis II; The Noachian Covenant." *Indian Theological Studies* 28(2), (1991): 155-165.
Barr, James. "Man and Nature – The Ecological Controversy and the Old Testament." *Bulletin of the John Rylands Library* 55(1), (1972): 9-32.
Bird, Phyllis A. "'Male and Female He Created Them' Gen. 1:27b in the Context of the Priestly Account of Creation." *Harvard Theological Review* 74(2), (1981): 129-159.
Clifford, Richard J. "Genesis 1-3: Permission to Exploit Nature?" *The Bible Today* 26 (1988): 133-137.
Coats, George W. "The God of Death: Power and Obedience in the Primeval History." *Interpretation* 29(3), (1975): 227-239.
Jobling, David. "'And Have Dominion …' The Interpretation of Genesis 1:28 in Philo Judaeus." *Journal for the Study of Judaism* 8(1), (1977): 50-82.
Limburg, James. "The Responsibility of Royalty: Genesis 1-11 and the Care of the Earth." *Word & World* 9(2), (1991): 124-130.
Limburg, James. "What Does it Mean to Have Dominion Over the Earth?" *Dialogue* 10(3), (1971): 221-223.
Parrish, V. Steven. "From Domination to Eco-Justice Rereading Selected Creation Texts in the Hebrew Bible." *Memphis Theological Seminary Journal* 29 (1991): 52-64.
Regensburger, Nancy. "Shepherding God's Creatures." *The Bible Today* 26 (1988): 138-140.
White, Lynn. "The Historical Roots of Our Ecological Crisis." *Science* 155(3767), (1967): 1203-1207.
Wildberger, Hans. *"Das Abbild Gottes." Theologische Zeitschrift* 21, (1965): 245-259.

Internet Articles

The Church of South India Department of Ecological Concerns, "Digital Bulletin Eco Activities 2021," [Available at: https://csi-synod.s3.ap-south-1.amazonaws.com/s3/1638450471229EcoBullettin-November2021-Final-WEB1638450470396.pdf], [Last accessed 10th December 2021].

11. The Churches' Responsibility to Develop Eco-Diakonia: A Reflection on Romans 8:19-23

Gloria Lita D. Mapangdol[1]

> [19] For the creation waits with eager longing for the revealing of the children of God; [20] for the creation was subjected to futility, not of its own will but by the will of the one who subjected it, in hope [21] that the creation itself will be set free from its bondage to decay and will obtain the freedom of the glory of the children of God. [22] We know that the whole creation has been groaning in labour pains until now; [23] and not only the creation, but we ourselves, who have the first fruits of the Spirit, groan inwardly while we wait for adoption, the redemption of our bodies. (Romans 8:19-23)

Introduction

Many Christians today are focused on working out their salvation and the salvation of what they refer to as the "lost souls." Others think the second coming of Christ will be hastened if more people get converted into their groups. Added to these is the presence of zealous prosperity gospel preachers who emphasise that the wealthier you become, the more blessed you are by God. These and many more have directly or indirectly led to the neglect and the abuse of other earthly life, the environment, the land and all of God's creation.

Let us bear in mind, however, that there are those who show concern for the environment and for other creatures, not so much for the sake of the environment or other creatures, but for economic profit or for human benefit. Ann Alexander tells us, for example, of people who protect animal habitat and species because they are important for medical studies. People do not pollute the river with chemicals because they might get cancer from drinking water. The idea that we should protect them because we benefit from them also becomes problematic as both may be used to justify the caring of the earth or the destruction of it.[2]

How can these anthropocentric views become problematic to the rest of God's creation, especially the nonhumans? I have no easy answers for this question but, in this essay, I reflect on how Romans 8:19-23 helps us to grapple with this problem even today in our situation, mindful of the gap between Paul's world and our world. In terms of the ethical implications of the text, I will be sharing about the plight of the indigenous peoples in my country, particularly on the effects of mining in their ancestral lands.

The Groaning of Creation in Romans 8:19-23

We are aware that Romans 8:19-23 has its own problems and some scholars would not be happy to consider it as an environmental mantra. Hunt, for instance, argues that extra caution is needed when appealing to Romans 8 as a sufficient piece of evidence of Christian environmentalism. Firstly, Romans 8 is theocentric and God subjecting creation to futility shows no indication of the liberating role of humans. Creation and humanity together are, however, encouraged to endure their suffering while waiting for God's deliverance. Secondly, Romans 8 is an eschatological narrative and that liberation is beyond the present world. Thirdly, the narrative is filled with ancient cosmological and mythological presuppositions that differ from

---

[1] Rev. Dr Gloria Lita Mapangdol currently serves as the President and Dean of St. Andrew's Theological Seminary (SATS), Quezon City, Philippines. She is also an ordained priest of the Episcopal Church in the Philippines. She teaches New Testament courses at SATS.

[2] Ann Alexander, "Groaning with Creation," *Church and Society* (Nov/Dec 2000): 69-84.

contemporary science. Hunt, herself, however, admits that while this may be fundamentally theocentric for Paul, this should also not imply that the narrative cannot support moral imperatives.[3] Indeed, with the advance of science and technology in this world of ours, there are challenges to how the text was originally interpreted. It can still remain theocentric and eschatological, but this time, more consideration is needed to the third party in the narrative, which is the creation or the nonhuman beings. Byrne says that in Romans 8, "creation" (*ktisis*) is understood by Paul as the "other-than-human" created world, which is intimately bound with the fate of human beings.[4]

Bauckham contends that while there are exegetical difficulties in referring to the text as Paul's environmental mantra, it is also undeniable that in Paul's narrative of God, Jesus, Israel, and the nations, he does not neglect the existence and importance of the nonhuman creation in that relationship. Paul talks about "the redemption of our bodies" in v. 23 because human bodies are our solidarity with the rest of creation and that the bodily redemption of believers accompanies the renewal of the created world. This solidarity, however, according to Bauckham, includes the "groaning" and the hope for future liberation or they are bound both in suffering and hope.[5] This is further strengthened if indeed, Paul, an Israelite, had in mind the mourning custom of the Jews. According to Braaten, mourning customs require the participation of the entire community in order to restore the mourner to their proper place in the social order.[6]

Two interesting things are mentioned here. The first is the liberation of creation, or their hope of redemption comes hand in hand with the redemption of human believers and vice versa. The second talks about the role of the whole community in the restoration of those who mourn or those who groan. I would like to understand that community here would also include the nonhuman beings who are part of God's creation. God is still in control of the relations, of the liberation, and of the restoration, but there is a silent call for human beings not to be mere passive expectators, but to be participants given their role as keepers and tillers of the land and the other creation (Gen. 1-2). The liberation and the restoration refer to the eschatological expectation we all hope for. This time, however, it is the whole of God's creation and not just us, human beings.

Another important point from Bauckham is his argument that the prophets of old spoke of the mourning of the earth. He especially mentioned Joel, in chapter 1, he speaks of the mourning of the ground (v.10), the domestic animals (v.18), the wild animals (v.20), as well as the farmers (v.11), the people (v.12), and the prophet himself (v.19). Created beings, apart from human beings also mourn mostly due to the devastation of nature. When they are not free to maximise their potentials, there is disaster. Having this in mind, Bauckham argues that creation's subjection to futility (v. 20) means "being prevented from fulfilling its purpose of flourishing and fruitfulness."[7] If Bauckham is right, then what prevents them from flourishing and bearing fruit? Joel seems to imply that the main reason was the invasion of a more powerful nation that destroyed the land (v. 6) and destroyed its natural resources like the vines and trees (v. 7) and dried the watercourses for the wild animals. It is the evil and greed of human beings that led to this. Was Paul implying the same in Romans 8? Is this not the same as liberating creation from its bondage (Rom. 8:21)? Is this not the same as the description of creation groaning in labour pains? I like how Bauckham puts it when he says that the "groaning" should not be only understood as an expression of "suffering" but also of "yearning in hope of redemption,"[8] which is closer to the reading of Joel.

---

[3] Cherryl Hunt, David G. Horrell, and Christopher Southgate, "An Environmental Mantra? Ecological Interest in Romans 8:19-23 and Modest Proposal for Its Narrative Interpretation," *Journal of Theological Studies* 59 (October 2008): 546-579.

[4] Brendan Byrne, "A Pauline Complement to Laudato Si'," *Theological Studies* 77(2), (2016): 308-327.

[5] Richard Bauckham, *The Bible in the Contemporary World* (Grand Rapids, MI: Eerdmans, 2015), 96.

[6] Laurie J. Braaten, "All Creation Groans: Romans 8:22 in Light of the Biblical Sources," *Horizons in Biblical Theology* 28 (2006): 131-159.

[7] Bauckham, *The Bible in the Contemporary World,* 98-100.

[8] Bauckham, *The Bible in the Contemporary World,* 101.

Moo raises an important point when, similar to Bauckham, he argues that, in Romans 8, the resurrection of the body seems to be the appropriate model for envisioning the material restoration of all creation. He explains this by claiming that for Paul, "creation cannot attain its telos unless and until humans to whom its fate is linked become who they are intended to be in Christ." Hence, the ethical imperative necessarily follows and this calls human beings to live as who they truly are as God's children. If this happens, it follows that nonhuman creation will begin to experience its liberation from futility and ruin. He adds that human beings' reconciliation with God also entails humankind's reconciliation with the earth and the other created beings. He quotes Jürgen Moltmann who says that "there is no fellowship with Christ without fellowship with the earth."[9]

Ethical Imperatives

While God is the initiator and the sustainer of all relationships, human beings cannot just be passive expectators. Our being created in the image of God does not put us on a pedestal over and above all the other creation, but it gives us a responsibility to be stewards and keepers of the rest of creation (Gen. 1-2). Yet, the groaning of creation puts into question our ability to be stewards and keepers. As Christians, this puts into question how we live our lives as children of God and as followers of Jesus. The hope of liberation and restoration of all of God's creation definitely entails ethical imperatives.

Indeed, it is impossible to not be affected by what is happening around us. Climate change, for instance, has given us enough challenges for a lifetime. The environment groans because of our neglect and mismanagement. However, we groan with them when they groan because we are also recipients of whatever happens to them: e.g. no trees, no water; polluted rivers, no fish, et cetera. As Moo contends, Romans 8 leaves us the challenge that "the whole of creation's fate is mysteriously bound up with the fate of one of its creatures."[10] From the beginning, God intended a balance of all created things, including human beings. Tipping this balance because of our disobedience and greed is very problematic. Moreover, when the process of liberation or restoration is exploited, disaster is likely to strike.

At a time when environmental disasters are affecting every community on this planet, what needs to be done? In a webinar on ecotheology, Professor George Zachariah emphasised the importance of naming the culprits. He argues that we cannot go on saying we are all responsible for the disasters when corporations and wealthy individuals enjoy wealth at the expense of the subaltern communities (the marginalised, the poor and oppressed communities). How can we say that we are all in the same boat or we are all equally responsible for this when 80% of the carbon emissions are from the industrial companies and yet the subaltern communities suffer much of the consequences even with a zero-carbon footprint?[11] Wherever we are, proof of the rape or what others call the colonisation of the land and the environment are evident. In a world of imbalance not only in the access to wealth, but the imbalance of taking responsibility for the degradation of the earth and all that lives on it, it is then natural to ask the question: what is the role of the church in all this? Or should we be passive expectators of what is to come and just mind our own business of saving our souls and the souls of others?

Application: Mining and the Indigenous Peoples in the Philippines

I cannot help but share the plight of the indigenous peoples (IP) in my country, being an indigenous woman myself. The IP communities are well-known for loving and protecting their ancestral lands. They have their

[9] Jonathan Moo, "Continuity, Discontinuity, and Hope: The Contribution of New Testament Eschatology to a Distinctively Christian Environmental Ethos," *Tyndale Bulletin* 61(1), (2010): 21-44.
[10] Moo, "Continuity, Discontinuity, and Hope", 29.
[11] George Zachariah, "Green Theology" (Virtual Lecture, Asia Theological Academy, 9th August 2021).

own rules and disciplinary measures, which sometimes come in the form of taboos, when it comes to protecting their land and their environment. There is a strong belief within the IP communities that whatever they do to the environment will be returned to them. If they take care of their environment, there is good fortune. If they will destroy, disaster may strike. Their relationship with the land and their environment is full of respect. This sometimes leads to resistance to any kind of development that destroys and exploits and rapes the land and all that is in it.

It cannot be denied that there are developments in these communities. For most, for example, electricity has reached the mountainous areas. Bridges were built to help their children cross rivers when going to school. The unavoidable use of plastic in homes and pesticides for a bountiful harvest were introduced. However, the negative effects of these developments to the community (people and environment) are minimal and are well-managed.

In most communities and countries around the globe, problems of environment, the land, and everything in it have to do with dominance, power, greed, conquest of the powerful over the powerless. It is not just the land or creation that is powerless, but the people close to them: the poor, marginalised, including the indigenous peoples who protect the land and the environment. So, when we deal with environmental problems, the issue also involves responding to the needs of the marginalised communities. In the Philippines, a group has come up with a map showing that almost all foreign big mining companies are located in lands of indigenous people.[12]

At first, I thought that this is perhaps because gold and other minerals are only found in these areas. Later on, I realised that it is probably because these marginalised communities have for centuries protected their land and environment against destruction and exploitation. Since the government has allowed the mining industries to flourish, however, these areas are now the targets of exploitation (the people, the environment, the land, and everything in it). The companies offer labour, and some indeed benefit from it by materially improving their lives. However, in general, the destruction of the environment lead to other disasters in the communities. The companies get their gold and run away with the profit, but the communities are left to suffer floods, erosions, pollution, and other disasters caused by the mining. These mining firms do not just continue to exploit these communities, but they also brainwash them into thinking that the land and other natural resources are there for their benefit and that it is such a waste not to maximise their potentials. Economic justice comes into play and this has led to resistance in most of the IP communities. The IP communities' relationship with nature is on the brink of disaster as nature now becomes an object to be exploited instead of being a part of their whole communal life. Alexander is correct when she contends that a healthy relationship with the earth is inseparable from economic justice. In fact, there is no just economic system that does not involve a just relationship with creation.[13]

It should be a given then for the Church to speak against irresponsible mining (if there is such a thing as "responsible" mining). The prophetic voice of the Church is much sought during this ecological crisis, but most often, it is not there. It is not so much because they do not care, but because a huge number of the flock is also benefitting from it. Such is a common dilemma in Philippine churches, particularly those located in indigenous areas where mining industries are located, not to mention the building of dams, all putting indigenous communities at risk. In mining, individuals and communities are employed and benefit from the industry, and so without offering any alternative to alleviate poverty, educating them of the dangers of mining usually fall of deaf ears. Churches sometimes end up becoming maintenance churches instead of dealing with the problems head on. It is a given fact, however, whether we admit it or not, that if our focus is the salvation of our souls and our economic security, other marginalised communities and creation are neglected and even suffer the consequences of our desires.

---

[12] From a MS PowerPoint presentation by Pia Malayao, Katribu (Kalipunan ng mga Katutubong Mamamayan ng Pilipinas).

[13] Alexander, "Groaning with Creation," 70.

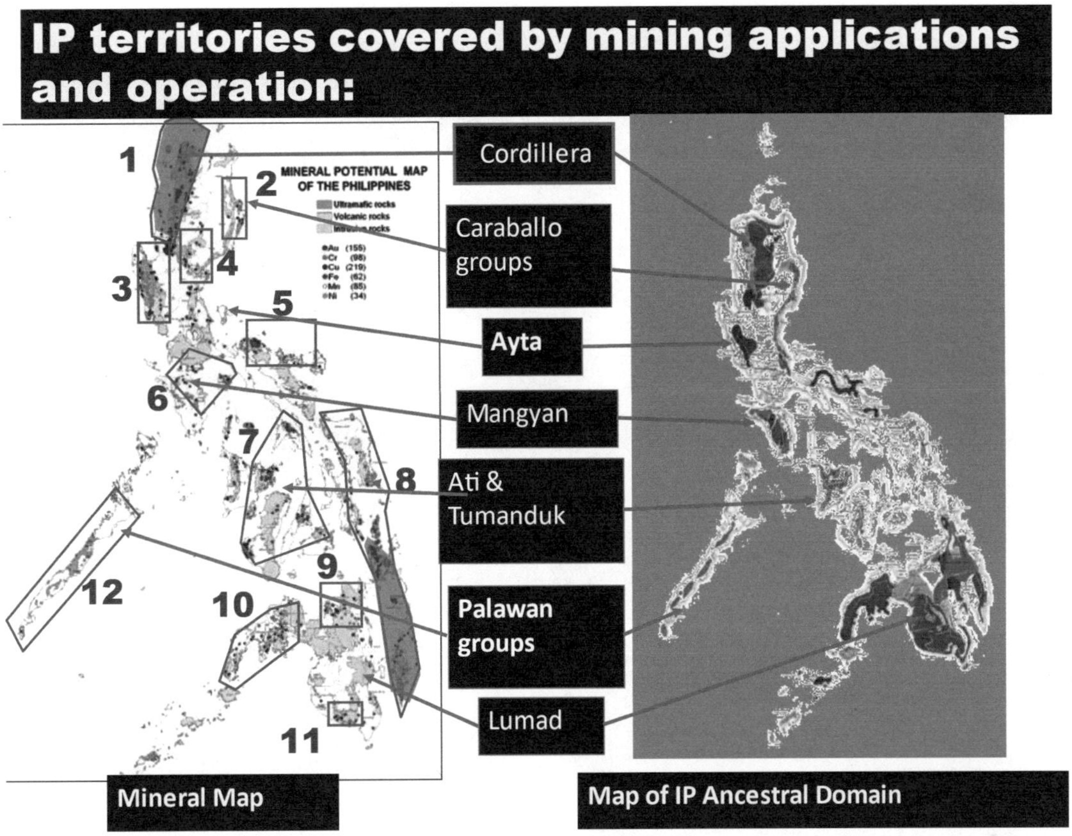

Figure 1: courtesy of Pia Malayao, Katribu

Any ecological problem will not be simply solved by passivity, believing that everything is God's plan. Christians who quickly respond this way are not getting at the root cause of the problem. Apart from that, they are absolving the sins of those who continue to plunder the earth and its riches at the expense of the subaltern communities like the Ips.[14] Hence, it is important to recognise the problems, name them, and do something about it as a community.

I am impressed by the presentation of IBON Foundation on the protection of the environment.[15] The chart below shows how large foreign companies plunder the environment and reap the benefits, leaving all the problems of garbage and pollution and destruction to the poor communities who own the land and live in the land. One of the striking recommendations for protecting the environment is "seeking the people's participation and consent, especially the indigenous communities, in managing and protecting the environment." This is often neglected because foreign companies are merely interested in the profit and they are thankful that they are allowed by the government to do so. They often forget that the indigenous

[14] George Zachariah, "Green Theology."
[15] IBON, "Protect the environment" 3rd August 2019 *IBON Foundation* [Available at: https://www.ibon.org/protect-the-environment/?fbclid=IwAR0gYvkcCUcGdS2zaw_SiRCmec0hV-F1tpGbEA_J44MXlif2xNT9kv_jQOg], [Last accessed: 28th January 2022].

peoples have every right to be part of any kind of development. The Church can participate in making sure that this is respected by any developer entering the sacred spaces of the indigenous people.

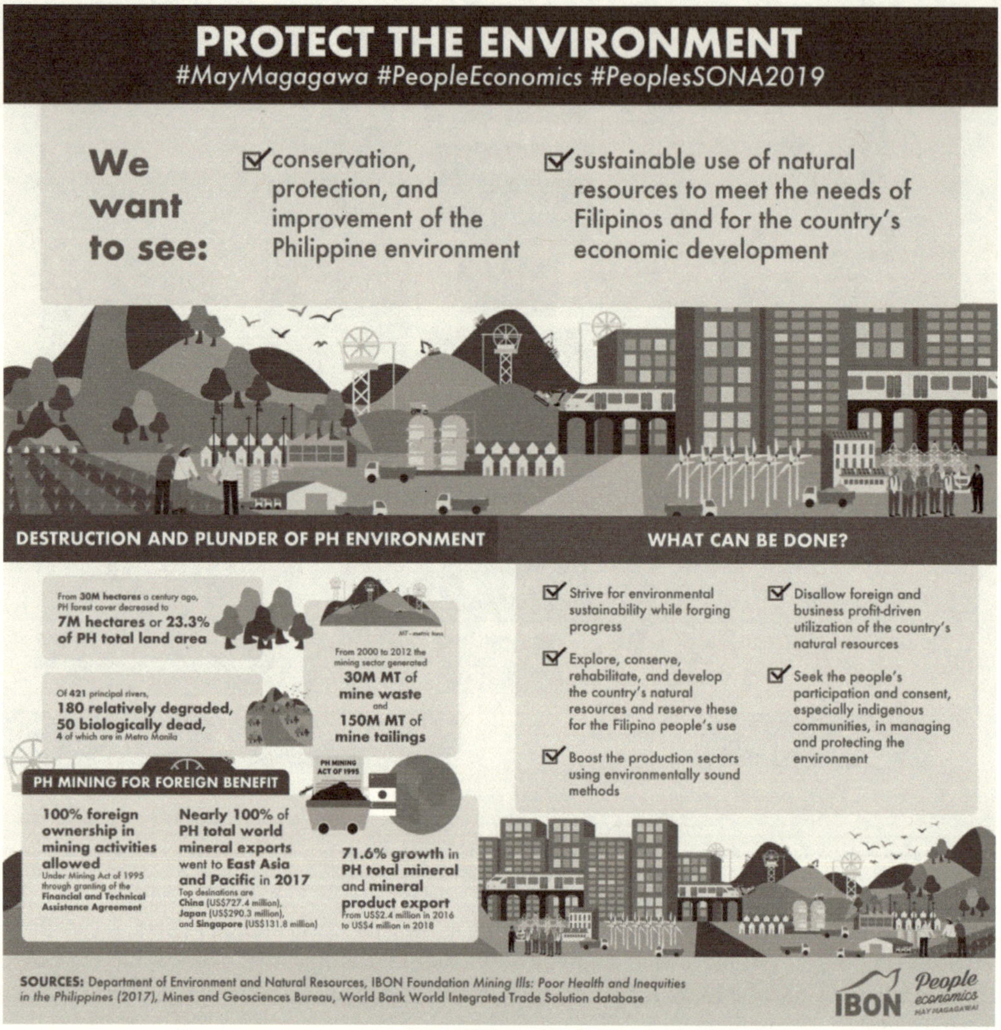

Figure 2: IBON Foundation

The Suffering of Creation as a Justice Issue

This leads to my conclusion that the groaning of creation is a justice issue. I agree with Bauckham and others who suggest that this groaning entails a liberation from bondage and suffering and letting creation maximise its potential. Someone does not just groan in pain just like that. And as with the body of Christ, if someone is in pain, we feel the pain and we groan with them. The same is true with the rest of creation. The issue of justice arises in the fact that something or someone must be responsible for the "groaning" and that liberation from this suffering is a moral obligation of the Church as the body of Christ. We often think of quick fixes. We organise tree planting activities or clean-up drives and we do it well. However, we cannot keep on cleaning and solving the problems brought about by rich companies who should be doing the cleaning and the tree planting themselves. In other words, those responsible for the environmental disaster should own up to their actions and do something about it. Otherwise, if they do not stop, part of the church's mission is not only to clean up the dirt of others, but also to cover up for the responsibilities of others.

What can be done? Let me quote from Figure 2 taken from the IBON Foundation: 1) strive for environmental sustainability while forging progress; 2) explore, conserve, rehabilitate, and develop the country's natural resources and reserve these for the Filipino people's use; 3) boost the production sectors using environmentally sound methods; 4) disallow foreign and business profit-driven utilisation of the country's resources; 5) seek the people's participation and consent, especially indigenous communities, in managing and protecting the environment.[16]

Now, these actions all sound great. However, going back to the earlier discussion in this paper, Romans 8 could also serve as a critique to the above-mentioned ethical imperatives. The words "sustainability," "reserve for Filipino people's use," and others still imply the anthropocentric idea of nature being there to serve humanity.

Conclusion

As Christians, there is a need to recover this communal relationship as God's creation and remind ourselves of God's plan. It was never an exploitative and destructive relationship, but one where everyone's beauty and potential are freely displayed, maximised, and appreciated. The Church has to continue to educate people concerning this relationship and to raise her prophetic voice against everything that tips the balance and that disturbs it, especially structures that cause unjust suffering to any of God's creation.

As believers in the resurrection, we can affirm with Luther that as the eschatological horizon looms nearer, those standing in solidarity with the martyred creation have good cause for rejoicing.[17] There is hope and this involves all of God's creation. However, a passive waiting and listening to the groaning and enduring the suffering does not seem to be the message of the text. As we continue to live our lives as Christians, let us be reminded by this quote from Jürgen Moltmann: "There is no fellowship with Christ without fellowship with the earth."[18]

Suggestions for Further Reading

Alexander, Ann. "Groaning with Creation." *Church and Society* (Nov/Dec 2000): 69-84.

Bauckham, Richard. *The Bible in the Contemporary World.* Grand Rapids, MI: Eerdmans, 2015.

Byrne, Brendan. "A Pauline Compliment to Laudato Si'." *Theological Studies* 77(2), (2016): 308-327.

Braaten, Laurie J. "All Creation Groans: Romans 8:22 in Light of the Biblical Sources." *Horizons in Biblical Theology* 28 (2006): 131-159.

Hunt, Cherryl, David G. Horrell, and Christopher Southgate. "An Environmental Mantra? Ecological Interest in Romans 8:19-23 and Modest Proposal for Its Narrative Interpretation." *Journal of Theological Studies* 59 (October 2008): 546-579.

Moo, Jonathan. "Continuity, Discontinuity, and Hope: The Contribution of New Testament Eschatology to a Distinctively Christian Environmental Ethos." *Tyndale Bulletin* 61(1), (2010): 21-44.

Tyra, Steven W. "All Creatures are Martyrs: Martin Luther's Cruciform Exegesis of Roman 8:19-22." *Westminster Theological Journal* 76 (2014): 27-53.

---

[16] IBON Foundation.

[17] Steven W. Tyra, "All Creatures are Martyrs: Martin Luther's Cruciform Exegesis of Roman 8:19-22," Westminster Theological Journal 76 (2014): 27-53.

[18] Quoted by Moo, "Continuity, Discontinuity, and Hope", 28.

12. WHO OWNS THIS EARTH BY THE WAY?
THE CHALLENGE OF REVISITING AND REFRAMING THE NOTION OF STEWARDSHIP

Muriel Orevillo-Montenegro[1]

The title of this essay is inspired by James H. Cone's talk "Whose Earth Is It Anyway?"[2] Here, Cone connects the degradation of the earth with racism. Environmental racism and ecological destruction injustice sadly continue because human beings behave like they are the owners of the earth.

"Smart City:" The City of Self-Proclaimed Demigods

As I write this essay, multi-sectoral protests – both physical and virtual – are going on in Dumaguete City, a small university town in Negros Oriental, in the Philippines.[3] They protested against the 174 hectares reclamation, an island to be constructed along the coastline of Dumaguete City. The mayor and majority of the city council, without prior consultation with the people, entered into an agreement with a contractor that has no track record of reclamation construction, along with a China state-owned company that has no license to operate in the Philippines.[4] The mayor entered into transactions as if he owns the city. This 174-hectare reclamation project would surely destroy the marine protected areas and Tañon Strait along the coast of Dumaguete and its neighbouring towns, an area which is a Protected Seascape. It is home to some ancient and endangered sea creatures.[5] The World Wide Fund for Nature (WWF) and local scientists confirmed that "14 species of marine mammals travel through the waters of Dumaguete to reach Tañon Strait."[6] This

---

[1] Muriel Orevillo-Montenegro is a lay feminist theologian, teacher-learner, and gardener. She was a youth worker and community worker before joining Silliman University Divinity School's faculty where she became the first female dean. She was the coordinator of Silliman's Justice and Peace Center. She holds degrees in agriculture and theological education from Silliman University and did her graduate and postgraduate studies at Union Theological Seminary in New York City. Her interests range from theology, ethics, liturgy, interreligious understanding, disability, ecology, and peace studies. She is a member of the Association of Women in Theology in the Philippines and the Asian Women's Resource Centre. She co-founded the Philippine Ecumenical Peace Platform (PEPP) that pioneered in calling the Government of the Republic of the Philippines and the National Democratic Front of the Philippines to resume the peace talks. Presently, she coordinates the Interfaith Cooperation Forum of Asia and the Pacific Alliance of YMCA based in Hong Kong.

[2] James H. Cone, "Whose Earth is it Anyway?" Cross Currents. [Available at: http://www.crosscurrents.org/cone.htm], [Last accessed: 28th January 2022].

[3] Zakarian Sarao, "Groups urge gov't to stop 'dump-and-fill' reclamation projects," *Inquirer.Net*, [Available at: https://newsinfo.inquirer.net/1468715/cso-collective-calls-on-national-govt-to-stop-approval-of-dumpfill-reclamation-projects], [Last accessed 6th July 2021].

[4] "Dumaguete's Scientists are Up in Arms against an Ambitious 174-hectare 'Smart City' Reclamation Project, *Tomorrow.City*, [Available at: https://tomorrow.city/a/dumaguetes-scientists-are-up-in-arms-against-an-ambitious-174-hectare-smart], [Last accessed 15th July 2021].

[5] Stacy K. Baez, Charlotte Grubb, Margot L. Stiles, and Gloria Ramos, "Love Letter to Tañon Strait," *Oceana* [Available at: https://oceana.org/sites/default/files/love_letter_final_singlepages_with_bleeds_editedsh.compressed_1.pdf], [Last accessed: 1st August 2021].

[6] Job Manahan, "Dumaguete reclamation to devastate nearby protected areas, marine biodiversity – conservation group," ABS-CBN News, 22nd July 2021, [Available at: https://news.abs-cbn.com/news/07/22/21/wwf-concerned-dumaguete-proposed-land-reclamation-project.] The mammals include the spinner dolphins, short-finned pilot whales, and dwarf sperm whales.

project would destroy both the ecological biodiversity and deprive the fisherfolks and small-scale businesses of their livelihood.[7]

The 2021 Report of the IPCC: Will the Nations take this Seriously?

The U.N. Intergovernmental Panel on Climate Change (IPCC) released an updated special report on 9th August 2021, on the impacts of global warming of 1.5°C.[8] The report seeks to strengthen the "global response to the threat of climate change, sustainable development, and efforts to eradicate poverty."[9] It expresses the "unequivocal" scientific consensus affirming the reality of anthropogenic climate change. It clarifies that a little increase in warming will bring life-threatening occurrences such as flooding, heatwaves, fire, melting of glaciers and ice sheets, irreversible thawing of permafrost, ocean warming, acidification, and deoxygenation. Scientists call on the world's attention to this alarming global crisis and act on it urgently. Swift action may still possibly put a cap on the current average warming of 1.1°C to the target of 1.5°C twenty years from now.[10]

The Call to Revisit Once Again the Concept of Stewardship

The Dumaguete 174-hectares reclamation is a blatant rejection of the Christian teaching of stewardship. Despite the warnings of the United Nation's IPCC in the past, the assault on ecology continues. Where has the concept of stewardship gone?

According to the Pew Research Center, Christianity is still the largest religion in the world with 2.3 billion adherents.[11] Christianity is expected to lead in promoting ecological justice. Yet, one wonders if Christianity made the impact in their practice of stewardship. It helps to revisit the concept of stewardship to make Christians take seriously the crisis of the Earth. Faith communities must see the implication of their practices in mitigating the rapid climate change. The Earth's crisis is a judgment on how believers understand themselves as stewards of God's creation.

Melzar: the Meaning of Steward in the Old Testament

Stewardship is about the duties and obligations of a guardian in "managing of something, especially the careful and responsible management of something entrusted to one's care." The word *melzar* (מֶלְצָר), a masculine noun of Babylonian origin (Daniel 1:11, 16),[12] has various biblical translations. The translations

---

[7] "Board of Trustees Re-Affirms Position of Silliman University on Reclamation," Silliman University, [Availale at: https://su.edu.ph/board-of-trustees-re-affirms-position-of-silliman-university-on-reclamation/], [Last accessed: 22nd July 2021].

[8] IPCC, "Summary for Policy Makers," *Special Report: Global Warming of 1.5°C*, IPCC, [Available at: https://www.ipcc.ch/sr15/chapter/spm/], [Last accessed: 10th August 2021].

[9] IPCC, *Special Report*;See also IPCC, "Climate change widespread, rapid, and intensifying – IPCC," 9th August 2021, [Available at: https://www.ipcc.ch/2021/08/09/ar6-wg1-20210809-pr/], [Last accessed: 10th August 2021].

[10] Cathleen O'Grady, "Climate change 'unequivocal' and 'unprecedented,' says new U.N. report," *Science,* 9th August 2021, [Available at: https://www.sciencemag.org/news/2021/08/climate-change-unequivocal-and-unprecedented-says-new-un-report], [Last accessed: 28th January 2022].

[11] Conrad Hackett and David McClendon, "Christians remain world's largest religious group, but they are declining in Europe," 5th April 2017, Pew Research Center [Available at: https://www.pewresearch.org/fact-tank/2017/04/05/christians-remain-worlds-largest-religious-group-but-they-are-declining-in-europe/], [Last accessed: 30th July 2021].

[12] *Brown-Driver-Briggs Hebrew and English Lexicon*, Unabridged, Electronic Database. [Avaiable at: https://hebrewcollege.edu/wp-content/uploads/2018/10/BDB.pdf], [Last accessed: 29th July 2021]. Henceforth, this will be referred as BDB to distinguish the e-book online from the hard copy.

include *melzar* as a guard,[13] as "steward,"[14] while others simply use "*Melzar*" as a proper noun (Gen. 15:2). Other versions translate *melzar* as a servant-heir (Gen. 15:3).[15]

The *Epitropos* and the *Oikonomos*

The New Testament introduces the Greek word *epitropos* (ἐπίτρποπος) as "steward or a manager" (Mt. 20:8). The *epitropos* is a trusted person who serves as an overseer of someone's house or property (Lk. 8:3) and a guardian.[16] The New Testament, however, has *oikonomos* (οἰκονόμος) as another word for steward.[17] The *oikonomos* also means a manager of a household, administrator, a trustee (Lk. 12:42; 16:1, 3, 8; 1 Cor. 4:2; Gal. 4:2). The *oikonomos* could also take a broader task as a public steward or as treasurer (Rom. 16:23). *Oikounomos* is a combination of two Greek words, *oikos,* and *nomos* (νόμος). *Oikos* (οἶκος, -ου, ὁ) means a house or dwelling (Mt. 9:6, 7; Mk. 2:1, 11; 3:20), or a household (Lk. 10:5; 11:17). *Nomos* means law, regulation, principle. Its verb form is *nemo* (νεμω), which means to divide and dispense,[18] and "to parcel out, especially food or grazing to animals."[19] Used differently from *torah* (תורה) as law, the Greek *nemo* is closer to the Hebrew verb *bin* (בין), meaning "to understand" and to the verb *bana* (בנה), to build.[20] These words may help us understand that stewardship is about understanding and following the law of equality and justice for the Earth and the earthlings.

Revisiting *Oikonomia* as Stewardship

The word "economy" in essence is the judicious administration and management of available resources. It comes from the Greek o*ikonomia* (οἰκονομία), a cognate noun of *oikonomos*. *Oikonomia* means "stewardship," referring to the management of a household (Lk. 16:2, 3, 4), and "due discharge of a commission, an apostolic commission to promote the Gospel (Eph. 3:2, 9; Col. 1:25).[21] Both *oikonomos* and *oikonomia* come from the root word *oikos*.

Oikos shares the same meaning with the Hebrew *bayith* (בית), which means a dwelling place, a habitation. Both *oikos* and *bayith* refer to those who live in the same house as a social unit, as *oikios* (οίκείος) – like family, clan, tribe, or relatives (Eph. 2:19-22), or descendants as an organised body (Gen. 18:19). *Bayith* also includes "everything on which one depends" (Gen. 39: 4; 44:1, 4; Job 8:14-15), and the shelter and abode of animals (1 Sam. 6:7, 10).

Two more cognates to *oikonomia* help us understand better the biblical thoughts on stewardship. One is *oiketerion* (οίκετερίον),[22] which also mean "household or dwelling place" and is connected with

[13] New International Version (NIV), New Revised Standard Version (NRSV), and Good News Bible (GNB).
[14] American Standard Version (ASV), and Revised Standard Version (RSV).
[15] W.F. Boyd, "Steward," in *Dictionary of the Bible*, edited by James Hastings (New York, Charles Scribner's Sons, 1909), [Available at: http://areopage.net/PDF/HBD/s.htm].
[16] Bill Mounce, "ἐπίτρποπος," in *Greek Dictionary,* [Available at: https://www.billmounce.com/greek-dictionary/epitropos], [Last accessed 18th July 2021].
[17] Mounce, "ἐπίτρποπος".
[18] Abarim Publications, "νομος," in *Biblical Dictionary: The New Testament Greek,* [Available at: https://www.abarim-publications.com/DictionaryG/n/n-o-m-o-sfin.html], [Last accessed 15th July 2021]. One must not confuse *nemo* with Greek σχιζω (schizo), meaning to split or divide.
[19] *Bible Tools: Greek and Hebrew Definitions*, "nomos," [Available at: https://www.bibletools.org/index.cfm/fuseaction/Lexicon.show/ID/G3551/nomos.htm], [Last accessed: 26th June 2021].
[20] Bible Tools "nomos".
[21] Bible Tools "nomos".
[22] Frederick William Danker et al. (eds), "οίκετερίον," in *A Greek-English Lexicon of the New Testament and Other Early Christian Literature*, 3rd ed. (Chicago and London: The University of Chicago Press, 2000), 694-96.

stewardship. Another more popular cognate among this family of words is *oikoumene* (οἰκουμένη), which refer to the inhabited world, the habitable earth (Mt. 24:14; Lk.2:10, 4:5; Rom. 10:16-18; Heb. 1:6).[23] *Oikoumene* is inclusive of all that dwells and inhabits the earth, including the human race.

All these keywords point to the notion of stewardship. These biblical words should have compelled Christians to appreciate the Earth as the dwelling of all earthlings. In this household, all earthlings must observe the law of fairness, equality, and justice to each other, and build to edify this dwelling place. So where did things go wrong?

The Marginalisation of the Oikonomia

Towards the end of the first century, the Deutero-Pauline writers tended to move away from the holistic understanding of *bayith and oikos* as the physical shelter and dwelling of human beings and animals. They limited *bayith* and *oikos* to the church as the "household of God" (Eph. 2:19; 1Tim. 3:15, 1 Pet. 4:17). This exclusive view blurs the image of *oikos* as the habitable dwelling for all earthlings. Consequently, the sense of the relationship between the human being and physical nature was relegated to the margins. Somehow, the faithful have unconsciously erased o*ikonomia* from memory. What remains of the memory of *oikonomia* and stewardship were mostly in terms of money, production, and consumption, while its essence of assuring equality to all earthlings is forgotten.

The Ambivalence and Vagueness of the Creation Story on Stewardship

Melzar, as steward does not appear in Genesis 1 and 2. Interpreters take the creation of the *ha-adam* (אדם), the human being, as outlined in Genesis 1. The last to be created, and created in God's image, the human being is deemed the crown of creation. Readers connect this with Psalm 8 that says, human beings are just "a little lower than God [...] given them dominion." This becomes the basis of anthropocentric interpretations of the text. The account of Genesis 1 complicates the concept of stewardship because the writer uses words that are not consistent with the meaning *melzar.* In the account of Genesis 1:26-28, we find the words *dominion* (*radah*) and *subdue* (*kabash*). These two powerful but harsh words, *radah* (רדה) and *kabash* (פכש) have a strong influence on *ha-adam* to rule over, dominate, and have dominion (*radah*) over the earth.[24] *Kabash* means to subdue, bring into bondage, to dominate, conquer, make subservient, tread down, and even to force a woman (Esth. 7:8).[25] These forceful, aggressive, violent tones and imagery of *radah* and *kabash* overshadow the sense of *melzar* as a steward, servant, being a guard, and trustee. This changes the posture of the human being into that of a conqueror.

Retrieving the Concept of Stewardship in Genesis 2

Genesis 2 seems to provide a counterpoint to Genesis 1:26-28. Verse 7 says God first created the human being (אדמ – *adam*) from the "dust of the ground" (אדמה – *adamah*)[26] before creating other earthlings. This chapter also has two keywords that shaped the concept of stewardship. They are *abad* (עבד), and *shamar* (שמר). *Abad* means to work, to serve, "to till" (Dt. 21:4 Ez. 36:9, 34),[27] and *shamar* means, "to keep, watch, preserve."[28] Some used the infinitive form of *abad* (לְעָבְדָהּ -le-av-dah) and *shamar* (וּלְשָׁמְרָהּ or ul-sham-rah)

[23] Bill Mounce, "οἰκουμένη," in *Greek Dictionary* [Available at: https://www.billmounce.com/greek-dictionary/oikoumene] [Last accessed: 26th June 2021].
[24] BDB, "רדה," 2240.
[25] BDB, "פכש," 1126. See also at https://hebrewcollege.edu/wp-content/uploads/2018/10/BDB.pdf.
[26] BDB, "אדמ, אדמה" 77-78.
[27] BDB, "עבד ", 1720.
[28] BDB, "שמר,"2517.

to translate them "dress it and to keep it." In some texts, *shamar* means "observe," in the sense of following the dictates of prudence, justice, kindness, wisdom (Is. 56:1; Hos. 12:7; Prov. 4:4, 5:2). Thus, biblical versions translate these words as follows:

"till and keep it." (NRSV)
"work it and take care of it." (NIV)
"dress it and to keep it." (KJV, ASV)
"tend and keep it." (NKJV)
"cultivate and keep it." (Amplified Bible)
"cultivate and care for it. (NAB-RE)

Note that in Hebrew, the "garden of Eden," the Earth, is a feminine word. So, Jeff A. Benner proffers that the translation of Genesis 2:15 should be:

> "And YHWH Elohiym took the man and he caused him to rest in the garden of Eden to *serve her and to guard her*." [29]

The ancient notion of the Earth as feminine resonates with the Indigenous People's view through their chant that says, "The Earth is our Mother, We must take care of her."[30] It highlights the concept of stewardship as serving the Earth. However, there is a glitch somewhere.

Genesis 2:23-24 says God created a helper for *ha-adam* by taking a rib from him. Hereafter, man (אִישׁ) as *ish* was distinguished from the woman (אִשָּׁה) as *isha*. The storyteller seemed to put the creation of *isha* as an afterthought in the creation process. Being created as a helper implies that *isha* is not quite an equal. This reinforces the idea that *ish* is superior to *isha* and *isha* is merely a servant of *ish*. This story presents the basis for androcentrism while providing also a thread connecting *isha* and Mother Earth. *Ish* conquered the Earth instead of guarding her, just like how he dominates *isha*. While the creation story in Genesis 1 projects violent anthropocentrism, Genesis 2 provides an underpinning for androcentrism. Both postures have reinforced the patriarchal cultural practices towards women and the Earth.

The Empire's Christianity and the Earth

An indigenous person, Telesforo Sungkit Jr, confronts the complicity of Christianity in the colonisation and imperial projects of the West. Coming from the Higaonon tribe of the Philippines, he wrote the poem, "I Higaonon" where he tells how Christians protrayed themselves as good while saying that the native is pagan and bad. Yet, the "good" Christian destroyed the trees that the native respected, grabbed their lands, their gold, and called their deity Migbaya, the devil.[31]

The Indigenous Peoples, for centuries, held on to spiritualities that are closely attached to the Earth. Yet, much of the destruction of the earth happens in the areas where they and other vulnerable peoples live. Science and technology brought about the notion of development at the expense of the Earth to feed the capitalist hunger for profit. The Earth ceased to be the habitable dwelling for the earthlings. She becomes a body to be vanquished. The appalling change from the reasonably stable climate during the 12,000 years of the Holocene period is now leading the Earth to the overwhelming alterations to the atmospheric, geologic,

---

[29] Jeff A. Benner, "Genesis 2: Syntax and Morphology," in *Ancient Hebrew Research Center,* [Available at: https://www.ancient-hebrew.org/studies-verses/genesis-2-syntax-and-morphology.htm], [Last accessed: 1st August 2021]. The prefix ל (L) means in וּלְשָׁמְרָהּ "to" – to serve. The suffix ה (ah) identifies the object of the verb as feminine. The garden as the object (the "her") is a feminine word.

[30] From the Higaonon tribe in the Philippines.

[31] Telesforo Sungkit, Jr., "I Higaonon," in *Cordite Poetry Review*, [Available at: http://cordite.org.au/poetry/philippines/i-higaonon/], [Last accessed: 14th August 2021].

hydrologic, biospheric, and other Earth systems. Greed leads to the anthropogenic activities, which define the Anthropocene.[32] The Earth has not reached the climate cap of 1.5ºC yet, but the Earth is already experiencing floods, heatwaves, fires, shorter cold, and longer warm seasons. A little increase beyond 1.5ºC of global warming will be catastrophic for Planet Earth and human life as a whole.[33]

Critical voices emerged in the 1960s, questioning the impact of Christianity on ecology. Prominent was that of the most cited Lynn Townsend White, Jr. To him, being anthropocentric, Christianity is culpable for encouraging science to conquer nature, leading to the ecological crisis. Western Christianity "not only established a dualism of man and nature but also insisted that it is God's will that "man [*sic*] exploit nature for his proper ends."[34]

Some disagreed with White. Andrew Basden argued that Genesis 1-2 has been mistranslated and misinterpreted. Like James Barr, Gerhard Von Radand others,[35] Basden benignly interpreted *radah* and *kabash*. Basden translates *radah* as "to rule with authority." God created human beings in God's image, then human beings reflect that godly image by managing the creation, "as God would want it to be."[36] God ordered human beings to rule with authority through responsible management. Others proffered that *radah* and *kabash* should be interpreted positively as careful service and caring for the earth. *Kabash* is not conquest. *Radah* and *kabash* also imply reflecting the kingly rule of God as taking responsibility and care for the well-being of the subjects. Basden proffered an affirmative view of *kabash* with the analogy of God, who like a parent, "subdue" the children to have peace in the family. He asserted that the text "seems to imply to subdue for the good of the things being subdued rather than for our own convenience, pleasure or resource."[37] Some suggested that the breadth of the words *radah* and *kabash* point to the necessities of settlement and agriculture.[38]

Basden's argument for *radah* and *kabash* looks plausible on the surface. However, the Old Testament also tells us that kings, even David, did not truly look after the well-being of the subjects, especially women. Solomon's projects destroyed the forests and scoured the Earth's bowels for precious stones. Doing a reality check, however, makes us see that such arguments sanitising *radah* and *kabash* did not translate into moral practice. To balance the notion of *radah* and *kabash* with *abad* and *shamar*, at attempt to reframe stewardship with other biblical concepts might help.

---

[32] Meera Subramanian, "Humans versus Earth: the quest to define the Anthropocene," in *Nature* (6th August 2019; correction 2nd October 2019), [Available at: https://www.nature.com/articles/d41586-019-02381-2], [Last accessed: 2nd August 2021].

[33] IPCC, *August 9, 2021 Press Release: Climate change widespread, rapid, and intensifying,* IPCC, [Available at: https://www.ipcc.ch/site/assets/uploads/2021/08/IPCC_WGI-AR6-Press-Release_en.pdf],[Last accessed: 10th August 2021].

[34] Lynn T. White, Jr., "The Historical Roots of our Ecologic Crisis," in Science 155 (1967) 1203-207. Reprinted in Mary Heather MacKinnon and Moni McIntyre (eds), *Readings in Ecology and Feminist Theology* (Kansas City: Sheed and Ward, 1995), 31.

[35] James Barr, "Man and Nature: The Ecological Controversy and the Old Testament," in David and Eileen Spring (eds), *Ecology and Religion in History* (New York: Harper & Row, 1974), 58. See also Gerhard Von Rad, *Genesis: A Commentary*, The Old Testament Library (Philadelphia: The Westminster Press, 1972), 60. Cited in Daniel J. Stulac, "Hierarchy and Violence in Genesis 1:26-28: An Agrarian Solution," 2nd November 2013, *Academia*, [Available at: https://www.academia.edu/5186990/Hierarchy_and_Violence_in_Genesis_1_26-28 An_Agrarian_Solution], [Last accessed: 25th July 2021].

[36] Andrew Basden, "Detailed Analysis of Radah," [Available at: https://kgsvr.net/xn/radah.analysis.html], [Last accessed: 2nd August 2021].

[37] Andrew Basden, "On the Interpretation of Four Hebrew Words: *Radah, Kabash, Abad, Shamar,*" [Available at: https://kgsvr.net/xn/discussion/radah2.html], [Last updated: 17th July 2016, accessed 2ndAugust 2021].

[38] Stulac, "Hierarchy and Violence in Genesis 1:26-28: An Agrarian Solution," 2.

Reframing the Picture? Or, Wearing New Lenses for Reading?

"Reframing" means putting a new frame for an old picture, which although it does not change the picture, changes the view of it somewhat. The concepts *radah* and *kabash, abad,* and *shamar* could not be removed from the scriptural pages, but perhaps a new frame could shift the Christian's perspective and take an ethical posture towards working for a "moral climate."[39] Adding a new element to the framed image could probably make the concept of *oikonomos* more compelling.

The Anthropocene, exemplified by human and Earth rights violations[40] are images of unpeace. Then, the broad concept of *shalom* (שָׁלוֹם) should be taken as an overarching vision. *Shalom* means peace, harmony among people, well-being, completeness, wholeness, and prosperity. The world cannot attain *shalom* when human beings violate the Earth. God's *oikos* – the Earth – needs stewards to be peacebuilders.

With the frame of *shalom* in the *oikoumene,* the habitable and inhabited Earth, the *oikodomos* may improve the old picture. It provides counterbalance to the callousness of *radah*, and *kabash*, and brings to the forefront the constructive meaning of *abad* and *shamar*. The *oikodomos* (οἰκοδόμος, ου, ὁ) is a builder. Its verb form, *oikodomeo* (οἰκοδομέω), has a long list of definitions. An *oikodomos* builds, constructs, rebuilds, edifies, strengthens, develops another person's life through acts and words of love, encourages repair, and even beautifies (Mt. 23:29; Mt. 16:18).[41] An *oikodomos* contributes to advancement in religious knowledge and a person's spiritual condition (1 Cor. 14:4, 17; 1 Cor. 8:1; 1 Cor. 8:10).[42] An *oikodomos,* as a peacebuilder, seeks to enable the household to do its tasks and live responsibly (Acts 9:31; 20:32). In light of the *oikonomos,* the *oikodomos* will improve our understanding of the steward's task in managing the affairs of a household on behalf of the owner. This debunks the usual interpretation of stewardship that follows the violent-prone concept of *radah* and *kabash.* The anthropocentric theology of stewardship and creation following the *radah* and *kabash,* along with *abad* and *shamar* is defective. It did not save the Earth from degradation. Instead, it has historically endorsed the plunder and rape of Mother Earth. It served as the basis for human beings to play gods or demigods, and abuse their power. The old concept of stewardship did not pay attention to human beings who embody the house destroyer, the *phtheiro* (Φθείρω) who destroys, corrupts, leads astray, and causes to perish. The *phtheiro* brings corruption to households and families, and are seducers of [married] women (1 Cor. 3:16-17;1 Cor. 15:33; 2 Cor. 11:3).[43] Its cognate, *oikophthoros* (οίκοφθόρος)[44] is the nemesis of the *oikodomos,* of *melzar.*

Unlike the household destroyer, the *oikonomos* as an *oikodomos* recognises that all things, everything – matter and spirit – are related, interconnected. As *oikodomos*, the *oikonomos/shamar* understands the principle that peacebuilding encompasses the wholeness and well-being of the whole Earth. The *oikodomos* seeks to be a "sign of healing and justice in the world,"[45] and to act as an agent of care (θεραπεία)[46] to heal the planet. The task of healing involves claiming the "power of anger in the work of love"[47] to dismantle

[39] Michael S. Northcott, *A Moral Climate: the Ethics of Global Warming* (Maryknoll, NY: Orbis Books, 2007).
[40] "Earth rights" is a term for organszations that takes the power of law and people power to defend human rights and environment.
[41] Bill Mounce, "οἰκοδομέω," *Greek Dictionary*, [Available at: https://www.billmounce.com/greek-dictionary/oikodomeo], [Last accessed: 25th July 2021].
[42] Mounce, "οἰκοδομέω".
[43] Mounce, "Φθείρω," *Greek Dictionary*, [Available at: https://www.billmounce.com/greek-dictionary/phtheiro], [Last accessed: 25th July 2021]. See also I Corinthians 3:17, "φθείρει and φθερεῖ," *Bible Hub*, [Available at: https://biblehub.com/interlinear/1_corinthians/3-17.htm], [Last accessed: 11th August 2021].
[44] Frederick William Danker, et.al. (eds), *A Greek-English Lexicon of the New Testament and Other Early Christian Literature,* 3rd edition (Chicago and London: The University of Chicago Press, 2000), 694-696.
[45] Letty M. Russel, "Signs of Healing and Justice: A Bible Study," in Letty M. Russel and J. Shannon Clarkson (eds), *Women's Ways of Being Church (*Geneva: World Council of Churches, 2005).
[46] Danker, et. al., 452.
[47] Beverly Wildung Harrison, *Making Connections: Essays in Feminist Social Ethics,* ed. Carol Robb (Boston: Beacon Press, 1985), 3-21.

abusive and violent cultures. The *oikodomos* takes the prophetic task of justice-making for the Earth and its defenders. Thus, the *oikodomos* is a builder of a peaceful society and practices the ethics of resistance to any political, economic, social, and cultural schemes that denigrate the rights of the Earth and the earthlings.

With *oikodomos* as a new element to frame the concept of stewardship comes the hope for a broader understanding and balance of life on the *oikoumene.*

What does it take to be Stewards in God's Oikoumene?

One can intellectually regurgitate on the ancient Hebrew and Greek words in the scriptures to understand the meaning of stewardship. Yet, a scientist warned that while scientific competence can be taught and learned, knowledge will have no impact if humanity refuses to take the truth that "character and faith is the responsibility of everyone."[48] Translating knowledge into moral practice is a challenge: "how would the principles [...] values (life-style priorities) be developed and efficiently practiced?"[49]

Environmentalists lamented that human beings exercise power over nature because they shaped God in their image. Human beings sadly assume they are the owners of God's creation. Humanity must see and recognise God in creation,[50] and restrain the self from "the danger of 'Play God Syndrome' tendency".[51]

Human beings should cultivate biophilic ethics and lifestyle that exemplifies "the passionate love of life and all that is alive."[52] It takes faith, character, and commitment. Christians could re-invent Christianity into an Earth-loving and liberating religion. They must remember that they are not the universe's centre, and muster the humility to acknowledge that they, too, are earthlings. In doing so, as latecomers of this planet, the Mother Earth – they would embody the original essence of stewardship, that is to *serve her and to guard her.*

Recommendations for Further Reading

Abarim Publications, "νομος." In *Biblical Dictionary: The New Testament Greek*, [Available at: https://www.abarim-publications.com/DictionaryG/n/n-o-m-o-sfin.html], [Last accessed: 15th July 2021].

Baez, Stacy K. Charlotte Grubb, Margot L. Stiles, and Gloria Ramos. "Love Letter to Tañon Strait." In Oceana.org, [Available at: https://oceana.org/sites/default/files/love_letter_final_singlepages_with_bleeds_editedsh.compressed_1.pdf], [Last accessed: 1st August 2021].

Barr, James "Man and Nature: The Ecological Controversy and the Old Testament." In David and Eileen Spring, Eds. *Ecology and Religion in History*, New York: Harper & Row, 1974. Cited in Daniel J. Stulac, "Hierarchy and Violence in Genesis 1:26-28: An Agrarian Solution," 2nd November 2013, *Academia*, [Available at: https://www.academia.edu/5186990/Hierarchy_and_Violence_in_Genesis_1_26-28 An_Agrarian_Solution], [Last accessed: 25th July 2021].

---

48 Marlon Rosendo Daza, "Understanding the Earth: Why do Calamities Arise?" Lecture at Silliman University Divinity School, 19th March 2014.

49 Ibrahim Udale Hussaini, "Sustainable Development and the Ethical Issue of Human Morality; an Overview," in *Academia Letters*, 2021 Article 456, [Available at: https://doi.org/10.20935/AL456], [Last accessed: 4th August 2021].

50 Ben S. Malayang III, "Keynote Address: Understanding Calamities and Disasters," Theological Consultation-Workshop on the Situation of Calamities and Disaster, Silliman University Divinity School, 18th March 2014.

51 Hussaini, "Sustainable Development", 4.

52 Erich Fromm, *The Anatomy of Human Destructiveness* (New York: Holt, Rinehart and Winston, 1973). Cited in "Biophilia hypothesis," *Brittanica,* [Available at: https://www.britannica.com/science/biophilia-hypothesis#ref1115990], [Last accessed: 14th August 2021]. Erich Fromm first used the word biophilia in 1964.

Basden, Andrew. "Detailed Analysis of Radah," *Writing on Christian Topics,* [Available at: https://kgsvr.net/xn/radah.analysis.html,] [Last accessed: 2nd August 2021].

— "On the Interpretation of Four Hebrew Words: Radah, Kabash, Abad, Shamar," [Last updated: 17th July 2016], [Available at: https://kgsvr.net/xn/discussion/radah2.html], [Last accessed: 2nd August 2021].

Benner, Jeff A. "Genesis 2: Syntax and Morphology." In *Ancient Hebrew Research Center*, [Available at: https://www.ancient-hebrew.org/studies-verses/genesis-2-syntax-and-morphology.htm], [Last accessed: 1st August 2021].

Bible Tools: Greek and Hebrew Definitions, "nomos," [Available at: https://www.bibletools.org/index.cfm/fuseaction/Lexicon.show/ID/G3551/nomos.htm], [Last accessed: 26th June 2021].

"Board of Trustees Re-Affirms Position of Silliman University on Reclamation." In Silliman University, [Available at: https://su.edu.ph/board-of-trustees-re-affirms-position-of-silliman-university-on-reclamation/], [Last accessed: 22nd July 2021].

Boyd, W.F. "Steward." In James Hastings, Ed. *Dictionary of the Bible* (New York, Charles Scribner's Sons, 1909). [Available at: http://areopage.net/PDF/HBD/s.htm].

Brown-Driver-Briggs Hebrew and English Lexicon, Unabridged, Electronic Database. Copyright © 2002, 2003, 2006 by Biblesoft, Inc. [Available at: https://hebrewcollege.edu/wp-content/uploads/2018/10/BDB.pdf], [Last accessed: 29th July 2021].

Cone, James H. "Whose Earth is it Anyway?" *Cross Currents* [Available at: http://www.crosscurrents.org/cone.htm], [Last accessed: 28th January 2022].

Danker, Frederick William, Ed. *A Greek-English Lexicon of the New Testament and Other Early Christian Literature*, 3rd edition. Chicago and London: The University of Chicago Press, 2000.

Daza, Marlon Rosendo. "Understanding the Earth: Why do Calamities Arise?" Lecture at Silliman University Divinity School, 19th March 2014.

"Dumaguete's Scientists are Up in Arms against an Ambitious 174-hectare 'Smart City' Reclamation Project, *Tomorrow City*, [Available at: https://tomorrow.city/a/dumaguetes-scientists-are-up-in-arms-against-an-ambitious-174-hectare-smart], [Last accessed: 15th July 2021].

I Corinthians 3:17. "φθείρει, φθερεῖ." *Bible Hub*, [Available at: https://biblehub.com/interlinear/1_corinthians/3-17.htm], [Last accessed: 11th August 2021].

Fromm, Erich. *The Anatomy of Human Destructiveness*. New York, Holt, Rinehart and Winston, 1973.

Hackett, Conrad and David McClendon, "Christians remain world's largest religious group, but they are declining in Europe," 5th April 2017, Pew Research Center, [Available at: https://www.pewresearch.org/fact-tank/2017/04/05/94hristians-remain-worlds-largest-religious-group-but-they-are-declining-in-europe/], [Last accessed: 30th July 2021].

Harrison, Beverly Wildung. *Making Connections: Essays in Feminist Social Ethics*, edited by Carol Robb. Boston: Beacon Press, 1985.

Hussaini, Ibrahim Udale. "Sustainable Development and the Ethical Issue of Human Morality; an Overview." In *Academia Letters*, 2021 Article 456, [Available at: https://doi.org/10.20935/AL456], [Last accessed: 4th August 2021].

Intergovernmental Panel on Climate Change. "Summary for Policy Makers." In *Special Report: Global Warming of 1.5°C,* IPCC, [Available at: https://www.ipcc.ch/sr15/chapter/spm/], [Last accessed: 10th August 2021].

— *Special Report: Global Warming of 1.5°C*, IPCC, [Available at: https://www.ipcc.ch/sr15/], [Last accessed: 10th August 2021].

— "Climate change widespread, rapid, and intensifying – IPCC," 9th August 2021. [Available at: https://www.ipcc.ch/2021/08/09/ar6-wg1-20210809-pr/], [Last accessed: 10th August 2021].

— "August 9, 2021 Press Release: Climate change widespread, rapid, and intensifying, IPCC, [Available at: https://www.ipcc.ch/site/assets/uploads/2021/08/IPCC_WGI-AR6-Press-Release_en.pdf], [Last accessed: 10th August 2021].

Malayang, Ben S. III. "Keynote Address: Understanding Calamities and Disasters." Theological Consultation-Workshop on the Situation of Calamities and Disaster, Silliman University Divinity School, 18th March 2014.

Manahan, Job. "Dumaguete reclamation to devastate nearby protected areas, marine biodiversity conservation group." *ABS-CBN News*, 22nd July 2021. [Available at: https://news.abs-cbn.com/news/07/22/21/wwf-concerned-dumaguete-proposed-land-reclamation-project.]

Mounce, Bill. "ἐπίτροπος," in *Greek Dictionary*, [Available at: https://www.billmounce.com/greek-dictionary/epitropos], [Last accessed: 18th July 2021].

—— "οἰκοδομέω." *Greek Dictionary*, [Available at: https://www.billmounce.com/greek-dictionary/oikodomeo], [Last accessed: 25th July 2021].

—— "οἰκουμένη." In *Greek Dictionary*, [Available at: https://www.billmounce.com/greek-dictionary/oikoumene], [Last accessed 26th June 2021].

—— "Φθείρω." *Greek Dictionary*, [Available at: https://www.billmounce.com/greek-dictionary/phtheiro], [Last accessed: 25th July 2021].

Northcott, Michael S. *A Moral Climate: the ethics of global warming*. Maryknoll, NY: Orbis, 2007.

O'Grady, Cathleen. "Climate change 'unequivocal' and 'unprecedented,' says new U.N. report," *Science*, 9th August 2021, [Available at: https://www.sciencemag.org/news/2021/08/climate-change-unequivocal-and-unprecedented-says-new-un-report], [Last accessed: 28th January 2022].

Russel, Letty M. "Signs of Healing and Justice: A Bible Study." In Letty M. Russel and J. Shannon Clarkson, Eds. *Women's Ways of Being Church*. Geneva: World Council of Churches, 2005.

Sarao, Zakarian. "Groups urge gov't to stop 'dump-and-fill' reclamation projects." *Inquirer.Net*, [Available at: https://newsinfo.inquirer.net/1468715/cso-collective-calls-on-national-govt-to-stop-approval-of-dumpfill-reclamation-projects], [Last accessed: 6th July 2021].

Subramanian, Meera. "Humans versus Earth: the quest to define the Anthropocene." *Nature* 6th August 2019; correction 2nd October 2019, [Available at: https://www.nature.com/articles/d41586-019-02381-2], [Last accessed: 2nd August 2021].

Sungkit, Telesforo Jr. "I Higaonon." In *Cordite Poetry Review*, [Available at: http://cordite.org.au/poetry/philippines/i-higaonon/], [Last accessed: 14th August 2021].

White, Lynn T. Jr. "The Historical Roots of our Ecologic Crisis." In *Science* 155 (1967) 1203-207. Reprinted in Mary Heather MacKinnon and Moni McIntyre, Eds., *Readings in Ecology and Feminist Theology*. Kansas City, KS: Sheed and Ward, 1995.

Von Rad, Gerhard. *Genesis: A Commentary, The Old Testament Library*. Philadelphia, PA: The Westminster Press, 1972.

13. THE SIGNIFICANCE OF LAUDATO SI' FOR ASIAN CHURCHES WITH SPECIAL REFERENCE TO THE "LAUDATO SI' YEAR" AND "ACTION PLATFORM"

Joshtrom Isaac Kureethadam SDB[1]

Laudato Si': A Paradigm Shift in Creation Care

Laudato Si' is widely recognised as "the most important environmental text of the twenty-first century."[2] As an article published in the prestigious scientific journal *Biological Conservation* in 2019 acknowledged, "after decades of declining interest in the environment, *Laudato Si'* may be catalysing societal transformation."[3] The encyclical has had a great impact on the collective imagination of the world precisely for the fact that it captured the dramatic urgency of the historical moment we are living in, namely, the threat to our very common home. As Pope Francis highlighted in the encyclical, "we need only take a frank look at the facts to see that our common home is falling into serious disrepair" (*Laudato Si'*, 61) and we may be condemning future generations to a home in ruins.

The paradigm shift brought about by *Laudato Si'* is most evident in the new language of "*integral ecology*" provided by Pope Francis. According to Pope Francis, "human life is grounded in three fundamental and closely intertwined relationships: with God, with our neighbour and with the earth itself" (*Laudato Si'*, 66). Our relationship with God and our neighbour inherently includes our relationship with mother Earth. *Laudato* Si' has highlighted in a very striking way "the cry of the earth and the cry of the poor". As the Pope writes, "a true ecological approach *always* becomes a social approach; it must integrate questions of justice in debates on the environment, so as to hear *both cry of the earth and the cry of the poor*" (*Laudato Si'*, 49).

Laudato Si' also fills a sort of theological lacuna that existed in the ecological discourse until very recently. Pope Francis affirms that the ecological crisis is not only about the collapse of the planet's ecosystems and biochemical cycles with a profound impact on human populations, especially on the poor, but is also ultimately a theological issue. Pope Francis offers a profoundly positive vision of the natural world, speaking of the "gospel" of creation, which is the title of the second chapter of the encyclical. The Pope cites his predecessor, Pope John Paul II, to remind Christians to "realise that their responsibility within creation, and their duty towards nature and the Creator, are an essential part of their faith".[4] (*Laudato Si'*, 64)

Pope Francis' invitation in *Laudato Si'* to listen to "the cry of the earth and of the poor" and to perceive the natural world as the "gospel of creation" has had a unique impact on the Asian Churches that continue to struggle in truly undergoing "the double baptism of Asia's poverty and religiosity" – to use an oft-quoted expression from the late Asian theologian Aloysius Pieris.

In the present article, I shall seek to highlight how Pope Francis' invitation to be attentive to "the cry of the earth and of the poor" is particularly relevant for the Asian context. I shall also reflect on the significance

---

[1] Joshtrom Isaac Kureethadam is Co-ordinator of the "Ecology and Creation" Sector in the Vatican Dicastery for Promoting Integral Human Development. He is also Chair of Philosophy of Science and Director of the Institute of Social and Political Sciences in the Faculty of the Salesian Pontifical University in Rome. He is also a member of the religious order of the Salesians of Don Bosco (SDB).

[2] Dale Jamieson, "Why Laudato Si' Matters," *Environment: Science and Policy for Sustainable Development* 57/6 (2015), 19.

[3] Malcom L. McCallum, "Global country-by-country response of public interest in the environment to the papal encyclical, *Laudato Si'*", *Biological Conservation* 235 (2019), 209.

[4] Pope John Paul II, *Message for the 1990 World Day of Peace*, 15: *AAS* 82 (1990), 156.

of the Laudato Si' Special Anniversary Year (2020/21) that was announced by Pope Francis to mark the fifth anniversary of the encyclical. It was indeed a moment of grace that found a special echo in the spiritually fertile land of Asia, the pantheon of the world's great religions. I will conclude by reflecting on the *Laudato Si' Action Platform* that was launched by Pope Francis at the close of the *Laudato Si' Year* and briefly articulate the promises and challenges it holds for the Christian communities in Asia. The Holy Spirit is indeed stirring faith communities to mobilise and act to renew the face of the Earth, in the current era of planetary emergency.

Listening to the Cry of the Earth and Cry of the Poor

Laudato Si', as Pope Francis himself has pointed out several times, is not a fashionable "green" text. It is a genuinely "social" encyclical that seeks to address the intimately linked cry of the earth and of the poor.

The cry of the earth continues to ring loudly in the multiple manifestations of the contemporary ecological crisis: droughts, floods and hurricanes, destruction of life-sustaining ecosystems and unprecedented levels of biodiversity loss, pollution of the land, atmosphere and water bodies, water scarcity, deforestation, and a thousand other ways that expose the travail and agony of Mother Earth. From the melting ice caps in the Arctic to the raging wildfires in the Amazon, from extreme weather patterns around the world to losing the biodiversity that sustains the very fabric of life, the multiple "cracks in the planet that we inhabit" (*Laudato Si'*, 163), are too evident and detrimental to be ignored any longer.

The poor are wailing too. Vulnerable communities around the world are currently the first and most disproportionately affected victims of ecological degradation. Citing from the pastoral letter of the Bolivian Bishops, he writes: "Both everyday experience and scientific research show that the gravest effects of all attacks on the environment are suffered by the poorest"[5] (*Laudato Si'*, 48). The Pope also decries the fact that on the global arena "there is little in the way of clear awareness of problems which especially affect the excluded" (*Laudato Si'*, 49). The poor are conveniently forgotten or ignored at the High Table of world affairs. Yet, as the Pope points out, "they are the majority of the planet's population, billions of people" (*Laudato Si'*, 49).

Integral ecology is about communal listening to both the groaning of the planet and of the poor. As Pope Francis notes in *Laudato Si'*, "the deterioration of the environment and of society affects the most vulnerable people on the planet" (*Laudato Si'*, 48). It is significant that while outlining the important and recurring themes of the encyclical in the introduction (*Laudato Si'*, 16), Pope Francis enumerates "the intimate relationship between the poor and the fragility of the planet" as the very first among them. Poignantly, such a concern is mentioned also in the closing paragraph of the encyclical, as we read in the concluding prayer: "the poor and the earth are crying out" (*Laudato Si'*, 240). The prominence awarded to this question is not just casual. The concern for the poor – and as the Pope mentions "the earth herself, burdened and laid waste, is among the most abandoned and maltreated of our poor" (*Laudato Si'*, 2) – is at the heart of the encyclical, and as it is evident by now, at the heart of Pope Francis' own personal vision and universal mission.

The current COVID-19 emergency has greatly amplified the cry of the earth and of the poor. The pandemic has revealed a fundamental truth that we have ignored for too long, namely, that we cannot be healthy unless our relationships with the planet and its ecosystems are healthy. Human health and planetary health are intimately linked. As Pope Francis reminded us in Laudato Si', we need to realise that we, "human beings are not completely autonomous" (*Laudato Si'*, 105). "We cannot interfere in one area of the ecosystem without paying due attention to the consequences of such interference in other areas" (*Laudato Si'*, 131). COVID-19, and other deadly zoonotic viruses of the recent past, are a clarion call to humanity to

[5] Bolivian Bishops' Conference, Pastoral Letter on the Environment and Human Development in Bolivia *El universo, don de Dios para la vida* (23rd March 2012), 17.

realise that we humans cannot exist and flourish if we destroy the very ecosystems that sustain us and the whole fabric of life.

The coronavirus emergency also made clear how, as in every crisis, the poor are the hardest hit. The COVID-19 emergency is turning out to be the worst global crisis since the Second World War. It is estimated that the economic fallout from the global pandemic could increase global poverty by as much as half a billion people – equivalent to 8% of human population. It would literally mean reversing a decade of global progress made on poverty reduction. Global poverty could increase for the first time since 1990, thereby posing a significant challenge to the UN Sustainable Development Goal of ending poverty by 2030. It is clear that while all of humanity will be affected by the current coronavirus emergency, it will hit the poor hardest.

> This virus affects us all, even princes and film stars. But the equality ends there. By exploiting the extreme inequalities between rich and poor people, rich and poor nations and between women and men, unchecked this crisis will cause immense suffering.[6]

The cry of the poor has been amplified particularly in Asia in the wake of the COVID-19 emergency. Who can forget, for example, what happened in India shortly after the first wave of infections? It was literally a "way of the Cross" for thousands of migrant brothers and sisters who staggered along highways, clasping tightly not only to their meagre possessions but also to their children, under the scorching summer sun, thirsty and hungry, as they attempted to get back to the safety of their native villages thousands of kilometres away. These brothers and sisters epitomised the poor and vulnerable, considered as mere labour within an economic system that plunders the planet and the bodies of people, the hapless victims of the throw-away culture that Pope Francis has vehemently denounced time and again.

The "cry of the earth and of the poor", epitomised in *Laudato Si'* and amplified in the COVID-19 pandemic, is painfully heard across Asia. The impacts of climate change through extreme climate events and the loss of biodiversity are particularly relevant for Asia. Many communities in Asia are already living through the climate emergency as typhoons, floods, droughts, landslides, and extreme weather events happen with alarming frequency and growing intensity. Asia, home to more than 60 percent of the global population, hosts some of the countries and regions most vulnerable to the climate crisis. Six of the ten nations at highest long-term risk are in South and Southeast Asia, regularly prone to impacts such as strong tropical cyclones and droughts. Billions of people living in cities and fishing communities along the coasts are exposed to sea level rise, flooding from extreme rainfall, and storm surges. Destructive activities such as mining, deforestation, plastic pollution, and illegal wildlife trade have only hastened the occurrence of these events and worsened their impacts.

The Laudato Si' Special Anniversary Year

Pope Francis is a man of surprises. On 24th May 2020, on the fifth anniversary of the encyclical, and as many nations around the world were being submerged by the early waves of the deadly pandemic, Pope Francis went on to announce a *Special Laudato Si' Anniversary Year*.

Why a special Laudato Si' Anniversary Year just five years after its publication? It has never happened with any other papal encyclical. A clue can be found in the very words of Pope Francis when he announced the anniversary year: "today is the fifth anniversary of the Encyclical *Laudato Si'*, with which we sought to call attention to the cry of the Earth and of the poor". He went on to invite "all persons of good will" to

[6] Oxfam – 9th April 2020.

celebrate the Special Anniversary Year running from 24th May 2020 to 24th May 2021 and "take care of our common home and our more fragile brothers and sisters."[7]

The Laudato Si' Special Anniversary Year was an invitation to listen and respond to the cries of the Earth and of the poor which have only gotten louder and more heart-wrenching since the publication of the encyclical.

The Laudato Si' Special Anniversary Year was in response to a third cry as well. To the cry of the Earth and of the poor, another cry has been joined in recent years, namely the anguished wail of our children and future generations. Pope Francis asks in *Laudato Si'*, "What kind of world do we want to leave to those who come after us, to children who are now growing up?" (*Laudato Si'*, 160). During the last few years, we have heard our own children reversing the question back to us and telling us very clearly that we have no right to steal their future. We have seen children taking to the streets around the world, in large and growing numbers, giving vent to their frustration about our apathy and inaction.

The coming decade is indeed crucial. We have been served a last call! We are the last generation that could possibly act in order to avoid the crossing of dire tipping points and avoid irreversible damage to our common home.

The Laudato Si' Special Anniversary Year announced by Pope Francis came as a ray of hope in the gloomy situation as presented above. As always, Pope Francis was moved by the deep faith that the Holy Spirit offers us a time of grace (*kairos*) in a moment of deep crises – ecological, social and economic, compounded with the health, migrant and food security crises. The Pope wanted the Special Laudato Si' Anniversary Year and the ensuing decade to be a time of grace, a true *kairos*, a decisive turning point for humanity to come together and act to save our common home before it is too late.

By announcing the Laudato Si' Special Anniversary Year, Pope Francis was auguring a "Jubilee for the Earth" which providentially was the theme chosen by the ecumenical steering board of the Season of Creation for 2020.[8] The Laudato Si' Year was to be a blessed and prolonged "Sabbath" period to heal and recover after centuries of abuse, exploitation and unfettered collective market greed to the detriment of the poor and the planet. It was a time to lift up the voice of creation and of our vulnerable brothers and sisters, our indigenous communities in particular, whose integral perspective of life is central to the collective journey ahead. It was an invitation to undergo a truly personal and communitarian "ecological conversion" translated into concrete actions to protect our common home and the most vulnerable among us.

The Special Anniversary Year began with the Laudato Si' Week (16th-24th May 2020) with hundreds of events – mostly webinars and online side events given the lockdown in many countries – and with thousands of participants. The Churches in Asia were most generous in responding to Pope Francis' invitation to celebrate the Laudato Si' Year. The Federation of Asian Bishops Conference organised a very well-attended webinar to mark the inauguration of the Laudato Si' Special Anniversary Year for Asia. Numerous initiatives took place during the Laudato Si' Year in Christian communities across Asia. There are be too many to enumerate here so we may mention only a handful.

Immediately after the announcement of the Laudato Si' Year, the Church in Bangladesh launched a campaign to plant 400,000 trees – an approximate representation of the population of Catholics in the country based on a "one Catholic one tree" principle – in an audacious initiative to celebrate the fifth anniversary of the encyclical. As expressed by Cardinal Patrick D'Rozario, Archbishop of Dhaka, the initiative was "to help the faithful strengthen their relationship with the creator, creation, and humankind."

[7] Pope Francis, *Regina Caeli,* 24th May 2020 The Vatican, [Available at: https://www.vatican.va/content/francesco/en/angelus/2020/documents/papa-francesco_regina-coeli_20200524.html], [Last accessed: 3rd February 2022].

[8] For access to the excellent ecumenical guide that was produced for the 2020 Season of Creation on the theme "Jubilee for the Earth" see: "Jubilee for the Earth Season of Creation 2020 Celebration Guide", *WCC* [Available at: https://www.oikoumene.org/sites/default/files/Document/SOC%202020%20Final%20Jubilee%20for%20the%20Earth.pdf], [Last accessed: 3rd February 2022].

The tree-planting drive was led by the eight Catholic dioceses in Bangladesh in collaboration with the Bangladesh Catholic Student Movement (BCSM), as well as the United Forum of Churches, with its 200,000 Christians of other non-Catholic denominations. In the end, nearly a million trees were planted during the Laudato Si' Year – double the original target! – and the initiative is bound to continue in a land where trees have been destroyed due to erosion, cyclones and deforestation.[9]

Another Asian country that responded with great enthusiasm to Pope Francis' invitation to celebrate the Laudato Si' Special Anniversary Year was the Philippines. Living Laudato Si' Philippines along with the Archdiocese of Manila and many others organised a special webinar on 24th May 2020 to mark the opening of the Laudato Si' Year.[10] Among the numerous initiatives undertaken by the Catholic Church in the Philippines was the blessing on 7th November 2020 of the "Laudato Si' Living Chapel" – the first of its kind in Asia. It is situated on a pilgrimage hill called Tagudtod sang Pangamuyo (Hill of Prayer), with a panoramic view of rice paddies and the majestic Mount Guiting-Guiting Natural Park in the background. The open-air Living Chapel was set up by the faithful community of Santo Niño Parish (Diocese of Romblon) in Sibuyan Island, under the leadership of Living Laudato Si' Philippines. Seven ecology ministers were solemnly commissioned in a ceremony to mark the inauguration of the Living Chapel who committed to become stewards of God's creation and take the message of Laudato Si' to each family in the parish.[11]

A third and final example from the hundreds of initiatives that were organised across Asia to celebrate the Laudato Si' Special Anniversary Year is from India. The communities of the Province of Hyderabad of the Salesians of Don Bosco – one of the largest Catholic religious orders which works mainly for the welfare of needy children and youth around the world – organised webinars during each of the months of the Laudato Si' Year. The first webinar of each month was to study and reflect on the content of the encyclical with the help of experts in the field, while the second webinar was praxis-oriented and highlighted concrete actions that could be done by communities to respond to the cry of the Earth and of the poor. Significantly, by the end of the Laudato Si' Year, all of the nearly forty religious communities in the province successfully managed to make the transition to solar energy in all their institutions![12]

Laudato Si' Action Platform: A People's Movement from Below

The most significant and longstanding fruit of the Laudato Si' Special Anniversary Year is the "Laudato Si' Action Platform" that was announced by Pope Francis on 25th May 2021 at the close of the Laudato Si' Year. Here are some excerpts from the video message of Pope Francis released during a special Press Conference at the Vatican on that day:

> We have a great responsibility, especially with regard to future generations. [...] I therefore renew my appeal: let us take care of our mother Earth; let us overcome the temptation of selfishness that makes us predators of resources; let us cultivate respect for the gifts of the Earth and of creation; let us inaugurate a lifestyle and a

---

[9] Bangladesh Laudato si' drive: "One Catholic One Tree" *Vatican News*, [Available at: https://www.vaticannews.va/en/church/news/2021-03/bangladesh-laudato-si-tree-planting-catholic.html], [Last accessed: 3rd February 2022].

[10] John Leo Algo, "Laudato Si' Goals Launched for Total Sustainability" 25th May 2020, *Living Laudato Si' Philippines* [Available at: https://livinglaudatosi.org.ph/laudato-si-goals-launched-for-total-sustainability/], [Last accessed: 3rd February 2022].

[11] Living Laudato Si' Philippines, "First 'Living Chapel' In Asia Rises In Romblon" 7th November 2022, *Living Laudato Si' Philippines*, [Available at: https://livinglaudatosi.org.ph/first-living-chapel-in-asia-rises-in-romblon/], [Last accessed: 3rd February 2022].

[12] Father Baly Yerramaneni, "Hyderabad Salesians Host 1st Laudato Si' Province Webinar", 11th July 2020, *Don Bosco India*, [Available at: https://www.donboscoindia.com/english/bis/default_ms.php?proid=5.0&newsid=9423], [Last accessed: 3rd February 2022].

> society that is finally eco-sustainable: we have the opportunity to prepare a better tomorrow for all. From God's hands we have received a garden, we cannot leave a desert to our children.
>
> Today I am pleased to announce that the *Laudato Si'* Year will result in a concrete action project, the *Laudato Si'* Action Platform, a seven-year journey that will see our communities committed in different ways to becoming totally sustainable, in the spirit of integral ecology.[13]

The Laudato Si' Action Platform is deeply inspired by the integral ecological vision of Laudato Si'. This is evident especially in the seven sectors that constitute the platform, the seven Laudato Si' Goals that inspire its journey, and the participatory Synodal path envisioned for its realisation. The entire process is ultimately motivated by a sense of urgency articulated in the seven-year journey and a movement that will expand exponentially during this critical decade.

Firstly, the Laudato Si' Action Platform embraces Pope Francis' vision of Earth as our common home and is inspired by the conviction that we need each and every segment of the common household to heal and rebuild our planetary abode. The Platform therefore invites the following sectors to undertake the journey of total sustainability: *Families and Individuals*; *Faith Communities* (Parishes, Dioceses, Basic Ecclesial Communities, etc.); *Educational Institutions* (Schools, Colleges, Universities, Seminaries, etc.); *Health and Healing* (Hospitals, Clinics, Care Centres, etc.); *Economy* (Businesses, Farms, Labour Unions, etc.); *Groups* (Movements, Organisations, Communication Centres, etc.); *Religious Orders* (Communities, Provinces, Orders, etc.)

Secondly, the Multi-Year Laudato Si' Action Platform is framed across seven "*Laudato Si' Goals*" – LSGs – (resembling the UN SDGs), which will serve as parameters for integral ecology in the spirit of *Laudato Si'*. The holistic goals reflect the gamut of Catholic social teaching, and each lists examples of various benchmarks to accomplish.

1. *The Response to the Cry of the Earth* is a call to protect our common home for the wellbeing of all, as we equitably address the climate crisis, biodiversity loss, and ecological sustainability. Actions could include the adoption of renewable energies and energy sufficiency measures, achieving carbon neutrality, protecting biodiversity, promoting sustainable agriculture, and guaranteeing access to clean water for all.
2. *The Response to the Cry of the Poor* is a call to promote ecojustice, aware that we are called to defend human life from conception to death, and all forms of life on Earth. Actions could include projects to promote solidarity, with special attention given to vulnerable groups such as indigenous communities, refugees, migrants, and children at risk, analysis and improvement of social systems, and social service programmes.
3. *Ecological Economics* acknowledges that the economy is a subsystem of human society, which itself is embedded within the biosphere – our common home. Actions could include sustainable production and consumption, ethical investments, divestment from fossil fuels and any activity harmful to the planet and the people, supporting circular economies, and prioritising care labour and protecting the dignity of workers.
4. *The Adoption of Sustainable Lifestyles* is grounded in the idea of sufficiency, and promoting sobriety in the use of resources and energy. Actions could include reducing waste and recycling, adopting sustainable dietary habits (opting for a more plant-based diet and reducing meat consumption), greater use of public transport, active mobility (walking, cycling), and avoiding single-use items (e.g. plastic, etc.).

---

[13] "Video Message of the Holy Father to mark the launch of the 'Laudato Si' Action Platform" 25th May 2021, *Vatican* [Available at: https://www.vatican.va/content/francesco/en/messages/pont-messages/2021/documents/papa-francesco_20210525_videomessaggio-laudatosi.html], [Last accessed: 3rd February 2022].

5. *Ecological Education* is about re-thinking and re-designing curricular and institutional reform in the spirit of integral ecology in order to foster ecological awareness and transformative action. Actions could include ensuring equitable access to education for all and promoting human rights, fostering Laudato Si' themes within the community, encouraging ecological leadership (students, teachers), and ecological restoration activities.
6. *Ecological Spirituality* springs from a profound ecological conversion and helps us to "discover God in all things", both in the beauty of creation and in the sighs of the sick and the groans of the afflicted, aware that the life of the spirit is not dissociated from worldly realities. Actions could include promoting creation-based liturgical celebrations, developing ecological catechesis, retreats and formation programmes, etc.
7. *Community Resilience and Empowerment* envisage a synodal journey of community engagement and participatory action at various levels. Actions could include promoting advocacy and developing people's campaigns, encouraging rootedness and a sense of belonging in local communities and neighbourhood ecosystems.

The Laudato Si' Action Platform Goals are closely entwined with the healing, restoration and regeneration of Asia, especially in the context of Community Resilience because it is the repair and building of relational tissue and the ecological framework of life that is the heart of being Church. To those most vulnerable to climate impacts, resilience is paramount. Just focusing on mitigation alone will not address how people will live their lives while coping with the impacts of global warming that are already happening and worsening day by day.

Thirdly, the Laudato Si' Action Platform commits itself to walk the "Synodal" path. The precarious state of our common home calls for and unified responses at all levels – local, regional, national and international. The Action Platform is being realised through partnerships at various levels. There is a Steering Board coordinating the journey at the international level along with Working Groups for each of the seven actors and involving hundreds of partners across the world. Analogously Steering Boards and Working Groups are emerging at the continental, national and regional levels. Asia was the first continent to set its own Steering Board and Working Groups to assist in the roll-out of the Laudato Si' Action Platform. The Platform is indeed giving rise to "a peoples' movement" – an alliance of all people of good will – for the care of our common home. As Pope Francis reminds us in Laudato Si', "All of us can cooperate as instruments of God for the care of creation, each according to his or her own culture, experience, involvements and talents" (*Laudato Si'*, 14). We need an alliance of people from churches, faith communities, NGOs and governments involved in ecological, economic, educational and political issues, and civil society, in general.

Fourthly, moved by the urgency to act in the current of planetary emergency, the Laudato Si' Action Platform is envisaged as an intense seven-year journey towards total sustainability in the spirit of integral ecology. Pope Francis opened the enrolment phase of the first cohort of communities and movements joining the Laudato Si' Action Platform on 14th November 2021 – the World Day of the Poor. The choice of the day was itself a powerful message, especially in the wake of 26th Conference of Parties in Glasgow (COP26), that the transformation of the world will begin from below and the peripheries and will be led by simple and ordinary people. It is envisaged that in 2022, a new group, hopefully double the number of the previous group, will begin their 7-year journey, and so on. This will go on for each of the coming years of the current decade. In this way, it is hoped that we arrive at the "*critical mass*" needed for radical *societal transformation* invoked by Pope Francis in *Laudato Si'*.

The Spirit Calling the Churches to Renew the Face of the Earth

It is significant that the encyclical *Laudato Si'* was issued on the day of the Solemnity of Pentecost in 2015, a day in which Christians all over the world commemorate the work of the Spirit of God in creation and in redemption. As generations of believers have prayed down the centuries, we too can pray today: "Send forth your Spirit O Lord and renew the face of the earth" (Ps. 104:30).

The renewal of Earth, our common home, is the mission to which the Holy Spirit is calling our Churches today. It is encouraging to see how the Spirit is indeed raising individuals and communities to respond to the epochal challenge that will determine the very fate of human civilisation and the flourishing of the rest of the biotic community. I would like to conclude with the words of Pope Francis.

> We are aware that the cries of the earth and of the poor have become even louder and more painful in recent years. At the same time, we also witness how the Holy Spirit is inspiring individuals and communities around the world to come together to rebuild our common home and defend the most vulnerable in our midst. We see the gradual emergence of a great mobilisation of people from below and from the peripheries who are generously working for the protection of the land and of the poor. [...]
>
> We rejoice too that faith communities are coming together to create a more just, peaceful and sustainable world. [...] Let us all rejoice that our loving Creator sustains our humble efforts to care for the earth, which is also God's home where his Word "became flesh and lived among us" (Jn. 1:14) and which is constantly being renewed by the outpouring of the Holy Spirit.

Suggestions for Further Reading

Bolivian Bishops' Conference, "Pastoral Letter on the Environment and Human Development in Bolivia" *El universo, don de Dios para la vida,* 23rd March 2012), 17.

Jamieson, Dale. "Why Laudato Si' Matters," *Environment: Science and Policy for Sustainable Development* 57(6), (2015), 19.

McCallum, Malcolm L. "Global country-by-country response of public interest in the environment to the papal encyclical, *Laudato Si'*", *Biological Conservation* 235 (2019), 209.

Pope John Paul II, *Message for the 1990 World Day of Peace*, 15: *AAS* 82 (1990), 156.

14. Environmental Stewardship and Creation Care as a Key Concern of the Global Lausanne Movement: Biblical Foundations, Key Initiatives and Future Perspectives

Las Newman, Ed Brown and Dave Bookless[1]

Introduction

The concept of *Integral Mission* has been part of the DNA of the Lausanne Movement since its founding in 1974. It was to be expected that an understanding of the gospel as being *both* evangelistic proclamation *and* social involvement[2] would expand to include creation care as well. Thus, Lausanne's Theology Working Group, in preparing for the Third Lausanne Congress which then was held in Cape Town, South Africa, in October 2010 included this statement in their advance report:

> Lausanne 1974 was a landmark for 20th century evangelicals in binding together the personal and the social dimension of the gospel in our understanding of holistic mission in relation to human need. Cape Town 2010 needs to call evangelicals to recognise afresh the biblical affirmation of God's redemptive purpose for creation itself. Integral mission means discerning, proclaiming, and living out, the biblical truth that the gospel is God's good news, through the cross and resurrection of Jesus Christ, for persons, and for society, and for creation. All three are broken and suffering because of sin; all three are included in the redeeming love and mission of God; all three must be part of the comprehensive mission of God's people.[3]

A significant outcome of the Cape Town Congress was the birth of the Lausanne Creation Care Network. It was a new initiative for the Evangelical Church and it emerged from one of the Congress's multiplex sessions, which boldly focused on the issue of "Creation Care and the Gospel". Attending the Congress and leading the charge was Sir John Houghton, co-chair of the Nobel Peace Prize-winning UN Inter-Governmental Panel on Climate Change (IPCC)'s Scientific Assessment Working Group. John Houghton was a renowned international atmospheric scientist, environmental advocate, and campaigner for creation care. The Congress Statement, *The Cape Town Commitment: Confession of Faith and Call to Action* included an emphatic assertion that "*creation care is a Gospel issue under the Lordship of Christ*". It further stated that "*urgent prophetic action is required*".[4]

As a follow-up to that plea at the Congress, the first global post-Congress consultation of the Lausanne Movement was held in the climate vulnerable region of the Caribbean in 2012. Against the background of a rising concern for the consequences of a global ecological crisis, the consultation sought to examine the

---

[1] Dr Las Newman is Lausanne Global Associate Director for Regions and Regional Director for the Caribbean. He organised and hosted the first Lausanne Global Consultation on Creation Care and the Gospel in Jamaica in 2012. He used to serve as president of the Caribbean Graduate School of Theology. Rev. Ed Brown is a Lausanne catalyst for creation care and the director and CEO of Care of Creation, guiding its work in the US and Tanzania. He grew up in Pakistan. Rev. Dr Dave Bookless is Director of Theology for A Rocha International and co-lead of the global Lausanne / World Evangelical Alliance Creation Care Network. He is also on the Church of England's Environment Working Group and the global Season of Creation Steering Committee. He was born and raised in India and has a deep appreciation for Indian culture and Indian Christianity.

[2] Melba Maggay, *Integral Mission: Biblical Foundations*, M-Series (Cape Town: Micah Global, 2007): 12.

[3] Thomas Schirrmacher, Peter Harris, and Christopher J. H Wright, "The Whole World: Part III of The Whole Gospel, The Whole Church, The Whole World", *The Whole Gospel, The Whole Church, The Whole World* (Lausanne Theological Working Group, with the WEA Theological Commissions, July 2010).

[4] See: *CTC* I-7-A; in Lausanne Movement, *The Cape Town Commitment*, [Available at: https://lausanne.org/content/ctc/ctcommitment#p1-7-A], [Last accessed: 30th March 2022].

theme and develop an action plan around it. This consultation produced a number of important initiatives, which are outlined below, including the Jamaica Call to Action.[5]

The global ecological crisis was manifesting itself with verifiable evidence of the destructive abuses of the urban, rural, industrial, marine, natural, and the built environment on every continent. In addition, advocacy groups and the global environmental and scientific community had become stronger in alerting the world to the increasing evidence of the impact of global warming on habitats, on land and oceanic environments, on major biodiversity loss and on endangerment of species, through human-induced climate change. Environmental impacts from such actions as deforestation, air pollution, and extreme weather events saw declines in agricultural outputs, threats to global food security, threats to global peace and security through cross-border resource conflicts, increase in climate refugees, increase in energy demands, consumption and insecurity. These strengthened the global concern.

On 18th June 2015, Pope Francis courageously pronounced his second encyclical – *Laudato Si'*: (*Praise Be to You*), *On Care For Our Common Home.* In this landmark document for the church and the world, Pope Francis made a direct link between the global environmental crisis and human care of God's creation. In that same year, December 2015, at the highly anticipated UN Climate Summit in Paris, the Small Island States (SIDS) of the Caribbean and the South Pacific (Oceania) campaigned for the world community to set an ambitious carbon emissions target of no more than "1.5 to Stay Alive". Paris 2015 was a watershed moment as 195 nations signed this Accord. The Evangelical community was well represented in Paris, with a hub and collaborative events including A Rocha International, Tearfund and CCOP (the Christian Climate Observers Program).

For an Evangelical Movement, the Jamaica Consultation on Creation Care and the Gospel in 2012 was very collaborative in design, with co-sponsors as partners. They included Tearfund, World Vision, A Rocha International, Eden Vigil, and the International Fellowship of Evangelical Students. As general collaboration continued, in 2015, the Lausanne Creation Care Network became The Lausanne/WEA Creation Care Network (LWCCN) when the World Evangelical Alliance (WEA) Creation Care Task Force formally joined the Network.[6]

The Lausanne/WEA Creation Care Network is led on the Lausanne side by Creation Care Catalysts Rev. Ed Brown (Creation Care Inc.), Rev. Dr Dave Bookless (A Rocha International), and Jasmine Kwong (OMF International), and on the WEA side by Dr Chris Elisara (WEA Creation Care Task Force) and Matthias Boehning (WEA Sustainability Center).

Reactions

Reactions to expressions of these concerns were swift and vocal. They came from climate sceptics, climate deniers, and politically motivated oppositional groups, including from the Church. Today, a decade later, faced with overwhelming scientific evidence and the lived experiences of catastrophic environmental disasters in the global north, south, east and west, due to climate change, declarations of "climate emergency" and cries of "Code Red for humanity" have emerged from governments, corporate business, and local communities. In 2021, the United Nations Climate Summit, COP 26, in Glasgow, Scotland, heard strident pleas and impressed upon the world community the urgent need to take drastic multi-level steps to avert impending catastrophic consequences of the global environmental crisis, and that inaction is not an option. The Lausanne/WEA Creation Care Network was present at COP 26 and shared in that call.

---

[5] See Lausanne Movement, "Creation Care and the Gospel: Jamaica Call to Action", St. Ann, Jamaica, November 2012, [Available at: https://lausanne.org/content/statement/creation-care-call-to-action], [Last accessed: 30th March 2022].

[6] See Lausanne/WEA Creation Care Network Website [Available at: http://lwccn.com/], [Last accessed: 30th March 2022].

Key Initiatives of the Lausanne/WEA Network on Creation Care (LWCCN)

A. Jamaica Consultation and Call to Action (2012)

The global consultation organised by the **LWCCN** in 2012 included theologians, church leaders, scientists, creation care practitioners, social advocates, and media practitioners, fifty-seven men and women from twenty-six countries from the Caribbean, Africa, Asia, Latin America, Oceania, North America, and Europe. They represented countries as diverse as Argentina, Bangladesh, Benin, the United Kingdom, Kenya, Papua New Guinea, Uganda, Singapore, Trinidad and Tobago, the USA and Canada. They met in Jamaica, from 29th October-2nd November, under the auspices of the Lausanne Movement, working in close collaboration with the World Evangelical Alliance. Needless to say, they were hosted by a country and region known for outstanding natural beauty and tropical radiance. The participants enjoyed, celebrated, and reflected on the wonder of God's good creation from biblical passages, including Genesis 1-3, Psalm 8, and Romans 8. These reflections informed prayers, discussions, and deliberations structured around the themes of **God's Word** (*Bible Reading*)**, God's World** *(Science)*, and **God's Work** *(Church and Mission)*. As it happened, the consultation convened on the eve of Hurricane Sandy, one of the deadliest hurricanes of the annual Atlantic hurricane seasons that devastated the Caribbean and the east coast of the United States. The destruction and loss of life was a startling reminder of the urgency, timeliness, and importance of the subject matter of the Consultation.

1. Call to Action:

The Consultation's statement, now known as The Jamaica Call to Action, was based on two primary convictions:

> Creation Care is indeed a "gospel issue" within the doctrine of the "Lordship of Christ".
>
> Humanity is faced with a pressing, urgent, and far-reaching crisis that must be resolved in our generation with "urgent and prophetic ecological responsibility".[7]

Based on these two convictions, the Jamaica Statement called upon the whole church, in dependence on the Holy Spirit, to respond radically and faithfully to care for God's creation, demonstrating our belief and hope in the transforming power of Christ. The Jamaica Statement called on the Lausanne Movement, evangelical leaders, national evangelical organisations, and all local churches to respond urgently at the personal, community, national. and international levels. The 10-point statement specifically called for:

1. *A new commitment to a simple lifestyle*. Recognising that much of our crisis is due to billions of lives lived carelessly, we reaffirm the Lausanne commitment to simple lifestyle,[8] and call on the global evangelical community to take steps, personally and collectively, to live within the proper boundaries of God's good gift in creation, to engage further in its restoration and conservation, and to equitably share its bounty with each other.

2. *New and robust theological work*. In particular, we need guidance in four areas:

> An integrated theology of creation care that can engage seminaries, Bible colleges, and others to equip pastors to disciple their congregations.

---

[7] See: *CTC* I-7-A; in Lausanne Movement, *The Cape Town Commitment*, [Available at: https://lausanne.org/content/ctc/ctcommitment#p1-7-A], [Last accessed: 30th March 2022].

[8] See Lausanne Movement, "Lausanne Occasional Paper: An Evangelical Commitment to Simple Lifestyle", March 1980, *Lausanne Movement Website*, [Available at: https://lausanne.org/content/lop/lop-20], [Last accessed: 31st March 2022].

A theology that examines humanity's identity as both embedded in creation and yet possessing a special role toward creation.

A theology that challenges current prevailing economic ideologies in relation to our biblical stewardship of creation.

A theology of hope in Christ and his Second Coming that properly informs and inspires creation care.

3. *Leadership from the church in the Global South.* As the Global South represents those most affected in the current ecological crisis, it possesses a particular need to speak up, engage issues of creation care, and act upon them. We, the members of the Consultation, further request that the church of the Global South exercise leadership among us, helping to set the agenda for the advance of the gospel and the care of creation.

4. *Mobilisation of the whole church and engagement of all of society.* Mobilisation must occur at the congregational level and include those who are often overlooked, utilising the gifts of women, children, youth, and indigenous people as well as professionals and other resource people who possess experience and expertise. Engagement must be equally widespread, including formal, urgent and creative conversations with responsible leaders in government, business, civil society, and academia.

5. *Environmental missions among unreached people groups.* We participate in Lausanne's historic call to world evangelisation, and believe that environmental issues represent one of the greatest opportunities to demonstrate the love of Christ and plant churches among unreached and unengaged people groups in our generation.[9] We encourage the church to promote "environmental missions" as a new category within mission work (akin in function to medical missions).

6. *Radical action to confront climate change.* Affirming *The Cape Town Commitment's* declaration of the "serious and urgent challenge of climate change" which will "disproportionately affect those in poorer countries",[10] we call for action in radically reducing greenhouse gas emissions and building resilient communities. We understand these actions to be an application of the command to deny ourselves, take up the cross and follow Christ.

7. *Sustainable principles in food production.* In gratitude to God who provides sustenance, and flowing from our conviction to become excellent stewards of creation, we urge the application of environmentally and generationally sustainable principles in agriculture (field crops and livestock, fisheries and all other forms of food production), with particular attention to the use of methodologies such as conservation agriculture.

8. *An economy that works in harmony with God's creation.* We call for an approach to economic well-being and development, energy production, natural resource management (including mining and forestry), water management and use, transportation, health care, rural and urban design and living, and personal and corporate consumption patterns that maintain the ecological integrity of creation.

9. *Local expressions of creation care.* We commend such projects which preserve and enhance biodiversity, along with any action that might be characterised as the "small step" or the "symbolic act", to the worldwide church as ways to powerfully witness to Christ's lordship over all creation.

10. *Prophetic advocacy and healing reconciliation.* We call for individual Christians and the church as a whole to prophetically "speak the truth to power" through advocacy and legal action so that public policies and private practice may change to better promote the care of creation and better support devastated communities and habitats. Additionally, we call the church to "speak the peace of Christ" to communities

---

[9] (*CTC* II-D-1B) in Lausanne Movement, *The Cape Town Commitment*, [Available at: https://lausanne.org/content/ctc/ctcommitment#p2-IID-1-B], [Last accessed: 30th March 2022].
[10] (*CTC* II-B-6) in Lausanne Movement, *The Cape Town Commitment*, [Available at: https://lausanne.org/content/ctc/ctcommitment#p2-2-6], [Last accessed: 30th March 2022].

torn apart by environmental disputes, mobilising those who are skilled at conflict resolution, and maintaining our own convictions with humility.

2. Call to Prayer

Each of the calls to action rest upon an even more urgent call to prayer, intentional and fervent, soberly aware that this is a spiritual struggle. Prayer must begin with lamentation and repentance for our failure to care for God's creation and for our failure to lead in transformational change at a personal and corporate level. Having tasted of the grace and mercies of God in Christ Jesus, through the enabling work of the Holy Spirit, and with hope in the fullness of our redemption, we pray with confidence that the Triune God can and will heal our land for the Glory of his name and the flourishing of His Kingdom.

B. Other Outcomes

In addition to the *Jamaica Statement on Creation Care and Call to Action*[11] from the Consultation in 2012, the LWCCN has seen the following outcomes:

1. *Development of a global campaign* joined by other evangelical organisations as partners, including Latin Link (Latin America), OMF (East Asia), LEAD-SIL (South East Asia), and EFICOR (India). The Campaign ran from 2014 to 2020, when it was disrupted by COVID-19. In that time, the campaign reached 140 countries. It was comprised of regional/national consultations on Creation Care with agencies engaged in church mobilisation. These have been held in *East Africa (Kenya), West & Francophone Africa (Ghana), Southern Africa (South Africa), Caribbean (Trinidad and Tobago), East Asia (Taiwan), Western Europe (France), Latin America (Peru), North America (Boston/California), Oceania (Australia), South Asia (Nepal),* and *South East Asia (Philippines).*The regional/national consultations followed the same programme structure as in 2012: God's Word (*Bible Reading*), God's World *(Science*), and God's Work *(Church and Mission)* with local/regional scholars and practitioners.

2. *Publication of a major book* on *Creation Care and the Gospel: Reconsidering the Mission of the Church,*[12] published in 2016, containing essays from the Consultation, case studies from the Global South, and invited contribution from other reflective practitioners.

3. *Follow-up Summits* have been convened with environmental scientists and practitioners, theologians, media practitioners, and international agencies as partners.

4. *Participation in international multilateral environmental gatherings* (UN Climate Conferences, Habitat, Biodiversity, etc) has been encouraged.

C. What Does the Lausanne/WEA Network On Creation Care Look Like Today?

1. It is a Global Campaign for *Creation Care and the Gospel of Jesus Christ* that seeks to mobilise the Global Church towards environmental reflection and action.
2. It is a campaign that centres on an *Appeal,* a *Lament,* and *Advocacy.*
3. It collaborates in environmental advocacy from a Christian perspective and issued an *Evangelical Call to Action on Biodiversity*[13] prepared for the UN Summit on Biodiversity in September 2020.
4. It hosted a *Creation Care at the Crossroads Summit 2020: Revisiting the Jamaica Call to Action* 10th-12th November 2020. The event was co-sponsored by the ***Loka Initiative*** based at the University of Wisconsin – Madison, the ***Fetzer Institute,*** the ***Nelson Institute*** at the University of Wisconsin-Madison, ***Care of Creation***, Inc, and ***A Rocha International***.

[11] Lausanne Movement, "Creation Care and the Gospel: Jamaica Call to Action", St. Ann, Jamaica, November 2012, [Available at: https://lausanne.org/content/statement/creation-care-call-to-action], [Last accessed: 30th March 2022].
[12] Robert S. White and Colin Bell (eds), *Creation Care and the Gospel: Reconsidering the Mission of the Church* (North Shore, MA: Hendrickson, 2016).
[13] World Evangelical Alliance, "Faith Call to Action for Biodiversity", WEA Creation Care Task Force Website, [Available at: https://www.weacreationcare.org/faith-biodiversity-call-to-action], [Last accessed: 31st March 2022].

5. As the COVID-19 public health pandemic persisted, a virtual follow-up Summit on *Creation at the Crossroads 2.0: Sharing Our Stories* was followed up from 25th-27th May 2021.
6. It publishes a monthly blog and e-newsletter *The Pollinator*.[14]

D. Facing the Future:

1. As the Lausanne/WEA Network on Creation Care (LWCCN) continues its Global Campaign to 2023, its vision is to:
(a) focus on some of the major challenges and threats facing humanity as a result of environmental degradation,
(b) encourage and mobilise Christian action towards fundamental change in behaviour regarding the environment, and
(c) develop further insights into what the global church (and the Evangelical church in particular) have to offer in dealing with issues of environmental justice and sustainable development of the world community.
2. In developing local and regional Creation Care networks the LWCCN will continue its collaboration and partnership with others:
(a) to further faith in the Lord of creation, engagement with a robust theology of creation and the environment that includes care for the poor and the most vulnerable,
(b) to enhance a Christian Spirituality that informs liturgy and practice, and
(c) to nourish a Christian view of Stewardship that encourages responsible moral action in personal, corporate, and political life.

Suggestions for Further Reading

Bauckham, R. *Bible and Ecology: Recovering the Community of Creation*. London: DLT, 2010.

Bookless, D. "The Evolution of Evangelical Environmental Engagement 1990-2016". *Crucible* (April 2017): 38-53.

—. "Jesus is Lord … of all? Evangelical Perspectives on Earthcare", in K. J. Kaoma, Ed. *Creation Care in Christian Mission*. Oxford, Regnum Books, 2016: 105-120.

—. "Christian Mission and Environmental Issues: An Evangelical Reflection". *Mission Studies* 25 (2008): 1-16.

—. *Planetwise: Dare to Care for God's World*. Nottingham: IVP, 2008.

Brown, E. R. *Our Father's World: Mobilizing the Church to Care for Creation*. 3rd Edn. Cambridge, MA: Doorlight Publications, 2018.

Brunner, D. L., Jennifer L. Butler and A.J. Swoboda. *Introducing Evangelical Ecotheology: Foundations in history, theology, scripture and praxis*. Grand Rapids, MI, Baker Academic, 2014.

Daneel, I. "Earthkeeping in Missiological Perspective: An African Challenge". *Mission Studies* 13(1), (1996): 130-188.

Gnanakan, K. *The Whole Gospel of God*. Bangalore: Theological Book Trust, 2014.

—. *God's World: A Theology of the Environment*. London: SPCK, 1999.

Harris, P. *Lausanne Occasional Paper #65c: Towards a Missiology of Caring for Creation*. Lausanne. 2010. [Available at https://lausanne.org/content/lop/towards-a-missiology-of-caring-for-creation-lop-63-c], [Last accessed: 31st March 2022].

—. *Kingfisher's Fire: A Story of Hope for God's World*. Oxford: Monarch, 2008.

Hodos Institute. EcoHodos: ecotheology, mission, and leadership/ EcoHodos: экобогословие, миссия и лидерство. 2021. [In Russian only; available through Kinigi Online https://knigionline.com/catalog/knygy/bogosliv-ya/religiyna-filosofiya/ecohodos-kobogoslovye-myssyya-y-lyderstvo-sbornyk-statey/ or by emailing Hodos Institute (info@hodosinstitute.com)].

Maggay, Melba. *Integral Mission: Biblical Foundations*. Cape Town: Micah Global, 2007.

[14] See LWCCN's website: http://news.lwccn.com/.

Moo, J. and D. J. Moo. *Creation Care: A biblical Theology of the Natural World.* Grand Rapids, MI: Zondervan, 2018.

Padilla De Borst, R. "God's Earth and God's People: Relationships Restored." *Journal of Latin American Theology: Christian Reflections from the Latino South* 5(1), (2010): 6-17.

White, R. S. and C. Bell, Eds. *Creation Care and the Gospel: Reconsidering the Mission of the Church.* Peabody, MA: Hendrickson, 2016.

Yoder, L. and R. J. (Sam) Berry, Eds. *John Stott on Creation Care.* Nottingham: IVP, 2021.

15. A Biblical-Theological Basis for Ecology: Reading the Bible in the Perspective of Harmony between Earth and Humankind

Chong Hun Pae[1]

Introduction

The significance of ecological theology was made clear to the world, as COVID-19 appeared and greatly impacted Christian theology. It turned out that the direct cause of COVID-19 was nature's counterattack on humans' destruction of nature.[2] In order to save human beings from the tragedy caused by nature's counterattack, this era is in need of an ecological theology that seeks coexistence with nature, rather than the development and abuse of it. The important elements in ecological theology are God, man, and nature. What is necessary for sound biblical ecological theology is to solve the question of how to establish the relationship between human beings and nature. While it is widely acknowledged that traditional anthropocentric theology has thrown the ecology into crisis, there are various solutions. One solution suggests ending humans' abuse of nature, while still acknowledging the human domination of nature. Another one is to equate human beings with nature by disregarding the uniqueness of human beings.

This article proposes a balanced reading of the Bible as the story of man and earth to establish a biblical bio-theology. The story of human beings should acknowledge human beings' stewardship over nature while reflecting on humans' distorted domination of nature. The story of the earth should not disregard nature as irrelevant to God or as a sacred object on its own, but as a space to experience God's presence.[3]

The Ecological Crisis and Rediscovery of Ecological Theology

Lynn White, Jr.,[4] who tried to attribute the ecological crisis to Christianity, criticised Christianity in two ways as follows: the first concerns the status of nature in relation to God. Christianity rejected the animistic worldview that the spirit dwells in all things in nature. Although White attributed the ecological crisis to Christianity, he saw Francis of Assisi as a person who identified, nature and man as brotherly companions by his actions, not seeing nature as an object of destruction.[5] By equating humans with nature, White attempts to save nature by blocking the possibility of humans destroying nature. His preference for an

---

[1] Rev Dr Prof. PAE, Chong-hun is an Ordained Pastor of the Presbyterian Church of Korea; Old Testament Scholar with a PhD, from Graduate Theological Union, USA; Former Faculty member at Daejeon Theological University, Korea; Presently teaching Old Testament at the Presbyterian University & Theological Seminary, Korea Th.M, Princeton Theological Seminary, USA. His publications include: *Wisdom from the Heaven: Canonical Understanding on Proverbs, Ecclesiastes and Job. Theory and Practice of Canonical Hermeneutics to Revitalize Korean Churches.*

[2] Alexander J. B. Hampton (ed), *Pandemic, Ecology and Theology: Perspectives on COVID-19* (New York: Routledge, 2020).

[3] John Stott describes as follows: 1) We will avoid the deification of nature. 2) We must avoid the exploitation of nature. 3) The correct relationship between human beings and nature is that of cooperation with God. John Stott, "Foreword," in R. J. Berry (ed), *The Care of Creation: Focusing Concern and Action* (Leicester, England: Inter-Varsity Press, 2000), 8-9.

[4] L. White, Jr. "The Historical Roots of Our Ecological Crisis," *Science* 155, no. 3767 (1967), 1203-1207. Reprint, R. J. Berry (ed), *The Care of Creation: Focusing concern and action* (Leicester, England: Inter-Varsity Press, 2000), 31-49.

[5] White, "The Historical Roots of Our Ecological Crisis," 41.

animistic worldview led him to adopt a pantheistic tendency in which the distinction between God and nature became vague.

The second criticism concerns the relationship between nature and humans. According to White, Christianity lowered the status of nature and matter by rationalising the human conquest and domination of nature as a matter of course based on an anthropocentric worldview. According to White, Christianity and humans are responsible for nature's destruction by man.[6] In reality, however, the ecological crisis is not due to Christianity, but rather due to the human desires that arose after the recent technological development and industrialisation. The direct cause of the ecological crisis can be attributed to the mechanical view of nature that was formed and developed by Descartes, Bacon, Newton, etc., and Darwin's theory of evolution, which preached the logic of competition and survival of the fittest.[7]

After White, discussions on ecological theology put an emphasis on nature. Some scholars assumed that the Bible equates nature with humans, not showing a negative attitude toward nature. This optimistic interpretation of the Bible is well demonstrated in the Green Bible.[8] Furthermore, there have been attempts to find a principle based on ecological justice beyond the usual Biblical texts.[9] Scholars participating in the Earth Project criticise the fact that the Bible is utilised too simplistically in ecological theology. Furthermore, some scholars believe that the Bible should be used more critically because the Bible does not always favour ecological theology. The problem with the Earth Project, which reads the Bible from the earth's point of view, is that it places its final authority on the principles of eco-justice formulated in and for dialogue with scientists, ecologists and people of other faiths, rather specifically from the perspective of the Bible or the Christian tradition.[10] For these principles to have an ecological basis for Christians, I believe that they must be grounded in the authoritative Bible and Christian tradition.[11]

A proper ecological theological interpretation of the Bible is not to choose in an either-or between humans and nature. It is understandable to emphasise the earth, against the anthropocentric theology that has been emphasised so far; however, it is only a temporary alternative to the ecological crisis to focus on the story of the earth while neglecting the story of humans. Sound biblical theology should be developed for ecological theology, which is to read the Bible as a balance between the story of man and the story of the earth. The story of man emphasises man's stewardship over nature, and the story of the earth regards nature as a space to experience God's presence.

Biblical Ecological Interpretation: The Balance between the Earth's Story and Man's Story

Ecological Bible reading implies that one is reading the Bible in a balanced way.[12] When reading the Bible as a story centred around humans, the following points are emphasised: 1) Humankind is the centre of the universe, and the earth needs man to cultivate it. 2) Humans are limited creatures made of the earth but, at the same time, they are differentiated from other living beings when they receive the breath of God. 3) The fates of the earth and living things depend on man's obedience to God's commands.

When reading the Bible as a story of the earth, the following points are emphasised: 1) The earth is a creature of God and a space where God is present. 2) The earth is the base of life with its vitality received

---

[6] White, "The Historical Roots of Our Ecological Crisis," 36-40.
[7] White, "The Historical Roots of Our Ecological Crisis," 36-40.
[8] *The Green Bible* (New York/London: HarperCollins, 2008).
[9] N.C. Habel, "Introducing the Earth Bible," in N.C. Habel (ed), *Reading from the Perspective of Earth* (The Earth Bible, 1; Sheffield/Cleveland, OH: Sheffield Academic Press/Pilgrim Press, 2000), 30.
[10] N.C. Habel, *Reading from the Perspective of Earth,* 24.
[11] David G. Horrell et el. (eds), *Ecological Hermeneutics: Biblical, Historical and Theological Perspectives* (New York, T & T Clark, 2010), 1-9.
[12] Fred Van Dyke et al. (eds), *Redeeming Creation: The Biblical Basis for Environmental Stewardship* (Downers Grove, IL: InterVarsity Press, 1960), 1-27.

from God and has the power to allow living things to exist and to survive. 3) Human beings, dependent on the earth, are entrusted with the authority to fill and conquer the earth and to rule over living things. Let us read the Bible with these differences in mind.

Creation Story (Genesis 1-2)

Genesis 1 should generally be read as a story of the earth, with the order of God, earth, and man in mind, rather than as the story of earth (Gen. 1:1-25) and the story of man (Gen. 1:26-31) being in constant struggle. Although it may appear that viewing humans as the image of God (Gen. 1:26-28) is anthropocentric, this is actually the story of the earth. Explanations of human interests aside, the story of the earth unfolds first, and only at the end does it include the story of humans. The subject in Genesis 1 is the creator of the heavens and the earth (vv. 1, 3, 9, 14, 20, 24, 26, 29). The earth does not have any divine powers by itself, but rather becomes a home for the birth and preservation of living things through God's creative work. The climax of creation is the rest of God during the Sabbath, not the creation of man. Creation consists of space (sky, land, and seas) and things that fill the space (light, birds, fish, and animals). From the third day, the vitality of the earth becomes prominent.[13] According to the command of God, space (heaven, earth, water) gives rise to life. The earth produces plants and animals (1:11-12, 24-25), the firmament makes the birds fly (1:20-21), and the water makes the fish alive (1:20-21).

Let's take a closer look at the role of Gen 1:26-28 in Genesis 1. This section is arguably the story of man. However, Gen 1:26-28 differs from Genesis 2 in that the former describes man in the context of the relationship between God and the earth. In other words, humans are not absent in the story of the earth but adequately play their own roles between God and the earth. After God created the earth and living things irrespective of human interests, God creates humankind on the sixth day. Humankind is introduced for the first time in relation both to the existing earth and living things. Although humans and other creatures are similar in that they are all blessed to be fruitful, multiply, and replenish the earth (Gen. 1:22. 28), the uniqueness of man is that, unlike other creatures, he was created in the image of God (1:26), to subdue the earth and to have dominion over all living things (1:28).

N.C. Habel emphasises that Genesis 1:26-28 is the story of man, while Gen. 1:1-25[14] is the story of the earth.[15] He asserts that unlike vv. 1-25, vv. 26-28 focus on the role of dominating and governing the earth. According to Habel, the term "*kabas (vbK)*" is used to mean "to subdue the earth" (Gen. 1:28). It does not only mean human power to rule over the earth, but also refers to a harsh control over the earth. He claims that this word does not suggest the shepherd nurturing the sheep. In Genesis 1:26-28, the story of man is seen as hierarchical and contrasts the earth with the human who has authority over the other creatures. According to Habel, the very command to "subdue the earth and have dominion over the living things" given to man in 1:26-28 has already been directed towards the dominion of abuse and exploitation.[16] He concludes that the human-centred theology of exploiting the land is the original claim of the Bible.

---

13 Mark G. Brett, "Earthing the Human in Genesis 1-3," in N.C. Habel (ed), *The Earth Story in Genesis* (The Earth Bible, 2; Sheffield/Cleveland, OH: Sheffield Academic Press/Pilgrim Press, 2000), 74-80.

14 Habel emphasises that 1:1-25 is the story of the earth: "1) the protagonist in the process of creation is the earth, not the entire universe or man; 2) If we remove the story of human creation in Genesis 1:26-30, the rest of the story is a coherent story about the earth that confirms its intrinsic value." N.C. Habel, "Geophany: The Earth Story in Genesis 1," in N.C. Habel (ed), *The Earth Story in Genesis*, 35. Walter Brueggemann says that Genesis 1 celebrates and emphasises the creation of man. Walter Brueggemann, *Genesis* (Interpretation; Atlanta: John Knox, 1982), 31-35.

15 NC. Habel, "Geophany: The Earth Story in Genesis 1," 46-47.

16 His study of Genesis 1 comes from the Earth Project focusing on ecological justice. He asserts that Genesis 1:26-28 is a text that distorts the earth story and legitimises human dominion over nature, but rather emphasises only the earth story.

However, this claim stems from a misunderstanding of this passage. It should be understood as a text emphasising the harmony between humans and nature through the presentation of the role of a shepherd who manages nature for good. Genesis 1 emphasises the harmony between the earth and man. The human authority given to humankind in Genesis 1:26-28 was an opportunity for the good for the earth and for living things, notwithstanding the potential for abuse by humans.

Genesis 1:26-28 is known as the text of man's domination of nature.[17] God decides to make man in God's image and creates man. The purpose of creating man is for him to have dominion over all living things on the earth (fish of the sea, birds of the sky, livestock, and all creeping things on the earth). God's making man in God's image involves "man's rule over living things."[18]

God blessed humans to "be fruitful and increase in number; fill the earth and subdue it" (Gen. 1:28) after he created man, and this blessing is similar to the blessings for other creatures (Gen. 1:22). Thus, humans are God's creation that should fill the earth, as should other creatures.

The word "subdue" (*kabas / vbK*) in this context is in relation to the earth. Habel asserts that this word refers to harsh domination over nature.[19] However, it is especially used in the Priestly Document (P) in the sense of "conquering" in relation to the earth (Num. 32:22, 29; Jos. 18:1; 1 Chr. 22:18).[20] The word "conquer" in these texts does not mean human exploitation of the land. It rather means that God, the Creator, resides in the land of Canaan, inhabited by the Gentiles, and that the land is filled with God's people and transformed into a holy land ruled by God. As such, Genesis 1:28 shows man, created by God, ruling over God's other creations on the land filled with God's presence. The word "*kabas*" here shows God's intention in commanding humans to conquer the land that God rules.

The final blessing is to "have dominion over (*radah-hdr*) the fish of the sea and over the birds of the sky and over every living thing that moves on the earth." The object of control is not only the earth, but all the creatures that live in all the space in the earth, such as the sea, the sky, and the earth. Of the two meanings of the verb *radah(hdr)*, which are "rule over" and "trample",[21] the meaning used in Genesis 1 is "to rule over." This word was originally used for kings and is part of the King's ideology of the ancient Near Eastern region, which sees the king as a divine being, however the word was later also applied to all human beings.[22] Humans, created in the image of God, were given the dominion to rule with justice over the creatures in the universe like a king. To rule over however does not mean to exploit, but to care for and to nurture. This is a concept that accompanies the authority of a royal responsibility, like that of a shepherd's (Ez. 34:1-4; Ps. 72:8-14). In Genesis 1:26-28, the power given to man is expected to be used to govern nature as a good king would govern a country. Although this power could in certain abusive cases lead to the destruction of the nation by an evil king, this is not the intention, goal nor fault of the Bible, but in human history, it is the responsibility of humans who have abused and distorted the proper authority of God-given rule.

---

[17] James Barr, "Man and Nature-The Ecological Controversy and the Old Testament," *Bulletin of the John Rylands Library* 55(1972): 9-32. Norbert Lohfink, *Theology of the Pentateuch: Themes of the Priestly Narratives and Deuteronomy* (Edingburgh: T & T Clark, 1994). Bernard W. Anderson, "Creation and Ecology," in Bernard W. Anderson, *Creation in the Old Testament* (Philadelphia/London: Fortress/SPCK, 1984), 152-71.

[18] C. Westermann, Genesis: Genesis 1-11 (Neukirchen-Vluyn: Neukirchener Verl., 1999), 146. Gerhard Von Rad, Genesis (London: SCM, 1972), 57-61.

[19] N.C. Habel, "Geophany: The Earth Story in Genesis 1," N.C. Habel (ed), *The Earth Story in Genesis*, 46. It is true that this word is used negatively in making a slave (Jer. 34:11; 2 Chr. 28:10; Ne. 5:5) and having sex with a woman by force (Ezra 7:8).

[20] BDB, 461. HALOT, 460.

[21] This has a functional meaning, "to tread the wine press" (Joel 3:13).

[22] B.W. Anderson, "Human Dominion over Nature," in Miriam Winter (ed), *Biblical Studies in Contemporary Thought* (Winchendon, MA: Greeno, Hadden Company, 1975), 111-113. P. Bird, *Missing Persons and Mistaken Identities: Women and Gender in Ancient Israel* (Minneapolis, MN: Fortress Press), 134-38. N. Lohfink, *The Theology of the Pentateuch: Themes of the Priestly Narrative and Deuteronomy,* 1-17.

Genesis 2:4b-25

The second creation story (Gen. 2:4b-25) is the story of humans. In this story, Adam is given the task of cultivating and protecting the land (Gen. 2:15). Carol A. Newsom argues that this text (Gen. 2:4b-25) is not an anthropocentric text as is commonly seen, but rather a text focusing on the solidarity between man and nature.[23] Its first part (Gen. 2:1-17) emphasises the creation and mission of man. Before man was created, the earth was imperfect, since there was no man to cultivate (*abad/db*) the earth.[24] When God created man, he used the earth, as He did with animals;[25] however, God breathed His breath of life into man's nostrils to make man a living soul (*nephesh haya/hYx; vp,n<*). The earth is the background of the creation of Adam and Eve and their activity in Genesis 2.[26]

The second half (2:18-25) describes the relation between humans and animals. Some scholars claim that humans and animals have an equal relationship without domination or subordination, since humans and animals have the same common ground.[27] However, even though man and other creatures are expressed with the same term in Hebrew (*nephesh haya/hYx; vp,n<),* the context of the text indirectly refers to the difference between man and other creatures. The word "nephesh hayah" is used not only here, but also to indicate living creatures on water (Gen. 1:20) and on land (Gen. 1:24, 28, 30), and all living creatures except humans (Gen. 9:12, 15, 16). Since the word "living creatures" is used for fish in the sea, birds in the sky, and things that move on the ground just like humans, it is hard for us to distinguish humans from other creatures only with the word "living creatures". Nevertheless, the context reveals the differences between humans and other living things. When God made man out of dust (Gen. 2:7a), man was not yet a living being, but man became a living being when God breathed life into him. Therefore, human beings are creatures of God's breath and came to be distinct from other living things.[28] In Genesis 2, humans and animals are not described to be in a conflicting or equal relationship.[29] Rather, human beings are dominant in their relationship with animals, as humans are in the position to give names to animals.

The Fall of Man (Genesis 3-4)

In Genesis 3, the relationship between man and nature is affected by the relationship between man and God. In Genesis 2, the only thing forbidden to humans is the eating the fruit from the tree of the knowledge of good and evil (Gen. 2:16-17). In Genesis 3, humans' violation of God's said ban changed the relationship between man and nature. Although man did not directly damage the earth, the earth was cursed when man disobeyed God by eating the forbidden fruit (Gen. 3:17). As the earth was cursed, only through toil could man eat food from it. Human labour was required for the production of food. In the Garden of Eden, the earth was originally supposed to give fruits as food for humans. However, due to the fall of human beings,

---

[23] Carol A. Newsom, "Common Ground: An Ecological Reading of Genesis 2-3," in N.C. Habel (ed), *The Earth Story in Genesis*, 63.

[24] Although the text is human-centred, it shows rain, fog, and rivers that appear on the ground (Gen. 2:5-6, 10-14), and the soil is used as a material to make animals and humans (2:7, 10).

[25] It is an appropriate observation that both humans and animals come from the soil and have a sense of solidarity as a predator. Carol A. Newsom, "Common Ground", 63.

[26] In Chapter 2, the understanding of the land differs from Chapter 1 in that it reveals an anthropocentric perspective. The land awaits man who cultivates it. It is also humans who cultivate and keep the garden. Carol A. Newsom, "Common Ground", 65.

[27] Carol A. Newsom, "Common Ground", 65-66.

[28] Newsom agrees with the views of scholars who presuppose that God also breathed life into animals. Carol A. Newsom, "Common Ground", 65.

[29] Newsom tries to understand humans and animals in Genesis 2 as partners without difference. Carol A. Newsom, "Common Ground", 65-66.

man can only eat the fruits of the human labour through sweating.[30] Man became an exploiter of the earth due to the fall of man. From then on, humans do not return to the Garden of Eden, but live on the earth as cultivators (Gen. 3:23). Genesis 3 is the story of man, but it tells us that the counterattack of the cursed earth has begun due to man's fall. Nature's first counterattack against human sin was to demand human labour and exhaust the vitality of the earth.

In Genesis 4, human sin and nature's counterattack further develop. Cain took Abel's life and shed his blood on the ground. This sin is also called the "second original sin," which contrasts with Adam's sin.[31] As a result of Cain's sin, the earth did not yield its produce no more, and Cain became a wanderer who could no longer dwell on the earth (Gen. 4:11-12). The earth, a victim of human sin, struck back against humanity. Due to Cain's sin, nature does not give birth and drives man from the earth. The tradition of Cain's sin, of the shedding of human blood, later leads to humankind being wiped from the earth by a flood (Gen. 6:13) and the land vomiting out its inhabitants (Lev. 18:24-25).

The Flood (Genesis 6-9)[32]

The story of Noah's flood (the "Flood") (Genesis 6-9) is a mix of human and earth stories. In the human story, the cause of the Flood is human sin. According to this story, the cause of the Flood is that all man's plans are evil (Gen. 6:5), which means that man's nature became evil. The goal of the Flood was to destroy mankind whose nature is evil (Gen. 6:7). Furthermore, because of man's wickedness, God decided to wipe out all living things along with man from the ground (Gen. 6:7). Humans became subject to judgment because they sinned, and other creatures that had nothing to do with human sin were also judged because of human sins. However, after God destroyed man with the flood, He said that man was evil from an early age (Gen. 8:21), implying that the flood could not restore man to the way he was before sin.

The story of the earth (Gen. 6:9-22) is different from the story of humans. The story of the earth emphasises the purity of the defiled earth without reference to man's inner goodness or evil. The cause of God's decision to bring the Flood is the corruption of the earth due to human violence. The reason for the decision to bring down the Flood in the earth story is not because of human nature's wickedness, but because the earth is full of violence (Gen. 6:11-13). This violence was caused by the bloodshed through life-killing murder.[33] Because human violence has polluted the earth, God expelled humans from the earth to purify the earth. It was forbidden to shed blood after the flood (Gen. 9:4-6), since the blood defiles the earth. The earth should be for God's presence. To purify the land polluted by violence, God used a flood to sweep away mankind and purify the earth. Just as Cain left the earth as a wanderer, humans were driven out of the earth for the earth's purification. The motive of the expulsion of humans from the earth due to the shedding of blood is taken up in Leviticus again (Lev. 18:24-25, 28).

Restoration of the Earth

When the earth is defiled, the key biblical methods of restoring the earth and its vitality are the Sabbath, the Sabbatical year, and the Jubilee. The Sabbath, the day commanded to stop working, was initially for humans, but gradually developed into a regulation also for the earth and animals (Deut. 5:14). In other

---

[30] J.B. Callicott, "Genesis and John Muir", in C.S. Robb and C.J. Casebolt (eds.), *Covenant for a New Creation: Ethics, Religion and Public Policy* (Maryknoll, NY: Orbis Books, 1991), 125.

[31] N. Lohfink, *The Theology of the Pentateuch*, 96-115.

[32] The text to be studied is the YHWIST story (Genesis 6:5-8; 7:1-5, 7, 10, 12, 16b-20, 22-23; 8:3b-3a, 6, 8-12, 13b, 20-22) and sacrificial (P) documents (6:9-22;7:8-9, 11, 13-16a, 21, 24; 8:1-2a, 3b-5, 7, 13a, 14-19; 9:1-17). Yawist's story emphasises the human story, while the sacrificial texts emphasise the earth's story.

[33] To J. Milgrom, violence is the origin of negativity because it kills life. J. Milgrom, "Priestly Source," in *ABD* 5: 456-457.

words, the concept of rest appears as the right of not only humans but also that of the earth and animals.[34] The Sabbatical year is the time when the earth, which has been depleted of its vitality for six years, recovers its earthly power and enters the presence of God at the seventh year (Ex. 23:10-11; Lev 25:1-7). Furthermore, the Jubilee is a system to return humans to the earth, alienated from the earth due to human social evil (Lev. 25:8-34). These laws preserve the divine holiness originally given to the earth by protecting it from human uncleanness.

The first attempt to solve human uncleanness is to restore the land in the seven-year Sabbatical year. The evils that could not be resolved in the Sabbatical year are only restored in the Jubilee year that comes after seven Sabbatical years. What the Sabbatical year and Jubilee years count as pollution in effect is a social or ecological sin that drives humans from the earth. In the rule of the Jubilee, the standard of restoration is to declare as God's the land distributed to the twelve tribes in the land of Canaan (Lev. 25:23), and to return to the land those who were expelled from the land by social injustice for 50 years, in order to bring restoration.[35] The Jubilee Law of the Old Testament prepares for the presence of God by emphasising the rest of the earth itself, unlike the fallow law in the Near East that simply prevents the depletion of the earth and preserves the productivity of the earth.[36]

Conclusion

Christianity must respond, with a theological basis, to the criticism that the cause of the ecological crisis is its own anthropocentric reductionism in reading its creation narratives. Some attempts are made to read the Bible only as a story of man while emphasising man's dominion and stewardship over nature, while others attempt a solution by opposing the voice of the earth with man. However, to solve the ecological crisis, the Bible must be read in a balanced way as a human story as well as a land story and story of nature.

To read the Bible in a balanced way as the story of humans and the story of the earth, the following points should be emphasised: 1) God is the Creator; 2) nature, as a creation of God, should not be deified. It is a space where all creatures can reside and experience God's presence; 3) humans, as creatures created by God, received the breath of God, became distinct from animals, and communicated with God. Humans are not equal to the earth but are the beings who rule and protect the earth. This principle is the basis for recovering the ecological crisis. The ecological crisis appears as nature's counterattack against human sin. The ecological crisis of modern society marked by COVID-19 is due to a mechanical worldview and technological civilisation that encourages human greed, and we must control human greed and strive for the restoration of humans and the land. We must recognise the proper relationship between God, earth, and humans. The story of the earth and the story of humans should be read in a balanced way together. We should recognise nature as an entity of coexistence rather than an object of exploitation, purify the earth from the sins caused by us, and try to restore the land based on the Jubilee spirit.

Suggestions for Further Reading

Anderson, B. W. Ed. *Creation in the Old Testament*. Philadelphia, PA: Fortress, 1984.
Bauckham, Richard. *Bible and Ecology: Rediscovering the Community of Creation*. London: Darton, Longman and Todd, 2010.

---

[34] Mark G. Brett, "Earthing the Human in Genesis 1-3," in N.C. Habel (ed), *The Earth Story in Genesis*, 79-80.
35 M. Weinfeld, "Sabbatical Year and Jubilee in the Pentateuchal Laws and their Ancient Near Eastern Background," in T. Veijola (ed), *The Law in the Bible and its Environment* (Gottingen: Vandenhoeck & Ruprecht, 1990), 39-62. J.S. Bergsma, *The Jubilee from Leviticus to Qumran: A History of Interpretation* (SVT 115. Leiden- Boston: Brill, 2007).
[36] J.P.M. van der Ploeg, "Studies in Hebrew Law," CBQ 12(1951), 248-59; B.A. Levine, *Leviticus* (JPSTC; Philadelphia: Varda Books, 1989), 272. Sun-Jong Kim, "Les enjeux theologiques des beneficiaires de l'annee sabbatique (Lev 25:6-7)," *ZAW* 122(2010), 38-43.

The Green Bible. New York/London: HarperCollins, 2008.

Habel, Norman C. Ed. *Reading from the Perspective of Earth, The Earth Bible, 1*. Sheffield/Cleveland, OH: Sheffield Academic Press/Pilgrim Press, 2000.

— *The Earth Story in Genesis, The Earth Bible 2*. Sheffield: Sheffield Academic, 2000. [Especially: Carol A. Newsom. "Common Ground: An Ecological Reading of Genesis 2-3," 60-72.]

Horrell, David G. Ed. *Ecological Hermeneutics: Biblical, Historical and Theological Perspectives*. New York, T & T Clark, 2010.

— *The Bible and the Environment: Towards a Critical Ecological Biblical Theology*. New York: Routledge, 2014.

Simkins, Ronald A. *Creator & Creation: Nature in the Worldview of Ancient Israel.* Peabody, MA: Hendrickson, 1994.

Van Dyke, Fred, David C. Mahan, Joseph K. Sheldon, and Raymond H. Brand. *Redeeming Creation: The Biblical Basis for Environmental Stewardship.* Downers Grove, IL: InterVarsity Press,1996.

Berry, R. J. Ed. *The Care of Creation: Focusing Concern and Action*. Leicester, England: InterVarsity Press, 2000.

16. The Ecological Relevance and the Meaning of the Land According to the Book of Psalms

Yifan Lu[1]

Introduction

The land theme runs through the Old Testament texts: from the land promises in narratives of the ancestors; through the possession of land and the distribution of land, the loss of land in the exile period, to the promises of a renewed return to the land in prophetic literature.[2] The land is not only a place to survive; through the land, people can also find their identities and memories. Land can evoke people's memories at any time, and it is again through the land that God even reminds Israelis that they have rebelled, so the land has a perceptual and spiritual atmosphere. It can be seen that land is a material that can satisfy human beings in material and spirituality. The land in the Old Testament is an important topic that is explicitly addressed in almost every book. The land as a bridge connects the people of Israel with God. They belong closely together in the Old Testament. The history of Israel is marked by the promise of land, occupied land, and the loss of the land.[3]

The Land is not just a place of settlement, nor is it purely an economically developed asset of agricultural development. The land is not even real estate that can be traded on the market. The land is often reduced to a stage background. Through God's promise and covenant grant, this land belongs to Israel, but this land is still God's land, and he maintains the moral right to use this land. The land is like a thermometer, assessing the relationship between Israel and God at any time. The land is like a measuring stick, measuring the social life of Israel and its relationship with God. The ecological concerns do not feature explicitly in the thinking of ancient Israel, but the narrative of creation has taught the Israelis how to govern the land and provide irrigation, therefore we can still explore the ecological values and goals in the Old Testament.

The Theme of Land in the Book of Psalms

The Psalter is a selected collection of 150 poetic texts of different genres. "The Psalter can shape the worldview of those who pray it, encouraging them to live within the earth rather than against it."[4] The psalms also take up the land theme in many different ways. Such land themes not only shape the historical retrospective in the Psalms or laments of the people, but are also received in other genres of the Psalms.

The main terms for land in Psalms are ארץ (190 times) and אדמה (6 times). אדמה means "ground, earth, land", "cultivated arable land" or "land ownership as opposed to non-cultivated land such as steppe or desert".[5] ארץ means "earth, ground, land", "property" and "area", usually in a political sense.[6]

---

[1] Ms. Yifan Lu was a Pastor in Chuzhou in China. She is now a doctoral candidate at Missionsacademy of University of Hamburg, Germany.

[2] Kathrin Liess, "Die auf JHWH hoffen, werden das Land besitzen" (Psalm 37,9) in *Jahr Buch für Biblische Theologie (JBTh)*, Band23: Heiliges Land: Neukirchener Verlag, 2009, 47.

[3] Liess, "Die auf JHWH hoffen, werden das Land besitzen", 47.

[4] David Rensberger, "Ecological use of the Psalms" in William P. Brown (ed), *The Oxford Handbook of the Psalms* (Oxford: Oxford University Press, 2014), 609.

[5] L. Köhler; W. Baumgartner, *Hebräisches und aramäisches Lexikon zum Alten Testament* (HALAT), Bd.1, Brill Deutschland GmbH, 1996, 14-15.

[6] L. Köhler; W. Baumgartner, HALAT, 87-88.

The concept of land is a starting point for communion with God.[7] The Communion with God describes it as the basis of the life of the person praying, and thus expresses the hope of salvation. "The updating in historical psalms and some lamentations, the historical review of the land concept of the land theme always aims at the meaning for the present and the concrete situation of the respective psalmist."[8] The Psalms of creation refers to a universal-cosmologic conception of land. In the historical Psalms, the conception of land is connected with the tradition of the covenant and particular understandings of the concept of land in a limited number of specific psalms.

Land in the Psalms of Creation

In the creation Psalms, the word ארץ usually is translated as "the earth". As declared in Psalm 24:1, "The earth is the Lord's, and everything in it, the world, and all who live in it", the God of Israel owns the entire universe. The earth belongs to God because God created it. "Creation" is an important theme in the Bible, because it touches the ultimate destination of humankind. Mankind was born in the earth, grew up in the earth, returns to the earth, because humans are dust (Gen. 3,19). The earth is the stage for humankind, and it is also the place where all living creatures live and move.

Psalm 104 not only pursues the themes of truth, goodness, and beauty but also emphasises the connection with the creator of the universe.[9] Psalm 104 begins and ends with the same phrase: "Bless the Lord, O my soul." It was used for collective worship and praise and admiration of JHWH as the king of all things in the universe (Ps. 104:1-4). Psalm 104 speaks from heaven to earth and it is like the poetic version of Genesis 1. Genesis records the sequence and process of JHWH's creation, but Psalm 104 focuses on the appreciation of the creature before it talks about JHWH's glory and power. On the other hand, the psalm not only points directly to the reality of the world but also makes hints at the existence of the angelic world (v.4). The world can see God's deeds, but cannot see God's essence; this subtly reflects the ancient Israel's view of God.[10]

From this poem, the reader can perceive the existence and deeds of an all-powerful God, see the splendid and beautiful universe, the space where animals and plants live, the society in which human labour and survival take place, and the peaceful coexistence and mutual coexistence of all living entities. It is not difficult to realise that everything God created is beautiful, and everything people should be grateful for and cherish. In Psalm 104, the universe observed by the poet is colourful. From space to earth, from high mountains and valleys to plains and grasslands, from small streams to the vast sea, from the sun and the moon and stars to wind, fire and thunder and lightning, from animals to birds, from beasts to crocodiles, from angels to humans, from vegetables to forests, from caves to mountains – all are filled with God's glory. Among them, the list of creatures mentioned is rich enough. God created the diversity of creatures according to their species,[11] but all of these depend on the "breath of life" given by God to live. Once God takes back their "breath", they immediately die and return to the dust. Because God is the only source of life, all kinds of creatures in the universe receive life from Him.[12] The breath (spirit) of God is a key presence and described as the creative source of life. Living creatures are diverse, but life is unique.

In this poem, the psalmist does not pay much attention to "human beings", but also summarises some ideas about them: 1) humans must work and rest on time (v.23). God's creation itself is a kind of great labour process, and the world should also regard labour as sacred; God is the God who gives rest, therefore people must be grateful and enjoy the rest he gives. 2) Human societies need to communicate with each

---

[7] Liess, "Die auf JHWH hoffen, werden das Land besitzen", 72.
[8] Liess, "Die auf JHWH hoffen, werden das Land besitzen", 72.
[9] Ronald A. Simkins, *Creation and Ecology: The Political Economy of Ancient Israel and the Environmental Crisis* (Eugene, OR: Cascade Books, 2020), 167.
[10] Simkins, *Creation and Ecology*, 168.
[11] Rensberger, "Ecological use of the Psalms", 618.
[12] Rensberger, "Ecological use of the Psalms", 618.

other. In the process of labour, people learn to help each other, to exchange and to share. Therefore, it promotes the increase of productivity and improves the life of human beings. 3) People have free will and can think. Therefore, they can both commit crimes but also they are capable of writing poems and praise. 4) Humans are created and loved by God, so God created production conditions and rich material life for them. However, sin does not come from God. Therefore, it is sin and evil that God wants to eliminate, but not the people He created.

Psalm 104 emphasises the daily life of the creatures and the care for them by the Creator.[13] The ongoing maintenance of the world is due to divine care, and all creatures are continuously dependent on the Creator. It is also clear that, in this Psalm, all the creatures are praising creatures, they are not set apart from other creatures but have their own particular roles.

Land in the Wisdom Psalms

In the wisdom Psalms, "Land" often functions as a metaphor for the encounter between JHWH and his people. In Psalm 37, land is granted to those whoועשה־טוב ביהוה בטח ("trust in JHWH, and do good", v. 3), who יהוה קוי ("wait for JHWH", v. 9), the ענוים ("meek", v. 11), מברכיו ("blessed by JHWH", v. 22), who־ועשה טוב מרע סור("depart from evil, and do good", v. 27), the צדיקים ("righteous" v. 29), and those who דרכו ושמר אל־יהוה קוה ("wait for JHWH, and keep his way", v. 34). The Land is promised to a group of good people. JHWH will reward them with the heritage of the land. This psalm reveals the obvious connection between the beneficiaries of the land and the poor and the righteous.

According to Psalm 37, the joy of living in the land (v. 11) correlates with the joy in JHWH (v. 4), thus the possession of the land is connected to the relationship with JHWH. This is about a lasting relationship with God of the righteous (צדקם) and the meek (ענוים). The focus of this Psalm is not on the promise of land addressed to the righteous, but on the validity of the relationship with God.[14]

The land is the inheritance of Israel; in the context of Psalm 37, the land can be understood as the property and habitat of JHWH's people. The main theme of this Psalm is the inheritance or the destruction of the land: the land serves as a metaphor for divine blessing and in later contexts possibly also as a symbol for eternal life.[15] The Psalm proclaims that the wicked will be cut off and the righteous and meek will take possession of the land. The righteous will inherit the land (ארץ-ירשו vv. 9, 11, 22, 29 and 34 ארץ-לרשת), always inhabit it (v. 27), and receive redemption and deliverance (v. 39-40).

The land is God's covenant gift as the place of a living and flourishing existence, in which case attention is drawn to the imbalance in people's access to its benefits.[16] This includes in particular the affirmation of the need to trust in JHWH and not to worry about the wicked. Both the activity of doing good and the attitude of hopeful trust are qualities that determine whether the land can be possessed or not.

In the wisdom Psalm, the idea of the land as JHWH's gift of salvation to his people runs through[17] and is unfolded together with the theology of the poor. The focus of the Psalm is on the possession of the land and can be interpreted as a promise and guarantee of land possession for the population group that has no means to acquire the land.[18] Psalm 37 describes this life situation of the poor and a life threat emanating from the evils being done. The land has become a target for looting, greed, exploitation by land occupiers. When the land becomes a commodity and God becomes an ornament, the land causes "amnesia". The

---

[13] Rensberger, "Ecological use of the Psalms", 619.

[14] Hans-J. Kraus, *Biblischer Kommentar Altes Testament (BK), 1. Teilband, Psalms 1-59* (Neukirchen-Vluyn: Neukirchener Verlag, 1978), 444.

[15] Kraus, *Psalms 1-59*, 440.

[16] Craigie, Peter C., *Word Biblical Commentary (WBC): Psalms 1-50*, 2nd Edition (Nashville, TN: Thomas Nelson, 2004), 300.

[17] Hossfeld, *Psalms 1-50* (NEB), 229.

[18] Erhard S. Gerstenberger, *Arbeitsbuch Psalmen* (Stuttgart: W. Kohlhammer GmbH, 2015), 101.

people then no longer think about where the land comes from, who is the owner of the land, and what responsibilities should be attached and respected by them. They also no longer look forward to the future and think that everything now "should be like this." The conviction that God will come as a judge is, as Erich Zenger points out, the ultimate hope of the weak and oppressed.[19] The judge will rescue them from the hands of the rich and powerful. This central theme of the Psalms has its roots in the Pentateuch. All sections of the Law contain exhortations and rules to help the poor (Ex. 20:10; Dt. 5:14). That God cares for the poor is also a central belief of the Psalmists. He is "A Father of the fatherless, a defender of widows" (Ps. 68:5).

The Land is thus not promised exclusively to the "poor", as is sometimes noted; rather, it seems obvious that these belong to a "group of good people". The Psalm thus presents the possession of the land as dependent on proper ethics.[20] Indeed, the psalmist asserts that right ethics will lead to blessings given by God, and the practice of wrong ethics will result in punishment and destruction. Although it may sometimes seem that those who live immoral and irreligious lives enjoy prosperity and success, the Psalm offers assurance that the ethic of retribution is alive and still functioning.[21] The morally upright will find comfort and, moreover, know that in the end the wicked will be destroyed, but only the righteous will be blessed.

Land in the Historical Psalms

In the historical psalms,[22] the land as a gift is an important aspect as well. The depictions of the history of Israel contain similar elements: the settlement in Egypt (Ps. 78:12; 105:23-25), the plagues (Ps. 78:43-51; 105:28-36), the crossing of the Red Sea (Ps.78:13; 106:9-11) and the guidance in the desert (Ps.78:52-53). The brief glimpse on traditional history stresses the land topic as the "land" is brought up in memorisation.

Psalm 78 for instance looks back at history in-depth and focuses on the different ways in which the people have tested JHWH and sinned against JHWH.[23] At this point, the story begins with a pedagogical expression (78:1; Dt.4:6) and is seen as a story of rebellious generations who did not live in the land (78:56). In this Psalm, the land is not the subject but the covenant gift of God. Verse 54 connects God's guidance to the land directly to the mountain of God, which YHWH has acquired for the Israelites. However, as Psalm 78 varies the formulations of Exodus 15:17 but does not explicitly mention the sanctuary, its sacred place, the mountain, is named as the target of the conquest of Land.[24] Verse 55 takes up this idea of a connection between the indigenous people of the country and connects this with the tradition of land distribution by casting out the measuring cords.[25] Psalm 78:55 linguistically modifies this idea by dividing the peoples themselves with the measuring cord and giving Israel as inheritance (נחלה).[26] Looking back on the historical deeds of YHWH, which also includes the land gift, the Psalm then calls on the people to trust in God and not to forget him.

---

[19] Gerstenberger, *Arbeitsbuch Psalmen*, 101.
[20] Eleuterio R. Ruiz, *Das Land ist für die Armen da: Psalm 37 und seine immer aktuelle Bedeutung* (Stuttgart: Verlag Katholisches Bibelwerk, 2015), 53.
[21] Ruiz, *Das Land ist für die Armen da*, 44.
[22] The psalm group (Ps. 77, 78, 105, 106, 135, 136) tells the experiences that Old Testament Israel had with its God. This story is recounted in poetic form and interpreted in various ways (Gärtner, Judith, *Die Geschichtspsalmen: Eine Studie zu den Psalmen 78, 105, 106, 135 und 136 als hermeneutischen Schlüsseltexte im Psalter*, Mohr Siebeck, 2012, 3). (Hossfeld, Zenger, Psalms 51-100.400). Although the genre of the introduction (vv. 1-8) is a teaching psalm, the whole psalm emphasised history.
[23] Patrick D.Miller, "The land in The Psalms" in Jacques T.A.G.M. van Ruiten and J. Cornelis de Vos (eds), *The Land of Israel in Bible, History, and Theology (*Leiden: Brill, 2009), 183.
[24] Liess, "Die auf JHWH hoffen, werden das Land besitzen", 54.
[25] Frank-Lothar Hossfeld and Erich Zenger, *Herders Theologischer Kommentar zum Alten Testament* (*HThKAT*)*: Psalmen 51-100*, 3rd Edition (Freiburg, Herder Publisher, 2007), 438.
[26] Liess, "Die auf JHWH hoffen, werden das Land besitzen", 55.

Land in the Psalms of Lament

The experience of the exile can be clearly felt in Psalm 137. The grief of the exile group links to the memory of Zion. Jerusalem had been conquered, the temple destroyed, and the people taken to a strange land far from Zion, their source of peace and security.[27] In exile, Israel lived without a land for a long time, and yet in the certainty and in the belief in the eternal value of the land promise.[28]

The use of the particles שם ("there" v. 1:3) is important here. The psalmist's local situation has since changed; he speaks directly to Jerusalem. For the exiled Jews, "there" refers to Babylon, the foreign land in which their enemies live in, and what they miss is the distant homeland Zion ("here").

The strange phrase נכר אדמת על does not just mean "abroad". The adjective נכר is used in almost all religious and cultic contexts and emphasises a contrast to YHWH (foreign god/foreign gods, Gen. 35:2,4; Dt. 21:12; 31:12; Jos. 24:20, 23; 1 Sam 7:3; Jer. 5:19 etc.).[29] That is why it is not translated here as "foreign country", but as "the foreign soil that foreign gods ruled". The foreign soil is determined to be unclean land, and the peoples of the foreign soil are also determined to be an unclean people. In the unclean land, one can only voice the complaint, but not the praise of JHWH.

The Psalm 85 begins emphatically with the verb שוב "You have pardoned your land". The Hebrew perfect tense interprets the past. One can state that salvation has happened. The turning point has been accomplished (שבות שבת). As a counterpart to the אתה (you of God), "your country", "Jacob", "your people" appear as beneficiaries of action. Salvation is for his land, for Jacob (v. 2).[30] Here, the favour of God meant restoration, because God turned away his wrath.

ארץ is a dwelling place which belongs to JHWH Himself. The term ארצך ("your land") is a land that God claims for himself (Ps. 60:8-10), the Holy Land, and then the name "Jacob", which is encountered more frequently in the Korah and Asaph Psalms and alludes to the people of God. ארץ here probably refers to the people of the land (a metonymy of the subject), parallel to "Jacob" in the second colon.[31] The prophetic books use some of these keywords repeatedly; "Jacob" is used for the restored nation in passages such as Isaiah 40:27; 41:14,21 and 42:24. The statement that God has restored the nation's fortunes is reflected in the praise of Psalm 126:1.

Psalms point out that the land belongs to God. In the book of Leviticus, it is also mentioned that people are only travellers and sojourners and that the land belongs to God. Therefore, it is not pleasing to God if people should pollute the land. Man only trusts the land, but the sovereignty lies in the hands of God. Man should not rely on the land, but on the God who gave it. Unfortunately, today, land properties have become a commodity.

Land Issues in the Chinese Context

China is an agrarian civilisation and its cultural roots are in the land, which nurtures civilisations, families, tribes and nations. The land is therefore the most important resource, which is why Chinese people have had a strong attachment to it since ancient times. Despite its vast size, China has a very limited land area *per capita*, which has led to the Chinese people's land complex being tied to their survival. Even Chinese funeral customs are mainly earth burials, believing that the deceased need to be put to rest into the earth for peace. Along with the rapid industrialisation and urbanisation process, a large amount of land in rural areas

[27] Gunther Wanke, *Die Zionstheologie der Korachiten in ihrem traditionsgeschichtlichen Zusammenhang* (Berlin: Töpelmann, 1966), 76.
[28] Jörn Kiefer, *Exil und Diaspora: Begrifflichkeit und Deutungen im antiken Israelitentum und in der Hebräischen Bibel* (Leipzig: Evangelische Verlagsanstalt, 2005), 287.
[29] Zenger, *Psalmen 51-100 (HThKAT)*, 691.
[30] Klaus Seybold, *Studien zu Sprache und Stil der Psalmen* (Berlin: De Gruyter, 2010), 125.
[31] Zenger, *Psalmen 51-100 (HThKAT)*, 530.

has been expropriated, resulting in many landless farmers and tragedies caused by unfair compensation for land expropriation and demolition or forced demolition. It is also true that the ecological environment has been sacrificed for the course of China's industrialisation.

In Leviticus 25:23, God says that "the land shall not be sold in perpetuity, for the land is mine". When land is changed from a gift to a commodity, it leads to exploitation and injustice, yet it is more important to have a clear understanding of land ownership (1 Kings 21:19), that land belongs to God, not to individuals or collectives, and that people only have the right to inhabit and use it, but not to abuse. The land needs to be managed as a place of righteousness and freedom. At the same time, man has an obligation to maintain the entire ecological environment. God will not give the blessing of fruitfulness when men defile the land (Jer. 3:1-2).

Conclusion

The psalms of creation focus not so much on exploitation within the human community, but extend an invitation to be aware of the earth and all of its inhabitants as objects of divine mercy. The fact that the universe is created should evoke the desire to be responsible for participating in the life of the created. To truly live in the reality of the created world requires not only an acknowledgment of the existence of the Creator, but also the reconciliation with the Creator's will. According to the Psalmist, the will of the Creator is to seek the continued well-being of the created world. The task of humanity is to rethink the relationship between humans and other creatures. The Psalmist's basic response to the recognition that the world was created is praise. Life, truly conditioned by joyful praise to the Creator, cannot at the same time continue to be exploitative and destructive to its very roots.

Therefore, the theme of Land in the Psalms also connects with issues of social justice by using certain metaphors and other rhetorical methods of describing the interrelationship between humans and God, humans and nonhuman creation. For example, Psalm 37 teaches about the promise that the righteous/poor will inherit the land. This implies not only a commitment for just judicial decision-making but also for fair governance, because it is the rule of the Creator to protect the weak from the strong and other creatures from the ravages of the "people". The strong tendency towards justice in the Psalms therefore implies not only justice between humans, but also justice between humans and other creatures within the whole of the created world.

Suggestions for Further Reading

Bauckham, Richard. *Living with other Creatures: Green Exegesis and Theology*. Waco, TX: Baylor University Press, 2011.

Brueggemann, Walter. *Hopeful Imagination: Prophetic Voices in Exile*. Philadelphia, PA: Fortress Press, 1986.

Fretheim, Terence E. *God and World in the Old Testament: A Relational Theology of Creation*. Nashville, TN: Abingdon, 2005.

Habel, Norman C. *The Land is Mine: Six Biblical Land Ideologies*. OBT. Minneapolis, MN: Fortress, 1995.

17. GOD'S CREATION AND CREATION CARE IN THE OLD TESTAMENT: PERSPECTIVES OF THE HOLY COVENANT (BERIT)

Li Xinnong[1]

The Hebrew Bible, which we are accustomed to call "The Old Testament", in fact is the deepest recourse of ecotheology. The covenant concept (בְּרִית bĕriyth for "covenant") is the most important topic in Old Testament theology and a core reference point for ecotheology. According to the Old Testament, God has established the covenant (or covenants) with his people and with all of the living creatures. The most significant contribution of Israel to this world is the monotheism which makes the world unique. The book of Genesis tells us that we have only one God who created this world. "Creation" and "covenant" are the two "columns" in our theological framework, the real foundations of our ecotheology and all our theological thinking falls under this umbrella. "Creation looks forward to the covenant, but the covenant serves the creation."[2] It is important to realise that the holy covenants between God and human beings are not agreements or administrations, but bonds. They bind people and all of the nonhuman creatures together. The living God brings life and order to a chaotic cosmos. We dwell in this living world and rely both on the living covenant and the living faith. Taking care of God's creation is our duty according to the holy covenants.

We have to rethink some main topics in our dogmatic theology from the perspective of ecotheology, and unpack their functions, related to concepts such as covenant, creation, the image of God, redemption, justification, amongst others.

The Living Covenant, the Living Hope: Covenant and Covenants

The most essential elements of the Bible are the holy covenants between God and the created world. This is the most basic and important relationship by which we recognise who we are, and understand what "the image of God" is. The covenant implies that humanity is not the central point of the cosmos as well as saying that humankind is not the maker of the heaven and earth. The Bible tells us that God actively made several covenants with the created world. The meaning and dimension of the holy covenants in the Bible are not temporary or finite. God, creating this world, brings us a living world, and God himself is a living Spirit from eternity to eternity.

In the light of ecotheology, the most precious action of God is to establish a covenant with Noah (and through Noah to mankind) and with all of the living things and the earth itself. This particular covenant is referred to as "the Holy Covenant" in this article. We are reminded that this covenant is "with every living creature that is with you, the birds, the domestic animals, and every animal of the earth with you, as many as came out of the ark, I establish my covenant with you, that never again shall all flesh be cut off by the waters of a flood, and never again shall there be a flood to destroy the earth" (Gen. 9:10-11, *NRSV*). Genesis 9:16 reveals to us that this covenant is "the everlasting covenant".

---

[1] The author is an assistant editor of *Nanjing Theological Review* and lecturer in the field of the Old Testament at Nanjing Theological Seminary.

[2] John E. Goldingay, *Old Testament Theology*, vol. 1 (Downers Grove, IL: InterVarsity, 2003), 101.

We can read the entire Torah as a covenant text.[3] As Dumbrell explains, "in Genesis 2 we are in effect told how this dominion mandate which is his within the covenant structure, is to operate."[4] Genesis 2:15-17 can be seen as a draft of a covenant which was established between God and the living beings. But humanity rebelled against God and broke this covenant. That "you shall die" (2:18, *NRSV*) means that humanity disturbs the normal relationship between God and human beings, for Adam did not die immediately.

The verses mentioned above focus on the term "renewal", for all of the covenants in the Scriptures are not dead promises, but are living relational realities. The account in Genesis 2:18 employs a very acute word "die" to announce the broken relationship, but, in Genesis 9, the key meaning is to have a new beginning. Thus, the Covenant with Noah is not entirely new, but is a renewal of Eden covenant. The former implied keeping life, and the latter declared the continuing love of God upon all of the living creatures.

Environment

Generally, the environment is defined as "the complex of physical, chemical, and biotic factors (such as climate, soil, and living things) that act upon an organism or an ecological community and ultimately determine its form and survival. The more efficient note about environment is the aggregate of social and cultural conditions that influence the life of an individual or community."[5]

To define environment in a secular way is quite different from what the Bible says about it. The authors of the Bible insert religious elements of meaning into the wholeness of the world. God the creator establishes covenants with his world, and the human being is the steward or representative who has dominion over the created world, while being himself a partial living element in the covenant relationship. Thus, to protect the so-called "environment" is to obey the holy covenants. The story of Eden and the following chapters of Genesis are a deep reflection of ancient Israel on the relationships between humanity and their "environment", a history which is unfinished. Human beings are sinners and their transgressions do not only harm other living creatures, but they break the holy covenants. Both our physical body and soul need renewal. To sin against our environment means to sin against God the creator.

We could call the "Old" Testament the "everlasting" covenant, whereas the "New" Testament can be called the story of the "extended" covenant. On one side, the resurrection of Jesus Christ brings benedictions and hope to our souls; on the other, it also brings sustainability and healing and reconciliation to the environment, including our physical body. Christ already reconstructed the cosmos. What is the essence of the covenants? It is this: God says to his people: "I will be your God, you will be my people." This is God's way of saying, "I love you." Just as the rainbow is the sign of the covenant with Noah, circumcision is the sign of the covenant with Abraham, the Sabbath is the sign of the covenant with Israel at Mount Sinai, we can regard our environment and all the objects surrounding us as the signs of God's holy providence and love. We should see the living hope on every leaf in the spring, for the holy providence and God's love are the main contents of the holy covenants. This is meaningful for the discussion of ecotheology.

The Living World, the Living Ecotheology: Redemption

The discussion mentioned above suggests to us to rethink and adjust the traditional conception of "redemption" and the ideas which are related to it, such as repentance, regeneration and sanctification.

---

[3] See John D. Levenson, "Idioms of Creation and Covenant", in Ben C. Ollenburger (eds), *The Flowering of Old Testament Theology* (Winona Lake, Indiana: Eisenbrauns, 1992), 438.

[4] W. J. Dumbrell, *Covenant and Creation* (Nashville, TN: Thomas Nelson, 1984), 35.

[5] Environment | Definition of Environment by Merriam-Webster [Available at: https://www.merriam-webster.com/dictionary/environment], [Last accessed: 1st Febrrary 2022].

> Whatever our views on the 1 Peter context may be, the section makes it clear that Noah's deliverance was regarded as a type of Christian redemption [...] Genesis 9 made it clear, as we have seen, that the covenant with Noah had the preservation of the created order in view, but this in itself is a redemptive exercise on the widest scale. The restoration of man is bound to affect his world and consistently with this, the New Testament asserts strongly that the redemption of the creature must involve the redemption of creation.[6]

God is not a dead God, but a living God. The revelation God gives to humans is given gradually. In the same way, our view of God should not be stagnant, but should evolve along with the times. As Christians, we are also part of society and our physical environment, and we cannot live in isolation from it. Rather the environment in which we live is eternally changing and developing in a forward direction. By taking care of the environment, we are taking part in the process towards a new creation and redemption as partners and friends of God just as Abraham did.

Righteousness

The holy covenants stretch over all people, Christians or non-Christians, human beings or other living creatures, even upon inanimate objects. "In the introductory chapters of Genesis, God blesses the birds and fishes (1:22), mankind (1:28), the Sabbath (2:3), and Noah (9:1). Once again Genesis' interest in procreation is evident, for God's blessing is linked with his command to 'be fruitful and multiply' in 1:22, 28 and 9:1."[7] How can we understand justice or righteousness in the light of ecotheology? From the perspective of Biblical theology, God is righteous, for God keeps all of the covenants which were recorded in the history of creation and redemption. Therefore, the concept of "righteousness" or "the image of God" does not mean a kind of steady existence or substance above the earth which used to be conceived in such a way in Greek philosophy, but it means that God is taking care of the created world with enthusiastic love forever. The action of creation is a kind of blessing. In my opinion, to be righteous is to forgive human beings for what they did to the "environment" in the sense of Noachian Covenant. This is the key word for a living ecotheology: that God's love never ends is showing that the Noachian covenant still has effect.

The Worldliness of the OT

Being justified sinners in status, we Christians should be the forerunners in the field of so-called secular ecology. We should not refuse or deny "worldliness" of the messages of the holy Bible which is more evidently testified with the Old Testament.

> The this-worldly perspective of the OT sounds a distinctive note for readers used to the predominant other-worldliness of the NT. [...] the worldliness of the OT as a whole reflects its conviction that humanity's redemption by God releases us to live in the world, which God created, not out of it.[8]

In a word, this world is the haven of our bodies and souls, every object surrounding us is included in our own "household". In the process of the changing world, creation and redemption are the two sides of a coin. Jürgen Moltmann, according to Wells, argues that we need to "avoid drawing a firm distinction between creation and redemption: theologies that do so tend to find it difficult to articulate such an affirming role

---

6 W. J. Dumbrell, *Covenant and Creation*, 41.

7 Gordon J. Wenham, *Story as Torah: Reading Old Testament Narrative* (Grand Rapids, MI: Baker Academic, 2000), 21.

8 Leslie C. Allen, *A Theological Approach to the Old Testament* (Eugene, OR: Cascade), 2014, 8.

for creation itself, since they tend to see everything through the lens of the Fall. By contrast, Moltmann says 'creation is aligned towards its redemption from the very beginning'."[9]

The Living Faith, the Living Future: Dualism

In our Chinese context, Christians who are doing ecotheology are facing some theological difficulties. On the one hand, some Christians used to treat the nonhuman natural creation as merely instrumental value in the process of redemption. Some people misunderstand the relationship between the Old Testament and the New Testament, by arguing in a simplistic manner that the former focuses on creation and the latter focuses on redemption.

> Many Christians today are infected with a form of Gnosticism, a heresy that plagued the early church. Gnostics believed our physical world, including the human body, is destined for destruction in the life to come. Only the spiritual will exist in heaven. Gnostics thought earthly matter is, at best, a divine mistake, and at worst, intrinsically evil. The Gnostic concept of salvation, therefore, focused on liberation from the body and birth into a purely spiritual world.[10]

Evidently, this kind of theological thinking is rooted in a potential dualism. On the contrary, we must treat the environmental degradation properly theologically. On the other hand, industrial development in China caused water and air pollution. In China, the concern for the environment dates back some 40 years, much later than international scientists developing this concern. "It is an endless enjoyment to fight against the heaven, it is an endless enjoyment to fight against the earth, and it is an endless enjoyment to fight against human beings."[11] This was a well-known anti-human and anti-ecological slogan in the past, but there are great changes today. We are trying to abandon goals that are unworthy of people.

The Good News

Chinese Christians have to keep a living faith that leads to a living future of our churches and our country. What is really the Good News for our people? What concretely is sin in China today? What is salvation? All of these questions must be resolved both in the light of special revelation and general revelation that will determine the direction of the ecotheological development in Chinese context.

Some vital clues are already expressed in the above-mentioned lines. Our relationship (that means the holy covenant) with God is not self-feeling-centred; it is God-centred. And God is faithful to all his promises made in the covenant. According to the Covenant with Noah, to encroach the living world is to sin against the created order, for "the created order itself reveals both the existence and the character of God. Given the biblical teaching that one's actions reveal one's being (Prov. 237; 27:19; Mt. 12:34; 15:18), since God created the world, one would expect the creation to reflect its Maker."[12] Yes, this world is the world of the Heavenly Father. Fifty years ago, I spent my childhood in my hometown, in a northern part in China. The water in rivers surrounding our village was clean enough so that I could catch fresh shrimp and eat them directly. This experience reminded me to depict an ecotheological portrait for myself then and now. The

---

[9] Samuel Wells (ed), *Christian Ethics: An Introductory Reader* (West Sussex: Blackwell Publishing, 2010), 316.
[10] Christopher T. Bounds, "God's Ongoing Redemption of All Creation", in Joseph Coleson (ed), *Care of Creation: Christian Voices on God, Humanity, and the Environment* (Fishers, IN: Wesleyan Publishing House, 2010).
[11] The sentence "Endless enjoyment to fight against heaven, against earth, against the human beings" was a well-known slogan and leading vision for Mao Tse-tung, which symbolized the start of the Cultural Revolution in China and was published in his first poster which was published on 05.08.1966 in the Newspaper The People's Daily; See: The People's Daily, August 5, 1966. p. 3.
[12] David W. Jones, *An Introduction to Biblical Ethics* (Nashville, TN: B&H Publishing Group, 2013), 33.

natural environment is not just "natural" but a precious gift for us. The Old Testament tells us that God placed his dwelling in people's midst (Lev. 26:11, Rev. 21:3). We not only meet God in church buildings, but in our environment. In my opinion, this is the very "Good News" and the greatest mercy for us. Do I have a real fear and reverence for God in the environment? All of us are outlaws under the thorough survey of ecotheology. Ignoring the ecological balance is destruction of God's creation. To respect the natural world is to respect our God.

Sanctification

Sitting in the clean and bright chapel, reading the holy Bible – most have become used to this being the normal religious life. All may think we already performed our duties before God and have kept a correct relationship with God. God's covenant-document however is in the midst of his people: his people formed as his covenant assembly. All of the objects surrounding us are included in this assembly, for we Christians are the representatives or stewards of God on earth. Our relationship with God is defined, established, guaranteed, and maintained by God.

We already recognised that Christians and non-Christians were both under the covenant made with Noah. We are performing the same duties in the realm of ecotheology. The Covenant with Noah is not merely "General Revelation", but also "Special Revelation". "General revelation [...] includes the created order, the conscience of man, and the events of history."[13] There are many wonderful instances in the Old Testament of a concern and interest in the whole natural world as a part of God's creation, independent of human beings. This idea is useful in understanding the concept and brief meaning of ecotheology. We can enlarge the religious function and the spiritual meaning of "sanctification" in the process of environmental protection. The life of humankind itself and the living world are mysterious. The only thing we can do is to humble ourselves before God the creator. In this process, the key ideas are obeying God's voice and keeping the Holy Covenant. This can also be understood as another kind of sanctification, for "We Christians affirm the universe and all it contains as God's creation. This affirmation means that the created world is good and holy."[14] According to the teachings of the Old Testament, the priests take roles as teachers and mediators in Israel's daily life. "When the priest delivered an oracle, he was passing on an answer from God; when he gave an instruction, a *tôrah*, and later when he explained the Law, the Torah, he was passing on and interpreting teaching that came from God."[15] We Christians are the priests before God and our Chinese people. The Chinese church has a long tradition of "lifting up the Bible". Lifting up the Bible and lifting up the sufferings of creation is a key mandate for Chinese Christianity.

For example, 17th June 2021 was the 27th "World Day to Combat Desertification and Drought". The year's global theme was "Restoring Ecology, Protecting Land, and reviving the Economy". China's theme was "Harmonious coexistence between Mountains, Rivers, Forestry, Woods, Lakes, and Grass".[16] In a recent issue, of *Nanjing Theological Review*[17] several articles were published focusing on an ecotheological theme. Behind the covenants, is the sovereignty of God. Theologically, we Christians entirely welcome what our government does, for a friendly and peaceful environment is a fundamental element for every person, including Christians.

---

[13] David W. Jones, *An Introduction to Biblical Ethics*.
[14] K. H. Ting, *Love Never Ends* (Nanjing: Yilin Press, 2000), 399.
[15] Roland de Vaux, *Ancient Israel*, Vol.2. (New York: McGraw-Hill, 1965), 357.
[16] 沙区变绿洲，福建沙化土地治理成效显著 18th June 2021, [Available at: http://fj.people.com.cn/n2/2021/0618/c181466-34781808.html], [Last accessed: 1st February 2022].
[17] See: *Nanjing Theological Review* Vol.3, 2021. This journal is the most important theological quarterly in mainland China.

The Image of God

Our relationship with God has a name: a covenant in which we Christians are also involved. The Covenant with Noah challenges us to abandon all self-centred, man-centred, feeling-centred thinking and living. The Image of God can be understood more clearly in the light of the Covenant with Noah which is the essential relationship between God and human beings. According to this covenant, human beings and their environment – the earth – are tied together as the community of being. Here, Salvation of God means the healing of creation. This is an ecotheological invitation to covenantal thinking and living.

> "Likeness to God means God's relationship to human beings first of all, and only then, and as a consequence of that, the human being's relationship to God. God puts himself in a particular relationship to human beings – a relationship in which human beings became his image and his glory on earth."[18]

Thus the protection and respect of the environment is the adherence of the Covenant with Noah. When Cain killed Abel, God asked Cain: "Where is your brother Abel?" (Gen. 4:9, *NRSV*). We also can ask ourselves in the same way: "Where is your environment?" For the environment and all of the living creatures are our partners in the pilgrimage to God.

Conclusion

In Psalm 147:15-20, the word and commandment of God are described as being sent to the earth to bring winter and springtime. The declaration follows that God showed his word unto Jacob, his statutes and his ordinances unto Israel. While Jesus was going and apostles were gazing up toward heaven, two angels said to them, "Men of Galilee, why do you stand looking up toward heaven?" (Acts 1:11, *NRSV*). All of us can grasp the main meaning of this question which is pointing the disciples towards the earth. Our environment is on the earth. This is an warning to us: we have to keep the Noachian Covenant, and take care of our environment as that is the great gift of God for human beings. This is the real testimony of Christians in the field of ecotheology.

Suggestions for Further Reading

Coleson, Joseph, Ed. *Care of Creation: Christian Voices on God, Humanity, and the Environment*. Fishers, IN: Wesleyan Publishing House, 2010.

Dumbrell, W. J. *Covenant and Creation*. Nashville, TN: Thomas Nelson, 1984.

Goldingay, John E. *Old Testament Theology*, vol. 1. Downers Grove, IL: InterVarsity, 2003.

Jones, David W. *An Introduction to Biblical Ethics*. Nashville, TN: B&H, 2013.

Moltmann, Jürgen, *God in Creation: A New Theology of Creation and the Spirit of God.* New York: HarperCollins, 1991.

Myers, N. and J. Kent. *Environmental Exodus: An Emergent in the Global Arena*. Washington DC: Climate Institute, 1995.

Wenham, Gordon J. *Story as Torah: Reading Old Testament Narrative.* Grand Rapids, MI: Baker Academic, 2000.

Wells, Samuel, Ed. *Christian Ethics: An Introductory Reader*. West Sussex: Blackwell, 2010.

Wright, C. J. H. *Old Testament Ethics for the People of God.* Leicester: InterVarsity, 2004.

[18] Jürgen Moltmann, *God in Creation: A New Theology of Creation and the Spirit of God* (New York: Harper Collins Publishers, 1991), 220.

18. Reconsidering Ecological Civilisation from a Chinese Christian Perspective[1]

Bryan K. M. Mok[2]

Introduction

Climate change mitigation or, more broadly, ecological crisis alleviation requires a wholesale change in policymaking and lifestyle which also requires a radical shift in perception. Thus, it is not only a scientific and political issue but has its cultural and religious dimensions. As American environmentalist James Gustave Speth indicates, a spiritual and cultural transformation is needed on top of scientific and technological solutions to rectify human exploitation of nature.[3]

To attain such a transformation, it is necessary to renew people's conception of nature.[4] In China, environmental scholars have attempted to substitute a symbiotic cosmology for the anthropocentric and triumphalist attitude towards nature since the mid-1980s. They put forward the notion of ecological civilisation, which stresses nature's innate value and envisages a harmonious human-nature relationship. In the early 2000s, the Chinese Communist Party (CCP) formally took this notion into its official agenda and declared it the major environmental policymaking principle. However, some philosophical and practical problems are yet to be settled. This calls for a critical examination of the term "ecological civilisation".

This chapter investigates the possible contribution of religion to ecological civilisation from a Chinese Christian perspective. Although the CCP is sceptical about religion, religion does play a crucial role in constructing an ecological worldview by offering comprehensive and normative pictures of the totality of the universe through symbolic representation.[5] Particularly, it argues that while the concept of ecological civilisation is closely related to Chinese religious traditions, an interreligious approach is necessary for a thorough understanding of the underlying worldview of ecological civilisation.

The Notion of Ecological Civilisation and its Development in China

Agricultural economist Ye Qianji first introduced the notion of ecological civilisation in 1984 to advocate ecologically sustainable agriculture. A decade later, ecological activist Roy Morrison conceived it a

[1] This essay is a shortened and edited version of an article of the author published under the same title; see Bryan K. M. Mok, "Reconsidering Ecological Civilization from a Chinese Christian Perspective," *Religions* 11, no. 5 (2020): 261, [Available at: https://doi.org/10.3390/rel11050261].

[2] Dr Bryan K. M. Mok is a Research Associate in the Centre for the Study of Religious Ethics and Chinese Culture, the Chinese University of Hong Kong (CUHK) and a Part-Time Lecturer in the Divinity School of Chung Chi College, CUHK. His primary research interests are religious environmental ethics and the intersection of religion and society. He has published several articles on religious and theological engagement in ethical, social, political, and ecological issues. kiemanbryanmok@cuhk.edu.hk.

[3] Christine Wamsler, "Contemplative Sustainable Futures: The Role of Individual Inner Dimensions and Transformation in Sustainability Research and Education," in *Sustainability and the Humanities*, ed. Walter Leal Filho and Adriana Consorte McCrea (New York: Springer, 2019), 360.

[4] J. Robert Cox and Phaedra C. Pezzullo, *Environmental Communication and the Public Sphere*, 4th ed. (Los Angeles, CA: SAGE, 2016), 12.

[5] Ernst M. Conradie, "Climate Change and the Common Good: Some Reflections from the South African Context," *International Journal of Public Theology* 4, no. 3 (2010): 273, [Available at: https://doi.org/10.1163/156973210X510857], [Last accessed: 3rd February 2022].

replacement of industrial civilisation in his book *Ecological Democracy*.[6] According to him, the core of ecological civilisation lies in its emphasis on the human embeddedness within nature. This shows that human flourishing depends on the conservation of a sustainable equilibrium of the biophysical sphere. In turn, it urges people to relinquish an unsustainable civilisation that is based on hierarchy, progress, and technique.[7] Recently, some scholars further develop this notion by contrasting it with industrial civilisation. Their contributions can be summarised in four points. First, ecological civilisation turns away from the reductionist materialism of industrial civilisation and stresses the symbiosis between human life and natural ecosystems. Secondly, it rectifies the error of unrestrained economic growth by advocating self-regulation and self-restraint on human consumption. Thirdly, it perceives human-nature relationship in terms of harmony, not domination. Finally, it envisages that the goal of economic activities should be sustainable development rather than profit maximisation.[8]

Ecological civilisation is closely linked to the Chinese context. First, many scholars in China claim that Chinese philosophy has a long tradition of ecological awareness, which is best demonstrated in the Confucian notion of the "unity of Heaven and humanity." Some of them uphold the centrality of this notion in Chinese ecological ethics. For them, Heaven is a symbol representing the totality of the universe. Thus, this notion can serve as a foundation of Chinese ecological ethics that balances the human-nature dualism in Western thought.[9] Ecological civilisation's proponents also seek to revive this philosophical tradition to create a sustainable future.[10]

Secondly, there is a hint of environmentalism in socialism. For instance, Marx and Engels considered that industrial capitalism is an important source of unsustainable exploitation of nature.[11] In *Capital*, Marx argues that capitalist production "disturbs the metabolic interaction between man and the earth."[12] Engels also suggests that "harmony with laws of nature" is a necessary condition for human freedom.[13] As socialism is China's official ideology, sustainability and harmony with nature are often supposed to be the guiding principle in environmental policymaking.

---

[6] Maurizio Marinelli, "How to Build a 'Beautiful China' in the Anthropocene: The Political Discourse and the Intellectual Debate on Ecological Civilization," *Journal of Chinese Political Science* 23, no. 3 (2018): 373, [Available at: https://doi.org/10.1007/s11366-018-9538-7], [Last accessed: 3rd February 2022].

[7] Roy Morrison, *Ecological Democracy* (Boston, MA: South End Press, 1995), 9-12.

[8] Arran Gare, "Toward an Ecological Civilization: The Science, Ethics, and Politics of Eco-Poiesis," *Process Studies* 39, no. 1 (2010): 5-38; Fred Magdoff, "Ecological Civilization," *Monthly Review* 62, no. 8 (2011): 1-25; Jiahua Pan, *China's Environmental Governing and Ecological Civilization* (Berlin: Springer Berlin Heidelberg, 2016), 29-50.

[9] Zhengrong She, *Zhongguo shengtai lunli chuantong de quanshi yu chongjian* [Interpretation and Reconstruction of the Chinese Tradition of Ecological Ethics] (Beijing: People's Publishing, 2002), 18-54; Qingju Qiao, *Ze ji caomu, en zhi shuitu: Rujia shengtai wenhua* [Bounties to Vegetation and Soil: A Confucian Ecological Culture] (Jinan: Shandong Education Press, 2011), 191-200; Zhou Wu, *Zhongguo gudai zhexue de sengtai yiyun* [Ecological Implications of Ancient Chinese Philosophy] (Beijing: China Social Sciences Press, 2012), 85-123; Xing Han, "Rujia tian ren yi ti guan yu shengtai wenming" [The Confucian concept of unity of heaven and humanity and ecological civilisation], in *Tian ren zhi bian: Ruxue yu shengtai wenming* [Distinction between heaven and humanity: Confucianism and ecological civilisation], ed. Liwen Zhang (Beijing: People's Publishing House, 2013), 323-34.

[10] Mette Halskov Hansen, Hongtao Li, and Rune Svarverud, "Ecological Civilization: Interpreting the Chinese Past, Projecting the Global Future," *Global Environmental Change* 53 (2018): 197, https://doi.org/10.1016/j.gloenvcha.2018.09.014.

[11] Jean-Yves Heurtebise, "Sustainability and Ecological Civilization in the Age of Anthropocene: An Epistemological Analysis of the Psychosocial and 'Culturalist' Interpretations of Global Environmental Risks," *Sustainability* 9, no. 8 (2017): 10, https://doi.org/10.3390/su9081331.

[12] Karl Marx, *Capital: A Critique of Political Economy*, translated by Ben Fowkes, vol. 1 (London: Penguin Books, 1990), 637.

[13] Magdoff, "Ecological Civilization," 20.

Thirdly, ecological civilisation has entered CCP's official agenda.[14] The Chinese government has included sustainable development and ecosystem improvement in their process of policymaking. This is visible in the four targets set in the CCP's 16th National Congress in 2002 and President Hu Jintao's call for improvements in ecological construction and education in 2005.[15] At the same time, Chinese officials endeavoured to propagandise ecological civilisation with reference to the Chinese tradition.[16] Eventually, ecological civilisation became a key political guideline in CCP's 17th National Congress in 2007 and was formally written into the constitution in 2018.[17]

It seems that the above three points have altogether put China at the forefront of ecological civilisation. Environmental philosopher Arran Gare even suggests that "[t]he world should follow the lead of China" in advocating ecological civilisation.[18] However, one needs to examine the official ecological discourse more carefully before making such a conclusion. Particularly, it is necessary to look closer into the relationship between ancient Chinese philosophy and the contemporary notion of ecological civilisation.

CCP's Official Discourses for Ecological Civilisation

Pan Yue, a CCP official, has published several articles concerning the theoretical basis of ecological civilisation. He attempts to prove that traditional Chinese culture can provide intellectual resources that Western philosophies lack. For him, Western civilisation is fundamentally anthropocentric, and industrialisation and capitalism have further made it unable to lead the world in environmental protection. In contrast, ecological conservation is an intrinsic part of Chinese culture, and Chinese civilisation is inherently in line with ecological civilisation. Particularly, the principle of "unity of Heaven and humanity" has made Chinese civilisation respect the intrinsic value of nature. In addition, the Daoist principle that "*Dao* (the Way) follows what is natural" has brought about an intersubjective unity between humankind and nature, whereas Chinese Buddhism has taught that all forms of life possess Buddha-nature and are thus of equal status.[19]

President Hu first adopted the notion of ecological civilisation in his report to the 17th National Congress. In the report, Hu requests the Party to firmly establish the idea of ecological civilisation in

---

[14] Chen Liu et al., "A Chinese Route to Sustainability: Postsocialist Transitions and the Construction of Ecological Civilization," *Sustainable Development* 26, no. 6 (2018): 742, https://doi.org/10.1002/sd.1743.

[15] Pan, *China's Environmental Governing*, 47-48.

[16] Heurtebise, "Sustainability and Ecological Civilization," 7-8; Hansen, Li, and Svarverud, "Ecological Civilization," 197-98.

[17] Qingzhi Huan, "Growth Economy and Its Ecological Impacts upon China: An Eco-Socialist Analysis," in *Eco-Socialism as Politics: Rebuilding the Basis of Our Modern Civilization*, ed. Qingzhi Huan (New York: Springer, 2010), 200; Hansen, Li, and Svarverud, "Ecological Civilization," 195.

[18] Gare, "Toward an Ecological Civilization," 6.

[19] Yue Pan, "Huanjing wenhua yu minzu fuxing" [Environmental culture and national revival], Ministry of Ecology and Environment of the People's Republic of China, 28th October 2003, [Available at: http://www.mee.gov.cn/gkml/sthjbgw/qt/200910/t20091030_180661.htm], [Last accessed: 9th April 2020]; Pan, "Shengtai Hexie Guan: Goujian Shehuizhuyi Shengtai Wenming" [Perspectives on Ecological Harmony: Constructing Socialist Ecological Civilization], *21st Century Business Herald*, 9th October 2006, [Available at: http://finance.sina.com.cn/review/20061001/22132961402.shtml], [Last accessed: 9th April 2020]; Pan, "Evolution of an Ecological Civilization," *Beijing Review*, 9th November 2016, updated 15th December 2016, [Available at: http://www.bjreview.com.cn/expert/txt/2006- 12/15/content_50890.htm], [Last accessed 9th April 2020]; Pan, "Shengtai wenming jiang cujin Zhongguo tese shehuizhuyi jianshe" [Ecological Civilization will Promote the Construction of Socialism with Chinese Characteristics], Zhongguowang, 23rd October 2007, [Available at: http://www.china.com.cn/policy/txt/2007-10/23/content_9108996.htm], [Last accessed 9th April 2020]; Pan, "Zhonghua chuantong yu shengtai wenming" [Chinese Tradition and Ecological Civilization], Renminwang, 15th December 2008, [Available at: http://env.people.com.cn/GB/8517913.html], [Last accessed: 9th April 2020].

society.[20] In his report to the next National Congress, Hu further puts constructing ecological civilisation into the overall framework of the national strategy that aims to "build a beautiful China." Besides, he also institutionalises ecological civilisation and urges the whole country to advance to a "socialist ecological civilisation."[21] President Xi Jinping largely retained this direction in his report to the 19th National Congress.[22]

It is noteworthy that President Xi published an article specifically on ecological civilisation in CCP's major theoretical journal, *Qiushi*.[23] This article shows his ambition to propagandise ecological civilisation as part of the CCP's political agenda grounded on traditional Chinese philosophy. However, a theoretical link between ecological civilisation and the Chinese tradition is missing. Slightly earlier, Pan Yue wrote another article that attempts to demonstrate the ecological awareness in ancient Chinese culture.[24] However, Pan does not explicate how the classic passages he cited can enlighten the contemporary construction of ecological civilisation. This shows that the Chinese official discourse may have taken for granted the ecological relevance of the Chinese classics. Yet, as Jean-Yves Heurtebise, a researcher in oriental philosophy, points out, Heaven in Chinese classics primarily refers to a universal law rather than the biophysical environment. Thus, the identity of Heaven with nature in a biophysical sense may be an anachronistic overinterpretation.[25] In fact, Pan's critics have already problematised this kind of appropriation of Chinese classics, which is said to be selective and reductionist.[26] Therefore, it is necessary to have a rationale that goes deeper into the cultural dimension of ecological civilisation.

Although ecological civilisation is not without philosophical difficulties in China, it is a useful means "to give a moral legitimacy to the enforcement of environmental regulations."[27] However, one needs to put it under the scrutiny of different religious traditions, for the ecological crisis is a global issue. Hence, it calls for a cross-cultural and cross-religious approach.[28] The transformation from industrial to ecological civilisation is something as large as a paradigm shift. It calls people to thoroughly reconceptualise their relationship with the biophysical universe and radically change their ways of living. This shift of perception and behaviour is religious, for it calls upon the conversion of core beliefs and values. Lynn White may have been mistaken about the historical roots of the ecological crisis, but he was right in indicating the significance of religion for environmental protection.[29]

---

[20] Jintao Hu, "Hu Jintao zai Zhonggong di shiqi ci Quanguo Daibiao Dahui shang de baogao quanwen" [The Full Text of Hu Jintao's Report Presented in the 17th National Congress of the CCP], www.gov.cn, 24th October 2007, [Available at: http://www.gov.cn/ldhd/2007-10/24/content_785431_4.htm], [Last accessed: 9th April 2020], sec. 4.
[21] Jintao Hu, "Hu Jintao zai Zhongguo Gongchandang di shiba ci Quanguo Daibiao Dahui shang de baogao" [Hu Jintao's Report Presented in the 18th National Congress of the Communist Party of China], www.gov.cn, 17th November 2012, [Available at: http://www.gov.cn/ldhd/2012-11/17/content_2268826_5.htm], [Last accessed: 9th April 2020], sec. 8.
[22] Jinping Xi, "Juesheng quanmian jiancheng xiaokang shehui, duoqu xinshidai Zhongguo tese shehuizhuyi weida shengli: zai Zhongguo Gongchandang di shijiu ci Quanguo Daibiao Dahui shang de baogao" [Determining the success of full-scale well-off society, winning the great victory of socialism with Chinese characteristics in the new era: report presented in the 19th National Congress of the Communist Party of China], www.gov.cn, 17th October 2017, [Available at: http://www.gov.cn/zhuanti/2017-10/27/content_5234876.htm], [Last accessed: 9th April 2020].
[23] Jinping Xi, "Tuidong woguo shengtai wenming jianshe maishang xin taijie" [Advancing the construction of ecological civilization in China to a new stage], *Qiushi*, 31st January 2019, [Available at: http://www.qstheory.cn/dukan/qs/2019-01/31/c_1124054331.htm], [Last accessed: 9th April 2020].
[24] Yue Pan, "Shengtai wenming jianshe de genben zunxun" [The Fundamental Adherence of Constructing Ecological Civilization], *Guangming Online*, 8th November 2018, [Available at: http://epaper.gmw.cn/gmrb/html/2018-11/02/nw.D110000gmrb_20181102_2-10.htm], [Last accessed: 9th April 2020].
[25] Heurtebise, "Sustainability and Ecological Civilization," 9.
[26] For example, see Hansen, Li, and Svarverud, "Ecological Civilization," 198.
[27] Heurtebise, "Sustainability and Ecological Civilization," 11.
[28] Liu et al., "Chinese Route to Sustainability," 747.
[29] Lynn White, Jr., "The Historical Roots of Our Ecological Crisis," *Science* 155 (March 1967): 1203-7.

Religion is fundamentally a system of symbols that structurally guides humankind to understand their existence and establishes powerful and abiding moods and motivations.[30] An important role of it is its provision of symbolic representations and visualised pictures of the totality of the world. These representations and pictures are the spiritual ground for realising ecological civilisation. They can take the form of stories, symbols, rituals, or even conceptual models. The key is that they connect people with different backgrounds and call them together to revolt against industrial civilisation that has misled people into taking modern consumerism as the best way of living.[31] The remain of this chapter will discuss the symbolic representation of the human-nature relationship in the Chinese tradition and bring Christian insights into the discussion.

***Qi* and *Li*: Confucian Thought on Human-Cosmic Unity**

Unlike Abrahamic religions, traditional Chinese thought has no idea of an external God who creates all that is and keeps them in order. Contemporary Confucian Tu Wei-ming states that the Chinese model of the world is founded on the belief in the continuity of being. The world is not a *creatio ex nihilo* but a result of impersonal cosmic forces. Existence requires no creator, and harmony needs no ordainer.[32] In this model, *qi* (or *ch'i*) – the vital force of the cosmos – is an essential notion in understanding how nature operates. *Qi* brings everything into unity, for every worldly being and entity is made of and consists of it. Thus, in the depth of reality, humanity and nature are one. In turn, *qi* makes the world a closed system of self-generating life processes. This system is not only an unbroken chain of being, but also a dynamic and organic whole. According to Zhang Zai (1020-1077), humanity is the offspring of the Father Heaven and the Mother Earth, and they together form a holistic and organic body. This is where the unity of Heaven and humanity gains its ecological meaning.[33]

Humanity has a naturalistic side. Both humankind and nature are made of *qi* and are bodily connected through it. In this sense, humanity is a modality of *qi*. However, humanity is also a unique outcome of *qi*.[34] Tu places this uniqueness of human nature in consciousness. With reference to Wang Fuzhi's (1619-1692) interpretation of the *Doctrine of the Mean*, Tu contends that humankind must keep enlarging and deepening their compassion to embody the whole cosmos. Only in this way can they follow the heavenly principle fully. Thus, humanity neither stands in a subject-object dichotomy with nature nor entirely merges into it. Rather, humankind forms one body with the myriad things in the cosmos through participation from within. The human mind, which is a refined and subtle form of *qi*, enables humankind to resonate with Heaven and Earth and the myriad things.[35] In a later article, Tu, with reference to Xunzi (310-235 BCE), further states that while all things consist of *qi*, only humankind has a sense of righteousness.[36] Hence, righteousness can be understood as a particular development of *qi*, which is the overall principle of human activities and behaviours.

---

[30] Clifford Geertz, *The Interpretation of Cultures* (New York: Basic Books, 1973), 90.
[31] Michael Northcott, "Sustaining Ethical Life in the Anthropocene," in *Creation in Crisis: Christian Perspectives on Sustainability*, ed. Robert S. White (London: SPCK, 2009), 226-29.
[32] Wei-ming Tu, "The Continuity of Being: Chinese Visions of Nature," in *On Nature*, ed. Leroy S. Rouner (Norte Dame, IN: University of Norte Dame Press, 1984), 113-18.
[33] Tu, 121–22; see also Mary Evelyn Tucker, "The Philosophy of Ch'i as an Ecological Cosmology," in *Confucianism and Ecology: The Interrelation of Heaven, Earth, and Humans*, ed. Mary Evelyn Tucker and John H. Berthrong (Cambridge, MA: Harvard University Press, 1998), 191-97.
[34] Shuo Dongfang [Hongxing Lin], *Cong Hengqu, Mingdao dao Yangming: Rujia shengtai lunli de yi ge cemian* [From Hengqu, Mingdao to Yangming: the flank of Confucian ecological studies] (Hong Kong: The Chinese University Press, 2005), 9.
[35] Tu, "Continuity of Being," 125-26.
[36] Wei-ming Tu, "Confucianism and Liberalism," *Dao: A Journal of Comparative Philosophy* 2, no. 1 (2002): 2, [Available at: https://doi.org/10.1007/BF02856993], [Last accessed: 3rd February 2022].

Tu's representation of the world as a self-generating life system reflects the traditional Confucian worldview. According to this worldview, the coming into being of all that is and the emergence of life is a result of the virtue of Heaven and Earth. It is a process similar to the growth of an organism.[37] As the human mind is a special form of *qi* that has a sense of righteousness, humankind is responsible to act righteously by following the *li* (principle) of Heaven. In neo-Confucianism, *li* connects with *qi* closely. In a sense, *li* can be seen as the neo-Confucian term of *Dao* (the Way).[38] While *qi* is the vital force of changes that runs throughout all that is and brings new things into being, *li* is the pattern of changes or the principle of *qi*.[39]

Michael Kalton, a scholar in comparative religion, argues that the neo-Confucian notion of *li* can provide a profound philosophical interpretation of the systems theory emerging in the late twentieth century. Since *li* carries normative content for life, it can offer a moral dimension to various systems, such as biosystems, ecosystems, and social systems. In traditional thought, *li* is the cosmological root of ideal humanity. This idea can plausibly renew our understanding of the evolutionary process. Systems theory, according to Kalton, has falsified the popular equation of evolution with "survival of the fittest." On the contrary, symbiosis is indispensable for fitting in an ecosystem because every existence in the world is in a web of responsive relationships with others. Humankind cannot survive without the support of other forms of life and the surrounding ecosystems. *Li* reveals that the well-being of each worldly body is dependent on the well-being of other bodies. It is thus the normative principle of the entire body of the cosmos and each of its parts.[40] Accordingly, the development of ecological civilisation hinges on how far humanity follows *li* and agrees with *qi*.

A question here is how humankind can be aware of *li* and follow through with it. According to Chinese thinker Dongfang Shuo (aka. Lin Hongxing), neo-Confucian Cheng Hao (1032-1085) claimed that all things in Heaven and Earth hold fast to *li*.[41] In other words, *li* is inherent in humanity as in the myriad things in the world. Dongfang further contends that according to Wang Yangming (1472-1529), *li* never falls outside human hearts. In Wang's thought, *li* is just another form of conscience. Furthermore, human conscience is the same as the conscience of inorganic entities, for the myriad things are of one body. Those who are benevolent can get rid of their selfish desires and see themselves in the same body as the myriad things.[42] Religious scholar and theologian Lai Pan-chiu adds that the virtue of *ren* (benevolence) is the key to connecting human conscience with the cosmic principle, for *ren* "constitutes some ontological continuity or unity between Heaven and humanity."[43] In short, humankind can appeal to their conscience to achieve unity with the myriad things, for conscience unites humanity and divinity and guides humankind to overcome selfish desires through the virtue of *ren*.

The previous discussion shows that Chinese culture is ecological not because some classic Chinese passages seemingly support the harmony of humanity and nature, but because it offers a world-picture that reveals the commonality between humankind and other cosmic beings. Whenever we do good to the well-being of nature, we do good to our well-being; whenever we harm nature, we harm ourselves. This cosmological picture gives a philosophical basis for ecological civilisation and offers an enlightening way to perceive our innate interdependence and shared destiny with nature. Instead of simply making

---

[37] Pan-chiu Lai, "The Christian Story of God's Work: A Chinese Christian Response," in *T&T Clark Handbook of Christian Theology and Climate Change*, ed. Hilda P. Koster and Ernst M. Conradie (London: T&T Clark, 2020), 481.

[38] Michael C. Kalton, "Extending the Neo-Confucian Tradition: Questions and Reconceptualization for the Twenty-First Century," in *Confucianism and Ecology: The Interrelation of Heaven, Earth, and Humans*, ed. Mary Evelyn Tucker and John H. Berthrong (Cambridge, MA: Harvard University Press, 1998), 82.

[39] Tucker, "Philosophy of Ch'i," 191-92.

[40] Kalton, "Extending the Neo-Confucian Tradition," 83-85.

[41] Dongfang, *Cong Hengqu*, 33

[42] Dongfang, *Cong Hengqu*, 57-82.

[43] Lai, "Christian Story of God's Work," 481.

propagandist claims, it is more important to change the people's hearts. The principle of *li* in Confucian philosophy may help achieve this by appealing to the benevolence and righteousness that lie within the human nature. The (neo-)Confucian thought on *qi* and *li* reveals that real ecological change should begin in the natural law within the human conscience.

Confucian philosophy has displayed an inward, self-referential, and humanistic understanding of the human-nature relationship. An advantage is its emphasis on the human potentiality of perfection. From a Chinese perspective, unity with the world and the myriad things is inherent in the human nature. This is not to say that human effort can by any means surpass or replace divine actions, for natural phenomena are seen as results of the heavenly mandate. However, whether these phenomena lead to blessings or disasters is not unrelated to human morality. Therefore, for the well-being of humankind and the myriad things, the crucial role of humankind lies in their moral and spiritual cultivation. One of the human tasks in the cosmos is to assist the divine work of sustaining and nourishing life by actualising the potential of humanity. By recovering the "true self" through appealing to conscience and righteousness, one can break away from the small self, which is occupied by selfish desires, and achieve a bigger self, which is in line with *li*.[44] This perspective offers a positive way of understanding human responsibility for constructing ecological civilisation.

However, this symbolic representation of the cosmic role of humankind needs to be complemented by other religious resources in the development of ecological civilisation. Particularly, one needs to question whether humanity can turn away from selfishness and follow *li* without any external assistance. If humanity can achieve harmony and unity with nature by activating their conscience, why has environmental degradation and climate change kept worsening? What hampers us to practice *ren* and follow *qi* and *li*? How can we overcome this predicament? The Christian tradition, which upholds the necessity of salvation from without, may provide a heuristic account that may further enlighten the construction of ecological civilisation.

On the Necessity of an External Saviour: A Chinese Christian Perspective

A primary difference between Christianity and Confucianism is the former's belief in an external saviour. Christians believe that humankind cannot break away from fallenness without the divine grace that was ultimately revealed in Jesus Christ. How can this worldview enrich the religious dimension of ecological civilisation? The Confucian approach to achieving human-nature unity is insufficient because it lacks a way to tackle human sinfulness and fallenness. Given the seriousness of environmental degradation in China and elsewhere, this matter is significant theoretically and pragmatically. Thanks to its appeal to divine intervention, the Christian perspective has the potential to rectify the major weakness of Confucian thought. In fact, Confucianism is a long-time dialogue partner of Chinese Christianity. Hence, a survey of how Chinese Christians have integrated Confucian thought into their theology may provide further insights into the philosophical depth of ecological civilisation.

Both Roman Catholicism and Protestant Christianity are among the five officially recognised institutional religions in China, alongside Buddhism, Daoism, and Islam.[45] Unfortunately, the ecological account of Chinese Christianity is relatively thin compared with Confucianism, Daoism, and Chinese Buddhism. Moreover, Chinese scholars often represent Christianity as an unecological religion. However,

[44] Lai, "Christian Story of God's Work," 481-83.

[45] Confucianism is not on the list because it is often not formally regarded as a religion, although it definitely offers a religious worldview. Nonetheless, Confucianism is recognised as one of the six major religions in Hong Kong.

in their endeavours to Sinicise Christian thought, Chinese theologians of different ages have demonstrated the possibility of constructing a Chinese ecotheology.[46]

The Church of the East (also known as *Jingjiao*) was the first Christian church that reached China. The inscription on the Nestorian Stele composed by Syrian missionary Jingjing (eighth century) was the first Christian documentation in China. In the inscription, Jingjing depicted Christ as God's alter ego divided from the Trinity. This triune God was said to be the ultimate mystery that has created all that is and generated Yin and Yang through the Holy Spirit. Humankind was commissioned to guard and cultivate nature, but Satan had made them turn away from their original nature and thus become unable to implement the task. As a result, Christ was sent to redeem the fallen humankind, and he accomplished his mission by overcoming Satan's plot through his death and resurrection.[47] While employing Chinese symbolic representation in his theology, Jingjing differed from Confucianism in two ways. First, although all beings came into existence through Yin and Yang, they were created by a creator who transcends and precedes the world. Secondly, the way for humankind to return to the original goodness depends on an external saviour. From its beginning, Chinese Christianity has been sceptical about any self-referential path of human-nature reconciliation.

These two distinctions between Chinese Christianity and traditional Chinese thought were also visible when Roman Catholicism entered China in the late sixteenth century. In answering why there needs to be a creator when *qi* and *li* can explain the self-generation of all that is, Yang Tingyun (1557-1627) argues that *qi* has no consciousness and *li* has no soul. Hence, *qi* and *li* alone are insufficient to explain the world's formation. This is because *qi* is just an arbitrary force, and *li* cannot produce matter. The order of the universe and the possibility of life illustrates that every entity and organism in nature comes from a creator.[48] Interestingly, Yang accepted the neo-Confucian idea of the unity of nature and humanity. As for the neo-Confucian philosophers, the myriad things and the human subject are of the same body. However, for Yang, this did not mean that humankind and natural entities are of the same substance.[49] They are different in nature, and yet the same in principle; different in faction, and yet the same in origin. In this way, Yang was able to preserve both human distinctiveness and their unity with nature. Concerning the necessity of a saviour, Yang contends that only the redemption brought by Jesus through the cross could cancel out human transgression of the divine mandate.[50] In other words, humankind inevitably transgresses the natural order of *qi* and *li* thanks to their sinful nature. Only salvation through Jesus Christ could rectify this problem and enable humankind to follow *qi* and *li* again.

The link between Christ's redemption and the human relationship with the natural world was largely overlooked in Protestant Christianity in China, at least until the indigenous theology of the Three-Self Patriotic Movement came on the scene. The notion of the cosmic Christ proposed by the bishop and theologian Ting Kuang-hsun (also known as K. H. Ting or Ding Guangxun, 1915-2012) reconnects Christology and soteriology with the wider universe. His notion of the cosmic Christ has two main principles: the extension of Christ's reign, providence, and love over the cosmos, on the one hand, and love as the core nature of Christ, on the other hand. Based on these two principles, Ting contends that Christ has

---

[46] For a concise summary of these efforts, see Pan-Chiu Lai, "God of Life and Ecological Theology: A Chinese Christian Perspective," *The Ecumenical Review* 65, no. 1 (March 2013): 74-78, [Available at: https://doi.org/10.1111/erev.12027.]

[47] Jingjing, "The Monument of the Propagation of the Luminous Religion from *Daqin* in China," in *Sino-Christian Theology Reader,* ed. Guanghu He and Daniel H. N. Yeung, Institute of Sino-Christian Studies Monographs Series 35 (Hong Kong: Institute of Sino-Christian Studies, 2009), 19-20, 23 (in Chinese).

[48] Tingyun Yang, "A Treaty for Removing Doubts (Daiyi Pian) (Excerpt)," in *Sino-Christian Theology Reader,* ed. Guanghu He and Daniel H. N. Yeung, Institute of Sino-Christian Studies Monographs Series 35 (Hong Kong: Institute of Sino-Christian Studies, 2009), 62-63 (in Chinese).

[49] Yang, "A Treaty for Removing Doubts," 68-69. In classical Chinese, the word *ti* 體 can mean both "body" and "substance." Yang attempted to differentiate these two uses of the word in his work.

[50] Yang, "A Treaty for Removing Doubts," 71.

been participating in the divine creation, and the goal of salvation is to make God's love, peace, and justice the principle of the cosmos. In the meantime, Christ is directing the process of history to that goal. Hence, salvation and redemption are not bound by the Christian church but spread all over the cosmos. In turn, the whole universe is under God's providence and Christ's reign.[51] In the light of Ting's cosmic Christ, it can be said that Christ has revealed the divine source of *qi* and *li*, and that salvation and redemption allow humankind to take part in the cosmic order properly.

It is important to note that none of the above Chinese theologians have dealt with ecology in the modern sense. However, their Christology does have ecological implications and potentials. Among the notable modern Chinese theologians, Wang Wei-fan (1927-2015) was perhaps the closest to a conscious ecotheology. Grounded on the concept of *shengsheng* (production and reproduction of life) in *I Ching* (also known as *Yi Jing*) and the inscription of the Nestorian Stele, Wang presents the Christian God as the source of *shengsheng*. Accordingly, Christ is the saviour and fulfiller of life, and those whom Christ redeemed shall see *sheng* (life) as the great attribute and the highest excellence.[52] Regrettably, Wang does not further develop this insight in another article concerning the Christian faith and the ecological crisis.[53]

Wang's interpretation of the Christian faith in terms of the perpetuating production and reproduction of life has provided important resources for reconsidering ecological civilisation from a Chinese Christian perspective. If *qi* is the vital cosmic force and *li* is its principle, God is the ultimate source of life. God gives, fulfils, and sustains life in the cosmos through *qi* and by *li*. However, sin has distorted *qi* and disabled humankind from following *li*. The impairment and loss of life due to environmental degradation by human activities is perhaps the most vivid demonstration of the effect of sin in our age. Humankind has failed in implementing the task of cultivating life. From a Chinese Christian perspective, Christ's redemption is the only way for humankind to return to the source of life and reconcile with *qi* and *li* by taking life as the top priority. Only in this way can *Shengsheng* be resumed, and life can go on. Thus, acknowledging the source of life and redemption by Jesus Christ, the God-man who has fulfilled and sustained life, is necessary for ecological civilisation.

Conclusion

The notion of ecological civilisation has demonstrated that a profound transformation of civilisation is necessary for its preservation. There are already too many signs pointing to the destruction of life as a consequence of industrial civilisation, which employs a laissez-faire approach to economic growth and excludes the well-being of other forms of life in nature. Ecological civilisation reveals human embeddedness in nature and dependence on other species. This reminds humankind that they must acknowledge their symbiotic relationship with other beings in nature and take actions to restrain economic activities. Life and civilisation can continue to flourish only if sustainable development is substituted for profit maximisation.

---

[51] Kuang-hsun Ting, "The Cosmic Christ," in *Sino-Christian Theology Reader,* ed. Guanghu He and Daniel H. N. Yeung, Institute of Sino-Christian Studies Monographs Series 35 (Hong Kong: Institute of Sino-Christian Studies, 2009), 205-7.

[52] Wei-fan Wang, "Shengsheng pian: nianyi shiji dui Zhingguo gudai shengsheng shenxue zhi zhaohuan" [A chapter on *shengsheng*: the call of the twenty-first century to the theology of *shengsheng* of ancient China], in *In the Wilderness for Two Decades: Selected Works of Wang Wei-fan (1979-1998)*, Ching Feng Series 19 (Hong Kong: Christian Study Centre on Chinese Religion and Culture, 2011), 106-10. The Chinese word *sheng* can mean "to produce, generate, conceive, or give birth to" as a verb and "life" as a noun, and duplication often has a sense of recurrence or perpetuation. Therefore, *sheng sheng* primarily refers to the perpetuated activity of life.

[53] Wei-fan Wang, "Ren yu dadi" [Humans and the earth], in *In the Wilderness for Two Decades: Selected Works of Wang Wei-fan (1979-1998)*, Ching Feng Series 19 (Hong Kong: Christian Study Centre on Chinese Religion and Culture, 2011), 84-92.

As discussed previously, a danger of the Chinese agenda of ecological civilisation is its lack of a comprehensive investigation into the depth of culture. To avoid being empty slogans, the construction of ecological civilisation requires a closer look into the ecological rationale of Chinese religious philosophy. Enjoying an official status throughout most of Chinese history, Confucianism has served as a backbone of the Chinese belief system. It thus may offer some important intellectual and spiritual resources for examining the notion of ecological civilisation. By interpreting neo-Confucian understanding of *qi* and *li*, contemporary Confucians have established a link between human self-cultivation and ecological practices. According to them, humankind can attain the unity of humanity and nature by appealing to our conscience. In terms of ecological civilisation, everyone can overcome the selfish desire intensified in industrial civilisation and market capitalism through moral and spiritual cultivation. This guides humankind to tune their way of living in accordance with *li* and thus attain harmony with *qi*.

However, the realities of environmental degradation and climate change in China and globally have made the Confucian optimism about human cultivation dubious. Under the circumstances, the Christian insistence on the necessity of a saviour from God does make sense. The legacies of Chinese Christian thinkers may provide resources to supplement the self-referential tendency of the traditional Chinese worldview. The construction of ecological civilisation requires humankind to restrain their economic activities and sacrifice individual and collective wealth. Moreover, to cater to the well-being of other species means that our living may probably become less convenient and comfortable. Negatively, Christian teachings remind us that humankind always fails to achieve self-limitation without divine assistance. It guards against any illusion that humankind can save themselves and the world from ecocide on their own. Humankind needs to confess their tendency to transgress *li* and hamper *qi*.

What positive contributions can this Chinese Christian perspective offer? It is important to note that salvation and redemption are not separated from creation in the Christian worldview. The doctrine of creation suggests that everything in the cosmos is from God and thus has a divine imprint. In the words of Pope Francis, creation "has to do with God's loving plan in which every creature has its own value and significance."[54] In turn, the salvation and redemption through Christ was a renewal of this plan. Thus, the Christian emphasis on the prevalence of sin and the necessity of salvation does not negate the possibility of human perfection and the endeavour to work for God's plan. In contrast, it proclaims the good news that, thanks to the life and death of Jesus Christ, "[a]ll of us can cooperate as instruments of God for the care of creation, each according to his or her own culture, experience, involvements, and talent," even though we are sinful.[55]

In this light, the Christian tradition has offered a paradoxical interpretation of the unity of humanity and the cosmos. While affirming the human responsibility to respect the value of other forms of life and take care of their well-being, it always denies the possibility for humankind to take up this responsibility by their effort. This paradoxical perspective reveals the importance of being critical of ecological practices and environmental policy-making.

In principle, the Chinese effort to promote ecological civilisation and CCP's move to take the notion into its agenda should be appreciated, especially because a top-down approach can be highly effective. If the construction of ecological civilisation leads to a culture that treasures symbiosis and sustainability, China can provide a successful model for the world to tackle the ecological crisis. However, there is still a long way to go. It requires radical changes in its mode of production and consumption, and these changes need the backup of profound ecological culture and spirituality. From a Chinese Christian perspective, the answer as to whether China can achieve this is both yes and no. It is a "yes" because balance, harmony, and

---

[54] Francis, *Encyclical Letter Laudato Si' of the Holy Father Francis on Care for Our Common Home*, the Holy See, 24th May 2015, [Available at: http://www.vatican.va/content/francesco/en/encyclicals/documents/papa-francesco_20150524_enciclica-laudato-si.html], [Last accessed: 15th April 2020], para. 76.
[55] Francis, para. 14.

unity are long regarded as the most important values in Chinese culture. In particular, Confucian thought has revealed the way to attain these values by self-cultivation. However, it is simultaneously a "no" because humankind is always bound by selfish desire. Not only the Bible says so, but the sheer fact of ecological destruction in China and in the world also vindicates such pessimism.

Without realising the no (our tendency to turn against what is good for both nature and humanity), humankind can never actualise the yes (our potential to attain unity with the cosmos); without affirming the yes (our task to cultivate life), we will easily fall prey to the no (despair and hopelessness). While ecological civilisation is perhaps just another of CCP's propaganda, it has the potential to rectify the fatal consequences of industrial civilisation. Different religious traditions have a role in nurturing – both constructively and critically – the best part of ecological civilisation with their spiritual wisdom. An insight that Chinese Christianity can offer is that, while humankind always fails to follow the principle of the cosmic force that gives and sustains life, the renewal brought by the ultimate source of life has empowered us to work for the well-being of all life.

Suggestions for Further Reading

Hansen, Mette Halskov, Hongtao Li, and Rune Svarverud. "Ecological Civilization: Interpreting the Chinese Past, Projecting the Global Future." *Global Environmental Change* 53 (2018): 195-203. [Available at: https://doi.org/10.1016/j.gloenvcha.2018.09.014].

Heurtebise, Jean-Yves. "Sustainability and Ecological Civilization in the Age of Anthropocene: An Epistemological Analysis of the Psychosocial and 'Culturalist' Interpretations of Global Environmental Risks." *Sustainability* 9, no. 8 (2017). [Available at: https://doi.org/10.3390/su9081331].

Kalton, Michael C. "Extending the Neo-Confucian Tradition: Questions and Reconceptualization for the Twenty-First Century." In Mary Evelyn Tucker and John H. Berthrong, Eds. *Confucianism and Ecology: The Interrelation of Heaven, Earth, and Humans.* Cambridge, MA: Harvard University Press, 1998. 77-101.

Lai, Pan-chiu. "The Christian Story of God's Work: A Chinese Christian Response." In Hilda P. Koster and Ernst M. Conradie, Eds. *T&T Clark Handbook of Christian Theology and Climate Change.* London: T&T Clark, 2020. 480-89.

Morrison, Roy. *Ecological Democracy*. Boston: South End Press, 1995.

Tu, Wei-ming. "Confucianism and Liberalism." *Dao: A Journal of Comparative Philosophy* 2(1), (2002): 1-20. [Available at: https://doi.org/10.1007/BF02856993].

Tu, Wei-ming. "The Continuity of Being: Chinese Visions of Nature." In Leroy S. Rouner, Ed. *On Nature.* Norte Dame, IN: University of Norte Dame Press, 1984. 113-29.

Tucker, Mary Evelyn. "The Philosophy of Ch'i as an Ecological Cosmology." In Mary Evelyn Tucker and John H. Berthrong, Eds. *Confucianism and Ecology: The Interrelation of Heaven, Earth, and Humans.*Cambridge, MA: Harvard University Press, 1998. 187-207.

19. THE ECOLOGICAL HERITAGE OF PROTESTANTISM FROM A CHINESE CHRISTIAN PERSPECTIVE[1]

Lai Pan-Chiu[2]

Introduction

The year 2017 marked not only the 500th anniversary of the Reformation(s),[3] believed to begin with the posting of Ninety-Five Theses by Martin Luther (1483-1546), but also the 50th anniversary of the publication of Lynn White Jr.'s (1907-1987) controversial essay "The Historical Roots of Our Ecological Crisis."[4] On the surface, these two events are unrelated. Many of the existing studies of the historical influence of the Reformation(s) focus on the ecclesiastical, theological, social, cultural, and political aspects, and knowingly or unknowingly omit the ecological aspect.[5] This omission may imply that the Reformation(s) made no significant contributions to the development of the environmental movement. However, this may also imply that the Reformation(s) had adverse effects on the natural environment, of which the heirs of the Reformation(s) are not aware of or prefer not to mention. The omission in any case may reinforce a popular impression that the Protestant heritage is fundamentally irrelevant to the contemporary environmental movement.

Against this negative impression concerning the ecological heritage of Protestantism, it seems rather paradoxical to say that Protestantism might have played a subtle yet important role in the promotion of environmental protection. As Mark R. Stoll points out, "[i]n Europe and in Anglophone nations, Protestant nations have tended to be greener in politics and policy than Catholic regions, and historically Reformed areas greenest of all."[6] Michael S. Northcott argues along the same lines:

> Majority-Protestant nations have taken the lead, as compared to Asian, Catholic European, and Latin American nations, in the last century and a half in advancing nature as the modern sublime, and in founding scientific and charitable societies for the study and protection of species and habitats.[7]

---

[1] This article is by permission re-published from: Christian Study Centre on Chinese Religion and Culture, Ching Feng, n.s., 19 (1-2), (2020): 21-47. The paper was previously presented at the conference: "Celebrating 500 Years of the Reformation: The Reformation's Culturally Transformative Influences and Impacts – European and Asian Cultural Perspectives," Hong Kong Baptist University, 22nd-23rd September 2017.

[2] LAI Pan-chiu (LAI Pinchao 賴品超) is professor in the Department of Cultural and Religious Studies, The Chinese University of Hong Kong.

[3] The term "Reformation(s)" (instead of "Reformation") is used in this essay to indicate the recent development in Reformation scholarship concerning the plurality of the Reformation(s). Although this essay focuses on Protestantism, especially Lutheranism, I refer to the Catholic Reformation as part of the Reformation(s) rather than "counter-reformation." See Carter Lindberg, *The European Reformations*, 2nd ed. (Oxford: Wiley-Blackwell, 2010), xii-xiii, xv.

[4] Lynn White Jr., "The Historical Roots of Our Ecological Crisis," *Science* 155, no. 3767 (10th March 1967): 1203-7.

[5] For instance, Thomas A. Howard and Mark A. Noll (eds), *Protestantism After 500 Years* (Oxford: Oxford University Press, 2016), and Alister McGrath, *Christianity's Dangerous Idea: The Protestant Revolution – A History from the Sixteenth Century to the Twenty-First* (New York: Harper One, 2007), neither of which lists entries for "ecology" or "environment" in its index.

[6] Mark R. Stoll, "Sinners in the Hands of an Ecological Crisis: Lynn White's Environmental Jeremiad," in Todd LeVasseur and Anna Peterson (eds), *Religion and Ecological Crisis: The "Lynn White Thesis" at Fifty* (New York: Routledge, 2017), 55.

[7] Michael S. Northcott, "Lynn White Jr. Right and Wrong: The Anti-Ecological Character of Latin Christianity and the Pro-Ecological Turn of Protestantism," in *Religion and Ecological Crisis*, 71, further details 67-71.

These arguments seem to suggest that the transformative influences and impacts of the Reformation(s) on the formation and development of environmental movements may be rather ambiguous and complicated, and thus deserve to be further explored, especially from a cross-cultural perspective. According to White, "Christianity is a complex faith, and its consequences differ in different contexts."[8] Following this view, as Protestantism has become global, one may examine the cultural impacts of Protestantism not only in a Western context but also in non-Western contexts. This essay, then, aims to examine the ecological heritage of Protestantism from a Chinese Christian perspective.

My argument divides into three main sections. The first section reviews the evaluation of the Protestant heritage in a Western context. It will start with a review of the Protestant heritage through a critical dialogue with White and, through a case study of H. Paul Santmire, illustrate how contemporary Protestant theology endeavours to evaluate and retrieve the ecological heritage of the Reformers' theologies. This section aims to show that, despite their overall tendency towards anthropocentrism, the Reformers' theologies include a certain potential for developing ecological theology. The second section sketches the cultural context of the Chinese reception of the Protestant heritage, especially the perception of the ecological heritage of Chinese culture and the negative impression of the ecological heritage of Christianity in contemporary China. This section aims to indicate that the dominant negative impressions of Christianity were partially influenced by White's criticism and reinforced by the Chinese understanding of the ecological heritage of Chinese culture. The third section includes an analysis of the anthropocentric soteriology widely shared among Chinese Protestant churches, a summary of the ecological discourses of Chinese Protestants, and a case study of a Chinese Christian theologian's evaluation and retrieval of the Protestant heritage. This section aims to show that even though Chinese Protestant churches were mainly influenced by the anthropocentric understanding of salvation championed by the Reformers, there are also significant attempts made by Chinese theologians to develop their ecological theologies by using their religious as well as cultural resources. However, the positive influences of the Reformers' theologies remain far from significant. Based on the discussion in these three sections, this essay concludes with a reflection on the ecological heritage of Protestantism.

Protestantism from an Ecological Perspective

It is interesting to note that although White appeared to be highly critical of Christianity, he came from a very strong Christian background. Being a son of an ordained minister, White was a devout Christian from the Reformed tradition and an occasional preacher, with a master's degree in theology from Union Theological Seminary.[9] Some scholars even commented that White's essay looked like a sermon rather than a scientific report.[10] Given White's religious background, one may wonder whether White's essay, which was slightly beyond his expertise in the relationship between religion and medieval technology, was religiously motivated – making a prophetic call for repentance or reformation.

In terms of content, White's essay seemed to identify the Judeo-Christian tradition in general as the historical root of the ecological crisis in the Western world. It also singled out Latin Christianity and the theme of human dominion in Genesis 1 as the major targets of his criticisms. Admittedly, White commented that "[e]specially in its Western form, Christianity is the most anthropocentric religion the world has seen."[11] For him, the solution could be either to "find a new religion or rethink our old one."[12] He did mention other religions, such as Zen Buddhism, as possible resources for a more environmentally friendly attitude, but in

[8] White, "The Historical Roots of Our Ecological Crisis," 1206.
[9] Elspeth Whitney, "Lynn White Jr.'s 'The Historical Roots of Our Ecological Crisis' after Fifty Years," in *Religion and Ecological Crisis*, 22, 24; also, Leslie Sponsel, "Lynn White Jr., One Catalyst in the Historical Development of Spiritual Ecology," in *Religion and Ecological Crisis*, 90.
[10] Stoll, "Sinners in the Hands of an Ecological Crisis," 47-48.
[11] White, "The Historical Roots of Our Ecological Crisis," 1206.
[12] White, "The Historical Roots of Our Ecological Crisis," 1206.

his view, this was not a viable option in modern Western society.[13] So, in the final analysis, the only viable option for White was to rethink the Christian tradition. That was the reason why he mentioned the example of St. Francis of Assisi (1181/2-1226), who affirmed the "equality of all creatures,"[14] to search for a more adequate response to the contemporary ecological crisis.

After the publication of his essay in 1967, White continued the debate in another essay published in 1973. He wrote:

> [A] man-nature dualism is deep-rooted in us [...] Until it is eradicated not only from our minds but also from our emotions, we shall doubtless be unable to make fundamental changes in our attitudes and actions affecting ecology. The religious problem is to find a viable equivalent to animism.[15]

In 1978, White published another essay, "The Future of Compassion," on the ecological issue in *Ecumenical Review*, a Christian theological journal published by the World Council of Churches. White explicitly calls his fellow Christians to solidarity with the natural world they belong to, noting that "we can sense our comradeship with a glacier, a subatomic particle of spiritual nebula. Man [sic] must join the club of creatures. They may help to save us from ourselves."[16] In other words, what White called for was not necessarily pre-Christian or non-Christian animism, but merely something functionally equivalent. This might be a Christian "animism" capable of cultivating a sense of solidarity between humankind and nature, as well as a compassionate attitude towards non-human creatures. In short, given the improbability of the wide acceptance of other religious traditions as cultural mainstream as well as a religious basis for addressing environmental issues in modern Western society, what White advocated, in effect, was not the abandonment of Christianity as a whole, but a reformation of Christianity, especially in its Latin form.

White's essay, which has been documented to be one of the most impactful essays published in *Science*, exerted tremendous influence on the discussion concerning religion and ecology, including the development of Christian ecological theology.[17] In 1979, Pope John Paul II named St. Francis the patron saint for people promoting ecology. The World Council of Churches also called for an "ecological reformation of Christianity."[18] So, given the motivation, contents, and impact of White's essay, we may interpret it as a call for repentance and ignition that unintendedly sparked an ecological reform in Christian theology. These impacts of White's essay may be reminiscent of Luther's Ninety-Five Theses, similarly written in the academic style of the day and calling for repentance, leading to dramatic transformations of Christianity such as the author could hardly have foreseen.[19]

Perhaps our major concern is neither the parallels/similarities between White's essay and Luther's Ninety-Five Theses, nor whether White's criticisms against Latin Christianity are valid, but more specifically whether White's criticisms apply to Protestantism, which is to a certain extent a descendent of,

---

[13] White, "The Historical Roots of Our Ecological Crisis," 1206.

[14] White, "The Historical Roots of Our Ecological Crisis," 1207.

[15] Lynn White Jr., "Continuing the Conversation," in Ian Barbour (ed), *Western Man and Environmental Ethics: Attitudes Toward Nature and Technology* (Reading, MA: Addison-Wesley Publishing Company, 1973), 62; quoted by Todd LeVasseur and Anna Peterson, "Introduction," in *Religion and Ecological Crisis*, 5.

[16] Lynn White Jr., "The Future of Compassion," *Ecumenical Review* 30(2), (1978): 106-107; quoted by LeVasseur and Peterson, "Introduction," in *Religion and Ecological Crisis*, 5-6.

[17] For details, see Whitney, "Lynn White Jr.'s 'The Historical Roots of Our Ecological Crisis' after Fifty Years," 18-31.

[18] See "Conference Calls for Ecological Reformation of Christianity," World Council of Churches, 7th April 2016, [Available at: https://www.oikoumene.org/en/press-centre/news/conference-calls-for-ecological-reformation-of-christianity], [Last accessed: 13th September 2017].

[19] H. Paul Santmire made a brief comparison between the two events. He found the parallels interesting but not very meaningful. See H. Paul Santmire, *Nature Reborn: The Ecological and Cosmic Promise of Christian Theology* (Minneapolis, MN: Fortress Press, 2000), 11.

as well as a rebellion against, Latin Christianity of the medieval period. If Latin Christianity is the most anthropocentric religion by far, does it mean that Protestantism is also anthropocentric and ecologically bankrupt? Did the Reformation(s) transform the ecological dimension of medieval Latin Christianity? If so, in what ways?

Based on his study of the role played by Christianity in the rise of environmentalism in America,[20] Mark R. Stoll criticises "White's ignorance of Presbyterianism's environmentalist heritage"[21] by pointing out that "a huge majority of leading American conservationists and environmentalists before 1970 came out of Reformed Protestantism."[22] Stoll argues,

> Considering that in 1906 Presbyterians constituted just above 6% of the population, the Presbyterian church has turned out an astonishing number of prominent preachers for nature and the environment, even if most wound up unchurched.[23]

Stoll names some famous environmentalists as illustrations – including not only those who are close relatives of ordained ministers, for example, John Muir, Robinson Jeffers, and Rachel Carson, but also those who are themselves ordained ministers, for example, William O. Douglas, Archie Carr, and "Holmes Ralston III" (*sic*; should read "Holmes Rolston, III").[24] Stoll also points to the New England Puritans, who were influenced by the Calvinistic ideal, as "the only sustainable, equitable settler society in America,"[25] suggesting that "White's own Reformed Protestant tradition may still have much to teach us."[26]

In a more balanced manner, Michael Northcott on the one hand admits that "for the most part, the Reformers did not repair the disappearance of nature from the story of salvation in Catholic culture and theology. On the contrary, the Reformers continued and, if anything, deepened the confining of the action of grace to humans"; for "the Reformers encouraged an individualistic and inward turn in religion towards the action of grace on the emotions and the mind and will of the believer" and "this resulted in the gradual desacralisation of nature in space and time in Protestant culture."[27] On the other hand, Northcott points out,

> Protestantism proved fertile ground for a new "turn to nature" as a subject in post-reformation art and as a source of moral redemption and spiritual inspiration for the inhabitants of early industrial cities and towns in the New World and in Europe.[28]

Apart from American environmentalism, which is rooted in the Protestant (especially Presbyterian) tradition, the idea of stewardship and the Calvinistic view that the earth remains the "theatre of God's glory" even after the Fall, are also examples of the "Pro-ecological Turn of Protestantism."[29] Besides, Northcott mentions the Puritans' attitude towards nature embodied in John Milton's literature, which not only depicts Eden as a beautiful, blissful, and harmonious paradise but also envisions salvation in terms of regaining that paradise rather than spiritually retreating from the world. In terms of actual practice and spirituality, the Reformed idea of redemption through encountering God's divinity in nature did inspire the preservation of wildernesses and the promotion of recreational hiking advocated by American environmentalists.

---

[20] Mark R. Stoll, *Inherit the Holy Mountain: Religion and the Rise of American Environmentalism* (Oxford: Oxford University Press, 2015).
[21] Stoll, "Sinners in the Hands of an Ecological Crisis," 51.
[22] Stoll, "Sinners in the Hands of an Ecological Crisis," 55.
[23] Stoll, "Sinners in the Hands of an Ecological Crisis," 48.
[24] Stoll, "Sinners in the Hands of an Ecological Crisis," 48.
[25] Stoll, "Sinners in the Hands of an Ecological Crisis," 56.
[26] Stoll, "Sinners in the Hands of an Ecological Crisis," 58.
[27] Northcott, "Lynn White Jr. Right and Wrong," 66.
[28] Northcott, "Lynn White Jr. Right and Wrong," 67.
[29] Northcott, "Lynn White Jr. Right and Wrong," 67-68.

Northcott thus concludes that White's critique of medieval Latin Christianity may be largely correct, but White fails to recognise that "Western Protestant Christianity had within it the seeds of a different trajectory."[30]

Case Study of a Western Protestant Theologian

Whereas Stoll and Northcott respond to White and offer their assessments of the Protestant (especially the Presbyterian/Reformed) tradition mainly from a cultural-historical perspective, H. Paul Santmire, a Lutheran pastor who has engaged in ecological theology for decades, offers his assessment of the Protestant (especially the Lutheran) ecological heritage mainly from a theological perspective. Fundamental to Santmire's analysis and evaluation of the ecological heritage of Christianity is the distinction between spiritual and ecological motifs. Whereas the ecological motif is nature-affirming, the spiritual motif is nature-denying, focusing on how the human soul may ascend to God.[31] These two motifs intertwined in the Christian tradition making it rather ambiguous concerning its ecological promise. Santmire's evaluation of the Reformation(s) is, to a certain extent, quite in line with his overall evaluation of Christianity.

Santmire admits that "The *pro me* of Reformation existential faith as a matter of course tended to produce an anthropocentric reading of creation texts as well as redemption texts."[32] However, although the Reformers did not essentially change the central concern of salvation of humankind inherited from medieval Christianity, they changed the direction of the question from "how we human beings can ascend to God" to "how God descended among us." With this fundamental shift, the Reformers focused on the relationship between God and humankind, without overlooking the power and the glory of God manifested in nature or human solidarity with nature. However, without directly causing it, the Reformers' preoccupation with human salvation also "helped set the stage" for the secularisation of nature.[33] Santmire thus concludes that, "[a]ll in all [...] the reformers never really solved the tension in their thought between the soteriological-anthropocentric focal point and the ecological-theocentric circumference."[34]

Unlike many scholars' exclusive focus on White's essay, Santmire notices that White's seemingly sweeping argument in the essay was based on his more detailed study of medieval science and technology, which belong to White's specialisation. According to White,

> [t]he emergence of Gothic art reflects a fundamental change in the European attitude toward the natural environment. Things ceased to be merely symbols, rebuses, *Dei vestigia*, and became objects interesting and important in themselves, quite apart from man's spiritual needs.[35]

In other words, the great cathedrals themselves were dramatic expressions of this new confidence in understanding and mastering nature.[36] This makes Santmire's proposals concerning how Christianity can become more ecological rather comprehensive. They do not only cover theological ideas or Biblical interpretations but also include church architecture as well as ritual.[37] In terms of the theology of nature, Santmire identifies himself with the "orthodox but innovative revisionist tradition," and among the

---

[30] Northcott, "Lynn White Jr. Right and Wrong," 68-71.

[31] H. Paul Santmire, *The Travail of Nature: The Ambiguous Ecological Promise of Christian Theology* (Philadelphia: Fortress Press, 1985), 13-29.

[32] Santmire, *Nature Reborn*, 29-30.

[33] Santmire, *The Travail of Nature*, 121-22.

[34] Santmire, *The Travail of Nature*, 132.

[35] Lynn White Jr., "Natural Science and Naturalistic Art in the Middle Ages," in *Religion and Technology: Collected Essays* (Berkeley, CA: University of California Press, 1978), 33; quoted by Santmire, *Nature Reborn*, 80.

[36] Santmire, *Nature Reborn*, 80.

[37] H. Paul Santmire, *Ritualizing Nature: Renewing Christian Liturgy in a Time of Crisis* (Minneapolis, MN: Fortress Press, 2008), 92-105.

"reformers," instead of the "apologists" or "reconstructionists."[38] In line with this approach and to counter the theology of ascent of the Gothic vision, Santmire attempts to retrieve Luther's theology of divine descent, especially the concept of the "cosmic Christ" and his emphasis on the divine immanence in nature as well as in the sacrament.[39] However, for Santmire, "[t]he legacy of the Lynn White thesis is therefore primarily this: the discourse of a new paradigm for theological thought about nature, extending our understanding of the love of God to nature."[40] From an ecological point of view, perhaps a more crucial issue is not the love of God for nature, but how His love for nature can be translated into human love for nature. Probably, for this reason, Santmire has to move on from Luther's theology of the divine presence to the spiritual tradition of Celtic Christianity for a vision of the togetherness of human and nonhuman beings in death and salvation.[41] Although a similar emphasis on togetherness between human and nonhuman beings, as Santmire points out, can be found in Tillich,[42] Santmire's exploration of the ecological potential of Celtic Christianity may indicate not only his ecumenical openness to other denominations but also his implicit admission of the under-development of this particular aspect in his Lutheran tradition.

The Chinese Perception of Christian Ecological Heritage

The dramatic increase over the last three decades in the number of publications concerning ecological/environmental issues is likely due to the present severity of China's ecological crisis. However, in many of these Chinese publications, Christianity is often stereotyped as an anthropocentric religion detrimental to the environment. For example, in a recently published book on cross-disciplinary studies of comparative literature, which includes chapters on the relationship between literature and ecology and literature and religion, Christianity or Christian culture is blamed not merely for the ecological crisis in the Western world, but also for the ecological disasters of humankind.[43] The book discusses American ecological literature and mentions merely the possible influence of German Romanticism without noticing its possible connection with Christianity.[44]

Contrasting with this extremely negative view of Christianity, some Chinese publications concerning ecological civilisation or environmental ethics evaluate Christianity in a more balanced manner.[45] Some of these publications recognise, particularly and positively, the Christian idea of stewardship and the ecological theologies articulated by some contemporary Western theologians.[46] However, these acknowledgements of Christian ecological theology are limited to its usefulness in guiding and encouraging Christian environmental practice in the West.[47] In other words, most of the relevant Chinese publications focus their discussions on Western Christian theology and its significance for Western society, rather than its relevance in the Chinese context. Even if Christianity is not to be rejected as ecologically bankrupt, the

---

[38] Santmire, *Ritualizing Nature*, 7-9.
[39] Santmire, *Ritualizing Nature*, 74-92.
[40] Santmire, *Ritualizing Nature*, 15.
[41] Santmire, *Ritualizing Nature*, 93-114.
[42] Santmire, *Ritualizing Nature*, 64-65.
[43] Gao Xudong 高旭東, *Kuaxueke yanjiu* 跨學科研究 [Cross-Disciplinary Study] (Beijing: Peking University Press, 2017), 137.
[44] Gao Xudong 高旭東, *Kuaxueke yanjiu* 跨學科研究, 144.
[45] For example, Yang Tongjin 楊通進 and Gao Yuyuan 高予遠 (eds), *Xiandai wenming de shengtai zhuanxiang* 現代文明的生態轉向 [The Ecological Turn of Modern Civilization] (Chongqing: Chongqing Publishing House, 2007).
[46] For example, Cao Mengqin 曹孟勤, *Renxing yu ziran: Shengtai lunli zhexue jichu fansi* 人性與自然——生態倫理哲學基礎反思 [Humanity and Nature: Reflection on the Philosophical Foundation of Ecological Ethics] (Nanjing: Nanjing Normal University Press, 2004), 67–78.
[47] For example, Wang Zhengping 王正平, *Huanjing zhexue: Huanjing lunli de kua xueke yanjiu* 環境哲學——環境倫理的跨學科研究 [Environmental Philosophy: Cross-Disciplinary Study of Environmental Ethics] (Shanghai: Shanghai People's Publishing House, 2004), 342.

Christian ecological heritage is still disregarded based on the assumption of its irrelevance to the Chinese context.

Given the fact that Christianity does not represent contemporary mainstream Chinese culture, it is quite natural for Chinese intellectuals to disregard the possible relevance of the Christian ecological heritage to the Chinese context. Assuming that the development of environmental ethics in the Chinese context would prove most effective if based on Chinese culture, some Chinese intellectuals endeavour to explore either Marxism or, more often, the Chinese cultural tradition as a possible source of ecological wisdom. The Chinese publications concerning ecological ethics or the environmental philosophy of Buddhism, Confucianism, and Daoism have mushroomed in the last two decades or so.

It is noticeable that Confucianism, Daoism, and Buddhism share a certain cosmic vision that emphasises the unity between humanity and nature. The idea of "forming one body with the myriad things of heaven and earth" (*yu tiandi wanwu chengwei yiti* 與天地萬物成為一體) is affirmed in Daoism, Confucianism, and Buddhism.[48] In terms of ethics, "having compassion towards all lives" (*cixin yu wu* 慈心於物) is part of the ethics advocated by Chinese popular religion.[49] According to Chinese Mahayana Buddhism, all sentient beings, including human and nonhuman beings, possess Buddha-nature. Some Chinese Buddhists further suggest that even trees and grass are sentient beings and possess Buddha-nature, and will eventually take part in the universal salvation and become buddhas.[50] This affirmation of the Buddha-nature of trees and grass, together with the assumption that plants are sentient beings with feelings, arguably became part of Chinese culture. A well-known example is that Zhou Dunyi 周敦頤 (1017-1073), a representative of Neo-Confucianism influenced by Buddhism to a certain extent, was known to have a strong love for life and refused to cut the grass outside the window of his study.[51] Nowadays, it is common to find the notice "Keep off the grass" (*buyao jianta caodi* 不要踐踏草地) on many university campuses and at tourist sites across Mainland China. Besides this, we may also find a more elaborated notice which reads: "Trees and grass have feelings. How could anyone crush them?" (*caomu youqing, tazhi heren* 草木有情, 踏之何忍). This affirmation of the Buddha-nature of trees and grass seems to function as the sort of ecological "animism" mentioned by White.

These seemingly "ecological" characteristics of Chinese religions might reinforce the stereotype or contrast that, where Christianity is one of the most (if not *the* most) anthropocentric religion and is thus ecologically bankrupt or irrelevant, Chinese religious tradition offers promising ecological wisdom. The contrasts between Christianity and Chinese religious tradition can be found not merely in doctrines, but also in actual practices. For example, Ciji 慈濟 (*Tzu Chi*), a Buddhist non-government organisation based in Taiwan and famous for its charity work, has launched many environmental protection projects. Its founder, a Buddhist nun named Dharma Master Cheng Yen 證嚴, articulates her ideas and suggestions for environmental protection in daily life.[52] It is fair to say that, in contrast to the recognised contributions of

---

[48] For a Christian ecological appropriation of this idea, see Lai Pan-chiu, "God of Life and Ecological Theology: A Chinese Christian Perspective," *The Ecumenical Review* 65, no. 1 (March 2013): 67-82.

[49] See, for example, *Taishang ganying pian* 太上感應篇 [Treatise on Response and Retribution]; English translation, [Available online at: https://archive.org/search.php?query=subject%3A%22%E5%A4%AA%E4%B8%8A%E6%84%9F%E6%87%89%E7%AF%87%E6%96%B0%E4%B8%AD%E8%8B%B1%E6%96%87%E7%89%88%22], [Last accessed: 13th September 2017].

[50] For a theological response to the Chinese Mahayana Buddhist view of universal salvation, see Lai Pan-chiu, "Reconsidering the Christian Understanding of Universal Salvation in Mahayana Buddhist Perspective," *Ching Feng, n.s.,* 12, no. 1-2 (2013): 19-42.

[51] See Chan Wing-tsit, trans. and comp., *A Source Book in Chinese Philosophy* (1963; Princeton, NJ: Princeton University Press, 1969), 462.

[52] See Zhengyan fashi 證嚴法師 (Dharma Master Cheng Yen), *Yu diqiu gong shengxi* 與地球共生息 [Symbiosis with the Planet Earth] (originally published in Taiwan, 2006; Shanghai: Fudan University Press, 2009).

Chinese Buddhism to environmental protection, the environmental actions taken by Chinese Christian churches are relatively rare and far from influential in Chinese society.

The Anthropocentric Soteriology of Chinese Protestantism

Other than the circumstantial factors mentioned above, the proclamation and practice of Chinese Christian churches might have reinforced the stereotype that Christianity is "anthropocentric" – in contrast to "eco-centric" but not "theocentric." The problem is particularly acute for Chinese Protestant churches, which were deeply influenced by the evangelistic and pietistic traditions of Protestant missionaries to China. The gospel proclaimed by most of these missionaries is mainly characterised by spiritual, individualistic, and anthropocentric salvation. Apart from this spiritual and individualistic interpretation of salvation, some missionaries and church leaders have emphasised the social and political relevance of Christian salvation, especially when China was in serious socio-political turmoil during the Republic period (1911-1949). However, the socio-political interpretations of salvation proposed mainly by Chinese Christian intellectuals such as Zhao Zichen 趙紫宸 (1888-1979) and Wu Leichuan 吳雷川 (1870-1944) were not very popular at the grassroots level. After all, these interpretations remained largely anthropocentric – emphasising human liberation and neglecting the liberation of nonhuman beings as well as the relationship between human and nonhuman beings. An illustrative example of this overall anthropocentric tendency of Chinese Protestantism is the translation of the Bible. Among Chinese Christians, John 3:16 is probably the most popular verse of the Bible. In the Union Version (*Heheben* 和合本), which was translated about a century ago and arguably remains the most widely used Chinese translation of the Bible, the Greek word *κόσμον* for "world" or "cosmos" was translated as *shiren* 世人 (people of the world, everyone) instead of *shijie* 世界 (world). The meaning is thus changed rather drastically from "for God so loved the world" into "for God so loved human beings." In this way, non-human creatures were implicitly excluded from the love of God. Similarly, the Union Version also translates *καινή κτίσις* (meaning new creation) of 2 Corinthians 5:17, another oft-quoted Biblical verse in Chinese Protestant churches, into *xinzao de ren* 新造的人 (newly created human being). These inaccurate translations or interpretations reflect the popularity of an anthropocentric understanding of salvation in the gospel promulgated by Protestant missionaries as well as church leaders in China.

The anthropocentric mistranslation or over-interpretation is not without Biblical grounds. For example, John 3:16 seems to suggest that all those who believe can be saved. If one believes that only human beings can understand the gospel and have faith, it is reasonable to assume that only human beings can be saved. A corollary is that since dogs and cats cannot understand the gospel articulated in human language, they cannot have faith in Jesus Christ, and thus cannot be saved anyway. This anthropocentric understanding of salvation is thus supported by the assumption that faith is a necessary condition or pre-condition for salvation. Eventually, the problem goes back to the Protestant doctrine of justification by faith. However, the ecological dimension has been largely neglected by Chinese Christians in their studies of the Reformers' thought.[53] Furthermore, due to certain cultural and political considerations, some leaders of the Three-Self Churches in mainland China have tended to "tone down" or "dilute" (that is, whenever possible, not to

[53] Some examples are: Andres S. K. Tang 鄧紹光 (Deng Shaoguang), ed., *Huidao genyuan qu: Fuyin xinyang yu gaijiao jingshen* 回到根源去——福音信仰與改教精神 [Back to the Root: Evangelical Faith and the Spirit of Reformation] (Hong Kong: Logos Publisher, 1999); Jason Hing-kau Yeung 楊慶球 (Yang Qingqiu), *Mading Lude shenxue yanjiu* 馬丁路德神學研究 [The Study of Martin Luther's Theology] (Hong Kong: Logos Publisher, 2002); Liu Linhai 劉林海, *Jia'erwen sixiang yanjiu* 加爾文思想研究 [Study of Calvin's Thought] (Beijing: China Remin University Press, 2006); Lin Hong-hsin 林鴻信 (Lin Hongxin), *Jia'erwen shenxue* 加爾文神學 [Calvin's Theology] (Taipei: Liji chubanshe, 1994).

mention) the doctrine of justification by faith.[54] Thus they have not deeply explored nor set out to reinterpret or problematise the doctrine of justification by faith for the Chinese context, not to mention its ecological significance.

Chinese Ecological Theologies[55]

If one surveys the Chinese publications on ecological theology, one may find that many Chinese studies of ecological theology are introductions to the views of contemporary Western theologians with or without elaborating their significance for the Chinese context. A typical example is a special issue of *Logos & Pneuma* on ecological theology published in 2002. The whole issue mainly consists of an introduction and translation of the theological works of James A. Nash, Rosemary R. Ruether, John B. Cobb Jr., Dietrich Bonhoeffer, and Paul Tillich.[56] In contrast to the attention paid to contemporary Western theologians, the ecological heritage of the Reformers has been largely neglected in the Chinese-speaking world. A similar omission of the Reformers' theologies can be found in a special issue of the *CGST Journal* on "Ecology and Christian Faith" published in 1999. Whereas the first two articles are apologetic as well as critical responses to White's thesis from philosophical-theological and Biblical perspectives respectively,[57] the next three articles explore ecological and related issues from three different perspectives. The third article advocates for an aesthetic approach to nature and draws support from both Christian tradition and the Chinese culture.[58] The fourth article surveys empirical studies concerning the relationship between economic growth and environmental protection without any theological analysis or comment.[59] The fifth article explicates the ethical issues involved in the controversies in the German-speaking world concerning animal rights.[60] The last article, which was authored by an environmental activist from Taiwan, affirms that our ecological discourses must be informed by contemporary environmental sciences. It also suggests that Chinese ecological theology should be rooted in the Chinese cultural context and make cautious reference to Western ecological theologies, which might provide some, albeit limited, inspiration.[61] Similar calls for exploring the Chinese cultural heritage, instead of the Reformers' theological heritage, in developing Chinese ecological theology can be found among some Hong Kong Christians engaging in environmental science and practice.[62]

---

[54] Deng Fucun, "The Basis for the Reconstruction of Chinese Theological Thinking," in Miikka Ruokanen and Paulos Huang (eds), *Christianity and Chinese Culture* (Grand Rapids, MI: William B. Eerdmans, 2010), 297-308, esp. 306-308.

[55] For a more detailed survey of Chinese Christian ecological discourses, see Lai Pan-chiu, "Ecological Theology as Public Theology: A Chinese Perspective," *International Journal of Public Theology* 11(4), (2017): 477-500.

[56] See *Logos & Pneuma* 道風 18 (Spring 2002): 11-146 (in Chinese, with abstract in English on 310-13).

[57] Carver T. Yu 余達心 (Yu Daxin), "Shengtai weiji xun huogen" 生態危機尋禍根 [The Roots of Our Ecological Crisis], *CGST Journal* 中國神學研究院期刊 26 (January 1999): 9–31; and Stephen Lee 李思敬 (Li Sijing), "'Shangdi xingxiang' yu 'guanzhi dadi'" 「上帝形象」與「管治大地」 [*Imago Dei* and *Dominium Terrae*], *CGST Journal* 26 (January 1999): 31-42.

[58] Samuel Sung-him Ho 何崇謙 (He Chongqian), "Shengtai shenxue: Ziran yu ziwo" 生態神學——自然與自我 [Towards an Ecological Theology: Nature and the Self], *CGST Journal* 26 (January 1999): 43-60.

[59] Kin-yip Louie 雷競業 (Lei Jingye), "Jingji chengchang yu huanjing baohu" 經濟成長與環境保護 [Economic Growth and Environmental Protection], *CGST Journal* 26 (January 1999): 61-79.

[60] Wilson Lee 李威信 (Li Weixin), "Dongwu quanli" 動物權利 [Animal Rights], *CGST Journal* 26 (January 1999): 81-99.

[61] Nancy C. M. Chen 陳慈美 (Chen Cimei), "Shengtai yu jiaohui: Yige Taiwan jingyan di huigu 生態與教會—— 一個台灣經驗的回顧 [Ecology and the Church: A Retrospectus of a Taiwanese Experience], *CGST Journal* 26 (January 1999): 81-120, esp. 113-14.

[62] See Ho Kin-chung 何建宗 (He Jianzong), "Duibi Rujia he Jidujiao de kechixu fazhan shiye" 對比儒家和基督教的可持續發展視野 [Contrast the Confucian and Christian Perspectives of Sustainable Development], in *Jidu zongjiao ji Rujia duitan shengming lunli* 基督宗教及儒家對談生命倫理 [Christian-Confucian Dialogue on Life and

It is noteworthy that these Chinese Protestant discourses on ecological issues were made by Christians from various academic and professional backgrounds, and they adopted a variety of approaches to ecological issues. However, many of them prefer to explore the resources from Chinese culture rather than the theological heritage of the Reformers. If one googles the Chinese words *Lude* 路德 (Luther) and *shengtai* 生態 (ecology), one may find very few Chinese articles with these two terms. One is a brief article referring to a "*Luther*an" theologian Joseph Sittler (1904-1987) rather than to "Luther" himself.[63] The other is a brief report of a conference related to ecology and it mentions one of Luther's prayers in passing.[64] A relatively more elaborate discussion concerning Luther's theology from an ecological perspective is a short section of a journal article published in 1995 surveying the Christian attitudes towards the earth. It is rather ironic that the author Aloisius Luis Gutheinz 谷寒松 (Gu Hansong) is a Jesuit from Austria working in Taiwan for many years but not a Chinese Protestant theologian.[65] Another ironic case relates to an international symposium held in Beijing in early September 2017 commemorating the 500th anniversary of the Reformation. The conference had three parallel sections for Christianity, Buddhism, and Islam respectively. According to the conference handbook, among the twenty-four papers presented in the section for Christianity, none of them addressed ecological issues, and the only paper related to ecological issues was about Chinese Buddhism and was presented at a parallel section for Buddhism.[66]

Based on the above survey, one may find that the Reformers' theologies did not have substantial transformative influences on the ecological discourses or culture of the Chinese Protestant churches, not to mention China as a whole. The Chinese Protestant churches seemed to inherit the anthropocentric view of salvation advocated by the Reformers without benefiting from the ecological heritage of the Reformation(s). The positive influences of the Reformers' theologies on Chinese Protestant ecological theologies are rather indirect (through some modern and/or contemporary Protestant theologians) and far from significant. In practice, many Chinese Protestant Christians would prefer exploring the ecological wisdom of the Chinese culture instead of retrieving the ecological heritage of the Reformers.

Case Study of a Chinese Protestant Theologian

Similar to Santmire, Lai Pan-chiu 賴品超 (Lai Pinchao), who is probably one of the few Chinese theologians who has published significant works about ecology,[67] is an ordained Lutheran pastor and attempts to evaluate the ecological heritage of Christianity, especially that of Chinese Protestant churches.[68]

Ethics], ed. Lai Pan-chiu 賴品超 (Hong Kong: Centre for the Study of Religion and Chinese Society, Chung Chi College, The Chinese University of Hong Kong, 2002), 127-38; and, Wong Fook-yee 王福義 (Wang Fuyi), "Zhongguo wenhua yu shengtai shenxue" 中國文化與生態神學 [Chinese Culture and Ecological Theology], *CGST Journal* 53 (July 2012): 79-108.

[63] See Chan Ka 陳嘉 (Chen Jia), "Jidujiao shengtai shenxue fazhan de beijing" 基督教生態神學發展的背景 [Background of the Development of Christian Ecological Theology], [Available at: http://digital.lib.hkbu.edu.hk/eco-religion/christian.php?cat=article&code=A2,] [Last accessed: 13th September 2017].

[64] See Wong Mei-fung 黃美鳳 (Huang Meifeng), "Yu Lude tongzhuo de shengtai gongyi" 與路德同桌的生態公義 [Ecological Justice at the Same Table with Luther], [Available at: http://hkci.org.hk/1351.html], [Last accessed: 13th September 2017].

[65] See Aloisius Luis Gutheinz 谷寒松 (Gu Hansong), "Shengtai shenxue yaosu" 生態神學要素, *Collectanea theologica universitatis Fujen* 神學論集 104 (1995): 231-78, [Available at: http://archive.hsscol.org.hk/Archive/periodical/ct/CT 104/CT104E.htm], [Last accessed: 13th September 2017].

[66] See the conference handbook of "Zongjiao gexin yu shehui fazhan: Zongjiao gaige 500 zhounian guoji luntan" 宗教革新與社會發展——宗教改革500周年國際論壇 [Religious Renewal and Social Development: International Symposium for the 500th Anniversary of the Reformation], Beijing, 4th-6th September 2017.

[67] Alexander Chow, *Chinese Public Theology* (Oxford: Oxford University Press, 2018), 130.

[68] For details, see Lai Pan-chiu 賴品超, "Shengdan, huanbao yu daocheng roushen" 聖誕、環保與道成肉身 [Christmas, Environmental Protection, and the Incarnation], in *Duoyuan, fenqi yu rentong: Shenxue yu wenhua de tansuo* 多元、分歧與認同——神學與文化的探索 [Plurality, Diversity, and Identity: Explorations of Theology and

For Lai, the mainstream Chinese Protestant churches emphasise salvation rather than creation and interpret both salvation and creation in an anthropocentric way. Furthermore, the Chinese Protestant churches tend to emphasise a forensic doctrine of justification by faith and interpret faith as a pre-condition for salvation, which is often understood in an anthropocentric as well as individualistic way. For ecological theology, the most crucial issue to be dealt with is soteriology rather than the doctrine of creation. Apart from his critique of the theological tradition embodied in the mainstream Chinese Protestant churches, Lai also attempts to explore viable alternatives within the Christian tradition. He mentions how the Anglican and Methodist/Wesleyan traditions, due to their appropriations of some insights from patristic theology, can affirm a more cosmic understanding of salvation rather than an exclusively anthropocentric one. Lai also notices that before the publication of White's essay, some Lutheran theologians, including Joseph Sittler and Paul Tillich, had already responded to the degradation of nature by emphasising the unity between creation and salvation, and by advocating for a cosmic and inclusive understanding of salvation which includes nonhuman beings as recipients of divine salvation.[69] Lai agrees with Santmire that there are some valuable ecological resources within the Christian tradition, including the Lutheran theological tradition. One question that remains, however, is how the seemingly anthropocentric doctrine of justification by faith is to be related to the salvation of nonhuman beings and interpreted from an ecological perspective.

Lai argues that *sola fide* refers to *sola gratia* as its ontological basis, as the formula "justification by grace through faith" indicates. If grace is based on God's free election and faith is a response to grace, God can take the initiative to bestow grace on those without faith or even on those attempting to reject God. This refers not merely to the "natural grace" (for example, sunshine and rain) given to both the just and the unjust (Mt. 5:45), but also the divine love embodied in the Incarnation. It is thus entirely legitimate to extend anthropocentric universal salvation, which covers both Israelites and Gentiles (Rom. 9-11), to a more cosmic universal salvation of the whole creation, which includes both human and nonhuman creatures travailing and waiting eagerly for God's salvation (Rom. 8:18-25). Furthermore, to overcome the anthropocentric tendency of understanding salvation exclusively in terms of the human soul, Lai proposes taking "healing" as a key soteriological metaphor. With this metaphor, one can affirm a multi-dimensional understanding of salvation which includes not only spiritual and psychological dimensions but also socio-political and physical dimensions referring to bodies of both human and nonhuman beings, as well as to the healing of the earth. Negatively speaking, the doctrine of justification by faith, which is supposed to apply mainly to human beings, does not exclude the salvation of nonhuman beings. Positively speaking, the doctrine of justification by faith (which implies the justification of sinners) can be illustrative of the unconditional character of the divine grace which is also the basis for the salvation of nonhuman beings. Lai even explores the implications of justification by faith for ecological practice and argues that the doctrine, which counters the culture of consumerism, may support a more environmentally friendly mentality as well as lifestyle. Lai concludes with a call for a more thorough exploration of the Christian tradition, which is also important for the development of ecological theology and should be accompanied by dialogue with other religions on ecological issues.[70] However, Lai's studies of ecological theology might not match his call very well.

Lai did elaborate on a multi-dimensional understanding of salvation in dialogue with Chinese religions in some depth;[71] however, his explorations of the Christian tradition have not exhausted the range of ecological heritage from the Reformers'. In addition to his general survey of contemporary ecological

Culture] (Xinbei: Chung Yuan Christian University Graduate School of Religion/Chinese Christian Literature Council (Taiwan), 2011), 277-98.

[69] Lai Pan-chiu, "Shengdan, huanbao yu daocheng roushen", 278-87.

[70] Lai Pan-chiu, "Shengdan, huanbao yu daocheng roushen", 288-98.

[71] Lai Pan-chiu, "Religious Diversity and Public Space in China: A Reconsideration of the Christian Doctrine of Salvation," in Simone Sinn and Tong Wing-sze (eds), *Interactive Pluralism in Asia: Religious Life and Public Space* (Leipzig: Evangelische Verlagsanstalt, 2016), 43-58.

theology,[72] Lai also published specific studies of prominent ecological theologians, for example, John B. Cobb Jr.,[73] as well as modern theologians who might be less famous in ecological theology, for example, Paul Tillich,[74] and even the ecological ethics of some pre-modern theologians, such as St. Thomas Aquinas.[75] However, unlike Santmire, Lai makes no notable attempt to explore the ecological significance of the Reformers, especially Luther. Lai's interpretation of *sola fide* and *sola gratia* outlined above is based primarily on his reading of Tillich's rather than Luther's theology. Lai prefers to explore ecological issues mainly through the lens of comparative studies or dialogue between Christian and Chinese religious traditions, advocating for a pluralistic and contextual approach to ecological ethics.[76] He is more interested in exploring how Chinese Christian ecological theology may articulate its Christology and anthropology through dialogue and even integration with Confucianism.[77] In a similar vein, Lai also appreciates the ecological wisdom of Chinese Buddhism, especially its emphasis on the inherent value of all sentient beings, and attempts to promote a mutually transformative dialogue or even collaboration between Buddhism and Christianity.[78] It is noticeable that the Reformers' theologies merely played a minor role in Lai's ecological discourses. Lai's case illustrates vividly that, in their explorations of ecological theology, Chinese Christian theologians might be more interested in Chinese cultural resources than the theological heritage of the Reformers.

Concluding Reflections

Based on the above discussion, one may get the impression that the ecological heritage of Protestantism is ambivalent, especially if one views it from a Chinese Christian perspective. On the one hand, the Protestant theological or doctrinal formulas developed during the sixteenth century were mainly anthropocentric, and the Reformers' anthropocentric soteriology did exert tremendous influences on Chinese Protestant churches. On the other hand, the efforts made by Western and Chinese theologians also indicate that certain useful ecological resources can be derived from the Reformers' theologies. However, taking Santmire's exploration of Luther's theology as an example, if one compares it with Chinese cultural resources, one may find that although there are certain interesting similarities, Chinese cultural resources appear to be ecologically more adequate than those of Luther. Due to the limitations of this essay, just a few observations or Chinese responses to Santmire are made here.

First, Santmire mentions how Luther enjoyed the wonder of nature by citing his exclamation: "If you really examined a kernel of grain thoroughly, you would die of wonderment."[79] Confucianism uses the word

---

[72] Lai Pan-chiu 賴品超, "Shengtai shenxue" 生態神學 [Ecological Theology], in *Xin shiji de shenxue yicheng, xiace* 新世紀的神學議程, 下冊 [Theology for the New Century, vol. 2], ed. Benedict H. B. Kwok 郭鴻標 (**Guo Hongbiao**) and Too Kin-wai 堵建偉 (Du Jianwei) (Hong Kong: Hong Kong Christian Institute, 2003), 423-51.

[73] Lai Pan-chiu, "Inter-religious Dialogue and Social Justice: Cobb's Wesleyan Process Theology in East Asian Perspective," *Asia Journal of Theology* 25(1), (April 2011): 82-102.

[74] Lai Pan-chiu, "Paul Tillich and Ecological Theology," *The Journal of Religion* 79(2), (April 1999): 233-49.

[75] Lai Pan-chiu 賴品超 and Wang Tao 王濤, "Zaisi Sheng Duomasi de shengtai lunli" 再思聖多瑪斯的生態倫理 "Reconsidering St. Thomas's Ecological Ethics," *Universitas: Monthly Review of Philosophy and Culture* 哲學與文化 37(11), (November 2010): 155-73.

[76] Lai Pan-chiu, "Inter-religious Dialogue on Environmental Ethics," *Studies in Interreligious Dialogue* 21(1), (2011): 5-19.

[77] Lai Pan-chiu, "Christian Ecological Theology in Dialogue with Confucianism," *Ching Feng* 41(3-4) (September-December 1998): 309-44; also, "Beyond Anthropocentrism and Ecocentrism: Eco-theology and Confucian-Christian Dialogue," *Ching Feng, n.s.*, 2(1-2), (2001): 35-55.

[78] See Lai Pan-chiu, "Buddhist-Christian Relations in China: A Christian Perspective," In Perry Schmidt-Leukel (ed), *Buddhist-Christian Relations in Asia* (St. Ottilien, Germany: EOS Verlag, 2017), 375-98.

[79] Martin Luther, *Werke* (Weimarer Ausgabe/Weimar Edition), XIX: 496; cited by Heinrich Bonnkamm, *Luther's World of Thought*, trans. Martin H. Bertram (Saint Louis, MI: Concordia Publishing House, 1959), 182; see also: Santmire, *Nature Reborn*, 70.

"*ren*" 仁 to refer to both the "kernel" of a seed of a plant and the cardinal virtue of benevolence, which characterises not only human nature or innate potential of human beings for benevolence, but also the heart-mind of Heaven and Earth that gives birth to and embraces both human and nonhuman beings.[80] Second, Santmire attempts to highlight the ubiquity or omnipresence of Christ's humanity in nature. According to Hua-yen Buddhism, Luther's interpretation may be closer to the dharma realm (*fajie* 法界) of "non-obstruction between principle and events" (*lishi wu'ai* 理事無礙) and may fall short of the highest dharma realm of "non-obstruction among events" (*shishi wu'ai* 事事無礙), which can also be expressed in terms of "one in all and all in one" (*yiji yiqie, yiqie jiyi* 一即一切, 一切即一) and is more in line with the worldview advocated by deep ecology.[81] Third, Santmire endeavours to reinterpret the Lutheran theological tradition to argue that "[he] can salute the maple tree in [his] front garden as a member of [his] own extended family."[82] Based on the Chinese idea of forming one body with the myriad things of heaven and earth, one may take a step forwards to recognise the maple tree as part of one's body rather than merely a member of one's own extended family. Besides, the Buddhist doctrine of the Buddha-nature of grass and trees can affirm the Buddha-nature of the maple tree as well as its potential for Buddhahood. Thus, one can have compassion toward this tree because we are "fellow-sufferers" as well as "fellow-pilgrims." That one has to take good care of the tree is not merely due to the moral example of the bodhisattva having mercy towards all living beings, but also the ontological view of dependent co-arising or non-duality between oneself and the other advocated by Buddhism. This would imply that the maple tree and oneself are inseparable parts of one body. Based on these comparisons, one may find that in terms of an idea or doctrinal formulation, the ecological resources of traditional Chinese culture are by no means inferior, and may in fact be superior, to the Lutheran heritage.

So, what can the heritage of Protestantism, especially the Reformers' theologies, contribute to the formulation of ecological theology in the contemporary Chinese context? Before exploring this question, one may have to address some of the challenges to the basic tenets of Protestant theology. There are at least two issues involved. First, the doctrine with an anthropocentric view of salvation together with the doctrine of justification by faith or *sola fide* seems to be inferior to a more cosmic or universalistic vision of salvation in some Chinese religious traditions, especially Chinese Buddhism. Second, with the motto *sola scriptura*, which concerns the methodology of theology, the question remains whether and how Chinese cultural resources can be used in ecological theology.

As regards the Protestant motto of *sola scriptura*, some observations have been made. First, the motto itself rules out the use of non-Christian or non-scriptural sources in Christian theology and thus does not support the development of ecological theology with Chinese characteristics. However, the motto itself is being challenged in the ecological context. White suggests that Daniel 3:57-90, which is presumably the song of three young men, should be used for grounding ecological responsibility, for it cites God's praises as declared by angels, heavens, waters, sun, stars, showers, dews, winds, mountains, seas and rivers, sea beasts, birds, etc., and "makes no distinction between categories of creatures."[83] However, if one applies the Protestant principle of *sola scriptura* strictly, this text could not be accepted as "canonical" because it is in the Septuagint (LXX) but not the Hebrew Masoretic text (MT). Thus, it is included in the Catholic Bible but excluded from the Protestant Bible. In other words, if one follows strictly and exclusively the Protestant principle of *sola scriptura*, Protestant ecological theology may be worse off. Ecological

---

[80] For details, see Chan Wing-tsit, "The Evolution of the Confucian Concept of *Jen*," *Philosophy East and West* 4(1), (1955): 295-319.

[81] See David Landis Barnhill, "Relational Holism: Huayan Buddhism and Deep Ecology," In David Landis Barnhill and Roger S. Gottlieb (eds), *Deep Ecology and World Religions* (Albany, NY: State University of New York Press, 2001), 77-106.

[82] Santmire, *Nature Reborn*, 73.

[83] White, "Continuing the Conversation," 61; cf. Christopher Cone, "Continuing the Conversation," *Religion and Ecological Crisis*, 108.

theologians seem to reject the exclusivist application of *sola scriptura*, as many of them make use of the findings from ecological or environmental science as well as various concepts or theories from different schools of thought, including process philosophy and the Gaia hypothesis. The use of non-scriptural or even non-Christian resources seems to be allowed as long as the authority of the Bible on matters related to human salvation is not challenged.

Second, the motto of *sola scriptura* also means the exclusion of any church authority or human tradition, and thus prevents taking any previous form of Christianity as absolute or eternal truth. This might allow the Reformers to take a critical stand on Latin Christianity, while imagining their reforms more radically, and allow contemporary Christians to reflect more critically on prevalent forms of Christianity from an ecological perspective. Similarly, based on the principle of *sola scriptura*, one can take a critical stand on the Reformers' theologies, including their anthropocentric understanding of salvation, and keep an open mind regarding the ecological insights from other Christian denominations and even non-Western cultural traditions.

Third, as White's critique of Genesis 1 and some biblical scholars' exposition of Genesis 2 may imply, perhaps not every part of the Bible (as well as interpretations of these parts) is equally adequate from an ecological point of view. This is reminiscent of not only Luther's doctrinal classification of the Bible, ranking the Book of James the least valuable and Romans and St. John's Gospel among the most valuable,[84] but also the Buddhist practice of doctrinal classification (*panjiao* 判教), which aims at ranking different scriptures as well as their doctrines according to their respective degrees of profundity or their functions at different stages on the way to Enlightenment.[85] One of the basic criteria shared by various schools of Chinese Buddhism is the distinction between Hinayana (small vehicle) and Mahayana (great vehicle). Whereas the former upholds an elitist view of salvation, the latter advocates a universalistic understanding of salvation. In some Buddhist schools, "universal salvation" may include all sentient (both human and nonhuman) beings. An interesting question is whether it is possible to apply a similar doctrinal classification to the Christian scriptures and Protestant theologies. For example, is it possible to rank anthropocentric theology, which rejects the participation of nonhuman beings in salvation, as "Hinayana" which is less "environmentally friendly" than the "Mahayana" which affirms the equal participation of humans and nonhuman beings in salvation? It is not necessary to apply a criterion external to the Bible to evaluate individual scriptures, for it can be an exercise of comparing critically the theological contents of different scriptures within the canon by using a criterion derived from the Bible itself.[86] This may allow contemporary ecological theology to take a more critical and flexible approach to the scriptures, including particularly those "Hinayana" or not so environmentally friendly parts.

To summarise, the heritage of *sola scriptura* is ambivalent. It may hinder the development of ecological theology, especially one with Chinese characteristics. However, it may also help theologians to become more critical of the not so environmentally friendly elements in Christian theology and even those in the Bible.

The case of the doctrine of justification by faith is similar. To borrow the parable or *koan* of "finger pointing to the moon" from Ch'an (Zen) Buddhism, the doctrine of justification by faith can be interpreted and received in various ways. Those with "Hinayana" mentality may misidentify the finger as the moon and understand the doctrine literally and negatively as a condemnation of those without faith and thus rule out the possibility of salvation of nonhuman beings. But for those with "Mahayana" mentality, the finger is

---

[84] See Martin Luther's "Preface to the New Testament 1545," [Available at: http://www.godrules.net/library/luther/NEW1luther_f8.htm], [Last accessed: 13th September 2017].

[85] See Mun Chanju, *The History of Doctrinal Classification in Chinese Buddhism: A Study of the Panjiao Systems* (Lanham: University Press of America, 2006).

[86] For a proposal for adopting the Buddhist method of doctrinal classification to rank the Christian scriptures, see Lai Pai-chiu 賴品超, *Dacheng Jidujiao shenxue* 大乘基督教神學 [Mahayana Christian Theology] (Hong Kong: Logos and Pneuma Press, 2011), 39-68.

also a signifier pointing to a greater truth or the ultimate truth beyond itself. According to this Mahayana understanding, the doctrine of justification by faith is a demonstration of and a signifier to *sola gratia*, which can be freely bestowed on all creatures according to God's will alone. This alone is sufficient to constitute the basis for the salvation of all creatures, including human and nonhuman beings, with or without faith. In other words, the doctrine of justification by faith as such is ambivalent concerning its ecological potentials.

For the articulation of Chinese Christian ecological theology, it must deal with the cultural, religious, or spiritual resources of Chinese religions as well as the Chinese religions themselves as living realities. According to Karl Barth (1886-1968), the doctrine of justification by faith is very important for reminding Christians, especially Protestants, that Christianity is comparable to a justified sinner. For Barth, Christianity as a human religion is not necessarily better than other religions. This applies not only to the practice but also to the doctrine of Protestantism. Christianity is a religion of grace. It is not due to its doctrine of grace, which can be articulated in similar or even more radical expressions in other religions, such as the True Pure Land Buddhism in Japan. That Christianity can be a true religion is entirely due to divine grace and election.[87] Moreover, God remains free to pronounce divine judgment against Christianity through other religions or political parties (for example, Russian Communism), human cultural heritage (for example, flute concerto), or even beautiful or sorrowful natural phenomena (for example, a blossoming shrub or a dead dog).[88] Barth's further elaboration of the doctrine of justification by faith may help Christians to become more humble and open towards ecological doctrines and practices of other religions, the ecological heritage of non-Western cultures, discoveries of environmental science, as well as ecological insights from natural phenomena. If Protestants find the practices and doctrines of other denominations or even other religions better than their denominational traditions, they should frankly and freely admit to this, and humbly listen and learn. This attitude, which is derived from the doctrine of justification by faith, can be beneficial to the development of Protestant ecological theology and practice, especially in the Chinese context.

If one understands Protestantism merely in terms of its origin in the sixteenth century, one may perhaps find it irrelevant to contemporary ecological concerns. However, if one understands Protestantism by looking at its developments,[89] especially its contemporary developments in and beyond the Western world, one may find that Protestantism has the potential to become an environmentally friendly religion. Paul Tillich made an interesting distinction between Protestantism and the Protestant principle. Tillich thought that, at any time in history, [historical] Protestantism (which was a historical movement originating in the sixteenth century) should be subject to the judgment of the Protestant principle (which is against the self-elevation of religion). With the Protestant principle, one may affirm that all historical forms of Christianity are relative and should be judged and reformed.[90] According to this understanding, the Christian churches should undergo continuing reformation as the slogan *semper reformanda* succinctly articulates. This makes Protestantism particularly receptive to the words of God, especially calls to repentance, including those coming from outside of the church walls, for example, that of Lynn White Jr. Perhaps the Protestant principle or the Protestant spirit of continuing reformation may be able to explain partially why, as a descendent of the "most anthropocentric religion," Protestantism may have transformative impacts on and

---

[87] See Karl Barth, *Church Dogmatics*, vol. 1, part 2, trans. G. T. Thomson and H. Knight (Edinburgh: T & T Clark, 1956), 280-361; also, Lai Pan-chiu, "Barth's Theology of Religion and the Asian Context of Religious Pluralism," *Asia Journal of Theology* 15(2), (October 2001): 247-67.

[88] See Karl Barth, *Church Dogmatics*, vol. 1, part 1, trans. G. W. Bromiley (Edinburgh: T & T Clark, 1975), 60.

[89] John Dillenberger and Claude Welch, *Protestant Christianity: Interpreted through Its Development* (New York: Charles Scribner's Sons, 1954).

[90] See Lai Pan-chiu, *Towards a Trinitarian Theology of Religions: A Study of Paul Tillich's Thought* (Kampen, The Netherlands: Kok Pharos Publishing House, 1994), 88-99.

contribute to the contemporary development of environmental movements. This may be a valuable, if not the most important, part of the Protestant heritage for the ecological age.

Suggestions for Further Reading

Conradie, Ernst M. and Hilda P. Koster, Eds. *T & T Clark Handbook of Christian Theology and Climate Change*. London: T & T Clark, 2020.

Hessel, Dieter H. and Rosemary Radford Ruether, Eds. *Christianity and Ecology: Seeking the Well-being of Earth and Humans*. Cambridge, MA: Harvard University Center for the Study of World Religions; distributed by Harvard University Press, 2000.

Jenkins, Willis. *Ecologies of Grace: Environmental Ethics and Christian Theology*. Oxford: Oxford University Press, 2008.

Martin-Schramm, James B. and Robert L. Stivers. *Christian Environmental Ethics: A Case Method Approach*. Maryknoll, NY: Orbis Books, 2003.

McFague, Sallie. *A New Climate for Theology: God, the World, and Global Warming*. Minneapolis, MN: Fortress Press, 2008.

Moltmann, Jürgen. *God in Creation: An Ecological Doctrine of Creation*. Translated by Margaret Kohl. London: SCM Press, 1985.

Northcott, Michael. *The Environment & Christian Ethics*. Cambridge: Cambridge University Press, 1996

Oelschlaeger, Max. *Caring for Creation: An Ecumenical Approach to the Environmental Crisis*. New Haven & London: Yale University Press, 1994.

Schaefer, Jame. *Theological Foundations for Environmental Ethics: Reconstructing Patristic & Medieval Concepts*. Washington, D.C.: Georgetown University Press, 2009.

Scheid, Daniel P. *The Cosmic Common Good: Religious Grounds for Ecological Ethics*. Oxford: Oxford University Press, 2016.

20. Life in the Spirit: Paul Tillich's Ecological Pneumatology in the Chinese Context

Keith, Ka-fu Chan[1]

Introduction

Both Christian religion and western philosophical traditions are criticised for anthropocentrism and dualism, which are regarded as the main causes of the global environmental crisis. The western dualistic conceptualisation, with its demarcation between transcendence and immanence, and a hierarchical mode of thinking, is now being challenged by movements, such as radical eco-egalitarianism, ecofeminism, the deep ecological movement and post-humanism. From these perspectives, the emergence of secularisation results in the divine absence from the world, and promotes a scientific-technological mindset which consolidates human rationality and subjectivity which, in turn, deepens the western ecological crisis.

However, the above, highly generalised picture is contrasted and corrected by many religious attempts and studies insisting that religion should not be regarded as bankrupt in dealing with the environmental crisis, but rather that it provides fruitful and promising resources for us to re-think the ecological question from a different angle. In this context, the east-west religious-ecological dialogue establishes a platform in which different religious traditions try to articulate the inter- and intra-textual readings of the other (as well as their own) in order to explore numerous potentialities and possibilities for ecological thinking.

This essay aims at examining the thought of Paul Tillich and of Confucianism, and tries to argue that both share a similar ontological and cosmic vision, which is relational, dynamic and universal in nature. I will firstly argue that Tillich's notion of sacramentality is ontological-universal in character and that this concept expresses the nature of the multi-dimensional universe which is based on his pneumatology. Likewise, in Confucian cosmogony, transcendence and immanence are interrelated within a dynamic and holistic whole in which the underlying principle of the universe is wholly embodied within the structure of the world.

Tillich's Pneumatological Sacramentality

Pneumatology, for Tillich, plays the decisive role to reconceive his entire theological project.[2] The interplay between Christology and pneumatology constitutes the theological methodological consideration in integrating the universality and particularity into the divine revelation and redemption. Thus, the being of God and the New Being manifested in Jesus as Christ are both well-grounded in the Presence of the Spirit as the unity of power and meaning. Secondly, Tillich is distinctive in his approach to correlate both the life universal and human life in particular with the divine Spirit. The Presence of the Spirit brings the self-transcendence of life in multi-dimensional unity. The Spirit, for Tillich, is not only regarded as the life-power and vitality of the different life forms, but also she dwells into the historical dimension of the multi-faceted levels of beings and reveals the fulfilment of the *telos* of all beings. In this sense, the term

---

[1] Prof. Dr. CHAN Ka Fu, Keith is a Professor at the Center for Judaic and Inter-religious Studies, School of Philosophy and Social Development, Shandong University, China. After completing the doctoral degree in the Chinese University of Hong Kong, he worked at the Institute of Sino-Christian Studies and Hong Kong Baptist University. Contact: keithchan@sdu.edu.cn.

[2] Keith, Ka-fu Chan, "Paul Tillich's Understanding of Theology: A Pneumatological Christological Perspective," Sino-Christian Studies: An International Journal of Bible, Theology & Philosophy, 20 (2015): 33-86.

sacramentality denotes the presence of the infinite in the finite, and the finite symbols points to the infinite. Tillich's idea of sacramentality is wholly and definitely pneumatological.

In his volume three of his *Systematic Theology*, Tillich expressed a dynamic and unifying perspective towards a multi-dimensional understanding of life. For him, the concept of "life" embraces different "dimensions" in which the interplay between potentiality and actuality is intertwined. Therefore, nothing should be reduced to a "thing" only. As he emphasised, "no thing in nature is merely a thing."[3] Nature is viewed neither as a scientific-technological object nor as a magical substance, but it is to be perceived theologically as "the finite expression of the infinite ground of all things."[4] On the one hand, Tillich strongly rejects the sacralisation of nature when he holds the realist interpretation towards the real structure of nature, even though, under the multi-dimensional unity of life, the infinite divine and the finite creatures are clearly distinguished but not separated. On the other hand, the innermost structure of nature as the form of the divine substance of the Spirit constitutes the theonomous attitude towards the universe in which the divine and the nature is interpenetrated. Tillich's "*infra Lutheranum*" background allows him to adopt the mutual indwelling of the two natures of Jesus Christ in whom the presence of the infinite in everything finite is theologically possible. God is the ground and the power of beings. Every being is grounded in the innermost part of God's being. Therefore, all objects or events become a medium functioning as a sacrament in which the transcendent is perceived to be present.[5]

Although Tillich emphasised that the character or quality of nature itself is closely related with the sacred power it symbolises, those qualities are only to be considered as the *bearer* of a sacred power. Nature is the object of Christian redemption. Therefore, the quality of the natural object is a necessary but not sufficient condition for becoming a sacrament. For Tillich, revelation and salvation are interchangeable. In volume one of his *Systematic Theology*, Tillich insisted that nothing is excluded from the participation in the ultimate ground of beings, and nothing is qualified and worthy in itself to represent the ultimate concern. In order to be the medium of the divine revelation, it should be also the object of divine redemption. This is the reason why the whole reality has become a medium of revelation but at the same time is never identified with the divine.[6] Tillich tends to accept nature as embodying a kind of symbolic character in revealing something ultimate.

For Tillich, the whole theology of sacramentality relies on a theology of the symbol in which the sacramental material is not only a sign, but also stands for a symbol that participates in what it signifies and is intrinsically related to what it expresses.[7] The theology of the symbol is closely related to his notion of self-transcending realism (*glaubiger Realismus*). As Tillich noted, "self-transcending realism is a universal attitude toward reality. It is neither a merely theoretical view of the world, nor a practical discipline for life [...] it is a basic attitude in every realm of life, expressing itself in the shaping of every realm."[8] This type of realism confirms the concrete form of nature as the embodiment of a spiritual power and meaning. Following Tillich's "*form-Inhalt-Gehalt*" framework for a theology of culture, the spiritual *Gehalt* reveals its power and meaning through natural forms and structures. Tillich insisted that "the new realism was not interested in the natural forms of things for their own sake, but for their power of expressing the profounder

[3] Tillich, *Systematic Theology* Vol.3 (Chicago, IL: University of Chicago Press, 1963), 34.
[4] Tillich, "Autobiographical Reflection," In Charles W. Kegley & Robert W. Bretall (eds), *The Theology of Paul Tillich* (New York: MacMillian)., 4.
[5] Tillich, "Nature and Sacrament," In James Luther Adams (ed), *The Protestant Era* (Chicago, IL: University of Chicago Press), 1948, 108.
[6] Tillich, *Systematic Theology* Vol.1 (Chicago, IL: University of Chicago Press, 1951), 118.
[7] Tillich, *Systematic Theology* Vol.3, 123.
[8] Tillich, "Realism and Faith," In James Luther Adams (ed), *The Protestant Era* (Chicago, IL: University of Chicago Press, 1948), 67. German original, "Über gläubigen Realismus," In John Clayton (ed), *Paul Tillich. Main Works/Hauptwerke* Volume 4 (Berlin: Walter de Gruyter, 1987), 193-212.

levels and the universal significances of things."[9] Through the given natural forms, this realism functions as symbolic embodiment and "tries to point to the spiritual meaning of the real by using its given form."[10] For this reason, Tillich rejected both the Catholic idea of transubstantiation, which transforms a symbol into a thing to be handled, and the reformed tradition of the sign character of the sacramental symbol.[11] Considering the Catholic side, nature as symbol representing spiritual power is not functioning as "*opus operatum*" in order to receive objective grace from the divine power and, considering the reformed side, Tillich argues that it is also not just a sign for the faith community to remember the divine saving event. In sum, nature as symbol participates in the power of what it symbolises, and therefore, it can be a medium of the Spirit.[12]

In Tillich's early demonstration of sacramental thinking, Christology and soteriology are linked with the power of a sacramental bearer. In order to attack magical and mythological usage, the Protestant tradition needs to bring nature into the context of the history of salvation, so that the demonic quality of nature is conquered in the New Being in Jesus Christ.[13] "Any sacramental reality within the framework of Christology and of Protestantism must be related to the New Being in Christ."[14] For Tillich, the New Being created by Jesus as the Christ is the new creation universe. Cosmic Christ as the New Being also represents the paradoxical character of the divine symbol in which "the absolute side of the final revelation, that in it which is unconditional and unchangeable, involves the *complete transparency* and the complete self-sacrifice of the medium in which it appears."[15]

However, the above Christological orientation is shifted into a pneumatological perspective in volume three of his *Systematic Theology*. In that work, Tillich tried to develop the doctrine of pneumatology in order to answer numerous criticisms on one hand, and to re-articulate his theological perspectives in the light of the doctrine of the Holy Spirit on the other. Although Tillich emphasised that the divine spirit is essentially correlated with the human spirit, it does not exclude the Spiritual Presence indwelling in the multi-dimensional unity of life. Given the rejection of dualistic and supernaturalist concepts, spiritual power and meaning manifest the "dimension of the ultimate" or "the dimension of depth."[16] Therefore, for Tillich, we have no reason to adopt the narrow sense of the concept of "sacramental" in which some particular objects and acts are qualified as the medium for the experience of divine spirit in a faith community. Rather, Tillich enlarged the sense of "sacramental" to cover *everything* in which the Spiritual Presence has been experienced.[17] The spiritual community "is free to appropriate *all* symbols which are adequate and which possess symbolic power."[18]

The Confucian Cosmogony

Generally speaking, the western dualistic conceptualisation is not found in the Chinese holistic and organic world view. Instead, the poles of transcendence and immanence integrate within each other to construct a more dynamic and developmental cosmic whole. The genuine Chinese cosmogony is that of an organic process, meaning that all of the parts of the entire cosmos belong to one organic whole and that all interact

---

[9] Tillich, "Realism and Faith," 193-212.
[10] Tillich, "Realism and Faith," 193-212.
[11] Tillich, *Systematic Theology* Vol.3, 123.
[12] Tillich, *Systematic Theology* Vol.3, 123.
[13] Tillich, "Nature and Sacrament," In James Luther Adams (ed), *The Protestant Era* (Chicago: University of Chicago Press, 1948), 102-103.
[14] Tillich, "Nature and Sacrament," 109.
[15] Tillich, *Systematic Theology* Vol.1, 151. [Emphasis mine].
[16] Tillich, *Systematic Theology* Vol.3, 113.
[17] Tillich, *Systematic Theology*, 121. [Emphasis mine].
[18] Tillich, *Systematic Theology*, 123. [Emphasis mine].

as participants in one spontaneously self-generating life process.[19] According to Tu Weiming, continuity, wholeness and dynamism are the three characters of the Chinese vision of the cosmos. The reality is regarded as a huge continuum that nothing is outside of. In rejecting dualistic thinking, nature is perceived under holistic thinking. The whole of reality is not static but vitality and dynamism of life always perform in a process-oriented way. In Neo-Confucianism, the dynamic ordering pattern (*li*) and the vital energies (*qi*) emanate from the ultimate Great (*taiji*). The latter performs as the basic structure and function of the cosmos and it penetrates into the former. Therefore, the ultimate principle of the universe is the ultimate One and it differentiates itself into the diverse structures and patterns in order to form different beings. In this context, the transcendent principle and the immanent forms are not dualistic but function as polar interaction. This philosophy of *Qi* becomes the focus in Zhang Zai's philosophy. *Qi* functions as the cosmic force to unite everything in the universe, and it is embodied in the human mind to embrace the pluralist and diverse conditions in everything into an integral whole.[20]

Nature is a relational whole in which human life and the rhythms of nature that sustain life in both its biological needs and socio-cultural expressions operate together. Everything in nature is interdependent, interrelated, dynamic and transformational. Nature, therefore, is inherently valuable and morally good. Value lies in the ongoing transformation and productivity of nature. Tu Weiming asserted that Confucian ontology is regarded as the continuity of being in which all modalities of being are organically connected.[21] Spiritual and material realms are co-related under the vital force. All beings, whether living or non-living, consist of this vital force. Without the concept of a creator God and the Christian idea of creation out of nothing, Confucian thought emphasises a spontaneously self-generating life process within which all beings, human and nonhuman, are integral parts of an organic continuum.[22] Under this way of thinking, humans and nature share the same cosmic creative force, so that a kind of kinship relationship develops between them.

Although nature has inherent value and embodies the normative standard for all things, it is not viewed from an anthropocentric perspective. In Confucianism, value is embodied within nature and lies in the ongoing transformation and productivity of nature. In this context, the Confucians do not view hierarchy as leading inevitably to domination. Rather, they see that value rests in each thing, but not in each thing in an individual. The Confucian vision of reality asserts that everything has its appropriate role and locationality. The use of nature for human ends must recognise the intrinsic value of each element of nature, but also its value in relation to the larger context of the environment. Each entity is considered not simply equal to every other; rather, each interrelated part of nature has a particular value according to its nature and function.[23] Hierarchy, for Confucianism, is seen as a necessary way for each being to fulfil its function. Thus, no individual has an exclusive privileged status. The processes of nature and its ongoing logic of transformation is the standard form that takes priority.

Human actualisation in cultural and ethical transformation is always embodied in the transformation process within the dynamic of nature. The great triad of Confucianism, heaven, earth and humans, signifies this understanding that humans can only attain their full humanity in relationship to both heaven and earth. This becomes an ontological-ethical foundation for a cosmological ethical system of relationality applicable to the spheres of family, society, politics and nature. Nature functions in this world view as parent to

---

[19] Weiming Tu, "The Continuity of Being: Chinese Visions of Nature," In J. Baird Callicott (ed), *Nature in Asian Traditions of Thought: Essays in Environmental Philosophy* (Albany, NY: State University of New York Press, 1989), pp.67-78.
[20] Jung-Yeup, Kim, *Zhang Zai's Philosophy of Qi: A Practical Understanding* (Lanham, MD: Lexington Books, 2015).
[21] Weiming Tu, "The Continuity of Being: Chinese Visions of Nature," 70.
[22] Weiming Tu, "The Continuity of Being: Chinese Visions of Nature," 70.
[23] Mary Evelyn Tucker, "Confucianism and Deep Ecology," In David Landis Barnhill and Roger S. Gottlieb (eds), *Deep Ecology and World Religions*. (Albany, NY: State University of New York Press, 2001), 131.

humans, providing sustenance, nurturing, intelligibility and guidance. In return, nature requires human respect and care. Human realisation is achieved by fulfilling this role of filial children to beneficent parents who have sustained life for humans. The human participation in the vast processes of nature has to be done in ways which are cultivating themselves in relation to nature's seasons and transformations.

Ecological Nature in Christian-Chinese Context

Tillich's pneumatology is multi-dimensional in character. The Holy Spirit is correlated with poly- and multi-faceted levels of numerous forms of life in our world. This cosmic and universal aspect of pneumatology makes a strong critique of the subjectivist understanding of the divine Spirit and the human spirit and challenges the traditional dualist concept in the western traditions which are generally regarded as the main cultural causes of environmental crisis. In Tillich's multi-dimensionality of life, different dimensions of life-forms (inorganic, organic, spiritual and historical) are capable of symbolising the divine; they are all potentially the bearer of divine manifestations in which the boundary of different forms of life blurs.

Likewise, in Confucian ecological thinking, nature is a relational whole. Everything in nature is interdependent, interrelated, dynamic and transformational. Nature, therefore, is inherently valuable and morally good. Value lies in the ongoing transformation and productivity of nature. Human beings as the centre of the universe share all the ontological power of the universe, and all powers of the universe are manifested in human beings. The existential ambiguity of human creativity is profoundly expressed in Tillich's pneumatology in the view that the human being is both the fulfilment and the potential destroyer of the universe. This ambiguous mixture points to the quest for pneumatological healing and divine redemption

Conclusion

We would conclude that the Christian idea of the pneumatological concept of nature and the Confucian cosmogony are providing potential religious-cultural resources for us to rethink our eco-religious-cultural worldviews. Through an intensified Christian-Confucian dialogue, nature should no longer be viewed as the object of the technological-scientific matrix, but as a kind of religious-aesthetic object, which is full of divine and holistic dimensions of power. All these findings direct us to rethink about the limits of the modern enlightenment project and to reconsider the role of the religious-cultural matrix in our age of environmental bankruptcy.

Suggestions for Further Reading

Moltmann, Jürgen.1985. *God in Creation*. London. SCM Press.

_____. 1992. *The Spirit of Life*. London. SCM Press

Santmire, H. Paul. 1985. *The Travail of Nature: The Ambigous Ecological Promise of Christian Theology*. Philadelphia: Fortress Press.

Tillich, Paul, 1963. *Systematic Theology*. Volume III. Chicago: University of Chicago Press.

Tu, Weiming. 1989. "The Continuity of Being: Chinese Visions of Nature," *Nature in Asian Traditions of Thought: Essays in Environmental Philosophy*. Ed. J.Baird Callicott. NY: State University of New York Press, pp.67-78.

Tucker, Mary Evelyn. 2001. "Confucianism and Deep Ecology,"*Deep Ecology and World Religions*. Eds. David Landis Barnhill & Roger S. Gottlieb. NY: State University of New York Press, pp.127-152.

21. Spiritual and Contextual Theological Resources for Resilience in Pacific Islands Communities: Choosing life – Affirming our Right to Live with Integrity of Creation

Lorine Tevi[1]

From the depths of my despair I call to you, Lord.
Hear my cry, O Lord, listen to my call for help.
Psalm 130:1-2

Fiji and the other islands of the Pacific are suffering in our struggle to survive and live life in its fullness. Whilst we too are experiencing the devastating COVID-19 pandemic, our islands are sinking, marine lives are diminishing, weather patterns are changing and villages are relocating because of climate changes. Here, too, as around the world, poverty is escalating, non-communicable diseases are increasing, drug addiction and deaths by suicide are staggeringly high, sexual abuse and exploitation particularly of women and children is alarming. The negative effects of secularisation particularly with regard to individualism are strongly felt, especially how it manifests as a loss of culture and caring community. Social media and electronic communication gadgets ever more dictate people's thinking and acting. Churches are becoming affluent and authoritarian whilst not serving the poor. There is a great deal of preaching and evangelising as well as increasing number of dwellers on the streets. This is an indication of spiritual poverty and spiritual death.

The above picture is very gloomy and results in despair and hopelessness, leading to what Gustavo Gutierrez[2] calls "premature and unjust death". Shall we continue to live this way? A fervent "No! No! No! No!" we shout.

Most of the Pacific Island communities are communities of faith. Most of them consist of Christians. They believe in a righteous, just and loving God who commands us to love one another. It is their faith in a living God that makes them to choose life and to nurture resilience in their communities. Resilience is nurtured and experienced because of the realities of life-threatening events from COVID 19, tropical cyclones and hurricanes, to heavy rainfall and earthquakes. We are crying deep inside. With these disasters, the anchor that we hold onto is our own faith in a living and loving God. We cry and pray from the depths of our being for the Lord to hear our crying prayer.

The Pacific people's prayer during moments of despair, at times with confession and conversion, sparked a new life as God encounters them and they personally encounter His son, Jesus Christ. They are affected and they know what is God's will for them. It is at this moment of encountering that the soul of people is affectively touched and an uplifting liberating spirit sparkles. It brings joy and, at times, even tears of joy are shed because of this profound encounter. God encounters them in the realities of their daily existence. There is mutuality in this encountering as we are partners with God in the ongoing process of creation. This profound mutual spiritual experience is the spirituality that nourishes, nurtures and develop resilience in Pacific communities. These spiritual encounters take place first as people in Pacific communities personally encounter Jesus Christ. What follows in the second stage is also to reflect theologically on the realities of their daily existence.

[1] Lorine Tevi was General Secretary for the Pacific Conference of Churches in the years from 1977-1981.

[2] Gustavo Gutierrez, *We Drink From Our Own Wells* (New York: Orbis Books, 1992).

They have *talanoa*[3] sessions of their faith with the realities of the sufferings and the struggles being faced. This is their theological reflection. What is God saying and how are they responding to God whom they believe as the God of their life, the God who responds to their prayer, their cry from the depths of their despair.

As part of their theological reflection, they consult their scripture, their Bible, to read and study what the God of history, the righteous, just and loving God, is telling them now. It is a *talanoa*, a conversation session and sharing with God on the realities of their daily existence. Thus, their spiritual encounter is followed by contextual theological reflection resulting in their authentic theology that serves as bedrock to their suffering and struggles. Both their spirituality and their authentic theology strengthen their communities as they share, study the bible together, pray and worship together gaining insights to sustain their faith for the struggle.

Thus, in villages and communities where persons of faith exist as a redemptive community of believers, there is both crying and praying to God from the depth of their being but also inspirations from God on how to face their sufferings, their struggles and to solve their life's issues. Together, they nourish, nurture and develop their resilient spirit and actions.

In 2010, Pacific Islands Association of Non-Government Organisations (PIANGO) held a seminar on the "Pacific We Want". Participants in one of the sessions included graduate students from the University of the South Pacific (USP), who had their field trip to Tuvalu, one of the atoll islands that is badly affected by climate change. They were asked what touches them in their field trip, in their journey. One of them loudly said, "their faith". The sharing and learning from that session inspired PIANGO to continue to advocating the role that Pacific Spirituality plays in the redemptive community of believers in the region. It was at the official adoption of the Pacific Island Development Forum (PIDF) Charter in 2014 at the Grand Pacific Hotel in Suva, Fiji, that one of the values was stated, which is embedded in the principles of the Charter instrument, namely "Affirming Pacific spirituality as a foundation of nurturing and building resilience in Pacific communities."[4]

At the 6th Assembly of the World Council of Churches (WCC), held in Vancouver in 1983, 34 years ago, a one-hour plenary session was held on the Pacific. At that time (indeed since 1975), PIANGO and the Pacific churches were in solidarity in their struggle for Pacific Islands self-determination and for a Nuclear Free Pacific. This was because of the atomic bomb testing of the French government in French Polynesia. The plenary hall heard the thunder of the Pacific Islands participants who shouted at the top of their voices:

IF IT IS SAFE,
DUMP IT IN TOKYO,
TEST IT IN PARIS,
STORE IT IN WASHINGTON,
BUT, KEEP MY PACIFIC NUCLEAR FREE

That plenary impacted the Assembly; the Lord encountered a good number of the participants, and the Pacific movement gained more solidarity with international ecumenical partners.

From 1975 onwards, civil society organisations began getting together to deal with issues of life and death in the region. This continued until today where COVID-19 and the negative effects of climate change

---

[3] Talanoa is a traditional word used in Fiji and across the Pacific to reflect a process of inclusive, participatory and transparent dialogue. The purpose of Talanoa is to share stories, build empathy and to make wise decisions for the collective good.

[4] Pacific Islands Development Forum, "Charter of the Pacific Islands Development Forum", *Pacific Islands Development Forum Website* (Suva, Fiji: PIDF, September 2015). [Available at: http://www.pidf.int/wp-content/uploads/2017/07/PIDF-Charter.pdf], [Last accessed: 1st April 2022].

are the main issues of the Pacific Islands. The churches still continue to play a major role in nurturing and developing resilience in Pacific communities based on the Pacific spiritualities and contextual theologies.

Like with the struggles for a Nuclear Free Pacific in the 1970s and 1980s, today, it is the pain, the agony, the suffering, the questioning, the hopelessness of how human beings are treating each other which is on our agenda as churches in the Pacific as we regularly experience the negative effects of climate change and COVID-19. The majority of Pacific Islanders are holding onto their faith in a righteous, just and loving God as their main weapon to combat world injustices.

A Call to a NEW EXODUS[5] was a resource book published 1982 by Lotu Pasifika of the Pacific Conference of Churches. It was written by Suliana Siwatibau, a biologist and activist from Fiji, and Davis Williams, Co-ordinator of Justice and Development programme of the Pacific Conference of Churches (PCC) from the Methodist Church of USA. The book has the story of the struggles, the data collected, the scientific explanation, the Bible study and the theological perspectives of the struggle and the movement. It was evident that the Pacific Island people have a strong faith in a loving God, the creator of the world, as they cry to their Lord from the depths of their being. Their spirituality was empowered with God's Holy Spirit which impels them to action. They collected data, engaged with participatory relevant Bible studies shared their stories and articulated their theological basis of action together.

1976 was the 3rd Assembly of the PCC held in Port Moresby, Papua New Guinea. It was a historical occasion when the Roman Catholic Bishop Council of the South Pacific, CEPAC, was accepted as full member of the Pacific Conference of Churches (PCC). PCC was the first regional ecumenical body that accepted Roman Catholics as full members. In that Assembly, "Integrated Human Development" and the "Nuclear Free Pacific" were two of the important outcomes of the gathering. A holistic and people centred development was the main goal. The church, civil society and government leaders all co-operated with each other.

In March 2001, a small group of less than 10 persons were called by the Pacific Desk of WCC as a small thinktank to go to Geneva to discuss "what is the alternative to globalisation". The sharing ended with an attempt to spell out the values of the Pacific Islands' family life, of which relationship, environment, spirituality and traditional economy were identified. The vision of "The Island of Hope",[6] a Pacific alternative to economic globalisation is the alternative as reported at this conference. The theological discussion continued and the book was published by WCC in 2001. It is the Pacific region's response to the ecumenical dialogue searching for an alternative perspective to globalisation. These values, identified and articulated by persons of faith and activists in their own professional fields, have been developed and are still being developed. Pacific spirituality is one of these values. The "Island of Hope" is being permeated with spirituality and a reflected theological position.

Today, as I continue to journey with this Pacific spirituality and theological reflection on it, I am grateful to the Almighty that as the essence and elements of Pacific Island spirituality it was affirmed that we choose to live but not to die and that we take our stand and affirm our right to live with the integrity of creation.

Our spirituality is springing from the depths of our faith and hope in a righteous, just and loving God. This gives us the courage, energy and joy to move forward. In the midst of the deadly effect of climate change and COVID-19, Fijian women of faith have accepted their moral responsibility to register, to vote and even to stand for the political election and spontaneously danced, Fijian style, in the church hall celebrating the freedom as they have to participate in the political decision-making of their nation. It is the spring of their spirituality experienced individually and co-operatively that empowered and impelled them to move on and to witness their faith publicly.

---

5 Suliana Siwatibau, *A Call to a New Exodus* (Havelu, Tonga: Lotu Pasifika Productions, 1982).

6 WCC, *Island Of Hope: A Pacific Alternative to Economic Globalisation*, Report of the Churches' Conference on Economic Globalisation (Papers presented 12th-18th August 2001, Nadi, Fiji, published June 2002), [Available at: https://www.ptc.ac.fj/fastpage/downloads/IsOfHope.pdf], [Last accessed: 1st April 2022].

As the journey of faith continues, the following are the essential features of Pacific spirituality and Pacific contextual theological reflection:

The Centrality of Jesus' Way of Living, his Suffering and the Victorious Event of the Easter Story

The personal encounter that the individual experiences with Christ is the centre. Christ touches the soul, the depth of one's faith and liberates one's life to live as God wills. The salvation act of God is experienced personally. The victory of the empty tomb is the hope and victory that a spiritual person lives with. One is impelled with God's spirit and moves all the way to live and to bring life in its fullness. One responds to the call of discipleship.

Scriptural and Biblical Based Spirituality

Reading the Bible with new eyes and ears is the new experience of being engaged in relevant and participatory approaches to study the scriptures. Women particularly are now beginning to take this approach as they seek enlightenment from the Word of God. Identifying and articulating their needs, studying the scriptures of relevant situations, reflecting theologically with God of what speaks to them, what that means to them and what inspiration for action they feel, is all part of their liberation experience.

Living with the Integrity of Creation

Living with the integrity of creation is the Pacific identity. Our land and our sea are part of us and we are part of them. Genesis 1:26-31 and Psalm 24:1-2 are embedded in our lives. The interconnectedness and interdependence of God's creatures impels us to embrace our down-to-earth spirituality and responsibility. In 1975, the Against Testing on Mururoa (ATOM) Committee[7] organised the first conference of the Nuclear Free Pacific at USP. The Young Womens' Christian Association was instrumental in organising the conference involving CSOs and the churches. It is only in the last two decades and particularly the last five years that all the different parts of the world have come together and collectively spoken up against the negative effects of climate change. Yet the Pacific Islands, half a century ago already, raised their voices to talk of connectedness and interdependence with God's creation.

Our faith is in a righteous, just and loving God, who has provided planet earth with sufficient resources to enable all people to live their lives with integrity. Unfortunately, selfishness and unjust development in the world results in an unbalanced and unjust sharing of the earth's resources that in turn creates a gap between the rich getting richer and the poor getting poorer.

Deconstructing Patriarchal Attitudes and Practices and Reconstructing the "Priesthood of all Believers" (Jer. 1:9-10, 1 Pet. 2:9)

The Pacific is the most religious region in the world; at the same time, it ranks amongst the worst in the world on certain social issues such as domestic violence and exploitation, particularly of women and children and increasing poverty. There are ways of worship and church practices that contribute to condoning these problems. They reveal a pattern of patriarchal theology and a way of life that places the male first and puts women and children as inferior and as second-class citizens. In 1979 at Malua in Western Samoa (as it was known at that time), the PCC and the WCC were sponsoring an ecumenical regional

[7] Walter Johnson and Sione Tupouniua, "Against French Nuclear Testing: The A.T.O.M. Committee", *The Journal of Pacific History* 11(4), (1976): 213-216. [Available at: https://www.jstor.org/stable/25168265], [Last accessed: 1st April 2022].

consultation on Justice, Peace and Integrity of Creation. The late Rev. Galuefa Aseta, who was then the Assistant General Secretary of PCC, stated that he agreed that the group most needing liberation are Pacific men. This was a profound statement at that consultation. Aseta was referring to the cultural and religious patriarchal theologies, ways of worship and practices that still exist in the Pacific today.

In a recent UN Spotlight Initiative to "eliminate violence against girls and women" from March 2021, it was reported:

> "We face the challenge that patriarchal attitudes and structural violence has been ingrained and reinforced in our culture and religious practice," said General Secretary of the Pacific Conference of Churches (PCC), Reverend James Bhagwan at the launch of Spotlight Initiative's Pacific Regional Programme in October 2020. "There is also a confrontational approach in engaging the church, in a region where over 90 per cent of the population identify as Christian and hold a worldview shaped by their faith, as agents of social transformation. As Churches, we have confessed our negative contribution to the structural violence enacted upon women of all ages and social status in the Pacific. Patriarchal structures of leadership and decision-making, biblical interpretation and attitudes towards women in faith communities have underpinned the psychological, emotional, physical, sexual and economic violence that Pacific women have had to endure." [...] Studies have shown that the Pacific region has some of the world's highest recorded rates of violence against women and girls, with almost two out of every three women impacted by physical or sexual violence in their lifetime – double the global average.[8]

The Biblical truth however teaches us that there is no discrimination; Jesus is not reserved for one part of humanity because we are all equal as sons and daughters of a loving, righteous and just God. Yet, certain traditional practices in the Pacific Islands also continue to contribute to this discrimination. Therefore, the relationships between Gospel and cultures need to be looked into in order to deconstruct patriarchal theologies, attitudes and practices and to plant a new style of the "priesthood of all believers", because we are all sons and daughters of a righteous, just and loving God.

We are All Partners with God in the Ongoing Process of Creation (Eph. 1:8-10)

The spiritual experiences of encountering Jesus Christ and in believing and seeing oneself as partner with God in the ongoing process of creation enables and inspires individuals and groups to covenant themselves with God so that unity in diversity will become a reality. Encountering Jesus Christ with spiritual experiences in every situation followed with contextual theological reflection on realities of daily needs and challenges is the path that needs to be encouraged and followed. In God's own timing, unity will take place. "All this wisdom comes from the Lord Almighty. The plans God makes are wise, and they always succeed" (Is. 28:29). This verse expresses the necessity of planning with God when one chooses to live one's life with integrity. Gustavo Gutierrez has expressed spirituality in love and hope of life when he says "A spirituality is a walking in freedom according to the spirit of love of life. This walking has its departure in encountering the Lord. The encounter is a spiritual experience, it springs from the Lord's initiative".[9]

I have stated above that the Pacific region is the most religious region of the world but is also performing worst on specific social issues. What is the matter? The challenge now is to work towards encouraging and promoting what Donald Dorr calls "Integral Spirituality".[10]

Integral spirituality is based on Micah 6:8: "The Lord has told what is good. What he requires of us is this: to do what is just, to share constant love, and to live in humble fellowship with our God." It is the

---

[8] See Donna Hoerder, "Faith Based Organisations' Commitment to Ending Violence Against Women and Girls", 8th March 2021, *United Nation Pacific* [Available at: https://pacific.un.org/en/115362-faith-based-organisations-commitment-ending-violence-against-women-and-girls], [Last accessed: 1st April 2022].

[9] Gutierrez, *We Drink From Our Own Wells,* 35.

[10] Donald Dorr, *Integral Spirituality: Resources for Community, Peace, Justice, and the Earth* (New York: Orbis Books, 1990).

necessary nourishment to sustain the faith journey in its mission in liberating individuals and groups to choose life. For an integral spirituality, it is necessary to have positive meaningful experiences in living the Kingdom of God in a redemptive community of faith.

The Pacific Islands people are crying, they are struggling, they are suffering, they are in agony and they are praying, crying to God from the depths of their despair.

We plea to the world and to those who will be spiritually empathising with us to stand in solidarity with the Pacific Islands people.

Suggestions for Further Reading

Pacific Conference of Churches (PCC) - website: https://www.pacificconferenceofchurches.org/

A New Voyage: Pacific People Explore the Future They Want'. The second consultation of Bread for the World partners in the Pacific, November 2011, in: https://www.brot-fuer-diewelt.de/fileadmin/mediapool/2_Downloads/Fachinformationen/Dialog/Dialog_11_a_new_voyage.pdf

PART III: LATIN AMERICA AND CARIBBEAN

22. THEOLOGICAL AFFIRMATIONS FOR LIVING TOGETHER

Marisa Strizzi[1]

Introduction

In the broad context of a global concern for the present and future of life on earth, this article will focus on the issue of human life and its impact on life in general. To that end, I will review specific information from a wide range of contemporary studies on this subject. In the light of that review, I will note down some theological aspects inspired by the sixteenth-century Reformation tradition as they appear, mainly, in the work of Martin Luther. In this way, I will seek to develop theological affirmations that illuminate an eco-diakonia for living together on a planet characterised by the manifestation of the phenomenon of life.

Inside a Big Map

The project of "big history" was introduced by David Christian, who defines it as a "modern creation myth"; as such, it is a way of giving meaning and orientation to contemporary human life.[2] As a "grand scientific metanarrative," big history integrates physics, chemistry, geology, biology, anthropology, cosmology, sociology, economics and history into a single narrative that portrays the development of the universe, the evolution of life and the course of humanity.[3] This approach thus provides an immense contextual map that, by situating the brief history of the species within the history of the universe, puts human beings "in their place" allowing us to observe that:

We are a tiny part of a larger event. Explaining the origin of humans from evolutionary theory, astrophysics, quantum physics and cosmology makes it necessary to start with the Big Bang, and, from there, to follow the emergence of new and different patterns of complexity. In other words, the succession of transitional moments from which something new is abruptly created and the whole system enters a new phase. Thus, the crossing of various thresholds takes us through the 13.7 billion year history of our universe, the 4.5 billion year evolution of our planet, the development of our species through 7 million years, and then to the 10,000 year accelerated drama of human civilisation.[4] Following Carl Sagan, if the Big Bang occurred on 1st January at midnight, we humans would appear on the cosmic calendar so recently that our recorded history would occupy only the last seconds of the last minute of 31st December.[5] We are newcomers to an immeasurable event.

We are made up of the very matter of the universe. To explain our constitution, one must think of electrons, quarks, protons, neutrons, hydrogen, helium, stars, galaxies, heavier elements, complex chemistry and planetary systems that gave rise to the formation of a small planet in a small solar system

---

[1] Dr Marisa Strizzi is a Professor in the Ecumenical Network for Theological Education, where she co-ordinates the Department of Theology and Interdisciplinary Studies. Contact: strizzimarisa@gmail.com.

[2] David Christian, *Maps of Time: An Introduction to Big History* (Berkeley, CA: University of California Press, 2004): 2-5.

[3] See Metanexus, "Explore Big History," 25th October 2011, *Metanexus Website*, [Available at: https://metanexus.net/explore-big-history/], [Last accessed: 17th March 2022].

[4] See "Explore Big History".

[5] Carl Sagan, *Dragons of Eden: Speculations on the Evolution of Human Intelligence* (New York: Random House, 1977): 13-14.

where the intricate phenomenon called "life" took place. Prokaryotic cells and symbiotic unions, eukaryotic cells and sexual reproduction, multicellular organisms… all of them introduced different forms of living entities: bacteria, fungi, algae, ferns, flowering plants and sponges, corals, worms, arthropods and vertebrates. Planet Earth and life have our species as one of very many possibilities. Thus, we share our chemistry with stars and planets, and our biological material relates us to bacteria, fungi, fish, reptiles, birds, ants, spiders, cats, dogs, apes and many others.[6]

As complex living organisms, we suffer and die. Given the general tendency of the universe toward disorder, living organisms could be described by their constant defiance of the second law of thermodynamics. They show, as Schrödinger would express, an astonishing ability to "continually suck order out of their environment."[7] Indeed, life introduced on Earth a new level of order and complexity and a great capacity to control and organise free energy, but this was achieved at the price of great fragility: *life introduced death*. As a species that is the product of a long evolution, *Homo sapiens* shares these aspects with other living organisms. With a highly sensitive nervous system, we feel physical pain; with a sophisticated capacity for flexible symbolic language and abstraction, we have an open horizon of mental possibilities. This makes us particularly prone to anxiety, distress and other forms of mental suffering, but also allows us to enjoy all its benefits. Finally, like all living beings, human beings die.

We are but one species bound to planet Earth along with many, many others. It is estimated that there are between 10 and 100 million different species on Earth, each consisting of many individual organisms.[8] Our species interacts with many of these species directly on an ongoing basis, at multiple levels and with different outcomes. The agricultural revolution marked a threshold in human evolution because we established a special co-dependent relationship with certain plants and animals. But, in many cases, the interaction with other species is much closer: numerous diseases are precisely an internal encounter with some of them, and our own body becomes the battlefield. Fortunately, other encounters obey symbiotic "agreements" and keep all parties healthy; these "contracts" are multiple and some of them continue – modified – after our death, when our bodies are only food. The number of bacteria living in our bodies outnumbers our body cells by ten to one.[9] The human microbiome shows how we harbour 100 trillion bacteria spread over our skin, conjunctivae, oral cavity, respiratory tract, stomach, intestines and genitals;[10] altogether it weighs about 1,500 grams and is considered another organ of the human body. The fact is that human beings are not alone, because alone we could not *be*.

Like all species, the human species is finite. Big history reminds us that "ever since Darwin, it has been clear that species are not eternal."[11] As biology observes, a species manages to establish itself when it finds a niche within the community of other species, extracting enough resources from the environment to be able to survive and reproduce successfully. The history of a species usually follows a characteristic pattern: *migration* allows it to expand its niche or exploit new regions; *innovation* leads to rapid growth until the lack of a resource critical to its life prevents it from growing further; this stage of *overexploitation* is sometimes followed by a catastrophic population *decline*. However, populations can increase again by

---

[6] See "Life", *Big History Project Website*. [Available at: https://www.bighistoryproject.com/chapters/3#], [Last accessed: 17th March 2022].

[7] Erwin Schrödinger, *What Is Life?* (Cambridge: Cambridge University Press, 1992): 73.

[8] Christian, *Maps*, 133.

[9] See American Society for Microbiology, "Humans Have Ten Times More Bacteria Than Human Cells: How Do Microbial Communities Affect Human Health?", 5th June 2008, *ScienceDaily*, [Available at: https://www.sciencedaily.com/releases/2008/06/080603085914.htm], [Last accessed 17th March 2022]; Leroy Hood, "Tackling the microbiome," *Science* 336(6086) (2012): 1209.

[10] A "microbiome" is "the ecological community of commensal, symbiotic, and pathogenic microorganisms that literally share our body space." J. Lederberg, y A.T. McCray, "'Ome Sweet 'Omics – a genealogical treasury of words," *Scientist* 15 (2001): 8.

[11] Christian, *Maps*, 133.

adapting more subtly to the opportunities and limits of their environment, and reach the *stabilisation* phase. A species may go through this cycle many times, but eventually the transformation of the environment – often because of other species – has fatal results, without allowing stabilisation. Then the species will go into *extinction*, even though it may leave descendants different enough to be classified as members of a new species.[12] If, as complex living organisms, we are bound to our share of suffering, pain and death, as a species we are destined to eventual extinction and/or mutation.

We developed an ability to make a great impact on our environment. Powerful brains and a precise and flexible symbolic language allowed us to interact and exchange ideas, fuelling a unique ability to create collective knowledge.[13] Increasing knowledge and technology allowed us to control resources and the environment, giving rise to increasingly complex civilisations. Very recently, after the year fifteen hundred, our societies began to spread and connect fully across the planet producing networks for the exchange of ideas, technology, goods and belief systems. The *agricultural*, *industrial* and *information* revolution brought us to a point in history where knowledge and technology are transforming everyday life by making unprecedented levels of comfort and well-being available. But, on the other hand, the energy we use and the food we produce have to sustain nearly eight billion human beings and require a huge share of the Earth's resources. We are having such an impact on the planet and all life on it that the various scientific communities identify this epoch, which began some 500 years ago, with our name: the Anthropocene.[14]

A Particular Species

Now, what dominant characteristics did the *anthropos* develop and how do they impact life on planet Earth? The big history gathers cold, amoral data. Entering the internal record of the life of the species makes it necessary to modify this broad focus to perceive closely the small, near stories. The work of feminist thinkers – including philosophers, biologists, social scientists and theologians – contributes significantly to the observation of particular aspects. Different readings produced from the Global South provide us with the specific g/local. So, we can detect:

A peculiar dominant profile. Anthropos understood itself as the centre of the universe. In fact, *he* established himself as the representative of the species, differentiating himself from its others: "gods, machines, animals, monsters, creepy crawlies, women, servants and slaves, and noncitizens in general."[15] The term "human" thus became an exclusive designation appropriated, preferentially, by specimens with specific traits: *Homo sapiens*, male, white, heterosexual, inhabitant of a perfectly functional body, with access to property, political participation and certain standards of education. Under the metaphysical alias of "subject", the human came to consider himself as the foundation of knowledge, the origin of truth claims, the guarantor of meaning and, consequently, an autonomous agent.[16] This profile of the human easily assumed the role of interpreter, owner and/or administrator of all his "others."

A particular way of connecting. The delimitation of the Anthropocene coincides with the development of a particular economic system. This system progressed from the momentum of the connections that human societies began to establish around the world around the year 1500. Globalisation, the discovery and

[12] Christian, *Maps,* 133-134.
[13] See "Humans," *Big History Project Website*, [Available at: https://www.bighistoryproject.com/chapters/4#], [Last accessed: 17th March 2022].
[14] Be this as a metaphor for this epoch or as a truly new geological era. On this discusión, see Liz-Rejane Issberner y Philippe Léna, "Antropoceno: la problemática vital de un debate científico," *El Correo de la Unesco* (abril-julio 2018): 7-9.
[15] Following Donna Haraway's clever list in *When Species Meet* (Minneapolis, MN: University of Minnesota Press, 2008): 9.
[16] See Celia Amorós, *Hacia una crítica de la razón patriarcal*, segunda ed. (Barcelona: Anthropos, 1991): 21-106 and María L. Femenías, *Sobre sujeto y género* (Buenos Aires: Catálogos, 2000).

exploitation of new resources and the increasing use of fossil fuels were driven by capital and the market.[17] The global connections that stimulated the human capacity for collective knowledge and innovation occurred, in fact, in contexts of colonial or imperial conquest and domination: the expropriation of lands and territories, the appropriation and exploitation of natural resources, human slavery, and cultural, racial, gender and religious imposition. The history of colonialism teaches us that ideas, goods and technologies were "traded," but the trade was anything but fair.[18] Thus, the networks of exchange in which ideas, technology, goods and belief systems began to be "shared" were akin to an economic system that responds to the dominant profile of the species and whose viciousness grows ever more complex as it extends over time.

A vicious impulse. Various critical studies affirm that there is a strong link between colonialism, capitalism and patriarchy.[19] Early feminist critique reveals the relationship involving the overexploitation of land, women and other species.[20] Moreover, as Marx himself noted, the history of capitalism and the species' capacity for innovation are linked, stimulating each other in a particularly powerful synergy.[21] Donna Haraway asserts that turning the whole world into commodities is the driving force of capitalism: "Indeed, remaking the world so that new opportunities for commodity production and circulation are ever generated is the name of this game."[22] At present, it is easily observable that the naturalised logic of "this game" involves associated elements that can only lead to an enormous impact on planetary life. Cynthia Moe-Lobeda thoroughly observes how late capitalism, a form of neocolonial domination, intends and presupposes unlimited growth in the production of goods and services; unlimited resources and services provided by the Earth; and an unregulated market of powerful actors. These actors have the freedom to do as they please with economic assets, such as carbon emissions or speculative investments that can lead to the collapse of national economies. In this horizon, state socialism does not offer an alternative option either; it is "yet another form of centralised economic power dedicated to growth and unaccountable to a democratic public."[23] Finally, this "game" is not without religious blessing. Marcella Althaus-Reid lays bare how capitalism, the market economy and the drive for neoliberal ideological globalisation find their foundation in the interplay of dominant theological and political discourses. And, as she rightly unpacks: "Economic desires run side by side with erotic desires and theological needs."[24] All theology accounts for the intimate connections between hegemonic sexual and socio-political constructs.

The architecture of a predatory planetary system. The dominant profile of the species is based on the design of a system of appropriation, extraction, exploitation and consumption from whose impact nothing and no one escapes. Patriarchal logic finds as necessary domination and slavery which, when articulated with capitalism, are placed at the service of capital accumulation, managing the interdependence and co-

---

[17] Christian, *Maps*, 364-405.

[18] As Samir Amin observes, colonialism and capitalism are inseparable, "Le colonialisme et le capitalisme sont inseparables," interview by Lucien Degoy, *l'Humanite*, 14 de diciembre, 2005, [Available at: https://www.humanite.fr/le-colonialisme-et-le-capitalisme-sont-inseparables-340582], [Last accessed: 17th March 2022].

[19] See Iris Hernández Morales, "Colonialismo, capitalismo y patriarcado en la historia y los feminismos de Abya Yala," *REPL* 3(1) (2020): 29-47.

[20] See María Luisa Cavana, Alicia Puleo and Cristina Segura (eds), *Mujeres y Ecología. Historia, Pensamiento, Sociedad* (Madrid: Almudayna, 2004).

[21] Christian, *Maps*, 357-59.

[22] Haraway, *When*, 45.

[23] Cynthia Moe-Lobeda, *Resisting Structural Evil: Love as Economic and Ecological Vocation* (Minneapolis, MN: Augsburg Fortress, 2013): 41-42 [42].

[24] Marcella Althaus-Reid, *Indecent Theology: Theological Perversions in Sex, Gender and Politics* (London: Routledge, 2000): 165-176 [166].

production of the fabric of life in terms of exploitation and hierarchy.[25] All that lives is especially affected, because climate change – generated by the planetary impact of the species – not only originates a problem for the human, creating a link of pan-human vulnerability, but also connects the human with the destiny of other species.[26] However, uncontrolled human activity not only endangers other species by the modifications inflicted on their environment, but also because human beings have become users and abusers of human and nonhuman species. Thus, if the logic of the game according to Marx was to mercilessly suck out the living human labour force, this now turned out to be only a part of the history of living capital. *Das Kapital* has effectively revealed itself as *Das Biokapital*.[27] The picture of an economic system of exploitation of the human by the human now appears much more nuanced and complex. Many of the "others," arbitrarily lumped together under the label "animals," have been brought into the game in a paradoxical way. On the one hand, as living material not only for food but for all kinds of experiments; they are mistreated, tortured, genetically manipulated to serve the needs of biotechnology and the cosmetics and pharmaceutical industries. An ill-constructed distinction between "human" and "animal" is used not only to delimit what is edible, but also to justify the perverse and massive genocidal torture inflicted on other species.[28] On the other hand, they are counted as consumed and consumers in the staggeringly profitable market of pets or "exotic commodities." In this game, they are commodities that consume commodities: food, products and services for their care mean big global business.[29] Likewise, the valuable plants that we humans learned to grow, care for and use are also part of the globally commoditised living species. In addition to the tangible resources they represent, biotechnology allows access to "plant genetic resources" and this generates a field of common property rules that puts the ownership of intellectual patents and rights over plant genetics in constant dispute. Here, the winners are increasingly exclusive private domains.[30] Agriculture – the first revolution of the species – became throughout the Anthropocene, in the hands of "biopiracy," a curse for the planet.[31] The first human societies intensified the use and care of certain plants and animals, establishing a relationship of co-dependence with them; the indigenous and peasant communities that safeguard this knowledge and care of the planet's biodiversity see their biocultures increasingly threatened.[32] The dynamics of capital and the market corrupt any possibility of fair relations.

Bar codes for life. There is yet one more aspect, which even Marx's worst nightmare could not have foreseen: the taking of "life as surplus value." Life has been drawn into the circuits of value creation, and the history of biotechnology is tied to the rise of neoliberalism as a political force and as economic policy.[33] The transformative and beneficial dimensions of contemporary biotechnology go hand in hand with an "imperative of violence that sustains neoliberalism's *promise of more and better life*."[34] Biotechnology is,

---

[25] See Vanesa Carsolio, "Claves para comprender la dimensión especista en la coproducción de la vida", *Revista Latinoamericana de Estudios Críticos Animales* 7(1) (2020): 381-398.

[26] Rosi Braidotti, *The Posthuman* (Cambridge: Polity Press, 2013): 111.

[27] Haraway toys with the idea of "a Marx equivalent [...] writing *Biocapital*, volume I, today"; *When*, 46.

[28] Mónica Cragnolini, "Políticas de la otredad: la cuestión animal", in H. Daniel Dei and Marisa G. Divenosa (eds), *La cuestión del otro en la filosofía, la política, la sociedad y la cultura* (Remedios de Escalada: Universidad de Lanús, 2017): 108-114.

[29] See Haraway, *When*, 45-67.

[30] See Carolina Roa-Rodriguez and Thom van Dooren, "Shifting Common Spaces of Plant Genetic Resources in the International Regulation of Property", *The Journal of World Intellectual Property* 11(3) (2008): 176-202 and Vandana Shiva, *Monocultures of the Mind* (Penang: Third World Network, 1993): 73-127.

[31] See Vandana Shiva, *Biopiracy. The Plunder of Nature and Knowledge* (Boston, MA: South End Press, 1997).

[32] Fausto Torrez and Elsa Nury Martínez, "La cuestión agraria y los desafíos actuales", *Revista América Latina en Movimiento* 541 (2019): 12-14.

[33] See Melinda Cooper, *Life as Surplus: Biotechnology and Capitalism in the Neoliberal Era* (Seattle, WA: University of Washington Press, 2008).

[34] Thus, in the context of debt imperialism, the contemporary pharmaceutical industry decides which countries have access to medicines and how, Cooper, *Life*, 12. (Emphasis mine).

in fact, a distinctive feature of the knowledge sponsored and exploited by contemporary capitalism: the Human Genome project, stem cell research, and biotechnological intervention on animals, seeds, cells, and plants. Rosi Braidotti observes, "advanced capitalism both invests and profits from the scientific and economic control and the commodification of all that lives"; moreover, they hunt for "the informational power of living matter itself."[35] In the Anthropocene, a global economic system designed by the human species intends to take over the miracle that occurred on Earth 3.6 billion years ago: Life, with a capital letter.

Cyber-connections. Archaeologists, palaeontologists, and palaeoanthropologists mostly agree that tool use is a defining characteristic of human beings. Our evolution is related to the use and development of tools: we are something like "natural-born cyborgs."[36] Fostering the human capacity for innovation, the species updates itself daily through its cyber-connections. Today, biotechnology, nanotechnology, computer and cognitive science enhance human life to the fullest. Technological devices are, in fact, extensions of our bodies: domestic machines, information and communication devices, prostheses and drones. Our relationship with technology has become a symbiosis and the boundaries between technology and our bodies are blurred in our everyday experience. However, the fact that we live in the age of advanced global capitalism means that all knowledge is promoted to be co-opted in the service of capitalism's own development.[37] We connect and communicate for different purposes, we access and provide information at the same time. We input our data and the market uses it to continually reshape itself and us. Technoscientific knowledge applied to the advancement of the global multimedia environment and ultra-sophisticated military technology are just examples of interrelated modes of appropriation that accompany the conversion of the ecosystem into a planetary production apparatus.[38] "Thus cyborgs not only includes the glamorous bodies of high-tech, jet-fighter pilots, or film stars" demystifies Braidotti, "but also the anonymous masses of the underpaid, digital proletariat who fuel the technology-driven global economy without ever accessing it themselves."[39] Human culture continues to increase innovation to unimaginable levels, improving and prolonging *some* lives and, at the same time, perfecting the global market for the technology of death.

Theological Affirmations

At this point, I formulate an obvious statement: Living together is not the fruit of a choice; *living* is *living together*. So, on this planet, with the characteristics of our species, what theological resources can illuminate an eco-diakonia founded on this inescapable cohabitation of the living?

We firmly believe that God has created us together with all creatures.[40] The life of our species is not of our species. We participate in the same miracle as millions of other species and are linked to them ever since we began and in ways that exceed us. Our Christian service to the planet testifies that life is immeasurable and that its manifestations are manifold.

Dust we are and to dust we shall return (Gen. 3:19). We who evolved by working the earth, we come from it; made from a "clod of dirt" and together with all creatures we share with this planet the matter that

[35] Braidotti, *The Posthuman*, 59.

[36] Taede Smedes, "Technology and Evolution: The Quest For a New Perspective", *Dialog* 44(4) (2005): 355.

[37] See Andrés Barreda, "El sometimiento capitalista de las tecno-ciencias", *Revista América Latina en Movimiento* 543 (2019): 5-8 and Vidushi Marda, "Inteligencia artificial: una perspectiva desde el Sur", *Revista América Latina en Movimiento* 545 (2019): 1-5.

[38] Adriana Franco, "La ciberguerra en la disputa intercapitalista," *Revista América Latina en Movimiento* 544 (2019): 13-16.

[39] Braidotti, *The Posthuman*, 90.

[40] "I believe that God created me together with all creatures," thus in the German original version of the *Small Catechism*: "Ich gleube, das mich Gott geschaffen hat sampt allen Creaturn." Martin Luther, *D. Martin Luthers Werke.* Kritische Gesamtausgabe (Weimar: Hermann Böhlaus Nachfolger, 1883-2009), 30.I:363,2.

shapes us.[41] We will return to the earth, nothing of our matter will be lost but the cycle of life will continue. Our "creation myths" affirm this.

The existence and subsistence of all life comes from God. The sustainment of human life depends on other forms of life, but the possibility of this vital exchange does not belong to us. Our theological traditions express themselves in an anthropocentric way; the emphasis is on human beings as beneficiaries of creation.[42] This, however, is far from embracing the anthropocentric perspective of the modern autonomous subject: everything is a gift from God and no one is capable of possessing or preserving their life or that of others for themselves.[43]

Our relationships are marked by sin. In all things we seek only ourselves and use which is good in a bad way. Others are only a means to our self-realisation. The evil of the curvature that we cast in our actions must never be ignored.[44]

The dominant profile of Anthropos thus denotes the structural sin of the species. The suffering of creation – which suffers innocently – is directly related to human abuse.[45] The suffering inflicted on the life of our own species rests on this same structure. The curvature – the closing in on oneself – not only responds to the sinful pursuit of the ego or of the subject, but to that of the species as a whole, taking asphyxia[46] to planetary proportions.

Only the cross allows us to see the suffering of all creatures. While the sciences give us cold, precise data on the evolution of life in the cosmos, only by learning Jesus Christ "and him crucified" (1 Cor. 2:2) we can "see creation as creation longing, groaning, in travail."[47]

Always by grace and through faith. Life and our part in it has salvation only through the flesh of God who lives, suffers and dies in Jesus Christ. The word about this unconditionality of the Risen One who was crucified, takes us out of our selfhood and saves us. This faith is the interruption of suffocating self-realisation; it is the opening to the other that tears us out of ourselves. Thus, the *oikos* of *eco*-diakonia refers to the different *eco*nomy of a new community: an *eco*nomy of grace, which does not close in on itself but remains open to the gift of otherness.

Calling things what they actually are. The theology of the cross continues to inspire our commitment: a diakonia that gets its hands dirty will not fail to make it clear that ecological justice seeks to care for the vital tissue of the planet and for that it needs to heal the rip of sin in this fabric. The fullness of life must be promoted even – and most especially – against the interests of our own sinful institutions. Refusing to play the game is an act of fidelity. Moreover, putting one's own life to change the game – for one of "open format and open access" in which every life counts – is all about this call. In this context, we can affirm that, "the theologians of the 'theologically correct' call evil good and good evil; the theologians of the cross call things as they really are."[48]

The faith of Jesus Christ opens life in a new format. If techno-science in the service of capitalism formats all that lives in a calculated way at the demand of the market, a "*fides Christo formata*" justifies and saves into a new format, an actual futural form of the human, of the world, of the cosmos.

---

[41] Martin Luther, "Lectures on Genesis," in Jaroslav Pelikan and Helmut Lehmann (eds), *Luther's Works* (Philadelphia, PA: Muhlenberg, 1955-1986), 1:83.

[42] Martin Luther, "The Large Catechism", in Theodore G. Tappert (ed and trans), *The Book of Concord: The Confessions of the Evangelical Lutheran Church* (Philadelphia, PA: Fortress, 1959), II.14-15.

[43] Luther, "Large Catechism", II.15-16.

[44] Luther, "Lectures on Romans", *LW*, 25:344-345

[45] Martin Luther, *Sermons by Martin Luther*, edited and translated by Nicholas Lenker (Grand Rapids, MI: Baker, 2000), 8:93,1

[46] Asphyxia is a condition of deficient supply of oxygen, in other words: suffocation.

[47] Luther, "Lectures on Romans", *LW*, 25:361

[48] Luther, "Heidelberg Disputation", *LW*, 31:40 (my adaptation).

We are, together with all creatures, the raw material of the future in God's hands. "[T]he human being in this life is the simple material of God for the form of their future life. Just as the whole creation which is now subject to vanity [Rom. 8:20] is for God the material for its future glorious form."[49] Commodified human algorithms pretend to design virtual futures from the repetition of closed presents and those futures only fit into "more of the same" and lead towards "extinction." God designs real futures from open presents where the play of life welcomes and protects the vulnerability of the different.

Suggestions for Further Reading

Althaus-Reid, Marcella. *Indecent Theology: Theological Perversions in Sex, Gender and Politics.* London: Routledge, 2000.

American Society for Microbiology. "Humans Have Ten Times More Bacteria Than Human Cells: How Do Microbial Communities Affect Human Health?" 5th June 2008, *ScienceDaily*. [Available at: https://www.sciencedaily.com/releases/2008/06/080603085914.htm], [Last accessed: 17th March 2022].

Amin, Samir. "Le colonialisme et le capitalisme sont inséparables". Entrevista por Lucien Degoy. *l'Humanité*, 14th December 2005. [Available at: https://www.humanite.fr/le-colonialisme-et-le-capitalisme-sont-inseparables-340582], [Last accessed: 17th March 2022].

Amorós, Celia. *Hacia una crítica de la razón patriarcal*. Second edition. Barcelona: Anthropos, 1991.

Barreda, Andrés. "El sometimiento capitalista de las tecno-ciencias". *Revista América Latina en Movimiento* 543 (2019): 5-8.

Braidotti, Rosi. *The Posthuman.* Cambridge: Polity Press, 2013.

Carsolio, Vanesa. "Claves para comprender la dimensión especista en la coproducción de la vida". *Revista Latinoamericana de Estudios Críticos Animales* 7(1) (2020): 381-398.

Cavana, María Luisa, Alicia Puleo and Cristina Segura, Eds. *Mujeres y Ecología. Historia, Pensamiento, Sociedad.* Madrid: Almudayna, 2004.

Christian, David. *Maps of Time: An Introduction to Big History*. Berkeley, CA: University of California Press, 2004.

Cooper, Melinda. *Life as Surplus: Biotechnology and Capitalism in the Neoliberal Era.* Seattle, WA: University of Washington Press, 2008.

Cragnolini, Mónica. "Políticas de la otredad: la cuestión animal", in H. Daniel Dei and Marisa G. Divenosa, Eds. *La cuestión del otro en la filosofía, la política, la sociedad y la cultura*. Remedios de Escalada: Universidad de Lanús, 2017.

Femenías, María Luisa. *Sobre sujeto y género. Lecturas feministas desde Beauvoir a Butler*. Buenos Aires: Catálogos, 2000.

Haraway, Donna. *When Species Meet*. Minneapolis, MN: University of Minnesota Press, 2008.

Hood, Leroy. "Tackling the microbiome". *Science* 336(6086) (2012): 1209.

Lederberg, J. and A.T. McCray. "'Ome Sweet 'Omics – a genealogical treasury of words". *Scientist* 15 (2001): 8.

Luther, Martin. *D. Martin Luthers Werke.* Kritische Gesamtausgabe. Weimar: Hermann Böhlaus Nachfolger, 1883-2009.

——. *Luther's Works.* Jaroslav Pelikan and Helmut Lehmann, general eds. Philadelphia, PA: Muhlenberg Press, 1955-1986.

——. "The Large Catechism", in Theodore G. Tappert, Ed and Trans. *The Book of Concord: The Confessions of the Evangelical Lutheran Church*. Philadelphia, PA: Fortress, 1959.

——. *Sermons by Martin Luther*, edited and translated by Nicholas Lenker. Grand Rapids: Baker, 2000.

[49] Luther, "Disputation Concerning the Human Being", *LW*, 34:138.

Marda, Vidushi. “Inteligencia artificial: una perspectiva desde el Sur.” *Revista América Latina en Movimiento* 545 (2019): 1-5.
Moe-Lobeda, Cynthia. *Resisting Structural Evil: Love as Economic and Ecological Vocation.* Minneapolis, MN: Augsburg Fortress, 2013.
Roa-Rodriguez, Carolina and Thom van Dooren. “Shifting Common Spaces of Plant Genetic Resources in the International Regulation of Property”. *The Journal of World Intellectual Property* 11(3) (2008): 176-202.
Sagan, Carl. *Dragons of Eden: Speculations on the Evolution of Human Intelligence.* New York: Random House, 1977.
Schrödinger, Erwin. *What Is Life? The Physical Aspect of the Living Cell.* Cambridge: Cambridge University Press, 1992.
Shiva, Vandana. *Biopiracy. The Plunder of Nature and Knowledge.* Boston, MA: South End Press, 1997.
Shiva, Vandana. *Monocultures of the Mind.* Penang: Third World Network, 1993.
Smedes, Taede. “Technology and Evolution: The Quest for a New Perspective”. *Dialog* 44(4) (2005).
Torrez Fausto and Elsa Nury Martínez. “La cuestión agraria y los desafíos actuales”. *Revista América Latina en Movimiento* 541 (2019): 12-14.

23. Justice by Faith and Ecojustice: Contours of a 'Life in the Spirit', in Contrast to the Spirit of the Unlimited

Daniel Carlos Beros[1]

To my brother and colleague, Dr Pedro Kalmbach *in memoriam*.

Introduction

The starting point of the following reflections is grounded in the thesis that identifies the "spirit of the unlimited" as an essential motive in the global dominant cultural regime under the rule of financial capitalism, and also sees its impact as responsible for the true ecocide that is taking place on our planet. Here we propose to show how, in the face of the deadly tyranny of the limitless, the community of faith has been promised in Jesus Christ the irruption of a "liberating limit," which inaugurates a new life in the Spirit (Gal. 5), manifested as a resistant and compassionate commitment to eco-justice. We will do so by conversing with analogous proposals about spirituality and "ecological conversion," as the one developed by Pope Francis in his Encyclical Letter *Laudato Si'*.

The Tyrannical Regime of Unlimited Exploitation

Our place in the world is the Southern Cone of South America. Here, the multinationals that control the extractive exploitation that they call "agro-industry" or "agribusiness", celebrate the virtual dissolution of the limits of the old Nation-States through the establishment of an alleged "United Soybean Republic".

Figure 1: República Unida de la Soja

[1] Daniel Carlos Beros is a Doctor in Theology, Professor and General Co-ordinator of the Ecumenical Network of Theological Education (REET, for its initials in Spanish) and Head of its Department of Systematic Theology and Ethics. Contact: danielberos@gmail.com.

However, the deceptive nature of this propagandistic fiction does not only consist in calling "republic" what in essence is a form of tyranny, a product of the imposition, in and from the sphere of agricultural production, of patterns dictated by companies mostly controlled by large international capital. If we pay attention to the ambivalent associations linked to the green colour with which the territory conquered by "soy" is represented, it becomes clear that it does not only refer to this vegetable. For, while deceptively suggesting respect for the environment (ecology), it refers in a veiled way to the "green bill", to the US dollar (economy) – authentic "object of desire" that fuels and unleashes the expansive dynamics of the crop, transformed into a commodity. In this way, the propaganda consummates a kind of farce. It does so by concealing the very serious mortgage left behind by the unlimited advance of the transgenic desert: plundered wealth, expropriated and poisoned peoples, devastated ecosystems, corrupted institutions. This is the violent and ruinous reality suffered by the peoples and the environment of our subcontinent because of the neocolonial cartographic transformation promoted based on proclamations such as "Soy knows no borders".

From our location and concrete experience in the southern part of the world – stricken by multiple forms of extractivism, plundering and exploitation – it is extremely relevant to pay attention to the symbolic and discursive operations around which the propaganda and marketing of companies such as *Syngenta* revolves. This topic allows us to note the recurrence of an essential motive of the globally dominant cultural regime, consisting in its reference to the *unlimited*, to that which *knows no limits*. It insinuates the spectral figure of an order that pretends to set itself up as absolute, and as such, seeks to appropriate all other otherness. In this respect, the leitmotif of a North American software company, *Netsuite*, specialising in finance and international trade, is particularly illustrative: "*One system, no limits*".[2]

The crucial significance of the "spirit of the unlimited" (i.e. of unlimited economic growth and individual consumption) in the context of our globalised civilisation, hegemonised by the powers of transnational financial capitalism, has found in various ways a prominent treatment in Pope Francis' Encyclical Letter *Laudato Si'* "On Care for our Common Home".[3] Of particular importance in this regard are a number of key paragraphs, in which the Argentine pontiff's text seeks to identify "the human roots" of the crisis (Chapter III), focusing on: "I. Technology: creativity and power",[4] "II. The globalisation of the technocratic paradigm",[5] "III. The crisis and effects of modern anthropocentrism".[6]

---

[2] Cf. Daniel C. Beros, "El límite que libera: la justicia 'ajena' de la cruz como poder de vida", in Martin Hoffmann, Daniel C. Beros and Ruth Mooney (eds), *Radicalizando la Reforma. Otra teología para otro mundo* (Buenos Aires: La Aurora; San José, Costa Rica: SEBILA, 2016): 221. A relevant observation, which makes it possible to roughly locate the historical matrix that first gave specific density to that motive, related to the remote origins of Western individualism and the spread of private property and money throughout Eurasia from about 800 BCE, points out that: "pre-Socratic philosophy, beginning in Miletus, the first fully monetarised polis, is essentially determined by the thought of the subject of money. Those thinkers – from Thales to Parmenides, but above all Anaximander, who produces the concept of the unlimited (*apeiron*) to designate the One in the Plural – consciously understand themselves as individuals. Their fundamental question aims at the One in the Plural, just as one can transform money into all commodities", Ulrich Duchrow, "El posicionamiento de Lutero hacia el individualismo del moderno sujeto del dinero", in *Radicalizando la Reforma*, 160.

[3] Francis, *Laudato Si'* (Vatican City: Vatican Press, 2015). [Available at: https://www.vatican.va/content/francesco/en/encyclicals/documents/papa-francesco_20150524_enciclica-laudato-si.html], [Last accessed: 18th March 2022].

In the different analytical-descriptive contexts of the factors that determine the current "ecological crisis", the pontiff resorts on more than 30 occasions to categories that revolve around a group of concepts that allude to (the loss or suppression of) "limits" and to the "unlimited" (or, equivalently, to the opposites "finite" and "infinite").

[4] Francis, *Laudato Si'*, 102-105.

[5] Francis, *Laudato Si'*, 106-114.

[6] Francis, *Laudato Si'*, 115-136. In one of the key passages of the chapter and of the encyclical as a whole (LS 106), it is possible to observe exemplarily the relevance that the question of the unlimited has in the papal discourse. It is emphasised therein that the fundamental problem is in "the way that humanity has taken up technology and its

The encyclical outlines a sort of "phenomenology of the spirit" of the unlimited. However, in characterising the phenomenon as a whole, a series of markedly rationalist notes prevail in its approach, which we suspect are related to its basic anthropological conception, indebted to the classical Western tradition. Therefore, from this perspective, in spite of any "fading" of human freedom,[7] *Laudato Si'* determines that "[w]e are always capable of going out of ourselves towards the other." For this reason, it explains that "the basic attitude of *self-transcendence*, breaking isolated conscience and self-referentiality is the root that makes all care for others and the environment possible, and that gives rise to the moral reaction of considering the impact caused by each action and each personal decision outside of oneself".[8] Within this framework, the magisterial text supports a correlative notion of sin, which remains on more of a moralistic plane, centred on the individual human person as a subject ("errors, sins, faults and failures").[9]

In contrast to this point of view, if we follow in the footsteps of the biblical and reforming tradition, we must emphasise that the "spiritual" motive identified at the "root" of the social and ecological crisis is expressed, above all, as a (limitless) *abysmal desire* for the unlimited – that desire which the New Testament calls "the lust of the flesh" (Gal. 5:13). In the present stage of civilisation, governed by technological and military power at the service of global finance, this desire has been strengthened and fed to such an extent that it has come to represent a real threat of annihilation of the human species and of innumerable forms of life on the planet – its first victims being the poorest peoples and nations, along with the rest of the earth's most vulnerable beings and environments.

In a transitional era, marked by the expansion of European mercantilism and colonialism, in the light of the Scriptures, Martin Luther described the hermetic closure of the human being in the economy of this unlimited desire as "curvature upon oneself" (*incurvatio in se ipsum*). And he unmasked its supposed capacity for "self-transcendence" for self-determination – in its deepest and most fundamental dimension – as the product and expression of the "enslaved will" (*servo arbitrio*). If this perspective is adopted, when speaking today of the human being as a subject, it is necessary to recover the etymological meaning of the Latin word *sub-iectum*: "placed under," "submitted," "subjected." For, in their blind surrender to the impure (limitless) "spirit of the unlimited," which the globally imposed system never ceases to update as infinite greed for capital and "natural resources," humans tyrannically *govern* the world *as* they are tyrannically *governed*. This is the paradoxical tyranny that, through multiple mediations, is very well described in the

---

development *according to an undifferentiated and one-dimensional paradigm*" [emphasis in original]. In relation to this, the letter states that this scheme corresponds to "the concept of a subject who, using logical and rational procedures, progressively approaches and gains control over an external object. This subject makes every effort to establish the scientific and experimental method, which in itself is already a technique of possession, mastery and transformation." And further on, it concludes, "This has made it easy to accept the idea of *infinite or unlimited* growth, which proves so attractive to economists, financiers and experts in technology. It is based on the lie that there is an *infinite* supply of the earth's goods, and this leads to the planet being squeezed dry *beyond every limit*" [emphasis ours].

[7] Francis, *Laudato Si'*, 105.

[8] Francis, *Laudato Si'*, 208. Translator's note: the English version of this quote from section 208 above is my translation of the official Spanish version used by the author. The structure of the official Spanish version of the *Laudato Si'* in this passage differs from that of the official English version. The author bases his arguments on the Spanish version of the *Laudato Si'*, and so the rendering provided here above allows the reader to understand author's insistence on "self-transcendence" in his arguments. The official English version published by the Vatican reads as follows: "Disinterested concern for others, and the rejection of every form of self-centredness and self-absorption, are essential if we truly wish to care for our brothers and sisters and for the natural environment. These attitudes also attune us to the moral imperative of assessing the impact of our every action and personal decision on the world around us." Other quotes in English from *Laudato Si'* are taken from the official Vatican English translation.

[9] Francis, *Laudato Si'*, 218.

papal encyclical letter, and which causes "sister earth, along with all the abandoned of our world, to cry out, pleading that we take another course".[10]

From our point of view, we can only express our gratitude for the very significant contribution of the Encyclical *Laudato Si'* and its vigorous promotion of a serious and urgent debate on the ecological crisis, its multiple aspects and consequences. However, if the diagnosis we sketched above about the current human and civilisational reality were to capture in essence "the real,"[11] we ask ourselves: how adequate is it to formulate a possible response from Christian spirituality to that cry and claim based on an appeal to the "basic attitude of self-transcendence" of human beings? Would we not thus run the risk of indirectly and involuntarily contributing to further cementing "the spirit of the limitless" by way of its religious or theological justification? If so, from where could we then expect "*another* course"?

Justice of Faith: Liberating Limit

In our opinion, a first and valuable indication in relation to this question can be offered by the testimony that opens the liturgy of Sunday worship in our own community of faith, the Evangelical Church of the Río de la Plata. There, the believers are invited to listen and confess with the psalmist the shared hope in the *coming*, in the *advent of God*: "From where will my help come? My help *comes* from the Lord, who made heaven and earth" (Ps. 121:2).[12]

From this perspective, sustained in the biblical tradition, the opening of the hermetic world of the human being and its institutions takes place in the event by which *God's own self breaks into it* by the power of *God's* Spirit, pronouncing the "Word of the Cross" (1 Cor. 1:18). In this Word, God's unprecedented love for the world is made manifest to us in God's *strange* wisdom and justice, in God's characteristic "madness": in God's unconditional solidarity with the "nobodies", women and men, victims of sinful humanity's unlimited desire for appropriation and domination; and at the same time, in God's unrestricted condemnation of the victimising powers, of those who seek to be "someone" or "something" by blindly surrendering themselves to this search.

Whoever by faith lets that Word and divine justice *of God* apply to themselves (Rom. 1:17), promulgated by the free judgment and decision of God in the resurrection of the Crucified One, justifies God in God's reasons (Ps. 51:4). Thus renouncing, without reservation or conditions, their own interests, calculations and arguments, they cease to live by their own judgments and possibilities, in order to live by the possibilities and justice of the One who vivifies the dead and calls into existence those things that were reduced to nothing, so that they may live (Rom. 4:17).

In this way, the justice of faith lives only from the alien, external and strange justice of the cross (*iustitia aliena crucis*);[13] precisely in this way, it lets "God be God" in God's Word and judgment,[14] consummated through God's own radical *self-limitation.* Through God's free self-abasement, moved by the "love of the cross, born on the cross", as Luther phrased it, the Spirit of grace establishes that "liberating limit" which manifests itself *per fidem* as the *power of life*: first of all, as grace for the afflicted, the violated, the exploited, but also – through a radical and penitent change of course, of fidelities and historical solidarities – for the

[10] Francis, *Laudato Si'*, 53.

[11] Martin Luther, "Disputación de Heidelberg (1518)", in Carlos Witthaus (ed and trans), *Obras de Martín Lutero (Tomo I)* (Buenos Aires: Paidós; Nueva York: El Escudo, 1967), 1:42.

[12] Cf. "Orden del culto de la Iglesia Evangélica del Río de la Plata. Orden del culto mayor" in *Culto Cristiano* (Buenos Aires: La Aurora, 1979).

[13] On this nodal theological concept, cf. Beros, "El Límite", 210, note 1.

[14] Thus are left behind those human beings who "are by nature unable to want God to be God. Indeed, they want to be God, and do not want God to be God", according to the acute and concise description offered by Martin Luther in Thesis 17 of the "Disputatio contra scholasticam theologiam" (1517). Cf. William R. Russell and Timothy F. Lull (eds) *Martin Luther's Basic Theological Writings: Third Edition* (1517 Media, 2012): 3-7.

former "indifferent" and "anguish-stricken". Thus, the triune God *creates* through this *via crucis* a redemptive path open in hope for those who live (and die) imbricated in the sacrificial violence that propitiates human sin through the idolatry of the unlimited.

Against the background of what has been said so far, it is worth returning to the dialogue concerning the proposals developed by the Encyclical *Laudato Si'* regarding the possible contribution of faith and Christian spirituality in the face of the growing aggravation of the ecological crisis. Particularly where the letter states:

> A spirituality which forgets God as all-powerful and Creator is not acceptable. [...] The best way to restore men and women to their rightful place, putting an end to their claim to absolute dominion over the earth, is to speak once more of the figure of a Father who creates and who alone owns the world. Otherwise, human beings will always try to impose their own laws and interests on reality.[15]

The paragraph cited above raises the link between God and the human problem of power, violence and limits, in a manner quite analogous to our own. However, we seem to be able to note a certain *christological* and *soteriological* "deficit" throughout the encyclical.[16] The "figure of a Father who creates and who alone owns the world" who would be as such the "best way to restore men and women to their rightful place, putting an end to their claim to absolute dominion over the earth," is also indebted to classical metaphysics of Greco-Latin style, sharing with that tradition – at least in virtue of our concrete question – all its ambivalent problematics.

Limiting ourselves to just two aspects, one might ask, on the one hand, if by returning to the concept of an "all-powerful God" in the aforementioned terms, there is not a danger of enabling a dynamic of mirrorlike feedback of that "will to power" that "knows no limit" in its questioned "self-referentiality." In our opinion, such a danger will exist to the extent that the diffuse pantocratic and patriarchal traits of this concept are not redefined with sufficient theological precision as the power of a Christ-like love, which manifests itself as such in its sovereign *self-limitation* and *weakness* (2 Cor. 12:9). For without such a redefinition, the notion proposed by the Encyclical would tend to backslide – as Ludwig Feuerbach warned – on the dialectical projection of a "*human*, all too human" (Friedrich Nietzsche) figure of the divine – which ultimately *empowers* that which in reality it intends to *disempower.*

And if, on the other hand, what we wish to propose is the "figure of a Father who creates and who alone owns the world," would we not run the risk characteristic of that kind of "iconic" mediation of the divine, about which the second commandment warns (Ex. 20:4)? This would be so insofar as its "representations" – devoid of the necessary *eschatological reserve* – are liable to be subjected to the subtle operations of "appropriation," manipulation and instrumentalisation, which are characteristic of that same unlimited will to power.

Life in the Spirit – In the Service of Eco-Justice

From the perspective that we have been developing, the "change of course" (*metanoia*, cf. Mk. 1:14), lies above all in "suffering" over and over again that *verbum crucis* (1 Cor. 2:2); "conversion" consists in "allowing oneself to be pulled into walking the path that Jesus walks, into the messianic event".[17] Those

---

[15] Francis, *Laudato Si'*, 75.

[16] Francis, *Laudato Si'*, 96-100. Within the framework of the Encyclical, Christological references are concentrated in section VII "The Gaze of Jesus" (sec. 96-100) of Chapter Two "The Gospel of Creation", where the rhetoric of the *exemplum of* the earthly Jesus as the archetype of a healthy bond with creation predominates, rather than that of the *sacramentum* as the mediator of salvation (an aspect not only restricted, but somewhat dissociated from the former).

[17] Dietrich Bonhoeffer, "Letter to Eberhard Bethge, July 18, 1944", in Dietrich Bonhoeffer, Christian Gremmels, Eberhard Bethge, Renate Bethge, Tödt Ilse and John W De Gruchy, "Letters and Papers from Prison", 1st English

who, through faith, allow the triune God to work in this way, give glory to God alone. Thus, they enter into an ineffable becoming, into a permanent renewal/revolution of their entire existence. Impelled by the Spirit of God, they open themselves to God's reign, to God's call to live a life in communion and solidarity with those they had lost, and now have found again in Jesus Christ: God and neighbour, beginning with the most neglected among other human beings and the suffering creation; for those who groan in ardent longing for the manifestation of the daughters and sons of God (Rom 8:18).[18]

Therefore, if we follow the trail of this reforming biblical theology, it is a matter of being incorporated into that "school of the Holy Spirit" in which Mary herself learned to testify that the God of the Promise, with the coming of God's justice and cruciform work, "to exalt them of low degree, to put down the mighty from their seats, in short, to break whatever is whole and make whole whatever is broken."[19] For only to those who unreservedly expose themselves to this concrete becoming in the history of God with God's people and creation, offering themselves as instruments of justice (Rom. 6:13), will also be given to indicate that *place* where it is possible to await the manifestation of the new in its transforming and renewing power: the new creature and creation of God in Jesus Christ (2 Cor. 5:17).

This *eschatological topos*, to which is associated the promise of the renewed irruption of the justice of God, is rooted there where the mutual witness of the Word of the Cross takes place – as a sacramental foretaste of a renewal that includes and is projected to the whole of creation. The form of life that is recreated again and again in it is made manifest decisively as a passive life (*vita passiva*); that is, as a life constituted *ex*-centrically, by "suffering" the cruciform Word through faith alone. Now, precisely because it is a creature of *that* Word (*creatura verbi*), and not of other words that it claims to say to itself, the community of faith is impelled to bear witness to the *advent* of the liberating divine justice promised to all creation.

This community will follow that vocation and calling, which constitute it as an *ekklesia* thanks to the justice *of faith*, through a broad, co-operative, *ecu*menical search for *eco*-justice. That is, in the concerted effort to articulate a renewed fidelity, solidarity and commitment to both the right to a dignified life for the poor (*eco*nomy) and the care of all creation (*eco*logy).[20] This resilient, compassionate and tangible witness, concretised in the different spheres in which it develops its personal and collective existence (church, politics, economy, education, culture, science, etc.), reveals the essential contours of its "spirituality," that is, of its life in the power of the life-giving and renewing Spirit of the "crucified messiah."

With regard to the contribution of Christian spirituality to an "ecological conversion,"[21] *Laudato Si'* emphasises the need to re-cultivate in people "adequate motivations," "interior motives;" and that such "virtues" be animated by a "mysticism" oriented on the "model" of Francis of Assisi.[22] Against the background of the previous paragraphs, it is worth noting that here, the aspects of the argumentation of the Encyclical that in our judgment are (at least partially) inconsistent, are projected in its *eschatological, pneumatological and ecclesiological* dimension. For by not pointing out with sufficient clarity the *critical-communicative* constitution of Christian "spirituality" and its ethical-moral expression (and not only its communitarian projection),[23] the very conditions of possibility of an authentic overcoming of the self-

edn. *Dietrich Bonhoeffer Works* (Minneapolis, MN: Fortress, 2010): 8, 480. [Available at: https://muse.jhu.edu/book/40174], [Last accessed: 29th November 2021].

[18] Cf. Francis, *Laudato Si'*, 53.

[19] Martin Luther and A. T. W. Steinhaeuser (trans), "The Magnificat (1521)", in *Works of Martin Luther* Vol. 3 (Albany, OR: Books for the Ages, 1997): 107-165, 110. [Available at: https://media.sabda.org/alkitab-8/LIBRARY/LUT_WRK3.PDF], [Last accessed: 6th December 2021). Cf. also Daniel C. Beros, "'Fuera de lo cual no se enseña otra cosa que apariencias y palabrería…' Algunas consideraciones sobre el significado de la herencia de la Reforma en América Latina", *Cuadernos de Teología* XXX (2011): 45-52.

[20] Cf. Guillermo Kerber, "Ética social ecuménica y la encíclica Laudato Si", *Didaskalia* 46 (2016): 55-72.

[21] Francis, *Laudato Si'*, 216-221.

[22] Francis, *Laudato Si'*, 10-12; 218.

[23] Francis, *Laudato Si'*, 219.

referentiality of the subjects remain somewhat inconsistent and diffuse, at least from the biblical-theological perspective sketched out here.

Final Thoughts

Returning to our place in the south of the world, we reiterate that we cannot but welcome the timely appeal of Pope Francis regarding the serious and urgent challenges posed by the civilisational crisis that humanity is going through – which, at the impulse of the (limitless) "spirit of the unlimited," threatens to destroy "our common home" (*oikumene*). Our critical remarks on certain elements of the philosophical and theological framework on which the arguments of his Encyclical Letter are based do not prevent us from celebrating other aspects of enormous value, which manifest a growing ecumenical convergence, such as, for example, those that propose the indissoluble relationship between justice for the poor of the earth and for the ravaged creation, the conviction that everything in the world is interconnected or the criticism of the "throwaway culture."

During the last decade, throughout "*Nuestra América*" (José Martí), a series of changes of political regimes have taken place, marked by the phenomenon of lawfare, the legal war,[24] about which the Argentine pontiff has also expressed his views.[25] In the light of such (geopolitical) events, it is essential not to dissociate social and environmental damage from the orchestrated imposition of pseudo-democratic regimes that – through extreme financial liberalisation, aggressive extractivist opening and excessive external indebtedness – sacrifice entire peoples and ecosystems on the altar of the "divinised market".[26] For such developments seek to re-edit in perpetuity the neocolonial drama, which continues to be perpetrated – at least in countries like Argentina – through the imperial imposition of an "agro-industrial" model that evokes *as a farce* the establishment of a "United Soybean Republic" beyond all limits and frontiers.

In this concrete situation, we Christians are called to explore in a committed, collaborative and "ecumenical" way *the form of life in the Spirit* that is the *fruit of the justice of faith,* striving for *eco-justice* at the regional and global levels. In virtue of that commitment, we are convinced that critically and constructively explore the significant contribution made by the papal document is very relevant, in particular its vision of an "integral ecology,"[27] its promotion of a broad process of dialogue – political, economic, spiritual and scientific – for "human wholeness"[28] and its joint search for an education and spirituality at the service of a "new way of life."[29]

Such an exploration will necessarily have to take place in multiple fields, contexts and *crucial* scenarios of historical reality, where the very possibility of life on earth is at stake today, with unusual drama – such as, for example, the fields of *politics, economics, law, health and culture.* When confronted with their enormous challenges, their painful urgencies and their intricate complexity, the truly decisive part of *our* contribution as individuals and Christian communities will lie in accepting with confidence the invitation inherent in the *alien* justice of faith to follow in the footsteps of the crucified messiah – the intimate friend of the poor and vulnerable, the lover of all creation – in each of them. For only in this way will we learn to verify – in the fulfilment of the mission of the universal church of Jesus Christ, on the one hand; and in the committed exercise of citizenship, on the other – with renewed hope, love and creativity what is "the good

[24] Andrés Scharager, "Más allá del Lawfare: avatares de la judicialización de las políticas públicas y los conflictos sociales en Argentina y América Latina", *Revista de Direito da Cidade* 12(1) (2020): 280-305.

[25] Cf. for example: "Papa a jueces panamericanos: trabajen por la justicia social y el bien común", 4th June 2019, *Vatican News* [Available at: https://www.vaticannews.va/es/papa/news/2019-06/papa-francisco-jueces-panamericanos-doctrina-social-franciscana.html], [Last accessed: 19th March 2022].

[26] Francis, *Laudato Si'*, 56.

[27] Francis, *Laudato Si'*, 137.

[28] Francis, *Laudato Si'*, 164.

[29] Francis, *Laudato Si'*, 202.

and perfect will of God" (Rom. 12:2) given with the coming of *God's* justice and peace to our "common home."

Suggestions for Further Reading

Adrianos, Louk *et al.* Eds. *Kairos for Creation. Confessing Hope for the Earth.* Solingen: Foedus, 2019.

Albareda Tiana, Silvia. "Aportaciones de la Laudato si' en el contexto de la Agenda 2030 para el Desarrollo Sostenible". *Scripta Theologica* 48 (2016): 443-462

Beros, Daniel C. and Pedro Kalmbach, Eds. *Riesgos y desafíos del actual modelo de producción agrícola. Un abordaje interdisciplinario.* Buenos Aires: Colección PPCC, 2018.

Dahill, Lisa E. and James B. Martin-Schramm, Eds. *Eco-Reformation: Grace and Hope for a Planet in Peril.* Eugene, OR: Cascade, 2016.

Hoffmann, Martin, Daniel C. Beros and Rut Mooney, Eds. *Radicalizando la Reforma. Otra teología para otro mundo.* Buenos Aires: La Aurora; San José, Costa Rica: SEBILA, 2016.

Lizarralde, Eusebio and Alfredo Salibian, Eds. *Ecoteología. Aportes desde el ecumenismo.* Buenos Aires: Dunken, 2013.

24. Ecotheological Narratives for a Planet in Code Red

Neddy Astudillo[1]

Introduction

Theologian Elizabeth Johnson has pointed out that during the first 1,500 years of Church history, nature was viewed as a loving creation (Gen. 1).[2] During this period, the church was governed mainly by a trinitarian mysticism (God-Human-Nature) that, although it was far from being perfect – for existing still within a dualistic, patriarchal and hierarchical world – it allowed people to see nature as a *living being*, with *rights* and also as a *theological locus.*[3]

In this sense, the church recognised that in nature, and with it, we know God's wisdom (Prov. 8), providence (Lk. 12:22-32),[4] glory (Ps. 19:1), and love (Jn. 3:16). For this reason, until that moment, the formation of theologians included the study of nature, in order to understand the mysteries of God for the good of the people. It was known that by leaving aside part of that Trinitarian mystique, our knowledge of God, nature and ourselves, remains incomplete.[5]

We also see that mystique of a communal nature in Scripture in some passages where nature comes to serve as a restorative and healing entity of the human being. In Revelation 22:2, we read about the tree of life and its role in healing the nations; in Ezekiel 47:2, the waters of God's temple flow, healing and giving life wherever they pass; in John 9:6-7, Jesus heals a blind man by spitting on the mud and sending him to bathe in the waters of the pool of Siloam. In all these texts, we also perceive the rest of nature as a living being, conscious and obedient to the will of God.

What Happened Five Hundred Years Ago?

Five hundred years ago, a process began in which the church stopped discerning the mysteries of the universe as a way of seeking our return to God (salvation) going hand in hand with nature. In both the Catholic and Reformed churches, this happened when their world views were confronted, and then enchanted, by the discoveries of modernity and the new modern science.

Although science managed to prove that the anthropocentric and hierarchical vision of the world, according to which the universe revolved around the earth, was a human construction, the church did not know how to dialogue with the new discoveries. If these had been positively assumed by a theology at the service of life, they would surely have had transformative social implications as they would have demanded

[1] Neddy Astudillo is an ecotheologian of Venezuelan origin. She is pastor of the Presbyterian Church (U.S.A.) and co-ordinator for Latin America of the organisation *GreenFaith.* neddy@greenfaith.org.

[2] The Hebrew word "*tov*", translated in Genesis 1:12, 18, 25 and 31 as the goodness of creation, can also be translated as the generator of life.

[3] Elizabeth Johnson, "Losing and Finding Creation in the Christian Tradition", in Dieter T. Hessel and Rosemary Radford Ruether (eds), *Christianity and Ecology: Seeking the Well-being of Earth and Humans* (Cambridge, MA: Harvard CSWR, 2000): 6.

[4] The Brazilian ecotheologian Ivone Gebara points out that when Jesus tells people to look at the birds and the lilies of the field, he is opening new paths of salvation that go beyond him, so that we find hope, wisdom to live, abundant life and salvation with their help. Ivone Gebara, *Intuiciones Ecofeministas. Ensayo para repensar el conocimiento y la religión* (Madrid: Trotta, 2000), 107.

[5] Johnson, "Losing and Finding", 6.

that the western man (male) relocate himself in the face of the universe, including women, indigenous communities, black and coloured communities.[6]

However, ecclesial leaders, like Pharisees in their time, preferred to reject or ignore such discoveries, making irrelevant the testimony of the church at a crucial historical moment for humanity. The world sustained in narratives and hierarchical practices continued to be legalised through the papal orders,[7] and was exported to the Americas by the reformers, along with the other forms of oppression: patriarchy,[8] racism, capitalism and colonialism. The last three, born at the same time, made the advance of the conquest possible.[9] The modern era would not have happened without the exploitation of African slaves, indigenous people, and the land.[10]

It is important to highlight this history because the racial disparities and hierarchies that facilitated the modern era and industrialisation, causes of the environmental and climate crisis,[11] are still present today. The tendency to place ourselves in relationships of dominance (male-female, human-nature) continues to this day, when the environmental and climate crisis – a product of human exploitation – requires us to critically review that past, to find corrections to the environmental and climatic crisis. This narrative of dominance operates by facilitating extractivism on indigenous lands, the creation of sacrificial zones,[12] and the contamination of economically and politically vulnerable communities;[13] promoting a sustained advance in consumption in rich countries, which is unattainable for the poor majorities – among other things, because the land simply cannot satisfy them, nor do the systems serve the benefit of the majority, but rather that of a few rich and ultra-rich people.

---

[6] The word "colour" refers here to the offspring product of the mixture between white, black and indigenous people. Even though race is a term invented after the beginning of European exploration and colonisation, systemic racism places people of colour, as referred to here, below "whites" and above "blacks". The caste system and colourism are still manifest, the product of this hierarchical narrative, non-existent in nature. For more information see: "Race", *Talking Glossary of Genetic Terms*, National Human Genome Research Institute, [Available at: https://www.genome.gov/genetics-glossary/Race], [Last accessed: 19th March 2022].

[7] The papal bull "was […] the legal principle used by every Protestant Christian group who made claims to Native land in North America, from the Episcopalians […] to the Puritans and Pilgrims […] and Lutheran immigrants who swept across the northern tier of the U.S." See Tink Tinker, "The Doctrine of Christian Discovery: Lutherans and the Language of Empire", *Journal of Lutheran Ethics* 17(2) (2017), [Available at: http://elca.org/JLE/Articles/1203], [Last accessed: 19th March 2022].

[8] Patriarchy was also a schema of work and objectification of boys, girls and women, by the church and by any other system. Its imposition gave rise to the modern era, colonialism, capitalism and racism.

[9] Columbus' impulse was trade. His goal was to travel to India in order to access spices, a product for the wealthy class of his time.

[10] Oppression and slavery existed throughout the world as class oppression; but it was never based on skin colour or "race" before then. Slavery was not necessarily perpetual, for life either. With the blessing of the church, racism took place in the Americas in a way that had not happened before. The church declared that neither the blacks nor the natives had a soul, until Bartolomé de las Casas (1542) travelled to Europe to advocate on behalf of the natives and convince the Pope otherwise. Black communities, however, were not so lucky.

[11] Cynthia C. Moe-Lobeda proposes: "Climate change may be the most far-reaching manifestation of white privilege and class privilege yet to face humankind. Climate change is caused overwhelmingly by the world's high-consuming people who are disproportionately descendants of Europe." Cynthia D. Moe-Lobeda, "A Haunting Contradiction, Hope, and Moral-Spiritual Power", in Lisa E. Dahill and James B. Martin-Schramm (eds), *Eco-Reformation, Grace and Hope for a Planet in Peril* (Eugene, OR: Cascade, 2016): 40.

[12] Cristian Arroyo, "Zonas de sacrificio en áreas prioritarias para la conservación", *Oceana*, 13th January, 2017, [Available at: https://chile.oceana.org/blog/zonas-de-sacrificio-en-areas-prioritarias-para-la-conservacion/], [Last accessed: 19th March 2022].

[13] Shashank Bengali, "Los países asiáticos toman acciones contra los residuos plásticos del mundo rico", *Los Angeles Times,* 18th June 2019, [Available at: https://www.latimes.com/espanol/internacional/la-es-los-paises-asiaticos-toman-acciones-contra-los-residuos-plasticos-del-mundo-rico-20190617-story.html], [Last accessed: 19th March 2022].

In these last five hundred years, we see that the Trinitarian mysticism, with regard to nature, has also been disappearing. This occurred in coincidence with the modern imposition of the definition of well-being and human development based on the access and accumulation of material goods, and no longer as a harmonious life with nature and with God. This vision of modernity is expressed in an analogous way in the discourse of current theology of progress: "the more goods and money you have, the more proof you have that God is blessing you."

Throughout later history, some theologians paid serious attention to developments in science; for example, reflecting on the implications of advances in fields as diverse as genetics or astronomy (including the Big Bang theory). However, the institutional church left to science, modernity and then the market the task of dealing with nature: of studying it, defining it and exploiting it – no longer to guide the people of God towards the path of salvation, but to promote "human development" in modern terms. By seeking God's revelation solely through Scripture, the written word of God, the Church abandoned its vocation of discerning the universe for the good of God's people, throwing nature overboard as a source of divine revelation and inspiration.

In this framework, nature, from being understood in a certain way as a subject (Dt. 10:14), began to be treated as a mere object. From being recognised as a living being (Mk. 4:39; Ps. 104:29), it became determined as an inanimate being, without a soul or spirit. From being recognised as having rights, instituted by divine will (Lev. 25), nature became ruthlessly exploited. From being considered as creation (Mk. 16:15), it came to be treated as a "natural resource". From being recognised as an authentic theological place (Job 12:7), it came to be seen as mere raw material, as a labour force absolutely subordinate to the terms of the market, the industrial revolution and human development framed in the hegemonic project of Western capitalism.

It is said that Calvin formulated the doctrine of the sovereignty of God as a reaction to medieval abuses and that, through him, the reformer wanted to warn that, regardless of what we human beings might do, God was above everything and everyone. The problem with this doctrine of God – analogous to the current interpretation of the famous mandate to "dominate" the earth (Gen. 1:28) – is that, in the context of the markedly hierarchical and dualistic Western culture, people easily came to conclude that God is *so* far above everything, that in reality God is *outside* of everything and everyone, even outside of nature.

From our point of view, this kind of theological reasoning leads to the fact that, in the current reality, marked by a deep environmental and ecological crisis, nature continues to be abandoned and the church continues to fail to manifest itself prophetically. Since the church stopped viewing nature as a theological place, it is not surprising that it has believed and taught that the most important part of our faith is our vertical relationship with God and not the way in which we relate to the rest of his creation.

More than Stewardship

From the first passages of Scripture (Gen. 2:15) to the last (Rev. 11:18), we hear a call and a warning to care for God's creation (Ps. 24:1). When we do not respect this calling, the harmonious order under which God created life is inevitably affected, and all creatures suffer the consequences (Jer. 14:2-7).

The current environmental and climate crisis requires us to acknowledge the mistakes we have made as a church and consequently to reform the narratives and theologies that have contributed to them. To become faithful to the environmental challenges facing the world today and to be part of the solutions that are required, we need to thoroughly review our values. The environmental and climate crisis is a new opportunity for the church. It means that we can no longer continue preaching, praying and singing to God in one way, and acting in society in another, which endangers the regenerative capacity of the earth, the most vulnerable communities and the next generations. Otherwise, our preaching, prayers and songs will only be like a "noisy gong or a clanging cymbal" (1 Cor. 13:1).

In a world where the climate has sustained the life of all creatures for thousands of years, but where human actions now threaten to such an extent that the "third rock from the sun can no longer be counted on for steady seasons of seedtime and harvest; for glacial waters feeding great rivers; for sea levels trustworthy enough to permit the building of great cities,"[14] our churches can no longer limit themselves to mere talk about stewardship. God's inescapable call also implies speaking out publicly and prophetically in order for governments to take the urgent measures necessary to mitigate and stop the most serious impacts of climate change.

In a world where there is still enough food for everyone, but millions of people suffer from hunger, where climate change threatens all with droughts and rising temperatures, we can no longer be content with increasing the size of our private food pantry at church. We must plant our orchards and gardens, and learn to eat what our soil produces. We must support fair trade and advocate for policies that protect farmers. We must exercise international law that leads rich countries to pay their ecological debt and give sanctuary to climate refugees who arrive at their doors, coasts or walls.

The history of colonisation, of the plundering of peoples and of the land has to stop. We must contribute to this from our simplest practices to the most complex endeavours, such as actively working to dismantle structural racism, responsible for the exploitation of our bodies and the earth. The role of the church is to share the good news of Christ with all creation (Mk. 16:15). The gifts have been delivered. The call is clear. Therefore, it is time to act.

An Outdated Ecotheology

"If God gave us the right to dominate the earth, nothing bad can happen that is not already prescribed. Therefore, if the climate is changing and the poles are melting, it is a sign of good news."[15] Even though more than 95% of the world's scientists agree that climate change is the result of greenhouse gas emissions produced by human activity from the rise of industrialisation to the present day, in the US, the evangelical majority believes that climate change is a sign of the end times, and not the result of our own actions.[16] Such belief ignores the reality that there are powerful companies financing this kind of thinking.

During a visit I made to a mining area in Guatemala, local people reported that extractive companies were financing churches that preach the same kind of message. The painful thing is that, even though communities are known to be impoverished by the same mining responsible for the contamination of their lands and rivers, this economic support – which weakens their ability to organise against the mining companies – is vital for them. For this reason, a theology like that, which interprets the environmental and climatic crisis as "good news," is expressed as a discourse on God and the divine at the service of death; this is evident when contrasted with the promise of "abundant life" embodied by the coming of Jesus (Jn. 10:10) and his clear call: "Go into all the world and proclaim the good news to the whole creation" (Mk. 16:15).

Faith in Action

When we read the story of Joseph and the dreams of the Egyptian Pharaoh in chapters 39 to 41 of the Book of Genesis, we see two men of different faiths, classes and cultures, who, faced with the divine

[14] Larry L. Rasmussen, *Earth-Honoring Faith: Religious Ethics in a New Key* (New York: Oxford University Press, 2013): 5.

[15] A common expression in widespread circles of the evangelical world in the Americas.

[16] Barbara R. Rossing, "The World is about to Turn: Preaching Apocalyptic Texts for a Planet in Peril", in Lisa E. Dahill and James B. Martin-Schramm (eds), *Eco-Reformation, Grace and Hope for a Planet in Peril* (Eugene, OR: Cascade, 2016): 142.

announcement of an unprecedented crisis, end up uniting to work for the common good. In a similar way, climate scientists today warn us of fluctuations in temperatures, stronger storms, longer droughts and floods, as an expression of a complex global phenomenon of an anthropogenic nature, which is already affecting biodiversity and endangering the most vulnerable communities on earth.

In the Genesis story, the announcement comes in time and the effort to respond (and interpret the dreams) required everyone's participation. Faced with a greater threat and challenge, such as the one posed by the climate crisis, we can assume that God is also being revealed. The search for understanding and achieving the common good requires that we put into action our gifts, organisational capacity, authority and leadership to guide the world, so that through all this, the glory of God also be manifested, even in the midst of crisis.

When asked if we still have time to reverse climate change or if our personal actions could have any substantial impact in making a difference, I answer that as people of faith we simply cannot ignore the crisis. We must each act according to our gifts and responsibilities. If even with our collective efforts we cannot avoid the worst of the climate crisis, it will not be because we did not try, nor because God did not come to warn us. We have tools at our disposal that we have not yet used, and it is time. For this reason, we may still have time to avoid a greater evil, but it will depend on each and every one of us.

As support, three ecotheological biblical reflections are proposed below, to be incorporated into our daily lives, and to allow ourselves to be transformed by them:

Stewardship[17]

Stewardship takes into account that we were created, man and woman, in the image of God, with a certain special status compared to the rest of creation. We were invited to be fruitful in it and to make use of everything that is in it. However, this special status does not grant us privileges against others, but is a call to service, just as Jesus himself did when he was among his disciples.

The psalmist recognises in the human being a certain privileged status, located in creation almost like a god. But when passing through the land, there are certain "rules" that we must abide by. The land is given to us with certain "instructions." A very important rule is that the land is God's, and we are outsiders. Our use of resources has a limit, it must be done in such a way that the most vulnerable communities also have what they need. Even when God seems to give us everything, we must choose the good – that is, life – and use resources to ensure the well-being of the next generations.

Eco-Justice[18]

The earth and human beings belong to God. Although we may have a special status in nature, the covenant that God made with Noah *also includes the rest of the creatures on earth*. The power of dominion over the earth does not separate us from it. Our sin produces alterations in nature. Our actions have consequences on it, since we are part of a whole, created in deep interrelation. Because of them not only humanity suffers, but also the earth and the animals of the field; even soils suffer.

We share the experience of suffering with all living creatures. That is why the promise of freeing ourselves from the slavery of sin with all creation is common to us. It expects us to manifest ourselves as sons and daughters of God doing our part, communicating the good news of Christ to all creation. Because the love and redemption that we receive in Christ *are not exclusive to human beings, but also include all of creation*. The biblical promise of the "new heaven" and the "new earth" shows that our salvation goes hand

[17] See, Gen. 1; Mt. 6; Lk. 22; Ps. 8; Lev. 25; Dt. 24 and 30:19.

[18] See, Gen. 9:1-17; Gen. 24:1-2; Is. 24:4-6; Jer. 3:2-5; Hos. 4:1-6; Joel. 2:18-27; Rom. 8:19-23; Mk. 16:15 and Jn. 3:16; Rev. 11:18.

in hand with the earth. Therefore, God's justice in the "new Jerusalem" includes the extermination of those powers that exploited and destroyed it. Creation also hopes for justice and liberation.

Ecospirituality[19]

Ecospirituality does not only recognise the special role that human beings have on earth, but also values the role of each creature. It puts the human being in a horizontal situation, recognising the role that each creature plays in protecting the regenerative capacity with which God created the earth.[20] For ecospirituality, it is not only the human being who serves the earth, but the former, in turn, *is served by* the latter; because we are earth. Ecospirituality recognises the presence of God as Spirit, inspiring, renewing, giving life to everything that exists. Nothing lives without being infused by the breath of God. Therefore, *the Holy Spirit is not just an experience of the church, but of all creation.* God equips each creature with gifts in order to fulfil God's divine will in, with and for God's creation.

It is the presence of the Spirit of God that makes it possible for us to know God both in the study of nature and in the study of Scripture. The earth is filled with the glory and wisdom of God, from the very beginning. Animals can also teach us, guide us, support us, so that God's will can be done in our lives. God is not limited to revealing Godself through human beings, but also is made present and speaks to us through nature. In it and with it, we live, feel and know God.

Final Thoughts

The ethicist, Larry Rassmusen,[21] has argued that in the present age, due to climate change, the church faces a challenge similar to that faced by the Israelites in exile (Ps. 137:1-4). They, like us, asked themselves: how are we going to live, how are we going to worship God, in a strange land? In case we fail to stop or mitigate climate change, our cry will be: how are we going to live in a hostile land, in which as humanity we have never lived?

Returning metaphorically to the passage of Joseph and the dreams of the pharaoh (Gen. 39-41), we could say that perhaps today some people are still trying to interpret "the dreams of the pharaoh" to understand what the scientists announce if we do not act immediately. Others may be dreaming, but the leaders responsible for interpreting them and drawing the necessary consequences do not understand their dreams, which is why it is necessary to look to other borders, communities, religions, cultures, who can help. There are those of us who are already sowing and saving seeds, enjoying good times, but aware of the even more difficult times that can come if we are not responsible for what we must take care of today. That is why we get involved in organisation, adaptation and mitigation actions, creating resilient communities. Many others are already in the middle of the storm, crying out for their lives and wondering if God does not care if they die by drowning (Mk. 4:36-41). These are climate refugees. Looking for new firm soils to live, sow, raise their children, they await the mercy of God, manifested in the solidarity of his people.

It is fair to say that, although the symptoms of climate change are currently being experienced across the planet, the responses must be different between those who suffer directly from its effects and those who are primarily responsible for the crisis.

Where are we? The time to act is now, supported by our faith and trust in divine providence, who loves God's creation and wants our good.

---

[19] See, Ps. 104; Prov. 8; Job 12:7; Gen. 2:7; 1 Kings 17:2-16.

[20] Although in some passages the Scriptures point out that human beings are special to God, in others we read that the destinies of both humans and animals are united. Any thought that denies this last aspect is pure "vanity" (Ec. 3:19).

[21] Rasmussen, *Earth-Honoring Faith*, 5.

Suggestions for Further Reading

Gebara, Ivone. *Intuiciones ecofeministas. Ensayo para repensar el conocimiento y la religión.* Madrid: Trotta, 2000.

—. *Longing for Running Water: Ecofeminism and Liberation*. Minneapolis, MN: Fortress, 1999.

Kerber, Guillermo. *O ecológico e a teologia Latino-Americana. Articulação e desafios*. Porto Alegre: Sulima, 2006.

Moltmann, Jürgen. *God in Creation.* Minneapolis, MN: Fortress, 1993.

—. *Dios en la creación. Doctrina ecológica de la creación.* Sígueme: Salamanca, 1990.

May, Roy H. *Ética y medio ambiente. Hacia una vida sostenible*. San José, Costa Rica: DEI, 2004.

Radford Ruether, Rosemary. "Eco-feminism and Theology", in David G. Hallman, Ed. *Ecotheology: Voices from South and North.* Maryknoll, NY: Orbis Books, 1994, 199-205.

—. *Mujer nueva, tierra nueva. La liberación del hombre y la mujer en un mundo renovado.* Buenos Aires: La Aurora, 1977.

25. Ecological and Integral Spirituality: A Latin American Perspective

Claudio de Oliveira Ribeiro[1]

Introduction

In this reflection, our objective is to offer the foundations of Latin American ecotheology as seen from the perspective of the pluralist principle.[2] We propose to contribute in the conceptual field to the confrontation of the main issues related to climate change, the protection of biodiversity, food security and an ethic of the sustainability of life. In this way, we hope to co-operate with the awareness processes of the churches and other groups that, from their testimony, are involved in ecological transformation, including climate justice, the protection of biodiversity and the care and defence of the integrity of creation.

The Need for a New Epistemology

Latin American theology, among other contributions proceeding from different places and contexts, has been a fundamental reference to envision a spirituality that values life, is sensitive to the care of nature and the poor, is open to the mysteries of the universe and is attentive to the main social and political challenges of the world today.

More specifically, in ecofeminist theological approaches, there is a search for new epistemological profiles taking into account the criticism of the anthropocentric, androcentric and patriarchal characteristics of Western culture, assimilated by theology. Such characteristics produce exclusionary effects, especially for women, black communities, LGBTQI+ groups, and various other subaltern groups. Latin American feminist ecotheology seeks not to be centred on the human being and therefore values the dimensions of everyday life that are always revealing of multiple realities of corporeality, also producing diversified experiences, both of resistance to oppressive systems, and of empowerment in the face of social challenges.

> For ecofeminism, the same system that subdues women also subdues nature. The guiding principle of domination is the same. The dominant power that permeates the different sectors, that oppresses and destroys, is the same. Therefore, it is necessary to analyse the interrelationship between the different power systems.[3]

The ecofeminist vision begins by demystifying the hierarchical, anthropocentric and androcentric visions of patriarchal epistemology since, due to its rather different perception of human beings and their relationship with the earth and the entire cosmos, it proposes a rather different epistemology.[4] Thus, its alternative view of knowledge is interdependent, integrating the spirit and the body, contextual, holistic, affective and inclusive. Knowing is not simply a rational and cognitive exercise, but a deeply personified experience and, in this sense, the woman's body is a crucial factor of knowledge.

Knowledge is a process that does not necessarily follow a linear and rectilinear pattern, but is open to the complexities, subjectivities and surprises that the reality of life possesses. Therefore, it is contextual, because a culturally conditioned type of knowledge cannot be imposed as the norm to be followed by all

---

[1] Claudio de Oliveira Ribeiro is a Methodist pastor and professor of Religious Sciences at the Federal University of Juiz de Fora (Brazil). cdeoliveiraribeiro@gmail.com.

[2] Claudio de Oliveira Ribeiro, *O princípio pluralista* (San Pablo: Loyola, 2020): 407-446.

[3] Anete Roese, "Ecofeminismo e sustentabilidade", in SOTER (ed), *Sustentabilidade da vida e espiritualidade* (San Pablo: Paulinas, 2008): 140.

[4] Ivone Gebara, *As águas do meu poço* (San Pablo: Brasiliense, 2005): 48.

people, groups and cultures. Contextual knowledge develops from local contexts before opening to a global perspective.

The dominant western epistemology is generally based on the experience of "western white men" and is presented as "universal knowledge," although it excludes large groups of people. It is hierarchical because it gives greater importance to intellectual knowledge than to other forms of knowledge that are articulated with experiences, narratives and subjectivities. Even the theology that methodologically started from social reality, has maintained a patriarchal, hierarchical and universalist character, because it has not taken sufficient distance from that traditional epistemology.

Interdependence and relationality are not exclusive dimensions of the human being, but extend to the earth and the cosmos itself. A deep and authentic recognition of our interdependence could transform our consciousness and our educational and political processes. Instead of the conquest of peoples or spaces, we would have the communion of all things, persons, groups and cultures. Egocentrism and individualism would give way to respect and care for the greater body, the planet as a whole.

This vision of interdependence has a sacred character that requires radical transformations in the ways of doing business, in the market economy and in international relations. And, not least, the "interdependence of knowledge should inaugurate a new page in the history of Christian theology, encouraging us to use a language that is more humble, more existential, more experimental and more open to dialogue."[5] Furthermore, "we must add an ecological perspective to the humanistic perspective of Jesus" and we need to abandon an anthropocentric Christianity and begin to visualise a "biocentric understanding of salvation."[6]

The fundamental question of an ecofeminist epistemology is to know through what experience a certain statement is related to reality. In this way, knowledge is the product of an inclusive and holistic circularity, in which people and groups, in their different cultures and places of passage, continue to add experiences that can alter the knowledge that was used at the starting point.

The central hypothesis of this epistemology is that the deepest experience we share is that of reciprocal interdependence between all the elements of the cosmos. As human beings, we are not only part of the whole, but the whole is also part of us, as the most recent and consistent discoveries in the natural sciences indicate. These reveal the complex interdependence between all life forms and show how evolution proceeds from an infinitely dense energy singularity and moves creatively and irreversibly toward increasing diversification. In this process, we are all part of the same source and, despite the existing plurality and differentiation, our original interdependence and affinity are maintained.

The sources of ecofeminist epistemology include emotions, affects and plural forms of subjectivity and recognise that reason has an important place in the process of knowledge production, but does not have absolute autonomy, especially in the body that we are. Similarly, the dimension of rationality cannot be completely isolated from other dimensions of our being. This set of human dimensions is embodied in everyday life; since this is almost always absent from social and theological analyses, it needs to be highlighted appropriately.

For this reason, ecofeminist epistemology recognises the diversity of experiences and their multiple expressions, without setting absolute limits on our ways of knowing. In this way, it reveals the relativity of all truths, including theological ones.

Humans in their Relationship with the Earth and the Cosmos – Limits and Possibilities

Despite the call for human participation in the process of recreating the world, the tasks of educational, political and theological-pastoral reflection in general must contribute to overcoming the centralism of the human being in creation, so as not to reinforce the justifications of the destructive forms of domination of

[5] Gebara, *As águas,* 54.
[6] Gebara, *As águas,* 183.

nature. "The understanding of creation as a totality and the concept of solidarity between human beings and creation lead, on principle, to a critical stance against the domination to which human beings subject created nature."[7]

In recent decades, analyses of the human condition have multiplied, especially regarding whether they can reach the depths of life or whether they are being reduced to forms of alienation, escapism and commercialisation. The loss of meaning of existence and the planetary risks of today have visible consequences. In general, it is possible to indicate some factors:

> (a) an emptying of the depth of being, especially as a result of consumerism, easy and mass religiosity, and the disposability of the popular masses in relation to social and economic processes;
> (b) the prevalence of domination and prejudice against the poor, racism in society and in churches, unjust relationships between men and women, violence and discrimination against LGBTQI+ groups, the precariousness of the lives of women, migrant populations, xenophobia, etc.
> (c) the depersonalising manipulation of the human being and the enhancement of massification processes;
> (d) the triumph of the cold calculation of data over the consideration of the person from the perspective of grace;
> (e) the cheapening of the gospel, since the religious sphere – once the governing body of human activity – has been privatised and relegated to the individual sphere or channelled into violent, sectarian and fundamentalist public expressions.

In addition, in a variety of explanations about the human being from simplified Greek philosophical formulations, humans are exposed to a division that does not correspond to the purposes of the Creator in relation to their creation. The human being is complete, holistic and cannot be divided into parts; it will be necessary to understand human beings in their most diverse manifestations, which translate an individuality that, in turn, must reflect the transcendent communion of the Creator with creation.

In the same way, God cannot be seen as one who abandons God's creation and offers theophanic spectacles in history. God must be understood as a participant in eternal recreation. This perspective challenges different ecclesial and political practices. The human being is part of creation and participates in God, who surrounds everything. Creation, in a certain sense, completes the divine existence, which makes the human being a participant of God in all of their being.[8]

However, contradictorily, the human being, mediated by economic and political structures that generate injustice, has placed itself in an aggressive and destructive position.

> Our systematic attack on all life systems is so profound that we have inaugurated [...] a new geological era: the Anthropocene. The human being (*anthropos*) [sic] has become hostile to life, the meteor of yesteryear that can profoundly damage the physical, chemical and ecological bases that sustain life on Earth, including the human species. They have shown that in addition to being homicidal and ethnocidal they can become ecocidal, biocidal and geocidal.[9]

To establish a theological critique of this perspective, a pluralistic anthropological basis is necessary. The multiplicity of the human is intensified with the diversity of cultures, with the different ways of understanding the biological and its multiple relationships with the dimensions of subjectivity, feelings and senses and, above all, with its relationship with cosmic dimensions.

---

[7] Nélio Schneider, "Solidariedade no sofrimento e na esperança em busca da relação justa entre o humano e o criado *coram Deo*", in Luiz Carlos Susin (ed), *Mysterium creationis: um olhar interdisciplinar sobre o universo* (San Pablo: Paulinas, 1999): 186.
[8] Claudio de Oliveira Ribeiro, "Por uma teologia da criação que supere os fundamentalismos", in Afonso Garcia Rubio and Joel Portela Amado (eds), *Fé cristã e pensamento evolucionista* (San Pablo: Paulinas, 2012): 133-154.
[9] Leonardo Boff, *Ecologia, grito da terra, grito dos pobres: dignidade e direitos da Mãe Terra* (Petrópolis: Vozes, 2015): 8.

> Thus, humanity is seen in Genesis as an expression of the Earth. Somehow, we are effectively created in a way that provides us with a special connection to the planet, formed from it, as if we were children of the Earth. We are Earth in which the breath has become immanent. We are the Earth become conscious in a new way. We are not above, but we are part of it. We are, consequently, called to live in a deep and conscious relationship with the Earth and its creative process. We reclaim our own humanity in our earthly restoration, in the recognition that we are part of the greater earthly community.[10]

In a century of development of technology and science in different fields, we experience, on the one hand, an excess of scientific production; on the other, we find immense existential voids that seem to reach all social classes, despite the religious effervescence that is currently being experienced.

The fact that religions have mostly emphasised the myths of "above" and the will of the gods, has generated religious forms that relegate the destiny of people's lives to those same myths or to their human religious representatives. From the dissatisfaction and reaction to this situation arises the interest in a new search for meaning and fullness of life that, in an effort to fill these "voids," is opposed to realities such as the commercialisation of religions – taken as consumer goods and religiously promoted support for the politics of "empires."[11]

The human being is better understood not only in the dimensions of history and social life, but in its complex and diverse relationship with the earth and the cosmos.

Relationality and Interdependence

Although not in a hegemonic way, a theoretical effort is taking place in the Latin American theological community to deconstruct images and systems in order to propose something innovative and different, namely, a new epistemology based on the experiences of poor communities. These initiatives have promoted a deconstruction and reconstruction of Christian symbols in the midst of oppression and violence, especially androcentric and patriarchal visions, but also in the midst of the vitality of the poor who manage to survive and even live with joy and festivity, even in the midst of pain and suffering.

Ecofeminist theology, for example, among its many challenges, seeks to question theological universals, generally false or ideological, and also to establish theoretical bases that facilitate practical connections between human beings and the cosmos. In the words of Ivone Gebara:

> My adherence to ecofeminism originated from observing the lives of poor women in the northeast (of Brazil) and living in a marginal neighbourhood. Specialised literature helped me expand my knowledge and refine my analysis. However, it was in coexistence that I realised the connection between the economic and social slavery of women and the slavery of the land in the hands of a few large landowners.[12]
>
> The ecofeminist perspective, an intimate articulation between a feminist line of thought about life and an ecological line, opens us not only to a real possibility of equality between women and men, from different cultures, but to a different relationship between us, with the Earth and with the entire Cosmos.[13]

The ecofeminist perspective highlights the collective dimension present in the reality of each person's life, which does not consist in mere autonomy but in relationality. This is not only anthropological, but also cosmic, since it is based on the fact that we are all part of the same mystery of life. The term 'relationality'

---

[10] Leonardo Boff and Marc Hathaway, *El Tao de la Liberación: Una ecología de la transformación* (Madrid: Trotta, 2014): 387.

[11] Ivone Gebara, *Mulheres, religião e poder: ensaios feministas* (San Pablo: Terceira Via, 2017): 15-69.

[12] Ivone Gebara, *Intuiciones ecofeministas: ensayo para repensar el conocimiento y la religión* (Madrid: Trotta, 2000): 24.

[13] Ivone Gebara, *Trindade, palavra sobre coisas velhas e novas: uma perspectiva ecofeminista* (San Pablo: Paulinas, 1994): 69.

refers to the vital forces that determine the mutual human connection and that of human beings with the earth. It is a fundamentally human and cosmic condition that acts as a force that unites us to the earth, as a reality that drives us towards ethical actions and authentic religious experiences. Relationality is at a deeper level than that of human consciousness.

The relationality and interdependence between people and between people and the earth must be recognised as important variables in the emergence of ethical actions. Through forms of experiential learning around human and cosmic interdependence, it is possible to rediscover the relationality of all life, which reinforces ethical attitudes of respect towards other people, groups and the great body of the cosmos.

This set of experiences can represent an impetus for qualitative social changes, starting with the formation of new forms of community life, marked by happiness and ecosocial justice. "The new self-understanding of the human being has to emerge from this interrelation and interdependence of nature, the person, other people and God, through that deep contemplation of the transcendent in nature."[14]

The Power of Renovating Life – the Broad Perspective of Salvation

To reverse the scenario of environmental destruction, it is necessary to elucidate a more substantially biblical perspective of salvation, which highlights its broad and integral dimension. Obviously, several theological efforts must be made, duly articulated with practical aspects, to make this new vision possible.

From a practical point of view, Leonardo Boff indicates the need for a new sense of global interdependence and universal responsibility:

> We must imaginatively develop and apply the vision of a new sustainable way of life at the local, national, regional and global levels. Our cultural diversity is a precious heritage and different cultures will find their own ways to make this vision a reality. We must deepen and broaden the global dialogue generated by the Earth Charter, as we have much to learn from the ongoing search for truth and wisdom.[15]

This perspective is based on the vision, indispensable for the future of humanity, of a spirituality that values life. "Conceiving the world as a 'Common House' and cultivating ecospirituality will contribute to strengthening an embodied and integrating mystique, an antidote to the growing escapist spiritualism with its dualistic tendencies."[16] This perspective allows us to perceive the natural, material and human world as living sources of energy and move towards a response to the call to communion between them.

The contribution of the Christian faith to ecospirituality is fundamental for personal, community and ecological integration, as well as being vital for the survival of the biosphere. An ecological spirituality has as a consequence "the re-enchantment of nature. Modern rationality has tried to exclude fantasy, desire, inventiveness, from religious experience [...] The latter celebrates the integration between human beings and nature, the communion between genders and a perichoresis between God and humanity."[17]

From these proposals, we want to make visible a spirituality that emphasises the value of life and is sensitive to the care of nature, perceiving in it the place of salvation, in the same way that we look at the human. It is a spirituality that, because it is ecological, defends the poor and learns from them, and that opens up to the mysteries of the universe and the world, relating them to the social and political challenges that life poses to us.

---

[14] Marlene Pereira, "Cada parte dessa terra é sagrada para o meu povo", in Luiz Carlos Susin and Joe Marçal dos Santos (eds), *Nosso Planeta, nossa vida: ecologia e teologia* (San Pablo: Paulinas, 2011): 219.

[15] Boff, *Ecologia, grito da terra,* 459.

[16] Murad, Afonso Tadeu, "Paradigma ecológico: gestão e educação ambientais", in SOTER (ed), *Sustentabilidade da vida e espiritualidade* (San Pablo: Paulinas, 2008): 61.

[17] Da Costa Junior, Josias, *O Espírito criador: teologia e ecologia* (San Pablo: Fonte Editorial, 2011): 65.

Faith as a Way of Being in Life

If, from the point of view of ethics and ecology, it is necessary not to be enslaved by forms of consumption and propaganda, from the religious point of view something similar should be sought. A new model of society would require a new understanding of the human being and their needs, and a new expression of God. Submitting ourselves to the patriarchal and exclusive pattern of society, clinging to creationist myths and the authoritarian will of the gods and goddesses of multiple religions – often created in the image and likeness of the human being – generates an uncritical, accommodating and inert attitude towards ideological forms of religion, secular forms of consumption and policies that are exclusivist and destructive of nature.

The gods of the past and present have occupied a fundamental place in people's lives, which requires overcoming the fear of losing the visions instilled by hierarchical religions, that is, those that receive orders from heaven or secret divine revelations. It is also necessary to seek new answers, because the current reality raises new questions. Thus, "the past will not be discarded, but the human flavour of it will be preserved, the flavour of good things, capable of sustaining our life."[18]

The plurality of human experiences and the alterity present in interpersonal relationships and between human beings and nature make a free and authentic faith possible, despite human ambiguities. "The experience of God, of God's grace and mercy, does not take place on another level than that of otherness, of the consciousness of the Other, of the corporeal-sexed reality, in short, of the human."[19]

This spirituality is expressed in practical and concrete areas of social and political life, and highlights the processes of defence of life, of social and economic justice, of human and land rights, of citizenship and of the dignity of the poor, the domain of the logic of selfishness both in the macro and systemic spheres as well as in daily and personal life.[20] Such spiritual perspective generates a space for social consciousness, otherness and co-existentiality, cordiality, humanisation and cosmic integration. It is the empowerment of life, not only of human life, but in all its most diverse forms of manifestation, and it is revealed as indispensable for the future of humanity and the earth, especially in the face of commercialisation, financialisation and exploitation of nature.

María Clara Bingemer, commenting on the Encyclical *Laudato Si*, highlights that the papal document:

> proposes a new idea of progress, not centred on an arrogant omnipotence of the human being, which gives itself the right to damage the planet it inhabits, forgetting that it is the common home of all. But a progress with a holistic and ecologically sustainable development, which is the founding act of a new civilisation.[21]

Since the last century, the World Council of Churches (WCC) has articulated various initiatives around justice, peace and the integrity of creation (JPIC).

> [The WCC] recognises that environmental impacts are historical in the trajectory of humanity, but the common home is experiencing a more serious moment than ever. A great new evil affecting creation is the world culture of exacerbated consumption, widely experienced and fostered by rich and developing countries.[22]

[18] Ivone Gebara, *Vulnerabilidade, justiça e feminismos* (São Bernardo do Campo: Nhanduti, 2010): 165.
[19] Maria Joaquina Fernandes Pinto, "Sexualidade e salvação: realidades opostas?" in Afonso Garcia Rubio (ed), *O humano integrado* (Petrópolis: Vozes, 2007): 258.
[20] Ver Sinivaldo Tavares, *Teologia da criação: outro olhar – novas relações* (Petrópolis: Vozes, 2010).
[21] Maria Clara Bingemer, "Louvor, responsabilidade e cuidado: premissas para uma espiritualidade ecológica", in Afonso Murad and Sinivaldo Tavares (eds), *Cuidar da Casa Comum: chaves de leituras teológicas e pastorais da Laudato Si'* (San Pablo: Paulinas, 2016): 180.
[22] Magali Cunha, "*Laudato Si'*: o eco papal de uma busca ecumênica", in Afonso Murad and Sinivaldo Tavares (eds), *Cuidar da Casa Comum: chaves de leituras teológicas e pastorais da Laudato Si'* (San Pablo: Paulinas, 2016): 123.

In more global religious terms, it is hoped that each spiritual tradition seeks within itself and in its own foundations the perceptions that may lead itself to a reverence for life, in the direction of an ethics of sharing and caring for life in its human and cosmic dimensions, to awaken to the vision that the sacred is present in history and in the cosmos.[23]

On the Latin American continent, "the ecological mystique of the aboriginal peoples, in the indigenous populations, is strongly present. For them, the ground we walk on is a sacred place. Mother Earth cares for and feeds all of her sons and daughters: plants, animals and humans. She offers us mountains and valleys, air, water and soil as gifts."[24]

To point to the renewing power of life, sectors of various churches in Latin America, together with different social forces, have been fighting for several decades against the devastating impacts of extractive industries, the destruction of tropical forests and the orientation towards monocultures by large-scale agribusiness. These actions require structural changes in agricultural policies, in water treatment and in the defence of the basic human rights of indigenous peoples and those who live on the outskirts of large cities. Such practices co-operate with, and at the same time reinforce, the construction of new expressions of spirituality.

Synthesis

The perspective we have presented opens up possibilities for an eco-diakonia whose theological foundations emphasise prophetic witness, Christian and interfaith social services, and joint ecumenical action to confront the roots of the global environmental crisis, the destruction of biodiversity and the health threats related to climate change at the local, regional and global levels.

Our vision emphasises the close relationship between historical projects and horizons of hope, values political processes, initiatives to promote human life in a broad sense and the preservation of the integrity of creation. It also allows the articulation of the most objective elements of faith and theological reflection, together with the most subjective elements that generate forms of spirituality committed to the reality of life and the destiny of the world.

Latin American ecotheology highlights relationality as an expression of the human in its interpersonal and collective relationships and in its broad and plural relationships with nature and the cosmos. Relationality has been understood both in the collective dimension present in the reality of each person's life and in the cosmic dimension, since the human is integrated into the immensity of the mystery that sustains life. This means that relationality refers to the vital forces that determine the mutual human connection and that of human beings with the earth. It is a fundamentally human and cosmic condition – it acts as a force that unites the human with the earth and drives the human to ethical actions and authentic and creative religious experiences.

Relationality reveals the fundamental epistemological question that constantly asks through what experience a certain statement is related to reality. This questioning deconstructs the conception of knowledge as a linear and power process and describes it as a circularity in which people and groups, in their different cultures and places of passage, continue to add experiences, especially everyday ones, that can alter the knowledge that was used at the starting point. It is an inclusive and holistic epistemology of fundamental importance for an integral and ecological spirituality that values life.

---

[23] Boff and Hathaway, *El Tao de la liberación.*

[24] Afonso Murad, "Ecologia, consciência e bem-viver", in Afonso Murad (ed), *Ecologia: um mosaico* (San Pablo: Paulus, 2016): 57.

Suggestions for Further Reading

Bingemer, Maria Clara. "Louvor, responsabilidade e cuidado: premissas para uma espiritualidade ecológica", in Afonso Murad and Sinivaldo Tavares, Eds. *Cuidar da Casa Comum: chaves de leituras teológicas e pastorais da Laudato Si'*. San Pablo: Paulinas, 2016: 169-181.

Boff, Leonardo. *Ecologia, grito da terra, grito dos pobres: dignidade e direitos da Mãe Terra*. Petrópolis: Vozes, 2015.

Boff, Leonardo and Marc Hathaway. *O Tao da libertação: explorando a ecologia da transformação*. Petrópolis: Vozes, 2012.

Costa Junior, Josias. *O Espírito criador: teologia e ecologia*. San Pablo: Fonte Editorial, 2011.

Cunha, Magali. "*Laudato Si'*: o eco papal de uma busca ecumênica", in Afonso Murad and Sinivaldo Tavares, Eds. *Cuidar da Casa Comum: chaves de leituras teológicas e pastorais da Laudato Si'*. San Pablo: Paulinas, 2016: 115-128.

Gebara, Ivone. *Mulheres, religião e poder: ensaios feministas*. San Pablo: Terceira Via, 2017.

—. *Vulnerabilidade, justiça e feminismos*. São Bernardo do Campo: Nhanduti, 2010.

—. *As águas do meu poço*. San Pablo: Brasiliense, 2005.

—. *Teologia ecofeminista: ensaio para repensar o conhecimento e a religião*. San Pablo: Olho d'Água, 1997.

—. *Trindade, palavra sobre coisas velhas e novas: uma perspectiva ecofeminista*. San Pablo: Paulinas, 1994.

Murad, Afonso. "Ecologia, consciência e bem-viver", in Afonso Murad, Ed. *Ecologia: um mosaico*. San Pablo: Paulus, 2016: 17-61.

—. "Paradigma ecológico: gestão e educação ambientais", in SOTER, Ed. *Sustentabilidade da vida e espiritualidade*. San Pablo: Paulinas, 2008: 39-62.

Pereira, Marlene. "Cada parte dessa terra é sagrada para o meu povo", in Luiz Carlos Susin and Joe Marçal dos Santos, Eds. *Nosso Planeta, Nossa Vida: ecologia e teologia*. San Pablo: Paulinas, 2011: 215-222.

Pinto, Maria Joaquina Fernandes. "Sexualidade e salvação: realidades opostas?" in Afonso Garcia Rubio, Ed. *O humano integrado*. Petrópolis: Vozes, 2007: 234-260.

Ribeiro, Claudio de Oliveira. *O princípio pluralista*. San Pablo: Loyola, 2020.

—. "Por uma teologia da criação que supere os fundamentalismos", in Afonso Garcia Rubio and Joel Portela Amado, Eds. *Fé cristã e pensamento evolucionista*. San Pablo: Paulinas, 2012: 133-154.

Roese, Anete. "Ecofeminismo e sustentabilidade", in Soter, Ed. *Sustentabilidade da vida e espiritualidade*. San Pablo: Paulinas, 2008: 135-172.

Schneider, Nélio. "Solidariedade no sofrimento e na esperança em busca da relação justa entre o humano e o criado *coram Deo*", in Luiz Carlos Susin, Ed. *Mysterium creationis: um olhar interdisciplinar sobre o universo*. San Pablo: Paulinas, 1999: 177-188.

Tavares, Sinivaldo. *Teologia da criação: outro olhar – novas relações*. Petrópolis: Vozes, 2010.

26. Eroecosophia of Territory-Bodies: Feminist Spiritualities in Resistance

Marilú Rojas Salazar[1]

Introduction

This article aims to rescue the *ero-eco-sophia* category as a vital element of the territory-bodies that exercise a subversive spirituality of resistance. It is especially related to the feminist struggles and defenders of the territories that are being exploited by the predatory logic of patriarchal, neoliberal capitalist, market systems. And it is articulated within the contexts of daily conflict throughout Latin America and the Caribbean.

Territory-Bodies

Our bodies are our first territory, which in turn inhabit another larger body, which is the earth. Both are our vital space which we inhabit, and in which we are located, move, are and co-exist. This is what our companions from the women's groups of defenders of territory-bodies affirm:

> [...] We recognise the territory in our bodies: when the places we inhabit are violated, our bodies are affected, when our bodies are affected, the places we inhabit are violated. These teachings were shown to us by women from many parts of Latin America, especially from the rural and indigenous world.[2]

There is no doubt that what happens in the territories is imprinted on the body: sadness over exploitation, anguish over pollution, violence and abuse. But there is also joy and passion within us and in our hearts, for trying to build and defend other worlds, despite so much violence. There is a vital connection between the cavities and caves of the earth and our body cavities. Because we have been created from that larger body, we are part of that vital body from which we have emerged.

We, the ecofeminist women, propose to weave connections between feminism, environmentalism, nature and territories, which allow us to look at the world in a more complete and sensitive way. We want to transform our lives by recognising that bodies are not only humans, but that we are a collective part of air-bodies, fire-bodies, plant-bodies, animal-bodies, mineral-bodies, microscopic-bodies, cosmic-bodies, ecosystemic-bodies. And recognising that we are in an interdependent relationship of bodies, which we conserve and of which we have memory. It is about memories and internal forces, which inhabit us in our corporeal cavities:

---

[1] Marilú Rojas Salazar is a Doctor in Systematic Theology from the Catholic University of Louvain, Belgium. She is a feminist theologian and Professor at the Ibero-American University of Mexico City and the Department of Religious Sciences. She is also a professor at the Theological Community of Mexico. She belongs to TEIFEM ([Women] Theologians and Feminist Researchers of Mexico). She is the director of *Sophias* journal, a founding member of the UPM Academy of Theology in Mexico, a member of the DARE (Discernment and Radical Engagement) of the Council for World Mission. She belongs to the TEPALI Network ([Women] Theologians, Pastors and Christian Leaders). saroma24@gmail.com.

[2] Colectivo Miradas Críticas del Territorio desde el Feminismo, *Mapeando el cuerpo-territorio. Guía metodológica para mujeres que defienden sus territorios* (Quito: CLACSO, 2017): 7.

> [...] but a stream would rise from the earth, and water the whole face of the ground – then the LORD God formed the human being from the dust of the ground, and breathed into their nostrils the breath of life; and the human became a living being (Gen. 2:6-7).[3]

According to the original myths of the Jewish and Christian monotheistic religions, the body is from its origin territory; that is to say that, according to them, we are part of a single body with the earth.

The cartographies of the body as territory are a research proposal of feminist theories, which help us to locate the areas of violence suffered by women and by the land; in the case of land, we analyse the extractivist policies that violate and wear it down. Feminist theologies are recovering the body as the theological place where grace, salvation and love take place. That is why it is important to eradicate all kinds of violence. However, the extractive, racist, sexist and elitist violence of the colonisation of the market by neoliberal capitalist logic has wreaked havoc on our territory-bodies; using rape, injustice and force, it has sought to seize bodies. And, for this, it has often used religious and political discourses of compliance, obedience and neo-fundamentalist submission.

Sexual abuse, feminicide, racism and sexism are some of the most common tools of invasion of the territory-body. By ignoring the rights of bodies and devaluing them as bodies that do not matter, they give them the category of garbage-bodies, bodies that do not deserve to be mourned, waste-bodies, thrown into clandestine graves. Such is the case in Mexico, where there are thousands of bodies missing or buried throughout the country, without the State seeming to care very much.[4] This reality has made the bodies of mothers and family members – which constitute especially women's bodies – to organise themselves in their search. Thus, they go from the condition of victims to that of a prophetic and subversive force, expressed by groups of women seeking bodies that deserve to be mourned, bodies that matter.

Philosopher Judith Butler, following work by Julia Kristeva, explains that there are abject bodies; that is to say, bodies that the heteronormative system of neoliberal capitalism considers junk-bodies. Capitalism, with its market logic, has colonised our bodies, categorising them as fat, black, Indian, mestizo, migrant, poor, "weird" or queer, sick, old, considered disposable, they do not count.[5] Bodies have been colonised by the market, fashion, medicine, biology and genetics. Before they were colonised by white-western-heteronormative Eurocentrism. Now the logic of necro-power deployed by necropolitics and necroreligions also categorises bodies as racialised – which is why it is urgent to decolonise the stereotype of the body as abjection (that is, as despicable or vile).

Ero-eco-sophia

Ero-eco-sophia is a concept that I have coined and I define it as the inner force that inhabits each territory-body and that positions us before life to face challenges. It is the political force of the search for the common good, which emerges from our individual and collective corporalities as bodies that deserve to be mourned, bodies that matter; and as bodies in a subversive political alliance, that take a stand in the streets to prophetically protest and demand justice.[6]

This inner force, which we call spirituality, arises from the desire for an immanent divine experience. It represents the passionate nuclear force, which unites the humanising trinity *eros-oikos-sophia* in opposition to the patriarchal market God. For that God proposes pornography as a material resource for sale, exhibiting the fragmented bodies and the obscenity of disposable bodies, especially those of women, girls and boys,

[3] TN: The author modifies the text slightly in order to insist on inclusivity. This rendition is based on the New Revised Standard Version of the Bible, but also incorporates modifications to represent the inclusivity that the author intended.

[4] The official figures, which speak of 80,000 missing Mexican persons, are evidently conservative figures.

[5] Judith Butler, *Cuerpos que importan. Sobre los límites discursivos del "sexo"* (Barcelona: Paidós, 2002).

[6] Judith Butler, *Formas de resistencia a la violencia de hoy. Sin miedo* (México: Taurus, 2020): 52.

LGBTQI+ people and migrants. All of them are considered territory-bodies in dispute by the patriarchal forms of hegemonic systems, such as neoliberal capitalism, Christianity and the market.

The ero-eco-sophianic trinity of the territory-bodies is constituted by *oikos-gaia* (house-earth) – that is not only a living being with rights, they also possess their passionate inner strength that inhabits and emerges from each passionate corporality (*eros*); and their own uncolonised wisdom (*sophia*), of which all the beings that inhabit them are participants – and this wisdom is episteme: situated knowledge. Hence, the concept "ero-eco-sophia". We recognise this prophetic force as a creative street-savvy, anti-systemic, anti-patriarchal, anti-racist and anti-colonial courage on the part of young feminists. This is expressed in the collapse of the "phallocentric sculptures," which bothers the dominant systems so much, as well as those who think like they do.

I position ero-eco-sophia as the feminist trinity, inhabiting diasporic and fragmented bodies, disposable bodies by the patriarchal market God, pornographic bodies used by consumer society and marketing. For the ero-eco-sophia is, in turn, the vital force of resistance that opposes oblivion and makes a clandestine memory resurface in the marginalised of history – who find pleasure in political hope, and yearn for the justice that does not finish arriving. The wise (*sophia*) force (*eros*) of the common home (*eco*) inhabits our bodies and all of creation. They converge in a hypostatic union, in which the three lovers have the burning desire to maintain a communion of correlation with all diverse people (sex-gender), overcoming homo-lesbo-transphobia. And they give rise to an interpenetration of cultures and races, which overcomes any xenophobia, thus showing the union of cosmic diversity in all territory-bodies.

The ero-eco-sophianic trinity recognises that the distinction is necessary for communion as an open reality, in which the three realities do not constitute a closed circle, but a spiral of persons, and that "diasporic bodies" – bodies despised for their sex, gender, raciality, social situation; fragmented or necrophilic bodies – are inhabited by this eroecosophianic consubstantiality. *Eros*, *oikos* and *sophia* are internal forces. Each one penetrates the others and lets themself be possessed by the others. Each one dwells in the other and opens outward from themselves, inviting the creatures of the universe to the divine life in full humanity. As a force inhabits our territory-bodies – not only human bodies, but all bodies of cosmic creation: air and earth bodies, plant and animal bodies, microscopic, human, celestial and terrestrial bodies – to enter into the recognition that divinity inhabits all creation and cries out for justice against the extractive principles of the territory-bodies.

Subversive Resistance: Our Feminist Spiritual Force

> Wisdom cries out in the street;
> in the squares she raises her voice.
> At the busiest corner she cries out;
> at the entrance of the city gates she speaks (Prov. 1:20-21).

The protest movements emerging in many parts of the world, especially in Latin America and the Caribbean, that cry out for a more just and equitable life and for the procurement of human rights, are the subversive prophetic forces that resist all neocolonial, racist, sexist, elitist and predatory forms of domination of the ecosystems of our "common home". If we understand spirituality as the way to situate ourselves in the face of life and its vicissitudes, the inner force that moves these street-savvy groups to oppose the prevailing systems of domination is a prophetic spiritual force of resistance.

These feminist spiritualities, which are articulated and expressed in a situated and contextual way, have the following characteristics: they are corporal, erotic, political, everyday, communitarian and sexual. That is why it is not a mistake to affirm that there is no single form of universal spirituality, but rather plural, diverse, intercultural and, therefore, interreligious spiritualities. If each territory-body has their inner spiritual strength and dynamism, which helps them to position themself before their vital environment, we cannot speak of spirituality as a human quality or characteristic. For each living being has that spiritual dimension because it is the work and likeness of its Creator. From what I have been arguing, I am not postulating a pantheism (everything is God), but a panentheism (God is in all creation). From an analogous understanding among our ancestral peoples, each living being has its own spirit: the spirit of the forest, of the earth, of plants, of animals. Human beings share that dimension or inner strength that helps us to seek the common good and that starts from within our corporeality to resist the logic of extermination.

The women who go out to protest in the streets emerge with their inner spiritual strength and, like the wisdom of the text of the biblical book of Proverbs, they cry out and raise their voices in the squares to demand a world without violence.

Queer/*Cuir*/Weird Ecofeminism

In 1994, Catriona Sandilands questioned the defence of territories from queer bodies. Since then, at least in the Anglo-Saxon world, a debate has developed that, starting from the idea of "queering ecofeminism", led to the proposal of a "queer ecology".[7] The concept *queer* is a word from the Anglo-Saxon world that means and evokes the "extravagant", weird, twisted or out of the norm. Queer theory has as one of its characteristics the decoloniality of bodies and diverse sexualities in relation to the heteronormative matrix:

> […] the problem of oppression based on sexuality is not limited to heterosexual / *queer* dualism. […] The biggest problem is the erotophobia of Western culture, a fear so strong that only one form of sexuality is openly allowed; only in one position; and only in the context of certain legal, religious and social sanctions.[8]

It has already been mentioned that erotica was and has been colonised by hegemonic patriarchal Christianity, confusing it with pornography and has been assigned the character of "sin" or of an anti-Christian category. The exclusion of erotica led to fundamentalist spiritualities of a somatophobic (body phobia), hedophobic (fear of experiencing pleasure) and egodistonic (rejection of one's own diverse sexuality) tendency with implications of alienation from the body or gender binarisms.

Decolonising erotica implies returning to the origin of its value as the capacity for deep knowledge, as an energy potentially present in our bodies. It favours the recovery of the power of the violated bodies and the prophetic-political force that emanates from the abject bodies: racialised, discriminated against and excluded due to poverty or sexually diverse orientation. Queer theology – or "*cuir*", in its most Latin American and Caribbean acceptation – aims to recover erotica as a diversity of relationships that emanate from divinity and make creative action possible, making all creation participate in its loving power. This participation enables each creature to come out of themself to meet the "otherness" called neighbour. According to the South Korean philosopher Byung-Chul Han, "eros tears the subject from themself and leads them out, towards the other."[9]

From queer feminism, it is pointed out that sex (supposedly biological, natural) is constructed in as culturally a binary way as gender is. Queer researcher Joan Roughgarden identifies various genders in certain animals and says that many species have three or four genders.[10] If we define culture by the existence of social structures, language, learning and affections, it is true that we can observe a lot of culture in animals and an abundance of affective and sexual relationships that escape heteronormativity.

---

[7] Andrea Speck, "Aportaciones desde la teoría queer al ecologismo en tiempos de extinción", *EL Topo*, 10th June 2019, [Available at: https://eltopo.org/aportaciones-desde-la-teoria-queer-al-ecologismo-en-tiempos-de-extincion/], [Last accessed: 22nd March 2022].

[8] Greta Gaard, "Toward a Queer Ecofeminism", *Hypatia* 12(1) (1997): 114-37.

[9] Byung-Chul Han, *La agonía del eros* (Barcelona: Herder, 2014): 6.

[10] Joan Roughgarden, *Evolution's Rainbow: Diversity, Gender, and Sexuality in Nature and People* (Berkeley, CA: University of California, 2004).

Assuming this perspective, ecofeminist theology is also posited as queer/*cuir*/weird in the recovery of diverse territory-bodies. As political theology, conceived as a critical continuation of feminist liberation theory, it is articulated through a multidisciplinary approach supported by Judith Butler's sexual theory, especially inspired by Marxist and poststructuralist philosophy, as well as decolonial critical theory. In this framework, its theoretical effort specifies a theological approach to diverse sexualities and is located in the area of systematic theology.[11] It starts from the principle that every human being is the image of Godde,[12] and that this image is their identity in flux; and therefore, from the recognition of the sacred in each living being that inhabits the planet and the cosmos, regardless of the sexual role that they perform – meaning by performatively repeated actions (performativity), recognised by tradition or by the conventionalism of a given society. It is enough for us to see, in this sense, how diverse the nature of bodies is in plant and animal species.

Sexuality, queer theories, and queer theology are very complex areas, but the three come together in an interdisciplinary way to free us from epistemic colonialisms, gender impositions, heteronormativity, and neoliberal policies that colonise bodies. Poor people's sexuality is seen as a problem, but rich people's sexuality is not judged that way. It is not the same to be gay, as to be a "pansy", or to be a lesbian, as to be a "tomboy". In all of this, there is an intersectional crossing of multiple oppressions: class, sexual orientation and race, which marginalises LGBTQI+ poor people twice or three times more than rich people, starting with the language used to address them. As Marcella Althaus-Reid observes, "the problem is usually the combination of desire and poverty."[13] Both are taboo subjects in the lives of poor people. Sexual violence among poor people is never taken very seriously, but the same is not true of rich people. As long as this idea does not change in society and in religious spaces, it will continue to be considered that way, as a "problem". As there is an obscene desire for control over the bodies and sexualities of poor people, for the use of these by neoliberal capitalist logic and by political agendas, which attempt to obtain power at the cost of sexuality and the impacted bodies of women and men considered non-heteronormative.

Queer/*cuir* theology questions such a position, and even questions feminist liberation theology itself, insofar as it has not taken into account the diverse sexualities of poor women, and poor people in general, out of an excess of "decency". For this reason, it has suggested establishing the category "indecent" as an epistemic principle of sexuality and desire in the daily life of poor people. In this sense, this category constitutes a principle of subversion of a heteronormative sexuality, which from the political and economic sphere colonises the bodies, desires and sexualities of poor people. The love of God or divine wisdom from the vision of queer theology emerges from the bodies that inhabit the peripheries of societies without any type of exclusion; it is a love that arises in people of the same sex and in those who express their love in filial relationships.

Queer or *cuir* theology finds its maximum expression in the diverse love of the divine trinity, because in the perichoretic relationship – understood as a non-hierarchical, but horizontal love relationship, between the three divine persons of the trinity – a profound plural and at the same time unique love is expressed.

> When we speak of "sexualising" and decolonising the Trinity we must acknowledge two themes. On the one hand, the plurality of the Trinity is the way to deal with mechanisms of colonialist activity, especially the disruption of the binary system (the number three is important as a symbol of disruption of the number two that marks the dichotomy). The term disruption is the radical subversion that pushes us to re-evaluate certain presuppositions. On the other hand, the multiple experiences of gender and the representations of sexuality in pursuit of the renewal of creation are expressed in the images of God, which always reflect the different plural understandings of humanity and of the whole of creation. And all these images must be on an equal footing with

[11] Marcella Althaus-Reid, *Indecent Theology: Theological perversions in sex, gender and politics* (London: Routledge, 2000): 7.
[12] TN: The author uses the Spanish "Di@s" in the original, instead of "Dios."
[13] Althaus-Reid, *Indecent Theology*, 137.

> each other, and not in hierarchical options or trapped in the truth / heresy binomial, since human beings do not have the right to tell God what God should or should not be.[14]

The metaphors of the "weirdness" or "twistedness" of God – who decides to love those considered non-persons – and of the relationship of God with "otherness" – which is neither static nor normative, but rather dynamic, flexible – allow us to approach the experience of Divinity and a theological reflection that takes God "out of the closet" (if by closet we understand the rigidity of a static, legalistic and judgmental God). Ángel Méndez Montoya explains for queer theology that this is not a concept only for sexually diverse people, but for those people considered non-people:

> Queer identity not only designates an affirmation or recognition of sexual diversity, but also opens up to the recognition and respect of everyone who lives on the peripheries of society: women, the poor, migrants, indigenous people, the homeless, the voiceless, those people who have been deprived of their agency. Queer are those identities indecent for a society that excludes them for not following the "decent" regulations imposed by supremacist and oppressive constructs.[15]

In this sense, Jesus of Nazareth was a "weird" or "indecent" man, who did not assume the stereotypes of hegemonic masculinity based on three principles: providing, protecting and impregnating. For the texts of the Gospels indicate that those who provided for Jesus with their goods were some women (Lk. 8: 1-3); they show that he was not able to protect himself (Mt. 27: 9), nor his followers; and they coincide in not mentioning if he had children. According to their testimony, Jesus was accused of being a glutton, a drunkard, and a friend of people of doubtful repute (Mt. 11:19). Jesus, a lawbreaker, also broke the hegemonic principles of masculinity of his time. He deconstructed himself, dying with an abject and garbage body. This is not denying the incarnation of Jesus in a male body, since queer feminists have no problems with that Christological reality as such. However, we do have problems with the interpretation that has been given to the male body of Jesus, according to which the fact that Jesus was incarnated as a male gives men a category of supremacy over women and over sexually diverse bodies. Therefore, the problem lies in the fact that there are not more men capable of deconstructing their hegemonic masculinity as did Jesus, who had to learn to embody a non-violent, non-patriarchal, non-hierarchical masculinity in the encounter with the women of his time.

Queer or *cuir* theology celebrates the weirdness of a God or Divine Wisdom that comes out of itself in a transgressive act (*cuir*), and is incarnated in a violated, temporary and limited body, such as that of the human being Jesus. An unlimited and infinite God, who becomes historical limitation and finitude, in a concrete corporeality is able to make his own body the table of enjoyment, unable to exclude anyone from his table, and less for reasons of race, sexuality or social categorisation.

Conclusion

Ecofeminist spiritualities in resistance are opening the way towards other forms of inclusion and relating with and within life environments. The political-social-cultural and religious contexts need to be analysed from other angles: neither dominant, nor patriarchal, nor sexist. That is why the resistances are calling for the exercise of decolonising Christian spirituality, and are proposing an inter-species, interdependent, subversive, corporeal, erotic and street savvy spiritual movement, since this is how prophesying has been since biblical times. We are challenged to the prophetic-political exercise in the daily life of our vital environment, if we do not want to be the end of the Anthropocene.

---

[14] Hugo Córdova Quero, "Sexualizando la Trinidad: aportes desde una teología de la liberación queer a la comprensión del misterio divino", *Cuadernos de Teología* 30 (2011): 67.

[15] Ángel Mendez Montoya, "Teología Queer", *Sofías. Revista Interdisciplinar de Teología Feminista* 2(4) (2016): 7.

Suggestions for Further Reading

Althaus-Reid, Marcella. *Indecent Theology: Theological perversions in sex, gender and politics*. London: Routledge, 2000.

Boheler, Genilma, Lars Bedurke and Silvia Regina De Lima Silva, Eds. *Teorías Queer y teologías: estar... en otro lugar.* San José, Costa Rica: DEI, 2013.

Butler, Judith. *Formas de resistencia a la violencia de hoy. Sin miedo*. México: Taurus, 2020.

—–. *Cuerpos que importan. Sobre los límites discursivos del "sexo".* Barcelona: Paidós, 2002.

Camps, Victoria. *El gobierno de las emociones.* Barcelona: Herder, 2011.

Colectivo Miradas Críticas del Territorio desde el Feminismo. *Mapeando el cuerpo-territorio. Guía metodológica para mujeres que defienden sus territorios.* Quito: CLACSO, 2017.

Córdova Quero, Hugo. "Sexualizando la Trinidad: aportes desde una teología de la liberación queer a la comprensión del misterio divino". *Cuadernos de Teología* 30 (2011).

Gaard, Greta. "Toward a Queer Ecofeminism". *Hypatia* 12(1) (1997): 114-137.

Han, Byung-Chul. *La agonía del eros*. Barcelona: Herder, 2014.

Martínez Andrade, Luis. *Ecología y teología de la liberación. Crítica de la modernidad/colonialidad.* Barcelona: Herder, 2019.

Mendez Montoya, Ángel. "Teología Queer". *Sofías. Revista Interdisciplinar de Teología Feminista.* 2(4) (2016).

Roughgarden, Joan. *Evolution's Rainbow: Diversity, Gender, and Sexuality in Nature and People.* Berkeley, CA: University of California, 2004.

Servitje Montull, María del Carmen, Ed. *Genealogía crítica de la violencia: Hacia la liberación del espacio político religioso del cuerpo de las mujeres.* México: Universidad Iberoamericana, 2020.

Speck, Andrea. "Aportaciones desde la teoría queer al ecologismo en tiempos de extinción". *EL Topo*, 10th June 2019. [Available at: https://eltopo.org/aportaciones-desde-la-teoria-queer-al-ecologismo-en-tiempos-de-extincion/], [Last accessed: 22nd March 2022].

27. THE OLD NATURE AND THE NEW CREATION

Néstor Míguez[1]

The Word and the Words

Let us begin by clarifying the concepts and words with which we designate this tension. Because the words we use, how we use them, and the underlying logic in the choice of terms also show the different ways in which we conceive of our relationship with divinity, with other human beings, and with the environment that surrounds us. These forms are inserted in the different cultural configurations, but also in the ways in which we present economic dynamics, socio-political constructions. Theo-logy, as its name indicates, is a construction of words on the Word, and in them are played out the dynamics of our complex interactions and their meanings. It is also a decisive point in ecumenical and interreligious dialogue, which on the American continents must take place fundamentally with the worldviews of native peoples.

Nature

The idea and concept of nature, with its long tradition and multiple meanings, entails a certain look at what surrounds us, how it originates and how it is governed. In its origin, the Greek concept (*fysis*) denotes the birth or formation of something, the development contained in the origin or the path by which it manifests itself.[2] Things, plants, animals, humans, exist and eventually grow "according to their nature." That is to say, there is an inherent condition in the thing itself. Thus, in the conception of Aristotle (according to Köster):

> The order of nature is absolutely valid and allows no operation of supernatural forces within it. Hence anything against nature, but only against it [...] as it mostly is, should be called a miracle. [...] On the other hand, nature is not just an object of scientific concerns; it is also an independently operating force which establishes a wise order in its own sphere.[3]

Later, in Stoic Hellenism, nature acquires a dimension of divinity, bordering on a certain pantheism. However, the distinction between nature and human law appears, as, on the one hand, that which is given, which emerges from the order of things, and, on the other, that which the human being disposes and establishes as different from that order, which makes another order, which emerges as "moral", as a custom that creates the *ethos* of co-existence. Nature and law then appear as entities, both necessary, but opposite, both in origin and function.

Finally, it is convenient to point out other myths where nature is a divine manifestation or is configured as a deity, or, even more, is itself a set of divine forces. The stars are celestial powers, and earth and sky are divinities. We can see this, with their differences, be it in the ancient Greek, Mesopotamian and Egyptian

---

[1] Néstor Míguez is an Argentine Doctor in Theology with a graduate degree in Social and Political Anthropology. He is Pastor and Professor Emeritus of Biblical Hermeneutics and Systematic Theology. He has been president of the Argentine Federation of Evangelical Churches, and held various positions in ecumenical organisations. He has collaborated with missions among native peoples and in the popular reading of the Bible in Latin America and is a member of the Presidency Council of the Permanent Assembly for Human Rights. nestormiguez@gmail.com.

[2] On this subject, at least as it is used in ancient philosophy and in the New Testament, I avail myself of the extensive and informed article by H. Köster, "*fysis*" in *Theological Dictionary of the New Testament Vol. IX* (Grand Rapids, MI: Wm. B. Eerdmans, 1977): 251-277.

[3] Köster, "*fysis*", 258-259.

myths, and also, with their particularities, in the cosmologies of the original peoples of our *Abya-yala* (later converted to America). In the Andean tradition, Inti (the sun), the Pachamama (the earth), the Achachilas (mountains, ancestors) are divinities. Other native cultures have, with slightly different names and characteristics, a similar understanding, with lunar deities and the presence of protective spirits of the jungle, of the rivers, of the different species.

For its part, the Hebrew language does not have any word that denotes the same thing; there is no concept of "nature" in that sense. For this reason, we will not find any reference to "nature" in the texts of the Hebrew Bible, although we will find the elements and dynamics that compose it. In the pseudepigraphic version of the Septuagint, already under Hellenistic influence, there are a few mentions of the term *fysis*, but always in the sense of something that responds to its own condition, or in the compound *parafysis*, alluding to what is done contrary to the natural disposition. Philo and Josephus, in their intention to assimilate Hebrew thought with Greek philosophy or Roman politics, will be the ones who will resort to the concept of nature, often linking it to the sexual drive "according to nature" or "contrary to nature".

We will not find the idea of nature in the New Testament either, in the sense given to it by the use of contemporary Hellenistic Greek. The word appears in Pauline writings, especially in the Letter to the Romans. In the case of the first chapter, it has the same meaning that we have seen in Philo. The same is true of the mentions in the letter of Judas. For he will say that those who do not have the law (of Moses) *by nature* follow the law (Rom. 2:14). In Romans 11, the metaphor about the salvation of the Gentiles, like the wild branch that is grafted into the good olive tree, resorts to that which is according to nature and which is outside of nature (*kata fysis* and *para fysis*). The sense of "the natural" is also used for the subject of hair in 1 Corinthians 11, again as given, that which is the peculiar quality of something, of a species or gender. That meaning is also given by 2 Peter 1:4 when he speaks of the "divine nature" in which we are participants by the messianic promise.

A more interesting occurrence is given in the Letter to the Galatians. There, Paul, in his discussion of freedom in Christ and slavery to the law, points out: "Formerly, when you did not know God, you were enslaved to beings that *by nature* are not gods. Now, however, that you have come to know God, or rather to be known by God, how can you turn back again to the weak and beggarly elemental spirits" (4:8-9).[4] The idea of submitting to the elements of this world appears as something parallel to submitting to the law. Was Paul referring to "the elements" in the sense of the four elements that, according to philosophy, make up the reality of the physical world? Or was it a reference to pagan deities?

But the concept of nature has been modified, especially through science and a positivist understanding. When we look at a current dictionary (in our case, that of the Spanish language) it offers us the following definitions of *naturaleza*:

> 1. *Principio generador del desarrollo armónico y la plenitud de cada ser, en cuanto tal ser, siguiendo su propia e independiente evolución.*
> 2. *Conjunto de todo lo que existe y que está determinado y armonizado en sus propias leyes.*
> 3. *Virtud, calidad o propiedad de las cosas.*
> 4. *Instinto, propensión o inclinación de las cosas, con que pretenden su conservación y aumento.*
> 5. *Fuerza o actividad natural, contrapuesta a la sobrenatural y milagrosa.*[5]

[4] Translator's note: The biblical quotes in English in this translation are taken from the New Revised Standard Version.

[5] 1. Generating principle of harmonic development and the fullness of each being, as such, following its own independent evolution; 2. Ensemble of everything that exists and that is determined and harmonised in its own laws; 3. Virtue, quality or property of things; 4. Instinct, propensity or inclination of things, with which they seek their conservation and increase; 5. Natural force or activity, as opposed to the supernatural and miraculous. *Diccionario de la Real Academia Española, ad loc.*

The *Cambridge Dictionary of the English Language* specifies the notion of "nature": "All the animals and plants in the world and all the features, forces, and processes that exist or happen independently of people, such as the weather, the sea, mountains, reproduction, and growth. [...] the force that is responsible for physical life and that is sometimes spoken of as a person".[6]

In both cases, the autonomy of that which is natural is pointed out and, in the case of the Royal Academy of the Spanish Language, it advances to explicitly oppose it, as Aristotle did, with the intervention of divine forces.

Creation[7]

Conversely, we have the concept of creation. Most of the cultures of antiquity have myths about the origins, generally linked to complex theogonies, where there are tangled struggles between primal deities, plurality of origins for the different elements, even differentiations between human beings. In some cases, although the narrative myths show this plot, later the liturgies simplify things and the idea of a creator God appears more strongly. We see this in the peoples of the first nations of America. *Qadta*, the great Father, is the creator God for the Qom of the Argentine Chaco. That creation is then cared for by the protective spirits that Qadta pours out over the earth. Among the Iroquois of North America, the following prayer is recorded:

> And this is what the Creator did. He decided, 'There will be plants growing on the earth. Indeed, all of them will have names, as many plants as will be growing on the earth. At a certain time, they will emerge from the earth and mature of their own accord. They will be available in abundance as medicines to the people moving about on the earth.' That is what he intended. And it is true: we have been using them up to the present time [...] And this too the Creator did. With regard to the plants growing on the earth he decided, 'There will be a certain plant on which berries will always hang at a certain time. I shall then cause them to remember me, the people moving about on the earth. They will always express their gratitude when they see the berries hanging above the earth.' And it is true: we see them when the wind becomes warm again on the earth; the strawberries are indeed hanging there. And it is also true that we use them, that we drink the berry water. That is what he did. And it is true: it comes to pass.[8]

The biblical account stands out for its sobriety in this regard. Perhaps, precisely, it seeks to differentiate itself from Mesopotamian theogonies. The creational poem that opens the biblical account, which reaches its final form in times after the Babylonian exile, is probably, among other things, a way of confronting these myths. It is certainly not a scientific description (as certain fundamentalisms confuse it), but a hymn of praise for the work of the creator.

Among the different words that various passages of Hebrew Scripture use for creation, the one that appears in the first verse of Genesis stands out: *barah*. This verb is used only for God, who by God's word alone creates and orders. This is how the power of God, capable of generating from the non-existent, stands out. (Psalm 33:9: "For God spoke, and it was came to be; God commanded, and it stood firm"). Everything that exists arises from that creative will, and therefore nothing that is made has the same original or divine character as the deity that creates it.

Israel surely reached this conception over the course of time. However, the Israelite experience of God is not primarily as author of the visible, but as liberator. "The connection between power in history and

---

[6] See https://dictionary.cambridge.org/es/diccionario/ingles/nature

[7] In this section, we base our arguments on José S. Croatto, *El hombre en el mundo I: Creación y designio comentario a Génesis 1.* (Buenos Aires: Ediciones La Aurora, 1974) and José S. Croatto, *Crear y amar en libertad. Estudio de Génesis 2:4-3:24* (Buenos Aires: Ediciones La Aurora, 1986). Also on W. Foerster, "*ktizo*", in *Theological Dictionary of the New Testament – Vol.VIII* (Grand Rapids, MI: Wm. B., 1966): 1000-1035.

[8] Wallace L. Chafe. "Seneca Thanksgiving Rituals", *Bureau of American Ethnology Bulletin* 183 (1961).

power as Creator is a very close one in the OT, for the shaping of history is also a creation, and the same words are used of it as are applied to the creating and fashioning of the world and man."[9]

This idea of a unique deity, creator out of nothing, will later also feature in the New Testament expression. The verb root of *ktizo* and its derivatives will be that which predominates in this sense, since like *barah* in the Old Testament, it will be used only for divine action. The root of *poieo* (to do) also appears with that sense.

The prologue of the Gospel of John is one among many expressions in this sense ("In the beginning was the Word, and the Word was with God, and the Word was God. He was in the beginning with God. All things came into being through him, and without him not one thing came into being" John 1:1-3). We will find similar expressions in each Gospel ("But from the beginning of creation, 'God made them male and female.'" Mark 10:6), in the Pauline writings ("for in him all things in heaven and on earth were created, things visible and invisible, whether thrones or dominions or rulers or powers – all things have been created through him and for him" Colossians 1:16), and in the other writings, including Revelations ("You are worthy, our Lord and God, to receive glory and honour and power, for you created all things, and by your will they existed and were created" Rev. 4:11), to cite just a few examples.

It is Paul who brings this theologumen into play the most. And it will reach its greatest expression in chapter 8 of the Letter to the Romans (8:21), where we find the idea "that the creation itself will be set free from its bondage to decay and will obtain the freedom of the glory of the children of God". In this way, he expresses the ambiguity that affects what is created, including the human being. It is the recognition that the very good creation of God suffers and is captive, and with it we human beings suffer, that "we await the redemption of our bodies." This hope is affirmed by the presence of the Messiah, since nothing "in all creation will be able to separate us from the love of God in Christ Jesus our Lord" (Rom. 8:39).

It is precisely this messianic presence in the midst of creation that will be the specific influence of the New Testament. God intervenes in history, as was the Israelite prophetic conviction, but not by revelations or extraordinary interventions, rather by getting into the space of creation, in time, and thus modifying the sense of the created space and time, the beginning of the promised "new creation". It is clearly expressed in the prologue of the Gospel of John:

> He was in the world, and the world came into being through him; yet the world did not know him. He came to what was his own, and his own people did not accept him. But to all who received him, who believed in his name, he gave power to become children of God, who were born, not of blood or of the will of the flesh or of the will of man, but of God. And the Word became flesh and lived among us, and we have seen his glory, the glory as of a father's only son, full of grace and truth (Jn. 1:10-14).

Also in Paul's theology: "Let the same mind be in you that was in Christ Jesus, who, though he was in the form of God, did not regard equality with God as something to be exploited, but emptied himself, taking the form of a slave, being born in human likeness. And being found in human form, he humbled himself and became obedient to the point of death – even death on a cross" (Phil. 2:5-8).

This messianic presence in the midst of creation establishes a new way of understanding the created world, which in reality means a "new" creation. The cures, resuscitations, the feeding of the multitude, and even the relationship of the messiah with the forces of the storm (Mk. 4: 37-41) are not "miracles", in the sense of interrupting the course of nature, but interventions in the created world in order to protect and safeguard life. They are not supernatural, but rather events that occur in the broad and complete scope of creation, showing its power. Jesus' expression in the sermon on the mount about wild lilies, or his observation about sparrows ("Are not five sparrows sold for two pennies? Yet not one of them is forgotten in God's sight" Lk. 12:6) show that this presence in creation is not limited to human history, but includes

[9] W. Foerster, "*ktizo*", 1006.

all life, all expression of that which exists. This significantly affects the theology of creation and is what invites us to differentiate the idea of creation from that of nature.

Between the Options

As we have seen, we find ourselves, in broad terms, fundamentally faced with three options: a) an understanding of nature as a self-governing entity, whose laws determine the being of beings and their dynamics; b) a certain identity of natural forces as deities, as divine powers, and the necessary respect for and worship of them in their preservation and care; and c) a concept of creation as a product of divine action, although distinct from its creator, in which God continues to act and, in the Christian vision, this creator chooses to be immersed in and for it, becomes creation in order to act from within creation itself, renewing it.

The three options are not absolute and, although in their strictest enunciation they seem exclusive, we can see, in a tour of Christian theology in its different moments and varieties, how each one of them in some way affected the thought and action of Christians and churches. Although the concept of creation is central, the presence of Jesus and Jesus' actions are inescapable in all theology that arises from the Christian faith. This was not always articulated in the same way, but rather according to differing understandings, and in relation to the various influences received from philosophy, science, or the interlocutors of the religious world.

Although we cannot cover all these lines in the brief space of this article, it is worth noting how they have influenced and nuanced theological thought. In some cases, this was through questioning certain statements that seemed central to Christian religiosity, and that had to be rethought in the light of scientific or philosophical criticism, and in others leading to manifestations that ended up hiding significant aspects of the faith, as happened with deism, on the one hand, or with a certain pantheism on the other.

The contributions of science, in its time, made it necessary to read creational stories in a different way, recognising complex, elusive elements and dynamics. That same science today alerts us to the dangerous derivations of certain modes of human action, the consequences of some productive models, the irresponsibility of a blindness regarding the limits that the same physical dynamics impose upon us. On the other hand, in astronomical studies and quantum physics, forms and situations are revealed to us in which the "laws" that were believed to be regular are not, and that the power of matter acts in unforeseen ways, at least unforeseen for the manner in which the human being has understood them until now.

This reality obliges us to overcome a conception of the "stopgap God", as Dietrich Bonhoeffer called it, in which religion rushes to give answers to scientific enigmas by resorting to "the work of God", as if the arcane of the divine were an answer to the unsolved riddles that are presented to us in the universe we inhabit. The divine mystery, at least in the New Testament understanding, is not the answer to the riddles of nature, but the potential of the messianic presence to be the way of salvation for the human being and the whole of creation. In this sense, faith in Jesus and the science that studies nature, do not oppose each other, but rather complement each other, they nourish each other with knowledge and hope.

Moving Beyond the Language of "Conserving Nature"

Thus, the idea of "conserving nature" is not adequate, it is not even good. Certain proposals, apparently well-intentioned, end up ignoring the very dynamics of the nature that they seek to take care of. The very condition of life and species is extinguished and renewed, has changed and is modified continuously, even long before the appearance of human beings. Even more so when human action itself has already and irreversibly modified certain conditions of life on the planet, and where it makes no sense – and in some cases it is not even possible – to go back. This does not mean ignoring the devastating action produced by some activities, and even less when this is aims to be done at the expense of caring for human life, for the goods necessary for future generations, ignoring the situation of poor people or putting at risk the weakest and most vulnerable human beings.

The traditional definition of culture, in the sense of what the human being does beyond nature, is also insufficient from that perspective. In addition, culture itself does not exist, but rather there are different cultural forms and modes which build different forms of relationship with the environment in which they live. The different cultures establish mediations that are ways of relating, of interaction, where the human being produces active exchanges, with each other, with the environment, with the transcendent (in the sense of what transcends and gives meaning to their own life, although they do not always do so in the form of religion or recognise it as divinity). Culture is what human beings do with nature; it is the form of our participation in the created world.

This interaction generates forms of coexistence, which we call politics, and ways of producing and distributing the goods necessary for subsistence, or to satisfy desires, which we call economics. But none of these are isolated or have independent forms: the meanings of power (politics) and value (economics) are also cultural constructions, marked by religious and ethical conceptions, gender situations, ethnic condition, philosophical, ideological and axiomatic views, among which are included the ways of understanding our place in the world, of our human condition within the totality of which we are part.

Moving Beyond the Language of Resources

Many of those forms that we elaborate, as peoples, as classes, social sectors, as persons, are destructive, since they are only guided by an egocentric, irresponsible self-perception, where politics and economics only serve our own personal or collective pride. Once again, language helps us discover the underlying conceptions. Thus, the dominant economy in the world today, capitalism, refers to the elements at its disposal as "resources", showing a utilitarian vision of nature, which constitutes a capital of which certain humans are considered the owner, a property of which they can make use and abuse, as Roman law said, to consume or destroy – and which capitalism is effectively destroying. But it goes even further, and through the financial market it creates fictions (financial resources) that, in truth, do not exist in the natural world, and through financial mechanisms, it controls and proposes to control not only the present but also the future, generating long-term obligations. It thus claims an almost divine power: "One system, no limits", as the advertising slogan of a company of financial management products says.[10]

Worse yet is when human resources or human capital are assessed, as if work, capabilities and human life itself are an entrepreneurial means to make a fortune, instead of the social and collective act of participation in the extension of life. When accumulation becomes an end in itself, and possession ceases to recognise the social meaning of every good entrusted to humanity, it ceases to understand itself as indebted to the creator, and to the totality of creatures, and one cannot expect but pain, injustice and destruction. This has also happened with other economic systems.

Other practices and cultures, on the other hand, attempt to know more deeply the relationships and spaces that they inhabit (and not only as science, but also as life wisdom), and thus seek to generate better living conditions, and join the creative task and the dynamic which affirms and projects the existence of all creation – what the Andean peoples call "good living", *Sumak kawsay*, in the Quechua language.[11] It is what springs from the creational account in Genesis: "God saw everything that he had made, and indeed, it was

---

[10] Netsuite, "Netsuite: One System, No Limits", *ExtendTech Website*. [Available at: https://extendtech.net/netsuite-erp-one-system-no-limits/], [Last accessed: 23rd March 2022].

[11] On "good living" and its theological impact, see, among others, my chapter "Together towards Life and Contemporary Latin American Theology", In Kenneth R. Ross, Jooseop Keum, Kyriaki Avtzi and Roderick R. Hewitt (eds), *Ecumenical Missiology: Changing Landscapes and New Conceptions of Mission* (Edinburgh: Regnum Edinburgh Centenary Series, 2016): 519-529.

very good" (Gen. 1:31). Thus, what creation offers us is something good, a benefit; the different elements that we have available are considered goods to be cared for and administered wisely, since those same assets are the ones that preserve and encourage life. The "good living", the gospel's offer of full and abundant life, does not consist in how much or little we can accumulate, but in the quality of our relationships, in how we love those around us, human or not. Thus, we give deeper meaning to our existence. It is what we call salvation, and it has a horizon of eternity.

Most of our actions and decisions, we must admit, participate partially in both orientations, they are loaded with the ambiguity typical of every human condition, of all creation that is shown to be both good and vital, while suffering from corruption, that awaits liberation and the new creation, but in the meantime it suffers with birth pains, and groans within itself (Rom. 8:22-23). The tension between the responsible care of the goods that we safeguard, and the response to certain economic needs or desires for expansion and comfort, is continuously manifested. The old nature and the new creation coexist in us, and thus envelop all that we are and do.

Towards the New Creation

What I would like to highlight in this trajectory is that the concept of creation, as an integrating axis, allows us to overcome certain antinomies and paradoxes of the relationship between the human being and the whole of creation. And this is shown par excellence as we see it in the logos embodied in the person of Jesus, in the deep conviction of the Christian faith, where humanity, divinity and nature coincide in their vital, creative, creating power.

Overcoming the distinction between nature and culture, between the law of nature and human law, between divine work and human action, is only possible when we consider our own actions as participation in the collective creative act that involves us in the divine project – what, in Jesus, is announced as the reign of God. Paul points out this understanding by saying that "if anyone is in Christ, there is a new creation (*ktisis*): everything old has passed away; see, everything has become new" (2 Cor. 5:17). In this way, the "old nature" (the old heaven and the old earth that pass) is being shaped according to the new creation, the old humanity "is clothed [...] with the new self, which is being renewed in knowledge according to the image of its creator" (Col. 3:10).

The canonical book of Revelation, in the final chapters, with its mythical-poetic language, its paradoxes and open images, provides us with an approximation to this vocation. There, the visionary sees "the new Jerusalem", and announces that the old things have passed away and all things are made new (21:1-4). However, this novelty does not mean ignorance of human work. Unlike the Genesis account, the space of human habitation is no longer the bucolic garden; it is now a city, and the city is, according to Genesis itself, human work. An invention originally seen as evil, but is now redeemed as a "holy city". The old opposition between country and city, between the rustic and the cultural, is overcome. Curious city, walled but with doors always open to all sides, with streets of crystalline gold, furrowed by a river that flows from the divine throne, gardens with trees that always bear fruit, at all times, and whose leaves produce healing.

Human history is not denied in the new creation, but assumed and transformed by the divine presence. The elements continue to be named with the names that humankind gave them, the portals bear the names of the tribes of Israel, and the foundations the names of the apostles (Rev. 21:12-14). The old and the new people of God are remembered and included. But it also includes all the peoples who recognise the creator God and who walk in this God's light. Power is reconfigured, since the monarchs bring their glory to this city, where this very same God will be their God and they will be God's people (Rev. 21:3).

Conclusion: To Be Inspired by New Creation to Become Beneficiaries Responsible to the Creator

This vision of the new creation, which recovers and redeems what we have contributed to this ambiguous human history, is what allows us to guide our actions in the life that we still have in this world of the old nature. It is part of the service we provide to God in the person of our brothers and sisters, and the entire common home that we inhabit (hence it is recognised as eco-diakonia). It is not simply a matter of preserving what exists, given that "nature" itself is constantly changing; it mutates according to, what seems to us, its own laws, but also beyond them and unexpectedly (the current pandemic is a clear example of this).

As we pointed out at the beginning, our conceptions and words are meaningful, they frame and guide our actions. It is not the same to speak of "resources" as of "goods", to use nature as a deposit of materials, or to participate in creation as something living and life-generating, which allows for good living. Considering ourselves as possessors does not produce the same effects as recognising ourselves as beneficiaries responsible to the creator. The Christian faith, rooted in biblical revelation, beyond all the historical deformations that it has suffered, is called to commit to this task and mission knowing itself as part of God's new creation in Christ Jesus.

Suggestions for Further Reading

Chafe, Wallace L. "Seneca Thanksgiving Rituals". In *Bureau of American Ethnology Bulletin* 183 (1961).

Croatto, José S. *Crear y amar en libertad. Estudio de Génesis 2:4-3:24.* Buenos Aires: Ediciones La Aurora, 1986.

—. *El hombre en el mundo I: Creación y designio, comentario a Génesis 1.* Buenos Aires: Ediciones La Aurora, 1974.

Foerster, W. "*ktizo*", In *Theological Dictionary of the New Testament – Vol. III.* Grand Rapids, MI: Wm. B. Eerdmans, 1966: 1000-1035.

Köster, H. "*fysis*", In *Theological Dictionary of the New Testament – Vol. IX.* Grand Rapids, MI: Wm. B. Eerdmans, 1977: 251-277.

Ross, Kenneth, Jooseop Keum, Kyriaki Avtzi, Roderick R. Hewitt, Eds. *Ecumenical Missiology: Changing Landscapes and New Conceptions of Mission.* Edinburgh: Regnum Edinburgh Centenary Series, 2016.

28. Religion, Nature and Health as Stimuli for Eco-Diakonia: Reflections from Hildegard von Bingen and Catherine von Bora

Márcia Blasi[1] and Valério G. Schaper[2]

Introduction

The relationships between religion and health have become antithetical and are permeated by conflicts of all kinds. In part, this was due to the fact that the relationship between health and disease came to be understood through the biological sciences and progressively managed through a set of medical techniques.[3] This transfer of the relationship between health and disease to the exclusive domain of the biological sciences and the growing predominance of medical techniques produced a progressive distancing between religion and health.[4] The consolidation of this process took place in the last four centuries. However, experiences prior to this period showed more complex and satisfying relationships between religion and health.[5]

In this article, we do not intend to treat the relationship between religion and health in a comprehensive way. Our purpose is more modest in scope and more specific in focus. We are interested in pointing out that the proximity between religion and health, in the period prior to their mutual estrangement, found one of its common denominators in the work of women. For a long time, before the advancement of medical science, women were in charge of caring for the sick in the family and the neighbourhood, diagnosing

---

[1] Márcia Blasi is Doctor of Theology (Faculdades EST), Master in Theology (Graduate Theological Union, Berkeley, CA/U.S.A.) and Professor in the Faculdades EST, where she co-ordinates the Program of Gender and Religion. She leads the Nucleus of Gender Investigation. retalhos13@hotmail.com.

[2] Valério G. Schaper is Doctor of Theology (Faculdades EST) and Professor in the Faculdades EST, where he co-ordinates the Institute of Sustainability for Latin America and the Caribbean. He leads the Nucleus of Investigation on Human Rights and the Nucleus of Studies on Contemporary Ethics. valerio@est.edu.br.

[3] Gil Sevalho, "Uma Abordagem Histórica das Representações Sociais de Saúde e Doença", *Cadernos de Saúde Pública* 9(3) (1993): 349-363; Dorothy Porter, *Health, Civilization and the State: a history of public health from ancient to modern times* (London: Routledge, 1999): 23-44; Marli Terezinha Stein Backes, *et al.*, "Conceitos de saúde e doença ao longo da história sob o olhar epidemiológico e antropológico", *Revista Enfermagem da UERJ* 17(1) (2009): 111-117. Taking up the instigating approach of the "medicalisation of life", proposed by Michel Foucault remains beyond our reading of this "management" process. Cf. Michel Foucault, *Microfísica do Poder* (Rio de Janeiro: Edições Graal, 1988): 69-128; 193-208.

[4] The different understandings of the disease-health relationship are the result of different conceptions of causality that define certain ways of interpreting reality and that generate specific forms of medical intervention. Cf. Georges Canguillen, *O normal e o patológico* (Rio de Janeiro: Editora Forense Universitária, 2009); Maria Amélia de Campos Oliveira and Emiko Yoshikawa Egry, "A historicidade das teorias interpretativas do processo saúde-doença", *Revista da Escola de Enfermagem da USP* 34(1) (2000): 9-15; Rita Barradas Barata, "Causalidade e epidemiologia", *História, Ciências, Saúde* 4(1) (1997): 31-49.

[5] See Harold G. Koenig, "Religion and Medicine I: Historical Background and Reasons for Separation", *The International Journal of Psychiatry in Medicine* 30(4) (2000): 385-398; Gary B. Ferngren, "Medicine and Religion: a historical Perspective", in Mark R. Cobb, Christina M. Puchalski and Bruce Rumbold (eds), *Oxford Textbook of Spirituality in Healthcare* (Oxford: Oxford University Press, 2012): 3-10; Darrel W. Amundsen and Gary B. Ferngren, "Medicine", in Gary B. Ferngren (ed), *The History of Science and Religion in the Western Tradition: An Encyclopedia* (New York: Garlando, 2000): 556-562; and Gary B. Ferngren, *Medicine and Health Care in Early Christianity* (Baltimore: John Hopkins University Press, 2009).

illnesses, creating and administering appropriate therapies and taking the necessary supplies from nature (natural remedies, food, et cetera).[6]

Thus, we intend to examine the relationship between religion, nature and health based on the contributions of two women at two different times in the Middle Ages. This approach is useful to identify the interweaving of the three theses that guide the focus of this article: a) The process of distancing between religion and health is relationally interwoven with the social construction process of the mechanisms that restrict the participation of women in medieval society.[7] b) In the two cases examined in the article, the women, through their resistance and resilience, were able to find gaps to develop and affirm their knowledge and skills, especially with regard to health,[8] in close connection with Christian spirituality. Indirectly, this reflection will make it possible to question the idea that, in the Middle Ages, Christianity as a whole represented a setback by attributing religious causes to illness and focusing on salvation more than on therapy.[9] c) The solutions developed by the women in the cases examined in the article, by reconciling religion, health, nature and Christian spirituality, represent significant contributions to contemporary eco-diakonia.

Two Singular Women in the Middle Ages

Although born four centuries apart, Hildegard von Bingen (1098-1179) and Catherine von Bora (1499-1552) had something in common. Both were daughters of the German-speaking rural lower nobility and confronted the social structure that assigned medieval women a subordinate role in society.

Strongly restricted to the roles they could play in the complex game of family institutions (from biological reproduction, through food and medical care, to economic reproduction), women never allowed themselves to be completely subjugated: "However, without being denied, this subordination often had to be justified, explained, in short, discussed. It was not at all a peaceful reality."[10]

Referred by their families to the religious life, Hildegard von Bingen and Catherine von Bora received a good formation in the Benedictine order. This aspect is not irrelevant. The rule of this order had some significant characteristics: a) it established, through the motto *ora et labora*, an adequate balance between work (cultivation of the land and study were considered work) and spiritual activities; b) it gave importance

[6] William L. Minkowski, "Women Healers of the Middle Ages: Selected Aspects of Their History", *American Journal of Public Health* 82(2) (1992): 288-295; Monica Green, "Women's Medical Practice and Health Care in Medieval Europe", *Signs* 14(2) (1989): 434-473; Montserrat Cabré, "Women or Healers? Household Practices and the Categories of Health Care in Late Medieval Iberia", *Bulletin of the History of Medicine* 82(1) (2008): 18-51.

[7] Paula M. Rieder, "The Uses and Misuses of Misogyny: A Critical Historiography of the Language of Medieval Women's Oppression", *Historical Reflections* 38(1) (2012): 1-18.

[8] We find this resistance in other women of the Middle Ages. The case of Trotula de Rugiero is often cited. Trotula was initially thought to be the name of a twelfth-century woman who widely practiced medicine and wrote important works. Trotula, however, is the name of a work that circulated in the twelfth century and that collected three important works on medicine, focused on women's health and that, quite possibly, were written by women from the city of Salerno, in the south of Italy. It has been reported that a significant group of women were engaged in obstetric practices in this region. Among them was a woman named Trota, about whom we know nothing and who probably wrote the second text of the mentioned work (*De curis mulierum* – On the cure of women), among other works, and whose medical practice was not limited to obstetrics. Monica Green, *The Trotula: A medieval compendium of women's medicine* (Philadelphia: University of Pennsylvania, 2001): 1-69.

[9] Oliveira and Egry, "A historicidade das teorias", 10; Sevalho, "Uma Abordagem Histórica", 353-354; Backes, *et al.*, "Conceitos da saúde," 113; Porter, *Health, Civilization and the State,* 42-44. Of course, it is not a question of completely discarding the cultural representations that have been established between illness and religion (sin).

[10] Christiane Klapisch-Zuber, "A mulher e a família", in Jacques Le Goff (ed), *O homem medieval* (Lisbon: Presença, 1989): 208.

to education (reading and writing in Latin); and c) it granted autonomy to the abbeys. Saint Benedict proposed a moderation of ascetic life, prescribing adequate rest and sufficient food.

In addition, dedication to work, beyond promoting discipline and fighting idleness, generated wealth for the order, administrative knowledge for the people involved and brought the Benedictine order closer to the people, making the abbeys provide an important social service by welcoming the poor, sick, crippled and afflicted.[11] Many of the characteristic elements of the order were well outlined in the personalities of these two extraordinary women.

In addition to their good intellectual training and their ability to read and write in the current language, Latin, both showed great administrative acuity. It should also be noted that the peculiar ethos of the Benedictine order, which combined a spiritual life, a good intellectual education, and the discipline derived from intense manual labour, engendered a spirit of leadership, which gave the church many popes and notables, such as Hildegard von Bingen and Catherine von Bora.

Thus, both found, in institutions of the same church, which in part promoted the legitimising discourse of the subordination of the "feminine condition", the space and the instruments that allowed them to break the limits of the imposed borders. Circulating along the border between acceptance and persecution, both knew how to demand respect and recognition. Obviously, this was not without conflict. A clear indication of this is the fact that both have remained forgotten for so long.

Another aspect of the medieval context that indicates the unique position of the two nuns concerns healthcare. At a time when it was believed that disease was caused by agents external to the body, medical care mixed the use of amulets, filters and exorcisms. Both Hildegard von Bingen and Catherine von Bora developed an intense phytotherapeutic practice and also made use of other well-known therapies of the time. Following the common practice of the order to which they belonged, they cared for people in need, especially the sick.

It should be noted, however, that phytotherapeutic practices, as well as the various therapies based on natural nutrition, represented one of the most inspiring aspects of the contributions of these two women. It is important to bear in mind that, in the medical practice and theory of Hildegard von Bingen, nature is not a mere ingredient or a simple resource, but rather, it is also about understanding health and nature as elements energised by spirituality.

Hildegard von Bingen, the Sibyl of the Rhine – Of the Heavenly and the Earthly: Her Integral Theology

Considering her work as a whole, it is evident that Hildegard von Bingen was responsible for significant theological work. Hildegard von Bingen did not limit herself to the mere transmission of mystical visions; after the exposition of her visions, she carried out an exegetical work on them, ordering them and relating them to themes of theology. In this case, the mystical experience did not mean the elision of Hildegard's subjectivity. In a sense, the way Hildegard elaborated her "awakened" visions brings her closer to the prophetic tradition.[12]

[11] "The Rule of the Order of Benedictine monks – one of the first in the West – in addition to regulating the daily life of monks and nuns, was concerned with health and the appearance of diseases. The result of this concern was the organisation of a system of medical assistance in the monasteries, with infirmaries for the monks (*infirmarium*), for the rich and noble (*domus hospitum*) and for the poor and pilgrims (*hospitale pauperum*), with the reproduction of the social order also existing outside the monasteries. They also had cells for doctors, the seriously ill, baths, a pharmacy, and a garden with medicinal herbs." Cybele Crossetti de Almeida, "Do mosteiro à universidade: considerações sobre uma história social da medicina na Idade Média", *Aedos* 2(2) (2009): 39.

[12] Due to her peculiar way of dealing with visions, Hildegard von Bingen was not, for some researchers on the subject, a mystic in the classical sense. She did not experience absences of consciousness when she had her "visions". She even had some restrictions regarding this kind of mystical experience, because she feared that this

Hildegard von Bingen elaborated a theology that, to use a popular expression, "spoke of heaven and earth", with the goal of their unification. Her allegorical image of the universe as a "cosmic egg," which appears in the third vision of the first part of her book, *Know the Ways of the Lord* (*Scivias*), sums up this understanding that runs through all of her theology.[13] In this "cosmic egg", the human being is a microcosm related to the macrocosm.[14] In turn, the central idea of her Book of Divine Works is to accentuate that profound unity of creation. Creation, seen in this way, is a reflection of the glory and love of God. In the human being, we find, in one way or another, a summary of the cosmic totality.

God made the elements of the world, and these elements are in the human being and the human being is elaborated by them. They are fire, air, earth and water. These four elements are intricately intertwined and linked together in such a way that none can be separated from the other, and thus they are at the same time contained in what is called the firmament.[15]

From this idea of an intricate unity between the human microcosm and the macrocosm of the universe, Hildegard von Bingen draws even deeper consequences. Since the totality is reflected in the human being, all changes in the macrocosm influence the human being and vice versa.[16] Thus, the nature of human life finds its explanation in the connection with the cosmos, which indicates that her theology significantly expands the relationships between the spiritual and physical dimensions.

The Theological Notion of "*Viriditas*"

The intimate and deep relationship between the microcosm and the macrocosm presupposes a delicate balance between the conduct of spiritual life and the correct relationship with everything that is arranged in earthly life. For von Bingen, events and physical suffering have a deep relationship with the imbalances of the soul for staying in harmony with the divine precepts, which also meant staying in harmony with the natural world. Breaking balanced relationships with nature leads to suffering and disease.

Disease, according to this conception, would be the result of an imbalance in the cosmic harmony that runs through the micro and macrocosms. Health was the "regeneration" of the "sources of life".[17]

unconsciousness would be an occasion for demonic forces to take possession of her person. However, she knew how to respect and encourage the nun Elisabeth von Schönau who, precisely, experienced these absences of conscience in her visions. See Maria Nogueira and Ana R. Cabral de Vasconcelos, "Hildegard von Bingen e Elisabeth von Schönau: a correspondência (Cartas 201-201r) entre duas místicas visionárias do século XII", *Trilhas Filosóficas* 13(1) (2020): 40-42.

[13] The image of the "cosmic egg", presented in the book *Know the Ways of the Lord* (*Scivias*), is now described in *The Book of Divine Works* as a "wheel". See Hildegarda de Bingen, *El libro de las obras divinas* (Madrid: Hildegardiana, 2013): 45, [Available at: http://www.hildegardiana.es/5pdf/libro_obras_divinas.pdf], [Last accessed: 23rd March 2022].

[14] Mark Atherton (ed), *Hildegard von Bingen: Selected Writings* (London: Penguin Books, 2001): 201.

[15] Hildegarda de Bingen, *Libro de las causas y remedios de las enfermedades* (Madrid: Hildegardiana, 2013): 28 (I,7), [Available at: http://www.hildegardiana.es/5pdf/causas_y_remedios.pdf], [Last accessed: 23rd March 2022]. It should be noted that, in this book, the issues of reproduction and human sexuality occupy a third of the content. Hildegard's language is direct, unusual for her time, and she describes in a very plastic way the sexual encounter between the man and the woman, establishing the equality between both and emphasising the importance of pleasure. Bingen, *Libro de Las Causas*, 55, 72-73, 89.

[16] In a certain way, in the thought of Hildegard von Bingen, it is possible to identify significant signs of a systemic conception such as the one that we find contemporaneously exposed, see for example, in Edgar Morin, *Introducción al pensamento complejo* (Barcelona: Gedisa, 1998).

[17] Albrecht Classen, "Introduction", in Albrecht Classen and Marilyn Sandidge (eds), *Mental Health, Spirituality, and Religion in the Middle Ages and Early Modern Age* (Berlín: Walter de Gruyter, 2014): 58.

In the dynamics of this balance, the notion of "*viriditas*" is present, a frequent theological concept in the work of Hildegard von Bingen.[18] The Latin term simply means "greenness or greenery", but also has the meaning of vigour. For Hildegard, it is not about the colour, but about the profound sense that "greenness" indicates a peculiar quality of that which is alive: the vigour or, more exactly, the inner force or the active principle that gives life or energy to plants, animals and humans. It is, therefore, a vital force that, flowing from God to the totality of creation, allows it to grow, mature, remain alive and reach the full actualisation of its potentialities.[19]

According to this approach, a single principle animates and sustains everything that exists. Its absence indicates a state of degradation of matter.[20] For Hildegard von Bingen, the medical procedures she prescribed, ranging from prevention – based on careful dietary prescriptions – to the administration of herbal therapies, were intended to activate and maintain *viriditas*. These procedures were not dissociated from Christian spirituality.

As Marder rightly observed, Hildegard von Bingen combines in her poetic language analogical and non-analogical references to *viriditas*, complicating the perception of this notion. This author defines her proposal as a psycho-physio-theology, in which the Holy Spirit – the active force of *viriditas* – functions as a "root shared by all creatures," being also their source of sustenance.[21]

Catherine von Bora – Homemade Medicine

The young nun Catherine von Bora had come to acquire a great knowledge about herbs and plants. She was in charge of taking care of the sick nuns and preparing the medicines in the monastery.

Once wife of Martin Luther, Catherine had a significant "home pharmacy" in her house, with medicines that she herself prepared. These were herbal preparations, teas, ointments for wounds and rheumatic pain, and for internal diseases. In addition, she had knowledge of massage techniques. Her knowledge was not only intended for her house and her family, but also for other people who needed it. Catherine prepared remedies and herbs to help Luther with his many physical and psychological ailments. She had a special talent for organising a diet, growing herbs, preparing poultices and giving massages.[22]

The couple's house, which Catherine turned into a pension, also welcomed people who needed special care. There, Catherine cared for the sick in times of plague, even remaining in the city when most of the population had fled.[23]

Knowledge about herbs and the use of plants was passed down among women from generation to generation. Was this a practice also among convents? Did Catherine know Hildegard's recipes and

[18] Hanna Strack, "Viriditas bei Hildegard von Bingen und ihre Bedeutung für eine Theologie des Blühens", *Hanna Strack Website,* [Available at: https://www.hanna-strack.de/user_files/test_1303107939_1778.pdf], [Last accessed: 23rd March 2022]. The author highlights the centrality of this notion in the thought of Hildegard von Bingen. The concept has some antecedents in theology, but finds a special parallel in its use by Gregory the Great (540-604) in his commentary on Job. Jeannette DiBernardo Jones, "A Theological Interpretation of *Viriditas* in Hildegard of Bingen and Gregory the Great", *Portfolio of the Department of Musicology and Ethnomusicology* 1 (2012), [Available at: https://www.bu.edu/pdme/jeannette-jones/], [Last accessed: 23rd March 2022].

[19] Barbara Newman, *Sister of Wisdom. St. Hildegard's Theology of the Feminine* (Berkeley, CA: University of California Press, 1987): 102; Dorothy Tran, *The Role of Womanhood in St. Hildegard's Medical Practices* (Waco, TX: Baylor University, 2019): 21.

[20] Bingen, *El libro de las obras*, 53, 126; Hildergarda de Bingen, *Libro de los Méritos de la Vida* (Madrid: Hildegardiana, 2014): 121, [Available at: http://www.hildegardiana.es/5pdf/libro_meritos_de_la_vida.pdf], [Last accessed: 23rd March 2022].

[21] Michael Marder, "Saint Hildegard's Vegetal Psycho-Physio-Theology", *Religions* 9(11) (2018): 2-3, [Available at: https://www.mdpi.com/2077-1444/9/11/353/htm], [Last accessed: 23rd March 2022].

[22] Roland H. Bainton, *Women of the Reformation in Germany and Italy* (Boston: Beacon, 1974): 29.

[23] Heloisa Gralow Dalferth, *Katharina von Bora: uma biografia* (Blumenau: Otto Kuhr, 2014): 44.

recommendations and did she put them into practice? These are important questions for further investigation.

Action

The results of the investigations carried out in this regard suggest that Catherine would not have written any theological treatise, hymn, text or prayer. The letters that she wrote to Luther or to other people have been lost. However, this should in no way be interpreted as an absence from theological debates. In a letter dated 4th October 1529, Luther shares with her the discussion surrounding the understanding of the Lord's Supper.[24] If Catherine did not participate in the theological conversations, her husband would be unlikely to waste his time describing the details of the disputes with other theologians.

Researchers agree, instead, that Catherine had a unique "theological" involvement in the Reformation movement:

> The "Black Cloister," an abandoned Augustinian monastery Katharina renovated [...] was her seminary and her church. That was where she "ruled" the large "congregation" that regularly occupied all of her 40 rooms and where she hosted meals for 30-40 on a regular basis and often banquets for as many as 120 people.[25]

Conclusion

As announced, this study has a very specific scope: it examines the contribution of two women to the topic of the relationship between religion (spirituality) and health and their connections with nature (creation) at different times in the Middle Ages.

Obviously, being an examination of the lives of two people, it is not possible to make generalisations. However, it has been possible to follow, from the biographies studied, the path reserved for women in the Middle Ages. It can be said that the two women's lives are exemplary in two senses: on the one hand, they confirm that the social role of women was very limited; on the other, they inform us that some women managed to overcome these limitations and trace alternative paths, creating important gaps in the rigid structure of medieval society.

It is possible, therefore, to infer that these women broke the initial delimitation of women's work in the area of health, and thus advanced towards other areas of medical knowledge, producing important theoretical and practical knowledge. It is also possible to conclude that they did theology in a singular register and that they were capable of maintaining the unity of the fields of knowledge that the growing rationalisation made an effort to separate.[26]

The resources obtained through the analysis of the works of the two women studied suggest that a specific gender sensitivity provided the opportunity for a peculiar perception of the relationship between the sacred, nature and human health. This sensitivity thus endorses the possible unification of two different fields of knowledge (health and religion), organising themselves around the human body.

---

[24] Dalferth, *Katharina von Bora*, 62-63.

[25] Kirsi Stjerna, *Women and the Reformation* (Malden: Blackwell, 2009): 61.

[26] Some of that historical resistance persists today in the midwives and medicine-women of the interior of Brazil. In addition to the expressed gender question, in Brazil these practices intersect with the racial question and with popular religiosity, adding more elements to the complex mosaic of connections between religion, gender and health. Cf. Marisete T. Hoffmann-Horochovski, "Velhas benzedeiras", *Mediações – Revista de Ciências Sociais* 17(2) (2012): 126-140; Iraci de Carvalho Barroso, "Os saberes de parteiras tradicionais e o ofício de partejar em domícilio nas áreas rurais", *PRACS: Revista Eletrônica de Humanidades do Curso de Ciências Sociais da UNIFAP* 2(2) (2009), [Available at: https://periodicos.unifap.br/index.php/pracs/article/view/34], [Last accessed: 23rd March 2022]; Dulce Santoro Mendes and Claudio São Thiago Cavas, "Benzedeiras e benzedeiros quilombolas – construindo identidades culturais", *Interações* 19(1) (2018): 3-14.

It can be inferred, in a preliminary way, that the body is theologised in such a way that, first, the deconstruction of a theology that morally associates the evils of the body as a punishment related to a sin takes place. After this deconstruction, the next movement allows us to reread the body and its ills in a new theological register. From this perspective, the corporeal and the spiritual come together in such a way that each of the two dimensions affects the other, generating an imbalance that results in the loss of "freshness", of vital energy and, to use Hildegard von Bingen's terminology, of viriditas. Thus, spiritual life, organic life, and inorganic life form a whole that can be reintegrated through the correct combination of foods, herbs, and therapies as inseparable aspects of the spiritual experience.

Being a knowledge and a practice that has flourished in Catholic and Protestant spheres, it also implies an integral spirituality with great ecumenical potential. Starting from the centrality that nature, as creation, occupies in the theological understanding and the medical-diaconal practice of both women, the potentiality gains strength here of a diakonia that does not take the care of nature as a task, but instead assumes it as the centre of actions that allow the person to rediscover the balance of health as part of their spiritual experience.[27]

Indirectly, these conclusions, albeit partial, allow us to suggest that these and other medieval theologians who dealt with theology and health make possible a new reading of the way in which Christianity thematised, at least in part, the relationship between disease and health, religion (spirituality) and nature (creation). Perhaps, it can also be said that the approach proposed by these theologians would also allow a reinterpretation of the relationship between health and disease beyond the notion of causality present in current epidemiological approaches. This opens a new front that could imply the redefinition or representation of what health is.[28] Diakonia finds within this approach the possibility of integrating the confrontation of all the ills that affect the health of people, especially the most vulnerable, within the framework of a Christian spirituality that takes the relationship with nature (creation) as a means of continuous worship, that of a prophetic, liberating and reconciling eco-diakonia of the relationship between the genders and with the totality of creation.

Suggestions for Further Reading

Cuyatti, Patricia and Valério G. Schaper. *Diakonia – The Transformation into the Hands of God.* Geneva: LWF, 2017.

Dalferth, Heloisa Gralow. "Katharina von Bora", in Claudete Beise Ulrich and Heloisa Gralow Dalferth, Eds. *Mulheres no movimento da Reforma.* San Leopoldo: Sinodal, 2017: 11-36.

Elst, D. Ver. "A powerful encounter: the relation between diaconia and spirituality". *Acta Theologica* 40(2) (2020): 342-359.

Furst, Lilian R., Ed. *Women Healers and Physicians: Climbing a Long Hill.* Lexington, KY: The University Press of Kentucky, 1999.

Nordstokke, Kjell. *Liberating Diakonia.* Trondheim: Tapir Akademisk Forlag, 2011.

World Council of Churches, *Ecumenical Diakonia* (Doc. No. 17 App). Bossey: World Council of Churches, 2017. [Available at: https://kirken.no/globalassets/kirken.no/smm/dokumenter/2019/wcc-ecumenical-diakonia-study-document.pdf], [Last accessed: 23rd March 2022].

---

[27] Ninna Erdgardh and Erik Lundströn, "The gender order of prophetic diaconia", *Diaconia* 8(1) (2017): 38-50, [Available at: https://www.vr-elibrary.de/doi/10.13109/diac.2017.8.1.38], [Last accessed: 23rd March 2022].

[28] Canguillen, *O normal*, 85-91; Barata, "Causalidade"; Oliveira y Egry, "A historicidade das teorias."

29. The Anthropocene in Salvation History

Lucio Florio[1]

Biogenesis Leading to the Anthropocene

A situation of profound modification of the biosphere began to occur due to human activity enhanced by technology, starting in full force with the Industrial Revolution. The transformation has taken on such dimensions that, from geology, this period has been named "Anthropocene",[2] explicitly admitting the emergence of a new geological era. This new stage of the planet consists of a period of alteration of the global system of structural interrelationships of the Earth by the work of *Homo sapiens*. The main elements that this alteration includes are: climatic modification; the massive loss of biodiversity – the sixth massive extinction of species;[3] the contamination of the land, sea and air; the erosion and degradation of soils and the radical transformation of ecosystems. After more than 3 billion years, the biosphere is subjected to a situation of extreme fragility. Paradoxically, the origin of such a situation is found in one of the beings that have appeared through the same evolutionary process: *Homo sapiens*.

The awareness that we are part of an evolutionary history of life has been consolidated almost at the same time that we are perceiving the dimensions of an ecological crisis that seriously threatens that history. With the knowledge of the life's past emerges a prospective vision of its possible end. On the one hand, since the eighteenth century and, especially, since the second part of the nineteenth century, the awareness that we are part of a common life history that dates back around 3.5 billion years has been consolidated. The idea of a common and evolutionary history of species and of the biosphere as a whole constitutes knowledge acquired by the scientific community.[4] Also, the position of the human being is clearly established within an evolutionary paradigm, considering it as one more link in the chain of evolutionary interaction, as a small point in the phylogenetic tree.[5] On the other hand, almost simultaneously with evolutionary perception, it has become evident that a critical moment in the evolutionary process has been reached. Indeed, in the same period in which the human being perceives him or herself as part of a complex and long history of the biosphere, they also know that they have entered a destructive stage of it. If the well-known graphic of the 24-hour clock is used to symbolise the history of the biosphere, it would be seen that the human being has only appeared in the last minutes and that in the last seconds (since the nineteenth century) there has been a great acceleration in the process of altering the planet, which heralds a highly troublesome second day.

---

[1] Lucio Florio is a Doctor in Dogmatic Theology from the Faculty of Theology of the Pontificia Universidad Católica Argentina (UCA). He is a researcher and teacher at the Faculty of Philosophy and Letters and at the Faculty of Theology of the UCA. He chairs the Foundation "Dialogue between Science and Religion" (DECyR) and the journal *Quaerentibus: Teología y Ciencia* (www.quaerentibus.org). He is a member of the International Society for Science and Religion (ISSR), the International Research Network for the Study of Science & Belief in Society (INSBS) and the Argentine Society of Theology (SAT). He is a Catholic priest, and collaborates in parishes of the City of La Plata, Buenos Aires, Argentina. lflorio.18@gmail.com.

[2] P. J. Crutzen and E.F. Stoermer, "The 'Anthropocene'", *Global Change Newsletter* 41 (2000): 17-18.

[3] Gerardo Ceballos, Paul R. Ehrlich, Anghony D. Barnosky, *et al.*, "Accelerated Modern Human-Induced Species Losses: Entering the Sixth Mass Extinction", *Science Advances* 1(5) (2015), [Available at: http://advances.sciencemag.org/content/1/5/e1400253], [Last accessed: 24th March 2022].

[4] See Douglas Futuyma, *Evolution* (Sunderland: Sinauer, 2010); see also the more popularly oriented work of Edward Larson. *Evolution* (New York: Modern Library, 2004).

[5] For an analysis of the theological implications of the phylogenetic tree, see Lucio Florio, "The Tree of Life: Philosophical and Theological Considerations", *Studia Aloisiana* 4(1) (2013): 15-27, [Available at: https://www.academia.edu/36099030/Lucio_Florio_The_Tree_of_life], [Last accessed: 24th March 2022].

A Theology that Incorporates Evolution and Ecological Crisis

This crossroads for the evolution of life needs to be reflected on by theology in an integrated way. Although the study of biological evolution and ecology has already become widespread in the scientific field,[6] it is not often that both evolutionary and threatened life are jointly addressed in the theological arena. On the contrary, there is a separate treatment: on the one hand, there is an important development on the theology of evolution; and, on the other hand, there is a growing production on ecotheology or ecological theology.[7] However, the joint approach, that is, of a theology of the evolutionary biosphere in crisis phase, is rare.

Indeed, the theology of an evolutionary creation is gradually entering the contents of the theology of creation in a good proportion of Christian theological centres. The discussion with evolutionary theories is part of a preparatory or historical step, assuming the evolutionary fact as something evident from the point of view of scientific rationality. This does not mean ignoring the existence of some theological centres that maintain a firm creationism. Their reasons may be that either they continue with a literal hermeneutic of the biblical texts, or they are in a critical position against haphazard and materialistic forms of neo-Darwinism that exclude any possibility of dialogue with theology. However, with these exceptions, most of the academic theology of the historical churches has incorporated the evolutionary perspective as part of the data contributed by scientific reason to think about revelation. For this reason, theology thinks of creation in the terms in which the astrophysical and biological sciences describe the history of the cosmos and the biosphere. But in parallel, theology addresses the ecological issue. This work forms the new discipline of *ecotheology*.

Now, the task of ecological theology is generally carried out in an anachronistic way, that is, without reference to the history of the life of which it is its most recent act. However, the biosphere has a history of which the Anthropocene is only one phase. For this reason, it is necessary to analyse biogenesis as a whole, also from a theological point of view. In other words, it is necessary to think theologically about the mystery of life as a long history of billions of years that is in a critical phase, the product of the excessive action of one of the species that appeared during the process. Indeed, *Homo Sapiens* is one more species, identifiable phylogenetically and taxonomically. However, human beings are also, for the biblical view, a privileged subject in the process. For this reason, the history of life is understood not only as creation but also as saving history. The human being is, in fact, image and likeness, recipient of the covenant, as well as the species in one of whose organisms the Son of God was incarnated. For this reason, for theology, biogenesis and noogenesis[8] qualitatively determine the history of salvation.

Ecotheology, therefore, must integrate the theology of evolution into its discourse. For this reason, the scientific disciplines on which it must be supported are evolutionary biology and ecology. Naturally, the disciplines involved need a philosophy that leads them to a meta-scientific level, in order to be suitable for a theological understanding. For this reason, a philosophy of biology and ecology act as a critical assumption of such ecotheological reflection. The epistemological level in which ecotheology is inscribed is that of an understanding of the created reality called "life", whose structure and form of manifestation in time are studied by evolutionary biology and, in its face of interrelated phenomenon, by the ecology. As

---

[6] In the abovementioned guide of Futuyma there is a point on environment and conservation ("Environment and conservation", in *Evolution*, 628-629) in which reference is made to the use of phylogenetic information, evolutionary biogeography and genetic methods to collaborate in conservation efforts. Nonetheless, there are publications explicitly aimed at relating both fields of study (e.g., the open access journal *Ecology and Evolution*, available at: https://onlinelibrary.wiley.com/journal/20457758).

[7] The Encyclical Letter *Laudato Si'* of Pope Francis gathers a good part of the theological and pastoral movement concerning environmental problems in a synthesis guided by the idea of a "common home" that the human being must take care of (Vatican City: Editorial Vaticana, 2015).

[8] Noogenesis is seen as the fourth stage of evolution, in which reflective thought (the noosphere) enters the world, along with human beings.

such, it is collected by the theological instance that is, at its core, an intellection of such a reality from the perspective of faith.

Theology of the Evolutionary Biosphere

The theories about a biological evolution broadened the framework of understanding life and the human. If, at some point, it was thought that the acceptance of evolution could lead to a decrease in the theological assessment of the human condition, today it is thought of in a different way. Many theologians consider that a process of evolution – haphazard in its mechanisms, but with a certain logical structure rooted in its genetic heritage – produced the human creature. This, from the angle of revelation, appears as the recipient of the covenant and as the subject of the incarnation. In other words, the cosmic and biological process came together in the man Jesus of Nazareth. This confluence was not the product of a coldly designed plan and applied through a mechanistic finalist process. On the contrary, it was a relatively open project, through a certain flexibility at once random and logical of life, created remotely in the initial Big Bang and emerged a few billions of years ago on planet Earth, until now the only one known with a biosphere. In such a process, *Homo sapiens* appeared in which the *Logos* was made present.

The theological vision of life, based on biblical revelation, speaks of life from the divine perspective using the knowledge of the time in which the texts were written. According to the Old Testament perspective, life is created, sustained, animated by the spirit of God, manifesting something of the splendour of its creator. God appears as the creator, through whose word a work was designed and carried out, a work of which no one knows its hidden places or origins (Job 28-29). But God is also the one who is always coming and, furthermore, who will have to root out life itself as a whole. For the New Testament, on the other hand, life acquires greater density, since through the incarnation and Easter not only the Son is integrated into the current of the biosphere, but he effectively provokes the cosmic and vital novelty to which the Old Testament alluded. Specifically, it is the Holy Spirit, who appears as the generator of the new reality of a life recreated from the paschal mystery. For its part, the Book of Revelation presents all living beings before the Lamb, symbol of the *Logos* made flesh, at the end of his biological and human cycle (Rev. 7:9-17).

The entire biblical vision is described with an intuitive idea of life. Obviously, there is no experimental or scientific analysis of the phenomenon, but rather a perception – deep and at times full of admiration – of a reality of which one is a part and which overflows in innumerable beings and forms. Contemporary science, although stammering when defining what exactly life is,[9] also offers an astonishing description of the plurality of beings and their history. In particular, the evolutionary explanation of life – without which, everything in biology would be meaningless[10] – makes it possible to discover God's creative and recreative action from an absolutely wonderful prism. We are part of the history of life, and the *Logos'* very self collects and prolongs that evolutionary historicity. According to the comprehensive picture prepared by Pierre Teilhard de Chardin, christogenesis would have been inserted in the vastness of the processes of cosmogenesis, biogenesis and noogenesis.[11]

---

[9] See Rafael Vicuña, "La complejidad molecular de la vida", in Sociedad Argentina de Teología (ed), *Discursos científicos y discursos teológicos. Creer en el contexto de los nuevos saberes* (Buenos Aires: Ágape, 2013): 55-78.
[10] Theodosius Dobzhansky, "Nothing in Biology Makes Sense Except in the Light of Evolution", *The American Biology Teacher* 35(3) (1973): 125-129. See Lucio Florio, "'En biología nada tiene sentido sino a la luz de la evolución'. Incorporación teológica de este principio biológico", *Revista de Teología* 52(116) (April 2015): 9-27.
[11] See Ignacio Nuñez de Castro, *Teilhard de Chardin: el hombre de Ciencia y el hombre de Fe* (Puebla: Cuadernos de Fe y Cultura, 2006): 8-14.

The *Logos* Became Biosphere

The statement in John 1:14a, that "the Word became flesh", has produced innumerable interpretations and theories over the past two millennia. For now, the expression means that the eternal Logos entered into creation, travelling the distance from divine to creaturely reality. For this reason, it can be said, that the Word was incorporated into the history of the matter and the life of the universe and planet Earth. The eternal Word was inserted into the same process that unifies the whole universe. In the man Jesus of Nazareth, he assumed the chemical elements originated in the Big Bang and discriminated during the process of composition of the stars. His body, started at the biological origin of the first Adam (Lk. 3:22-28), comes from the clay of the universe: it is "stardust", made of matter forged in the heat of stellar foci.

Furthermore, Jesus of Nazareth is, as a living being, a product of biogenesis. For this reason, the expression of the Johannine prologue could be translated as: "the Word became life". It can also be said that through his body runs the genome of "Adam", the first man to appear in an indecipherable instant less than a million years ago, probably somewhere in East Africa. His genetic heritage depends on that stream of humanity that has reached Mary and, through her, even himself. Moreover, his living being is part of an extremely complex flow of life, in a phylogenetic history that goes back millions of years. Jesus is therefore part of the same evolutionary history of the biosphere.

The christological claims of the history of Christianity can be thought of in a biotheological perspective.[12] Thus, for example, the affirmation of the Council of Chalcedon (451) on the two natures of Christ, which indicates that Jesus of Nazareth is truly human and God (DS 302)[13] acquires a greater density of meaning when the human is thought of in an evolutionary key. That is, when the human condition of Christ is understood not as a reality that appeared in the very recent past, prepared almost ad hoc for the incarnation, but as a living entity, the product of millions of years of history and intertwined with a network of beings who share with it their condition as living beings. In such a vision, it makes sense to break down the affirmation of the incarnation in this way: *the Logos became life, that is, biosphere, genomic structure, predator and prey, breathing, instinctive, sensory, mammal, hominid, part of an ecosystem, neuronal being, empathetic, gregarious, etc.*[14]

Theology of the Anthropocene: A Phase of Salvation History

The appearance of the human being meant little from the phylogenetic aspect: only the emergence of one more species among many others, in a certain way irrelevant in planetary history.[15] However, from the ontological dimension, its emergence implied the novelty of an unprecedented dimension in the biosphere: the noosphere,[16] the world of the human that includes culture. The expression "noosphere" highlights the positive connotations of the appearance of the human on the planet (socialisation, communication, art, etc.).

---

[12] Lucio Florio, "Life and Evolution: Why Theology Matters", in Luca Valera and Juan Carlos Castilla (eds), *Global Changes: Ethics, Politics and Environment in the Contemporary Technological World* (Cham, Switzerland: Springer, 2020): 131-138.

[13] This formula has been questioned for its lack of integration of the historicity of Jesus Christ, which would lead to the exclusion of the biological history of the man Jesus. However, a hermeneutic of the formula allows it to be considered in what it intended: to specify the double dimension of Christ and the unity without confusion of his natures. See Sergio Zañartu, "Reflexiones sobre la fórmula dogmática de Calcedonia", *Teología y Vida* 39 (1988): 155-184.

[14] Lucio Florio, *Teología de la vida en el contexto de la evolución y de la ecología* (Buenos Aires: Ágape, 2015): 20.

[15] This is how Teilhard de Chardin mentioned it, as an almost imperceptible appearance in its origins. See Gustave Martelet, *E se Teilhard dicesse il vero* (Milan: Jaca Book, 2007): 31.

[16] For a presentation of the bio-philosophical thought of Teilhard de Chardin, see Ignacio Nuñez de Castro, "The Bio-Philosophy of Teilhard de Chardin", in H. Del Riego (ed), *God Seen by Science: Anthropic Evolution of the Universe* (Madrid: Universidad Pontificia de Comillas, 2008): 99-126.

Instead, the term "Anthropocene" highlights the disturbing dimension of anthropic activity in the evolutionary course of the biosphere.[17] If the expression noosphere is optimistic, Anthropocene is, to say the least, dramatic. The Anthropocene detects that the phenomenon of globalisation has caused a profound deterioration for all living beings. It is not an insignificant fact that the animals that are having the best fortune in this anthropic empire are the domestic ones, that is, those integrated into the field of relations of the *Homo sapiens* species.[18]

The biosphere, therefore, experiences a phase of planetary domination by one of the many species in its phylogenetic history, characterised by massive destructive activity of Homo sapiens. This demands, as has been pointed out, an integrally evolutionary and ecological thinking of the period of the planet's history.[19] Theology can provide a fruitful perspective for other disciplines. For biblical revelation, God has manifested Godself in a history of the universe, of life and of the human species.[20] This is the reason why the biosphere, with its long history, must be included within the history of salvation.

Under this perspective, the theological category of salvation history can be thought of as part of a cosmic and biological history, of which the Anthropocene would represent its last link.[21] The timeline is as follows: *history of the universe – history of the biosphere – human history – history of salvation.*[22] These stages configure the conceptual framework to carry out a theological approach to the biosphere in its current phase, characterised by the modification of its physical, chemical and biological systems. The unprecedented situation of the biosphere, situated in the context of an evolutionary creation centred on the Covenant, demands a multidimensional reading that integrates the perspectives of diverse disciplines. Indeed, *Homo sapiens*, which appeared after a long evolutionary history, is the same "Adam" symbolically described in Genesis as the image and likeness of God, and the species in which the Logos was incarnated and in whom the Holy Spirit inhabits and acts. It is the same human being – created, evolved, redeemed and destined for participation in divine life – which is causing the destruction of their own habitat, the biosphere, itself the subject of a long and complex evolutionary history.

As part of the substantiation of this type of approach, it must be added that only a theological reception of the environmental crisis based on an evolutionary theology of creation allows us to retake the link between creation and soteriology, intrinsic to biblical texts. Indeed, just as biblical faith in creation arose in close connection with faith in the saving God, an ecological theology would remain incomplete without a link to soteriology.[23] Ultimately, God's creative project is that of a creation which transforms not only of the human being but of the universe as a whole. The ecological crisis is presented as a critical moment of

[17] See Richard Monastersky, "Anthropocene: The Human Age", *Nature* 519 (2015): 144-147, [Available at: https://www.nature.com/articles/519144a], [Last accessed: 24th March 2022].

[18] See Richard Francis, *Addomesticati. L'insolita evoluzione degli animali che vivono accanto all'uomo* (Torino: Bollati Boringhieri, 2016): 14.

[19] See José R. Dadon, "Los modelos científicos sobre el origen de la vida y sus consecuencias ambientales", *Quaerentibus. Teología y Ciencias* 7 (2016): 121-126, [Available at: http://quaerentibus.org/assets/q07_los-modelos-cient%C3%ADficos....pdf], [Last accessed: 25th March 2022].

[20] See on the subject Jorge Papanicolau, *Cristología cósmica* (Buenos Aires: Epifanía, 2005). Also, E.M. Conradie (ed), *Creation and Salvation. Vol. 2: A Companion on Recent Theological Movements* (Münster: LIT, 2012).

[21] Although the concept of "history of salvation" has been subjected to numerous questions, it is still useful to refer to the historical continuity of the salvific project, regardless of the narrative fissures of biblical traditions. See Gerhard Lohfink, "La 'storia della salvezza'. Uno esempio di sfoggio del concetto di storia della salvezza negli ultimi decenni", in *Le nostre grandi parole* (Brescia: Paideia, 1986): 87-104.

[22] This type of schema is totally indebted to P. Teilhard de Chardin and his categories of cosmogenesis, biogenesis, noogenesis and cristogenesis. However, it is also connected with the exegesis of the 20th century that placed the first eleven chapters of Genesis as a prologue to the history of salvation, surpassing literal readings. In this way, the history of salvation is presented as beginning with the creation of the universe, regardless of the way it occurred.

[23] This is the perspective of the aforementioned volume, edited by Conradie, *Creation and Salvation.*

this design.[24] The human being, a central creature in the idea of biblical creation, emerges as a being endowed with the possibility of irreversible damage to its habitat, thus conditioning the final purpose of the salvific project. But, at the same time, the human being appears as an agent who can resume their place as an administrator and co-creator and guide the ecological process towards an instance of fullness, according to the New Testament perspective, which postulates the novelty of creation and of the human being renewed by the Holy Spirit.

The Christian thinkers of the first centuries coined the expression "economy" to designate the plan of God administered in history. The expression uses the root *oikos*, meaning house, just like the word "ecology". Although ecological concerns were not on the minds of these early Christian theologians, the unity between creation and recreation was (obviously, within the horizon of the worldview of their time).[25]

The saving economy is an attempt to put into words God's plan, which includes creation and redemption. Under this concept, the situation of ecological crisis can be integrated. Indeed, ecology describes the interrelationships of living beings with their environment. It is, therefore, a description of the part of creation that, in the current period, has entered a phase of crisis, produced by the free activity of human beings. For this reason, the ecological question constitutes a part of the dynamics of human and cosmic salvation. The ecological crisis appears then as a phase of the economy of salvation. In the language of H. U. von Balthasar, it would be one more act of the salvific action in the "theodrama";[26] in that of Teilhard de Chardin, a critical moment of the biogenesis and noogenesis within the framework of christogenesis.

Conclusion

The geological category Anthropocene describes a phase of the planet Earth, characterised by a massive intervention of *Homo sapiens* on its lithosphere, atmosphere, hydrosphere and biosphere. As such, it allows for framing the anthropocentric dimensions of the environmental crisis, while making it possible to see it in a historical perspective. For these reasons, this focus offers a platform of thought for ecological theology. Biblically rooted theology can incorporate into its vision of the "economy" or "salvation history" the new phase to which the history of the biosphere and of *Homo sapiens* itself has arrived. The latter, in addition to be one more living being, is a special dialogue partner of the God of revelation. As such, human beings are called to collaborate in the economy of salvation, which has known a long cosmic and biological history, and which is in a critical state, at least in the Earth's biosphere. The human theological mission seems to be intimately linked to a lucid and responsible collaboration with the Spirit that wants to make a new creation from the evolutionary biosphere.

Suggestions for Further Reading

Arnould, J. "Evolución y finalidad: Una invitación a reintroducir a Cristo en el discurso sobre la creación". *Communio* 3 (2002): 53-69.

Deanne-Drummond, C. *Eco-theology.* Winona, MN: Saint Mary's Press, 2008.

---

[24] See Niels Gregersen and Ulf Görman (eds), *Design and Disorder: Perspectives from Science and Theology* (Bodmin, Cornwall: T&T Clark, 2001).

[25] The cosmic dimension of the economy of salvation was already present since the theology of the Holy Greek Fathers. In this regard, see K. Duchatelez, "La notion d'économie et ses richesses théologiques". *Nouvelle Revue Théologique* 92(3) (1970): 267-292, especially, 280-283.

[26] Hans Urs von Balthasar, *Theodramatik* (Benziger, Einsiedeln: Johannes-Verlag, 1973). See also Raymund Schwager, *Erbsünde und Heilsdrama: im Kontext von Evolution, Gentechnologie und Apokalyptik* (Münster: LIT, 1997) [trans. to English: *Banished from Eden: Original Sin and Evolutionary Theory in the Drama of Salvation* (London: Gracewing, 2006)].

Florio, L. "El planeta Tierra ha sido hospitalario para la vida. ¿Lo seguirá siendo en el futuro?" in Cecilia Avenatti de Palumbo, Ed. *Hospitalidad: encuentro y desafío.* Buenos Aires: Ágape, 2021: 195-216.
Florio, L. *Ciencia y religión. Perspectivas históricas, epistemológicas y teológicas.* Salta: Eucasa, 2020.
Florio, L. "Ecología y teología", in V. Figueroa Clérici, Ed. *Crisis ecológica. Apuntes para una ecología integral.* Salta: EUCASA, 2020: 78-92.
Florio, L. "Una creación evolutiva y una biosfera amenazada. Perspectivas bíblicas y teológicas". *Estudios Trinitarios* 1 (2012): 105-143.
Galleni, L. "Is Biosphere Doing Theology?" *Zygon* 36 (2001): 33-48.
Haught, J. *Cristianismo y ciencia. Hacia una teología de la naturaleza.* Santander: Sal Terrae, 2009.
Löning, K. and E. Zenger. *In principio Dio creo. Teologie bibliche della creazione.* Brescia: Queriniana, 2006.
Plašienková, Z. and L. Florio. "Ideas inspiradoras de Teilhard de Chardin para la educación en un tiempo de crisis ecológica". *Quaerentibus: Teología y Ciencias* 8 (2017): 100-112.
Svampa, Maristella and Enrique Viale. *El colapso ecológico ya llegó. Una brújula para salir del (mal) desarrollo.* Buenos Aires: Siglo XXI, 2021.
Van Huyssteen, J. W. *Alone in the World? Uniqueness in Science and Theology.* Grand Rapids, MI: The Gilford Lectures, 2006.

30. Pentecostalism: Spirituality, Body and Creation

Abiud Fonseca[1]

Introduction

This work sets forth theological and anthropological foundations that offer the possibility for Pentecostal spirituality, specifically in its Latin American expressions, to be an area where a culture of co-existence between human beings and creation may be configured. I begin by doing a self-critical exercise on the noticeable lack of an ecological conscience in the faith practice of contemporary Pentecostalisms; to later argue that, in one of its distinctive practices – the corporeal experience with the Holy Spirit – there exist key elements for the reconfiguration of the believer-nature relationship.

This essay is not intended to be exclusive to the practice of the Pentecostal faith. Rather, the criticisms of the modern rationalist paradigm, which arise from the Pentecostal experience, can serve, from diverse religious and spiritual expressions, to reconsider the place of the body in theology, the divine dynamism and the agency of what is nonhuman in the conception of the God-human relationship. And thus, to explore new ways of living spirituality which do not relegate eco-diakonia to mere sporadic actions, but instead assume it as a fundamental basis. Ecological awareness and action can be an epistemic substrate of the Christian faith.

Pentecostalism and Ecological Consciousness: Lack and Opportunity

Some time ago, I participated in a dialogue with anthropologists and sociologists on how to recognise alternatives to development in ways of life that have not been completely absorbed by the developmental discourse of modern capitalism. The dialogue was carried out under the premises of the Latin American theoretical proposal of post-development.[2]

The assignment I had received was to analyse and discuss whether in emerging Christian religious expressions, such as Pentecostalism, thoughts or actions are being articulated that allow them to be recognised as alternatives to development. It was not an easy task. I used the proposals of Latin American anthropologists Arturo Escobar[3] and Gustavo Esteva,[4] who postulate that a way of life is an alternative to development, when three significant axes can be identified in it:

- A notion about history that differs from the idea of the linear temporal continuum that modern logic has constituted.
- Ethical bases that go beyond individuality, because they are constituted from an ideal of community life.

---

[1] Mg. Abiud Fonseca is professor of Systematic Theology and Old Testament at the Seminario Sudamericano Semisud. He is a theologian and anthropologist researching Latin American Pentecostalism and an ordained pastor of the Church of God in Ecuador. afonseca@semisud.edu.ec.

[2] A current of thought, mainly Latin American, whose main representatives are Arturo Escobar and Gustavo Esteva. This current does not intend to displace or oppose developmental discourse, but, from a critique of modernity and capitalism, to propose alternatives of parallel thought.

[3] Arturo Escobar, "El 'postdesarrollo' como concepto y práctica social", in *Políticas de economía, ambiente y sociedad en tiempos de globalización*, coordinated by Daniel Mato (Caracas: Facultad de Ciencias Económicas y Sociales, Universidad Central de Venezuela, 2005): 17-31.

[4] See Eduardo Gudynas, "Debates sobre el desarrollo y sus alternativas en América Latina: una breve guía heterodoxa", in *Más allá del desarrollo: grupo permanente de trabajo sobre alternativas al desarrollo* (Quito: Abya Yala; Fundación Rosa Luxemburgo, 2011): 21-53.

- A more symmetrical relationship between society and nature, as opposed to the asymmetry in favour of society limited to the way of life of modern societies.

Initially, it seemed delusional to me to place the practices of Pentecostalism in any of these questions. However, after reviewing my own experiences in Pentecostal spirituality and accessing abundant studies on Latin American Pentecostalisms, I was able to realise that Pentecostal life has grounds common to the first two aspects of alternatives to development.

About the first: From an anthropology of Christianity, Joel Robbins argues that founding Christian experiences, such as conversion, imply ruptures – even dramatic ones – from the cultural continuum.[5] In Pentecostalisms, in addition to this rupture, ecstatic experiences, such as the baptism in the Holy Spirit, are experienced as a rupture of the temporal continuum.[6] In these practices of embodiment of divine reality, temporal linearity is suspended in and from the body. The baptism in the Holy Spirit is a corporeal ecstasy that re-creates the experience of Acts 2, implying a temporal-spatial break performed mainly during the liturgy. The Pentecostal theologian, Bernardo Campos assures us that "in its process of socio-religious foundation, the pentecosting community carries out a kind of an-historical migration through which it places itself 'congenially' at the very centre of the Pentecost event, as if to reproduce it."[7] From the timeless bodily experience,[8] Pentecostal spirituality symbolically configures its own specificity.

Concerning the second, since the studies by Walter Hollenweger,[9] it has been noted that the communitarian dimension of the Pentecostal faith experience is fundamental in its spirituality. Theologian and historian, Carmelo Álvarez comments about community in Pentecostalism: "in the face of a hostile, unjust and precarious society, the Pentecostal community of faith becomes a 'community of meaning.' It is a charismatic community, where life in the Spirit flows and makes itself felt."[10]

However, after embarking on a search, I had to acknowledge that the third axis is almost indistinguishable or even absent in the practice of Pentecostal faith.

Prior to this dialogue, I participated in a huge convention of one of the largest Pentecostal denominations in Ecuador and, indeed, there was not the slightest reflection on the ecological issue. Moreover, it became clear that practice in favour of environmental care is really neglected. As is usual in these concentrations, there was an excessive use of electrical energy, an unnecessary accumulation of garbage, disproportionate increase in the decibels of the sound system, indiscriminate sale of foods that cause contamination, and, in addition, it was enthusiastically promoted that this form of socialisation should to be reproduced in local liturgies.

What was conspicuously constant in that event was the rereading of Chapter 2 of the Acts of the Apostles. In up to three presentations I attended, that was the reference text. The outstanding theme of the mentioned biblical passage was the irruption of the Holy Spirit during the Feast of Pentecost.

What does this text say that is so often reread, memorised, and appropriated by Pentecostals? I will quote from the 1960 Reina Valera version of the Bible, as this is the most commonly used in Latin American Pentecostal congregations:

---

[5] Joel Robbins, "El pensamiento de la continuidad y el problema de la cultura cristiana: Creencia, temporalidad y la antropología del cristianismo", *Apuntes de Investigación: Oficios y Prácticas,* 18 (2010): 111-144.

[6] Simon Coleman, "'Right Now!': Historiopraxy and the Embodiment of Charismatic Temporalities", *Ethnos Journal of Anthropology* 76(4) (December 2011): 426-447.

[7] Bernardo Campos, "Lo testimonial: un caso de teología oral y narrativa", in Carmelo Álvarez (ed), *Pentecostalismo y liberación: Una experiencia latinoamericana* (San José, Costa Rica: DEI, 1992): 128.

[8] Bernardo, Campos, *El principio pentecostalidad: la unidad en el Espíritu, fundamento de la paz* (Salem, OR: Publicaciones Kerigma, 2016): 147.

[9] Walter Hollenweger, *El pentecostalismo: Historia y doctrinas* (Buenos Aires: La Aurora, 1976).

[10] Carmelo Álvarez, "Lo popular: clave hermenéutica del movimiento pentecostal", in Carmelo Álvarez (ed), *Pentecostalismo y liberación: una experiencia latinoamericana* (San José, Costa Rica: DEI, 1992): 94.

> And suddenly a sound came from heaven like the rush of a mighty wind, and it filled all the house where they were sitting. And there appeared to them tongues as of fire, distributed and resting on each one of them. And they were all filled with the Holy Spirit and began to speak in other tongues, as the Spirit gave them utterance (Acts 2:2-4).[11]

The Pentecostal reading has made some semantic emphases in this passage that, with the advance of Pentecostalism, have served to discursively support the experience of the baptism in the Holy Spirit and its corporeal manifestations, such as speaking in tongues or glossolalia.

These semantic emphases bear significant weight on the symbolic construction of the Pentecostal faith, and could become a more than optimal substrate for developing a spirituality that reconciles the human being with nature. However, the question arises, why have the majority of Latin American Pentecostal and non-Pentecostal expressions not been able to generate that awareness?

In what follows, I am going to reflect on the ecotheological possibility that I distinguish in the Pentecostal rereading of Acts 2, the foundation for the Pentecostal life of faith. However, I will leave the stipulated question open, since I consider that the various Christian confessions, starting from their own experiences, are the ones who should answer it, from a recognition of their lack of ecological awareness.

The use of Acts 2 by the preachers at the convention had up to three common elements that confirm the semantic emphases I mentioned. The presentations had different nuances, but what converged was:

- *The body*: Pentecostal spirituality vindicates the corporeal aspects of ecstatic experiences, based on the significant value attributed to the assertion: "they […] began to speak in other tongues" (Acts 2:4).
- *The Spirit*: Pentecostal pneumatology maintains that the intervention of the Holy Spirit is foundational for the life of faith, assuming as a correlate the phrase: "they were all filled with the Holy Spirit" (Acts 2:4).
- *The power*: Pentecostals consider that the action of the Spirit is an energetic irruption experienced sensorially. Which is testified by the phrase: "And suddenly a sound came from heaven like the rush of a mighty wind" (Acts 2:2). I note that in this emphasis there are at least two natural elements: the sky/heaven[12] and wind.

The Body in the Pentecostal Experience: Place of Possibility for a Pentecostal Ecotheology

The first semantic emphasis made by the Pentecostal interpretation of Acts 2 indicates that the action of the Holy Spirit must be experienced bodily. The so-called classical Pentecostalisms,[13] that come from the revivals in the American South, went so far as to establish that, according to Acts 2, the initial evidence of the baptism in the Holy Spirit is glossolalia. In other words, if there is no ecstasy, it cannot be said that there has been an action of the Holy Spirit on the believer.

So, for Pentecostals, the human-God relationship is more highly validated when it is felt bodily. This conviction alters what has been determined by Western Christianity, heir to the Thomasian ontology and, also, what has been established by modern Cartesian logic. These ideas consider the relationship of the human being or the subject with the other, as primarily a relationship of knowledge, therefore, rational. For the Pentecostal, the human experience with God is mainly corporeal, therefore, sensitive and affective.

In Pentecostalism, experiencing God bodily does not mean that one is having an experience with an empirical, factual or tangible, and therefore knowable object; rather, it is a corporeal experience with the

[11] TN: The most similar English rendition of the text cited by the author is from the Revised Standard Version.
[12] Translator's note: In the original Spanish of this essay and of the verse quoted from Acts 2:4, the word is "cielo" which means both "heaven" and "sky," and thus refers to a natural element that the word "heaven" does not.
[13] Allan Anderson, *An Introduction to Pentecostalism: Global Charismatic Christianity* (Cambridge: Cambridge University Press, 2004): 39-62.

nonhuman and the non-tangible. This capacity of the body of the person of Pentecostal faith opens up the possibility of making a connection with current ecological interests.

Body and Affective Social Relationship with Nature

One of the great problems that the modern Western worldview is generating is the environmental crisis. This crisis is based on the modern conception that the relationship between human beings and nature is an asymmetric relationship.[14] The human being is understood as a subject and nature is defined as an object. Thus, nature, an object, has become a resource that can be used by the human being, a subject. So, from this conception of the relationship between human being and nature, the conceptual idea has been generated that the reality of nature lies in its tangible objectivity.

Contemporary ecology is nourishing itself from the worldviews of aboriginal peoples, thus encouraging a deconstruction of modern logic on the relationship between human beings and nature. This process begins by ceasing to think of nature as an object or as merely a resource at the complete disposal of human beings – which does not mean that it is a subject, because the subject is also an ontological construction. Rather, it means that nature is indefinable, self-generating, self-sustaining. Byron Calo, an indigenous Pentecostal leader, affirms that nature is "everything, an uncatchable everything."[15]

Thus, if we continue to assume that the body must respond to its conscious and cognitive capacities to perceive only the objectified and conceptualised, the corporeal experience will be valid only when it occurs in relation to the tangible, and it will be knowledge when the object is rationally configured. Accordingly, nature cannot be more than a thing or a resource. In contrast, in the worldviews of indigenous peoples, the body also has the ability to experience the non-tangible. For this reason, the experience with nature cannot be only an experience marked by the knowledge acquired by the subject about the object; rather, it has to be a sensitive and affective bodily experience, in which she is mother, sister, strength, power, everything and more.

Similarly, the body of the person of Pentecostal faith, who feels the nonhuman and the non-tangible, constitutes a great possibility for subverting the rationalist principles that dominate us and that are causing the accelerated destruction of our common home.

Pentecostal Body and the Recreations of its Affective Social Relationship

In Pentecostalism, a reconfiguration of the sensitivity of the body over rationality takes place. There are many reasons that can be articulated to support this idea. I will propose only two in what follows:

First, Pentecostalism has constituted and even symbolically recognised its origins in the corporeal protest against the absolutisations of the cultural mediation of the gospel of Christ.[16] In other words, the Pentecostal movement recognises that its historical beginning occurred when the body became a place and agent for the construction of its relationship with God, leaving behind the certainty that dogmatic conclusions or theological rationalisations offered for determining the relationship with God.

While for most Christian organisations the foundational milestones are the signing of minutes, presentation of speeches, wars won, political triumphs, meetings convened, regulations adopted; for Pentecostals, the original milestone is the moment when the body felt the Spirit of God and overflowed into

[14] Maristella Svampa, "El Antropoceno como diagnóstico y paradigma. Lecturas globales desde el Sur", *Utopía y Praxis Latinoamericana* 24(84) (2019): 33-54.
[15] Byron Calo, "Ecología en el cristianismo pentecostal indígena de Ecuador," (paper presented at the *Programa Intensivo de Desarrollo Ministerial Ecosistencia: De la preservación a la coexistencia*, Quito, Semisud, 2019).
[16] Juan Sepúlveda, "El principio pentecostal. Reflexiones a partir de los orígenes del pentecostalismo en Chile", in Daniel Chiquete and Luis Orellana (eds), *Voces del Pentecostalismo Latinoamericano: Identidad, teología e historia* (Concepción: RELEP, 2003): 14.

emotional and non-rational expressions. The revivals around the world in the first decade of the twentieth century[17] are moments recognised as the beginnings of Pentecostalisms due to the lived experiences of ecstasy.

Second, the preferred setting for the corporeal Pentecostal experience with God is the liturgy or worship. The evaluation that the Pentecostal believer makes of a liturgical service depends on whether or not the presence of God was felt. And how does one know that this presence has been made manifest? Through the collective ecstatic manifestation, expressed in groans, cries, falls, ecstasy. Speaking in tongues is the culminating experience, because, in this ecstasy, the Pentecostal believer asserts that they have not only felt the Spirit bodily, but even that the Spirit has spoken bodily.

But how can the body perceive the Spirit, if the Spirit is neither a body nor a tangible object, but is spirit? From rational principles, it can be argued that – in the Pentecostal experience – Pentecostals "fantasise" from their affective bodily perception and call their "fantasy" Spirit, because it is not possible for the body to feel realities that are not knowable or recognisable by reason.

This assertion could be inverted in the question posed by the phenomenology of the body: Why do realities have to be recognisable by reason? Why does the sensibility of the body have to be governed by the authorisation of reason so that only then the certainty of the experience can be ascertained? The North American anthropologist Thomas Csordas argues that human existence cannot continue to be understood in the duality between thought and emotion, where thought is greater. Hence, it is not about turning emotion into a kind of embodied thought, but it is simply emotion.[18]

The body that perceives realities beyond the tangible is a body with the ability to develop an affective relationship with what is objectified by the rational paradigm. This is a great opportunity to establish new relationships between human beings and nature. Anthropologists Tim Ingold, Roy Wagner and Eduardo Viveiros de Castro assure, from their ethnographic studies, that the greatest contribution that modern societies can learn from native peoples is the redemption of the centrality of the body in social life. Because, among these peoples, the body can feel more than know. Csordas also asserts that this contribution can be found not only in native peoples, but also in dissident spiritualities, such as the Catholic charismatic movements and Pentecostalisms.[19]

And if it is possible to feel more than to know, the great phenomenologist Maurice Merleau-Ponty assures us that at last we will have acknowledged that the body is not just a vehicle of reason and, therefore, another object. Since the human being is not a being *in* the world, a notion that has distanced us from nature; rather, the body is the human being as *being-of-the-world*.[20]

The Spirit: Divine Dynamism in the Pentecostal Experience

The second semantic emphasis of the Pentecostal re-readings of Acts 2 highlights that the most experienceable representation of the divine is the Spirit. For a bodily experience with God to be sensitive and affective, there is no better way to conceive of God than as spirit.

The person of Pentecostal faith feels the Holy Spirit bodily, and it is not by chance that it is the Spirit, because the Spirit shows and demonstrates the dynamism of the divine. For the Pentecostal believer, it is more valuable to feel that which is dynamic and relational of God than to think or reproduce some articulated concept of God.

---

[17] Vinson Synan, *The Holiness-Pentecostal Tradition: Charismatic Movement in the Twentieth Century* (Grand Rapids, MI: William B. Eerdmans, 1997).

[18] Thomas Csordas, "Embodiment as a paradigm for Anthropology", *Ethos* 2(1) (March 1990): 37.

[19] Thomas Csordas, *Embodiment and Experience* (New York: Cambridge University Press, 1994).

[20] Maurice Merleau-Ponty, *Fenomenología de la Percepción* (Barcelona: Planeta, 1993): 98.

In other words, implicit in the Pentecostal experience is a critique of theological ontology that, following the concern for essentiality, has historically asked: What is God? Thus, for the Pentecostal faith, God matters more for that which is perceptible of God's presence than for the unsearchable essence of God.

The Spirit conceived by the Pentecostal believer is a reality in motion. This is highly significant, because movement implies indeterminacy and indeterminacy requires imagination. Imagination leads us to constant invention, argues anthropologist Roy Wagner. Invention is the recreation of reality,[21] and it is not the same as fantasy, which is the simulation of an unreality.

Pentecostal theologian Frank Macchia argues that "The Spirit is the 'go-between God' and, as such, baptises people into a realm of relationships shaped by divine love."[22] In other words, in Pentecostalism, the baptism in the Spirit is not an experience to learn more about God, cognitively and conceptually. Rather, baptism, being a baptism in the Spirit, implies immersing oneself in an experience in which God is giving God's self. And God, who is a gift, is given in the body of the believer. Therefore, baptism in the Spirit is also baptism in affection or in love.

This baptism in love is fundamental for the understanding and adoption of a community life as the social foundation of Pentecostalisms. And this is because the irruptive arrival of the Spirit sensitises the believer mainly in their emotions and affections.

In my research, I have conducted multiple interviews with Pentecostal brothers and sisters. In all of them, the narration of the baptism in the Spirit was also a setting for reliving bodily a new experience with the Spirit. It is common to hear people of the Pentecostal faith tell their stories and say: "I am telling you and when I do it, I feel the Spirit again" (crying, goosebumps, sensations).

The question then arises, how could this contribute to a greater ecological awareness in Pentecostal life?

A first point to formulate a possible answer arises from the affirmation of the philosopher Stéphane Vinolo who, based on the postulates of the phenomenologist Jean-Luc Marion, argues that, preferring to experience the dynamism of the divine rather than knowing a monolithic concept of God, is to open oneself to the possibility of – even – refounding our principles of life, allowing us to pass from ontology to phenomenology.[23] And this implies moving from the concept to the relationship.

Through this route, the perceived reality would not be a definite object, determined to give it a definite use, but rather it would be an experienceable, that is living, reality. The Pentecostal conception of God as dynamic reality or Spirit, gives Pentecostalism the opportunity to also rethink the reality of nature so that it is not restricted to being a mere profitable object – a matter that is already noticeable in indigenous Pentecostalisms.

Secondly, if the Spirit is God in movement, movement is movement when it is perceived. If a tremor is not perceived, it is not trembling. And all perception implies, then, relationship. For the Pentecostal experience, it is fundamental to assume God, first of all, as a felt relationship. Thus, the notion of God-Spirit, is giving way to conceive of God rather more as movement. Some phrases that I have heard from people who have lived the experience of the baptism in the Holy Spirit are: "the Spirit seized me", "it came to me and shook me", "it was the Spirit that touched me", "it enveloped me", "I couldn't stop moving, it was the Spirit."

For ecotheology, it is also fundamental to recognise God as movement, because that implies that the entire world, created and sustained by God, is also movement. Ultimately, this is the foundation for understanding that life cannot be appropriated, summarised, monopolised, stigmatised, homogenised by any human power. Rather, dynamic life is, and is in, everything.

---

[21] Roy Wagner, *The Invention of Culture* (Chicago: The University of Chicago Press, 2016).

[22] Frank Macchia, *Baptized in the Spirit: A Global Pentecostal Theology* (Grand Rapids, MI: Zondervan, 2006): 152.

[23] Stéphane Vinolo, *Jean-Luc Marion: La fenomenología de la donación como relevo de la metafísica* (Quito: Centro de Publicaciones de la PUCE, 2019): 153-176.

The text of Genesis 1:2 describes how the movement of the Spirit becomes the movement that makes everything exist. And the text of Genesis 2 again insists on the movement of the breath as the foundation of the living. So, to perceive the Spirit as God moving, is to perceive the world also in movement.

This is congruent with what the North American anthropologist Tim Ingold proposes, when he reflects on the world closed within what has already been imagined of it – but that would be a world that "would not leave room for life or imagination." Ingold interpellates saying: "Let us, then, follow the threads of correspondence wherever they may lead us. Let us toast to the proliferation of loose ends!"[24] Because it is not the same to live in an imagined world as in an imaginable one. The imagined world is exhausted in the determinate, while the imaginable world is one that is in motion. Nature in motion is imaginable; nature without movement is appropriable, usable and disposable.

The Pentecostal notion of the Spirit as the dynamism of the divine, lived out in bodily experience, is another powerful possibility for building an ecological consciousness.

The Power of the Spirit that Breaks Forth From "the Sky/Heaven Like Wind"

The third semantic emphasis that the Pentecostal interpretation makes in relation to the Acts 2 account emphasises that the transformative bodily experimentation of the baptism in the Holy Spirit is due to an action where the power of the Spirit is displayed. The use of the term power does not correspond to sociopolitical theorising, especially of a Foucaultian orientation, but has a meaning more linked to the physical: to the capacity and energetic intensity for doing something.

The Pentecostal believer assumes that what is felt in his or her bodily experience is due to the fact that the Holy Spirit has not only moved, but has released God's divine force generating an overflowing bodily reaction. According to Acts 2, that power came from the sky like a wind. The Pentecostal readings of this text emphasise more the divine impetus and, although they have noticed the presence of two natural elements such as the sky and the wind, they only recognise them as useful instruments for the arrival of the power of the Spirit.

People of Pentecostal faith have as emblematic this story showing the sky and the wind as agents of the action of the Spirit. Unfortunately, the rationalist principles that govern our way of perceiving the world have made us understand that the mention of the sky and wind in this text gives expression only to a simple metaphor.

On the basis of the recognition of the body as a social experience with the world, and of the Spirit as a vital movement, Pentecostalism has the opportunity to broaden its conception of nature. This includes, as an example, understanding that this passage is presenting the sky and the wind as realities with agency.

Our way of life has an urgent need to resort to the knowledge of indigenous and peasant peoples, who have a symmetrical relationship with nature. Because they do understand life from the dynamics that nature has: the skies, the mountains, the winds, the thunders are nature interacting socially. Therefore, if the text of Acts 2 says that the Spirit came like a wind, from these original worldviews it can be understood that the vital action of nature does not symbolise the action of God, but rather is the action of God.

The French anthropologist Philippe Descola emphasises that, in the Amazonian peoples, the action of nature is not a metaphor. Rather, it is a metonymy. So, saying that the Spirit came like the wind does not have the same meaning for an indigenous inhabitant as for one of the city. For the first, the wind can *be* the Spirit while for the other, the wind only symbolises the Spirit.

---

[24] Tim Ingold, "Conociendo desde dentro: reconfigurando las relaciones entre la antropología y la etnografía", *Etnografías Contemporáneas* 2(2) (2015): 230.

Conclusion

If Pentecostal spirituality presents broad possibilities thanks to the centrality of the body and the indeterminacy of the dynamism of the Spirit, why cannot the person of Pentecostal faith read the wind beyond the metaphorical?

The question is bigger: if we Pentecostals have an excellent substrate for redefining the relationship between human beings and nature, why don't we do it? It would be very daring to simplify this answer into a determinism that says: "This is why!" or "it is because of that!" However, I am going to end this brief reflection by articulating critical opinions about what is posed in this question, starting from another account from the same book of Acts: "Now when Simon [a magician from Samaria] saw that the Spirit was given through the laying on of the apostles' hands, he offered them money" (Acts 8:18).

The body may be shown to be central to the Pentecostal experience, but for the power schemes of Western culture, the body is a desired good. And it cannot be denied that the Pentecostal experience, like many other forms of life that generate subversions to the discourse of the dominant culture, is subsumed in it.

The body, in Pentecostalism, is presented as the place and agent from which new meanings of the human-God relationship are being reconfigured. Therefore, the body can also be the place from where Pentecostalism has the great opportunity to redefine the relationship between human beings and nature. Yet that same body has become an area of dispute, because it is a body desired by those who want to control it in order to resolve their interests for dominion.

Simon, the magician, saw that the bodies of those who believed in Jesus, back in Samaria, lived an experience with the Spirit, after the apostles laid on hands. And it did not occur to him to experience that movement of the Spirit bodily; rather, he wanted to instrumentalise the dynamism of the Spirit, in order to achieve a higher status himself. He wanted to dominate bodies, appropriate them. So, it is one thing that the body of the Pentecostal believer perceives the Spirit moving and generates new configurations of their relationships; and quite another, that the Spirit moves only when "the anointed shepherd" desires it.

Throughout its history, Pentecostalism or Pentecostalisms – specifically the Latin American ones – in their local expressions, situated in particular contexts, have shown that the possibilities of subverting, from the body, the dominations of society are specified in distinct practices of their faith. In this way, Pentecostalisms have the challenge of continuing to find in their own spirituality the opportunities to promote greater transformative and saving actions of humanity and the world, such as the formation of an ecological conscience and the concomitant ecological practice. However, Pentecostalism must be well aware that its main value, the body, must be constantly protected and liberated from the oppressive forces of this world; because the body is also a place in which multiple dominations are played out.

This interpellation can be extended to the various Christian confessions that have made theological evasions of the body as the primary place of experience with God. Perhaps, if we subvert a little more the dominant logocentrism in our faith, which has looked at the body with suspicion, or has used it as a useful tool for the deployment of power, we can also reconfigure the human-nature relationship, and live in a more capacious way our experience with an infinite divinity, which exists dynamically in the infinity of nature.

Suggestions for Further Reading

Álvarez, Carmelo. "Lo popular: clave hermenéutica del movimiento pentecostal", in Carmelo Álvarez, Ed. *Pentecostalismo y liberación: una experiencia latinoamericana*. San José, Costa Rica: DEI, 1992: 89-100.

Anderson, Allan. *An Introduction to Pentecostalism: Global Charismatic Christianity*. Cambridge: Cambridge University Press, 2004.

Calo, Byron. "Ecología en el cristianismo pentecostal indígena de Ecuador." Paper presented at the *Programa Intensivo de Desarrollo Ministerial Ecosistencia: De la preservación a la coexistencia.* Quito: Semisud, 2019.

Campos, Bernardo. "Lo testimonial: un caso de teología oral y narrativa", in Carmelo Álvarez, Ed. *Pentecostalismo y liberación: Una experiencia latinoamericana.* San José, Costa Rica: DEI, 1992: 125-145.

Campos, Bernardo. *El principio pentecostalidad: la unidad en el Espíritu, fundamento de la paz.* Salem, OR: Kerigma, 2016.

Coleman, Simon. "'Right Now!': Historiopraxy and the Embodiment of Charismatic Temporalities". *Ethnos Journal of Anthropology* 76(4) (December 2011): 426-447.

Csordas, Thomas. *The Sacred-Self: A Cultural Phenomenology of Charismatic Healing.* Berkeley, CA: University of California Press, 1997.

Csordas, Thomas. *Embodiment and experience.* New York: Cambridge University Press, 1994.

Csordas, Thomas. "Embodiment as a paradigm for Anthropology". *Ethos Journal of Anthropology* 2(1) (March 1990): 5-47.

Descola, Philippe. "Términos, relaciones, categorías", in *Más allá de naturaleza y cultura.* Buenos Aires: Amorrortu, 2012: 344-359.

Escobar, Arturo. "El 'postdesarrollo' como concepto y práctica social", in Daniel Mato, Ed. *Políticas de economía, ambiente y sociedad en tiempos de globalización.* Caracas: Facultad de Ciencias Económicas y Sociales, Universidad Central de Venezuela, 2005: 17-31.

González, Oscar, Ghillean Prance, and A. J. Swoboda. "La iglesia pentecostal como un aliado potencial para la conservación en los trópicos latinoamericanos". *Razón y Pensamiento Cristiano* 7(2) (2018): 1-12.

Gudynas, Eduardo. "Debates sobre el desarrollo y sus alternativas en América Latina: una breve guía heterodoxa", in *Más allá del desarrollo: grupo permanente de trabajo sobre alternativas al desarrollo.* Quito: Abya Yala; Fundación Rosa Luxemburgo, 2011: 21-53.

Hollenweger, Walter. *El Pentecostalismo: Historia y doctrinas.* Buenos Aires: La Aurora, 1976.

Ingold, Tim. "Conociendo desde dentro: reconfigurando las relaciones entre la antropología y la etnografía". *Etnografías Contemporáneas* 2(2) (2015): 218-230.

Macchia, Frank. *Bautizado en el Espíritu: una teología pentecostal global.* Miami: VIDA, 2008.

Merleau-Ponty, Maurice. *Fenomenología de la Percepción.* Barcelona: Planeta, 1993.

Robbins, Joel. "El pensamiento de la continuidad y el problema de la cultura cristiana: Creencia, temporalidad y la antropología del cristianismo". *Apuntes de Investigación: Oficios y Prácticas* 18 (2010): 111-144.

Sepúlveda, Juan. "El principio pentecostal. Reflexiones a partir de los orígenes del pentecostalismo en Chile", in Daniel Chiquete and Luis Orellana, Eds. *Voces del Pentecostalismo Latinoamericano: Identidad, teología e historia.* Concepción, Chile: RELEP, 2003: 13-28.

Smith, James K. A. *Thinking in Tongues: Pentecostal Contribution to Christian Philosophy.* Grand Rapids, MI: Eerdmans, 2010.

Svampa, Maristella. "El Antropoceno como diagnóstico y paradigma. Lecturas globales desde el Sur". *Utopía y Praxis Latinoamericana* 24(84) (2019): 33-54.

Synan, Vinson. *The Holiness-Pentecostal Tradition: Charismatic movement in the Twentieth century.* Grand Rapids, MI: William B. Eerdmans, 1997.

Vinolo, Stéphane. *Jean-Luc Marion: La fenomenología de la donación como relevo de la metafísica.* Quito: Centro de Publicaciones de la PUCE, 2019.

Vondey, Wolfgang. *Beyond Pentecostalism: The crisis of global Christianity and the renewal of the theological agenda.* Grand Rapids, MI: Eerdmans, 2010.

Wagner, Roy. *The Invention of Culture.* Chicago, IL: The University of Chicago Press, 2016.

31. "The Earth *is* the Lord": Towards an Ecospirituality for the Caribbean

Anna Kasafi Perkins[1]

> The earth is special, the land is special, the land is true wealth [...] I have a story to tell, to tell women, men, the young, and students, to cherish our natural environment [...] to share the value in loving a life that is so simple and natural and royal [...] and just working and living in harmony with one another, and finding time to celebrate earth and life. So it is all in the concept of Rastafari.[2]

It is well known that RastafarI[3] have a special love for the natural world – creation without interference (*iration*),[4] nature, the earth and all living things – which expresses itself in an *ital* livity, that is, "a spirituality and the teachings that inform it".[5] Little research has been undertaken, however, to systematically explore the rich and textured theological and ethical resources which ground Rasta livity-spirituality.[6] Such resources could contribute to an ecospirituality or ecological spirituality for the Caribbean. Indeed, Powell identifies an "ital hermeneutic", which is a distinct and innovative exegetical approach emerging from Rastafari that offers a "radical reinterpretation of spiritual resources [...] to place the unity of creation at the centre of interpretation".[7]

This chapter frames an ecumenical ecospirituality for the Caribbean grounded in the ital hermeneutic on which the Sixth Principle of RastafarI – "Ital: The Natural Way"[8] – emerges, in dialogue with theological resources from Caribbean Christian traditions. It explores the theological meanings of the RastafarI declaration that "the Earth *is* the Lord!"[9] This statement is a deliberate reworking of Psalm 24:1, in the King James Version (KJV), the favoured Bible of RastafarI. It reads: "the earth *is* the Lord*'s* and the fullness thereof" (Ps. 24:1). In removing the possessive and making it a declarative, such a reworking functions both to demonstrate the Rasta word power through which they expose language's oppressive and liberative

---

[1] Dr Anna Kasafi Perkins is a Jamaican Roman Catholic theologian. She is adjunct faculty at St Michael's Theological College and Seminary, and senior programme officer in the Quality Assurance Unit at The University of the West Indies, Regional Headquarters, Jamaica. She teaches and researches in ethics, justice, popular culture, sexuality, theology, scripture, and quality assurance. anna.perkins@uwimona.edu.jm.

[2] Akilah Jaramogi, Rastafari co-founder of the Fondes Amandes Community Reforestation Project (FACRP) in Trinidad. See Diana J. Fox and Jillian M. Smith, "Stewards of their island: Rastafari Women's Activism for the Forests and Waters in Trinidad and Tobago-Social Movement Perspectives", *Resilience: A Journal of the Environmental Humanities* 3 (2015-2016): 142-168.

[3] The Pronominal "I" has a particular meaning in RastafarI; it captures the self-understanding of RastafarI, especially in the concept of I-n-I, which speaks to the presence of the divine in Black people. The centrality of the "I" is RastafarI is captured in the way it is written by some scholars and this is the way it is used in this discussion, except if from a direct quote.

[4] Joseph Powell, "Ital Hermeneutics: The Innovative Theological Grounding of Rastafari Dietary (Ital) Practices", *Black Theology* 19(1) (2021): 32-52.

[5] Powell, "Ital Hermeneutics", 34.

[6] Anna Kasafi Perkins, "Heartbless and Mek a Trod: Meditation on a Rasta Spirituality for justice and peace", in Fernando Enns, Upolu Luma Vaai, Andrés Pacheco Lozano, and Betty Pries (eds), *Transformative Spiritualities for the Ecumenical Pilgrimage of Justice and Peace* (Geneva: WCC Publication, 2021/2022) (forthcoming).

[7] Powell, "Ital Hermeneutics", 33.

[8] Winston Williams [Ras Ishon], "The Seven Principles of Rastafari", in Rex Nettleford and Veronica Salter (eds), *Rastafari* (Caribbean Quarterly: The University of the West Indies, 2008): 17-24.

[9] Joseph Owens, *Dread: The Rastafarians of Jamaica* (London: Heinemann, 1976 [1982]): 146.

possibilities as well as their power to reread and reclaim the Bible from the experience of the oppressed.[10] Their strategic (re)reading "discommode[s] the messenger and oppressor and secure[s] liberation for the oppressed through Rasta biblical reasonings and reggae chants against the Babylon system (corrupt social, political, and economic systems in Jamaica and the West)".[11]

Their apparently pantheistic declaration moves beyond the recognition of the Earth as simply a divine creation to identify the Earth with Jah in a manner that critiques some contemporary approaches to environmental ethics, which have failed to capture the imagination of a broad cross-section of Christians. Arguably, some ways of doing environmental ethics have "yet to make compelling arguments that moral concern for the Earth and its ecosystems are integrally related to the practice of Christian faith; [they have] yet to successfully persuade Christians that all creation is a community of moral significance".[12] As such, religiously grounded and morally persuasive environmental ethics may perhaps then be termed an ecospirituality.

The moral and theological meaning and implication of "the earth *is* the Lord" will be fleshed out in reference to some of the writings of the Antilles Bishops of the Caribbean and the Jamaica Baptist Union, which demonstrate the moral and religious significance of the environment to Christian faith. Such a dialogue between Rastafari and Christian thought and practice is possible given some shared perspectives, while the differences serve to challenge, deepen and inform.[13]

This article will highlight practical examples of morally responsible action shaping such a burgeoning Caribbean ecumenical ecospirituality. Undertaking the exposition of an ecospirituality is an important and ongoing task in Caribbean theological circles as there has been a lack of sustained theological writing on the ecological crisis by Caribbean thinkers.[14] In particular, there has been little research on the ecological perspectives of RastafarI, which can make a significant contribution to a uniquely Caribbean ecospirituality, from which valuable insights outside of the dominant spaces can be found.[15] This exercise is necessary, therefore, to make a contribution to the larger interrelated global conversation on environmental justice or integral ecology, as Pope Francis refers to it.[16]

---

[10] Nathaniel S. Murrell, "Wresting the Message from the Messenger: The Rastafari as a Case Study in the Caribbean Indigenization of the Bible", in R. S. Sugirtharajah (ed), *Voices from the Margin: Interpreting the Bible in the Third World* (Maryknoll, NY: 2006): 169-188.

[11] Murrell, "Wresting the Message", 174.

[12] Keith Warner, "Franciscan Environmental Ethics: Imagining Creation as a Community of Care", *Journal of the Society of Christian Ethics* 31(1) (2011): 143-160.

[13] Fox and Smith, "Stewards", note, for example, the sharing of core principles and resonances between Rastafari and non-Rastafari in Trinidad, the latter being influenced by the Black Power Movement.

[14] Christopher Llanos, "Caring for the Earth and Plutonium Shipment: A Response to the Ecological Thought of the Antilles Episcopal Conference", in Anna Kasafi Perkins, Donald Chambers and Jacqueline Porter (eds), *Justice and Peace in a Renewed Caribbean: Contemporary Catholic Reflections* (New York: Palgrave MacMillan, 2012): 219-231. Grenadian Baptist pastor Vonnie James makes a similar point, calling out the churches in Grenada, in particular, for their lack of engagement in the issues concerning climate change. See Vonnie James, "The Dialogue: A Call for Faith Groups in Grenada to Join the Conversation on Climate Change (CC)" (Unpublished manuscript, 2020).

[15] One apparent exception to this is Kadamwe K'nife, "Rastafari: An Ethic for Sustainable Development: Insights from Deep Ecology" (Paper presented at the International Association of Cultural Studies Conference, The University of the West Indies, Mona, 6th July 2008).

[16] Pope Francis, *Laudato Sí* (Vatican: Libreria Editrice Vaticana, 24th May 2015).

Irituality (Spirituality) and Ecospirituality

Spirituality is not a univocal concept. While I have argued elsewhere that RastafarI may well reject any notion of spirituality,[17] South African Ras Yada Tafari argues for a Rasta *irituality* (spirituality).[18] According to Tafari:

> *Irituality* is nothing more than just *sound ethics* and *just environment* where it rises up [...] In other words, [it] is the mastering of the individual to bring his mind under the control of *irits* [spirits] (emphasis added).[19]

There is an important individual spiritual journey in Rastafari, which leads to philosophical conclusions and practices that may be highly individualised and heterogeneous.[20] Rastafari have no "correct way" in which they are called to believe (orthodoxy) and practice (orthopraxis). As such, caution needs to be exercised in categorising aspects of Rastafari belief and practice. Nonetheless, it is possible for Middleton to assert, "Among Rastafari, livity is spirituality".[21] Middleton quotes Jamaican dub poet Yasus Afari from the 2001 documentary, *Ras tafari*, in which he defines "spirituality" in communitarian terms as "a network that links us all together onto our source, the Creator."[22] Rastafari livity, therefore, fosters "creational fraternity", that is, heightens "humanity's divinely mandated duty as stewards of Selassie's creation".[23] It grounds itself in "a fundamental appreciation and valuation for all life on earth".[24]

Similarly, Mountlouis maintains that livity is a spirituality, especially among the Bobo Shanti mansion of RastafarI.[25] Indeed, Mountlouis argues that the Bobo Shanti "had to create their own philosophical discourse to counteract the mainstream narrative of spirituality."[26] This recognition of the *iritual* in the RastafarI livity is a first step in delineating a Rastafari spirituality. As such, "ecological spirituality is a resolute way whereby humankind gives the lordship of creation back to the Creator – to whom it belongs – and assumes responsibilities as custodians of the earth."[27]

Furthermore, there is an implicit relationship between ecology and spirituality that is captured in the term ecospirituality; that is, "there is a spiritual dimension to ecology and that spirituality is indissociable from ecological concerns."[28] (Choné does point out that it is possible to pursue spirituality inside or out of any religious context, and even without believing in God; this indicates the need to interface with the non-religious, another important yet overlooked conversation partner).[29] At the same time, ecospirituality should necessarily be ecumenical and interreligious. Care for the environment cuts across denominational borders; Christian communities need to therefore engage ecumenically to prevent doctrinal differences from

[17] Perkins, "Heartbless".
[18] Ras Yada Tafari, *Rastafari Is: The Truth and King of Righteousness* (Durban, South Africa: Isalem Publications, 2007/2014).
[19] Tafari, *Rastafari Is*, 18.
[20] Powell, "Ital Hermeneutic."
[21] Darren J. Middleton, *Rastafari and the Arts: an Introduction* (London and New York: Routledge, 2015): 163.
[22] Middleton, *Rastafari and the Arts*, 163.
[23] Middleton, *Rastafari and the Arts*, 163.
[24] Powell, "Ital Hermeneutic," 33
[25] Nathalie Mountlouis, "Lords and Empresses in and out of Babylon: The EABIC community and the dialectic of female subordination" (PhD diss, University of London, 2013).
[26] Mountlouis, "Lords and Empresses", 154.
[27] Emmanuel Orok Duke, "From Christian spirituality to eco-friendliness", *International Journal of Humanities and Innovation* 3(1) (2020): 34-38.
[28] Aurélie Choné, "Ecospirituality", in Aurélie Choné, Isabelle Hajek and Philippe Hamman (eds), *Rethinking Nature: Challenging Disciplinary Boundaries* (Abingdon: Routledge, 2017): 38-48.
[29] Anna Kasafi Perkins, "Theological Literacy and the Strange(r) Stranger: Theological Education and the Non-religious Believer", *The First*, 1st May 2020. [Available at: https://catholicethics.com/forum/theological-education-and-the-non-religious-believer/], [Last accessed: 27th March 2022].

presenting a barrier to the ecospiritual quest. Similarly, the care for the earth needs collaboration from people of all faiths, who inhabit the same Earth, the same home (*oikos*).

It is our common responsibility to care for the earth, as the Antilles Bishops of the Caribbean remind us.[30] Therefore, differences in religious allegiance or (no religious allegiance) should not be allowed to hinder collaborative efforts to care for the earth either.[31] Hence, ecological spirituality needs also to engage interreligious partners.[32]

"The Sixth Principle of RastafarI: Ital: The Natural Way"

RastafarI vision of the relationship between spirituality and ecology is complex and multifaceted. It is rooted in how they see nature and divinity. They see nature as a powerful and dynamic force, which can be destructive or creative. Nature is the source of divine judgment against those opposed to it. Natural phenomena like lightning and thunder and other natural phenomena manifest the judgment of Jah. Indeed, "Rastas take manifest delight in beholding a thunderstorm, for they see it as the immediate working of Selassie's judgment".[33]

At the same time, nature and the fruits of the earth are considered as a gift of the Father "for the healing of the nation".[34] This perspective is not only of ganja, "the weed of wisdom," but to all of nature, whether animal or plant, all of life. So, generally, "with almost the force of doctrine,"[35] Rastas reject artificial things (additives, preservatives, and processed foods) and some prefer to consume food in as raw a state as possible. Fundamentally, Rastas believe that "all on the planet in its natural form is exactly as Jah intended it and as such cannot be improved upon, only degraded, when processed or altered by humanity".[36] Consuming such artificial items leads to degraded physical and nutritional status, but also spiritual denigration as well. On the individual level, such consumption "interrupts [the] connection with Jah and creational forces, it places a block in the way".[37] Furthermore, such plant-based dietary practices fosters being "more spiritually in tune with Jah,"[38] who also consumed a completely plant-based diet. Of course, abiding by this tenet is practically challenging for many Rastafarians, particularly those who do not have the means to plant their own food. "Necessity often takes precedence over dietary proscriptions".[39] And, it has connections with other movements such as veganism, raw veganism and other sustainable ways of eating.

The Earth is the Lord's

Psalm 24:1 is popular in Christian discussions on the environment. Duke, for example, references it in the context of the creative tension he identifies in Judeo-Christianity between domination and stewardship of the earth (Gen. 1:28-30; 2:15). He argues that the divine command is to treat the earth with special love as

---

[30] Antilles Episcopal Conference (AEC), *Caring for the Earth – Our Responsibility: An Invitation to Reflection (CFTE)*. Port of Spain: Antilles Episcopal Conference Secretariat (April 2005). [Available at: http://aecbishops.org/caring-for-the-earth-our-responsibility/], [Last accessed: 27th March 2022].

[31] Duke, "From Christian Spirituality."

[32] James, "The Dialogue".

[33] Owens, *Dread*, 145.

[34] Barry Chevannes, "Rastafari: towards a new approach", *New West Indian Guide/Nieuwe West-Indische Gids* 64(¾) (1990): 140.

[35] Chevannes, "Rastafari", 140.

[36] Powell, "Ital Hermeneutics", 39.

[37] Powell, "Ital Hermeneutics", 39.

[38] Powell, "Ital Hermeneutics", 45.

[39] Obiagele Lake, "Cultural Ideology and RastafarI Women", in Michael Barnett (ed), *Rastafari in the New Millennium: A Rastafari Reader* (Syracuse, NY: Syracuse University Press, 2014): 222-238.

co-master of the earthly environment with the Creator (Gen. 1:28-30). Such mastery of the ecosystem does not imply degradation, however.

> [C]are for the environment is a concern for Christian spirituality because it belongs to God as one reads in Psalm 24:1: "The earth belongs to the Lord and everything in it". Consequently, ecology and spirituality constitute an item in the contemporary study of religion, given that creedal convictions can encourage eco-friendly behaviours.[40]

Former president of the Jamaica Baptist Union (JBU), Stephen Jennings, in his "Greetings" for the *Environmental Stewardship Series*, a manual prepared in response to the Union's biennial sub-theme, "The Call to Stewardship", placed the verse within the context of an ecological theology.[41] Jennings argues it is "an updated and systematic way of reflecting on a strand of biblical thought contained in verses such as Psalm 24:1".[42] These powerful insights, he maintains, should form the bedrock of Christian faith as much as other doctrinal statements. Deepening biblical and theological understanding should be accompanied by practical demonstrations of accountable environmental stewardship by Baptists and members of the religious community. The JBU have engaged in several such practical demonstrations of accountable environmental stewardship alongside the Environmental Stewardship manual. The manual is itself an ecumenical project including the scholarship of renowned theologians, climate researchers, human rights activists, and environmental scientists. Other noteworthy efforts have included the Sunday School series[43] and the Carbon fast for Lent 2015.[44] Unit Two of *Living the Word Caribbean Bible Lessons* focused on Environmental Stewardship.

The Antilles Episcopal Conference (AEC), the Roman Catholic Bishops pastoring the English-, Dutch- and French- (except Haiti) speaking Caribbean, similarly called upon Psalm 24:1 in their opening discussion on stewardship in their 2005 pastoral, *Caring for the Earth.* They discuss stewardship in a broader sense beyond building up the Church community through sharing time, talent and treasure as they had done in a previous pastoral. This stewardship involves the care of creation, which is God's gift and the primary sacrament of God's love. To take responsibility for creation, with a thankful mindset, is an important part of what it means to be created in God's image.[45] In such a stewardship context, the AEC point out that it is important to be reminded and to proclaim to the world that "the earth and its fullness is the Lord's". Human beings are in the world not as owners but as tenants and stewards. The Christian understanding of stewardship therefore involves responsibility for the integrity of creation.

The AEC return to the verse again in § 33 of the pastoral, where, in discussing elements of a contemporary Christian Spirituality, they emphasise that the Judeo-Christian interpretation of the creation story in Genesis is "that the world and everything in it were made by God, is sustained by Him, and *belongs to him*".[46] The Bishops point out that the truth of this is maintained by both Jews and Christians when they

---

[40] Duke, "From Christian Spirituality", 34.

[41] Stephen Jennings, "Greetings," Rochelle Walters, et al. (eds), *Environmental Stewardship Series* (Kingston, Jamaica: Jamaica Baptist Union and Environmental Foundation of Jamaica, 2009).

[42] Jennings, "Greetings".

[43] Thanks to my doctoral student Elecia Myers for sharing both the *Environmental Stewardship Manual* and the *Caribbean Bible Lessons* with me. Elecia has an important chapter in the manual, "How the Environment Works" to which Dr Barry Wade provides a theological response.

[44] Thanks to Rev Marvia Lawes, who shared the information on the Carbon Fast. Rev Lawes, a womanist Baptist pastor, also has a chapter on the theological perspectives on the importance of forests in the JBU environmental manual.

[45] AEC, *Caring for the Earth*, § 1.

[46] AEC, *Caring for the Earth*, § 33, emphasis in the original.

pray the Psalms. The AEC then explicitly quote Psalm 24:1 and conclude, "God is sovereign of all that exists and has instilled in every creature, including humans, laws and purposes that must be observed".[47]

The Earth is the Lord

Rastafarians, on the other hand, as an expression of their innovative and distinctive mode of biblical exegesis, drop the possessive from "Lord's" to state, "The earth *is* the Lord and the fullness thereof"; they see earth and nature as a unity and "both are identified with the Lord: 'that is how I would say God again: God is nature'".[48] "[T]he Almighty's whole *being* extends down to the smallest in creation, as he is demonstrated to be akin to them and amongst them".[49] This perspective has resonances with feminist theologian Sallie MacFague's model of the world (cosmos) as "God's body".[50] Similarly, Dancehall artiste Tanya Stephens, who demonstrates in her oeuvre the impact that Rastafari has had on the Jamaican worldview, likewise speaks of God as everything.[51]

As I argue, in relation to Tanya, the Rasta perspective appears at first glance to be pantheistic, where creation and God are said to be one and the same.[52] God is everything and so everything is God. There is no separation or distinction between God and God's creation. This is consonant with the RastafarI belief in a divine that is man in the person of Jah, HIM Haile Selassie I. God is a Black man so Black man is God.[53] Such a pantheistic vision immediately raises the question of how nature is to be treated, including and especially Black men? Should everything be worshipped – wind, trees, seas, Black men? Is some form of idolatry not implicit in such a dogma?

However, perhaps the vision is more panentheistic than pantheistic. Panentheism frames the declaration of "God is iration" in a more nuanced way that recognises everything that exists is *in* God even as God is beyond everything that exists. The Almighty dwells in all iration and this energy which imbues creation is present in humanity. Humanity becomes divine through this union with Jah's divine energy.[54]

If God is embodied, then our relationship with God must be similarly enfleshed.[55] This captures anew the way God moves in the world. Rasta argues that Judeo-Christianity tends to perceive a distinction between self and body which is paralleled in the separation between the divine and the natural world. Such a distinction has allowed African people to be denigrated. Such a distinction has allowed the earth to be mistreated. Their complexly panentheistic position pushes beyond such separation and calls for a deepened interdependence between divinity and the natural world. In claiming an identity between nature and divinity, they call for nature to be treated with the special love and regard divinity deserves. Bodies – all bodies, but especially Black bodies – must be treated differently, respectfully, as if they mattered. It requires treating our own bodies as temples which should not be defiled.[56] Our own embodiment must be taken seriously, especially Black bodies, Rastafari bodies, which are among the most denigrated in the Caribbean. This calls for a new way of seeing creation which leads to a new way of seeing God – an ecological theophany.[57]

---

[47] AEC, *Caring for the Earth*, § 33.
[48] Owens, *Dread*, 145.
[49] Powell, "Ital hermeneutic", 46.
[50] Sallie MacFague, *The Body of God: An Ecological Theology* (Minneapolis, MN: Fortress, 1993).
[51] See Perkins' discussion of Tanya Stephens' song, "You keep looking up," in Anna Kasafi Perkins, "Epilogue: A Bunch of Righteous Freaks: Tanya, God, Christians and the Bible", in Adwoa Onuora, Anna Kasafi Perkins and Ajamu Nangwaya (eds), *Rough Riding: Tanya Stephens and the Power of Music to Transform Society* (Kingston: The University of the West Indies Press, 2021): 252.
[52] Perkins, "Epilogue: A Bunch".
[53] I note that this identity between Black men and God does not extend to Black women.
[54] Powell, "Ital Hermeneutics."
[55] MacFague, *The Body of God*, i.
[56] Powell, "Ital Hermeneutics."
[57] MacFague's metaphor of God's body is also a call to seeing the world differently.

Mother Earth, Earth Mother

Rastas accept, without contradiction, that the earth is also "the loving mother", who is to be treated with respect.[58] Jamaican RastafarI dub poet Yasus Afari captures this well: "The earth is our mother and our friend!//We are the children and the friends of the earth, of the earth, of Mother Earth".[59] Akilah Jaramogi expresses similar sentiments as she recites: "Environmental destruction affects all mankind. Cherish Mama Earth is my plead [sic]. Love Mama Earth. Save Mother Earth."[60]

There is clearly an incipient ecofeminist dimension to the RastafarI perspective which may not be immediately recognised. The symbolism of the Earth as Mother/Mother Earth, who gives birth and sustains all life, including human life, makes this dimension present even as it may obscure it at the same time. The mistreatment of the Earth is akin and related to the mistreatment of women, but some Rasta may not recognise this as it is arguable that RastafarI expresses the hegemonic masculinities of Babylon, which legitimises male dominance and female subordination.[61] "Ecofeminism focuses on the lost connection between the domination of women and domination of the earth. The same patriarchal structures which have kept in place the domination of one sex by the other have also permeated thinking on the environment".[62] Indeed, patriarchal culture has defined women as "closer to nature", with resulting false equations as: "Female is to male as nature is to culture"; female and nature are the less valuable in the four. So, women are falsely said to be closer to matter, the body/flesh, earth, sexuality, and other bodily processes. (Hence the ease with which nature can be feminised as Mother.) All the assumed weaknesses, inferiority, and proneness to sin that accompany these characteristics are then said to be found women. The male is, therefore, closer to and identified with the higher realms of spirit, mind, progress, and culture. These beliefs shape social constructions such as the gendered division of labour; women's roles have been tied to "the basic sustenance of life – feeding, bearing, bringing to birth and caring for the young, nursing and caring for the sick, young and elderly – cleaning".[63]

Unsurprisingly, Rasta generally reflects these Babylonian patriarchal ideas about women, which are oft-repeated and as often unchallenged. Arguably, the negative portrayals of women reside in the wider Jamaican culture but are amplified in peculiar ways in RastafarI given the centrality of the Bible in day-to-day living. Interpretations of the Bible encourage portrayals of women as responsible for sinfulness, lust, and corruption.[64] The use of terms like "Mother Earth" may well be part of the linguistic containment of women, sustaining male privilege and subordinating women. Indeed, such fondness for the use of this term may exemplify "how women are deified in the abstract and derogated in reality".[65]

Yet, women, including Rasta sistren, have been involved in and at the forefront of the environmental movement in the Caribbean. Fox and Smith presented the case of a RastafarI woman-cofounded and -led community NGO in Trinidad, the Fondes Amandes Community Reforestation Project (FACRP).[66] In this community movement, which is has been in progress for over thirty years, there is the intersection of four discrete movements – Black Power, Rastafarianism, women's and environmental – through which it "strives to confront and move beyond the interlocking structural inequalities of race, gender, class and

[58] Owens, *Dread*, 146.
[59] Yasus Afari, "The Earth is Our Friend," [poem]. [Available at: http://www.yasusafari.com.http://www.yasusafari.com/index.asp?pageid=457445], [Last accessed: 27th March 2022].
[60] Fox and Smith, "Stewards", 164.
[61] Imani Tafari Ama, cited in Fox and Smith, "Stewards".
[62] Mary Grey, "Ecofeminism and Christian Theology", *The Furrow* 51(9) (September 2000): 482.
[63] Grey, "Ecofeminism", 482.
[64] Imani Tafari Ama," Resistance Within and Without: Reasonings on Gender Relations in RastafarI", in Michael Barnett (ed), *Rastafari in the New Millennium: A Rastafari Reader* (New York: Syracuse University Press, 2014).
[65] Lake, "Cultural Ideology", 235.
[66] Fox and Smith, "Stewards", The FACRP website is available at https://facrp1.webs.com/ [Last accessed: 27th March 2022].

religious oppression as well as ethnic divides and ecological devastation".[67] Among the activities, which the award-winning FACRP is involved in, are tree planting, forest fire prevention, environmental education, advocacy, partnering and even protest against the very government and corporations with whom it partners. Under the leadership of Jaramogi, the community was transformed; community members transformed from marginalised squatters to recognised eco-activists.

Towards a Caribbean Ecumenical Ecospirituality

In summarising the broad elements of a Caribbean ecumenical ecospirituality shaped by the distinct perspectives of RastafarI, I draw on the work of Franciscan theologian Keith Warner.[68] Warner argues that such an ecological spirituality uses scripture as an ethical resource; it engages scripture in a fashion that is open to contemporary questions and ways of knowing. Such is clearly the case in engaging with the ital hermeneutic and the experiences of women, including Rasta sistren, who are often in the forefront of environmental efforts.

Second, this ecospirituality accords creation theological and moral significance. Indeed, perhaps the Rastafarian Movement's most important contribution to ecospirituality is its theological and moral valuing of all creation as blessing, as judgement, as imbued with and by the Lord, and, importantly, even *as* the Lord. Importantly, "Since creation has a religious purpose: it bears God; it communicates God; it prompts human beings to journey into God; it praises God independently of human beings. Once creation is understood to bear religious significance, it readily follows that one recognises creation as morally significant".[69] Put another way, nature is sacramental and human beings are called on in myriad of ways to protect and care for the environment by conserving energy, reducing pollution, treating the vulnerable justly, eating naturally and sustainably, etc.[70] Furthermore, if nature communicates anything about God, it emphasises that it has inherent value that is not dependent on human beings. This approach can attenuate the radical anthropocentrism of contemporary Christian thought, for it undermines the sharp ontological division between humanity and the rest of creation assumed by many modern Christians.

Third, recognising the religious significance of creation calls for the exercise of the moral imagination in environmental ethics. It provides the moral motivation from which moral action readily follows.

Food for Thought

In closing, MacFague offers three "house rules" as we contemplate and commit to an ecumenical ecospirituality: "take only your share, clean up after yourself, and leave the place in good repair for others." Easily said. How do we get there? And how do we help others to get there? Two practical resources are found in the Carbon Fast and the *Living the Word Caribbean Bible Lessons*.

For Lent each year, a Carbon Fast could be engaged. The challenge is to look at the choices we make each day and discern their impact on the environment, and our fellow citizens locally and globally. We can then take some small steps to reduce our carbon dioxide output and to directly care for the environment. In the process, we could renew our relationship with God, each other, ourselves, and the rest of Creation.

Living the Word Bible Lessons for Easter 2020 contains lessons on Stewardship of the Environment, which are geared for adults, but could easily be adapted for all age groups. The lessons are structured around

---

[67] Fox and Smith, "Stewards", 158-59.

[68] Warner, "Franciscan Environmental Ethics."

[69] Warner, "Franciscan Environmental Ethics", 150.

[70] Nathaniel Samuel Murrell, "Introduction: The Rastafari Phenomenon", in Nathaniel Samuel Murrell, William David Spencer and Adrian Anthony McFarlane (eds), *Chanting Down Babylon: The Rastafari Reader* (Kingston, Jamaica: Ian Randle, 1998).

key verses of scripture ("Bible Focus"), a "Key Verse", central truth to be remembered ("Bible Truth"), a question for individual reflection ("Life Question"), an extended teaching on the Bible ("What does the Bible teach?"), a poetic item ("That's Life"), and a "Reality Check". A very useful activity is "My Environmental Audit", which helps us to see how to improve conduct to honour God in the way we treat the environment.

Suggestions for Further Reading

Antilles Episcopal Conference (AEC). "Pastoral on Stewardship and the Revitalisation of Parish Life in the Caribbean (SRPL)". Port of Spain: Antilles Episcopal Conference Secretariat, 2003. [Available at: http://aecbishops.org/wp-content/uploads/2019/01/Stewardship-and-the-Revitalization-of-Parish-Life-in-the-Caribbean-converted.pdf], [Last accessed: 27th March 2022].

___. "AEC Declaration on Climate Change". Port of Spain: Antilles Episcopal Conference Secretariat, 8th June 2015. [Available at: http://aecbishops.org/aec-statement-declaration-on-climate-change/], [Last accessed: 16th December 2021].

Diocese of Jamaica & The Cayman Islands. "Christians urged to take part in carbon fast during Lent". *Carbon Fasting: Diocese of Jamaica & The Cayman Islands Website.* 27th February 2017. [Available at: http://www.anglicandioceseja.org/?p=8146], [Last accessed: 27th March 2022].

Living the Word Caribbean Bible Lessons, Easter Issue 2020 (Phase 4, Vol 14, No. 2). Kingston, Jamaica: Caribbean Christian Publications Ltd, 2020.

Jamaica Baptist Union. *Environmental Stewardship Series*. Kingston, Jamaica: Jamaica Baptist Union, 2009.

Section II

Concepts and Profiles of Creation Care and Eco-Diakonia in Different Regions and Denominational Traditions

Part I: Africa and the Middle East

32. "The Welfare of the Earth is our Welfare": The Work and Ministry of AACC in Eco-Diakonia and Creation Care

Lesmore Gibson Ezekiel[1]

Introduction

Ecumenical reflections and actions leading to robust initiatives that will demonstrate the imperative of creation care are crucial. They bring to the fore the facts of biblical and theological foundations of the creator God who has invited humanity to serve as stewards and servants of the earth. The bulk of human activities seem to show that the stewardship responsibility has been neglected because of greed. The earth is constantly under attack, plundered and raped by those with responsibility to care for it. Such gruesome acts are no doubt responsible for the what today is described as "ecological crisis". This makes it apt to bring to mind and action the prayer of the Rev. Ken Carter:

> O God, maker of Heaven and Earth, of all that is seen and unseen:
> You place us in your Creation, and you command us to care for it.
> Your works declare glory and splendour, and you call us to praise and reverence.
> Where we have degraded or destroyed Earth's bounty, forgive us.
> Where we have taken beauty and majesty granted, have mercy upon us.
> Where we have become estranged from creatures, we share this planet with, Grant us your Peace.
> Renew us in the waters of baptism.
> Refresh us with the winds of your Spirit, and sustain us with the Bread of Life.
> In the name of Jesus Christ and for the sake of the New Creation, we pray. Amen.[2]

The prayer brings to mind the necessity to always confess our dishonest acts towards creation and our constant need for forgiveness by the Creator-God. The earth and all that are in it belong to God but God chose to give humanity responsibility of caring for all that has been created. Humanity's quest for even the things that are not needed leads to egregious acts towards creation. Humanity has abandoned its role of a caregiver and turned to that of an exploiter. This certainly calls for genuine metanoia, repentance from the heart and complete change of attitude going forward.

The All Africa Conference of Churches (AACC) at a Glance

The All Africa Conference of Churches (AACC), *Conférence des Églises de toute l'Afrique* (CETA) is an ecumenical fellowship that represents more than 140 million African Christians drawn from the Protestant, Anglican, Orthodox and African Indigenous Churches. It has a membership of 204 national churches,

---

[1] Lesmore Gibson Ezekiel serves as the Director of Programmes at the All Africa Conference of Churches (AACC). He previously served as Director for Peace, Diakonia and Development at AACC. He holds a PhD in Ministerial Studies with emphasis in Ecumenical Theology, Missiology, Religion and Governance from University of KwaZulu-Natal South Africa. He also holds three postgraduate degrees, including a Masters of Advance Studies in Ecumenical Studies from University of Geneva, Switzerland. He is an ordained minister of Lutheran Church of Christ in Nigeria (LCCN).

[2] Ken Carter, "Prayer of Confession for Earth Day and the Festival of God's Creation", April 2012, *Re-Worship Blog*, [Available at: https://re-worship.blogspot.com/2012/04/earth-day-prayer-of-confession.html], [Last accessed: 31st March 2022].

Christian councils and institutions in 43 African countries. AACC has its head office in Nairobi, Kenya. There is a regional office in Lomé, Togo. AACC also has an office in Addis Ababa, Ethiopia, which serves as its Liaison Office to the African Union. The Desmond Tutu Conference Centre in Nairobi is an affiliate of the AACC.

Historically, an ecumenically dedicated Presbyterian, Sir Dr Francis Akanu Ibiam, together with other likeminded African ecumenists initiated and convened a conference of Christian organisations and churches in Africa that took place in the year 1958 at St Anne College, Ibadan, Nigeria. The conference laid the foundation for the formation of the All Africa Conference of Churches (AACC). Mobilisation continued among churches in the continent with support from founding mission agencies in Europe, the United Kingdom and North America.[3] This eventually led to the first assembly of the AACC in April 1963 in Kampala, Uganda. The theme of the first assembly was "Freedom and Unity in Christ". The delegates addressed the colonial situation in the spirit of African-nationalism that permeated the political scene of the continent at the time. The delegates identified themselves with the aspirations of the peoples of the continent towards development of dignity and a mature personality in Christ and exhorted the churches "to participate wholeheartedly in the building of the African nation". The AACC has accompanied the churches in their engagement in the decolonisation and nation-building processes. It played a significant role in the dismantling of apartheid in Southern Africa. The journey towards unity and freedom initiated at Kampala has continued through the assemblies that followed. This is marked by the various themes of the subsequent assemblies. The themes were formulated to address issues of the time and to stimulate further engagement within the framework of the prophetic roles of the churches in Africa.[4]

Thus, the AACC continues to accompany the churches of the continent towards addressing relevant issues that confront the continent. It has and continues to create potent platforms for collective ecclesial voices and collective ecumenical actions at different levels. Its foundational programmes are theology, peace and development, ecclesial leadership development, interfaith relations, women and gender justice issues, youth engagements, and ecumenical growth. Core issues on its agenda include social, economic and ecological justice, peace building, addressing life-denying theologies, population and demographic impediments, gender inequity, health and wholeness (HIV/AIDS), diakonia accompaniment and advocacy actions related governance, ethics and morality. The AACC continues to engage in different processes of strengthening ecumenical relationships and co-operation in the continent and globally by building and sustaining fraternity with the churches, national councils, sub-regional fellowships, with other continental bodies and global movements to ensure coherent networking and co-operation for the good of the created earth.

Eco-Diakonia and Creation Care as an Ecumenical Imperative for the AACC and Churches in Africa

Africa as a continent is endowed with human and natural resources that are enough to take of all its needs. As Mahatma Gandhi once said, "the earth provides enough for every person's need, but not enough for every person's greed."[5] The continent is faced with numerous challenges which are mostly caused by humanity and lead to disastrous outcomes. Wars and violent conflicts have continued to socially dislocate hundreds of thousands of people. Natural disasters have continued in some regions unabated. These are not unconnected to the effects of climate change. The AACC, at its 11th Assembly that took place from 2nd-7th July 2018 in Kigali, Rwanda, reaffirmed its unwavering commitments to mobilising churches and councils

[3] John Mbiti, "All Africa Conference of Churches", in Erwin Fahlbusch and Geoffrey William Bromiley (eds), *The Encyclopedia of Christianity*, Vol. 1. (Grand Rapids, MI: Wm. B. Eerdmans, 1999): 40-41.

[4] Efiong Utuk, *Visions of Authenticity: The Assemblies of the All Africa Conference of Churches 1963-1992* (Nairobi: AACC, 1997).

Jeffrey Sachs, "Need Versus Greed", 28th February 2011, *Project Syndicate Website* [Available at: https://www.project-syndicate.org/commentary/need-versus-greed-2011-02], [Last accessed: 31st March 2022].

within the continent to join efforts with state and non-state actors in addressing the ecological crisis. This commitment transformed itself into a resolution of the Assembly as a demonstration that AACC is not taking issues of climate change and its attendant consequences lightly. The resolution was translated into the five-year organisational strategy of the AACC. Climate change and care for creation and the environment constitute major thematic areas in the strategy.

The consequential impact of climate change on the continent is monumental, even though the continent contributes least to the climate catastrophe. Africa continues to bear the brunt of the devastating effects of climate change. There is no part of Africa that has not suffered losses because of the climate crisis. The devastating impact of climate change is manifested in the rising sea levels in the coastal regions leading to serious flooding that has destroyed lives, properties and sources of livelihood of many households. The World Meteorological Organization (WMO) Secretary General, Petteri Taalas, lamenting the havoc caused by climate on the continent of Africa said, "Climate change is having a growing impact on the African continent, hitting the most vulnerable hardest, and contributing to food insecurity, population displacement and stress on water resources. In recent months we have seen devastating floods, an invasion of desert locusts and now face the looming spectre of drought because of a La Niña event. The human and economic toll has been aggravated by the COVID-19 pandemic."[6] Taalas has captured succinctly the existential threats of climate change on the vulnerable population of the continent. In order not to be guilty of minimising the affected population to the vulnerable groups, no one can deny one's own responsibility. Food insecurity affects all regardless which social category a population falls within.

Eco-diakonia is a critical component of ecumenical witness and ministry. The *Dictionary of the Ecumenical Movement* defines diakonia as "the responsible service of the gospel by deeds and by words performed by Christians in response to the needs of people."[7] The displaced and vulnerable populations need to be attended to. The diakonia imperative compels the churches and ecumenical entities to respond to those affected by natural disasters in their moment of dire need. Biblically speaking, John 10:10 alongside Luke 4:16-21 and Matthew 25:31-46 evidently point to a vision and practice of diakonia as the churches' embodiment of God's reign to come with its promise of life, justice and peace and God's preferential option for the poor as theological and ethical criteria for the way forward. These texts should serve as the motivation and inspiration needed by the church as an institution and individual Christian to deliberately get involved in diakonia. The AACC accompanies the affected populations through the member churches and councils and through capacity building initiatives. A number of member churches and representatives of councils participated in capacity-strengthening programmes on diakonia. The programmes challenged churches to be intentional in putting in place institutional mechanisms that respond to the plights of the people affected by emergencies.

Creation care is crucial in legitimising the ministry and witness of the church. Biblical narratives call for authentic stewardship. The notion of stewardship addresses the misleading idea of exploiting the environment. It is countercultural to the culture of greed and excessive desire for wealth accumulation. The AACC emphasises the need to reject the notion of extreme greed that often leads to unbridled exploitation of nature and at the expense of human populations. A penchant for material acquisition continues to be responsible for the plundering of the ecosystem where biodiversity is constantly under severe threat. Jeffrey Sachs, disturbed by the reality of greed leading to the superlative robbing and raking of nature, bemoans that, "if greed dominates, the engine of economic growth will deplete resources, push the poor aside, and drive us into social, political, and economic crisis. The alternative is political and social co-operation, both within countries and internationally. There will be enough resources and prosperity to go around if we

---

[6] UN Climate Change News, "Climate Change Is an Increasing Threat to Africa", 27th October 2020, *UN Climate Change Website,* [Available at: https://unfccc.int/news/climate-change-is-an-increasing-threat-to-africa], [Last accessed: 31st March 2022].

[7] Art "Diakonia", in: Nicholas Lossky a.o. (eds): Dictionary of the Ecumenical Movement, WCC Publications 2002, Geneva, p. 305ff

convert our economies to renewable energy sources, sustainable agricultural practices, and reasonable taxation of the rich. That is a path to shared prosperity through improved technologies, political fairness, and ethical awareness."[8] The AACC works to enlighten its constituency to understand the nexus between economic and ecological injustice. Injustice in any of the two dimensions impacts the other, thereby leading to devastating outcomes for humanity and nature. This understanding will certainly spur individual Christians and the churches to challenge systems and structures that oppose the fullness of life for the vulnerable population. The AACC has and will continue to strengthen the capacity of member churches and councils to work and advocacy for a just society.

Welfare of the Earth, our Welfare: A Theological Motif for Ecumenical Engagement for Climate Justice

In preparation for its participation in COP26 in Glasgow, United Kingdom, the AACC convened a roundtable for faith leaders drawn from different African countries, most of whom were from AACC constituency with representatives of other faith communities. The roundtable was to take place in Addis Ababa in May 2021 with a driving theme, "The Welfare of the Earth is our Welfare". In the statement that was issued at the end of the roundtable, the faith leaders identified as key demands for COP26: "We, the faith leaders in Africa, guided by our religious teachings and in recognition that we are close to the grassroots that bear the brunt of the devastating impact of climate change state unequivocally that Climate Change remains a serious existential threat facing humanity. This is not what Creator God intended for all creation. We are obligated by our life-affirming faith to demand from State and Non-State Actors to stand shoulder-to-shoulder with a sense of urgency to respond to the effects of climate change."[9] The faith leaders were mindful of their spiritual and moral responsibility to caution humanity, particularly those within their faith communities, to refrain from immoral acts that negatively impact nature. They were cognizant of their responsibility of being a voice of the voiceless, who are the bulk of those who suffer most from the effects of climate change. The Christian sacred texts admonish believers that, "Speak up for those who cannot speak for themselves, for the rights of all who are destitute. Speak up and judge fairly; defend the rights of the poor and needy."[10] The faith leaders collectively affirmed that no one of them has a reason not to be actively involved in actions for climate justice including creation care. This is in recognition that humanity is part of the ecosystem benefitting from what nature gives. This is, of course, connected to the understanding that all people, the universe, the Earth and all its components have a value in itself and are naturally connected to each other for their mutual good.

The Christian belief system makes clear that the world is God's marvellous gift to human and nonhuman creation, and that God's offer of life is graciously providing abundance for all the created earth. This notion of the world as God's marvellous gift is rooted in the understanding that the world and all that is within it is God's good creation as explicitly written in Psalm 24:1. The understanding is that nonhuman creation is a valued and equal part of God's creation, just as we, human beings, are also valued and equal members of the created-earth by God. God intended for us to live in relationship with each other and God's creation. This is about a relationship of serenity and vitality. The biblical creation narrative affirms God's love for all the earth that is inclusive of creation and humanity as a whole. Our authentic response to God's love for creation is our unwavering care for and stewardship of the earth. Good stewardship leads to a reciprocal relationship between people and the earth. The reciprocity is seen in the way and manner that humanity appreciates and nourishes the ecosystem and biodiversity that benefits human beings the most. Seemingly, human beings must recognise this as a fact that humanity depends on the earth and, therefore, they are

[8] Jeffrey Sachs, "Need Versus Greed", 28th February 2011, *Project Syndicate Website* [Available at: https://www.project-syndicate.org/commentary/need-versus-greed-2011-02], [Last accessed: 31st March 2022].
[9] AACC Statement on Climate Change – Key Asks for COP 26, Addis Ababa, 20th May 2021.
[10] Proverbs 31:8-9, New International Version.

obligated to take care of it. Responsible stewardship is demonstrated through human care of creation and care for fellow humankind. This is further affirmed by the need for human beings to recognise that the earth is a balanced and diverse domain where responsible stewards function as partners with, rather than as rulers over, the Earth and thereby would be able to sustain its balance and diversity. In essence, stewardship means a shift in our understanding and relationship with creation from being rulers over creation to becoming partners caring for all creation as entrusted by God of life.[11]

Sacred People, Sacred Earth: Our Call

In conclusion, the theological and ethical tasks of answering climate change and environmental degradation are demanding and should not be seen as fallacious although denialist conspiracy theories have continued to be circulated in Africa which propagate that climate change in essence is not a cause for panic. These denialist perceptions are also found among people who claim to be professing a living faith. It is most unfortunate that despite the obvious fact that the impacts of climate change are tremendous, they have chosen the path of disbelief. AACC as a faith-oriented organisation intends to intensify its campaigns and engagements to counter misleading messages and convictions on climate change in the continent of Africa and in African Christianity. AACC will collaborate with organisations, institutions and agencies with similar mission and objectives to mobilise sacred people to preserve, conserve and protect the sacred earth as we all share and enjoy life in its fullness as promised by the living God of the ecosystem and biodiversity.

People of faith must deliberately be involved in activities that mitigate the effects of climate change. They must support and contribute in concrete ways to climate change adaptation interventions to be resilient communities in Africa, while calling on governments, multilateral organisations, financial institutions, and multinational corporations to do the needful in combating threats to our common home. Multinational corporations and financial institutions must refrain from financing fossil fuel generation in any significant quantity. All organisations, institutions and agencies should reject acts that desecrate and destroy nature by walking the talk on policy implementation and commitments made during different of parties and other related events. The ecclesial community and ecumenical movements should not stop from its prophetic engagements of calling all people and institutions to renounce consumerism in its entirety and embrace modesty in all ramifications of lifestyle that does not exploit and inflict injuries on nature, thereby inflicting pains and sufferings on vulnerable populations.

Suggestions for Further Reading

Ezekiel, Lesmore Gibson and Jooseop Keum, Eds. *From Achimota to Arusha: An Ecumenical Journey of Mission in Africa*. Geneva & Nairobi: WCC Publications and Acton Publishers, 2018.

Houghton, John. *Global Warning: The Complete Briefing*. 4th Edn. London: Cambridge University Press, 2012.

Sachs, Jeffrey. "Need Versus Greed", 28th February 2011, *Project Syndicate Website* [Available at: https://www.project-syndicate.org/commentary/need-versus-greed-2011-02], [Last accessed: 31st March 2022].

[11] Lesmore Gibson Ezekiel, "Mission as Transforming Discipleship: An African Missio-Discourse", in Lesmore Gibson Ezekiel and Jooseop Keum (eds), *From Achimota to Arusha: An Ecumenical Journey of Mission in Africa* (Geneva & Nairobi: WCC Publications and Acton Publishers, 2018): 158.

33. Ecological Crisis and Climate Change as a Theological Challenge in Francophone Africa

Samuel Frouisou[1]

Introduction

In a globalised world, sometimes called the "global village", it's easy to think that everyone should conform to the prevailing culture. In this regard, those who do not conform or who resist one or other dominant culture are treated as "barbarians" or "uncivilised". In this sense, African societies, as a whole, are also faced with various challenges to adapting their political, economic, socio-cultural and religious systems of organisation to the new world order, and if not, they simply disappear. This is why, in most African countries, there is nowadays a great confusion as to the actions to be taken, especially when faced with the ecological crisis and climate change as a challenge to the well-being of the entire creation.

In other words, the problem of the ecological crisis and climate change as a challenge in Francophone Africa lies at the centre of the debates which affect deeply and completely the integrity of human life as a whole. More so than in the past, the question of the ecological crisis and that of climate change are linked to the polysemic concepts of well-being or common good for all, as the very survival of the human species is at stake. The consequences of such a crisis will very negatively affect those African societies who are still lagging behind, because they are unbalanced by both endogenous and exogenous forces.

It should also be remembered that it was the dominant civilisations of Judeo-Christian and Arab-Muslim origin, who set up the systems of exploiting natural resources during the periods of historical encounters between the different peoples on the earth. But the results of such enterprises, as we now know, are recurring evils, from which the whole of creation currently suffers: these evils are environmental degradation, pollution, desertification, climate change, famine, and also the availability and judicious distribution of arable land. These challenges are closely linked to the issue of sustainable development, a subject of a declaration adopted by the United Nations General Assembly in September 2015.[2]

What can or should be the contribution of African Christian theologians in the context of this crisis today?

The main objective of this chapter is to underline the importance of community life and the expression of solidarity in Francophone Africa on the one hand, and on the other, to evaluate the effects of the different encounters between the world civilisations in Africa historically. This is so because in Africa we do not speak of "wealthy", "developed", or "prosperous" countries apart from regarding community life. The African concept of "Ubuntu" excludes any individualism, any egoism, and any exploitation of nature or of human beings. From African perspectives each life is sacred, therefore the notions of "wealth", "prosperity", and "development" take up different meanings.

This article will first present three conceptions of the world as an attempt to explain the biblical advent of a new heaven and a new earth (according to the Book of the Revelation of John 21:1-5). Secondly, it will present the current context of the ecological crisis as a challenge. Finally, it will present the role and the importance of prayer as an attempt to manage the effects of ecological crisis and climate change from an African perspective.

---

[1] Rev. Professor Samuel Frouisou is the General Secretary and Director of Doctoral School and Head of the Department of History and Religious Sciences of the Faculty of Protestant Theology and Religious Sciences of the Protestant University of Central Africa in Yaoundé-Cameroon.

[2] At the heart of the 2030 agenda, 17 Sustainable Development Goals (SDGs) were set in September 2015. They cover all the development issues in all countries such as climate, biodiversity, energy, water, poverty, gender equality, economic prosperity, peace, agriculture, education, just to name but a few.

Biblical Concepts of a New Heaven and a New Earth

How can we tackle the problem of the ecological crisis within the framework of an inter-convictional, ethical and theological dialogue, capable of bringing together and integrating the whole of humanity in its physical and spiritual environments?

How can mankind reverse the process of corruption and the pollution of the physical environment, which seems to be irreversible nowadays? How should human beings deal with the multidimensional damage which their actions are causing to planet earth? And how can or should human beings act in accordance with the vision of creation account in the book of Genesis?

The convictions based on the accounts of the revealed religions of Abrahamic origin, namely, Judaism, Christianity and Islam, present three different avenues of research and visions, with a view to the restoration of the original creation, named "Tikkun Olam"[3] in the Jewish tradition, as the earth groans under the destructive effects of the combined actions of sin and greed in human beings.[4]

The Iconographic Vision of the World as a Possible Solution for the Restoration of Creation

An icon is defined as a way of perceiving, understanding and representing the elements of nature in their interactions. It is, in fact, the conception whereby every element created by God, every element that has the breath of life in it, is holy (see Psalm 150:6). In other words, when our heart is sensitive to this reality of things, our eyes are open to clearly discern the beauty of created things, as will say Abba Isaac, The Syrian.[5]

Icons restore and reconcile; they remind us that we are not the only creatures of God, living in the cosmos; they offer us possibilities to correct our destructive cultures. Icons reveal to us what the real value of all of God's creatures really is, and why God created them. Icons engage us, or rather engage our theological convictions in a perspective of faith in the advent, or in the realisation of the kingdom of heaven on earth. The icons help us distance ourselves from philosophical considerations which differentiate the material from the spiritual, the temporal from the eternal, and the created from the uncreated.

This is why in Christianity, the doctrine of the incarnation is at the heart of iconography (see Psalm 45:2; John 1:1-18; Romans 8:18-22). For Christians, the whole of creation is an icon. Because "nothing is for nothing before God," Irenaeus[6] would say. This is why in the icons, the rivers have a human form, as well as the sun, the moon and the stars that God has created (see Psalm 8:4-8).

The Liturgical Vision of Creation

When we consider the impact of the actions of human beings on their physical environment, we are often far from realising that these actions are really damaging to the ecosystem. In their daily actions, human beings behave like simple tourists, extra-terrestrials whose survival would be totally independent of that of the earth, from which they nevertheless draw all the resources necessary for their existence. Taking a closer look at this, we realise that human treatment of the environment carries the germ of original sin, that is to

[3] In the teaching of Judaism, Tikkun Olam recalls any activity aimed at improving the harmonious state of the original creation. Tikkun Olam also means that the world was created good; its Creator intentionally provided an opportunity to improve the state of his work. All human activities should be considered as opportunities to accomplish this mission. As such, any person, regardless of their social status, can and should be associated with Tikkun Olam: child or adult, student or entrepreneur, industrialist or artist, social worker or merchant, political activist or environmentalist, or any other person here among us, who fights against the deterioration of creation, in view of its restoration.

[4] See Hosea 4:3 and Romans 8:22.

[5] Le Syrien, A. I., *Light through Darkness: Orthodox Spirituality* (Maryknoll, NY: Orbis Books, 2004).

[6] Irenaeus lived in the 2nd Century, he wrote a number of books, the most important of which is *Contre les hérésies dénonciation et réfutation de la gnose au nom menteur,* traduit par le Moine Adelin Rousseau (Amazon Books, 2001).

say, the pride and disobedience of humanity, instead of the responsibility vis-à-vis the creation of God, as defined in the book of Genesis 1 and 2.[7]

The liturgy is precisely an exaltation of the communion between God, the peoples and the things which God has created. For it is through the liturgy that God is celebrated in his creation, as well as by humans, trees, birds, stars, and the moon (see Psalm 19:1). Thus, if we forget that our life is a liturgy which consists of imploring God for the renewal of our cosmos polluted by our irresponsible actions, we are far from being those creatures that God made a little inferior to himself.

The Ascetic Vision of the World as a Solution to the "Ecological Crisis"

Asceticism should not always be understood as contempt, the flight from the material realm for the benefit of the spiritual. Lynn White, in an article titled, "The Roots of Our Ecological Crisis," notes the following: "The Eastern Saint Contemplates; the Saint of the West acts; the Latins thought that sin was moral evil, and that salvation should be found in good behaviour. […] The implications of Christianity in the conquest of nature should therefore come more easily from the West."[8] It appears, according to this author, that a contemplative vision of nature is more sober and gentle, in terms of the impact on creation, than an aggressive action. Therefore, to have an ascetic view of the world in order to solve the problem of the ecological crisis is to learn to offer, to share and to reconnect with one's fellow human beings and with nature at the same time. It is also to move away from our selfishness and to love other creatures through the love of God the Creator.

If our ecological commitments should leave the field of theoretical and convictional dissensions, to take shape in concrete actions, we will have to follow these three models mentioned above – models which are complementary in our search for solutions to our environmental problems; namely the biblical model, the ascetic model and the sacramental model.

According to the ascetic model, the solution to the "ecological crisis" comes from putting into practice the following three "Rs", namely: Renunciation, Repentance and Responsibility.

1. *Renunciation* consists of using material goods with parsimony and intelligence. It is about living simply, and simply living.
2. *Repentance* is about confessing, i.e. to confess that we have abused of the land, and by doing so, having failed in our vocation to cultivate and keep the land safe from any harm (see Genesis 2:15).
3. *Responsibility* is about engaging with the ways in which we respond to "the call of God", in the face of the challenge of preserving his creation. We are called to surrender to the wisdom and love of God who wants us to be responsible for the renewal of his creation, according to the Revelation to John 21 and Paul's Letter to the Romans 8.

Thus, one of the major challenges to be taken up by the Christian churches in Africa lies in taking into consideration the word of Jesus: "Give them food yourselves" Matthew 14:16b, and putting into practice "Give us this day our daily bread" (Mt. 6:11).

Meeting the challenges of sustainable development, in the current context, will mean dealing with the issues of climate change, food security and the management of creation from a pastoral and theological perspective. Hence the following question is important for us: how do we train men and women, capable of giving their best for the cause of the poor, the hungry and those left behind in the "global village"? What are the tools or arguments that African Christians need, which can enable them to feed themselves, and to ask God for the daily bread for those among us who are in need?

---

[7] La Bible, Edition bilingue, Français et Anglais, 1-4.

[8] Lynn White Jr, "The Historical Roots of Our Ecological Crisis," *Science*, no. 3767 (1967): 1203-07.

The Current Context of the Ecological Crisis as a Theological Challenge of Holistic Well-being in Africa

In a report published by Nagel Institute of Calvin College 2014 on the theme: "Engaging African Realities", African leaders including Ministers of Worship, University Lecturers, Theologians, Philosophers, Researchers in Social Sciences and Natural Sciences, have committed the Churches to train men and women capable of addressing the "current challenges of sustainable development".[9]

After more than half a century of autonomy, most of their theological and pastoral training seminaries, for example, continue to operate on the basis of traditional Christian doctrines and practices, established by the founding missionary societies. Training in these theological institutes and faculties is carried out as if they were training people to meet the needs of people from the nineteenth century.[10] This should no longer be the case, because as C. Peter Wagner acknowledges, "Seminaries previously functioned like dental schools or police academies. The job market is closed to those who haven't been to the approved schools. When this was the case, seminaries had an established constituency and they could function almost indefinitely. No longer [is this the case]."[11] Thus, given the new context, theological and pastoral training institutes in Africa must adapt to the new situation[12] in order to meet the current challenges of humanity threatened by multidimensional crises.

This all-out crisis that African Churches are currently going through is reflected and partly caused by the fact "that theological seminaries are no longer considered above all as institutions for the training of pastors, but as places of discussion and the study of religion."[13]

The Role and Importance of Prayer in the Management of the Ecological Crisis and Climate Change

Praying for daily bread means meeting the current challenges of climate change, food security and the problems of the earth. This is because "prayer is risky; it commits the one who prays to follow it up with a corresponding action."[14] Sometimes people might tend towards the following: "The problems of hunger in the world are so overwhelming that we are tempted to think, like the disciples: 'Send them away', or as the rich man: 'Send Lazarus beyond the grave', to warn my brothers." Knowing the answer that Jesus gave to

---

[9] Joel Carpenter and Nellie Kooistra, "Engaging Africa, Report, June 2014", Nagel Institute for the Study of World Christianity, Nagel Institute of Calvin College, NY.

[10] In the 19th century, the "Religious Awakening" crossed all of Europe. Protestant Revival and Catholic Renewal constitute the most proselytising form of Western Christianity. Groups praying for missionaries sent to the world by mission societies, notably the London Mission (LMS) founded in 1795 and the Basel Mission founded in 1815, multiplied. Baptists, Reformed, Lutherans, Independents came together for the Mission. But in the field of the Mission, misunderstandings emerged, and quickly, we witnessed the establishment of biblical and pastoral training structures, in accordance with the particular doctrines of the missionary churches. Here, special emphasis is placed on the spiritual formation of local personnel; over there, it is a workforce in the service of the "missionary-trader-settler" that preoccupies those responsible for the formation. See also the excellent articles by Joseph Ki-Zerbo, "The influence of Western cultural models on African societies", and by Michel Sauvetre, "Des Écoles, Pourquoi faire?" In Flambeau *Spécial Éducation*, Nos 34-35, May-August, 95-108 and 111-127, respectively, Cle, Yaoundé, 1972.

[11] Wagner C. Peter, Churchquake! (Ventura, CA: Regal Books, 1999), 223.

[12] In a context of multidimensional crisis where voices are being raised increasingly in favour of a holistic training of pastors, theologians and social workers, it becomes more than urgent for the theological and pastoral training to include in its curricula, in addition to the purely spiritual teachings, subjects such as: Study of the natural environment, Population growth, Environmental management, Technology and environment, etc. See also the excellent works by Joe Holland and Peter Henriot, SJ, *Social Analysis: Linking Faith and Justice* (Maryknoll, NY: Orbis, 1984); and James Cochrane, John de Cruchy and Robin Petersen, *In Word and Deed, Towards A Practical Theology for Social Transformation* (Pietermaritzburg: Cluster Publications, 1991).

[13] James Cochrane, John de Cruchy and Robin Petersen, *In Word and Deed*, 1991.

[14] "To all of you", in *Give Us Today Our Daily Bread,* Eleventh General Assembly of the LWF, Study Materials, Day Two, 2007, 7.

these two concerns, “Give them food yourselves” and, “Your brothers have prophets and preachers with them on earth, let them listen to them”, we should emphasise especially on prayer in all our actions in favour of holistic development.

According to Martin Luther,[15] “God gives bread to all men, even to the wicked, and this regardless of our prayer.” However, in this prayer, we ask that God gives us a grateful heart so that we can receive our daily bread with thanksgiving.

When asked what is meant by the expression ‘daily bread’ contained in the 4th request of the Lord’s Prayer, Luther answered: “all that is necessary for the maintenance of the body and of life, food and clothing, home, fields, cattle, money and all goods, a good husband, good children, faithful servants, just supervisors, good government, favourable seasons, peace, health, order, honour, good friends, friendly neighbours […]” This petition comes right in the middle of a series of seven different prayer requests. It should also be noted that, of these seven requests of the Our Father, it is the only one which is concerned with the material needs of humankind. It is therefore quite clear that, in the Lord’s Prayer, emphasis is placed more on spiritual blessings than on material ones, for six of the seven requests made are in favour of spiritual needs. But, in our prayers, we often reverse the order. Six of the seven requests that we make to the Lord are generally for temporal needs. Is this not the preoccupation with wanting to own the material riches of this world that often leads us to selfishness: everything for myself and nothing for others? Is it not the desire to accumulate material wealth for ourselves that makes us actors in the destruction of our own natural environment?

In terms of purely economic development, it is important to remember that relations between Africa and the outside world were essentially characterised by what Jean Yves Carfantan[16] and Charles Condamines called “the aid that makes you hungry”. It is no secret that the exclusive or one-sided system of commerce between the metropolis and the colony, also known as the “colonial pact”, consisted essentially of the development of the colony for the sole benefit of the metropolis.

The introduction of currency, money, also called Mammon in biblical language, in the colonial economy favoured the imbalance of the mechanisms of production and distribution of goods in African societies, because according to Jean Marc Ela, money “carries with it the crisis of traditional socio-economic balances”.[17]

In order to better understand the situation that African people are living in today, it must be noted that, since we have been made to believe that having a lot of money in the bank is the real sign of wealth, of social success and that human essence depends on what they own, everyone fights hard for money and always focuses on money. But for what results? For the budgets of African nations, which increase year after year simultaneously with the economic growth of these nations, which still are always described as underdeveloped? If so, why is Africa experiencing a food crisis when, at the same time, it is recognised as one of the continents potentially rich in arable land?

In a survey carried out by Jean Yves Carfantan and Charles Condamines on the causes of hunger in Third World countries including African countries, the French attribute the causes of hunger in the Third World to bad governance: “They are hungry because they are badly governed and incapable of living in a democracy”.[18] But if we follow the current debates on the issue of bad governance and the poverty of the African populations, the current givers of lessons in democracy and governance are not exempt from criticism.

---

[15] Martin Luther, *La foi des Eglises luthériennes Confessions et catéchismes*, Textes édités par André Birmelé et Marc Lienhard, Editions du Cerf (Paris: Editions Labor et Fides, Genève, 1991), 309.
[16] J.Y. Carfantan, *Vaincre la faim, c'est possible* (Paris: Seuil, 1983).
[17] J.M. Ela, *L'Afrique des villages* (Paris: Karthala, 1982), 13.
[18] J.Y. Carfantan, *Vaincre la faim*, 5-6.

Pastoral Dimensions of Prayer for "Daily Bread" in Africa

The responsibility of the Church in the management of material, financial and spiritual resources in Africa and in the world is no longer to be demonstrated.

As spiritual guides of the people of God, pastors usually are regarded as being above all lay people of prayer. The time they spend with God in intercession on behalf of His people makes them increasingly aware of the harsh realities of human life in this world, general, and in Africa, in particular. By devoting oneself to the activity of prayer, the pastor has a deeper understanding of the struggle that Christians have, to meet their daily needs. Prayer makes us aware, not only of the needs of others, but also of our own needs. In this sense, we pray the 'Lord's Prayer', not only when we are together for a worship service where we recite this model prayer, but also and above all, when we formulate specific prayers in favour of the poor who live among us. The pastor, and the Christian community of which they are leader, pray to ensure that all the poor and hungry will receive what they need, to nourish their bodies, and that together, we are satisfied, both materially and spiritually.[19]

The passages which deal with the theme of "Christ the bread of life", without being explicitly formulated in the form of a prayer, are found as examples, in John 6:1-11 Jesus feeds five thousand men; in John 6:25-40, he presents himself as the "bread of life"; in John 10:7-16, he tells the story of the labourer who works for his belly, and the good shepherd who leads the sheep into the green pasture and gives his life for them.

In explaining the Lord's Prayer to the faithful, pastors should draw the attention to the important aspects of this prayer, aspects which relate to the question of the availability of 'bread' and its equitable distribution to members of the community.

The Seventh Commandment that says, "Thou shall not steal", also has important implications for the distribution of material wealth in the world today. We must not forget that, from its beginnings, the Church has always cared for the poor and the disinherited, working for a certain social revolution. According to Acts 4:32, it is said that: "No one claimed that any of their possession was their own, but they shared everything they had".

In the history of Christian Church, the fundamental question of sound stewardship of the means with which God blesses humanity was of great concern to everyone. The question of property and material possessions was at the heart of the debate over the role the Church should play in the social, political and economic spheres. Inspired by the narratives of Genesis 1:26 and Genesis 2:15, Popes Francis and Bonaventure developed the concepts of "stewardship without property", to address the problem of corruption and mismanagement of property of the Church in the 13th century. In this same perspective, the Protestant Reformation of the sixteenth century has revived it, by reinterpreting the biblical notion of "vocation" in order to revalue human work as a divine call through which each one exercises his talent for the well-being of all.

The churches' witness must take on a diaconal dimension, the pastor sometimes then being considered as a servant in the Church or, even as a servant of the Church. This has profound concrete and practical implications.

Practical Dimension of "Give us our daily bread" in Africa

Like Christ, the pastor should avoid being served or to be served to the detriment of others. It should be noted, however, that the temptation for pastors to seek service is often very great, despite many scriptural warnings against them (Read 1 Peter 5:1-4).

---

[19] To be "materially full presupposes concrete actions aimed at producing material goods such as food, drink, clothing and shelter from the effects of weather". But, for Jesus the creator, He is already taking care of it. In other words, the prayer of the Christian must always precede the actions and not the contrary, as in Matthew 6:25-34. If, in this article, we focus on the concept of prayer, it is precisely to explain the importance of this activity (prayer is a priority activity in the life of believers), in relation to the concrete actions that Christians must lead for their testimony in the world.

There are cases of abuse of authority or mismanagement noted among pastors, where they were driven by bad management structures, resulting from organisational systems that do not promote sharing, solidarity, and collegiality, while the pastoral ministry on the contrary is defined in the Holy Scriptures, as a collegial ministry. In some so-called traditional churches, pastors are even cited as mainly serving selfish and partisan interests to the detriment of the interests of the whole Church, and especially of the weakest among us. But if the Church wants the pastor to fully play their role of servant of the community itself, it will also be necessary to accept that they are a servant in this same community, that is to say, they must be given the necessary means of service that is required of them.

In the struggle to give "bread" to all, one must not forget that the Lord himself has promised to bless his Church with all the necessary gifts that we need to function as a community of brothers and sisters, sharing all in common, according to 1 Corinthians 12:18-27.

Conclusion

The profound changes that we are witnessing in Africa affect all walks of life. But the religious or spiritual aspect seems to be the most determinant.

While it is not true to say that African culture is primarily spiritual, whereas that of the West is primarily materialistic,[20] there still is a way to make a distinction between the two visions of the world, namely, the African vision of the world, the Ubuntu concept, and the Western world visions.

The universe according to an African is a field of forces in perpetual dialectical interaction in search of new balances. Aware of this dynamism and being part of this universe, the African participates fully in the achievement of harmony within their physical and spiritual environment. This explains the African's attitude of reverence towards the elements of nature, an attitude in which Western civilisation saw more an anti-progress and inactive spiritualism.

Seen in this light, the notion of sustainable development for postmodern societies has become a top priority, a pressing necessity that affects all areas of human life. But the motives that lead to it are multiple and vary according to the field in which one is positioned. For some, only the contribution of the so-called exact or experimental sciences count in order to achieve the goal for development. For others, all contributions, wherever they come from, are of equal importance, provided that they lead us to meet the challenge of realising the goals of sustainable development.

In order to give back to humanity its true dimension which thereby places it at the centre of any process of sustainable development, it is the task of Christians, committed to the search for practical solutions, to meet the challenges of an ecological crisis, in close relation with deviant theologies linked to very controversial and polysemous notions of holistic well-being and the preservation of God's creation.

Suggestions for Further Reading

Carfantan, J.Y. *Vaincre la faim, c'est possible*. Paris: Seuil, 1983.

Carpenter, Joel and Nellie Kooistra. "Engaging Africa, Report, June 2014", *Nagel Institute for the Study of World Christianity*. New York: Nagel Institute of Calvin College, 2014.

Cochrane, James, John de Cruchy and Robin Petersen. *In Word and Deed, Towards A Practical Theology for Social Transformation.* Pietermaritzburg: Cluster Publications, 1991.

Ela, J. M. *L'Afrique des villages*. Paris: Karthala, 1982.

Hamidou Kane, Cheikh. *L'Aventure Ambigüe*. Paris: Union Générale des Editions, 1961.

Ki-Zerbo, Joseph. *Histoire de l'Afrique noire.* Paris: Hatier, 1978.

---

[20] Cheikh Hamidou Kane, in his novel, *L'Aventure Ambigüe*, especially 83-86, treats Islam as an African religion and contrasts it with Western culture, which he calls very materialistic, with "Islamised" Africa, which he strongly qualifies as spiritualist.

La foi des Eglises luthériennes Confessions et catéchismes. Textes édités par André Birmelé et Marc Lienhard, Paris: Editions du Cerf; Genève: Editions Labor et Fides, 1991.
Wagner, C. Peter. *Church quake!* Ventura, CA: Regal Books, 1999.

34. African Ecumenical and Diaconal Approaches to Ecological Crisis Mitigation

James Amanze[1]

Introduction

This essay examines African ecumenical and diaconal approaches to ecological crisis mitigation today. The need to mitigate the effects of the ecological crises facing Africa is not only a matter of urgency but it is also a matter of absolute necessity. Failure to stop the ravages of ecological degradation will lead to the extinction of humanity itself and the rest of creation. This paper begins by looking at the ecological crisis globally and Africa in particular. To substantiate the point that Africa is indeed experiencing ecological crisis, some examples are given from a number African countries. After this, some of the causes are examined that are believed to cause environmental degradation in Africa. A lot of these factors evolve around the need for economic growth and the misinterpretation of the theology of "domination" of nature as narrated in Genesis 1:26-30. Finally, the author considers what to be the best ecumenical and diaconal approaches in the efforts being made towards mitigating the negative impacts of the ecological crisis in Africa today.

Ecological Crisis – A Global Phenomenon

Maurice F. Strong, in *Redeeming the Creation*, stated that the world is facing a crisis as a result of the damage "we are inflicting on our earth's environment and life-support systems in the pursuit of our economic and development goals".[2] The ecological crisis is of such magnitude that, for a number of years now, world leaders and ecumenical organisations have been making relentless efforts to come up with policies and programmes that can put a stop to the contemporary destruction and turmoil of the ecosystem in order to preserve it for future generations. In the contemporary world, ecological issues are considered not only in local terms but also in global terms. It has been established that the earth should be conceived as a single home in which life is interconnected. In this regard, damage, waste and greed in one place diminish life in other places. It is held, for instance, that warming of the global atmosphere, while caused primarily by the fossil fuels burned by affluent societies in the Northern Hemisphere, threatens a rise in sea levels and changes in weather patterns which cause global consequences. In the same way, preserving fresh water and controlling toxic waste requires not only local and regional solutions but also international action.[3] Africa is one of the continents which is currently experiencing the negative effects of ecological crisis that needs urgent mitigation using all means available.

---

[1] Professor James Nathaniel Amanze, St. Augustine Theological School, P. O. Box 769. Gaborone, Botswana, is a Retired Professor in Systematic Theology at the University of Botswana in the Department of Theology and Religious Studies. He holds a PhD in Religious Studies (University of London), MA in Theology (Oxford University), BA Honors in Theology (Oxford University), Bachelor of Social Science (University of Malawi) and Diploma in Theology (Makerere University). He has carried out extensive and intensive research both in Malawi and Botswana primarily in the areas of contextual systematic theology, ecumenical theology and African Traditional Religions. He has served as Chairman of the Association of Theological Institutions in Southern Africa (ATISCA 1994-1998), as African Representative in the World Conference of Theological Institutions (WOCATI-2008-2010) and Secretary/ Treasurer (2010-2015). Professor Amanze is currently serving as Executive Secretary of ATISCA. Contact: amanzejames@gmail.com or amanzejn@ub.ac.bw.

[2] Maurice F. Strong, "Foreword" in Wesley Granberg-Michaelson (ed), *Redeeming the Creation* (Geneva: WCC Publications, 1992): iii.

[3] Granberg-Michaelson, *Redeeming the Creation*, 12.

Ecological Crisis in Africa and the Need for Mitigation

Africa is at a crossroads; one road leads to self-extinction, the other leads to self-preservation. Obaji M. Agbiji has observed that many parts of Africa are currently experiencing the severe effects of environmental degradation arising from extensive exploitation carried out by multinational companies.[4] In the same vein, K. Mwambazambi has opined that although Africa has not contributed much to global climate changes, it is, certainly, among the continents that have been impacted negatively by climate change. It is noted that more than 180 million people will suffer from the consequences of climate change in Sub-Saharan Africa.[5] This point has been made more forcefully by George K. Kiarie, who has noted that environmental crisis is experienced in many countries in Africa from North to South and from East to West.[6] A few examples of the magnitude of the ecological crisis in Africa will suffice here. Kiarie, writing about ecological degradation in Kenya, has documented the disappearance of thick forests, trees on the mountains, fish and aquatic life in rivers and lakes, wild animals, reduced water levels in dams and the degradation of beautiful features that captivate the eye.[7]

Kenya is, of course, not the only country in Africa which is experiencing the dire consequences of ecological destruction. Several countries in Africa are going through the same experience. For instance, Grain W. Malunga noted that "Malawi's high population density and the dependence of Malawians on agricultural production, in the absence of other economic opportunities, led to alarming rates of environmental degradation. The result has been deforestation, decreased soil fertility, increasing erosion, water depletion, loss of biodiversity and increasing pollution. These poor environmental conditions are exacerbated by poverty. In order to subsist, a high proportion of the population relies on the exploitation of natural resources as firewood and fish stocks."[8]

Nigeria is experiencing a similar crisis where the key issues facing the country include land degradation, deforestation, water and air pollution, intensive grazing, over-cultivation and continued urbanisation,[9] a picture that is also replicated in South Africa. Brett Smith has indicated that, in South Africa, the mining of the countryside has been a major cause of the country's ecological crisis. The solid waste produced in the mines are discarded in enormous dumpsites. These contain radioactive uranium which, when inhaled, induces serious health conditions like lung cancer.[10] It has also been observed that, in Angola, ecological crisis is worsening. The main problems reported include, among others, land abuse, desertification, loss of forests, impure water, soil erosion, the disappearance of endangered species such as elephants, Vernay's

---

[4] Obaji M. Agbiji, "Religion and Ecological Justice in Africa: Engaging value for community as praxis for ecological and socio-economic justice", *HTS Theological Studies*, online version, 71(2) (2015): 5.

[5] K. Mwambazambi, "A theological view of environmental protection in Africa", *Skrifling*, online journal, 45(4) (2011). [Available at: http://www.scielo.org.za/Scielo.phphttp://www.scielo.org.za/scielo.php?script=sci_arttext&pid=S2305-08532011000400007&lng=en&nrm=iso], [Last accessed: 2nd March 2022].

[6] Wesley Granberg-Michaelson (ed), *Redeeming the Creation* (Geneva: WCC Publications, 1992) 12.

[7] George K. Kiarie, "Environmental Degradation: What is the role of the church in environmental conservation in Kenya from 1963-2019", *Studia Historiae Ecclesiasticae*, online version, 46(2), Pretoria (2020): 2.

[8] Grain W. Malunga, "Foreword" in *Malawi State of Environment and Outlook Report: Environment for Sustainable Economic Growth,* Lilongwe: Ministry of Natural Resources, Energy and Environment, Malawi Government, 2010, iii. [Available at: https://www.unep.org/resources/report/malawi-state-environment-and-outlook-report-0], [Last accessed: 2nd March 2022].

[9] UNEP, "Nigeria: National Policy on the Environment (Revised 2016)", 7. [Available at: https://leap.unep.org/countries/ng/national-legislation/national-policy-environment-revised-2016], [Last accessed: 2nd March 2022].

[10] Brett Smith, "South Africa: Environmental Issues, Policies and Clean Technology", 30th July 2015, *AZO Clean Tech* [Available at: https://www.azocleantech.com/article.aspx?ArticleID=561], [Last accessed: 2rd March 2022].

climbing monkey and the black rhinoceros. The list of endangered animals, birds and plants is almost endless![11]

Another example of ecological crisis can be drawn from Ghana where air pollution causes the premature death of nearly 16,000 people while more than half of the deaths from pneumonia in children under five is associated with air pollution. Again, it is held, that water pollution causes significant damage to equivalent to 3% of the GDP while plastics pollution is increasing to crisis proportions. Added to these environmental issues are poor land management, deforestation, artisan gold mining, coastal erosion and flooding, climate change to name but a few.[12]

Who is to Blame for the Ecological Crisis in Africa?

Ecological crisis in Africa can be blamed on several factors. One of these is the African people themselves. Akin L. Mabongunje in "The Environmental Challenges in Sub Saharan Africa" has argued that the people of the African region are highly irresponsible towards the environment and look to the international community to save them from themselves. According to Mabongunje, "Africa finds itself now afflicted by the consequences of inappropriate policies, endemic political instability, inability to manage its economies effectively and an increasingly hostile external economic milieu".[13] Interestingly, this indictment of the African people as being responsible for the degradation of the ecosystem, stands in sharp contrast with the traditional African values of conservation of nature. This means that the main factors that lead to ecological crisis in Africa are primarily external. As we shall see below, anthropological research in Africa both in the past and in the present shows, unequivocally, that the African people are by nature conservationists. They live "in communion" with nature thereby assuring its conservation and preservation for future generations.

The African Peoples' Theology of "In Communion" with Nature

It is important to point out that, in traditional Africa, the environment occupies a very special place in the life and work of the African people. It is engraved in their spiritual and religious systems. In the absence of legal frameworks to protect the environment, like those found in western societies, many African communities have belief systems and practices that prevent people from degrading nature by imposing ethical injunctions in the form of taboos which, if broken, have immediate disastrous consequences. As a result, the relationship between nature and human beings in most African societies is one characterised as being "in communion" with nature and not "dominating" nature. In this regard, the aspect of being "in communion" with nature has ensured the preservation of landmarks such as forests, hills, as well as endangered animals, birds and other natural resources. As a result, the continent of Africa has been able to conserve vast natural resources for millions of years.[14]

One of the most important and significant elements in the conservation of natural resources in Africa has been the role played by African Traditional Religious beliefs, practices and spirituality. Anthropological research testifies to the fact that Africans are environmentally user friendly. In Africa, land and its environs are considered as one of the most precious gifts God gave to humankind because people are born in it, live on it, and are buried in the bosom of the mother earth. God is conceived as the sole owner of the land who

---

[11] "Angola-Environment" *Nations Encyclopedia*, [Available at: https://www.nationsencyclopedia.com/Africa/Angola-ENVIRONMENT.html], [Last accessed: 2nd March 2022].
[12] Sanjay Srivastavaagata and Ewa Pawlowska, "Ghana: Balancing economic growth and depletion of resources" 26th September 2020 *World Bank Blogs* [Available at: https://blogs.worldbank.org/africacan/ghana-balancing-economic-growth-and-depletion-resources], [Last accessed: 2nd March 2022].
[13] Akin L. Mabongunje, "The Environmental Challenges in Sub-Saharan Africa" *African Technology Forum* 8(1) (1995): 1, [Available at: http://web.mit.edu/africantech/www/articles/EnvChall.htm] [Last accessed: 2nd March 2022].
[14] James N. Amanze, "From dominion to in communion: Ecotheology from an African perspective", *Anglican EcoCare Journal of Eco Theology* 2 (2016): 11.

has entrusted it to the living through the living-dead who are considered as "guardians of the land". According to Geoffrey Parrinder, land is generally considered sacred in Africa for it belongs to the earth-spirit and to the ancestors as well as the living community.[15]

It is generally held among African scholars that the African people understand themselves as living "in communion" with nature. Therefore, all elements of creation – land, plants, animals, non-living things and humanity – are knit together. Their common origin is God himself. Africans understand themselves as part of God's creation. As a result, their life is lived in community.[16] Dominique Zahan has intimated that the natural tendency of African religion is to maintain a close contact with the cosmos. He has further noted that the African people's close relationship with nature explains the existence of natural landmarks that are scattered throughout the African continent through which the African people communicate with the divine to ensure its continued existence".[17]

One of the dominant views among the African people is that, in order to live in harmony with nature, the natural world must be protected from all forms of defilement. This is because defilement of the land such as cutting trees unnecessarily generates a state of "hotness" which is the antithesis to "coolness". Hotness, it is believed, leads to drought which is a form of punishment from God. There is a general belief among the African people that for the land to be useful to human beings, it must remain constantly in the state of ritual coolness. This generates good health, material prosperity, harmony, peace, social order, spiritual blessedness and most important of all rain.[18] It is strongly believed that land has been given to human beings as a gift from God. In this regard, human beings do not possess the land as their own personal property to be used at will but act as trustees of it.[19] Thus the environment in many African communities is protected by unwritten traditional laws which are based on the beliefs and practices of traditional religions and not on rules enforced by the government.

Evan Zuesse in his anthropological study of the Lele people, who live on the southern fringes of the Congo Forest, established that, among this group of people, conservation of nature is not only desirable but it is also mandatory. According to Zuesse, the Lele people have beliefs and religious practices that promote social cohesion, solidarity and harmony among the people and the environment.[20] John Mbiti has indicated that many African people have sacred forests where they perform religious ceremonies for a variety of needs such as rain, fertility of the land, childbearing, peace and the like. Certain trees in the forest, where sacrifices, offerings and prayers are made, are considered sacred. In most cases, such forests are protected and thus become a sanctuary of plants, birds, and animals. This is the case, for example, among the Chewa of Southern Malawi who locate the land of the departed in the woods and forests. They also have special forests where they pray for rain in times of drought.[21]

Great respect for the environment is also shared by several people groups in Southern Africa. This is the case among the Batswana of Botswana where the conservation of trees is not only sanctioned by the letter of the law but also by indigenous religious beliefs. The chiefs are considered custodians of the environment. They represent the will of the ancestors and God. In traditional Africa, their word is law *de facto* and *de jure.* It is believed among several ethnic groups in the country that certain trees are associated with the fertility of the land. Therefore, cutting them can bring bad omens to the harvest. It can also cause hailstones, thunder, lightning, and very strong wind that can destroy houses, crops and cause injury and death to

---

[15] Geoffrey Parrinder, *Religion in Africa* (Harmondsworth: Penguin, 1969): 53.

[16] Amanze, "From dominion to in communion", 13.

[17] Dominique Zahan, *The Religion, Spirituality and Thought of Traditional Africa* (Chicago: University of Chicago Press, 1979): 20.

[18] James N. Amanze, *African Traditional Religion and Culture in Botswana* (Gaborone: Pula Press, 2002): 303.

[19] Amanze, *African Traditional Religion*, 303.

[20] E. M. Zuesse, *Ritual Cosmos* (Athens: Ohio University Press, 1979): 63-64.

[21] James N. Amanze, *African Traditional Religion in Malawi* (Blantyre: CLAIM, 2002), where this has been discussed in detail.

people.[22] In the same way, there are certain animals, which are considered sacred therefore cannot be killed indiscriminately. Such animals include the giraffe, the buffalo, the python, the eland, the gemsbok to name a few. The main purpose of this prohibition is to protect such animals from extinction.[23]

Mention should also be made here regarding the importance of water. Water is very scarce in Africa. Therefore, it has high religious value to the African people. Zahan has indicated that springs, streams, rivers, lakes and ponds constitute the great aquatic temples of African religions. The theological significance of water is evident in the religious life and thought of the Azande people of Sudan. According to Evans-Pritchard, the Azande attribute to springs the idea of death and rebirth.[24] Michael Gelfand has noted that, among the Shona people of Zimbabwe, water is associated with life. It purifies, restores, cleanses and regenerates. Water is the universal mother, the essence and soul of life.[25] Therefore, it must be used responsibly and conserved for future generations.

Ecological Crisis Caused by the Failure of Developmental Polices

It should be noted that a great number of recent studies have pointed out that the current environmental crisis experienced globally is a result of the failure of development traditionally understood as "economic growth". Wesley Granberg-Michaelson has argued that development envisaged in the form of "economic growth" has had its catastrophic cost in the form of rising temperature of the globe's atmosphere, the deterioration of its ozone layer, the poisoning of its waters and the loss of its soil. These effects, although caused chiefly by the Global North, are being felt globally particularly in the Global South.[26] I concur with Herman Daly who has argued that the concept of development as "economic growth", particularly when it threatens the carrying capacity of the environment, is not helpful at all. Such economic growth and expansion is tantamount to "anti-economic" because it is a growth that impoverishes rather than enriches people in real terms. Such anti-economic growth makes it harder to eliminate poverty, protect the biosphere and, theologically, such affluent growth is sin.[27] The challenge here is that growth, as perceived in contemporary terms, focuses on the present at the expense of future generations. In the words of Daly, "our ability and inclination to enrich the present at the expense of the future and of other species is as real and as sinful as our tendency to further enrich the wealthy at the expense of the poor [...] If it is a sin to kill and to steal, then surely it is a sin to destroy carrying [...] capacity of the earth."[28]

The view that misconceived economic growth of development has been the chief cause of environmental degradation has been voiced by a number of other scholars. Mwambazambi has observed that "Global warming, the depletion of ozone layer, the degradation of the soil due to deforestation, erosion, desertification and the pollution of the water and atmosphere are [...] the outcome of human industrialisation in pursuit of economic interests without care for the environment."[29]

Misinterpretation of the Theology of "Domination" of Nature

One of the things that have been blamed for the degradation of ecology is the theology of "domination" of nature by human beings. In Genesis 1:26-30, God gave to human beings the authority to "be fruitful and multiply [...] have dominion over the fish of the sea, over the birds of the air, and over every living thing that moves on the earth [...] every herb that yields seed [...] every tree [...] every beast [...] everything that

22 Amanze, *African Traditional and Culture*, 305.
23 Amanze, *African Traditional and Culture*, 310.
24 Zahan, *The Religion*, 20.
25 Michael Gelfand, *Shona Religion* (Cape Town: Juta Company, 1962): 151.
26 Granberg-Michaelson, *Redeeming the Creation*, 4.
27 See Granberg-Michaelson, *Redeeming the Creation*, 5.
28 Granberg-Michaelson, *Redeeming the Creation*, 5-6.
29 Mwambazambi, "A theological view".

creeps on earth in which there is life". The theology of "subduing" and "dominating" nature, it is argued, is one of the factors that have led to the wanton destruction of the environment by human beings on the understand that God gave them absolute authority to use natural resources as they wish.[30] Interestingly, the misinterpretation of the theology of "domination" of nature has, to some extent, undermined the intrinsic goodness of creation which in Genesis 1:31 God declared as very good.

The theology of human beings as the "crown" of God's creation put humanity at the centre of the world. This anthropocentric view of the world is a leading factor of ecological crisis in the world today. Its grave consequences are such that they are threatening the very existence of humanity itself and therefore needs to be rejected by arguing that human beings are part of the complete whole.[31] The report of the theology group from the ecumenical meeting at the Rio Earth Summit in Brazil, which was held in 1992, affirmed the goodness of God's creation and the intrinsic worth of all beings and recommended the adoption an "eco-centred" theology of creation, which emphasises God's Spirit in creation and human beings as an integral part of nature".[32] This view is in line with Obaji M. Agbiji's hypothesis according to which human beings should view their uniqueness amongst other creatures as conferring on them a responsibility to maintain the created order as creatures "in community with other creatures thereby interdependence between them becomes rather inevitable".[33]

The Ecumenical and Diaconal Approach Towards the Mitigation of Ecological Crises in Africa

Having discussed the nature and extent of the ecological crisis in Africa as well as its causes, in this section of the paper, we shall discuss the ecumenical and diaconal mitigation of the negative effects of the ecological crisis from an African perspective. This paper recommends the "spiritual model" in which the churches and faith communities are the chief actors. Boutros Boutros-Ghali, former General Secretary of the United Nations, once said that human beings should not only love their neighbours as they love themselves, but they must also love the earth. There is a need to live in a spiritual relationship with the world. Human beings must build a new ethical and political context to live and act with the earth.[34]

I concur with Boutros-Ghali that human beings should love the environment as they love themselves. For this is the best way that can lead to the conservation of the ecosystem. Borrowing a leaf from Emilio Castro, former General Secretary of the WCC, the churches must, ecumenically, bring Jesus Christ into the equation of nature conservation. In other words, the churches should "bring the faith of belonging to the body of Christ, following the one through whom the whole world has been claimed by God's redeeming love."[35] The churches' ecumenical and diaconal role should be aligned with the theology of "in communion" with nature. It is a theology based on "inter-relationships" between God, human beings and nature as expressed in African spirituality. This is in line with the spirituality of African Traditional Religions which is essentially "relational" and not "hierarchical". It is characterised by co-operation, harmony, solidarity, and interdependence as encapsulated in the African philosophy of *Ubuntu* (personhood). At the highest degree of abstraction, *Ubuntu* defines the spiritual relationship that exists between the living-dead, the living, those yet to be born, nature and God. It has been noted by several scholars that an "ecotheological" or "relational" model rests upon the deep understanding of the unbreakable interdependent relationship that exists between God, humanity, and the whole of creation.[36]

Agbiji has intimated that the concept of "in community" in the context of Africa can contribute tremendously towards a more significant engagement of ecclesial communities in environmental and

[30] Granberg-Michaelson, *Redeeming the Creation,* 51-52.
[31] Granberg-Michaelson, *Redeeming the Creation*, 53.
[32] Granberg-Michaelson, *Redeeming the Creation*, 53.
[33] Agbiji, "Religion and ecological justice in Africa", 5.
[34] Granberg-Michaelson, *Redeeming the Creation*, 25.
[35] Granberg-Michaelson, *Redeeming the Creation*, 38.
[36] Granberg-Michaelson, *Redeeming the Creation*, 56.

economic justice issues. This is because, in Agbiji's words "in an African view of the world, the word community, refers to more than a mere association of isolated individuals". The term itself suggests bondedness. It refers to the act of sharing and living in communion. Agbiji has identified *ubuntu* as one of the elements that glues African societies together for *ubuntu* represents the deep sense of being human in African world view. It encapsulates respect for any human being, human dignity, the sanctity of human life, collective sharedness, obedience, humility, solidarity, caring, hospitality, interdependence and communalism with each other and with nature".[37]

According to Agbiji, communalism insists that the good of all determines the good of each individual and the welfare of everyone depends on the welfare of all. But what is even more important is the fact that Africans do not live for themselves, but they live for the community. The essence of communalistic approach to life is that it fosters and enhances the well-being of the whole community in a much broader sense. It encompasses social-cultural, economic, moral, political, religious, environmental, and ecological aspects.[38] Agbiji has noted further that some aspects of African cultural and religious life are life-affirming. These include, among others, protection of streams and rivers that provide water to the community, protection from deforestation, the practice of shifting cultivation, preservation of farmlands, the protection of animal, aquatic, and plant life. All this is done to promote the existence of corporate existence whereby each member of the community seeks the wellbeing of the present and future generations.[39]

This is in line with Leonard Boff's contention that all life, human and nonhuman, is bound together in a covenant of the three divine persons of the Trinity in one God. The universe lives within this communion which is celebrated in the sacrament of life.[40] In order to mitigate the negative effects of ecological crisis in Africa the churches must, therefore, promote the "theology of integration", a "relational theology" or, better still, a "theology of in communion" because this can be very empowering ecumenically to the people of the African continent. The churches, as one, must act and speak with one voice conscientising people regarding the importance and significance of the environment for the people now and those yet to be born. This conscientisation should be done through preaching, catechetical teaching and theological education in schools, colleges, and universities.[41]

In agreement with Granberg-Michaelson, the author is of the view that, while it is true that the ecumenical movement cannot offer technical expertise to faith communities, it is also true to say that the churches in their diaconal ministry can offer their moral and ethical expertise, clarifying the choices available to policy makers and governments and encouraging them to uphold values and standards which treat the earth as the common and precious gift from God to all.[42]

The author agrees with the recommendation made by the Africa Diakonia Consultation to the peoples of the African continent. At a meeting, held in 1989, it was recommended that the churches, in their diaconal ministry, should create programmes that address environmental issues such as tree planting, prevention of bush fires, protection of wildlife, soil and water conservation, control of communal grazing and shifting cultivation.[43] In this regard, churches were encouraged to speak out against excessive exploitation of natural resources that impoverishes ecology and take steps to encourage and work with peoples in its preservation.[44] In the same breath, it was recommended that ecological issues should be an important agenda in the churches' diaconal service. The churches should, ecumenically, urge governments in Africa to be more

[37] Agbiji, "Religion and ecological justice in Africa", 10-11.
[38] Agbiji, "Religion and ecological justice in Africa", 11.
[39] Agbiji, "Religion and ecological justice in Africa", 11.
[40] See Granberg-Michaelson, *Redeeming the Creation*, 56.
[41] Granberg-Michaelson, *Redeeming the Creation*, 65.
[42] Granberg-Michaelson, *Redeeming the Creation*, 68.
[43] *Diakonia: Towards Christian service for our time (*Geneva: The Africa Desk of the World Council of Churches Commission on Inter-Church AID, Refugee and World Service, 1990): 57.
[44] *Diakonia: Towards Christian service for our time,* 57.

vigilant against the use of chemicals and pesticides that may be harmful to humans and the environment generally.[45]

This view has been reiterated by Kiarie, who has emphatically noted, and I agree with him, that the churches should, ecumenically, condemn ecological degradation as sin. But above all, it must also provide instructions on environmental issues. It must teach the faithful that the entire universe belongs to God and that human beings must protect the earth as one way of fulfilling God's will on earth. They must care, watch and preserve the environment both in words and in action on God's behalf.[46]

Conclusion

In conclusion, this paper discussed ecological crisis in Africa and the various forms that this is taking. It began by discussing the global nature of the ecological crisis, after which it gave a detailed account of the ecological crisis in Africa that is threatening the very existence of the African people. The paper also discussed the factors that are causing the ecological crisis in Africa, chief among which are the need for economic growth and misinterpretation of the theology of domination as expressed in Genesis 1:26-30. Finally, the paper discussed what the author considers to be the best ecumenical and diaconal strategies in the efforts being made to mitigate the negative impacts caused the degradation of the environment by human beings in Africa today. This will ensure not only the survival of the human race but also the whole creation which, in Genesis 1:31, God saw was very good.

Suggestions for Further Reading

Agbiji, Obaji M. "Religion and ecological justice in Africa: Engaging value for community as praxis for ecological and socio-economic justice". *HTS Theological Studies*, online version, 71(2) (2015).

Amanze, James N. "From dominion to in communion: Ecotheology from an African perspective". *Anglican EcoCare Journal of Eco Theology* 2 (2016).

——. *African Traditional Religion in Malawi.* Blantyre: CLAIM, 2002.

——. *African Traditional Religion and Culture in Botswana.* Gaborone: Pula Press, 2002.

Gelfand, Michael. *Shona Religion.* Cape Town: Juta Company, 1962.

Granberg-Michaelson, Wesley. *Redeeming the Creation: The Rio Earth Summit: Challenges for the churches*. Geneva: WCC Publications, 1992.

Kiarie, George K. "Environmental degradation: What is the role of the church in environmental conservation in Kenya from 1963-2019". *Studia Historiae Ecclesiasticae*, online version, 46(2) (2020).

Mabongunje, Akin L. "The Environmental Challenges in Sub-Saharan Africa". *African Technology Forum* 8(1) (1995). [Available at: http://web.mit.edu/africantech/www/articles/EnvChall.htm] [Last accessed: 2nd March 2022].

Malunga, Grain W. "Foreword". In *Malawi State of Environment and Outlook Report: Environment for Sustainable Economic Growth.* Lilongwe: Ministry of Natural Resources, Energy and Environment, Malawi Government, 2010.

Mwambazambi, K. "A theological view of environmental protection in Africa". *Skrifling*, online journal, 45(4) (2011). [Available at: http://www.scielo.org.za/pdf/ids/v45n4/07.pdf], [Last accessed: 2nd March 2022].

Parrinder, Geoffrey. *Religion in Africa.* Harmondsworth: Penguin, 1969.

Smith, Brett. "South Africa: Environmental Issues, Policies and Clean Technology". 30th July 2015, *AZO Clean Tech* [Available at: https://www.azocleantech.com/article.aspx?ArticleID=561], [Last accessed: 2rd March 2022].

[45] *Diakonia: Towards Christian service for our time*, 57.

[46] Kiarie, "Environmental degradation", 6.

Zahan, Dominique. *The Religion, Spirituality and Thought of Traditional Africa*. Chicago: University of Chicago Press, 1979.
Zuesse, E. M. *Ritual Cosmos.* Athens: Ohio University Press, 1979.

35. She Was Living in a Forest: Lessons on Christian Mission for Environmental Care from African Rural Women

Eunice Kamaara[1]

Introduction

Before colonialism and the attendant re-introduction of Christianity in the vast land that is now known as Africa, the inhabitants lived in indigenous forests with low levels of greenhouse gas (GHGs) emissions. Everything (religion, culture, politics, economics et cetera) was integrated into a holistic way of life, like an indigenous forest, an ecosystem. There was no proselytisation. Religion was to be lived, not professed. To be born was to live and to live was to be spiritual. Everybody was living in the Forest, not owning it, not claiming it, just depending on it and, likewise, the Forest depending on the people. For they were clear that nobody owns the Forest. Then Christian missions came and hostilities and divisions emerged, even within denominations. Consequently, creation started groaning as the indigenous gave way to the exotic. To restore relationships, Christian and the broader religious ecumenism was born. This movement has been a great success, thanks to the top-down approach of the WCC, ACC, and NCCK found in urban areas but more to the bottom-up approach driven especially by local rural African women merely living their day-to-day lives as will be illustrated in this piece. The top-down ecumenical movement and the entire international community has lessons to learn from this population for the successful response to the current environmental crisis, this major threat to humanity. While changes in weather patterns and in ecological systems have always occurred, these were slow until technological advancements drastically changed human activities from subsistence relying on rudimentary tools to mass profit-driven industrial production. Since then changes in weather patterns have become much more dramatic and far-reaching. These rapid, massive, and extensive changes in weather patterns is popularly known as climate change (Jackson and Jerome, 2021).[2] The Christian mission of spreading the gospel is dynamic because the gospel is always interpreted in the context of the realities of the day. Care for creation is the most urgent action for the Church's pastoral care today.

But who is the Church? The word Church has multiple meanings. It may refer to a building or just a space dedicated to the worship of God; a body of Christian worshippers; the governance structures of a Christian group; Christian leadership; and it may refer to the entire body of Christians globally. In this context, we use the word to mean two groups: 1) ordinary African rural women who act as the Church witnessing Christ through environmental stewardship in their day-to-day life, and 2) the leadership of the

[1] Eunice Kamaara, a professor of African Christian Ethics at Moi University, Eldoret, Kenya, is an ethicist with over thirty years of experience in holistic health development, participatory research and practice. She has expertise in mainstreaming Gender & Diversity for Justice and Inclusivity in interdisciplinary and transdisciplinary research and is passionate about translating research findings into practical development through policy influence and community engagement. She has consulted for the All Africa Conference of Churches (AACC), World Council of Churches (WCC), the World Bank, United States Agency for International Development (USAID), the United Nations Population Fund (UNFPA), Templeton World Charity Foundation (TWCF), and the Institute of Development Studies/Partnership for African Social Governance Research (PASGR), and has served on international boards of Church World Service, Theological Book Network, and currently, on Médecin Sans Frontières Ethics Review Board and has more than 100 publications. She co-directs the African Character Initiation Programme, a community-based and community-participatory organisation on mentorship of adolescents for health and values, recognised by the World Health Organization among the Top 30 2019 Africa Health Innovations. See: http://innov.afro.who.int/innovators/professor-eunice-kamaara-25. Eunice is Presbyterian by birth, Roman Catholic by marriage and Catholic by choice.

[2] For simple but comprehensive, free and downloadable resources on environmental care and what to do about it see *The Good Guides* e-books available at https://www.joingoodside.com/.

Christian ecumenical movement who are challenged to take lessons from African rural women on environmental stewardship. To illustrate the success of Christian ecumenism and of Christian environmental stewardship, we use the case of a particular African rural woman brought up by a strict African indigenous couple who later became a first-generation Presbyterian couple and who is now flourishing. The basic argument is that the urgent need to respond to the current environmental crisis is at the core of the mission of the Church in the 21st Century.

This paper is structured into four sections. This first section is an introduction. The second session provides the experience of an African rural woman as she lives her day-to-day life in the forest. This provides the socio-historical and cultural backdrop against which the African Church has played out ecumenism which would then inspire environmental response. As observed by O'Callaghan:

> Christian faith is that the former is itself the fruit of a historico-cultural process deeply influenced by Christian faith. In many ways modern culture is an elevated, sophisticated one, containing a great variety of precious anthropological insights and strengths, with a surprising adaptability and openness to absorb, to clarify and to unite.[3]

Although women make up the great majority of practising Christians in Africa, they remain invisible and voiceless because their participation is limited to less powerful positions of implementing rather than making decisions. We apply Diverse Critical Literacy (DCL) theory[4] to privilege these ordinary rural African women in the margins in order to amplify their voices and the critical roles that they play in Christian mission. Thereafter, we provide an analysis of the case in the third section, and finally make some conclusions.

Mwari wa Mbugua, an African Christian Rural Woman Lives On, in the Forest

Mwari wa Mbugua had fallen and lay down in the forest. She did not show any sign of distress, or pain. Perhaps, consistent with her character, she kept her pain hidden from her family. She seemed calm, courageous, full of hope and in full control of her mind and spirit. She calmly listened to the sound of the wind, seemingly consciously and patiently waited to be lifted up high on wings.

On the contrary, she was not in charge of her body. She seemed to have let go of it after the fall. She could not even talk, not with the ventilator in her mouth. Instead, she gestured with her hands. The gestures clearly and consistently suggested: 'If you would surround the bed I am lying on, we would pray together so that I can bid you goodbye and go away." Sooner than later, she would have no control of her body whatsoever.

My siblings and I would not take the last part of the message. We prayed as requested but ignored the part about goodbye and her going away. However, she persisted. Every time two or three people surrounded her bed at the corner of the Intensive Care Unit, she faithfully repeated the gestures. Then, the full diagnosis came. She had advanced anaplastic thyroid carcinoma – one of the most aggressive and lethal cancers. After the doctor explained the diagnosis to her, she changed the last of her gestures. Instead, of merely pointing to the ceiling with finger, she now flapped her arms up and down before pointing. The message sank in. She was feeling light enough to fly rather than walk or ride.

We had no choice but to escort her to the "airport". We organised for her Presbyterian minister to come pray with us. The minister kindly turned it into Holy Communion. Although my siblings and I were soaked in tears throughout this last "meal", we managed to sing *Tukutendereza,* a worship and adoration song that is synonymous with the great Presbyterian revival of the 1970s, to which our mother ascribed. The song

[3] Paul O'Callaghan, "Cultural challenges to faith: a reflection on the dynamics of modernity", *Church, Communication and Culture,* 2(1) (2017), 25-40: 25.

[4] Melissa Steyn, "Critical Diversity Literacy: Essentials for the Twenty-First Century". In Steven Vertovec (ed), *Routledge International Handbook of Diversity Studies*. London: Routledge, 2015. 379-389.

seemed to put her into a sleep mode, nay, a flying mode, and in a few hours' time, her organs started to let go. Her primary doctor, a Muslim pulmonologist, soon confirmed this; Mwari wa Mbugua had flown away – a most beautiful transition of a most beautiful person who had lived a most beautiful life. And so, she lives on. In the Forest.

Mwari wa Mbugua was born into a forest – literally and metaphorically. Literally, she was born in Molo Forest, Nakuru, to Mbugua wa Regeru and Mwari wa Runyiri. Our grandparents long transitioned to the land of no return but my memory of them remains intact. Mbiti's concept of the living dead makes sense.[5]

Slightly less than an hour's drive north-west of Nairobi is Baraniki, Kikuyu. This ridge, a stone's throw away from the Thogoto Mission area, holds some of the fondest memories of my childhood. During most school holidays, my siblings and I lived with our maternal grandparents and would traverse much of the mission area running errands for them. Today, the mission area comprises the famous Church of Torch, Kikuyu High School, Musa Gitau Primary School, Alliance High School, The Presbyterian Hospital, Thogoto Teachers College and the Presbyterian University among other landmarks.

The Church of Torch remains a breath-taking feature. Designed by a Scottish architect, Bernard P. Gaymer, and built in the middle of a dark indigenous forest over a period of five years (1928-1933), the Church was expected to light, not just the surrounding forest, but the entire dark continent that Africa was perceived to be, with the spirit of the Good News of Jesus Christ.

What is today called Kikuyu High School was a few years back called Kikuyu Day High School. Before that, it was Mambere, the first school (described by some as the cradle of education in Kenya). Jomo Kenyatta, James Gichuru and Musa Gitau, the first African church minister, studied here. These people would chase mental darkness from the minds of indigenous Kenyans. Directly opposite Kikuyu High School is the Presbyterian University of East Africa, a stone's throw away from there is the Alliance High School (twin schools, one for boys and one for girls), and a few kilometres away is Thogoto Teachers College – built later on for advanced formal education. This was the first mission school to which the first indigenous Kenyans were to learn the three Rs of basic education: reading, writing and arithmetic (usually said as "reading, writing, and 'rithmetic").[6] While the Church lit the spirit, the schools were designed to chase mental darkness out of the minds of locals.

Immediately next to the Church of Torch is the PCEA Kikuyu Hospital (well-known for its specialty in ophthalmology and orthopaedics). To date, this hospital would attend to the physical needs of persons from far and wide.

My mother and her siblings referred to their dad by the nickname Muthingi (foundation) because he was one of the earliest of the first-generation African Christian converts in this early mission area in Kenya. We, my siblings and I, call him Guka (grandfather). Guka was a direct descendant of Waiyaki wa Hinga: his mother, Nyanginya, after who I am named, was one of the wives of Waiyaki wa Hinga. The clan of Waiyaki wa Hinga lost much of their land to the Church of Scotland to give room to the mission area, leaving Guka and his siblings to share a small piece at the edge of the forest. Waiyaki wa Hinga's attempt to resist costed him his life. He was buried alive in Kibwezi, upside-down. Upon his death, his children were dispersed before they returned to Kikuyu to share a small piece of land on the edge of the forest. However, that is a story for another day.

Guka went to live in Lamu along the Kenyan coast. He was a typical indigenous African man who wore his identity with pride and gratitude. But identities and moralities are complex and never static. While in Lamu, Guka converted to Christianity and returned to the Kikuyu mission area. With others in his family who had "toed the line", Guka was rewarded with the land in Baraniki, lessons on how to read, write and count, and an apprenticeship in masonry. He was among the people who built the Church of Torch. Later, he became the caretaker of the entire mission area, around which he rode a bicycle. By the early 1970s,

[5] Mbiti JS (1969) *African Religions and Philosophy*. Nairobi: Heinemann educational Books, page 10.
[6] See: https://en.wikipedia.org/wiki/The_three_Rs

Guka retired to manage his own quarry as he volunteered to take the gospel to children at the Dagoretti Approved School.

Figuratively, Mwari wa Mbugua, was living in a forest. With indigenous Africans as her parents, she adopted the African worldview into which she was born. This was an indigenous African brought up before Kenya became a British colony, and instilled in her was an indigenous African worldview where everything is related to everything else and life is one interconnected whole. Religion, culture, politics, economics were integrated into one whole way of life, and both living and the non-living are distinguished only by their different stages in the process of life. In this worldview, a good life is characterised by healthy relationships among all as in the forest. This explains my mother's philosophy of life "*weka wega niwe weika, wka uru, niwe weika*" (when you do good, you do it to yourself; when you do bad, you do it to yourself).

We have heard this statement compared to Ubuntu philosophy[7] so many times from our mother that we believe if she was talking at the point of her transition, these would probably have been her last words to her descendants.

Since Muthingi converted, our mother naturally went to Mambere where she learnt basic literacy. Although she grew up as a strict Presbyterian with no association whatsoever with acenji, she did not change her philosophy.

Figure 1: Our Mother's Farm: The Forest

Fast forward to when I grew up in Ngemwa village ikinu in Kiambu County where my mother moved after marrying our father. Our father was a Christian. He prayed with us and taught us some Christian songs which remain indelible in my mind. However, I don't know our father enough because we didn't get to see

[7] A. Shuttle, *Ubuntu: An Ethic for New South Africa* (Pietermaritzburg: Cluster, 2001).

him much. Much of what I remember are the many beatings we got from him to manage childhood unruliness. Typical of fathers in those days, our father worked and lived away from home coming home for a night or two probably once a month. The opposite is true of our mother. I can confidently say that I know her. We lived side by side – seemingly almost every minute. The hours spent in primary school seemed short compared to the hours spent with our mother on our family farm, the Forest. It is on this family farm that I saw my mother change from zero associations with Roman Catholic families to making friends with Catholic women and hosting them and sharing meals in her house. I have recounted this in another paper so I won't dwell on this here. Here I would like to focus on our mother's farm, the farm on which she toiled and brought up her big family who escorted her to the "airport". The Forest in which I was born and brought up. It provided little income but adequate subsistence. My father paid fees – no mean feat for so many children very closely spaced that there was one in almost every class from standard 1 to Form 4. This is where my mother taught me how to live, but more importantly, how to die that life may flourish. Rather than describe, I sketch the farm as I reconstruct it from my memory growing up in the 1970s.

Analysis

An analysis of the sketch above provides key lessons on environmental management. Let's start from the south moving up towards the north. Internationally, the UN recommends that countries should ensure a 10% forest cover in the fight against climate change especially from GHG emissions. Kenya has a 7% forest cover and seeks to raise this to 10% by the end of 2022. Our mother's farm has a forest cover of close to 50%. Nonetheless, forest cover is not merely about having trees. As observed by various scholars on ecosystems, public dialogue has emphasised tree planting without due regard to what trees need to be planted and where.[8] This is dangerous for care of creation. Our mother's forest cover is an indigenous forest. This is the kind of forest that allow all species of creation to enjoy their natural habitats where species are dependent on each other. In this forest, my brothers would hunt antelopes and hares and roast them for us on an open fire.

After the forest, let us cross the river. While I was growing up, this river was flowing with a lot of water-enough for us to learn how to swim. Today, a small seasonal river is all that remains, resulting from climate change. Along the riverbanks, my mother would plant arrowroots, sugar cane, tomatoes, and sweet potatoes. These are indigenous foods that would provide light meals for our family.

Past the arrowroots, the farm had a section with maize, banana plants, beans, and vegetables. A mixture of maize and beans boiled to taste interchanged with ugali (mealie from the maize) would provide regular meals for the family. On rare occasions like Christmas Day, there would be rice and chapatti for the family. Apart from the indigenous forest, our mother's farm has exotic trees scattered all over. These she would cut for domestic fuel needs but also for sale as wood and timber. A variety of indigenous vegetables, kales, onions and other vegetables would be scattered across the farm not to mention roots like cassava and yams. Other trees scattered across our mother's farm are fruit trees– mangos, oranges, guavas, custard apples, different kinds of berries, passion fruits, among others and plants of so many different kinds. At any one time, there would be some fruit in season on our mother's farm. Banana trees would also be scattered all across the farm. I found it amazing to observe how banana trees quickly grow into groups. This is necessary for their flourishing. The roots mesh into a complicated network that, in spite of their weights and single stems, it was not common to find a banana tree felled by the wind. Like an ecumenical family, the trees draw their strength from each other. In an email message condoling with me after my mother's death, Ernst Conradie appreciated that a forest is a perfect image of being ecumenical "where the one tree keeps the other tight because their roots are deeply intertwined."[9]

---

[8] J.W. Veldman, et al. "Tyranny of trees in grassy biomes". *Science*, 347(6221) (2015): 484-5.

[9] Ernst Conradie, Personal correspondence with the writer.

A portion of the land would be reserved for coffee trees, a legacy of British colonialism and a mark of neocolonialism. It was illegal to cut coffee trees or to plant anything else in the coffee farms. But our mother had exotic trees including fruit trees inside the section in which she grew coffee.

Behind the family house would be at least one dairy cow that provided milk for family consumption as well as for sale. A few goats would be in a pen next to the cow shed. Our father roasted one of these at least twice a year –on every Christmas and on another holiday that nobody seemed to know what it marked – it's been a well-kept secret.

This farm turns out to be the classroom in which our mother was the teacher from whom I learnt how to live a worthy life – life spent in healthy relationships. Much more importantly, I learnt how to die with conviction that to die is to live and let live. Consider the way that a grain of wheat has to die for it to bring forth new life (John 12:24-26). The farm is my basic frame of reference every time I think of environmental management. It presents blending of the old and new (indigenous/exotic forest; indigenous and modern worldview) into a forest that may be compared to ecumenism. I am committed to replicating it in my small corner of the forest. This is how I interpret the concept of "think global, act local".

Key Lessons

The Christian call to mission, specifically to pastoral care, is dynamic and complex, understood only in the context of its socio-historical and cultural background. At the beginning of the 21st century when climate change is undeniably a major threat to human life, creation care and eco-diakonia are key. The success registered by the Christian ecumenical movement, following top-down but also bottom-up approaches, provides lessons for the mission of the church today on creation care and eco-diakonia. From bottom-up approaches, we learn that in the mundane action of day-to-day life, African rural women live out the gospel of healthy relationships and interdependence of all creation. Clearly, top-down approaches need to engage and support bottom-up approaches for success in creation care and eco-diakonia.

Suggestions for Further Reading

Jackson, L., and Lauren Jerome. *The Good Guide to Learning about Climate Change* Toronto: Goodside, 2021. [E-book available at https://www.joingoodside.com/] [Last accessed: 7th February 2022].

O'Callaghan, Paul. "Cultural challenges to faith: a reflection on the dynamics of modernity". *Church, Communication and Culture,* 2(1) (2017): 25-40.

Shuttle, A. *Ubuntu: An Ethic for New South Africa*. Pietermaritzburg: Cluster 2001.

Steyn, Melissa. "Critical Diversity Literacy: Essentials for the Twenty-First Century". In Steven Vertovec, Ed. *Routledge International Handbook of Diversity Studies*. London: Routledge, 2015: 379-389.

Veldman, Joseph W., Gerhard E. Overbeck, Daniel Negreiros. Gregory Mahy, Soizig Le Stradic, G. Wilson Fernandes, Giselda Durigan, Elise Buisson, Francis E. Putz and William J. Bond. "Tyranny of trees in grassy biomes". *Science*, 347(6221) (2015): 484-5.

36. The Missing Link: Women of Faith as Advocates of Climate Justice

Rosinah Mmannana Gabaitse[1]

This paper seeks to locate African women of faith within the conversation and dialogue regarding climate change which the United Nations has named the "defining issue of our time."[2] The earth, our home, is changing due to human misactions, hence conversations about climate change are urgent.[3] The title is very broad, and I will narrow it to discuss women of faith in Africa even though, of course, Africa is a whole continent and not homogeneous as it has diverse cultures and practices. However, I am using Africa as a context to denote a geopolitical reality and shared common experiences. I can therefore, make some generalisations in this paper even though I will be using examples from the Botswana setup where I am based. Further, the faith I reference in this paper is Christianity so that the "women of faith" here refers to Christian women. Occasionally, I will refer to women who follow traditional/indigenous religions but that will be specified. The paper is divided into four parts. The first part will be a brief discussion of what climate change is. The second part will look at the impact of climate change on the environment, including on humans. The third part will discuss the role of humans in mitigating climate change. The fourth part will propose strategies through which women can mitigate climate justice by drawing insights from women in Botswana who have been engaged in efforts to preserve the environment.

Introduction

"We as indigenous women and indigenous peoples, believe it's vital to consider our knowledge to prevent and adapt into climate change."[4] The above quotation by Tarcila Rivera, from Peru, makes a strong but broad claim by women from the developing world that whilst the world is frantically searching for answers to respond to the challenges posed by climate change to the global community, indigenous women possess knowledge that can contribute to a solution were it to be considered. This is a very bold, yet positive claim which has to be taken seriously. The aim of this paper is to explore the contributions that can be made by women in addressing the threats to life that emanate from climate change.

Climate change is evident in a number of global environmental changes. The most recent past has witnessed severe heatwaves in parts of Africa. For example, severe heatwave activity occurred in southern Africa in 2019, with temperatures exceeding 45°C in parts of Botswana, South Africa, Zimbabwe and Mozambique. One does not need to be a scientist to tell that the climate is changing. Citizens, especially women and children, do experience and feel climatic changes and they have a role to play in order to reverse or to prevent the catastrophe that comes with climate change. This paper observes that women are easily organised through the church because of their faith and commitment to this institution. The church therefore cannot stand aloof from issues of climate change. Kapya Kaoma noted that:

---

[1] Dr. Rosinah Mmannana Gabaitse is Senior Lecturer at the UB Department of Theology and Religious Studies at the University of Botswana in Gaborone, Doctor of Philosophy.

[2] The United Nations. [As found on: https://www.un.org/en/global-issues/climate-change], [Last accessed: 7th February 2022].

[3] D.E. Sherkat and C.G. Ellison. "Structuring the religion-environment connection: identifying religious influences on environmental concern and activism". Journal for the Scientific Study of Religion 46 (2007): 71-85.

[4] Tarcila Rivera. Quoted by "8 Quotes That Emphasize Why We Should Celebrate & Support Women Land Defenders For Earth Day" *Global Fund for Women*, 20th April 2018. [Available at: https://www.globalfundforwomen.org/latest/article/8-quotes-women-land-defenders-earth-day], [Last accessed: 7th February 2022].

> African Christianity should respond aggressively to the challenges posed by the recurring ecological crisis. The ever-growing population, soil erosion, pollution, and deforestation are not just ecological issues – they are gospel issues as well.[5]

The question at the heart of this paper is what women can do to mitigate against climate change. The truth is that women, especially women of faith, more than men are missing/absent in the dialogue on climate change, yet they are a critical stakeholder to the conversation because they are the most affected by the effects of climate change. Because of the inequalities between men and women, whenever there is a humanitarian crisis women suffer the most. Before I answer the question at the heart of this paper, it is necessary discuss the role that human beings are playing in exacerbating climate change.

Human Beings and the Causation of Climate Change

The majority of climate scientists are unanimous that climate change is happening now. Science has become more irrevocable than ever before. From its beginning, the earth has always warmed and cooled naturally and the climate continuously changes. However, the difference between natural climate change and what is happening now is the sheer scale of the changes that are taking place in a very short space of time. The earth is now warming faster than at any point in recorded history and this has led scientists to argue that human beings are behind the rapid changes in the climate. The Intergovernmental Panel on Climate Change (IPCC) notes that it is unequivocal that human influence has warmed the atmosphere, ocean and land.[6]

Human beings started to seriously impact the climate some two hundred years ago with the Industrial Revolution mostly through the burning of fossil fuels for energy, industrial processes and transportation. Since then, huge quantities of greenhouse gases have been and are still being released into the atmosphere. According to the National Academies, greenhouse gases are at their highest levels in at least 400,000 years and they continue to rise.[7] The Royal Society and National Academy of Sciences in the US noted that the present level of atmospheric carbon dioxide concentration is almost certainly unprecedented in the past million years, during which time modern humans evolved and societies developed.[8] The IPCC notes that in 2019, atmospheric carbon dioxide concentrations were higher than at any time in at least two million years.[9]

The Effects of Climate Change on the Environment and Humanity

The National Academy of Science in the US reports that human health is affected by climate change due to "heat stress, increased air pollution and lack of food due to droughts or other agricultural stresses."[10]

---

[5] K. Kaoma, *The Creator's Symphony: African Christianity, the Plight of the Earth and the Poor*. Pietermaritzburg: Cluster, 2015: 15.

[6] IPCC, *Climate Change 2021: The Physical Science Basis Summary for Policymakers* Working Group I Contribution to the Sixth Assessment Report of the Intergovernmental Panel on Climate Change. Geneva, Switzerland: IPCC, 2021. [Available at: https://www.ipcc.ch/report/ar6/wg1/downloads/report/IPCC_AR6_WGI_SPM_final.pdf], [Last accessed: 7th February 2022].

[7] Amanda Staudt, Nancy Huddleston, and Sandi Rudenstein (eds), "Understanding and Responding to Climate Change – Highlights of NATIONAL Academies Reports", *The National Academies of Sciences* October 2005 [Available at: https://www.preventionweb.net/files/2276_climatechangefinal.pdf], [Last accessed: 7th February 2022].

[8] The Royal Society & National Academy of Sciences. *Climate Change: Evidence & Causes.* The Royal Society & National Academy of Sciences, 2020: 9. [Available at https://royalsociety.org/~/media/royal_society_content/policy/projects/climate-evidence-causes/climate-change-evidence-causes.pdf], [Last accessed: 7th February 2022].

[9] IPCC, *Climate Change 2021.*

[10] Staudt et al, "Understanding and Responding to Climate Change", 14.

According to the UN, climate change is the single biggest health threat facing humanity.[11] Its impacts are already harming health through air pollution and diseases. About 90 per cent of the world's population breathes polluted air, largely resulting from burning fossil fuels. In addition, the UN Climate Change News of 15th February 2018 says, "The large-scale extraction of natural resources, climate change and environmental degradation are advancing at an unprecedented pace, undermining the livelihoods of millions of women and men, particularly in the developing world."[12] Data shows that the effects of climate change are disproportionately dispersed. While it affects all regions of the world, the developing world is impacted more because it relies heavily on the natural environment, has poor infrastructure and the least resources to mitigate its impacts. Most people in Africa, in particular, already live on the front lines of pollution, disaster, and degradation of natural resources and land. For them, adaptation is a matter of sheer survival. Furthermore, climate change is becoming a security threat. It is likely to produce numerous socio-political problems that are likely to weaken states and societies. Already Africa has a history of resource and political conflicts. Climate change could exacerbate territorial and border disputes. Climate change should best be viewed as a threat multiplier that exacerbates existing trends, tensions and instability.[13]

What these extreme weather changes have done is increased migration drastically, particularly in Africa, as people move from drought prone poorer countries and regions to more affluent and resilient ones. Of the 5 135 000 forcibly displaced persons identified by the International Organization for Migration across six countries in Central and West Africa, 4%, or approximately 180 700 individuals were displaced by natural disasters.[14] The Internal Displacement Monitoring Centre (IDMC) reported 649 448 new disaster-induced displacements in West and Central Africa, mainly due to flooding.[15] Furthermore, climate change is becoming a security threat. It is likely to produce numerous socio-political problems that are likely to weaken states and societies. It is clear that, as a developing continent, Africa is adversely affected by climate change and its manifestations much more than other regions.[16]

These climatic changes not only affect humans, they have enormous impacts on the environment too. Many animal and plant species are disappearing from the face of the earth because they cannot cope with the increase in temperatures. Climate change is contributing to "increased and spread of infectious diseases such as malaria because of the expansion of mosquito habitat and range."[17] Scientists associate climate change with greater risks of zoonotic diseases. For some contagions, increases in temperatures or rainfall can affect the life cycles of either the pathogen or its vector – the intermediate species that spread the disease from the original host to humans.[18] Flooding can lead to the spread of waterborne diseases. As the geographic ranges of mosquitoes and ticks expand, they carry diseases to new locations. Warmer temperatures and higher rainfall increase habitat suitability for biting insects and the transmission of vector-borne diseases such as malaria and yellow fever. There has been an increase in heat-related deaths in some regions of the world. In many rural areas of the developing world, the majority of residents depend on traditional plant-based medicines for basic health care. The destruction of biodiversity is leading to the disappearance of medicinal plants, depriving millions of people of critical medicines.

---

[11] United Nations, "Climate Action Fast Facts" UN website, [Available at: - https://www.un.org/en/climatechange/science/key-findings#temperature-rise], [Last accessed: 7th February 2022].
[12] UN Climate Change News, "Gender Equality Crucial to Tackling Climate Change" UN 15th February 2018, [Available at: https://unfccc.int/news/gender-equality-crucial-to-tackling-climate-change-un], [Last accessed: 7th February 2022].
[13] Institute for Security Studies. *The Impact of Climate Change in Africa.* Pretoria: Institute for Security Studies, 2010: 7. [Available at: https://www.files.ethz.ch/isn/136704/PAPER220.pdf], [Last accessed: 7th February 2022].
[14] International Organization for Migration, "Migration, Environment and Climate Change", *IOM* website, [Available at: https://www.iom.int/migration-environment-and-climate-change.
[15] World Meteorological Organisation. *State of the Climate in Africa* Geneva, Switzerland: WMO, 2019: 19.
[16] D. Jamieson, "Climate Change, Responsibility, and Justice", *Science and Engineering Ethics* 16 (2010): 431-445.
[17] Staudt et al, "Understanding and Responding to Climate Change", 16.
[18] United Nations, "Climate Action Fast Facts".

Therefore, it goes without saying that climate change is a threat to creation as a whole; humans, animals, and the entire ecosystem. However, despite the urgency of the situation and the reality of the threat caused by climate change, not everyone is involved and invited to the high table where conversations are taking place regarding climate change, its causes and impacts and how to mitigate them. Government officials, NGOs, coalitions of organisations and secular activists, who are mostly elite males, are at the table trying to resolve the impacts of climate change, leaving behind a critical mass of women on the ground who are disproportionately affected by the crisis. Yet they have vast knowledge and skills for adaptation that they have been practising for the longest of time. Therefore, it is critical that women are part of the conversations about climate change, as they are the most affected.

Women as Agents of Climate Justice

Patricia Espinosa, UN Climate Change Executive Secretary is on record lamenting the absence of women in climate change discussions:

> For the Paris Agreement to succeed, women and girls must be fully involved in climate policy. When we include women in climate solutions, we see enhanced economic growth and the outcomes are more sustainable [...][19]

I concur with Espinosa that women must be involved as valuable conversation partners as they have been during the fight to reduce HIV stigma, fighting inequalities and supporting the vulnerable members of society. Women of faith are critical in the endeavour to resolve the impacts of the climate crisis because they are at the forefront of feeding their families. Although this is a stereotype regarding gender roles, at the moment most women are focused on feeding their families and making sure that there is food on the table.[20] Even though women are the majority, in most countries, they are usually ignored when it comes to issues of development yet they "play important roles in the different areas of development, such as education, health, commerce and industry, agriculture, the informal business sector etc., to mention a few. However, their participation in the various sectors is negatively affected by numerous cultural, social, economic, political and legal barriers.[21]

Perhaps and most importantly, women constitute a large percentage of the world's poor. Further, the majority of the women in Africa are active in agriculture, tilling the land and for a long time, women in agriculture have had a good relationship with their land, using sustainable agricultural practices. It follows that they feel and see the reality of climate change on a daily basis. They do not need to be told how to preserve nature because they are the *de facto* experts in sound and sustainable agricultural practises. In fact, they should be telling the world what sustainable land use practises look like.

Drawing from Cultural Resources

Women who follow traditional Botswanan indigenous religions are more likely to respect the taboos associated with land and the environment than men. This is because of strong cultural opinions that associate women's bodies with uncleanliness and even pollution of the land. For instance, women are not to enter farms when they have lost a spouse because they carry some dark energy associated with death and that energy kills crops.[22] Men, on the other hand, do not have such taboos; they enter lands at any time, even after losing a spouse. Women are more policed to respect the taboos associated with the environment than

---

[19] UN, "Gender Equality Crucial to Tackling Climate Change".

[20] While feminists are still pushing for dissolving gender roles, this is the reality on the ground. In as much as this is a stereotype regarding women, in the real world women do worry and work the land to produce food for their families.

[21] M. Bolaane, et al. *Botswana Women Write*. (Pietermaritzburg: University of KwaZulu-Natal Press, 2019): 519.

[22] J. Amanze, *African Religions and Culture in Botswana* (Gaborone: Pula Press, 2002): 35.

their male counterparts.[23] It is also taboo to cut trees, such as the *Motsweri* tree which takes a long time to grow, but men cut it when they prepare the land for commercial farming, hence adding to the climate crisis. In addition, as much as women use firewood for cooking and energy, they reforest and this is a good practice as it not only keeps trees intact, but obviously more trees are good for drawing down greenhouse gases from the atmosphere. Furthermore, women produce goods using environmentally friendly and biodegradable products such as grass to produce mats and baskets instead of using products such as plastic that pollute the environment. Women also preserve food for use during drier seasons such as meat and fruits such as melons and berries using solar energy which is obviously good for the atmosphere. Women also cook fresh foods to feed their families and this alone uses less heat in contrast to men who cook on a larger scale for the market, which emits carbon dioxide, black carbon and other gases into the atmosphere. Moreover, Batswana women are engaged in horticulture[24] to produce food for sustenance and they often use simple handheld tools such as hoes and spades to till the land, plough, plant and harvest. All this equipment is environmentally friendly since they produce no carbon dioxide. While there is evidence that agriculture contributes to the production of greenhouse gases such as methane and nitrous oxide, subsistence horticulture seems to be producing little or at least less greenhouse gases compared to commercial farming where heavy farm machinery and equipment are used. From these examples, men more than women tend to pollute the earth, while women tend to contribute to the healing of the earth. This means that, if climate change education can be afforded by these women, they can be more sensitive to climatic change risks, much more so than men.

The Role of Women of Faith in Mitigating Climate Change

There is an ongoing misconception that women of faith, especially those in the church, are not concerned and cannot make a difference on the issues of climate change because it is a complex subject. Nothing can be further from the truth. The combination of their daily experiences of working on the land, their indigenous beliefs and attitude towards the land and their Christian belief in the stewardship of creation qualifies them to a chair at the discussion table. They may not be "experts" in the sense of knowing the finer scientific details, but they are acutely aware of the realities of climate change because it is impacting their daily lives through heat waves, severe flooding, low rainfall and cyclones. Granting that it is a complex subject, when women of faith are educated, however, they can easily engage in promoting more environmentally sustainable lifestyles. This being said, successful conversations on climate change require not only indigenous wisdom, they require the presence of African Christian women also drawing from the doctrines and theologies of the Bible. Studies show that women are the majority in churches; they are a critical mass in terms of the numbers as well as representations, so, the church is female.[25] Hitherto, women have been a silent, if not silenced, majority everywhere, even in their churches, yet, they are to all intents and purposes defining the church and therefore should be invited to the table for discussions on climate change.

There are a couple of strategies that can be employed by Christian women to respond to the climate crisis and promote sustainable use of the environment. I will discuss them in turn.

The Bible has some transformative environmental doctrines that emphasise a concern for nature/creation and how to protect it from harm and degradation. The Bible also speaks highly of how the vulnerable members of society must be taken care of. Both of these doctrines call for Christians to be stewards and

---

23 Amanze, *African Religions*, 36.

24 O. Mackett, "Female farm holding in Botswana's agriculture industry". *Agrekon*, 60(3) (July 2021): 317-334.

25 D. Ramodibe, "Women and Men Building Together the Church in Africa." In M.M. Fabella and M.A. Oduyoye (eds), *With Passion and Compassion: Third Women Doing Theology* (Maryknoll, NY: Orbis Books, 1996): 14-21.

caretakers of the world that God created; humans, living and non-living things.[26] As stewards, Christians are to speak against human misactions that threaten the existence of the earth because the earth belongs to God, the creator. Here, I want to highlight four texts that are transformative and can be used to form a solid doctrine against human misactions that cause climate change.

> Genesis 2:15. And the Lord God took the man, and put him into the garden of Eden to dress it and to keep it.
> Psalm 24:1. The earth is the Lord's, and everything in it, the world, and all who live in it.
> Psalm 19:1. The heavens proclaim the glory of God, the skies display his craftsmanship.
> Job 12:7-10. But ask the animals, and they will teach you, or the birds in the sky, and they will tell you; or speak to the earth, and it will teach you, or let the fish in the sea inform you. Which of all these does not know that the hand of the LORD has done this? In his hand is the life of every creature and the breath of all mankind.

Genesis 2:15 and Psalms 24 give human beings responsibility to care for the environment without dominating it.[27] Psalms 19:1 basically speaks against the contamination of the sky because if that happens, the sky will not display God's beauty. Job 12:7-10 affirms that all of God's creation is valuable and reveals something about God. The call for Christians is clear – there shouldn't be anything that risks damage to creation because then what will reveal God?

Now these texts can be used as models/strategies to mitigate against climate change risks. The models of stewardship, of keeping the skies clear so that they display God's craftsmanship and of celebrating all created things should be enhanced so that women of faith (who, again, are the majority of church-goers) embrace the care of the environment as a faith, justice and Gospel issue. Women of faith can be an asset and a resource in that they are driven by faith – faith that the world was created good and must be protected from degradation and harm.

Christian women can broadcast the care of the environment and live by being intentional about climate change mitigation through applying sustainable land use patterns because God commands them to keep God's creation intact and good. These models/strategies can serve as a reminder that, if they fail to care for the environment, they are disobedient to God. Women can use the above texts to be conscious that if the environment is hurt, they – women and children – will be the most affected. Since the church is moved by justice which focuses on the vulnerable, the women should be empowered to appreciate that nations will starve and their families will starve if humanity does not take care of the environment. There is need to be intentional about increased literacy on how climate change is manifested through weather patterns that disrupt food availability and how food production may harm the most vulnerable members of the communities. Women of faith are committed to justice, justice for small people and vulnerable members of the society. If they are educated on what climate justice is and how it is a Gospel issue, they will care for the environment knowing that the effects of non-action can be heavy on the vulnerable. If women are given education regarding the effects of climate change, they will manage climate-related risks with intentions and purpose. If women of faith are educated that human misactions towards the earth are injustice towards the perfect world that God created, they can be taught strategies to reduce carbon footprints.

Women of faith, therefore, need to engage and be engaged in theological reflection on what the Bible teaches about creation and the environment so that they are able to come to the climate change conversation armed with a theology that challenges anthropocentrism which is at the root of environmental problems and, ultimately, climate change. There is hardly any active preaching/teaching or a developed theology

---

[26] Presbyterian Mission Agency, "Earth Care Congregations", *Presbyterian Mission Agency Website.* [Available at: https://www.presbyterianmission.org/ministries/environment/earth-care-congregations/], [Last accessed: 8th February 2022].

[27] I am not ignorant of the Genesis 1 creation story which is problematic in that it seems to licence/ calls humanity to dominate and subdue creation. There are a lot of more other texts that balance it and calls humans to be stewards of Gods' creation. And other essays in this handbook explore the ideas of Genesis 1 in detail, including the words "dominion".

about the value of creation and climate change among African Christians, yet the Bible is very rich in this area. If Christian women are educated about the intersectionality of caring for the environment and the theology of stewardship and the beauty of creation, they can contribute more to promote the protection of the ecosystem. Armed with Christian doctrines of stewardship and convinced that the created world is displaying God's works and every created being is valuable, women of faith can be advocates of climate change justice. And if they are given proper spaces at the table, women of faith can also help governments to reach their targets and engage in environmental activism with intent and purpose. Women of faith are already a massive social capital in our African contexts and they are already highly motivated on issues related to the preservation of the earth. Therefore, it is only right that they are more visibly involved in mitigating climate change.

Conclusion

It is evident that climate change is a growing problem that is threatening the wellbeing of the whole world. Therefore, it requires every member of the earth community to be involved especially those in the margins and women. I do not see governments and churches making any headway on this matter without engaging women's contribution and wisdom. Institutions and ecumenical bodies have been doing amazing work in response to the challenges of climate change, but the dangers of a total collapse of the environment is still a looming reality. I have argued in this paper that the slowness in progress is accounted for in part by the failure to engage women in their numbers in the struggle for climate justice. However, taking into consideration that the church has been entrusted with stewardship and most of its African members and leaders are women, the impact of its work on climate justice will be felt more strongly if women are brought to the forefront of this work. For the church to push the industrialists, the owners of multinational companies which are behind pollution of the planet, and the leaders of government who have to devise and implement policies churches and societies will require more visible participation and input from the wisdom and courage of women.

Suggestions for Further Reading

Agang, S.B. Ed. *African Public Theology*. Nigeria: Hippo Books. 2020.

Amanze, J. *African Religions and Culture in Botswana.* Gaborone: Pula Press, 2002.

Ayre, C and E. Conradie. *The Church in God's Household.* Pietermaritzburg: Cluster, 2016.

Bolaane, M.M.M., Mary S. Lederer, Leloba S. Molema and Connie Rapoo, Eds. *Botswana Women Write.* Pietermaritzburg: University of KwaZulu-Natal Press, 2019.

Clayton, L. *Wangari Maathai: Get to know the woman who planted trees to bring change.* United Kingdom: Capstone, 2020.

Conradie, E and D. Field. *A Rainbow Over the Land: a South African Guide on the Church and Environmental Justice.* Wellington, South Africa: Western Cape Provincial Council of Churches, 2000.

Institute for Security Studies. *The Impact of Climate Change in Africa.* Pretoria: Institute for Security Studies, 2010. [Available at: https://www.files.ethz.ch/isn/136704/PAPER220.pdf], [Last accessed: 7th February 2022].

IPCC, *Climate Change 2021: The Physical Science Basis Summary for Policymakers* Working Group I Contribution to the Sixth Assessment Report of the Intergovernmental Panel on Climate Change. Geneva, Switzerland: IPCC, 2021. [Available at: https://www.ipcc.ch/report/ar6/wg1/downloads/report/IPCC_AR6_WGI_SPM_final.pdf], [Last accessed: 7th February 2022].

Jamieson, D. "Climate Change, Responsibility, and Justice". *Science and Engineering Ethics* 16 (2010): 431-445.

Kaoma, K. *The Creator's Symphony: African Christianity, the Plight of the Earth and the Poor.* Pietermaritzburg: Cluster, 2015: 15.

——. *God's Family, God's Earth: Christian Ecological Ethics of Ubuntu.* Zomba: Kacheri Books. 2013.

Mackett, O. "Female farm holding in Botswana's agriculture industry". *Agrekon*, 60(3) (July 2021): 317-334.

Nuernberger, K. *Prosperity, Pollution & Poverty. Managing the Approaching Crisis*. Pietermaritzburg: Cluster, 1999.

Presbyterian Mission Agency. "Earth Care Congregations". *Presbyterian Mission Agency Website.* [Available at: https://www.presbyterianmission.org/ministries/environment/earth-care-congregations/], [Last accessed: 8th February 2022].

Ramodibe, D. "Women and Men Building Together the Church in Africa." In M.M. Fabella and M.A. Oduyoye, Eds. *With Passion and Compassion: Third Women Doing Theology.* Maryknoll, NY: Orbis Books, 1996: 14-21.

The Royal Society & National Academy of Sciences. *Climate Change: Evidence & Causes.* The Royal Society & National Academy of Sciences, 2020. [Available at https://royalsociety.org/~/media/royal_society_content/policy/projects/climate-evidence-causes/climate-change-evidence-causes.pdf], [Last accessed: 7th February 2022].

Sherkat, D.E. and C.G. Ellison. "Structuring the religion-environment connection: identifying religious influences on environmental concern and activism". *Journal for the Scientific Study of Religion* 46 (2007): 71-85.

Staudt, Amanda, Nancy Huddleston and Sandi Rudenstein, Eds. "Understanding and Responding to Climate Change – Highlights of NATIONAL Academies Reports", *The National Academies of Sciences* October 2005 [Available at: https://www.preventionweb.net/files/2276_climatechangefinal.pdf], [Last accessed: 7th February 2022].

Uejio, C.K., J.D. Tamerius, K. Wertz and K.M. Konchar. "Primer on Climate Science". In G. Luber and J. Lemery, Eds. *Global Climate Change and Human Health*. San Francisco, CA: Jossey-Bass, 2015.

UN Climate Change News, "Gender Equality Crucial to Tackling Climate Change" *UN* 15th February 2018, [Available at: https://unfccc.int/news/gender-equality-crucial-to-tackling-climate-change-un], [Last accessed: 7th February 2022].

Warmback, A. *The Church and Ecological Justice*. Pietermaritzburg: Cluster, 2017.

World Meteorological Organisation. *State of the Climate in Africa.* Geneva, Switzerland: WMO, 2019.

37. Youth Redefining Ecotheology: A Narrative of a Young Lutheran Theologian from Nigerian Context

Barde Cham Benedict[1]

> And why do you worry about clothing? Consider the lilies of the field, how they grow; they neither toil nor spin, yet I tell you, even Solomon in all his glory was not clothed like one of these. But if God so clothes the grass of the field, which is alive today and tomorrow is thrown into the oven, will he not much more clothe you – you of little faith? (Mt. 6:28-30).

Introduction

Growing up as a child in north-eastern Nigeria, the relationship between humanity and other creation used to be "fun". It was "fun" because we grew up without any sense of creation care. Although in Sunday School we were taught about creation as the handiwork of God given to humanity for sustenance (Gen. 1:29-30), we were not shown at that same early stage in life the flip side of the coin which entails creation care (Gen. 2:15). All that we saw and cared for about the creation was food. And, because of poverty, food insecurity and the growing population, every household tried to secure what was needed before it was too late. For example, firewood was the major (if not the only) means of cooking energy in those days so, as early as 4:00am, we would leave home for tree cutting. Because of this daily practice, trees which we used to get to in no distant journey and in good quality and quantity became difficult to get. It got to the point where we had to trek for about two hours before reaching any trees we could cut down. This was done without any effort to plant new trees. I do not know how many hours people trek for today before getting a tree to cut down for firewood because of the devastating effect of human activities on the vegetation. This is what Moses Audi calls "raping the environment."[2] Yet "even today about 60 percent of the developing world's peoples are dependent upon trees for their energy."[3]

The best description of such ecology is exploitation, which was not caused by the biblical dominion given to humanity as claimed by some ecotheologians,[4] but rather it is a result of the fall from general perspective and some level of ignorance in some contexts. When I understood the divine mandate on creation care and the ecology in photosynthesis for example, my perspective towards vegetation changed greatly. It dawned on me heavily that caring for vegetation is not only caring for my life, but also caring for the entire community in which I live and beyond. It became clear that vegetation serves greater purposes in my life than food, because, without the oxygen they produce, breathing is not possible. No wonder that in the creation order God created vegetation first before humanity.

Multiple approaches were employed in the struggle for eco-justice from different works of life toward mitigating the threatening nature of the challenges posed by global ecological crises like climate change and environmental degradation. These solutions should not be approached with an attitude of competition but rather in a complementary spirit such that all hands are on deck in dealing with a problem caused by all

---

[1] Barde Cham Benedict is an ordained Pastor with Lutheran Church of Christ in Nigeria; a lecturer in the Biblical Theology Department, Bronnum Lutheran Seminary Yola, Nigeria, and PhD student in the Theological College of Northern Nigeria Jos, Nigeria. barde.benedict@gmail.com

[2] Moses Audi, "The Theocentric Approach", In Adetoye Faniran (ed), *Theology of Creation and Environment* (Ogbomoso: International Council for Higher Education, 2019): 172.

[3] Adetoye Faniran, "Biocentric Approach", In Adetoye Faniran (ed), *Theology of Creation and Environment* (Ogbomoso: International Council for Higher Education, 2019), 215.

[4] Ably represented by Jurgen Moltmann in *God in Creation: A New Theology of Creation and the Spirit of God* (Minneapolis, MN: Fortress Press, 1993), 26.

hands. This is because "the multidimensional nature of the challenges being addressed"[5] in ecology requires a multidimensional approach, multiple efforts and contributions for it to be mitigated reasonably.

Ecotheology is defined as "religious thought and action concerning the relationship between human beings and the natural world."[6] From the biblical approach of this endeavour, many eco-theologians from twentieth century to date made some significant contributions in establishing a biblical thought on the relationship between human beings and the rest of the creation. This article seeks to make a similar yet new contribution from a biblical-contextual lens in strengthening and continuing the fight for ecological justice.

The Unclothed Creation

Ecotheologians unanimously affirmed the devastating effect of the fall of humanity not only on the image and likeness of God in humanity but also on the entire creation – living and non-living things. For example, the earth on which all vegetation stands and thrives was cursed because of the fall (Gen. 3:17-18). One then sees how Noah's generation brought another devastating consequence to creation because of sin, where God destroyed humanity, animals and vegetation in the deluge, sparing only the Noah's family and the different species of animals in the ark (Gen. 6-7). Audi affirms the position of Faniran and Lateju regarding the effect of the fall on creation, "the fall of man in the Garden of Eden affected the creation of God, even though God purposed to preserve it."[7] He further sees the effect of the fall in the negative attitude of humanity toward creation which limits "the value of nature to human utility without consideration for its preservation and effective management."[8] In this overexploitation of the environment, a sense of care and responsibility is completely missing or neglected. Humanity lacked love and mercy toward creation in their selfish endeavour to make better their lives at the expense of the environment. This leads to what I call "unclothing the creation" that was beautifully "clothed" by God at creation before the fall – an inference drawn from the above text. The Greek words *periballo*[9] and *amphiennymi*[10] that were used in this pericope both have the generic meaning of "to cloth" or "to adorn", that is, "to put on clothing to adorn the outward form of something". It can be clothing or adorning a person or, as used in the text, adorning the grass (creation) to make it beautiful and attractive. This does not only reveal God's care in clothing creation but also the beauty and glory of the cloths with which God adorned creation.

This beautiful clothing of creation was destroyed by human activities and leaving the creation "unclothed." The ecological crisis we are facing today comes as a result of "unclothing creation" in many ways. The beauty and goodness of the creation that Genesis 1:25 and 31 declare is now made ugly and wicked due to this "unclothing." Deforestation is an "unclothing" of the land which destroys the natural beauty of the land and opens it for devastating erosion thereby destroying lives and properties. The depletion of the ozone layers, which is predominantly caused by human activities, is an "unclothing" of the creation, which is now the major cause of myriads of dangers to human life which has effects on the weather, human health, animals, plants, agriculture, sea levels and more. Indeed, "the global ecological crisis, including climate change, is human-induced."[11]

---

[5] S. A. Kolawole, "Biblical and Theological Strategy for Sustainable Earth", In Adetoye Faniran (ed), *Theology of Creation and Environment* (Ogbomoso: International Council for Higher Education, 2019), 225.

[6] Panu Pihkala, "Ecotheology and the Theology of Eating: Convergences and Controversies," *Religion and Food*, Scripta Instituti Donneriani Aboensis, 26 (2015): 64-81.

[7] Audi, "The Theocentric Approach", 173.

[8] Audi, "The Theocentric Approach", 173.

[9] "περιβαλλω" in: Horst Balz/Gerhard Schneider (eds): *Exegetical Dictionary of New Testament*. PC Study Bible V5. CD-ROM.

[10] "ἀμφιεννυμι" in: Horst Balz/Gerhard Schneider (eds): *Exegetical Dictionary of New Testament*. PC Study Bible V5. CD-ROM.

[11] LWF Twelfth Assembly, *Public Statements and Resolutions* (Windhoek: LWF, 2017), 13.

Matthew 6:28-30 gives us an astounding revelation about the state of the environment (represented by the grass in the text) at the creation. Jesus makes reference to this fact in encouraging his disciples to trust God for their material and day-to-day needs. The use of the beauty of environment (in its admirable state) as the basis for trusting God for material clothing clearly reveals the original state of creation as God intended, created and desires to sustain and preserve. Since the mandate of the new creation is that of restoring what the fall had destroyed, the church as the community of new creation ought to reflect this experience on the entire creation. "Our new creation is the beginning of a cosmic renewal, a renewal as comprehensive as was the original creation."[12] The environment needs to also experience some renewal as a testament to the reality of the new creation. "In every way we can, it is the church's duty to show and share the reality of new creation in the midst of the old."[13]

Re-Clothing the Creation

The first thing God did to Adam and Eve after the fall was to cover their nakedness using animal skins: "*And the LORD God made garments of skins for the man and for his wife, and clothed them*" (Gen. 3:21), which was a physical clothing for the sinful humanity, a typology of the divine clothing brought to humanity in the redemptive work of Christ. Paul alludes to this reality "*As many of you as were baptised into Christ have clothed yourselves with Christ*" (Gal. 3:27, cf. Rom. 13:14). Despite our sinfulness, this clothing gives us the beautiful cover and adornment through which God looks at us and through which we are able to commune with God who is holy. This clothing does not only ensure our relationship with God but even with one another as Paul charged the Colossians: "*As God's chosen ones, holy and beloved, clothe yourselves with compassion, kindness, humility, meekness, and patience. Bear with one another and, if anyone has a complaint against another, forgive each other; just as the Lord has forgiven you, so you also must forgive. Above all, clothe yourselves with love, which binds everything together in perfect harmony*" (Col. 3:12-15, cf. 1 Pet. 5:5). Since the church is saved and "re-clothed", what about the rest of creation? As humanity was instructed to keep and take care of the environment in the first creation, the new creation re-echoes afresh this call, mandate and order on the church that the creation would be re-clothed. Samuel Peni Ango asserts (as quoted by Kolawole) that:

> Since the fall of man, his ability to treat the environment in accordance with God's commands became distorted along with other moral failings. It also follows that when God provided salvation for man from sin, man's ability to obey God's commandments was restored. Therefore, it is to be expected that redeemed man should have a greatly enhanced tendency and ability to treat the environment in a responsible manner.[14]

It is possible to conceive and speak of this level of God's care revealed in Matthew 6:28-30 as concerning only the humanity that was made in the image and likeness of God. But this is not true from the gospel text above. In the text, God also clothes the grass of the field (creation) as he clothes the humanity. For example, the field was beautifully "clothed" by trees and grasses of different kind, the stratosphere was gloriously "clothed" with an ozone layer at creation. The gospel text makes a mind-blowing revelation of the extent of God's 'clothing' the grass of the field as even better than King Solomon's adornment and glory: "even Solomon in all his glory was not clothed like one of these". "Solomon's wardrobe fades into insignificance beside the simple beauty of a flower."[15] In this comparison, one may get an idea that God's care for the

---

[12] John M. Frame, *Systematic Theology: An Introduction to Christian Belief* (Philipsburg: P&R Publishers, 2013), 191.
[13] Mark Hopkins, "Transforming Christian Attitudes to Creation Care: A Perspective from Public Theology", In *TCNN Bukuru Journal of Transformational Theology*, vol. 2 (2021): 88-89.
[14] Kolawole, "Biblical and Theological Strategy for Sustainable Earth", 230-231.
[15] Joe Kapolyo, "Matthew", In Tokunboh Adeyemo (ed), *Africa Bible Commentary* (Nairobi: WordAlive, 2006), 1123.

grass is better and greater than humanity as far as clothing is concern. If this is how our heavenly Father cares about the beauty and adornment of the creation, the question we may ask is: how are we (his children) supposed to care for the creation?

One of the fundamental principles underscoring the New Testament ethics on the faith community, as revealed in the Sermon on the Mount, is "so that you may be children of your Father in heaven" (Mt. 5:45). Becoming children of our heavenly Father includes love and care for creation – "to value it as he does, and to do our level best to live in harmony with it and restore its beauty."[16] It becomes a responsibility on the church to care for the creation in a way and manner that God cares for it. This is what Paul refers to as "imitating God" (Eph. 5:1), a call he made to the Ephesian church regarding the love which brings forth sacrificial service. Unless the church cares for what God cares for holistically and to the degree in which God cares, we still have much to imitate of God, particularly in regards to creation care. The idea of the Escapists who think that "The God who redeems us has little to do with the God who created the world"[17] is rather misleading and deceptive. The redemptive clothing the church receives which ensures a harmonious relationship with God and humanity should also complete the circle by ensuring a better and healthy relationship with the environment. "God is to be manifest in us not only in reverence for human life but also the nonhuman creation."[18] This is because "ecology implies total interconnectedness of creation, and this connectedness is not strange to biblical teaching."[19] Danny McCain reiterates the church's responsibility toward the environment, "The Christian attitude toward the environment is one of protection from further injury and rebuilding and restoring of that which has been damaged and destroyed."[20] This is the clarion call that the church must harken to today so as to re-clothe the environment, restoring its beauty and glory. "We must restore all of the natural things that have been perverted, abused and polluted."[21]

How would the church achieve living up to this grave and important responsibility of re-clothing the creation in a systematic, progressive and generational manner? The Lutheran World Federation Twelfth Assembly's Public Statement and Resolution on Climate Change and Mark Hopkins' article[22] gave some important suggestions, namely: education, advocacy, and creation care projects.

Education is key to every transformation and meaningful development be it spiritual, economic, social and even ecological. "The foundation or basis of human actions can largely be traced to the form of education or information, both formal and informal to which the people are exposed."[23] There is a need for the church in Africa to be deliberate in educating her teeming members about creation care using all the available platforms and programmes. Formally, theological seminaries and church-owned institutions are enjoined to integrate creation care into their curriculums and lessons so as to deliberately inculcate this concern on the minds of the new generation of leaders for the church and society. Informally, church teaching programmes like Sunday preaching, mid-weeks, Bible Studies, Sunday School classes, baptism and confirmation classes, and subgroup activities should bear witness to the reality of climate change and creation care. "At the denominational level churches should set in place structures to ensure that creation care is mainstreamed right down to the congregational level [...] communicating creation care as an integral feature of the Gospel through all available means to all sectors within churches."[24]

---

[16] Hopkins, "Transforming Christian Attitudes to Creation Care: A Perspective from Public Theology", 89.

[17] Ernst Conradie, "The Environment", In Sunday Bobai Agang (ed), *African Public Theology* (Bukuru: ACTS, 2020), 165.

[18] Ken Gnanakan and Adetoye Faniran, "Anthropocentric Approach", In Adetoye Faniran (ed), *Theology of Creation and Environment* (Ogbomoso: International Council for Higher Education, 2019), 201.

[19] Gnanakan and Faniran, "Anthropocentric Approach", 198.

[20] Danny McCain, *We Believe: An Introduction to Christian Doctrine* Vol. 1 (Bukuru: ACTS, 2004), 114.

[21] McCain, *We Believe: An Introduction to Christian Doctrine* Vol. 1, 111.

[22] Hopkins, "Transforming Christian Attitudes to Creation Care: A Perspective from Public Theology", 77-92.

[23] Ken Gnanakan and Adetoye Faniran, "Anthropocentric Approach", 190.

[24] Hopkins, "Transforming Christian Attitudes to Creation Care: A Perspective from Public Theology", 90.

The church should engage in constant advocacy for creation care and protection and climate justice. The church's vanguardism for creation care should be taken to the front doors of political leaders, traditional leaders and institutional leaders so as to ensure all hands are on deck for this noble and holy task. "The Assembly calls upon the member churches to advocate for environmental care and protection [...] to integrate these goals and engage governments and national or local organisations for the implementation of the Sustainable Development Goals (SDGs)."[25] In order for the church to model this message, there is need for the church to embark on creation care projects so as to combine activism with practical actions. This can be in the form of tree planting, good management of waste, protection of biodiversity, and the like. This will go a long way to ensuring creation care and protection. "Christians have a duty to look after the creation God has saved along with us; indeed, this is a core feature of Christian witness to the kingdom of God."[26]

Conclusion

It is crystal clear that the world is at a crossroads now considering the alarming danger and threads posed by the growing ecological crisis. The unclothing of creation makes its nakedness gloomy for human existence and well-being. Biodiversity is at the brink of extinction due to irresponsible human behaviours and activities. The hope of reversing this catastrophe lies in the collective response from all persons: big and small, rich and poor, leaders and members, male and female, religious and nonreligious, government and nongovernmental, educated and non-educated. The church in Africa has the needed demography, resources and theology with which to lead this noble and holy campaign. Unclothing what God has clothed is a bad stewardship and irresponsive to the first task given to humanity in the creation, that is keeping and caring for creation. The beauty of creation must be preserved, conserved, protected and restored. The beauty and glory of human life is directly proportional to the beauty and glory of the life of other parts of creation.

Suggestions for Further Reading

Adeyemo, Tokunboh, Ed. *Africa Bible Commentary*. Nairobi: WordAlive, 2006. [Especially Joe Kapolyo's chapter: "Matthew"].

Agang, Sunday Bobai, Ed. *African Public Theology* Bukuru: ACTS, 2020. [Especially Ernst Conradie's chapter: "The Environment"].

Faniran, Adetoye, Ed. *Theology of Creation and Environment.* Ogbomoso: International Council for Higher Education, 2019. [Especially chapters: Moses Audi. "The Theocentric Approach"; Adetoye Faniran. "Biocentric Approach"; Ken Gnanakan and Adetoye Faniran. "Anthropocentric Approach"; and S.A. Kolawole. "Biblical and Theological Strategy for Sustainable Earth"].

Frame, John M. *Systematic Theology: An Introduction to Christian Belief.* Philipsburg: P&R Publishers, 2013.

Hopkins, Mark. "Transforming Christian Attitudes to Creation Care: A Perspective from Public Theology", *TCNN Bukuru Journal of Transformational Theology* 2 (2021): 77-92.

LWF Twelfth Assembly. *Public Statements and Resolutions.* Windhoek: LWF, 2017.

McCain, Danny. *We Believe: An Introduction to Christian Doctrine.* Vol. 1. Bukuru: ACTS, 2004.

Moltmann, Jurgen. *God in Creation: A New Theology of Creation and the Spirit of God.* Minneapolis, MN: Fortress, 1993.

Pihkala, Panu. "Ecotheology and the Theology of Eating: Convergences and Controversies". *Religion and Food*, Scripta Instituti Donneriani Aboensis, 26 (2015): 64-81.

---

[25] LWF Twelfth Assembly, *Public Statements and Resolutions*, 13.

[26] Hopkins, "Transforming Christian Attitudes to Creation Care: A Perspective from Public Theology", 77.

38. Interreligious Engagements on Climate Change Adaptation: Walking the Talk of Interfaith Relations

Margaret Makafui Tayviah[1]

Introduction

Christianity and Islam are monotheistic religions and these religious groups revere God as the creator of the universe. Christians and Muslims are enjoined in the Bible[2] and the Qur'an[3] to care for the environment and be stewards of God's creation. Since that creation, the environment has undergone several positive and negative transformations. Some of these negative transformations have caused severe damage to it thereby leading to unbearable changes in the climate. Therefore, humankind has been entrusted with the task of protecting the ecology, treating the climate justly and safeguarding the biodiversity by adopting ethos to sustain the created order. Since Christians and Muslims are charged in their Holy Books to be stewards and caretakers of God's creation, it is imperative that the two faith groups co-operate and collaborate to fight against the global abuse of the environment. Both religions have the duty and the responsibility to care for God's creation and this is a good foundation for interfaith engagement and for joint religious action to tackle the root causes of the global environmental crisis, biodiversity destruction and climate change with their attendant health hazards on local, regional and global levels. This article seeks to assess the situation in Ghana in terms of what Christians and Muslims have done and are doing concerning their care for God's creation as well as their joint actions in the adaptation to climate change. This article will also advocate closer cooperation and collaboration between the two faith groups to strengthen their fight against climate change in Ghana.

Religions as Caretakers for the Environment

Many religious traditions have regard and concern for God's creation and the environment. Hence, any consequences of climate change and its adverse effects on the lives of humans necessitates a common call for concern and care.[4] The term climate change has been defined to be "all human activities, directly or indirectly that alters the composition of the global atmosphere over a period of time."[5] Climate change threatens human life as well as the environment. Yet, since climate change is human-induced, it will need an all-inclusive and global action to fully address its situation. Religious people need to be constantly reminded of the need to be good stewards of the environment and thus help mitigate any negative acts that affect it. No single religious body/tradition or state can curb the issues and threat of climate change effectively but it takes the effort and enhanced co-operation and collaboration of all states and religious traditions to be responsible for the care of the environment. Thus, a common task and responsibility of all humanity. It is important to begin with that religious people deepen their understanding of each other's

---

[1] Dr Margaret Makafui Tayviah is a lecturer in the Department of Religious Studies at the Kwame Nkrumah University of Science and Technology (KNUST), Kumasi, Ghana. She is a member and currently the Area Advisor of the Ghana Committee as well as the Anglophone West Africa coordinator of the Programme for Christian-Muslim Relations in Africa (PROCMURA) which has its Central Office in Nairobi, Kenya. Her publications are in the areas of Islamic studies and Christian-Muslim Relations. makafui2007jub@yahoo.com

[2] Genesis 1:28; Genesis 2:15.

[3] Surah 2:30-39; Surah 33:72, Surah 56:11, 88.

[4] WCC, "Interfaith Statement on Climate Change: Climate, Faith and Hope: Faith Traditions Together for a Common Future", [Available at: https://www.oikoumene.org/resources/documents/interfaith-statement-on-climate-change], [Last accessed: 8th February 2022].

[5] *United Nation Framework Convention on Climate Change*, Article 1, Paragraph 2, 1994.

religious traditions, ways of life and appreciate each other's spiritual values concerning the care for the environment.

Many groups have actively engaged with global climate agencies and civil society organisations on anthropogenic climate change. Such engagement has occurred at the highest levels, involving popes, UN Secretary Generals, national leaders, and monarchs.

Christianity and the Environment

The issue about the duty to care for God's creation has set many people thinking. The deterioration of the environment by mostly human activity has resulted in questions such as who takes responsibility for the environment? How should humans care for creation? These questions and many more call for the need for the Church to place more emphasis on the Christian principle of environmental stewardship. According to Norman Geisler, a Christian theologian and philosopher, the Christian perception of the environment suggests that natural resources should be respected and put to proper use.[6] This assertion confirms how the Bible expects Christians to relate with the natural environment.[7] The Bible also commands humankind to be stewards of the environment by taking good care of it for their good and as reverence to God. From the Christian point of view, humankind, then, is supposed to be the keeper of the earth because it is a duty entrusted by God the creator.[8] It is therefore necessary for man to be more responsible in his treatment of the environment.

The Biblical worldview of creation stipulate two phrases, "to have dominion" and "to till and keep" which need much attention in contemporary times. Although these phrases have been interpreted in many ways, there is the need to re-examine them in order to assess its impact on Christian life as far as stewardship of the environment is concerned. Genesis 1:26 and Genesis 2:15 are Bible verses people have ascribed the stewardship of creation to man. The most popular words deduced from these verses is to "have dominion", to "till" and "keep". This makes the Church, if not all religious groups, to agree to the submission that the earth and everything in it needs proper management since humankind would be accountable to God concerning it.

To Have Dominion

In Genesis 1:26, God's plan and intention for creating humankind is clearly stated:

> Then God said, let us create man in our image, after our likeness; and let them have dominion over the fish of the sea and over the birds of the air and over the cattle and over all the earth, over every creeping thing that creeps upon the earth.[9]

This verse points out that God created everything that exists, including humans. He further gives humans the mandate to take care and control all that He has created. Christians believe that the word "dominion" as used in the text indicates that they have been given authority and power by God over the world. This suggests a divinely assigned "responsibility of stewardship" to take good care of all that God created. From this point of view, the word "dominion" could also be understood as to take care, look after, respect, protect and control.[10] Thus, Christians believe that humans have been tasked with the responsibility to care for the environment, not to misuse it, and to keep it in good condition for posterity.

---

[6] Norman Geisler, *Christian Ethics* (Grand Rapids, MI: Baker, 2010), Kindle Edition: 315.
[7] Deuteronomy 29:19.
[8] Godfrey J. Ucheawaji and Loveday C. Onyezonwu, "'Dress and Keep' the Garden: Environmental Stewardship as a Biblical Motif for the 'Great Commission'". *AAMM* 9 (2014); 57.
[9] Genesis 1:26 (RSV).
[10] Bible Society, "The Environment and Stewardship". *American Bible Society*, 2006: 3.

To Till and Keep It

In Genesis 2:15, the Christian principle of environmental stewardship was clearly established and states that: "The Lord God took the man and put him in the Garden of Eden to 'till it and keep'."[11] According to Berry Sam, this verse provides a moral attitude of respect for the environment, which would lead to environmental sustainability.[12] To Berry, "the verse is the heart" of the Christian understanding of environmental stewardship. He highlights that, to "till" is about the responsibility of humans to work rightly and manage the earth using the natural resources given by God. To "keep" as used in the verse is about respect and control which gives humans the opportunity to control and manage the natural resources so that they are renewed and restored for future generations.

The Issue of Dominion

It appears that one of the most misunderstood and most misapplied words in caring for the environment is "dominion". Both David Rhoads and Marvin Tate argue that Christians have distorted the meaning of dominion in Genesis 1:28, which has caused the reckless exploitation of creation due to human activities.[13] The concept that gave humankind responsibility over creation has rather caused them to dominate and destroy. Thomas Aquinas likewise argues that, "as the plants make use of the earth for their nourishment, and animals make use of plants, and man makes use of both plants and animals. Therefore, it is in keeping with the order of nature, that man should be master over animals."[14] Lynn White agrees with Thomas Aquinas' position when he indicated that Genesis 1:28 is human-centred and, therefore, humans have the right to use any creature for their benefits.[15] However, White states that, "what people do about their ecology depends on what they think about themselves in relation to things around them. Human ecology is deeply conditioned by beliefs about our nature and destiny (religion in this case)."[16] According to Nancy Opstad Weldon, White saw some depravity in the Christian theology, which allows some Christians to unfairly treat the environment. For Weldon, it was in this view that White applauds some religious groups like the Hindu and adherents of African traditional religions who attached themselves directly with the environment.[17]

On the other hand, John Calvin has it as: "let him who possesses a field, so partake of its yearly fruits, that he may not suffer the ground to be injured by his negligence, but let him endeavour to hand it down to posterity as he received it, or even better cultivated [...] let everyone regard himself as the steward of God in all things which he possesses."[18] Walter Brueggemann added that the idea of dominion is to be understood as nurturing the environment and not exploiting it.[19] In spite of all these lofty ideas, yet humans continue to cruelly destroy the very environment for selfish ends.

---

[11] Genesis 2:15

[12] Sam Berry, *A Christian Approach to the Environment*. (London: The John Ray Initiative, 2005): 1-2.

[13] David M. Rhoads, "Stewardship of creation," *Currents in Theology and Mission* 36, no. 5(2009): 1; Marvin E. Tate, "An Exposition of Psalm 8," *Perspectives in Religious Studies* 28 (2001): 344

[14] Thomas Aquinas, *Summa Theologica*. Translated by Fathers of the English Dominican Province (New York, NY: Benziger Brothers, 1947): 96.

[15] Lynn White, Jr., "The Historical Roots of Our Ecological Crisis", *Science* 3767 (1967): 155.

[16] White, "The Historical Roots of Our Ecological Crisis", 155.

[17] Nancy Opstad Weldon, "A Biblical Hermeneutic for Dominion: Domination vs Stewardship", *Obsculta* 9(1) (2016): 75.

[18] John Calvin, *Commentary on Genesis*, translated by. John King, M.D. (Grand Rapids, MI: Christian Classics Ethereal Library, 1578)

[19] Walter Brueggemann, Terence E Fretheim, Jr, Walter C Kaiser, Leander E. Keck (eds), *The New Interpreter's Bible: Genesis to Leviticus*, Volume 1 (Nashville, TN: Abingdon, 1994), 346.

The Bible and the Environment

God declared in John 1:3 and Colossians 1:16-17 that all things were made through Him as it was first captured in Genesis 1:1. God then reveals His attachment to the environment by how He feels about the animals in Isaiah 43:20-21 ("the wild animals honour me, God"). In the words of God in Job 12:7-10, animals and things in the world are meant to teach people things unknown to them as well. It is with this view that God admonished the Israelites (Lev. 25:23-24) not to sell their land permanently because the land belongs to God; man is just a tenant. God added that humans are to redeem any land they get hold of. This position was taken further in Ezekiel 34:2-4 when God warned the people against taking care only of themselves and leaving the animals and other creatures. The verse adds that there will be judgment on whoever does not heal the environment. A comparative analysis of the contemporary environmental crisis and the history of Israel (Is.2:4-6) reveals that the majority of the environmental crisis is caused by human action/inactions. For God, the earth dries up and withers, the world languishes and withers, the exalted of the earth languish because people have disobeyed the laws of nature (Is. 2:4-6). This connotes that people are destroying the creatures of the world by defiling the land (Jer. 2:7). On this note, God will destroy whoever destroys the earth (Rev. 11:18).

Christian Organisations and the Environment

Many Christian organisations and councils have met to discuss issues pertaining to Christians being stewards of the earth. For instance, the World Council of Churches (WCC) met in 2014 to discuss climate change in light of Christian faith as a means of giving hope to the world. Anchored in their faith, the participants showed concern about climate change as a threat to life, for they admitted the gift of the environment by God and the need to care for it.[20]

It has been observed that many Christians have responded to the harm caused to the land by human actions and have released policy statements, declarations, resolutions, and pastoral letters to provide a theological foundation for Christian stewardship concerning environmental protection. Since it is generally believed that God created the world and entrusted it in the hands of humankind as "caretakers and stewards", Walter Brueggemann argues that "the recovery of creation as the horizon of biblical theology encourages us to contribute to the resolution of the ecological crisis".[21] In other words, theology deduced from the Bible urges Christians to care for the environment.

Russell Butkus also submits that creation is centred on God and there is the need to acknowledge that.[22] Butkus further argues that as far as Christian stewardship is concerned, creation has not ended and is still ongoing. Thus, God created humankind and gave them the ability to procreate (continue creating); God entrusted the world in the hands of humans to continue creating as well. God sees creation as a relational entity in a harmonious manner where each depends on the other and has an appropriate place to function as created and designed. This idea dawns on Christians to see to it that all things are kept in their original position for it to function well. For instance, deforestation has impacted changes in climate since trees are not planted to replace them. It has been observed in some parts of Ghana where rivers have dried out because of the cutting of trees along the riverbank.

---

[20] WCC, "Ecumenical movement, Climate, Faith and Hope: Faith Traditions Together for a Common Future", 2014 [Available at: https://www.oikoumene.org/news/ecumenical-organizations-set-to-promote-climate-justice-at-cop-20], [Last accessed: 27th June 2021].

[21] Walter Brueggemann, "The Loss and Recovery of Creation in Old Testament Theology", *Theology Today* 53 (1996): 188.

[22] Russell A. Butkus, "The Stewardship of Creation", *Moral Landscape of Creation* (Waco, TX: The Center for Christian Ethics at Baylor University, 2001): 20. [Available at: https://www.baylor.edu/ifl/christianreflection/Creation.pdf], [Last accessed: 9th February 2022].

According to Douglas Hall, "the steward is one who has been given the responsibility for the management and service of something belonging to another, and his office presupposes a particular kind of trust on the part of the owner or master."[23] The key words in Hall's definition on stewardship is responsibility, management, service and master. From the key words, it can be said that caring is being concerned about something which is not for the caretaker and that they will render an account to the rightful sometime to come. So, basically, stewardship is taking care of someone's property. It is in this vein that Russell Butkus said the term steward was linked to Israel's kings as they ruled on God's behalf and they are responsible to God on the throne.[24] People must look at life beyond themselves and think about others. This would help to reduce the harm caused to the environment if we get to know the negative effect it is going to have on the life of others.[25]

Church-based Projects

Many church denominations are helping in the fight against climate change and some of them have instituted some avenues to help in this course. Taking the argument from a worldwide perspective, most churches are reducing their carbon footprint by engaging in energy efficiency programmes and purchasing renewable energy. In the US, the *Episcopal Church* paved the way with its award-winning *Episcopal Power and Light Campaign* that was expanded into an interfaith initiative: *Interfaith Power and Light* reached 28 states in the US and unites more than 4,000 congregations in reducing the devastating effects of global warming by conducting energy audits and purchasing green power. In Germany, the ecological management programme "*The Green Rooster*" has been developed to apply the official European Ecological Management and Auditing Scheme (EMAS) issued by the European Commission to the context of the churches.[26]

In Ghana, most Christian leaders have expressed their support for caring for the environment. This can be witnessed in the recent "Green Ghana" project that was launched by the President of the country, Nana Addo Dankwa Akuffo Addo which saw several churches participating in it. The Most Rev. Charles Gabriel Palmer-Buckle (the Catholic Archbishop of Cape Coast), submitted in his speech during the Arbor Week of the Catholic Church, that coincided with the Green Ghana exercise at Anomabo in the Central Region, that the Catholic Church will plant one million trees every year to help in greening Ghana. He indicated that "In fact, we are going to continue and we intend for the whole month of June, the rainy season, to have contributed, at least, one million trees in the Catholic Church, nationwide, to the Green Ghana Project of 5 million trees." This conforms to the Catholics Arbor Week instituted in the 1980s, a week that is set aside to plant trees and care for the environment. The church believe that they are part of nature, which propel them to have feeling for nature as one of them.[27]

Pastor Dr Kwame Kwanin Boakye (the President of Northern Ghana Union Mission of the Seventh Day Adventist Church [SDA]), also indicated that the SDA Church and its members have fully embraced the Green Ghana Project aiming at planting 500,000 trees. He added that the course of making Ghana green is not one man's business but a collective responsibility.[28] On the part of the Church of Pentecost, its Chairman Apostle Eric Nyamekye, submitted that "By planting trees, we are giving more life to the nation because the tree is life,"[29] and this applies to humans depending on nature and vice versa.

---

[23] Douglas John Hall, *The Steward* (Grand Rapids, MI: Wm. B. Eerdmans, 1994), 32.
[24] Butkus, "The Stewardship of Creation", 19.
[25] Psalm 119:36.
[26] Michael C. Slaby, *Generating the Renewable Energy of Hope: An Earth Charter Guide to Religion and Climate Change* (Costa Rica: Earth Charter International, 2008), 11.
[27] See: https://www.myjoyonline.com/archbishop-palmer-buckle-calls-for-sustenance-of-green-ghana-project/
[28] See: https://citinewsroom.com/2021/06/sda-church-targets-500000-trees-to-support-green-ghana-project/
[29] See: https://www.myjoyonline.com/the-church-of-pentecost-kick-starts-1-million-tree-planting-project/

In the same vein, the Methodist Church of Ghana led by its Presiding Bishop, the Most Rev. Dr Paul Kwabena Boafo, threw the support of the Methodist Church in planting 1.4 million trees. This is in agreement with the Church's position on the importance of trees and vegetation to sustain human life.[30]

The above examples from the Catholic, SDA, Church of Pentecost and Methodist Churches in Ghana bring to light the efforts Christians in the country are making as their contribution to fulfilling their biblical obligation of caring for the world as instructed by God.

Islam and Climate Change

Islam has a deep sense of respect and consideration for the natural environment.[31] According to the Qur'an, Allah created everything on the earth for humankind.[32] The earth was God's gift *(ni'mah)* to humans but with conditions. Nevertheless, the way humankind strives to maintain and keep this gift is a test that shows the measure of acts of worship *(ibada)* in a way that is pleasing to Allah. Although the Qur'an speaks so much about man keeping and caring for the environment, the issue of climate change is still a problem among Muslims in the world today. This is because even though the Qur'an admonishes Muslims not to waste, spend or consume anything excessively,[33] in contemporary times, the issue of climate change involves Muslims as well. It was the practice (Sunnah) of the Prophet Muhammad, that whenever he sent soldiers out for a military campaign, he cautioned them not to cut trees, kill animals, destroy farm produce of the enemies, not to kill children and women no matter what.[34] The Qur'an states that Allah created man and elevated him and has entrusted in his care what is in the sea and on land.[35] The Qur'an also speaks of Adam's creation to be Allah's vicegerent on earth[36] when the earlier occupants (*jinns*) were spreading *fasad* (wrongdoing). It states that:

> Remember˺ when your Lord said to the angels, "I am going to place a successive ˹human˺ authority on earth (*khalifah*)." They asked (Allah), "Will You place in it someone who will spread corruption there and shed blood while we glorify your praises and proclaim your holiness?" Allah responded, "I know what you do not know.[37]

The above surah and many others in the Qur'an suggest that Allah made man a vicegerent and gave humankind the responsibility of conservation, protection and preservation of the environment.[38] Man was expected to treat the environment better than the *jinns* did.

The hadith also gives many instances of how the prophet Muhammad encouraged Muslims to care for and protect the environment. For instance, the Prophet forbade cursing animals, tormenting animals and killing them for sport.[39] Thus, the task of humankind to preserve the environment is a form of worship.

The Qur'anic view holds that everything on the earth was created for humankind. It was God's gift (*ni'mah*) to us, but a gift with conditions nevertheless. The tests are a measure of our acts of worship (*ihsan*) in its broadest sense. That is living in a way that is pleasing to Allah, striving in everything we do to maintain the harmony of our inner and outer environments. It is based on these common scriptural injunctions on

---

[30] Lydia Kukua Asamoah, "Methodist Church to plant 1.4 million trees to support Green Ghana Project", Ghana News Agency 8th June 2021, [Available at: https://www.gna.org.gh/1.20889432], [Last accessed: 9th February 2022].
[31] Mawil Y. Izzi Dien, "Islamic environmental ethics, law and society". In J.R. Engel and J.G. Engel (eds), *Ethics of Environment and Development* (London: Belhaven, 1990): 189-198.
[32] Surah 4:125, Surah 55:1-5.
[33] Surah 17:26.
[34] Sahih Muslim, Book 32 on Virtues and Good manners.
[35] Surah 17:70.
[36] Surah 2:30.
[37] Surah 2:30.
[38] Surah 6:38.
[39] Sahih Muslim (Book 21, Chapter 11, Number 4810).

both Christians and Muslims that this article encourages religious people to engage with each other to curb issues in climate change.

The Principle of *Khalifa* (Vicegerent)

The principle of *khalifa* establishes a tripartite relationship between the Creator, humankind and creation. This principle holds that God created everything for humankind and appointed humankind as vicegerent (*khalifa*) on earth.[40] Thus humankind is tasked with a moral responsibility of being a trustee (*amanah*)[41] and humankind will be accountable for their actions.[42] As a vicegerent (*khalifa*) on earth, humankind has the right to use the earth and everything within the earth to help humankind. Humankind's rights and responsibilities toward the environment are summarised by the Qur'anic word *khalifa* (viceroy, steward, representative).[43] Since humans are God's representatives and stewards on earth, they are charged to act and live responsibly in this world by maintaining, tending and caring for it but not to destroy the environment.[44]

The Qur'an and the Environment

The Qur'an outlines moral ecological guidelines for humankind so that we will not be wasteful and extravagant[45] but will 'walk modestly' on the earth.[46] However, the environment, which was created by God, is now suffering degradation and climate change. Muslims must remind themselves always about their role to maintain and safeguard the environment. Since everything in God's creation is for humans, the question is whether to develop it or destroy it. Surah 26:32 encourages Muslims to cultivate, conserve and exploit nature so that it can be beneficial to humans. The Qur'an teaches humankind to maintain and care for nature and the environment. Surah 21:107 states "and We have not sent you except for (a) mercy for all creatures." Having mercy on nature is to help in the implementation of preserving and maintaining nature. Therefore, Muslims are charged to respect nature and be responsible towards nature as stewards.

Christians and Muslims Efforts in Mitigating Climate Change

Christians and Muslims in Ghana are known to relate well as they practice the "dialogue of life"[47] in their everyday life. At the national level, Christian and Muslim leaders have found ways to make their adherents understand the need to engage and relate to each other on matters of common concern including health, education, social amenities, politics and safeguarding the environment. Caring for the environment is a priority for the government of Ghana and many religious groups because the negative impact and effects of climate change makes everyone vulnerable, therefore, there is the need for everyone – citizen or religious adherent – to adopt measures to minimise the impact of climate change. It is also important for everyone to be concerned about climate change and climate variability since it may pose serious challenges to national development. It is for this reason that the government of Ghana has come up with the National Climate Change Policy to resolve and to lessen the potential hardships that climate change impacts may pose to the

---

[40] Surah 2:30; Surah 6:167.
[41] Surah 33:72.
[42] Surah 55:59.
[43] Suwar 2:30, 35:39.
[44] Suwar 2:36; 67:15.
[45] Surah 6:141
[46] Surah 25:63
[47] Dialogue of life is a form of inter-religious dialogue and relations, which commonly takes place at any place and any time. This makes people attend school together, work together, live together irrespective of their religious background.

sustainable development of the country. The policy provides strategic directions and coordinates issues of climate change in Ghana, bearing in mind its linkages with the country's development.[48]

In order to intensify the role of harmonising and coordinating the implementation of the National Climate Change Policy, the Ministry of Environment, Science, Technology and Innovation works in close collaboration with the National Development Planning Commission and other major stakeholders. It is important to note that the success of the implementation of the National Climate Change Policy is not the singular responsibility of central government but also depends on the involvement and participation of all relevant stakeholders, including the private sector, NGOs and civil society and religious organisations.[49]

In relation to the above, 11th June 2021 was designated as Green Ghana Day by the Ministry of Lands and Natural Resources with a target to plant and nurture 5 million trees across the country. Every government sector, religious bodies and individuals took part in this Green Ghana Day project.

The Way Forward

Climate change affects everyone irrespective of one's religion. It calls for a conscientious effort to act on the measures put in place to mitigate climate change. It is evident that many religious groups believe that God made man a vicegerent and steward to care for the environment. Thus, religious groups can engage each other by raising greater awareness about climate change. Religious groups can invoke the injunctions of their scripture towards the care for the environment as they do so and raise awareness for the greater population. Religious groups can also use socio-technological measures to reduce carbon emissions thus making sure that energy is conserved in religious buildings. Religious leaders can also remind their followers of their lifestyles through religious school teachings and messages during religious services on the need to care for, protect, conserve and safeguard the environment. Religious people must also make a point to act on what is to be done in their various scriptures concerning safeguarding the environment. Finally, there is the need for interfaith co-operation on climate change mitigation. Since we need the co-operation of each other in every walk of life, there is also the need for religious people to co-operate and collaborate with each other to mitigate climate change.

Conclusion

Religions are major social actors and institutions with considerable influence, therefore human-induced climate change must be the focus of all religions in a bid to mitigate it. The global fight against climate change calls for a collective effort. For this reason, religion should not be misconstrued as a substitute of science in its effort to eradicate this common enemy. But rather religion should be understood in its role as a divine consecration of the bond that humans have with nature. In this sense, religion and science can effectively complement each other to minimise the adverse effects of climate change in communities. There is no better time to walk the talk in our engagements towards climate change than now.

Suggestions for Further Reading

Books

Aquinas, Thomas. *Summa Theologica*. Translated by Fathers of the English Dominican Province. New York, NY: Benziger Brothers, 1947.

Berry, Sam. *A Christian Approach to the Environment*. London: The John Ray Initiative, 2005.

[48] *Ghana National Climate Change Policy* (Accra: Ministry of Environment, Science, Technology and Innovation, 2013) [Available at: https://www.un-page.org/files/public/ghanaclimatechangepolicy.pdf], [Last accessed: 9th February 2022].

[49] *Ghana National Climate Change Policy*

Bible Society. "The Environment and Stewardship", PowerPoint Presentation. Philadelphia, PA: American Bible Society, 2006. [Available at: https://educationresources.biblesociety.org.uk/common/pdf/ks3/CEV/Environment%20and%20Stewardship/Environment%20and%20Stewardship%20main%20resource%20-%20CEV%20powerpoint%20version.pptx], [Last accessed: 9th February 2022].

Brueggemann, Walter, Terence E Fretheim, Jr, Walter C Kaiser, Leander E. Keck, Eds. *The New Interpreter's Bible: Genesis to Leviticus*, Volume 1. Nashville, TN: Abingdon, 1994.

Butkus, Russell A. "The Stewardship of Creation," *Moral Landscape of Creation* (Waco, TX: The Center for Christian Ethics at Baylor University, 2001): 20. [Available at: https://www.baylor.edu/ifl/christianreflection/Creation.pdf], [Last accessed: 9th February 2022].

Calvin, John. *Commentary on Genesis*, tr. John King, M.D. 1578.

Geisler, Norman. *Christian Ethics.* Grand Rapids, MI: Baker, 2010.

Thangaraj, M.T. *The Common Task: A Theology of Christian Mission.* Nashville, TN: Abingdon, 1999.

United Nation Framework Convention on Climate Change, 1994.

Chapters in an Edited Book

Izzi Dien, Mawil, Y. "Islamic environmental ethics, law and society". In J.R. Engel and J.G. Engel, Eds. *Ethics of Environment and Development.* London: Belhaven, 1990: 189-198.

Sewe-K'Ahenda, Nduku, E., and S. Weldon, Eds. *Stewardship of God's Creation: A Catholic environmental toolkit for catechism and seminarians*. Nairobi: CUEA Press, 2014.

Journal Articles

Brueggemann, Walter. "The Loss and Recovery of Creation in Old Testament Theology". *Theology Today* 53(2) (1996): 177-190.

Koehrsen, Jens. "Muslims and climate change: How Islam, Muslim organizations, and religious leaders influence climate change perceptions and mitigation activities". WIREs Climate Change 12(e702) (2021): 1-19. [Available at: https://wires.onlinelibrary.wiley.com/doi/epdf/10.1002/wcc.702], [Last accessed: 9th February 2022].

Rhoads, David M. "Stewardship of creation". *Currents in Theology and Mission* 36(5) (2009): 335-340.

Tate, Marvin E. "An Exposition of Psalm 8". *Perspectives in Religious Studies* 28(4) (2001): 343-359.

Ucheawaji Godfrey J. and Loveday C. Onyezonwu. "'Dress and Keep' the Garden: Environmental Stewardship as a Biblical Motif for the 'Great Commission'". *Asia-Africa Journal of Mission and Ministry*, 9 (2014): 15-63

Weldon, Nancy Opstad. "A Biblical Hermeneutic for Dominion: Domination vs Stewardship". *Obsculta* 9(1) (2016): 75.

White, Lynn. "The Historical Roots of Our Ecological Crisis." *Science*3767(155) (1967): 1203-1207. [Available at: https://www.cmu.ca/faculty/gmatties/lynnwhiterootsofcrisis.pdf], [Last accessed: 24th June 2021].

39. CLIMATE ACTION, AFRICAN TRADITIONAL WISDOMS AND LAUDATO SI

Obiora F. Ike[1]

> An ounce of action is better than tonnes of theory.
>
> Igbo wisdom, Nigeria

Overview – Sustainability as Framework for Enhanced Quality of Life for All

This paper seeks to add voice to the urgent discussion for the redemption of Creation, Ecotheology And Our Environment through an understanding and integration of indigenous African thought and wisdom in modern thinking. The paper puts forward a practicable stakeholder orientation of African worldviews towards building a more sustainable and humane ecology using the traditions of the Igbo people of Nigeria with its religious and cultural values known as the "Omenala" as a guiding thread. We also attempt to bring these African philosophies into a unifying voice, devoid of ideological interests across cultures to reflect reasoning and practices that embedded within them respect for life, the protection of the environment and respect for the sacredness of the earth and the entirety of nature – visible and invisible. Listening to African voices by reflecting on its past traditions, wealth of values, priceless qualities and cultural-rational reasoning in respect of preserving the environment would bring some contribution to this ongoing global dialogue and search for ecological sustainability promoted by the SDG Agenda 2030 of the United Nations.

For generations, Africans, and this applies to other traditions and cultures, developed a deep spiritual sense of stewardship over creation with practiced actions of preservation that protected planet, people, nature and the world of flora and fauna and mammals. The advent of colonial, modern industrial and recent technological, financial and dominant political interests with foreign business-minded exploitative practices destroyed much of these cosmo-visions. In view of current efforts to salvage the common values of humanity and secure a new deal for nature, people and climate, Catholic Social Teaching complements African worldviews on ecotheology as expounded in the Encyclical Letter, *Laudato Si'* of Pope Francis, published on 18th June 2015. The appeal by Pope Francis in the profoundly religious and scientific document *Laudato Si'* for climate action summarises the planet as our "*Common Home*". The first step towards addressing this issue is the call for immediate action with "*ecological conversion*". This encompasses social justice and spiritual responsibility.

The science is clear that we are now accelerating towards tipping points as past few years have gone down as the hottest in history. The ozone layer is thinly veiled. Catastrophic rainfalls continue to cause havoc with winds and tornadoes unknown to humanity a century earlier. Small states living on islands could go under the ravaging seas and oceans within a century as Mauritius and others in this category suffer from devastating impacts of climate change. It is a matter of life and death for many people and nations. Global warming affects ecosystems as well as human health, livelihoods, food security, water supply and economic growth in many ways.

It is no longer news that the agenda for realising SDG13 ("Take urgent action to combat climate change and its impacts") which is abbreviated in the 13th Sustainable Development Goal as *Climate Action* formed the basis for the world's biggest UN Climate Summit Pact COP26 which was held in Glasgow in November

---

[1] Msgr. Prof. Obiora Ike is Roman Catholic Professor of Ethics and Intercultural Studies at the Godfrey Okoye University in Enugu State, Nigeria. He is the Founding Director of the Catholic Institute of Development, Justice, Peace and Caritas (CIDJAP); Chairman of Umuchinemere Pro-credit Microfinance Bank Limited; Chairman of the Enugu State Economic Advisory Committee. He is currently the Executive Director of the Geneva-based Global Ethics Centre.

2021. They are already a moment in history. The climate movement's slogan reads "*The time to act is now*". All nations today have an urgent challenge to scale up climate ambitions, introduce carbon tax for redistribution, give stimulus programmes to save the climate with reduction in emissions. There is need to listen to the call of activists who work for the protection of the poorer peoples and nations, and even minimum polluters, yet bear the brunch of negative consequences. The worst is yet to come, but the time to act is now.

In the ongoing dialogue and universal conversation towards finding a proper balance between individual freedoms and community welfare in their attitude to planet, nature and environment, discussions have arisen around the use and abuse of human and natural resources which threatens all, thus the growing desire for an all-round environmental sustainability. The challenges and effects of climate change are common knowledge nowadays.

Moving to action beyond lip service is of uppermost importance to reflect the global common good in policies that guide the economy, society, technology and the way we live in a growing, complex but interrelated world. The era of ideologies and models of unbridled consumerism with an endless productive cycle of capitalism, built around big numbers and big data as a measure of human progress is coming to an end as it has grossly destroyed the human and planetary ecology. The core idea of sustainability originally was regarding natural resources, where long-term environmental preservation was the focus. Today, the term is applied in many disciplines including economic development, environment, food production, energy, consumerism and lifestyle. This term raises controversy as well as challenges for present generations to meet the needs of today without hindering the ability of future communities to meet theirs. Sustainability refers to doing something with the long-term view in mind and decisions made with a consideration of human activities into the future. The goal is typically towards preserving quality interactions with the local environment, the social system and the economy. Examples abound where communities seek economic development approaches that benefit the local environment and improve overall quality of life for many and for all.

Sustainable development provides a framework under which communities can use resources efficiently, create efficient infrastructure, protect and enhance quality of life, and create new businesses to strengthen their economies. On the other hand, a sustainable community is achieved by a long-term and integrated approach to developing and achieving a healthy community, by addressing economic, environmental, social and cultural issues.

Fostering a strong sense of community and building partnerships and consensus among key stakeholders are also important elements of making development sustainable. Gradually, policies of nation-states and activities of the various levels of any society, including corporations, are measured against their sustainability. This involves taking account of the costs to the environment and depletion of natural resources as well as the economic cycle of production – that is the use and disposal of products maintained indefinitely without denuding resources or damaging the environment or society. It includes some effort by each individual person to improve on their treatment towards our common home, involving ensuring that actions of their institutions and businesses comply to these standards, can begin with a mental shift and change of attitude in the use of the goods of the earth.

An African Narrative to Environment and Climate Concerns

There are at least two sides to every narrative. One side may not necessarily present the whole story, but it is a valid contribution and helps to get the whole picture. The reality of Africa is more complex than the "*outsider clichés*" would have it described. Africa is not simply a "*continent of hunger and heat, nor is it the land of the dark-skinned people whose religion, culture, politics, art and history is uncivilised and primitive*". It is even difficult to treat the continent as one piece, even though some generalisations are allowed as applicable. History teaches that Africa is that continent where humankind first began, where art, religion and philosophy commenced, and where civilisation and culture first arose.[2]

One is always amazed at the complexity and diversity of human cultures, each distinct by virtue of its historical evolution, making it structurally unique and original. Theories of development have often neglected the cultural and spiritual dimension of the human person. In the complexity and sophistication of our modern societies, it is possible to have lost track of the basic and simple values that give life meaning, including ethics.

The African narrative starts with a spiritual dimension and understanding of space and time as gift and mystery from the divine who is creator and first principle. It is this principle and worldview that is embedded in culture, ever dynamic and yet constant, transmitted through generations. Such education guides the values of people, which affect the structures of the economy, politics, society, religion, ethics and technology. This African narrative, embedded mainly in values and beliefs, goes beyond codified legal instruments or laws and impacts people's attitudes to climate concerns and the environment.

These values include respect for the divine and the sacred; respectful use of trees and animals according to the needs of life; divination of the stars and the planet as sacred and to be preserved; respect for life and community consciousness; respect for elders; keeping one's promise; honesty at all times; justice and fairness in dealing with others; keeping to agreements and cultural norms above private needs; putting the interest of the community over private and individual interests; avoidance of conflicts; a culture of transparency, disclosure and accountability; preservation of the common good; the protection of all life and the environment of nature; prudence in speech and not harming others; contentment and absence of greed.

Our search therefore is to rediscover these inherent traditional values and principles of sustainability, subsidiarity, and solidarity and apply them to modern models of a global culture that speaks of Corporate Governance, Corporate Social Responsibility, Business Ethics, climate justice, environmental protection in order to maintain best practices within an African milieu. We thereby establish the integral nature of African cultural and religious values considered as ethical values in the protection of the planet – our common home.

An Integral Approach to the Environment – Past, Present and Future

African philosophies teach that the individual exists within the context of their social existence, with responsibility at three levels of existence:

1) The present-living, meaning the community in which the business operates, the employees who work within the corporation, the suppliers, the consumers, the environment, and the entire world community.
2) The living dead, meaning the cultures and ancient traditions of the people in whose communities the businesses operate, as well as where they market their goods and services. This would mean recognition of our heritage from previous generations, and include respect for the diversity and plurality of the world.
3) The yet-unborn, meaning responsibility towards future generations, particularly in the use of the world's natural resources and therewith a recognition that ownership of these natural resources cannot be absolute. It would also recognise the responsibility of every business to the sustainable management of nature's gifts.

This vision of the world imposed some cyclical guide for responsible and sustainable management of resources with future generations in mind.[3]

---

[2] Cf. F. O. Ike and N.N. Edozien, *Understanding Africa – Traditional Legal Reasoning as a Basis for Culturally Rooted and Sustainable Development* (Enugu, Nigeria: CIDJAP, 2001): 1-4.

[3] Obiora F. Ike, *Freedom is more than a Word: On Potentialities for Development in African Culture* (Enugu, Nigeria: CIDJAP Press, 1998).

Omenala (culture of the land) linked the past, the present and future in one continuum offering a basis for understanding the dimensions of sustainability much clearer as cultural (past), social (present) and ecological (future). The three levels of existence in Igbo Logic, Igbology, offer an important principle and philosophy in understanding the interplay between community and individual; forces of nature and nurture; religion and business; the environment and humanity; and generally helps us better understand various factors and values that ensured sustainability and stakeholder participation among traditional African peoples. It provided a valuable foundation for problem-solving in modern times.[4]

Omenala, understood as the entire way of life of the people (past, present and future), is the traditional law in African societies, a central thread guaranteeing the protection of life and property, the harmony of members of society among themselves and with nature, their linkage to the divine through the ancestors and the deities. In various African cultures and among the traditional Igbo people of Nigeria, land (nature), human resources and material wealth (capital) signified more than just factors of production. Land, for instance, was a goddess "Ala" "Ani" – *"the Earth Deity"*. It was the earth deity that determined customs and traditions (*Omenala*), much of which was the promotion and protection of all life, a transgression of which (*Nso Ala*) was punished by Ala, the Earth deity. Taking the Igbo people of Nigeria as an example, land, including water, mineral resources, animals, animate and inanimate beings were all creatures of Chukwu (God) who made them all for a purpose according to religious interpretations and these were all interlinked. Indeed, in Igbo cosmology, all nature visible and invisible live and relate to each other as ordered by Chukwu. They manage their relationship according to the guidance of Chukwu such that their common destines were interlinked. Any imbalance triggered tragic consequences and the destiny of the individual, the community and entire environment were all interlinked.[5]

Some lessons from African wisdom towards achieving climate justice in the present global situation include:

- Doing something with the long-term perspective in mind.
- Making decisions with consideration of its impact on humanity, ecology and the future.
- Meeting the needs of the present generation without compromising the ability of the future generations to meeting theirs.
- The balance between the community concerns and the individual aspirations, made manifest in the concept of communal ownership of land and water and natural spaces.

Each member of the clan was considered as a stakeholder. This ensured equity in economic affairs, since opportunity and access for all was guaranteed. An individual could own property but because of the intrinsic ties between the individual, the family and ultimately the community, ownership of property is understood as a social mortgage.

The wisdom thought here is essential: *"it belongs to me but I belong to the community"*. Whatever property was acquired by the individual was based on the individual right of access and use, in a proximate but not ultimate sense. Members of the extended family were empowered as stakeholders and co-owners of the individual and his/her/their enterprise, and participated actively at different levels in the management of the political, social, cultural and economic life of their community. As stakeholders, they were co-responsible for the success of the business alongside community life, ensuring that business and public interests were managed by members of the community, thus promoting values of solidarity and subsidiarity.

The Igbo attitude to the ownership and management of wealth and property exposes a deeply spiritual, yet secular understanding of the interconnectedness of the universal destination of created goods. The traditional Igbo interplay of the secular and the sacred ensured that ethical considerations were an intrinsic

[4] Obiora F. Ike, *Tradition, Toleranz und Diskurs*, Kongress Paper: Ethik in der Demokratie – Demokratie in der Ethik, der Internationalen Vereinigung. This corresponds to the findings of the Frankfurt Hohenheim Guidelines and the work of other rated and respected schools of thought such as the Project Group, Ethical-Ecological Rating/Oekom Research AG, Hoffmann/Scherhorn (eds) and their Implementation via the Corporate Responsibility Rating (Schriftenreihe zur oekologischen Kommunikation, 8, 2nd extended edition, Oekom Verlag, Frankfurt, 2003).

[5] A. Afigbo, *Ropes of Sand, Studies in Igbo History & Culture* (Oxford: Oxford University Press, 1981), 6.

part of economic life. Deriving from the traditional Igbo ownership and management traditions are the humanist principles of solidarity and self-reliance (subsidiarity), which manifest as guiding principles and as the starting point for a modern economy. In traditional society, there was a profound sense of the sacred intrinsically woven into society's communal way of life.

It is said that every people have a culture, a way of life that links their past to the present and the future. Even though culture is not static but steadily dynamic, some of the elements that provided rationality for cultural practices in the past may have disappeared in the face of modern realities of migration, new technologies, scientific discoveries, and wars to mention but a few ingredients. Nonetheless, there is need to enhance the linkage and sustainability of cultural developments and its interpretation at least on the levels of principles that identify these societies even in the face of a modern age. In the African milieu, whether amongst an agricultural people or nomadic tribes, culture (Omenala) provided a proper foundation for a sustainable economy where the preservation of the environment, the enhancement of principles of equity and fair play and the promotion of an economy that recognises both individual interests and communal protection existed alongside each other.

Community Concerns and the Common Good Precede Individual Interests

African philosophies and cultures centre on community, well-expressed in the phrase *'I am because we are, and since we are, therefore I am.'*[6] This is a cardinal point in understanding an African view of the relationship between planet, people and environment, or between individual, personal priorities and the common good. African communal consciousness means that:

> [O]nly in terms of other people does the individual become conscious of his or her own being, his or her own duties, his or her own privileges and responsibilities towards himself or herself and towards other people. When he/she suffers, he/she does not suffer alone but with the corporate group. When he/she rejoices, he/she rejoices not alone but with his/her kinsmen, neighbours or relatives whether dead or living. When married, he/she is not alone neither does the wife belong to him alone; so also the children belong to the corporate body of kinsmen even if they bear only the father's name. Whatever happens to the individual, the individual can only say 'I am because we are, and since we are, therefore I am'.[7]

The individual exists as part of the community, not "apart" from it. This formed the basis for social responsibility that include the past (ancestors) and the yet-unborn. It is also the basis for continuity and sustainability. The typical African wisdom thought is "*It belongs to me but I belong to the community*". This guaranteed property relations and usage of temporal goods which ensured that ownership rights existed and were respected, yet limited by overall social concerns and communal purposes so that every member of the community, beyond the immediate family including the kith and kin, benefitted. This sense and recognition of community found expression in the daily lifestyle of people where loyalties of kinship, clanship, language, culture, politics, religion and economy converged to create social groups recognised as stakeholders. Property relations in traditional Igboland were guided by a philosophy that supported the common good. As such, absolute ownership of land and other means of production was discouraged. This was an important factor in ensuring the sustainable use and management of natural resources, and the protection of the stakeholder interests at three levels of existence.

In other words, any young person who consciously cuts off from the community and develops as a successful individual in the modern or sometimes, individualistic and autonomous sense, is no longer a person in the African sense no matter the degree of individual prowess. If such an individual is to survive to some degree, the person must quit the village and begin existence somewhere else. No matter how prosperous such a person eventually becomes, one is presumed to miss something in one's personality when

---

[6] J.S. Mbiti, *African Religions and Philosophy* (London: Heinemann, 1975), 108-9.

[7] Mbiti, *African Religions and Philosophy*, 108-9.

existing apart from the community. It is only in re-establishing the link with one's kith and kin, which is actually part of oneself, that one can once more be a person, i.e. the "full self".[8]

The New Testament of the Christian Bible contain such practices (see for instance Acts of the Apostles, chapter Three: the story of Ananias and Saphira). Humans become who they are only through their relationship with others. One's individuality would be understood in and through one's social relations. Being in a community is a constitutive element of the human make-up.[9] The individual was recognised as deriving their existence and relevance as a member of the community. In other words, wealth had significance when it was used responsibly to further community interests and not hoarded only for individual use. This furthered social responsibility at the individual and corporate level.

Not Only Humans are Part of the Community But the Entire Nature

In many African cultures, belief systems maintained that all natural resources belong to Chukwu (the Supreme God) who ceded management thereof to Ala, the earth deity. The ancestors were thought to have obtained the traditions and customs of the land (referred to as Omenala) from Ala. A modern interpretation of this may be the acknowledgement of nature and natural resources, including air and water, as a gift to be used, managed and held in trust. This is an important element often lacking in modern business management where the pursuit of private interests inadequately recognises responsibilities towards the use of natural resources. There is an urgent need for businesses to manage with greater responsibility the natural resources, which actually belong to the entire human community.

The Igbo Omenala (customs and tradition) was handed on from one generation to the next generation just as the earth Ala upon which the Omenala was anchored. As such, the responsibility to preserve and sustain the tradition of the African Igbo and the natural resources, including land, plants, animals and entire nature for future generations was transmitted as culture, taught and understood as an intrinsic part of being a community member with the rights of usage of land: that is the conduct of business and daily life. Those presently-living, meaning the community to whom the individual belongs; the ancestors who are past custodians and referred to as the living-dead, but from whom tradition and culture derives their continuity; and the yet unborn who ensure that the future is guaranteed.[10]

Life and existence are view in Igbo metaphysics as a continuum that extends beyond the demise of the material self. Central to this religious world-view is the belief in Chukwu (Chi Ukwu – the great God), who is the author of life and is the absolute owner of all things that exist in all creation, whether visible and invisible. Chukwu fashions and carries the world; owns the universe and sends the sunshine and the rains at various times for the good of creation. Chukwu makes the crops grow and is the source from which people derive their Chi (destiny, soul, luck, identity). Since the Igbo believe in Chukwu as merciful, they believe Chukwu allows lesser spirits, the dead ancestors (living dead) and humankind to manage the created universe as stewards.

What emerges from this Cosmo vision is interconnectedness between the spiritual realities and the material; between the sacred and the secular; between the past, present and future. It is an integral worldview where although God is the absolute owner, human beings and other spirits are sub-delegated to act on behalf of Chukwu in the ownership and management of goods of the earth.

There exists in African traditions, the moral consciousness of the individual in their existence as a part of the community upon which actions and behaviour were judged right or wrong. The principle or sense of togetherness extends to include both the temporal and the spiritual sphere: "*not only the living but also the*

[8] see: F.H. Bradley, *Ethical Studies, Essay II: Why Should I Be Moral?* 2nd Edition (Oxford: Clarendon Press, 1927).
[9] see: J.P.C. Nzomiwu, *The Moral Concept of Justice Among the Igbos* (Lateran University Rome: Alfonsiana, 1977): 39.
[10] see: E.A. Isichei, *History of the Igbo People* (London: Macmillan, 1976): 3.

living dead, the ancestors, the Supreme Being, and the entire spiritual world are interconnected".[11] There is no room for rugged individualism as every person is related to the other, making possible a deep common solidarity and loyalty. Even natural objects are interrelated as symbols of each other; thus nature and the environment are included in its concept of stakeholders. The rights of usage of natural, human and capital resources are accepted in traditional society together with implied responsibilities towards the providers of these factors of production, whom we call stakeholders. The stakeholders of a business include the host community, the host country and associated society, culture and environment. In an increasingly global world, it is easier for companies to shirk responsibilities when they are "foreign" business. This has had significant and disastrous consequences and there is need to emphasise the moral obligations of capital, and address the increasing imbalance between the three factors of production: land, labour and capital. Business decisions should not be taken solely in the interests of rewarding the providers of capital with a higher rate of return at all costs.

As such, the communal ownership structures and corresponding participatory management practices of the Igbo were embedded in specific ethical value propositions. These can be found in the principles of subsidiarity and solidarity, which provide for us an overlap with Catholic Social Thought in the body of which these principles are expressly defined.

Sustainability is Linked to Solidarity and Subsidiarity Concerns

Sustainable coexistence in traditional African society could best be understood as the continuity of historicity, defined as the linkage of the past, the present and future. Such thinking takes a view of the past as the guarantor of the present and as the basis for the future. It provides strong arguments and long-term foundations for a more grounded and rational basis which seeks to promote a sustainable world for everybody. In this context, the UN defined sustainability as "*building upon the resources and heritage of the past generations, to meet needs of the present generation without compromising the ability of future generations to meet their own needs*".[12]

According to these ethical principles of subsidiarity and solidarity as embedded in the Igbo worldview, subsidiarity implies that each person (private interest) exists individually and that small groups or levels of authority have competencies of responsibility at that level. The classical definition of this principle is found in the Papal Encyclical, *Quadragessimo Anno* (QA) of Pope Pius XI:

> Just as it is gravely wrong to take from individuals what they can accomplish by their own initiative and industry and give it to the community, so also it is an injustice and at the same time a grave evil and disturbance of right order to assign to a greater and higher association what lesser and subordinate organisations can do. For every social activity ought of its very nature to furnish help to the members of the social body, and never destroy or absorb them [...] Therefore, those in power should be sure that the more perfectly a graduated order is kept among the various associations, in observance of the principle of 'subsidiary function', the stronger social authority and effectiveness will be, the happier and more prosperous the condition of the state.[13]

The principle of subsidiarity presupposes the principles of solidarity and the common good, but is not identical with them. That society must help the individual is a clear statement of the solidarity principle, which emphasises mutual connection and obligation. The distribution and delimitation of the competence to be considered in this help fall to the subsidiarity principle. The point being made here is that African traditional religion is essentially a philosophy and a spiritual way of life, which permeates, pervades and

[11] see: E. Isichei, *A History of the Igbo People* (London: Macmillan, 1976): 3.
[12] United Nations, UNEP, Rio Earth Summit, 1992; Cf Brundtland Commission on Environment and Development. *Our Common Future*. (Oxford: Oxford University Press, 1987).
[13] Papal Encyclical 'Quadragesimo Anno' No 79; [Available at: https://www.vatican.va/content/pius-xi/en/encyclicals/documents/hf_p-xi_enc_19310515_quadragesimo-anno.html].

animates the traditional social institutions, norms and celebrations. Every Igbo ritual act of the peoples of south-eastern Nigeria, including sacrifice, dance and festival had a philosophy or idea behind it. In other words, action was motivated based on values, which involved a basic belief, a philosophy, an underlying principle or an idea. These values thus generated actions and behaviour, which in turn influenced individuals and groups.

1. Stakeholder Orientation Beyond Simply Shareholder Value

The African philosophy of: "*I am because we are, and since we are, therefore I am*" clashes with modern values of a world economy dominated by the liberal capitalist practices, where the human person has become a factor of production – simply – a labourer who does a paid job and is relieved when not needed. The labourer is a cog in the wheel of the production process. Here, the interests of stakeholders other than shareholders- are neglected and side-lined. Such questions as what is the responsibility of businesses and their managers to shareholders, *and* stakeholders?; what mechanisms could be put in place to guarantee a balance between the pursuit of private interests of management or shareholders and public interests including those of the environment, society, host communities, employees, etc.?, do not arise as such where the responsibility of businesses and individuals only to shareholders is recognised and acted upon. In recognising the existence of the much larger group of stakeholders to include shareholders, employees, host communities, customers, suppliers, and the environment as well as society and humanity at large, businesses could and should realign their private interests to ensure that sustainability (at the cultural, social, environmental and economic levels) becomes an agenda alongside that of profit-making.

Finally, traditional African economies, with communal structures, implied certain ownership and management structures which promoted social responsibility, equity and sustainability. These structures, which promoted equitable access instead of accumulation of wealth, have been criticised as being the cause for why Africa has not been able to launch herself economically on the world stage. Refuting this critique is not the object of this paper. Rather it is to say that the African concept of communal ownership and participatory management structures put forward a business model that promotes sustainability and balances private (business) and public interests. It would be seen that there was a tension between the individual and the community on matters of ownership in the Igbo culture. Indeed, this tension did and does still exist. However, a balance was sought for and achieved in such a way that individual ownership of property was a natural, valid and necessary expression of the right to acquisition. Possession and control did not however assume an absolute dimension but were restricted within the limits imposed by their social function. This original African tradition of communal ownership does in fact correspond to a Christian conception of the world and of life. Writing in *Laborem Exercens* in 1981, John Paul II states that "Christian tradition has never upheld the right to private property as absolute and untouchable. On the contrary, it has always understood this right within the broader context of the right to common use of the goods of creation. The right to private property is thus subordinated to the right to common use and to the fact that goods are meant for everyone."[14]

The Igbo understanding of ownership is practically demonstrated in the life of its people centuries before this Christian teaching was formulated. In summary, this research examines ownership and management structures of traditional Igbo businesses based on ethical values of subsidiarity and solidarity. It understudies and promotes African traditional values which, applied to modern issues of sustainability and the corporate governance function, offer as a solid basis to establish a fair and sustainable future for individuals, communities and societies. In this context, I argue that our generation would do better by building upon the resources and heritage of the past generations, to meet needs of the present generation without compromising the ability of future generations to meet their own needs.

---

[14] *Laboram Exercens* 1981, No (34), [Available at: https://www.vatican.va/content/john-paul-ii/de/encyclicals/documents/hf_jp-ii_enc_14091981_laborem-exercens.html].

2. Property Considered a Social Mortgage

One of the most fundamental cultural, social and economic realities in Igbo culture, as is found in many other African societies, is the basic understanding of property as a natural right and therewith a human right, for the satisfaction and protection of the needs of the individual, the family and the clan as a whole. Property is the basis of wealth and the Igbo tradition of communal ownership makes everybody a stakeholder and not just strangers in their own community. Although an individual has the right to own property, and in fact does own some property, it is the family and the entire community, which ultimately owns the individual because he or she is tied to this community in an intrinsic manner. In traditional society, whatever the individual acquired as private property (farm products, animals, skills, utensils, clothing) was based more on the right of 'access' and of 'use' in a proximate but not ultimate sense. Igbo culture and tradition understood ownership to mean the possession, authority and control of and over something by an individual, a community and the ancestors, which implied a spiritual bond. The destiny of the individual and the community was often interlinked.

Since private property was necessary for the security, life and survival of the family, it was understood as a "social mortgage", emphasising the right of access to which every member of the community was entitled. This meant that, in traditional society, ownership had an intrinsically social function which it has retained until today. The division of *haves* and *have-nots* in society was avoided by ensuring every member of the community had access to factors of production, including land, according to their need and entrepreneurial ability. The exclusive usurping of property rights by a few lucky enough to access capital, and corresponding marginalisation and exploitation of the rest of society was generally not possible. In modern society, much of this has changed but the lessons and values remain.

Possession and control did not however assume an absolute dimension but were restricted within the limits imposed by their social function. This original African tradition of communal ownership does in fact correspond to a Christian conception of the world and of life. Writing in *Laborem Exercens* in 1981, John Paul II states that "Christian tradition has never upheld the right to private property as absolute and untouchable. On the contrary, it has always understood this right within the broader context of the right to common use of the goods of creation. The right to private property is thus subordinated to the right to common use and to the fact that goods are meant for everyone."[15]

Lessons from *Laudato Si*

The main contribution of Pope Francis to the climate crisis in the Encyclical Letter *Laudato Si* is a call to ecological conversion by all actors. This ecological conversion encompasses ecological equilibrium, social justice, and spiritual responsibility, and it calls for immediate action.

Laudato Si brings the wisdom found in African cultures and other traditions into sync with Christian teaching, calling the earth our common home. To tackle global environmental degradation, Pope Francis uses the evidence of natural sciences and the frightening results made available by the scientific community to say that the earth which is our "sister now cries out to us because of the harm we have inflicted on her by our irresponsible use and abuse of the goods with which God has endowed her".[16] He argues that we now see ourselves as Lords and masters entitled to plunder the earth at will. It is an unprecedented document in its adoption of scientific concepts and terms, thus establishing the new concept of integral ecology within the churches' social thought.

This addresses the need to integrate social justice and spiritual responsibility in each person's attitudes and actions. This call is based on biblical foundations grounded in the incarnate Word, Jesus Christ (Jn.

---

[15] Pope John Paul II, *Laboram Exercens*.

[16] Pope Francis, *Laudato Si.* No.2 [Available at: https://www.vatican.va/content/francesco/en/encyclicals/documents/papa-francesco_20150524_enciclica-laudato-si.html].

1:1). It takes on the faith of entire humanity for a better world for all and finds theological and philosophical considerations with ethical and scientific reflections that point to the need for a change of lifestyle in how humanity relates with the entire ecology of space and time and nature. The Pope argues that a "very solid scientific consensus indicates that we are presently witnessing a disturbing warming of the climatic system, a rise in the sea level and an increase of extreme weather events."[17]

He re-iterates a religious vision of "sister earth" which Africans call by another female name "Mother Earth" with an urgent plea for action. "Humanity is called to recognise the need for changes of lifestyle, production and consumption".[18] "Yet, we are called to be instruments of God our Father, so that our planet might be what he desired when he created it and correspond with his plan for peace, beauty and fullness".[19]

Even though Catholic Social Teaching decrees the "universal destination of all earthly goods and a social mortgage on property, for the first time, Pope Francis points to the climate as being "a common good, belonging to all and meant for all".[20] He defines it at the global level as "a complex system linked to many of the essential conditions of human life".

The crucial section of Laudato Si makes it clear that poverty is not a side issue to the ecological problem but an essential part of it. He therefore argues that "the earth's resources are also being plundered because of short sighted approaches to the economy, commerce and production. The loss of forests and woodlands entails the loss of species which may constitute extremely important resources in the future, not only for food but also for curing disease and other uses".[21] Pope Francis is bold and states that "we cannot be silent witnesses to terrible injustices if we think that we can obtain significant benefits by making the rest of humanity, present and future, pay the extremely high costs of environmental deterioration".[22] Indeed, "we cannot overlook the huge global economic interests which under the guise of protecting (biodiversity) can undermine the sovereignty of individual nations. There are proposals to internationalise the Amazon, which only serve the economic interests of transnational corporations".[23] He calls for a revolution, saying "all of this shows the urgent need for us to move forward in a bold cultural revolution"[24] and to stop boiling down human knowledge to the purely instrumental dimension while ignoring ethics. This will require a fresh vision and new responsibility in the face of new challenges. To the political class, the Pope issues some invitation and clear words calling on politicians to act. "Politics must not be subject to the economy, nor should the economy be subject to the dictates of an efficiency-driven paradigm of technocracy. Today, in view of the common good, there is urgent need for politics and economics to enter into a frank dialogue in the service of life, especially human life".[25]

Finally, in a critique of global injustices perpetrated against the vulnerable through unethical practices that exploit the planet's resources, the Pope calls for an attitudinal change, a Metanoia for all persons. "In the present condition of global society, where injustices abound and growing numbers of people are deprived of basic human rights and considered expendable, the principle of the common good immediately becomes, logically and inevitably, a summons to solidarity and preferential option for the poorest of our brothers and sisters".[26]

---

[17] Pope Francis, *Laudato Si.* No.23.
[18] Pope Francis, *Laudato Si.* No.23.
[19] Pope Francis, *Laudato Si.* No.53.
[20] Pope Francis, *Laudato Si.* No.23.
[21] Pope Francis, *Laudato Si.* No.32.
[22] Pope Francis, *Laudato Si.* No.36.
[23] Pope Francis, *Laudato Si.* No.38.
[24] Pope Francis, *Laudato Si.* No.114.
[25] Pope Francis, *Laudato Si.* No.189.
[26] Pope Francis, *Laudato Si.* No.158.

The words addressed to the market and to unbridled consumerism are also apt in the context of this paper: "since the market tends to promote extreme consumerism in an effort to sell its products, a change in lifestyle could bring healthy pressure to heart on those who wiled political, economic and social power".[27]

The teachings of the remarkable document of *Laudato Si* thus provides a solid basis for a global new value system and attitudinal change which are in resonance with traditional African wisdom systems such as in Igbo culture, laying the fundamental ground for a style of production and consumption, of the economic, the agricultural as well as the mobility concepts of society which have to dramatically change if the life opportunities of future generations are to be respected on this planet.

Suggestions for Further Reading

Afigbo, A. *Ropes of Sand, Studies in Igbo History and Culture*. Oxford: Oxford University Press, 1981.

Amecea Pastoral Institute. *Human Response to the Call of God.* Kenya: Gaba Publications, 1979.

Bradley, F. H. *Ethical Studies, Essay II: Why should I be Moral?* 2nd Edition. Oxford: Clarendon, 1927.

Ike, Obiora. "Tradition, Toleranz und Diskurs". *Kongress Paper: Ethik in der Demokratie – Demokratie in der Ethik*, der Internationalen Vereinigung Deutsch-sprachiger Moraltheologen und Sozialethiker, Münster, Germany, 1997.

Ike, Obiora. *Freedom is More Than a Word: On Potentialities for Development in African Culture.* Enugu, Nigeria: CIDJAP, 1998.

Ike, Obiora and N.N. Edozien. *Understanding Africa Traditional Legal Reasoning, Jurisprudence and Justice in Igboland*. Enugu, Nigeria: CIDJAP, 2001.

Isichei, E. *A History of the Igbo People*. London: Macmillan, 1976.

Mbiti, J. S. *African Religions and Philosophy*. London: Heinemann, 1975.

Nnoli-Edozien, Ndidi. "Ownership and Management Structures of Traditional Igbo Business with inherent values of solidarity and subsidiarity: African Values Applied to Modern Issues of Sustainability and Corporate Governance". Doctoral Thesis. August 2006, Frankfurt University, Germany. Printed by CIDJAP, Enugu, 2008.

Nzomiwu, J.P.C. *Concept of Justice Among the Igbos*. Rome: Lateran University, 1977.

Pope Francis. *Laudato Si*, Encyclical Letter – The Earth Our Common Home. Vatican: Vatican Press, 2015.

Pope John Paul II. *Laborem Exercens*, Encyclical Letter (On Human Work). Vatican: Vatican Press, 1981.

Pope John Paul II. *Solicitudo Rei Socialis*. Vatican: Vatican Press, 1988.

Pope Pius XI. *Quadragesimo Anno*. 15th May 1931. Roma: AAS, 1931.

Smith, A. *The Wealth of Nations*. London: Ward Lock, 1838.

Project Group, Ethical-Ecological Rating/oekom Research AG, Eds. *Ethical Ecological Rating: The Frankfurt–Hohenhėim Guidelines and their Implementation via the Corporate Responsibility Rating*. Schriftenreihe zur ökologischen Kommunikation, 8, 2nd extended edition. Munich: Oekom Verlag, 2003.

Rawls, J. A. *Theory of Justice*. Oxford: Oxford University Press/Harvard University Press, 1971.

The Vatican. *Catechism of the Catholic Church*. Vatican: Libreria Editrice Vaticana, 1994.

World Commission on Environment and Development. *Our Common Future*. Oxford/New York/Toronto: Oxford University Press, 1987.

[27] Pope Francis, *Laudato Si.* No.203-206.

40. Healing of Creation for Sustainable Development in the Context of East Africa

Ernest William Kadiva[1]

Africa is known to be the richest continent in all natural resources: continuous, renewable and non-renewable. It is believed that the continent's natural resources have the potential to feed the entire globe for many generations to come. Nations outside Africa are benefiting immensely from Africa's natural wealth. Industrialised nations of the west have been enjoying them for long time, and now China has also begun to focus more on Africa because of the untapped resources with which the continent is richly endowed. However, despite all these natural resources, Africa is known as the poorest continent.[2]

The majority of Africa's natural world heritage sites are worse off today than when they were admitted to the prestigious world heritage list. Alexander Crummell, more than 150 years ago, said: "There seems to me to be a natural call upon the children of Africa to come and participate in the opening treasures of the land of their fathers."[3] His words are appropriate for Africans today for he spoke not only of literal treasures such as gold, uranium or diamonds, but of cultural treasures as well. The "treasures of the land" abound in Africa's cultures, its peoples and in all that the continent has to offer.

Also W.E.B. Dubois stated that "one thing is sure and that is the fact that since the fifteenth century these ancestors of mine and their other descendants have had a common history, have suffered a common disaster and have had one long memory [...] It is this unity that draws me to Africa."[4] But the memories of what Africans contributed to African culture and development are sinking in the sand because of modernisation and globalisation.

All resources on the earth are finite. However, resources are exploited very quickly once a society discovers their utility. The underlying cause of this exponential use is the tremendous growth of human populations and technology which make use of the resources. However, these efforts usually soon encounter what is termed the "Law of Diminishing Return" in economics, which points to the fact that increasing efforts to extract resource produce progressively smaller amounts/returns.[5] This results in increased depletion of resources. Production declines exponentially because the most easily extracted concentrations of the resource become exhausted. "Historically, societies respond to an increase in resource prices by switching to another resource. England switched from wood to coal as energy when forests were decimated and more recently to oil because it is cheaper. The series of bubbles shown in England has often been repeated elsewhere and with other resources, as societies have tended to switch from one unsustainable

---

[1] Rev Dr Ernest William Kadiva is a United Evangelical Mission (UEM) Deputy Executive Secretary for the Africa region and ordained pastor of the Evangelical Lutheran Church in Tanzania Eastern and Coastal Diocese since August 2002. He served in different capacities including a chaplain of Azania Front Cathedral, and a deputy general secretary for administration, human resources and estate affairs. In 2014, he was a member of Tanzania special parliament assembly for constitutional review. Rev Kadiva conducting missional leadership training programmes for clergy and lay ministers and holds a Doctoral of Ministry from Luther Seminary in the USA, Master's degree in theology from Bossey Institute Geneva, Bachelor of Divinity from Tumaini Makumira University, and Bachelor of Commerce from Dar es Salaam University. Contact details: revkadiva@hotmail.com, kadiva-e@vemission.org.

[2] "Africa: Why the richest continent is also the poorest" [Available at:http://mugishagwe.blogspot.com/2011/02/why-is-africa-richest-continent-but.html, September 5, 2008], [Last accessed: 14th February 2022].

[3] Alexander Crummell, *The Relations and Duties of Free Colored Men in America to Africa: A Letter To Charles B. Dunbar Of New York City* (Hartford: Press Of Case, Lockwood and Company, 1861).

[4] W.E.B. Dubois, "The Concept of Race", in Eric J. Sundquist, *The Oxford W.E.B. Dubois Reader* (New York: Oxford University Press, 1996): 87.

[5] "Principles and Approaches to Natural Resources Management" [Available at: https://vackmedia.blogspot.com/2019/01/principles-and-approaches-to-natural.html, January 21, 2019], [Last accessed: 14th February 2022].

resource to another."[6] The only way to break this ''cycle of unsustainable use'' is to switch to sustainable uses by putting a halt to natural resources depletion which is the aggregated sum of net forest depletion, energy depletion, and mineral depletion.[7]

The issue of creation crisis is evident everywhere. Evidence abounds of the steady destruction of creation as manifested in atmospheric changes, air and water pollution, loss of species, use of pesticides and the tearing down of rainforests and declining soil fertility. Already the world has witnessed her impacts at both local and global levels, from melting ice sheets to an increase in storm events. The impacts of drought and increased disease are affecting and will continue to affect God's community.

The Destruction of Creation: Its Roots and Impact

Having made the above explanations, let us now turn to the key roots and impacts of creation destruction in East Africa in order to discover ways and means of healing it for sustainable development. The key driving factors for the destruction of creation have some ethical, religious, political and economic implications and root causes. According to Byaruhanga, the destruction of creation occurs when there is a distortion or damage in the physical, chemical or biological characteristics of air, land and water. This has harmful effects upon human life and that of other living species and our industrial processes, living conditions and cultural assets, which in the long run will also lead to waste or deterioration of our raw material resources.[8] The destruction of creation can impose many negative impacts on living organisms.

Historical Roots

From the prehistory period, most African traditional societies had effective preservation systems which helped them to regulate patterns of resource use and abuse. In their traditional settings, people evolved taboos, superstitions and common rights and formulated laws to improve stewardship of the God's creation. However, the advent of Christianity and colonialism in Africa disrupted African cultural and traditional religions, which had previously promoted a system which allowed mutual co-existence between human beings and creation and nature. This affirmation is supported by John Mbiti, who maintained that the coming of Christianity and Colonialism brought a confrontation between Christianity and African Cultures, which resulted, in what he called a "cultural clash".[9] Writing on the environmental crisis, Mika Vahakangas underlines the claim of many African theologians that missionary theologians brought an unbiblical dichotomy between the sacred and the secular, which is alien to the African traditions.[10] This dichotomy resulted in a polarisation between nature and humankind, instead of seeing humankind as part of nature. The causes of creation destruction in many parts of East Africa attest the validity of Mbiti and Vahakangas' claims. For example, the coming of Christianity abolished cultural taboos and traditions that once helped to preserve creation. Christianity brought new courage and hope of life to all who joined it. Christianity not only declared superiority over traditional religions but also paralysed them. Following this change of

---

[6] Michael L. Mckinney, Robert M. Schoch, Logan Jonavjak, Grant A. Mincy (eds): Environmental Science. Systems and Solutions, Sixth Edition, chapter 6.6. *Patterns of Resource Depletion.* Burlington: Jones and Bartlett Learning, 2021. page 164

[7] Paul Afra, *Natural Resources Management* (Tabora, AMUCTA TANZANIA, 2016. [Available at: https //www.academia.edu/26476177/NATURAL_RESOURCE_MANAGEMEN_BY_PAUL_AFRA_PUBLISHED_BY_AMUCTA_TABORA_TANZANIA], [Last accessed: 14th February 2022].

[8] See Karungi T. A. Byaruhanga, "The Church's Role in Environmental Protection", in Joseph Agbasiere and B.K. Zabajungu (eds), *Church Contribution to Integral Development* (Eldoret, Kenya: Amecea Gaba Publications, 1989): 230.

[9] John S. Mbiti, *An Introduction to African Religions* (London: Heinemann, 1975): 191.

[10] Mika Vahakangas, "The Environmental Crisis in light of the Cross", in J.N.K. Mugambi and Mika Vahakangas (eds), *Christian Theology and Environmental Responsibility* (Nairobi: Acton, 2001): 112-113.

attitude brought by Christianity, Christians found it no longer necessary to respect traditional taboos and sacred sites. They started to cut down trees regarded as sacred and they encroached on and plundered places where a god was believed to live (because of being the source of water) just to prove that the god was not there.

Pollution

Pollution is another facet of the destruction of creation. Pollution in this article refers to inappropriately disposed waste materials. Urban dwellers in cities generate a huge amount of refuse or waste. This refuse comes from residential places, commercial, administrative and industrial activities. Although such refuse or waste cannot be practically avoided, it contributes to destruction of creation and the distortion of the aesthetic outlook of cities, if not properly disposed of. The problem of waste management is a big challenge in East African cities. Cities do not currently have the technological and skills capacity for a comprehensive waste management system; and hence fail to dispose properly of the waste they generate. The piles of garbage around factories and markets are shocking, while mountains of waste in the official dump areas are still growing. Thus, the safe and effective disposal of waste becomes increasingly difficult and a priority issue for African communities.

The efforts of the governments to handle waste particularly in urban areas have not significantly improved. Meanwhile, there are many District Commissioners and Municipal Authorities, which take part in improving urban sanitation. They have contracted companies for the collection of refuse. The city authorities have set points where refuse is deposited, ready for collection for final disposal. In some municipalities, there are complaints about the inconsistency of the collection of the waste, making routines difficult. This results in decomposition of refuse particularly in the markets, which starts to smell, and attracts rodents and flies. Another complaint is that the collection of the refuse is done manually with shovels and rakes by men without gloves who accompany the vehicles. Another pathetic situation is about the final dumping sites where the refuse is not being properly sorted and are simply dumped unguarded. This attracts street children and poor dwellers to scavenge at the dumping areas hoping to find valuable things. See the picture below.

Figure 1: a photo if people rummaging on a landfill

The consequences for many poor people are communicable diseases such as cholera and other related diseases. Other incidents result from the birds picking up pieces of unprotected refuse. Birds then drop them back to the living compound, which affects not only humans but also other domestic livestock such as chickens.

The numerous markets are the worst areas of ecological issues and unhygienic conditions because of the huge amounts of accumulated rubbish they generate. People literally walk, eat and trade very close to waste. From our own observation, this problem is further complicated by a number of factors, such as the people's attitude towards environmental sanitation, the lack of adequate information and the unenforceability of strict measures to control the haphazard dumping of waste. Most people understand creation preservation as preservation of forests and tree planting not the inhabited and urban areas. Therefore, for too many people, sanitation issues are not part of the understanding and practice of creation preservation.

Deforestation

Deforestation is another issue of great significance for creation care in Africa. Deforestation is the removal of a forest or standing trees where the land is thereafter converted to a non-forest use. Currently, deforestation consists of the clearing of trees and bushes for farming and building without concurrent measures for replanting. One of the major causes of deforestation in East Africa is the conversion of forest to agricultural land, both for large-scale agriculture (including ranching and cash crops) and for subsistence agriculture. Investors are acquiring substantial areas of land for commercial forestry, cultivation of biofuels and other crops. As a result, the competition for land and water increases, fuel wood and charcoal forests face degradation. Commercial logging and timber production is often carried out in an unsustainable way for profit without concern for the long-term outcome.

The effects of deforestation in Tanzania are quite serious. It is maintained that only 37.7% or about 33,428,000 hectares of Tanzania is forested, of which only 0.7% (240,000 hectares) is classified as primary forest, the most biodiverse type including and carbon-dense form of the forest. Between 1990 and 2010, Tanzania had lost an average of 403,350 hectares or 0.9% of forests per year and in total, in those 20 years, Tanzania lost 19.4% of its forest covering around 8,067,000 hectares.[11] Forests are ecologically, economically and culturally important at local and global levels. The loss of forests therefore has a number of serious consequences. Forests help to prevent soil erosion and impede water flows, soil nutrient loss. Loss of forest also leads to increase in floods and climate change.

There is evidence that the increased cost of electricity in East African countries creates an increased demand for charcoal as an "alternative" source of energy, which in turn exacerbates tree cutting leading to continued deforestation. I have witnessed sacks of charcoal line the main roads from both Arusha and Dodoma to Dar es Salaam waiting to be sold. Following the rise of electricity costs, the police and natural resources officers have encountered hundreds of sacks of charcoal, harvested illegally and are captured by authorities every day. This shows the magnitude of the problem of environmental degradation, which is part and parcel of the destruction of creation.

According to Betsy Mason, "Although it's tempting to blame the (Kilimanjaro) ice loss on global warming, researchers think that deforestation of the mountain's foothills is more likely the culprit." She went further in saying that forests at the base of Kilimanjaro have been steadily disappearing for decades. "Without the forests' humidity," she reports, "previously moisture-laden winds blow dry. No longer replenished with water, the ice is evaporating in the strong equatorial sunshine."[12] They found that the ice on Mount Kilimanjaro has shrunk from about twelve square kilometres in 1912 to about two square kilometres today. That is about an eighty percent reduction in the ice. Scientists say the ice will be gone by 2025 if it continues to melt at its current rate.[13] The mountain is also one of the wonders of God's creation and also a prominent tourist attraction in East Africa and thus leads to national income through tourism.

---

[11] Misitu ni Mali-Forest is Wealth, Vol. XI No. 4 October-December 2019.

[12] James Taylor, "Nature Debunks Kilimanjaro Glacier Myth", 1st February 2004, *The Heartland Institute*, [Available at: https://www.heartland.org/news-opinion/news/nature-study-debunks-kilimanjaro-glacier-myth], [Last accessed: 13th February 2022].

[13] James Taylor, "Nature Debunks Kilimanjaro Glacier Myth".

Figures 2 and 3 show Mount Kilimanjaro as it was before the destruction of the creation and after the ongoing destruction of creation

Deforestation also leads to desertification, commonly thought of as the expansion of the true desert into areas previously capable of agriculture production. However, it is best to think of desertification as a "sustained reduction in the biological productivity of land"[14] particularly in dry lands. In some regions of East Africa, desertification has reached catastrophic proportions.

Desertification has contributed to soil erosion, gully erosion and floods hence an increase of land degradation. It is reported that the ecological impact of desertification in Tanzania includes decline in soil fertility, loss of biodiversity, and loss of most arable land. There is evidence in East Africa that most former arable lands are dried up without her natural vegetation's vitality and diversity. Because of desertification, there was low rainfall in most parts of East Africa and therefore there are more and more cases of serious food shortages, leading to a loss of subsistence livelihoods which directly connects to poverty, malnutrition, forced movements or migrating from unproductive land to more productive land.

Poor Agriculture Methods

In East Africa, agriculture is regarded as the backbone of the economy. The vast majority of the people in East Africa depend directly on the healing of creation for their livelihood. Agricultural activities depend on the changes of the weather or rain seasons. If the weather is not favourable due to factors like desertification, deforestations, droughts and others; agriculture production is likely to be unfavourable. Sibuga argues that the deficit caused by the approaches of modern agricultural methods brings a lot of environmental

[14] See Mike Hulme and Mick Kelly, "Exploring the Links Between Desertification and Climate Change" *Environment: Science and Policy for Sustainable Development* 35(6) (July/Aug 1993): 4-45.

destruction in Africa.[15] Because of a lack of modern farm implements, most poor people in East Africa opt for poor farming methods such as bush-burning which is used as a means of clearing vast land ready for planting. Cultivation of vast land through bush-burning as done by poor farmers has encroached upon and destroyed wildlife reserves which previously had rich and unique species of animals and plants.

Figures 4-8: photos of desertification in East Africa

Figure 9: a photo of degraded land from bush-burning.

[15] K.K. Sibuga and K.P. Sibuga, *Principles of Crop Production* (Dar es Salaam: Educational Books Publishers, 1987): 11.

Taking into account that most of the people who depend on agriculture for their survival are rural people, and that most natural vegetation is found in rural areas, an enormous destruction of natural vegetation is because of these poor farming methods.

There is also the phenomenon of the reduction of tree cover and cultivation on steep slopes without terracing which contributes to high rates of soil erosion in highland regions across East Africa. Cultivation close to forest reserves leads to deforestation because of that fact that the encroachment of forests reserves is having a direct impact on surface water supply and has virtually turned vast areas into waste lands. A vivid example of this is the encroachment in the Shengena forest and Kilimanjaro forest, which once were regarded as sacred.

Shifting cultivation is another farming method which leads to the destruction of creation. This practice involves clearing of bushes and burning them down. Once bushes are cleared, the result is deforestation. Burning bushes kills a lot of flora and fauna, including the micro-organisms which keep the soil fertile, leading to soil.

Most rural livestock herders use fire for many purposes. It can be used to clear trees and shrubs hence allow the growth of sward of grass. Burning can destroy the habitat of the tsetse flies, and other insects and pests. They claim that tsetse flies have caused many cattle deaths and veterinary services have been either too expensive or unavailable. Fires may also be used to burn grass that has become too fibrous to procure the growth of a green flush of more nutritious and palatable grasses.

The solution for the current destruction of creation caused by poor farming methods requires a multi-dimensional approach. Therefore, awareness, education and control of standards of farm implements are crucial in the efforts toward healing creation for.

Mining

The leaking of toxic materials from mining into the rivers, streams and aquifers has been often reported. Experts have frequently warned that once the ground water is contaminated, it is extremely expensive and difficult, sometimes even impossible, to clean again. Despite activists' efforts, data shows that the dumping of toxic materials is still growing and affecting inhabitants living around the mining areas. Mining developments produce mineral waste and air pollution. Gloria Mafole Policy Analyst of Christian Council of Tanzania (CCT) revealed that only about 15% of people living around the mining areas in Tanzania have knowledge about the side effects of the toxic materials they are exposed to. Chemicals and other waste products go directly into water bodies without treatment, causing damage to the ecosystem and contaminating drinking water supplies.

Figure 10: People mining

Causes and the Impact of the Creation Crisis Globally

The book *Ecological Debt* describes how the debt accrued by Northern, industrial countries towards the Global South has resulted into resource plundering, environmental damage and the occupation of the environmental space.[16] The root causes of ecological debt, which are behind the creation crisis in East Africa, have a long history. Cecil Rhodes outlined the main purpose of colonial economy as follows: "we must find new lands from which we can easily obtain raw materials and at the same time exploit the cheap slave labour that is available from the natives of the colonies. The colonies would also provide a dumping ground for surplus goods produced in our factories."[17] This situation echoes with the side effects of unequal terms of trade.

> Ecological debt is increasing under a system of unequal terms of trade wherein southern countries are forced to export goods at prices that do not take into account the social and environmental impacts of their extraction and production. Extraction of natural resources (e.g. petroleum, minerals, marine, forest and genetic resources) in order to pay external financial debt is destroying the basis of survival of Southern peoples.[18]

National obligations to pay external debts and their interests have aggravated the creation crisis in East Africa. The Southern countries are pressured through structural adjustment programmes to export more and more products in order to serve their debt and interest payments. It is equally important to note that the high interest rates that are engendered by the present global financial system serve to undervalue the future by way of creation concerns being discounted in favour of the present.[19] There are direct relations between the ecological debt and the financial debt wherein huge projects are financed through external lending by international financial institutions with little consideration of their social and creation crisis impacts.[20]

The ecological costs associated with the funded projects are profound and often irrevocable. These include the disturbance to terrestrial and aquatic habitats and, consequently, the irreversible loss of sensitive flora and fauna; the erosion and/or flooding of prime agricultural lands that are crucial to food sovereignty; the pollution and drying up of rivers, streams and aquifers; and the increased incidence of natural disasters such as earthquakes.[21]

K.C. Abraham in his article, "A Theological Response to the Ecological Crisis", affirms that; in the past, nature was seen as an object for ruthless exploitation by "developers" and scientists for the "good" of humans. Little thought was given to the perils of creation destruction.[22]

It is both the responsibility of governments in some industrialised as well as emerging countries (e.g. South Africa, Brazil, China) to change their course. All EU country governments have signed the Kyoto protocol and the EU has very strict CO2 reduction goals with its EU Green Deal project. However, there are several Non-EU countries which have signed Kyoto and Paris agreements, but have since left them (like US) or did not formulate ambitious goals (China and Russia).[23] "Some of these agreements have set medium

---

[16] Rogate Mshana, "Preface", in Athena L. Peralta (eds), *Ecological Debt: The Peoples of the South are the Creditors* (Quezon City, The Philippines: Troika Press, 2009), v.
[17] Mshana, "Preface", vi.
[18] Mshana, "Preface", vi.
[19] Peralta, *Ecological Debt*, 5.
[20] Peralta, "Introduction to Ecological Debt", in *Ecological Debt*, 5.
[21] Peralta, "Introduction to Ecological Debt", 7.
[22] By Francis Ng'ambi, "Dams on the Zambesi River as Sources of Ecological Debt to the People of Mozambique", in *Ecological Debt*, 66.
[23] Switch 2 Green, "The EU Green Deal – a roadmap to sustainable economies", Switch 2 Green Website. [Available at: https://www.switchtogreen.eu/the-eu-green-deal-promoting-a-green-notable-circular-economy/], [Last accessed: 14th February 2022].

and long-term targets for the implementation of their policies, which are not enough to stop damage to the environment."[24]

The international financial institutions also bear a lot of responsibility for creation degradation because they finance resource extraction while paying little attention to the social and environment consequences of these practises. The situation is made acute by the water crisis. Major and unprecedented droughts and floods have caused a lack of access to drinking water and sanitation.

Figure 11: water scarcity

The Healing of Creation in East Africa

The healing of creation is not something that will happen overnight. What is needed is an analytical looking at factors that contributed, and are still contributing, to the destruction of creation. We have to look at our governmental policies and interrogate whether these talk to preservation of creation and respect of our good culture as Africans. We need to stand up against a system in our societies and in our religions that continues to fail to acknowledge the goodness of creation and the relevance of human efforts for healing it. Five principles are important for implementing healing of creation as major principle for sustainable development in Eastern Africa.

1) The tendency to heal our creation should not be the tendency of placing too much blame on the developed nations or colonialists. It is an undeniable fact that the colonialists benefitted a lot from Africa's resources and they still do even now. But the fact also is that proper leadership in most African nations since independence has been lacking. For example, Tanzania is the sole country in the world where the mineral and stone of Tanzanite is found but Tanzania itself is not the main exporter of it.[25]
2) We need better systems of governance, economic stability and consequently great progress supported by the availability of large reserves of resources.
3) We need meaningful, peaceful and democratic elections that will create stability in each country which in turn will propel sustainable development.
4) We need respect both for people's rights and nature's rights. Denying people rights and acting against peoples' interests is widespread in African countries. It is only free people, people with rights,

[24] Rogate Mshana (ed), *Poverty, Wealthy and Ecology: Latin America & Caribbean Perspectives* (Geneva: World Council of Churches, 2009): 5.

[25] Dodgson, Lindsay, Tanzanite: how Tanzania can profit from mining its rare stone: [Available at: https://www.mining-technology.com/features/featuretanzanite-how-tanzania-can-profit-from-mining-its-rare-stone-4698401//], [Last accessed: 14th February 2022].

responsible citizens, who can participate in the development and in the protection of the nature and heritage. It is difficult to heal our creation in a nation which is full of corruption, greed and injustice.

5) Our sustainable development and the survival of future generations depends on a common commitment to key goals for a healed creation. Therefore, we also need a political will from those industrialised countries who have been a catalyst for the persistent destruction and degradation of creation. We also need a reinterpretation of our faith; it was through the misinterpretation of faith and through collective and individual misbehaviour that we have participated in the process of creation destruction, rather than participating in the healing of creation that God requires.[26]

The fundamental theological and biblical principles for healing creation should be developed and understood. Healing of creation emanates from the scripture, both Old and New Testaments. The scripture reveals that God is the Creator of all that exists, the creation and that He has declared that "it was good" (Gen. 1:3; 1 Tim. 4:4).[27] Human beings, bearing the image of God and as an integral part of creation, should imitate the concern of God for maintaining and taking care of the earth.[28] We recognise the need to develop a new theological understanding and interpretation of the biblical tradition on the aspect of healing of creation. For God is the Creator, the source of Life, the Lord, who created the heavens and stretched them out. He spread the earth and what comes from it (Is. 42:5a). The goodness of God's creation and the intrinsic worth of all beings and human beings as an integral part of nature (Gen. 1:2, Ps. 104) needs to be affirmed. Instead of dominating nature, humans have the responsibility to preserve and properly cultivate the earth, and to work with God for the sustainability of the planet.[29] Churches remind us that "the earth is the Lord's and all that is in it, the world, and those who live in it" (Ps. 24:1). In Christ, "the creation itself will be set free from its bondage to decay and will obtain the freedom of the glory of the children of God" (Rom. 8:21).[30]

Conclusion

The article analysed the root causes and the impacts of environmental destruction in East Africa. The article revealed that the ongoing degradation results from human activities and has given rise to the depletion of non-renewable resources, loss of the biodiversity through rapid destruction of habitats, erosion of top soil through unsustainable agriculture and forestry practices, pollution of air by toxic emissions from industries and water pollution. The article revealed that the problem of creation destruction affects both the physical health and general well-being of society. Women and the poor bear a heavy burden from degraded creation. In this article, the communities which bear the cost of creation destruction and degradation are the poor who are pushed away due to weak ownership rights. The article observed that the current global economic structure not only vandalises creation but also enlarges the gap between the haves and the have nots, leaving the majority of the Global South in abject poverty and excluded from meeting their basic human needs. The article argues that the healing of creation is everybody's responsibility and can only be met through joint efforts of all levels of the society. It requires collaboration, synthesis and interconnectedness with government, stakeholders and faith-based organisations locally and globally.

According to evidence presented on the global causes of creation destruction both the rich and the poor are to blame for the creation crisis. Furthermore, the article discussed how the rich nations have heavily contributed to the global creation crisis. This gives the heavy responsibility to invest a sizable amount of

[26] Michael Kinnamon (ed), *Signs of the Spirit, Official Report Seventh Assembly (*Geneva: World Council of Churches, 1991): 55.

[27] Kinnamon, *Signs of the Spirit*, 56.

[28] Kinnamon, *Signs of the Spirit*, 56.

[29] Wesley Graberg-Michaelson, *Redeeming the Creation, The Rio Earth Summit: Challenges to the Churches* (Geneva: World Council of Churches, 1992): 78.

[30] Kinnamon, *Signs of the Spirit*, 56.

capital and effort into healing the issues, especially those factors which have led humans into plundering the earth's resources.

To address the issue of corruption, there needs to be collective effort of the government and religious institutions. If the prevailing trend continues then the issue of creation protection and healing for sustainable development will be difficult, both for the urban and rural poor. Religious organisations and government have the potential resources to inspire commitment and the collective will of the people despite corruption and other malpractices. The teachings of the religious or faith-based organisations have proved to create awareness, transform and inspire practical commitment and bring about a change in people's behaviour and attitude towards sin. If the religious organisations manage to address the issue of creation destruction as sin, requiring people to repent, there can be a positive response in terms of healing creation of sustainable development.

Suggestions for Further Reading

Hallman, David G. "Climate Change and Ecumenical Work for Sustainable Community", in D.T. Hessel and Larry L. Rasmussen, Eds. *Earth Habitat: Eco-injustices and the church's response.* Minneapolis, MN: Fortress, 2001: 125-134.

—. "Ethics and Sustainable Development", in David G. Hallman, Ed. *Voices from South and North.* Geneva: World Council of Churches, 1994: 264-283.

—. *A Place in Creation: Ecological Visions in Science, Religion and Economics.* Geneva: World Council of Churches, 1992.

Meadows, Donella H., Dennis L. Meadows, Jørgen Randers and William W. Behrens. *The Limits to Growth: A Report for the Club of Rome's Project on the Predicament of Mankind.* New York: Universe Books, 1974.

Kabugumila, Alice. "Tanzania Women's Response to the Environmental Crisis", in J.N.K. Mugambi and Mika Vahakangas. Eds. *Christian Theology and Environmental Responsibility.* Nairobi: Acton, 2001: 64-73.

Mshana, Rogate, R. Ed. *Wealth Creation and Justice: The World Council of Churches Encounters with the World Bank and the International Monetary Fund.* Geneva: World Council of Churches, 2003.

Otim, J.J. *The Taproot of Environmental and Development Crisis in Africa.* Nairobi: ACLCA, 1992.

Sibuga, K.K. and K.P. Sibuga. *Principles of Crop Production.* Dar es Salaam: Educational Books Publishers, 1987.

World Commission on Environment and Development. *Our Common Future: From One Earth to One World.* Oxford: Oxford University Press, 1987.

World Council of Churches, *Caring for Creation: Call to the Latin American Churches.* Church and Society, Document 6. Geneva: World Council of Churches, 1988.

—. *Integrity of Creation – An Ecumenical Discussion*, Granvollen, Norway, February 25-March 1988. Geneva: World Council of Churches/Church and Society, 1989.

41. The Role of Pentecostal Churches for Strengthening Ecological Principles and a Foundation for Pentecostal Contribution to Creation Care

Mangaliso Matshobane[1]

Introduction

This essay discusses the role of Pentecostals in strengthening ecological principles by plotting the journey from its fundamentalist roots to its current position on ecotheology. The journey is long and winding, starting from the anthropomorphic ideals of human dominance over creation, influenced by apocalyptic eschatological views which render the conversation on creation-care void. The breakthrough came when Pentecostals refocused on their pneumatological theology which led them to a conversation about the role of the Spirit in creation. The essay discusses the ecotheological perspective of Pentecostals using their four tenets of Christ as saviour, healer, baptiser in the Spirit and coming king. The essay uses Osmer's theoretical framework[2] of describing what is going on in eco-Pentecostal theology, interpreting why it is going on, then reflecting normatively on what should be going on and finally proposing pragmatic ways to improve the involvement of Pentecostal churches on creation-care. A Pentecostal hermeneutical approach on biblical theology is proposed as a strategy to engage Pentecostal churches in creation-care.

Pentecostalism is arguably the fastest growing religious movement in the world. Anderson says that, by 2012, there were over 612 million Pentecostal/Charismatics in the world.[3] This number is inclusive of independent churches known as Neo- Pentecostalism and Neo-charismatics and African Initiated Churches (AICs). The greater percentage of Pentecostals comes from the Southern Hemisphere (Latin America and Africa). There is also a significant percentage in Asia. "Within the past thirty years there has been an estimated 700% increase in the number of Pentecostal believers who represent about a quarter of the world's Christian population and a two-thirds of all Protestants".[4] If these statistics are anything to go by, the planet stands to benefit if the global Pentecostal movement can play a role in strengthening ecological principles.

The Pentecostal church is fairly new to the discussion on ecotheology. This is partly due to its alignment and adaption of the fundamentalist position on creation in the earlier years of the 20th century (1920 and 1930).[5] This alignment was beneficial to Pentecostals who found the collaboration with fundamentalists helpful in defending the credibility of the scriptures on God and the creation against liberal and modernist attacks.[6] The alignment with fundamentalists has unfortunately played a great influence in making

---

[1] Mangaliso Matshobane is a founder and an ordained Apostle of an Independent Pentecostal Church, named Community Church, based in South Africa. He is a board member of a professional body for clergy in South Africa called an Association for Christian Religious Practitioners (ACRP, acrpafrica.co.za). He is also a PhD graduate in Practical Theology at the University of Pretoria in South Africa, PhD research on Pastoral Succession in Independent Pentecostal Churches.

[2] Richard Osmer, *Practical Theology: An Introduction* (Grand Rapids, MI: Eerdmans, 2008).

[3] Allan Anderson, *An Introduction to Pentecostalism: Global Charismatic Christianity*, 2nd edition (Cambridge: Cambridge University Press, 2014): 3-5.

[4] Allan Anderson, Michael Bergunder, Andre Droogers and Cornelis van der Laan (eds), *Studying Global Pentecostalism: Theories and Methods* (Berkeley, CA: University of California Press, 2010): 2.

[5] Amos Yong, "Poured out on all creation!? Searching for the Spirit in the Pentecostal Encounter with Science". in Amos Yong (ed), *The Spirit Renews the Face of the Earth: Pentecostal forays in science and theology of creation* (Eugene, OR: Wipf and Stock, 2009): xiv.

[6] Gerald King, "Evolving Paradigms Creationism as Pentecostal Variation on a Fundamentalist Theme", Amos Yong (ed), *The Spirit Renews the Face of the Earth: Pentecostal forays in science and theology of creation* (Eugene, OR: Wipf and Stock, 2014). King elaborates on the history of Pentecostals and fundamentalists collaboration against the modernist biblical higher criticism that is undergirded by Darwin's argument of evolution.

Pentecostals socially and environmentally indifferent.[7] The latter was promulgated by a premillennial apocalyptic view which purports that the world will come to an end in a cataclysmic fashion where creation as we know it will be destroyed. It is this kind of eschatological view that has influenced conventional Pentecostalism to become indifferent to environmental responsibilities.[8] The other contributor to the negative view of Pentecostals on creation-care is the fundamentalist position on the six days, young earth creation which rejects the evolutionary science of the old age earth.[9] This rejection of evolutionary science of creation has also caused the rejection of caring for the creation especially in view of climate change.[10] It is also unfortunate that Pentecostals did not involve themselves in the early conversations on creation care with ecumenical groups, due to their suspicion of such forums to be pursuing a liberal agenda.[11]

One of the main contributors to this indifferent perspective is the exegesis of Genesis 1:28 where God gives mankind dominion over creation. Pentecostals take their cue from fundamentalists in their definition of dominion, which is taken literally, assuming to give mankind dominance or rulership over creation. Humanity is seen as the centrepiece of creation and therefore has the right to dominate all creation as a "God-given resource for unlimited human use."[12] This anthropocentric perspective of creation has created a hierarchical relationship between humanity and nature which has led to the degradation of the environment by humans.[13] The anthropocentric perspective is the dominant factor that features in the main tenets of Pentecostal theology, which present Christ as saviour, healer, baptiser in the Spirit and coming king.[14] These theological tenets will be discussed from an ecotheological perspective within a theoretical framework of Osmer. The latter will help us to describe *what is going on* traditionally in Pentecostal churches on creation-care; to give an interpretation on *why is it going on*; to find the normative of *what should be going on* and to propose a pragmatic strategy on *what can be done* to ensure that Pentecostal churches contribute in strengthening ecological principles for creation-care.[15]

It is important to firstly establish what is going on within Pentecostal circles in reference to ecotheology and, where possible, to give reasons on why it is going on, before proposing the role that Pentecostal churches can and should play.

What is Going On and Why?

As indicated in the introduction, I will begin my discussion from an eco-theological perspective using the four tenets of Pentecostal theology to establish the traditional, normative and practical view of Pentecostals on creation-care. Firstly, we will discuss Christ as Saviour.

---

[7] Shane Clifton, "Preaching the Full Gospel in the context of global environmental crises", In Yong, *The Spirit Renews the Face of the Earth*, 118.

[8] Al Truesdale, "Last things First: The impact of Eschatology on Ecology", *Perspectives on Science and Christian Faith,* 46(2) (1994): 116-122.

[9] Clifton, "Preaching the Full Gospel", 120.

[10] Clifton, "Preaching the Full Gospel", 120.

[11] Cecil Robeck, "Pentecostals and the Apostolic Faith: Implications for Ecumenism", *PNEUMA: The Journal of the Society for Pentecostal Studies* 9(1) (1987): 61-84.

[12] Paul Maltby, "Fundamentalist Dominion, Postmodern Ecology", *Ethics and Environment* 13(2) (2008): 119-141.

[13] Matthew Tallman, "Pentecostal Ecology: A Theological Paradigm for Pentecostal Environmentalism", in *Yong, The Spirit Renews the Face of the Earth*, 140.

[14] Donald Dayton, *Theological roots of Pentecostalism* (Peabody, MA: Hendrickson,1987).

[15] Richard Osmer, *Practical Theology: An Introduction* (Grand Rapids, MI: Eerdmans, 2008).

Christ as Saviour

Traditional View

Pentecostals have traditionally viewed salvation from an anthropocentric perspective. The saving of souls has always been prioritised over the "saving of the soil."[16] Pentecostal theologians agree that the traditional view of salvation that is exclusively for humans to the neglect of creation has been more prominent within Pentecostal circles.[17] Pentecostals place a high value on evangelism such that social action (like feeding the poor, taking care of orphans et cetera) is viewed as a tool to evangelise the individuals who are being served. If social action has to ultimately lead to evangelism, it will be difficult for Pentecostals to comprehend how environmental action can produce similar results.[18] This dualistic view that separates between the spirit and nature is informed by the influence that Greek philosophy (Stoicism) has had on Christian tradition, in general, instead of the Judeo-Christian tradition that is fundamental to Christianity which emphasises stewardship of creation where dualisms do not exist.[19]

Normative View

Yong proposes a view of salvation that is multidimensional, namely: a salvation that is personal, material, social, cosmic, eschatological, family-oriented and ecclesiastical.[20] We'll focus here on cosmic salvation which refers to the salvation of all creation. This understanding is also confirmed by the Pauline writings where he states that creation waits eagerly to be delivered from its groans and labours.[21] Hubbard-Heitz discusses how traditional Pentecostals associated certain spaces (clubs, movie theatres and saloons) with activities of sin. The intention, therefore, is to transform those spaces into sacred spaces through preaching the message of salvation.[22] If spaces can be seen as needing transformation through salvation, then the sins of ecological domination and oppression on creation are not excluded from atonement. The latter should motivate Pentecostals to seek for spaces that are ecologically unfriendly and convert them into healthy ecological havens.[23]

Pragmatic View

A teaching that focuses on redefining human dominance over creation as a way of stewardship from a Pentecostal theological perspective must be newly developed and taught in Pentecostal theological schools. When pastors of churches have been taught correctly, they will in turn teach their congregations an environmental inclusive theology. The role of a pastor as an instructor of truth in Pentecostal circles is highly valued and yields a lot of influence especially among Neo-Pentecostals also known as Charismatic-Pentecostals.[24] Arguably, the first pronouncement of a Pentecostal view on ecology was by the Dutch

---

[16] Aaron Jason Swoboda, "Eco-Glossolalia: Emerging Twenty -First Century Pentecostal and Charismatic Ecotheology", *RuTh* 9(2) (2011): 101-116.

[17] Tallman, *Pentecostal Ecology*, 132; Clifton, "Preaching the full gospel", 120; Aaron Swoboda *Tongues and Trees: Toward a Pentecostal Ecological Theology. Journal of Pentecostal Theology* Supplement 40. (Blandford Forum, UK: Deo, 2013): 193.

[18] Clifton, "Preaching the full gospel", 122.

[19] Veli-Matti Kärkkäinen, "The Greening of the Spirit: Towards a Pneumatological Theology of the Flourishing of Nature", in Aaron Swoboda (ed), *Blood Cries Out: Pentecostals, Ecology, and the Groans of Creation* (Eugene, OR: Pickwick, 2014): 87.

[20] Yong, *The Spirit poured out on all flesh*, 95.

[21] Romans 8:19-22 NKJV

[22] Brandon Hubbard-Heitz, "The Devil Suicide: Early Pentecostal Hermeneutics of Space and their Ecotheological Implications", in Aaron Swoboda (ed), *Blood Cries Out: Pentecostals, Ecology, and the Groans of Creation*(Eugene, OR: Pickwick, 2014), 35.

[23] Brandon Hubbard-Heitz, "The Devil Suicide", 37.

[24] Maria Frahm-Arp, *Professional Women in South African Pentecostal Charismatic Churches* (Leiden: Koninklijke Brill NV, 2010), 67.

theologian Jean-Jacques Suurmond in 1988 who advanced an argument on an ecological lifestyle which encompasses three interconnected dimensions of life: personal, ecclesiological and universal ecologies.[25] This interconnected holistic approach is the focus the Pentecostal church must take when teaching congregants to be sensitised to ecological issues.

Christ as Healer

Traditional View

The traditional view of Pentecostals on the work of Christ as a healer has always been anthropocentric.[26] This is because Pentecostals have always linked healing with salvation, therefore, they view it as attainable by means of the atonement for mankind.[27]

Normative View

Harold Hunter challenged this anthropocentric perspective on healing, arguing that it should involve all of creation, including "the sick and dying environment."[28] The zeal that Pentecostals have demonstrated in administering gifts of healing can easily make them pray for creatures other than humans. This was demonstrated by William Branham, a well-known charismatic healing evangelist of his time, who prayed for an opossum.[29] If Pentecostals can stretch their faith in this manner, they can also extend their faith to pray for the healing of all creation.

Pragmatic View

Pentecostals can learn how to extend their theology of healing to other creatures by studying the example set by the African Indigenous churches of Zimbabwe, called the Association of African Earth-keeping Churches (AAEC), which in the broader sense can be classified as Pentecostal because of their pneumatic nature.[30] These churches have developed a liturgy in their tree planting ceremony of confessing ecological sins followed by a planting of trees.[31] Another ground-breaking work on creation-care, from which Pentecostal churches can learn is Harold Hunter's article "Pentecostal healing for God's sick creation". Hunter, a Pentecostal scholar, challenged Pentecostals to understand healing not just from an anthropocentric view but also from an all-creation perspective, where all of creation, including humans, can be healed.[32] Such literature can form a basis onto which Pentecostal churches can develop bible study curriculum thus beginning a conversation that will lead to a practice of healing the creation.

---

[25] Jean-Jacques Suurmond, "Christ King: A Charismatic appeal for an Ecological Lifestyle", *Pneuma* 10 (1988): 26-35.

[26] Clifton, "Preaching the 'Full Gospel", 122.

[27] William Menzies and Robert Menzies, *Spirit and Power: Foundations of Pentecostal Experience* (Grand Rapids, MI: Zondervan, 2000): 160.

[28] Clifton, "Preaching the Full Gospel", 131.

[29] William Branham, "God's cure for an Opossum", *Voice* 3(6) (September 1955): 3-11.

[30] Maria Frahm-Arp, *Professional Women in South African Pentecostal Charismatic Churches* (Netherlands: Koninklijke Brill NV, 2010): 48. When referring to various groups within the Pentecostal movement and their interpretation of the work of the Holy Spirit whether they are classical Pentecostal, Zionist, Apostolic churches or Pentecostal Charismatic groups including contemporary neo- Pentecostals, Frahm-Arp calls them a "Complex of Pneumatically Sensitive Expressions of Christianity (CPSEC)".

[31] M.L. Daneel, "African Independent Churches Face the challenge of Environmental Ethics", in David Hallman (ed), *Ecotheology Voices of South and North* (Geneva: World Council of Churches, 1994): 247-263.

[32] Harold Hunter, "Pentecostal Healing for God's Sick Creation", *The Spirit and Church*, 2 (2000), 145-167.

Christ as Baptiser in the Spirit

Traditional View

Traditionally, Pentecostals view the Holy Spirit as exclusively active in humans, particularly in believers and not in unbelievers, let alone in any other creature.[33] They base their Pentecostal experience of the infilling of the Spirit with the evidence of speaking in other tongues, from the passage of Acts 2, which at face-value looks like it is anthropocentric.

Normative View

Pinnock's work on the *Flame of Love* helped both Protestants (Moltmann) and Pentecostals (Macchia) to understand the role of the Spirit not only at creation but as a power which continues to relate to creation. He indicates that the role of the Holy Spirit in creating the earth out of nothing (*creatio ex nihilo)* must not overshadow the continual work of the Spirit creation (*creatio continua)*.[34] Some Pentecostals affirm the role of the Spirit in creation as proposed by Pinnock and further argue that the role of the Spirit in creation should not be separated from the role of the Spirit in salvation.[35] The same Spirit who created is still the same Spirit who is present in redemption.

Pentecostals are further challenged by the theology of Jürgen Moltmann on kenotic pneumatology: the Spirit who suffers with the creation as he did in the incarnate Christ.[36] This means that the Trinity empties itself through the Holy Spirit who identifies with the on-going groanings of creation as it awaits its redemption.[37] Some Pentecostals have gone on further to advocate the role of the Holy Spirit not only in creation but in nature, calling it the pneumatological theology of nature, juxtaposed with the role of the Holy Spirit in creation, also known as a pneumatological theology of creation.[38] The former is based on an argument for the involvement of the Spirit in nature, using the metaphorical language of scripture where the Spirit and natural elements are used together: "tongues of fire", "the wind of the Spirit".[39] Swoboda further develops the role of the Holy Spirit as uniting both the creation and the church through baptism, which is a central doctrine of Pentecostals.[40] The Spirit who baptised the early church in Acts 2, is the same Spirit who was hovering over primordial chaos in Genesis 1:2; therefore, the Spirit-baptised church must care for the Spirit-baptised creation.[41]

Pragmatic View

There is a need to approach this subject from scriptural records that place the Holy Spirit in relation with creation. Pentecostals being keen observers of the scriptures will appreciate the number of biblical texts that highlight the involvement of the Spirit with creation, which in any case formulates their pneumatological theology.[42] These biblical texts must then be interpreted within an ecotheological perspective to highlight the role of the Holy Spirit in creation. When this has been established, Pastors of

---

[33] Steven Studebaker, "The Spirit in Creation: A unified Theology of Grace and Creation Care", *Zygon* 43 (2008): 943-960.
[34] Clark Pinnock, *Flame of Love: A Theology of the Holy Spirit* (Downer's Grove, IL: IVP, 1996): 49-72.
[35] Studebaker, "The Spirit in Creation", 953.
[36] Jürgen Moltmann, *The Trinity and the Kingdom: The Doctrine of God*, trans. Margaret Kohl (Minneapolis, MN: Fortress, 1993): 119.
[37] Peter Althouse, "Implications of the Kenosis of the Spirit for a creational Eschatology: A Pentecostal Engagement with Jürgen Moltmann", in Amos Yong (ed), *The Spirit Renews the Face of the Earth: Pentecostal forays in science and theology of creation* (Eugene, OR: Wipf and Stock, 2009): 156.
[38] Amos Yong, "Introduction: Poured out on all creation! Searching for the Spirit in the Pentecostal Encounter with Science", in Yong, *The Spirit Renews the Face of the Earth*, xix-xx.
[39] Yong, "The Spirit Poured Out On All Flesh", 267.
[40] Swoboda, "Eco-Glossolalia", 11-13.
[41] Swoboda, "Eco-Glossolalia", 13
[42] Swoboda, "Eco-Glossolalia", 12.

Pentecostal churches must then teach a pneuma-ecological theology where the congregants are called upon to invite the Holy Spirit to be poured out and "renew the face of the earth."[43] The Pentecostal church, in its teaching, must draw from the history of its theologians who have been advancing a pneumatological ecotheology. In 1996, the work of Clark Pinnock, alluded to above, became a turning point in Christendom on the significant role of the Holy Spirit in creation and it set a tone for an ecotheology that is pneumatologically understood.[44] Macchia, gave a positive review of the work of Pinnock, from a Pentecostal perspective.[45] He noted that Hollenweger, a Pentecostal scholar, in his classical work *Creator Spiritus*, sought to point Pentecostals in the direction of the work of the Spirit in creation.[46] The conversation of the Spirit in creation has always been in the foundation of the church but latent and dormant. It is the responsibility of the church to re-open this conversation.

Christ as Coming King

Traditional View

A traditional Pentecostal view of eschatology is influenced by the fundamentalists who subscribe to a dispensational premillennial view of an end of the world in a cataclysmic fashion.[47] This view has caused Pentecostals not to entertain any discussion on creation care because of their apocalyptic view of eschatology.[48] Their view of eschatology has mostly been anthropocentric where the future is seen in terms of eternal life, and as a result, their engagement with the social, political and environmental issues of this age is lacking.[49]

Normative View

Peter Althouse, a Pentecostal scholar, discusses at length Moltmann's view of eschatology and affirms his view of a transformational eschatology.[50] The latter refers to the fact that, although Christ died physically and was buried, at resurrection, his body was transformed. In the same way, the earth which is presented in the scripture as "passing away" then again as "a new heaven and a new earth", does not refer to the annihilation of the earth but rather its renewal, as it was also the case with the flood.[51] Moltmann provides classification of eschatology into four areas: personal eschatology which focuses on eternal life, historical eschatology focuses on the kingdom of God, cosmic eschatology focuses on the creation, then lastly divine eschatology focusing on the glory of God.[52] Moltmann further argues that eschatology cannot be exclusively reduced to the human context without involving their environment because they are intrinsically connected.[53] Pentecostals must therefore not see eschatology in the light of cessation of creation but must

---

[43] Psalm 140:30.
[44] Clark Pinnock, *Flame of Love: A Theology of the Holy Spirit* (Downer's Grove, IL: IVP, 1996).
[45] Frank Macchia, "Tradition and the Novum of the Spirit: A Review of Clark Pinnock's Flame of Love", *Journal of Pentecostal Theology* 6 (1998): 31-48.
[46] Walter Hollenweger, "Creator Spiritus: The challenge of Pentecostal Experience to Pentecostal", *Theology* 81(679) (1978): 32-40.
[47] Robby Waddell, "Revelation and the (New) Creation: A Prolegomenon on the Apocalypse, Science and Creation", in Yong, *The Spirit Renews the Face of the Earth*, 35.
[48] Al Truesdale, "Last Things First: The Impact of Eschatology on Ecology", *Perspective on Science and Christian Faith* 46(2) (1994): 116-122.
[49] Waddell, "Revelation and the New Creation", 31.
[50] Peter Althouse, "In appreciation of Jürgen Moltmann: A Discussion of His Transformational Eschatology", *Pneuma* 28(1) (2006): 28.
[51] Douglas Moo, "Nature in the New Creation: New Testament eschatology and the environment", *Journal of the Evangelical Theological Society* 49(3) (2006): 466-469.
[52] Jürgen Moltmann, *The Coming of God: Christian Eschatology* (Minneapolis, MN: Fortress, 1996).
[53] Jürgen Moltmann, *Science and Wisdom* (Minneapolis: MN: Fortress, 2003): 71.

view it in the context of a pneumatogical theology that focuses on the Spirit who gives life and transforms the earth.[54]

Pragmatic View

Pentecostals must intentionally study other eschatological views in order to migrate from a premillennial apocalyptic view of eschatology which promotes an annihilation of the universe and embrace a transformative eschatology which is eco-friendly. The eschatological theology of a transformational eschatology advanced by Moltmann,[55] needs to be taught in Pentecostal theological schools and churches. This transformational eschatology can be taught from a Pentecostal perspective which has been ably reviewed by Althouse,[56] who also attests to the fact that "Moltmann's eschatological theology is helpful for constructing a Pentecostal ecotheology."[57]

Now that we have discussed the ecotheological perspective of Pentecostals based on their theological tenets, we will then discuss what the church ought to be doing to strengthen ecological principles.

What Should Be Going On?

The Role of the Church

The Pentecostal church must correct the faulty exegesis of Genesis 1:28 where dominion has been given to mankind by God, for stewardship, not for dominance.[58] Humanity has a delegated responsibility to look after the earth and its resources as expressed by Genesis 2:15. Pentecostal-Charismatics in Africa define dominion as a delegated authority given to man by God to continue the work that God had started in creation and to handle creation in the same way that God would handle it.[59] In other words, mankind must take their pattern of dominion from God whose pattern encompassed the fruitfulness and benefit of all creation and not just humans, hence the blessing of fruitfulness was firstly given to other creatures before mankind as clearly written in Genesis 1:22. There must be earth-stewardship activities that the church mobilises its congregants to deliberately engage in, so as to promote awareness within the church and the community, including but not limited to waste recycling projects and tree planting ceremonies.

The Pentecostal church must leverage on its rich pneumatological theology and particularly the interaction of the Spirit with creation. Yong brings a fresh perspective on the discussion of ecotheology that is pneumatologically inclined. His main perspective is on the metaphorical ecological language used in relation to the Spirit, based on Acts 2:2-3, 19, 20. On the day of Pentecost, there were "sounds of a rushing wind", "tongues of fire" and also "the sun turned into darkness and the moon to blood".[60] His argument is

---

[54] Clifton, "Preaching the Full Gospel", 132.

[55] Jürgen Moltmann, *Ethics of Hope*. Translated by Margaret Kohl. (Minneapolis, MN: Fortress, 2012): 16.

[56] Peter Althouse, "Pentecostal Eco-Transformation: Possibilities for a Pentecostal Ecotheology in light of Moltmann's Green Theology", in Aaron Swoboda (ed), *Blood Cries Out: Pentecostals, Ecology, and Groans of Creation* (Eugene, OR: Pickwick, 2014): 116-132.

[57] Althouse, "Pentecostal Eco-Transformation", 122.

[58] Douglas John Hall, *Imaging God: Dominion as Stewardship* (Grand Rapids, MI: Eerdmans, 1996); Robby Waddell, "A Green Apocalypse: Comparing Secular and Religious and Eschatological Visions of the Earth", in Aaron Swoboda (ed), *Blood Cries Out: Pentecostals, Ecology, and Groans of Creation* (Eugene, OR: Pickwick, 2014): 139; Alistair Petrie, *Releasing Heaven On Earth: Removing the Barriers to Effective Evangelism, Revival and Lasting Transformation* (Lancaster, LA: Sovereign World, 2000). Petrie is a Pentecostal Charismatic author who is not writing from an academic perspective but a devotional perspective from a background of a group associated with dominion theology. It is significant to note that he writes about the role of stewardship that the people have over the land.

[59] Kwabena Asamoah-Gyadu, "God's laws of Productivity, Creation in African Pentecostal Hermeneutics", in Yong, *The Spirit Renews the Face of the Earth* (Eugene, OR: Wipf and Stock, 2009): 185-186.

[60] Amos Yong, *The Spirit Poured Out On All Flesh: Pentecostalism and the Possibility of Global Theology* (Grand Rapids, MI: Baker Academic, 2005): 267.

that the use of ecological language (wind, fire) to describe the Spirit is not a random coincidence but an indication of an inseparable relationship between the creation (sun, darkness, moon) and the Spirit.

This ecological language as found in the Bible text is an entrance point the Pentecostal church can use in drawing its congregants into a conversation on creation-care. The literal interpretation that most Pentecostals use when exegeting scripture (which in some cases can be incorrectly used as is the case with Genesis 1:28 on dominion) can serve as an easy point of entrance to convince an average Pentecostal of creation-care. Whereas most Christian traditions rely on a systematic theology when exploring their belief in God, Pentecostals rely on a biblical theology which "tends to be descriptive, inductive and as diachronic as possible."[61] They prefer to draw their instruction and inspiration straight from the biblical text rather than through a processed analysis found in biblical commentaries; as a result, a few Pentecostal scholars of systematic theology have based their work largely on biblical theology.[62]

What Can Be Practically Done?

It is against this background that Pentecostal churches must highlight biblical texts that are connected to an ecological framework even if the language used is metaphoric. Some of the most evident biblical texts that can be a basis for creation-care based on the four tenets of Pentecostal theology are:

Colossians 1:19-20

For it pleased the Father that in Him all the fullness should dwell, and by Him *to reconcile all things to Himself*, by Him, whether *things on earth or things in heaven*, having made peace through the blood of His cross.

This scripture refers to Christ as Saviour of all creation not just humans.

2 Kings 2:21

Then he went out to the *source of the water*, and *cast in the salt there*, and said, "*Thus says the Lord*: '*I have healed this water*; from it shall be no more death or barrenness.'" So the *water remains healed* to this day, according to the word of the Elisha which he spoke.

This scripture relates to Christ as Healer of all creation not just humans.

Genesis 1:2

The *earth* was without form, and *void*; and darkness was on the face of the deep. And the *Spirit* of God was *hovering* over the face of the *waters*.

Psalms 104: 30

You send your *Spirit*, they are *created*; and you *renew* the face of the *earth*.

These scriptures relate to Christ as Baptiser in the Spirit for all creation not just humans.

Revelations 22:1-2

And he showed me a *pure river of water* of life, clear as crystal, proceeding from the throne of God and of the Lamb. In the middle of its street, and on either side of the river, was the *tree of life*, which bore *twelve fruits*, each tree yielding its fruit every month. The *leaves of the tree* were for the *healing of the nations*."

This scripture relates to Christ as Coming King not to annihilate but to transform the earth.

These biblical texts and many others like them can be used by Pentecostal churches to facilitate a conversation among congregants and communities on creation-care. These conversations will then lead to

[61] Keith Warrington, *Pentecostal Theology: A Theology of Encounter* (London: T&T Clark, 2008): 185.
[62] Warrington, *Pentecostal Theology*, 186.

action plans that will make Pentecostal contributions of great significance to the planet, given its global stupendous growth.

Pentecostal churches must also seek to acquaint themselves with the ecotheological conversation that has been going on for over 40 years in ecumenical circles and bring their flavour and flair in the fight against climate change.

Conclusion

This essay highlighted the fundamentalist roots of Pentecostal churches due to their collaboration against a modern liberal agenda that attacked the biblical creation narrative. This collaboration, as much as it was a positive resistance at that time, unfortunately affected the perception Pentecostals had on science in general including climate change proponents, as an anti-biblical campaign against the creation narrative. The fundamentalist apocalyptic view of eschatology came as a package of the collaboration and made Pentecostals indifferent to the concept of saving the earth. There was no point in discussing creation-care when creation was going to be annihilated in a cataclysmic fashion. The breakthrough came when Pentecostals asserted themselves in their pneumatological theology which set them apart from fundamentalists.[63] Ecotheological voices started emerging within Pentecostals and began to shape an eco-Pentecostal theology.

The essay has attempted to discuss creation-care using Pentecostal tenets of theology as a basis to show how ecotheology can emerge within the belief system of Pentecostals. The essay discussed creation-care using Osmer's theoretical framework to highlight the traditional, normative and pragmatic views of Pentecostal perspectives on ecotheology. This exercise highlighted what has been done so far, what is currently being done and what still needs to be done in bringing the contribution of Pentecostals on par with the rest of the ecumenical family.

Finally, a Pentecostal hermeneutical approach to scripture has been proposed as a model that Pentecostal churches can use to facilitate a conversation on ecotheology that can challenge Pentecostal churches to engage more actively in strengthening ecological principles in their ministry praxis.

Suggestions for Further Reading

Althouse, Peter. "In appreciation of Jürgen Moltmann: A Discussion of His Transformational Eschatology". *Pneuma: The Journal of the Society for Pentecostal Studies* 28(1), 2006.

Pinnock, Clark. *Flame of Love: A Theology of the Holy Spirit.* Downer's Grove, IL: IVP, 1996.

Studebaker, Steven. "The Spirit in Creation: A unified Theology of Grace and Creation Care". *Zygon* 43, 2008.

Suurmond, Jean-Jacques. "Christ King: A Charismatic appeal for an Ecological Lifestyle". *Pneuma: The Journal of the Society for Pentecostal Studies* 10, 1988.

Swoboda, Aaron. "Tongues and Trees: Toward a Pentecostal Ecological Theology". *Journal of Pentecostal Theology* Supplement 40, 2013.

Swoboda, Aaron, Ed. *Blood Cries Out: Pentecostals, Ecology, and Groans of Creation.* Eugene, OR: Pickwick, 2014.

Yong, Amos. *The Spirit Poured Out On All Flesh: Pentecostalism and the Possibility of Global Theology.* Grand Rapids, MI: Baker Academic, 2005.

Yong, Amos, Ed. *The Spirit Renews the Face of the Earth: Pentecostal Forays in Science and Theology of Creation.* Eugene, OR: Wipf and Stock, 2009.

[63] Clifton, "Preaching the Full Gospel", 118.

42. Theological Motivations behind Conservation of Church Forests in Ethiopia

Abate Gobena[1]

Introduction

Most community perceptions directly, or indirectly, rely on their respective religions, cultures and taboos. For most cultures, religion is one of the very important factors in defining what is conceived of as right or wrong. Religions, cultures and taboos can have a relationship, direct or indirect, with nature and affect the management of ecosystems.[2] Christianity forwards the conservation of natural biodiversity through the provision of ethical models in order to live with nature respectfully. The Ethiopian Orthodox "ተዋሕዶ *Tewahido*"[3] Church (EOTC), in this respect, has played a significant role in the religious, socio-cultural and politico-economical life of the people of Ethiopia. EOTC is an indigenised integral Christian Church of Ethiopia and one of the oldest Christian churches.[4] It is a founding member of the World Council of Churches (WCC) and All African Conference of Churches (AACC). It has played a great part in influencing and shaping Ethiopian culture. The Church, for centuries, was considered as the dominant framework through which Ethiopia could be understood.[5]

Forests have the richest biodiversity of all the terrestrial ecosystems and harbours up to 90% of the world's terrestrial biodiversity. They are also very important storehouses of genetic material for biodiversity conservation.[6] Loss of forest cover and its biodiversity is a growing global problem. Deforestation accounts for more than one-sixth of greenhouse gas emissions globally and this is particularly severe in Africa as forests are in decline across the continent.[7] Forest biodiversity is increasingly threatened due to

---

[1] Fr. Abate Gobena is a Lecturer at Sankt Ignatios College (Stockholm School of Theology), PhD Candidate at University College Stockholm, and serving priest of the Ethiopian Orthodox Tewahido Church in the UK and Sweden. He has a BTh from Holy Trinity Theology College (Addis Ababa, Ethiopia), where he has also taught; a BSc in Agro-Engineering & Mechanization (Hawassa University, Ethiopia); an MA in Sustainable Development (Middlesex University, UK); an MSc in Biodiversity Conservation (Gottingen University, Germany), and an MSc in Forest and Nature Management (Swedish University of Agriculture Sciences, Sweden); and previously worked as a Coordinator of Integrated Rural Development Projects (IRDPs) at EOC-DICAC in Ethiopia; Rural Policy Intern at campaign to Protect Rural England (CPRE) in London, UK.

[2] C.S. Negi, "Religion and Biodiversity Conservation: not a mere analogy", *International Journal of Biodiversity Science & Management* 1(2) (2005): 85-96.

[3] It is *Gi'iz* (Ethiopic), which literally means "united", used to denote the doctrinal stand of EOTC in line with the Oriental Orthodox Christology. There are several references in Gi'iz (Ethiopic) to better understand some terms crucial to this paper. The transliteration applied in this paper is based on the one used in *Acta Aethiopica* (see Rubenson, 1976: 413-414), which is preferred for the purpose of simplicity. Some popular words whose spelling has already been widely accepted, are used as they are.

[4] T. Tura, et al. "Holy Hills Role in Biodiversity Conservation and Mountain Management: Implication of Multi-Purpose Ethiopian Orthodox Tewahido Church in Sustainable Mountain Conservation". *Journal of Resources Development and Management* 28 (2017): 20-32.

[5] R. Pankhurst, *A Social History of Ethiopia*. (Addis Ababa: IES, AAU; ELM Publications, 1990); S. Ancel and E. Ficquet, *The Ethiopian Orthodox Tewahido Church and the Challenges of Modernity: Understanding Contemporary Ethiopia.* (London: Hurst, 2015): 63.

[6] E. Kelbessa and A. Girma, *Forest Types in Ethiopia: Status, Potential Contribution & Challenges* (Addis Ababa: Forum for Environment, 2011): 89.

[7] Jinzhuo Wu, Wenshu Lin, Xuanyi Peng, Weiguo Liu, "A Review of Forest Resources and Forest Biodiversity Evaluation System in China", *International Journal of Forestry Research* 209 (2013): 1-7; N. Adams, "Faith in Development: Buddhism and Forest Conservation in Southeast Asia". *World Faiths Development Dialogue*, 22nd

anthropogenic activities and this alarming loss is mainly caused by rapid population growth, which in turn results in extensive forest clearing for cultivation, exploitation of forests for fuelwood and construction materials without proper replanting.

Forests in Ethiopia – A Brief Historic Account

Ethiopia is a country of great geographical diversity. Altitudes range from the Afar Depression (130 metres below sea level) to the highest peak at Ras Dejen (4,620 metres above sea level). Biomes range from equatorial desert to hot and cool steppe, and from tropical woodlands and rainforest to warm temperate and cool highlands.[8] Because of this geographical diversity, Ethiopia's forest resources are diverse and the country is regarded as one of the most important countries in Africa in its floral and faunal resources.[9] There is no organised record regarding forest and vegetation in Ethiopia, except some indirect references in homilies of saints and the notes of some travellers and historians. Therefore, there is no reliable information on the extent and the location of the past, or indeed present, natural forest cover in Ethiopia.[10] In Ethiopia, several studies have been carried out to estimate forest cover and its change in different parts of the country; however, little is known about the types and the dynamics and also comparable information for the whole of Ethiopia is not available.[11]

The conditions observed by travellers like Francesco Alvarez,[12] James Bruce[13] and other visitors from the medieval to the early modern period, paired with current trends of forest utilisation, enable us to make a tentative reconstruction of the process of deforestation in the past.[14] Based on the travellers' accounts, hagiographic sources and the existing behaviour of people towards forests and vegetations vindicate that there is "no doubt that Ethiopia was densely wooded country in ancient and not so remote times."[15] About 40% of the land area was covered with high forests at the turn of the 19th century. However, this reduced to less than 3% in 2000, and over two million ha of forest were lost between 1990 and 2005, with an average annual loss of 140,000-200,000 ha.[16] Dry Evergreen Montane Forest originally occupied a large area in the northern, central highlands of Ethiopia,[17] but it has been considerably depleted and only remains on some isolated highlands and mountain chains, mostly in churchyards and monastery grounds.

April 2014. [Available at: https://berkleycenter.georgetown.edu/posts/buddhism-and-forest-conservation-in-southeast-asia], [Last accessed: 16th February 2022].

[8] E. Kelbessa and A. Girma, *Forest Types in Ethiopia: Status, Potential Contribution and Challenges*. (Addis Ababa: Forum for Environment, 2011): 5.

[9] A.A. Abunie and G. Dalle, "Woody Species Diversity Structure and Regeneration Status of Yemrehane Kirstos Church Forest of Lasta Woreda, North Wollo Zone, Amhara Region, Ethiopia", *International Journal of Forestry Research* 7 (2018): 1-8: 1.

[10] S. Chojnacki, "Forests and the Forestry Problem as Seen by Some Travellers in Ethiopia", *Journal of Ethiopian Studies* 1(1) (1963): 32-39.

[11] Negasi Solomon, Hadgu Hishe, Ted Annang, Opoku Pabi, Isaac K Asante and Emiru Birhane, "Forest Cover Change, Key Drivers and Community Perception in Wujig Mahgo Waren Forest of Northern Ethiopia", *Land* 7(1) (2018): 1-16; Chojnacki, "Forests and the Forestry Problem".

[12] G.W.B. Huntingford and C.F. Beckingham, *A True Relation of the Lands of the Prester John, being the narrative of the Portuguese Embassy to Ethiopia in 1520, written by Father Francisco Alvares* (London: Hakluyt Society, 1961).

[13] J. Ballantyne, *Travels to Discover the Source of the Nile, in the Years 1768-1773 By James Bruce of Kinnaird*, 2nd Ed. (Edinburgh: Ruthven, 1804).

[14] Chojnacki, *Forests and the Forestry Problem*.

[15] H. F. Mooney, *The Need for Forestry in Ethiopia*. (Addis Ababa: University Press, 1955): 15.

[16] M. Bekele, "Forest Plantations and Woodlots in Ethiopia: A Platform for Stakeholders in African Forestry", *African Forest Forum* 1(12) (2011): 1-56; B. Bishaw, "Deforestation and Land Degradation in the Ethiopian Highlands: A Strategy for Physical Recovery", *Ethiopian E-Journal For Research And Innovation Foresight* 1(1) (2009): 5-18.

[17] Kelbessa and Girma, *Forest Types in Ethiopia*.

Church Forests

Amidst successive waves of deforestation and depletion of forest biodiversity, however, unique and valuable natural forest remnants have survived in monastic territories and around churchyards of EOTC. While forests in most other areas have been completely destroyed and converted into farms and grazing lands over centuries, in the northern highlands of Ethiopia, patchy remnants of old-aged Afromontane forests are found almost only around the churches. Any visitor to rural Ethiopia often notices the patches of trees atop many of the hills, usually churches enveloped in a forest. "These wooded hilltops", as described by Allen-Rowlandson, "often in an otherwise treeless landscape, are mostly in Ethiopia's northern highlands, home of the Ethiopian Orthodox *Tewahido* Church."[18] EOTC has long history of planting, protecting and preserving trees.[19] The area covered by church forests varies dependant on the area of land owned by a parish or a monastery, and these may range from a minimum of a couple of hectares up to hundreds of hectares.

Figure 1: Aerial photo of a typical Ethiopian Orthodox Church surrounded by forests.

The primary purpose of churches and monasteries is to serve as places for prayer, worship and meditation, burials and eternal rest of bodies as well as centres for gatherings and festivals. Along with their primary purposes, the churches also provide valuable, often unique and secured habitats for plants and animals. The native forest and forest biodiversity in the central and northern highlands of Ethiopia are almost confined to the sacred groves associated with the Ethiopian Orthodox parish churches and monasteries.[20] For this reason, forests around churches are considered as the last remnant forest patches in

[18] T.Allen-Rowlandson, "The Forestry Example of the Ethiopian Church", *National Religious Coalition on Creation Care* (2003) [Available at: http://nrccc.org/PDF/The-Forestry-Example-of-the-Ethiopian-Church.pdf], [Last accessed: 16th February 2022].

[19] T. Tura, T. Soromess, M. Argaw and S. Leta. "Holy Hills Role in Biodiversity Conservation and Mountain Management: Implication of Multi-Purpose Ethiopian Orthodox Tewahido Church in Sustainable Mountain Conservation", *Journal of Biodiversity and Environmental Sciences* 5 (1), 179, 2017.

[20] R. Aerts et al. "Conservation Of The Ethiopian Church Forests: Threats, Opportunities And Implications For Their Management", *The Science of the Total Environment*, 551-552 (2016): 404-414.

this part of the country.[21] Church buildings and their compounds are considered to be sacred places used exclusively for sacramental prayers. Forests and their biodiversity found in churches and monasteries survived from degradation for the reason they are parts of these sacred grounds and as they share the sacredness of the church.[22] This allowed many endangered forest and other species to survive in areas where their habitat has otherwise been lost.[23]

Motives Behind Conservation of Church Forests

Ethiopian Orthodox tradition relied on the authority of biblical, patristic, liturgical and hagiographic sources as the basis of instructions for the faithful in their life of worship in the church as well as their social interaction elsewhere. In this respect, the main reason for the survival and continued conservation of church forests is achieved as a result of the teaching and instructions of the church, derived from scriptural sources and practices directly or indirectly dictated by the "ቅዱሳት መጻሕፍት *qiddusat meṣahift*" (sacred scriptures).

Biblical Motivations

The Holy Bible is the core for Christian teaching. The faith and order of EOTC, as for other Christian churches, stemmed from the Holy Bible, the Old and New Testament books and their interpretations. All the written and oral traditions and practices in EOTC anticipate their origins back in the phrases of the books of the Bible and their exegetic meanings. Teachings and practices of the Church, directly or indirectly, are sourced from, backed by, or related to the Holy Bible. The Bible states that entire world is God's creation and the purpose of creation is to proclaim God's glory.[24] He can be seen in the forests of the mountains, the waters of rivers and lakes, wild lives of the forests, fishes and whales of the sea, etc. The Holy Bible also tells us that God reveals Himself through creation saying: "For since the creation of the world His invisible attributes are clearly seen, being understood by the things that are made, even His eternal power and Godhead, so that they are without excuse".[25] God not only reveals Himself through nature but also speaks through creation. The message from the mouth of a donkey, in human words, is God's speech to Balaam.[26] The Whale was obedient and carried Jonah for three days and three nights and transported him to the port of Nineveh[27] and this was God's speech to His people. The plagues sent on Pharaoh when he refused to let the Israelites go were God's speech via His creations. Water turning to blood, frogs, lice, flies, livestock pestilence, boils, hail, locusts and darkness were God's message to Pharaoh to free the Israelites.[28] Based on such biblical accounts and their exegeses, the EOTC teaches that God speaks through the creation. This link between the Creator and the creation, through which He reveals Himself, can be regarded as a basis for the eco-ethical theories and practices in the church.

---

[21] A. Wassie, "Opportunities, Constraints and Prospects of the Ethiopian Orthodox Tewahido Churches in Conserving Forest Resources: The Case of Churches in South Gonder, Northern Ethiopia". MSc Thesis. SLU (2004).; A. Wassie and M. Lowman, "Saving Ethiopian Church Forests and their Biodiversity: Report of Tree Foundation Project" *Tree Foundation* (February 2014). [Available at: http://treefoundation.org/2014/03/14/overview-church-forest-project-in-ethiopia/], [Last accessed: 16th February 2022].

[22] It is worth noting here that, even though this expression of sacred spaces is consistent with sacred forests in other contexts; this does not mean that the EOTC faithful consider individual trees sacred.

[23] V. Votrin, "The Orthodoxy and Sustainable Development a Potential for Broader Involvement of the Orthodox Churches in Ethiopia and Russia", *Environment, Development and Sustainability* 7(1) (2005): 9-21.

[24] Psalms 19:1; H. Rolston, "The Bible and Ecology" *Journal of Bible and Theology* 50 (1996): 6-26.

[25] Romans 1:20.

[26] Numbers 22:23.

[27] Jonah 1:17.

[28] Exodus 7:14 to 11:10.

Liturgical Motivation

EOTC is one of the sacramental churches that have ancient rites where "the ancient liturgical traditions can be traced".[29] Liturgy is the most celebrated of all services of the church, which is conducted every day all year in almost all the parishes and monasteries. The Ethiopian Orthodox liturgy is composed in a way that it can be read, recited and/or sang by the clergy and the laity alternatively.

PEW Research Centre, in its survey on the Orthodox populations, indicates that 98% of the interviewees respond that religion is important to them. In addition to this, nearly 80% of the population go to church weekly to attend services,[30] mainly liturgical or Eucharistic service. Such a service, attended by the vast majority of the faithful, with a participatory nature and frequent celebration, creates a great opportunity of acquainting many people with the contents of the texts and the internalisation of them by participants. This will considerably impact guidance and the shaping of behaviours and practices. The life and character of an Orthodox Christian is in large measure shaped, nourished, and enriched by the liturgy or worship in the Church. In the liturgy, the Orthodox Christian is in constant touch with the fundamental truths of the faith.[31] It is suggested that a common worship life, as experienced in liturgical or Eucharistic service, has the potential to shape and inform the participant's ethical thinking.

Liturgical materials of the church encompass the ecological dimension and vision. One of the main themes of the liturgical book is the relationship of God, the Creator, with His creatures (humans, animals and plants) and their environment. An extract from the preparatory section of an Ethiopian Orthodox Liturgy, for instance, recited by the priest as: "remember, O Lord, the plants and the seeds and the fruits of every year, to bless them and make them abundant."[32] This prayer is followed by an affirmative reply of the deacons and the people saying: "amen! *kyrie eleison*" which means "O Lord have Mercy upon us". Likewise, the deacon implores "for the fruits of the earth we beseech, that God may grant the earth her fruits for sowing and for harvest"[33] is also replied with similar affirmative phrase by the people as "amen! *kyrie eleison*".

The EOTC's liturgy comprises an official compilation of 14 and 7 unofficial anaphora. In the Anaphora of St Basil the Great, for example, there is a set of prayers allocated to be recited by the deacon, the Laity and the priest respectively. Let's read the three sets:

> **Deacon:** "Pray for the rain, the wind of the sky, the fruit of the earth, seed, plants, the fruit of the trees and also the vineyards, and for every fruitful tree in the entire world, that Christ our God will bring them into perfection in safety and peace and forgive us our sins."
>
> **Laity:** "O Lord have Mercy upon us, O Lord spare us, O Lord have mercy upon us."
>
> **Priest:** "[…] give graciously, rain and suitable weather and the fruit of the earth and bless the trees/herbs"; "Bring them up according to their measure that they may grow and prosper through your grace. You make the face of the earth to rejoice, water her furrows, let her grain be abundantly multiplied and make ready her seed-time and harvest".[34]

---

[29] S. Hable-Sellassie and T. Tamrat, *The Church of Ethiopia: A Panorama of History & Spiritual Life*. (Addis Ababa: Ethiopian Orthodox Church, 1970).

[30] J. Diamant, "Ethiopia: An outlier in the Orthodox Christian world", *Pew Research Center* (28th November 2017). [Available at: https://www.pewresearch.org/fact-tank/2017/11/28/ethiopia-is-an-outlier-in-the-orthodox-christian-world/], [Last accessed: 16th February 2022].

[31] A.C. Calivas, "The Sacramental Life of the Orthodox Church", *Greek Orthodox Archdiocese of America* (3rd September 1998). [Available at: https://www.goarch.org/-/the-sacramental-life-of-the-orthodox-church], [Last accessed: 16th February 2022].

[32] EOTC, *The Liturgy of the Ethiopian Orthodox Tewahedo Church* (Addis Ababa: TPH, 2010): 82-3.

[33] EOTC, *The Liturgy,* 56-7

[34] EOTC, *The Liturgy,* 270.

Christians who partake in these liturgical prayers will recognise that it is the will of God for the natural biodiversity to grow, prosper and abundantly multiply. Furthermore, the above prayers, in turn, impart sense of duty on the faithful, who frequently partake in these services, to care for the environment and avow for themselves and commit to live responsibly within the environment as stewards of God's creation. When the laity respond, "O Lord Mercy up on us", it implies that the sins they repent for and seek forgiveness also include "ecological sin".

Ascetic and Hagiographic Motivation

To help us understand the contribution of ascetic motivation, it is worthy to consider the Ethiopic concept of monastery and monastic. Monastery, in Gi'iz language is termed as "*ገዳም gadam*", which is literally defined as forest, desert or wilderness.[35] After monasticism achieved great prominence in the church, the term was used as the name for a "convent of monks and nuns or important centre of prayers and ascetic dedication". In almost all of the monastic literature or hagiographic sources, ascetics are praised as saints and their places of devotion (monasteries) depicted as centres of sanctity. Likewise monastic life is also regarded as the way of holiness. Ascetic figures are frequently described with suffices "*ገዳማዊ gedamawi*" (the Monastic) and admired with phrases: "*ኮከበ ገዳም kokebe gedam*" (star of the forest/of the monastery), "*ማኅቶተ ገዳም mahitote gedam*" (light of the forest/of the monastery).[36]

In the Ethiopian Orthodox tradition, monastic wilderness is considered to be living far from settlements of people in order to unbound oneself from social bondage, which will potentially be source of temptations and distractions. Ascetics, therefore, detach themselves from the external world and dwell in the monastic wilderness in an attempt to enhance their relations with God and avoid the distraction from the world. The notion of monastic wilderness, through detachment from and resentment to the world, is captured in its Ethiopic expression as "*ዓለም በቃኝ alem beqqagn*" (I have had enough of the world, I have withdrawn)[37] used by those who choose to become ascetics, monks or nuns. The hermits, monks and nuns who chose such a life and decide to lead solitary life in the monastery are named "*መናኝ mennagn*" (who left the world). Since the ascetics live with great abstinence in terms of fasting and leading a very simple life, they are characterised by the acts of self-denial and are termed as "*ጸዋሚ ṣewami*" (one who fasts), "*ተኀራሚ teharami*" (who abstains), "*ባኅታዊ bahitawi*" (who lives in solitude), and "*ዝጉኀዊ ziguhawi*" (who enclosed himself from the external world). Contrary to the over-exploitation of the ordinary community who compete for resources in cutting trees, hunting wild lives for food, shelter and surplus of wealth, for ascetics the utilisation of natural resources in their surroundings is insignificant and cause no harm to biodiversity. For this very reason, monasticism is praised for its eco-friendly way of life.

Monastic fathers devote themselves not only to the care for human beings but also to all creatures including animals and plants. Ascetic holiness, therefore, has a positive relationship to the care and preservation of natural biodiversity. The exemplary life of ascetics and other saints is recorded in hagiographies[38] and remained as reference for others to imitate the saints' life of abstinence and peaceful co-habitation with all creatures, which in turn, will help biodiversity conservation. Hagiography of St Gebre Menfes Qiddus, for instance, states that the Saint "lived with lions and leopards; they bowed for him, slept

[35] K. Kifle, *Meshafe Sewasiw Wegiss Wemezgebe Qalat Haddis*. (Addis Ababa: Artistic Printers, 1948): 302.

[37] G. Haile, *Voices from Dabra Zamaddo: Acts of Abba Bartalomewos and Abba Yohannes.* 45 Miracles of Mary. Aethiopistische Forschungen 79. (Wiesbaden: Harrassowitz Verlag, 2013).

[37] I. Orlowska and P. Klepeis, "Ethiopian Church Forests: A Socio-Religious Conservation Model under Change", *Journal of Eastern African Studies* 12(4) (2018): 674-695.

[38] Hagiography is one of the most important genres of the Ethiopian Christian literature, which includes "*ገድለ ሰማዕታት gedle sema'itat*" (acts of martyrs) and "*ድርሳነ ጻድቃን dirsane ṣadqan*" (homily of saints). The complex corpus of Ethiopian hagiographical texts can be grouped in to two broad categories: translations and original compositions. Translations are from Greek, Syriac and Arabic languages and the original works are compiled by Ethiopian authors. (For more details, please see: S. Hummel, *Ethiopian Hagiography – A Particular Case of the Rewriting of a Holy Monk's Life*. (Hamburg: Hiob Ludolf Centre for Ethiopian and Eritrean Studies, 2016): 2.)

under his feet, obeyed his words".[39] Another hagiography, Acts of St Bertelomewos of Zemedo, states that "he embraced leopard with his arms".[40] In addition, many ascetic saints such as St. Samuel of Waldiba, St. Binyam of Begemidr and St. Anbes of Hazelo have lions each to aid them to travel.

The hagiographies describe not only the saints' care and harmonious cohabitation with wild animals, but also their role of taming them for inter-species peaceful cohabitation. The Acts of St. Hara Dingil, for instance, states that the Saint saved a certain hare from a leopard who chased her to prey upon. This hagiography describes that the leopard obeyed the Saint's word – "God didn't allow you to kill and eat her"[41] – and never attacked her again. There is another hagiographic inspiration, which states that the ascetic saints enhanced a peaceful human-animal relationship in the surrounding community out of their monastic wilderness. The Acts of St. Yosef of Lasta, for instance, states that the Saint reconciled local farmers with a flock of monkeys in the area.

Figures 2-5: (Clockwise from top left): Icons of St Gebre Menfes Qiddus with his 60 lions and 60 leopards; St Yosef of Lasta reconciling a farming community with monkey herds, St. Samuel of Waldiba using lions for travel; St Bertelomewos of Zemeda cuddling a leopard in his arms.

In EOTC, there is a tradition of reading such hagiographic texts during the pre-liturgical services, whenever there are Eucharistic services. Additionally, it is also prayed mostly on Sundays, the saints' monthly and annual feast days in monasteries, and read on the pulpit before and after every liturgical (eucharistic) service. In the processional celebration and reading, parishioners or pilgrims congregate

[39] EOTC *Gedle Gebre Mensfes Qiddus: Gi'iz 'na Amarigna* (Addis Ababa: TPH, 1999/2000):8.
[40] Haile, *Voices from Dabra Zamaddo*, 18, 142.
[41] EOTC, *Gedle Abune Hara Dingil: Be Gi'iz 'na Be'Amarigna.* (Addis Ababa: Birana, 2009/2010): 63-64.

around the pulpit to listen attentively and receive their blessing. For example, the Act of St Gebre Menfes Qiddus starts with an order that "all the priests, deacons and the people (men and women, elderly and children) listen to this book of great importance, book of life and salvation", and continues to order them and let them take part (share) the blessings of the Saint".[42] Icons of saints have a special place in the church. They are not simple pictures but are the focus of meditation during prayers and worship. So hagiographic readings and iconic displays create motivation and inspiration in shaping the behaviours of the faithful in their treatment of church forests.

Conclusion

An Ethiopian Orthodox parish church or monastery usually appears to be enveloped in forests. These church forests are considered to be extensions of the church and the church's sacredness is believed to be extended to its yards and compounds. The entire church ground with its sacred topography consisting of the space immediately surrounding the main church building as far as the boundary of the church compound. The church forest is also considered to be there to respectfully cover and shelter the church. There is a famous Ethiopian expression saying: "*ጽሕም የሌለው መምህር፣ ዐጸድ የሌለው ደብር ሳይከበር ይኖራል*" literally translated as, "a church without forest and a priest without beard will not receive the due regard". For this reason, church forests are strongly linked with the honour and respect of the church, and this extends to mean that the respect to a church is related to the density of the forest in which it is enveloped.

People take inspiration from sacred scriptures, the Holy Bible or hagiographies, which then continuously influence the human-nature relationship, more specifically to the reverence given to church forests and the preservation of them from deforestation. Church grounds are tranquil places of worship, sanctuaries of saints and eternal rest places for bodies, and forests add extra worth. This sense of respect is derived from the theological justifications deduced from biblical, hagiographic and liturgical sources. The teachings and practices of saints are regarded as a guideline in the life of subsequent monastic communities as they are directly inherited as spiritual treasures. The lives of saints, therefore, has impact on the contemporary practical orientation through the hagiographic readings and iconic representations in the church.

In summary, we can say that the Ethiopian Orthodox theology and activities based on these theological instructions become basis for the eco-ethical thoughts and practices to spare the natural biodiversity in and around churches and monasteries from depletion, and keep them intact from ancient times until the present day.

Suggestions for Further Reading

Abunie, A.A. and G. Dalle. "Woody Species Diversity Structure and Regeneration Status of Yemrehane Kirstos Church Forest of Lasta Woreda, North Wollo Zone, Amhara Region, Ethiopia". *International Journal of Forestry Research* 7 (2018): 1-8.

Adams, N. "Faith in Development: Buddhism and Forest Conservation in Southeast Asia". *World Faiths Development Dialogue*, 22nd April 2014. [Available at: https://berkleycenter.georgetown.edu/posts/buddhism-and-forest-conservation-in-southeast-asia], [Last accessed: 16th February 2022].

Aerts, R. *et al*. "Conservation of the Ethiopian Church Forests: Threats, Opportunities and Implications for their Management". *The Science of the Total Environment* 551-552 (2016): 404-414.

Allen-Rowlandson, T. "The Forestry Example of the Ethiopian Church", *National Religious Coalition on Creation Care* (2003) [Available at: http://nrccc.org/PDF/The-Forestry-Example-of-the-Ethiopian-Church.pdf], [Last accessed: 16th February 2022].

Ancel, S. and E. Ficquet. *The Ethiopian Orthodox Tewahido Church and the Challenges of Modernity: Understanding Contemporary Ethiopia.* London: Hurst, 2015.

[42] EOTC, *Gedle Gebre Menfes Qiddus: Gi'iz 'na Amarigna.* (Addis Ababa: TPH, 1999/2000): 8.

Bekele, M. "Forest Plantations and Woodlots in Ethiopia: A Platform for Stakeholders in African Forestry". *African Forest Forum* 1(12) (2011): 1-56.

Bishaw, B. "Deforestation and Land Degradation in the Ethiopian Highlands: A Strategy for Physical Recovery". *Ethiopian E-Journal For Research And Innovation Foresight* 1(1) (2009): 5-18.

Calivas, A.C. "The Sacramental Life of the Orthodox Church". *Greek Orthodox Archdiocese of America* 3rd September 1998. [Available at: https://www.goarch.org/-/the-sacramental-life-of-the-orthodox-church], [Last accessed: 16th February 2022].

Chojnacki, S. "Forests and the Forestry Problem as Seen by Some Travellers in Ethiopia". *Journal of Ethiopian Studies* 1(1) (1963): 32-39.

Diamant, J. "Ethiopia: An outlier in the Orthodox Christian world". *Pew Research Center* 28th November 2017. [Available at: https://www.pewresearch.org/fact-tank/2017/11/28/ethiopia-is-an-outlier-in-the-orthodox-christian-world/], [Last accessed: 16th February 2022].

EOTC. *The Liturgy of the Ethiopian Orthodox Tewahedo Church.* Addis Ababa: TPH, 2010.

EOTC. *Gedle Abune Hara Dingil: Be Gi'iz 'na Be'Amarigna.* Addis Ababa: Birana, 2009/2010.

EOTC. *Gedle Gebre Mensfes Qiddus: Gi'iz 'na Amarigna.* Addis Ababa: TPH, 1999/2000.

Hable-Sellassie, S. and T. Tamrat. *The Church of Ethiopia: A Panorama of History & Spiritual Life.* Addis Ababa: Ethiopian Orthodox Church, 1970.

Haile, G. *Voices from Dabra Zamaddo: Acts of Abba Bartalomewos and Abba Yohannes.* 45 Miracles of Mary. Aethiopistische Forschungen 79. Wiesbaden: Harrassowitz Verlag, 2013.

Hummel, S. *Ethiopian Hagiography: A Particular Case of the Rewriting of a Holy Monk's Life*. Hamburg: Hiob Ludolf Centre for Ethiopian Studies, 2016.

Kaplan, S. "Hagiographies & the History of Medieval Ethiopia". *History in Africa* 8 (1981): 107-123.

Kelbessa, E. and A. Girma. *Forest Types in Ethiopia: Status, Potential Contribution and Challenges.* Addis Ababa: Forum for Environment, 2011.

Negi, C.S. "Religion and biodiversity conservation: not a mere analogy". *The International Journal of Biodiversity Science and Management* 1(2) (2005): 85-96.

Orlowska, I. and P. Klepeis. "Ethiopian Church Forests: A Socio-Religious Conservation Model under Change". *Journal of Eastern African Studies* 12(4) (2018): 674-695.

Pankhurst, R. *A Social History of Ethiopia*. Addis Ababa: ELM, 1990.

Reynolds, T. W. "Changes in community perspectives on the roles and rules of church forests in northern Ethiopia: evidence from a panel survey of four Ethiopian Orthodox communities". *International Journal of Climatology* 11(1) (2017): 355-387.

Rolston, H. "The Bible and Ecology". *Journal of Bible and Theology* 50 (1996): 6-26.

Solomon, Negasi, Hadgu Hishe, Ted Annang, Opoku Pabi, Isaac K Asante and Emiru Birhane. "Forest Cover Change, Key Drivers and Community Perception in Wujig Mahgo Waren Forest of Northern Ethiopia", *Land* 7(1) (2018): 1-16.

Tura, T., T. Soromess, M. Argaw and S. Leta. "Holy Hills Role in Biodiversity Conservation and Mountain Management: Implication of Multi-Purpose Ethiopian Orthodox Tewahido Church in Sustainable Mountain Conservation". *Journal of Biodiversity and Environmental Sciences* 5 (1), 179 (2017): 28-32.

Votrin, V. "The Orthodoxy and Sustainable Development a Potential for Broader Involvement of the Orthodox Churches in Ethiopia and Russia". *Environment, Development and Sustainability* 7(1) (2005): 9-21.

Wassie, A. "Opportunities, Constraints and Prospects of the Ethiopian Orthodox Tewahido Churches in Conserving Forest Resources: The Case of Churches in South Gonder, Northern Ethiopia". MSc Thesis. SLU (2004).

Wassie, A., and M. Lowman, "Saving Ethiopian Church Forests and their Biodiversity: Report of Tree Foundation Project". *Tree Foundation* February 2014. [Available at: http://treefoundation.org/2014/03/14/overview-church-forest-project-in-ethiopia/], [Last accessed: 16th February 2022].

Wu, Jinzhuo, Wenshu Lin, Xuanyi Peng, Weiguo Liu. "A Review of Forest Resources and Forest Biodiversity Evaluation System in China". *International Journal of Forestry Research* 209 (2013): 1-7.

43. The House of God: The Orthodox Church in the Middle East and the Environment

Bassam A. Nassif[1]

> Bless the Lord, O my soul! O Lord my God, You are very great [...] You are clothed with honour and majesty [...] You covered it with the deep as with a garment [...] The waters stood above the mountains [...] By them the birds of the heavens have their home [...] The trees of the Lord are full of sap, The cedars of Lebanon which He planted [...]" (NKJV, Psalm 104:1-16).

Introduction

The semantics of this psalm reveal the deep connection that the human beings living on Planet Earth have with their *oikos*. Anyone reading this Psalm would imagine the Prophet David standing beside the Forest of the Cedars of God in North Lebanon, overlooking the Holy Valley, which in Aramaic is called "Qadisha". The cedars of Lebanon are mentioned 103 times in the Scriptures. The semantics of this psalm reveal a deep connection between God, humanity, and the Earth. Walking down the valley of Qadisha, one can easily discover not just the wildlife, but remnants of holy lives found in dozens of natural caves which were inhabited by persecuted Christians. These caves became places of refuge and temples of divine worship. These natural temples are adorned with the aromatic gardens home to rich biodiversity on both sides of the overflowing Qadisha River. Walking behind the mountains of Lebanon, as the sun rises, one can smell the incense rising from wild roses, and hear the symphonic band of hundreds of bird species, forming together a mystical natural song of praise offered to the Creator. The earth is indeed the house of God (Psalm 24:1).

In the twentieth century, the Middle Eastern countries became a site of political, ethnic, and religious wars, ravaging not only human beings but also the natural habitat. Wars bring with them all kinds of deadly sins, attacking the organic unity between God, humans, and the environment. They are not just crimes committed against humanity, exterminating human life with lethal weapons, but also against ecology, destroying the environment with air, land, and sea pollution. Being one of the largest legal owners of land in the Middle East, the Orthodox Church carries Her stewardship mission, since she believes that this work maintains peace in the *oikos* between human beings and the rest of God's creation. Although her work is unknown to many, the Church continues to faithfully carry her mission, by word and deed. The property under Her care became reserves to protect biodiversity in Lebanon and Syria. This article surveys the environmental advocacy taken by the hierarchs, theologians, organisations, and parishes of the Orthodox Church in order to preserve the Church's large lands of forests and other natural habitats and remain faithful to Church's mission of stewardship and expand Her engagement in environmental advocacy and ecological sustainability.

Theological Advocacy

Facing various wars and destruction, hierarchs and clergy have acknowledged the urgency of the situation and called for immediate action. Their words are based on a rich legacy of the Orthodox Church's theological thought about creation and ecology. The late Patriarch of Antioch and All the East, Ignatius IV

[1] Fr. Bassam Nassif is the Associate Professor of Pastoral Theology and Marriage Counselling at the Saint John of Damascus Institute of Theology, University of Balamand in Tripoli, Lebanon. His research addressing contemporary pastoral challenges facing the Orthodox Church is concerned with embracing the modern human sciences within pastoral theology and patristic anthropology, leading to the formation of a therapeutic and holistic pastoral care approach.

of Thrice Blessed Memory (1920-2012), was a pioneer in steering the attention of the Church to be concerned with the environmental crisis. In March 1989, Patriarch Ignatius IV issued a warning to the international community about the ecological crisis. In an exceptional address made in Lausanne, Switzerland, in response to an invitation from the Conference of Catholic Bishops of Switzerland and the Federation of Swiss Protestant Churches, Ignatius IV called all humanity to unite in a common effort not just to save the earth but to enliven it. He clearly and emphatically stated that the world is experiencing an ecological crisis because of an initial spiritual crisis in humanity. He affirmed that a renewed personal relationship with God and His creation is the only way to solve this environmental crisis. He called humanity to conversion and repentance, saying: "Nothing will happen unless our personal and liturgical prayer, our sacramental life, our asceticism regain their cosmic dimension."[2]

Being personally well-informed in the writings of Eastern saints such as Ephrem and Isaac the Syrians, John the Damascene, and Maximus the Confessor, Ignatius IV gave a précis of their writings on Creation. He emphasised that humanity has been entrusted with the riches of the earth and given a key role of reconciliation. For Ignatius IV, the transfiguration of nature begins with the transfiguration of the human being. Therefore, if sin led to the disfiguration of man, holiness leads to the transfiguration of man, for "If any man is in Christ, he is a new creation" (2 Cor. 5:17).

One of the most prolific writers and theologians of the Church, Archimandrite Thomas Bitar, the Abbot of St. Silouan Monastery in North Lebanon, has made several contributions to the issue of ecology and the theology of the environment. Since the monastery has large pieces of land, the Abbot worked on sustainable agricultural development of the monastery's lands, yielding increased agricultural productivity. For him, if humans love the earth with the love of God, earth will treat them as its own masters, and they need not impose themselves on it. He explains that if man walks in the Word of God, grace is bestowed upon him, making him master of the earth. Otherwise, if the human being is not obedient to God, grace leaves them and the curse is unleashed. Hence, humanity's behaviour towards the earth and nature is strongly influenced by their relationship with God.

As grace wanes, the earth becomes cursed because of human sin (Gen. 3:17). However, the earth regains its glory through humanity's communion with God (Lev. 26:3). Fr. Thomas' conclusion is spiritual. He declared: "Nature cannot be healed anymore with tools invented by humans imprisoned by human passions. Nature cannot be healed unless humanity is first healed."[3]

Thus, the theological view on the present crisis defines it as a spiritual crisis in humanity. Sin is the ultimate polluter of the world. The exploitative mentality of human selfishness and self-gain is a sin that leads all creation to dust and ashes. On the other hand, living in Christian holiness leads all people to a renewed relationship with God and His creation, thus solving this environmental cosmic crisis.

Church-Wide Pastoral Directives

The current Patriarch of Antioch and All the East, John X, continues to think theologically and practically on the various ecological concerns and is developing plans for environmental sustainability. The Patriarch issued a pastoral letter upon his enthronement, 17th February 2013, in which he addressed the Church's commitment to participate in endeavours towards solving the ecological crisis and encouraged establishing new policies that formulate an ethics of sustainable development in society. He said:

---

[2] Patriarch Ignatius IV of Antioch, "Three Sermons: A Theology of Creation; A Spirituality of the Creation; The Responsibility of Christians", *The Orthodox Fellowship of the Transfiguration* 12th March 1989. [Available at: http://www.orth-transfiguration.org/], [Last accessed: 17th February 2022].

[3] Archimandrite Thomas Bitar, "The Earth and Us", *Holy Trinity Family* 27th July 2014. [Available at: http://www.holytrinityfamily.org/], [Last accessed: 17th February 2022]. [Arabic].

> We have already developed, in our Antiochian Church, a long-term plan concerning the preservation of the environment. We will try to put these environmental projects into practice. We shall also try to widen participation in these local and global initiatives, for the whole creation is called to praise God.[4]

On 10th October 2019, the Holy Synod of Antioch, presided over by Patriarch John X in Balamand Monastery called for the clergy to preach about the sacredness of God's creation and to hold educational sessions in parochial schools, youth organisations, diocesan high schools, and the University of Balamand. It also issued the following statement about ecological concerns and the deteriorating environmental crisis:

> The Holy Synod calls for courageous living options that respect the environment and reduce the greed of consumption that dominate nature for quick and easy profit. The Synod also asks the governments to enforce policies that guarantee the prospects for future life and contribute to protecting the access by future generations to the goods of the earth.[5]

Liturgical Initiatives

After the recommendations of the pan-Orthodox conference on the environment (Academy of Crete, 5th-11th November, 1991), 1st September has been, in Antioch, a day of prayer for the preservation of the environment. In 1999, Metropolitan Ephrem of Tripoli and Koura,[6] composed the following troparion as a supplicatory prayer for God's mercy on creation:

> You who have created all things out of nothing, save your creation which became corrupt, and grant your creature made out of the dust of the ground tears of repentance to water the dry land, for you have promised your beloved ones a new earth and a new heaven, and many eternal blessings.[7]

This prayer resonates with the prophetic words of Isaiah speaking about the eschatological expectations related to nature (Is. 65:17-25).

Metropolitan George Khodre, the former Archbishop of Byblos and Botrys (Mount Lebanon), was a pioneer in establishing a fixed liturgical rite for the day of creation. He published on recycled paper a booklet containing a liturgical service of supplication for the preservation of God's creation to be prayed on the first of September every year. This liturgical text asks God for help, to grant a favourable climate, an abundance of the fruits of the earth as food, and peaceful times.[8] This booklet of supplications along with a paper icon of Christ blessing creation was freely distributed to every household in the parish. Khodre wanted to expand the petition of the *Great Ektenia* found in almost all liturgical services, "For healthful season, for abundance of the fruit [...]", so that it would include a reminder of the role of Christians in protecting the environment.

Social and Political Advocacy

Since Beirut is the capital of Lebanon and home to governmental institutions and political leaders, the Archdiocese of Beirut plays an important role in Lebanese advocacy, especially in educating about the need

[4] Patriarch John X of Antioch and All the East, *Pastoral Letter* (Damascus, Syria: The Greek Orthodox Patriarchate of Antioch and All the East Publications, 2013): 12-13.
[5] Holy Synod of Antioch, "Synodal Statement." 10th October 2019, *Antioch Patriarchate* [Available at: https://www.antiochpatriarchate.org/en/page/statement-issued-by-the-holy-synod-of-antioch-balamand-october-10-2019/2279/], [Last accessed: 10th November 2020].
[6] At that time, he was Archimandrite and Abbot of the Archangel Michael Monastery in the town of Baskinta, Mount Lebanon.
[7] Archimandrite Ephrem Kyriakos, "Troparion of the Environment", *Annour Magazine* 5(56) (2000): 258. [Arabic].
[8] For the publications of George Khodre see: http://georgeskhodr.org/en/category/articles/

to preserve the environment. On 4th September 2019, in his keynote address at the inauguration of a new garden in the city of Beirut, the Archbishop of Beirut said:

> The human being, although created in the image of God, has forgotten that love is the way to exercise control, so he became oppressively dominant over nature without love [...] Greed has darkened human hearts, and made the site of high rise building a source of admiration [...] We need these green pastures for our psychological and physical well-being. Furthermore, there is a great need for us to inaugurate libraries for the purpose of educating our people to free themselves from the pollution of technology. In this way, we offer back creation to God as He intended it to be, that is in His image and likeness.[9]

In another homily given on 1st January 2010, the Metropolitan of Beirut spoke about the sacredness of the environment and its preservation. He asked each family to make a new year's resolution to care for the plants on their balconies, and to be careful about wasting water and power. He called for an end to the killing of birds, the cutting of trees, and the incineration of garbage. Each Orthodox Christian, he said, ought to be a friend of the environment, using renewable energy sources, such as the wind, water, and the sun to generate power as alternatives to the polluting power-plants. In a country that does not respect its citizens, Audé called for people to be educated to respect nature because, in this way, each human being will be educated to respect each other's freedom and human rights.[10]

On 4th August 2020, the disastrous explosion occurring at the Beirut seaport made the situation even worse. The particles emitted during the blast were contaminants and affected public health. All these factors have exacerbated mental health issues in the Lebanese population and especially among the Orthodox Christians living in this country. Metropolitan Elias Audé decried the situation in his address to the graduates of the four high schools run by the Archdiocese of Beirut. He described the environmental peril in Lebanon as a kind of a holocaust, a war waged to exterminate human beings, as follows: "Our environment today is perishing because of the human selfish mentality [...] Germs increased to the point that human health deteriorated [...] The mental and physical health of our children is in dire danger."[11]

Parochial Initiatives

Metropolitan George Khodre encouraged priests to develop environmentally friendly parishes through recycling projects and various environmental activities organised by the faithful, such as planting trees, flowers, and cultivating gardens around the churches. In this way, the parish a model to be imitated in the houses of the faithful. In Metropolitan's view, God is present in the universe through various ethical, artistic, and scientific discoveries. Christians, therefore, should not exclude scientific solutions to the global challenges facing humanity. He called Christians to break into and overcome the world and share in its historical transformation. He affirms that the world is transformed by holiness, but this holiness should not be limited to one's individual life. It ought to be actualised in the transformation of the world. This is achieved through exchange or participation. This participation needs to be in a spirit of self-effacement, humility, and love. In other words, he called upon all to listen well to the voice of science especially in terms of the scientific solutions to ecological problems, and to participate in all initiatives, endeavours, and activities proposed by governmental agencies and non-governmental organisations to increase awareness

---

[9] Metropolitan Elias Audé of Beirut, "Opening of Metropolitan Elias Audé Garden in Beirut", 4th September 2019. *Lebanon 24* [Available at: https://www.lebanon24.com/news/wedding-events/575365/lebanon24-article], [Last accessed: 14th December 2020]. [Arabic].

[10] Metropolitan Elias Audé of Beirut, "Homily on the New Year", 1st January 2010. [Available at: http://afedmag.com/web/ala3dadAlSabiaSections-details.aspx?id=405&issue=&type=4&cat=], [Last accessed: 14th December 2020]. [Arabic].

[11] Metropolitan Elias Audé of Beirut, "We are Living in the Most Polluted Countries", 2nd July 2019. *El Nashra* [Available at: https://www.elnashra.com/news/show/1327103], [Last accessed: 15th December 2020]. [Arabic].

of ecological concerns, the need for the preservation of the environment, and how to act in environmentally sustainable ways.[12]

As part of the sustainable development initiatives in Mount Lebanon, Khodre encouraged the Youth movement (MJO) of Mount Lebanon to establish a project entitled "Recycle for Education" in which schoolbooks are recycled, and through this recycling, school tuition fees for needy students are paid. Parishioners were invited to bring their schoolbooks to each prayer service and drop them in a recycling box set up at the doors of churches.[13]

In addition, Metropolitan Elias Audé of Beirut has established policies to promote environmental awareness and raise ecological consciousness in the Archdiocesan educational and medical institutions, not only in the religious education classes and the curricula of school courses, but also in St. George's University Medical Hospital.

Sustainable Development Programmes in Syria

As part of its efforts to be an active participant in initiatives to preserve the environment, in 2014, the Patriarchate of Antioch, in partnership with the Syrian government, organised the first national conference on education for, and the ethics of, Sustainable Development in Syria. The conference included a series of workshops in schools to form environmental clubs, promote awareness of environmental issues, and teach sustainable development and lifestyles.

Additionally, the Patriarchate of Antioch established the Department of Ecumenical Relations and Development whose primary focus and work are education for sustainable development and the environment. This Department has been an effective and trustworthy collaborator with the Ministry of the Environment in Syria and with various Islamic organisations to formulate several projects and action plans, such as water and garbage recycling in several schools in Damascus.[14] The Department has set up a Geographic Information System database of land owned by the Patriarchate in Lebanon and Syria to help ensure that church lands are being properly managed and agricultural plans are sustainable. It has also promoted the use of water-saving devices in all Church institutions and in all Orthodox homes.[15]

Educational Initiatives in Lebanon

In 2007, the University of Balamand, an educational institution founded by the Patriarchate of Antioch, became the first university in Lebanon to own and run a natural reserve. This reserve was made possible by the gift of a large piece of land from one of the faithful of the Orthodox Church, Dr Farid Karam in Kaftoun, a village in North Lebanon. Dr Karam donated the reserve to the University of Balamand as a testimony to his love of nature. He intended the reserve to be a place of cultural and environmental activities, and that it would maintain and enrich the existing ecosystem and biodiversity of the area. Students and researchers from the Faculty of Sciences conduct studies on the flora and fauna in the reserve. These studies contribute

[12] Metropolitan Georges Khodr of Lebanon, *L'Appel de l'Esprit: Église et Société* (Paris: Les Editions Cerf, 2001); 7-11; "Technology and Social Justice", In *Church in the World: Christian Views on the Commitment to Earth Issues*, edited by Georges Khodr, Gregory Haddad, Hector Dwaihy, Antoine Makdissy (Beirut: Annour Publications, 1973), 126-153. [Arabic].

[13] *Annour Magazine,* "Environmental News" 6(70) (2014): 323-324. [Arabic]. *Annour* (*The Light* in English) is a widely known church magazine of the Orthodox Youth Movement (Mouvement de la Jeunesse Orthodoxe or MJO). It has dedicated the yearly issue of September to scientific articles about the environment and the effects of various pollutions.

[14] Melhem Mansour, "Orthodox Christianity and Education for Sustainable Development", in Rick Clugston and Steve Holt (eds), *Exploring Synergies between Faith Values and Education for Sustainable Development* (San José, Costa Rica: Earth Charter I Secretariat, 2012); 33-34.

[15] Mary Colwell, Victoria Finlay, Alison Hilliard, and Susie Weldon (eds), *Many Heavens, One Earth: Faith Commitments to Protect the Living Planet* (Bath, UK: Alliance of Religions and Conservation, 2009): 18, 20.

to the preservation of its species and the sustainable use of resources from natural ecosystems, such as water resources and wildfire protection.

In 2008, the Patriarchate of Antioch asked the University of Balamand's Institute of the Environment to further advance the Church's commitment to environmental preservation by developing a seven-year plan to effectively care for the environment and study the possibility of implementing a sustainable development plan for the Church's lands.[16] This plan offered several strategies for environmental protection and sustainability. These strategies can be implemented in the parishes of the Orthodox Church in Lebanon and Syria under the leadership of their hierarchs. The strategies propose the use of proper expertise, with modular incremental movement and achievements, while setting benchmarks, within the framework of seven themes touching different environmental problems within the Middle Eastern context: environmental education, sustainable agriculture, water efficiency, waste management, energy efficiency, climate change, and advocacy.

In addition, the St. John of Damascus Institute of Theology at the University of Balamand, a school of theology that educates students in undergraduate, graduate, and doctoral programmes, will incorporate courses about the preservation of the environment in its academic curricula and internal life of students.

Conclusion

Living in a land adorned by divine beauty but filled with conflicts and wars, the Orthodox Church stands as a Christian witness calling for reconciliation between humankind, creation, and God. This reconciliation brings about peace, the peace that breaks down the walls of hostility between human beings and the whole creation. The Church has welcomed various scientific initiatives as proposed solutions to the ecological crisis. It has made use of both individual holiness and social participation as a means of healing creation in Christ.

In light of this rich theology and engagement, the Orthodox Church in Lebanon and Syria carry the responsibility and the unique vocation to lead the quest for local solutions to environmental problems to preserve creation, the house of God. The Church leads a creative work of environmental sustainability through making use of scientific knowledge and technological innovations in practical local initiatives, and in promoting educational advocacy and liturgical renewal.

Suggestions for Further Reading

Annour Magazine. A Special Issue on the Environment. 6(70) (2014). [Arabic]

Ignatius IV, Patriarch of Antioch. "Three Sermons: A Theology of Creation; A Spirituality of the Creation; The Responsibility of Christians". 12th March 1989. *The Orthodox Fellowship of the Transfiguration.* [Available at: http://www.orth-transfiguration.org/], [Last accessed: 4th December 2020].

John X, Patriarch of Antioch and All the East. *Pastoral Letter*. Damascus, Syria: The Greek Orthodox Patriarchate of Antioch and All the East Publications, 2013.

Nassif, Fr. Bassam A. "The Church of Antioch: Creation and Environmental Sustainability". In Christina Nellist, Ed. *Climate Crisis and Sustainable Creaturely Care: Integrated Theology, Governance and Justice*. Cambridge: Cambridge University Press, 2021.

UN News. "Beirut Facing Acute Environmental Crisis, Warns UN Energy Specialist". 1st September 2020. *UN News* [Available at: https://news.un.org/en/story/2020/09/1071462], [Last accessed: 1st December 2020].

Walker, Andrew and Costa Carras, Eds. *Living Orthodoxy in the Modern World: Orthodox Christianity & Society*. Crestwood, NY: St Vladimir's Seminary Press, 2000.

[16] Colwell *et al, One Earth.*

44. "One God, Maker of Heaven and Earth, and of All Things Visible and Invisible": Teachings on Creation from "For the Life of the World. Toward a Social Ethos of the Orthodox Church"

Ecumenical Patriarchate[1]

§73 In the Church's central symbol and declaration of faith, the Nicene-Constantino-politan Creed, Orthodox Christians confess "one God, maker of heaven and earth, and of all things visible and invisible." Scripture affirms that "God saw everything that was made and, indeed, it was very good" (Gen. 1:31). The word for "good" (*kalos*) in the canonical Greek text connotes more than just the value of a thing, and more even than its mere moral acceptability; it indicates that the world was also created as, and was called to be, "beautiful." The Liturgy of St James affirms this too: "For the one God is Trinity, whose glory the heavens declare, while earth proclaims his dominion, the sea his might and every physical and immaterial creature his greatness." This profound belief in the goodness and beauty of all creation is the source and substance of the Church's whole cosmic vision. As Orthodox Christians sing at the Feast of the Theophany: "The nature of waters is sanctified, the earth is blessed, and the heavens are enlightened [...] so that by the elements of creation, and by the angels, and by human beings, by things both visible and invisible, God's most holy name may be glorified" (From the Great Blessing of the Waters). St Maximus the Confessor tells us that human beings are not isolated from the rest of creation; they are bound, by their very nature, to the whole of creation.[2] And when humankind and creation are thus rightly related, humanity is fulfilling its vocation to bless, elevate, and *transfigure* the cosmos, so that its intrinsic goodness might be revealed even amidst its fallenness. In this, God's most holy name is glorified. Nevertheless, human beings all too often imagine themselves to be something separate and apart from the rest of creation, involved in the material world only insofar as they can or must exploit it for their own ends; they ignore, neglect, and even at times willfully reject their bond to the rest of creation. Again and again, humankind has denied its vocation to transfigure the cosmos, and has instead disfigured our world. And ever since the birth of the industrial age, humanity's capacity for harm has been relentlessly magnified. As a result, we today find ourselves faced with such previously unimaginable catastrophes as the increased melting of ice-caps and glaciers, rain and rivers running sour from pollution, pharmaceuticals tainting our drinking-water, and the tragic reduction or even extinction of many species. Over against all the forces – political, social, and economic, corporate and civic, spiritual and material – that contribute to the degradation of our ecosystems, the Church seeks to cultivate a truly liturgical and sacramental path to communion with God in and through his creation, one that necessarily demands compassion for all others and care for all of creation.

§74 The work of cosmic transfiguration requires great effort, a ceaseless striving against the fallen aspects of humanity and of the world; and the embrace of this labour requires an ascetic ethos, one that can reorient the human will in such a way as to restore its bond with all of creation. Such an ethos reminds Christians that creation, as a divine gift from the loving creator, exists not simply as ours to consume at whim or will, but rather as a realm of communion and delight, in whose goodness all persons and all creatures are meant to share, and whose beauty all persons are called to cherish and protect. Among other things, this entails working to eliminate wasteful and destructive uses of natural resources, working to

[1] See the full text of "Life for the World", released on 27th March 2020 from the Ecumenical Patriarchate in: https://www.goarch.org/-/life-of-the-world-thurs; or in: https://www.goarch.org/social-ethos; see also: https://orthodoxtimes.com/for-the-life-of-the-word-toward-a-social-ethos-of-the-orthodox-church-is-now-available-online/.

[2] Maximus the Confessor, Mystagogia 7 PG 91.684, in *Maximus Confessor: Select Writings* (New York, NY: Paulist Press, 1985): 196.

preserve the natural world for the present generation and for all generations to come, and practicing restraint and wise frugality in all things. None of this, however, is likely possible without a deep training in gratitude. Without thanksgiving, we are not truly human. This, in fact, is the very foundation of the Church's Eucharistic understanding of itself and of its mission in the world. When humanity is in harmony with all of creation, this thanksgiving comes effortlessly and naturally. When that harmony is ruptured or replaced by discord, as it so often is, thanksgiving becomes instead an obligation to be discharged, sometimes with difficulty; but only such thanksgiving can truly heal the division that alienates humanity from the rest of the created order. When human beings learn to appreciate the earth's resources in a truly Eucharistic spirit, they can no longer treat creation as something separate from themselves, as mere utility or property. Then they become able truly to offer the world back up to its creator in genuine thanksgiving – "Your own of your own we offer to you, in all and for all" (From the Anaphora in the Divine Liturgy of St. John Chrysostom) – and, in that act of worship, creation is restored to itself: everything assumes again its purpose, as intended by God from the beginning, and is to some degree arrayed again in its primordial beauty.

§75 The Church understands that this world, as God's creation, is a sacred mystery whose depths reach down into the eternal counsels of its maker; and this in and of itself precludes any of the arrogance of mastery on the part of human beings. Indeed, exploitation of the world's resources should always be recognised as an expression of Adam's "original sin" rather than as a proper way of receiving God's wonderful gift in creation. Such exploitation is the result of selfishness and greed, which arise from humanity's alienation from God, and from humanity's consequent loss of a rightly ordered relationship with the rest of nature. Thus, as we have repeatedly stressed, every act of exploitation, pollution, and misuse of God's creation must be recognised as sin. The Apostle Paul describes creation as "groaning in pain along with us from the beginning till now" (Rom. 8:22), while "awaiting with eager longing" (Rom. 8:19) "the glorious liberation by the children of God" (Rom. 8:21). The effects of sin and of our alienation from God are not only personal and social, but also ecological and even cosmic. Hence, our ecological crisis must be seen not merely as an ethical dilemma; it is an ontological and theological issue that demands a radical change of mind and a new way of being. And this must entail altering our habits not only as individuals, but as a species. For instance, our often heedless consumption of natural resources and our wanton use of fossil fuels have induced increasingly catastrophic processes of climate change and global warming. Therefore, our pursuit of alternative sources of energy and our efforts to reduce our impact on the planet as much as possible are now necessary expressions of our vocation to transfigure the world.

§76 None of us exists in isolation from the whole of humanity, or from the totality of creation. We are dependent creatures, creatures ever in communion, and hence we are also morally responsible not only for ourselves or for those whom we immediately influence or affect, but for the whole of the created order – the whole city of the cosmos, so to speak. In our own time, especially, we must understand that serving our neighbour and preserving the natural environment are intimately and inseparably connected. There is a close and indissoluble bond between our care of creation and our service to the body of Christ, just as there is between the economic conditions of the poor and the ecological conditions of the planet. Scientists tell us that those most egregiously harmed by the current ecological crisis will continue to be those who have the least. This means that the issue of climate change is also an issue of social welfare and social justice. The Church calls, therefore, upon the governments of the world to seek ways of advancing the environmental sciences, through education and state subventions for research, and to be willing to fund technologies that might serve to reverse the dire effects of carbon emissions, pollution, and all forms of environmental degradation.

§77 We must also recall, moreover, that human beings are part of the intricate and delicate web of creation, and that their welfare cannot be isolated from the welfare of the whole natural world. As St Maximus the Confessor argued, in Christ all the dimensions of humanity's alienation from its proper nature are overcome, including its alienation from the rest of the physical cosmos; and Christ came in part to restore to material creation its original nature as God's earthly paradise.[3] Our reconciliation with God, therefore, must necessarily express itself also in our reconciliation with nature, including our reconciliation with animals. It is no coincidence that the creation narrative of Genesis describes the making of animal life and the making of humanity as occurring on the same day (Gen. 1:24-31). Nor should it be forgotten that, according to the story of the Great Flood, Noah's covenant with God encompasses the animals in the ark and all their descendants, in perpetuity (Gen. 9:9-11). The unique grandeur of humanity in this world, the image of God within each person, is also a unique responsibility and ministry, a priesthood in service to the whole of creation in its anxious longing for God's glory. Humanity shares the earth with all other living things, but singularly among living creatures possesses the ability and authority to care for it (or, sadly, to destroy it). The animals that fill the world are testament to the bounty of God's creative love, its variety and richness; and all the beasts of the natural order are enfolded in God's love; not even a single sparrow falls without God seeing (Mt. 10:29). Moreover, animals by their very innocence remind us of the paradise that human sin has squandered, and their capacity for blameless suffering reminds us of the cosmic cataclysm induced by humanity's alienation from God. We must recall also that all the promises of scripture regarding the age that is to come concern not merely the spiritual destiny of humanity, but the future of a redeemed cosmos, in which plant and animal life are plentifully present, renewed in a condition of cosmic harmony.

§78 Thus, in the lives of the saints, there are numerous stories about wild beasts, of the kind that would normally be horrifying or hostile to human beings, drawn to the kindness of holy men and women. In the seventh century, Abba Isaac of Nineveh defined a merciful heart as "a heart burning for the sake of the entire creation, for people, for birds, for animals [...] and for every created thing."[4] This is a consistent theme in the witness of the saints. St Gerasimos healed a wounded lion near the Jordan River; St Hubertus, having received a vision of Christ while hunting deer, proclaimed an ethic of conservation for hunters; St Columbanus befriended wolves, bears, birds, and rabbits; St Sergius tamed a wild bear; St Seraphim of Sarov fed the wild animals; St Mary of Egypt may well have befriended the lion that guarded her remains; St Innocent healed a wounded eagle; St Melangell was known for her protection of wild rabbits and the taming of their predators; in the modern period, St Paisios lived in harmony with snakes. And not only animals, but plants as well, must be objects of our love. St Kosmas the Aetolian preached that "people will remain poor, because they have no love for trees"[5] and St Amphilochios of Patmos asked, "Do you know that God gave us one more commandment that is not recorded in scripture? It is the commandment to love the trees." The ascetic ethos and the Eucharistic spirit of the Orthodox Church perfectly coincide in this great sacramental vision of creation, which discerns the traces of God's presence "everywhere present and filling all things" (Prayer to the Holy Spirit) even in a world still as yet languishing in bondage to sin and death. It is a vision, moreover, that perceives human beings as bound to all of creation, as well as one that encourages them to rejoice in the goodness and beauty of the whole world. This ethos and this spirit together remind us that gratitude and wonder, hope and joy, are our only appropriate – indeed, our truly creative and fruitful – attitude in the face of the ecological crisis now confronting the planet, because they alone can give us the willingness and the resolve to serve the good of creation as unremittingly as we must, out of love for it and its creator.

---

[3] Maximus, *Ambiguum* 41. PG 91.1305CD. See *On Difficulties in the Church Fathers*, vol. 2, 103-121.

[4] Abba Isaac the Syrian, Ascetic Treatises [In Greek] 62, Holy Monastery of Iveron, Mount Athos, 2012, 736

[5] *Prophecy* 96.

45. THE STRATEGIC ROLE OF ACT NATIONAL FORUMS AND NATIONAL COUNCILS OF CHURCHES IN PUBLIC ADVOCACY FOR CLIMATE JUSTICE, CREATION CARE AND SUSTAINABLE DEVELOPMENT IN AFRICA

Bob Kikuyu and Julius Mbatia[1]

Over the years, faith-based organisations have been a catalyst for change in various communities with myriad initiatives on health, livelihoods and responding to humanitarian disasters. Their religious convictions have not only contributed to international development work but provided hope to many across the world. This has seen the emergence of an interesting paradigm where, increasingly, the world appreciates the unique role that faith beliefs and values play in inspiring, informing, catalysing, and sustaining meaningful, responsive, and transformative development. Equally, change has occurred within these organisations.

In addition to building a wealth of knowledge and experience on humanitarian responses and development paradigms and dynamics, faith-based organisations are ramping up efforts beyond mainstream development programming. They are raising a voice that ardently challenges power imbalance, systemic discrimination, marginalisation, poor governance and injustice through advocacy.

The question here is whether and how the church can be more than a respondent and become an advocate for its communities. Whereas the church has excelled in hearing the cries of the affected and afflicted, it has not been as effective in attending to the deeper issues that cause the cries, and to become a voice that calls for change. Some would call it a prophetic voice, defining it as the voice that speaks "truth to power" by challenging institutions and individuals who propagate injustices that disadvantage and marginalise communities. Walter Brueggemann suggests, "The task of prophetic ministry is to nurture, nourish, and evoke a consciousness and perception alternative to the consciousness and perception of the dominant culture around us".[2]

The role of the church and affiliated faith-based organisations in public advocacy may very well be both a voice as well as a stirrer of emotions that alert the community to the danger of slumber and obsequiousness. The level of trust that society bestows on these institutions is of immense value to advocacy. This trust dates back centuries and time has allowed them to assert their roles in spiritual vitality, life counsel and encouragement. As in governance, faith institutions that have withstood the test of time are those that have had functioning structures and evolve in a manner that affirms their relevance to the changing needs of society. Owing to their unique position in society, these institutions have a moral imperative to offer true and unwavering advice, call out unfair acts in development, creation care, society, culture and keep alive societal ethos. Their voice is deemed impartial, one necessary to bring humanity back on track where waywardness sets in. As such, immense possibilities for faith institutions to advance advocacy and cause change exist. However, maximising on them requires the appreciation that their faith identity and advocacy as a concept are mutually reinforcing. While international development is seemingly a secular discipline, these organisations need to acknowledge that their identity, faith values, and conviction offer an important constituent in how they put mainstream advocacy approaches to work.

---

[1] Bob Kikuyu is the Global Theology Advisor for Christian Aid, a faith-based international Humanitarian and Development organisation. He also co-ordinates the Collaboration Research Project for the WCC and ACT Alliance. He has over 18 years of pastoral experience with churches. He is based in Nairobi, Kenya. bkikuyu@christian-aid.org.
Julius Mbatia is the Global Climate Advisor for ACT Alliance, a faith-based humanitarian and development umbrella body. He is part of the Kenya Youth Climate Network and has previously worked for Christian Aid and the Pan African Climate Justice Alliance. He is based in Nairobi, Kenya.

[2] Walter Brueggemann, *The Prophetic Imagination* (Minneapolis, MN: Fortress, 2018).

Leveraging Faith in Advocacy

Advocacy is a useful means to deliver people's aspirations of a just world and the pursuit of common good. National Councils of Churches and ACT forums have a crucial role in how advocacy is organised to deliver aspirations of communities that rise above social and climate change impacts. A foundational pillar for advocacy efforts by these institutions is the uniqueness of their place as faith institutions in society. The entire advocacy cycle must maximise on the mobilisation capacity – trust and access characterising their existence. These are critical levers around which various advocacy strategies can be pieced together.

National Council of Churches and ACT forums have social mobilisation capabilities. Churches offer a critical mass that can serve as the starting point for mobilising for change within the context of climate change. The church constituency can drive ripple behaviour change in society through advocacy. Whilst leveraging this mobilisation capacity would offer quick wins in advancing social and environmental change, it is counterintuitive to assume that such wins are guaranteed if efforts to concretise the advocacy voice are not pursued.

To build strong justice advocates, National Council of Churches and ACT Forums must employ various tactics to marshal an influential faith voice and movement. An inward-looking strategy to catalyse active engagement by the church is needed if a causal sequence in the larger society is to be triggered by people of faith. In this context, churches can be viewed as fertile ground to root the inspiration and urgency to meaningfully tackle economic and climate justice including through strategic public advocacy. Such a strategy would need to recognise the importance of providing ecumenical insights and emphasis on climate justice while availing mainstream knowledge around thematic or general issues through sensitisation. This will deliver knowledge and ignite a moral conviction for the church to be a powerful justice advocacy agent, in turn leading a social movement for climate and social justice and action. The United States Conference of Catholic Bishops captured this well.

> This attention to the environment also must reflect the special concern for the poorest members of the human community, as poverty and environmental degradation often go hand in hand. God created the bounty of the earth to be shared among all of his children, equitably and justly, and he commands us to be stewards of this great creation. To embrace our role as stewards of God's creation, we must employ "restraint and moderation in the use of material goods, so we [do] not allow our desire to possess more material things to overtake our concern for the basic needs of people and the environment." In fulfilling these duties, we promote a focus on authentic development, encouraging the economic and spiritual advancement of the poorest people on earth as a means to living out our Catholic faith.[3]

Mobilisation efforts must be complimented by a powerful advocacy messaging that is rooted in the realities of local communities and contexts. The imperative to urgently act on the climate crisis is to safeguard the lives, livelihoods, and rights of those vulnerable to climate change impacts, a problem they have least contributed to. The same too for economic justice. Dismantling global to local power imbalances, systemic inadequacies and structural hurdles that impede access to effective policies and solutions becomes a major advocacy ambition.

National Council of Churches and ACT Forums are faith institutions that communities entrust with the mandate to take on the economic and climate struggle on their behalf at all levels of governance. In addition to these agencies having a leeway to build social movements for justice, they have internal capacities to engage in strategic lobbying at policy levels. Their years of impactful work in humanitarian and sustainable development, and identity as faith-based organisations wins them favour with policy makers, governmental development practitioners and political leaders giving them "unspoken" access to power and decision-making spaces.

---

[3] The United States Conference of Catholic Bishops, "Why Does the Church Care About Global Climate Change", 2014 *United States Conference of Catholic Bishops Website* [Available at: https://www.usccb.org/resources/why-does-church-care-about-global-climate-change], [Last accessed: 28th March 2022].

Engaging Indigenous Knowledge for Creation Care

During the IUCN congress held in France in September 2021, Ledama Masidza, a delegate from the Global South, commented:

> Nature-based solutions have been around for a long time. So, in that context, they are not nature-based solutions […] just a solution. And because it is something that has been practised for a long time not only in our area but if you go to many other areas around the world, to the communities, to the rural areas, to the indigenous people where they are, nature-based solutions are just the solutions where they are.[4]

The point he raises is critical – that people have solutions that work for them where they are especially when it comes to environment and creation care. What is critical is whether, and to what extent, outsiders recognise the solutions of people to their challenges where they are, and work with the communities using those solutions.

Whilst the localisation agenda pushes for more resources – mainly financial to be allocated to local NGOs and development actors, very little is said about utilising local knowledge. Instead, the line taken is that of capacity building, and bringing in knowledge and expertise from external sources. We need to more diligently pursue development and care of creation through using sustainable local solutions. And indeed, most local solutions have been sustainable, probably more sustainable than imported solutions because they have been derived from locally developed knowledge.

ACT members and churches are well-placed to advocate for the use of local solutions using indigenous methods. The international NGOs allied to the ACT Alliance can and should support the place and use of local solutions. They can support the research of methods used and strengthen how they are applied in local situations. They can help to generate the data and evidence where these local solutions are being used and succeeding. Just like other solutions, where they fail, they can find ways in which these indigenous epistemologies can be improved. Even more, the churches and NGOs can promote confidence by highlighting and proposing the use of these local methods and solutions to the government and donor institutions. This partnership provides a fertile seedbed for nurturing local knowledge and solutions for creation care.

A respect for local environmental epistemology comes by listening and trusting the local people in this regard. The churches as centres for the community are centres for some of these epistemologies. Furthermore, the support and use of local knowledges promotes the use of local resources, whether human or otherwise which means they are sustainable and affordable. The effort and energy used in transfer of knowledge is almost minimal because it is already locally appreciated. This gives value and dignity to the community.

Time for Localisation in Deed

The localisation agenda was touted as a reforming model for sustainable development as well as taking care of the need for appropriate resource allocation. Localisation has at its core the understanding that those closest to the crisis or challenge at hand have a better understanding of the context and should therefore be mandated with designing and mostly implementing the response. The collaboration between churches and ACT members is suited for the development of localisation because ACT members have committed to it and churches are open to it. The faith language that is shared between the two is an added benefit when this is considered.

---

[4] Ledama Masidza, "IUCN Congress 3-10 September: Nature's Role in COVID recovery", IUCN Conference 2021: Conference highlight video, *Vimeo, uploaded by Earth Negotiations Bulletin* 15th September 2021, [Available at: https://vimeo.com/605671974], [Last accessed: 28th March 2022].

The COVID-19 pandemic highlights the need for advancing the localisation agenda. To stem the spread of the pandemic, many countries instituted lockdowns which meant that not only offices were shut but movement was restricted. Many areas of need were isolated, and the work of NGOs was severely paralysed. Mostly local NGOs and churches were also cut off from donor support at a time when they had to take on a greater responsibility. It is likely that those local faith organisations and NGOs whose capacity had been built were able to respond more effectively to the needs of affected communities during the pandemic. But it also indicates the need for the localisation to be strengthened.

Capacity building needs to be considered alongside local knowledge. It should lead from firefighting to sustainability where local organisations such as churches and local NGOs are strengthened and enabled to manage the crises which affect them. In these times, when people are experiencing extreme climate crises with increasing frequency, the focus should not just be on the humanitarian response but also on mitigation using local knowledge and solutions. There should be a deliberate effort to see their primary role move from being first responders in times of crisis to first enablers to avert a crisis. Where there is sustainable development, there is less scope for a humanitarian crisis. However, most critical is the danger to force local actors into the international actors' image, which takes away from the reason that we have sought localisation. Olivia Wilkinson and Florine de Wolfe have added:

> From an international perspective, there are advantages to including local actors in humanitarian, development, and peace activities. These advantages at the international level are coupled with advantages for local actors that come in the form of being treated as equals and having the opportunity to build their organisational capacity to respond to crises. The humanitarian system is complex and increasingly standardised, which makes it difficult for local actors to adhere to its requirements. It could be a mistake to ask local actors to follow the same norms, standards, and procedures as international organisations. Doing so, may undercut their ability to work flexibly and in remote regions, some of the very attributes international actors seek. Strict donor compliance regulations can result in a loss of diversity and a lack of long-term thinking; two criticisms levelled at international humanitarian aid organisations.[5]

A Refreshed Look at Collaboration between ACT and NCCs

The World Council of Churches (WCC) and the Lutheran World Federation (LWF) were the founders of the ACT Alliance with the intention that it serves as their humanitarian and development agency. Speaking recently, the Acting General Secretary of the WCC stated that the relationship between WCC and ACT Alliance had significantly changed. "When ACT Alliance was formed, many referred to the WCC as its parent," said Rev. Prof. Dr Ioan Souca, acting general secretary of the World Council of Churches in his opening remarks. "Today we are siblings, serving the churches side-by-side as an expression of unity and common witness."[6]

Yet in between the founding and the current state, there has been competition for resources, duplication of programmes, and other competing agendas. Nevertheless, there have also been efforts to talk through these challenges and find solutions to the areas of contestation and to strengthen the areas of agreement. As part of the process, the Malawi Consultation of 2014 resolved that a Reference Group be formed to attend to this challenge in the relationship. One of the activities was to conduct research on collaboration between the two bodies, essentially between churches affiliated to the WCC and ACT members to learn how to

---

[5] Florine de Wolf and Olivia Wilkinson, *The Triple Nexus, Localization, and Local Faith Actors: The intersections between faith, humanitarian response, development, and peace*. (Washington DC; Copenhagen: Joint Learning Initiative on Faith and Local Communities; DanChurchAid, 2019): 10. [Available at: https://jliflc.com/wpcontent/uploads/2019/10/TripleNexus_SouthSudan_ReviewOfLiterature.pdf], [Last accessed: 28th March 2022].

[6] Rev. Prof. Dr Ioan Souca, "ACT Alliance Electronic Assembly opens with the theme of youth and climate", 29th November 2021, *Act Alliance Website.* [Available at: https://actalliance.org/act-news/act-alliance-electronic-assembly-opens-with-the-theme-of-youth-and-climate-justice/], [Last accessed: 28th March 2022].

better collaborate between them. The research is ongoing in Malawi and Cameroon using projects where the collaboration is working successfully. However, it is worth noting how an ACT member and the National Council of Churches of Kenya expressed their collaboration, taking note of how they worked with clergy and people at the grassroots.

> In the month of April 2020, NCCK with support from Dan Church Aid (DCA) collaborated with North Rift Economic Bloc (NOREB) to increase the level of awareness of community members on the COVID-19 disease at the grassroots by utilising clergy and community organisers. This was done through a series of activities that included a translation of COVID guideline materials to local dialects; printing of posters and stickers for distribution to villages; recording of short video clips of religious leaders offering messages of hope shared on various mainstream and social media platforms; and purchase and distribution of 500 cartons of bar-soap, 20 cartons of sanitisers, 6,000 face masks and 120 buckets for hand washing in public spaces in Elgeyo Marakwet and Baringo Counties.[7]

Kitui County in Kenya is one of the driest and most drought prone areas in Kenya and has suffered some of the worst effects of extreme climate events. When Christian Aid, an ACT member, partnered with the Anglican Development Services in the region, one of the foremost things they chose to do was to build sand dams. These dams were used to trap water from the short rains that fell. The local community then piped the water to their nearby farms. When the rains ceased, the community dug wells in the sand thus ensuring there was still a source of water even when it was dry around them. This simple method using local solutions contributed to a significant change in the communities where the dams were situated. "Built of sturdy concrete and stretching wide across the river, ADSE's sand dam means the community can wave goodbye to those long walks to collect water. Rainwater is collected in the sandy riverbed and piped to nearby fields. The result is flourishing crops which can feed a family or be sold at market."[8]

With the ongoing WCC/ACT Collaboration Learning Project, it is fitting that collaboration between the WCC and ACT members has edged towards an examination of the collaboration between the ACT country forum members and the churches. This is a significant departure from looking at collaboration only at the high organisation level. The WCC is an umbrella body of churches and, therefore, there is the need to be talking with churches on the ground. ACT Alliance is an umbrella body of INGOs who have local representation in countries where they work. The conversation needs to grow at this level. This welcome departure from the traditional way of focusing organisational collaboration only at the high level is much needed and will help to deliver change where it is most needed – at the grassroots.

Conclusion

The voice of justice, reason, and fairness rooted in faith and conviction can prevail over injustice. It is impossible to have a better world while people of faith remain silent and disengaged in making the world a better place. Unlike time-bound advocacy projects and programmes, our faith is continually alive demanding that our advocacy is always kept alive for there is no alternative to a faith advocacy voice. Our hope for a better future is only practical if we act in the present. People of faith must engage in the various discourses of the world if injustice in our societies is to be uprooted and good is to overcome evil. How much better to do it in collaboration as churches and ACT members strengthen each other. For as the saying goes, if you want to walk fast, walk alone; if you want to walk far, walk with others.

---

[7] National Council of Churches Kenya, "NCCK COVID-19 Response Activities in The North Rift", 17th May 2020, *NCCK Website*, [Available at: https://www.ncck.org/ncck-covid-19-response/], [Last accessed: 28th March 2022].
[8] Christian Aid News Update, "Four Things the Kalawani Community of Kenya Want You To Know – In Photos", 22nd August 2016, [Available at: https://news.christianaid.org.uk/four-things-the-kalawani-community-in-kenya-want-you-to-know-in-photos-4564b49efd0], [Last accessed: 28th March 2022].

Suggestions for Further Reading

Act Alliance. "Global Strategy for ACT Alliance 2019-2026". 10th October 2018. *Act Alliance Website.* [Available at: https://actalliance.org/wp-content/uploads/2018/10/10-Global-Stategy-2019-2026.pdf], [Last accessed: 28th March 2022].

Act Alliance. "WCC, ACT Alliance pilot 'learning process' in Malawi and Cameroon to strengthen collaboration". 21st April 2021. Act Alliance Website. [Available at: https://actalliance.org/act-news/wcc-act-alliance-pilot-learning-process-in-malawi-and-cameroon-to-strengthen-collaboration/], [Last accessed: 28th March 2022].

WCC. "WCC central committee lifts up resources for ecumenical diakonia and other programmes", 16th February 2022, *World Council of Churches Website* [Available at: https://www.oikoumene.org/news/wcc-central-committee-lifts-up-resources-for-ecumenical-diakonia-and-other-programmes], [Last accessed: 28th March 2022].

WCC. "Church organizations explore ways of strengthening relationships". 10th September 2014. Malawi Consultation between WCC and ACT Alliance 2014. *World Council of Churches Website* [Available at: https://www.oikoumene.org/news/church-organizations-explore-ways-of-strengthening-relationships], [Last accessed: 28th March 2022].

PART II: ASIA AND PACIFIC

46. ECO-JUSTICE AND ECO-DIAKONIA – AN IMPERATIVE FOR CREATION CARE: PERSPECTIVES AND INITIATIVES FROM CCA

Mathews George Chunakara[1]

Eco-justice is an imperative for the care of creation. The fundamental principle of eco-justice affirms that ecological justice is integral to social justice, and that without ecological justice there can be no social justice. Although both concerns are deeply rooted in Christian social thought and theological emphasis, greater attention has hitherto been focused on Christian social teaching and practice, with specific emphasis on social justice. The term 'eco-justice' was coined by two American Baptist leaders, Richard Jones and Owen Owens, in the early 1970s. However, since that time it has been argued and articulated in Christian circles that preferring to work for ecology instead of against or alleviating poverty, or vice versa, is not an ideal perspective or choice, because the predicament demands that one chooses both. In the days when these were considered mutually exclusive priorities, the question posed was: is caring for the environment incompatible with working for social justice? The two Baptist leaders argued that ecology and justice were intertwined, and they started to promote the conjoined word 'eco-justice' to emphasise and reflect on those connected needs.

During the past half a century, this additional emphasis gained momentum and the impetus shaped the contemporary environmental movement. Subsequently it was also affirmed that eco-justice, climate justice, economic justice, racial justice and intergenerational justice were all connected, and dependent on each other. An American Presbyterian ethicist, William E. Gibson, who had initiated a campus ministry programme headquartered at Cornell University, gave the affirmation that eco-justice seeks "the well-being of all humankind on a thriving Earth."[2] Gibson, who wrote persuasively and encouraged others to reflect in-depth on this subject, practiced what he preached, inspiring many to follow these principles in daily life and chosen work. He motivated a network of individuals and institutions to counteract earth-destroying habits by caring for ecological integrity together with socio-economic justice, for the good of all.

In 1985, Gibson wrote an elaboration of the nine-word definition, making it clear that a thriving earth is necessary for the health and prosperity of humans. He also affirmed that eco-justice calls for humans to practice, "a way of living within the natural order that is fitting: respectful of the integrity of natural systems and of the worth of nonhuman creatures, appreciative of the beauty and mystery of the world of nature."[3] In other words, 'eco-justice' aims to promote the well-being of all humankind on a thriving earth. As a target to achieve the goal, eco-justice retains and reinforces commitment to justice in the social order; it affirms justice to human beings, and is inseparable from right relationship and stewardship with all God's creation and justice to all God's creation. Eco-justice also bonds ecological sustainability with a thriving earth.

---

[1] Dr. Mathews George Chunakara is the General Secretary of the Christian Conference of Asia (CCA). He was Director of the Commission of the Churches on International Affairs of the World Council of Churches CCIA / WCC in Switzerland

[2] William E. Gibson (ed), *Eco-Justice – The Unfinished Journey* (New York: State University of New York Press, 2004).

[3] William E. Gibson, "Eco-Justice: New Perspective for a Time of Turning," in D. T. Hessel (ed), *For Creation's Sake: Preaching, Ecology, and Justice* (Philadelphia: Geneva Press, 1985), 15-31, also quoted in: http://www.ecojusticenow.org/resources/Eco-Justice-Ethics/Eco-Justice-Ethics-(Brief-Overview).pdf.

Social justice and ecological ethics have been the focus of the ecumenical diakonia promoted by the ecumenical movement for a long time. The subsequent emergence of the neoliberal trend warranted the need for shifting the emphasis to the interaction between creation and humanity. Environmental movements in many parts of the world started echoing their demand for ecological justice. It was affirmed that ecology and economy are inseparable perceptions of *oikos* – the household of God – which necessitate the church's role in participating in God's mission to protect and promote justice in creation. The churches around the world and the ecumenical movement as a whole started to realise that eco-justice is not merely an ethical issue or a political demand. The struggle for eco-justice is an expression of the spirituality of resistance.

Eco-Justice in the Household of God

The meaning and scope of the household of God and its interconnectedness with various spheres of life and with better stewardship emphasises the principles of eco-justice. The basic components and parameters envisaged as essentials for dwelling in the household of God with better stewardship are deeply rooted in eco-justice. 'Dwelling in the household of God' is often debated and interpreted differently. The Australian Catholic Mary L. Cole, in a study on 'Dwelling in the Household of God: Johannine Ecclesiology and Spirituality',[4] explores its meaning. Cole describes what it means for God to make a dwelling in the human community and depicts the characteristics of 'household', leading to a deeper grasp of the divine *economia* ('the order of the household') and *ecologia*, a term suggesting the communal living and inter-relationships that make up the life of the household. She emphasises the fact that "no instance of the universe of God's creation exists in an atomized isolation from the whole." Professor of Theology Anthony Kelly opines that the focal symbol / metaphor of the household chosen by Mary L Cole, with its ecclesiological and spiritual resonances, enables her to highlight the communal nature of the inter-relationships existing between God and Christian believers. Mathai Zachariah, a prominent Indian ecumenical leader and spokesperson of wider ecumenism in the last century, was of the opinion that for a balanced household situation, "economy and ecology must work in cooperation, rather than in combat and this can happen only if justice is done to all the inhabitants of the earth." Such a balanced situation can be sustained only through a better stewardship in the *oikos*. This is what Larry Rasmussen, Professor of Social Ethics, also conveys when he argues that, "Environmental justice is also social justice and all efforts to save the planet begins with hearing the cry of the people and the cry of the earth together." [5]

The thesis of Rasmussen's *Earth Community, Earth Ethics*[6] is that without an earth ethics governing humankind, the possibility of creating a world community in harmony is weak. The concept and philosophy of earth ethics to create a community in harmony is not a modern phenomenon. It has been emphasised in all ages and in all cultures, especially in different religious traditions. The Vedic teachings of the ancient Indian tradition perceives God's presence through nature. The perception of the motherly dimension of nature is very prominent in Hindu religious teachings and spirituality. Mountains, caves, rocks, forests, trees, plants, healing herbs, rivers, streams, and lakes are an integral dimension of the spiritual heritage of Hindu religion. The ancient church fathers constantly remind us about the spiritual dimension of the integrity of the creation. The Cappadocian Fathers teach that God first creates the world and beautifies it like a palace, and then leads humanity into it. The Nicene creed affirms that the Father is the "Creator of heaven and earth and of all things visible and invisible," the Son "He through whom all things were made," and the Holy Spirit, the "Creator of life." St. Basil the Great wrote, "We should understand in the creation the original cause of the Father as a founding cause, the cause of the Son as a creative one, and the cause

[4] Mary L. Coloe, *Dwelling in the Household of God: Johannine Ecclesiology and Spirituality*, a Michael Glazier Book published by Liturgical Press, 2007 by the Order of St. Benedict, Collegvielle, Minnesota.
[5] Larry Rasmussen, *Earth Community Earth Ethics (Ecology & Justice)* (Maryknoll: Orbis Books, 1989), 291.
[6] Larry Rasmussen, *Earth Community Earth Ethics (Ecology & Justice)* (Maryknoll: Orbis Books, 1989).

of the Spirit as an implementing one." An orthodox perspective on creation emphasises the Patristic views on the value of creation as seen through a Trinitarian lens:

> The value of the creation is seen not only in the fact that it is intrinsically good, but also in the fact that it is appointed by God to be the home for living beings. The value of the natural creation is revealed in the fact that it was made for God, i.e. to be the context for God's incarnation and humankind's deification, and as such, the beginning of the actualization of the Kingdom of God. We may say that the cosmos provides the stage upon which humankind moves from creation to deification. Ultimately, however, the whole of the creation is destined to become a transfigured world, since the salvation of humankind necessarily involves the salvation of its natural home, the cosmos.

A prayer from the Coptic Orthodox liturgy reminds us about the spiritual dimension of eco-justice:

> Bless, O Lord
> The plants, the vegetation, and the herbs of the field,
> That they may grow and increase to fullness and bear much fruit.
> And may the fruit of the land remind us of the
> spiritual fruit we are to bear.

The household of God destined on the basis of eco-justice and the foundation of proper order and management of the *oikos* affirm collaborative living, rightful relationships based on equality, security and harmony, the indispensable components of human existence. Samuel Rayan, a prominent Asian Roman Catholic theologian, conveys this message more explicitly when he argues that basic human equality forbids concentration and privatisation of the resources of God's earth. The earth is God's provision for his entire family on this planet. This is what the church fathers call '*ta koina'*, common goods destined for the benefit of everyone. It is not *'ta idia'*, the fruit of somebody's labour.

The church fathers articulated the principle of stewardship in the household of God of a common universe where earth, air, light, and water are the essential enablers of life, and of which nobody may be deprived, or forced radically to depend on somebody else. This is the essence of eco-justice. However, life in the household of God today is in danger as ecological balance is in peril. Archbishop Anastasios of Albania, who reflects on global concerns, elucidates the crisis of identity in the household of God when stewardship is not nurtured. He says that the conditions created by our global, technological culture has given rise to a terrible crisis in people's sense of their own legitimacy. Although human beings were created in "God's image", as St. Gregory of Nyssa expresses, they degenerated into "an ugly mask" when they abused their own nature by rejecting a koinonia of love with God. The acid test of authentic diakonia is its response to the need for reinforcing the struggle against all forms of injustices, including efforts towards upholding the values of eco-justice.

In ecumenical circles, until the early 1960s diakonia was meant to respond only to the consequences of poverty. However, as the struggling Christian communities began to develop their own biblical theological methodology, the prophetic content of the diaconal praxis started to become evident. Today, in the changing global context and the changes or shift in emphasis and priorities in the ecumenical and ecclesiastical realms, the emphasis of diakonia and its practical applications have been shifted from its original vision. Eco-justice also has emerged as a prime concern of the vision of diakonia in the present changing contexts. The Fifth World Conference on Faith and Order noted the interrelationships between diakonia and koinonia:

> The church as koinonia is called to share not only in the suffering of its own community but in the suffering of all; by advocacy and care for the poor, needy and marginalized; by joining in all efforts for justice and peace

within societies; by exercising and promoting responsible stewardship of creation and by keeping alive hope in the heart of humanity.[7]

Today, responsible stewardship of creation in the context of eco-justice has become an integral concern of the churches and the ecumenical movement. A prayer from the Church of Norway's liturgy is an example of a call for better stewardship aimed at sustaining eco-justice:

O God, we use more than what is ours,
Therefore your creation is suffering.
We consume the resources of the earth
at the expense of the poor and the oppressed.
We are prisoners of consumption
and we confess that we do not want to get out of our captivity.
We seek security by possession.
We steal from those coming after us.
We know that the earth is fragile, but this knowledge paralyses us.
As we do not want to commit ourselves
our proclamations are not credible
As we do not want to be a part of a change
Others have to live in despair.[8]

Asian Initiatives through CCA on Eco-Justice and Eco-Theology

Ecological crisis is the ground reality in many parts of Asia, with its impacts being manifested in many ways. The negative effects of climate change on deforestation, destruction of habitat and biodiversity, radioactive and hazardous wastes, water quality and supply, energy exploration and development, pesticides and food security, and environmental health have been escalating despite some attempts to redeem the situation. The ramifications of these challenges cross national borders and may affect economic, political, and cultural relationships on a vast geographic scale in many parts of Asia. The result of these would cause innumerable Asians to suffer due to the devastating effects of cyclones, floods, earthquakes, drought, acute water shortage, and rise in atmospheric pressure and temperature, which would further result in more heat waves. Many Asians and most Asian countries are victims of environmental destruction. Several studies and surveys in recent years illustrate the magnitude of such devastations in Asia.

The Asian Development Bank studies revealed that:

- Asia occupies 30% of the world's land mass, but 40% of the world's disasters occurred in the region in the past decade, resulting in a disproportionate 80% of the world's disaster deaths. More than 2,200 natural disasters struck Asia in the past 20 years, claiming close to one million lives, with the following six mega-disasters accounting for three-quarters of fatalities: Japan's 2011 earthquake/tsunami (20,000 deaths), the 2004 Indian Ocean tsunami (more than 200,000 deaths), Myanmar's 2008 Cyclone Nargis (140,000 deaths), Bangladesh's Cyclone Gorky in 1991 (140,000 deaths), China's 2008 earthquake (90,000 deaths), and Pakistan's 2005 earthquake (75,000 deaths).
- Asia is home to 75% of the world's population that lives at risk due to the increase in devastating floods every year.

---

[7] From the Faith and Order study on costly unity: Par 3; in: https://archived.oikoumene.org/en/resources/documents/commissions/faith-and-order/vi-church-and-world/ecclesiology-and-ethics/costly-unity.

[8] Prayer from the Church of Norway. Reproduced by ECEN for Creation Time 2004; in: https://www.coursehero.com/file/p2j78m2/Source-A-Service-of-Worship-The-Earth-is-the-Lords-United-Church-of-Canada/.

- In 2018, several Asian countries suffered natural disasters due to heavy rain and flood. The most flood-affected regions and areas in Asia last year were in Kerala State in India, and Irrawaddy Delta areas in Myanmar. A dam in Lao PDR collapsed on 24 July, 2018; Typhoon *Mangkhut* hit massively in Taiwan on 16 September 2018, and Typhoon *Ompong* struck the Philippines on 17 September, 2018. The ground reality now is that a vast number of people in Asia are the worst hit when natural disasters strike.
- In 2018, as well as in the immediate past years, earthquakes destroyed the lives and security of people in countries such as Indonesia, Nepal, Japan, Pakistan, and China, etc.

Ecumenical Responses: Early Initiatives by CCA

Ecological crisis was not considered a serious problem in many developing countries in the world for a long time. Most of them considered poverty as their most pressing problem and environment related issues were considered only as an issue of the industrialised Western or Asian countries. The interconnection between poverty and environmental degradation was rarely addressed or acknowledged at that time. As early as the 1990s more serious efforts were made to identify and highlight specific instances. A conference on Ecology and Development held in India stated how the poor and impoverished were affected by ecological crisis in the Indian context.

> While all are affected by the ecological crisis, the life of the poor and marginalised is further impoverished by it. Shortage of fuel and water adds particular burdens to the life of women. It is said that the tribals are made environmental prisoners in their own land. Dalits, whose life has been subjected to social and cultural oppression for generations, are facing new threats by the wanton destruction of natural environment.[9]

The Christian Conference of Asia and many of its member churches and councils have been taking ecological concerns seriously for several decades. They have been responding to ecological crises as a justice issue out of their strong theological and faith convictions. CCA's direct involvement in raising eco-consciousness and addressing environmental degradation started as early as the 1970s. CCA identified and advocated, mainly through the programmes of the Development and Service Desk, for ecological issues to be seen as justice issues.

During the first half of the 1970s, several Asian countries started facing serious environmental issues. The newly introduced economic trade and industrial policies of several Asian governments were adding more environmental problems in the respective countries. For example, the Japanese government pursued a 'Project of Reforming the Japanese Islands' that aimed at a drastic change of industrial structure. Heavy chemical industry was encouraged on the one hand, while primary industry was deliberately downsized on the other. As a result, environmental pollution started increasing; the sea and the air of Japan became polluted by chemical and nuclear materials. The agricultural policy of the Japanese government since the 1960s encouraged farmers to leave farming and become industrial workers, which resulted in farmers incurring huge amounts of debt. Japanese companies were also responsible for increasing environmental pollution in several other Asian countries in those days. Several countries in Asia started experiencing ecological problems such as deforestation, greenhouse effect, acid rain, influx of chlorofluorocarbons, desertification, and natural disasters. CCA's Development and Service Desk and the Urban Rural Mission programme Desk continuously challenged the then existing development models and called for broader interfaith actions and coalitions to promote and protect the environment, and stop the exploitation of natural resources under governmental patronage.

---

[9] Daniel Chetti (ed.), *Ecology and Development* (Madras: BTESSC & Gurukul, 1991), 96.

Tropical forests in several Asian countries were destroyed in order to sell timber to affluent countries so as to earn foreign exchange to repay national debts, and provide land for cattle grazing and cash crops, which also helped to earn export revenue. In Bangladesh environmental problems manifested themselves in different forms of natural disasters such as flood, cyclone, tornado, drought, river erosion and water pollution. Due to water contamination, the availability of fresh water fish has been drastically reduced. In a country like Bangladesh, where 75 % of the total protein supply comes from fish, the overall nutritional supply to a vast number of poor people was hampered. Starting from the 1970s, the frequency of ecological disasters increased tremendously with widespread devastation due to global ecological degradation. The CCA started collaborating with the Christian Commission for Development in Bangladesh (CCDB), a social development wing of the National Council of Churches in Bangladesh, which was initiated by the World Council of Churches in the early 1970s for raising eco-consciousness in the country.

Indonesia started facing large-scale deforestation from the 1970s, especially after starting gigantic industrial projects. Indonesian churches and the national ecumenical council, the Communion of Churches in Indonesia (PGI), came forward at that time with a development policy calling on churches to participate based on their faith convictions. Since the 1980s, Indonesian churches have taken various efforts to raise eco-consciousness among church officials as well as assist people in improving ways of meeting their needs, such as providing agricultural skills and sustainable farming. Korean churches, together with other faith-based organisations, took the initiative in the 1980s in addressing the environmental degradation in Korea due to heavy industrialisation and in educating the public about the ecological crises faced by the country. The trend of deforestation supported by the military junta of Myanmar, shifting of cultivation, over-exploitation of fish in order to generate foreign exchange, mining and destruction of natural resources were all common policies of the Myanmar's military government for many years. It was in such a context that the Myanmar Council of Churches initiated certain programmes to assist the people in rural areas to teach them about reforestation, systematic use of soil and soil conservation, and organic farming. A CCA member church, the Myanmar Baptist Convention (MBC), also introduced such programmes in almost all MBC local congregations in 1980s.

During those years, several Asian countries started constructing several new dams. It was also during that time that a large number of Asian governments started readily allowing multinational companies to be engaged in the search for raw materials through large-scale mining, deforestation and clearing of lands for developing agribusiness. Large-scale logging industries allowed by the governments resulted in deforestation in many Asian countries in 1970s and 1980s. The CCA initiated, supported and facilitated several studies during this time, and consistent support was extended to the people's movements that emerged in several Asian countries to resist these maldevelopments and their negative impacts. CCA started focusing on ecological and environmental problems in Asia, and took the initiative to address these concerns. CCA's efforts to sensitise the people through its member churches and councils helped facilitate eco-consciousness and assisted in the mobilisation of the affected communities and people.

Regional Consultation on Ecology and Development

CCA articulated its convictions in a more systematic way through various study consultations and seminars with the participation of church leaders and representatives of concerned groups in the 1990s. Those programmes were aimed at educating more and more people to be concerned about the relationships between the environment and economic development as the core issue. A regional consultation organised by CCA on Ecology and Development (13-18 July 1992) was held in Chiang Mai, Thailand, where the participants adopted a statement in which they called for the need to redefine the concept of 'development' and emphasised the need to change the patterns and trends of present development practice.

> We met as representatives from churches to consider the impact of human activity and development on the environment, following the UN Conference on the Environment and Development (UNCED) Earth Summit… As Christians we have become aware of the damage that is being caused to the earth – God's creation – by humankind. Our meeting recognises the need for reflection on the purpose of God for creation and on our relationship with the natural world.[10]

The Chiang Mai consultation heard stories of the commonalities in terms of the environmental situations in various Asian countries: depletion of the once abundant resources, particularly that of forests, commercial demands on natural resources due to the commercial demands for export trading and agricultural products, degradation and destruction of the various related ecological systems – deforestation, loss of biodiversity, and extinction of many animal and plant species due to destruction of their habitat, land/ soil erosion, water and air pollution – which further aggravated rural and urban poverty in each country. The 1992 Chiang Mai consultation found depletion of rainforests to be a widely discussed issue, and ecological consequences and cultural alienation imposed upon the indigenous populations emerged as one of the most crucial issues in the environmental concerns of Asia. It was also observed by participants who represented various Asian churches that the growing tourism industry was another environmental hazard.

Consultation on 'Churches' Response to Environment in Asia

A second consultation organised by CCA in 1995 on 'Development and Environment: Churches Response to Environment in Asia' was held in Jakarta and examined people's spirituality and ecology, stating, "It is through creation that God liberated the world from chaos and total disorder. It is the spirit of God that moved over waters and formed the earth that became a systematic and harmonious environment."

The Jakarta consultation further observed:

> Faith, which is rooted in Judeo Christian heritage was awakened by the ecological crisis and we have begun to make a connection between faith and the fate of nature. Anchored to our understanding of biblical analysis, theological heritage and our knowledge of the environment and our ecological endeavours, a new dimension of faith is fashioned that gives reverence to the creator by caring for the creation.[11]

The Jakarta consultation further observed that in relation to 'sustainable development' in Asia, which was undergoing industrialisation and rapid urbanisation, the concept of development must be defined.

Inter-Religious Consultation on 'Climate Change: A Challenge to Sustainable Development in Asia'

An inter-religious consultation organised by CCA in Kyoto, Japan, from 30 November to 5 December 1998, brought together representatives from various religions on a common platform with several ecumenical organisations. The Kyoto consultation analysed and reflected on the responses of religions and society, with the perspectives of peace with justice and integrity of the creation. The consultation was a breakthrough in terms of building effective interfaith coalition to promote advocacy on climate change and environmental degradation.

---

[10] 'Report of the Consultation on Environment and Development Christian Conference of Asia' (Osaka: CCA, 1993).

[11] Nathan and Martha Knoll (eds.), *Church, Environment, Development in Asia, Christian Conference of Asia* (Hong Kong, 1995).

The consultation expressed concern on the growing destruction caused to the eco-system through unsustainable lifestyles that promoted aggressive accumulation of wealth, massive consumption and jet speed mobility. A statement adopted by the participants of the Kyoto consultation noted:

> One of the major impacts of this process, euphemistically called economic growth, has been a massive use of fossil fuels with the emission of greenhouse gases that have been disrupting the climate system with a vengeance, a fact that is fairly well documented and affirmed overwhelmingly by scientists all over the world. Although the poor do produce greenhouse gas emissions, they do as a result of emissions from poorly insulated homes. These 'survival emissions' are qualitatively different from the 'luxury emissions' of the industrialised countries of the North.[12]

Living Together in the Household of God in Asia

The CCA's systematic approach in sensitising the Asian churches with proper theological undergirding was more evident during the 14th General Assembly of CCA held in May 2015. One of the most pertinent foci of the Assembly was on Asian realities, with the biblical theological emphasis on household of God and the challenges faced in emerging socio-economic, environmental and political contexts. CCA organised a series of study consultations and seminars in conjunction with the 14th General Assembly based on the main theme of the Assembly, 'Living Together in the Household of God'. The theological consultations, seminars and study conferences organised by CCA at the national, sub-regional and the Asia regional levels shared eco-theology and its significance in addressing the challenges in the household of God.

Life Giving Agriculture for Sustainability in God's *Oikos*

Another important area that saw CCA's direct involvement in articulating and facilitating the practical application of ecological concerns was in initiating and organising a series of study consultations on 'Life Giving Agriculture for Sustainability in God's *Oikos*'. The CCA organised the first Asian Life-Giving Agriculture (LGA) Forum in the early 2000s and subsequently CCA, together with Korean Christian Life Giving Agriculture Forum (KCLGAF), organized several consultations of the Life Giving Agricultural Forum in different countries in Asia and tried to develop it as a movement of the people and a way of life that relates to livelihoods – the land, forest and water are gifts of God to all on earth. LGA is a living philosophy based on the theology of life. It is a life-enhancing process grounded in faith and nurtured in a culture of sharing, caring and loving.

Through LGA, CCA conveys the message that the present dominant development model of agriculture is corporate and market-driven. It is capital intensive, export-oriented, mono-cultural with profit as its motive. It compels farmers to use genetically modified seeds, pesticides, and chemical fertilizers. This leads to soil degradation, loss of indigenous seeds, bio-diversity and concentration of lands in the hands of a few. It restricts diversity of agriculture based on the food patterns that are dictated by fast-food companies, increases occupational losses, displacement, drought and migration. Decades of these unsustainable agricultural practices have led to the erosion of cultures, and of traditional knowledge and sustainable agricultural systems.

This ecumenical forum on 'Life Giving Agriculture' aims to identify problems and constraints faced by small farmers and consider alternative approaches to agriculture in the Asian context. It also seeks to strengthen existing solidarity networks and establish new ones at the regional, national and congregational levels. Theoretical and practical inputs geared towards supporting ecologically-friendly agricultural

---

[12] Report of Consultation on Climate Change: A Challenge to Sustainable Development in Asia (Hong Kong: CCA, 1998).

activities such as globalization and its impact on small farmers in Asia, sustainable agricultural technologies and agro-ecological practices, crisis of agriculture after the Fukushima disaster, pursuit for alternative energies and agriculture, the cooperative movement, fair trade, case studies and sharing of experiences from Asian communities are to constitute the focus of the forum.

Over the years, CCA facilitated the participation of its member churches and councils from countries such as South Korea, Japan, the Philippines, Indonesia, Malaysia, Thailand, Sri Lanka, Myanmar, Cambodia, Laos, India, Nepal and Bangladesh in the LGA Forum. Now the Korean counterpart, KCLGAF, has been entrusted with the responsibility of coordinating the Forum on a bi-annual basis on behalf of the Asian ecumenical family.

Response to *Laudato Si*

The CCA and the Federation of the Asian Bishops' Conferences (FABC) jointly organised a study seminar to study Pope Francis' encyclical on the environment and human ecology – *Laudato Si*. The seminar was held in Medan, Indonesia, in July 2016 and was hosted by CCA member church HKBP. Several issues and themes related to ecology and environmental concerns were addressed from an Asian theological perspective. Representatives of different traditions of Asian churches including representatives of Asian Evangelical Alliance attended the seminar.

Renewal and Restoration of the Creation: Thematic Emphases of CCA's Major Events

In 2019 and in 2020, CCA scheduled three major events with the thematic focus on renewal and restoration of the creation.

Congress of Asian Theologians (CATS) – IX on 'Reconciliation, Renewal and Restoration of Creation: Divine Initiative and Human Imperative'

The CATS, a major Asian theologians' summit which is organised on a triennial basis, originally started in 1997. The theme of CATS-IX which was held in Indonesia in August 2019, focused on 'Reconciliation, Renewal and Restoration: Divine Initiative and Human Imperative'. Various issues related to eco-theology, ethics of sustainability and stewardship of the creation were part of the deliberations of CAT-IX. Approximately 120 Asian theologians, including Asian theologians in diaspora, attended the summit.

Asian Ecumenical Women's Assembly (AEWA) on 'Arise, Be Awake to Reconcile, Renew and Restore the Creation'

An Asian Ecumenical Women's Assembly (AEWA), a major ecumenical Asian women's event, was organised by CCA from 21 to 27 November 2019 in Hsinchu, Taiwan. The theme of AEWA was 'Arise, Be Awake to Reconcile, Renew and Restore the Creation'. The AEWA was an opportunity for Asian women to articulate theological perspectives with specific feminist emphasis on creation and eco-theology.

Eco-School on Living in Harmony with Nature

As part of global ecumenical family's engagement in addressing ecological issues affecting the planet and people, the Christian Conference of Asia organised and facilitated a training programme, an Eco-School, jointly organised by the WCC and the CCA.

About thirty young people from eleven countries attended the training which was held at the CCA headquarters in Chiang Mai, Thailand, from 4 to 17 November 2019. The theological undergirding emphasised during the deliberations underscored life in all its fullness and emphasised a God who assures and expects wholeness of life for all his creation. It was also emphasised that God inspires and challenges us to live in harmony with nature and to actively engage in the redemption and restoration of creation, acknowledging the plurality that defines co-existence, the kinship of the 'unequal' and the common dwelling house of all who appear different yet are intrinsically the same (and also the understanding that the ecclesia is to be the living example of an alternate life style that affirms life).

A major concern addressed by the participants based on their local experiences in the Asian context was that water, a gift of God, a public good and a fundamental human right for all, must not be privatized. The budding Asian ecumenists and church leaders were empowered to be involved in advocacy on eco-justice.

General Assembly Theme 2023 with Focus on 'God, Renew Us in Your Spirit to Restore the Creation'

Asian church delegates meet once every five years as a major representative gathering of CCA for its General Assembly. The 15th General Assembly, to be held in 2023, will focus on the theme 'God, Renew Us in Your Spirit to Restore the Creation'. An assembly is an occasion to initiate several pre-assembly events as part of the preparations. All such initiatives and events will focus on the same theme, which are opportunities to take the message of the assembly, especially the theme of the General Assembly, to the grassroots. The theological emphases delivered and shared, especially through Bible studies, thematic presentations and other discussions, will be based on the theme 'Renewal and Restoration of the Creation'. The assembly theme focusing on God's creation will be a major impetus for sensitising the members of the Asian churches at the grassroots levels.

Involvements of Asian Churches in Local Contexts in Addressing Ecological Concerns

In comparison with the recent past, more and more Asian churches are directly involved in responding to, and articulating, their theological convictions on ecology, sustainability of the creation and the need for living together in the household of God in the present day. The churches, including local congregations, are more and more involved in emphasising eco-theology and also involved in the practical application of a sustainable ethics of development. 'Eco-friendly churches / congregations', as well as the idea of encouraging 'green churches', have become mottos of many Asian churches. We receive reports from CCA member churches and related institutions, including theological education institutions in countries such as India, Sri Lanka, Bangladesh, Thailand, the Philippines, Indonesia, South Korea, Japan, and Taiwan, that are directly involved in promoting eco-friendly churches.

In some Asian countries, Christian institutions and organisations have major involvement in promoting ecological and environmental concerns, as well as advocating for better stewardships of God's creation. The Climate Technology Park initiated in Bangladesh by the Christian Commission for Development in Bangladesh (CCDB), the social development arm of the Protestant Churches in Bangladesh and a partner of CCA and WCC, is an extremely creative initiative. Bangladesh is one of the poorest countries in the world where a large number of people are affected for a major part of the year by floods and typhoons. The objective of the initiative is to demonstrate low-cost technologies related to climate change adaptation and mitigation that can be replicated at the community level, in both urban and rural settings in Bangladesh. The project is being implemented with the support of the Bread for the World and the Federal Ministry for Economic Cooperation and Development in Germany. Over a period of time, the facility will become a learning centre as well, which would facilitate knowledge generation and capacity building for those working on climate change in Bangladesh and beyond. The park will be a space where visitors, especially children, students, teachers, practitioners and policy makers can learn about technologies from a range of different options, bringing together traditional indigenous ones as well as newer technologies.

The National Christian Council of Sri Lanka (NCCSL), a member of the council of CCA, has been trying to sensitise members of NCCSL churches about the concerns for the well-being of their neighbours and a responsibility to care for the creation. The NCCSL also promotes the understanding of sustainability in its broadest contexts and motivates them to educate people to minimise the impacts on the environment in all their activities.

The Malankara Mar Thoma Syrian Church in India, especially the supreme head, the late lamented Dr. Joseph Mar Thoma Metropolitan, had been urging for an all-out effort to protect and preserve the environment for the survival of humankind. He had often called upon members of his church to realise how the environment was being destroyed by vested interests, posing a danger to society, and asked them to reflect on the devastating situation created by people and so take remedial measures. He called for responsible stewardship in protecting the environment, and encouraged people to take the initiative to protect the environment, including rivers and trees.

The Church of South India (CSI) has been involved in a Green Church Campaign which encourages parishes to incorporate ecological concerns in their order of worship and include both advocacy and direct action for eco-justice and the integrity of creation in missional activities. The CSI published 'Earth Bible Sermons' to provide sound theological backing for the Green Church Movement, with the aim of teaching the members about the faith aspect of environmental ministry.

Member churches of CCA in the Philippines have been engaged in responding to environmental issues, especially by participating in people's struggle to protect resources necessary for their subsistence. They have been part of the struggle of the people against the neoliberal policies designed by the Philippine government to encourage the mining of nonferrous metals by multinational corporations. Mining, an activity with substantial potential for environmental degradation in the Philippines, deprives the poor of their livelihood. The churches in the Philippines have taken a stance opposing mining as an activity that may harm the poor by degrading the environment upon which they depend for their livelihood and thus further impoverishing them.

CCA's Environmental Protection Guidelines and Policy

The CCA has officially introduced a set of environmental protection guidelines and policies with the aim of reducing waste by initiating recycling programmes within the office – including the recycling of paper, cardboard, beverage containers, plastic containers, and other materials that are accepted by a recycling provider. As per this policy, CCA purchases environmentally responsible products that have been selected based on criteria including: toxicity, durability, use of recycled or re-furbished materials, reduced energy and/or water consumption, reduced packaging, and ability to be recycled, refilled or re-furbished at the end of its useful life. The CCA also promotes efficient use of resources throughout our facility, including water and energy, and there are ongoing efforts to avoid unnecessary use of hazardous materials and seek alternatives whenever feasible. These guidelines and policies help CCA in continually striving to improve environmental performance, as well as in educating staff and participants of CCA programmes on relevant environmental issues. CCA is also committed to the establishment of a green procurement policy, minimal use of water and energy, and minimal use of hazardous and toxic substances found in the office.

Towards Developing a Systematic Culture of Eco-Consciousness and Eco-Theology in Asia

Over the past quarter of a century, there have been many serious attempts and initiatives to create awareness among people to be more environmentally conscious and environmentally friendly. The notion of responding to the ecological crises has been a central concern of churches in different parts of the world, especially in the West, which has started reflecting on it from a Christian eco-theological perspective. However, there is still a significant part of the population that is not aware of the importance of taking care of the environment in which they live, and many people do not know even the buzzwords 'going green' and being 'environmentally friendly'. Being environmentally conscious can mean something different to each person because it is a broad term that describes many different behaviours, cultural patterns, and guidelines that exist to reduce or minimize environmental degradation. There are many different ways people can make changes to safeguard their environment. Being eco-friendly on a personal level can mean changing those aspects of one's routine, lifestyle and attitude which are not helpful in protecting the environment. Being environmentally conscious is an ever growing and a continuous learning process which could focus on different ways of protecting the environment. Being aware of the problem and helping to educate others are the best ways to be an environmentally friendly person in a congregation or a member of any organisation. The church can contribute significantly and effectively to mobilising more environmentally friendly people through congregations. The church in Asia has a responsibility to nurture and inculcate theological values among the members of each congregation. A church which emphasises eco-theology can articulate faith convictions in a more authentic and convincing way.

Eco-theology addresses various forms of environmental issues from theological perspectives. Though it is generally considered to still draw on the authority of the Bible and the Christian tradition, cco-theology has deeper roots and not just in Christianity. In a multi-religious and multi-cultural Asian context, ecological concerns should be taken up as a common concern and cause of adherents of all faiths. In order to protect the household of God and the entire creation, all religions should come forward and contribute their spiritual resources and values. The Christian world often limits their theological perceptions within the orbits of Christian spirituality or theology and interprets it from a common Christian heritage. In this context, what Andrew Spencer from Oklahoma Baptist University observes is relevant. He pointed out that,

> Still, the relative dearth of focus on central Christian doctrines and the radical revision of the message of Scripture bring into question the trajectory of eco-theology. Based on the current emphases of eco-theology, it is not clear whether the next generation of disciples of an eco-theological Christianity can present a coherent witness to the gospel of Christ.[13]

Eco-theology is considered a contextual theology in Asia, and it is slowly gaining momentum in academic circles. However, more systematic efforts need to be initiated to make people understand the value of eco-consciousness from a theological basis. More concrete steps and actions need to be initiated by Asian churches and the ecumenical movement in the future with more precise practical approaches rather than focusing on, or repeating, outdated theological jargon. Norman Habel has expressed his views on theological conjectures of eco-theology and six eco-justice principles developed in the Earth Bible Project,[14] an international project that was initiated in Australia. In spite of considerable literature on eco-theology and eco-spirituality, it became very apparent that few scholars had undertaken a serious attempt to interpret the biblical tradition from an ecological perspective. No explicit ecological hermeneutic had been developed. While many read the biblical text with a view to understanding ecological topics, few have sought to read the tradition from the perspective of Earth or the Earth community. The principles articulated below are concerned with ecology in general, and ecological concerns linked to the Bible in particular are more meaningful and relevant in developing a new eco consciousness and eco-theology in Asia:

---

[13] Andrew J. Spencer, 'Beyond Christian Environmentalism: Eco theology as an Over-Contextualized Theology, *Themelios*, Volume 40 Issue 3 December 2015; see also: https://www.thegospelcoalition.org/themelios/article/beyond-christian-environmentalism/.

[14] Norman Habel, "Introduction," in Norman C. Habel and Peter L. Trudinger (eds), *Exploring Ecological Hermeneutics* (Atlanta: Society of Biblical Literature, 2008), 2.

The principle of intrinsic worth: the universe, Earth and all its components have intrinsic worth/value.

The principle of interconnectedness: Earth is a community of interconnected living things that are mutually dependent on each other for life and survival.

The principle of voice: Earth is a subject capable of raising its voice in celebration and against injustice.

The principle of purpose: the universe, Earth and all its components are part of a dynamic cosmic design within which each piece has a place in the overall goal of that design.

The principle of mutual custodianship: Earth is a balanced and diverse domain where responsible custodians can function as partners with, rather than rulers over, Earth to sustain its balance and a diverse Earth community.

The principle of resistance: Earth and its components not only suffer from human injustices but actively resist them in the struggle for justice.

Suggestions for Further Reading

Website of CCA: https://www.cca.org.hk/

Church, Environment, Development in Asia: A report of the workshop on Environment and Development: Church's Response to Environment in Asia (Jakarta, 1995). Published by CCA Development and Service.

Creation and Spirituality: Asian Women Expressing Christian Faith through Art: A result of the First Consultation of Asian Christian Women Artists (Hong Kong, 1992), jointly sponsored by the Asian Christian Art Association and CCA Women's Desk. The volume captures the reflections of artists around the issues of: images of women, spiritual journey of the artist, and solidarity with people. Edited by Rebecca Lozada and Alison O'Grady.

47. Eco-Theological Reflections and Praxis on Organic Farming and Biogas in Indonesia

Petrus Sugito[1]

So whether you eat or drink or whatever you do, do it all for the glory of God. (1 Corinthians 10: 31)

Eco-Farming and Energy: Brief Reflections

'Farming' can be categorized as one form of 'whatever one does' from the above passage from his word. Thus, there is a normative responsibility in "doing it for the glory of God". What is the relationship between 'farming' and "doing it for the glory of God"?

Referring to the opinion of Pastor Agatho Elsener[2] regarding the organic understanding that, "each organ serves an organism, and each organism serves all its organs," it can be understood that organic 'farming' is a vehicle in glorifying God. The method of organic farming with the principles and techniques as described in the book is very pro-life as God is very pro-life. According to the love of God, he does not will for humanity to perish, rather he has willingly sacrificed himself so that humanity can live eternally. Organic farming is very pro-life centered, as can be seen from Pastor Agatho's summary that humanity should read messages from nature which should be imitated in humanity, including:

1. I work so that all can develop and support my development;
2. Each person supports the community, and all the community faithfully supports its citizens;
3. Each citizen supports the government, and the government serves each citizen;
4. Organic vegetables improve our health, and we support nature to produce healthy vegetables.

Seen through the Christian 'lens', humanity is in a key position to determine whether its actions are more oriented towards harm, destruction, and death (in other words, they are pro-death), or whether their actions are oriented towards sustainability, continuity, harmony, and life (in other words, are pro-life oriented). This statement differs from Psalm 8: 4-10.

> 4 what is mankind that you are mindful of them, human beings that you care for them?
> 5 You have made them a little lower than the angels and crowned them with glory and honor.
> 6 You made them rulers over the works of your hands; you put everything under their feet:
> 7 all flocks and herds, and the animals of the wild,
> 8 the birds in the sky, and the fish in the sea, all that swim the paths of the seas.
> 9 Lord, our Lord, how majestic is your name in all the earth!

The above passage is a reflection from David, who is traditionally believed to be its author, regarding the identity of humans before God and amongst his other creations. Humanity amongst his other creations is essentially the same, namely being a 'command'. However, as a 'command', that possesses a distinction as, "You have made them similar to God." The King James translates this as, "For Thou has made him a little lower than the angels." Man and woman as 'creation' stands just below God's angels, and then the other creatures follow. The distinction of humankind is not just in standing amongst God's other creations, but also in the completeness given by him in the creation of man and woman. He "has crowned us with

---

[1] Petrus Sugito is a pastor of GKJTU or Javanese Protestant Church from North Central Java. Currently works in United Evangelical Mission as Deputy Executive Secretary for Asia.

[2] Agatho Elsener, Pioneer of the Organic Way of Living (VCD), Bina Sarana Bakti, Centre for Organic Development.

glory and respect." Intellect, feelings, heart and conscience represent the completeness inherent in humankind so that they may maintain and show their 'nobility' and 'respect'.

In addition, God gives power over other "works of God's hand." "You made them rulers over the works of your hands; you put everything under their feet." 'Power' is defined as competence, authority, strength; to govern and develop other creations in the scope of creating civilization, prosperity and harmony between humankind and earth. The phrase "power tends to corrupt" has become commonplace as humankind tends to misuse its power to exploit nature. This in Christian theological perspective is due to sin in humankind. However, God wishes not to lament his or her sin, but rather for humankind to live with new hope, through an incarnation of a new life by imitating Jesus in the spirit of salvation. If we are relating this issue to the understanding and practise of farming, it becomes clear that farming needs to be done in line with nature, and that we need repentance and obedience to dutifully use the 'power' given to humankind in a respectful way in managing nature.

The Integral Mission of the Church

Today, many churches reinterpret the definition of their mission as one that is of an integral nature. The Micah Network[3] declares the integral mission of the church as follows:

> Integral mission…is the proclamation and demonstration of the gospel…Our proclamation has social consequences, and our social involvement has evangelistic consequences. Justice and justification by faith, worship and political action, the spiritual and the material, personal change and structural change belong together.[4]

John Stott in *Christian Mission in Modern Society* states that, "Human beings are spirit and soul and body – living in community. The good news of Jesus is good news for human beings in their totality."[5] If taken into the context of the Gereja Kristen Jawa Tengah Utara in Indonesia (GKJTU), this church very clearly has committed to an integral mission as stated in the following call:

> Gereja Kristen Jawa Tengah Utara (GKJTU) is called to create a fellowship with Jesus Christ, Head of the Church, and all organs of the Body of Christ, that is the Holy and Universal Church, as well as other Oikumene fellowships. With this fellowship, GKJTU has been called to witness and/or preach the gospel, namely the good

---

[3] The Micah Network is a network group of over 500 social organizations for Christian poverty and justice; churches and individuals; 300 of them are full members and 200 are honorary members; spread through 80 countries through the world. The foundation of this Network is based on Micah 6:8 "He has shown you, O Mortal, what is good. And what does the Lord require of you? To act justly and love mercy, and to walk humbly with your God." See: https://www.micahnetwork.org/resources/micahnetworkdeclarationonintegralmission/
The Network was founded in 1999 and headquartered in England with 3 key objectives, including:

1. Strengthen the capacity of members in establishing a biblical basis in responding to the needs of the poor, and the oppressed.
2. Encouraging a deepened understanding of the integral mission to be able to speak louder and more effectively, referring to characteristics of the Church's mission to proclaim and demonstrate the love of Christ to the world according to what is needed.
3. Advocacy for and with the poor as a manifestation of voicing the prophetic voice and influencing leaders and policy makers in society to fulfil the rights of the poor, and the oppressed, and free the weak, and the poor.

[4] see: Micah Declaration on Integral mission (2001), in: With your God." See: https://www.micahnetwork.org/resources/micahnetworkdeclarationonintegralmission/ Page 1

[5] John Stott, *Christian Mission in the Modern World. What the Church should be doing now!* (Leicester: IVP, 1975).

> news that saves people; and based on love of serving each other in all aspects of human life in this world (John 13:1-20;14; Matt. 22: 37-40; 28: 19).[6]
>
> Fellowship, witness and service are done for the glory of God's name.[7]

This call is then manifested in one of the missions of the church's strategic development goals which is defined as the 'mission of creation', understood as follows:

> The church has a duty from God to care for and preserve all of creation for the benefit of all creation. This mission includes various aspect of life: social, cultural, political, and ecological. The objective of this mission is the creation of a new heaven and earth.

This implies that the church must take up the responsibility to 'restore' creation that has been damaged due to humanity's actions and take part in the transformation process into a new creation. To conduct this mission, the church must be able to 'open its eyes', seeing critically the various damages that have been caused. Next, the church must open up and work together with any and all parties to prevent and repair this damage. The natural and socio-cultural damage caused by humanity's greed must become an issue of serious importance for the church.[8]

While this is the foundation of the church's reflection on its ecological engagement, it has implemented a concrete program to support farmers to return to organic farming methods as part of its commitment to integral mission according to the biblical vocation: "Do not conform any longer to the pattern of this world, but be transformed by the renewing of your mind..." (Romans 12: 2)

Sharing on Eco-Praxis in Organic Farming and Renewable Energy

Organic Farming

Chlaodhius Budhianto and Wiwid Widiasmoko[9] stated that 2008 represented the first milestone for GKJTU in developing organic farming. This involvement represents a manifestation of the GKJTU's mission regarding the integrity of creation. In this framework, GKJTU sees that the agricultural world possesses a large role in the process of environmental destruction. The usage of a wide variety of hazardous chemicals contained in several synthetic chemical substances proves to be not only dangerous for the environment, but also has a negative impact on human health. Concerned about these conditions, GKJTU conducted several training sessions on organic farming at the presbytery and congregational levels.

At this moment, GKJTU's involvement in developing organic farming is already more than a decade old. Throughout this decade, plenty of events have happened in the development of organic farming activities. The continuity of eco-theological praxis with and for the younger generations is also very much a major concern. One of the forms in which this is implemented is in the form of a community: 'Surga Farm.'

---

[6] GKJTU or Javanese Protestant Church from North Central Java is a small protestant church headquartered in Salatiga, Central Java, Indonesia. Most of the congregations are in villages. Therefore, most of the congregation members are farmers.

[7] Tata Dasar GKJTU bab II pasal 4.

[8] Rencana Induk Pengembangan 2003-2028 Gereja Kristen Jawa Tengah Utara hal. 73. (Javanese Protestant Church from North Central Java; Development Master Plan 2003 – 2008, 73).

[9] Chlaodhius Budhianto and Wiwid Widiasmoko in Resiprositas Kiprah Oikomene dan Kemitraan Gereja Kristen Jawa Tengah Utara (Reciprocity of Oikomene's Donations and Partnership with the Javanese Protestant Church from North Central Java), Salatiga 2021.

Surga Farm represents an effort in finding new ways of organic farming in GKJTU. Different from other organic farming groups present in the Kopeng class, the development of this organic farming in GKJTU is done by this specific community. Surga Farm is a forum for organic farmers in the Merbabu Valley. Farmers which joined together in this community are GKJTU organic farmers who are present in the presbytery of Kopeng and Getasan. Surga Farm does not have relationships with other organic farming organizations that used to exist because its members are different from those of previous farming organizations.

As a group, Surga Farm started from a string of organic farming tuitions given by Pastor Chlaodhius Budhiantoin in 2019. After the training, participants understood that conventional farming systems (fertilizer and chemical substance-based farming) are unhealthy. The conventional farming system not only destroys nature, but also creates agricultural products that are filled with fertilizers and chemical residues, which are of course highly dangerous for human health. Conventional farming has also made many farmers feel that they are no longer independent. They have become dependent upon the agricultural industry, starting from the use of fertilizers, seeds, and the marketing mechanisms of chemical industries.

In addition to these understandings, each participant has been made aware that they are farmers that have many limitations, but also have rich responsibilities to spread the gospel of God's Kingdom through what they do, namely in the world of agriculture. For members of the Surga Farm community, farming is not just a livelihood but also a vehicle for presenting the signs of God's Kingdom. The Surga Farm community understands the signs of God's Kingdom in very elementary and simple forms. The term '*Syalom*' or peace is a key term used in the Surga Farm for understanding and communicating God's Kingdom.

Syalom or peace will happen once all of the living creation can live together in harmony. When this principle is translated into the agricultural world, there must be cooperation between the soil and plants, humans and animals (livestock and various micro-organisms). In this cooperation between soil and plants, humans support the soil, plants and animals, and in turn the animals will support humans with a fertile soil and with many plants. When this harmonic cooperation between the three elements is maintained and preserved, *syalom* can be felt by the farmers.

Renewable Energy: Biogas

Witono[10] states that 2007 was the beginning of GKJTU's biogas program which started in the Sion Getasan Orphanage. Biogas is the result of the organic waste fermentation process which consists of methane (CH4) 55 – 75%, carbon dioxide (CO^2) 25 – 45%, nitrogen (N^2) 0 – 0.3%, hydrogen (H^2) 1 – 5%, hydrogen sulphide (H^2S) 0 – 3%, oxygen (O^2) 0.1 – 0.5%, and water vapor.[11]

At that time, a biogas reactor was built measuring 18 m3, utilizing the waste from 12 cows in Makaryo's stable. The reactor was constructed with a fixed dome design (two domes / old design). The resulting gas was used to fulfill the cooking needs of the orphanage which took care of 30 children. The biogas saved the usage of 2 12kg elpiji containers each month.

Five years later, Yayasan Sion as the GKJTU's charity arm, made acquaintances with partners concentrating on biogas energy development, namely Yayasan Rumah Energy with its Biogas Rumah Tangga (BIRU) (Household Biogas) program. This introduction led to a partnership to provide training for more expertise for biogas production for Yayasan Sion field staff (including this author). Limited financial assistance was also made available for the development of biogas for families to fulfil their daily energy needs.

Witono stated that he was trained to build a fix dome biogas reactor for household usage measuring $4m^3$, $6m^3$, $8m^3$, $10m^3$, and $12m^3$. The strength and durability of the biogas reactors means that they are able to

[10] Witono in Resiprositas Kiprah Oikomene dan Kemitraan Gereja Kristen Jawa Tengah Utara (Reciprocity of Oikomene's Donations and Partnership with the Javanese Protestant Church from North Central Java), Salatiga 2021
[11] Burke, 2001

last up to 30 years or more. Yayasan Sion was then made a Construction Partner Organization (CPO) by Yayasan Rumah Energy.

With the motto *"Olah limbah jadi berkah"* (convert waste into blessings) the Household Biogas program began to garner the community's attention as capacities were adjusted with the number of livestock and the daily cooking needs of each household. At least two cows can provide the main ingredient for a biogas reactor with a capacity of $4m^3$ fulfilling daily needs.

This program turned out to have an impact on GKJTU's outreach in the renewable energy field, as many institutions and academics have entrusted the construction and training of biogas facilities to Yayasan Sion. Between 2012 and 2020, Yayasan Sion has established many partnerships with a number of churches and higher education institutions.[12]

Since this program has started, no less than 30 people have been trained in becoming builders for biogas developments. They are now present in Sumatra and Java. This newfound skill has created a potential job sector for biogas builders. In 2017 Yayasan Sion received the appreciation of becoming the best Construction Partner throughout Central Java from Yayasan Rumah Energy for construction quality, fulfilling national standards.

Another impact of the biogas program is the encouragement of new businesses internally and externally. Yayasan Sion has developed a biogas workshop unit, producing basic biogas tools including main pipes, mixers, dome malls and manometers, which are also sold to construction partners. The construction of biogas ovens cannot be done yet, thus requiring the construction to be ordered from the factory based in East Java.

Biogas users have also found creative ways of utilizing biogas energy as a new form of business in the middle of the pandemic, including coffee shops. Meanwhile the production of slurry fertilizer is utilized as a medium for growing vegetables, organic fertilizer as a medium for growing mushrooms, and the production of fish feed pellets and for worm cultivation. Thus, the integration of the biogas program is highly supportive in saving the environment and heading towards a zero-waste organic waste management.

Up to November 2020, the biogas program has built roughly 200 biogas units with household sizes ranging from $4m^3$ to $12m^3$. No less than 1,000 people have become beneficiaries of waste utilization training, utilizing organic waste from various sources including animal feces, soy waste, and water hyacinth waste.

The benefits of biogas energy are not only economic and agricultural, but also include education. Biogas installations have been built by GKJTU, and some of them have become references for schools of all levels (from elementary to higher education) to conduct comparative studies and introduce the benefits of biogas. Other impacts of biogas have been the development of communal awareness, namely in the slopes of Merbabu and Merapi ,to reduce the consumption of firewood that was previously used as raw materials for daily cooking needs.

In terms of financing, roughly 70% of reactors that have been built are self-funded by communities; the remaining 30% are subsidized through stimulants. GJKTU always educates about the benefits of the program that ultimately belongs to the community and becomes part of saving the environment.

The education process is carried out on a continuous basis through brochures, farmer gatherings, and medias (including Facebook and Instagram) to capture the large potential for the development of the biogas program for communities in the near future, especially with the increasing number of livestock owned by

---

[12] Church institutions: BNKP and HKBP; higher education institutions: UNDIP, Polines, UNS, Universitas Muhamadiyah Magelang, UKSW; government: Program PNPM (PNPM Program), Dana Desa (Village Fund), Dinas Lingkungan Hidup Kab Semarang (Semarang Regency Environmental Services Agency); private sector: Exxon Mobil in providing training for handymen and waste utilization, Yayasan Truka Jaya (GKJ) and German University students in practicing water hyacinth waste utilization in Rawa Pening.

communities – for example, in Central Java alone there are 2 million cattle, 4 million goats, and 41 million chickens.13

According to data from YRE, the total number of biogas units built throughout Indonesia as per 10th September 2020 totals 24,945 units spread over 12 provinces in Indonesia, meaning that we are still very far from the expectations of reaching 23% of renewable energy by 2025. The main obstacle for further biogas development are the relatively high construction costs. Also, the knowledge of the benefits of biogas as an alternative energy still is not fully understood by communities living within rural and mountainous areas, requiring continuous socialization in areas that have potential.

In addition to the potential from livestock waste, there are still many other sources of biogas which have yet to be developed, including water hyacinths present in the Rawa Pening lake. If this can be developed, it would represent one of the largest contributions in saving the mangrove habitat. For this reason, the initiative to start building biogas from water hyacinths as a pilot project began in 2018.

Other potential sources include household organic wastes in cities, which are often abandoned and create air pollution, and subsequently illness. For this reason, Sion is working together with Universitas Negeri Sebelas Maret (Sebelas Maret State University) in the Karanganyar Regency, building a biogas reactor in the middle of a densely populated area precisely above the village landfill. Waste is sorted where organics are selected as a source of biogas energy and can then be utilized by seven families.

Through the strengthening of connections and partnering, Sion always tries to create new initiatives in the development of this program. For example, at the end of September 2020, with YRE Sion created an innovation in the form of mini household biogas (biomiru) as a solution to rising material prices and also for communities who do not have livestock. Biomiru's size is smaller, roughly 2m^3, and utilizes household organic waste to create a fire which lasts for about one hour for cooking. It is hoped that this innovation can be used in city areas with household organic waste.

> Energy represents a basic need for humanity in fulfilling needs. Humans cannot rely only on a single energy source. Breakthroughs are required through alternative energy to fulfill this need, one of which is biogas. Sion has started by taking local steps, which definitively will have global impacts. The utilization of biogas energy reduces CO^2 gas emissions by 465.5 kg every year per reactor.[14] With the Gereja Kristen Jawa Tengah Utara Church in Indonesia (GKJTU), we have become an agent of change in saving the environment through this program.

Suggestions for Further Reading

Agatho Elsener, Pioneer of the Organic Way of Living (VCD), Bina Sarana Bakti, Centre for Organic Development. (Filed note when the author visited to the Bina Sarana Bakti on May 17, 2014.

Chlaodhius Budhianto and Wiwid Widiasmoko in Resiprositas Kiprah Oikomene dan Kemitraan Gereja Kristen Jawa Tengah Utara (Reciprocity of Oikomene's Donations and Partnership with the Javanese Protestant Church from North Central Java), Salatiga 2021.

Witono in Resiprositas Kiprah Oikomene dan Kemitraan Gereja Kristen Jawa Tengah Utara (Reciprocity of Oikomene's Donations and Partnership with the Javanese Protestant Church from North Central Java), Salatiga 2021

Rencana Induk Pengembangan 2003-2028 Gereja Kristen Jawa Tengah Utara hal. 73. (Javanese Protestant Church from North Central Java; Development Master Plan 2003 – 2008.

Tata Dasar GKJTU (Church Constitution of Christian Church from North Central Java).

[13] https://www.suaramerdeka.com/news/baca/128841/potensi-populasi-hewan-ternak-di-jateng-dan-daerah-lainnya-masih-bisa-ditingkatkan.

[14] See: www.biru.or.id.

https://www.suaramerdeka.com/news/baca/128841/potensi-populasi-hewan-ternak-di-jateng-dan-daerah-lainnya-masih-bisa-ditingkatkan.
https://www.micahnetwork.org/resources/micahnetworkdeclarationonintegralmission/
www.biru.or.id

48. Creation Care as a Theme in Chinese Christianity – Beginnings, Obstacles and Potentials

Theresa Carino[1]

Introduction

The article will look at the broader ecological context in contemporary China and the urgency for eco-diaconal engagement by Chinese churches. It will draw on the experience of Amity Foundation, one of the largest FBOs in China today, that was established by Bishop K.H. Ting in 1985 in Nanjing, China. At the same time, it will try to provide an overview of China's struggle over the last two decades to mitigate the negative consequences of rapid industrialization that has led to severe land degradation, air and water pollution, through legislation and religio-cultural means. This will entail a brief exploration of the idea of 'ecological civilization' and some of its roots. Last but not least, the article will provide some reflections on how the religious sector in China can work ecumenically to reinforce the momentum for sustainable development and a green economy.

Environmental Degradation and Failure of Legislation

Environmental degradation was most rapid in the 1980s and 1990s as China embarked on an economic growth trajectory that relied on Foreign Direct Investment (FDI), labor intensive, polluting industries and the extensive use of coal for energy. While China has made great strides in environmental and biodiversity restoration in the last two decades, attempts at strengthening laws and regulations for environmental protection have consistently met with challenges at the level of implementation. In the last few decades, most analysts agree that the enforcement of existing laws have generally failed mainly because of the emphasis on maintaining the gross domestic product (GDP) and high economic growth. Laws were violated more often than not, especially in industry and at the local levels as officials tried to maintain growth figures by tolerating polluting practices at community and corporate levels.

Environmental legislation, no matter how stringent, has been unable to prevent the environmental situation from deteriorating. In recent years, the disputes caused by environmental pollution have increased 20% yearly but less than 1% of these cases chose litigation to resolve these disputes.[2] This proves that environmental issues are more than simply legal issues – they are also political, social, and philosophical issues. Important factors include the role of capital, interest groups, the development model and an anthropocentric worldview and values.[3] Policy makers realized that normative values had to be promoted or advocated using religio-cultural sources such as Confucianism, Daoism and Buddhism in order to motivate climate action. This gave rise to the idea of ecological civilization.

---

[1] Theresa Carino is Senior Research Consultant and Adviser to the Amity Foundation in its international relations.

[2] Zhihe Wang, Huili He and Meijun Fan, "The Ecological Civilization Debate in China: The Role of Ecological Marxism and Constructive Postmodernism—Beyond the Predicament of Legislation" in *Monthly Review* (Nov 1, 2014), 2. Accessed at https://monthlyreview.org/2014/11/01/the-ecological-civilization-debate-in-china/.

[3] Zhihe Wang et al, Ecological Civilization Debate, 2.

Ecological Civilization and Chinese Religio-Cultural Sources

Chinese philosophy has been regarded as having a long tradition of ecological awareness, which is best demonstrated in the ancient concept of the 'unity of heaven and humanity' (*tian ren he yi*).[4] According to the Daoist classic *Daodejing*, human beings shall be in harmony with the Way (*Dao*) of Heaven (*Tian*), for their well-being is dependent on the latter.[5] Chinese scholars concur that the concept of the 'unity of heaven and humanity' is one of the most important resources for proposing a Chinese perspective of ecological ethics. Heaven is seen as a symbol that represents the totality of the universe. Thus, they believe that this emphasis on the unity of humanity and the universe can serve as a foundation of Chinese ecological ethics that balances the dualism between humanity and nature in Western thought. In turn, ecological civilization in China seeks to revive this philosophical tradition to create a sustainable future.[6]

In the domestic debate on ecological civilization, two movements are now recognized as having had an influence on the concept of ecological civilization: one has been the zeal for Chinese resources and traditions and the other is the Influence of Alfred North Whitehead's process theology. Chinese environmentalists find 'constructive post-modernism' attractive as it refers to a pluralistic but integrative thinking, worldview, and practice. It is postmodern not in the sense of being anti-modern, but rather of trying to build upon the best aspects of modernity and tradition, thus creating new ways of thinking.[7] It can guide China towards a path of development that does not simply imitate Western models, but which helps China and others to "move in the direction of an ecological civilization."[8]

Ecological civilization is seen as being different from industrial civilization in four ways. First, it rejects a materialism that instrumentalizes nature for human purposes and stresses the importance of a symbiosis between human life and natural ecosystems. Second, ecological civilization rectifies industrial civilization's error of unrestrained economic growth by advocating self-regulation and self-restraint on human consumption. Third, it suggests that the human relationship with nature should emphasize harmony, not domination. Finally, it envisages that the goal of economic activities should no longer be output and profit maximization but rather, sustainable development.[9]

The institutionalization of 'ecological civilization' as a working concept has taken several decades to accomplish. 'Sustainable development' entered the agenda of the Communist Party of China (CPC) and the Chinese government in 1995. The government began to include 'sustainable development' and ecosystem improvement into the policymaking process, evident in the four targets set during the 16th National Congress of the CPC in 2002 and the call of President Hu Jintao for improvements in ecological construction and education in 2005. Ecological civilization became a *key* political guideline of the CPC in its 17th National Congress in 2007 and was formally written into China's Constitution in 2018.[10]

---

[4] Bryan K. M. Mok, "Reconsidering Ecological Civilization from a Chinese Christian Perspective," Centre for the Study of Religious Ethics and Chinese Culture (Hong Kong: The Chinese University of Hong Kong). Accessed at *Religions 2020*, 11, 261; doi:10.3390/rel11050261 www.mdpi.com/journal/religions.

[5] Bryan Mok, Reconsidering Ecological Civilization, 3.

[6] Bryan Mok, Reconsidering Ecological Civilization, 3.

[7] Zhihe Wang, et. al, Ecological Civilization Debate.

[8] Zhihe Wang, et.al., 6. It should also be noted that well received talks in China include John Cobb's "China Is the Place Most Likely to Achieve Ecological Civilization," David R. Griffin's "The Ecological Crisis: Could China Save Civilization?," Philip Clayton's "Science and Religion as Servants of Ecological Civilization," David Schwerin's "Green Is Golden," Cliff Cobb's "The Practical Steps to Achieve Ecological Civilization," Michael Perelman's "An Ecological Future: Marx and Wu-Wei," and Mary Evelyn Tucker's "Confucianism and View of Nature.

[9] Bryan Mok, 3.

[10] Bryan Mok, 3.

Roots of Creation Care in Contemporary Chinese Christianity

How is eco-theology understood in Chinese Protestant churches? Among churches in mainland China, two theologians most associated with reflections on 'Creation Care' in the last 30 years have been Bishop K.H. Ting and Rev Wang Weifan. With an Anglican background and theological education at Union Theological College in New York in the 1940s, K.H. Ting was much influenced by western liberal theology. He has also incorporated the idea of the 'Cosmic Christ' in his reflections on the environment.

Taking into account the multi-cultural and multi-religious context of Chinese civilization, K.H. Ting's view is inclusive and provides a broad framework of Christian understanding that encourages, justifies and promotes ecumenical, inter-faith and inter-sectoral cooperation in addressing sustainability and climate change issues. By 1990, as the founding Chair of Amity Foundation, Ting had begun attending international ecumenical meetings on the environment. Approaching the problem from a global viewpoint, he saw pollution as mainly coming from the industrialized, developed countries and causing great harm in the developing ones. In 1990, he had presciently said:

> The work of healing the planet has grown beyond the work of a single factory, region or nation. We can only approach it from a global standpoint. There is a very unjust state of affairs in the world today – the majority of pollution comes from the industrialized developed countries and many developing countries reap a great deal of harm from this.[11]

He highlighted the impact of climate change as an issue of social justice:

> Cutting down the forests, polluting the air, contributing to the rise in the earth's temperature are also forms of murder, though not as obvious as shooting someone. Ignoring the ecological balance is destruction of God's creation; it leads imperceptibly to the deaths of countless innocent people. The natural world is suffering and cries out to us.[12]

In contrast to Ting, Wang Weifan had an early education steeped in Chinese philosophy and ethics. In his theology, he incorporated traditional Chinese ideas of ecology and the cosmos, rooting eco-theology in Chinese cultural soil. Wang is considered by some as the most notable in demonstrating how traditional Chinese culture may be integrated with ecological theology. One of the key concepts in Wang's theology is 'creative creativity' (*Sheng sheng*).[13] Recognized as a key concept in Confucianism, *Sheng sheng* is derived from the *Book of Change*.[14]

Wang Weifan takes *Sheng* as an important contact point between Christianity and Chinese culture and suggests that, "in line with the principle of *sheng sheng*, the Christian God is to be understood as a God of originating lives, sustaining lives and renewing lives. According to this view of God's continuing creation, salvation can be understood in terms of the renewal of creation."[15] A practical implication of Wang's theology of creative creativity is his emphasis on social ethics and ecological responsibility.[16]

---

[11] K.H. Ting, "Caring for God's Creation: Speech at the Global Consultation on Development and the Environment, Moscow, 1990" in K. H. Ting, *Love Never Ends* (Nanjing: Yilin Press 2000), 400.
[12] K H. Ting, 401.
[13] Lai Panchu, "Harmonious Society and Environmental Protection" in Theresa C. Carino (ed), *Christianity and social development in China* (Hong Kong: Amity Foundation 2014), 107.
[14] Lai Panchu, 107-8.
[15] Lai Panchu, 107-8.
[16] Lai Panchu, 107-8.

Reforestation and Renewable Energy

Reforestation and the promotion of renewable energy have been among Amity's best practices in relation to climate change over the last 36 years. In the early 1990s, with funding from ecumenical partners, Amity undertook important reforestation projects in Guangxi, in partnership with local government officials, that eventually caught the attention of the provincial government and became replicated on a much larger scale. Renewable energy such as biogas and solar energy were promoted in remote areas of China as part of poverty alleviation. In Hunan, Amity partnered with local governments to promote the use of biogas projects in communities where cattle and pig raising were commonly practiced. In Tibet, solar stoves were distributed to communities to provide renewable energy for cooking.

Renewable energy projects involving biogas and mini-hydros had a significant impact on local communities in the Philippines through South-South exchanges between Amity and the Philippines-China Development Resource Center. Filipino engineers from Manila, Cebu and Davao were trained at the Biogas Training Center in Chengdu in the mid-1990s leading to the setting up of community-based biogas projects in Cebu and Mindanao.[17]

Even though church engagement in social services was not officially endorsed by the Chinese government until 2003, by the late 1990s the Amity Foundation was able to involve the participation of the Hunan Christian Council in water, environmental and renewable energy projects. In many of these projects, local governments gave their support, helping to coordinate the fuller participation of local villages and counties, thereby raising awareness of local communities on the importance of renewable energy in protecting the environment. One notable impact of these projects was a marked reduction in the cutting of trees for fuel.

Christian Engagement in Environmental Conservation

In the last decade, despite earlier hesitations, Chinese urban congregations have gradually grown to appreciate the necessity of environmental conservation. For instance, the church in Suzhou, a mega urban center in Zhejiang Province, has been holding annual bazaars and fundraising for philanthropic projects that encourage the sale of recyclables. These annual events are accompanied by lectures in the local church about the need for caring for God's creation. One interesting feature of these annual bazaars is that they are publicly announced through a noisy parade of the church's brass band marching through public thoroughfares. The noise and fanfare usually attracts residents in neighborhoods surrounding the church who are welcomed to the bazaar regardless of their religious or non-religious backgrounds. Funds raised are used to install water systems in water-scarce areas for marginalized communities.

Engaging Christian Entrepreneurs in Creation Care

According to Cui Wantian, who founded Shengshang, a faith-based organization dedicated to raising levels of social involvement among Christian entrepreneurs:

---

[17] Aileen Baviera, "Prospects for Cooperation and Partnership between Philippine and Chinese Non-profit organizations: The PDRC and IIRR Experience" in *Strategic Issues in Philippines-China Relations: Comprehensive Engagement* (Manila: PDRC, 2000). See also Theresa C. Carino, "Beyond Borders: Amity's South-to-south Exchanges" in Katrin Fiedler and Zhang Liwei (eds), *Growing in Partnership: The Amity Foundation 1985-2005* (Hong Kong: Amity Foundation 2005).

> The mission of Shengshang is to enable entrepreneurs to apply the right beliefs, values and ethics in business operations, to promote corporate integrity and sustainable development and to ultimately contribute to the moral upliftment of the entire community.[18]

It teaches an environmental philosophy based on Christian ethics, in which the world is viewed as God's creation that is to be preserved and protected by human beings. One of its goals is to impress upon entrepreneurs the need to counter environmental degradation and pollution through improved management of company operations, supply chains, products, and services, so that their environmental impact can be reduced to a level possible for natural recovery and waste absorption. This is considered an important moral obligation and responsibility to be undertaken by enterprises. Entrepreneur trainees are brought on environmental study tours to European countries. As a result, some trainees have modified their own behaviors and lifestyles.

Cui gave examples to illustrate this:

> One of those who ran a coal-mining firm decided to shut it down because of the harm it had done to his hometown and resolved to turn to clean energy. Another entrepreneur launched a public welfare project by setting up a trading platform for people to sell secondhand commodities at a very low price or to give them away for free to those in need. Thus, commodities can be reused and recycled, reducing the consumption of resources. Currently, the number of platform users has exceeded 50,000.[19]

Recent ecumenical projects related to climate change include an FCC-sponsored (Friends of the Church in China) 'Waste Management Training' project in Yunnan Province. In 2018, an Amity staff member spent time in the UK learning more about British environmental projects. FCC has subsequently supported Amity's 'Yunnan Rural Waste Management Project' that focuses on preserving the environment of the Wa minority community through waste management training in Cangyuan. Likewise, the Green Life project, supported by NMS (Norwegian Mission Society), is an activity started by a church in Changsha last year, aimed at protecting the environment. The church has started a recycling center on its premises, carries out environmental protection training and collects unwanted food for redistribution to the poor in the community.

Walk for Living Water

This is an advocacy project begun in 2012 as a result of research carried out on Amity's water projects in China. The research highlighted the serious water crises in China, demonstrating how water sources were increasingly being depleted by mining industries and the widespread use of chemical fertilizers in agriculture. In remote communities, traditional sources of clean drinking water are being contaminated by unrestricted animal husbandry or drying up due to over-use or deforestation. It has become increasingly difficult for local communities to access new water sources. Polluted drinking water has contributed to ill-health, higher mortality rates, lower agricultural productivity and in some cases, village relocations.

In response to the need for locating new sources of water for seriously affected communities, Amity Hong Kong began to raise funds for water projects by mobilizing students from church-run secondary schools in Hong Kong, encouraging students to make a 'walk for living water' by taking part in a mini-walkathon. The Annual Walkathon soon gathered interest and momentum as students learned more about the water crisis, how they could reduce water wastage and to care more about how their behavior and

---

[18] Cui Wantian, "Faith, Values and Entrepreneurship in Contemporary China" in Zhuo Xinping, Qiu Zhonghui, Philip Wickeri and Theresa Carino (eds), *Toward a shared sustainable Future: Religions, Values and Ethics* (Hong Kong: Amity Foundation 2018), 180-82.

[19] Cui Wantian, 182-83.

lifestyles can have consequences for the environment and the planet as a whole. The advocacy component has gained strength as more students, teachers, schools and colleges in Hong Kong became involved.

Youth Solidarity and Advocacy for Global Climate Equity

Funds raised were used to build much-needed water systems in remote villages, not only in China, but more recently in Nepal, Myanmar, Cambodia and the Philippines. Not to be deterred during the Covid-19 pandemic, Amity organized advocacy events that brought students together in virtual gatherings to have discussions with beneficiaries of the water projects. Through such interactions, the youth learned about poverty conditions in these countries.

Observing the positive impact of having clean drinking water in villages highly inspired the youth to connect with the global challenge of climate change and lack of clean water access. Individuals are now approached to take on personal challenges for themselves and find groups willing to support this through raising funds for people affected by climate change and bringing them water access.

Amity has advocated for global climate equity by connecting the challenge of global warming to a personal challenge. It is educating Hong Kong students in an engaging way and raising their awareness of the climate change crisis. The youth are challenged to transform their lifestyles, to reduce their carbon footprints and to think of different ways of doing this. Quite a few volunteered to be 'ambassadors' for water conservation. Others took on personal challenges to modify lifestyles and behavior. Some offered to reduce their carbon footprint by consuming less meat while others committed to using more public transportation, recycling and reducing water wastage. More are now joining the call for governments to attain carbon neutrality by 2050, using social media to reach their peers.

Learning from Other Religions: Daoism and a Green China

The Chinese Daoist Association in China has been engaged on issues related to deepening the understanding of religious traditions and the natural environment. This includes understanding myths of creation, views of non-human animals or ethical texts on how human beings should act in this world.[20] The association has also promoted 'green practices' and produced policy statements and action plans on environmental issues from the late 1990s onwards.[21] The Daoist Ecological Temple Network has started many campaigns to reduce carbon emission. For instance, ten years ago, people who visited Daoist temples would usually burn a massive amount of incense sticks. The Daoist 'three incense campaign' urged followers to burn only three simple electric incense sticks per temple, an environmentally friendly action that also follows the Daoist principle of simplicity. Today, this has become the practice of almost all Daoist and Buddhist temples in China.

Conscious that meat consumption and livestock raising have been one of the largest contributors to climate change, the Daoists have returned to their tradition of abstaining from meat on the first and fifteenth day of each month, as offerings and sacrifices made to honor 'heaven'. Daoists have started a vegetarian fasting campaign whereby the 'good days for fasting' are clearly marked in a calendar. If this traditional practice takes hold over a large part of the country, it could result in a significant reduction of meat consumption across the country. James Miller in his book on Daoism as a 'Green Religion' shows how Daoism can provide some answers and viable responses to the environmental challenge that can lead to sustainability. Beyond what Daoism can contribute, Miller poses the question: "What can moderns learn

[20] James Miller, *China's Green Religion: Daoism and the quest for a sustainable future* (New York: Columbia University Press, 2017), 5.
[21] James Miller, *China's Green Religion*, 5.

from Asian civilizations in order to examine whether they allow a more viable cosmological foundation for sustainability?"[22]

Conclusion – The Need for An Ecumenical, Multi-Faith, Global Approach

The need for such a broad and encompassing perspective was strongly emphasized by K.H. Ting. In a speech delivered at a 1990 global consultation on 'Development and the Environment' held in Moscow, Ting had emphasized the multi-cultural and multi-religious context of China and the importance of working with people of different faiths and of no faith:

> Among China's one billion people, there are Buddhists, Muslims, Taoists and Christians, both Catholic and Protestant. Our religious beliefs are all different, but when it comes to the environment, we all feel this is an important question tied to the continued existence on this planet of our common humanity.[23]

He continues:

> To safeguard our earth, we need to unite with others who have the same goal. Anywhere you look, there are religious believers and non-believers, or those who believe differently from ourselves. But in matters of faith we can have mutual respect. Toward all those who are involved in improving the environment and developing the economy, we should be welcoming, grateful, supportive and cooperative. We express this idea in one short phrase in Chinese: "Seek the common ground while reserving differences."[24]

This affirms the view that the religious sector has tremendous resources to contribute. Inter-faith dialogue and cooperation, mutual learning and joint advocacy are goals to aim for. As we have seen, policies and legislation are important but for them to be fully implemented, public involvement is necessary and essential. Christians need to work ecumenically to ensure that care for creation is realized in the face of the 'impending disaster' to our planet and ultimately to ourselves.

Combating global climate change requires the public to take practical actions. It has become a top priority in China to mobilize public participation in tackling climate change. Chinese researchers have noted the changing perceptions of the Chinese public in combatting climate change. In the last decade, surveys taken both internationally and nationally indicate there is a growing interest among the Chinese population in taking action such as changing lifestyles to mitigate environmental pollution and destruction, and even to pay more for products that are environmentally friendly.[25]

Integrating Theology with Practice

Mainstreaming eco-theology, climate justice and food security concerns as integral components in Christian leadership formation both in formal theological education as well as in non-formal programmes of Christian diaconia and development training is a major challenge and task for Amity Foundation and churches in China.

Since 2017, Amity has cooperated with faculty at Nanjing Union Theological Seminary (NJUTS) and Jiangsu Seminary to conduct courses on diaconia, with the aim of helping students integrate the biblico-

---

[22] James Miller, *China's Green Religion*, 141.

[23] K.H. Ting, Caring for God's Creation, 399.

[24] K.H. Ting, 399.

[25] Binbin Wang and Qinnan Zhou, *Climate change in the Chinese mind: An overview of public perceptions at macro and micro levels.* Lorraine Whitmarsh, and Mike Hulme (eds) First published: 09 April 2020. Accessed at https://wires.onlinelibrary.wiley.com/doi/10.1002/wcc.639.

theological understanding of diaconia with its practice. Such an integrative approach is expected to contribute to the strengthening and sustainability of diaconal practice in churches. Since the start of 2019, both seminaries have begun separately offering courses on diaconia which have attracted much interest from students.

Amity has cooperated with NJUTS (the only national level Christian seminary in China) on diaconia training at the 'Summer Academy on Diaconia' since 2017. The jointly held training program incorporates theological and biblical foundations for diaconia, with international and local theologians as resource persons, as well as scholars and experts on development and social services in China. These courses were attended by church leaders, pastors and lay social service practitioners as well as seminary students. In 2019 alone, Amity facilitated 24 capacity-building sessions targeting church social service volunteers and Christian Councils of 20 cities in six provinces, with more than 1,500 volunteers participating in the program. These local level training sessions have helped develop supportive networks linking churches across provinces and can become an important platform for raising environmental awareness in churches.

In the 'Wuppertal Call: Kairos for Creation' from 2019,[26] Ernst Conradie raises the key contradiction between sustainable growth and climate change mitigation: can we offer a viable alternative growth concept? He notes that an alternative growth concept is still under- or ill-defined and indicators for growth measurement are politically not agreed upon. What kind of growth within the 'planetary boundaries' do we want? The world seems to be still far from an international agreement for binding environmental obligations. There is a UN Council for Human Rights, but there is not yet a parallel UN Council for Environmental Obligations and Rights of Nature.

Seeking viable and sustainable 'alternatives' to the present system is clearly a formidable challenge and an urgent task. In a world where market forces dominate, can 'sustainability' become something seen as beneficial and 'profitable' for humankind? What is a green economy, a green environment and a green society and can religions contribute more? As noted earlier, in the last decade in China, the growing negative impact of climate warming on local populations, both urban and rural, have contributed to a rise in understanding of the relationship between unsustainable industrial growth, unrestrained human consumption of the earth's resources and humanitarian disasters. As the effects of climate change become increasingly dire there is an undisputable urgency for ecumenical and inter-faith collaboration to be part of the global effort to reverse this trend. While there is still a long way to go, Chinese Christians are sharing hope in the future by undertaking environmental projects that attempt to restore green areas lost to desertification, for instance, and working ecumenically with Buddhist organizations.[27] We need to set aside our differences and focus on saving the environment as it is tied to the continued existence on this planet of our common humanity.[28]

Suggestions for Further Reading

Ampony, Godwin, Martin Buscher, Beate Hofmann, Felicite Ngnintedem, Dennis Solon and Dietrich Werner (eds), *International Handbook on Ecumenical Diakonia.* Oxford: Regnum, 2021.

Carino, Theresa C. (ed) *Christianity and social development in China.* Hong Kong: Amity Foundation 2014.

---

[26] https://www.brot-fuer-die-welt.de/fileadmin/mediapool/2_Downloads/en/20_About_Us/Wuppertal_Kairos_for_Creation_Publication_01.pdf.

[27] The Shanghai YMCA has been working on restoring and revitalizing land lost to desertification in Inner Mongolia, in an interfaith project with the Shanghai Buddhist Association of China. Jianrong Wu, Zhaozhen Ma and Ruomin Liu, "Diaconia across borders: Interfaith cooperation – a case study of Shanghai YMCA and YWCA in China" in Godwin Ampony, Martin Buscher, Beate Hofmann, Felicite Ngnintedem, Dennis Solon and Dietrich Werner (eds), *International Handbook on Ecumenical Diakonia* (Oxford: Regnum 2021), 236-37.

[28] K.H. Ting, Caring for God's Creation, 399.

Miller, James. *China's Green Religion: Daoism and the quest for a sustainable future*. New York: Columbia University Press, 2017.

Ting, K. H. *Love Never Ends*. Nanjing: Yilin Press, 2000.

Wang, Zhihe, Huili He and Meijun Fan, "The Ecological Civilization Debate in China: The Role of Ecological Marxism and Constructive Postmodernism—Beyond the Predicament of Legislation" in *Monthly Review*, Nov 1, 2014. https://monthlyreview.org/2014/11/01/the-ecological-civilization-debate-in-china/

Zhuo, Xinping, Qiu Zhonghui, Philip Wickeri and Theresa Carino (eds) *Toward a shared, sustainable future*: *The Role of Religion, Values and Ethics.* Hong Kong: Amity Foundation, 2018.

49. On the Concepts and Forms of Engagement for Ecological Transformation in Churches in China

Ruomin Liu[1]

Dismal Personal Experiences and Observations

About 30 years ago, as most of the other children in the countryside in China, I was enjoying swimming in small rivers, ponds and lakes during the summertime. Our parents worked in the farms and even took water for drinking directly from the rivers after working. Nowadays almost nobody does this anymore, since the rivers and ponds are terribly polluted. The third longest river of China is totally polluted, let alone the smaller rivers, lakes and ponds.[2]

My parents are now living in a small town in south China, and they have to cycle for two hours or drive for 30 minutes to fetch their daily drinking water – as do all of the other 300,000 people around the town, even though there is tap water at home. For many years the people in the city have known that the river around the city has been polluted by mining factories and other industries alongside the river.

Seventeen years ago, Nanjing Union Theological Seminary, the national theological seminary in China, began to look for a site to construct a new campus in order to take on more and more theological students. The first time I visited the site, it was a beautiful farmland of rice field. Nowadays the same area is coved by thousands of high concrete buildings, and there is a university town of 15 universities and colleges nearby.[3] That it just a tiny example of the rapid urbanization in China.[4] The urbanization rate has increased steadily over the last few decades, while in the same period both the natural and the social ecological balances have been heavily changed and hugely disturbed.

Transformation of Theological Concepts: The Continuity of Creation and Redemption as the Theological Foundation for Ecological Responsibility

There were many different kinds of mission societies in China and their theological backgrounds were different. Even though the fundamental theological thoughts since the nineteenth century have always been

---

[1] Dr. Ruomin Liu is a head of Studies at Missionsakademie of University Hamburg.

[2] In Yale University's 2012 Environmental Performance Index, China is one of the worst performers (ranked 116 out of 132 countries) with respect to its performance on changes in water quantity due to consumption, including industrial, agricultural, and household uses. Jonathan Kaiman wrote in *The Guardian*, "The head of China's ministry of water resources said in 2012 that up to 40 percent of the country's rivers are "seriously polluted", and an official report from the summer of 2012 found that up to 200 million rural Chinese have no access to clean drinking water." Chang in his article in 2015 listed the really troubling facts about China's water quality: 70% of the rivers and lakes are polluted, 90% of underground water in cities is affected, approximately 300 million citizens in China have no access to clean water – see Ramond Nobu Chang, "Water polluted in China is our of control," https://rnobuchang.wordpress.com/2015/04/13/water-pollution-in-china-is-out-of-control/ (August 20, 2021). "China's lakes are often affected by pollution-induced algae blooms, causing the surface of the water to turn a bright iridescent green. Yet even greater threats may lurk underground. A recent government study found that ground water in 90% of China's cities is contaminated, most of it severely." Jonathan Kaiman, "Chinese environment official challenged to swing in polluted river", https://www.theguardian.com/environment/2013/feb/21/chinese-official-swim-polluted-river (August 20, 2021).

[3] "Jianning University Town", https://zhidao.baidu.com/question/44249876.html (August 20, 2021).

[4] According to the Seventh Population Census conducted in 2020, about 63.9% of the total population in China lived in cities in 2020. "Degree of urbanization in China from 1980 to 2020", https://www.statista.com/statistics/270162/urbanization-in-china/ (August 20, 2021).

a large influence among Chinese Christians, the division between Christians and nonbelievers, the gap between church and society, and the isolation of the pious community remained a common phenomenon amongst a lot of church communities. Theological reflections on political issues and social care rarely played a strong role in the teaching and preaching of the churches – let alone ecological issues. The church and its theology in China in this sense is not yet well 'cultivated', or in another word, it is still 'unhealthy'.[5]

K.H. Ting (1915-2012), who was the president of Nanjing Union Theological Seminary from 1952 to 2010, and also the chairperson of the National Christian Council and the National Three-Self Patriotic Movement (the highest umbrella organizations of the Protestant Church in China) from 1981 to 1996, initiated a movement for 'theological renewal'. The goal of the movement was further development of the church in China in order to provide for 'running the church well' and for an *aggiornamento*, i.e. adaptation to the socialist society, so that believers may really engage in social issues. Thus, the church was to be brought in line with the spirit of the times. In 2000 in his last published article, Ting explained the aims of this movement and described the need for this *aggiornamento*:

> We are beginning to realize that theological renewal is a necessary and fundamental issue for running the church well, a crucial among many weighty issues facing the church. We live in a socialist society. This being the case, how will our students adapt if we keep to the status quo of the 19th and 20th centuries, mechanically copying all the traditional ways received by the Western missionary movement? [...] Our future vision of the Chinese church is one that is rich in a theology that respects reason and is more suited to Chinese socialist society. It will be one that can help believers to establish a more harmonious and reasonable faith and witness.[6]

In his lecture at the 90th anniversary of the 4th May Movement[7] in 1999 at the Nanjing Union Theological Seminary (where the author was present as a junior student), Ting emphasized that theology is not only a

---

[5] Ruomin Liu, Vom Christentum in China zum chinesischen Christentum. Die Sinisierung und ihr gesellschaftliches Ziel, in Interkulturelle Theological Theologie, 1/2021, Evangelische Verlagsanstalt, Basel 2021, 139. Evaluating the influence of missionaries and mission movement in China since the nineteenth century is a controversial topic, and there are two extreme opinions. One group criticizes the movement of mission in China – for example, Zhang Zhigang echoes the opinion of Luo Guangzhong (1920-2011), former chairman of the National Three-Self Movement of the Protestant Church in China. He writes, "Modern Christianity was introduced to China in the 19th century and had made certain contributions to Chinese society. Unfortunately, the introduction of Christianity was inseparable from the invasion of China by imperialism and was caused by colonialism and used by imperialism." Guangzhong Luo, "Qianshi Buwan Houshi Zhishi" (Not forgetting the past, a guide for the future – a review of historical facts about imperialists using Christianity to invade China), Zhongguo Zongjiao Wenhu Chubanshe: Beijing 2003, 2. Another group recognizes the contribution of missionaries and mission society to the civilization of China. Recently, Yuyu Chen, Hui Wang and Se Yan, in their article, "The Long-Term Effects of Protestant Activities in China", pointed to the deep impact of Protestant activities in China, such as on education, rights for women, health care etc. Yuyu Chen, Hui Wang and Se Yan, "The Long-Term Effects of Protestant Activities in China," http://mpra.ub.uni/muenchen.de/53531 (August 20, 2021).

[6] K.H. Ting, "My View of These Fifty Years," in Janice and Philip Wickeri (eds.), *A Chinese Contribution to Ecumenical Theology* (Geneva: WCC Publications, 2002), 112-113. K.H. Ting, "On the Last 10 Years," in *Tianfeng*, no. 23 (2008), 1. Wickeri comments: "In Ting's understanding, theological reconstruction has been an extension of running the church well, for a well-run church should have its own theology, one that enables it to respond to the times. That theology should bear witness to God's love, confront Christian fundamentalism, play down the differences between believers and nonbelievers and give greater attention to social involvement. There is also a need for 'mutual adaption' between Christianity and Chinese society in order to facilitate the mission of the church and contribute to society. Ting's own theology has been a useful corrective to the narrow one-sidedness of Chinese evangelicalism, which has tended to close the church off from its social and cultural milieu." Philip Wickeri, *Reconstructing Christianity in China. K. H. Ting and the Chinese Church* (New York: Maryknoll, 2007), 376.

[7] The May Fourth Movement originated in the student protests in China against the Treaty of Versailles on May 4, 1919. China sided with the Allies in World War One and hoped for the abrogation of the Unequal Treaties and non-recognition of Japan's 21 demands of 1915. These hopes were not fulfilled by the treaties. The May Fourth

pure science for the scholars in theological institutes, but also has a political dimension, related to the specific Chinese context. Theology relates to the current world and the social challenges of today: "Theology is a more meticulous form of politics." This needs to be reflected on carefully. However, traditional theology as inherited and influenced by the West, has had a strong exclusionary effect, particularly in the style of sermons. For this reason, Bishop Ting argued that it is necessary for theologians to reflect deeply on the current Chinese situation and take a critical stance.

"Theology is a more meticulous form of politics." This can be understood with Dietrich Bonhoeffer's famous motto, "Theology is a tool to struggle."[8] Thus theology is a tool to help identify the wrong, the unkempt thoughts or unhealthy theologies within the church, and to support the church in its spiritual struggle.[9] Moreover, it is also an instrument to call erring churches to the truth. Furthermore, theology can train human self-criticism in relation to God's good-will and therefore contributes to recognizing and taking on social responsibility.

But we have to ask more precisely, theology is a tool for what? If it is an instrument of struggle, against what do we have to struggle? Ting has stated that the movement of renewal has to be directed "against absurd fundamentalist currents" in the Chinese church in order to adapt it to socialist society. The fundamentalist currents, in Ting's view, refer to a predominant theology of fear and a strong separation between Christians and non-Christians. As Monika Gänßbauer pointed out in *Party State and Protestant Church*:

> [Ting] justified the need for the movement by arguing that many Christians in China, especially in the countryside, still held strongly conservative theological views, some of which dated back to the preaching of Western missionaries. In the countryside, a theology of fear and a strong separation of Christians from non-Christians often still prevail. Such Christianity is incapable of entering into a dialogue with religious scholars and intellectuals in China. He sees himself as a 'liberal theologian' and his vision is that the Chinese church will one day have a 'wonderful, liberal theology'.[10]

Since the 1950s, Ting had repeatedly criticized these 'absurd' fundamentalist currents of theology in China.[11] In the 1980s, he also extended his criticism to a distorted perception of the relationship between creation and salvation which affects the division between Christians and nonbelievers. At that time, however, Ting had not yet dealt with ecological issues directly. In seeking a meaningful dialogue with atheism, Ting urged a positive view of humanity, believers and nonbelievers, and encouraged Christians in China to take responsibility for nature and society. He counselled Christians to see creation and redemption as equal parts of God's whole plan of salvation. He writes:

Movement is considered the first mass political movement in Chinese history and thus serves as a point of reference for identification and legitimation for many political movements to this day. See Dewang Zhang, *The History of the May Fourth Movement*, Harbin 2011 (Chinese).

[8] Thus Bonhoeffer himself also describes theology as, "an aid, a means of struggle, not an end in itself." Dietrich Bonhoeffer, *Theologie und Gemeinde*, in *Dietrich Bonhoeffer Werke Band 16*, Gütersloh 1996, 496.

[9] "Bonhoeffer's understanding of theology, if we briefly summarize the preceding, places theoretical endeavor at the service of ecclesiastical practice. Proclamation and faith-obedient following of Christ can be seen as cornerstones of his theology, which can be found in the individual aspects that follow, as well as in the description of theology as reflexive and descriptive tracing of the given contents of faith." Gerhard Ludwig Müller, ‚Bonhoeffer's Theology. Ein Ort katholischer Theologie heute', in J. Außermeier; G. Maria Hoff (Hrsg.), *Dietrich Bonhoeffer – Orte seiner Theologie*, Ferdinand Schöningh: Paderborn/München/Vienna/Zürich 2008, 36.

[10] Monika Gänßbauer, *Parteistaat und Protestantische Kirche. Religionspolitik im nachmaoistischen China*, Lembeck: Frankfurt am Main 2004, 147-148.

[11] Chloë Starr, *Chinese Theology: Text and Context* (New Haven: Yale University Press, 2016), 185ff.

> Christ is Lord of both creation and redemption....The New Testament recognizes Christ's creation and it also recognizes his redemption. This is one and the same Christ and creation and redemption are a unity, not an opposition. There are not two gods each tending to his own.[12]

In 2009, theologian and long-time Professor at Nanjing National Theological Seminary, Chen Zemin (1917-2018), articulated in his last open lecture, 'I Still Have Something to Say', a major encouragement for the younger generation of Chinese theologians to take up different kinds of ethical issues in Chinese society. The key argument was that, "Christ is cosmic in his nature. And God's work of creation is ongoing."[13]

> I hope that through the joint efforts of all those who are theologically versed and have a direct or indirect relationship with Jinling [Nanjing Union Theological seminary], a group of theological researchers will emerge who will join the church, focus on society, and look to the future and academic theological scholars be sincerely benevolent, true, just, humble and servant.[14]

Though these issues continue to be widely debated in the Chinese church, more and more theologians in China accepted this as the theological foundation for ecological responsibility – that Christians have to take up social responsibility and care for God's creation.

Political and Social Engagement: A Successful Case

China is the world's second-largest producer of municipal solid waste and a recycling regimen is long overdue. In the year 2004, one Christian member of the National Committee of the Chinese People's Political Consultative Conference and the Vice-President of the national Three-Self-Patriotic-Movement of Christianity in China, Rev An Xinyi, submitted his proposal, 'Call on the Government to Make greater Efforts to Properly Deal with the Problem of Waste' to the national congress.[15] This proposal then was adopted by the national congress and widely promoted, thereby showing that there was room for Christians to play a public role on building ecological harmony in Chinese society.

An Xinyi stated, "Cities have gradually established urban waste collection, transportation and treatment systems, but they are not yet perfect. During urbanization, attention should be paid to improving the urban ecological environment and improving the level of urban waste treatment." He made people aware of several problems and difficulties in the collection, transportation and disposal of garbage in China, including: that often management cannot keep up with working demands; transportation equipment is relatively backward; garbage transfer facilities in some places are insufficient; and garbage transportation vehicles are outdated. Problems also often exist in the further processes: the classification of garbage is also outdated; people's environmental awareness is still relatively poor; and the recycling technology and the resource utilization are not highly developed. In addition, many of the garbage treatment facilities are not up to standard and fail to meet the technical standards promulgated by the state in 2001.[16]

---

[12] K H. Ting, 'Creation and Redemption', in Janice and Philip Wicheri (ed.), *A Chinese Contribution to Ecumenical Theology. Selected Writings of Bishop K. H. Ting* (Geneva: WCC, 2002), 103.

[13] Zemin Chen, 'I Still Have Something to Say', in *Chinese Theological Review* 25, FTESEA, Philadelphia 2013, 154.

[14] Ibid, 153f.

[15] 'An Xinyi, member of the National Committee of the Chinese People's Political Consultative Conference, called for improving the level of urban garbage disposal', https://www.solidwaste.com.cn/news/26059.html (August 20, 2021).

[16] 'An Xinyi, member of the National Committee of the Chinese People's Political Consultative Conference, called for improving the level of urban garbage disposal', https://www.solidwaste.com.cn/news/26059.html (August 20, 2021).

An Xinyi therefore recommended to intensify the reform and opening up of the sanitation industry, including the investment in and operation of sanitation services, as well as the construction of garbage projects and the implementation of the right to operate garbage disposals. According to him, it is important to formulate laws and regulations for separate waste disposal and resource recycling systems and also to improve the hazardous waste treatment system, in order to prevent hazardous wastes (listed in the 'National Hazardous Waste List') from being mixed into the domestic waste treatment systems.

The official proposal was accepted by the central committee conference and the central government finally set out waste sorting plans in March 2017, which aimed to recycle 35% of waste in 46 major cities of China by 2020. In March 2020, the State Council further issued a plan to make sorting of domestic waste compulsory. Produced by the National Development and Reform Commission and the Ministry of Housing and Urban-Rural Development, it would put in place legislation and standards for waste sorting by the end of 2020, piloting compulsory sorting in ten or more cities before other cities followed suit.[17]

Educational Programs for Environmental Ethics

Fourteen years previously, at the academic conference, 'The Chinese Christians and the Harmony Society', an article was published by the author explaining responsibility for the protection of the environment according to the theology of creation:

> Human beings have generally recognized that ecological problems have threatened their own survival and that climate change is the biggest currently challenge to the humanity. As Christian, we must urgently take responsibility to promote the movement of environmental protection among all people, not only theoretical issues, but also practical engagement.[18]

Christianity is not a religion isolated from the world. God is the creator of the all creature, both the visible and the invisible things, and every Christian is not 'raptured' after conversion to exist apart from the world, but still lives in the world because we have the responsibility to be disciples of Christ in this visible world. Both stewardship and discipleship are therefore marks of our identity. Our Lord also told us that we are "light and salt" (Mt 5:14) of the earth, and that we have to fulfill our social and ethical responsibilities in this world. Concern for the environment is also one of our ethical responsibilities as Christians. In China, there is a strong positive meaning to be able to guide more than 40 million Christians with the Christian concepts of ecology. As Christians, we must consider what role the church and Christians will play in the construction of a harmonious society.[19]

Christian ethics has always been an important subject at Nanjing Union Theological Seminary in China. Since 2004, together with Raymond Whitehead from Canada, we have provided a course on Theological Ecology for senior students of the bachelor program and also students of the master program. As a result of this, there have always been some students working on the issues of theological ecology and environment protection.

In addition, other lecturers from Nanjing Union Theological Seminary have also made a contribution to promote Christian perspectives on engagement in environment protection. Following the traditional understanding of what it means be a Chinese Christian, ecological dimensions can also be highlighted in

---

[17] 'China is sorting its household waste problem', https://chinadialogue.net/en/pollution/9812-china-is-sorting-its-household-waste-problem/ (August 20, 2021).

[18] Ruomin Liu, 'The Christian Ecological Responsibility according to the Theology of Creation', *The Academic Annual of Taiwan Baptist Theological Seminary*, Taiwan Baptist Theological Seminary: Taipei 2007, 59.

[19] Ibid, 60ff.

the three key pillars of Chinese Christian existence: faith, worship and preaching, as reflected upon in the following.[20]

Ecological Renewal of the Liturgical Texts for the Lord's Supper: Emphasizing the Community between Humanity and Nature

As theological educators in China, we believe that, "liturgical texts contain theological presuppositions about God, about humanity, about the ordering of creation, about the relationship between people, and between people and God."[21]

During worship we restate what sort of God it is that we serve. For example, the very common traditional exclamation, "Lord have mercy," is not a hopeful request, nor a command, but a pre-fulfilled request made in the knowledge of a merciful God derived from promises in the gospels and validated by the experience of worshippers. Certain language choices serve to establish the distinctions in the relationship, most obviously by traditionally reserving 'Thee/Thou/Thine' for God, after it had fallen out of use; or by using epithets for God which are not used of humans (or even heavenly beings), such as ineffable, almighty, immortal etc. These assertions are more than descriptions – they re-state for the community what sort of God it is who hears and answer our prayers, and the worshippers learn through the liturgical exclamation for their daily life.

Since 2014 I have promoted the renewal of the liturgical texts through the course 'Ecclesiology and Liturgy' at Nanjing Theological Seminary. Michal Welker writes about the renewal of liturgical text for the Lord's Supper"

> As 'gift of creation', bread and wine are not simple 'gifts of nature'. This means that there is no bread and wine without the successful communion of human beings with each other and with nature. This comes to expression in seed-time and harvest, and the processes that produce bread as a daily means of nourishment and wine as a festive drink.[22]

With the purpose of promoting the theological ecology, the following sentences were added to the Eucharistic liturgy:

> ...Receiving bread (congregation standing): You take it and eat it. This is a gift from God the Father, the creator of all things. The wheat originally grown in the field, the Father made it sprout, root, grow, and the laboring farmers, cultivated, harvested. Now it is made into the bread. As the Lord Jesus himself taught us on the night in which he was betrayed, this is the body of the Savior Jesus Christ, who was given up for your sins. May the Lord Jesus strengthen you in true faith until eternal life. ...
>
> Receiving the cup (the congregation stands up): Take it and drink it. This is the gift of God the Father who created the heavens and the earth. The grapes originally are grown in the valley, the heavenly father told them to grow: and the gardeners cultivated, picked, and fermented them into a festival drinking. Present to the Lord now, as our Lord himself taught: This is the blood of the Savior Jesus Christ, which was shed on the cross to forgive your sins. May the Lord Jesus strengthen you in faith until eternal life."

---

[20] Cf. Joseph Tse-Hei Lee, 'Preaching (傳 chuan), Worshipping (拜 bai), and Believing (信 xin): Recasting the Conversionary Process in South China', in Richard Young (ed.), *Asia in the Making of Christianity: Conversion, Agency, and Indigeneity, 1600s to the Present*, Brill 2013, 81ff.

[21] Juliette Day, 'Liturgical language and the liturgical text', https://www.thepastoralreview.org/issues/36-past-issues/2012/november-december-2012/68-liturgical-language-and-the-liturgical-text (August 20, 2021).

[22] Michael Welker, *Was geht vor beim Abendmahl?* Gütersloher Verlagshaus, Gütersloh 1999, 70f.

Ecological Dimensions in Churches' Arts

Hymns on the care of creation

Fortunately, there are many Chinese hymns which thank and praise God for creation, and offer insights into the nature of God based on the wonders of the natural world. Several of them are included in the *New Hymnal Book*, published by China Christian Council (CCC) in 1983. The hymnal book is popular among Christians in China, since there is only one official published hymnal book and so every congregation in China sings the hymns from this book.

Some hymns explicitly remember the creation of God:

> Long before the universe was formed, The Lord God revealed His grace. God our Father heavenly lights did make, Sun, moon and star, ass for our sake. …[23]

Some hymns sing high praise to the great beauty of His nature:

> Nature glows with colors rare, Poet's verse blooms from his pen, heavenly pours forth its music pure, God shows new art to all men. …[24]

Some hymns also revoke the 'new vision' of heaven and earth as the will of God:

> … View our country being touch by the Creator's brush. By God's grace fertile plains, Swift rivers, high peaks bold. …Until the day when work's done, New heaven and earth we see.[25]

Christian painting and its contribution to ecology

There are some talented Chinese Christian artists with some exceptional works – even some books published in Europe and the USA have taken paintings from China for cover designs! Some church events have also taken drawings by Chinese Christians for posters (for instance, the works of Dr. Qi He).[26] However, human figures seem to be almost everywhere dominant in paintings, and the harmony between humankind and nature (which was the most important issue in traditional Chinese painting art) plays almost no role in Christian art. The relationship between humanity and nature certainly has been a dominant theme in traditional Chinese paintings, which together with traditional Chinese culture has influenced the world for thousands of years with its art, philosophy, technology, food, medicine and performing arts. The idea of harmony with nature underlies many aspects of Chinese culture, from calligraphy and painting to architecture and medicine.

"Oriental thought stresses the interaction between humans and nature, and thinks that the two should be integrated with each other. This is quite different from Western thought which regards humans as the center of the world."[27] From its beginning, Chinese painting has gone through great development to emerge as an independent cultural form which has experienced many years of sophistication. Therefore, it has had an indispensable contribution to the development of the Chinese humanistic spirit. Having greatly enriched the spiritual connotation of Chinese traditional culture, and having an important positive significance for

---

[23] Shengjie Cao, 'Long before the universe was formed', *The New Hymnal*, The New Hymnal Editorial Committee of National China Christian Council, China Christian Council, Shanghai 1983, 9. Cf. 6, 7, 12, 25, 30, 31, 33, 309.
[24] Y.L. Yang, 'Nature glows with colors rare', *The New Hymnal*, The New Hymnal Editorial Committee of National China Christian Council, China Christian Council, Shanghai 1983, 13. Cf. 14, 17, 21, 22, 26, 27.
[25] Zemin Chen, 'Creator's artistic brush', *The New Hymnal*, The New Hymnal Editorial Committee of National China Christian Council, China Christian Council, Shanghai 1983, 178.
[26] https://www.heqiart.com/.
[27] Bi Nan, 'Artist explores the relationship between humans and nature', http://covid-19.chinadaily.com.cn/culture/art/2016-07/12/content_26057597.htm.

the progress of the society, traditional Chinese painting therefore should also be an issue for the Chinese Christian art, for the movement of Sinicization to be promoted.[28]

Ecological education through social-media

Recently environmental challenges have also been aggravated by the extensive use of face masks during COVID-19. Wearing masks has become a global requirement to stop the spread of COVID-19, although they do have one drawback, as they can become disastrous for the environment – the TNT they are made from takes between 400 and 450 years to break down. That is why health authorities the world over are concerned about this new type of environmental pollution.

Waste from the masks has increased across the world, as people have not been following appropriate disposal methods for used masks. This has created a new environmental challenge, and many developing countries have no appropriate waste collecting methods. "There is a dramatic rise in the generation of plastic waste during the COVID-19 due to the increased use of face masks and change in customer preference to single use mask due to the hygienic problems."[29]

Some pastors in China have had a clear vision to help people learn more about disposal of masks and protecting the environment. Among the Wechat-goups,[30] some pastors regularly posted information and suggestions on how to dispose of masks and gloves.[31] For example, the materials should be placed into two small plastic bags – one inside the other – tied firmly, and then thrown away with general domestic waste. If the materials have been in contact with an infected person, take extra care and write 'Risk of Contamination' on the bag.

No Conclusion, But a Tiny Example

I live with my family in Hamburg. Before Christmas every year, my children always ask whether there is any possibility of buying a Christmas tree. However, I always refuse! Customers spend €20 – €40 to buy a tree for two or three weeks, yet the trees are 10 or 20 years old. For this reason I refuse to buy a tree of green branches for Christmas.

---

[28] Cf. Ruomin Liu, ‚vom Christentum in China zum chinesischen Christentum. Die Sinisierung und ihr gesellschaftliches Ziel', in Interkulturelle Theologie, 1/2021, Ev. Verlag und Basileia Verlag, Basel

[29] https://www.sciencedirect.com/science/article/pii/S2667010021000184
L. Patrício Silva, J. C. Prata, T. R. Walker, D. Campos, A.C. Duarte, A. M. V. M. Soares, D. Barcelò, T. Rocha-Santos, 'Rethinking and optimising plastic waste management under COVID-19 pandemic: policy solutions based on redesign and reduction of single-use plastics and personal protective equipment', *Sci. Total Environ.*, 742 (2020), Article 140565.

[30] So almost all pastors in China have been appreciating the benefits of digitalization and the possibilities of mobile communication for more than ten years, but never as much as they have since the beginning of the year 2020. The corona virus SARS-CoV-2 has crippled large parts of China since the measures taken on 23 February 2020. Many companies remained closed because employees did not have to return or remained in quarantine. And even short purchases can become a risk. In many cities, after 'Defense Condition 1', people were not even allowed to go outside from their own homes. All conferences, meetings, even spring festival parties were cancelled. All religious sites also had to remain closed. Thanks to the Internet and mobile communications, Christians in China have still been able to celebrate services, but all have had to stay at home. This increases the time available and the need to attend Bible circles and worship services via apps even more often than usual. The local churches either have developed their own apps or have rented a stake in social communication apps from the telephone companies. Almost all pastors have their own WeChat IDs (WeChat is a Chinese chat service for social networks, comparable to WhatsApp, but with considerably more functions). The age of mobile communication certainly offers new opportunities for evangelization in China. For example, there is an app that was developed by a group of young Chinese Christians which offers users not only church news and information about the parishes but also a liturgical calendar, religious music and audio books, videos, prayer of the hours, Bible reflections and chat groups.

[31] https://mp.weixin.qq.com/s/uIziRaPgS1V-ugOlERPBUQ.

Climate change is not only caused by a single group of the world's population; it is not only the responsibility of one nation. Climate change relates both to the unjustified unlimited global trade system, as well to individual consumer behavior in all the countries of the world. Therefore our ecological ideals, our moral standards in our daily life, as well as our corrupted culture, needs to be challenged and changed. But as God's love to his creation never ends, our responsibility also never ends, since we are his disciples and witnesses.

Suggestions for Further Reading

Changxing Wu (ed.), The theological Ecology. The Academic Annual of Taiwan Baptist Theological Seminary 2007, Taiwan Baptist Theological Seminary: Taipei 2007.

Katrin Fiedler (Hrsg.), Ökologische Perspektiven in China. Beiträge aus Kultur, Religion und Zivilgesellschaft, Evangelisches Missionswerk in Deutschland: Hamburg 2011.

Chloë Starr (ed.), Chinese Theology: Text and Context, Yale University Press, New Haven 2016.

Anthony E. Clark (ed.), China's Christianity: From Missionary to Indigenous Church, Brill: Leiden/Boston 2017.

50. Further Contextualization of Chinese Christianity from an Ecological Perspective

Manhong Lin and Xuebin Zhou[1]

As scholars have pointed out, the root causes of the ecological crisis largely come from anthropocentrism, alienation of science and technology from nature and related alienation of consumption, the capitalist system, and religions.[2] What lies behind the causes are the distorted relationships between human beings and nature, the exploitation of national resources in the course of the development of human society, and excessive human greed and selfishness. To properly handle the human-nature relationship and to restrain human uncontrolled selfish desires is a key to environmental protection and human development, which needs to be understood as ecological sustainability. This paper mainly aims to propose a relevant ecological view from a Chinese Christian perspective by drawing on the resources from the biblical creation story, the ecological wisdom of ancient Chinese philosophers, and current Chinese theory on the construction of an ecological civilization to contribute to the global Christian discourse on ecological sustainability. Constructing such a theory and encouraging Chinese Christians to take up their ecological responsibilities can also be regarded as an effort for fostering further contextualization of Chinese Christianity from an ecological perspective.[3]

A Chinese Christian's Integral Ecological View

Chinese Christian churches, from the Reconstruction of Theological Thinking in 1998 till the present, have experienced further contextualization by renewing their theological thinking so that the "basic [Christian] faith will be expressed in terms that are more accessible and more reasonable" to Chinese Christians.[4] The theological reflections on ecology will not undermine the faith tradition of Chinese Christians, but rather strengthen their faith in God and have it transformed by integrating the ecological wisdom in Chinese culture and the theory of national ecological civilization into the Christian view of God's relationship with all of God's creation.

Rooted in the Ecological Interpretation of the Bible

As mentioned, religion is deemed as one of the root causes of the ecological crisis. Among religions, Christianity is further accused of its theoretical support for anthropocentrism, particularly by its creation

---

[1] Rev. Dr. Manhong Lin is Associate General Secretary of the China Christian Council (CCC), Director of the Theological Department of CCC&TSPM (China Christian Council and the National Committee of the Three-Self Patriotic Movement), Academic Dean and Professor of Christian Ethics of Nanjing Union Theological Seminary (NJUTS). Mr. Xuebin Zhou is Lecturer of English and Theology of Worship of NJUTS.

[2] Wang Xiaobin, "sheng tai wei ji zhong de zong jiao ze ren" [Religious Responsibilities in Ecological Crisis], *zong jiao yan jiu* [Religious Studies], no. 3 (2015): 279.

[3] The term "further contextualization of Chinese Christianity" in Chinese 基督教中国化 (*ji du jiao zhong guo hua*) refers to the process of making Chinese Christian Church Chinese in such areas as doctrine, church governance and ministry. Although alternative translations like "Sinicization of Chinese Christianity" are often seen in publications, the official translation recognized by the China Christian Council is the "further contextualization of Chinese Christianity."

[4] K.H. Ting, "Theology Adapting to a Changing Culture," in *God Is Love: Collected Writings of Bishop K.H.Ting* （CO: Cook Communications, 2004), 451-452.

story. Some Christian have eco-scholars also self-reflected about this accusation. For instance, Lynn White, an American historian, states that the Christian theology and culture of the Middle Ages where God is thought to be outside the creation makes available an unholy material space, thereby justifying the utilitarian view of nature as a resource pool.[5] Jürgen Moltmann also points out that the root of ecological crisis lies in the "modern view of God." According to Moltmann, since the Renaissance, due to the lopsided emphasis on divine omniscience and omnipotence, God has been seen as having withdrawn to the transcendental realm after having created the heavens and earth and alienated himself from the creation. Consequently, human beings, bearing the image of God, mistakenly claim themselves to be masters of nature like God. The ever-increasing desire and power of humankind distances human beings from nature, even causing them to be in opposition to nature.[6]

Does the creation story indeed support an anthropocentrism or is it simply misinterpreted? How to depart from the 'modern view of God' and establish a proper 'view of God' that is conducive to eco-sustainability? To answer these questions, we must revisit the biblical creation story for a brief investigation on the God-human-nature relationship.

First, according to the order of creation in Genesis, nature is created before human beings, and therefore nature and all creatures cannot originate from human will, nor can human beings be the center of the world. Meanwhile, all created things of every kind are good in the eyes of God (Gen. 1:11-25). Thus, nature derives its intrinsic value from the fact that it demonstrates the beauty and goodness recognized by God the creator. It is also endowed with the inherent right for survival and thriving. Moreover, all creatures are in the inclusive love of the creator rather than being at odds with one another, which indicates and demonstrates a kind of beauty and goodness of all creation, rendered not by human will, but God the creator.

Second, God cares for all creatures in a covenantal relationship. After the flood, God makes a covenant not only with Noah's family, but also with all the living creatures that come out of the ark (Gen. 9:9-11). Although God graciously gives human beings all kinds of living things as food, this does not mean that human beings have the right to treat animals abusively. Rather, human beings are supposed to "know the needs of their animals" as the righteous would do (Prov. 12:10). Human beings should govern the whole earth like servants with awe in their hearts towards the creation of God, for God is the common master of humankind and nature.

In addition, the teaching of Sabbath in the Bible also reveals God's love for all creatures. The biblical tradition of the Sabbath is proposed by Moltmann as a way out of the ecological crisis. Moltmann believes that Sabbath has three mutually related layers of implications. God's Sabbath is God's rest from his work and God is dwelling in all things and all things in God; God's Sabbath also makes all things in heaven and on earth rest; the Sabbath of all things allows all creatures to live in the way that they are meant to, fitting their own kinds and following their own needs without being threatened and assimilated by nothingness.[7] As the result of Sabbath, the land is preserved, animals and plants are cared for, human strength is renewed and the entire ecosystem develops in a harmonious manner.

Thus, the ecological stance represented in the biblical creation story is far from anthropocentric. God the creator, the sole master is truly, fully and impartially present with all creatures, including humankind. There is a continuous, purposeful, and ultimate salvific relationship between God and the whole creation which is implied in the Sabbath. The ecological view for Chinese Christians should correspond to such ecological revelation in the Bible.

---

[5] Michael S. Northcott, "Ecology and Christian Ethics" in Robin Gill (ed.), *The Cambridge Companion to Christian Ethics* (Cambridge: Cambridge University Press, 2012), 221.

[6] Jürgen Moltmann, *su shi zhong de shang di* [Gott im Projekt der modernen Weit], trans. Zeng Nianyue (Taiwan: Ya Ge Publishing, 1999), 12; Li Lei, "sheng tai wei ji de zong jiao gen yuan-mo er te man sheng tai si xiang lun shu" [The Religious Roots of Ecological Crisis- Jürgen Moltmann's Ecological Thoughts], *zi ran bian zheng fa yan jiu* [Studies in Dialectics of Nature] (September 2004): 17.

[7] Li Lei, "sheng tai wei ji de zong jiao gen yuan-mo er te man sheng tai si xiang lun shu," 18.

Drawing on Chinese Traditional Ecological Wisdom

The formulation of an ecological view of Chinese Christians needs to also draw on the ecological ethics of the excellent tradition of Chinese culture. In the thoughts of classical Confucianism and Taoism, we can roughly see the following two aspects of ecological thoughts in Chinese traditional culture:

First, Chinese traditional culture emphasizes human beings' harmonious coexistence with nature in compliance with the laws of nature. For instance, Confucius' thoughts of "knowing the heavenly will" (知天命 *zhi tian ming*) and "fearing the heavenly will" (畏天命 *wei tian ming*) not only pertain to human ethics but also reveal the ethics of heaven, earth and nature. The "heavenly will" proposed by Confucius refers to the laws of nature, including the laws of heaven, earth and humankind. It is fundamentally an objective and irresistible natural law. Therefore, knowing the heavenly will means the same as abiding to the natural law. A wise person, according to Confucius, behaves in line with the time of a day as well as the movement of the sun and the moon. A wise person does not rely on divination to distinguish fortune from misfortune but simply follows the laws of heaven and earth.[8] Knowing and respecting the heavenly will and not violating the laws of nature constitute the theoretical cornerstone of Confucius' ecological ethics.

Additionally, "knowing the heavenly will" and "fearing the heavenly will" are applied to distinguish the virtuous people (君子 *jun zi*) from the small people (小人*xiao ren*) as "the superior man is quiet and calm, waiting for the appointments of Heaven, while the mean man walks in dangerous paths, looking for lucky occurrences [*sic*]."[9] Virtuous people, with awe of the heaven, behave cautiously to stay in harmony with other human beings and with nature. By contrast, small people have no fear of the heaven. As a result, the small people, desperate to achieve their selfish ambitions, disregard the laws of nature and wantonly harm the relationship between human beings and nature. Therefore, it is justifiable to propose that the majority of crises in today's world, including the ecological crisis, have something to do with the absence of the fear of the heavenly will or the heavenly decrees.

Hsün-tzu (荀子ca.298 – ca. 238 B.C.), another representative figure of Confucianism, also stresses that people should respect the laws of nature. He puts forward the ecological thesis that "the natural law is constant." (天行有常 *tian xing you chang*). He writes, "the natural law is eternally constant. It does not survive for the sake of Yao (尧), nor does it cease to be because of Jie (桀). Fortune will come about when natural laws are observed in governing nature, otherwise misfortune will fall upon the land."[10] That is, nature operates according to certain laws, not depending on human will. It will be auspicious and smooth therefore if society adapts to the laws of nature with correct governing measures; if nature is treated with the wrong measures, severe disasters will appear.

Similar to Confucianism, Taoism states that people should conform to nature. Lao Tzu claims that, "the knowledge of constancy is enlightenment." (知常曰明 *zhi chang yue ming*). He says, "All things work together. I have watched them reverting and have seen how they flourish and return to their roots. This is stillness, a retreat to one's roots, or even better, return to the heavenly will, which is to constancy. The

[8] Tomohisa Ikeda, "ma wang dui han mu bo shu zhou yi zhi yao pian shi wen xia" [Annotations on the "Yao" Passage of the Mawangdui Han Silk Manuscripts of the Book of Changes], tran. Niu Jianke, *zhou yi yan jiu* [Studies of Zhouyi], no. 2 (1997):11.

[9] Confucius, "Ju Yi," in *Zhong Yong* 14 [The Doctrine of Mean 14], trans. James Legge, https://www.sacred-texts.com/cfu/conf3.htm. As regards the translations of "君子 *jun zi*" and "小人 *xiao ren*," there are quite a few translations in English publications such as "superior man," "gentleman" and "noble man" for "*jun zi*" which denote the moral character of a person who follows the heavenly will; "inferior man" and "petty man" for "*xiao ren*" which refers to someone who behaves against the heavenly will. In this paper, "*jun zi*" is translated as "virtuous people" and "*xiao ren*" as "small people" except for their equivalents in direct citations.

[10] Hsün-tzu, "Tian Lun" [On Heaven], *Hsün-tzu*, https://ctext.org/xunzi/tian-lun. Yao is one of the five worthy tribal leaders of the early ancient times. Jie is said to be a cruel and corrupt king of Xia Dynasty (ca.2070-ca.1600 B.C.).

knowledge of constancy is enlightenment and not knowing it is blindness that works evil."[11] For Lao Tzu, "knowing the constancy" (知常 *zhi chang*), that is, knowing the laws of nature, generates wisdom, whereas ignorance of natural law leads to confusion and disaster.

At the same time, Taoism highlights the equal symbiosis between humankind and nature. In Lao Tzu's words, "The *Tao* is great, and so are the heaven, the earth, and the human. Within the realm, these four are great; the human but stands for one of them. Human conforms to the earth, the earth to the heaven, the heaven to the *Tao*, and the *Tao* to its own nature."[12] Lao Tzu believes that the *Tao* is the noumenon of all things, and is the reality that cannot be sensed. It follows its own nature. Nature is not only a moral law but also a universal law that governs heaven, earth and humankind. Therefore, the *Tao*, the heaven, the earth and the human are all equally noble and belong to the realm of the cosmos, which drastically differs from what anthropocentrism implies.

Second, in Chinese classical culture, human beings are not thought to be passively related to nature but using it in a restraint manner and out of human love for nature.

Confucius' saying that, "The wise find pleasure in water; the virtuous find pleasure in hills" (知者乐水，仁者乐山 *zhi zhe le shui, ren zhen le shan*) reflects this ecological sentiment and is employed as one of the Confucian moral codes to cultivate the character of a virtuous person. Moreover, Confucius' view of ecological conservation is explicitly demonstrated in sayings such as, "The Master angled, but did not use a net. He shot, but not at birds perching [*sic*]" (钓而不纲，弋不射宿 *diao er bu gang, yi bu she su*), and, "He who aims to be a man of complete virtue in his food does not seek to gratify his appetite, nor in his dwelling place does he seek the appliances of ease [*sic*]" (君子食无求饱，居无求安 *jun zi shi wu qiu bao, ju wu qiu an*). In Confucius' view, it is against the benevolence (仁 *ren*) to fish with a net and to shoot the birds in nest as these will lead to the depletion of natural resources, and thereby endangering the survival of those who make a living by fishing and hunting. Similarly, if people eat too much and live too comfortably, they will inevitably overconsume land space and building materials.[13] To put the above sayings in modern words, human behaviors like these violate the sustainable utilization of ecological resources.

Likewise, Mencius's idea of "benevolence for people and love for things" (仁民爱物*ren min ai wu*) also calls for human charity towards nature.[14] Mencius argues that the concrete performance of benevolent people lies in being able to "treat with the reverence due to age the elders in your own family, so that the elders in the families of others shall be similarly treated; treat with the kindness due to youth the young in your own family, so that the young in the families of others shall be similarly treated" (老吾老，以及人之老；幼吾幼．以及人之幼,*lao wu lao, yi ji ren zhi lao, you wu you, yi ji ren zhi you*).[15] In the same way, loving things are construed as giving grace to all things in the world, as a result of which the view of sustainable utilization of resources is proposed in Mencius' writing. On one occasion, Mencius says to King Hui:

> If the seasons of husbandry be not interfered with, the grain will be more than can be eaten. If close nets are not allowed to enter the pools and ponds, the fishes and turtles will be more than can be consumed. If the axes and bills enter the hills and forests only at the proper time, the wood will be more than can be used.[16]

---

[11] Lao Tzu, *Tao Te Ching* 16, trans. R. B. Blakney (NY: New American Library, 2007), 89.
[12] Lao Tzu, *Tao Te Ching* 25, 89.
[13] The Confucian quotations in this paragraph are taken from *Confucius Analects*: 6-21, 7-26, 1-14, trans. James Legge, https://ctext.org/analects.
[14] James Legge trans., "Jin Xin I-45," in *Mencius,* https://ctext.org/mengzi/jin-xin-i.
[15] James Legge trans., *Liang Hui Wang Shang* [King Hui of Liang 1A.3], https://ctext.org/mengzi/liang-hui-wang-i.
[16] James Legge trans., *Liang Hui Wang Shang* [King Hui of Liang 1A.7].

That is to say, if we farm according to the farming season, fish properly and cut trees according to the rules, there will be an inexhaustible supply of grain, aquatic products and timber.

Taoism also bears such ecological wisdom of conservation. Lao Tzu says, "The mean man pays the highest price; the hoarder takes the greatest loss; a man content is never ashamed, and self-restrained, is not in danger: he will live forever [*sic*]"[17] 甚爱必大费，多藏必厚亡，故知足不辱，知止不殆，可以长久(*shen ai bi da fei, duo cang bi hou wang, gu zhi zu bu ru, zhi zhi bu dai, ke yi chang jiu*). Lao Tzu believes that only when a person knows how to be content with what is given, can he or she not be humiliated; when a person knows enough is enough, he or she will not encounter danger, so that long-term peace and sustainable resources will be maintained.

To conclude, like the ecological wisdom of the Bible, Chinese traditional culture represented by Confucianism and Taoism emphasizes the equal symbiosis between humankind and nature under the rule of the common heavenly will or natural law. Moreover, Chinese traditional culture expresses the deep love of human beings for nature and the ardent pursuit of the harmony with all things in nature, which is particularly evident in Chinese traditional art, such as classical brush painting and gardening. The common ecological themes in the Bible and Chinese culture provide Chinese Christians' ecological engagement with a rationale and a vehicle of articulation.

The Theory of the National Ecological Initiative of China

The undergoing ecological initiative of the Chinese government, especially its theory, enriches Chinese Christians' understanding of ecological protection. The theory of the national ecological initiative is composed of a scientific view of nature, of green development, of ecological livelihood, of an ecological system, of an ecological legal system and of an ecological common interest of the world.[18]

The scientific view of nature promotes harmonious coexistence between human beings and nature. Human beings are required to respect and safeguard nature as they are interconnected members of the common life community, an ecosystem which also includes mountains, rivers, forests, fields, lakes and grasslands. The scientific view of nature is an extended connotation of the common destiny of humankind, as well as a further interpretation of the law of natural development from the perspective of ecological civilization.

The view of green development is derived from the 'Two-Mountain Thesis' of President Xi Jinping, who metaphorically compares the relationship between development and ecological protection to that between "gold mountain, silver mountain" (金山银山 *jin shan yin shan*) and "green waters, green mountains" (绿水青山 *lv shui qin shan*).[19] Scholars further elaborate on the three layers of implications of the thesis. First, environmental protection should be balanced with economic development, and one cannot lose sight of the other. Second, when contradiction occurs between socio-economic development and ecological protection, decisive choices must be made in favor of the environment. Third, environmental protection contributes to enhancing human livelihood. A sound ecological environment constitutes part of the welfare of the people. Not only is it required to meet the people's social and economic needs, but also to ensure the people's opportunities and rights for thriving.

To achieve the national ecological vision, the rule of law must be implemented. This view of ecological rule of law is the concrete embodiment of the principle of governing the country by law in the construction

---

[17] Lao Tzu, *Tao Te Ching* 44, trans. R. B. Blakney (NY: New American Library, 2007), 114.

[18] Li Xin and Cao Hongjun, "xi jin ping sheng tai wen ming si xiang de he xin gou cheng ji qi shi dai te zhen" [the Core Structure of the Ecological Thoughts of Xi Jinping and Its Characters], in *hong guan jing ji yan jiu* [Macroeconomics], no.6 (2019): 5-15.

[19] President Xi Jiping first put forward the 'Two-Mountain' thesis in 2005 when he was then Secretary of the Zhejiang Provincial Committee of Communist Party of China.

of ecological civilization. Meanwhile, the ecological initiative in China calls for global collaboration and reciprocal participation in addressing regional and global issues such as climate change, deforestation and environmental justice for the sustainable development of the world.[20]

Overall, the current ecological initiative in China inherits the wisdom of ancient Chinese ecological ethics and responds to the requirements of the new era. The harmonious coexistence between human beings and nature rejects the anthropocentrism and the overcorrection of naturalism in theory. It acknowledges the need of a wholesome development of human beings and brilliantly represents the dialectical relationship between socio-economic development and environmental protection. Obviously, the national ecological initiative provides Chinese Christians with opportunities for further engaging in environmental protection and foster the process of further contextualization of Chinese Christianity.

Upgrading the Ecological Engagement of the Chinese Christian Churches

The ecological wisdom in the Bible, the ecological thoughts in classical Chinese culture and the ecological initiative in today's China – all of these contribute to the church's development of ecological theology and practice in the process of a further contextualization of Chinese Christianity.

The Chinese Protestant Churches have been exploring approaches to integrating the biblical and cultural resources into church ecological teachings. For instance, in 2019, the Chinese Christian Council (CCC) and Three-Self Patriotic Movement (TSPM) set 'Cherishing God's Creation and Building a Better Life Together' as the theme of sermon exchanges for the preaching team for promoting the Reconstruction of Chinese Theological Thinking. The preachers delved into the scripture for ecological wisdom and helped believers understand that the harmonious coexistence with nature was as important as personal salvation. More than that, preachers were encouraged to exposit on the ecological teachings of the Bible in a way the Chinese audience found easier to accept by employing materials such as Chinese sayings, philosophical quotations and folk stories.

Additionally, churches, seminaries and regional Christian Councils (CCs) TSPMs have regularly launched environmental programs and actively participated in and contributed to the national and regional ecological initiatives. For instance, some churches put special days like the Tree-planting Day, International Water Day and Earth Hour on the church calendar for prayer meetings and special worship services to enhance the congregations' ecological awareness. A number of urban churches regularly host charity sales, flea markets and church donations for the congregants to recycle life supplies such as clothes, books and printers. Christian churches take these programs as both environmental projects and church discipleship programs, helping church people to lead a simple and yet caring life.

The Chinese Protestant Churches also reach out to social programs of ecological protection. Chinese Christians are often seen visiting the cleaners on the street in hot summer days, offering beverages and towels to pay their respect to those who work hard in harsh conditions to create agreeable surroundings. Meanwhile, Chinese Christians participate in inter-faith projects for environmental protection. In July 2019, Christians and Taoists in Yunan Province launched the 'Safeguarding the Lake Dian (滇池 *dian chi*)'

[20] This section on the theory of the national construction of ecological civilization is based on the following materials: Lian Fu, Zhao Jianbin and Mao Lixia, "xi jin ping sheng tai wen ming si xiang de he xin nei han, jian she zhi xiang he shi xian lu jin" [the Core Implications, Visions and Paths of the Ecological Civilization Thoughts of Xi Jinping], in *xi bei nong ling ke ji da xue xue bao* [Journal of Northwest A&F University (Social Science Edition) (January 2021): 1-9; Wu Huaiyou and Chen Xinkang, "xi jin ping sheng tai wen ming si xiang de he xin yao yi" [The Core Meaning of the Ecological Civilization Thoughts of Xi Jinping], *zhong guo she hui ke xue bao* [Chinese Social Sciences] (June 24, 2021, Special Edition); Li Xin and Cao Hongjun, "xi jin ping sheng tai wen ming si xiang de he xin gou cheng ji qi shi dai te zhen" [the Core Structure of the Ecological Thoughts of Xi Jinping and Its Character].

program. They walked side by side along the lake to pick up rubbish from the lake bank, inspiring citizens to jointly protect the environment.[21]

In the future, Chinese churches should go further to incorporate ecological protection into international exchanges. Chinese churches need to share more with overseas church organizations and friends the theories and practices of China's ecological civilization initiatives and the churches' involvement. At the same time, the Chinese churches should continue to learn from the experience of overseas partners through ecumenical dialogues and global projects of organizations such as the World Council of Churches, in areas such as climate change, water conservation, biodiversity and grain issue. Moreover, Chinese churches should also become more conscious of eco-injustice and eco-imperialism which Bishop K.H. Ting's refers to as an "unjust state of affairs," when rich countries develop and safeguard their own economic interests at the expense of developing countries' natural resources and environments.[22]

Conclusion

The formulation and development of the ecological view is of great significance for Chinese Christian churches to engage in further contextualization of Chinese Christianity. Ecologically speaking, it is a process that involves renewing the Church's theological reflections on ecology by synthesizing the ecological wisdom in the Bible, the gems in Chinese traditional culture and the theory of the national ecological civilization while preserving Christian uniqueness. This integral view of ecology advocates reasonable and sustainable use of natural resources as it promotes the interdependence and interconnection between all creatures of God, including heaven, earth and humankind, which follow the universal will of heaven.

As Chinese Christians are becoming aware of their ecological calling to be caretakers of the earth, they are becoming more involved in national and regional ecological initiatives, as well as ecumenical dialogues and collaborations on environmental issues with a view to making contributions to the global Christian discourse on ecological sustainability through their distinctive theological reflections and dynamic church ministries.

Suggestions for Further Reading

Confucius. "Ju Yi." In *Zhong Yong* 14 [The Doctrine of Mean 14]. Translated by James Legge. https://www.sacred-texts.com/cfu/conf3.htm (accessed 23rd February, 2022).

Hsün-tzu. "Tian Lun" [On Heaven]. In *Hsün-tzu*. https://ctext.org/xunzi/tian-lun (accessed 23rd February, 2022).

Lao Tzu.*Tao Te Ching.* Translated by R. B. Blakney. NY: New American Library, 2007.

Li, Xin and Cao Hongjun. "xi jin ping sheng tai wen ming si xiang de he xin gou cheng ji qi shi dai te zhen" [the Core Structure of the Ecological Thoughts of Xi Jinping and Its Character]. *hong guan jing ji yan jiu* [Macroeconomics], no.6 (2019): 5-15.

Li, Lei. "sheng tai wei ji de zong jiao gen yuan-mo er te man sheng tai si xiang lun shu" [The Religious Roots of Ecological Crisis-Commentaries on Jürgen Moltmann's Ecological Thoughts]. *zi ran bian zheng fa yan jiu* [Studies in Dialectics of Nature] (September 2004): 16-18.

Legge, James, trans. "Jin Xin 1-45." In *Mencius*. https://ctext.org/mengzi/jin-xin-i (accessed 24th February, 2022).

[21] Daojiaozhiyin[the Voice of Taosim] (1 July, 2019), "*yun nan sheng dao xie xie tong sheng ji du jiao liang hui kai zhan zhi yuan xun he huo dong*" [Joint Voluntary Lake Patrol by Taoists and Christians in Yunan Province], https://www.daoisms.org/article/sort028/info-39779.html.

[22] K.H. Ting,"Caring for God's Creation,"in *God Is Love: Collected Writings of Bishop K.H. Ting* (CO: Cook Communications, 2004), 341.

Legge, James, trans. *Liang Hui Wang Shang* [King Hui of Liang I]. https://ctext.org/mengzi/liang-hui-wang-i (accessed 24th February, 2022).

Moltmann, Jürgen. *su shi zhong de shang di* [Gott im Projekt der modernen Weit]. Translated by Zeng Nianyue. Taiwan: Ya Ge Publishing, 1999.

Northcott, Michael S. "Ecology and Christian Ethics" in *The Cambridge Companion to Christian Ethics*. Edited by Robin Gill. Cambridge: Cambridge University Press, 2012.

Ting, K.H. *God is Love: Collected Writings of Bishop K.H. Ting*. CO: Cook Communications, 2004.

Tomohisa Ikeda. "ma wang dui han mu bo shu zhou yi zhi yao pian shi wen xia" [Annotations on the "Yao" Passage of the Mawangdui Han Silk Manuscripts of the Book of Changes II]. Translated by Niu Jianke. *zhou yi yan jiu* [Studies of Zhouyi], no. 2 (1997): 6-19.

Wang, Xiaobin, "sheng tai wei ji zhong de zong jiao ze ren" [Religious Responsibilities in Ecological Crisis]. *zong jiao yan jiu* [Religious Studies], no. 3 (2015):279-283.

Zhao Jianbin and Mao Lixia. "xi jin ping sheng tai wen ming si xiang de he xin nei han, jian she zhi xiang he shi xian lu jin" [the Core Implications, Visions and Paths of the Ecological Civilization Thoughts of Xi Jinping]. *xi bei nong ling ke ji da xue xue bao [Journal of Northwest A&F University (Social Science Edition)]* (January 2021): 1-9.

51. The Relevance of Eco-Diakonia in the Context of Palm Oil Industry in Indonesia – The Church Engagement towards Palm Oil Sustainability

Jenny Purba[1]

Introduction

Palm Oil is like the military – patches of black and green, with its spines, sharp like the blades of bayonets, its fruit hard and round like bullets, red like blood – it kills people. These words are how the community in one tribe in Papua symbolizes palm oil or *sawit* in Bahasa. Severe water pollution, endemic loss of biodiversity, and extensive deforestation have endangered the live of the forest people due to the large-scale expansion of palm oil monoculture. According to their belief, one is never alone in the forest but palm oil likes to be alone. It is considered as a selfish and solitary being, a plant without family and friends, because palm oil will never allow any plants or animals living together surround them.[2] This is the image of palm oil agribusiness plantation in Indonesia, which is different from what I experienced during my visit in November 2021 to Cameroon. There I witnessed palm oil which could be living together with bananas, coconut, casava and other plants and animals. The mega project of agribusiness in Indonesia has forced the *sawit* to turn into a selfish plant.

Corporations with the state have promoted agribusiness as a means to integrate rural communities into a modern lifestyle. Apparently, this industry has promoted economic development, infrastructures and modernization in some areas. Negatively, however, it has caused the community, indigenous people, laborers and smallholders to become cornered and to face serious unintended social, cultural, economic, and environmental implications.

Whose rationality matters and how do we find balance between humans and non-humans in this palm oil context? How do we find the balance between ecology, economy, society and culture?

The Palm Oil Industry in Indonesia

Elaeis guineensis originated in West Africa and has become one of the most profitable commercial high-tree crops. The earliest archeological evidence found in an old Egyptian tomb suggests that people have been cooking with palm oil for up to 5,000 years in the tropical zones of West and Central Africa.[3]

A mature palm can reach a height of 20 meters. Trees start to produce fruit about three years after planting and can live up to 50 years old. Due to the decline in yield and difficulty in harvesting, they are usually replanted after 20-25 years. Once harvested, the fresh fruit bunch must be processed within 48 hours, so access to a mill is a significant factor in determining where palms can be commercially established. It is essential to coordinate harvesting and processing operations to be geographically close with a reliable transport infrastructure.[4]

---

[1] Jenny Purba is an ordained pastor of the Simalungun Protestant Christian Church (GKPS) in North Sumatera, Indonesia, with a PhD in Diaconic Science from the Institute of Diakonic Management, Bethel, Germany.
[2] Sophie Chao, "In the Shadow of the Palm: Dispersed Ontologies among Marind, West Papua," *Cultural Anthropology* 33 (November 12, 2018), https://doi.org/10.14506/ca33.4.08, 622-641.
[3] Joshua M. Linder and Rachel E. Palkovitz, "The Threat of Industrial Oil Palm Expansion to Primates and Their Habitats," in Michel T. Waller (ed), *Ethnoprimatology* (Developments in Primatology: Progress and Prospects) (Cham: Springer International Publishing, 2016), https://doi.org/10.1007/978-3-319-30469-4_2, 21.
[4] IUF, "Background Document an Overview of the Palm Oil Sector: Countries and Companies" (Global Palm Oil Conference, Bogota, Colombia: IUF, 2015), 4-5.

The introduction of palm oil to Southeast Asia began in 1848 when the Dutch planted four seedlings in the Buitenzorg Botanical Garden, today Bogor, Indonesia, two of which came from the Amsterdam Botanical Garden and two from the Bourbon Island. Six years after that, the first Malaysian oil palm plantation was established in Kuala Selangor, Malaysia, using Deli origin seedlings.[5] The first large-scale plantation was launched in 1911 in the Deli province in Sumatera by a Belgian plantation entrepreneur Adrien Hallet with planted areas that reached 110,000 hectacres, after it was discovered that oil palms planted in Sumatera were more productive than in Africa.[6] In the early 2000s, the palm oil industry expanded rapidly in Indonesia and Malaysia in response to the global demand. Both countries account for 90 percent of all global exports of palm oil, forming one of the largest agricultural clusters in the world.[7]

Due to its significant contribution to Indonesia's economy, the Indonesian government has set a production target of 40 million tons crude palm oil (CPO) by 2020. Apparently, this target was fulfilled successfully. The areas have increased three-fold from 2.9 million hectares in 2000 to more than 8,6 million hectares in 2019.[8] The production has also increased significantly, from 19.4 million tons in 2008 to 45.8 million tons in 2019.[9] Palm oil makes an important contribution to the Indonesian economy contributing to economic growth, poverty alleviation and income distribution within society. Palm oil has succeeded in lifting 2.6 million rural Indonesians from poverty.[10] As a labor-intensive sector, palm oil has employed up to 7.8 million laborers.[11]

Palm oil occurs in two main products: crude palm oil (CPO) and palm kernel oil (PKO). CPO is mainly used for the food industry, as detergent, and as oleo-chemical plant, while PKO is mainly used for the chemical and animal feed industry. The major market destination of Indonesian palm oil export are India, European Union and China. The world demand for palm oil has climbed in the last two decades with the increasing global population and the globalization of agriculture. The accelerating of oil palm expansion has also been in line with the increasing global market demand for alternative energy, such as biofuel.[12]

For the next decade, the increasing demand for palm oil production will remain high due to the growth of the world population, which has led the industry to seek new, low-cost frontiers in Africa and Latin America. West Africa appears to be the location for the next expansion wave in palm oil, for both plantation and processing facilities, because of the apparent availability of land, relatively cheap labor, and governmental policies that encourage such expansion – in countries such as the Republic of Congo, Ghana, Nigeria, and Liberia.[13]

---

[5] K. P Prabhakaran Nair, *The Agronomy and Economy of Important Tree Crops of the Developing World* (London: Elsevier Science Limited, 2010), http://www.sciencedirect.com/science/book/9780123846778, 219.

[6] Paul H Kratoska, *South East Asia, Colonial History: High Imperialism (1890s-1930s)* (London: Routledge, 2001), 40.

[7] Valeria Giacomin, "The Emergence of an Export Cluster: Traders and Palm Oil in Early Twentieth-Century Southeast Asia," *Enterprise & Society* 19, no. 2 (June 2018): 272–308, https://doi.org/10.1017/eso.2017.10, 272-274.

[8] Data from Statistics Indonesia, BPS RI, 2019, available access on 08.10.2020 in official website https://www.bps.go.id.

[9] Data from Statistics Indonesia, BPS RI, 2019, available access on 08.10.2020 in official website https://www.bps.go.id

[10] Amzul Rifin et al., "Assessing the Impact of Limiting Indonesian Palm Oil Exports to the European Union," *Journal of Economic Structures* 9, no. 1 (December 2020): 26, https://doi.org/10.1186/s40008-020-00202-8, 2.

[11] Herry Purnomo et al., "Reconciling Oil Palm Economic Development and Environmental Conservation in Indonesia: A Value Chain Dynamic Approach," *Forest Policy and Economics* 111 (February 1, 2020): 102089, https://doi.org/10.1016/j.forpol.2020.102089, 1.

[12] Koesnadi Wirasaputra and Rukaiyah Rofiq, *Biofuel, a Trap, Notes from the Heart of Sumatra: Jambi, Riau and South Sumatera* (Indonesia: Setara Jambi, 2009), 2-4.

[13] IUF, "Background Document an Overview of the Palm Oil Sector: Countries and Companies" (Global Palm Oil Conference, Bogota, Colombia: IUF, 2015), 16-18.

The expansion of the industry in Africa is encouraged in order to develop rural areas and poverty reduction. I argue that corporations are reluctantly showing their responsibility towards sustainability with regard to this issue, because they are inclined to expand their business to other countries with less regulation and concern about sustainability to secure their businesses.

Challenges and Issues of the Palm Oil Industry in Indonesia

The proliferation of oil palm plantations in Indonesia has become the subject of political and environmental debates. Supporters are praising the crop as the catalyst for rural economies, contributing to economic development. Others are concerned about the potentially serious unintended social, economic and environmental impacts. Below are some descriptions of challenges around the palm oil industry in Indonesia.

Palm Oil and Ecological Issues

Oil palm expansion has been associated with rainforest clearing. Approximately 18 million hectares of tropical rainforest in Indonesia has been deforested and commercialized.[14] In Sumatera and Kalimantan over 10 million hectares of peatland has been degraded.[15] The conversion of forests for palm oil plantation has been associated with the loss of biodiversity, including orang-utans and the Sumatran Tiger.[16] Palm oil is a poor replacement for the natural tropical forest and fails to support biodiversity. Oil palm plantations can only feed up to 20% of the mammals, reptiles and birds in the rainforest.[17] It has caused a reduction in species richness by 83%. The species richness of forest butterflies has been reduced by 79-83%, and of birds-species by 73-77%.[18]

Forest fires are raging across over 4 million hectares and cause social and health impacts, as well as creating enormous amounts of greenhouse gas emissions with far-reaching environmental and economic consequences.[19] 2.6 million hectares of Indonesian land were burned between June and October 2015.[20] Palm oil production brings about various types of environmental pollution caused by forest and peat fires. All of these consequences due to unsustainable oil palm practices have further burdened communities in many locations.[21]

Socio-Economic Issues

Besides the ecological aspect, palm oil expansion draws criticism in terms of its socio-economic impact and human rights violations. Smallholders, plantation workers and indigenous people are marginalized through different structures and processes. The impact on human rights mainly occurred during the early

---

[14] Marcus Colchester, *Promised Land: Palm Oil and Land Acquisition in Indonesia: Implications for Local Communities and Indigenous Peoples* (Bogor, Indonesia: Sawit Watch, 2006), 12.

[15] Stephen Khan, "Indonesia Sets a Carbon Time-Bomb," *The Conversation*, September 25, 2013, accessed October 10, 2021, https://theconversation.com/indonesia-sets-a-carbon-time-bomb-17216.

[16] Obidzinski et al., "Environmental and Social Impacts of Oil Palm Plantations and Their Implications for Biofuel Production in Indonesia", 25.

[17] Jan Willem van Gelder, *Greasy Palms: European Buyers of Indonesian Palm Oil* (The Netherlands: Friends of the Earth, March 2004), 17.

[18] Lian Pin Koh and David S. Wilcove, "Is Oil Palm Agriculture Really Destroying Tropical Biodiversity?" *Conservation Letters* 1, no. 2 (2008): 60–64, https://doi.org/10.1111/j.1755-263X.2008.00011.x, 2-4.

[19] Norman Jiwan, Bambang Hero Saharjo, and Jeffri Saragih, *Development of Palm Oil Plantation Based on Greenhouse Gases Critical Perspectives* (Bogor: Sawit Watch, 2009), https://www.loc.gov/item/2012330588/, 19.

[20] Ann Jeannette Glauber et al., "The Cost of Fire," *World Bank*, February 2016, https://openknowledge.worldbank.org/handle/10986/23840, 1.

[21] Truly Santika et al., "Does Oil Palm Agriculture Help Alleviate Poverty? A Multidimensional Counterfactual Assessment of Oil Palm Development in Indonesia," *World Development* 120 (April 28, 2019): 105–17, 106.

development of land acquisition and plantation. Vulnerable groups such as women and children were predominantly affected. As a result, resentment and dissatisfaction led to land conflicts in palm plantations. In 2008 there were around 513 land disputes, closely monitored and documented as they pertain to abuses of human rights between palm oil companies and local communities in Indonesia.[22]

Even though palm oil is produced to meet the food demands in the global market, palm oil is associated with the food crisis and was accountable for 75 percent of the rise in food prices.[23] Many rice plantations have been converted to palm oil in Indonesia and the oil palm plantations have also disrupted the mutual aid system in Indonesia, *Gotong Royong*, an important feature of the Indonesian community.

Cultural-Anthropological Issues: Indigenous People

Indonesia has about 50 to 70 million indigenous people,[24] which account for about a quarter of the country's population.[25] The widespread expansion of land has prevented people from accessing resources, such as land for food crops that are used to meet basic needs and livelihoods, and from generating income, as well as participating in their cultures. The Principle of Free, Prior, and Informed Consent (FPIC) has been recognized but not implemented by the Indonesian government, impacting landless people groups devastatingly.[26] This FPIC is similar to Indonesia's principle of 'consultation and consensus' or *musyawarah dan mufakat*. Failing to fully respect the rights of local communities to their lands is the root cause of violent conflicts between and within communities. Such conflicts also present severe risks to plantation companies, investors and the state. Enhanced regulation of the oil palm, informing people on the long-term aspects of the conversion, and helping people remain connected to the community is very important. In addition, the embeddedness to local traditions and traditional institutions such as traditional knowledge, customary rules, norms and daily life values should be preserved. The connectedness with nature and of traditional beliefs with nature will lead to a positive appreciation of natural ecosystems.[27]

Balancing Ecology, Economy, Society and Culture

Disparate assessments of the costs and benefits of the palm oil industry illuminate the complexity of this issue. In calculating the costs and benefits of palm oil proliferation, others postulated that the economic and non-economic costs of the expansion of this industry outweigh the benefits. The ecological degradation caused by the economic benefit is unjustified. If palm oil expands at the current rate until 2025, the physical and monetary costs of palm oil expansion will exceed the benefits to the society because compromises exist not only between the environment and the economy, but also between social and cultural issues. The

---

[22] Marti Serge, *Losing Ground: The Human Rights Impacts of Oil Palm Plantation Expansion in Indonesia* (England: Friends of the Earth, LifeMosaic and Sawit Watch, 2008), 8-9.

[23] Raquel Moreno-Peñaranda et al., "Stakeholder Perceptions of the Ecosystem Services and Human Well-Being Impacts of Palm Oil Biofuels in Indonesia and Malaysia," in Kazuhiko Takeuchi et al. (eds) *Biofuels and Sustainability: Holistic Perspectives for Policy-Making*, Tokyo: Springer Japan, 2018), 133–73, https://doi.org/10.1007/978-4-431-54895-9_10, 145-47.

[24] https://www.iwgia.org/en/indonesia.html#:~:text=Indonesia%20is%20the%20home%20of,to%2070%20million%20Indigenous%20Peoples.

[25] Human Rights Watch, *"When We Lost the Forest, We Lost Everything": Oil Palm Plantations and Rights Violations in Indonesia* (United States: Human Rights Watch, 2019), 4-5.

[26] Saurlin Siagian, Amin Siahaan, and Nur Khairani, *The Loss of Reasons. Human Rights Violations in the Oil-Palm Plantations in Indonesia* (Indonesia: Lentera Rakyat, September 2011), https://docplayer.net/35527548-The-loss-of-reason-human-rights-violations-in-the-oil-palm-plantations-in-indonesia-saurlin-p-siagian-amin-siahaan-buyung-nur-khairani.html, 36.

[27] E.L. Yuliani et al., "Forest or Oil Palm Plantation? Interpretation of Local Responses to the Oil Palm Promises in Kalimantan, Indonesia," Land Use Policy 96 (July 2020): 104616, https://doi.org/10.1016/j.landusepol.2020.104616, 2.

suggested solution to this problem is that poor governance in oil palm management issues should be resolved, as well as reconsideration of the attitudes of local governments promoting oil palm expansion. The need for good governance to regulate oil palm expansion in Indonesia is urgently required to halt the forest conversion.[28]

Indonesia's ongoing challenge is to balance economic growth and efficiency with agricultural policies that benefit rural poor livelihoods and smallholders. The need to balance ecology, economic and socio-cultural aspects in this sector is crucial. The score of Indonesia on the sustainability palm oil index of 35.02% indicates that this balance is still disturbed and that Indonesia's palm oil is less sustainable.[29] This indicates that economics aspects are prioritized over social and ecological aspects. From the outset, Indonesia's main priority has been more likely to be dominated by economic aspects. When the development plans continue to be concerned only with one aspect, Indonesia will face ongoing problems and conflicts in the long run. There is a crucial need to achieve basic principles of palm oil sustainability – how to use its economic benefits, while minimizing ecological and social cultural costs. Sustainability can be achieved only when economic growth, environmental protection and improvement and equity go hand in hand.

A question then arises about who is actually responsible for addressing sustainability. There is a lack of collaboration between business, states and society towards palm oil sustainability. Business is believed to have an enormous potential to do good in the world. The influence of politics, political parties and policy makers should not be underestimated. Society also should be involved to reach a sustainable world. Unfortunately, limited participation, limited capacity building of society, limited partnership, inadequate engagement of stakeholders can all be a hindrance towards achieving sustainability. We cannot rely on the government alone. Hence, fostering a more effective relationship between business, politics and society to achieve goals crucial to sustainable development is necessary. A revolution of consciousness at every level of society, in institutions, organisations and government, is crucially needed.

There is a greater need for proactive policy formulation and operative management by every stakeholder, as well as for more cooperation and synergy. It is evident that this commodity has contributed to Indonesia's economic strength, and without it, the country would suffer greatly. Sustainable palm oil which is fair to workers, communities, indigenous people and ecology must continue to be instigated.

The Church's Engagement in the Palm Oil Industry

The church needs to broaden and strengthen cooperation and collaboration with multiple actors or players by describing the changing landscape of diaconal action. A church needs strong partnership to build on strengths and overcome challenges. The dialogue in the ecumenical movement can be a dialogue within the church and with the others outside the church.

In the context of palm oil and the economic tensions, we can find different rationalities from the different actors. We need to construct a more uniting paradigm that embraces the differences while respecting the different languages and rationalities at the same time. In order to build strong stakeholder networks, there needs to be a shift from caritative diakonia towards networks-based diakonia.

The dialogue that engages all actors in-depth on critical issues, particularly palm oil, must guide future ecumenical cooperation. Churches need to build a network, form alliances across denominations and religions, encourage participation, and invite inter-disciplinary perspectives from economic, ethical, management, leadership and even political backgrounds. Diakonia is dealing with multiple issues, problems

[28] Anggraini and Grundmann, "Transactions in the Supply Chain of Oil Palm Fruits and Their Relevance for Land Conversion in Smallholdings in Indonesia", 391-93.
[29] Petir Papilo et al., "Sustainability Index Assessment of Palm Oil-Based Bioenergy in Indonesia," *Journal of Cleaner Production* 196 (September 2018): 808–20, https://doi.org/10.1016/j.jclepro.2018.06.072, 818.

and actors. By such encounters with other stakeholders, transformation could possibly happen and there may be more hope for finding an integrated solution.

The development of an integrated policy for palm oil should be aimed at serious and balanced attention to both economic, social, cultural and environmental aspects. Any development which is more concerned with one aspect than with other will cause further problems in the future. Therefore, strategic steps are needed at each level of engagement, from micro to global scopes.

The micro level's actor is the individual/personal or community on the local level. On the meso level, we are dealing with institutions or organizations. One example is how a business formulates its own corporate ethics or corporate governance principles. The macro-level is broader because it deals with society and the state. The state will determine the economic policies and ethics, and political governance will be found at this level. The global level relates to global society, where there is a vision to formulate global or international economic ethics, or to formulate global governance or global policies.

Cooperation, coordination, and synergy among all stakeholders and related institutions are required to develop a sustainable palm oil industry. Decisions about the location of palm oil plantations until now have been determined more by economics than environmental compatibility. Therefore, other aspects need to be taken into consideration in future decisions.

Diakonia, present in the public sphere, takes seriously the fact that society has become pluralistic. Nevertheless, it does not mean that diakonia cannot show where it originates through biblical narratives and church traditions. However, to build cooperation with other groups, it is essential to use alternative language, such as that of human dignity, in order to reflect on the creation of human beings in God's image in the midst of a pluralistic world. Without denying its basis in Christian faith reflecting the love of God, diakonia can also acknowledge and express its values in other languages.

In public life the engagement between economy and theology is not always easy. Theology and economics speak in different languages, using different concepts and contrasting modes of analysis, and focus, to some extent, on quite different goals, priorities, and questions. Often these differences hinder fruitful engagement. We also admit that sometimes it is too easy for church leaders to pronounce on economic matters without adequate grounding, and theologians initiate most of the conversations about theology and economics.[30]

Both sides need each other – economists need theologians and vice versa. Economists find it hard to see the bigger picture, especially some of the moral and spiritual flaws in contemporary economic life. One example is the purely materialistic criterion assessment, focussing simply on growth of gross domestic product (GDP). Economists need to see the wider picture and what is happening in the world. Theologians need economists in regard to the socio-economic context – they need the competencies of economists in order to understand and address their concerns.

Though we are conscious that religions alone cannot remedy the earth's environmental, economic, political, and social problems, they can offer what manifestly cannot be attained by only using monetary plans, political programs, or legal regulations alone: a change in the internal orientation, the mentality, the consciousness, the 'hearts' of humans, and a conversion from a wrong direction to a new orientation for life which is needed for all. Humankind urgently requires social and ecological reforms; however, it desires spiritual reform just as urgently.[31]

---

[30] James K. Smith and J. David Richardson, "Economists, Theologians, and Globalization: An Exchange," *The Association of Christian Economists* 56 (2010), http://christianeconomists.org/2010/12/28/faith-economics-fall-2010/, 14-18.

[31] Peter Singer, *One World: The Ethics of Globalization*, 2nd ed (New Haven: Yale University Press, 2004), 238.

Stakeholders and Partners

According to the Saint Gallen management model, stakeholders are a group of people, organizations, or institutions, regardless of whether they are organized or not. They are all affected by the company's value-added activities and sometimes even value-destroying activities. It is not only the actors who make demands on the organization but also the broader actors from individuals, communities or organizations, who have participated in the creation of organizational value in some ways and are affected by the organization's influence. There are five categories of stakeholders which are the organizational relevant representatives of different environmental spheres and controversies.[32]

The first category comprises suppliers and customers. The second comprises investors or professional communities who provide significant financial and non-financial resources to an organization. The third comprises government agencies and providers of public infrastructure services. In this group, research and educational institutions and expert communities are involved. The states, including Indonesia and other countries, are the target of stakeholders in eco-diakonia. The fourth comprises social movements, mass media, and NGOs. They have to become a partner of the church to communicate with other target actors and institutions. With these stakeholders, the church builds a solid network to work together.

The last category comprises the population groups and the stakeholders directly and indirectly affected by organizational value creation, which cannot articulate and raise their concerns because they lack the necessary resources, skills, instruments or rights. They are involved in the extraction of raw materials or disposal activities in the value creation chain. However, they have not been granted rights in the appropriate economic, political and cultural contexts. This also includes other groups of people, such as infants, the sick or disabled, future generations, animals, and plants. In the palm oil industry, they are the smallholders, indigenous people, and the forest.[33]

To reach the aim towards a more sustainable palm oil industry, diakonia and the church cannot operate alone. The pluralistic world has offered us a possibility for pluralistic partnerships as well. The table below shows an extended scheme of multi-layered collaboration possibilities with various partners on different levels that the church can cooperate with.[34] Thus, eco-diakonia can unfold its full potential in strategic partnerships for dialogue, lobbying and advocacy work and political-ethical explorations.

Pluralistic Partnerships in Eco Diakonia

Liberal Economic Partnership	Pluralistic Partnership: Palm Oil Sustainability Council
Economic Experts	Economic Experts: Corporations, retailers, manufacturers, World Bank, finance institutions, Asian Development Bank, Palm Oil Association in Indonesia (GAPKI)
Employer	Employer
Unions	Unions
	Communities, smallholders, laborers, indigenous people and their organizations
	Organizations of the common good: churches and diakonia institutions

[32] Rüegg-Stürm, Johannes and Grand, Simon, *The St. Gallen Management Model: English Translation of the Fourth Generation of the German Text* (Haupt Verlag AG, Bern, 2016), 76-78.
[33] Ibid., 76-78.
[34] Table adapted from Martin Büscher, *Marktwirtschaft und kontextuelle Ökonomie: wirtschaftsethische Grundlagen zur Weiterentwicklung der Ordnungspolitik* (Wiesbaden: Dt. Univ.-Verl, 2000), 244.

	Churches, organizations and faith-based organizations: Christian Conference of Asia (CCA), World Council of Churches, MISEREOR, Brot für die Welt, Diakonie Deutschland, Lutheran World Federation (LWF), ACT-Alliance, Vereinte Evangelische Mission (VEM), and other organizations
	Women's organizations and NGOs
	Consumer organizations
	Environmental organizations and NGOs
	Labour organizations
	World organizations: United Nations, OECD, USAID, WTO, ILO
	Ministry of Labor, Ministry of Economics, Ministry of Agriculture, Ministry of Agrarian Affairs and Spatial Planning, Ministry of Villages, Development of Underdeveloped Areas and Transmigration of the Republic of Indonesia, Ministry of Education Regional, Provincial, and National Government
	Academic institutions: universities, schools, research and development agencies

In the operative management these partners need to work together to find solutions for a sustainable palm oil industry in Indonesia with the empowerment and advocacy strategies at all levels, from micro to meso, macro and global levels.

Closing Remarks

The church is one of the important actors which has a potential impact on the future of the palm oil industry, its sustainability principles and its global market. The church's responsibility towards palm oil sustainability characterizes diakonia as an integral part of church life and its integrity. The church cannot act alone to succeed in its mission to find the balance between all aspects of sustainability. The church should network with other civil society groups to hold the government accountable to the people. The church needs to bridge between society, business, and the state. In the palm oil context in Indonesia, the church will provide insights to the Indonesian government on the importance of human rights and ecology in decision-making and national economic development plans and policies. Moreover, the church can contribute to the dialogue between theology and green economy. It encourages the business to be responsible, assisting marginalized people and putting ecology as their primary concern.

Suggestions for Further Reading

Büscher, Martin. *Marktwirtschaft und kontextuelle Ökonomie: wirtschaftsethische Grundlagen zur Weiterentwicklung der Ordnungspolitik* (Wiesbaden: Dt. Univ.-Verl, 2000).

Büscher, Martin and Beate Hofmann. "Multirationales Management in diakonischen Unternehmen-Hermeneutische Grundlegung eines diakoniewissenschaftlichen Paradigmas," in *Diakonische Unternehmen Multirational führen: Grundlagen - Kontroversen - Potentiale*, heraugegeben von Beate Hofmann and Martin Büscher (Baden-Baden: Nomos, 2017).

Corley, R. H. V. and P. B. Tinker. *The Oil Palm*, 5. ed. (Chichester: Wiley-Blackwell, 2016).

Jiwan, Norman. "The Political Ecology of the Indonesian Palm Oil Industry: A Critical Analysis," in Oliver Pye and Jayati Bhattacharya (eds.), *The Palm Oil Controversy in Southeast Asia: A Transnational Perspective* (Singapore: ISEAS, 2012).

Rüegg-Stürm, Johannes and Simon Grand. *The St. Gallen Management Model: English Translation of the Fourth Generation of the German Text* (Bern: Haupt Verlag, 2016).

Schedler, Kuno and Johannes Rüegg-Stürm. "Strategies for Dealing with Multiple Rationalities." in Kuno Schedler and Johannes Rüegg-Stürm (eds.), *Multirational Management: Mastering Conflicting Demands in a Pluralistic Environment* (Basingstoke: Palgrave Macmillan, 2014).

Starnitzke, Dierk. *Diakonie in biblischer Orientierung: biblische Grundlagen - ethische Konkretionen - diakonisches Leitungshandeln* (Stuttgart: Kohlhammer, 2011).

52. Relationality, Creation Care, and Eco-Diakonia in Pasifika Communities

Upolu Lumā Vaai[1]

Introduction

Eco-diakonia in the Pasifika[2] communities differs slightly from that of other regions. This is because Pasifika Creation[3] care cannot have life unless relationality becomes its underpinning philosophy. In this context, at the heart of eco-diakonia is 'life for all'. This chapter looks at how the Pasifika communities understand and care for Creation from an eco-relational perspective. Critical to this chapter is understanding first the philosophical foundation of why Pasifika people think in such a way when it comes to Creation. The chapter aims to highlight some of the key principles, initiatives, and theological reconstructions mainly from the perspective of the Pasifika churches.

Relationality

In Pasifika, all of life is an assemblage of relationality. In the beginning there was relationship. Relationality is in our blood. We came into being through relationships, and it is through us that relationships will flow and continue. The goal of relationality is life, meaning 'life for all'. Because of the centrality of life, therefore, as Pasifika people we don't just understand, we understand according to the rhythms of relationships. We don't just interpret, we interpret life and texts through the lens of relationships. Relationality is the interpretive key to life and wellbeing for the whole. While cultures and identities are incredibly diverse in Pasifika, a region gifted with so many languages, cultures, and identities, relationality is their common cultural and spiritual threat. Thus, relationality functions as the ultimate point of reference for understanding life and the world.

However, relationality can also be abused and manipulated if not handled well, especially within the context of communal settings where sometimes autonomy and freedom are overlooked, or in the context of the individual where profit and gain is hoisted at the expense of the whole community. Relationality is complex and one must understand the nuances and dynamics of culture, language, and spiritualities in a context that relationality is applied to, or we miss the point altogether. Pasifika is a 'context-based' region and therefore relationality (or any other concept) must be carefully cognised and grasped.

Despite this diverse complexity, relationality has overarching principles that mould the corporate identity of the people and directs decision-making and daily activities. It is important to highlight these relational principles as they form the ground in which many Pasifika communities understand Creation care and eco-diakonia. I will mention only three.

---

[1] Upolu Luma Vaai is a son of the land. He grew up in both inland and coastal rural villages in Samoa, connected daily to the mana of the eco-relational cultures and philosophies of the dirt communities. He is the Principal and Professor of Theology & Ethics at the Pacific Theological College, Suva, Fiji, the first and only tertiary regional ecumenical institution of the Pasifika churches since 1965. His research interests are the Trinity, eco-relational theologies, indigenous relational philosophies, and Pasifika postcolonial studies.

[2] I use the word 'Pasifika' throughout this chapter, except when it is part of a quotation, as it encompasses a new inclusive and decolonial consciousness that challenges a more colonial compartmentalised and simplistic framing normally reflected in the word 'Pacific.'

[3] I capitalise Creation since in the Pasifika communities, it is the central focus and source of life. It is a 'relational whole' inclusive of the human being, even God through the Spirit. Therefore, relationship with Creation precedes all other relationships. Such relationship represents the highest good, informs beauty, and directs praxis.

The Kinship Principle

Most Pasifika communities have a Creation-centred focus of life. This means that their perception of life is first and foremost shaped by their relationship to the land and ocean.[4] It is based on the worldview that Creation is grounded on a deep living connection of the cosmic *Aiga* (cosmic extended family).[5] This is realized in the fact that in most of these communities, they believe that the Creation and all its ecosystem is *flesh, bones*, and *blood.* Kinship relationship and knowledge is critical in promoting stability and ecological wellbeing for communities. The kinship principle reminds people that Creation is a cosmic-community with deep cosmic genealogical interdependent connections. In this respect, ecology is always cosmological and relational.

In many Pasifika Creation stories the human is being perceived as a child of a cosmic union. Therefore, human identity is defined by this cosmic genealogy. Captured in the words of Tui Atua from Samoa,

> I am not an individual; I am an integral part of the cosmos. I share divinity with my ancestors, the land, the seas and the skies … I belong to my family and my family belongs to me. I belong to my village and my village to me … This is the essence of my sense of belonging.[6]

The same sentiment is also echoed in the words of Jean-Marie Tjibaou from Kanaki New Caledonia who said, "I am never undivided. I cannot be individual. The body is never a principle of individualization. The body is always a relationship."[7] This is why the notion of ownership is controversial when it comes to understanding what we normally call 'resources' in the development space. This is because we do not own the land and the ocean. Rather it is the land and ocean who own us. Thus, these are not meant to be 'resources'.

This relational cosmic kinship is displayed for example in how the *Itaukei* communities in Fiji continue to give place to their totems as symbolic of their cosmic ecological identities, where each person inherits from his/her clan or tribe a *tree* representing the land, a *fish* representing the ocean, and a *bird* representing the sky. The same eco-integrated view of life is present in most Pasifika cultures.

The 'Whole of Life' Principle

The kinship principle gives Pasifika people a broader cosmological perspective of life when it comes to decisions on economic and social development, as opposed to the dominant anthropological perspective of life, which has become a major force in the anthropocene epoch. They see things as a whole as opposed to seeing things in binary compartments, a narrative promoted by colonialists which still shapes the current dominant development narratives that continue to destroy Oceanic lands and oceans.

The 'whole of life' principle[8] recognizes the multi-strand dynamics of interwoven strands of the mat of life such as universality and particularity, communality and individuality, human and Creation, the living and the dead, tangible and intangible, secular and spiritual, and the seen and unseen. It emphasises the

---

[4] For more information on the Pasifika idea of kinship, see Christina Toren and Simonne Pauwels (eds.), *Living Kinship in the Pacific* (New York: Berghahn, 2015), in particular Unaisi Nabobo-Baba's chapter one on the mutual implication of kinship.

[5] *Aiga* in the narrow sense refers to a social unit in the village comprised of immediate family members and kinship. In the broader sense this is a holistic Pasifika concept that refers to the cosmic extended family inclusive of land, ocean, peoples, ancestors, and spirits/gods that constitute wholeness of life.

[6] Tui Atua, "In Search of Meaning, Nuance and Metaphor in Social Policy," in Tamasailau M. Sualii-Sauni et al. (eds.), *Su'esu'e Manogi: In Search of Fragrance* (Wellington: Huia, 2018), 103–20, 105.

[7] *Cibau Cibau: Jean-Marie Tjibaou* (Nouvelle-Caledonie: Agence de developpement de la culture Kanak, 1998), 28.

[8] Pacific Theological College, *A Covid-9 Wellbeing Statement: Rethinking Health from a Theological and Pasifika Cultural Perspective* (Suva: Pacific Theological College 2021), 4-5. Also available online, https://www.oikoumene.org/news/pacific-theological-college-publishes-a-covid-19-wellbeing-statement.

both/and way of thinking. Because of this 'whole of life' principle, there is intentional fluidity in life. Relationality is not a system. It is life. All of reality is constituted by relationality, by dynamic flows of relationships in an infinite multiplicity of becoming.

In other words, life is never rigid. Even knowledge is not stagnant, since it is deeply connected to the flow of time and ecological space. There are no centres. This principle decentralizes the human-centric development narrative. Relationality is embracing and inclusive. Creation is key in the sense that knowledge, spirituality, and wellbeing are dependent on its wellbeing. Thus, a relational approach to Creation is a 'whole of life' imperative.

The 'We Are' Principle

Following the kinship and the 'whole of life' principles, because we are part of the eco-relational whole, therefore, the cosmos is primary, a relational reality that precedes all realities, including the anthropological reality. To say that cosmology precedes anthropology sets the foundation to affirm human responsibility and deep solidarity towards Creation.

In this regard, we as humans cannot exist on our own. *We are, therefore we live.*[9] While the kinship principle informs us of the philosophy of life that underpins our cosmic identity, the 'we are' principle informs us of the collective actions to steward such identity.[10] While the kinship principle focuses on Creation identity, the 'we are' principle focuses on care and eco-diakonia. The former focuses on living relationally, that any human story is only a dimension of a larger cosmic story, the latter focuses on living responsibly. Because cosmology is a relationship and not just about systems of chromosomes and sets of natural rules, the 'we are' principle calls for a move beyond mere interactions and correlations to recognizing everything as Aiga, an extended family responsible for one another. The 'we are' principle invites the questions: What can we do together to survive as an Aiga? What is our responsibility to our ecological *flesh, bones*, and *blood*? How can we save our ecological neighborhood from the 'we have' tendency of the dominant development narrative?

Pasifika Eco-Theologies

Since the 1960s, the Pasifika churches through the Pacific Theological College (PTC) in Fiji established as one of its hallmarks being a reservoir of Pasifika indigenous knowledge grounded on the philosophy of relationality. PTC is a regional theological institution founded by the Pasifka churches in 1961 and was established in 1965. It was the first degree-offering regional educational institution in the region that trained church and religious leaders for the Pasifika mission. It was also the first institution to emphasise indigenous contextual theologies to reclaim the importance of a creation-centred faith for the church. Some of the theologians from PTC at the forefront of igniting passion for a Creation-centred faith were Sione 'Amanaki Havea, Sevati Tuwere, Winston Halapua, Amaamalele Tofaeono, to name a very few, who were either former principals, lecturers, or alumni of PTC.

Sione 'Amanaki Havea, former Principal of PTC, claimed in his *Coconut Theology* (1987) that the coconut as a gift from God to the Pasifika communities is able to assist in reconstructing a theology of God that is 'down to Earth'. The coconut is symbolic of a never-ending cycle of life that begins from the Earth, grows to the skies and bears fruits, then it rolls down again "to the lowest possible level," bringing "food,

[9] Upolu Lumā Vaai, "Pacific Spirituality and Changing the Climate Change Story," in Sherrie M. Steiner and James T. Christie (eds.), *Religious Soft Diplomacy and the United Nations: Religious Engagement as Loyal Opposition* (Lanham: Lexington Books, 2021), 241-258. See also Upolu Lumā Vaai, "We are therefore we don't have," in Upolu Lumā Vaai and Unaisi Nabobo-Baba (eds.), *The Relational Self: Decolonising Personhood in the Pacific* (Suva: University of the South Pacific and the Pacific Theological College, 2017), 283-84.

[10] Upolu Lumā Vaai, "Lagimalie: Covid, De-Onefication of Theologies, and Eco-Relational Well-being," in Jione Havea (ed.), *Doing Theology in the New Normal* (London: SCM Press, 2021), 209-221.

drinks, husks, shells, money and industry" for community sustenance and economy.[11] Coconut theology not only reaffirms the Creation-centred focus of Pasifika theologizing, that everything in life is connected to the land, it also reaffirms the coconut identity and images of Pasifika peoples rooted in lands and cultures.

Sevati Tuwere, former Principal of PTC, developed his *Vanua theology* as an impetus to drive the importance of a more relational and communal understanding of *vanua*, which not only means land, but also means community. The two cannot be understood separately. A Christian community can only be defined in relation to the land, taking Fiji back to its cosmological identity.[12] Winston Halapua, one of the first graduates of PTC in the late 1960s, introduced his *Moana theology* or *Theomoana* as an ocean way of doing theology, acknowledging the fact that while *moana* refers to the ocean(s), it is also a holistic symbol of embrace that is ecological and cosmologically focused.[13] Amaamalele Tofaeono, former student and lecturer at PTC, developed his *Aiga eco-theology* to highlight the point that Creation is a diverse and relational ecological Aiga that affirms both the creating and redeeming love of God in all Creation.[14]

Apart from these theologians, it is the common assumption that any Pasifika theology is deeply ecological in many ways. This is based on the fact that when Pasifika people theologise, they speak from a holistic perspective simply because of the life-centred focus and orientation of their thinking and cultures. This includes, for example, not separating ecology from God, or theology from life. In the words of Cliff Bird from the Solomon Islands, a former student and lecturer of PTC, "The life of which Pacific theologians speak is not compartmentalized but is one complete whole," that includes "life in relationships and inter-relationships with and between people, between people and their immediate environments, and between people and the divine."[15] This would be disappointing to those who normally look for departmental specifics when it comes to God-talk, since most Pacific theologies transcend the normal compartmentalised and departmental mindset of the Western mainstream theological discourse. Eco-theologies cannot be redemptive and inclusive until we focus on addressing this tension between the 'whole of life' fluid approach and a compartmentalised approach in theological discourse.

Pacific Household of God

In 2013 in the Pacific Conference of Churches assembly held in Honiara in the Solomon Islands, the Pasifika churches were urged to deeply reflect on renewing the ecumenical movement in the region. Some of the questions raised were: "Who are we, as an ecumenical family, in this new century? To whom and to what should we owe the reservoir of our Christian compassion, our resources on justice, the burden of our identity as cultured Christians, ad our moral responsibility?"[16] The questions point to the need to ensure that a new ecumenical story would respond effectively to the urgent task of understanding and critically addressing the root causes of injustices, in particular climate change and environmental destruction in the region.

In 2017, Pasifika church leaders decided to change the vision and foundational image of the regional ecumenical movement from 'unity in the Body of Christ' to the 'Pacific Household of God'. The decision was a response to the 2015 call to 'Rethinking the Household of God in the Pacific' by the churches with

[11] Sione 'Amanaki Havea, "Christianity in the Pacific Context," in Sione 'Amanaki Havea (ed.), *South Pacific Theology* (Oxford: Regnum Books, 1987), 11-15.

[12] Sevati Tuwere, *Vanua: Towards a Fijian Theology of Place* (Suva: University of the South Pacific, 2002).

[13] Winston Halapua, *Waves of Embrace: Sacred Perspectives from the Ocean* (Norwich: Canterbury Press, 2008).

[14] Ama'amalele Tofaeono, *Eco-Theology: Aiga – The Household of Life, A Perspective from Living Myths and Traditions of Samoa* (Erlangen: Erlanger Verl. für Mission und Ökumene, 2000).

[15] Cliff Bird, "Integrity of Creation," in Kenneth R. Ross, Katalina Tahaafe-Williams, and Todd M. Johnson (eds.), *Christianity in Ocean* (Edinburgh: Edinburgh Press, 2021), 329-340, 334.

[16] Tevita Havea, "A Vision of Our Pacific Household," in James Bhagwan, Elise Huffer, Frances Vakauta, and Aisake Casimira (eds.), *From the Deep: Pasifiki Voces for a New Story* (Suva: Pacific Theological College, 2020), 3.

its two aims: (a) renewal within and amongst the churches, and (b) affirming the contribution of churches to the renewal of the Pasifika societies.[17] The first means seeing with fresh eyes and minds the mission of God entrusted to us and what God is calling us into, and the second is rediscovering afresh God's love and vision for the created world.

At the heart of this rethinking and renewal is that the leaders envisioned a new ecumenical story to respond to the serious concerns on the environmental destructive practices. These are driven by the dominant neoliberal economic paradigm that continues to extract and wound lands and ocean. The shift of imagery implies (a) a shift from unity to relationality as the underpinning and driving force of the Pasifika ecumenical movement, (b) enhancing the sense of ownership of the ecumenical household by the churches, (c) greater development on ecumenical cooperation on development, ecological, and social justice issues, (d) rethinking the churches regional ecumenical institutions, their structures and management, and (e) revision and development of theological education and mission.[18] It was in the same meeting that the church leaders resolved to, "adopt relationality as the defining concept, framework and focus of the ecumenical movement in the Pacific."[19]

The Pacific Household of God – its ecumenical shift – was endorsed by the Pacific Conference of Churches assembly in Auckland in 2018. Part of the rethinking strategy is establishing what is called the Pacific Ecumenical Community (PEC) of the Pacific churches, responsible for the restructuring and renewing of the regional ecumenical institutions such as the PCC secretariat, PTC, and the South Pacific Association of Theological Schools (SPATS). This is not just for more cooperation but most importantly for efficiency and effectiveness in serving the ecumenical movement in the region. In addition, part of the ecumenical shift is transitioning PTC to become the Pasifika Communities University with its 'whole of life' vision to ensure this new Pacific Household of God direction is channelled through education.

Reweaving the Ecological Mat

In 2017, the Pacific Theological College (PTC) embarked on an initiative titled 'Reweaving the Ecological Mat' (REM)[20] in partnership with the Pacific Conference of Churches (PCC) and the Oceania Centre for Arts, Culture and Pacific Studies of the University of the South Pacific, with the support of individuals and partners. It uses the concept of 'reweaving' and the metaphor of the 'mat' to tell a story of hope about our ecology and development. The initiative is a self-determination strategy aimed at weaving a Pasifika story about us, our ecology and development; a story of hope in the midst of a depressing system of *onefication*[21] that continues to produce discouraging statistics on physical and mental health, poverty and inequality, impacts of climate change, environmental destruction due to over-logging and reliance on extractive industries, depleting fish stocks and changes in lifestyle, spurred on by consumerism and the 'more and more' ethic of the current development model and measures.

---

[17] Pacific Conference of Churches and Pacific Theological College, *Rethinking the Household of God in the Pacific: Ecumenical Rethinking and Renewal* (Suva: PCC and PTC, 2015).

[18] Pacific Conference of Churches and Pacific Theological College, *Sowing a New Seed of Pacific Ecumenism: Statement of Basis and Resolution* (Nadi: PCC and PTC, 2017), 1.

[19] *Sowing a New Seed*, 3.

[20] See_ https://ptc.ac.fj/oceanic-laca/quarter-one-issue/reweaving-the-ecological-mat/; https://www.oikoumene.org/events/reweaving-the-ecological-mat-pacific-voices-for-a-new-creation; https://iefworld.org/node/1123.

[21] *Onefication* is a term that I coin to represent a system underpinned by the logic of the 'singular one'. This logic is often manifested in the term 'oneness' which aims at glorifying one at the expense of many, centralizing and controlling benefits and resources under one culture, one economic system, or one people at the expense of many including the Earth. This is the opposite of 'unity' which is about the relational plural one. See Vaai, "Lagimalie, Covid, De-Onefication of Theologies," 209-212.

The REM is a unique and Pasifika grown initiative. It addresses the physical and mental health of Pasifika peoples, the environmental challenges and disasters facing Pasifika communities, and the models and indicators of development, and social and political relations that are detrimental to the wellbeing of Pasifika communities. It draws from three main sources central to Pasifika people: (a) indigenous knowledge (philosophy, spirituality and art); the Christian Bible, theology and spirituality; and local knowledge and experiences. The initiative offers a framework – an ecological framework for development or EFD – and three strategies: (a) ecological indicators as measures of national wellbeing; (b) ecological integration of national accounts as complementary to the Gross National Product (GDP); and, (c) research and education at community, national and regional levels, to help reweave those strands of the mat that are torn in Pasifika communities. At the core, the initiative is about the sustainable development and wellbeing of Pasifika communities, and their Ocean, lands, rivers, animals, and flora and fauna and forests. It offers a holistic sustainable approach that will enable Pasifika communities to progress into the future, assured of themselves and their place in the world.

The REM initiative is driven by the belief that the region can and should determine its own future, drawing from the richness of its diverse spirituality, religious and indigenous traditions, its worldviews, and experiences and lessons of present realities in development. For most Pasifika communities, ecology means the myriad intricate relationships of people, land, forests, rivers and sea, and the norms that govern, connect and link them into a web of sustaining life and meaning. Much of this framing relates to how communities are to relate to their natural environment and the governing norms on the sustainable use of land, forests, rivers and sea resources. It emphasizes the interdependent view of the human person's place in creation and their reliance on the natural environment for sustenance and conversely their responsibility to protect and conserve.

The REM initiative aims at achieving three things: (a) research and produce a 'Household' framework for development; (b) seek alternative measures for our islands' health and wellbeing; (c) produce well researched publications for education on the 'Household' framework for development. The initiative has grown into an ecological and wellbeing movement in Pasifika. It has created a renewed thirst for alternative models and the culture of hope for the Pasifika communities, which continues to follow the spirit of ecological concern of the Pasifika churches in the past years, as outlined in some of its key documents, such as the *Island of Hope: An Alternative to Economic Globalisation* (2001), which speaks of the importance of creating an "alternative to the project of economic globalisation which entails domination through an unjust economic system" and reaffirming the importance of prioritising "relationships, and celebrating quality of life and values human beings and creation over the production of things."[22] The same ecological concern is outlined in the many PCC statements such as the *Otin Tai Declaration* (2004),[23] the *Moana Declaration* (2009),[24] and the *Tokatoka Declaration* (2016),[25] with all three focusing on climate change and the call to action for ecological wellbeing and climate resilience.

More recently REM developed three key publications from a church and ecumenical perspective to assist the Pasifika region in terms of rewriting its story of development. First, the *Reweaving the Ecological Mat Framework: Towards an Ecological Framework for Development* (2020)[26] book introduces an ecological Pacific household framework of development grounded in theological and Pasifika indigenous spiritualities.

[22] Pacific Conference of Churches, *Island of Hope: An Alternative to Economic Globalisation*, 5, https://www.oikoumene.org/sites/default/files/Document/dossier-7.pdf.
[23] See in: Martin Robra and others: Climate Change, WCC Geneva 2005, 41f. https://www.oikoumene.org/sites/default/files/Document/Climate_Change_Brochure_2005.pdf.
[24] See: https://www.oikoumene.org/resources/documents/pacific-church-leaders-statement.
[25] See: https://actalliance.org/publications/tokatoka-declaration/.
[26] See publication Reweawing the Mat Framework; in: https://drive.google.com/file/d/1f1kamvePGZjv_gtl1l6lsFlhOncyAEdv/view.

Second, *Ecological-Economic Accounts: Towards Intemerate Values* (2020)[27] provides an alternative indicator to measure economic growth that should accurately reflect the holistic worth of the Pasifika communities' understanding of ecology and to complement the mainstream GDP.

And thirdly, the *From the Deep: Pasifiki Voices for a New Story* (2020)[28] offers the gift of Pasifika cultural and faith resilience under Covid-19 with the message that the ecological crisis faced by the world today cannot be solved by scientific and technical knowledge alone – it needs the contributions of indigenous and faith-based ecological frameworks to assist with finding solutions. REM is also now incorporated as part of the Pacific Islands Forum *2050 Strategy for the Blue Pacific Continent*[29] to assist Pasifika island countries in creating a more holistic development narrative that protects and safeguards lands and oceans.

Eco-Relational Theologies and Eco-Diakonia

This spirit of political, ecological, and educational self-determination is captured in the words of one of the elders of the Pasifika ecumenical movement and a founding father of the state of Papua New Guinea.

Our history did not begin with contact with the Western explorers. Our civilisation did not start with the coming of the Christian missionaries. Because we have an ancient civilisation, it is important for us to give proper dignity and place to our history. We can only be ourselves if we accept who we are rather than denying our autonomy… Now that we are finally connected with the world, we suddenly see ourselves through the world mirror. Will we see our own true size images, or will we see ourselves in the images and the shadows of others? Will we see ourselves in the long shadows of the dwindling light and the advanced darkness of the evening dusk, or will we see ourselves in the long and radiant rays of the rising sun? We can choose, if we will.[30]

As mentioned above, by shifting to the Pacific Household of God, the Pasifika communities hope to "give proper dignity" and "proper place to our history" by investing again in the importance of relationality that is foundational to a life-centred approach. This invites the churches to move beyond the confines of eco-theologies to eco-relational theology grounded in the relational cultures of the Pasifika people and in the relational Trinitarian story of the 'life-giving' economy of God who was culturally enfleshed. But Incarnation is not just a teaching about a *flesh-bearing God.* If flesh connotes ecological relationship and kinship, at least from a relational perspective, then we can affirm therefore that all of God is realized in that which is ordinarily cosmological (not just human).

The problem with many eco-theologies is that they sometimes overlook the basic foundational principle that makes ecological and environmental protection possible, that is, relationship. The following highlights the differences between eco-theology and eco-relational theology from a Pasifika relational perspective. But they also highlight the fact that if we are serious about eco-diakonia, then eco-relational theology is an imperative shift.[31]

a. While eco-theology is a theology of ecology, focusing on environmental crisis, eco-relational theology is a theology of relationships (cosmic), focusing on the whole/multi-dimensional relationships that constitute life. The ecological crisis is a crisis of relationships. "Creation for

[27] See: Arnie Saiki: Ecological-Economic Accounts: Towards Intemerate Values; in: https://drive.google.com/file/d/1OcaA8w_1NtE_g3w4iuEzvmLV53iRNV_E/view.
[28] https://drive.google.com/file/d/1WzdXAoFeUyRXPxKveE_651ki5IuW3W5U/view.
[29] https://www.forumsec.org/2050strategy/.
[30] Bernard Narokobi, cited by Jean Zorn, "In Memory of Bernard Narokobi," http://intersections.anu.edu.au/pacificurrents/zorn_memorial.htm.
[31] See my discussion of eco-relational theology in the chapter "Faith and Culture", in *Christianity in Oceania*, 235-246.

Oceanic peoples is about livelihoods, wellbeing, and wholeness of life."[32] In this regard, eco-relational theology urges eco-diakonia to put emphasis on the primacy of the interconnectedness of life.

b. While eco-theology emphasizes a shift from *humanity to space* ("in the beginning was space"), eco-relational theology is about a shift from *space to relationships and the spiritualities that make up space* ("in the beginning was relationship"). Space is made up of multiple relationships. Even the sacred spaces assumed by extractive industries as empty are full of relational dynamics and ancestral presence. Eco-relational theology focuses on the critique of the systems of relationships (political, economic, religious, gender, etc) that collapse eco-relational connections and destroy creation.
c. While eco-theology sometimes is too empirical and scientific, eco-relational theology argues that God and human are integral and intrinsic to ecology. Eco-relational theology urges for the *dirtification* of not only our theologies of God but also our own relationship with Creation. Being integral means reclaiming the importance of dirtified thinking and living, which is normally part of the Pasifika daily economic and life activities. Because life is eco-relational, everything is connected to the dirt, a synonym for land, ocean, people, and grassroots communities.[33]
d. While eco-theology sometimes treat ecology objectively, eco-relational theology allows us to be integral and to see emotions and hear the unspoken language of that which is not human, such as trees, land and ocean. In Samoa, for example, when a mother tree or a hub tree is cut, the word used is *oia*, meaning "the whole forest cries in pain." This is why ecology including theology cannot be treated objectively, as the whole forest will be affected from cutting just one tree. The role of theology is to theologically feel those emotions and prophetically speak of such ecological pain. In Kiribati, in the light of the Kiribati island wisdom, *kana teutana ao katuka teutana*, meaning 'eat a little and leave a little' this eco-relational wisdom is symbolic of the importance of cosmological *en-otherness*, of always having other relationships as part of our consciousness. It is a critique of not only the digestive monarchs and creators of digestive systems that promote 'eat all and leave nothing' but also of the objectification of our theological discourse.
e. Eco-relational theology upholds that ecology can only be understood through its mutual interweaving and entanglement with all, including the reuniting of the *oikos triplets* of ecology, economy, and oikoumene. For eco-diakonia to work, the *oikos triplets* must be mutually and harmoniously intertwined. Economy without ecology is aggressively capitalist. Oikoumene without ecology is brutally human-centric. And economy without oikoumene is cruelly secular.
f. While eco-theology claims that stewardship is about '*caring for*' ecology, eco-relational theology argues that stewardship is about '*deep connection*'. To '*be there*' and to '*be caring*' for Creation should start with the resolve to '*be with*'. We can honestly love and care for Creation only if we are deeply connected to it. Creation care is a relationship, not a duty.

Conclusion

All of life is relational, deeply interwoven with the cosmos. Therefore, we are eco-relational beings. Because relationality is at the heart of the Pasifika way of doing things, in particular the grassroots communities, eco-diakonia and Creation care cannot work in communities unless we frame and understand it in the way they understand and perform it, created and tested throughout centuries. Eco-diakonia must be from the ground-up, communities-based, deeply connected to the philosophy of *cosmic living relationships* to be effective and transformative. The continuing challenge is how this relational perspective

---

[32] Bird, "Integrity of Creation," 334.

[33] Upolu Lumā Vaai, "A Dirtified God: A Dirt Theology from the Pasifika Dirt Communities," in Jione Havea (ed.), *Theologies from the Pacific* (New York: Palgrave Macmillan, 2021), 15-30.

would contribute to deconstructing and reconstructing salvation history, especially the tension between the Creation-centred narrative and the redemption-centred narrative.

Bibliography

Halapua, Winston, *Waves of Embrace: Sacred Perspectives from the Ocean*. Norwich: Canterbury Press, 2008.

Havea, Jione (ed.), *Theologies from the Pacific*. New York: Palgrave Macmillan, 2021.

Pacific Theological College. "A Covid-9 Wellbeing Statement: Rethinking Health from a Theological and Pasifika Cultural Perspective." https://www.oikoumene.org/news/pacific-theological-college-publishes-a-covid-19-wellbeing-statement

Ross, Kenneth R. Katalina Tahaafe-Williams and Todd M. Johnson (eds), *Christianity in Oceania*. Edinburgh: Edinburgh University Press, 2021.

Tofaeono, Ama'amalele, *Eco-Theology: Aiga – The Household of Life, A Perspective from Living Myths and Traditions of Samoa*. Erlangen: Erlanger Verl. für Mission und Ökumene, 2000.

Tuwere, Sevati, *Vanua: Towards a Fijian Theology of Place*. Suva: University of the South Pacific, 2000.

Vaai, Upolu Lumā and Unaisi Nabobo-Baba (eds.), *The Relational Self: Decolonising Personhood in the Pacific*. Suva: University of the South Pacific and the Pacific Theological College, 2017.

Vaai, Upolu Lumā and Aisake Casimira (eds.), *Relational Hermeneutics: Decolonising the Mindset and the Pacific Itulagi*. Suva: University of the South Pacific and the Pacific Theological College, 2017.

World Council of Churches. "The Island of Hope: A Pacific Alternative to Economic Globalisation." https://www.oikoumene.org/sites/default/files/Document/dossier-7.pdf

Suggestion for Further Reading

Bird, Cliff, Arnie Saiki, and Meretui Ratunabuabua (eds.), *Reweaving the Ecological Mat Framework: Toward an Ecological Framework for Development*. Suva: Pacific Theological College, 2020.

Halapua, Winston. "Theomoana: Towards a Tikanga Theology," in Nasili Vaka'uta (ed.), *Talanoa Rhythms: Voices from Oceania*. Massey: Masilamea Press, 2011, 102-110.

Havea, 'Amanaki Sione (ed), *South Pacific Theology*. Oxford: Regnum Books, 1987.

Bhagwan, James, Elise Huffer, Frances Vakauta, and Aisake Casimira (eds.), *From the Deep: Pasifiki Voces for a New Story*. Suva: Pacific Theological College, 2020.

Toren, Christina and Simonne Pauwels, eds. *Living Kinship in the Pacific*. New York: Berghahn, 2015.

Tui Atua. "In Search of Meaning, Nuance and Metaphor in Social Policy," in Tamasailau M. Sualii-Sauni et al. (eds.)m *Su'esu'e Manogi: In Search of Fragrance*. Wellington: Huia, 2018, 103–20.

Vaai, Upolu Luma. "A Dirtified God: A Dirt Theology from the Pasifika Dirt Communities." In *Theologies from the Pacific*, edited by Jione Havea, 15-30. New York: Palgrave Macmillan, 2021.

———. "Faith and Culture." In *Christianity in Oceania*, edited by Kenneth R. Ross, Katalina Tahaafe-Williams and Todd M. Johnson, 235-246. Edinburgh: Edinburgh University Press, 2021.

———. "From Atutasi to Atulasi: Relational Theologising and Why Pacific Islanders Think and Theologise Differently." In *Theologies from the Pacific*, edited by Jione Havea, 235-250. New York: Palgrave Macmillan, 2021.

———. "Lagimalie: Covid, De-Onefication of Theologies, and Eco-Relational Well-being." In *Doing Theology in the New Normal,* edited by Jione Havea, 209-221. London: SCM Press, 2021.

———. "Pacific Spirituality and Changing the Climate Change Story." In *Religious Soft Diplomacy and the United Nations: Religious Engagement as Loyal Opposition*, edited by Sherrie M. Steiner and James T. Christie, 241-258. Lanham: Lexington Books, 2021.

PART III: LATIN AMERICA AND CARIBBEAN

53. JOINED THROUGH THE UMBILICAL CORD: TALE OF *NANA OLOGWADULE* (MOTHER EARTH)

Jocabed R. Solano Miselis[1]

> "*Ai ye, degi ye, Nana burba, bala midewe neggi, Nue iddo malo, Degi*" – Brother, sister, the sacred knowledge is in Mother Earth, it is in the cosmos. Listen well. It is so.

In the ancestral language of the *Gunadule* people, one of the hundreds of peoples in *Abya Yala*,[2] the *sagla* is heard singing the above phrase, which frames the heart of *Gunadule* spirituality: its relationship with Mother Earth, *Nabgwana*, nourished by the way in which the people "cosmolive"[3] with *Nana* and *Baba* (God).

It is the movement of the *Ruach* that has been blowing for thousands of years among the *Gunadule*, showing us from their life ethic what it means to live recognising that we are part of Mother Earth and that our union with her allows us to live in balance and harmony. It is through the sacred songs that we receive the teachings of the path of *Nana* and *Baba* (God) to live a life ethic of care, defence and recognition of Mother Earth in everyday life.

In this writing, through the sung Tale of *Nana Ologwadule*, I would like to make a brief analysis of the ways in which the *Gunadule* people live their relationship with Mother Earth and then ask what their theology proposes to the church and to society.

Nana Ologwadule[4]

The Tale of Ologwadule

At first everything was dark. A darkness so dense, as if two hands were squeezing one's eyes. There was no sun, there was no moon, the stars were not born. Then *Babdummad* (Great Father) set out to create the earth, *Nandummad* (Great Mother) set out to create the earth. When *Baba* formed *Nabgwana*, he also lit the sun, moon and stars. *Baba* radiated the earth; *Baba* illuminated the face of the mother. The earth was

---

[1] Jocabed R. Solano Miselis (playerjrsm@gmail.com) belongs to the *Gunadule* nation of Panama. She was born in the time of medicinal plants. She is the director of *Memoria Indígena* and completed a master's degree in interdisciplinary theology at the Community of Interdisciplinary Theological Studies (CETI) and at Carey Theological College of Canada.

[2] TN: *Abya Yala* is the Guna term for "land in its full maturity" (see "Abiayala" below near the end of the Tale of *Ologwadule*). It is one of the most ancient ancestral terms recorded that refers to the lands that have become the Americas. In the late twentieth and early twenty-first centuries, it has become a commonly used term amongst many indigenous rights movements of this continent.

[3] The concept describes the intrinsic relationship of the *Gunadule* people from their wisdom and relationship with *Nana* and *Baba*, Mother Earth, and the communities of living beings. It is used in contrast to "cosmovision," or "world view", which is a Western term that determines the source of knowledge from what is observed, while indigenous peoples posit *cosmoliving,* or *world experience*. See Patricio Guerrero Arias, "Corazonar desde el calor de las sabidurías insurgentes, la frialdad de la teoría y la metodología," *Sophia* 13 (2012): 208. See, by the same author, *La chakana del corazonar* (Quito: Editorial Universitaria Abya Yala, 2018).

[4] *Nana Ologwadule* is one of the ancient sung stories of the *Gunadule* nation. Here, an excerpt from the song is presented.

an image and a trace that spoke of the presence of *Baba*, of the presence of *Nana*. Mother Earth took the following names: *Ologwadule, Oloiiddirdili, Nabgwana, Olobibbirgunyai, Olowainasob*. *Baba* made it like this, *Nana* made it like this: *Babdummad* spread the mass of gold at the root of *Ologwadule* and fixed to it columns and trunks of gold vigorously tied with solid gold reeds. *Baba* knew that she would carry a heavy burden and provided her with a solid foundation. *Baba* and *Nana* worked together. When he had spread the layer of gold, *Babdummad* planted all kinds of flowers on it; she planted countless species of basil, red, blue, yellow; and made them all open their blades, and it was *Oloduddagibi*. Everything was gold, everything was silver; and they rejoiced. It was all one big celebration. *Baba* and *Nana* brought the flowers to life and they moved.

When we say this, it means that they were our own images; they embodied our lives. As *Nana Ologwadule*, mother earth, was completed, our spirits were also taking her form, defining themselves according to her rhythm. Because, thanks to her, we would be human beings; from her, we define ourselves. *Baba* then spread out another layer of gold. *Baba* and *Nana* worked in unison. This time *Baba* used the blue gold. *Nana* used the blue silver. They wrapped *Nana Ologwadule*'s face again. *Baba* reattached the blue gold columns and arches with solid blue gold reeds. *Baba* scattered the seeds and made the range of flowers and mint bloom. The flowers rejoiced; so it was a big celebration. And *Nana Ologwadule* gradually took her final form. *Babdummad* worked and formed the contours of mother earth, flooding her with joy, covering her with gold. *Nandummad* worked with *Babdummad* and together they covered *Ologwadule* with fine gold, with fine silver. The second layer was done. *Baba* proceeded to cover *Ologwadule* with the third layer of gold. He took yellow gold for this coat. He did the same process as the previous ones and *Ologwadule* was hardened like this yellow gold, yellow silver.

For the fourth layer, *Baba* used red gold. *Ologwadule* was clothed in red gold. In all its breadth the flowers danced, the basils of red gold danced. *Baba* thus strengthened the great nanny *Ologwadule*. He tied the pillars of gold to her. Then the river was born. And *Ologwadule* slowly came to her fullness. It was no longer formless, but solid and compact: *Abiayala*, *Oloburganyala*.

Nana Ologwadule poured out the stream of waters. The current of the river emitted its moan in the entrails of the mother and in her bark the seeds, the vines, sprouted. Greenery arose and the mother's body was filled with beautiful and robust trees with their varied colours. And that's why we call her mother. Mother Earth, *Nana Olobibbirgunyai*, *Baba* constituted her as the protector and defender of everything that rocks, moves, lives and rests on her. The sun itself is under her care, the moon, the stars, the winds, the rain, the abysses, the large and small animals. *Baba* and *Nana* left with her, from her inception, flower seeds of all kinds, but only when the time was right, and in the due course of their development, they sprouted, invigorating and blushing *Nana Ologwadule*'s cheeks.

Analysis of the Text

The story we have just reproduced develops a narrative full of metaphors. To understand it, one must understand the thought forms of the *Gunadule* nation. For the *Guna* people, everything that exists on Earth has life. Therefore, the Earth is a living being that feels and thinks. That is why the stories about its origin are narrated through characters as if they were human beings.

The text begins by pointing out that, at the beginning, everything was dark. This tells us that we do not know how the birth of the Earth and the Sun happened. What we do know is that Mum and Dad created them. And that, in this process, *Ologwadule* has been maturing.

When *Ologwadule* is spoken of in other narrations, it is pointed out that she was *Mago*'s partner and this may confuse many, since the use of metaphor and symbols are a fundamental part of the stories of the ancestral peoples. In them, poetry, art, images and beings are brought into play in order to "reveal" enigmas of culture and the cosmo-existence of the peoples. It is not easy for the Western mentality – for which even spiritual knowledge assumes a "linear" character – to understand this, at least initially. In ancestral peoples, such knowledge attends to non-linear, complex perspectives.

In the *guna* stories, *Mago* is the Sun and *Ologwadule* is the Earth. We do not know the mystery of this process, but *Mago*, before being Sun, when he was a boy, was the birth that became Sun. And in the case of *Ologwadule*, she was the Earth that, in her beginning process, was a girl. Both complemented each other, *Mago* and *Ologwadule*, the Sun and the Earth. Although we do not know how the Sun and the Earth came to be, we do know that the Great Father and the Great Mother (*Babdummad-Nandummad*) are their origin.

In *Gunadule* theology, the manifestation of the Divinity is understood as Mother and Father. And both complement each other. In the words of theologian, Aiban Wagua:

> everything subsists from a system of complementarity. Guna complementarity emerges from their own credibility motives: Baba-Nana, co-creators of the universe. That is to say that the spirituality, supported by its understanding of God as Mother and Father, sustains in practice the relationships between men and women as beings that complement each other and that community cannot be created without understanding this sense of complementarity. The relationship with the Earth and the Sun is understood in the same way.[5]

A comment that helps us better understand this sense of complementarity is expressed by the Igwanabiginya *sagla* (1897-1989): "In this sense, the universe has not been created, but co-created from a parity of forces: man/woman, female/male."[6] Therefore, the creation of the Earth comes from *Baba* and *Nana*. From the creation of the Earth and the Sun, the other stars were also born.

In *Ologwadule's* story, the emphasis falls on the creation of Mother Earth, where we are also told that human beings are an image of her. That is to say, we are little Mother Earth, because we carry in us the elements of the Mother. This makes a difference in relation to the concept of the "common home" that others use to refer to the Earth. Theologian Marilú Rojas Salazar says:

> The Greek term has traditionally been interpreted as a common house, only this concept, in my opinion, has two underlying epistemic problems. On the one hand, it evokes the patriarchal house and the hierarchical relationships that are established in it from the stratified kyriocentric model even to the slaves. On the other hand, the house is an object that can be sold or bought through the logic of the market, that is, it also functioned as an economic-social unit in ancient Greece. In this model, the *pater familias*, a white, rich, Hellenic and free man, exercised his sovereign authority as owner of the *oikos*, thus generating a patrilineal line from the oldest man to the youngest, always establishing patriarchal hierarchies. Women, children, slaves were a kind of "goods" or belongings of the *pater familias*.[7]

The indigenous peoples of *Abya Yala* have understood since ancient times through their spirituality and, as we delve into their wisdom, we are getting to know this richness present in the midst of the different nations of *Abya Yala*. The God of life breathed out their breath and has been present in these lands. That is to say, the *nega* (house) has a "hearting" of a living being and, therefore, constitutes a multiunit in itself, where human beings participate in the cosmic community. Life, as a sacred text, enlightens us to live in harmony with others in our *nega*. The latter is presented as a different concept from the western one of house-*oikos*. The *nega* is interpreted in relation to Mother Earth and, from there, it constitutes another fabric.

---

[5] Aiban Wagua, interview by Jocabed Solano Michelis, 25th September 2020.

[6] Aiban Wagua, *Los gunas entre dos sistemas educativos* (Panamá: Proyecto EBI Guna; Fondo Mixto Hispano Panameño, 2005): 9.

[7] Marilú Rojas Salazar, "Diversidad eroecosofiánica como categoría epistémica decolonial de los cuerpos abyectos ante los fundamentalismos religiosos", in Comisión 'Saberes' of the Red TEPALI (eds), *Las teologías feministas frente al fundamentalismo religioso* (Vitória, Brasil: Editorial Unida, 2020): 273-274.

Memory of the Earth and its Influence on the Daily Life of the Gunadule People

From the whistling of birds, from the moaning of wild animals, from the sob of trees (*dumbirgessu*), from the whisper of *Ologwadule*, we learn to live in harmony. We learn with the senses. Each story, each dance, the language, the food, the relationships, the silence and much more, form or deform a nation. This is well known to the grandparents in the *Gunadule* nation. So, since ancient times, they have worked so that the new generations can continue singing, and not die.

The great importance of spirituality lies in the fact that our political actions emanate from it. We do not separate public life from private. And we do not disintegrate the life of the sacred from the life of the secular. The whole of life is sacred. Every act, no matter how small, is a political act.

The highest ethic of the *Gunadule* nation is community life. Without that community, we are beings alienated by our selfishness. In the songs, we are reminded of this so that we do not forget and do not repeat the stories of regret that we have lived when we have not been able to recognise the importance that one has for the others and of the others for one.

Therefore, when we go to one of the sacred places of the *Gunadule* people, which is called the *ommagenednegga*, we know that it is important to pay attention. We listen to the *sualibgan-Suwaribga*[8] when they warn us: *Gabidamalarggenueiddomalargge* (Pay attention! Do not fall asleep!). Because it depends on this song for the community to understand well what our behaviour should be. Thus, we join the heart of the Great Father, the Great Mother, the heart of *Ologwadule* and we remember the memories of the Earth, of our grandmothers and grandfathers, their celebrations, struggles, laments, hopes, and cries of resistance.

It is a moment that we live in community, where co-existence is not only passive, because we actively listen to the voice of God, of Mother Earth, of the cosmic community and we recognise that Mother and Father have been there. There, we are invited to listen to what they tell us through the Memory of the Earth. The secret of the *Gunadule* people has been that we listen to God (*Nana* and *Baba*) through the voice of *Mamá* (Mother Earth) as an invitation to live in harmony.

That is why we see the influence of the memory of the Earth in everything we do: from the birds, we learned to dance. One day, the children who were looking at the sky noticed that the birds were circling and they began to do the same. But they also learned to walk as birds walked, mimicking their steps and jumping, and they saw that the birds looked united as if they were holding each other by linking arms. So the children did the same. From the birds, we also learned to defend ourselves against the threats that we experienced. In the *Gwibloni*[9] season, which is the time of the warrior birds, they defend the territory with their own lives, they fly in flocks. And we, the *Gunadule*, learned from them to defend ourselves, we know that we must live as a family, that we have to defend ourselves from the threats that want to dismantle our identity. In ancient times, we defended ourselves from the genocide carried out by the conquerors; in February 1925, we rose up against the Panamanian state that wanted to "civilise" us.[10] The hegemonic systems have tried to impose their ideologies, economically and politically, religiously and culturally. It has been hundreds of years of resisting and uprising, loving the Earth, defending the autonomy of the territory.

The birds taught us the best strategy, but they also taught us and showed us the dangers. Through their gurgles and whistles, they heralded good times or warned to prepare to face an extremely dry season. When *gigga*[11] flew very low and almost brushed against a person and with desperate shrieks, it presaged something

---

[8] *Suwaribgan*: custodians or guardians of the community, people in charge of putting order in the communities and warning the people who listen to the *saglagan* in the *gunadule* general house of congress.

[9] *Gwiblonii*: in this month, due to the abundance of butterflies, the birds (*gwiblo*) come down. They fly in flocks. In the Gregorian calendar, it would be October.

[10] The Revolution of 1925, undertaken by the *Gunas* against the Panamanian state.

[11] *Gigga*: a messenger bird that, for the *Gunadule* people, warns about danger.

very unpleasant, a surprise that could be violent; but if it gurgled with slow and deliberate whistles, it was a sign of a pleasant message, maybe there was a herd of peccaries a short distance away.[12] We, the *Gunadule*, relate the combat and the message as signals to be alert.

The Earth is sacred and is inhabited by other living beings with which we maintain a harmonious relationship. This is how we plant timber trees such as *binnuwar* (wild cashew), *gaobanwar* (mahogany), *urwar* (cedar), *nugnuwar* (ceiba). Canoes are a sign of autonomy for the Gunadule people because they are used for work and daily transportation. Trees are among us and interacting with them gives us life. Therefore, most of the territories in the *Gunadule* nation are not inhabited by the *Gunadule*, as they are full of trees and medicinal plants.

Medicinal plants are sacred texts that tell us about health, strength, energy, vital air that we can breathe to live. Medicinal plants are female and are our great protectors. Memory tells that *Inabundorgan* went down late at night, while the evil spirits slept. And when they woke up, they heard thousands of female voices singing beautiful melodies and they were the plants. That is why, before uprooting the medicinal plants, we converse with them, and Mother and Father are invoked along with them.[13]

Indigenous knowledge about medicines is ancestral – it has been transmitted from generation to generation. An *inaduled* claims to be "a *duleina* dreamer" and recalls that "I learned everything from my ancestors and for 20, 30 years and I continue to learn other treatises, and I did not study for 10 years, as happens in *wagas* universities.[14] Our forest is a true university, there we practice and extract *ina* (medicine)." Another *inaduled* comments that "ancestral knowledge in our *ina* does not exist, the ancestral is the present, it always exists [...] because our *ina* is an entire health system that has been kept alive thanks to the effort and defence that we have made through the centuries." It is a timeless wisdom, it is a wisdom that comes from *Nabgwana* – Mother Earth.[15]

Some Implications for the Church

Gunadule hermeneutics is a proposal from the heart of Mother Earth. Their theology invites us to know from their stories how God's path has been in their memories. This leads us to know them, and from this knowledge, to know ourselves, to recognise ourselves, and to know the indigenous face of God. From missiology and in the pastoral care of the churches, *Gunadule* theology challenges us to ask ourselves how much of this tells us about the specificity and particularity of indigenous peoples as the people of God, who have special gifts that allow us to learn to live in harmony with all created beings, including human beings.

The importance of the voice of Mother Earth in daily life and the revelation of *Nana* and *Baba* to Mother Earth and in Mother Earth, lies precisely in the fact that God is not only revealed on Earth, but to her. And this propitiates a decolonising turn, because it conceives of the Earth as a living being, which receives the gift of life, co-creates with God, produces, regenerates, renews, and provokes. For she is ancestor, prophet, healer and body of God. This body of God expresses love, compassion, community, reciprocity, the relationship between the cosmic community, the power, the strength, the energy of the *Ruach* in it. Through cyclical and spiralling time, it is immanent and transcendent, but it also encompasses life at all times, transcending the dimensions of life and the cosmos.

From this perspective, *Gunadule* theology opens up other possibilities for us to understand Christology, pneumatology, creation stories. It invites us to walk in the mystery of God, which has no beginning or end, because its rhythm unfolds in a spiral. The interpretation of God in the *Gunadule* people is not articulated from a patriarchal system, since each person is important in the *Gunadule* community. For example, the

---

[12] Atilio Martínez, *El legado de los abuelos* (Panamá: Equipo EBI Guna, 2012): 71

[13] Martínez, *El legado.*

[14] *Wagas*: foreigner, ladino, not-*guna*, not-indigenous.

[15] Martínez, *El legado.*

house of the *Gunadule* people is one of the strongest structures from a political and spiritual point of view. As it expresses the complementary, integral and holistic conception that characterises the *Gunadule* people. In this framework, each act, however small it may seem, affects the harmony of life. Therefore, the task of *Gunadule* life is relevant and significant when doing *Gunadule* theology.

Hence, the invitation to Christians is to continue knowing, listening, recognising, dialoguing, to continue the path of a profound quest by those who embrace the faith of Jesus from their identity. And, in the case of the *Gunadules* as *guna*, to do it from the narrative that feeds the life of the people, which enhances and enriches their maturation as the image and likeness of God.

It is essential to value the narrative contribution of indigenous peoples and respect their theologies about the memory of the Earth. They allow us to have a broader picture of the grace and diversity of God in the world, inviting us to dialogue on the path of encounter and mediation. A path oriented towards world experience, which allows us to open ourselves to other worlds of possibilities in the understanding of biblical texts, which enrich and ferment an intercultural church.

It is necessary to recognise this liberating reading from the indigenous peoples. And to recognise the sacred texts of the indigenous peoples as a space of experience of these indigenous peoples in their relationship with the memory of the Divinity and of the Earth. This implies opening a path to deepen the faith of the indigenous ancestors as a meeting for dialogue, which allows recognising the indigenous face of the Divinity.

This should provoke in the global church an attitude of listening, of humility, to dialogue as peers and not seeking to impose submission, believing that there is only one truth about God. It is the invitation of the communities that allows us to dialogue and not the other way around. It allows us to walk with the indigenous peoples, being aware that they are the main actors in their own struggles. This includes the current agendas for the vindication of their territories against systems of death – such as extractivism, megaprojects, mining, monocultures, among other phenomena that cause the climate emergency – which are realities that affect the Earth and the crops.

The indigenous faces of God speak to us of the gift of community vocation that indigenous peoples have, given and revealed to each people in a specific way. They propose their own way of walking united, in the same way that the baby is joined through the umbilical cord with his mother. In this way, we can live the healing process of our body-territories, being healed by *Nana* and *Baba* on Mother Earth.

Suggestions for Further Reading

Congreso General Kuna. *Anmar igar (Normas Kunas)*. Panamá: Congreso General Kuna, 2001.

RIBLA. "La Palabra se hizo India". *Revista de Interpretación Bíblica Latinoamericana* 26 (1997).

Guerrero Arias, Patricio. *La chakana del corazonar*. Quito, Ecuador: Editorial Abya Yala, 2018.

—. "Corazonar desde el calor de las sabidurías insurgentes, la frialdad de la teoría y la metodología". *Sophia* 13 (2012): 199-228.

Martínez, Atilio. *El legado de los abuelos*. Panamá: Equipo EBI Guna, 2012.

Memoria Indígena. "Conclusiones del encuentro Lima 2015". 28th October 2015. *Memoria Indigena Website.* [Available at: https://memoriaindigena.org/conclusiones-del-encuentro-lima-2015/], [Last accessed: 8th May 2022].

Rojas Salazar, Marilú. "Diversidad eroecosofiánica como categoría epistémica decolonial de los cuerpos abyectos ante los fundamentalismos religiosos", in Comisión 'Saberes' of the Red TEPALI, Eds. *Las teologías feministas frente al fundamentalismo religioso*. Vitória, Brasil: Editorial Unida, 2020: 269-280.

Solano Miselis, Jocabed. "Las narrativas como resistencia política. La experiencia de la nación guna", in Priscila Barredo Pantí and Nicolás Panotto, Eds. *Juventudes: Otras voces, nuevos espacios. Confrontando la teología y la misión*. México: FTL, 2018.

Solano Miselis, Jocabed. "Voces indígenas: Fortaleza espiritual de los pueblos de Abya Yala. Dulamar gagga: anmar burba gangued Abya Yalagi". *The Global Church Project* 2018. [Available at: https://theglobalchurchproject.com/jocabed-spanish/], [Last accessed: 8th May 2022]

El sueño de Dios en la creación humana y en el cosmos. Memory of the IV Simposio Latinoamericano de Teología India, Lima (Perú), 28th March-2nd April 2011. Bogotá, Colombia: CELAM, 2013.

Ventocilla, José, Heraclio Herrera and Valerio Núñez. *El Espíritu de la tierra: Plantas y animales en la vida del pueblo Kuna*. Quito: Abya Yala, 1999.

Wagua, Aiban. *En defensa de la vida y su armonía*. Panamá: Proyecto EBI Guna y Fondo Mixto Hispano Panameño, 2011.

—. *Así lo vi y así me lo contaron*. Panamá: Fondo Mixto Hispano-Panameño de Cooperación, 2007.

—. *Los gunas entre dos sistemas educativos*. Panamá: Proyecto EBI Guna; Fondo Mixto Hispano Panameño, 2005.

54. "To Hear Both the Cry of the Earth and the Cry of the Poor":[1] Contribution from the Original Peoples of the Amazon Towards a Holistic and Integral Ecology

Birgit Weiler[2]

The pastoral-theological reflections that I will develop below intend to gather significant contributions from the original peoples that provide important insights for guiding the ecumenical commitment to an integral and holistic ecology, and the care for the "common home". In turn, these contributions will guide an eco-diakonia in times of climate emergency and acute ecological crisis in the Amazonian region and globally.

The Amazon, Rich in Diversity and of Great Beauty

When beginning reflections on the Amazon, it is important to keep in mind that the entire region covers an immense area of almost 7,500,000 km^2, of which approximately 5,500,000 km^2 are covered by forests.[3]

The Amazon biome has existed for more than 30 million years and is home to the largest and most diverse rainforest in the world. In the Amazon "everything is connected."[4] Thanks to the multiple connections and interactions between the diverse species of living beings, including fungi and microbes, that co-exist in this ecosystem, the Amazon rainforest is "exceptional and irreplaceable."[5]

Of the 30 million people who live in the Amazon, almost a million belong to native peoples. There are about 400 indigenous peoples in the region, who have "their own cultural identities and land management practices."[6] The growing migration from rural areas to urban areas has generated a multicultural reality in the Amazonian cities. Given its great diversity, it is important to highlight that there are many Amazons.

The Amazon Biome: Crucial for the Stability of the Global Climate

The Brazilian expert in biodiversity, ecosystems and climate, Carlos Nobre, who has studied the Amazon for more than 40 years, was one of the consultants of the Amazon Synod (2019). Along with a group of international experts, he developed a scientific framework to safeguard the Amazon. The experts placed great emphasis on the fact that the Amazon "plays a fundamental role in global water cycles,"[7] since the rivers of the region contain one fifth of all the fresh water on our planet.

---

[1] Francis, *Laudato Si'* (Vatican City: Vatican Press, 2015): sec. 49.

[2] Birgit Weiler (weiler.mms@gmail.com), of German nationality, is a member of the Congregation of Medical Missionary Sisters and has lived in Peru since 1988. She is a theologian and professor in the Department of Theology at the Pontifical Catholic University of Peru (PUCP). She is also a member of the team of theologians of the Episcopal Council of Latin America (CELAM) and of the Ecumenical Dialogue Team of the Pan-Amazonian Ecclesial Network (REPAM).

[3] Científicos de los Países Amazónicos y Socios globales, "Un marco científico para salvar la Amazonia," presented at the Special Assembly of the Synod of Bishops for the Panamazonian region, 30th September 2019, [Available at: http://www.synod.va/content/sinodoamazonico/es/noticias/un-marco-cientifico-para-salvar-la-amazonia-por-cientificos-de-l.html], [Last accessed: 8th May 2022].

[4] Francis, *Laudato Si*, 91.

[5] Camila Costa, "'La gran mentira verde': cómo la pérdida del Amazonas va mucho más allá de la deforestación", *BBC News Mundo*, 13th February 2020, [Available at: https://www.bbc.com/mundo/noticias-america-latina-51303285], [Last accessed: 8th May 2022].

[6] Científicos, *Un marco*, 2.

[7] Científicos, *Un marco*, 2.

The scientists also identified a system of so-called flying rivers, which play an important role in generating rainfall in much of South America. These "carry huge amounts of water vapour from the lower Amazon which in turn discharge rain to tropical glaciers," to the higher reaches and valleys of the Andes, "and provide the water supply for large cities like Bogotá, Quito, Lima and La Paz."[8]

The data collected by Nobre and his team since 1975 clearly prove that the Amazonian tropical forest and its ecosystems are essential for maintaining the climatic balance not only in the Amazon and Latin America, but also for the planet. In addition to very efficiently recycling water, the forest is also a huge carbon drain. Of the total carbon absorbed each year by the forests of our planet, the Amazon rainforest retains between 20% and 25%.[9] However, its great biodiversity and its fragile ecological balance mean, in turn, a great vulnerability of the territory and its inhabitants.

The Amazon: Close to a Dangerous Breaking Point

The Amazon biome is being increasingly affected by the multiple devastating impacts on its ecosystems, setting up a dangerous dynamic in which both factors reinforce each other. Such impacts are caused by massive extractive activities, aimed at exploiting its multiple renewable and non-renewable natural resources. Some examples are oil, gas and minerals (particularly gold, legally and illegally); agribusiness, with its extensive monocultures, and hardwood felling (largely illegal), among others.

In addition, it is necessary to point out the impact generated by the continuous expansion of the infrastructure required for extractive activities and the transportation of raw materials, the construction of hydroelectric dams to satisfy the growing demand for energy. Large projects, mostly extractivist, are often planned and implemented without prior and informed consultation with the affected indigenous peoples, although national and international laws prescribe it.

It is also worth mentioning the contamination of rivers and other water sources, as well as the soil, due to oil spills and the activities of companies and residents. In addition to high contamination by toxic waste, throughout the Amazon, there is a problem of enormous production of non-bio-agreeable garbage, especially in urban areas where the majority of the Amazonian population currently lives.

The increasing mass deforestation is contributing a lot to global warming. In the Amazon region, it is observed with concern that the dry seasons are lengthening and that the droughts are becoming more intense. As a result, tree mortality is increasing. This is a serious sign that the tropical forest is weakening and has less capacity to withstand the multiple stress factors to which it is exposed.

The Amazon is like a mirror of the serious ecological, socio-economic, political and cultural problems at the global level, and of their many interrelationships. Despite its increasingly alarming situation, since 2019 deforestation figures have been rising significantly. In this annual period, 2.4 million hectares of Amazonian forest were lost due to logging;[10] this corresponds to an area slightly smaller than the territory of Israel (22,145 km^2).

According to the scientists from Nobre's group, we are very close to the point of no return, where 50% or 60% of the entire Amazon forest could be transformed into an extensive savannah. In the documentary *Breaking Boundaries*, Joan Rockström, Director of the Potsdam Institute for Climate Impact Research (PIK), warns that within 15 years the tropical forest in the Amazon could begin to emit carbon into the

[8] Científicos, *Un marco,* 3.
[9] Científicos, *Un marco,* 4.
[10] See Costa, "La gran mentira verde".

atmosphere, thereby contributing to global warming.[11] This would have disastrous consequences for the Amazon, as well as for South America, the Caribbean and the global climate.

In the Amazon, a close connection can be observed between a violent attitude and practice towards nature and towards people, because "we have only one heart."[12] Due to the violent reality, which includes neo-extractivism[13] and its multiple harmful impacts, "the cry of the earth and the cry of the poor"[14] arises from the Amazon, a cry that needs to be heard and heeded. It is a scream of pain and resilience; at the same time, it is a hopeful sign that in the midst of these harsh and threatening realities, there is still life and not just the silence of death.

Among the communities most affected and threatened by the current climate emergency and the aggravated ecological crisis are those that already live in very precarious conditions of poverty and extreme poverty, as well as high vulnerability. This is especially true for the communities of indigenous peoples and the African diaspora. The truly dramatic situation of the Amazon region calls for an integral and holistic conversion,[15] that is pastoral, ecological and synodal.[16] In particular, the original peoples have much to teach and offer us in this process of conversion and deep transformation, which the critical state of the Amazon demands.

Contributions of the Indigenous Peoples in the Face of the Crisis: Comprehensive Worldview, Ecological Wisdom and Good Living (Buen Vivir)

For a long time, scientists have told us that everything in our world is connected. In the Amazon, this is not just abstract knowledge, but a notion that arises from the life experience of Amazonian communities, both indigenous and of the African diaspora. For many peoples and communities in the Amazon, especially for the original peoples, this understanding of reality does not represent something new but is deeply rooted in their worldview.

These peoples perceive the cosmos as a vast and complex web of relationships characterised by continuous interactions, intercommunications and interdependence, as well as by the flow of energy. In their understanding, life is lived in relationship and bonding with others, including other nonhuman living beings in relation to the earth and the territory. Human beings are part of this great fabric of life and have a significant role within it. At the same time, they have the deep notion and conviction that not only human persons but also other living beings act, and in that sense, they are all agents. This is true even for the smallest and seemingly insignificant elements, such as microbes and fungi. In the understanding of the native peoples, there is no "dead matter," rather everything is alive and full of energy, including rivers, forests, hills and mountains. As Pope Francis emphasises in the *Exhortación Querida Amazonia*, from "the original peoples, we can learn to *contemplate* the Amazon region and not simply analyse it, and thus

[11] Rockström, Johan, *Ten years to transform the future of humanity*, *TED Talks*, October 2020, [Available at: https://www.ted.com/talks/johan_rockstrom_10_years_to_transform_the_future_of_humanity_or_destabilize_the_planet (tiempo 2:43-2:51)], [Last accessed: 8th May 2022].

[12] Francis, *Laudato Si'*, 92.

[13] Extractivism – already practiced since colonial times – continues in the present, but adapting to current socio-political and economic conditions. That is why we speak of *neoextractivism*.

[14] Francis, *Laudato Si'*, 49.

[15] General Secretariat of the Synod of Bishops, "Final Document – The Amazon: New paths for the Church and for an integral ecology", 2019 sec. 17-19, [Available at: http://secretariat.synod.va/content/sinodoamazonico/en/documents/final-document-of-the-amazon-synod.html], [Last accessed: 8th May 2022].

[16] Synod, FD, sec. 20; 41; 65; 86.

appreciate this precious mystery that transcends us. We can *love* it, not simply use it, with the result that love can awaken a deep and sincere interest."[17]

For the peoples of the Amazon in general and the original peoples in particular, the territory has a great meaning not only in the material sense but also in the symbolic, affective and religious sense. According to them, "(i)n the Amazon, life is inserted into, linked with and integrated in territory."[18] In turn, the territory is for them a "place of meaning for faith or the experience of God in history."[19] There, "the reserve of life and wisdom for the planet is manifest, a life and wisdom that speaks of God."[20] In the understanding of the native peoples, the Amazonian territory teaches us something essential: "(n)o parts of the Amazon territory can subsist on their own", rather they support each other through multiple interconnections and interactions, "forming a vital whole."[21]

For all these reasons, among indigenous peoples, in general, the territory is not perceived as an economic good or capital with which it is possible to increase financial profits through its partial or total commercialisation. Rather, the conviction and the norm that the territory should not be sold predominates. However, companies often try to undermine this conviction through corrupt practices towards some members of the communities in order to break the cultural tradition and thus gain access to the land.

As different investigations show, the concerns and efforts of indigenous peoples to defend their territories against extractivist activities are based on reality. They clearly indicate that extractivism is in no way sustainable and that it is not economically profitable either, if all the ecological and social costs it generates are included in the balance.

Predatory extractivism, with its strong negative impacts, is a main cause of the increasing degradation and destruction of the Amazon.[22] For this reason, in the Amazon Synod, it was categorically expressed: "Faced with the pressing situation of the planet and of the Amazon, integral ecology [...] is the only possible path, because there is no other viable route for saving the region."[23] It is necessary "to hear both the cry of the earth and the cry of the poor."[24]

Nobre emphasises that to safeguard the Amazon forest, its ecosystems and biodiversity, as well as Good Living (*buen vivir*) for the different population groups in the region, an integral ecology and "bioeconomy" is needed.[25] This consists of an innovative way of understanding and practicing economy; it is based on activities that ensure the necessary income for a life in decent conditions and, at the same time, keep the Amazon forest "standing" by applying strict sustainability criteria to all its dimensions.

Great wisdom is expressed in the concept of Good Living (*buen vivir*) of the native peoples of the Amazon and elsewhere. Good Living is the result of a continuous cultural action that requires continuous personal and community work that aims at becoming aware of attitudes and actions. As Good Living always goes hand in hand with "good doing" and has to do with "good living together". This impacts relationships with others, starting with the family (clan) and the community. Other key dimensions of Good Living are reciprocity, solidarity and the constant search for balance and harmony in relationships with other members

[17] Francis, *Querida Amazonia* (Vatican City: Vatican Press, 2020), sec. 55. (The emphasis is original).
[18] General Secretariat for the Synod of Bishops, *Instrumentum Laboris* (Vatican, 17th June 2019), sec. 19 and 21, [Available at: http://secretariat.synod.va/content/sinodoamazonico/en/documents/pan-amazon-synod--the-working-document-for-the-synod-of-bishops.html], [Last accessed: 9th May 2022]. This "Working Document" which served as the basis to start the work in the Amazon Synod, gathers multiple contributions from the Amazonian peoples in the territorial consultations that took place prior to the Synod. More than 80,000 people participated in this process.
[19] Synod, IL, sec. 19.
[20] Synod, IL, sec. 19.
[21] Synod, IL, sec. 21.
[22] Synod, FD, sec. 67
[23] Synod, FD, sec. 67.
[24] Francis, *Laudato Si'*, 49.
[25] Científicos, *Un marco,* 7.

of the human community, with God or the Divine, and also with other living beings in nature. It is not acceptable to only use the land, but it is also necessary to provide it with services; for example, through the reforestation of a part of the forest or the care and non-pollution of water. The same goes for community relations, which must be based on a mutual giving and receiving of goods and services. This also includes persistent community work to overcome the *machismo* existing in many groups and to promote justice and non-violence in gender relations. As stated by many members of indigenous peoples, there should be no one "excluding nor excluded, and that among all of us we can forge a project of full life."[26] It reminds us and makes concrete the life in fullness promised by Jesus (Jn. 10:10).

Buen vivir is a dynamic conception that continues to be created in response to changing historical and socio-cultural contexts and in dialogue with other native peoples as well as with non-indigenous populations. As Eduardo Gudynas says, "it is a category in permanent construction."[27] Based on his research, Gudynas affirms that *Buen vivir* questions "the rationality of current development, its emphasis on economic issues and the market, its obsession with consumption, or the myth of continued progress [...] [emphasising] the quality of life."[28] With this concept, many leaders and members of indigenous peoples strongly criticise "the reductionism of presenting development as economic growth", insisting that "alternatives to development" must be construed.[29]

In his reflections, Gudynas emphasises that Good Living is an integral concept. He shares his observations that, for many members of the indigenous peoples, values such as solidarity, community and the common good continue to be relevant in their lives. Many strive to practice these values, even confronting increasingly difficult socio-cultural conditions.

On the other hand, in the face of certain ideas and images that idealise life in indigenous communities, it is necessary to critically point out that, even in the most remote communities, the influence of urban consumer culture is growing, along with its pronounced individualism. Furthermore, among the native peoples, the coherent practice of Good Living requires a continuous spiritual commitment, which appreciates the wisdom and values that are rooted in the concept with the purpose of transmitting them to the younger generations. For many men and women leaders who, because of their commitment to defend the rights and territory of their peoples, have suffered serious threats from different mafias, the spirituality and values linked to this practice are a source of courage, inner strength and resilience. This concept is very significant from the very fact that, throughout the year 2020, in the Amazon every other day an indigenous leader was assassinated for their commitment to Good Living.

Facing the sociocultural, economic and ecological crisis, as well as the critical situation in the Amazon, the native peoples on the peripheries of the centres of power open up new horizons for us based on their conceptions of Good Living. We need their ecological wisdom or *oiko-sofía* in order to carry out the necessary cultural revolution.[30] In other words, a courageous and profound transformation of our societies in the face of the neoliberal practice of the economy, which is seriously contributing to social and environmental degradation. Although it has emerged in rural contexts, the concept of Good Living contains valuable inspirations and significant questions for other contexts.

There are important points of contact between Good Living and the Christian faith. I want to outline several key aspects that arise in an intercultural and interreligious dialogue with indigenous peoples. In a rereading of our Christian theological and spiritual sources, it is noted that both Good Living and the Reign [or Kingdom] of God point towards a fuller life for all human beings and not only for some. Both Good

---

[26] Synod, IL, sec. 12.
[27] Eduardo Gudynas, "Buen vivir: Germinando alternativas al desarrollo", *América Latina en Movimiento* 462 (2011): 1-20.
[28] Gudynas, "Buen Vivir", 2-3.
[29] Gudynas, "Buen Vivir", 3.
[30] Francis, *Laudato Si'*, 114.

Living and the Christian faith are deeply relational: both sharpen the awareness that "everything is related". From this understanding, the Encyclical *Laudato Si'* emphasises that "(w)e are faced not with two separate crises, [...] but rather with one complex crisis which is both social and environmental. Strategies for a solution demand an integrated approach."[31]

Safeguarding the Amazon: An Urgent Need for Global Solidarity and *Effective* Alliances

An integral ecology demands a profound transformation of our societies towards true sustainability in all dimensions, which must take place at the local, regional and global levels, and requires networks of solidarity and shared commitments. For the Amazon, this means, among other things, that it is necessary to take the transitional steps away from an economy based mainly on extractivism towards a truly sustainable, biodegradable and circular economy.

Since global conditions are intertwined, safeguarding the Amazon has to be a shared commitment. Given the urgency of preventing us from reaching breaking points, a much more intense and firmer global commitment is imperative. The peoples of the Amazon are fully aware that they will not be able to deal effectively with the serious problems in their territories alone. They have asked the Christian churches to be their allies in the defence of their rights, and in denouncing the attacks against the health and life of the communities and their leaders, the lack of demarcation of their territories, as well as the predominant "predatory and ecocidal" economic model.[32] The churches are called to be prophetic and, together with the indigenous peoples, "to face the unlimited exploitation of our common home and its inhabitants."[33] This also implies insisting, before the authorities of the State and the companies, on the fact that local peoples must be the main interlocutors in dialogues about projects of various kinds that are sought to be implemented in their territories. From these people "we have the most to learn, to whom we need to listen out of a duty of justice [...]. Their words, their hopes and their fears should be the most authoritative voice at any table of dialogue on the Amazon region. And the great question is: 'What is their idea of 'good living' for themselves and for those who will come after them?'"[34]

The serious problems of the Amazon are linked to lifestyles, consumption and economic practices promoted or stimulated from elsewhere, especially in the Global North and in the "North" of each country in Latin America. Many agricultural products, hardwoods and minerals that are imported by the countries of the North from the Amazon, are causing the deforestation of vast areas of tropical forest. It is crucial that corporations assume their responsibility for the entire market chain and, with it, for the conditions in which products are generated and transported – in addition to questions of ecological, climate, social, cultural and gender justice. It is also of great importance that consumers and collaborators in co-operative projects consciously choose to effectively promote and support projects in the Amazon that contribute to promoting the transition from extractivism to an economy based on an integral ecology. Here, the Christian churches with their solidarity networks can contribute a lot.

Furthermore, Christian churches, together with communities and institutions of other religions, can collaborate significantly in promoting greater awareness of the urgency of safeguarding Amazonian forests and all tropical forests.[35] We are currently facing strong climatic changes in all regions of the world that have led to a "climate emergency", as many scientists attest. We are approaching several breaking points

---

[31] Francis, *Laudato Si'*, 139.
[32] Synod, FD, sec. 46.
[33] Synod, FD, sec. 67.
[34] Francis, *Querida Amazonia*, sec. 26.
[35] An inspiring example of this is the Interfaith Rainforest Initiative, see "New Hope for World's Tropical Forests as Christian, Muslim, Jewish, Hindu, Buddhist, Daoist Leaders Join Indigenous Forest Guardians to Launch Global Effort to End Deforestation", Press Release, 19th June 2017, [Available at: https://www.interfaithrainforest.org/s/iri_press_release.pdf], [Last accessed: 9th May 2022].

much faster than expected.[36] In this unprecedented situation, religions are called to contribute all that they can "towards an integral ecology and the full development of humanity."[37]

In the Amazon, this is already happening and has yet to continue through ecumenical and interreligious dialogue and collaboration aimed at putting an integral ecology into practice. This implies caring for the "common home" and the common goods that include the climate[38] and the Amazon biome. This is also vital for recognising the historical debt with the native peoples because of their colonisation and the "ecological debt"[39] with all the peoples of the Amazon, together with the need to promote, in alliance with many other actors, greater ecological and climate justice globally.

The Pan-Amazonian Ecclesial Network (REPAM) is committed to living this commitment in an ecumenical, interreligious and intercultural way, as well as in a strategic alliance with the Co-ordinator of the Indigenous Organisations of the Amazon Basin (COICA) and in co-operation with the Pan-Amazonian Social Forum (FOSPA). Collaboration with members of the indigenous peoples and of the African diaspora provides the opportunity to learn more about how to relate to others on equal terms and how to "overcome the various colonising mentalities and to build networks of solidarity,"[40] sustainability and eco-diakonia. In this way, the Christian churches, in alliance with the native peoples and many other actors, can work together to ensure that "the central role of the Amazon biome for the equilibrium of the planet's climate"[41] will be recognised and supported globally. This is vital for taking care of the Amazon, which is a significant part of our common home, entrusted by God to us. Since we have received the call to do so by bearing witness to our faith in God who is "lover of Life" (Wis. 11:26) and of God's covenant with all living beings on earth (see Gen. 9:12).

Suggestions for Further Reading

Boff, Leonardo. *Una ecología integral: Por una eco-educación*. Valencia: KHAF, 2020.

—. "Transición ecológica hacia una sociedad biocentrada". *América Latina en Movimiento,* 21st June 2020. [Available at: https://www.alainet.org/es/articulo/207397], [Last accessed: 9th May 2022].

Guridi, Román. *Ecoteología: hacia un nuevo estilo de vida*. Santiago, Chile: Ediciones Universidad Alberto Hurtado, 2018.

Lenton, Timothy, Owen Gaffney, Stefan Rahmstorf, Katherine Richardson, Johan Röckström, Hans Joachim Schellnhuber, and Will Steffen. "Climate Tipping points – too risky to bet against". *Nature* 575 (2019): 592-595.

Rosa Salazar, Marilú. "La pertinencia de la teología ecofeminista y su incidencia política ante el feminicidio y el ecocidio actual". *Revista Iberoamericana de Teología* 16(30) (2020).

[36] See report of the Intergovernmental Panel on Climate Change, "Climate change widespread, rapid and intensifying", Press Release, 9th August 2021, [Available at: https://www.ipcc.ch/2021/08/09/ar6-wg1-20210809-pr/], [Last accessed: 9th May 2022].
[37] Francis, *Laudato Si'*, 62.
[38] Francis, *Laudato Si'*, 23.
[39] Francis, *Laudato Si'*, 51.
[40] Francis, *Querida Amazonia*, sec. 17.
[41] Synod, FD, sec. 68.

55. Socio-Environmental Justice: The Earth and the Table as Theological Places

Juan Javier Pioli[1]

Introduction

In this article, we will show how life experience is a key element for building theological thought, especially when we talk about Creation Care. At the *Centro Emmanuel* of Colonia Valdense, Uruguay,[2] we believe that the practices and daily experiences of all people can serve as material that renews and gives meaning to reflections on ecotheology. Through trial and error, we try to build a contextualised reflection, a discourse that gives meaning to our practices, and a practice that renews and feeds that discourse. Eco-diakonia and ecotheology are two "doings" that feed off and constantly challenge each other. In this dynamic, the *Ruach* of God mysteriously operates.

Although our experiences cannot be transplanted, we can "tell them" and share knowledge, essays and illusions. We do it with the conviction that this narrative can, through the *Ruach* of God, inspire other dreams.

Our Tables

We like to say that the history of the *Centro Emmanuel* was woven around the table. Not because every important event happened over lunch, but because our dreams and aspirations became visible in that space.

In a very synthetic way, we can say that the *Centro Emmanuel*[3] was born more than sixty years ago as an ecumenical space for spiritual retreats. It arose inspired by the European experiences of *Taizé* or *Grandchamp* and, little by little, it became a space for the theological formation of church members. Between the sixties and seventies, the *Centro* participated in a time of great ecumenical dialogue, permeated by significant movements in our region's history: the activity of ISAL (the abbreviation in Spanish of Church and Society in Latin America), the impact of liberation theology and explorations in the field of popular education. In the mid-eighties and after a long dictatorship, the return to democracy redefined old dreams and generated new queries: thus, the idea of starting an ecological farm flourished.

In recent decades, the *Centro* has become a reference point for agroecological production, by creating networks between families in rural areas, supporting training and the exchange of knowledge. There is also a commitment to raising awareness among the general population, building bridges with organisations in civil society and other religious institutions. In line with this objective, *Centro Emmanuel* accompanies churches in their processes of incorporating the socio-environmental dimension as an important element in theological reflection, which generates new prophetic voices and diaconal practices. This has led the *Centro Emmanuel* to position itself as a leading actor in ecotheology as well as in agroecology. These dimensions have renewed our way of thinking about theological formation and biblical interpretation, revitalising intergenerational work, retreats and camps.

---

[1] Juan Javier Pioli (teologia@centroemmanuel.org) is a graduate in Theology from the University Institute – ISEDET – and taught history at the Instituto de Profesores Artigas. He currently works as the theological secretary at the Centro Emmanuel (Colonia Valdense, Uruguay) and teaches in secondary and technical-professional education. He is a member of the Evangelical Waldensian Church of the River Plate.

[2] See "¿Qué es el Centro Emmanuel?", *Centro Emmanuel* [Available at: https://centroemmanuel.org/quienes-somos/], [Last accessed: 9th May 2022].

[3] See also: https://centroemmanuel.org/

All this has been possible, to a large extent, thanks to the tables where we have been fed. In them, the ritual of food has the magical power to transform: bread can become a gesture, sharing a round of *mate* can generate ideas,[4] table talk becomes an invitation. How many relationships, projects, and ideas result from the shared table? How often has the community meal been a propitious place for a miracle, multiplication, consolation, for listening, or inspiration?

The Table as a Mirror

"Good God, heavenly Father, thank you for the material bread and the spiritual bread" – I heard an old farmer from the coast of the Paraná River saying this many times. He said it in verse before having lunch, there, where the water runs majestically, dragging with it colours, vegetation and sediments from the heart of our continent. This was an expression of spirituality, a form of piety typical of the agricultural colonies formed by Protestant immigrants who arrived in our region in the first decades of the twentieth century.

Although today we could reformulate some parts of that sentence, a very important element appears within it when thinking about our practices of commensality (the act of eating together or table fellowship/"Tischgemeinschaft"). Shared food allows a meeting between two dimensions of the human being; it satisfies two vital and interdependent needs: that of energy and nutrition, and the opportunity for sociability and bonding. Commensality is, in the daily cycle, a moment in which we not only eat what is on the plate; we also generate or reinforce a relationship, a link with those around us. By incorporating food, we also integrate bonds, stories, emotions. More than consuming, we incorporate, and that which is passed through the senses is added to the body to be processed. It remains *in corpore*. That is why we give thanks for daily bread, in its many forms and materials.

We then believe that commensality is a culturally significant ritual in which we can reconnect with the social, affective and spiritual. In the words of Patricia Aguirre:

> Commensality is the human way of eating, sharing with others according to certain values that give meaning to that food and that sharing. We don't eat just to feed ourselves, we eat because that food makes sense within the framework of social representations about who we are and why we are here.[5]

In our experience, these spaces of commensality were the moments in which some of the most valuable projects of the *Centro Emmanuel* emerged. In our River Plate culture, the lunch ceremony has its own liturgy, a set of more or less negotiable rules that give food a meaning that is both sacred and profane. At the end of the meal, the table talk can be a relaxed ritual, sometimes eternal, in which the anecdote and the joke can be interspersed with deeper conversations. In this dynamic, the colloquiality of the table talk generates a climate of trust and openness in which good things often mature. Ideas, initiatives, resources that needed a time of trust, the warmth of the table and the awakening of the senses can emerge and become reality.

On the other hand, a good reason to reaffirm the value of the table as a theological place is explained by the ways in which that space makes visible the ways in which we relate to all of creation. The table is not only a space for building social ties, but it is also a mirror in which a form of relationship with nature crystallises, the source from which our food is obtained. Where does what we eat come from? How much energy did its production and transportation demand? Is it seasonal food, canned food, has it gone through industrialisation processes? In what part of the elaboration do we participate? What processes did it go

---

[4] *Mate* (*mah'-tay*) is a traditional South American infusion prepared with dried leaves of yerba mate (*Illex paraguariensis*) and hot water. It was traditionally consumed by the Guaraní and Tupí indigenous peoples; in the Spanish conquest, it was adopted by the settlers. Currently, it is consumed mainly in Argentina, Uruguay, Paraguay and southern Brazil.

[5] Patricia Aguirre, *Una historia social de la comida* (Buenos Aires: Lugar Editorial, 2017): 318-319.

through before reaching our table? Do we know who planted, transported, prepared this food? What forms of spirituality underlie our ways of eating?

During her visits to the *Centro Emmanuel*, Nancy Cardoso reminded us of the importance of food as a space for exchange and bonding, but also as a "place" in which forms of production and distribution of resources become visible:

> Eating is a fundamental act of exchange with the world, a fundamental representation of belonging to a culture, an exercise in choosing elements and the permanence of species and agreements between different elements. [...] [Food] reveals a way of being in the world, and of establishing exchanges with the environment and culture, both in permanence and in adaptability and creativity.[6]

In reality, the ritual of commensality is a mirror of our world, a performative representation in which interpersonal relationships, forms of power, production relationships, traditions and knowledge, techniques and technology related to obtaining food are made visible.

Land and Humanity

It took many years for agroecology to become an identity element of the *Centro Emmanuel*. Some perseverance was also necessary to achieve this recognition by civil society, and the same also for the churches to see it as a form of diakonia and testimony. It was then that ecotheology emerged as a complementary field (we would almost say symbiotic with agroecology), which has the possibility of questioning people from different religious traditions, fields of work, formation and militancy.

On the other hand, the work in ecotheology and agroecology helped us to rescue a dimension and a form of sensitivity that our theological traditions had marginalised. Thus, in the dialogue with family producers, during the intergenerational camp meetings, in what people were looking for when they arrived at the *Centro Emmanuel*, and in our own quests, we began to notice that the land was a central element. We discovered that the earth was not only a topic of theoretical discussion, it was also a source of theological inspiration, a "place" charged with meaning, in which sensory experience and memory were of vital importance.

Thus, we began to work closer to the land, and our dynamics, camp proposals and reflections incorporated that dimension. Along this path, when playing, lying in the grass, working or walking barefoot, the experience of the land generated a crossroads with our corporeality. We then came to understand that ecotheology was not a unilateral, declaratory and eminently rational discourse, but rather a conversation, a dynamic marked by attentive listening and exchange. And in this dialogue, the land also becomes an interlocutor, who can "speak" through sensory experience, memory, and the voice of the other.

But the earth as a theological place is not our invention. In fact, the land is a central component in most biblical accounts. Although the Bible tells us about the relationship between God and God's people, this relationship includes the earth as a protagonist that has often been made invisible. In both the Old and New Testaments, the earth is a fundamental actor in understanding the meaning of several texts, because it is the place – or the body – on which many signs are produced. It is the object of a promise or a punishment, blood is shed on it and it is a disputed territory; the earth can be a source of food, shelter and protection; an object of play or distraction; a bed on which to rest; a place from which clean water flows; it can be inundated or arid. In the Bible, the land is laid bare after the battle and looting, it can also become a garbage dump, a vineyard or a wheat field, it can even be used to heal, to teach or to represent states of mind (throwing dirt on one's head, shaking off the dust et cetera).

[6] Nancy Cardoso Pereira, "Recetas de Vida: en la cocina con Elías y Eliseo", *RIBLA* 66(2) (2010): 51-52.

For all this, both in the Bible and in our own existence, the earth is an element that intervenes in that link between God and humanity. In the Bible, the earth can appear in different ways: only as a setting ("they went to Gethsemane"), as part of the message ("but other seeds fell on good ground"), or as an object of action ("he made a little mud and smeared it"). Although our readings ignore it, the land is there, giving meaning to the message. The big problem arises when the earth is made invisible, generating interpretations of the texts that "take it out of the equation" (spiritualising, moralistic, disembodied readings), and thus nurturing a spirituality that renounces sensorial experience, corporeality and the sense of participation in the land. By forgetting the land as a theological place, the human being becomes separated from it and forgets that human existence depends on the integrity of creation.

But it is not enough to talk about "the promised land", or to be thankful for "the fruits of the earth that God gives us." Sometimes our theologies, our liturgies and our diaconal practices reproduce idealised images of the earth, which lose sight of the complex power relations that are woven around it, which are manifested in forms of unjust possession or appropriation, subjugation, deprivation, exploitation or speculation.

In the Scriptures, we also find hints of a rather problematic relationship with and around the earth. For example, we have the policy of deportation practiced after the fall of Jerusalem, which only left in Judah the "poorest people of the land" (2 Kings 24:8-17). The ruling elites and the economically relevant sectors were forced to go into exile in Babylon, which annexed the territory of the Hebrew State into its empire. So the land, which was previously the possession of local elites, the object of rivalries and speculation among the Judeans, now becomes a foreign possession. Ironically, those who could previously assert their power over the land are torn from it. The poor, on the other hand, can remain, but in a relationship of submission and alienation. The land no longer belongs to one or the other: "Our inheritance has been turned over to strangers, our homes to aliens. […] We must pay for the water we drink; the wood we get must be bought" (Lam. 5:2, 4).

In the New Testament, the relationship with the land is also marked by tensions. Babylon has passed; now the territory has been annexed to the Roman Empire, which implements its own administration and government, creating alliances with local elites. The gospels will show that this stability is based on a situation of privileges and abuses. If we focus on the land and the use that is given to it, we see that a very important part feeds the armies and sustains a productive system that works for the empire, the court of King Herod, the Roman dignitaries and the priests of the temple. The widows and the sick wait, and those who have nothing to eat pick grain where they can.

As we have seen, the land is a central element when thinking about power relations, the economy and human subsistence. But the link we establish with the land is also an axis that structures our culture. It gives us identity. This relationship is so intimate, that although we do not notice it, it is present in the word that defines us as a species. The word "humanity" has its origin in the Indo-European languages and its root relates it to the term "*humus*", the richest portion of the earth in terms of nutrients and the presence of life. The Romans borrowed this root to refer to our species, creating the term *humanus*: "that which comes from the earth". Interestingly, the Judeo-Christian tradition also preserved a creation myth according to which God created the human being – *adam* – from the earth – *Adamah* (Gen. 2:7; 3:19; Ecc. 12:7).

Why does it seem so necessary in the Bible, as well as in many cultures, to insist on this relationship between land and humanity? Perhaps this question is a clue, a path that allows us to explore the link that exists between our destiny as humanity and that of the earth as soil, memory, source of inspiration. This sense of unity should also lead us to affirm that social justice and environmental justice are two interdependent practices.

Environmental Justice, Social Justice

Some years ago, the team at the *Centro Emmanuel* developed a definition of ecotheology with which we continue to feel a deep identification: "ecotheology is dialogue and conversation, it is God with God's feet on the ground, it is the Bible as compost for the soil: it is the possibility of interpreting, reading, and rereading our relationship with Creation. And it is the pursuit of integrity."[7]

This definition is traversed by the question about justice. When we talk about climate change, the problems associated with monoculture, the contamination of watercourses or the treatment of waste, deep down we are asking ourselves about justice. Contrasting this reality with the idea of what is fair to us, we see a contradiction.

Normally, these issues are addressed as environmental problems. However, in our journey, we have learned that environmental problems are not separate from social issues. It is not only the river that is polluted, there are those who drink that water. Additionally, we have learned that environmental problems, when they hit the social fabric, do not hit everywhere in the same way. There is a close relationship between the violence exerted on creation, and the violence experienced at the social level.

That is why we choose to speak of ecotheology as a commitment to socio-environmental justice. Because both bodies – the one of creation and the social one – are closely related. A few examples suffice to illustrate this idea, first taken from local, current events and then another from the biblical text. Firstly, we know that the use of synthetic chemical fertilisers is among the causes that have led to the contamination of watercourses. Uruguay boasted of pristine nature and good health, yet the problem became an issue on the public agenda when the beaches and water treatment plants began to be invaded by greenish stains. What looked like a stain from a distance, looked like a suspension of particles up close. What looked like dirty water up close has been shown to contain a toxin that can cause skin allergies, and respiratory and gastrointestinal disorders.

The scientists announced that they were cyanobacteria, organisms that live naturally in the water; they reproduce at an accelerated rate when the temperature and nutrients increase. Precisely, these nutrients runoff from excess fertilisers applied to crops, dairy farms, feedlots and from the sewage from towns and cities. Every summer, these eutrophication processes in the watercourses and reservoirs not only make purification processes more expensive and affect tourism,[8] but they also impact those who don't have access to other sources of drinking water, those who don't have the resources to buy bottled water or a home filter, and those who flock to urban beaches or creeks instead of swimming pools at clubs and hotels.

Something similar occurs with the so-called fumigated schools or with neighbourhoods built on land contaminated with lead. Who suffers this problem first? The children of dairy farmers, laborers and small producers who go to rural schools; the children from the peripheral neighbourhoods where no one wants to go; those relocated from the marginal neighbourhoods. They are the ones who will have lead poisoning, respiratory diseases, "rare allergies", oncological diseases with healthcare costs that they will not be able to afford.

In biblical texts, we can also find overwhelming situations in which the social and the environmental are intertwined. In 2 Kings 6: 24-31, we find a disturbing situation, perhaps one of the harshest that humans can encounter. The king of Syria has besieged the city of Samaria and after three weeks of blockade, resources are becoming scarce. At the time, it was a frequent military practice to siege walled cities as a

---

[7] Juan Javier Pioli (ed), *Por una cultura del cuidado de la vida: memorias de un seminario sobre diaconía y desarrollo sostenible (ODS)* (Colonia Valdense, Uruguay: Centro Emmanuel, 2018): 57-58.

[8] The eutrophication process refers to the contamination of aquatic ecosystems due to the effect of excess nutrients from human activity, causing the hyperproliferation of cyanobacteria. See G. Chalar, "Dinámica de la eutrofización a diferentes escalas temporales: Embalse Salto Grande (Argentina-Uruguay)", in G. Tundisi, T. Matsumura-Tundisi and C. S. Galli (eds), *Eutrofização na América do Sul: Causas, conseqüências e tecnologias de gerenciamento e controle* (Rio de Janeiro: Instituto Internacional de Ecologia e Gerenciamento Ambiental, 2006): 87-101.

strategy to force a surrender. A well-supplied city can hold out, but if the surrounding fields are razed, the flow of food is cut off, or the water supply is affected, the besieged is thrown into demoralising desperation.

In this story, there are two women who embody the most agonising part of the situation. Torn by famine, they agree to kill one woman's son in order to devour him and survive. The second was then to offer her son on a later day, but she hides him. Then the pain of mourning mixes with the pain of hunger and outrage at the broken pact: "Give up your son and we will eat him," says the first mother. Then, infuriated, she claims her right before the king. But he, instead of assuming an attitude of responsibility, tears his clothes and blames Elisha for the situation.

On this occasion, ambitions unleashed a climate of war with an unquestionable environmental impact. We know that warfare always leaves an ecological debt. Now, who are the people most affected by this crisis? Whose are the bodies that fall first in the trench of hunger and famine? The siege of the city, the lack of resources and the devastated land do not affect everyone equally. The king walks through the city and has clothes to tear as a sign of mourning, while two women tear the flesh of their children so as not to die. Where are the chiefs of the city, the merchants, the military chiefs, the religious leaders, and the king's court? Surely, they haven't eaten their children; surely, they have something in reserve. Because the environmental crisis is very respectful of social differences.

When we talk about "environmental problems" we must remember that the impact of our practices on the body of creation does not affect all people in the same way. Furthermore, when the most vulnerable make their cry heard, the powerful may tear their clothes in public display and get all the attention.

That is why we must talk about socio-environmental problems, because the social body and the body of creation cannot be dissociated. It is not possible to question the environmental crisis if we do not take into account the forms of oppression or helplessness that fall on the most vulnerable people. This key to reflection could also be applied to the current global situation, when we are going through a pandemic in whose genesis we could identify large environmental imbalances, the shifting of agricultural frontiers, the retreat of forests and wetlands, the loss of biodiversity, urban overcrowding and that of animal production. As in Samaria, today the environmental crisis, hunger and disease hit the world population unequally. While some may tear their clothes off in video streams or on Instagram, others experience the tearing of the social and community fabric, that of their economies, and even that of their own bodies.

Therefore, both in ecotheology and in eco-diakonia, it is essential to remember the intimate relationship that exists between the social and environmental fabric. Social justice and environmental justice are two threads with which the same system, the same *oikos*, is woven, which cries out from the depths of the earth.

Suggestions for Further Reading

Aguirre, Patricia. *Una historia social de la comida.* Buenos Aires: Lugar Editorial, 2017.

Alves, Rubem. *Estórias de quem gosta de ensinar – O fim dos vestibulares.* San Pablo: Papirus, 2000: 141-146.

Cardoso Pereira, Nancy. "Recetas de Vida: en la cocina con Elías y Eliseo". *RIBLA* 66(2) (2010): 50-65.

Chalar, G. "Dinámica de la eutrofización a diferentes escalas temporales: Embalse Salto Grande (Argentina-Uruguay)", in G. Tundisi, T. Matsumura-Tundisi and C. S. Galli, Eds. *Eutrofização na América do Sul: Causas, conseqüências e tecnologias de gerenciamento e controle.* Rio de Janeiro: Instituto Internacional de Ecologia e Gerenciamento Ambiental, 2006: 87-101.

Ferrer, Pablo Manuel. "Tierra, memorias y olvidos en el Nuevo Testamento". *Saberes a la Mesa* 1 (2021): 3-10. [Available at: https://centroemmanuel.org/revistasam/], [Last accessed: 9th May 2022].

Hillmann, Mónica, Guillermo Long Bertinat, Raquel Malan, J. Javier Pioli, Silvana Schaffner, Santiago Wirth Ricca. "De ciclos y ciclos: propuesta de reflexión en Ecoteología". *Centro Emmanuel Website.* [Available at: https://centroemmanuel.org/de-ciclos-y-ciclos-propuesta-de-reflexion-en-ecoteologia/], [Last accessed: 9th May 2022].

Long Bertinat, Guillermo, J. Javier Pioli and Silvana Schaffner. "Como el jardín: espiritualidad y trabajo de la tierra." *Saberes a la Mesa* 1 (2021): 15-19. [Available at: https://centroemmanuel.org/revistasam/], [Last accessed: 9th May 2022].

Pioli, Juan Javier, Ed. *Por una cultura del cuidado de la vida: memorias de un seminario sobre diaconía y desarrollo sostenible (ODS).* Colonia Valdense, Uruguay: Centro Emmanuel, 2018.

56. A Call to Value What Is Invisible: Epistemological Changes for an Ecological and Feminist Theology

Arianne van Andel[1]

Introduction

Is there a link between the exploitation of nature and the discrimination against women? Is this link reflected in theology? In their search for an answer to this question, my students usually mention that both nature and women aren't "seen" and that neither is recognised as important in today's socioeconomic system. This invisibility implies an undervaluation and even indifference regarding the abuse to which both are subjected. The word "invisibility" is striking, as it has to do with a conscious proactive act. It is closely associated to epistemology because what we value arises from what captures our gaze. The act of rendering something or someone "invisible" means that we do "not see," or "look the other way," because we don't value the object or the person. Our values, in turn, are connected to our beliefs.

The Chilean lawyer, Ezio Costa writes that, although ecological consciousness has grown over the last decades, "this hasn't yet translated into social, economic and legal systems that reflect the challenges we face."[2] I have the impression that the same occurs with theology. Although we are increasingly aware of the invisibilisation of creation and of women in the dominant Christian narratives, this awareness hasn't translated into a profound change in our epistemology or ways of being church. In this article, I explore some root causes of the invisibilisation of nature and women in many theologies, and I suggest some new practices that emerge from experiences in Latin America that may help us to understand and value what was made invisible.

Feminism and Ecology

Ecofeminism, a word coined by the sociologist Françoise D'Eaubonne in 1974, addresses the ideological connection between the exploitation of nature and the discrimination of women within the prevailing hierarchical and patriarchal system. The Spanish philosopher Alicia Puleo summarises this connection as follows:

> To comprehend the encounter between feminism and ecology, it is important to realise that feminism was able to show that one of the legitimising mechanisms of the patriarchal system has been the naturalisation of "Woman", in other words, women are perceived as the manifestations of an essence [...]. The feminine essence has been defined as the Other in contrast with fully human, as Otherness, as Nature, Cyclical Life, nearly unconscious. Conversely, Man has been thought of as the complete human being, as Reason, Mind, Spirit, Culture.[3]

---

[1] Arianne van Andel (ariannevanandel@gmail.com) is a Dutch ecotheologian from the reformed tradition, Co-ordinator of Training in the organisation Otros Cruces (Other Crossings) and of the Interreligious and Spiritual Alliance for the Climate (AIEC) in Chile. She is an organizational coach, a fellow of GreenFaith, a teacher of Theology in the "Comunidad Teológica Evangélica" (CTE) and the Methodist Seminary in Santiago de Chile and an activist in the Civil Society for Climate Action network (SCAC) and the "Mesa Ciudadana sobre Cambio Climático".

[2] Ezio Costa Cordella, *Por una Constitución Ecológica. Replanteando la relación entre sociedad y naturaleza* (Santiago de Chile: Catolonia, 2021): 18. Translation by the author.

[3] Alicia H. Puleo, *Claves ecofeministas. Para rebeldes que aman a la Tierra y a los animales* (Madrid: Plaza y Valdés Editores, 2019): 26. Translation by the author.

Drawing from this text, we can say that the invisibility of women and nature stems from the dualistic thinking characteristic of Modernity, which separates culture from nature, mind from body, reason from emotions, associating the second part of the binary with femininity. What we see and value are culture, mind and reason, as they have been defined since the Enlightenment in Europe. The view of a dualistic hierarchy led to the invisibility of the facet that is not a point of reference, which includes nature and women.

Three Instances of Invisibility Within the Churches

The Christian tradition, historically inclined to dualist thinking due to what Rabbi Sacks calls "Plato's Ghost,"[4] has adopted the dualisms of Modernity, and has legitimised them by adding the dualism of spirit/soul and body, and sacred/profane. The sacred and spiritual dimension was linked to culture, mind, and reason, associated with masculinity, and more highly valued. The undervaluation, if not outright disregard, for nature and women, as well as other groups associated with nature, such as indigenous people or Afro-descendants represents a tremendous deviation from the spirit of the gospel. We need to become aware of what we have habitually learned to consider as secondary. We can only deconstruct the hierarchical dualisms in theological thought if we look at reality from a different light.

After many years of reflecting and working to address the climate crisis and ecofeminist theology in church settings in Latin America, I have reached the conclusion that many churches still struggle to consider the ecological crisis as a cross-cutting issue in Christian mission, let alone connect it with equality between men and women. My perception is that we have not been able to fully address the epistemological component of our disconnection from nature because this would require a spiritual conversion, a change in language and symbols as well as in habits. I perceive this disconnection in the churches in three areas.

1) Invisibility of Nature and Land

Although an increasing number of theologians assume that theology of creation deserves a place alongside theology of salvation, they are rarely accorded the same level or integrated. Caring for nature is still considered to be an earthly task, disconnected from our spirituality. As I expressed in another article:

> We praise the marvels of God in nature, without associating them to our physical selves or the streets where we live. Ecology is associated with trees, herbs, plants, and flowers and less with buildings, the economy, and our lifestyle: transport, energy, or diet. We continue to see the work of taking care of creation as a responsibility for something "external" to us, not as part of our "self-care."[5]

In some Evangelical churches, eschatology still serves as a barrier that prevents people from taking seriously the idea of care for the Earth. "In the end we only reside in this land as foreigners and strangers (Lev. 25:23), and all is focused on the New Jerusalem, not this Earth," concluded a student.

This invisibility tells of abstraction and idealisation. To talk about care for creation, for our common home, calls for a view from the outside, which, in reality, we can never have. It is difficult to make this view concrete and to know and value the land of which our local churches are a part, its characteristics, its climate, its soil, and its water sources. And although we speak about Jesus' incarnation, we do not easily visualise our own bodies as an integral part of nature, including the way we are being affected by the degradation of the nature that surrounds us.

---

[4] Jonathan Sacks, *The Dignity of Difference. How to Avoid the Clash of Civilizations* (New York: Continuum, 2002): 45-66.

[5] Arianne van Andel, *Teología en Movimiento. Ensayos eco-teológicos y feministas para tiempos de cambio* (Miami: JUANUNO1 Ediciones, 2021): 238. Translation by the author.

In Chile, six areas have become known as "sacrifice zones." These are largely low-income communities that are heavily industrialised with the promise of "progress," and disproportionally affected by environmental contamination.[6] The churches in those zones have not engaged and lifted their voices to support the population's struggle. This is an example of how many churches live their mission disconnected from the natural place in which they are located.

On the other hand, in biblical interpretation, we do not usually address the characteristics of the territories present in the narratives and the link between the condition of the earth and the human quests and concerns that are described. Although the voice of the earth is present in the texts, we have a hard time listening to it, as we tend to prioritise the human side of the history.

2) Invisibility of the Public Sphere

Stemming from the previous point, we still perceive a reluctance in the churches to engage in debates in the public sphere beyond issues related to individual morality. This reflects the relegation of religion to the private sphere as the result of Modernity and the interpretation of the Lay State as a rigid separation of the churches from public concerns. Moreover, it is an indication of a certain individualism that has penetrated theology, in which the individual behaviour of the members of the church has become more central than the role of the community in its environment.

The positioning of the churches in the public sphere is ambiguous. While women also were excluded from the public sphere, the most conservative churches uphold positions that assert a traditional gender role, and control over women's bodies. Churches that do take a social role in society in the public sphere generally do so in charitable activities, positioning themselves in the same role relegated to women in society: as caregivers. The social projects in which churches are involved mainly concern providing shelter to the homeless, migrants, and support for women who suffer violence.

Thus, they have an important presence in providing refuge, but less in the political struggles that question a system that sustains those injustices: a system that not only denigrates people but also destroys ecosystems. The socioenvironmental problems are evident in the public space and are related to political decisions. In the case of environmental conflicts, movements in defence of the land arise, a space in which churches can play a role. Moreover, it is striking to see numerous women leaders in these movements in Latin America.

3) Invisibility of Everyday Life and Caregiving

As is well-known, faith communities in Latin America are mostly sustained by women, who take charge of caregiving tasks in the community. The gender roles that have been naturalised in our private life are replicated in many churches. The women prepare the coffee, cook, clean, keep the place in order and organise the care for and work with the children, the elderly and physically challenged persons. Although these tasks may be valued by the community, generally they don't have the same weight as the liturgies, education, pastoral missions, or church council meetings. Women are underrepresented in spaces of hierarchy and decision-making.

The climate crisis affects women much more severely than men because of the roles that women have in securing the basic necessities in the families. It is women who take the responsibility when there is a lack of resources; this scarcity is associated with and exacerbated by the climate crisis. It is women who take their children to the doctor, who take care of the sick and elderly. The book *Reflections on Feminism and Ecology in Quarantine*, a compilation of discussions of a group of ecological feminists in Chile, shows

[6] Van Andel, *Teología en Movimiento*, 140.

the different areas in which the ecological crisis impacts women differently than men. Access to water, food, energy, housing, work and care are examples.[7]

Animal raising and care is also traditionally a task for women, and it has been harshly affected by extractivist interventions in the territory, such as mining, in Bolivia. A testimony from Poopó in Bolivia indicates as follows:

> The grazing and care of the animals, as an essentially feminine task, has been heavily affected by the arrival of these operations. The death of 30 heads of cattle due to water pollution is a heavy blow for a rural family, an economic problem that overburdens women, exposing them to great vulnerability and poverty on account of the lack of resources. This type of deprivation shows clearly how the invasion of extractivist activities limits the capacity for self-determination and the full development of the indigenous population, mainly women, as it impedes the generation of basic resources and their own means.[8]

Daily caregiving activities are much present in church communities. Many churches are places of care and prayer for the personal lives of their members, but the concrete caregiving tasks continue to rely mainly on women. As María Pilar Aquino says: "For Latin American feminist theology, everyday life has been the main sphere that produces and reproduces social asymmetrical relationships that act against women in an organised way."[9]

To materialise an "eco-diakonia," a service of the churches to the integrality of the ecosystems and to the people as an integral part of nature, we are called upon to include and integrate earth and land, the public sphere and our everyday life into our discourse, activities, and liturgy. In what follows, I will offer a few ideas on how we can accomplish this integration process.

Towards the Integration of the Earth and Land-Body

The integration of the earth first of all implies reconnecting to the place in which we are situated. Within the premises of the churches themselves, this may include starting a community vegetable garden or planting a tree and looking after it together. Many environmentally conscious communities strive to recycle, or to stop using single-use plastics, or limit the use of paper. The incorporation of plants instead of disposable flowers, as part of the liturgical decoration is an important gesture. These are small steps that can sow a new culture.

A next level would be to leave our buildings and explore the neighbourhood or the surrounding land. What environmental challenges does our zone face? Can we support actions and projects of a group or local government? Is it possible to change our energy source to renewables or share it with neighbours? Is it possible to start a recycling programme in our church, or help neighbours to bring their waste to a distant recycling station? Some churches teach others how to use a compost bin or help clean streams or beaches.

In addition to these actions that many churches have already undertaken, feminist theology has indicated that in order to reconnect with the earth we need to reconnect with our own "naturalness": our bodies. This is a more sensitive issue in an ecclesial culture that still focuses heavily on "the word" and "rational reflection". Although in charismatic spaces, emotions are given free reign and expressions of the body are allowed, they are often cathartic, and aimed at connecting with God, not with ourselves.

---

[7] Coordinadora Feminista SCAC, *Reflexiones sobre Feminismo y Ecología (en cuarentena)* (Santiago: Ediciones Böll, 2021).

[8] Colectivo de coordinación de acciones socio ambientales y Colectivo CASA, *Despojo de agua por Mineria y el impacto en Las mujeres. Diagnóstico del despojo de fuentes de agua por minería estatal y transnacional* (Junin: Casa Colectivo, 2018): 24, [Available at: https://colectivocasa.org.bo/wp-content/uploads/2020/09/despojo-agua-por-mineria-impacto-en-las-mujeres.pdf], [Last accessed: 10th May 2022].

[9] María Pilar Aquino y Elsa Tamez, *Teología feminista latinoamericana* (Quito: Ediciones Abya-Yala, 1998): 58.

A repressive culture in regard to our body has also influenced the emergence of abuses, which sometimes make the churches more cautious about opening to the subject. There are many fears associated to valuing the integrality of our bodies, our emotions, intuitions and instincts. As we have already pointed out, these aspects are readily labelled as feminine, with the intention to devalue them. However, unless we accept our naturalness in all its dimensions, we will not be able to reconnect with nature and with other species, which share our ability to feel.

Embarking on our connection with the earth, we can reflect on the way in which physical places have determined our bodies: what memories do our hands contain, where have our feet walked, what smells, senses, and sounds connect us with specific places? There is a richness to sharing the wisdom that we have gathered thanks to the places in which we spent part of our lives, each one from their own singular experience. However, here we also encounter the experiences of violence inflicted upon the territories where we have lived, which is, at the same time, violence against our bodies. As the anthropologist Francisca Fernández writes:

> Women have mobilised to stop predation and dispossession, demanding and proposing alternatives to the current development model in order to eradicate, in turn, the violence against women associated with it (Segato, 2003a). In this way, the fight for territorial recovery is also the fight for the sovereignty of our bodies.[10]

Would it be possible in the liturgy to incorporate moments to reflect on how our body is feeling? Do we feel cold, heat, pain, anger, fatigue, tension, desire to move or be still, desire to sing and dance, or to be silent? Could we express our resonances with nature? Ecologist Joanna Macey suggests that we initiate our process of approaching the earth from an attitude of gratitude for what nature offers us every day, but also honouring our pain for its deterioration. She proposes creating moments or even places of mourning for the losses of species and ecosystems that we see, either around us or in the news.[11] Churches can host such moments and create such spaces. The pandemic is also a consequence of the imbalance of ecosystems: we can visualise our pain due to the losses caused by these and other diseases as an expression of the earth's pain in ourselves.

Finally, we can see the Biblical text itself as "body" or "earth", as was suggested in 1995 by Nancy Cardoso, who expressed the reflections of the First Latin American Encounter of Biblical Women:

> We see in history that the body has been the most important space for oppression and appropriation of women – as well as other dominated groups such as indigenous and blacks: rape, aggression, denial, abuse, manipulation, idealisation. For this very reason, the body cannot be left out of a reading that asks about gender relations. Life or death manifest through our bodies. Recovering concrete bodies is a fundamental part of affirming concrete and sensual life.[12]

In the text itself, the land is present, as are women, although there is no direct reference to them. We can analyse contexts and read between lines, to listen to the experience of the land and the bodies, visibly and invisibly present, about which the text narrates.

---

[10] Francisca Fernández Droguett, "Extractivismo y patriarcado: la defensa de los territorios como defensa de la soberanía de los cuerpos", in Soledad Rojas Bravo (ed), *Violencia estructural y feminismo: apuntes para una discusión* (Santiago de Chile: Red en contra de la Violencia contra las Mujeres, 2019): 35, [Available at: http://www.nomasviolenciacontramujeres.cl/wp-content/uploads/2019/09/Violencia-Estructural-y-Feminismo.pdf], [Last accessed: 10th May 2022].

[11] Joanna Macey and Christopher Johnstone, *Active Hope: How to Face the Mess We're in without Going Crazy.* (California: New World Library, 2012). E-book, Chapter 3 and 4.

[12] Nancy Cardoso Pereira, "Presentación. Pautas de una hermenéutica feminista de la liberación", *RIBLA* 25 (1997): 5-6, [Available at: https://www.centrobiblicoquito.org/images/ribla/25.pdf], [Last accessed: 10th May 2022].

Food is ubiquitous in Biblical texts. Bread and wine can be the starting point of a connection with agriculture. In Argentina, the commercialisation of transgenic products is being considered. "Transgenic wheat: for our daily bread?" Rosa Muñoz posed this question, referring to the Lord's Prayer.[13] In light of the climate crisis, it is urgent to ask ourselves: what do we eat in the community? Can we practice preparing foods from local agriculture, or can we become vegetarian? And who prepares the meals in our community? When we thus reflect on the Biblical texts by taking the earth and the bodies of the people as point of departure, integration with the public space will automatically emerge.

Towards an Integration of the Public Sphere

Integrating the public space in our actions as churches does not mean separating ourselves from our spiritual tasks. On the contrary, our spirituality can lead us to another form of involvement in the public space. "What is happening confronts us with the urgency of advancing in a courageous cultural revolution," says Pope Francis in the Encyclical *Laudato Si'*.[14] A cultural and spiritual perspective is much needed in the midst of political struggles, not with the intention to evangelise, but to humanise. Rather than impose our beliefs on others, a pastoral attitude of listening and support is required. We do not need to reinvent the wheel, but as churches we must be present.

Churches can be spaces where the dichotomy between the private and public space is overcome, since they both combine a small-scale personalised community, and are part of traditions present throughout the land, and linked internationally. This is an ideal situation for exercising influence on the climate crisis, since it provides a global view combined with articulation among specific territories. Through our traditions, we experience that we are one humanity and, through our local churches, we can realise our mission in contexts with concrete public challenges.

In what follows, I give some examples from my own experience of the integration of the public space that we have sought in Chile. The Ecumenical Coalition for the Care of Creation (CECC), a network that brings together 12 Christian communities, decided to focus on supporting territorial struggles. At the end of 2018, the network held an event to express solidarity with the organisation "Mujeres de Zonas de Sacrificio en Resistencia" (Women of Sacrifice Zones in Resistance). They travelled to Quintero-Puchuncaví where they formed a circle of silence – a form of protest inspired by active non-violent movements – on the beach opposite one of the country's most polluting thermoelectric plants.[15]

In 2019, motivated by the UN COP25 climate conference, which was to take place in Chile, communities of different religions and spiritualities formed the Interreligious and Spiritual Alliance for Climate (AIEC). The network acted in the public space to express a unified voice of concern and pressure towards the conference, while respecting the diversity of its members. The network formed an alliance with the Civil Society for Climate Action (SCAC) and held its celebrations in the same venue where the rest of civil society organised their discussions parallel to the conference.[16]

The AIEC continues its work and, as the network does not have an institutional or hierarchical structure, many women have taken leadership roles. The network tries to be participatory and works horizontally.

---

[13] Rosa Muñoz Lima, "Trigo transgénico: ¿para el pan nuestro de cada día?" *DW*, 14th April 2020, [Available at: https://www.dw.com/es/trigo-transg%C3%A9nico-argentino-para-el-pan-nuestro-de-cada-d%C3%ADa/a-55276310], [Last accessed: 10th May 2022].

[14] Francis. *Encyclical Letter: Laudato Si': On Care for Our Common Home* (Vatican City, June 2015): 114.

[15] See CECC, "Acción Ventanas" Youtube video, 5:21, 18th December 2018, [Available at: https://www.youtube.com/watch?v=AyIKzcgGR3Y&ab_channel=Coalici%C3%B3nEcum%C3%A9nicaporelCuidadodelaCreaci%C3%B3n], [Last accessed: 10th May 2022].

[16] For more information on the CECC, see Coalición Ecumécia por el Cuidado de la Creación, Facebook, https://www.facebook.com/ceccchile, and on the AIEC, see Alianza Interreligiosa y Espiritual por el Clima, Facebook, https://www.facebook.com/AIECChile.

Thus, ecology expresses itself first in the recognition of the biodiversity among us. The political dimension can be found in the ability to visualise a different world, based on the recognition of the dignity of each one of us and the intrinsic value of the living world of which we are part.

Towards the Integration of Everyday Life in Spirituality

Feminist theology has emphasised the need to reintegrate everyday life as an essential aspect in theological thought. As we have already pointed out, daily life is very present in communities of faith, but it is not normally seen as a source of spirituality. The Judeo-Christian tradition tends to see history as a linear path of progress, and in this path the "cyclical" pattern, strongly present in nature, as well as in our daily routines, has been separated from the transcendent, and has even been labelled as "pagan".

Many daily livelihood practices are the responsibility of women and are generally not viewed as spiritual. However, this is not the case everywhere. In monastic traditions, both in Christianity and in other traditions, cleaning tasks, preparing food, and washing clothes are practiced as moments of meditation and exercises in mindfulness. In these communities, such apparently mundane chores comprise special moments that are carried out by men and women alike. Everyday life and care can be part of a community's spirituality, as elements in the search for a caring culture, beyond traditional gender roles.

In the integration of everyday life, the community learns to listen to what we really need to live. Less projected in the future and the destiny of our soul, we can pay attention to the body and soul integrated in the here and now and learn from the limits that are present in us. Unlimited consumption is an illusion that is assumed by idealisation. Appreciating more what it means to assure our daily bread, create order out of chaos, and care for the healing of our bodies, we can practice sobriety, the simple life in which many women have been an example. It is those women, especially older women, who know how to repair clothes, reuse things, revive plants.

What is at stake in this valorisation of the everyday life in spirituality is nothing less than the search for a new form of economy, the economy of care. We have to prevent this economy from becoming the exclusive task of women. Women are not "naturally more wired" for these tasks, but they have been mostly in charge of those tasks, and therefore their experience can teach us the way forward. In Chile, I think of the embroiderers of resistance patchwork tapestries, the women who organise the soup kitchens, the women who take their children to the protests, those who work in the community vegetable gardens, those who take care of the sick in shelters, those who fight for the water, the earth and the air. In the churches, these women can teach us all how to overcome the dualisms that separate us from nature.

Conclusion

An ecological and feminist theology seeks a reality in harmony with nature and with equality between men and women. It is a quest that arises from the conviction that the two are intrinsically linked. Achieving this cultural and spiritual shift implies valuing reality differently, also in our churches. Integrating nature and land, our bodies, the public space, and everyday life as a place of spirituality are all steps that can ground theology and save it from essentialisms and idealisms. In the end, regarding reality in a new way, and valuing the intrinsic dignity of nature and women means returning to who we really are: people of the earth.

Suggestions for Further Reading

Andel, Arianne van. *Teología en Movimiento. Ensayos eco-teológicos y feministas para tiempos de cambio*. Miami: JUANUNO1 Ediciones, 2021.

Aquino, María Pilar and Elsa Tamez. *Teología feminista latinoamericana*. Quito: Ediciones Abya-Yala, 1998.

Cardoso Pereira, Nancy. "Presentación. Pautas de una hermenéutica feminista de la liberación". *RIBLA* 25 (1997): 5-6, [Available at: https://www.centrobiblicoquito.org/images/ribla/25.pdf], [Last accessed: 10th May 2022].

Colectivo de coordinación de acciones socio ambientales and Colectivo CASA. *Despojo de agua por Minería y el impacto en Las mujeres. Diagnóstico del despojo de fuentes de agua por minería estatal y transnacional*. Junin: Casa Colectivo, 2018. [Available at: https://colectivocasa.org.bo/wp-content/uploads/2020/09/despojo-agua-por-mineria-impacto-en-las-mujeres.pdf], [Last accessed: 10th May 2022].

Costa Cordella, Ezio. *Por una Constitución Ecológica. Replanteando la relación entre sociedad y naturaleza*. Santiago de Chile: Catalonia, 2021.

Coordinadora Feminista SCAC. *Reflexiones sobre Feminismo y Ecología (en cuarentena)*. Santiago: Ediciones Böll, 2021.

Droguett, Francisca Fernández. "Extractivismo y patriarcado: la defensa de los territorios como defensa de la soberanía de los cuerpos", in Soledad Rojas Bravo, Ed. *Violencia estructural y feminismo: apuntes para una discusión.* Santiago de Chile: Red en contra de la Violencia contra las Mujeres, 2019: 29-38. [Available at: http://www.nomasviolenciacontramujeres.cl/wp-content/uploads/2019/09/Violencia-Estructural-y-Feminismo.pdf], [Last accessed: 10th May 2022].

Francis. *Encyclical Letter Laudato Si': On Care for Our Common Home.* Vatican City: Vatican Press, June 2015.

Macey, Joanna and Christopher Johnstone. *Active Hope. How to Face the Mess We're in Without Going Crazy*. San Franscisco, CA: New World Library, 2012. E-book.

Muñoz Lima, Rosa. "Trigo transgénico: ¿para el pan nuestro de cada día?". *DW*, 14th April 2020. [Available at: https://www.dw.com/es/trigo-transg%C3%A9nico-argentino-para-el-pan-nuestro-de-cada-d%C3%ADa/a-55276310], [Last accessed: 10th May 2022].

Puleo, Alicia H. *Claves Ecofeministas. Para rebeldes que aman a la Tierra y a los animales*. Madrid: Plaza y Valdés Editores, 2019.

Sacks, Jonathan. *The Dignity of Difference. How to Avoid the Clash of Civilizations*. New York: Continuum, 2002.

57. New Scientific Paradigms, Biocolonisation and Latin American Ecospirituality

Juan Carlos Valverde Campos[1]

Introduction

It is difficult to understand and it is even painful to have to admit that, despite being in the preludes of the sixth mass extinction,[2] economic interests continue to prevail over the urgent need to change course in order to save the planet and, with it, life itself in its rich diversity.

No longer can any discipline feel excluded, nor can religions and spiritualities. The latter play a fundamental role in this context and must provide renewed energies that allow the human being to make the leap towards new, simpler lifestyles, in harmony with all members of the life system and less dependent on the transfer of goods, many of them unnecessary.

An imperative ecology of attentiveness must be put in place. The neoliberal economic system has won every corner of the planet and ruthlessly spreads its tentacles, numbing conscience and critical thinking through a fierce publicity barrage that imposes consumption as a necessity. This system generates unconscious human beings, dormant, without their own thought; there are really only few who have been and are capable of escaping from this lethal dynamic that is corroding us from within. The ecology of attentiveness proposes a "struggle against apparatuses of attentional enslavement," in order to obtain free human beings, capable of deciding for themselves.[3]

The economic system that we have created has realised that, at this point in time, all discourses must be impregnated with ecology. It has now been colonised by the financial elites that rule the world, making us believe that their proposals are also and above all "green", proposing a sustainable or tenable development. The human being that these elites desire is the same and nature continues to be a reservoir for the *homo consumericus*.[4] But that is not all; sadly, church structures have also been taken over by the spirit of capitalism. Its administrative and pastoral structures maintain and sustain excessive consumption and its theological bases respond to a hierarchical order marked by an excessive anthropocentrism, if not by an execrable androcentrism. In close relationship with classical science that proposes a stable universe, based on laws to be discovered, religions propose a world created by a clockmaker god who put it in motion and then retired to his celestial chambers. This god has characteristics similar to those of the human being that he created: namely, almighty, omniscient, and increasingly removed from the world.

The challenges seem obvious; the task is arduous. It involves launching the boat into deep waters, leaving dry land and daring to rethink everything that has been established as the foundation of religions.

---

[1] Juan Carlos Valverde Campos (juancavalcam@hotmail.com; juan.valverde.campos@una.cr) is a member Professor of the Ecumenical School of Religious Sciences of the National University of Costa Rica. He obtained a Bachelor of Theology and a Master of Biblical Theology from the Catholic Institute of Paris and a doctorate in Philosophy of Religion from the University of Strasbourg, France.

[2] See Michel Magny, *Aux racines de l'anthropocène. Une crise écologique reflet d'une crise de l'homme* (Lormont: Le Bord de l'Eau, 2019): 150.

[3] Yves Citton, *The Ecology of Attention,* trans. Barnaby Norman (Cambridge: Polity Press, 2017): 179.

[4] Neologism to describe consumerist people introduced by Gad Saad in *The Evolutionary Bases of Consumption* (Oxfordshire: Routledge, 2007) and by Gilles Lipovetsky in *Le bonheur paradoxal. Essai sur la société d'hyperconsommation* (Paris: Gallimard, 2006).

Old and New Scientific Paradigms

The science that we know, cite and defend was born in a precise time and place. Jacques Monod (1910-1976) presents the new science in biblical terms: "The ancient covenant is in pieces; man knows at last that he is alone in the universe's unfeeling immensity, out of which he emerged only by chance."[5] The ancient covenant seems to have come to an end to give way to a new covenant without mysteries, without gods, without souls. The new great prophet – Newton – has supplanted the previous one – Moses – as affirm Prigogine and Stengers.[6] Modern science, with its retinue of clergymen, breaks the dialogue with "nature" and places itself outside of it, as an attentive, objective and indifferent spectator, seeking to identify the laws that govern it. Modern science was constituted against the nonhuman world, denying its complexity and its becoming, in the name of an eternal, fixed, stable and knowable world, which must be dominated and from which all its riches must be extracted. There is no longer a community or temple in which to appease fears; the search now takes place in fortresses or laboratories, lofty and sacred sanctuaries of the new humanity. The prevailing rationality has eliminated all mysteries and has discarded the Mystery.

The prevailing scientific paradigm is a "*revealed* science, definitive," say Prigogine and Stengers.[7] A mystery is gradually revealed to the *man* of science, whose task is to decipher, little by little, the stable operation of this amazing machine called the universe. "Classical science always postulates the monotonous stupidity of the world it interrogates," these authors sustain.[8] It draws a cold, dead world, starved for originality, without a soul; and it describes its servants as self-sufficient, rational, indifferent, lonely beings and, above all, precise observers of a dynamics previously set in motion. Classical science assigns scientific knowledge the task of "dissipating the apparent complexity of phenomena, in order to reveal the simple order that they obey," says Edgar Morin.[9]

However, a new model or paradigm makes its way, little by little, in the tangle of confusing proposals that prevail today. This model is committed to complex thinking, to another "new science,"[10] which conceives reality as a network of relationships and not as closed entities independent of each other. If the classical paradigm orders, pursues disorder and reduces reality to laws; the new paradigm sees in agitation, chance, chaos, contradiction, interdependence, uncertainty, complexity and solidarity, the authentic forms of organisation of the universe.

In this new vision of things, human beings are completely immersed in the world that they investigate. There are connections, and not laws, that produce unexpected new worlds. The universe is not a machine, it is a living organism in constant evolution and expansion, capable of self-regulation.[11] The new paradigms of science conceive the Earth and all it contains as living beings integrated into great biological processes. Nature is returned to its rightful place in life's adventure and human beings return home.

---

[5] Jacques Monod, *Chance and Necessity,* trans. Austryn Wainhouse (New York: Vintage Books, Random House, 1972): 180.

[6] Ilya Prigogine and Isabelle Stengers, *Order out of Chaos: Man's New Dialogue with Nature,* trans. Alvin Toffler (New York: Bantom Books, 1984): 76.

[7] Prigogine and Stengers, *La nouvelle alliance. Métamorphose de la science* (Paris: Gallimard, 1979): 129. [TN: the author translates directly from the original French. The English edition changes the phrasing, so the quotation here is also translated into English directly from the original French. The emphasis is original.]

[8] Prigogine and Stengers, *La nouvelle alliance*, 92-93. [TN: Again, the author translated from the original French. The English edition, Prigogine and Stengers, *Order out of Chaos,* changes the phrasing. The translation shown here is directly from the French.]

[9] Edgar Morin, *Introducción al pensamiento complejo* (Barcelona: Gedisa, 2001): 21.

[10] "Scienza nuova," says Morin. See Morin, *Introducción al pensamiento complejo*, 71.

[11] James Lovelock, *La terre est un être vivant. L'hypothèse Gaïa* (Paris: Flammarion, 1993): 31-32.

On "Traditional" Theologies

Boaventura de Sousa Santos defines classical or traditional theologies as "non-hegemonic forms of globalisation put at the service of a vaster and, yes, hegemonic, globalisation: the globalisation of neoliberal capitalism, colonialism and patriarchy."[12] Traditional theologies, willingly or unwillingly, have put themselves at the service of neoliberal societies, paying homage to their hegemonic principles and values. Theological discipline, and with it also religions, has succumbed to the eloquent discourse of modern science, thus transforming its founding bases.

This traditional science loves a static, fixed, mechanical universe, without any possibility of creativity. It believes in a human being external to the observing world, an exalted, omniscient and all-powerful human being, identical to the one proposed by Christian theology and religions. In 1967, Lynn White Jr published in Science magazine an article – an inescapable reference – on Christian anthropocentrism: "Christianity is the most anthropocentric religion the world has known."[13] Anthropocentrism took root thanks to a particular vision of itself founded on a conception of God. The human being (not so other creatures!) was created in the image and likeness of God. Being *imago Dei* has led to the construction of a singular, bombastic, extraordinary *imago hominis*, which also grants authorisation to do whatever *he* wants.[14]

The old paradigm has limited Christian spirituality to the relationship between human beings and God: the cosmos has not been an essential part of it. The Christianity that has reached the Latin American continent and that still prevails in our days, has conveyed a spirituality that despises materiality – therefore, the cosmos itself – and insists on an extra-temporal and personal encounter with God.[15]

Overcoming these fragmentations and dualisms is, without a doubt, a challenge that must be taken up with courage by theologies and religions in Latin America.

New Theologies and Biocolonisation

In the process of the colonisation and evangelisation of the Latin American continent, many voices were silenced to impose a new social and religious order. With the sword of the colonisers also came the cross of classical or traditional theology. The sad celebration of 500 years of evangelisation of what they used to call the New World became the perfect occasion to awaken thousands of voices that have multiplied and wish to rebuild our society, saving the still smouldering remains of civilisations, thoughts and millennial theologies, valid and valuable worlds.

Time has passed. Meanwhile, women, indigenous peoples, Afro-descendants, immigrants, all those people who feel excluded, both from neoliberal capitalist society and from churches, Christian or not, raise their voices asking to be heard. Not only do they bravely criticise the ancient sclerotic schemes transmitted by the governments of the day and the hierarchies of the churches, they also propose new paths. Thus, for example, feminists observe that to Western Christianity was revealed a male god with well-defined attributes and qualities: almighty, omniscient, and transcendent. The Brazilian theologian, Ivone Gebara, recognises the triune God, one and multiple, in the very organisation of the life of the universe, in the movement of continuous creation. This is the Triune God who is also present in the diversity of peoples and cultures, in the "plurality that constitutes us as a human group" and also in the individual personal reality.[16]

---

[12] Boaventura de Sousa Santos, *Si Dios fuese un activista de los derechos humanos* (Madrid: Trotta, 2014): 42.

[13] Lynn White, Jr, "Les racines historiques de notre crise écologique", in Dominique Bourg and Philippe Roch (eds), *Crise écologique, crise des valeurs? Défis pour l'anthropologie et la spiritualité* (Geneva: Labor et Fides, 2010): 19.

[14] Douglas John Hall, *Etre image de Dieu* (Paris: Cerf, 1998).

[15] Louis Bouyer, *Histoire de la spiritualité chrétienne*, 4 vols. (Paris: Cerf, 2011).

[16] Ivone Gebara, "La Trinidad vista desde una perspectiva ecofeminista", in Rosemary Radford Ruether (ed), *Mujeres sanando la tierra. Ecología, feminismo y religión según mujeres del Tercer Mundo* (Santiago: Sello Azul, 1999): 36.

The First Nations have become the faithful witnesses of despised traditions that thought of the world as a home of which we are all members in equal parts and that must be respected in order to live in harmony. We recall the wise words of Chief Seattle:

> Every part of this earth is sacred to my people. Every shining pine needle, every sandy shore, every mist in the dark woods, every clearing and humming insect is holy in the memory and experience of my people. The sap which courses through the trees carries the memories of the red man. [...] We are part of the earth and it is part of us. The perfumed flowers are our sisters; the deer, the horse, the great eagle, these are our brothers. The rocky crests, the juices in the meadows, the body heat of the pony,.and man – all belong to the same family.[17]

The new paradigm that is emerging requires a complete review of our Latin American reality. In this context, the critique of Eurocentric expressions is fundamental. These become, with the passage of time, a new form of coloniality. European knowledge has been considered superior and worthy of credibility, unlike that which is produced in Latin America. For this reason, it is important for a critical theory to begin to be elaborated, with the Latin American reason and heart, of ecotheology and ecospirituality that takes into account the remaining fragments of the colonising genocide.

To refer to the permanent interference of colonial powers in ecological discourses, Juan Camilo Cajigas-Rotundo proposes the term biocoloniality.[18] Indeed, capitalism has incorporated the concern for the environment into its approaches, in order to preserve power. Biocolonisation manifests itself in the weakening and neutralisation of significant international agreements based on the influence of corporate elites and dominant transnational companies over national states and multilateral organisations, as in the case of the UN Convention on Biological Diversity. Or in its plain and simple instrumentalisation, as occurs with Intellectual Property Rights established by the WTO. Patents have also become the great business of the century; the new owners of life have begun a new process of colonisation as cruel, inhuman and heartless as the previous ones.

This same biocoloniality of power manifests itself in many ways in the field of theology and spirituality.[19] The imposing, exclusivist, misogynistic and universalist discourses of the ecclesiastical hierarchies that ignore or do not want to recognise the theological and spiritual pluriverse are an indisputable mode of colonisation. Gebara understands politics as a way to organise life and to dominate and control people's existence. Thus understood, politics "are strongly present in the theologies that are assumed by Christian churches";[20] for this reason, the "dreaming of changing theology and rebuilding a plural Church seems audacious, but it is a political act of justice, fundamental in the process of establishing more egalitarian human relations."[21] The hegemonic discourses thus become creators of subjectivity and places where the biocoloniality of power operates through the colonisation of the imaginary. The ecotheological reflections of many churches are subject to the ecclesiastical "androcracy" that has caused

---

[17] Chief Seattle, "Letter from Chief Seattle to President Pierce [1885]", [Available at: https://www.pick-upau.org.br/site_english/world/indian_charter/indian_charter.pdf], [Last accessed: 10th May 2022]. We are aware of the historicity questions associated with this letter. For our purposes, its content is important.

[18] Juan Camilo Cajigas-Rotundo, "La biocolonialidad del poder. Amazonia, biodiversidad y ecocapitalismo", in Santiago Castro-Gómez y Ramón Grosfoguel (eds), *El giro decolonial. Reflexiones para una diversidad epistémica más allá del capitalismo global* (Bogota: Siglo del Hombre Editores; Universidad Central, Instituto de Estudios Sociales Contemporáneos; Pontificia Universidad Javeriana, Instituto Pensar, 2007): 169-194.

[19] Nicolás Panotto offers a very complete and interesting synthesis of the progressive transformations of theology in the light of postcolonial studies; see Nicolás Panotto, "Descolonizar lo divino. Aportes para una teología poscolonial del campo religioso latinoamericano", in Laura Catelli and María Elena Lucero (eds), *Materiales (pos)coloniales y de la (de)colonialidad latinoamericana* (Rosario: UNR Editora. Editorial de la Universidad Nacional de Rosario, 2014): 143-55.

[20] Ivone Gebara, *Condimentos feministas a la teología* (La Habana: Caminos; Montevideo: Doble clic, 2019): 70.

[21] Gebara, *Condimentos feministas a la teología,* 70.

and continues to cause so much damage to life on the planet. The church hierarchy continues to colonise female bodies, as a metaphor for conquering the planet. With finesse, Gebara points the way: "Replacing the God of the 'big eye;, controller of our bodies, for a gaze of mercy towards one another, for education in the richness of diversity, for shared social and political responsibility, is the great challenge that still needs to be accepted by the Christian churches."[22]

The biocoloniality of power is ratified in the treaties signed between the churches and the states, wanting to perpetuate, in this way, an imaginary and a patriarchal and top-down status that subjects some to others.[23] Latin American theology and spirituality must courageously renounce and censor the discourses and treaties signed between powerful hierarchies that establish biocoloniality and prevent the continent from assuming its own spiritual identity.

Theology and religions have walked hand-in-hand with classical science, we have already noticed this. The time has come that, just as a part of the scientific community has felt the call to retrace the paths of the old paradigm, and has done so despite the consequences that this represented, so also it must happen within theology and religion, very much in spite of the certain consequences which will necessarily be incurred.

In the new paradigm, God is an indescribable Mystery from which emanates an Energy that flows in everything that exists. It is in everything, but it is not exhausted in the parts. With the death or disappearance of beings, the energy that runs in them returns to the cosmos, to integrate the total Energy.

In the new paradigm, "nature" ceases to be the scenario in which the salvation of the human being is played out. Matter is good in all its extremes, there is no original sin but an "original grace" that is life itself,[24] with its unpredictable results, uncertainties, risks and dangers. This life is not an illusion nor is it a function of another, eternal and perfect. The world is not a peripheral thing, it is mother and womb in constant expansion and evolution.

The new cosmological, and therefore also theological, paradigm requires a different vision of the human being, a member like all the others of nature: neither superior nor alien to the world, simply different.

Conclusions for a Latin American Ecospirituality

To achieve better living conditions for everyone requires an inevitable change in our ways of being and especially of being in the world. We propose a spirituality that recovers the soul, lost, abandoned and neglected by academic discourses and religious practices.

Recovering animism does not mean seeing gods everywhere; it means being able to perceive the Life that is present in that which surrounds us. Recovering animism means recognising the importance of territory, of the land that shelters us and in which we sink our roots. It implies simplicity,[25] harmony, order, respect, meaning and primacy of community.[26]

---

[22] Gebara, *Condimentos feministas a la teología,* 54-55.

[23] These treaties can be implicit or explicit. Many churches, Roman Catholic or not, have interest-based agreements with local governments. For example, Brazil signed a concordat with the Vatican; the Political Constitution of Costa Rica is openly Catholic; France, despite being a secular state, offers scholarships to study theology (in one of its regions – the Grand Est – there is the possibility of teaching religion in schools and colleges if students and families so wish); etc.

[24] José María Vigil, "Desafíos de la ecología a las religiones", *Franciscanum* 154 (2010): 214.

[25] We defend the urgency of adopting a voluntary simplicity; see, amongst others, Serge Latouche, *Vers une société d'abondance frugale* (Paris: Mille-et-une-nuits, 2011); Paul Ariès, *La simplicité volontaire contre le mythe de l'abondance* (Paris: La Découverte, 2011); Serge Mongeau, *La simplicité volontaire, plus que jamais...* (Montréal: Ecosociété, 1998).

[26] In the sense of the "earth ethic" of Aldo Leopold. See Aldo Leopold, *Almanach d'un comté des sables* (Paris: Flammarion, 2000): 255-84.

Animist spirituality believes in *creatio continua*, against the fixity of some religious, philosophical and scientific tendencies. It rejects a creation theology in which the Creator made all things, set them in motion, and then withdrew to his heavenly abode. It rejects the idea of an immutable, almighty, omniscient, and eternal Creator with human form, features, and capabilities.[27] It also disapproves of the theological notion of eternal natural laws that mechanistic science reinforces. The natural world is indeterminate, spontaneous, and creative.

For most of the European spiritual theologies, spirituality is forged in the depths of the individual, ignoring the territories. Latin Americans have had and have to fight for the territories because they have been plundered, the place where they live and everything it contains has been usurped. Our ancestors had to give up their territories by submitting to the cross and the sword. Visible and invisible beings inhabited them, constitutive relationships were established in them that fed and traversed everyday life. The territory does not belong to anyone, it is the common space where life multiplies. Therefore, there is no spirituality without territory and the spirituality of a Latin American person cannot ignore pain, suffering, and poverty. The lack of resources to have a minimally dignified life will radically mark the search for transcendence, the meaning of life, the way to hope, and to understand salvation.

A new history of spirituality must be written and thought from the emerging worlds, from the territories that have been and continue to be violated, disrespected and reduced to objects of exploration and exploitation. Spirituality cannot and should not be built or thought by forgetting the territory where it is located.

Suggestions for Further Reading

Accossatto, Romina. "Colonialismo interno y memoria colectiva. Aportes de Silvia Rivera Cusicanqui al estudio de los movimientos sociales y las identificaciones políticas". *Economía y sociedad* (2017): 167-181.

Boff, Leonardo. *Ecología: Grito de la tierra, grito de los pobres*. Madrid: Trotta, 2011.

Bourg, Dominique. *Une nouvelle terre.* Paris: Desclée de Brouwer, 2018.

Camus, Albert. *L'homme révolté.* Paris: Gallimard, 1965.

Capra, Fritjof. *La trama de la vida. Una nueva perspectiva de los sistemas vivos*. Barcelona: Anagrama, 2002.

Castro, Augusto. *El desafío de pensar diferente. Pensamiento, sociedad y naturaleza.* Buenos Aires: CLACSO, 2018.

Cornejo-Alvarez, Alfonso. *Complejidad y caos. Guía para la administración del siglo XXI*. Mexico: Ediciones Castillo, 1997.

Egger, Michel Maxime. *La Terre comme soi-même. Repères pour écospiritualité.* Geneva: Labor et Fides, 2012.

Escobar, Arturo. *Sentir-penser avec la terre. L'écologie au-delà de l'Occident.* Paris: Seuil, 2018.

Gebara, Ivone. *Intuiciones ecofeministas. Ensayo para repensar el conocimiento y la religión*. Madrid: Trotta, 2000.

Murad, Alfonso Tadeu and Germán Roberto Mahecha Clavijo, Eds. *Ecoteología. Un mosaico*. Bogota: San Pablo, 2016.

Ness, Arnæ. *Ecologie, communauté et style de vie*. Bellevaux: Editions Dehors, 2013.

Panikkar, Raimon. *La intuición cosmoteándrica. Las tres dimensiones de la realidad.* Madrid: Trotta, 1999.

Sheldrake, Rupert. *Una nueva ciencia de la vida. La hipótesis de la causación formativa.* Barcelona: Kairós, 2011.

[27] Raimon Panikkar rejected the idea of Creator as a kind of ontological degradation. More details in Raimon Panikkar, *La puerta estrecha del conocimiento* (Barcelona: Herder, 2009): 117 and following pages.

——. *L'âme de la nature.* Paris: Albin Michel, 2001.
Sousa Santos, Boaventura de and María Paula Meneses, Eds. *Epistemologías del Sur (Perspectivas).* Madrid: Ediciones Akal, 2014.

58. Towards an Ecotheology Incarnated in a Political Ecodiakonia

Jorge Weishein[1]

> Diakonia is a proposal that is contrary to the spiritualisation of people's needs, contrary to welfare that creates dependency and maintains the status quo; contrary to the individualisation of problems and solutions, to the institutionalisation or delegation of compassion to specialists outside of community life.[2]

What Are We Talking about When We Talk about Diakonia in Latin America?

The Enlightenment, extolling reason as an instrument for the construction of knowledge, and the constitution of the person as a subject based on knowledge, broke with the integral paradigm of medieval training (organised on the basis of the "*quadrivium*" represented by the schools of Arts, Medicine, Law and Theology).[3] Starting in the nineteenth century, the enlightenment paradigm began to be organised according to a binary model, made up of the sciences and humanities: "the former, dedicated to empirical research and hypothesis testing; the second, in charge of hermeneutical understanding."[4]

This paradigm of knowledge has assimilated into the theology and ecclesiology of the Christian church in modern history, accompanying its reflection and its practices. In this sense, "due to the denial of the churches or the impossibility of integrating the practical approaches to diakonia that arose mainly from Pietism, circles and societies were formed that were dedicated to charitable and missionary work. Diakonia found its place outside of institutional churches."[5]

While during the 19th and 20th centuries theology was characterised by a strongly phenomenological, rationalist and orthodox stamp, diakonia – because of its articulation with the grass-roots and its practical expression – was driven by a piety of feelings, influenced by experiences of the faith in absolute solidarity with others, mostly outside the institutions of the churches. This diakonic experience is a revealing spiritual event as a manifestation of Christ present in the need of another. Introduced largely by Pietism, such an event will organise the understanding of Protestant Christian diakonia until the post-war period of the 20th century in the West.[6]

The case of the Protestant churches of the Lutheran tradition (or Lutheran-Reformed) in the southern cone of Latin America is no exception.[7] A series of theological efforts within its ranks have attempted to rethink diaconic praxis based on the theology of the cross and certain elements of the pietistic tradition.

---

[1] Jorge Weishein (jorge.weishein@horadeobrar.org.ar) is a theologian and social worker, a pastor of the Evangelical Church of the River Plate, a member of the co-ordination team of the Pastoral for the Promotion of Creation Care (PPCC) and of the team of the Protestant Foundation of Diakonia *Hora de Obrar*.

[2] Rodolfo Gaede Neto, *A diaconia de Jesus: Contribuição para a fundamentação teológica da diaconia na América Latina* (São Leopoldo: Sinodal; São Paulo: CEBI e Paulus, 2001): 186.

[3] Hilde De Ridder-Symoens (ed), *Historia de la Universidad en Europa. Volumen I: Las Universidades en la Edad Media* (Bilbao: Servicio Editorial de la Universidad del País Vasco, 1994). For a brief review of the work in Spanish, see Maria Dolors Baena Tostado's review. [Available at: http://www.ub.edu/geocrit/b3w-135.htm], [Last accessed: 11th May 2022].

[4] Pedro Giordano, *Sistema-mundo moderno: emergencia, funcionamiento normal y decadencia. X Jornadas de Sociología. Facultad de Ciencias Sociales, Universidad de Buenos Aires* (Buenos Aires: UBA, 2013).

[5] Ekkehard Heise, "Diaconia e espiritualidade", *Estudos Teológicos* 39(3) (1999): 232.

[6] Ekkehard Heise, "Diaconia e espiritualidade…", 233.

[7] Sonia Skupch, "¿Una teóloga en el Siglo XVII?" in Sonia Skupch and David Cela Heffel (eds), *Reflexiones y recursos para conmemorar los 500 años del movimiento de la Reforma* (Buenos Aires: Comunión de Iglesias de la Reforma, s.f.): 111-118.

Luther, following the experience of Moses, understands that God's revelation is indirect, God can only be seen from behind, although God hears and sees the suffering of God's people (Ex. 3:7). It is only possible to recognise God "through suffering and the cross", and it is there that he can be found in the suffering and the cross of Christ, but also in the suffering and the cross of those who follow him, both of which go hand in hand. In this way, Christ reveals reality through the cross and, in that reality, he reveals God in all that lays bare the hidden face of the glory of the world.

> The cross of Christ is not just any cross; it is the cross of God in this world. At this crossroad it becomes clear how things intervene between God and the world. Therefore, every relationship with God must take into account the reality revealed by the cross of Christ. Only those who are situated in suffering and the cross can recognise God. God wants to be understood in *visibilia*, which according to Luther includes "humanity", "impotence" and "madness". God recognises God's self in concealment, "in the humility and shame of the cross" (WA 1,362,12s). In the crucified Christ, God is manifested in concealment. "We live in the concealment of Christ [sic] [God], that is, in the naked trust of his mercy." (WA 1,357,3ss).[8]

The theology of the cross directs the gaze of diakonia towards humanity, impotence and madness where God is revealed. This diakonia generates uncertainty among those who are attached to a secure life, and confronts all their values: "Because the gospel destroys that which is, it causes the powerful to fall, wisdom is brought down and they are turned into nothing, impotence, madness, because the gospel teaches humility from the cross (WA 1,617, 7)."

This theology of the cross is subsumed in the conception of institutional and communitarian diakonia of the Protestant churches of the region from the theological elaboration of their commitment to social justice. However, diakonia never finished establishing itself as a theological discipline in their theological schools, nor did it succeed in establishing itself as an established ministry in these Protestant churches. Therefore, this theological tradition is integrated into the history of the church in Latin America with permanent difficulties of articulation between theology and ecclesiology, on the one hand, and in the midst of the profound post-war social transformations and the incarnation in the popular field of liberation theology, on the other.

In summary, we can affirm that what Lutheran theology understands by service in the name of Jesus performed by the justified sinner is defined by liberation theology as the practice of committed faith.[9] In this sense, the understanding that diakonia integrates the commitment of faith with the militancy for social justice within the framework of international treaties in general, and of human rights in particular, is widely used in our churches.

The struggles for gender equality and the protection of the environment have recently introduced commitment and advocacy for gender justice and environmental justice in the diakonia of the churches. Such struggles question the current development of the world-system from a historical-critical perspective and put in tension the theology and ecclesiology of the churches in the region.

Environmental Diakonia: In What Context?

In the field of knowledge, a whole series of transformations are recognised that generate the conditions for these changes to crystallise in different ongoing processes and institutions.

Olivier Mongin maintains that humanity had the first globalisation in the 15th to 17th centuries during the Middle Ages, at the beginning of the Renaissance, arising from the great discoveries and the formation of a network of cities, connected through maritime trade. The second globalisation took place in modernity

---

[8] Martin N. Dreher, "Redescubriendo la teología de la cruz de Martín Lutero en el contexto de la teología de la liberación", *Revista Espiga* 16(33) (2017): 68.
[9] Martin N. Dreher, "Redescubriendo…," 70.

during the 18th-20th centuries with the Industrial Revolution, as a result of the technological advances promoted by the different industrial policies of the states and nations in the West and the East. This author places the third globalisation at the end of the twentieth century and the beginning of the twenty-first, based on the digital technological revolution and the fusion of regional economies in a single global economic regime.[10] In this period, from the dismantling of Eastern Europe, the neoliberal capitalist regime was consolidated, which tends to reduce states and reconfigure public policies in the service of free market competition based on new production patterns. This impacts the entire production chain by making the process and the labour market more flexible, as well as products and consumption patterns.

> This process, driven by microelectronic-based technology, computer science and robotics, requires new forms of structuring financial services and commercial innovations, a fact that has been generating and deepening an enormous inequality of development between regions, sectors, *et cetera*, in addition to substantively modifying the notions of space and time.[11]

In this framework, the chains of companies gathered in world holding companies are expanding, controlling multilateral financial organisations and states, defining public policies and seriously putting at risk with their extractivist and deregulated exploitation model both the living conditions of the population and survival itself. The adjustments in public finances and the flexibilisation of labour rights led to structural poverty and job insecurity for the vast majority of the population. All of this is justified in a discourse focused on efficient production, which should – supposedly – promote the quality of work and the quality of life.

Currently, there is talk of a fourth revolution underway, which is transforming life in the world: biotechnology. The overexploitation of natural resources and its impact on access to and control of these production inputs has led to this new world revolution. Biotechnology is the engine of development for the new modality of sustainable economic production.

> The accelerated progress of biotechnology is driving the bioeconomy, a recent label for an old concept: economic activity that develops products and services, using primarily renewable biological resources, efficiently and sustainably. It is closely linked to the concepts of green economy and circular economy, and implies that we must be able to live within the limits of what the planet can provide, and preserve it for future generations.[12]

However, these revolutions reach different regions of the globe at different times and under dissimilar conditions, with a varied impact on diverse countries. The last century of the industrial age was accompanied by a series of serious global crises. There is consensus that, in this period, the capitalist system generated three great global crises that transform reality and the global worldview, with its distinctive complexities and regional expressions. This idea had its origin in the conceptual matrix of international political economy, and was registered as a global and systemic crisis that affected all orders of life, making it unsustainable.

> Unlike the stock market crisis of 1929, the energy crisis produced by the black gold embargo made by the Organization of Petroleum Exporting Countries in 1973-1974, or the repeated crises due to excessive external

[10] Olivier Mongin, *La condición urbana: La ciudad a la hora de la mundialización* (Buenos Aires: Paidós, 2006): 174-176.
[11] Marilda Iamamoto, *El servicio social en la contemporaneidad: Trabajo y formación profesional* (San Pablo: Editora Cortez, 2003): 45s.
[12] Rafael Anta, "Biotecnología: ¿llegamos a tiempo a esta revolución?" *Banco Interamericano de Desarrollo,* 10th March 2020, [Available at: https://blogs.iadb.org/innovacion/es/biotecnologia-bioeconomia-desarrollo-america-latina/], [Last accessed: 11th May 2022].

indebtedness in the 1980s, later interpretive proposals arose from the 2007 financial crisis in the United States around a "triple crisis": financial, energetic, and environmental.[13]

In these last few decades, in Latin America, two collective reorganisations of knowledge and resources in this context of crisis have acquired great relevance: ecofeminism and the ecotheology of liberation. Ecofeminism, articulated above all from the central countries, in dialogue with Latin American feminist movements, questions the asymmetries of power between men and women and also raises a fundamental epistemological change, putting tension on the paradigm of hegemonic knowledge: "Ecofeminism is about connectedness and wholeness of theory and practice. It asserts the special strength and integrity of every living thing."[14]

For his part, from the ecotheology of liberation, the Catholic theologian Leonardo Boff, in the 80s and 90s, proposes a holistic approach in his problematisation of the social injustice in which the poor people of Latin America live, with a whole series of articles and books in which he integrates sociological and historical reading with an environmental and systemic perspective.[15] This new epistemological approach in liberation theology is multidimensional and intersectional, integrating different disciplines with the complexity of reality, orienting its analysis and proposals towards the collective creation of a paradigm of care.

> A subsistence perspective necessarily requires a multidimensional or synergistic approach to solving problems. It is based on the recognition that the diverse systems of domination are interconnected and that problems cannot be solved in isolation or with a mere technological fix. In this way, social problems (patriarchal relations, inequality, alienation, poverty) must be solved together with ecological problems. This interconnectedness of all life forms on earth, of problems and solutions, is one of the most important revelations of ecofeminism.[16]

In this dialogue, the so-called "communitarian feminism" is configured with strong articulation with indigenous traditions and original spiritualities of Latin America. Such traditions, linked to the preservation of the environment, are self-understood both in their projection towards civil responsibilities and as religious practices in honour of their deities. This dialogue calls into question the liberal rationalist feminism or the "rationalist and class feminism that has been built under a depoliticised and deterritorialised gender reading [...] that from their discourses deny the modern colonial mode of production".[17] In this sense, Ivone Gebara points out:

---

[13] Jorge Ceja Martínez (ed), *Vivir en la encrucijada: Crisis civilizatoria. Dimensiones críticas, perspectivas y alternativas* (Guadalajara, México: Centro Universitario de Ciencias Sociales y Humanidades, 2018): 8.

[14] Ynestra King, "The Eco-Feminist Imperative", in Leonie Caldecott and Stephanie Leland (eds), *Reclaiming the Earth: Women Speak Out for Live on Earth* (London: The Women's Press, 1983): 10. See also María Mies and Vandana Shiva, *El Ecofeminismo. Exponentes y Posturas Críticas* (Barcelona: Icaria-Antrazyt, 1997).

[15] At the present time, the decline in the public impact of leftist political movements is notorious after years of military dictatorships and the installation of neoliberal discipline in democratic states, through multilateral organisations, with strong repression of social organisations. The theologian Leonardo Boff, besieged from Rome by the Congregation for the Doctrine of the Faith due to the use of sociological instruments – associated with the Marxist perspective – in his theological productions, opts for a new, broader, spiritual and socio-environmental integral perspective, in which he goes from problematising the social reality of the poorest and the need to transform the church, to putting into discussion the way of inhabiting and living in the world in which the poorest are those who suffer the most from the exploitative nature of the system and the need to change the way of living in the world in order to survive and live together. See Fernando A. Zapata-Muriel and Marta Lucía Martínez-Trujillo, "Ecoteología: aportes de la teología y de la religión en torno al problema ecológico que vive el mundo actual", *Revista Producción + Limpia* 13(1) (2018): 92-105.

[16] Maria Mies and Vandana Shiva, *Ecofeminismo*… 120s.

[17] Ángela Erpel Jara (ed), *Mujeres en Defensa de Territorios: Reflexiones Feministas frente al Extractivismo* (Santiago de Chile: Fundación Heinrich Böll, 2018): 8s.

> Ecofeminism as a social thought and movement basically refers to the ideological connection between the exploitation of nature and the exploitation of women within the hierarchical-patriarchal system. From a philosophical and theological point of view, ecofeminism can be considered as a wisdom that tries to recover the ecosystem and women. These were relegated by the patriarchal system, and particularly by modernity, to be a force for the reproduction of labour – "blessed wombs" – while nature became an object of domination for the increase of capital […][18]

This historical struggle for the liberation of a whole system of exploitation in which the communities of Latin America live, from a decolonial and gender perspective, constitutes the deepest challenge for the diakonia of the church in the region, which is articulated by Protestant churches in their diaconic commitments for environmental justice and gender justice.

In the same way, this paradigm also challenges the states, which are mostly organised by modern liberal logic. Since it provides them with a critical perspective and an alternative rationality for the design of public policies.

> It questions and allows to rethink the conventional concept of "social protection", being itself only one of the dimensions of caring, and also admits the possibility of being approached as a "right" in itself and in a multidimensional way: the right to be cared for, to take care of oneself, of others, of everything that exists, to decide whether or not to take care of oneself and under what conditions, distancing ourselves from the anthropocentrism customary in our culture. A dilemma for intervention strategies and current policy approaches: taking care of the citizen and the environment at the same time, as a whole.[19]

The dimension of social problems, their complexity and intersectionality, requires the joint work of countries with social organisations and movements in order to unite forces at the local level, but also at the level of worldwide articulation, through multilateral organisations, in order to develop an overall vision at a global level.

Systemic Global Articulation and Diaconic Theology

In 2015, the UN General Assembly agreed on "Sustainable Development Goals," which expects results by 2030.[20] The Agenda is organised into 17 goals, integrally and indivisibly linked to 169 objectives, covering the economic, social and environmental spheres.

The Sustainable Development Goals (SDG) propose to work on 17 aspects of the global reality: poverty, hunger, health, education, women's autonomy, sanitation, energy, economic development, innovation, equal opportunities, infrastructure, lifestyle, climate change, ocean pollution, biodiversity, institutional strengthening and international co-operation. This set of objectives is integrated in such a way that it is difficult to disengage them, given the complex network of causes and consequences in which they intertwine or contradict each other.

The Agenda is extremely ambitious and of great value since it makes visible a painful and pressing global reality. However, the Agenda has both diplomatic value and a lack of critical analysis. For it

[18] Ivone Gebara, *Intuiciones ecofeministas: Ensayo para repensar el conocimiento y la religión* (Madrid: Trotta, 2000). See also: Grupo venezolano ecofeminista de investigación y acción "LaDanta LasCanta", "De la teología al antiextractivismo: ecofeminismos en Abya Yala", *Revista Ecología Política* 54 (2017): 37-43, [Available at: https://www.ecologiapolitica.info/?p=10152], [Last accessed: 11th May 2022].

[19] Silvia Gattino and Andrea Milesi, *Paradigma del cuidado: una nueva mirada para pensar las políticas de protección social y las estrategias de intervención* (Villa María, Córdoba: Universidad Nacional de Villa María, 2013): 2.

[20] United Nations, "17 Goals to Transform our World", *UN Sustainable Development Goals Website*, [Available at: https://www.un.org/sustainabledevelopment/], [Last accessed: 11th May 2022]

presupposes material and political conditions for an active role on the part of the states while at the same time it does not have resources for its application. This obliges the Assembly of countries to require the contributions of the central countries and the most concentrated economic actors worldwide, both because of their direct responsibility in the socio-environmental impact of their economic activity and also because of the need to have their financing. In many cases, these countries have not signed basic international agreements or treaties that allow any kind of commitment to be considered in relation to these objectives. At the same time, these objectives do not adequately integrate the historical advances in environmental and human rights matters that were achieved within the UN itself by their respective portfolios. This is the case with the recommendations for an agroecological transition of the Food and Agriculture Organization of the United Nations (FAO), which has an extensive long-standing global network. These disarticulations at the multilateral level itself, added to those of the state structure itself, strongly challenge social organisations in their interventions at the territorial level by becoming, in many cases, guarantors of rights (something that is, in reality, a task that cannot be delegated by the State).

Social organisations, including faith-based organisations (FBOs), have acquired a strategic role in the generation of public policies and in the promotion and defence of human rights. As agents for the implementation of public policies, the FBOs are constituted as demanders and interlocutors of the states, which leads them to confront the gaps generated by the governmental administrations with their own ecclesial management. As a consequence, they suffer in different fields and at different levels (legislative, communicational, financial, etc.), from the conditioning of local concentrated groups and from the pressures of foreign economic groups and multilateral organisations on public policies.

In this scenario, it also becomes necessary to recover collective memories that revalue international agreements and documents resulting from historical struggles, as is the case of the 10 elements of agroecology,[21] published by FAO in dialogue with environmental organisations around the world. This document aims to advise countries in the formulation of public policies in the agroecological transition for the preservation of biodiversity and the survival of our ecosystems. The document proposes ten elements that are not consecutive nor linear, but are intertwined with each other in an integral way. The proposed model indicates ten criteria for an agroecological transition process, namely:

1. Diversification of production and food;
2. Agricultural innovations recovering local knowledge;
3. Synergies between food systems, production and the ecosystem;
4. Innovative agroecological practices with fewer external resources;
5. Agricultural production with less economic and environmental costs;
6. Balance between people, communities and ecosystems;
7. Human and social values in defence of livelihoods, equity and well-being;
8. Development of healthy and diversified diets according to the culture and food traditions of each place;
9. Responsible management of soil and natural resources at different scales;
10. Circular and solidarity economies reconnecting producers and consumers.

The current international, national and local scenario calls us as Protestant churches to elaborate a theology that can transfer to the spiritual area of families – at a level of theological rationality and in the language of faith – approaches and strategies for the proclamation of the reign of God and God's justice, in a relevant and current way. In this foundational work, it is possible to recover some guidelines for the development of an ecotheology that meets the institutional prophetic demand and the injustices experienced in the communities that cry out to heaven.

---

[21] Food and Agriculture Organization of the United Nations. *The 10 Elements of Agroecology: Guiding the Transition to Sustainable Food and Agricultural Systems* (Roma: FAO, 2018).

In the search to put into dialogue a technical framework, which organises the reality in which we live, with the theological approach, which assigns a meaning from the biblical perspective, we connect to the history of salvation to nourish ourselves with its worldview and its symbols, and thus imagine new practices for a living testimony of the presence of God in our midst.

We propose ten principles for a comprehensive ecotheology:

1. The Spirit of God creates human life from the earth (Gen. 2:7; cf. 6:5-7).
2. The environmental crisis is a symptom of a spiritual malaise throughout the *oikoumene*.
3. The objectification of nature as an instrument and means of production relativises creation and distances creatures from God (sin).
4. The idea of Paradise as personal success leads to accumulating and reduces salvation in the reign of God to material satisfaction.
5. The ultimate purpose of creation is to guarantee the communion of everything among all in order to extend the fullness of life to all humanity.
6. Human beings are passing through the world and do not have property in the reign of God, so that they do not own anything, but at the same time they are responsible for everything.
7. The profession is the incarnation of God's call in the world to exercise love of neighbour for the benefit of all creatures alike.
8. God places children as the criteria of life for living the life created in the reign of God.
9. Ecumenical exchange is a testimony of unity in Christ and a sign of transformation for the world.
10. The Church is not at the service of the State, nor is the State at the service of the Church, but both are at the service of the reign of God.

With these ten principles identified in this path of reflection, together with the communities of faith, we continue to build diakonia following in the footsteps of our Lord Jesus Christ. When referring to the privileges of the powerful of the world, Jesus expressly stated that "among you it should not be so" (Mk. 10:43) – even though he taught that public obligations should be honoured. However, upon seeing the people "like sheep without a shepherd, he felt compassion for them" (Mt. 9:36) and asked us to "love our neighbour as ourselves" (Mt. 22:39) without excusing ourselves with theological interpretations or for "lack of mercy" (Mt. 9:13), but always seeking "the reign of God and God's justice" (Mt. 6:33).

Suggestions for Further Reading

Cervantes-Ortiz, Leopoldo. "Koinonía y Diaconía: Sus vínculos profundos". *Lupa protestante.* 5th June 2013. [Available at: https://www.lupaprotestante.com/koinonia-y-diaconia-sus-vinculos-profundos/], [Last accessed: 11th May 2022].

Esquivel, Juan Cruz and Fortunato Mallimaci. "Religión, medioambiente y desarrollo sustentable, la integralidad en la cosmología católica". *Revista Estudios Sociales* 60 (April 2017): 72-86.

Federación Luterana Mundial. *Diaconía en Contexto. Transformación. Reconciliación. Empoderamiento. Una contribución de la FLM a la comprensión y la práctica de la diaconía*. Francia: DMD/FLM, 2009.

Gligo, Nicolo. *La dimensión ambiental en el desarrollo de América Latina*. Santiago: CEPAL, 2001.

Mejía, Milton, Ed. *Diaconía, desarrollo sostenible y paz. Testimonios de la Iglesia Presbiteriana en Colombia*. Barranquilla: Ediciones Corporación Universitaria Reformada, 2020.

Programas Justicia y diaconía, Comunidades justas e incluyentes, y "Misión y evangelización" del Consejo Mundial de Iglesias. "Perspectivas teológicas sobre la diaconía en el siglo XXI." Sri Lanka, 2012. [Available at: https://www.oikoumene.org/es/resources/documents/theological-perspectives-on-diakonia-in-21st-century], [Last accessed: 11th May 2022].

Richter Reimer, Ivoni. "Economía de Dios y diaconía. Estrategias de esperanza para el mundo (Mateo 25:31-46)". *Revista de Interpretación Bíblica Latinoamericana* 39 (2001/2): 115-129.

59. Towards a Transforming Eco-Diakonia Method: Case Studies in Cuban Ecclesial and Ecumenical Centres

Carlos E. Ham[1]

In memory of Paulo Freire on the occasion of the centenary of his birth (1921-2021)

Introduction

The present article focuses on transformative eco-diakonia. "Through its diakonia, the Church witnesses to God's purpose in Jesus Christ and participates in God's mission. In its diakonia, the Church follows the way of its Servant Lord who claimed that he came to serve and not to be served (Mk. 10:45) […]"[2] "This mission of God is dynamic and inclusive of all people and forces that uphold the sanctity and integrity of God's creation".[3] The fusion of these two quotes defines what we call eco-diakonia – the ecological quality of diakonia, which is transformative – to creatively address one of our current main challenges, namely, preserving the integrity of God's creation.

Taking into account the relevance of this interconnection between the ecological aspect of diakonia and transformation, here I propose a method of transformative eco-diakonia, with a double meaning. On the one hand, diakonia is transformative (adjective) for both those who serve and those who are served; on the other hand, it points out the various interdisciplinary characteristics that help to transform (verb) diakonia. Thus, we will observe how eco-diakonia transforms and at the same time is transformed, in a recurrent process of mutual development, towards the construction of fair and inclusive communities.[4]

To design this *method of transformative eco-diakonia*, we draw on Paulo Freire's popular education method, especially on his classic book *Pedagogy of the Oppressed.* In relation to this work, Amanda Levin and colleagues maintain:

> A product of its circumstances and time, Freire's *Pedagogy of the Oppressed* […] reveals the writer's critical focus yet does not explicitly articulate gender or environmental inequalities within a movement for liberation […]. Focused on counteracting socio-economic and cultural oppression, Freire recognises humanity's dependencies upon, and interrelationships with, our natural environment, suggesting that conquering oppression empowers "human hands which work, and working, transform the world."[5]

---

[1] Carlos Emilio Ham (cehams@gmail.com) has been pastor of the Presbyterian-Reformed Church in Cuba for more than forty years. He joined the staff of the World Council of Churches (WCC) in March 2001 in various capacities, including Executive of Diakonia and Latin America-Caribbean. In June 2015, he was installed as Rector and Professor of Mission and Diakonia at the Evangelical Seminary of Theology of Matanzas. He received his doctorate in theology from the Free University of Amsterdam (2015).

[2] WCC, "Theological Perspectives on Diakonia in the Twenty First Century. Document adopted at the World Council of Churches Conference on Theology of Diakonia, 2012", in *Resource Book WCC 10th Assembly, Busan 2013* (Geneva: WCC Publications, 2013): 2.

[3] WCC, "Theological Perspectives", 2.

[4] Carlos Ham, "Empowering Diakonia: A Model for Service and Transformation in the Ecumenical Movement and Local Congregations" (PhD diss., Free University of Amsterdam, 2015), 10.

[5] Amanda Slevin, *et al.*, "Lessons from Freire: Towards a Pedagogy for Socio-Ecological Transformation", *Adult Learner*: *The Irish Journal of Adult and Community Education* 1 (2020): 78-79, [Available at: https://files.eric.ed.gov/fulltext/EJ1272318.pdf], [Last accessed: 11th May 2022].

The method of transformative eco-diakonia will include two basic notions from the work of Freire, namely, *conscientisation* and *praxis*. In regards to the first, it is worth noting that:

> Problem-posing education [...] begins with *conscientização* (conscientisation) as "learning to perceive social, political and economic contradictions, and to take action against the oppressive elements of reality." [...] Freire later elaborated on conscientisation as critical awareness of the material, social, political, cultural and ideological conditions in which we find ourselves [...].[6]

Therefore, in seeking conscientisation, exegesis of the particular context is essential. Regarding the last aspect (praxis), the same authors point out that:

> A Freirean-influenced pedagogy for socio-ecological transformation begins with critical consciousness-raising, reflection and action, progressing to a stage of "permanent liberation" underpinned by ideals of justice, respect equality, and sustainable living with each other and within planetary boundaries.[7]

Now, since Freire's logic addresses the "secular" world, when it comes to diakonia, I think there is a vital and explicit component that must be added from a biblical-theological point of view, which I call normativity. Such normativity is expressed in a spirituality of commitment, and in view of our diaconal mission, it underlines that we are empowered by the Spirit to serve as co-creators with the Creator God. As Leonardo Boff notes, citing Antoine de Saint-Exupéry and highlighting an "ethic of the land":

> we need to understand each other with reciprocity; the human being only becomes a reality together with other human beings, in love and friendship, however, human beings do not unite only by coming closer to each other, but by fusing together in the same divinity. We are thirsty. In a world turned into a desert, we thirst to find comrades with whom to share the bread [...].We have such a great need for a God...[8]

Normativity comes "from a standard or norm, particularly of behaviour and therefore has ethical connotations. It is a commanding point of reference, of taking stances, which provides meaning for the actions of a particular group. It is expressed in human core values, principles, and standards of comportment, in the judgment of what is important in life. In the Judeo-Christian tradition, it is rooted in the authority of the biblical text."[9]

But it is also grounded on our theological foundation, which provides the necessary vision towards a critical dialogue between our Judeo-Christian faith and the experience of our respective contexts, as the relevant paradigm for the churches to serve "the least of these" (Mt. 25:40).

Hence, vision and normativity, conscientisation and formation, and praxis and networking are the three legs of this tripod, called the *transformative eco-diakonia method*. All three factors interrelate holistically with each other in an interdisciplinary manner.

This article applies this *method* to the Cuban context. Cuba, as a tropical island nation, is increasingly affected by the impact of climate change, with increasingly frequent and intense storms. This phenomenon constitutes a key driver of poverty and an inhibitor of sustainable development, causing loss and damage, displacement and conflict.[10]

---

[6] Slevin *et al.*, "Lessons", 81.

[7] Slevin *et al.*, "Lessons", 82.

[8] Leonardo Boff, "Life of the Spirit and Ethics of the Earth and Antoine de Saint-Exupéry", *Leonardo Boff*, 20th February 2016, [Available at: https://leonardoboff.org/2016/02/20/life-of-the-spirit-and-ethics-of-the-earth-and-antoine-de-saint-exupery/], [Last accessed: 11th May 2022].

[9] Ham, "Empowering Diakonia", 10.

[10] See *National Environmental Strategy* 2019-2026, 18, [Available at: http://repositorio.geotech.cu], [Last accessed: 11th May 2022].

Covering the three components of this method, I will share the examples of four ecumenical organisations, reflecting on how they address this environmental crisis, namely the Evangelical Theology Seminary (SET),[11] the Martin Luther King Jr Memorial Centre (CMMLK),[12] the Christian Center for Reflection and Dialogue (CCRD),[13] and ACT Alliance-Cuba.[14]

These entities apply the principles of the Sustainable Development Program of the Council of Churches of Cuba (CIC) – to which they all belong – seeking to promote ecclesial spaces for participation that promote sustainable local development with gender equality, as a testimony of the Christian faith. Among its lines of action are raising awareness for the social commitment of the churches; the training of local development actors; the promotion of sustainable agriculture and food sovereignty; the care and protection of the environment; the diffusion of local alternative technologies; the training of gender promoters, and support for local development initiatives.[15]

All of this work dates back to the 1990s, when the Cuban economy practically collapsed and the churches became more active in social engagement. With the support of several foreign partners, the CIC created the Project Coordination and Advisory Department (DECAP) and the Medical Commission. The DECAP "undertook food security, ecology, energy, and church programmes."[16] In those "pioneering" days, we also created and co-ordinated the Commission for Life, which gave diaconal work a biblical-theological basis, with a very strong ecological component.

Vision and Normativity

Evangelical Theological Seminary

An interesting biblical-theological principle for eco-diakonia is the doctrine of creation which, according to Adolfo Ham:

> has been neglected lately because theology has focused its unilateral emphasis on anthropology. The problem has been because this doctrine of the human being has not been developed in a holistic way, neglecting, as such, the whole creation. Thus the ugly irony, nowadays, is that the human being is destroying God's creation. Furthermore, we cannot base our doctrine of the human being solely on Gen[esis] 1-3, which, like the whole book of Genesis, was written after the prophets wrote, who presented a more holistic cosmovision.[17]

---

[11] SET, founded in 1946, is the ecumenical theological seminary of the island (See SET Cuba website, [Available at: http://www.setcuba.org], [Last accessed: 11th May 2022]).

[12] CMMLK, founded in 1987, is an organisation of Christian inspiration in which the Cuban people and churches contribute prophetically to the solidarity of their country and their communities (See CMMLK website, [Available at: https://cmlk.org], [Last accessed: 11th May 2022]).

[13] CCRD, founded in 1991, is an inclusive organisation, of Christian principles. It promotes spirituality, human dignity, human rights and conflict resolution through reconciling dialogue (See CCRD website, [Available at: https://www.ccrdcuba.org], [Last accessed: 11th May 2022]).

[14] The ACT Caribbean Forum was launched in Cuba in 2018, made up of ACT members in Cuba, the Dominican Republic and Haiti. (See "CIC presente en articulación para la gestión de riesgo de desastres", CIC [Available at: https://consejodeiglesiasdecuba.org/index.php/category/act/], [Last accessed: 11th May 2022]).

[15] See "Programa Desarrollo Sostenible", *Consejo de Iglesias de Cuba*, [Available at: https://consejodeiglesiasdecuba.org/index.php/programa-desarrollo-sostenible/], [Last accessed: 11th May 2022].

[16] Caridad Massón Sena, "El Movimiento Ecuménico en Cuba. Sus estrategias contra la pobreza en los últimos 20 años", in Genaro Zalpa and Hans Egil Offerdal (eds), *¿El reino de Dios es de este mundo?: el papel ambiguo de las religiones en la lucha contra la pobreza* (Bogotá: Siglo del Hombre – CLACSO, 2008): 285.

[17] The most important biblical passages studied are OT: Gn. 1:1-2.4a (document P); 2:4b-7 (document J); Job 26:12s; 38:8-11; Ps. 74:s; 89:10s; 104:5-9; Pr. 8:29; Is. 27:1; 51:9-11; NT: Jn. 1:1-5; Acts 17:24-28; 1 Cor. 8:6; Rom. 1:19-

Here, we highlight three normative aspects that can illuminate and guide our efforts in eco-diakonia today: (1) a holistic understanding of creation as a communion, involving human beings with creation and integrating the divine community of the Trinity; (2) a call to be co-creators with the Creator; and (3) a demand, as co-creators, to pursue not domination, but "justice, peace, and the integrity of creation."

Christian Centre for Reflection and Dialogue

Our ecotheology is based on a liberating and holistic vision of the earth. Consequently, we defend respect for the planet and its diversity, ecological integrity, and social and economic justice for peoples. These indicate some of the themes that synthesise an ethic of care and use of nature's resources from hermeneutic-theological elements centred on the action of God in the history of the human being and therefore in nature, in creation.[18]

In the parables, which were the pedagogical method par excellence of Jesus, the New Testament refers to events related to agricultural cycles, where words such as sowing, harvest, weeds, mustard seed, fig tree, vineyard, sun and rain appear, among others. They reveal how the life of Jesus and the model that he proposes to us with reference to the reign of God, is an invitation, a challenge for the human being to enter into harmony with themself and with the rest of the cosmos.

ACT Alliance-Cuba

The earth and all it contains are gifts from God, and all people are called to participate in the ongoing creation, preservation, and maintenance of God's creation. Transformational development works to preserve, maintain and regenerate natural resources, drawing on everyone's knowledge and practices, and promoting the use of appropriate technologies.

Excessive consumption and lack of distribution of available resources by some members of the family of God (both in the North and in the South) prevent other people from enjoying their rights. Transformational development will promote conscientisation, attitude change and action within communities with excess resources and capacity to bring about change.[19]

Conscientisation and Formation

Evangelical Theological Seminary (SET)

Even though we recognise that we must deepen and emphasise it more, the ecological theme is present in a transversal way in our study plan, particularly in the "chair of systematic and contextual theology." Ecotheology and climate justice has been the theme chosen for the celebration of our "annual theological meeting" between our seminary and Toronto's Knox College, in February 2020, under the title "Confessing hope for the earth."

In regular SET courses, diakonia is taught by the Department of Mission and Diakonia (i.e. diakonia as global *missio Dei*). Since 2013 and under the co-sponsorship of the Evangelical Seminary of Theology (SET), the Martin Luther King Jr Centre (CMMLK) and the Diakonia Area of the Council of Churches of Cuba (CIC), the Cuban School of Diakonia was created. In it, the ecological theme is a transversal axis of the five meetings of each academic year.

20; 8:19-22; Col. 1:15-20; Heb. 1:1-3, class notes from Adolfo Ham, who was a professor at the Evangelical Seminary of Theology.

[18] Texts such as Gen. 1:26-28, Is. 30:23-26 and Is. 35:2, although they offer more of an administrative, management and care of nature reading, they do not authorise us human beings to behave in an anti-ecological way.

[19] "Our understanding of development", *ACT Alliance*, 2013, 2. [Available at: https://actalliance.org/wp-content/uploads/2015/07/Our-Understanding-of-Development_ENGLISH.pdf], [Last accessed: 11th May 2022]

Martin Luther King Jr Memorial Centre (CMMLK)

Since 1998, the CMMLK began to implement an educational-methodological accompaniment to the organisation of experiences related to community environmental training, promotion and management. Over the years, various popular educational workshops linked to environmental work experiences have been implemented, mainly in the educational, scientific-cultural and agricultural fields. It has participated in different spaces for reflection and debate on ecology and environmental work convened by both secular and ecumenical institutions. With the spaces for diaconal formation, they have collaborated with the Ministry of Science, Technology and Environment, the Council of Churches of Cuba and the Evangelical Seminary of Theology of Matanzas, particularly in the School of Diakonia, among others.

The main learnings of the Centre in this field have been:

1. Accompaniment of experiences as a process of mutual and symmetrical learning, of teaching by learning, of learning by teaching.
2. Implementation of practical experiences: we have learned that diaconal work in general and that of eco-diakonia in particular, requires the implementation and practical testimony of knowledge in concrete experiences that transform the subjects and the environmental reality in which they have incidence.

Christian Centre for Reflexion and Dialogue (CCRD)

The CCRD has been working on eco-diakonia since its foundation. Its proposals aim at raising awareness of environmental issues, focused especially on children and youth, through community interventions.

Environmental education as a model is vital for promoting moral values based on love, harmonious co-existence, responsibility, austerity, respect, equity, sustainability and solidarity in caring for the environment. It must begin at an early age and continue permanently throughout human life.

Ecological Integrity as an educational model and method must have as premises:

1. Protecting and restoring the integrity of the earth's ecological systems, with special concern for biological diversity and the natural processes that support life.
2. Avoiding harming creation, and when our knowledge is limited, proceeding with caution.
3. Adopting models of production, consumption and reproduction that safeguard the regenerative capacities of the earth, human rights and the well-being of the community.
4. Promoting the study of ecological sustainability and sponsoring the open exchange and extensive application of the knowledge acquired.

ACT Alliance-Cuba

ACT Alliance has a "Sustainable Development Training Unit" in Cuba that implements, together with the Cuban Council of Churches, the "Cuban Communities for Sustainable Development."[20]

For example, progress has been made in training regarding assessed risks and an action/measure plan has been prepared with the participation of the community, aimed at eliminating or reducing the identified vulnerabilities. This facilitates the empowerment of the community based on a participatory debate for planning the most important measures in the short term.

Congregational diaconal teams must conduct pre-plan exercises for emergency and disaster preparedness and response. In the end, these teams must have defined their strengths and weaknesses to deal with various emergency and/or disaster situations.

[20] See María Luisa Navas-Zorrilla, *Cambio Climático-Mitigación-Adaptación-Gestión del Riesgo de Desastres. Unidad Formativa de Desarrollo Sostenible* (La Habana: CIC, 2001).

Praxis and Networks

Evangelical Theological Seminary

Finally, our seminary continues to promote this awareness, research and training on climate justice, through:

1. National and international conferences, seminars, workshops, from a biblical-theological and interdisciplinary perspective.
2. Intentional, systematic and profound inclusion of the ecological theme in the various programmes and academic activities.
3. Research and advocacy among faith-based organisations in order to engage them, highlighting the specific contribution of climate justice in the realm of a spirituality of commitment to creation.
4. Strategic alliances with other institutions of the theological or secular academy in the country and abroad, with innovation in content and research methodologies.
5. Specific tasks such as a responsible administration of creation.

Martin Luther King Jr Memorial Centre

The CMMLK develops practical processes such as training, communication and educational accompaniment, integrated into the work in eco-diakonia, as part of the missiological action of accompaniment of the centre and its networks. As such, it involves practical experiences developed from a systemic approach, which require interaction and mutual contribution within community environmental management. This grassroots work has the dual purpose of deconstructing hierarchical ecological perceptions and practices and transforming attitudes and lifestyles that do not contribute to the sustainability of present and future life.

These processes suppose: (1) The participatory, pedagogical, didactic and methodological conception of popular environmental education; (2) perspectives such as those of "popular environmentalism or environmentalism of the poor", as opposed to the "worship of wildlife" and the "eco-efficiency gospel"[21] and (3) the ecotheological perspective based on co-responsibility towards all the forms of existence of creation, with the right to exist beyond their usage value.

Christian Centre for Reflexion and Dialogue

The CCRD collaborates both with churches and Christian institutions, including seminaries, centres and the Council of Churches of Cuba (CIC), as well as with Cuban research institutions, universities, and secular organisations, including the Ministry of Science, Technology and Environment (CITMA), the Ministry of Agriculture, the Ministry of Education and local governments.

Among the topics or areas of participation that they address are:

1. Avoidance of actions that negatively affect the environment, and promotion of measures for their mitigation.
2. Incorporation of natural and traditional medicine, as well as healthy eating.
3. Care for and enrichment of soils with natural methods.
4. Rational use of water with emphasis on saving measures.
5. Stimulation of actions focused on recycling and reusage.

Beyond its multiple causes, we see the lack of an environmental culture as a primary factor in the emergence of environmental problems. These include indiscipline, negligence, indolence, and many other

[21] See Ramachandra Guha and Joan Martínez-Alier, *Varieties of Environmentalism: Essays North and South* (London: Earthscan, 1997) and Joan Martínez-Alier, *The Environmentalism of the Poor: a study of ecological conflicts and valuation* (Cheltenham: Edward Elgar, 2002).

issues that have so much to do with the customs of people, and therefore belong to the field of morality. Networking contributes to creatively and effectively addressing these challenges.

ACT Alliance-Cuba

As well as trying to prevent climate change, ACT also adapts to this critical situation, which involves knowing the current transformations, as well as those expected and likely, and preparing the communities in the best possible ways to face them.

An important aspect of their collaborative efforts focuses on disaster risk reduction as a key to sustainable development. Risk management policies and practices must be based on an understanding of all its dimensions of vulnerability, capacity, exposure of people and assets, characteristics of hazards and the environment.

The methodology used by the Alliance with the CIC to assess disaster risk unfolds in four stages: (1) organisation and approach; (2) information gathering; (3) community risk analysis; and (4) socialisation of the evaluation and the action plan in the community.

Conclusion

As is expressed in the LWF Study Paper on "Diakonia in Context":

> From a theological point of view, transformation is a reminder of God's constant renewal of creation (Latin: *creatio continua*), as every morning we experience that the darkness of night is transformed into the light of a new day breaking forth. As people of God, we see transformation as God's gracious gift for which we owe praise and service.[22]

In the "darkness" of today's world, which is experiencing a profound ecological crisis, increasing impoverishment and polarisation, consumerism and the commodification of life, among other issues, due to neoliberal systems, churches are called to be co-creators with the God of life, helping to bring light to creation.

To carry out this effort, in this article, we have explored the method of transformative eco-diakonia, with its three steps of vision and normativity, awareness and training, and praxis and networking, and we have analysed four case studies in ecclesial and ecumenical centres from Cuba.

We are seeking: a "*koinonia*, a community beyond the narrow boundaries of the churches […] which marks its presence in the world. Diakonia, therefore, is not an end in itself, but rather an instrument used by God, together with others, to build an inclusive and just community, an *oikos*, a household in which the entire creation is included, enjoying the fullness of life intended for all."[23]

Suggestions for Further Reading

ACT Alliance, "Our understanding of development", *Act Alliance Website*, 2013. [Available at: https://actalliance.org/wp-content/uploads/2015/07/Our-Understanding-of-Development_ENGLISH.pdf], [Last accessed: 12th May 2022].

[22] Lutheran World Federation, *Diakonia in Context. Transformation, Reconciliation, Empowerment,* edited by Kjell Nordstokke (Geneva: LWF, 2009): 44.

[23] This thought is based on the report of the WCC general secretary at the time, Philip A. Potter, to its 6th Assembly, held in Vancouver, Canada, in 1983. [Available at: https://www.oikoumene.org/en/about-us/organizational-structure/general-secretary/since-1948], [Last accessed: 12th May 2022].

Boff, Leonardo. "Life of the Spirit and Ethics of the Earth and Antoine de Saint-Exupéry". *Leonardo Boff Website*, 20th February 2016. [Available at: https://leonardoboff.org/2016/02/20/life-of-the-spirit-and-ethics-of-the-earth-and-antoine-de-saint-exupery/], [Last accessed: 11th May 2022].

Guha, Ramachandra and Joan Martínez-Alier. *Varieties of Environmentalism: essays North and South.* London: Earthscan, 1997.

Ham, Carlos. "Empowering Diakonia: A Model for Service and Transformation in the Ecumenical Movement and Local Congregations." PhD diss., Free University of Amsterdam, 2015. [Available at: http://dare.ubvu.vu.nl/handle/1871/53516], [Last accessed: 12th May 2022].

Lutheran World Federation. *Diakonia in Context. Transformation, Reconciliation, Empowerment.* Geneva: LWF, 2009.

Martínez-Alier, Joan. *The Environmentalism of the Poor: a study of ecological conflicts and valuation.* Cheltenham: Edward Elgar, 2002.

Massón Sena, Caridad. "El movimiento ecuménico en Cuba. Sus estrategias contra la pobreza en los últimos 20 años", in Genaro Zalpa and Hans Egil Offerdal, Eds. *¿El reino de Dios es de este mundo?: El papel ambiguo de las religiones en la lucha contra la pobreza*. Bogotá: Siglo del Hombre – CLACSO, 2008.

Ministerio de Ciencia, Tecnología y Medio Ambiente. "Enfrentamiento al Cambio Climático en la República de Cuba: Tarea Vida", 2017. [Available at http://repositorio.geotech.cu/jspui/bitstream/1234/2864/1/Plan de Estado para el Enfrentamiento al Cambio Climático en la República de Cuba %28Tarea Vida%29.pdf], [Last accessed: 13th May 2022].

Navas-Zorrilla, María Luisa. *Cambio Climático-Mitigación-Adaptación-Gestión del Riesgo de Desastres. Unidad Formativa de Desarrollo Sostenible*. La Habana: CIC, 2001.

Slevin, Amanda, Roxanne Elliott, Rosie Graves, Colleen Petticrew and Alexandra Popoff. "Lessons from Freire: Towards a Pedagogy for Socio-Ecological Transformation", in *The Adult Learner: The Irish Journal of Adult and Community Education* 1 (2020). [Available at: https://files.eric.ed.gov/fulltext/EJ1272318.pdf], [Last accessed: 13th May 2022].

World Council of Churches. "Theological Perspectives on Diakonia in the Twenty First Century. Document adopted at the World Council of Churches Conference on Theology of Diakonia, 2012", in *Resource Book WCC 10th Assembly, Busan 2013*. Geneva: WCC, 2013.

60. Prophetic and Ecological Diakonia: Agricultural Production, Economy and Environmental Sustainability in the River Plate Region

Álvaro Michelin Salomón[1]

Introduction

Let me make a brief autobiographical reference. I was born and raised in Pueblo Miguelete, Colonia Department, Oriental Republic of the Uruguay. Miguelete is one of the agricultural colonies founded by Waldensians in 1909. My paternal grandparents were founders of the colony and my father, Gino, was an agricultural producer, as well as an official of the local agricultural co-operative. My father dedicated himself to extensive agriculture (wheat, barley, corn, sunflower, sorghum) and livestock (cows, steers and sheep). The prevailing type of production led him to make use of the technology provided, for example, with the purchase of professional seeds, the use of agrochemicals and agricultural machinery. Despite being considered a middle-class producer, my father went through times of financial hardship, specifically when he decided to retire. That is when Lelio, my older brother, and his wife decided to settle in the town, leaving Montevideo, the capital of the country.

An agricultural profitability that allows the support of one or several families, without a guaranteed monthly income, presupposes facing an important financial risk in addition to requiring a certain business administration capacity of one's own. Of course, for this there are specialists who advise on profitability and production with greater market advantages (internal or external). Production costs can be very high and, in many cases, this requires acquiring debt in the banking system. Crops and the sale of livestock offer possibilities to pay debts and add a return that allows families to continue living off the land. The purchase of agricultural machinery requires an investment effort that not every producer is in a position to make.

In a period of about twenty years, the value of a hectare of land multiplied by ten (in dollars!) in the most productive areas of Uruguay, including in the Department of Colonia. This is an indicator of how difficult it is today to acquire land in the country for producing according to agricultural exploitation under the technological parameters imposed by the international market.

In what follows, I will offer a series of theses, articulated on the basis of the well-known Latin American hermeneutical method *see, judge, act*, which seeks to outline some guidelines for the promotion of a prophetic and ecological diakonia in and from our River Plate regional context.

See

Thesis 1: *The current model of agricultural production based on bioengineering and the high technology of agricultural machinery, oriented towards exports to the central countries, promotes an increasing process in the concentration of wealth.*[2]

Colonialism remains a reality throughout the so-called Global South, even though it has changed its configurations over the centuries. Currently, its dominant forms are cultural and economic colonialism,

---

[1] Álvaro Michelin Salomon (alvaro.michelin.salomon@gmail.com) is a Waldensian Pastor, Doctor of Theology from the University Institute – ISEDET (Buenos Aires) and Professor of Practical Theology at the Ecumenical Network of Theological Education (REET). He studied at the Protestant Faculty of Theology at the University of Tübingen, Germany.

[2] See Carlos Duarte, *Soja y monocultivos: una mirada pastoral* (Buenos Aires: Iglesia Evangélica del Río de la Plata, 2013): 9-11.

which maintain and seek to deepen both epistemological subalternity and economic-financial dependence on peripheral societies.

The proposed statement is not a mere assumption but a consistent general interpretation of the conditions and dynamics that shape the reality of countries such as Uruguay and Argentina, among others. Given the specific characteristics of both nations, agricultural production has historically been and continues to be a backbone of their asymmetric integration into neocolonial globalisation, presided over by the powers of international financial capital. Within this framework, a production model based on the technological developments of bioengineering and the use of sophisticated agricultural machinery prevails, which is fundamentally oriented towards export to the central countries.

In line with this production model, if a family of several children intends to continue living from rural activity, they will have to risk taking out bank loans in order to buy machinery, supplies and, if necessary, to acquire larger areas of land. But the high risk of loans is daunting for most. In the worst case, the family will decide to sell their property, or rent the field and dedicate themselves to another activity. Since not all producers are in a position to acquire land, only those whose capital allows them to risk what the majority cannot, will buy. Then the trend will be the concentration of land – and wealth – in fewer hands.

Thesis 2: *In the world of agribusiness, the rise in the value of land and agricultural machinery due to an obsessive search for productivity at all costs, makes access to land ownership increasingly exclusive.*[3] *This also implies the expulsion of thousands of people from the countryside to small, medium and large towns, and even abroad.*[4]

The cost of agricultural machinery is not consistent with the average profitability of rural producers. The land itself is worth a lot, but if a farmer sells their property, what do they do next? Globalisation leads to an ever-increasing rise in the costs of agricultural inputs, but not to equalising the living conditions of those who work the land or those who want to work it.

The rural exodus, which is not new, has been presented as something inevitable. Only in a few traditional farm production regions is life in the countryside still a real possibility for families. However, where there once was agriculture, livestock or dairy activity, it is rare that the production be transformed into a farm activity that requires a much smaller number of hectares. The depopulation of the countryside has been projected into the overpopulation of the big cities.

Thesis 3: *If this model is maintained indefinitely over time, without the introduction of rational planning of the national and regional economy, as well as the world economy, large sectors of the population will not find a decent and adequate habitat, since there will not be enough time for governments to implement the development of the infrastructure of towns and cities.*[5]

Despite the arrival in Latin America of popular governments (years ago) and – in cases such as Brazil with the drastic decrease in poverty – poverty and extreme poverty still continue to be the greatest social problems in the region. If the countryside does not offer more possibilities of life for thousands of families, they must move somewhere else; therefore, the implementation of housing plans in towns and cities becomes an urgent need. But families also need jobs, health care and access to education. It becomes not just a question of where to live, but how to live. Therefore, the entire economy of a country is at stake, and

[3] See Bettina Müller, "El modelo extractivista de agronegocios en el marco político-económico actual", in D. Beros and P. Kalmbach (eds), *Riesgos y desafíos del actual modelo de producción agrícola. Un abordaje interdisciplinario* (Buenos Aires: Pastoral de Promoción del Cuidado de la Creación): 17.

[4] See Tamara Perelmuter, "El agronegocio en la economía regional", in *Riesgos y desafíos,* 34.

[5] See Guillermo Kerber, "Ecoteología y cambio climático: perspectivas ecuménicas", in E. Lizarralde and A. Salibián (eds), *Ecoteología. Aportes desde el ecumenismo* (Buenos Aires: Dunken, 2013): 35.

thus, due to the financial needs of countries with dependent economies, it is essential to find fair and accessible credit solutions (or subsidies?) from the central economies.

Thesis 4: *The concentration of wealth and the impoverishment of a large part of the population are producing problems that are very difficult to resolve in the short and medium term, concerning combating misery, poverty and unemployment.*[6]

This is linked to what was expressed in relation to Thesis 3. If *global* solutions are not adopted to these problems of *global interest*, planet earth will continue to be so divided that it will be impossible to avoid the permanent flow of *migrations* from smaller economies to richer ones.

Argentina and Uruguay, as well as Brazil, Paraguay and Chile, have been countries populated by European immigrants for many decades. The minority autochthonous populations began to co-exist with the foreign contingents. In the case of Argentina, particularly since the 1970s, immigrants from neighbouring countries have been received. With the economic crisis unleashed recently in Venezuela, the countries of the Southern Cone have become recipients of thousands of people of Venezuelan origin who are looking for work and stability. But large sectors of the population continue to be submerged in poverty and marginality. Is this just a *local or regional* issue?

Judge

Thesis 5: *For the Bible, even if we consider the creation stories of Genesis 1-2, the earth is not owned by humanity but by God, its creator.*

The concept of stewardship or administration of God's creation by the human being is central in the biblical conception. It must be understood in close connection with the Old Testament prophetic critique of the over-exploitation and grabbing of the land, as well as of poor and excluded people (widows, orphans and foreigners), including animals, as a source of profound inequalities, of economic, social and ecological violence in ancient Israel.[7]

Thesis 6: *The dominion of the human being over creation in the Genesis 1:26 story is not equal to indiscriminate exploitation but to the care, good use, and protection of creation.*

The human being, created in God's image and likeness, has not been established in creation to set themselves up as god, but to act in God's name. They do not replace God but represent God in the world. Their mission is not to do what they want with their habitat but what God wants for creation: that it live, endure and serve as a common home for all generations and species of life, including human life. Therefore, the use of the air, sun, water and earth should not be a cause of division in humanity, but rather of solidarity and inclusive complementation of forces, as a concrete way of glorifying and praising the creator.

Thesis 7: *Jesus Christ assumed the creation of God as the habitat not governed by mercantilism but by the grace of God. What he called the "reign of God" is precisely when God governs our existence including the areas of work, economy, nature and interpersonal bonds.*

Jesus Christ taught us to live, serve, and transform our integral existence giving a transcendent meaning to what we do, and to form faith communities in Jesus' image and likeness. His death on the cross marks our liberation from sin, injustice and death; his resurrection opens us to the perspective of hope that we only find in God, the Creator and Re-Creator of all things. We hope, pray and work for "*new heavens and a new earth, where righteousness is at home*" (2 Pet. 3:13).

---

[6] See Adolfo Boy, "En Argentina abunda de todo menos los sueños", in *Ecoteología,* 139.
[7] See for example, Is. 1:10; 8:21; 29:18; 58:6-7; Am. 2:6; 4:1; cap. 5.

As the Church of Jesus Christ, then, we are echo to the new creation that has already become present in the risen Jesus. Our faith must not be limited to experiencing an individual and private bond with God, for this would be to limit what God can do too much. The mission that lies before us has creation as its general scenario, as the human environment, the society in which we live, and as neighbours those who, from their Christian definition or not, do their best to preserve creation because they manifest themselves in solidarity with the present and future generations.

Act

Thesis 8: *The churches must proclaim their prophetic voice in the face of this situation that crosses borders and societies, in order to join those organisations that also seek a better future, especially for the large excluded sectors.*

In this increasingly interdependent world, where not only the *dependent* economies need the larger economies, but the latter also need the former to maintain their condition as such, the greatest social problems of the countries of the periphery should not be just a matter of these countries but of global interest. Just as the large seed corporations, many international industries of agricultural machinery and the production of agrochemicals do not have borders, it cannot be claimed that poverty, marginality, school desertion and the lack of health infrastructure in Latin American countries do. With this, I argue that *poverty and marginality* are not issues only of Latin America and for Latin America, but a problem of global interest. Economic dependence is not only a problem for our countries but for the world. "Our" poverty and "our" marginality are not the private property of this region of the world, but crimes against humanity. It is true that there are local and national responsibilities, but things should not stop there. For if it is not understood that we are part of a whole and that, therefore, when a member suffers, the other members also suffer (I Cor. 12), the churches will not make a voice heard that is different from the majority of social, political and economic voices.

Thesis 9: *The River Plate Protestant churches, located in rural contexts – especially those that were born with the agricultural colonies – depend financially to a great extent on the contributions of church members who live in the countryside. Rural producers accustomed to the prevailing production model do not easily find the possibility of assuming an alternative model of ecological production. Furthermore, the socio-economic and political environment does not help at all. This situation does not relieve the churches of, but rather challenges them to redouble, their prophetic and pastoral commitment.*[8]

To cover their expenses and contributions for pastoral care, Protestant congregations assume their financial responsibility (stewardship) based on contributions from church member families. A good part of this production is based, in many regions, on the production of soybeans.

Many soy producers are members of the Waldensian Church and the IERP (Evangelical Church of the Río de la Plata), and thus these churches receive their offerings or contributions largely from the profitability of this crop. So, as churches, it is not easy to promote radical measures against soy production. Notwithstanding this, both churches have made an effort to develop important initiatives in favour of an *ecological conversion of agricultural production*. This is a long-term process, and an indispensable debate.

Thesis 10: *It is possible to seek the gradual establishment of a new model of agricultural production, of working the land.*

---

[8] In this sense, it is worth highlighting the action developed by the Centro Emmanuel in Colonia Valdense, Uruguay, an agroecological and retreat centre for theological, ethical and social studies, supported by the Evangelical church of the Río de la Plata (IERP), the Methodist in Uruguay (IMU) and the Waldensian churches.

This model will be based on the offering of facilities for ecological production, within the horizon of a new internal and international trade that prioritises the defence of the land, the entire environment and the right to work by those who do not have the initial capital to start their own production.

The idea of developing ecological agricultural planning, based on productive diversity, has to stop being an unreachable utopia and become a social and economic programme under the care of local, national and regional political forces. Not all the production of the countryside will be extensive agriculture, or livestock, or dairy. There are other ways to produce on smaller land surfaces. But for this purpose, the creation of co-operatives and production and marketing networks must be promoted.

In addition, it is necessary to create local, national and regional markets that make it possible to commercialise the products. Soft loans must be made available to new producers; likewise, raising awareness among private and state banks so that they offer new possibilities of access to micro-credits or short and medium-term credits. Such initiatives should be framed in state policies. If the state does not see it that way, the churches have the responsibility to show the state the need that the most defenceless and poorest sectors have to access new production possibilities.

A Final Word

The ecological responsibility of the churches is not something optional but part of their integral mission in society. A prophetic and ecological diakonia will be possible when, by word and action, we bear witness to God's will that we be faithful stewards of creation.

As churches, we have to see, judge and act, serving in the world so that it is the inclusive house in which no one is left out. Produce enough, consume enough, distribute enough, and work so that future generations don't complain about us for destroying their life chances.

Suggestions for Further Reading

Beros, Daniel and Pedro Kalmbach, Eds. *Riesgos y desafíos del actual modelo de producción agrícola. Un abordaje interdisciplinario*. Buenos Aires: Pastoral de Promoción del Cuidado de la Creación, 2018.

Boff, Leonardo. *Ecología: grito de la tierra, grito de los pobres*. Madrid: Trotta, 2011,

Burghardt, Anne, Ed. *La creación no se vende*. Geneva: Lutheran World Federation; Leipzig: Evangelische Verlagsanstalt, 2016.

Duarte, Carlos. *Soja y monocultivos. Una mirada pastoral*. Buenos Aires: Iglesia Evangélica del Río de la Plata, 2013.

Gorbosth, Maike, Christopher Morck, Verónica Flachier and Elias Wolff, Eds. *Agua: don de Dios, derecho humano y bien común. Reflexionar, orar y actuar: Una afirmación ecuménica*. Quito: Consejo Latinoamericano de Iglesias, Red Ecuménica del Agua y Consejo Episcopal Latinoamericano, 2015.

Kerber, Guillermo. "Ecoteología y cambio climático: perspectivas ecuménicas", in E. Lizarralde and A. Salibián, Eds. *Ecoteología. Aportes desde el ecumenismo*. Buenos Aires: Dunken, 2013: 24-38.

Lizarralde, Eusebio and Alfredo Salibián, Eds. *Ecoteología. Aportes desde el ecumenismo*. Buenos Aires: Dunken, 2013.

Lovelock, James. *La venganza de la tierra. La teoría de Gaia y el futuro de la humanidad*. Buenos Aires: Planeta, 2007.

Francisco. *Laudato Si'*. Vatican City: Editora Vaticana, 2015.

Mendoza, Rolando, Alfredo Salibián, Christa von Hillebrandt de Andrade and Fernando Oshige. *Cristianos. Mayordomos de la creación*. Quito: Consejo Latinoamericano de Iglesias, 1993.

Moltmann, Jürgen. *El futuro de la creación*. Salamanca: Sígueme, 1979.

Sánchez Cetina, Edesio. "Creación, redención y sustentación". *RIBLA* 80(2) (2019): 99-109.

Müller, Bettina. "El modelo extractivista de agronegocios en el marco político-económico actua", in D. Beros and P. Kalmbach, Eds. *Riesgos y desafíos del actual modelo de producción agrícola. Un abordaje interdisciplinario.* Buenos Aires: Pastoral de Promoción del Cuidado de la Creación, 2018: 16-23.

Perelmuter, Tamara. "El agronegocio en la economía regional", in D. Beros and P. Kalmbach, Eds. *Riesgos y desafíos del actual modelo de producción agrícola. Un abordaje interdisciplinario.* Buenos Aires: Pastoral de Promoción del Cuidado de la Creación, 2018: 33-45.

61. Socio-Ecological Diakonia and Climate Justice – Perspectives Inspired from the Laudato Si' Encyclical

Humberto Ortiz Roca[1]

Point of Departure

In the light of the gospel and the social thought of the church, in communion with a community-based pastoral, a pastoral (or pastoral ministry) of creation care is called to promote a just, reconciled, fraternal society, in solidarity with and from the leading role of poor and excluded persons, in harmony with creation, a sign of the reign of God.

This ministry thus responds to the challenge of being prophetic witnesses of Jesus Christ in the world, servants of a church that is near, where in communion, women and men, contribute to the construction of the reign of God; where people live with dignity, appropriate use is made, and the goods of creation are respected for the common good towards a fraternal, solidary, reconciled, just and democratic world.[2]

This is part of our mission as Christians and believers, because "'Our sister, mother earth' is our common home and the place of God's covenant with human beings and with all creation."[3] This presents us with the task of building justice in solidarity with the poorest people, leading us to a special commitment to and with those who suffer from climate change, defending their rights, their dignity and their empowerment, from a perspective of solidary, integral human development.

In social action, communities of faith help during and in the aftermath of environmental disasters and carry out innumerable projects on all continents, especially those dedicated to promoting adaptation to and mitigation of climate change, sustainable agriculture and agroecology, the circular economy, prevention and management of risks in disasters, and awareness raising. In all this, we seek to become spokespersons for the cries of the most vulnerable and affected people, so that their situations and proposals are addressed by the highest local, national and international institutions.

Poor People Bear the Brunt of Environmental Degradation and Climate Change

Climate change may frustrate decades of efforts for economic growth and poverty reduction.[4] However, it is not about choosing between curbing climate change or fighting poverty and hunger; on the contrary, action against climate change is essential to effectively confront poverty, hunger and malnutrition. All of this is even more significant in the current context of the pandemic caused by COVID-19, since they are processes that are deeply interrelated.

---

[1] Humberto Ortiz Roca (apresidente@iglesiacatolica.org.pe) is assistant to the President of the Peruvian Episcopal Conference and is a member of the team "Nuevas Economías y Buen Vivir" of the Secretariat for Latin America and the Caribbean of Caritas (SELACC).

[2] See "Proceso de definición de la Misión y Visión" (Documento de Planificación Estratégica, Costa Rica, SELACC, November, 2015).

[3] CELAM, *V General Conference of the Episcopate of Latin America and the Caribbean. Concluding Document.* Aparecida, 13th-31st May 2007 (Bogotá: CELAM, 2007), sec. 125.

[4] Caritas Internationalis, *Agencias Internacionales de Desarrollo. Documento de Reflexión* (Vatican City: Caritas Internationalis, 2018).

Climate change not only seriously hampers the reduction of poverty, but also puts at risk the survival of the most vulnerable sectors of humanity and, due to the damage caused to natural resources and biodiversity, fundamentally threatens the survival of the planet itself.[5]

In recent decades, bishops from various continents have drawn attention to its effects, especially on the poorest people, groups and nations.[6]

Climate change alters weather patterns, profoundly affecting agricultural seasons, forests, fishing and livestock, all of which make it difficult for most people to access food. This situation of food insecurity causes growing precariousness and implies flagrant violations of fundamental human rights, such as the right to food, to life, to health and to the development and well-being of peoples. Today, almost a billion people do not have access to enough food to live well and climate change threatens to aggravate this situation in the context of the pandemic.

With the increase in ecological refugees, there is a real possibility that the advances in poverty reduction of the last decades will be lost, during which it was possible for a greater number of people to access basic services in areas such as health, education, transportation, as well as access to employment; these services have experienced acute precariousness in the context of the pandemic.

The poorest people, especially women, children, youth and adolescents, as well as older adults in rural or forest areas, who have contributed the least to global warming, are the most affected by climate change. Likewise, these are the people and groups that have the least means to cope with the negative effects. On the other hand, they also have no voice or representation in political decision-making, at virtually any level.[7] According to the Pontifical Academy of Social Sciences, 40% of the poorest people suffer the greatest impacts of this phenomenon.[8]

Climate change poses a threat to all of humanity, given the costs of inaction, which are projected to increase, as the necessary mitigating and restorative action continues to be postponed – something that has been highlighted with alarm by the United Nations Secretary-General.[9] The most recent estimates put the annual costs at some $1.2bn (1.6% of global GDP), with projections that this amount will more than double by 2030, if the current trend is not reversed. With recent disasters, which have affected entire communities (forest fires, floods, etc.), the impacts are being felt all over the world.[10]

---

[5] "Carta de Obispos de América Latina y el Caribe a la V Cumbre ALC-UE, Lima, 15 de mayo de 2008", *Con nuestro Perú*, 20th May 2008, [Available at: https://www.connuestroperu.com/actualidad/pronunciamientos/2060-carta-de-obispos-de-america-latina-y-el-caribe], [Last accessed: 14th May 2022].

[6] See United States Conference of Catholic Bishops, "Renewing the Earth: An Invitation to Reflection and Action on Environment in Light of Catholic Social Teaching. A Pastoral Statement of the United States Catholic Conference, 14th November 1991". [Available at: https://www.usccb.org/resources/renewing-earth], [Last accessed: 14th May 2022]; also, Council of Bishops' Conferences of Europe, *A Christian View on Climate Change* (Saint Gallen: COMECE, 2011): 19.

[7] CELAM, "Declaración final del seminario sobre crisis financiera internacional, cambio climático y su impacto en los pobres, Lima, 3rd-7th May 2009". [Available at: https://vidadelacer.org/index.php/comisiones/justicia-paz-ecol/1343-seminario-sobre-crisis-financiera-internacional-celam], [Last accessed: 14th May 2022].

[8] See "Statement of the Joint PAS/PASS Workshop on Sustainable Humanity, Sustainable Nature: Our Responsibility", *The Pontifical Academy of Social Sciences*, [Available at: http://www.pass.va/content/scienzesociali/en/events/2014-18/sustainable/statement.html], [Last accessed: 14th May 2022].

[9] See Nicholas Stern, "Fostering Growth and Poverty Reduction in a World of Immense Risk" (Webinar organised by the International Monetary Fund and the Global Resources Institute, 2nd April 2013), [Available at: https://www.wri.org/events/2013/04/fostering-growth-and-poverty-reduction-world-immense-risk], [Last accessed: 14th May 2022].

[10] "Climate Vulnerability Monitor, 2nd Edition. A Guide to the Cold Calculus of a Hot Planet", *DARA*, [Available at: http://daraint.org/climate-vulnerability-monitor/climate-vulnerability-monitor-2012/], [Last accessed: 14th May 2022].

Climate change is a huge constraint to genuine development in all its dimensions. However, *integral sustainable development* is essential for mitigating and adapting to climate change.

The Current So-Called "Development Model" is the Main Cause of Environmental Deterioration

Although it is true that the causes of these precarious life situations are multiple and complex, both the concrete experience and the analysis of experts from different fields of knowledge show that the fundamental cause of the problem is anthropogenic, and requires reflection and action from faith, because the care of the common home is at stake, a charge of the Creator to humanity.

The conventional model of economic growth is based largely on the consumption of energy based on oil, gas and coal. However, this pattern, coupled with the excessive profit motive of an irresponsible extractive activity, is clearly unsustainable, both for the Global North and South.

> Preserving nature is very often subordinated to economic development, with damage to biodiversity, exhaustion of water reserves and other natural resources, air pollution, and climate change. [...] Latin America [...] is affected by the warming of the earth and climate change caused primarily by the unsustainable way of life of industrialised countries.[11]

The production model of our current societies is based on consumerism and the rapid increase in business profits, which has led to a serious ecological imbalance: excessive consumption of non-renewable raw materials, noise, visual and atmospheric pollution, disappearance of species and climate change. This so-called "development model" is the "breeding ground" of the current crisis.[12]

In addition, environmental degradation is directly linked to poverty and social exclusion: poverty and "ecological misery" are inseparable.[13] There can be no ecological harmony in a world of unjust social structures. And, conversely, extreme social inequalities cannot lead to environmental sustainability, since "everything is interconnected" on earth, our common home.[14] All this is not only an *economic and environmental issue*, "the ecological crisis is a moral issue."[15]

Let Us Build an Alternative Vision

From a Christian perspective, it is necessary to take into account:

- A vision of the universe that substantiates human responsibility and accountability for the destiny of the earth, our planet;
- A consistent respect for human life, and for all forms of life that unfold throughout creation;
- A vision that affirms the ethical sense of global interdependence and the common good that is now dimensioned in a global common good;
- An ethic of solidarity that promotes fraternal co-operation and fair sharing in the world community;

---

[11] CELAM, *V General Conference*, sec. 66.

[12] CELAM, "Declaración final".

[13] See about the Pastoral Letter of 1988 of the Bishops of the Philippines on the ecological crisis in *Justice écologique 2011-2016, Reflexion 1 Developpement et paix*, [Available at: https://www.devp.org/fr/], [Last accessed: 14th May 2022].

[14] See Francis, *Laudato Si'* (Vatican City: Editora Vaticana, 2015).

[15] John Paul II, "Peace with God the Creator, Peace will All of Creation. Message of H.H. Pope John Paul II for the celebration of the World Day of Peace, January 1, 1990", sec. IV, 15, [Available at: https://www.vatican.va/content/john-paul-ii/en/messages/peace/documents/hf_jp-ii_mes_19891208_xxiii-world-day-for-peace.html], [Last accessed: 14th May 2022].

- The understanding of the universal destination of the goods of creation, which requires the equitable use of the planet's natural resources;
- The preferential option for poor people that encourages the search for a just and sustainable world;
- A concept of genuine integral human development in solidarity that guides progress that is respectful of human dignity and of the limits of material growth based on a dignified life.[16]

This alternative vision requires a socio-environmental policy aimed at finding true solutions to the integral ecological problem that we currently face.

Socio-Environmental Justice is Necessary[17]

The Lord tells us: "Blessed are those who hunger and thirst for righteousness, for they will be filled" (Mt. 5:6).

The sense of *justice* entails actions and attitudes that interrelate all those involved, taking into account the equality of rights, respect, care for each other, full inclusion. And when referring to the "socio-environmental" question, we take into account what Pope Francis says:

> It is essential to seek comprehensive solutions which consider the interactions within natural systems themselves and with social systems. We are faced not with two separate crises, one environmental and the other social, but rather with one complex crisis which is both social and environmental. Strategies for a solution demand an integrated approach to combating poverty, restoring dignity to the excluded, and at the same time protecting nature.[18]

Therefore, when the problems that affect humanity are considered, it must be taken into account that everything is interrelated, everything is integrated with each other:

> Today, however, we have to realise that a true ecological approach *always* becomes a social approach; it must integrate questions of justice in debates on the environment, so as to hear *both the cry of the earth and the cry of the poor.*[19]

Socio-environmental justice is deeply interrelated with integral ecology.

Human and Social Justice

The question of human and social justice raises the need for us to analyse the context in which peoples in general suffer the consequences of a predatory model, which mainly seeks profit and wealth at all costs; of a model that leaves aside the care of the goods of creation and the rights of the persons and peoples that inhabit the communities, many of which subsist since time immemorial and ancestral, contributing to the preservation of the goods of creation for humanity and the planet as a whole.

It is about confronting the situations of injustice that cause these predatory processes to destroy the ecosystem and the communities who inhabit it, especially the most fragile and vulnerable, affecting the peoples who often cannot make their voices heard or are simply not taken into account. This configures an

---

[16] United States Conference, "Renewing", sec. 3.

[17] This section is based on the axis "Justicia Socio-Ambiental y Buen Vivir" of the *Declaración fundacional de la Red Eclesiástica PanAmazónica*, "Pan-Amazonía: fuente de la vida en el corazón de la Iglesia, Brasilia, 12th September 2014", [Available at: https://jesuitas.lat/redes-sociales/documentos/cpal-social/declaracion-de-la-creacion-de-la-red-eclesial-pan-amazonica-repam-pan-amazonia-fuente-de-vida-en-el-corazon-de-la-iglesia], [Last accessed: 14th May 2022].

[18] Francis, *Laudato Si'*, 139.

[19] Francis, *Laudato Si'*, 49 (italics are original).

unfair situation, not only because it reduces their chances of life, making them victims of global phenomena, such as climate change, but also because it ignores the immense contribution that these communities and peoples have been making to conserve and maintain biomes, cultures and ancestral knowledge. All of them have great value both for the peoples themselves, as well as for humanity as a whole, since from their worldviews they propose alternative lifestyles, which will allow the continued life of the human species on the face of the earth and the planet itself.

That is why Pope Francis draws our attention when he says:

> Since the world has been given to us, we can no longer view reality in a purely utilitarian way, in which efficiency and productivity are entirely geared to our individual benefit. Intergenerational solidarity is not optional, but rather a basic question of justice, since the world we have received also belongs to those who will follow us.[20]

Environmental Justice

The Encyclical *Laudato Si'* insists on the conviction that caring for the environment is an act of recognition of the Creator and the Creator's work: "Together with our obligation to use the earth's goods responsibly, we are called to recognise that other living beings have a value of their own in God's eyes: 'by their mere existence they bless him and give him glory.'"[21]

Environmental justice works for the livelihoods of the people and those who inhabit the biomes to maintain their context, validity and contributions to life. This is also social justice, given that it is based on the recognition of the rights of peoples, on their defence and integral development, and on the deep appreciation of their contributions to the human family from time immemorial until today, in perspective and looking forward.[22]

The obsessive search for profit and power, and the disrespect for Mother Earth, lead to the belief that there are owners/proprietors of the biomes. This is why Pope Francis reminds us:

> We have come to see ourselves as her lords and masters, entitled to plunder her at will. The violence present in our hearts, wounded by sin, is also reflected in the symptoms of sickness evident in the soil, in the water, in the air and in all forms of life. This is why the earth herself, burdened and laid waste, is among the most abandoned and maltreated of our poor; she "groans in travail" (Rom 8:22). We have forgotten that we ourselves are dust of the earth (Gen. 2:7); our very bodies are made up of her elements, we breathe her air and we receive life and refreshment from her waters.[23]

Climate Justice

Socio-environmental justice requires climate justice, since it is necessary to contain global warming below 2°C,[24] taking into account what was agreed at COP 21, that it should be less than 1.5°C. This requires agricultural practices and technologies that increase productivity in a sustainable way, contributing to food security and promoting resilience.[25]

---

[20] Francisco, *Laudato Si'*, 159

[21] Francisco, *Laudato Si'*, 69

[22] See Benedicto XVI, *Caritas in veritate* (Vatican City: Editora Vaticana, 2009),

[23] Francis, *Laudato Si'*, 2.

[24] See the reflexions of the *ad hoc* Working Group on the Durban Platform for Enhanced Action (ADP), "Reflections on progress made at the fifth part of the second sesión" (ADP.2015.5. Informal Note, 7th July 2014).

[25] See United Nations – Subsidiary Body for Scientific and Technological Advice, "Report of the Subsidiary Body for Scientific and Technological Advice on its fortieth session, held in Bonn from 4 to 15 June, 2014," [Available at: https://unfccc.int/resource/docs/2014/sbsta/eng/02.pdf], [Last available: 14th May 2022].

It is urgent to materialise these intentions and agreements through a serious commitment, backed by adequate financing, leading to a definitive change in production and consumption patterns. All political decision-makers, international organisations and civil society must move towards a new social contract, which includes the environment and considers the impact of actions or inactions on future generations, since we have reached a point of no return. This cannot wait any longer!

- It is necessary to promote greater ecological and social responsibility of companies through the development of policies that guarantee responsible and sustainable business practices.[26]
- Mandatory requirements must be established for a greater focus on due diligence of companies regarding their social and ecological impacts.

Necessary Consciousness-Raising About the Care of the Goods Of Creation and the Promotion of Initiatives at all Levels

In Latin America and the Caribbean, the bishops and pastoral agents have valued the contribution of the encyclical *Laudato Si'* to the discussions, problems and alternatives of the climate crisis in our continent. This, with irrefutable theological foundations and a solid scientific base, has pointed out the urgencies, has valued the still weak results in the decisions of the highest authorities of the continent, and has called attention to the need to act promptly and change course towards a new lifestyle. This encyclical has had a great influence on the process and conclusions of the Pan-Amazonian Synod of October 2019, highlighting the need to work for integral ecology from social action and evangelisation in intercultural dialogue, especially with native peoples. These reflections and proposals are also evident in the challenges posed by the recent Ecclesial Assembly, held at the end of November 2021.

There is no doubt that it is urgent:

- To deepen the training processes of pastoral agents and allies in the care of the goods of creation and the transformation of social conflicts in the perspective of integral ecology;
- To accompany the processes already initiated for the defence of collective rights (prior consultation, environmental health, right to territory, water, bilingual intercultural education, among others).

It is also necessary:

- To give support to the pastoral agents of the communities that are facing socio-environmental conflicts in the perspective of the transformation of conflicts, highlighting emblematic cases, for which it is necessary to offer advisory services and accompaniment to dioceses, parishes and communities that thus request it;
- To develop practical experiences (experiential workshops) with pastoral agents and community leaders to face the problem of climate change in the light of the gospel, the social teaching of the church and the monitoring of local, national and international agreements (especially in what was agreed at COP 21);
- To promote initiatives to defend the quality of life from an integral ecology in the face of the problems of poverty, inequality, lack of work, especially in the most impoverished areas, from community

---

[26] Pontificio Consejo «Justicia y Paz», "La vocación del líder empresarial. Una reflexión", September 2012, [Available at: http://www.iustitiaetpax.va/content/dam/giustiziaepace/VBL/Vocacion%20esp_VBL.pdf], [Last accessed: 14th May 2022].
[TN: The Pontifical Council "Iustitia et Pax" has been merged with the Discatery for Promoting Integral Human Development. Available in English on the internet is the fifth edition of the Spanish language document that the author of this essay used: Discatery for Promoting Integral Human Development, "Vocation of the Business Leader: A Reflection," fifth edition, November 2018, accessed February 26, 2022, [Available at: https://www.humandevelopment.va/content/dam/sviluppoumano/pubblicazioni-documenti/documenti/vocation-of-the-business-leader-5th-edition/The%20Vocation%20of%20the%20Business%20Leader%20EN.pdf], [Last accessed: 14th May 2022].]

organisations and those of the solidarity economy, recognising and recovering the efforts of the ecclesial and local communities for the care of the goods of creation;
- To become aware both locally (micro) and nationally and globally (macro) that we have the ethical and theological imperative to contribute to the construction of a fairer and more supportive society. This involves processes "from below" as well as incidences in global instances, which constitute new areopaguses in which a prophetic voice needs to be heard.[27]

We emphatically reiterate that it is a false dilemma to choose between curbing climate change or fighting poverty and hunger. On the contrary, action against climate change is already an indispensable contribution to eradicating hunger, malnutrition and poverty, even more so in the current context of the COVID-19 pandemic.

Areas of Work to Deepen or Start

As faith-based organisations, we can act together in concrete actions from local spaces that are aimed at:
- Forming pastoral agents and social leaders for climate justice and care for creation;
- Strengthening specific pastoral actions and their articulation with other pastoral actions in the perspective of a joint and integral pastoral;
- Carrying out joint work in co-operation with other institutions and in civil society networks with which we share a common vision and fundamental values;
- Developing a voice and public advocacy in favour of fair policies that guarantee rights at the local, national and global levels.

In conclusion, we can say that the planet is currently groaning "in labour pains," that the cry of the earth and of the poor clamours out to heaven, demanding forceful answers. Our "common home" and those who inhabit it are at serious risk due to the maintenance of a pattern of exploitation solely oriented around the goal of profit at all costs. In the perspective of good co-habitation on the planet, we must orient ourselves towards a true integral and supportive human development, based on socio-environmental justice, on the sacred care of the goods of creation. An ecumenical socio-ecological diakonia as a service to humanity in current times must urgently contribute to this.

Suggestions for Further Reading

Assis, Raymundo Damasceno, *et al*. "Carta de Obispos de América Latina y el Caribe a la V Cumbre ALC-UE, Lima, 15 de mayo de 2008". *Con nuestro Perú,* 20th May 2008. [Available at: https://www.connuestroperu.com/actualidad/pronunciamientos/2060-carta-de-obispos-de-america-latina-y-el-caribe], [Last accessed: 14th May 2022].

Benedicto XVI. *Caritas in veritate.* Vatican City: Editora Vaticana, 2009.

Caritas Internationalis. *Agencias Internacionales de Desarrollo. Documento de Reflexión*. Vatican City: Caritas Internationalis, 2018.

CELAM. *V General Conference of the Episcopate of Latin America and the Caribbean. Concluding Document*. Aparecida 13th-31st May 2007. Bogotá: CELAM, 2007.

CELAM. "Declaración final del seminario sobre crisis financiera internacional, cambio climático y su impacto en los pobres, Lima, 3-7 mayo de 2009." [Available at: https://vidadelacer.org/index.php/comisiones/justicia-paz-ecol/1343-seminario-sobre-crisis-financiera-internacional-celam], [Last accessed: 14th May 2022].

Council of Bishops' Conferences of Europe. *A Christian View on Climate Change.* Saint Gallen, COMECE 2011.

---

[27] See CELAM, V Conferencia.

DARA. "Climate Vulnerability Monitor, 2nd Edition. A Guide to the Cold Calculus of a Hot Planet." *DARA Website*, [Available at: http://daraint.org/climate-vulnerability-monitor/climate-vulnerability-monitor-2012/], [Last accessed: 14th May 2022].

Discatery for Promoting Integral Human Development. "Vocation of the Business Leader: A Reflection," fifth edition. November 2018, [Available at: https://www.humandevelopment.va/content/dam/sviluppoumano/pubblicazioni-documenti/documenti/vocation-of-the-business-leader-5th-edition/The%20Vocation%20of%20the%20Business%20Leader%20EN.pdf], [Last accessed: 14th May 2022].

Francis. *Laudato Si'*. Vatican City: Editora Vaticana, 2015.

John Paul II. "Peace with God the Creator, Peace will All of Creation. Message of H.H. Pope John Paul II for the celebration of the World Day of Peace, January 1, 1990". *Vatican Website*. [Available at: https://www.vatican.va/content/john-paul-ii/en/messages/peace/documents/hf_jp-ii_mes_19891208_xxiii-world-day-for-peace.html], [Last accessed: 14th May 2022].

Justice écologique 2011-2016. Reflexion 1, Developpement et paix. [Available at: https://www.devp.org/fr/], [Last accessed: 14th May 2022].

Pontifical Council "Iustitia et Pax." "La vocación del líder empresarial. Una reflexión." September 2012. [Available at: http://www.iustitiaetpax.va/content/dam/giustiziaepace/VBL/Vocacion%20esp_VBL.pdf], [Last accessed: 14th May 2022].

Red Eclesiástica Pan Amazónica. "Pan-Amazonia: fuente de la vida en el corazón de la Iglesia, Brasilia, 12 de septiembre de 2014". [Available at: https://jesuitas.lat/redes-sociales/documentos/cpal-social/declaracion-de-la-creacion-de-la-red-eclesial-pan-amazonica-repam-pan-amazonia-fuente-de-vida-en-el-corazon-de-la-iglesia], [Last accessed: 14th May 2022].

Stern, Nicholas. "Fostering Growth and Poverty Reduction in a World of Immense Risk". Webinar organised by the International Monetary Fund and the Global Resources Institute, 2nd April 2013. [Available at: https://www.wri.org/events/2013/04/fostering-growth-and-poverty-reduction-world-immense-risk], [Last accessed: 14th May 2022].

United Nations – Subsidiary Body for Scientific and Technological Advice, "Report of the Subsidiary Body for Scientific and Technological Advice on its fortieth session, held in Bonn from 4 to 15 June, 2014." [Available at: https://unfccc.int/resource/docs/2014/sbsta/eng/02.pdf], [Last accessed: 14th May 2022].

United States Conference of Catholic Bishops. "Renewing the Earth: An Invitation to Reflection and Action on Environment in Light of Catholic Social Teaching. A Pastoral Statement of the United States Catholic Conference, November 14, 1991". [Available at: https://www.usccb.org/resources/renewing-earth], [Last accessed: 14th May 2022].

Section III

Trends, Key Issues and Best Practise Models for Creation Care and Eco-Diakonia

PART I: AFRICA AND MIDDLE EAST

62. FULLNESS OF LIFE AND HARMONY WITH NATURE: A MODEL FOR ADDRESSING CLIMATE CHANGE AND MIGRATION IN SOUTHERN AFRICA

Buhle Mpofu[1]

Introduction

This contribution drew on my previous research to propose an African model for an environmental response which presents a potentially constructive theological approach to care of creation. Exploring the African worldview, this model illustrates how the concept of unity between 'self and the entire *Kosmos*' in African worldview presents a potentially constructive African theology of ecology which should address environment induced migration challenges in Africa. In order to address migration of people displaced by floods, drought and other climate challenges, it is proposed that humanity should restore harmony with nature in order to attain fullness of life – *oikodome* – by extending the notions of healing, reconciliation and restoration to human interactions with nature.

One of my recent publications 'Pursuing fullness of life through harmony with nature: Towards an African response to environmental destruction and climate change in Southern Africa,' made the following observation as its central thesis:

> … nature has become violent with humanity, because we have been violent with nature. The implications of this is that destructive human activities lead to destructive natural disasters. It is my view that excessive and exploitative human economic activities affect harmony in nature – and all things are competing or at war with each other and humanity is at the centre of this disharmony.'[2]

In order to address climate change challenges, this contribution suggested that we need to take human relations with nature seriously and drew on the notions of 'cultural landscapes' and 'eco-theology' to underscore the significance of the African worldview in addressing the disharmony that has been created by excessive exploitation of natural resources. The thesis of this contribution underscored the argument that '…nature has become violent with humanity, because humanity has been violent with nature.'[3] At the time of writing this contribution, heat waves were causing fires that left a trail of destruction on Europe, with lives and properties lost.[4]

---

[1] Buhle Mpofu is a lecturer of Religion and Mission studies within the Faculty of Theology and Region at the University of Pretoria in South Africa. Mpofu did his Post-Doctoral Fellowship with the University of KwaZulu-Natal, School of Religion, Classics and Philosophy and is also an ordained minister with the Uniting Presbyterian Church in Southern Africa (UPCSA), with a background in ecumenical work and served as the General Secretary of the African Communion of Reformed Churches (ACRC). Contact email: buhle.mpofu@up.ac.za

[2] Mpofu, Buhle, 'Pursuing fullness of life through harmony with nature: Towards an African response to environmental destruction and climate change in Southern Africa', *HTS Teologiese Studies / Theological Studies* 77, no. 4 (2021): 1-8.

[3] Mpofu, 'Pursuing fullness of life', 6.

[4] For example, see News 24, *Greek heatwave: Seven deadly European summers*. Accessed 13 August 2021 from: https://www.news24.com/news24/world/news/greek-heatwave-seven-deadly-european-summers-20210802.

Responding to Climate Change

Climate change and its devastating impact is now a global phenomenon and there are ongoing discourses on its responses in various countries. The Food and Agricultural Organisation (FAO)[5] is responsible for monitoring the impact of "diverse challenges, including rapid population growth and urbanisation, changes in patterns of food consumption, globalisation of the agriculture sector, economic crises, the impacts of environmental changes, including climate change…."[6] This report also states that "many agricultural systems are becoming less productive and some plants and animal species disappearing."[7] Therefore, the impact of climate change is affecting the agricultural production with devastating social and economic consequences which include food security, displacement of communities, drought, heat waves and floods. For example, in Southern Africa, the impact of climate change has been felt through the El Nino drought in 2015, which left a devastating trail of destruction in the region and affected the livelihoods of many people in Zimbabwe, Mozambique, Malawi and Zambia. This was followed by cyclone Dineo, which caused damage to agriculture and destroyed homes in Mozambique and parts of South Africa's North-west province.[8] It is for this reason that a recent United Nations scientific report[9] warned that climate change is "code red for humanity", highlighted how human activities are impacting on the climate in "unprecedented and sometimes irreversible ways",[10] and stated there is an urgent need to cut carbon emission from green house gases in order to stabilise rising temperatures.

> Climate change has become a major concern for the international community. Among its consequences, its impact on migration is the object of increasing attention from both policy-makers and researchers. Yet, knowledge in this field remains limited and fragmented.[11]

During the COVID-19 lockdown period in 2020, carbon dioxide and methane levels increased, despite reduction in global economic activity as most non-essential services were forced to shut down. According to Sheree Bega,[12] most of these emissions are attributed to human activities which are "predominantly, although not entirely, from biogenic sources as wetlands and ruminants of cattle and sheep."[13] Global economic activity also contributes to climate change through industrial pollution and carbon emissions and despite COVOD-19 lockdowns, there were no significant changes in global carbon emissions. According to the National Oceanic and Atmospheric Administration (NOAA), carbon levels are now higher than any

[5] Food and Agriculture Organisation (FAO), 'International Regulatory Co-operation and International Organisations: The Case of the Food and Agriculture Organization of the United Nations (FAO)', 2016, accessed 13 August 2021 from: https://www.oecd.org/gov/regulatory-policy/FAO_Full-Report.pdf, 15.

[6] FAO, 'International Regulatory Co-operation', 15.

[7] FAO, 'International Regulatory Co-operation', 20.

[8] Conradie, Ernst, 'Praying for rain? Reformed perspectives from the Southern African context', in S.G. Brown, E. Chitando & E. Conradie (eds.), 'Praying for rain? African perspectives on religion and climate change', *The Ecumenical Review* 69, No. 3 (2017): 315–326. https://doi.org/10.1111/erev.12295, 319.

[9] McGrath, Matt, 'Climate change: IPCC report is 'code red for humanity'', accessed 13 August 2021 from: https://www.bbc.com/news/science-environment-58130705.

[10] McGrath, *Climate change*, 1.

[11] Piguet, Étienne, Pécoud, A., and de Guchteneire, P. *Migration and Climate Change: an Overview* (Oxford: Oxford University Press, 2010). Accessed 17 April 2021 from: https://environmentalmigration.iom.int/migration-and-climate-change overview#:~:text=Climate%20change%20has%20become%20a,field%20remains%20limited %20and%20fragmented.

[12] Bega, Sheree, 'Carbon dioxide, methane levels surge despite Corvid-19 lockdowns', 2021. Available at: https://mg.co.za/environment/2021-04-16-carbon-dioxide-methane-levels-surge-despite-covid-19-lockdowns/?utm_term=Autofeed&utm_medium=Social&utm_source=Facebook&fbclid=IwAR1jKHhakZL4Kgauzl CwWJC5lG-gqrWHBm_jkPLadA2B2pwVRu1FMH3P9aE#Echobox=1618575479. Accessed 17 April 2021.

[13] Bega, *Carbon dioxide, methane levels surge*, 1.

time in the past 3.6 million years when concentrations ranged from about 380 to 450 parts per million (ppm).[14] These developments have impacted on the movement of people in most parts of the world, as they seek safety from flood-prone areas and search for pastoral land – especially in Africa, where most rural communities rely on agricultural land. As Luo *et al* have rightly observed:

> Climate change is a greater driver of change in population exposure to river floods than socioeconomic development, because both the frequency and intensity of river floods is expected to increase due to climate change in many areas. This phenomenon would expand flood-prone areas, and make floods more likely to occur in those areas more often.[15]

Given the above challenges, this contribution proposes an African model for a harmonious relationship between humanity and all of God's creation as means to attain just, equitable and sustainable communities who care for creation. I will now illustrate this model and demonstrate how the concept of unity between 'self and the entire *Kosmos*' in the African worldview presents a potentially constructive African theology of ecology which should address environment induced migration and other climate challenges in Africa and the world.

An African Model for Harmony with Nature

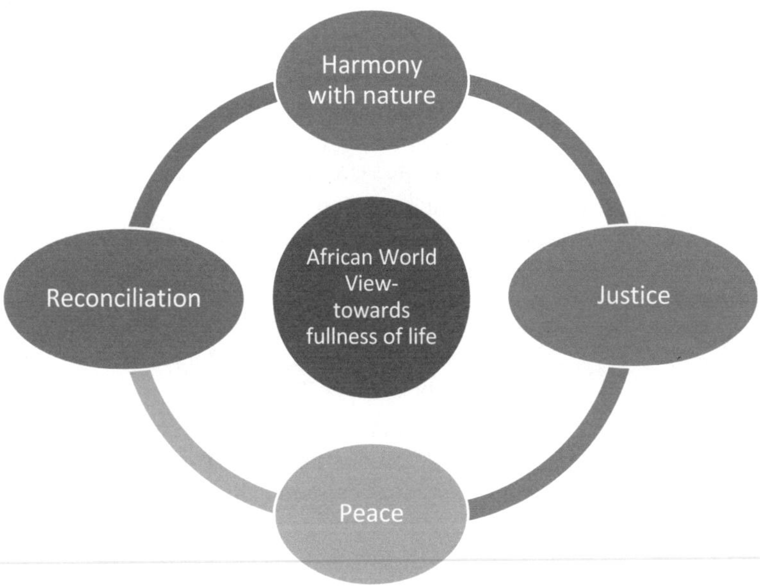

Figure 1. A model for harmony with nature

[14] Mavrokefalidis, Dimitris, 'Scientists warn CO2 levels in 2020 were 'higher than anytime in the last 3.6m years', *Energy Live News*, 2021. Accessed 17 April 2021 from: https://www.energylivenews.com/2021/04/12/scientists-warn-co2-levels-in-2020-were-higher-than-anytime-in-the-last-3-6m-years/.

[15] Tianyi, Luo, Maddocks A., Iceland C., Ward P., and Winsemius H. 2015. 'World's 15 Countries with the Most People Exposed to River Floods'. *World Resources Institute (WRI).* Available at: https://www.wri.org/blog/2015/03/world-s-15-countries-most-people-exposed-river-floods. Accessed 18/04/2021.

It is important to mention this model was informed by concepts which were developed in the article, 'Pursuing fullness of life through harmony with nature: Towards an African response to environmental destruction and climate change in Southern Africa'.[16] The thesis of this paper was that nature has become violent with humanity, because we have been violent with nature. I argued that there is no harmony in human engagement with nature and that the created order is now at war with itself in ways that impact on the 'equilibrium' of nature.

African Worldview

At the heart of this model is the African worldview – as demonstrated in the diagram above – and this is an ideology that underpins the pursuit of a harmonious relationship between humanity and the created order of the universe in the proposed model. In Africa, life is understood through a concept of '*ubuntu*' (humanity) which places emphasis on '*umuntu ngumuntu ngabantu*' – which literally means 'a person is a person because of other people'. This construction considers individuals within a community as a collective. People are not viewed as individuals, but individuals who are in relationship with their community and the world around them. This approach has emphasis on collaborative unity between humanity, spirituality and the material world (nature) as highlighted by Forster:

> [T]he essential unity between self and others, as well as the self and the entire *Kosmos*, is a vitally important aspect in relating the African world view to an integrated approach to consciousness.[17]

Africans understand their relationships in community with each other and the world around them. If we appreciate that in Africa people are not considered individually, but in relationship with the community, the world of nature around them and the unseen spiritual beings or God, it is therefore important that we develop holistic models of care for creation which are grounded on the understanding that God's created order places humanity at the centre of having dominion (Genesis 1:26). However, such dominion should be sustainable and fruitful (Genesis 1:28) so that the blessing of God will translate to a peaceful and harmonious relationship with all of God's creation. It is for this reason that this contribution extends the notions of justice, peace and reconciliation to explore the possibility of a world reconciled with itself through harmonious relationships for all of God's creation.

Justice, Peace and Reconciliation

In a way that resonates with this proposed model, the All Africa Conference of Churches (AACC) located the program of Climate Change under *Peace, Diakonia and Development* within its strategic plan[18] in a document that outlines key focus areas highlighting programmatic goals and interventions for member churches to, among other things:

> …educate members churches on the challenge of environmental and climate Justice and the imperatives of an eco-theology in African contexts…[by] address[sing] issues of land and water justice, creatively engage with UN Agenda 2030 and African Union 'Agenda 2063: The Africa We Want', equip churches to monitor implementation and hold their governments accountable … advocate for churches' commitment to economic

---

[16] Mpofu, 'Pursuing fullness of life', 1.

[17] Forster, Dion A., 'A generous ontology: Identity as a process of intersubjective discovery, An African theological contribution', *THS Teologiese Studies/Theological Studies* 66, no. 1 (2010): 82. https://doi.org/10.4102/hts.v66i1.731.

[18] All Africa Conference of Churches (AACC), *AACC Strategy:2019-2023* (Nairobi: AACC Publications, 2019), 13.

> justice in the continent, equip churches to monitor governments borrowing (ethical decision-making) [and] address issues of corruption.

It is ironic that this document links ethical decision-making with the challenge of corruption which is prevalent in the African context, where economic exploitation of resources leads to environmental destruction. The implication of this is that the AACC affirms the idea that climate change challenges, in part, emanate from human greed characterised by unethical environmental exploitation. Dealing with such challenges will require a broadened approach which encompasses the concepts of justice, peace and reconciliation within the context of human interactions with nature. It is for this reason that the AACC strategically locates the programme of climate change within the broader developmental agenda of *Peace, Diakonia and Development*. Some pillars of the program extend to the following key areas:

- Encouraging churches to have disaster preparedness and management systems (effective early warning systems).
- Assisting churches to play a proactive role in preventing potential conflicts (e.g. related to land, water and other natural resources).
- Facilitating reconciliation and mediation initiatives.
- Encouraging churches to include the issue of migration and human trafficking in the church agenda.19

Notably, this approach does not isolate natural disasters from the environmental socio-economic disruptions which emanate from unethical economic practices. For example, when multinational corporations engage in unethical industrial practices which destroy the environment, affected communities usually lodge legal claims sometimes creating tensions between companies and local communities. This is common in mining activities where communities suffer consequences such as destroyed livelihoods, poor health, environmental degradation and displacement. Under such circumstances, pursuit of justice, peace and reconciliation become arbitrary means to restore harmony. Therefore, the agency of religious communities in environmental justice and sustainability must be linked to collaborations which seek to address human conditions that are a result of violent and unethical environmental practices.

This approach is also reflected in the Word Council of Churches (WCC)'s Pilgrimage of Justice and Peace Program,[20] which calls on its member churches to:

> ...work together in a common quest, renewing the true vocation of the church through collaborative engagement with the most important issues of justice and peace, healing a world filled with conflict, injustice and pain.[21]

For the WCC, working together means that member churches will pursue healing and restoration of the world as means to attain peace and justice. When the environment is destroyed, pain is inflicted, not just on the environment, but also on the poor people whose livelihoods are destroyed, are displaced from their communities and are then forced to migrate in search of better living conditions. Therefore, there is a need for awareness regarding the impact of climate change in ways that help faith communities to appreciate and empower communities to become "people who know the story they are part of."[22] Christopher Wright is one of the few Western scholars who approaches the mission of God's people from a perspective informed by the African world view, as he defines God's people as "people who care for creation" and uses this hermeneutical approach to emphasize that redemption is God's plan for all of God's creation.[23]

---

[19] AACC *Strategy*, 12.
[20] World Council of Churches (WCC), 2017, *Pilgrimage for justice and peace*, accessed 13 August 2021, from https://archived.oikoumene.org/en/what-we-do/ pilgrimage-of-justice-and-peace, 441.
[21] WCC, *Pilgrimage for justice and peace*, 441.
[22] Christopher Wright, *The mission of God's people* (Grand Rapids: Zondervan, 2010), 35.
[23] Wright, *The mission of God's people*, 35.

For Wright, the church's mission should be holistic and encompass all human endeavours from the perspective of God's plan for redemption. It is for this reason that Wright develops his theology of the People of God's mission from themes which include: For God, For Us, Forever;[24] God's Glory as the Goal of Creation,[25] Human Life and Creation Integrally Bound Together,[26] The Earth Suffers with Us,[27] and God's Redemption Incudes Creation.[28] Thus, Wright underscores the significant observation that:

> Creation is not just the disposable backdrop to the lives of human creatures … we are not redeemed out of creation, but … part of redeemed creation itself … God will vindicate the oppressed, restore wholesome relationships, and bring peace and justice to earth.[29]

Harmony with Nature – A Model towards Fullness of Life

The above discussion underscores the fact that God's redemption involves all of his creation and by implication, when the earth (creation) suffers violence, we (humanity) also suffer with (or from) creation because we are not yet redeemed out of creation. Wright's emphasis on a collective destination for both humanity and nature underscores how his theology approaches humanity and the created universe as integrally 'bound together' within the broader framework of God's created redemptive purpose. This approach resonates with Biblical concepts of '*shalom*' which goes much further than the common understanding of 'peace', as can be discerned in a closer analysis of the Old Testament prophets' vision for the future which God intended. For examples of how these different aspects of 'shalom' or 'wholeness' are articulated in the Bible, see Micah 4:1-5, Isaiah 65:17-25, Jeremiah 31:2-14, and Ezekiel 34:11-31.[30]

It is important to highlight that God's purpose with creation was to maintain an orderly and harmonious world, and that this is better encapsulated or reflected within the African worldview. For Africans, the created universe is comprised of both seen and unseen, that is the spiritual world and spirit beings – human beings, plants, animals, mountains, waters, and all that is in the world in its entirety. This is the rationale behind a common African belief that, "through the laws of nature and various spiritual forces, as well as human customs and institutions, God sustains and upholds the world. Thus, he maintains an orderly and harmonious world so that all can perform their own duties in it."[31]

Therefore, in order to maintain harmony within the created order of the universe, humanity should seek to live peacefully and justly, not just with one another, but also with all living things (both those that are seen and those that are not seen). All of creation must enjoy peace and order with each other – human being, plants, animals, rivers and seas together with the unseen world – God, the ancestors and spirit beings. As I have demonstrated elsewhere,[32] this understanding is paramount to African practices where there are times when it is necessary for individuals, families or community groups to perform certain rituals as a way to restore the equilibrium in creation or to influence change in a particular state of affairs – this is considered as seeking of healing, or reconciliation, prosperity, asking for a blessing, or even seeking guidance.[33] This model for harmony with nature is a significant contribution in that it lays a foundation for integrating new

---

[24] Wright, *The mission of God's people*, 52.
[25] Wright, *The mission of God's people*, 53.
[26] Wright, *The mission of God's people*, 54.
[27] Wright, *The mission of God's people*, 55.
[28] Wright, *The mission of God's people*, 55.
[29] Wright, *The mission of God's people*, 56.
[30] Galpin, Mark, 'Moving from vision to practice: making fullness of life practical', *Micah Global: 6th Global Consultation* (Lima: United Mission to Nepal, 2015), 6. Accessed 13 August 2021 from: https://www.globalconnections.org.uk/sites/newgc.localhost/files/papers/fullness_of_life_galpin.pdf.
[31] Forster, 'A generous ontology', 83.
[32] Mpofu, 'Pursuing fullness of life', 8.
[33] Forster, 'A generous ontology', 37.

scientific perspectives on the natural world with traditional African and theological perspectives in developing a new hermeneutical or theological paradigm towards an African 'constructive eco-theology' which facilitates interrelationships between humanity and nature as means to explore African community-based, life-affirming and transformative responses to environmental destruction.

Conclusion

This proposed model for a reconciled and harmonious relationship between humanity and nature is grounded on the idea that in Africa, people are not considered individually, but in relationship with each other as a community and the world of nature around them, including the unseen spiritual beings. It is therefore necessary to emphasize that this understanding of '*ubuntu*' underscores the epistemological basis for an African eco-theology that is grounded on the collective unity between humanity, their spirituality and the material world around them.

The models and concepts of development for a response to the environmental crisis should take African values and spirituality seriously. This includes faith communities interventions and discourses of developmental agenda which are often motivated by moral ideals and notions of virtue taken from religious communities. Although there is a tendency for political instrumental engagement with 'faith-based' communities to motivate for Western-centred notions of development, these notions often conflict with alternative concepts of development devised by religious communities such as 'human flourishing' or 'fullness of life.' These intersections highlight conflicting concepts where local, traditional or globalised religious ideas and practices clash with scientifically informed methodologies, as evidenced in African Traditional Religions. Therefore, there is a need for contextually informed models of development that place African values at the centre of human interactions.

For Further Reading

All Africa Conference of Churches (AACC), *AACC Strategy:2019-2023* (Nairobi: AACC Publications, 2019)

Bega, Sheree, 'Carbon dioxide, methane levels surge despite Corvid-19 lockdowns', 2021. Available at: https://mg.co.za/environment/2021-04-16-carbon-dioxide-methane-levels-surge-despite-covid-19-lockdowns/?utm_term=Autofeed&utm_medium=Social&utm_source=Facebook&fbclid=IwAR1jKHhakZL4KgauzlCwWJC5lG-gqrWHBm_jkPLadA2B2pwVRu1FMH3P9aE#Echobox=1618575479

Conradie, Ernst, 'Praying for rain? Reformed perspectives from the Southern African context', in S.G. Brown, E. Chitando & E. Conradie (eds.), 'Praying for rain? African perspectives on religion and climate change', *The Ecumenical Review* 69, No. 3 (2017): 315–326.

Piguet, Étienne, Pécoud, A., and de Guchteneire, P. *Migration and Climate Change: an Overview* (Oxford: Oxford University Press, 2010)

Food and Agriculture Organisation (FAO), 'International Regulatory Co-operation and International Organisations: The Case of the Food and Agriculture Organization of the United Nations (FAO)', 2016, https://www.oecd.org/gov/regulatory-policy/FAO_Full-Report.pdf, 15.

Forster, Dion A., 'A generous ontology: Identity as a process of intersubjective discovery, An African theological contribution', *THS Teologiese Studies/Theological Studies* 66, no. 1 (2010)

Galpin, Mark, 'Moving from vision to practice: making fullness of life practical', *Micah Global: 6th Global Consultation* (Lima: United Mission to Nepal, 2015)

McGrath, Matt, 'Climate change: IPCC report is 'code red for humanity'', *BBC News*, https://www.bbc.com/news/science-environment-58130705.

Mpofu, Buhle, 'Pursuing fullness of life through harmony with nature: Towards an African response to environmental destruction and climate change in Southern Africa', *HTS Teologiese Studies / Theological Studies* 77, no. 4 (2021): 1-8.

News 24, *Greek heatwave: Seven deadly European summers.* https://www.news24.com/news24/world/news/greek-heatwave-seven-deadly-european-summers-20210802.

Tianyi, Luo, Maddocks A., Iceland C., Ward P., and Winsemius H. 2015. 'World's 15 Countries with the Most People Exposed to River Floods'. *World Resources Institute (WRI).*

Mavrokefalidis, Dimitris, 'Scientists warn CO2 levels in 2020 were 'higher than anytime in the last 3.6m years', *Energy Live News*, 2021

World Council of Churches (WCC), 2017, *Pilgrimage for justice and peace*, accessed 13 August 2021, from https://archived.oikoumene.org/en/what-we-do/ pilgrimage-of-justice-and-peace

Wright, C.J.H., *The Mission of God's People* (Grand Rapids: Zondervan, 2010)

63. Eco-Justice and Food Sovereignty – Perspectives of SAFCEI's Work in Southern Africa

Francesca de Gasparis[1]

The Southern African Faith Communities' Environment Institute (SAFCEI)[2] is a faith-based environmental organisation, comprised of people of many faiths united in diversity through a common commitment to cherish the earth. Based in Cape Town and working across the SADC region, SAFCEI supports faith leaders and communities in fulfilling their environmental and socio-economic responsibility, in order to bring about a more sustainable future. This includes people in leadership positions in their faith structures, laypersons, local congregations, and the wider community. Through collaboration, networking, research and action, the organisation seeks to raise environmental and climate change awareness, engage in influencing policy and ethical guidelines, and encourage environmental responsibility and action-taking.

By supporting faith environmental networks, SAFCEI assists the exchange of ideas and sharing of best practice in terms of environmental justice. A multi-faith organisation, it draws on the perspectives of a diverse range of faiths in implementing its vision. People of different faiths are brought together to work on the cross-cutting issues that they as 'earthkeepers' have in common, whether local – such as tree planting along a riparian zone in Malawi – or global – such as drafting a statement on climate change from people of faith in Africa for COP26. Through engagement, interfaith partnerships are formed, as people work together to achieve environmental sustainability. SAFCEI has established contacts with councils of churches and other faith-based organisations throughout Southern Africa – in Angola, Botswana, Lesotho, Malawi, Mozambique, Swaziland, Tanzania, Zambia, and Zimbabwe – and stretching further across the continent to Uganda.

The role of faith leaders in society at this time of chaotic environmental devastation and the Covid-19 pandemic has never been clearer. Faith leaders are not only the custodians of their environment and champions of those most vulnerable in society, they also have a moral imperative and standing in their communities to be able to advocate for policy change to the powers on the African continent and beyond. In following the ethics and values of their respective faiths, they are able to petition for local environmental solutions that rehabilitate the planet and promote sustainable livelihoods, because this is both the morally right thing to do and what science tells us needs to be done.

SAFCEI aims to empower faith leaders to stand up and make their voices heard by providing credible and independently verified science-based information with a focus on understanding the nexus between good governance, a stable society, and environmental responsibility. We build capacities, so faith leaders are better able to advocate and teach their communities, and take action collectively.[3]

A high percentage of people in Southern Africa practice a religion, with at least 86% of South Africans adhering to the Christian faith,[4] and this affords faith leaders status and allows them to assume the role of educating and informing their constituents. They bring a voice of reason and are widely recognised by both

---

[1] Francesca de Gasparis is the Executive Director of the Southern African Faith Communities' Environment Institute (SAFCEI). SAFCEI is a multi-faith environmental organisation committed to supporting faith leaders and their communities in Southern Africa to increase awareness, understanding and action on eco-justice, sustainable living, and climate change.

[2] See: https://safcei.org/.

[3] Ngonidzashe Edward, Kate and Geoff Davies, Francesca de Gasparis, 'Ethical Perspectives on interfaith approaches for ecological transformation in Southern Africa', in Cornelia Füllkrug-Weitzel and Dietrich Werner: *Ethics for Life. Voices from Ecumenical Partners on a New Paradigm of Life and Society* (Bread for the World: 2019), 173-182.

[4] See: https://www.indexmundi.com/south_africa/religions.html.

governments and civil society as playing a vital role in the achievement of (accountable and transparent) governance and eco-justice. Their role in society during crises, including the Covid-19 pandemic, demonstrates their ability to influence decision-making on issues that affect their communities and the natural environment, including urgently responding to environmental degradation and the climate crisis.

The Intergovernmental Panel on Climate Change (IPCC) report[5] obtained in late June 2021 by the Agence France-Presse (AFP) paints a devastating scenario if we do not adopt transformational change of our behaviour and practices, including a transition from industrial farming practices and the exploration and extraction of environmentally-damaging fossil fuels. The report gives stark warnings of species extinction, unliveable heat, widespread disease, rising sea levels, floods, wildfires, storms, and ecosystem collapse at the current trajectory of temperature rise due to greenhouse gas emissions from human activity.

The Southern African region finds itself at the brunt of these changing weather patterns and erratic climate conditions. Already, early signs of climate change are being experienced in our region. Much of South Africa has experienced drought from late 2018, including severe multi-year droughts in the Northern Cape, Karoo, and elsewhere, negatively affecting food security and social cohesion in the region. In 2020 drought continued in the Eastern Cape, while Western Cape and northern areas in South Africa and Zimbabwe had excessive rainfall. Science predicts that previously naturally occurring variations in temperature, drought and rain will be more and more erratic and extreme in intensity and length as global temperatures continue to rise.

Despite evidence of this unravelling, the predominance of industrial agriculture and fossil fuel extraction continues unabated in Southern Africa. This 'business as usual' approach is encouraged by the very same governments who have signed the Paris Agreement and committed to reducing damaging climate crisis impacts through their nationally determined contributions (NDCs). Governments remain intransigent, despite impassioned speeches at COP26[6] urging them to change the way of doing so that we can keep temperature rise predicted to 1.5 Celsius, which is the maximum limit for allowing for liveable conditions for much of the region.

Large industrial farming, whether large monoculture crops or livestock to feed our vast appetite for meat, is one of the largest contributors to the rise in global temperatures, as it releases vast volumes of greenhouse gases both in forest destruction and methane from farmed animals. Additionally, such farming practices reduce the capacity of the soil and vegetation to continue to provide vital carbon 'sinks' that fix carbon from the atmosphere. Regionally, industrial production of food causes large-scale environmental degradation and pollution, and spreads disease. The chemical fertilisers and pesticides utilised in monocropping run off into soils and waterways. The excessive waste from factory farms pollutes soil, water and air, depleting the natural environment. Food production and consumption methods contribute to the climate crisis, with increasing drought,[7] flooding and extreme weather patterns across the Southern African region, which in turn affect crops.

Factory farming also represents harsh industrial practices, in which animals are commodified. It is "a form of intensive agriculture designed to maximise profits using as few resources as possible … [where] large numbers of animals are confined in small spaces, which often means keeping [them] indoors for the

[5] Paris AFP, 'Crushing climate impacts to hit sooner than feared: draft UN report', *France 24*, June 23, 2021, https://www.france24.com/en/live-news/20210623-crushing-climate-impacts-to-hit-sooner-than-feared-draft-un-report.

[6] UN Climate Change, 'Speech: Mia Mottley, Prime Minister of Barbados at the Opening of the #COP26 World Leaders Summit', November 1, 2021, video, https://www.youtube.com/watch?v=PN6THYZ4ngM.

[7] See: https://www.iol.co.za/business-report/economy/kzn-food-security-in-state-of-disaster-zikalala-ee39484b-7639-4b44-9f32-a6a56f5fbbc4.

duration of their lives."[8] Harsh confinement includes battery cages and gestation or farrowing crates, almost completely restricting the movement of cows, sheep, pigs and hens.

South Africa is the thirteenth largest emitter of fossil fuels globally through its coal power plants. It is also a business leader in industrial food production that expands throughout Southern Africa and further north, via business supermarket and other chains, farming practices, ideologies about food systems and development. The rapid industrialisation of food systems and the impact on the African continent's ecosystems and human consumption patterns is a massive environmental and ethical challenge, and there is a direct correlation between unsustainable consumption and the climate crisis. The need is urgent to challenge the way in which food is produced, as the continent of Africa is the most vulnerable to climate change impacts,[9] due to its climate system and ongoing dry and warm conditions, and because it is under-developed. We need to challenge the predominance of industrialised food systems that weaken localised agri-food systems and accelerate the decline of indigenous food systems – destroying social and cultural practices, thereby denying all beings the right to a fulfilling life.

The centralised and highly concentrated industrial food system across the region means the poor are only able to access bad quality food. Food insecurity is understood as a situation where people do not have continuous physical or economic access to nutritious and safe food, as the distance to food access grows to the extent that communities are placed in food poverty which is then further exacerbated by climate impacts. The lack of food, particularly quality food, contributes to malnutrition and leads to hunger, poverty, and unemployment in rural communities. Chronic hunger has increased year-on-year since 2014. In sub-Saharan Africa,[10] 57% of the population cannot afford a healthy diet, and over 19% are malnourished. This chronic crisis is only set to get worse as governments continue to invest in top-down solutions promoted by businesses and corporate interests.

Prevailing socio-cultural norms commonly limit the ability of women[11] to exercise power and autonomous decision-making, disadvantaging them in accessing productive resources, innovative technologies, market information, financial services, and education and training. Although women play a vital role in growing,[12] processing and marketing food in developing countries, they have less access to assets, training and opportunities than men, and thus earn considerably less. Industrial farming and approaches that favour large-scale farmers and landowners have the potential to exacerbate women's poverty in integrated cash economies. The barring of girls and women from achieving their full potential inhibits progress to achieving productive, resilient and sustainable food systems that the region needs. Addressing gender inequalities is also key to overcoming the negative impacts of the Covid-19 pandemic on rural livelihoods, given that women play a crucial role in maintaining household food security.

Of particular concern to SAFCEI is the funding by the Bill and Melinda Gates Foundation of so-called 'green revolution technologies' through the Alliance for a Green Revolution in Africa (AGRA). Founded in 2006, it has received about one billion US dollars in donations – with two-thirds coming from the Gates Foundation, according to Timothy Wise, senior adviser at the Institute for Agriculture and Trade Policy.[13]

---

[8] The Humane League, 'Factory farming: what it is and why it's a problem', *THL*, December 1, 2020, https://thehumaneleague.org/article/what-is-factory-farming.

[9] See: https://www.iol.co.za/saturday-star/climate-change-apocalypse-17462385.

[10] See: https://www.who.int/news/item/13-07-2020-as-more-go-hungry-and-malnutrition-persists-achieving-zero-hunger-by-2030-in-doubt-un-report-warns.

[11] See: https://reliefweb.int/report/world/gender-inequalities-and-food-insecurity-ten-years-after-food-price-crisis-why-are-women.

[12] See: https://www.fao.org/3/x0171e/x0171e02.htm.

[13] Timothy Wise, 'The Gates Foundation's "Green Revolution" in Africa: Agribusiness Wins, Small Scale Farmers Lose', *Timothy A. Wise* (blog), July 15, 2020, https://www.timothyawise.com/blog/the-gates-foundations-green-revolution-in-africa-agribusiness-wins-small-scale-farmers-lose.

African governments, driven by AGRA's influence, have created tariff agreements and tax incentives that subsidise large agribusiness and worsen the crisis. Over 15 years, AGRA has restructured seed laws in favour of a limited range of genetically modified 'certified seeds' owned by corporations, which require inorganic fertilisers, must be repurchased for every planting, and force monocropping. In Africa, 80% of 'noncertified' seed comes from millions of smallholder farmers who recycle and exchange an open-source knowledge bank of fertile seeds. Industrialised farming undermines indigenous knowledge and community traditions, such as the saving and sharing of seeds. Coercing communities to embrace industrial farming through seed and other policy changes at the national government level is not a solution to poverty.

AGRA was founded on a promise to meet certain anti-poverty benchmarks by 2020. Data from AGRA's target countries, however, shows no significant alleviation of poverty. In fact, according to Wise, data shows a 30% *increase* in food insecurity.[14]

Access to adequate, agency-enabling food is a central tenet for the realisation of human and environmental rights. In the Southern African region where SAFCEI works, the majority of the population rely on food system-related activities, and primary livelihoods are directly dependent on natural resources, including clean water, healthy soils and air, and adequate sun and shade. However, at the same time, many people – and animals, and the environment – are exposed to food system-related injustices and unsustainable production and consumption practices, and lack the full realisation of their rights to adequate food and nutrition, which fundamentally compromises human capabilities, as well as individual and collective development.

African faith leaders are witnessing the negative impact of industrialised farming to the land and the well-being of their communities. They are calling for a shift to sustainable and agroecological farming that works in local contexts for people and does not harm the land. SAFCEI's response is to champion an ecosystems approach to food sovereignty and climate change, by promoting agroecology and opposing factory farming, industrial agriculture and GMOs. It supports calls for an equitable and sustainable food system in Africa, which is not to the detriment of small-scale producers and the plentiful availability of seed varieties. The Institute also supports a shift away from the ill treatment of animals. Likewise, the Evangelical Church in Germany (EKD),[15] in tackling the issue of livestock husbandry, writes of the challenge of dealing with fundamental ethical questions which surround the agrarian economy, animal ethics, veterinary medicine, economic efficiency and food culture. Although the industrial model of livestock agriculture delivers cheaper food, the environmental and public health bill and ill-treatment of animals bred for food is significant.

SAFCEI has led faith leader advocacy efforts concerning nationally determined contributions and food systems in the region. A notable success has been an African faith leader sign-on letter to the Bill and Melinda Gates Foundation by nearly 500 faith representatives and their supporters, and smallholder farmers, which challenges the Foundation's support for intensive industrial scale agricultural expansion that is undermining country level farming policies for traditional farming practices, such as seed banks and indigenous food crops, and ultimately heightens the ecological crisis and increases vulnerability of communities to climate change. Delivered in May 2021 to the Foundation, the letter delivered a strong message, declaring that "the Gates Foundation's support for the expansion of intensive industrial scale agriculture is deepening the humanitarian crisis."[16] The letter – shared beyond the region, more broadly in

---

[14] Ibid.

[15] Evangelische Kirche in Deutschland (EKD), *Livestock and Fellow Creatures! Animal Welfare, Sustainability and the Ethics of Nutrition from a Protestant Perspective* (EKD, September 2019). Available at: www.ekd.de/en/Texts-802.htm.

[16] Available at: https://safcei.org/wp-content/uploads/2020/09/Gates-Foundation-appeal-from-SAFCEI-African-faith-Leaders-September-2020.docx.pdf.

Africa and further afield – is a rallying point for the promotion of agroecology by the faith community and will continue to be a strong advocacy tool for some time to come.

SAFCEI has joined an African-wide and international group of NGOs, faith leaders and civil society groups who are campaigning against the corporatisation of seeds and farming in Africa. Food and climate justice-related faith networks have grown, and SAFCEI is linking these with civil society actors. It has entered a number of significant agroecology-related fora, including as a member of the Alliance for Food Sovereignty in Africa (AFSA), and dynamic spaces such as the Agroecology group in South Africa.

The Covid-19 crisis has intensified food insecurity and hunger globally and exposed the failings of a profit-driven, industrialised agriculture and food system. The pandemic saw already impoverished people across Southern Africa barred from work and the means to earn a basic income. SAFCEI was able to respond by providing a series of online workshops for faith leaders in order to encourage food resilience in communities. Faith leaders were provided with the information and resources to be able to assist their respective faith communities to grow their own food in order to avoid dependence on food relief. Training initiated on food gardens was well received and participants utilised the learnings and participated in measuring their eco-footprint. Additionally, the provision of small grants has alleviated immediate hunger and faith leaders have been able to purchase inputs to enable a number of food growing initiatives to alleviate hunger needs.

The urgency of climate change requires an undoing of industrial food systems and business as usual, and recognition of the need for justice to be central to development objectives. If global food systems are to become sustainable, then input-intensive crop monocultures and industrial-scale feedlots must become obsolete. Despite the Gates Foundation slogan that 'all lives have equal value', the needs of the poor and the earth are not met by AGRA's failed 'green revolution'.

As people of faith, we believe philanthropic efforts should fund initiatives that walk alongside local communities to ensure self-determination. In this case, smallholder farmers should be able to secure land tenure and have a real stake in the agricultural policy negotiations that impact them. People in Africa are often depicted as poor and without resources, but concepts such as agroecology, permaculture, and organic farming are in line with traditional customs and African wealth in the form of cultural and ecosystem knowledge. The West can learn a lot from this knowledge and practice.

Suggestions for Further Reading

Books

D'Silva, Joyce & Litt, D. *Religion and Factory Farming. A Briefing by Compassion in World Farming.* (Godalming: Compassion in World Farming, 2015). Available at: https://www.ciwf.org.uk/media/7425967/compassion-2015-religious-views-on-factory-farming.pdf.

Merritt, Jonathan. Green Like God: Unlocking the Divine Plan for Our Planet (Nashville: FaithWords, 2010).

Pollan, Michael. *The Omnivore's Dilemma* (New York: The Penguin Press, 2006).

Rosenberg, Alan. *Agroecology: The Promise of Future Flourish* (Bio-Green Books: 2020). For chapter titles, see: https://www.lindros.co.za/what-we-do/books/agroecology-the-promise-of-future-flourish/.

Safran Foer, Jonathan. *Eating Animals* (Boston: Little, Brown and Company, 2009).

Shiva, Vandana. *Stolen Harvest: The Hijacking of the Global Food Supply.* (Boston South End Press, 200) [and other books by the same author].

Singer, Peter. *Animal Liberation* (New York: Ecco Press, 2001).

Online Resources

Capra, Fritjof. 'Industrial Agriculture, Agroecology, and Climate Change: Contrasting practices that exacerbate climate disruption with those that build resilience and support health'. *Center for*

Ecoliteracy, 11 February 2015, available at https://www.ecoliteracy.org/article/industrial-agriculture-agroecology-and-climate-change.
Factsheets are available online at IFOAM – Organics International: https://www.ifoam.bio/resource-library.
Further resources are available online at FiBL: https://www.fibl.org/en/info-centre/publications-fibl-en.

64. Responding to the Fifth Mark of Mission – The Green Anglicans Movement

Rachel Mash[1]

Introduction

Across Southern and East Africa, 'Green Anglicans' are on the move, planting trees, promoting rocket stoves, installing water tanks, planting vegetable gardens, fighting plastic pollution and advocating against fossil fuel companies. What is this movement and why is it growing?

Background: The Impact of Climate Change in Southern Africa

The movement began in the Anglican Church of Southern Africa, which consists of six countries – South Africa, Eswatini (Swaziland), Lesotho, Angola, Mozambique and Namibia. Across our Province, the impacts of Climate Change are causing devastation.

In 2019, Cyclone Idai slammed into Mozambique, destroying almost 90 of the city of Beira, which will now go down in history as the first major city to be completed devastated by climate change.[2] The cyclone produced nearly a year's worth of rain in just a few days. Over the last century the ocean has risen nearly 30 centimetres,[3] leaving Beira now below sea level. Aerial photographs of the devastation showed a vast inland sea, with homes and harvests destroyed.

Namibia, the driest country south of the Sahara, suffered a devastating drought. In Northern Namibia, many people do not have a bank account, they save via their herd of cattle for the children's education, their daughter's wedding, their pension scheme etc. It was reported that older men became suicidal when they had to slaughter their cattle and lost their entire life savings.

All of the countries in our Province are experiencing severe effects of climate change. In Eswatini, Swaziland, the schools were closed because due to the drought there was no water for toilets. Cape Town became the first major global city to be faced with 'Day Zero' when all water taps would have been turned off.[4] The citizens rallied and reduced water consumption by 50% and were able to stave off that day until the rains came.

Drought, severe weather events and sea level increase are the immediate effects of climate change. Climate change has severe health implications, affecting clean water and air, food security and secure shelter.[5] There are also indirect effects – fewer children are in school due to malnutrition, many leave for

[1] Rev Dr Rachel Mash is the Environmental Coordinator of the Anglican Church of Southern Africa (South Africa, Eswatini, Lesotho, Namibia, Mozambique and Angola).

[2] Fernando, Amos, 'First city completed devastated by Cyclone Idai', *Relief Web* (Mar 2019) https://reliefweb.int/report/mozambique/first-city-completely-devastated-climate-change-tries-rebuild-after-cyclone-idai.

[3] see: https://climateknowledgeportal.worldbank.org/country/mozambique/impacts-sea-level-rise#:~:text=Currently%2C%20the%20annual%20rise%20is,to%20months%20or%20even%20decades.

[4] Welch, Craig, 'Cape Town running out of water', *National Geographic* (Mar 2018) https://www.nationalgeographic.com/science/article/cape-town-running-out-of-water-drought-taps-shutoff-other-cities.

[5] J Myers, T Young, M Galloway, P Manyike, T Tucker, 'A public health approach to the impact of climate change on health in southern Africa – identifying priority modifiable risks', *The South African Medical Journal* Vol 101, No 11 (2011), 817-722; in: http://www.samj.org.za/index.php/samj/article/view/5267/3674.

larger cities where they may then face xenophobic attacks or fall into crime out of desperation. Girls are at risk of sexual harassment, having to walk longer and longer distances to find water.

Response of the Church

What then has been the response of the Anglican Church of Southern Africa? The Fifth Mark of Mission has been identified as, "to strive to safeguard the integrity of creation and sustain and re-new the life of the earth."[6] We need to respond spiritually, then with local action and then with advocacy.

Step One: Spiritual Response

The starting point for our ministry is a spiritual change.

> I used to think the top environmental problems were biodiversity loss, ecosystem collapse and climate change. I thought that with 30 years of good science we could address those problems. But I was wrong. The top environmental problems are selfishness, greed and apathy … and to deal with those we need a spiritual and cultural transformation and we scientists don't know how to do that.[7]

In order to combat climate change and biodiversity loss, we need to change hearts. We must start with lament, recognising that the integrity of creation is being destroyed, the web of life is unravelling.

The devastation of God's creation has been undergirded with a Western theology which arrived with colonialism. This theology of dominion is based on verses such as Gen 1.28: "Fill the earth and subdue it. Rule over the fish in the sea and the birds in the sky and over every living creature that moves on the ground." We saw creation as a resource to be exploited, rather than a web of life to be treasured and protected. However, the first commandment that we were given as human beings was to work the land and take care of it (Gen 2:15). This we have failed to do and now living topsoil has been eroded, forests have been cut down and the rivers polluted. So the church must rise up and "renew the life of the earth".

In order to bring about this spiritual change it is important that we train clergy to look again at the Scriptures, by running eco-theology courses and eco-retreats. Recognising the key role of young people, we have developed materials for Sunday School (Ryan the Rhino[8]) and youth (Care for Creation).[9]

We provide liturgical resources for important environmental days such as World Water Day, World Environment Day and others.

One of the most significant actions that we have taken as a Province is to embrace the 'Season of Creation'. In our liturgical calendar we have times of the year when we consider God the Son (at Easter and Christmas), and God the Spirit (at Pentecost). But when do we consider what the Scriptures are telling us about Creation? So, for the last eight years we have provided appropriate materials for the Province.[10] The Season of Creation is a growing ecumenical movement now supported by the WCC, Lutheran World Federation, Global Catholic Climate Movement, A Rocha and others to promote the Season on a global

---

[6] "Anglican Communion, Five Marks of Mission" https://www.anglicancommunion.org/mission/marks-of-mission.aspx

[7] Gus Speth, a former US advisor to Bill Clinton on climate change is said to have made this statement. See: http://winewaterwatch.org/2016/05/we-scientists-dont-know-how-to-do-that-what-a-commentary/.

[8] Mash, Rachel, *Ryan the Rhino Sunday School Manual* (Cape Town: Anglican Church of Southern Africa Network, 2016) http://www.greenanglicans.org/wp-content/uploads/2013/08/CARING-FOR-CREATION-RYAN-THE-RHINO.pdf.

[9] Mash, R, *Care for Creation Youth Manual* (Cape Town: Anglican Church of Southern Africa Network, 2018), available at https://www.greenanglicans.org/wp-content/uploads/2019/05/care-for-creation-youth-manual-1.pdf.

[10] Anglican Church of Southern Africa Environmental Network, 'Liturgical Resources', http://www.greenanglicans.org/resources/liturgical/.

level. The Season of Creation runs from the first of September (World Day of Prayer for creation) until 4th October (St Francis Day).[11]

In our worship, we remember that God speaks to us through creation, even though we are often so enclosed in our four walls that we don't listen (Psalm 19-:1-2): "The heavens declare the glory of God; the skies proclaim the work of his hands. Day after day they pour forth speech, night after night they reveal knowledge." So we encourage people to take services outside – holding church in creation. When we look at Jesus' spirituality we find that he often prayed on the mountain, especially at times of stress. This has been a particularly important step during COVID as it increases the number of people who can attend church and keeps the congregation much safer.

With drought now becoming ever more frequent in our Province we have been reminded anew about the sacredness of water. We have looked again at the meaning of baptism – we become members of the family of God through the sacred waters of baptism. We have prepared Lenten materials on water, and run conferences on water justice. The Bible is full of references to water that restores, revives, cleanses and heals, and there are in fact 722 verses in the Bible that talk about and mention water! Baptised by the sacred waters, we must be guardians of all water. All of us know the river in which Jesus was baptised, the Jordan, but the majority do not know where the water came from that was used at our baptism – it simply 'came out of a tap'. So we encourage churches to do research and to adopt their own 'Jordan River', their own sacred river that should be protected and kept clean.

During the season of Lent, many people choose to abstain from a personal luxury such as alcohol or chocolate. We need to make this broader, and call for a fast for the earth, when we abstain from practices that cause damage to the earth. Every year we provide a calendar with 40 actions on different themes that can reduce our footprint. For instance, saving water, or buying a cloth bag for shopping, taking shorter showers or having meat-free Mondays. Once they have done a specific action for a month, for many people it then becomes part of their life-style going forward.[12]

Step Two: Local Action

If you do not start with spirituality, the danger is that a few activists will get involved and then burn out. If you start by a change of heart, then people will become involved out of love for God and creation, clearly seeing the strength of the Biblical call.

Nelson Mandela once said, "If you speak in a language that a person understands, you speak to their head, but if you speak in their mother tongue, you speak to their heart."[13] It is important to find ways of speaking of environmental actions in ways that connect with our spirituality – for instance, instead of 'eco-system restoration' or 'environmental actions', refer instead to 'renewing the face of the earth' or 'caring for creation'. In this way you speak to people's hearts.

Depending on the context there are many actions that can be taken.

Tree planting. When we started tree planting, we found that sometimes the trees would die because after initially being excited to plant a tree and take a photo with the bishop, nobody was then committed to watering it. So we have now moved from tree planting to tree *growing.* Trees need to be nurtured and watered for two years until the roots reach the water table. We have also linked tree planting with spiritual rituals – for instance, young people have a tree sapling blessed at confirmation, trees are planted at baptisms, marriages, birthdays and patronal festivals. Hashtag #birthdaytrees is becoming popular!

This year memorial trees have become very important as so many people were not able to attend funerals. We have indeed discovered that "the leaves of the trees are for the healing of the nations" (Rev 22:2). Some

---

[11] Season of Creation: www.seasonofcreation.org.

[12] Lenten Fasts for the Planet: http://www.greenanglicans.org/lent-fasts/.

[13] Lakar, Itziar, 'Mandela was right, the foreign language effect', *Mapping Ignorance* (Feb 2014), https://mappingignorance.org/2014/02/03/mandela-was-right-the-foreign-language-effect/.

dioceses are creating seedlings nurseries so that planting trees becomes accessible and affordable. It is also very important that the trees are indigenous, or else they may be water-guzzlers or reduce the biodiversity in that area.

Plastic. We are told that by 2050, there will be more plastic in the oceans than fish.[14] Our rivers and streets are clogged with single-use plastic which has been thrown away. The starting point is to encourage people to 'refuse' plastic. We run a 'bring your own bag' campaign and encourage changes such as stopping the use of bottled water etc. We are also encouraging clean-ups, and for churches to do recycling. With the clean-ups, if you clean up today, by the following week rubbish will have been dumped again, so we are claiming back areas which have become dumpsites by planting succulents or shrubs after the clean-up. Then we can say, "Refuse, reduce, reuse, recycle, REJOICE!"

Reduce our footprint. Individuals, families and congregations are encouraged to do an audit of their use of water, fuel, electricity and paper. In this way they can see where savings can take place. COVID has assisted us greatly in reducing our footprint, as people are now much more tech savvy and can use Zoom meetings instead of petrol. Air travel has also reduced drastically. Many dioceses have now gone practically paperless for meetings, and churches are sending out the bulk of pew leaflets electronically, just printing a few for the elderly or those without cell phones.

Catering. We are encouraging environmental practices for church functions, ideas that can be also used at home, such as reducing meat consumption, not using bottled water, and restricting Styrofoam take-aways or plastic cutlery. The church can set up a composting scheme and make a commitment to reduce waste. Even though the Mothers Union has passed a resolution to stop using Styrofoam at large events, it is still difficult to get that to be implemented everywhere, as for example people have got so used to the fast life-style of giving out take-aways at funerals without washing up dishes.

Home food gardens.With the huge increase of food insecurity, COVID showed us that it is wrong to have church land lying unused. So many churches are training people to grow their own food. If churches give out food parcels, they are encouraged to give them out with seeds or seedlings so that people can make a start at food growing. This brings blessing as people are empowered. We also teach that this forms part of our spiritual life, not something that we just 'do', since we are made in the image of God, we are co-creators with God.

One of the most significant actions we have taken was to 'Green the Canons',[15] meaning that environmental ministry has now been added to the role of the task of the incumbent, church wardens and parish council. A report must be given at vestry meetings on the environmental actions of the parish.[16]

Step Three: Advocacy

Proverbs 31: 8 declares, "Speak up for those who have no voice" – actually, they have a voice, the problem is that they are not being listened to! Advocacy seeks to tackle the root causes of an issue. If we look at the example of plastic, we can see that oil companies are planning to increase the sales of plastic, because they need to find an outlet for their oil as sales to car owners begins to fall.

Advocacy seeks to tackle the root causes of a problem. Plastic polluters such as Coca Cola want the individual to bear responsibility for the mess that the company is creating. And so, important as clean-ups are for protect biodiversity, we must become involved in stopping the increasing production of plastic.

[14] Kaplan, Sarah, 'By 2050 there will be more plastic than fish in the sea', *Washington Post* (Jan 2016), https://www.washingtonpost.com/news/morning-mix/wp/2016/01/20/by-2050-there-will-be-more-plastic-than-fish-in-the-worlds-oceans-study-says/.

[15] Canons (constitution) of the Anglican Church, https://anglicanchurchsa.org/canons/.

[16] See 28.4 (a) https://anglicanchurchsa.org/canons/chapter-c28-pastoral-charges/.

During COVID we have seen that more and more plastic has been used. Green Anglicans has become involved as one of the partners in a civil society campaign to ban single use plastics.[17]

We are facing two burning advocacy issues in our Province from fossil fuel companies. In Namibia a Canadian oil company, ReconAfrica, bought rights to do exploratory drilling in a vast 35,000 km^2 region of the Kavango Basin in the north of the country. This area is environmentally sensitive, and supplies water to the Okavango Delta. The Delta is one of the seven natural wonders of Africa and a protected World Heritage and key biodiversity area. Concerns have been raised about the rights of indigenous people being abused and the potential damage to groundwater – Namibia is the driest country south of the Sahara. The required public participation process was not complied with, and the local Namibian paper that reported on the story was sued by ReconAfrica.[18]

Bishop Luke Pato, the Bishop of Namibia, raised the issue with the church. A petition, signed by all the Anglican bishops of Southern Africa, was also signed by two of the archbishops of Canada and handed over to the Consulate of Namibia. An interfaith partner, Kairos Africa, presented the petition to the headquarters of Recon in Vancouver, and a silent protest was held on the steps of St George's Cathedral. What was fascinating to see was how the press had been fairly silent on the issue (no doubt for fear of being sued), but they were able to report on the bishops' petition as they could do so without the fear of being sued.[19]

In Northern Mozambique, a local insurgent group known as 'Al Shabaab' has been terrorizing local villages in areas being drilled by Total.[20] Bishop Ernesto Manuel, the Bishop of Nampula. pleaded with investors to take their money out of fossil fuels and instead invest in renewable energy.

> Fossil fuel investments increase climate change and impacts on those most vulnerable, and also destabilise communities. We have seen how over 700,000 people in Northern Mozambique have been displaced – many fleeing for their lives in terror from insurgents. Dozens have been beheaded, even children as young as 12. This violence only occurs in the areas where gas prospecting is taking place. Locals are not consulted and nor do they benefit, only suffering the impacts of rising prices, pollution and loss of land. We plead with the international community – take your money out of fossil fuels and invest in renewable energy which is decentralised, benefits local people and does not contribute to climate change.[21]

Advocacy is often defined as acting to, "Speak up for those who have no voice" (Prov 1: 31). In reality, all people impacted by climate change and fossil fuel extraction have a voice, the problem is that no-one is listening. Our task is to amplify their voices so that they can be heard.

Step Four: Creating a Movement

What has allowed the Green Anglican movement to spread so far? There are several factors at play.

There is no doubt that young people are the key factor in the growth of the movement. In 2016 a youth conference on climate change was held in Lusaka which brought together the youth of the Anglican Church of Southern Africa with the youth of Central Africa (Malawi, Botswana, Zimbabwe and Zambia). The

---

[17] 'South Africa makes steps to ban all single use plastic', *Averda* [accessed 14 Sep 2021] https://averda.co.za/news/south-africa-makes-steps-ban-all-single-use-plastics/.

[18] Musheko, T., 'Canadian Oil driller threatens to sue the Namibian', *The Namibian* (Feb 2020), https://www.namibian.com.na/208788/archive-read/Canadian-oil-driller-threatens-to-sue-The-Namibian.

[19] Bega, Sheree, 'Stop Oil and Gas drilling in Namibia's Kavango basin immediately says the Anglican Church', *Mail and Guardian* (March 2021), https://mg.co.za/environment/2021-03-08-stop-oil-and-gas-drilling-in-namibias-kavango-basin-immediately-anglican-church/.

[20] 'Bishop Manuel live on BBC World News', *MANNA* (Mar 2021) https://vimeo.com/523707142.

[21] Buchanan, James, 'Faith Institutions divest from fossil fuels and call for just recovery ahead of G7 and COP26', *Operation Noah* (May 2021), https://operationnoah.org/news-events/news/press-release-faith-institutions-divest-from-fossil-fuels-and-call-for-just-recovery-ahead-of-g7-and-cop26/.

young people realised that they faced the same challenges and so committed to working together to spread the movement.

A couple of years later, youth from Southern Africa attended the CAPA (Council of Anglican Provinces of Africa)[22] youth conference in Nairobi and the vision was caught by the youth of the Anglican Church of Kenya (ACK).

Social media has allowed the movement to spread, even during COVID, as we could still hold online services to share information and challenges. Individual actions do not lead to transformational change, but networked actions lead to change, and social media allows people to feel that they are part of a larger movement.

Finally, it is a movement and not an institution, so people can get involved in the way that they feel called to, and in ways that fit the needs of their context. Whether it is planting trees, doing clean ups, starting food gardens, investing in solar, campaigning against fossil fuel companies and single use plastic, we all know that God has called us to be part of a movement working to renew the life of the earth.

Let us go then and "preach good news to the whole of creation" (Mark 16:15).

Websites for Further Information

The Green Anglican site www.greenanglicans.org
Season of Creation www.seasonofcreation
Anglican Communion Environmental Network https://acen.anglicancommunion.org/

Suggestions for Further Reading

Conradie, Ernst, *Christianity and Earthkeeping: In Search of an Inspiring Vision*. Vol. 16. (African Sun Media, 2011).

Valerio, Ruth, *Saying Yes to Life: The Archbishop of Canterbury's Lent Book 2020* (London: SPCK, 2019).

Mash, Rachel, *Renewing the Life of the Earth, Christian Discipleship and Environmental Action* (Cambridge: Grove Books, 2021); https://grovebooks.co.uk/products/id-2-renewing-the-life-of-the-earth-christian-discipleship-and-environmental-action.

Mash, Rachel, 'The Green Anglican Movement and Climate Change', in *World Scientific Encyclopedia of Climate Change*, 257-260 (2021); see: https://www.worldscientific.com/doi/abs/10.1142/9789811213946_0032.

Mash, Rachel, *Care for Creation Youth Manual* (Cape Town: Anglican Church of Southern Africa Network, 2018); https://www.greenanglicans.org/wp-content/uploads/2019/05/care-for-creation-youth-manual-1.pdf.

Mash, Rachel, *Ryan the Rhino Sunday School Manual* (Cape Town: Anglican Church of Southern Africa Network, 2016); https://www.greenanglicans.org/wp-content/uploads/2013/08/CARING-FOR-CREATION-RYAN-THE-RHINO.pdf.

Mash, Rachel, 'A time to pray and act', in *Scottish Episcopal Institute Journal* 3.4 (2019): 117-123.

[22] Council of Anglican Provinces of Africa, https://capa-hq.org/.

65. Ecumenical Responses in the Time of Climate Change: The Case of Zimbabwe

Sostina Takure[1]

Climate change is increasingly becoming a threat to socio-economic performance in Zimbabwe. The occurrence of climate change in Zimbabwe and the world over is no longer a debatable issue. In Zimbabwe rural communities are the most vulnerable due to livelihoods dependent on rain fed agriculture. The rural population has less access to information and data regarding the climate change trends as well as resilience options. At the same time, climate change governance and coordination is mainly anchored around metropolitan cities, hence it is monopolized at a national level. There is also less involvement and inclusion of the youths in decision-making, resource allocation and policy influence at national level, yet 68% of the country's population are youths. As climate change impacts become more frequent and intense, the resilience of communities has been impacted mostly as a result of poor adaptive capacity, including impacts from loss and damage. Climate variability and change consequently place smallholder farmers, who have less adaptive capacity, in a precarious situation, since they must cope with recurrent droughts, mid-season dry spells, flooding, hailstorms and cyclones. Rural communities also depend on goods and services provided by our natural ecosystems, but unfortunately these have not been spared from threats posed by climatic variability. This therefore implies that approximately 70% of Zimbabwe's rural population is highly vulnerable to climate change. With increasing global surface temperatures, the possibility of more droughts and increased intensity of storms, floods, and heat waves is already a reality for Zimbabwe.

Government of Zimbabwe Response to Climate Change: International Regional and National Policies Agreements and Treaties

The Government of Zimbabwe (GoZ) is progressively committed to addressing the threatening reality of climate change. At the highest level of governance, the minister who heads the Ministry of Environment, Climate Change, Tourism and Hospitality Management shows enthusiasm and energy in pushing the climate change agenda in all government sectors. Such levels of engagement are also extended to the international and regional bodies such as UNDP, UNFCCC, Earth Day Network and Green Climate Fund. It is important to also note that the government is progressively becoming alert to the reality of climate change and its effects, thereby heightening the level of climate change sensitivity, and instilling a sense of responsibility that cuts across all parts of the Zimbabwean population. Through the Ministry of Agriculture, for example, smallholder farmers are getting a boost in terms of their capacity through upskilling initiatives such as the Pfumvudza/Intwasa scheme,[2] a scheme designed to promote resilient agriculture and maximize land yield with the least available moisture content. This, among other key interventions, has seen the nation building increasing adoption and efficiency of the concept of increasing food security and income for smallholder farmers.[3] It is also against the understanding that smallholder agriculture, a major driver of

[1] Sostina Takure is an experienced development practitioner with many years of working in the non-profit organization management industry and in strategic planning and program development. She has a Masters in Development Studies from University of KwaZulu Natal and Master in Philanthropy and Social Entrepreneurship focused on Social Entrepreneurship from Università di Bologna. Currently she serves as ACT Zimbabwe Coordinator.

[2] the Pfumvudza/Intwasa programme is a low input sustainable agriculture approach to enhance household food and nutrition security which is adopted in Zimbabwe, see: https://allafrica.com/stories/202110140400.html

[3] https://www.herald.co.zw/govt-to-mechanise-pfumvudzaintwasa/.

Zimbabwe's economy, is primarily rain-fed throughout the country. Broadly it can be highlighted that the government has taken positive steps in demonstrating leadership through showcasing solutions promoting climate resilient agriculture and food systems, protecting, and halting and reversing land degradation and biodiversity loss.

As part of the government of Zimbabwe's fight for climate and environmental justice, since 2013 Zimbabwe has been a party to the Ramsar Convention on Wetlands, which seeks to protect and preserve wetlands. Local laws, including the 2006 Environmental Management Act and the Environmental Assessment and Ecosystem Protection Regulations of 2007, provide for the protection of wetlands.

While these noble efforts can be duly noted and applauded, there is also evidence that suggests that not enough is being done to educate citizens, policymakers, and local and national government authorities on the importance of wetlands and on strengthening mechanisms for their protection. Evidence suggested through a critical source referred to as Harare Wetlands Trust, lack of appreciation of the importance of wetlands, coupled with poor urban planning and insufficient regulation, has resulted in the destruction of Harare's wetlands through mostly illegal construction on wetlands that feed into Lake Chivero, Harare's only water source. Illegal housing construction projects on the wetlands in Harare and Chitungwiza had turned the wetlands into 'concrete jungles'. The 2020-21 rainy season also laid bare the vulnerable state of citizens and their infrastructure should they fail to adhere to government standards that prohibit the development of any forms of housing on wetlands. In the long run the adverse effects of such reckless degradation have been seen to impact the right to clean water, which impacts the rights to health and life. This serial reaction is a point to trigger the government to take urgent action to protect wetlands and stop the ongoing and unprecedented degradation putting them at serious risk.

Zimbabwe has crafted its own National Climate Change Response Strategy (2014) and this has grown in popularity and practical embrace in the past four years, with multiple actors from the private sector and NGOs bringing their input to the table. Zimbabwe has also developed its National Climate Change Policy (2016), and this document continues to be aligned to key sectors of the economy and social fundamentals such as the gender aspect. Youth involvement and youth participation are becoming considerably evident, with the Ministry of Education introducing Education 5.0 framework that allows scholars to undertake action-oriented research that improves the livelihoods of communities in the face of imminent negative impacts of climate change.

Church Involvement in Fighting Climate Change

Climate change commentaries have been pervasive amongst all religious groups that can be identified in the world. For example, the Roman Catholic Church, through Pope Francis's *Laudato Si*,[4] the Lambeth Declaration on Climate Change issued by the Anglican Communion's bishops,[5] and an Islamic Declaration on Global Climate Change signed by Muslim leaders at the International Islamic Climate Change Symposium.[6] In 2015 came a Hindu Declaration on Climate Change,[7] a Buddhist Climate Change Statement

---

[4] *Encyclical Letter Laudato Si' of The Holy Father Francis on Care for Our Common Home* available at http://www.vatican.va/content/francesco/en/encyclicals/documents/papa-francesco_20150524_enciclica-laudato-si.html.

[5] *Lambeth Declaration 2015 on Climate Change* available at https://www.churchofengland.org/sites/default/files/2018-11/CCB_Lambeth-declaration-2015-on-climate-change.pdf.

[6] *Islamic Declaration on Global Climate Change* available at https://cambridgecentralmosque.org/wp-content/uploads/2020/03/writings-climate-declaration-mwb.pdf.

[7] *Hindu Declaration on Climate Change* available at http://www.hinduclimatedeclaration2015.org/english.

to World Leaders,[8] and a Rabbinic Letter on the Climate Crisis[9] was also developed to indicate the role of various players in the climate change discourse. Since the ratification of the Paris Accord, religious advocacy has continued to grow, as evident in 2016 where a number of prominent evangelical leaders issued a new Evangelical Call to Action,[10] and the Methodist Church updated its Book of Discipline to include a section explicitly calling for global climate stewardship.[11] The past five years have seen most of the world's religions coalescing around the common goal of advocating for action to address climate change, though this has faced some setbacks. Learnings from the United Methodist Church[12] uphold the climate justice call for faith actors to introduce change. The church emphasizes that clergy and laity should use the letter and accompanying resources to preach and teach on care for creation as part of members' discipleship. The faith community calls upon members to prayerfully explore lifestyle changes as individuals and faith communities that would reduce greenhouse gas emissions and support a cleaner, healthier future. In addition, the faith body calls for responsible bodies to support communities impacted by climate change, as well as those currently dependent on fossil fuel extraction and production as they transition to a new energy economy.

Intimate awareness creation (that can be simply understood as awareness created based on friendship and familiarity) is a key ingredient for advancing a climate change mitigation agenda. The reality of climate change should be made known. Faith-based leaders, the private sector and civic organizations should take it as a duty to enlighten their members on the dangers of climate change. This is where intimacy comes in, as the information should come from the leader to the led. This should be done on a regular basis during congregational services, meetings, fellowship and so on. The emphasis of this awareness should be on the practical ways and actions that can be taken to reduce carbon dioxide emission. Also, this method of awareness has more prospects for the eco-sustainability campaign. This is seen in the fact that any injunction given on the platform of religion tends to attract more compliance and obedience from adherents. Therefore, it is assumed that if Christian leaders actively participate in the campaign against climate change, the desired success would be achieved.

Ecumenical Climate Action Project

Zimbabwe faith actors are at the forefront in both policy advocacy and practical action to address climate change. The Ecumenical Climate Action Project was an incubator project created to support the major church bodies in Zimbabwe and develop a consortium on climate change, attract funding for it and develop the necessary coordination and implementation mechanisms to implement climate change initiatives, building on the gains of the historic COP21 Agreement. The aim of the union was to create a unifying platform for ecumenical bodies to engage on climate change issues through a range of coordinated actions, inclusive of: mass mobilization for action, lobby and advocacy, research, and initiating community based adaptation initiatives. The ecumenical consortium played an important role in lobbying the international community to fulfill longstanding demands by the faith community for the implementation of the Paris Agreement, Lima Work-Plan on Gender, and the Warsaw International Mechanism for Loss and Damage. It worked to encourage state parties to make drastic cuts to emissions, increase funding to help developing countries to take decisive climate action both in terms of mitigation and adaptation, establish clear fixed

[8] *Buddhist Leaders Call to World Leaders on Paris* available at https://unfccc.int/news/buddhist-leaders-call-to-world-leaders.

[9] *A Rabbinic Letter on the Climate Crisis* available at https://theshalomcenter.org/civicrm/petition/sign?sid=17.

[10] *Climate Change: An Evangelical Call to Action* available at http://www.christiansandclimate.org.

[11] *The Book Of Discipline of the United Methodist Church* available at https://www.ctcumc.org/files/fileshare/2016-book-of-discipline.pdf.

timelines for achieving gender-responsive climate policy, and transfer sound mitigation and adaptation technologies and know-how to developing countries.

Disaster Risk Reduction and Humanitarian Assistance

In 2018 Cyclone Idai hit Zimbabwe's Manicaland Province, resulting in loss of lives and livelihoods. One of the major learnings from the cyclone was that the country's disaster management structures were at best weak, if in fact they were even in existence. Part of the Forum's initiatives with regards to advancing the work of climate justice has been to support the Department of Climate Change through capacitating local officials on disaster preparedness and response. Part of the objectives of the training workshops were to develop community disaster risk preparedness plans and align district climate change profiles to the climate discourse. Faith and traditional leaders were part of these trainings, as they are the community gate-keepers – equipping them ensures sustainable, community-driven initiatives and is bound to increase community safety, as disasters can hit when government officials might not be present in the communities to act. Efforts towards risk mitigation and adaptation integration were also a product of the assistive tools developed by the trainers and populated by the local teams attending the trainings.

The church in Zimbabwe is a strong welfare institution and a provider of community social safety nets. It also exists to provide solidarity and assistance to survivors of climate disasters. The church in Zimbabwe has been at the forefront in providing safe shelter to displaced people. Through the appeal system, Action by Churches Together in Zimbabwe has been able to respond by providing food and unconditional cash transfers to millions of victims of protracted droughts and floods. The Forum has also built houses for cyclone victims, as well as providing them with psychosocial support.

Faith Leaders' Environmental Advocacy Training

Faith leaders have a crucial role to play in shaping community attitudes and behaviour. For them to cascade positive behaviour, they need to be equipped with information that reinforces such. The Faith Leaders Environmental Advocacy (FLEAT)[13] training is the flagship program of SAFCEI. SAFCEI is a multi-faith organisation which draws on the perspectives of different faiths in implementing its vision. Zimbabwe implements these FLEATs, targeting multi-faith actors including Catholics, Protestants, African Apostolic Churches, Quakers, Muslims and Pentecostals. This holistic interfaith approach ensures that no one is left behind and that the same message is shared across the faith community, reinforcing positive behaviour when it comes to environmental stewardship. These trainings are contextualised to ensure that they respond to the challenges of the trained faith leaders.

Zimbabwe struggles, especially with deforestation and land degradation due to illegal mining, curing of tobacco, and poor waste management – among other factors. The FLEAT trainings equip faith leaders with information on how to advocate for the introduction and adoption of alternative sources of energy to replace use of firewood in communities, for example. This is done through community dialogue and education on the effects of deforestation. Trained faith leaders have gone on to host community waste management hubs in their communities, including small income generating projects that use waste. Some have held tree planting Sundays in their churches, as well as hosting community clean-up campaigns.

---

[13] See: https://safcei.org/apply-now-to-join-our-faith-leader-environmental-advocacy-training-in-malawi/.

Afforestation and Environmental Clean-up Exercises

Between 1990 and 2015, Zimbabwe lost 36% of its forest cover at a rate of 9% per decade.[14] Destruction of natural habitats, pressure from human settlements and poaching have decimated wildlife populations, particularly those of endangered species. The ACT Zimbabwe Forum has been working with the faith community to plant trees in all areas that have lost vegetation and also at new sites, upon the advice of the environmental management agency. These tree planting exercises ensured the participation of faith actors in mobilizing communities to plant trees and in assisting them in the actual planting. Schools and health institutions have been roped in, as well as afforestation centers, to ensure that they become green zones. Land degradation and pollution are leading problems, and the Forum works with young people in carrying out environmental clean-up campaigns as a way of stewarding the environment. During these clean up campaigns, trained faith leaders educate the youth on climate change and the role they can play in rolling it back and in caring for creation.

Building Community Resilience and Adaptation

Climate change is exacerbated by the increased frequency of droughts, late season onset, veld fires and less capacity utilization of renewable energy. Rural communities are the most vulnerable, due to having livelihoods dependent on rain fed agriculture. The same population also has less access to information and data regarding the climate change trends, as well as fewer resilience options. ACT Alliance Zimbabwe Forum, in partnership with the Ministry of Environment, Climate, Tourism and Hospitality Industry, is undertaking a learning and skills development project comprised of workshops in ten districts from eight provinces across the country. These workshops target young people from rural communities and seek to raise awareness on climate change, enabling them regarding climate change adaptation and providing mitigation strategies with a tactical sensitivity to their contexts, geographical location and cultural background. The project will continue focusing on the identified opportunities for green businesses and various environmentally friendly practices of living. To support contextual community resilience and adaptation, the Forum partnered with academic institutions to carry out research on how communities are affected by climate change and how they are coping. The results from the research now inform the Forum programming.

Policy Support

The Zimbabwe Forum has a strong working relationship with all stakeholders addressing climate change in the country. One critical stakeholder is the Department of Climate Change, which oversees all work done by partners on climate change. The Forum has worked with the department to influence policy and support the cascading of information to rural areas that are marginalised when it comes to policy input. The Forum works to provide multi-stakeholder dialogue platforms where different stakeholders meet with the Climate Change Department to provide their input on new legislation – for example, the National Climate Policy and the reduction of emissions bill. This ensures that no one is left behind as the country plans to reduce emissions and tackle climate change. Several dialogues were conducted with multiple stakeholders on how best forum members and affiliated partners could influence policies and support communities to participate in the development and adoption of climate change policies at national and community levels, whilst also aiding the government to meet its national and international climate change obligations. The Forum has also supported multi-stakeholder consultations before and after the Conference of Parties international summits. This is to ensure that the national commitments receive input from all sections of the country.

---

[14] https://www.kas.de/c/document_library/get_file?uuid=6dfce726-fdd1-4f7b-72e7-e6c1ca9c9a95&groupId=252038.

Conclusion

Zimbabwe, like most countries in the global South, is not spared from the impacts of climate change. From a domestic level, the government has made progress in domesticating many of its international obligations to fight against climate change. However, the implementation of these policies does not inspire much confidence. As such, stakeholders such as Christian leaders have a part to play in taking up the responsibility of joining the war against the impacts of climate change.

There are some entry points that can be utilized to address the gaps prevalent in the fight against climate change and these include:

- Advocacy. Coordinated efforts at global, regional, national, and local levels. The World Council of Churches' advocacy initiatives have been systematically integrated with those of regional and national ecumenical bodies. There has been an important synergy between the World Council of Churches and member churches on sharing information, resources and collaborative advocacy. Locally continued capacity-building of faith-based organizations such as youth, women's groups, etc., remains crucial
- Education (Inclusive Curriculum). There is need for more 'integrated missions'. Faith-based educational institutions and platforms, and theological and religious education programmes, need to integrate doctrinal training with emerging issues such as climate change, gender issues, poverty and development issues, and environmental theology. Curriculums at seminary colleges must include modules on climate change so that faith leaders are equipped at entry level into ministry.
- Research and Publication. Faith based research on ecological protection and increasing accessibility to climate change materials/documents, for example in libraries, will be integral for research work to be undertaken.

Suggestions for Further Reading

Andrew Mushvishi Mash, 'Govt to mechanise Pfumvudza/Intwasa', *The Herald* 25 April 2022, in: https://www.herald.co.zw/govt-to-mechanise-pfumvudzaintwasa/.

Encyclical Letter, *Laudato Si' of The Holy Father Francis on Care for Our Common Home*, available at http://www.vatican.va/content/francesco/en/encyclicals/documents/papa-francesco_20150524_enciclica-laudato-si.html.

Lambeth Declaration 2015 on Climate Change, available at https://www.churchofengland.org/sites/default/files/2018-11/CCB_Lambeth-declaration-2015-on-climate-change.pdf.

Islamic Declaration on Global Climate Change, available at https://cambridgecentralmosque.org/wp-content/uploads/2020/03/writings-climate-declaration-mwb.pdf.

Hindu Declaration on Climate Change, available at http://www.hinduclimatedeclaration2015.org/english.

Buddhist Leaders Call to World Leaders on Paris, available at https://unfccc.int/news/buddhist-leaders-call-to-world-leaders.

A Rabbinic Letter on the Climate Crisis, available at https://theshalomcenter.org/civicrm/petition/sign?sid=17.

Climate Change: An Evangelical Call to Action, available at http://www.christiansandclimate.org

The Book of Discipline of The United Methodist Church, available at https://www.ctcumc.org/files/fileshare/2016-book-of-discipline.pdf.

Konrad Adenauer Stiftung (KAS), 'Climate Change in Zimbabwe. Facts for Planners and Decision Makers Berlin 2015', in: https://www.kas.de/c/document_library/get_file?uuid=6dfce726-fdd1-4f7b-72e7-e6c1ca9c9a95&groupId=252038

66. THE CONTRIBUTION OF A NATIONAL ACT FORUM AND ITS MEMBERS TO ECO-DIAKONIA IN TANZANIA

Modest Pesha[1]

Introduction

Action by Churches Together (ACT) Tanzania Forum is a member of ACT Alliance, a coalition of more than 140 churches and church-related organizations engaged in humanitarian, development and advocacy working together in over 120 countries. It was established in January 2010, working to create positive and sustainable change in the lives of poor and marginalized people regardless of their religion, politics, gender, race or nationality in keeping with the highest international codes and standards. Around 75% of ACT Alliance members are from the Global South. ACT Tanzania Forum membership consists of nine members made of three local church related members that are Evangelical Lutheran Church in Tanzania (ELCT), Christian Council of Tanzania (CCT) and Tanganyika Commission for Refugee Service (TCRS), and six international members that include Norwegian Church Aid (NCA), ACT Church of Sweden (Act CoS), Church World Service (CWS), Evangelical Lutheran Church of America (ELCA), Finnish Evangelical Lutheran Mission (FELM) and Mission 21 (M21).

Dyke et *al* (1996) asserts that, "The most basic, and most serious, of our environmental problems are those which threaten basis systems of our planet's life support".[2] The impact of an eco-diakonia consciousness and commitment which has been left behind by faith actors is climate change. This has a growing impact on the African continent, hitting the most vulnerable hardest, and contributing to food insecurity, population displacement and stress on water resources.

In recent months we have seen devastating floods, an invasion of desert locusts and droughts. The human and economic toll has been aggravated by the COVID-19 pandemic.[3]

In the same respect, H.E. Josefa Leonel Correia Sacko, Commissioner for Rural Economy and Agriculture of the African Union Commission, asserts that science-based climate information is the foundation of resilience building, a cornerstone of climate change adaptation, as well as an oasis for sustainable livelihoods and development. The State of Climate Report for Africa has, therefore, a critical role to play in this respect, including informing our actions for achieving the goals of the Africa Agenda 2063.

Many African countries are faced with developmental challenges, such as limited access to market, lack of competitiveness, fragile economic development, high poverty levels, limited analytical and technical capacity and data availability. These challenges are exacerbated by the continent's limited ability to manage climate change. Dyke et al. (1996) state that God has not left creation merely to fend for itself. Except for a few exceptions, the church has paid much attention to God the Creator but little attention to God the Sustainer.[4] Dyke's conception lies in the conformity of God the Creator with God the Sustainer of the

[1] Rev. Modest Pesha is the National Coordinator of ACT Alliance, Tanzania Forum.

[2] Dyke, Fred Van, Mahan, David C., Sheldon, Seph K. and Sheldon, Raymond H. *Redeeming Creation. The Biblical Basis for Environmental Stewardship* (Downers Grove: IVP, 1996), 19-20.

[3] Said by Petteri Taalas, the Secretary-General, World Meteorological Organization (WMO). See, 'World Meterological Organization: Mozambique cyclones are "wake-up call," says WMO', 29 May 2019 in: https://public.wmo.int/en/media/press-release/mozambique-cyclones-are-%E2%80%9Cwake-call%E2%80%9D-says-wmo

[4] Dyke at al., 16.

creation. The implication is obvious that the God who brought the creation into being is the same God who wants the creation to be sustainable.

Africa has enormous opportunities to contribute to the global efforts in combating climate change. All 54 countries have signed the Paris Agreement and have ratified the ambitious Nationally Determined Contributions (NDCs). However, most INDCs submitted by African countries were hastily put together and, in most cases, did not take long term effects on national development goals into consideration. 2020 NDCs are a key starting point for Paris processes that are meant to track progress and inform countries in updating their climate goals over time (reflected in NDCs with progressively enhanced ambition every five years). Although the Paris Agreement has established a global goal on adaptation with a view to contributing to sustainable development, current efforts at implementing NDCs, including those in Africa, have not attached much importance to adaptation and resilience building. The role of adaptation is crucial for climate action in an African context, including enhanced means of implementation – particularly finance and capacity building.

As climate change impacts become more frequent and intense, the resilience of communities has been impacted due to poor adaptive capacity, in particular impact from loss and damage. According to Elsdon, the number of poor people is rising, and with it the gap is widening between them and the better-off.[5] Despite these challenges, the African region is demonstrating leadership in showcasing solutions promoting climate resilient agriculture and food systems, protecting smallholder farmers, and halting and reversing land degradation and biodiversity loss. However, such solutions are few in number and need scaling up through the efforts of government, businesses, ecumenical fraternities, entrepreneurs, scientists, the media, youth and women. This underscores the need for increased financial flow to the region in order for climate ambition and action to keep pace with Africa's development efforts.[6]

This article focuses on showing the contribution of ACT Tanzania Forum through local and international members in practical engagement with issues of climate justice, care for creation and advocacy work for the protection of biodiversity.

Rationale for Care of Creation

The aim of this article is to contribute to IHCCE in providing an arena for learning from one another in terms of inter-contextual exchange, where the art of providing care with dignity, love with justice, and compassion with advocacy for the vulnerable, has risen up the agenda. With IHCCE, the role of churches, church related actors and interfaith actors in the Global South to contribute as actors for ecological transformation, climate justice, protection of biodiversity and ethics of sustainability will be underlined. Elsdon asserts that 'justice', 'peace' and the 'integrity of creation' are the theological titles of ecumenical programmes designed to awaken churches around the world to these coupled threats to the equality (and even the future viability) of human life.[7]

Care for creation and eco-diakonia have become new umbrella terms indicating prophetic witness, social Christian or interfaith services and joint ecumenical action to tackle root causes of the global environmental crisis, biodiversity destruction and climate change related health threats on both local, regional and global levels.

---

[5] Elsdon, Ron, *Greenhouse Theology: Biblical Perspectives on Caring for Creation.* England (Oxford: Monarch, 1992), 220.

[6] https://unfccc.int/news/climate-change-is-an-increasing-threat-to-africa.

[7] Elsdon, 219.

Definition of Terms

Diakonia. The RSV renders 'deacon' only in Phil. 1:1 and four times in 1 Tim. 3, but the Greek word thus represented, *diakonos* (generally in the AV 'minister' or 'servant'), occurs some 30 times in the New Testament, and the cognates *diakoneō* ('to minister') and diakonia ('ministry') occur between them a further 70 times. Basically, *diakonos* is a servant, and often a table servant, or waiter. In the New Testament, however, the word never quite loses its connection with the supply of material needs and service (Rom. 15:25, 2 Cor. 8:4).[8]

According to the Lutheran World Federation (LWF) contribution to the understanding and practice of diakonia; transformation, reconciliation and empowerment (2009), diakonia is a theological concept that points to the very identity and mission of the church. Another is its practical implication in the sense that diakonia is a call to action, as a response to challenges of human suffering, injustice and care for creation. The present use of the word has largely been shaped by how Christians have tried to be faithful to the biblical call to be a neighbours throughout the history of the church.[9]

Eco-Diakonia. It is in this respect a call to action in the ministry (*diakonia*) of safeguarding the ecological systems in which each servant (*diakonos*) must pay full commitment to the function of ministering (*diakoneō*), the same as devotion to the ministry of God the Creator.

Contribution of ACT Tanzania Forum Members to Eco-Diakonia

The forum joint workplan is the result of individual forum members' workplan in respective thematic areas where climate justice is cross-cutting. Individual member operations are linked to climate justice and eco-diakonia. Climate smart projects are part of climate justice interventions carried out to build capacity of communities for climate change adaptation and resilience. The following are the contributions of the ACT Forum member to eco-diakonia.

Climate, Environment and Food Security

The Christian Council of Tanzania (CCT) is the host organization of the forum, implementing adaptive and mitigative approaches in six regions across the Tanzania mainland and Zanzibar, through climate smart projects for responsive resilience and adaptation community capacity building. Through community initiatives such as IR-VICOBA, PAMOJA and IGAs, CCT enables communities to strongly address climate change related hazards by being responsive and adaptive. Over 15,000 trees have been planted, at the same time as promoting the best agricultural practices through Faming God's Way (conservation agriculture). Five districts have adopted this and over 2,400 IR-VICOBA members are practicing the method as an adaptive measure to curb the effects of climate change, whilst also improving household income.

CCT promotes climate friendly energy consumption. Energy saving stoves have been produced for beneficiaries' households to facilitate the use of limited energy with the aim of protecting the environment, and over 1,500 families have adopted the technology. The CCT solar energy project promotes the use of solar energy for lighting, cooking, irrigation and business, and 400 households have been reached with the technology. CCT also promotes best food storage practices as a way to cut down the post-harvest challenges faced by farmers with the aim of improving food security.

---

[8] Marshall, Millard, Packer, Wiseman (Eds), *New Bible Dictionary* 3rd Ed (Leicester: IVP, 1996), 61-162.

[9] 'Diakonia in Context: Transformation , Reconciliation and Empowerment. An LWF Contribution to the Understanding and Practice of Diakonia', Geneva 2009, in: https://www.lutheranworld.org/sites/default/files/DMD-Diakonia-EN-low.pdf.

By the year 2010, Africa will be the fastest growing continent on earth, surging from its present 701 million to over one billion. Yet in the 1980s total African food production actually decreased in the face of devastating drought which ravaged the center of the continent.[10]

Along with direct interventions, the organization also advocates for climate change at policy level. It participated in the development of National Climate Change Response Strategy 2021/2026 and Nationally Determined Contributions (NDCs).

Climate Smart and Renewable Energy

Norwegian Church Aid (NCA) is a forum international member. Among other projects is the integration of Climate Smart Agriculture (CSA) technologies and practices in SHE projects in Tanzania. Drip irrigation for the use of less water in order to ensure high productivity and profits in a small area is another intervention focusing on care for creation and eco-diakonia. The project includes activities such as the use of organic material during bed making, crop rotation including the planting of legumes, and mulching to reduce evaporation (hence less water and weed growth). Other activities include the use of organic fertilizers for improving soil fertility for agriculture, research and development by the world vegetable center (AVRDC), use of improved breeds for productivity, pest and disease resistance and better flock health management to reduce pests and diseases.

Improved feed is used so that animals produce more protein with less feed and lower emissions. Poultry feeds are made locally by entrepreneurs, and poultry is recognized for being among the 'greenest' meats, using up less resources and emitting less greenhouse gases than larger livestock. All these activities are contributing effectively to care for creation, promoting sustainable livelihoods and climate justice.

Food Adaptation and Mitigation Practices to Climate Change

The Evangelical Lutheran Church in Tanzania (ELCT), a local ACT Forum member, has been responding to climate change and creating awareness for adaptation and resilience to communities. In the agriculture sector food security has been adopted by communities in order to address food shortages, through the use of improved crops and breeding livestock for drought and pest tolerance. Schaefer asserts that, "Religious communities can play pivotal roles by reminding their members about traditions that can guide their attitudes, thoughts, and actions during this age of widespread ecological degradation".[11] As a result, knowledge of the relationship between effective food production to ensure household food security and a well-conceived ecology is vital.

In interventions to ensure eco-diakonia is exercised, ELCT promotes the use of improved soil and water conservation measures, water harvesting and the use of alternative environmental user-friendly sources of energy such as using energy saving stoves and solar power. As a result, living costs are cut down, contributing to poverty alleviation. ELCT commitment to promote integrity of creation in its new five-year strategic plan (2021-2025) is also one of the church responses to eco-diakonia that lead to the integration of afforestation programmes into the local government authorities' plans and budgets.

Climate justice sustainability interventions, including afforestation, are a prerequisite if the world is to envision a future where care for creation will be a fundamental role for everyone. Elsdon argues that a wrong relationship with creation flows from a wrong relationship with the creator.[12] In this regards, ELCT nurtures young believers toward environmental concerns through their confirmation classes by planting

---

[10] Dyke et al., 17

[11] Schaefer, James, *Theological Foundations for Environmental Ethics: Reconstructing Patristic and Medieval Concepts* (Washington: Georgetown University Press, 2009), 1.

[12] Elsdon, 185.

trees. This is made a priority to integrate the teachings of the church (doctrine) and eco-diakonia from an early age, at a stage if life when climate action can be profound. The church and other faith-based organization are striving to raise a generation in which the destruction of the creation is among other sins to avoid. According to Dyke at al, "The human species has no doubt sinned against the environment, but it has also sinned against itself – and God – which is why stories of redemption still possess power, even in an ecological age."[13] ACT Forum members consider the engagement of youth and children in climate action and gender equality in line with other faith-based advocacy roles from the grassroot levels.

Building Community Resilience for Climate Change Adaptation and Mitigation

Tanganyika Commission for Refugee Service (TCRS) is a local ACT forum member promoting food security by enhancing sustainable agriculture (including the cultivation of drought-coping higher yield crop varieties) and food storage. This project addresses the adverse effects of climate change using a value chains approach that honours nature. This initiative meets both vulnerable community priorities and needs, without compromising the future generation's ability to meet their own needs and take into account issues of healthy environment, economic profitability and social values. This project aims to enhance women, men, boys and girls to attain improved resilience for climate change, whilst also enjoying their rights. In addition, it aims to enable women and girls to realize their rights and attain sustainable wellbeing through self-employment and improved social services (livelihoods, water sanitation, and food security), responsive leadership and environmental sustainability.

The organization also educates communities in sustaining environmental sanitation to minimize the effects of epidemic diseases by the construction of sanitation and hygiene facilities at household and institution level. Community awareness is also raised, and knowledge about environment preservation matters is strengthened, including agro-forestry, forest management, conservation agriculture and the use of alternative affordable clean energy. Awareness creation and training on gender (GBV prevention), human rights and social justice to enhance gender equality and equity is implemented to contribute effectively to climate justice and eco-diakonia. The organization also facilitates communities to diversify livelihoods through entrepreneurship activities and by managing community-based fund reserves through a Village Community Bank (VICOBA) as an income source for poverty alleviation. The Village Government Leaders (VGL) are strengthened in their capacity to be accountable and responsible in disaster situations and related emergencies.

Conclusion

This article has described the role of the ecumenical ACT Forum Tanzania in the area of the churches witness for care for creation, climate justice and protection for biodiversity. One international and three local members have been sampled to show the various interventions implemented in Tanzania communities in areas of capacity building and policy influencing for climate justice.

Tanzania, being part of the Global South, needs the back-up of the forum to join the government initiatives toward care for creation. Such back-up is a fundamental prerequisite in which to provide a prophetic voice of the church for eco-diakonia as ecumenical action to tackle the root causes of the global environmental crisis, biodiversity destruction and climate change related health threats on both local, regional and global levels. The IHCC and eco-diakonia will cast light on what has been implemented and more interventions still needed to address the challenges associated with ecological destruction. The IHCC will also be a benchmark of where we have reached and where we still need to be in the role of eco-diakonia for sustainable livelihoods for both human beings and ecology.

---

[13] Dyke et al., 81.

Recommendations

In order for the sustainability of Eco-Diakonia and care for creation to be sustainable, a more joint and coordinated effort by all stakeholders towards adaptation and mitigation of climate change effects is required – FBOs, NGO, governments, international organizations and individual persons should take responsibility. Taking stock of successful interventions, learning and promoting adaptation of the best outcomes in local contexts should be our fundamental prerequisite. However, some interventions have failed or produced lesser output due to limited financial resources for their implementation. Therefore, soliciting more financing to support programs that support environmental (climate) advocacy issues should be a priority of all practitioners. The forum recommends for advocacy on the implementation of national climate change policies and commitments (nationally, regionally, continental and internationally) such as the National Climate Change Response Strategy 2021/2026 and the Nationally Determined Contributions (NDCs).

Exploring potential renewable energy sources that target the low-income bracket households such as promoting the clean cooking stove, so as to help to reduce the pressure on deforestation due to energy for domestic use (clean energy for all), is another yardstick for creation care. It should be a multi-sectoral task, building community environmental resilience and addressing systematic vulnerability at all levels, including ecumenical forums. The forums recommend the promotion of conservation agriculture (Farming God's Way), especially in dry areas, which is a good adaptation strategy for farmers. To ensure care for creation is the responsibility of everyone and that 'no one is left behind', the forum recommends the reduction of import duties, as well as taxes, on solar equipment with the aim of promoting the use of solar energy that could also be used in kitchen solutions. Sub-Sahara Africa is most suitable for solar energy as it has long sunny days.

Suggestions for Further Reading

Dunlap, Thomas R, *Faith in Nature: Environmental as Religious Quest* (Washington: University of Washington Press, 2004)

Dyke, Fred Van, Mahan, David C., Sheldon, Seph K. and Sheldon, Raymond H. *Redeeming Creation. The Biblical Basis for Environmental Stewardship* (Downers Grove: IVP, 1996).

Elsdon, Ron, *Greenhouse Theology: Biblical Perspectives on Caring for Creation.* England (Oxford: Monarch, 1992), 217-224.

Marshall, Millard, Packer, Wiseman (Eds), *New Bible Dictionary* 3rd Ed (Leicester: IVP, 1996).

Schaefer, James, *Theological Foundations for Environmental Ethics: Reconstructing Patristic and Medieval Concepts* (Washington: Georgetown University Press, 2009).

67. Eco-Diakonia as Joint Christian Action in the Understanding and Practice of the Church in Eastern Democratic Republic of Congo

Katsirabwenge Musongya Christine and Kambale Jean-Bosco Kahongya Bwiruka[1]

Introduction

Ecologically, the Democratic Republic of Congo (DRC) is a real paradise known for its dense tropical forests, which represent 47 percent of tropical African forests, the second largest tropical rainforest ecosystem after the Amazon. This vast rainforest is also home to some of the world's most spectacular wildlife, including gorillas, chimpanzees, forest elephants, and a multitude of bird varieties and insects. Regarding global warming, the Congo forest plays an important role in slowing down global climate change because it absorbs greenhouse gases, preventing them from being released into the atmosphere.

Demographically, more than 80 million people depend on this forest for their livelihoods from farming, hunting and harvesting of wild fruits and vegetables, edible oils, timber, and other essential products. This demographic growth, as well as the new industry over-exploitation by large companies, increases pressure upon the forest, the fertile land and the soil resources through unsustainable exploitation practices, thereby leading to the aggravation of poverty and the food insecurity of rural communities.[2] It is suggested that two to three animal or plant species disappear every day and, among them, some plants that could have contained necessary elements for producing medicines.

How far is the Christian community in eastern Congo aware of this rapid change and would they be ready to join their efforts to save the earth? This chapter highlights the daily practice of Christians in environmental protection and relates this commitment to the understanding of 'serving God' through the stewardship of creation.

Christian Awareness of Climate Change

In a recent article, Kambale Kahongya Bwiruka stated that for many Christians in the Central Africa region, protecting the environment has largely been seen as development programs and projects that come from outside, inspired mostly by governments, and only sometimes motivated and rooted in the local practices and traditions, such as protection of particular areas, species, farming according to seasons circle, etc. According to his observation, Christians have not thoroughly integrated environmental protection as a spiritual task and a responsibility towards the divine creation. He acknowledges, however, that only a few

---

[1] Katsirabwenge Musongya Christine is Head of the Department of Diaconia and Development of the Baptist Church in the Democratic Republic of Congo (CBCA), with a Master of Art in Diaconia and Management at the IMADM (2013), Bachelor of Health Institution Management (2004) and Diploma of Technics of Sewing (1999). Professor Rev. Dr Kambale J.-B. Kahongya Bwiruka (Dem. Rep. Congo) is an ordained pastor of the Baptist Church in Central Africa (CBCA), with a PhD in Intercultural Theology and Missiology from the Kirchliche Hochschule Wuppertal / Bethel in Germany. He serves as a professor in universities and as UEM-Advocacy Officer for Africa Region, and is an author of articles and books.

[2] See also https://www.fao.org/in-action/forest-landscape-restoration-mechanism/our-work/countries/democratic-republic-of-congo/en/.

Christians engage in such activities with an awareness of contributing to carbon dioxide emission reduction, and therefore mitigating the rise of global warming.[3]

Yet the Christian community in eastern Congo should consider 'serving ecology' (Eco-Diaconia) as a priority, in the same vein as to 'serve or worship God'. It can be a dangerous and risky game, thinking that it is up to someone else to take the initiative to stop the uncontrolled exploitation of the natural resources in the eastern part of Democratic Republic of Congo, to think that others will reduce air pollution. Why should Christian communities in the region integrate this task as a spiritual responsibility and therefore join efforts in fulfilling eco-diaconal duty?

Biblical Foundations of Eco-Diaconia

In the Christian tradition, the ecological issue is not a new theme. The biblical narrative of creation in Genesis 1:1-2, 1-4 and Genesis 2:4b-3, 24, as well as many of the Davidic Psalms, illustrate the greatness of creation and highlight the relationship between human beings and nature.[4] Even talking about the human body's cycle, in Genesis 3:19, God told Adam that his body would return to the ground when he died because out of it he was taken: "(…) for dust you are, and unto dust you shall return." For Yvon Christian Elenga, what many tend to overlook in this sentence is the ecological aspect, that God was describing a fundamental part of the carbon cycle. He argues that if God created us in his image and gave us domination over the works of his hands, over what belongs to him as a craftsman, then this tells us how we were supposed to exercise this domination: in the manner of God, acting for God! All our interactions with what God has created, whether animate or inanimate objects, must therefore consist of acting in God's way, and in a way which corresponds to God's love.[5]

If the task of mankind is to 'keep and cultivate' the garden, then this is not only a physical task, but much more a spiritual one. In fact, in Hebrews, the verbs 'to cultivate' (*'avad*) and 'to keep' (*samar*) both have a religious connotation, to 'keep' the commandments of God. Then the verb to cultivate and to work can have the meaning of 'worshiping' or 'serving God' in reference to the activity of the Levites in the tabernacle erected in the desert, or in the temple of Jerusalem. Priests were required to 'guard' the sanctuary, and in particular, to preserve the purity of the holy place from any profane defilement. The authority of human beings, delegated by God, and their vocation to fill and cultivate the earth, to identify, to name and to protect the living beings, is also worship to God. Therefore, it is criminal for humanity to misuse the dominion power and to be responsible for damage caused on the earth instead of taking care of it.[6]

The laws of the Old Testament, enunciated by Moses and recalled by the prophets, highlight the connection between the earth, its fruitfulness, and the moral as well as the religious obedience of God's people. The people of Israel were to keep the Sabbath, one day a week, and not work on that day. For these men and women that rest was a sign of their dependence on the Lord, of their faith in God who could provide for their needs, even when they rested. It was a reminder to them that they were creatures limited in time and space and that they had to respect their limits, as well as those of other creatures, including the animals they worked with.

The earth itself had to 'enjoy its Sabbaths' in order to bear more fruits. But when these commandments were transgressed, the earth, literally 'vomited' the inhabitants (Leviticus 18:27). This means the earth does not support over-exploitation by human beings, as this makes the earth sick. It suffers the effects of human

---

[3] Kambale J.-B. Kahongya Bwiruka, 'Leanings of UEM-Churches in Eco-Diakonia Commitment in Central and Eastern Africa' (article in section IV in this volume).

[4] Mulago gwa Gikala, *The Traditional Religion of the Bantu and Their Worldview* (Kinshasa: Faculté de Théologie Catholique de Kinshasa, 1980), 126.

[5] Yvon Christian Elenga, S.J., *Creation and Vision of Man: An African Reading of Laudato Si'* (Abidjan – Costa do Marim: Instituto de Teologia Da Companhia from Jesus, 2016), 136.

[6] *The Bible and Ecology*, https://lire.la-bible.net/reflexion/la-bible-et-l_ecologie.

disobedience to God's laws. This close link between obedience to God, the favorable climate, the fertility of the earth and the abundance of crops is clearly mentioned in the statement of blessings and curses, especially in Leviticus and Deuteronomy. In short, the solidarity among creatures ensures the safeguarding of the whole creation. How do churches carry out the service of ecology in this region?

The Eco-Diakonia Concept and Practice of the Baptist Church in Central Africa

After the Roman Catholic Church, the Baptist Church in Central Africa (CBCA) is the largest Protestant church in the Eastern part of the Democratic Republic of Congo. In ecological commitment, still it deserves to be mentioned as second, followed by the Seventh Day Adventist Church.

For the CBCA, the concept of ecology is part of the fulfilment of the holistic mission of the church. This mission considers the spiritual salvation of human beings but also cares for the creation. However, this ecological concept is not yet fully developed in academic discourses; rather, it is visible in a practical way, as Father Christian Ndoki put it.[7] It is a way of living and entering into a relationship with the world, while respecting it. It is lived as practice and experience.

In fact, the practice of Eco-Diakonia has a long tradition in all the three missionary churches (Roman Catholic Church, Seventh Day Adventist Church and the Baptist Church in Central Africa). This practice goes back to the days of the first missionaries (for the Baptists in 1927-1959). It involves all social categories of people in the church and it is carried out by all departments.

For example, in the Baptist church, while the development department integrates Eco-Diakonia into its agricultural programs, the women's department integrates it in their program of financially empowering women. Youth and children departments, on the other hand, apply Eco-Diakonia in the celebration of the annual Youth Climate Action Day. On the side of the advocacy department, Eco-Diakonia is addressed in the promotion of renewable energies, as well as in advocating for the protection of indigenous peoples' lands. This is observed conjointly in the three large churches just mentioned, although to be more specific, this article will focus more on the Baptist church.

Although many activities related to Eco-Diakonia are fully implemented conjointly by different churches, the theological conceptualization of the theme has not yet been elaborated, and therefore is not yet fully integrated in the church liturgy. In another article, Kambale Kahongya elaborates on more reasons why Christians in the Baptist church have not yet understood that careering for the creation is a spiritual responsibility. Amongst some of the kerygmatic reasons he mentions is the high focus on human-centered soteriology and eschatology,[8] leading to in the mind of many Christians in eastern Congo that somehow the whole creation seems to be excluded from the salvation process it has been waiting for (as stated in Romans 8:19-22 by the Apostle Paul.[9]

Nevertheless, for two decades now some Baptist theologians have started to focus research on eco-theology in academic way. This shows the important development of connecting faith and the welfare of the creation. This is what Kathleen Quiring supports when stating that protecting the planet is vital to a

[7] Father Ndoki, a Jesuit, from the Democratic Republic of Congo, engineer in agriculture and rural development, Professor at the Faculty of Agricultural and Veterinary Sciences of Loyola University in Congo. Responding to question: 'Why can't we echo gestures of respect for the environment as we have echoed barrier gestures against Covid-19?': https://www.vaticannews.va/fr/afrique/news/2020-10/l-ecologie-l-affaire-de-tout-le-peuple-africain.html

[8] Kambale J.-B. Kahongya Bwiruka, 'Eco-Theology in an African Perspective: Why the Delay to Embody Eco-Theology in African Christianity?', In Louk Andrianos, Michael Biel & al (eds.) *Kairos for the Creation. Confessing Hope for the Earth* (Solingen: Foedus-Verlag, 2019), 121-131.

[9] "For the anxious looking out of the creature expects the revelation of the sons of God. For the creation has been made subject to vanity, not of its will, but by reason of him who has subjected [the same], in hope that the creature itself also shall be set free from the bondage of corruption into the liberty of the glory of the children of God".

Christ-centered life.[10] It is also the conviction of Fidon Mwombeki when he states that "the welfare of the earth is our welfare".[11] In this regard, the Baptist church experiences Eco-Diakonia in planting trees and flowers, promoting clean energy and caring for all creation.

Tree and Flower Planting

Initially, the tradition of planting trees on church lands was not inspired by the idea of reducing carbon dioxide emissions. It was instead part of the traditional culture of marking boundaries on the land to protect it from land grabbing. Thus, since the time of the missionaries all the lands of churches, hospitals and schools were surrounded by trees. Later on, for the sake of investment and construction of infrastructure, trees were planted, but this time within the boundaries of the land, to produce building materials or for economic reasons, as they could be sold as wood or as planks.

Another use of trees is as domestic charcoal and firewood, and also in the manufacture of bricks and tiles. These activities have been performed, until now, by Christians as well as non-Christians. Every year youth and children have been learning to implement these activities in collaboration with other members of the United Evangelical Mission (UEM) during the celebration of the Youth Climate Action Day in December.

Apart from ordinary trees, the church has developed the tradition of planting fruit trees (avocado, orange, lemon, mango, banana, guava, etc.) on its land. All these tree varieties, beyond the fact that they contribute to the reduction of poverty and improve the health of the population, contribute enormously to reduce carbon dioxide emissions. As an ecological impact that people can directly notice, the rainfall has increased during the year, even in regions which were not previously covered by tropical forest.

Flower Garden in the Liturgy and Worship

Until the 1990s, the CBCA planted flowers around church buildings. These flowers were used to decorate churches during worship but also had a liturgical role, especially in wedding celebrations. On the eve of a wedding, the bride would collect a bouquet of flowers while the bridesmaids[12] were also collecting a large quantity of flowers in a basket that they would then spread on the ground in front of the couple during the liturgical procession. This glorious ceremony has remained a hallmark of the Baptist Church. Unfortunately, due to the influence of modernity and the excessive use of synthetics and plastic materials, natural flowers tended to disappear and are being replaced by artificial ones. As a result the flower gardens are slowly being abandoned for lawns. How can this change from natural flowers to artificial ones be explained?

It seems that the reason is found in a weak theological and liturgical valuation of flowers. Indeed, by using natural flowers in decoration of pulpits, the ornament of weddings and even funeral ceremonies, the church did not develop a permanent and coherent theological content to appreciate and to crystallize the role of flowers in Christian worship.

In fact, the use of flowers and other elements of the creation in decorating the place of worship is not just a simple aesthetic human desire. Rather, for humans it is their recognition of being part of God's worshipers among the multitude of the whole creation – human and non-human. This global worship generates an agreeable perfume in the face of the creator and lord of the universe, as expressed by the Psalmist" "The heavens declare the glory of God, and the expanse manifests the work of his hands" (Psalm

---

[10] Kathleen Quiring, 'What Does Jesus Have to Do with the Environment?', www.theguardian.com, 6 October 2014.

[11] Fidon Mwombeki, General Secretary of the All Africa Conference of Churches, interpreting the prophecy of Jeremiah in regards to the protection of the nature during the session of COP 26 UN-Climate Summit in Glasgow on 8 November 2021.

[12] The bridesmaids were called *Watupa Maua*, which means those who spread the flowers.

19). In this joint worship echoes the divine refrain of the beauty, which punctuates the creation liturgy: "...God saw that it was good..." (Genesis 1).

Returning to the use of flowers in wedding ceremonies, it can be admitted today that flowers more or less universally symbolize love – love that gives itself to the beloved and love that is proposed. However, flowers also symbolize the beautiful communion of the couple, which through the marriage mixes the perfumes generated by both and produce a new attractive and romantic smell (Genesis 2:22-25; Song of Songs 2:10-17). In addition, flowers are the symbol of joy and happiness released like a perfume by the couple all around them. However, the perfume can only survive thanks to a permanent refreshing of the flower. Therefore watering is a mandatory task, without which the flower withers, dries, and dies.

This symbolism is theologically very deep. The flower of love in any relationship, whether human or divine, survives through its daily maintenance. Nothing is won in advance or definitively. This is what makes the use of artificial flowers completely absurd and wrong. Artificial flowers do not have the capacity of either growing or regenerating, or even generating perfume. They are static and represent just a fake beauty, a fake life, a dead reality that has already expired. In 'Eco-Diakonia language', artificial flowers are just dangerous waste that kills the church environment, both in worship joint communion with the whole creation, and in the lack of lively love in relationships.

Finally, when flowers accompany us to death, they remind us both on the shortness of our earthly life (life cycle, joy of life, suffering in life, human activities, etc. Psalm 103:15-16), but also of hope for the future through the resurrection (John 12:23-25). Therefore, due to ecological concerns, churches have many theological justifications to permanently maintain the use of natural flowers in the liturgy, as well as in Eco-Diakonia, which is one of the daily expression of the Christian faith.

Legacy of the Indigenous Traditional Technology

The CBCA has members from several ethnic groups, and each one develops a particular traditional art and technology. Among these peoples are the pygmies, called also Batwa in Rwanda, who are the very first indigenous people in Central Africa. They are the owners of the culture of ceramic art. Learning from them, the women's department of the CBCA is now implementing an ecological program consisting of producing and disseminating improved cooking stoves.

This initiative came from the Anglican Church in Rwanda which through the Rural Development Interdiocesan Service (RDIS) has developed this technology to a semi-industrial level as a carbon credit project. The project consists of producing and distributing the ceramics improved cooking stoves and water filters which contribute tremendously to the reduction of carbon dioxide emissions. In Rwanda, the project started in 1991, but was scaled-up in 2015. The goal is to improve the living standards of households and to reduce the strain on natural resources. Today, the number of improved cooking stoves produced annually is 30,000, with a budget of €750,000.00. For such a capacity the project requires a staff of 87, which provides significant job creation for women and youth. The environmental impact of this production is that one improved cooking stove reduces emissions by 1.62 tons of carbon dioxide per household per year. Just the 30,000 stoves produced and distributed in Rwanda annually would reduce about 48,600 tons of CO_2 per year. Considering that these stoves are designed to last longer than ten years, the emission reduction in that period would be roughly 486,000 tons. These calculations are based only on Rwandan production and would increase if the production of Baptist women in DR Congo was taken into consideration.

Promoting Renewable Energy

The CBCA operates in an area where the sun shines the whole year. Therefore, thanks to the partnership with the UEM, since the 1980s the church has taken the opportunity to develop the installation of solar panel systems in hospitals, schools, universities, and some church buildings, offices, etc. Currently, through the financial capacity building of SACOSS system and small credits, many members have successfully installed solar panels on their houses. This clean energy is used for lighting, charging phones, running radios, televisions and other household electronic equipment. Even in some parishes solar energy is used to empower musical and electronic equipment during church services.

Recently the CBCA has discovered the biogas system associated with stall farming. Two pilot projects are installed in Vayana and Kitsimba Districts, located on a high altitude in the eastern part of the town of Butembo, in the territories of Beni and Lubero in the DRC. Both districts are bordered on the eastern part by the Virunga National Park in the Rift Valley, which extends to the border with Uganda in the further east.

In the years 1970-1990, the region was the main producer of vegetables (carrots, beets, cabbages, onions, garlic, leeks, soups, potatoes, etc.) which fed most of the east of the country, including the northern province, especially the cities of Bunia, Isiro and Kisangani. Cereals such as wheat, finger millet, corn and other products like fish, pig and rabbit meat were the specialties of the Kyondo-Luhotu and Masereka region. These activities contributed to the economy in the area, and particularly in the construction of the cities of Butembo and Beni.

However, as the fertility of this region boosted the rapid increase of its population, this simultaneously created a demographic pressure manifested by two phenomena. Firstly, there was an increase of the population in the neighboring regions where the CBCA operates, such as the districts of Mambowa, Maboya, Beni and Vuyinga, but also in Virunga National Park, a protected reserve along the border with Uganda. The young population moved there to acquire more space for farming and ranching. Secondly, in the region of Vayana and Kitsimba, cultivable space was greatly reduced and is no longer sufficient, even for a small family of approximately six members.

With this high density, a field that could have once fed a family of ten must now as the children grow up be divided into small lots, so that each of them gets a small space to feed their own small family. So, over the decades, the land (which never increases in size) runs out of steam through overexploitation and so becomes sterile. This situation generates land conflicts for the control of land between members of the same large family.

Although the population of the region is traditionally of pastoral vocation, still there are no livestock farms due to insufficient land being available. For this reason, it is not surprising to run into a whole herd grazing in the middle of a road! This straying of domestic animals leads to the destruction of field crops and creates permanent conflicts between herders and farmers.

Hydroelectric Dam

The CBCA is not simply limited to small domestic initiatives. It has larger ambitions in terms of energy production, having built a hydroelectric dam to supply schools, universities, hospitals, churches and homes in Ndoluma and Kitsombiro towns. This project has inspired other people to create cooperatives for building small hydroelectric power stations. In a country where the state is completely absent in the construction of infrastructures, it is only the church that remains the credible institution on which society can rely.

Conclusion

Despite the absence of a systematic, scientific and theological elaboration of the concept of eco-diakonia within the CBCA, there is a common practical experience of all the groups in the church in the form of a development program implemented in the framework of social commitments.

This commitment is part of the understanding of the holistic mission which considers salvation as a global and integral reality. The salvation of Jesus proclaimed by the church is not limited to freeing the human being from the slavery of sin, but much more it aims to improve their living environments, to provide them with abundant life (John 10:10).

However, the abundant life is not for the benefit of human beings alone, but rather it must integrate all the creation. This is why the service that Christians render to themselves in improving their own well-being, through the protection of the environment, should be theologically elaborated, in order to establish the link between 'serving God' – in the sense of worshiping him – and 'taking care of the creation' – in the sense of continuing the work of God, the creator.

Since the Baptist church as well as the Roman Catholic Church and the Seventh Day Adventist Church together promote the abundant life in their practices, there is a need to join their efforts in integrating the whole creation in their respective theological discourses and liturgical practices of their respective churches.

In this way, all Christians, as well as the whole church, will recover the true value of 'serving or worshiping God in partaking in his own holy work'. Like the Apostle Paul wrote to the Ephesians, "What you revere without knowing it is what I announce to you" (Acts 17:23b); so too will the Christian community in the region discover that, without knowing it, they have laid the practical foundations of Eco-Diakonia through development programs. This theological understanding will encourage more people to join with the spiritual motivation, i.e. the mission of protecting the creation.

Suggestion for Further Reading

Kambale J.-B. Kahongya Bwiruka, 'Leanings of UEM-Churches in Eco-Diakonia Commitment in Central and Eastern Africa' (article in section IV in this volume).

Kambale J.-B. Kahongya Bwiruka, 'Eco-Theology in an African Perspective: Why the Delay to Embody Eco-Theology in African Christianity?', In Louk Andrianos, Michael Biel & al (eds.) *Kairos for the Creation. Confessing Hope for the Earth* (Solingen: Foedus-Verlag, 2019), 121-131.

Mulago gwa Gikala, The Traditional Religion of the Bantu and their Worldview (Kinshasa: Faculté de Théologie Catholique de Kinshasa, 1980).

Yvon Christian Elenga, S.J., *Creation and Vision of Man: An African Reading of Laudato Si'* (Abidjan – Costa do Marim: Instituto de Teologia Da Companhia from Jesus), 2016.

'La Bible et l'écologie', (sans auteur) in, *Lire la Bible, Alliance biblique universelle*, in: https://lire.la-bible.net/reflexion/la-bible-et-l_ecologie.

Father Ndoki, interview on 'Why can't we echo gestures of respect for the environment as we have echoed barrier gestures against Covid-19?' – see https://www.vaticannews.va/fr/afrique/news/2020-10/l-ecologie-l-affaire-de-tout-le-peuple-africain.html.

Kathleen Quiring, 'What Does Jesus Have to Do with the Environment?', www.theguardian.com, 6 October 2014.

Fidon Mwombeki, 'The Welfare of the Earth is our Welfare', COP 26 UN-Climate Summit in Glasgow on 8th November 2021 on https://www.youtube.com/watch?v=bUHcaVJCiPY

Ernst M. Conradie (ed.), *Creation and Salvation*, Vol.1 (Münster: LIT Verlag, 2012).

https://www.fao.org/in-action/forest-landscape-restoration-mechanism/our-work/countries/democratic-republic-of-congo/en/

68. The Green Church Concept in the Anglican Church of Rwanda – A New Eco-Diaconal Paradigm

Jered Kalimba[1]

Introduction

The whole world is nowadays passing through traumatic calamities of climate. This disorder makes people aware of having failed their responsibilities of protecting God's creation. Indeed, our climate has changed tremendously – the normal cycle of rain and dry season is no longer, and our rivers, lakes and seas are becoming more dry. Humanity is anxious due to the climate's caprice and dangers that they themselves have given rise to. People forgot their role of stewardship and failed indubitably in their responsibilities. The Anglican Church of Rwanda (EAR) is raising its prophetic voice, reminding men and women of their duties towards the creation. She is sensitive and feels concerned for protecting the environment, attempting many ways to fight against the factors that destroy our earth. She is doing her best to change our earth again into the original Garden of Eden. In this essay we are going to show some practical models conceived by this church to keep the greenness of the earth and therefore to protect the creation of God. We will be referring to three points particularly under the headings, 'Theology of Creation', 'Changing the Deteriorated Eden into a Paradise', and 'Models of Practice in the Anglican Church of Rwanda'.

About Theology of Creation

God, Master of the universe is the Creator of all that exists.[2] He created humanity in his own image and all the beings were created in an unequal perfection. However, the creation was degraded by sin and humans were the first actors of that deterioration. Nevertheless, through the coming of Jesus in this world, the creation recovers its original state.

The creation is made by the Word of God. The word pronounced by him has the power of action which is the first source and the driving strength of all beings. God has to only speak; his voice has the power of action. As Saint Augustine explained, "Every day, God contemplated his creation; he saw that by its arrangement, his work was good and very harmonious. He gave to the whole creation a more achieved beauty than the perfection of each element taken singularly."[3]

The creation was made from nothing (ex-nihilo) by the Word of God. Humankind has to respect this order of God because life is rooted in God. All these beings satisfy our God because they constitute the cradle of life and the locus of the fullness and fulfilment.

The human being represents the wonder of the whole creation. He and she are made in God's image. Humankind has to lead animals and plants and to take care. Men and women are made responsible as managers and stewards of the creation of God. Humankind has to dominate, protect, respect and engage safe relations with creation. Unfortunately, sin changed the life in the Garden of Eden. It is no longer a

---

[1] Rt Rvd Dr Jered KALIMBA has been the Bishop of Shyogwe Diocese since June 1997 and Dean of Bishops since 2018 in the Anglican Church of Rwanda. He is also Lecturer of Contextual Ethics at the Protestant Institute of Arts and Sciences (PIASS) at Huye and the East African Christian College (EACC), Kigali. He is a member of Protestant Council of Rwanda (CPR) and President of RDIS (Rural and Development Inter-Diocesan Service).

[2] Genesis1:1-30.

[3] Saint Augustine, Confessions (Paris: Edit Gallimard, 1993), 454. See also Genesis 2:8-25; Genesis 3:1-24; Isaiah 32:15-17; Ezekiel 47:1-12; Romans 8:18-21.

paradise; the ground is cursed and brings thorns and thistles. Adam has failed, he is naked and Eden lost its beauty. The second Adam, Jesus, will bring a new Eden and make it as the first was.

The prophets and certain passages in the New Testament express the promise of universal peace made by reconciliation between all the living beings. That peace proclaims not only the absence of wars, injustice, and violence, but also abundance and fullness in the natural location – the desert shall be converted into paradisical garden, and bitter water shall be changed into sweet water and shall nourish plants, whose leaves shall keep their greenness without any sign of fading.

The Anglican Church of Rwanda (EAR) is founded on the word of God. As the Bible recommends, her determination is to bring back Eden and its greenness. She is teaching peoples to take up their responsibilities towards the environment until the coming of Jesus for the redemption of the whole of creation. We affirm with Larry Rasmussen that,

> Earth-honoring faith is discipleship, a calling and a praxis... all species, the earth, the waters, and the air are good, since they are integral parts of the planet which sustain their shared existence ... Since creation is good, God entrusted it to human beings, humans are God's stewards. Central to the theology of creation is the notion of stewardship ... God declares that creation is good. There is a divine imperative for humans to take care of creation.[4]

Changing the Deteriorated Eden into a Paradise

The creation is sick, our environment is losing its greenness and this disease can only be secured by humankind who serves as the promoter. This creation's sickness needs a doctor indeed, and men and women have indeed the cure in their hands.

The eco-diaconal example of the Bugesera region in Rwanda could help us to understand how people can intervene and save their environment. Bugesera has many lakes, but before the 1994 Tutsi genocide, the water reduced and some lakes even became totally dry. The churches, in collaboration with the current government, put effort into fighting erosion by creating terraces and taking out sands that were drying up the rivers, planting grasses on the edges of lakes and building large dams to conserve water across the whole of East Rwanda. Within a short time, the lakes' water returned and now this region is enjoying the vegetation and freshness of the climate brought about by the new strategy. Not only plants, but also farming and tree planting were revitalized, animals flourished and now the life is once again enjoyable in Bugesera.

From this illustration it becomes clear that people are changing their minds and playing their role regarding the environment. Our earth could be transformed into a paradise and keep its greenness forever. Men and women are stewards of the environment and have to preserve the creation of God by protecting resources from destruction. It is time for humankind to stop causing disorder and destruction. Many animals and plants have disappeared and been degenerated due to humanity's caprice and spirit of dominance and destruction. It is human beings who are responsible for water and air pollution, for throwing away toxic waste and plastic anywhere and anyhow. Thanks to the government of Rwanda for completely banning the use of plastics! Thanks also to the churches that fully supported this noble idea of plastic eradication.

To bring back the original Eden greenness, people have to stop exploiting the land and the mineral resources without balance. All the good soil is lost through our rivers; erosion is making our land naked, and in the end we will transform it into it a desert. Thanks to the Anglican Church, who joins the Rwandan government's efforts fighting against the effect of erosion in this country of thousand hills by forming terraces across those hills.

---

[4] Rasmussen, Larry, *Earth-Honoring Faith: Religious Ethics in a New Key* (Oxford: Oxford University Press, 2014), 24.

The EAR is training people to take care of and advocate for animals and plants. She also teaches people to avoid burning bushes and forests, as this is destroying a large amount of our fauna and flora. The church also educates people to abandon and fight against the pollution of our rivers and lakes due to waste and dead bodies thrown into them. In this anti-pollution line, all cars have to use electricity, and public transport also has to be converted in this move towards fossil-free energy supplies.

The reflection and practice of Christian ethics also needs to challenge science that is shamefully denaturing the creation by various manipulations, in particular genetic engineering. Humankind has become more egocentric and exploits only for their own interests, without balancing this with the wellbeing of other creatures.

The EAR has to raise its voice and tell people to stop all this destruction in order to bring back the dignity of both human beings and the greenness of the Garden of Eden.

Practical Models in the Anglican Church of Rwanda

Plantation of trees

Rwanda is an over-populated country depending mostly on agriculture. Deforestation increases due to efforts to avail more land for farming and building houses. As a result the greenness reduces day by day.

One of the major strategies to protect our environment and keep its greenness is to plant and preserve trees. EAR has encouraged Christians to plant more trees. The Rwandan government also has a well-developed policy on environment conservation. There is even a popular song exhorting Rwandans to 'cut one and plant two'. EAR counts more than 3,000 chapels or churches spread throughout Rwandan villages, and every chapel has her own plot of land. Since 1979, the church began to teach people how to establish tree nurseries of different species. Every year, the tree-planting project has distributed and helped to plant more than 200,000 tree seedlings for fruit and agro-forestry. Each tree nursery has 25,000 seedlings for agro-forestry, trees for fruit, for timber, for firewood and soil conservation, livestock fodder, income generation, shade etc. Some are planted in community woodlots, others in public places such as on road belts.

EAR leads this project through the Rural Development Inter-Diocesan Service (RDIS), a faith based organization owned by the church. RDIS serves nearly half of the Rwandan population in the southern and western provinces.

Stoves and water filter project

This project is a Carbon Credits for Emission Reduction (CCER), aiming to improve the living standards of households and reduce the strain on natural resources through the distribution of Improved Cook Stoves (ICS) and Ceramic Water Filters (CWF). EAR implements this project through RDIS, addressing poverty eradication by capacity building and training villagers. Cutting down of trees for firewood and charcoal is reduced, and according to research by RDIS workers, the improved stoves and water filters project has had a good impact on economic growth and environmental protection. It is affordable for rural communities, reduces carbon emissions and poverty, saves money, forests and time in cooking, and diminishes respiratory and eye diseases (due to reduced smoke exposure).

Improved stoves and water filters are made locally by trained villagers who use clay from the Shyogwe diocese valley. The beneficiaries are playing a major role in environmental protection by reducing emissions. Community members are also trained on how to install, maintain and repair the stoves. RDIS affirms that this project is financially viable and can generate a significant volume of carbon credits.

EAR via RDIS is financially and technically supported by Makerere University of Uganda, United Evangelical Mission in Germany, Bread for the World, Klima-Kollekte and the Ministry of Environment in Rwanda. EAR is raising awareness to many people in Rwanda, and also in East African countries and churches aiming to see many using these stoves and water filters for the same purpose.

Waste management

EAR through RDIS is also concerned with waste management, or waste reduction, the preferred approach in preventing environmental degradation. African cities, towns and shopping centres are growing rapidly and hygiene and sanitation are questionable. Therefore, the health of people is affected due to the poor collection, treatment, transportation, storage, and eventual disposal of waste. The beneficiaries of the project are church's training centres, guest houses, schools and health centres. Special training is given to managers and personnel and youth, and in particular to those who are able to influence others. Special waste bins and related waste management policies are distributed to these institutions.

The bins were conceived and designed by RDIS workers and made locally by carpenters from Gitarama Parish, Shyogwe Diocese. Bins are composed of three compartments: organic and compostable materials, non-recyclable waste and recyclable bottles and plastics. They were also sold by the affiliated companies of RDIS and Anglican Church institutions such as schools, health centres and guest houses. Looking forward, EAR wishes to transform the waste into land fertilizers and briquettes used for burning stoves and water filters

Urumuli iwacu: light at our homes – the solar home system

This project is a response to the challenge that Africa has 500 million people who still do not have access to energy. They use firewood or kerosene for lighting or cooking. In Rwanda, only 40.5% have regular access to energy. This lack of electricity constitutes a vacuum in the development of Africa and Rwanda.

Urumuri iwacu is a project for supplying Solar Home Systems. This is a joint project of the Presbyterian Church of Rwanda (EPR), the EAR, the dioceses of Butare, Cyangugu, Kigeme and Shyogwe via Rural Development Inter-Diocesan Service (RDIS) and One For the Climate.[5] The project aims to provide electricity to homes living far from the existing grid lines. Those homes are confronted with problems such as lack of access to communication tools (for example computers and mobile phones), children are hindered from doing their homework, and many households still use firewood or oil lamps and kerosene to lighten their houses, therefore contributing to the environmental destruction.

This lack of electricity is a challenge for remote areas and a handicap for some services requiring electricity. Solar Home Systems contribute greatly in the development of the country in general and households in particular. If solar energy substitutes or reduces the use of kerosene and firewood, this would have several long term impacts on both single families and on the entire community. It would decrease sickness or death by indoor pollution, decrease the cost of healthcare, children could do their homework more regularly and thus increase levels of education and the generation of employment. Solar energy is cheaper, saving money, and unused firewood for lighting reduces deforestation.

Conclusion

We conclude by taking this opportunity to thank the EAR with close collaboration of RDIS for their good stewardship and hard work towards the respect and dignity of creation. We address also our appreciation to this church for rising up her prophetic voice and speaking loudly about climate change, and for all the initiatives started that the church is smartly caring on. We hope that all the activities of preventing the effects of climate change done by EAR may be practical models to lighten many African communities.

[5] An international organization which works with churches in Rwanda. It connects people around the world to take community action on climate change through investments in renewable energy.

Suggestions for Further Reading

Augustine, *Confessions* (Paris: Edit Gallimard, 1993).

Feinberg, John S. and Feinberg, Paul D., *Ethics for a Brave New World*, 2nd Edition (Wheaton: Crossway Books , 2010).

Gustafson, James, *Ethics from a Theocentric Perspective*, Volume I (Chicago: University of Chicago Press, 1983).

Habel, Norman C., 'Earth-Mission, the Third Mission of the Church', *Currents in Theology and Mission* 37, no.2, 2010.

Motte, Jochen and Parlindungam, Andar, '"Mission Still Possible?": Global Perspectives on Mission Theology and Mission Practice: Contributions to a Conference of the United Evangelical Mission 20 Years After Internationalization', Dumaguete, Philippines, June 26th - June 30th, 2016 (Foedus Verlag 2017).

Rasmussen, Larry, *Earth-Honoring Faith: Religious Ethics in a New Key* (Oxford: Oxford University Press, 2014).

RDIS Organization, contribution to CO_2 Emission Reduction, website: www.rdis.org.rw and http//www.twitter.com/RDISforRwanda

Appendix

Planting trees

The church preparing trees from the nursery to be distributed to the community

The church encourages the youth to plant trees to care for environment

Stoves and water filters

Energy saving stoves from the furnace

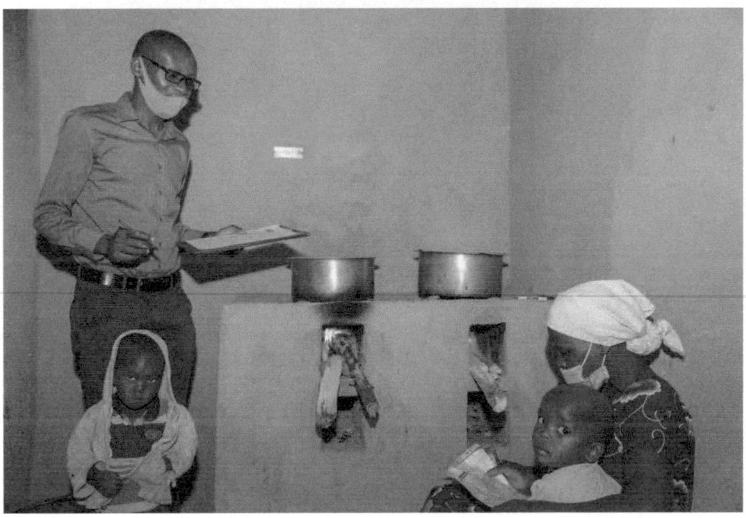

Community benefiting from the installed energy saving stoves

Water filters to be distributed to the beneficiaries

Happy people after receiving the water filters from the church

Waste management system

Solar Home System

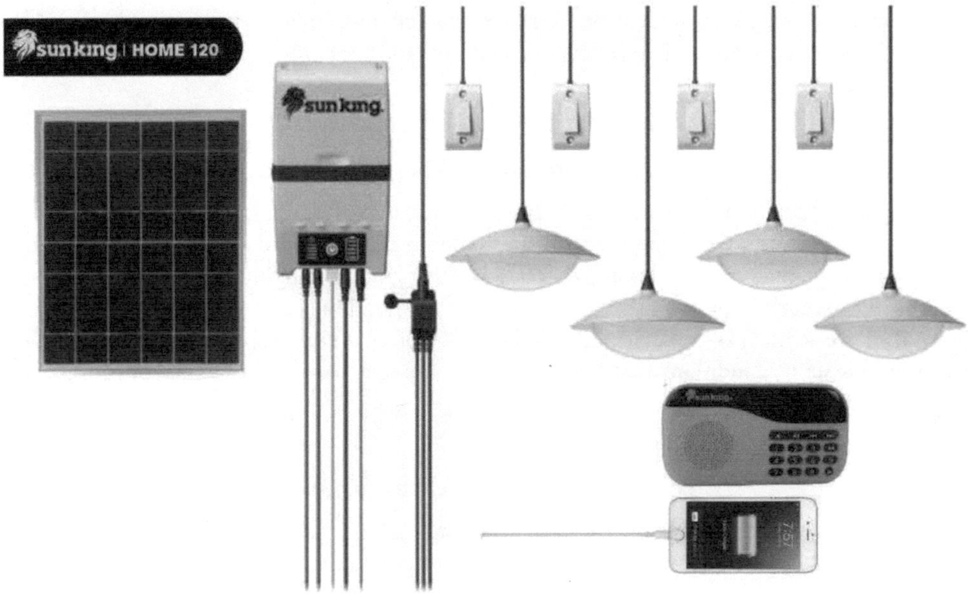

This light system is helping a lot of people who cannot access electricity from the grid

69. The Contribution of Religions for Peace Interfaith Youth Network on Climate Justice in Africa

Agathe Sagne and El hadj Magezi[1]

Introduction

The issues of climate change and environmental degradation have attracted the attention of the entire human family in recent decades, but it could be argued that awareness alone is not enough. Concrete action must be taken before it is too late as climate change and environmental degradation are the greatest threats facing humanity. These consequences can be mitigated if resolutions on climate change and environmental degradation are implemented at all levels.

This paper proposes the concepts of 'common good' and 'religion' as a framework to address the contribution of the interfaith youth network in preserving the environment; it also calls for a re-evaluation of the engagement of religious leaders on issues related to the environment. In this paper, the term environment will be used to refer to nature, land, climate and the common home – these are a common good and must be respected and protected by all.

Conceptual Clarification and Meaning of the Common Good

The 'common good' refers to those facilities – whether material, cultural or institutional – that the members of a community provide to all members to fulfill a relational obligation they all have to care for certain interests that they have in common.[2] It can be defined as the set of public interests shared by a community as a whole, such as security, justice, peace etc. The common good thus aims to promote the well-being of the individual in the context of the wider community. It is from this perspective that we can define the common good as a set of conditions that facilitate social life and enable individuals or groups to achieve their goals and perfection more fully and easily.

The Environment as a Common Good

The environment is that free space shared by all living beings. Moreover, the environment is not only shared by humans, but by all living species as a heritage. It is the very cradle in which all kinds of life, including human life, is born, nurtured, nourished and preserved. Pope Francis presents the environment as a common good that belongs to all and is meant for all, since, according to him, "everything is interconnected".[3]

---

[1] Ms. Agathe Mossane SAGNE is the Youth Representative in African Council of Religious Leaders-Religions for Peace. She is a Senegalese by nationality who comes from a strong Catholic family. Her career started with the Young Catholic Students (YCS) where she also joined the YCS National Team of Senegal in 2007. From being Secretary in charge of information, communication and documentation, she ended up being responsible for projects and programs after being in charge of training at national level. She also worked with YCS at the university level and currently serves as regional coordinator of IYCS Africa. El hadj Magezi, the second author, is co-chair of the African Interfaith Youth Network (AIYN) of Religion for Peace, together with Agathe Mossane Sagne (2016-2021).

[2] https://plato.stanford.edu/entries/common-good/

[3] https://www.vatican.va/content/francesco/fr/encyclicals/documents/papa-francesco_20150524_enciclica-laudato-si.html

Religion and Environment

All religions agree that nature is divine and should be treated as such. As a marker of identity across borders, religion influences many environmentally relevant behaviours. It is therefore essential to recognize its contribution in addressing environmental challenges.

Through the establishment of faith-based non-governmental organizations, the world's religions have helped to stimulate the debate on environmental protection and sustainable development. However, given the urgency of the climate crisis, the world would benefit most from the considerable influence of religious leaders who recognize that climate action has become a sacred duty and at the same time a full-fledged mission in their evangelistic work.

So, what should be done? Strengthen religious teachings and initiatives on environmental protection? Mobilize young religious leaders?

It is clear that if the considerable influence of religious leaders is harnessed, they can help the world to take important steps to avoid climate disasters due to environmental degradation. Young religious leaders can be very instrumental in leading the way.

In this article, we would like to share some of the initiatives of the African Council of Religious Leaders – Religions for Peace (ACRL – RfP) and Africa Interfaith Youth Network (AIYN) across Africa in mobilizing youth from different faiths to carry out various environmental activities.

The AIYN was launched in 2006 in Dar-es-Salaam, Tanzania, as a platform to connect young religious leaders from different countries in Africa and mobilize joint and concerted actions on some of the issues facing Africa and specifically young people.

The AIYN harnesses the energy and commitment of young religious leaders from around Africa to advance its mission of multi-religious cooperation for peace. Through these diverse groups of young religious leaders, the AIYN mobilizes young people to address some of the most pressing issues – contributing to peace building, fighting poverty and care of the earth.

Africa Interfaith Youth Network (AIYN) Success Story / Best Practices

As a strategic priority, AIYN is committed to mobilizing its members and contributing to the Sustainable Development Goals (SDGs) including: Responsible Consumption and Production, Climate Action and Life on Earth.

AIYN members undertook environmental campaign activities to raise awareness, as well as engaging their communities on the need to act urgently for the care of our common home. In this article, here, we will focus on the AIYN members' local initiatives in the Democratic Republic of Congo, Kenya and South Africa.

The Welcoming the Other: Clean, Pray and Collaborate Initiative

The *Welcoming the Other: Clean, Pray, Collaborate* was an initiative of Religions for Peace Global Interfaith Youth Network (GIYN). This was a one-day global awareness multi-religious campaign to encourage safe, clean, and environmentally friendly places of worship in celebration of United Nations Environmental Program World Environment Day. The idea was that the youth from different faith communities collaborate on activities in the different places of worship, including mosques, synagogues, churches and temples, and so learn from each other about each faith tradition, as well as deliver much needed services for the religious sites.

With the support of ACRL – RfP, AIYN in collaboration with the Kenya Interfaith Youth Network (KIYN) implemented the *Welcoming the Other: Clean, Pray Collaborate* initiative in two places of worship: the St. Paul's Chaplaincy and Chapel and the Kenyatta University Masjid in Nairobi. The initiative aimed to provide the interfaith youth with an opportunity to be in different places of worship from their own. The objectives of the cleanup exercise included:

- Promoting interfaith harmony among religious youth and learning different faith traditions take on the protection of the environment.
- Volunteer and provide cleaning and maintenance assistance to the places of worship.
- Commemorate the United Nations World Environment Day.

At Saint Paul's Chapel, the AIYN members attended a Sunday mass together with parishioners. The mass celebrant included the theme of welcoming the other in his sermon of the day, but also recognized the AIYN members' presence and appreciated their presence in the church service. After the mass, the members were joined by the university students, high school students and even the Sunday school children in the cleaning of the main building and the restrooms. After the cleaning activity, the AIYN members and the parish youth met to share the concepts of welcoming the other, interreligious dialogue and above all learning to live together, to tolerate each other and to learn from each other – the only way to counter religious extremism.

At the Kenyatta University Masjid the AIYN members were joined by university students for the mosque cleanup exercise. After the cleaning, members together with the university students and a few Muslim children joined the noon Muslim prayers which were led by Sheikh Khan a member of the AIYN. There were five other sheikhs who had also attended. The sheikhs included the theme of welcoming the other and how to live peacefully and harmoniously. The Muslim brothers and sisters had a great experience of having Christians in the mosque during the cleaning and during the prayers. In the afternoon after the prayers, the members joined by the sheikhs and university students held a discussion which was mostly about welcoming the other, peace, eradication of extremism and radicalization, morality and humanity.

The *Welcoming the Other* initiative in Kenya strengthened the capacity of young religious leaders to once again demonstrate their willingness to take an active role in this global effort to preserve the environment driven by their faith.

The Interfaith Youth Climate Forum in South Africa (IYCF)

The IYCF was initiated out of the *Our Earth, Our Responsibility Campaign* by Religions for Peace International Global Interfaith Youth Network, aimed at educating, engaging and impacting the communities. This was a global multi-religious youth-led campaign aimed at mobilizing young religious believers and people of goodwill to protect the earth from the ravages of climate change and its effects on the poor and vulnerable communities.

The main goal of the IYCF was to educate the community on climate change, to empower the voice of the youth and to impact the earth, the local communities and people's lives in a positive way. The activities included capacity building on the aspects of religion and spirituality with climate change as the main focus.

Since 2016, The IYCF organized activities such as: Tree Planting Ceremony and Faith Campaign with Sukyo Mahikari and community clean-up of Durban; Social Media Awareness with School Children – to emphasize youth participation in the fight against climate change; participation on the global Climate Change Sit-In to demand that decisions makers act now; donating and planting indigenous trees at schools, churches, mosques and temples; organizing an educational school tour on climate change to educate school kids on climate change and how religious scriptures, prayer and meditation through spirituality from various religions can be used to combat climate change through a multi-religious call to action.

The IYCF also carried out activities such as the Religions for Peace Youth Climate Festival. This initiative consisted of inviting schools, other youth organizations and various environmental companies to a festival which promoted healthy and sustainable living, and included talks by various religious leaders and presentations from environmental companies. Earth meditations were also organized, with music and poetry creating awareness of religious scriptures with regard to climate change. It was also an opportunity to promote the campaign and combat climate change at grassroots levels.

Democratic Republic of Congo Interfaith Youth Network Community Outreach and Awareness

As part of the multi-faith alliance that aims to stop deforestation of the rainforests with the leadership of religious leaders, the Congo National Interfaith Youth Network (NIYN) is involved in education and advocacy initiatives for the protection of the Congo rainforest, which is the core mission of the Interfaith Rainforest Initiative (IRI). The youth activities included:

- Awareness campaigns on environment cleansing in neighborhoods, to sensitize communities on the importance of the care of the environment by recycling waste and discouraging the use of plastic packaging.
- Teacher's training was organized and 'Friends of Nature' clubs were created in schools. with the main objective of creating spaces where students and their teachers can gather, share and discuss environmental issues.

Lessons Learned

These initiatives created a space for learning through awareness and education, promoting changes of mindsets and lifestyle towards the earth. The actions also created the building of friendships, and a sense of community and networking through a common goal for the protection of the earth by bringing together the AIYN members and communities from different faith backgrounds. The time spent together was an important moment in breaking down religious misconceptions and myths among the youth. From these different initiatives, we learned and acknowledge the following:

- The need for unity among the youth from different faith communities.
- How learning and a humbling experience opens up one's mind to being part of a different religion.
- The reduction of hostilities among the youth by understanding each other as humanity.
- A general appreciation for the work undertaken by the caretakers of places of worship, who ensure that worshippers commune in a clean and tidy environment.
- The satisfaction of community service and giving back to the community and the diversion of self-interest to the good of the society.
- That care of the environment is a God-given duty.

As a case of the welcoming others initiative, the youth were enthusiastic about being part of the initiative in visiting other places of worship for the first time.

Challenges

Covid-19 halted most of the youth initiatives and youth are now faced with other life challenges, such as a disrupted school year, unemployment, health crises and financial difficulties. It became difficult to mobilize youth for environmental activities, as other things became a priority for survival. However, the AIYN managed to conduct some online activities, like Twitter conversations on environmental issues to maintain the ongoing commitment of the youth in raising awareness on climate change and the urgency to act.

Recommendations

Youth must participate actively in the battle with climate change. However, we believe that if we plan environmental activities that would be more fun and engaging, it would allow youth to take an active leadership position or role to advocate for the care of our common home. This will encourage them to get interested and excited about it, to learn, lead and engage on a deeper level, even more so when the call comes from religious leaders. They are the people on whom young people rely most – their role therefore becomes indispensable in further mobilizing and inspiring initiatives for the care of the earth. Activities can be planned around promoting not only religion, spirituality, and climate change, but also employment and education through the technical and financial support of the religious leaders and institutions. That will make youth initiatives more sustainable and create a positive impact on society.

Recommendations for Further Reading

Religions for Peace: Key Strategic Priority: Sustainable Environment, in: https://www.rfp.org/priority-sustainable-environment/

African Council for Religious Leaders: African Position Paper on Protecting the earth and sustainable development, in: https://www.acrl-rfp.org/acrl-rfp-programs/protecting-the-earth-and-sustainable-development/

Interfaith Rainforest Initiative: Country website, factsheet and position paper on DRC Congo, in: https://www.interfaithrainforest.org/democratic-republic-of-the-congo/

Columbia Climate School: State of the Planet – Vegard Skirbekk, Alexander de Sherbinin, and Susana Adamo: How religion influences our relationship with the environment; 15 October 2020, https://news.climate.columbia.edu/2020/10/15/religion-influences-relationship-environment/

Vegard Skirbekk, Alex de Sherbinin, Susana B. Adamo, Jose Navarro, und Tricia Chai-Onn: Religious Affiliation and Environmental Challenges in the 21st Century, in: Journal of Religion and Demography Oct 2020, Online Publication, in: https://brill.com/view/journals/jrd/7/2/article-p238_5.xml

70. The Foundations and Practical Implications of the Ecological Work of the Church of Pentecost in Ghana

Emmanuel Anim[1] and Emmanuel Awudi[2]

Introduction

The twenty-first century has witnessed the emergence of many zoonotic diseases, including Severe Acute Respiratory Syndrome (SARS), Middle East Respiratory Syndrome (MERS), H1N1, Bird Flu, Lassa fever, and Ebola. Though speculative, the recent outbreak of Covid-19 has also been linked to the animal market in Wuhan City in China.[3] The destruction of habitats, both terrestrial and aquatic, and the poisoning of the food web has some consequences on both human and other-than-human lives. For instance, Allison M. Howell and Karim K. Koroma note that prior to the outbreak of Ebola in 2014, extensive destruction of forest areas occurred impacting wildlife habitats in Guinea, Liberia and Sierra Leone.[4] Thus, from the fall of the first couple, humanity has been empowered, especially by modern technology, to unleash several forms of ecocide on other-than-human creation to the extent that creation is losing its initial awe, beauty, dignity, and goodness.

Aside from some major ecological challenges that cut across the globe, Africa is of one of the continents plagued with major eco-crises such as the influx of electronic wastes, open defecation, inappropriate disposal of plastics, and deforestation. Rapid population growth, coupled with the demand to meet the needs of the population, has had dire consequences on the use of natural resources. The United Nations Education, Scientific and Cultural Organisation (UNESCO) in 2017 avers that, "Africa's population is estimated at 1.1 billion and according to United Nations forecasts, it will rise 2.4 billion, or nearly one-third of the world's population by 2050."[5] This rapid growth in human population within the continent puts pressure on the limited natural resources. For J.O.Y. Mante, it has caused untold hardship, sufferings and death on the people in Sub-Saharan Africa.[6]

Though scientists around the globe are working hard to mitigate the impact of eco-crises on all creation, their efforts seem not to be yielding the desired results. In this paper, we propose that religion, especially Christianity, is the last resort in tackling this menace globally. Samson Gitau posits that, "If Christians were to treat the environment as they possibly treat the Lord's Supper, that is, with faith and awe, the battle against environmental degradation would become less menacing".[7] Despite this realization, Pentecostalism,

---

[1] Emmanuel Anim holds the dual responsibility as the acting Pro-Vice Chancellor and the Director of School of Theology, Ministry, and Leadership at the Pentecost University in Ghana. He holds a PhD in Pentecostalism from All Nations Christian College in the United Kingdom.

[2] Emmanuel Awudi is an Adjunct Lecturer at the Pentecost University and a District Pastor with the Church of Pentecost in Ghana. He is a PhD candidate at the Akrofi-Christaller Institute of Theology, Missions and Culture, Akropong, Ghana. His focus is on African Pentecostal Eco-theology, Religion and Sustainable Development.

[3] Jason Gale, 'Delayed Wuhan Report Adds Crucial Detail to Covid Origin Puzzle', August 2021, Accessed 29 September 2021, https://www.bloomberg.com/news/features/2021-08-17/where-did-covid-come-from-report-on-infected-wuhan-wild-animals-sheds-new-light.

[4] Allison M. Howell and Karim Kelvin Koroma, 'The West African Ebola Virus Outbreak: Context, Response and Christian Responsibility – The Experience of the Wesleyan Church of Sierra Leone', *Journal of African Christian Thought,* Vol. 18, No. 1 (June 2015), 4-17 (6-7).

[5] UNESCO, 'Demographic Growth', 2017 29, Accessed February 2019, http://www.unesco.org/new/en/africa-department/priority-africa/operational-strategy/demographic-growth/.

[6] J.O.Y. Mante, *Africa Theological and Philosophical Roots of Our Ecological Crisis* (Accra: Sonlife Press, 2004), 14.

[7] Samson Gitau, *The Environment Crisis; A Challenge for African Christianity* (Nairobi: Acton Publishers, 2000), 3.

which is the fastest growing Christian tradition in Africa and a major force to reckon with in world Christianity,[8] has not devoted much attention to tackling this menace. Their influence in the conservation of biodiversity is minimal. Rather, their hermeneutical principles have been a source of worry to some ecologists like Ben-Willie Kwaku Golo and Emmanuel Anim.[9] Both Golo and Anim blame the prosperity gospel of Pentecostals and neo-Pentecostals for the ecological crises that Africa is facing.

The Church of Pentecost, which is the fastest growing Pentecostal tradition, realizing the church's potential for influencing every sphere of life with Christian principle and values, has in recent times engaged in some activities towards reclamation of degraded lands, environmental cleanliness and awareness creation on the preservation of biodiversity. In this paper, we bring to the fore the experience of the Church of Pentecost (CoP) in championing creation care in Ghana from 2018 to 2021.

Possessing the Nations

In the late 1930s, James McKeown (the founder of the Church of Pentecost) and some of his Ghanaian converts were praying when the vision of the church given was birth through prophesy.[10] The vision was that through the Church of Pentecost, the Gospel of Christ would reach the ends of the world. This vision became clearer and fully operational upon the assumption of office by the current chairman of the church in 2018, Apostle Eric Nyamekye. The vision, which is dubbed Vision 2023, is 'Possessing the Nations' – equipping members to transform every sphere of life with Christian values and principles.[11] This vision is similar to Kwame Bediako's explanation of the Great Commission. He states:

> The Great Commission, therefore, is about the discipling of the nations, the conversion of the things that make people into nations – the shared processes of thinking, the shared common attitudes, worldviews [including the worldviews of nature], perspectives, languages, cultural and social and economic habits of thought and behaviour and practice – all those things and the lives of the people in whom those things find expression – all that is meant to be within the call of discipleship. Nationality itself is brought within the purview of discipleship.[12]

Thus, transforming every aspect of life, including the ecosystem, is part of Possessing the Nations agenda. The initial idea was to organise a campaign to educate members of the church and the rest of the citizenry on environmental cleanliness. However, new ideas begun to emerge at every stage of the campaign. The impulse was derived from a peace campaign launched to promote peace in the run-up to the 2016 elections in Ghana. The church's concern was that because Ghana is the headquarters of the church,

[8] Allan Heaton Anderson, *Spirit-Filled World: Religious Dis/Continuity in African Pentecostalism* (Cham, Switzerland: Palgrave Macmillan, 2018), 3.

[9] Ben-Willie Kwaku Golo has cited the neo-Pentecostals' prosperity gospel (maximizing profit to the detriment of the environment) as a contributory factor to the degradation of the ecosystem. Ben-Willie Kwaku Golo, 'The Groaning Earth and the Greening of Neo-Pentecostalism in Twenty-First-Century Ghana' *PentecoStudies* Vol.13, No.2 (2014), 197-216 (204). Accessed 5 May 2017. http://dx.doi.org/10.1558/ptcs.v13i2.197. Similarly, Emmanuel Anim avers that the interpretation of dominion by Africa's neo-Pentecostals has encouraged them to lay siege of some sacred sites which were protected with primal worldviews (Emmanuel Anim, 'The Gods are dead and Now We are in Charge! The Hermeneutical Crisis in Africa's New Christianity and its Effect on the Environment and Sustainable Development', a conference paper presented at the international conference 'Between Cosmology and Community: Religion and Sustainable Development' at the Humboldt – Universität Zu Berlin on July 5 2019).

[10] Joshua Yirenky-Smart, *Pentecost from Jerusalem to Asamankese: The Journey of Pentecost and the Untold Story of Pastor James McKeown and The Church of Pentecost (1937-1982)* (Accra, Ghana: Pentecost Press Limited, 2017), 95.

[11] The Church of Pentecost, *Vision 2023: Five-Year Vision Document for The Church of Pentecost Covering the Period 2018-2023* (Accra, Ghana: Pentecost Press Limited, 2019), 9.

[12] Kwame Bediako, 'What is the Gospel', *Transformation Journal* Vol.14, No.1 (Jan/March 1997), 1-4 (4).

anything the marred the peace of the country affects the CoP worldwide. Thus, the peace campaign was launched in every district within the country.

After successful elections, leadership saw the need to use the same strategy to promote environmental cleanliness and to organise clean-up exercise. The campaign was launched at the Kokomlemle branch of the church in Accra on 22 November 2018. The launch of the campaign, which was attended by representatives from all regions in Ghana as well as government officials, was followed by a clean-up exercise on 8 December 2018 at Kasoa, a suburb of the capital city, Accra. After the launch at the national level, all areas and districts[13] of the church were expected to launch the campaign and follow this up with a clean-up exercise. Other branches of the church in the over 100 countries across the globe were mandated to also initiate programmes that were geared towards the reclamation of lands.

A Theology Was Born

Though the campaign was successful and the clean-up exercises well attended few days after, the entire environment where the exercise was carried was soon in a mess again. The General Secretary of the Church, Apostle Alexandra Nana Yaw Kumi Larbi, one of the principal officers of the church who took part in the clean-up exercise, drove through the same stretch of road to accompany the chairman on a familiarization meeting with pastors and laity of the church at Kasoa on 8 December 2018. He lamented that the whole place was in a mess after only three days. He blamed it on the attitude of the people and thus, before the people could have a clean environment, there was the need for them to change their attitudes. So from 2018 onwards, the environmental campaign has become an annual event. Also, in 2021 the leadership of the church decided to embark on a tree planting exercise which coincided with the government of Ghana's agenda of planting five million trees across the length and breadth of the country. The church was able to plant 627,000 seedlings out of the one million seedlings targeted.[14]

After a careful reflection on the problem, the Principal of the Pentecost Theological Seminary (now School of Theology Ministry and Leadership – Pentecost University), Apostle Dr. Emmanuel Anim, and the seminary faculty decided to introduce a course which would help train both the laity and the ministers of the church on how scripture speaks to eco-care and eco-mission. The leadership of the seminary realized that if the root of the ecological crises was not tackled, the church would engaged in its annual environmental campaign followed by clean-up exercises, but the menace would persist. There was the need for members of the church to realize that cleaning one's environment should not be just an event but a lifestyle. Therefore, in 2019 eco-theology was introduced, with the vision of assisting pastoral students to identify the roots of Africa's ecological crises, build knowledge of a biblical perspective and acquire practical skills to enable them to respond as African Christians to environmental issues in their communities. This course was welcomed by both students and faculty members, and so far three batches of pastors have taken the course. The first group of ministerial students to receive training in eco-theology was the 2017/2018 batch, and their training received attention in the church's official magazine, *Pentecost Fire.* Felix Brakatu reported in the magazine with the headline, 'Ministerial students undergo eco-theology training programme':

> The training which took place from October 15 to 18 2019 at the Centre for Ministerial Formation of the School of Theology, Mission and Leadership at the Pentecost University College, was intended to help the students appreciate the theology that underpins the Creation Care Campaign of the Church of Pentecost. … The course which was handled by Pastor Emmanuel Awudi, covered areas like Biblical Foundations for Creation Care and

[13] In the CoP setting, an area is manned by an apostle/prophet or evangelist who has several other pastors under him who man the districts, with several other locals known as assemblies.

[14] The church planted 627,000 seedlings out of its target of 1 million due to the inability of the Forestry Commission of Ghana to supply the quantity the church needed.

Redemption of Creation, Roots of Ecological Crisis, Creation Care from the African Traditional Perspective, and the African Green Church Model. The students were tasked to prepare and present what was termed, 'Green Sermons', sermons that speak to eco-care and eco-mission.[15]

By introducing the eco-theology course, the vision was to alter participants' worldviews about creation and how they treat them. Harvey Sindima argues that, "How we think about the world affects the way we live in it. In particular our understanding of nature – our cosmology – affects the way we understand ourselves, the way we relate to other people, and, of course, the way we relate to the earth and other forms of life".[16] Therefore, to tackle the root of Africa's ecological crisis, one needs to engage the worldview of the people. By May 2021, three batches of ministerial students had been trained in eco-theology. The course has also been added to the curriculum for the training of elders of the church, starting from September 2021.

Aside from the introduction of eco-theology curriculum at the seminary, the National Discipleship and Leadership Training Committee introduced topics on environmental conservation and awareness creation in its manual for the training of lay leaders of the church. In addition, Bible study topics were introduced in the 2019 and 2020 Bible Study Guides for the church, while topics on the conservation of biodiversity were also introduced in the daily devotional guides of the youth ministry of the church.

Lay Leadership Training

The leadership of the church saw the need to move eco-mission from the periphery to the mainstream mission. Thus, topics on creation care were introduced in the training manuals for lay leaders. The Lay Leadership Training School was introduced in 2010 to train the laity about the doctrines of the church, the responsibilities of the laity and other vital topics. The manual for leaders in Advanced Level 3, which was prepared in May 2018 for the training of church leaders August 2018, included topics on creation care such as, 'Taking Care of Our Father's Property', 'Environmental Pollution and its Effects', 'Assembly Bye-Laws, Regulations, Principles and Personal Responsibility', and 'Sanitation & Pollution – My Personal Commitment'.[17] This helped to create some form of awareness among leaders who attended that particular class to appreciate and propagate the message that environmental cleanliness and the conservation of biodiversity is a biblical mandate.

Bible Study Guides

In connection with tackling the worldview of the members of the church, the National Discipleship and Leadership Development Committee (NDLDC), which is responsible for developing Bible study materials for the church, added themes on creation care in both the 2019 and 2020 Bible Study Guides. The 2019 Bible Study Guide has topics such as 'Land Pollution: A Challenge to Practical Christianity', 'Consequences of Pollution', Possessing the Nation by Obeying Environmental Laws', and 'Personal Commitment to Addressing Sanitation and Pollution Challenges'.[18] Also, the topic for week 22 Bible Study

---

[15] Felix Brakatu, 'Ministerial Students Undergo Eco--theology Training Programme', *Pentecost Fire,* Issue182 (September – December 2019), 28.

[16] Harvey Sindima, 'Community of Life: Ecological Theology in African Perspective' in Charles Birch, William Eakin and Jay B. McDaniel (eds.), *Liberating Life: Contemporary Approaches to Ecological Theology* (Eugene, OR: Wipf and Stock Publishers, 1990), 137-144 (137).

[17] National Discipleship and Leadership Development Committee, *Lay Leadership Training Manual: Advanced Level 3* (Accra, Ghana: Pentecost Press Limited, 2018), 48-69.

[18] The Church of Pentecost, *Bible Study & Home Cell Guide 2019* (Accra, Ghana: Pentecost Press Limited, 2019), 65-79.

for 2020 reads, 'Environmental Care, Our Responsibility'.[19] It discusses the responsibility of Christians in caring for creation. Using the text Deuteronomy 23:9-14, the writer explained the responsibility of Christians to keep their environments clean, adding that God inhabits a clean environment.

Youth Devotional Guide

In the light of getting the message of ecological care to the grassroots, the youth ministry within the church introduced topics on creation care into its annual devotional guide, *Streams of Living Water 2021*. This devotional guide has 14 scripts dedicated to ecological care. The main topic is captioned, 'Plastic Society', with seven sub-topics for Monday 20 to Sunday 26 September. The topics discussed include 'The Goodness of God's Creation Reversed', 'Guard Creation Just as God Guards You', and 'What Does the Torah Say about Pollution'. The seven other topics which were meant to find alternatives to the use of plastics and other practices that endanger the ecosystem were intended for Monday 11 to Sunday 17 2021. Also included were topics on alternative livelihoods to illegal mining, lumbering and sand winning, and alternatives to the use of inappropriate agricultural methods.[20]

Emerging Articles

The editorial of issue 181 of the church's magazine, *Pentecost Fire* was also dedicated to issues of environmental care.[21] The role of the human species among other species was spelt out in the editorial. The writer indicated that creation care is a biblical mandate spelt out in Genesis 2:15. Thus, human beings were created in the image of God to care for the other species.

Aside from the editorial, articles have been published in different issues of the church's magazine, all geared towards the education of members of the church on maintaining the balance in the ecosystem. The church's official website, lso published some articles on creation care to educate the public.[22] One of such articles was titled, 'When Creation is Denied its Sabbath'.[23] This was written with the intention to educate readers on the consequences of neglecting the responsibility of caring for creation.

Sponsorship of Students

One minister with the CoP has been sponsored by the church to read for a Master of Art in Theology, Masters of Theology (MTh) and a PhD with a special focus on eco-theology. He is currently researching the possibility of developing an African Pentecostal eco-theology with lessons from scripture and the ecotheologies of some indigenous African churches, and working as an assistant / adjunct lecturer at the School of Ministry, Theology and Leadership at the Pentecost University, assisting the faculty to teach eco-theology at the Ministerial Formation Programme and the Elders Training Programme.

---

[19] The Church of Pentecost, *Bible Study & Home Cell Guide 2020* (Accra, Ghana: Pentecost Press Limited, 2020), 57-58.

[20] The Church of Pentecost – Youth Ministry, *Streams of Living Water 2021: A Daily Devotional Guide* (Accra, Ghana: Pentecost Press Limited, 2021), 336-345.

[21] Isaac Annor, 'Restoring the Lord's Beautiful Garden on Earth', *Pentecost Fire Issue 181* (May – August 2019), 3.

[22] https//www.cohhq.org.

[23] Emmanuel Awudi, 'When Creation is Denied its Sabbath,' April 2020, Accessed 30 September 2021, https://thecop.org/when-creation-is-denied-its-sabbath/.

Results

The church has witnessed massive participation of its members in the annual clean-up and tree planting exercises from 2018 to 2021. Also, members of the church are beginning to appreciate the need to care for creation, to keep their environments clean, and to conserve biodiversity. Airtime was given on the church's official television and radio for experts to broadcast messages tailored to eco-conservation.

Conclusion

This paper concludes that religion, especially Christianity, is the last hope of the world to save the groaning creation. Christians need to appreciate that Christ's vision of bringing the good news to the marginalized in society should be extended to the vulnerable creation. This is in appreciation of the fact that the marginalized in our society today include flora and fauna, aquatic organisms, the air, land, mountains and water bodies being treated with disdain. There are many scriptures that speak to ecological care and ecological mission, but most Christians are yet to appreciate them. There is the urgent need for the pulpit to be used to teach the pew about the conservation of biodiversity as a biblical mandate. Pentecostals need to lead the way to convert and conserve sacred forests, instead of condemning and destroying them.

Environmental degradation cannot be solved with only clean-up campaigns and exercises, since the root cause is the deep-seated worldview of humanity that creation is meant for their survival, thus leading to the commodification of all creation. The solution is to tackle worldviews about nature, since these worldviews determine how they handle creation. Looking at the filth in Africa and how the environment is fast depleting, there is an urgent need for all church traditions to come on board to tackle the menace. The CoP cannot do it alone, but with its agenda of possessing the nations, they are required to sell these ideas to other Pentecostal churches and other church traditions.

Recommendations for Further Reading

Anderson, Allan Heaton. *Spirit-Filled World: Religious Dis/Continuity in African Pentecostalism* (Cham, Switzerland: Palgrave Macmillan, 2018).

Anim, Emmanuel. 'The Gods are dead and Now We are in Charge! The Hermeneutical Crisis in Africa's New Christianity and its Effect on the Environment and Sustainable Development', a conference paper presented at the international conference 'Between Cosmology and Community: Religion and Sustainable Development' at the Humboldt – Universität Zu Berlin on July 5 2019.

Annor, Isaac. 'Restoring the Lord's Beautiful Garden on Earth', *Pentecost Fire Issue 181.* May – August 2019, 3.

Awudi, Emmanuel. 'When Creation is Denied its Sabbath,' April 2020. Accessed 30 September 2021, https://thecop.org/when-creation-is-denied-its-sabbath/

Bediako, Kwame. 'What is the Gospel?' *Transformation Journal* Vol.14, No.1 (Jan/March 1997), 1-4.

Brakatu, Felix. 'Ministerial Students Undergo Ecotheology Training Programme.' *Pentecost Fire,* Issue182 (September – December 2019).

Gale, Jason. 'Delayed Wuhan Report Adds Crucial Detail to Covid Origin Puzzle.' August 2021, Accessed 29 September 2021, https://www.bloomberg.com/news/features/2021-08-17/where-did-covid-come-from-report-on-infected-wuhan-wild-animals-sheds-new-light

Gitau, Samson. *The Environment Crisis; A Challenge for African Christianity* (Nairobi: Acton Publishers, 2000).

Golo, Ben-Willie Kwaku. 'The Groaning Earth and the Greening of Neo-Pentecostalism in Twenty-First-Century Ghana. *PentecoStudies* Vol.13, No.2 (2014), 197-216. Accessed 5 May 2017. http://dx.doi.org/10.1558/ptcs.v13i2.197.

Howell, Allison M. and Koroma, Karim Kelvin. 'The West African Ebola Virus Outbreak: Context, Response and Christian Responsibility – The Experience of the Wesleyan Church of Sierra Leone.' *Journal of African Christian Thought,* Vol. 18, No. 1 (June 2015), 4-17.

Mante, J. O. Y. *Africa Theological and Philosophical Roots of Our Ecological Crisis* (Accra: Sonlife Press, 2004).

National Discipleship and Leadership Development Committee. *Lay Leadership Training Manual: Advanced Level 3* (Accra, Ghana: Pentecost Press Limited, 2018).

Sindima, Harvey. 'Community of Life: Ecological Theology in African Perspective' in Charles Birch, William Eakin and McDaniel, Jay B. (eds.). *Liberating Life: Contemporary Approaches to Ecological Theology* (Eugene, OR: Wipf and Stock Publishers, 1990), 137-144.

The Church of Pentecost – Youth Ministry. *Streams of Living Water 2021: A Daily Devotional Guide* (Accra, Ghana: Pentecost Press Limited, 2021).

The Church of Pentecost. *Bible Study & Home Cell Guide 2019* (Accra, Ghana: Pentecost Press Limited, 2019).

The Church of Pentecost. *Bible Study & Home Cell Guide 2020* (Accra, Ghana: Pentecost Press Limited, 2020).

The Church of Pentecost. *Vision 2023: Five-Year Vision Document for The Church of Pentecost Covering the Period 2018-2023.* (Accra, Ghana: Pentecost Press Limited, 2019).

UNESCO. 'Demographic Growth', 2017 29. Accessed February 2019, http://www.unesco.org/new/en/africa-department/priority-africa/operational-strategy/demographic-growht/

Yirenky-Smart, Joshua. *Pentecost from Jerusalem to Asamankese,: The Journey of Pentecost and the Untold Story of Pastor James McKeown and The Church of Pentecost (1937-1982).* (Accra, Ghana: Pentecost Press Limited, 2017).

71. Eco-Theological Perspectives in East Africa

Loreen Maseno[1]

Introduction

The East Africa region comprises several states with a diversity of economic, political, and familial types, beliefs and practices. There are large towns and urban centres throughout the region. There are also many lesser towns that have attracted mixed immigrant populations from the countryside and from which modern Christian and syncretistic movements have spread out into the rural areas. Peoples in the region are influenced by Christianity, Islam and traditional local religions.

The term 'eco-theology' is a shortened form of 'ecological theology'. It has been suggested that the words 'ecological theology' was most likely to have been first coined by John Cobb in the mid-twentieth century. Later in 1961, it was given greater attention by Joseph Sittler calling on the WCC for a more comprehensive and cosmic-centered Christology with attention to a more cosmic soteriology.[2] Thereafter, in 1963, it grew in popularity in the context of the United States National Council of Churches (NCC) supported Faith-Man Nature Study Group. This study group was focussed on transforming Christian attitudes toward nature.[3] Celia Drummond suggests that the possibility of combining the concerns of the environment and an understanding of God allows for an eco-theology. To her, eco-theology is that reflection on different facets of theology which take their bearings from cultural concerns about the environment and humanity's relationship with the natural world. In general, eco-theology is a particular expression of contextual theology that emerges in the particular context of environmental awareness.[4]

Eco-theology considers ecological practices, which have been suggested to include stewarding the land, decrying species loss, recycling, and learning how to love God's creation. By doing these, they all imply humanity may be here for a while and must take a greater responsibility in stewarding earth's ecosystem. One theme within eco-theology is that of creation. A core focus has been to affirm the goodness of creation, that it has integrity as a whole, and that God is implicated, involved, within or with the dynamic of creation.

East Africa

Eastern Africa is that part of sub-Saharan Africa comprising two regions. The first is East Africa, made up of Kenya, Tanzania, and Uganda. The second region is the Horn of Africa, made up of Somalia, Djibouti, Eritrea, and Ethiopia. Geographically, Eastern Africa consists of plateaus and has some of the highest elevations in the continent. Two striking highlands are in Ethiopia and Kenya. At the same time, the volcanic massif of Kilimanjaro, the highest mountain in Africa, is located in the north eastern region of Tanzania. East Africa has parallel rift valleys that run through the region. The Great Rift Valley extends from the Red Sea, southward across the highlands of Ethiopia and Kenya and continues on into Tanzania, whereas the Western Rift Valley curves along the western borders of Uganda and Tanzania. Countries in

---

[1] Senior Lecturer Department of Religion, Theology and Philosophy and Research Fellow, Department of Ancient and Biblical Studies, UNISA.

[2] Steven C. Bouma-Prediger, *The Cosmic Christ: The Christology of Joseph Sittler* (2021 Hope College), in: https://digitalcommons.hope.edu/faculty_publications/945/

[3] See Lucas F. Johnston, *Religion and Sustainability: Social Movements and the Politics* of the Environment (Equinox: Sheffield, 2013), 55. See also James Livingston and Francis Fiorenza, eds. *Modern Christian Thought*, vol. 2 (Upper Saddle River: Prentice Hall, 2000), 333. This is also brought to focus by Michael Kinnamon, *Can a Renewal Movement Be Renewed?: Questions for the Future of Ecumenism* (Grand Rapids: Eerdmans, 2014), 48.

[4] Celia Deane-Drummond, *Eco-Theology* (London: Darton, Longman and Todd, 2008), x.

the region have a regional intergovernmental organisation of six states, comprising Burundi, Kenya, Rwanda, South Sudan, Tanzania and Uganda, with its headquarters in Arusha, Tanzania. This regional intergovernmental organisation is named the East African Community (EAC).

East Africa contains several geographical and cultural areas, with an immense variety of societies, languages, and religions. East African peoples are traditionally farmers and livestock herders, living together with others along sea coasts engaging in fishing. The peoples of East Africa have been impacted by Christianity, Islam and traditional local religions which remain active in almost every part of the area.

Diversity of Eco-Theological Perspectives in Context

Since eco-theology is contextual in nature, there are varieties that emerge from various contexts. Eco-theology from the West is simplistically what Deane-Drummond suggests to be those that could be broadly considered 'Western', which address individualism and consumerism of the modern life. This eco-theology weaves together the social and political strands of human life, evolving in dialogue with current political and social disputes. On the other hand, eco-theology from the East borrows a lot from the Orthodox tradition, which places emphasis on a liturgy that is much more conscious of participation by the whole of the created order in its theological reflection. This eco-theology shows the possibility of a life of simplicity and prayer, generating alternative ways of living.[5]

There is a global variety of the discourse summarised by Deane-Drummond as follows. Eco-theology from the North resists a wrongful attachment to technology in the name of progress. It encourages lifestyles attune with the natural world and processes. At the same time, it often does not consider global poverty, oppression and the suffering of the planet.[6]

Eco-theology from the South where East Africa is situated, is embedded in the cry for justice, placing development and ecology in balamce. The rampant loss of biodiversity happening in the developing countries causes many social, economic and political injustices that lead to wide scale humanitarian crises. It follows that the poor and marginalized who depend most immediately on the health of ecosystems are severely affected by the collapse of the natural systems that sustain life and society in the developing countries. Therefore, eco-theology from the South takes another step in that it challenges modernisation and enlarges the liberation theology agenda so that it capture the indigenous cultural reflections rooted in environmental practice.[7]

Christian Eco-Theology in East Africa

According to Conradie and Koster,[8] Christian eco-theology includes a collective response by Christian communities to the environment and climate change. In what follows, this essay shall use examples from Christian denominations in East Africa to demonstrate their action on creation care, following through what has been suggested as four roles of eco-theology.

Conradie and Koster contend that among mainline churches in the Global South, the Christian eco-theology which is emerging is having certain key roles, some of which include the following:

[5] Deane-Drummond, *Eco-Theology*, 67-68.
[6] Deane-Drummond, *Eco-Theology*, 43.
[7] Deane-Drummond, *Eco-Theology*, 45-55.
[8] Conradie Ernst & Koster, Hilda (eds.) *Christian Theology and Climate Change* (London: T&T Clark, 2019), 336-339.

(A) First, addressing the problems of environmental degradation and climate change.[9] Eco-theology, when well understood and put in practice within the various Christian communities, has the potential of reducing tree felling, wrong land use and encouraging a robust tree planting cycle within the community which in some way has a positive impact on climate change.

In addressing the problems of environmental degradation, the Archbishop of the Anglican Church of Kenya, Jackson Ole Sapit notes that:

> The Anglican Church of Kenya seeks to ensure that Christians obey the commandments of God. God commanded man to tend to the Garden of Eden and to honour him by preserving the environment. The Psalmist attributes God as the mover and author of what we see and do not see in the environment. And man has been enlisted to support in the care of the Environment. As the Anglican Church, we are working to ensure that we keep God's command. We also want to remind people that trees are part of living things and respond to situations and if we are pro-life, we must preserve all aspects of creations.[10]

In essence, the archbishop is directing the membership of his church to address the problems of climatic change, with the full view that it is the mission of the church to care for creation and leave the world behind as a better place for coming generations.

In Burundi, the efforts to reduce tree felling and plant many trees has been stepped up. The role of eco-theology among the Anglicans in Burundi bears fruit in several ways, since the planting of trees to mark special occasions such as confirmations, baptisms and weddings remains an increasingly popular practice in many areas, long after it was suggested and promoted by young Green Anglicans.

The province of Burundi is going a step further and is looking to plant one tree for every one of the 10 million-strong population of the country. The church hopes to reach its 'One Person, One Tree' goal within the next five years. Here the move is designed to protect and maintain forests and improve the environment. A report showed that the planting of trees on a hillside provided security for the refugees living in Rutana[11] and had resulted in a transformed environment not only for the Tanzanian refugees who have made it their home, but also for wildlife, including monkeys and partridges.[12]

(B) The second role of eco-theology in East Africa is that it gives the language for which we can speak of God and God's activity in creation and the planet within the parameters of God talk. Speech about God and his care for all creation has to be crafted in human language and able to be disseminated for the good of the environment. It is noted that although theological languages are highly symbolic, there are crucial insights and analyses about greed, sin, integrity, right relations, sacrifice, justice, solidarity, resistance, hope, goodness, beauty, wisdom, wonder and more.[13]

The Encyclical Letter *Laudato Si*[14] domiciled in the Catholic Church paid attention to the desire to move from concerns about the cracks in the planet that we inhabit[15] and the important hope placed on entering into dialogue with all people about our common home.[16] The Bukoba Diocese in Tanzania also had a plan that predated *Laudato Si*, which was a three-year project to make faith and the Word of God engines for

---

[9] Kate Davies and Ngonidzashe Edward, 'A Southern African Response to Todd LeVasseur and Bernard Zaleha', in Conradie Ernst & Koster, Hilda (eds.), *Christian Theology and Climate Change* (London: T&T Clark, 2019), 132-135.

[10] The Anglican Church of Kenya https://www.ackenya.org/archives/6033 viewed on 1st August 2021

[11] *Rutana* is a town in southern Burundi. It lies west of Mount Kikizi, one of the highest mountains in the nation.

[12] The Anglican Church in Burundi https://www.anglicannews.org/news/2016/12/anglican-church-of-burundi-to-plant-10-million-trees-in-five-years.aspx/ Viewed on 23rd July 2021.

[13] Heather Eaton, 'Working with climate scientists', in Conradie Ernst & Koster, Hilda (eds.), *Christian Theology and Climate Change* (London: T&T Clark, 2019), 25.

[14] Pope Francis, *Laudato si. Letter encyclical on caring for our common home* (Vatican Press, 2015).

[15] *Laudato si,* 163.

[16] *Laudato si,* 3.

restoration of nature and poverty eradication.[17] Many dioceses across the country were already running environmentally related projects to support farmers in the regions of Tanzania. The encyclical adds that both everyday experience and scientific research show that the gravest effects of all attacks on the environment are suffered by the poorest.[18] Therefore, in *Laudato Si* Catholic leaders have been strengthened to engage with political leaders across the continent to ensure that social and economic policies take into account both the cry of the earth and the cry of the poor.[19]

(C) Third, eco-theology provides an ethical framework which speaks to and promotes ideas and praxis within the Christian communities. The structure and support for environmental care is ably crafted within. According to the Anglican Church of Kenya bishop,

> The Green Anglican Movement was adopted through a synod resolution back in 2017, bringing on board all the bishops as our Green Movement Ambassadors and Champions. The intention was to ensure that all the bishops cascaded the conversation downwards through their diocesan synods and have it implemented in the local churches. This is because the local church is where the ministry is delivered, and the action is. We already have dioceses that have anchored conservation in their core mission agenda. And we view this not as a developmental agenda but as a mission mandate. We are also working with theological institutions to develop the theology of conservation as spiritual a core mandate. Conservation points us to our creator, who established our interdependence with nature. Nature sustains our existence by providing for what we need. And we have a moral responsibility to take care of the environment.[20]

(D) Fourth, although eco-theology has not been sufficiently mainstreamed in the Global South, eco-theology is able to express environmental responsibility, stewardship and caring for creation.[21] For example, the Lutheran World Federation (LWF) 12th Assembly passed a 'Resolution on the Commercialization and Commodification of Creation' which encourages member churches to become more theologically grounded in their teaching on human dignity, our identity as creatures, our relationship to the land and the value of creation.[22] LWF is committed to advocating for climate justice, and equipping member churches to care for creation. The LWF sustains this work by promoting a faithful, ecological sense of being human, and a creation-oriented spirituality that shapes the way we worship and live out our Lutheran tradition for the well-being of all creation.[23] In Uganda, the Lutherans consider that biodiversity matters because each of God's creatures has value in itself, and because maintaining diversity in mutuality is the key to sustaining healthy ecosystems and societies. The projects undertaken in areas such as Northern Uganda by the Lutherans are aimed at environment conservation and restoration. They do this by sensitizing populaces about environmental conservation and the dangers of environmental degradation, offering many tree seedlings for planting to restore the lost vegetation, and the limited provision of solar systems to influence masses to adopt clean, natural, renewable energy.[24]

---

[17] http://www.arcworld.org/downloads/Tanzania-Bukoba-Diocese-Summary-Sep2012.pdf viewed on 2nd August 2021.

[18] *Laudato si*, 48.

[19] '*Laudato si* in Africa', https://www.ncronline.org/news/earthbeat/laudato-si-takes-root-africa-much-urgent-work-remains viewed on 1st August 2021.

[20] The Anglican Church of Kenya interview with the presiding Archbishop, https://www.ackenya.org/archives/6033 viewed on 1st August 2021.

[21] Ibid, 133-135.

[22] See https://2017.lwfassembly.org/en/resolution-commercialization-and-commodification-creation.

[23] The Lutheran World Federation, eco-theological studies https://www.lutheranworld.org/content/ecotheological-studies viewed on 2nd August 2021.

[24] See https://uganda.lutheranworld.org/content/people-northern-uganda-uphold-environmental-conservation-106 viewed on 20th October 2021.

In Uganda, LWF works through a variety of programs to help people, both young and old, achieve their rights and develop sustainably. They help local grassroots and district structures to organize and manage areas such as livelihoods, water and sanitation, health, and environmental management.[25] Through their teachings in Lutheran seminaries and congregations across Uganda, the goal of eco-theology is seen to apply these lenses to the way they read the Bible, practice their faith and express the liberating grace for all creation that is the heart of Lutheran tradition.

Varieties of Eco-Theological Perspectives in East Africa

This section serves primarily as an overview, examining trends and thus setting the background on the emphasis observable from various traditions. In the past five decades, theologians have picked up the call to reclaim alternative theological traditions in various ways. At the core of this call was the attempt to develop a closer relationship between the divine and nature, a matter that is more common in the history of Christianity and today is widely emphasized in eco-theology circles. In Christian eco-theology, there are various theologies which have been developed, such as Roman Catholic eco-theology, Orthodox eco-theology, Protestant eco-theology, Protestant/Charismatic eco-theology, ecofeminist eco-theology etc.[26]

This variety is thanks to a multiplicity of voices, clustered together in diverging schools of thought within contemporary Christian eco-theology that each recognize insights that are indeed authentically Christian but cannot be readily harmonized with each other. Some of these varieties defend Christian ecological practices and their historical, theological and ecclesial traditions.

Roman Catholic eco-theology in East Africa lays an emphasis on creation theology, the dignity of all creation, and liberation theology of the earth. The *Laudato Si* makes clear the profound view of the human as a radically inter-relational creature with all creation and states that the human person grows more, matures more and is sanctified more to the extent that he or she enters into relationships, going out from themselves to live in communion with God, with others and with all creatures.[27] In this way these relationships express on their own the Trinitarian dynamism which God imprinted in them when they were created.

As seen within the Anglican communion, Protestant and Evangelical eco-theology emphasized eschatological hope, social zeal, and biblical theology.[28] This survey of the Lutheran and the Anglican communities draws sharp focus on biblical theology in relation to creation care and its applicability in the related societies of East Africa.

Pentecostal Eco-theology in East Africa lays emphasis on the pneuma,[29] a reading of contemporary environmental concern as a response to the prophetic voices of the non-human nature, and in that sense can be seen as a movement of the Holy Spirit. Pentecostal pneumatology presents the Holy Spirit as an abiding and active presence in the whole of creation. Further, when humans live in tune with the Spirit's work, they are empowered to live in ways that fosters the flourishing of all created life.[30] Some defend Christian

---

[25] The Lutheran World Federation Uganda Program https://www.lutheranworld.org/content/uganda viewed on 1st August 2021.

[26] A response from a related discussion was the need to further deepen through a study, to avail the prevalent eco-theologies from the various Christian traditions, see how they speak to each other and how their differences play out.

[27] Pope Francis, *Laudato Si* (Vatican City: Libreria Editrice Vaticana, 2015), 209-10.

[28] Loreen Maseno, 'Prayer for Rain: A Pentecostal Perspective from Kenya', *The Ecumenical Review*, 2017, Vol 69: 336-347.

[29] Loreen Maseno, 'An African Response to Christopher Vena', in Conradie Ernst & Koster, Hilda (eds.), *Christian Theology and Climate Change* (London: T&T Clark, 2019). See also Aaron Jason Swoboda, 'Tongues and Trees: Towards a Green Pentecostal Pneumatology' unpublished PhD thesis (University of Birmingham, 2011).

[30] Christopher Vena. 'Working with Pentecostal and Evangelical Forms of Christianity', in Conradie Ernst & Koster, Hilda (eds.), *Christian Theology and Climate Change* (London: T&T Clark, 2019).

ecological practice and its historical, theological, and ecclesial traditions. Still other theologians have responded by constructing an eco-theology on a biblical or theological level.[31]

Conclusion

As shown in this survey, eco-theological perspectives in East Africa are varied. While in search of a reliable eco-theology, Kate Davies and Ngonidzashe Edward propose that a credible Christian eco-theology should stand the test in terms of the following criteria.[32] First, that it is culturally relevant. In this case, any eco-theology has to address the human context and needs to be applicable in a culture. It therefore ought to be able to appropriate the cultural artefacts and contents in order to be robust and valid. The examples from East African Christian denominations on the role of eco-theology fall neatly in place with the premise that these must be culturally relevant and rooted within a given context.

Second, it ought to be sensitive to the context of the wider Christian community. The Christian community has to be taken into consideration in order to be credible. The Lutheran denomination in East Africa demonstrated the sensitivity to context. The related Christian tradition ought to inform the understanding of God's work on the planet.

Thirdly, developing such a theology would promote a purposeful ideological orientation for sustainable ecological engagement and praxis, finding expression in public worship, sermons, prayers and pilgrimages. However, eco-theological perspectives in East Africa continue to provide links between the living and creation, between the earth, the physical nature and the spirit world, as they carry out the various ritual practices in their contexts. This includes the idea that communities and species coexist alongside each other and need each other and the mutual dependence does not allow for total independence.[33] Eco-theological perspectives in East Africa therefore show us how best we can be citizens in the land community of our earth and how we can have a reasonable and healthy impact on the world we live in.

Recommendations for Further Reading

Davies, Kate and Ngonidzashe Edward. 'A Southern African response to Todd LeVasseur and Bernard Zaleha', in Conradie Ernst & Koster, Hilda (eds.), *Christian Theology and Climate Change* (London: T&T Clark, 2019), 132-135.

Deane-Drummond, Celia. *Eco-Theology* (London: Darton, Longman and Todd, 2008).

Eaton, Heather, ' Working with Climate Scientists', in Conradie Ernst & Koster, Hilda (eds.), *Christian Theology and Climate Change* (London: T&T Clark, 2019).

Ernst, Conradie & Koster, Hilda (eds.) *Christian Theology and Climate Change* (London: T&T Clark, 2019).

Johnston, Lucas. *Religion and Sustainability: Social Movements and the Politics of the Environment* (Sheffield: Equinox, 2013).

Kalu, Ogba. 'Preserving a Worldview: Pentecostalism in the African Maps of the Universe', *PNEUMA: The Journal of the Society for Pentecostal Studies,* 2002. 24(2):119-122 [https://doi.org/10.1163/15700740260388009].

[31] Loreen Maseno, ,Towards an African Inculturated Sophiology: The Case of African Wisdom Traditions from Myths for Ecological Concerns', in Celia Deane-Drummond and Heinrich Bedford-Strohm (eds.), *Religion and Ecology in the Public Sphere* (London, T&T Clark, 2011), 125-138.

[32] Kate Davies and Ngonidzashe Edward, 'A Southern African response to Todd LeVasseur and Bernard Zaleha', in *Handbook of Christian Theology and Climate Change* (Jahr: T&T Clark, 2020), 132-135.

[33] Micheal Northcott, 'Artificial persons against nature: environmental governmentality, economic corporations, and ecological ethics', *Annals of the New York Academy of Sciences* 1249 (2012), 104-117 [https://doi.org/10.1111/j.1749-6632.2011.06294.x], 108.

Kinnamon, Michael. *Can a Renewal Movement Be Renewed?: Questions for the Future of Ecumenism* (Grand Rapids: Eerdmans, 2014).

Livingston, James and Francis Fiorenza (eds.) *Modern Christian Thought*, vol. 2 (Upper Saddle River: Prentice Hall, 2000).

Maseno, Loreen. 'The Ogiek Indigenous People, Land Rights and the Environment', in Green MC, Harun, M. (eds.), *Law, Religion and the Environment in Africa* (Stellenbosch: Africa Sun Media, 2020).

Maseno, Loreen. 'An African Response to Christopher Vena', in Conradie Ernst & Koster, Hilda (eds.), *Christian Theology and Climate Change* (London: T&T Clark, 2019).

Maseno, Loreen. ‚Prayer for Rain: A Pentecostal Perspective from Kenya', *The Ecumenical Review*, 2017. Vol 69: 336-347.

Maseno, Loreen. 'Towards an African Inculturated Sophiology: The Case of African Wisdom Traditions from Myths for Ecological Concerns', in Celia Deane-Drummond and Heinrich Bedford-Strohm (eds.), *Religion and Ecology in the Public Sphere* (London: T&T Clark, 2011).

Northcott, Michael, 'Artificial persons against nature: environmental governmentality, economic corporations, and ecological ethics', *Annals of the New York Academy of Sciences* 1249 (2012), 104-117 [https://doi.org/10.1111/j.1749-6632.2011.06294.x], 108.

Pope Francis, *Laudato Si* (Vatican City: Libreria Editrice Vaticana, 2015).

Swoboda. Aaron Jason. 'Tongues and Trees: Towards a Green Pentecostal Pneumatology', unpublished PhD Thesis (UK: University of Birmingham, 2011).

Vena, Christopher. 'Working with Pentecostal and Evangelical Forms of Christianity', in Conradie Ernst & Koster, Hilda (eds.), *Christian Theology and Climate Change* (1London: T&T Clark, 2019).

Zizioulas, John D, *Being as Communion: Studies in Personhood and the Church* (Crestwood: St Vladimir's Seminary Press, 1993).

72. The Role of African Independent Churches on Ecological Principles for Land Use, Eco-farming and Nutrition Standards

John Gichimu[1]

The Organization of African Instituted Churches (OAIC) is an Association of African Independent Churches founded in 1978 in Cairo. The terms African Independent or African Instituted Churches (AICs) are used for a large number of heterogeneous faith communities across Sub-Saharan Africa. The OAIC understands an AIC as a church that acknowledges Jesus Christ as Lord, and which has either separated by secession from a mission church or an existing African independent church, or has been founded as an independent entity under African initiative and leadership. The first AICs were formed as popular Christian movements to preach the Gospel and to protect African values and forms of society against the impact of colonialism, and negative and overly restrictive aspects of the missionary-founded churches. They saw their churches as forerunners of a new, reformed, and more humane form of society that was both African and Christian, and would replace the colonialism that had deprived African people of their initiative, freedom, and sense of self-worth. The OAIC serves the member churches through the Program for Theology and Ministerial Formation (PTMF); the Livelihoods Program; the Just Communities Program; and the Community Health Program.

The Program for Theology and Ministerial formation is in place to reach out to the thousands of ministers in the member churches with appropriate theological education. This is done in cognizance of the identity, context and mission of African Independent Churches in relation to their founding visions.

The OAIC is involved in rural settings through the Livelihoods Program. The program is currently implementing a food security project which is aimed at reaching 400,000 households in East Africa and over 1,000 congregations and members of farmers' organizations. It is anticipated that the program will have a wider outreach to other regions of Africa, replicating success stories from East Africa. The process focuses on improving agricultural production and nutrition at household levels. The church congregation is at the center of the implementation, together with the catchment community that surrounds the congregation. The process involves community mobilization and organization for:

1. improved production (with sustainability at the center);
2. nutritional outcomes;
3. improved household incomes;
4. post-harvest management;
5. collective marketing;
6. influencing public policy.

The OAIC through the Just Communities Program is also involved in the mobilization and organization for Social Accountability. This is aimed at enabling churches to play a role in enhancing the civic competencies of the citizenry.

The Community Health Program works to empower congregations in the rural settings and informal settlements of urban centers to provide leadership on responding to health issues in communities.

---

[1] John Njeru Gichimu is an Archdeacon in the African Independent Pentecostal Church of Africa (AIPCA) which was founded in 1920s in Kenya during the Gikuyu nationalist movements. He has worked at the organization of African Instituted Churches (OAIC) since 1995 as a Facilitator for Theological Education by Extension (TEE) and currently the Director Programme for Theology and Ministerial Formation. He is a holder of Master of Arts in Mission Studies from Birmingham University UK.

These all are inspired by the biblical vision: “Do not dwell on the past. See, I am doing a new thing! Now it springs up, do you not perceive it? I am making a way in the desert, and streams in the wasteland” (Isaiah 43: 18 -19).

Background of Livelihoods and Food Security

The mantra of the Organization of African Instituted Churches strategic plan, “Visions for better world, abundant life for all in community,” entails that as followers of Jesus Christ we are called to respond firmly to poverty, poor health, and the breakdown of African cultural and social systems. Jesus’ own first public utterance, “The Spirit of the Lord is upon me, therefore he has sent me to bring good tidings to the poor …” (Luke 4: 18-19) invites us to take such action. Again, in the parable of the last judgement, we are told that we will be judged according to how we responded to the hungry, the thirsty, the naked and the stranger amongst us (Matthew 25: 31).

The OAIC has a long experience of working with rural church congregations of member churches and farmers’ organizations at community level to reach the small-holder farmers to enable them to increase their production and hence to provide better access to adequate food and enhanced financial incomes. The Livelihood Program began with providing capacity on HIV-AIDs by strengthening the ability of congregations and community based organizations (CBOs) in the provision of care and support services for those infected or affected by the scourge. Currently, the program scope of livelihood activities covers a wide range of agro-activities; food production, livestock rearing, bee keeping, and fish farming.

Ecology

There is no doubt that ecological transformation towards sustainability involves the capability to intervene into ongoing community, congregation, institutional and technological transformation processes, as well as providing transformative knowledge in various different settings including household level.

AICs are homegrown African churches. As followers of Jesus Christ, we are called to respond with conviction to the challenges, such as entrenched poverty or the breakdown of African cultural and social systems, that require groups to organize themselves in order to confront these challenges.

Consequently, African agriculture relies heavily on the ecosystem’s resources making these resources critical assets to the survival of agricultural communities. It is important that global agreements and their implementation mechanisms set up in response to climate change recognize this sensitivity of African agriculture to negative climate events. On the other hand African farmers have a duty of care for the environment and in particular to mitigate the factors that lead to these negative climate events. Abuse of ecosystem resources through inappropriate crop and animal husbandry and other practices such as the clearing of tree cover and reclaiming wetlands can lead to serious land degradation. Declining yields in turn lead to new cycles of abuse of ecosystem. To strengthen farming, the organization works to enable member churches and community based organizations (CBOs) to promote farming methods that are eco-friendly.

This is done by integrating farming with planet husbandry practices:

1. Farmer’s knowledge and practice of using farming activities to take good care of natural resources and the planet.
2. Clear understanding by smallholder farmers of the sustainable use of natural resources and the wellbeing of current and future generations.
3. Model farms and farmer organizations should specifically set out to achieve the goal of securing food and nutrition while aiding natural resource and environment regeneration.
4. Practices that are planet friendly include better soil conservation, increasing efforts for farm tree cover and water conservation.

Farmers Resource Persons (FRPs) Experiences

Whereas FRPs are the catalysts for change in the ecological transformation, the community and its environment are the context in which ecological transformation occurs.

In traditional societies, the community was self-sufficient to ensure the preservation of the community. This was not to a state of well-being of the individual, but relating to harmony and responsibility within the wider community.

The basic concepts of ecology include the following:

1. All living organisms and the environment they live in are mutually reactive, affecting each other in various ways.
2. Environment plays a major role in the critical stages of the life cycle of the species, including human beings.
3. The species react to the environmental changes and adjust themself.

To be able to succeed in the ecological transformation, FRPs need to be able to recognize these patterns and understand the ecological context in which the transformation needs to occur. Now it is time to change emphasis to facilitating the community to achieve their own objective.

OAIC builds the capacity of national FRPs (drawn from congregations of member churches and community farmer organizations) who through multiplier effect trains more FRPs and form a national team of FRPs. The team trains Lead Farmers (LFs). The LFs trains households (HHs) from congregations and community. FRPs, LFs and HHs establish model farmers for demonstration during training. The team also establishes demonstration farms for raining and seed banks.

Uganda FRPs

In order to mitigate levels of environment degradation and associated adverse effects on climate change for rain-fed agriculture, the FRPs work with farmers on the following:

- Empowering and building the capacity of farmers on plants which can fix nitrogen in soils.
- Agro-forestry by planting trees which can encourage bee keeping for cross pollination, especially OPV's open pollinated varieties.
- Emphasis on the use of green manure.
- Plants which fix nitrogen in soils and also act as fodder for animals.
- Encouraging our farmers to practice soil and water conservation on their lands in order to avoid soil erosion.
- Planting long term fruit trees, which produce fruits for income generating and conservation of the environment.

Moreover, farmers are practicing organic farming with the use of composite manure and rearing animals which provide dung and urine for manure preparations. Manure is then taken to gardens, from where we get food for humans and feeds for animals. From animals we get animals products for humans, and animals again give us dung and urine for manure preparations.

Thus, ecological transformation has already started supporting food and nutrition security and if fully adopted in future food and nutrition, security will be attained and we shall have agricultural sustainability because practices themselves are sustainable.

Tanzania FRPs

When climate is uneven, then it affects the growing of crops and rearing of livestock thus resulting in food insecurity. Ways to manage climate change consist of:

- mobilization of communities on effects of climate change;

- training farmers to practice agroforestry;
- training farmers to preserve natural and planted forest;
- training farmers on measures needed to minimize climate change.

Kenya FRPs

Farmers Resource Center Gambogi Vihiga: ecological transformation here is a tremendous opportunity to reinvent farming in line with principles of social justice and care for the environment. Solidarity and earth-friendly activities must be developed to jumpstart and sustain this transition, which is a necessary step forward. Humanity must restore the balance between human activities and caring for creation. Food security is primarily associated with socioeconomic as well as environmental conditions of the ecosystem.

- Discourage farmers from burning charcoal that results in decimating trees, while on the other hand it provides readily livelihood.
- Encourage farmers to apply conservation farming principles:
    - early planting;
    - minimum tillage;
    - soil cover after planting;
    - digging small holes before planting, hence putting a mixture of compost manure and ash before planting seeds;
    - when planting trees, e.g. fruit trees, to prepare recommendable holes depending on what type of the tree – if it's a mango tree, you should have a hole of 3x3 feet and space of 5 meters from one tree to the other;
    - preparing our own compost manure of green leaves and dry residues from the garden after harvesting, i.e. crop stems of maize, millet and sorghum;
    - crop rotation is a must to every farmer.

We encourage our farmers to sign a commitment form of agreement to promise us how many trees they will plant every season.

Agroforestry

We advise farmers to have their own small tree nurseries in order to cut the cost of buying tree seedlings.

- Trees on boundaries – these can be used as true fences when necessary.
- Home steads – trees grown around the homestead as wind break and for shade use.
- River banks – specific trees grown to protect against river bank erosion and catchment areas.
- Terraces – trees stabilize the terraces and provide organic matter and leaves decompose.
- Slope areas – trees are planted on the contour hedges which create barriers against soil creep and prevent soil erosion.
- Napier grass and other grass which can be used for animal feeds and prevention of soil erosion.

All the above are important for the following:

- conservation of moisture;
- improvement of soil structure;
- control of soil erosion;
- source of plants nutrients – retention of nitrogen in the soil.

What is the Basis for Engagement?

1. The fact that many African Independent Churches still hold worship services under trees is a clear indication of how AICs understand ecology to be a resource given by God, hence worthy of caring.

2. The appreciation of God's creation as a source for livelihoods. That is the reason the soil is cared for and in return it brings forth livelihood to the people.
3. Using environmental resources, i.e. the various types of plants that can be used for soil health and as pesticides is an appreciation and celebration of what God has provided in his creation.
4. The establishment of community seed banks is a response to the need for re-plantable seeds, and consequently a type of agriculture that relates to God's order where seeds are re-planted and seeds are shared within a community.
5. AICs' visions for a better world as a motivating factor for their action for the transformation of families and communities.
6. The congregation at the local level as a structure for mobilizing communities.

Conclusion

In every culture there is intuitive knowledge of how to relate with nature for posterity. The experiences of AICs in livelihoods traverse both traditional and technical methodologies of caring for environment. It is obvious that human endeavours to care for the environment is reciprocal for the care the environment takes for humans. We must resolve to be good earth-keepers now more than ever before to avert the danger that has come with climate change.

Suggestions for Further Reading

Agroecology: Key Concepts, Principles and Practices (Penang: Third World Network, 2015).

Colin, A., Pimbert, M., Kiss, C. (2015). *Building, defending and strengthening agroecology, a global struggle for food sovereignty.* Centre for Agroecology, Water and Resilience and Centre for Learning on Sustainable Agriculture. Coventry University (UK) and ILEIA (The Netherlands), 2015.

FAO website: "10 key elements of Agroecology": https://www.fao.org/agroecology/database/detail/en/c/1128220/

Farmers Resource Persons (FRPs) Reports to OAIC Secretariat 2018/2019 (Unpublished).

George, P. T. & Jafri, Afsar. *Handbook on Agroecology: Farmer's Manual on Sustainable Practices* (2014), see https://ag-transition.org/?initiative=handbook-on-agroecology-farmers-manual-on-sustainable-practices.

Serrat, Olivier. *The Sustainable Livelihoods Approach* (2008) ,see: https://www.adb.org/sites/default/files/publication/27638/sustainable-livelihoods-approach.pdf.

Taggar, KTH. Ecological Sustainability, Planetary Boundaries, Environmental Objectives, Environmental Quality Objectives (2015), see: https://www.kth.se/en/om/miljo-hallbar-utveckling/utbildning-miljo-hallbar-utveckling/verktygslada/sustainable-development/ekologisk-hallbarhet-1.432074.

73. Churches in Rwanda: Promoters of Ecological Justice

Gloriose Umuziranenge[1]

General Introduction

Rwanda is a small landlocked country of 26,338 km^2 located in the central-eastern part of Africa. It shares boarders with Uganda in the North, Tanzania in the East and Southeast, Burundi in the South and Democratic Republic of Congo in the West. It is one of the highest population densities in Africa (1,060 / sq mile) and its population was estimated at 12.79 million in 2019.[2] It is predicted that the population will increase to 26 million by 2050, with a population density of 987 people per square kilometre. Urbanization is increasing at 4.4% per year, with over 1 million people living in the capital city, Kigali. As pressure on the land increases, urbanization will increase, and urban centres will expand. If this urbanization is properly managed and coupled with industry and services, it can be an instrument for wealth creation. Alternatively, there is a risk of urban slums developing and creating associated health and social problems. Job creation, education, health care and social protection are all needed to address population growth, while urban areas must be high density and resource efficient to support a growing skilled workforce.

Therefore, Rwanda's future socio-economic development is uncertain as its population grows and the climate changes, causing pressure on land, water, food, and energy resources. Rwanda is experiencing severe consequences of climate change, especially in rural areas. The consequences include heavy rains causing widespread flooding, severe soil erosion, landslides, crop and livestock loss, and destruction of road infrastructure and property countrywide and, in some instances, the highest cost of the loss of human life.[3] In addition, it threatens agricultural production. Impacts associated with climate change have been found to be a main challenge for rural poor farmers dominating the agriculture sector due to their limited adaptive capacity at coping with these impacts.[4] Therefore, in rural areas where people depend on agriculture, farmers face substantial risk of crop failure and famine when drought hits.

The Ministry of Disaster Management and Refugees (MIDIMAR) from January to end of April 2018 recorded 95 people dead and 195 injured. Disasters damaged 4,560 hectacres of crops and destroyed 370 houses. They destroyed 12 roads, 7 churches, 18 bridges and killed 700 livestock.[5] According to the study conducted to assess the impact of climate change on food security in Rwanda (the case of Bugesera District), decline in the food crop productivity has been found to be the main result of extreme climatic events.[6]

In Rwanda, the majority of the population are believers in one of the existing religions. The dominant religious group is Catholics, who represent 44% of the resident population of the country. The second most prevalent religious group are Protestants (38%), while other religion groups are made up of Adventists (12%), Muslims (2%) and Jehovah's Witnesses (1%). While those with no religious affiliation represent

---

[1] Dr. Gloriose Umuziranenge is Head of Department of Natural Resources and Environmental Management at Protestant Institute of Arts and Social Sciences: u.gloriose@gmail.com

[2] National Institute of Statistics of Rwanda (NISR), 'Population Projections Fourth Rwanda Population and Housing Census', Thematic Report, 2012.

[3] REMA, 'The Assessment of Economic Impacts of the 2012 Wet Season Flooding in Rwanda' (Kigali: 2013).

[4] MINAGRI, 'Plan for the Transformation of Agriculture in Rwanda – Phase III', Ministry of Agriculture and Animal Resources (Kigali: 2013).

[5] https://reliefweb.int/report/rwanda/midimar-supported-and-comforted-population-affected-disasters.

[6] Rwanyirizi and Rugema, 'Climate Change Effects on Food Security in Rwanda: Case Study of Wetland Rice Production in Bugesera', *Rwanda Journal* 1 (1) (2013), 35–51.

2.5%, adherents of the traditionalist/animists and of other religions each represent less than 1% of the population. Thus, Christian religious groups represent 95% of the population of Rwanda.[7]

African countries, including Rwanda, have commonalities in a number of areas, such as value systems, beliefs, and practices. These countries used to have traditional practices of conserving the environment – for example, where forests were considered to be sacred areas for the invocation of the sacred powers of the supreme beings, forbidden areas associated with worships and so on. Different African communities have strong indigenous knowledge that they used in the past and that can still be used to conserve forests and biodiversity. For example, in some communities it was forbidden to enter the forest without permission and the culture forbade any member of the community from cutting down trees for firewood or any other purpose.

Before the colonial era, Rwanda was categorically a nation-state, with people sharing the same religious beliefs, traditions, customs, and speaking the same language (Kinyarwanda) – in short, sharing the same culture. Rwandan society was inherently linked to the forest, which hid (was the space for) great lessons concerning rites, ancestral customs, taboos, arts, crafts, music, dance etc. In Rwanda, cutting of certain tree species is seen as a taboo, as well as killing of indigenous animals such as primates, elephants, leopards, birds. This conservation culture emphasized the symbiotic and interdependent relationship between people, plants and animals. It is for these reasons that cultural values are an essential component of every society, and they act as checks and balances in the management of natural resources.[8] Due to cultural values given to some natural sites, few ecosystems which have been safeguarded by the local population are still observed. This is especially the case for the natural forest of Cyamudongo. Some species which have almost disappeared in the natural environment are also found preserved in the gardens of traditional healers, and in the enclosures and gardens of certain individuals, according to the cultural value of the plant.[9] Because of the cultural norms and values associated with the sacred forest, this has led to non-exploitation and therefore conservation of some forests in Rwanda and some parts of Africa. However, to consolidate their power, colonizers and missionaries have, from the outset, sought to blot out the identity and collective memory of Rwandans. Thus, many traditional cultural practices such as worship of ancestors were described as wild and pagan, and in some places trees and sacred places were destroyed just like in other African countries. With globalization, the cultures, good practices and values of African countries have been lost when they should instead guide the local communities in making their resources, such as forests, part of their lives with feelings of ownership and pride.

Why Ecological Justice?

According to Schlosberg,[10] justice is identified with a person's abilities or substantive opportunities in being able to acknowledge different functioning. The ability approach in this manner offers an understanding of distributive equity, capabilities, recognition, participation, and procedural justice. Therefore, social justice includes the designation of rights, goods and freedom in a general public, social and financial fairness,

[7] National Institute of Statistics of Rwanda, 'Fourth Population and Housing Census. Thematic Report: Socio-cultural Characteristics of the Population', 2012.

[8] Irakiza, R., Vedaste, M., Elias, B., Nyirambangutse, B., Serge, N.J. & Marc, N., 'Assessment of traditional ecological knowledge and beliefs in the utilisation of important plant species: the case of Buhanga sacred forest, Rwanda', *Koedoe* 58 (1) (2016): a1348. http://dx.doi.org/10.4102/koedoe.v58i1.1348.

[9] Munyaneza. E., et al., 'The role of cultural practices in the conservation of biodiversity in Rwanda', 2009.

[10] Schroeder, R., Martin, K. S., Wilson, B., & Sen, D. 'Third world environmental justice', *Society and Natural Resources*, 21(7) (2008): 547-555. See https://www.academia.edu/28968705/Third_World_Environmental_Justice; David Schlosberg, 'Justice, Ecological Integrity and Climate Change', in Thompsen, *Ethical Adaptation to Climate Change. Human Virtues for the Future* (MIT Press, 2012), 165-183, see: https://www.academia.edu/1613920/Justice_Ecological_Integrity_and_Climate_Change

recognizing the role of everyone, promotion of capabilities for better functioning, as well as inclusion in the decision making process.

In Nancy Fraser's three-dimensional account of justice,[11] redistribution, recognition, and representation are highlighted. According to Fraser's understanding, injustices in natural resources management and conflicts may arise when decision makers ignore the voice of community members and reject their ability to participate. Therefore, conservation and development strategies require guaranteeing equity as equality of interest and consider social plans that allow all persons to take part as companions in social life. Thus, the increase of community participation and their involvement improves equity and empowerment of the community,[12] while inequity in engagement processes lead to disputes and conflicts among different actors.[13] The implementation of different policies and initiatives relating to the conservation of protected areas should consider the voice and consultation of the local community, otherwise social injustices at intersecting scales can occur and lead to the social exclusion of the global poor.[14]

Environmental justice and community empowerment are closely interlinked. In this regard, it is worth describing how scholars conceptualize the previously mentioned terms before showing how they are related. Environmental justice is a concept which can be defined in different perspectives by different scholars. It can be seen as a process of dealing with all justice related issues in environmental management through distributive and procedural dimensions.[15] With regard to justice, the environmental justice approach, 'eco-justice', challenges both humanity's destruction of the earth and the abuse of power which results in environmental damage, with poor people suffering the greatest impact.[16]

On the one hand, the distributive dimension is concerned with equity as regard to dealing with people's outcomes in social exchanges.[17] It concerns mainly the distribution of costs and benefits among communities living in the protected areas. On the other hand, procedural justice is related to the procedures and processes.[18] This is concerned with the extent to which communities are involved in the process of decision-making.[19] Regarding community participation, Pretty gives a model of participation indicating different forms of participation.[20] They include manipulative (through unelected representatives), passive (receptive of information), consultation, material incentives, functional (by serving to achieve external project goals) and interactive participation. Though no form can fit all contexts, interactive participation might be important in regard of considering the needs of concerned people and organizations or systems.[21]

---

[11] Fraser, N, *Scales of Justice: Reimagining Political Space in a Globalizing World, New Directions in Critical Theory* (Cambridge: Polity Press, 2008).

[12] Reed, M. S., 'Stakeholder participation for environmental management: a literature review', *Biological conservation*, 141 (10) (2008): 2417-2431.

[13] Leciejewski, M., & Perkins, H. A., 'Environmental justice in Appalachia: Procedural inequities in the mine permitting process in Southeast Ohio', *Environmental Justice*, 8 (4) (2015): 111-116.

[14] Fraser, N., 'Injustice at Intersecting Scales: On Social Exclusion and the Global Poor', *European Journal of Social Theory*, 13 (3) (2010): 363-371.

[15] Ikeme, J., 'Equity, environmental justice and sustainability: incomplete approaches in climate change politics', *Global Environmental Change*, 13 (3) (2003): 195-206.

[16] Conradie, E.M., 'How can we help to raise an environmental awareness in the South African context?', *Scriptura* 82 (2003): 122-138; http://dx.doi.org/10.7833/ 82-0-903.

[17] Brashear, T. G., Brooks, C. M., & Boles, J. S., 'Distributive and procedural justice in a sales force context: Scale development and validation', *Journal of Business Research* 57 (1) (2004): 86-93.

[18] Sheppard, B.H., Lewicki, R.J., & Minton, J.W., *Organizational Justice: The Search for Fairness in the Workplace* (New York: Lexington Books, 1992).

[19] Svarstad, H., Sletten, A., Paloniemi, R., Barton, D. N., & Grieg-Gran, M., 'Three types of environmental justice: from concepts to empirical studies of social impacts of policy instruments for conservation of biodiversity', in *Assessing the Role of Economic Instruments in Policy Mixes for Biodiversity Conservation and Ecosystem Services Provision: Report for the Policymix Project* (Oslo: Norwegian Institute for Nature Research, 2011).

[20] Pretty, J., 'The many interpretations of participation', *Focus*, 16 (1995): 4-5.

[21] Reddy, G.N., *Empowering Communities through Participatory Methods* (Delhi: Manak Publications, 2002).

In the context of conservation, procedural environmental justice regards how people living in protected areas are empowered to make decisions regarding conservation policies as well as their own development projects. As indicated earlier, environmental justice is closely related to community empowerment. The relationship is described based on two dimensions of environmental justice. First, equity in cost and benefits from natural resource management is a means of social and economic empowerment of the local community.[22] For example, tourism revenue sharing is a tool for not only engaging surrounding communities, but also contributes to their socio-economic development.[23]

Community participation is considered as a tool for empowerment, building beneficiary capacity, increasing effectiveness in the desire to share costs, and improving the efficiency and success of the projects. People should have the relevant assets and instrumental freedoms (representation and consultation) to achieve different needs, including human assets (health and education), natural assets (having access to resources), and physical assets by access to the infrastructure. Communities are not only empowered by providing incentives but also through involvement in the decision-making process.

With procedural environmental justice, people are empowered to become agents of change. They are expected to be independent and make decision on their own by building trust in such a way that they can empower themselves.[24] It is important to note that participation in decision-making is a crucial element to ensure sustainable development processes and create an influence on norms and value.[25] The involvement of the locals including women, youth and other groups, is a driver to the success of development initiatives to avoid social injustices at intersecting scales that can occur and lead to the social exclusion of the global poor. Thus, environmental justice (distributive and procedural) is a means through which population surrounding protected areas may be economically and socially empowered.

Biblical Perspectives on Environmental Care

The issue of environment deterioration and its consequences has ethical and spiritual dimensions, among others. The biblical concept of creation and stewardship by human beings clearly teaches that 'human beings' are responsible for taking care of God's creation (Genesis 2:15). Theologically, this means that salvation brought by Jesus Christ does not only send us to be witness to others, but rather and more importantly to take care of God's creation in its wholeness. Hence, the church of God is called and sent to sensitize the community for the change of attitudes and practices towards the environment.[26] In addition, religion is cultural language which people in Rwanda understand well because they are deeply embedded into religion systems and rationalities. With Christianity being a majority, a better understanding of its scriptures can help this sensitization. However, in this paper let me confine myself to the Christian responsibility for environmental conservation.

Christians believe that God created the universe, everything created belongs to God, not us, God gave human beings the responsibility to care for it, and that a good Christian is the one who protects the environment. He created male and female, blessed them, and said:

---

[22] Walpole, M. J., & Thouless, C. R. 'Increasing the value of wildlife through non-consumptive use? Deconstructing the myths of ecotourism and community-based tourism in the tropics', *Conservation Biology Series* 9 (2005): 122.
[23] Imanishimwe, A., Niyonzima, T., & Nsabimana, D., 'Contribution of Community Conservation and Ecotourism Projects on Improving Livelihoods and Sustainable Biodiversity Conservation in and around Nyungwe National Park (NNP)', *J Tourism Hospit*, 7 (363) (2018): 2167-0269.
[24] O'Neil, T., & Domingo, P., *The Power to Decide: Women, Decision-making and Gender Equality*. (London: The Overseas Development Institute, 2015).
[25] Mensah, J., & Casadevall, S. R., 'Sustainable development: Meaning, history, principles, pillars, and implications for human action: Literature review', *Cogent Social Sciences*, 5 (1) (2019): 1653531.
[26] National Institute of Statistics of Rwanda, "Fourth Population and Housing Census. Thematic Report: Socio-cultural characteristics of the population", 2012

> Have many children, so that your descendants will live all over the earth and bring it under their control. I am putting you in charge of the fish, the birds, and all the wild animals. I have provided all kinds of grain and all kinds of fruit for you to eat; but for all the wild animals and birds I have provided grass and leafy plants for food. (Genesis, 1)

The Lord God placed humans in the Garden of Eden to cultivate and guard it. Unfortunately, in proudness of wanting to be like God, human beings rebelled, and one of the consequences of human rebellion is the rejection of being God's stewards. Humans have destroyed the creation of God to the extent that even human beings are in turn destroying themselves. Indeed, in so much as it has neglected the socio-ecological implications of its teachings, Christianity has a certain responsibility in helping to bring about the ecological crisis, despite also holding within itself the potential to provide a robust foundation for socio-ecological actions linking social justice and ecological health as the essence of environmental justice.[27] This concept is linked to the principles of eco-theology in connecting the pain of people to degraded ecosystems, seeking to alleviate both human pain and ecological degradation.[28] Since environmental problems are very serious issues in Rwanda and the Bible stresses God's concern for the environment, religious philosophy ought to have the option to address current emergencies and crises by offering progressively natural and socially sustainable initiatives and choices.

Green Churches in Rwanda

In 2000, Rwanda was recovering from almost a decade of war and genocide against the Tutsi since 1994 which had left the country isolated and devastated. The country adopted its development guide policy, 'Vision 2020', as a mechanism to accelerate economic development and to reduce the number of people living in poverty.[29] The government of Rwanda, as any of the African countries where faith-based organizations and churches predominantly offer social services such as healthcare, education and social cohesion, has involved faith-based organizations and churches in the development of both documents – the consultation resulted in the adoption of the 'Vision 2020'.[30] To this day the Christian churches are members of the local 'Joint Action Development Forum' (JADF).[31]

Similarly, to their Catholic counterparts, Protestant missionaries and independent churches after them have also run interventions aiming at the transformation of populations around the stations. Common interventions include schools and health facilities, as well as community development programmes such as improved agriculture, craft, water, and sanitation, among others. Churches and Christian organisations are very active in education, health, and community development. They own and run schools and institutions of higher learning, health facilities and community initiatives.[32] According to Maurice, in 2015, half of the primary and secondary education schools were owned by churches, as well as approximately 30% of the health facilities (health centres and hospitals) either privately or in partnership with the government.[33]

---

[27] Dawson, N., Grogan, K., Martin, A., Mertz, O., Pasgaard, M., & Rasmussen, L. V., 'Environmental justice research shows the importance of social feedbacks in ecosystem service trade-offs', *Ecology and Society*, 22 (3) (2017).

[28] Hrynkow, C. W., 'Greening God? Christian Eco-theology, Environmental Justice, and Socio-Ecological Flourishing', *Environmental Justice*, 10 (3) (2017): 81-87.

[29] Republic of Rwanda, 2012, 2.

[30] National Poverty Reduction Programme and Ministry of Finance and Economic Planning 2002, 34.

[31] Republic of Rwanda: Office of the Prime Minister, 7/20/2015., pp. 54, 55, 71.

[32] Tharcisse Gatwa and Laurent Rutinduka (eds.), *Histoire du christianisme au Rwanda. Des 562rigins à nos jours.* Yaoundé (Cameroun): Éditions CLÉ 2014.

[33] John Maurice, 'Faith-based organisations bolster health care in Rwanda', *The Lancet World Report*, Vol.386, Issue 9989, 123-124, July 11, 2015, in: https://www.thelancet.com/journals/lancet/article/PIIS0140-6736(15)61213-2/fulltext.

The Protestant churches which this paper focuses on are heirs of the sixteenth century Reformation that has been diverse in its shape, giving rise to Lutherans, Anglicans and Calvinists (Presbyterians); and from the revivals, Methodists, Baptists, and Pentecostal churches that nurtured the missionary movement of the eighteenth and nineteenth centuries.

The first protestant missionaries in Rwanda were German, established in East Africa; they arrived in Rwanda in 1907 from Tanganyika. They were authorised by King Musinga to start activities in Zinga and Kirinda in 1907, in Rubengera in 1909, and in Remera Rukoma in 1912. Second in in the evangelisation of Rwanda after the Catholic white fathers of 1900, the German missionaries were then forced to leave the country in 1916 when their country was defeated in Africa. Their stations were taken over in 1921 by the Belgian Society of Protestant Missions in Congo, until 1959 when they gave autonomy to the local church, known today as the Presbyterian Church of Rwanda.[34]

Contrary to the Roman Catholic Church, where Caritas coordinated social services, most Protestant churches organise the interventions locally in the community with the local congregations, with little or no coordination from the regional or national hierarchy and national church coordination – except in the Presbyterian Church in Rwanda (EPR) and the Anglican Church in Rwanda (EAR), who have diaconia and mission and development departments.[35]

On the track of dealing with climate change effects in Rwanda, Protestants churches were not left behind. The Protestant University of Rwanda, in a partnership with United Evangelical Mission (UEM), stated an environmental awareness program to help underserved communities shape their knowledge with regards to environmental protection, especially climate change mitigation and adaptation measures as a matter of environmental justice, as well as a biblical perspective with regard to environmental care. In fact, 80 participants from Protestant churches received training to help address local environmental, health, and economic challenges, thanks to UEM who supported the implementation of this activity. The training has been held at PIASS since January 2017 in consecutive phases. It is aimed at improving the knowledge and skills of church members, mostly from the Anglican and Presbyterian churches, with information about mitigating and adapting the effects of climate and its consequences on human welfare – especially on food security in Rwanda, waste management and sustainable development goals, as well as learning from what other practitioners have done in environmental protection related matters. Participants were church leaders, Mothers' Unions, Protestants schools' directors, and church development officers.

The partnership between the Protestant University of Rwanda (PUR) and UEM created a working group with the emphasis on the connections between environmental justice and the role of Protestant churches and how they can integrate environmental justice and trainings in their strategic planning. The training facilitated collaboration between churches and environmental justice stakeholders, and it strengthened the capacity of communities and church-based organizations to engage in environment advocacy and awareness in planning. Training offered knowledge to the participants and made them able to respond to nature conservation in their communities. It was expected that, at the end of each training, the trainees would be able to explain the consequences of human actions on the deterioration of the integrity of creation, articulate theological and biblical insights on the place of human beings in the created world and their responsibility as stewards of God in taking care of creation, and argue the role of Christians in sensitization, advocacy, and practices for the integrity of the created order.

Climate Change Training Program at Protestant University of Rwanda

[34] Gatwa, T. & Rutinduka, L., *History of Christianity in Rwanda, from Beginning to Present Day: An Ecumenical Perspective* (Yaoundé: Editions CLE, 2013).
[35] Protestant University of Rwanda (PUR) 2017, 172.

Scenes from Climate Change Training Program at Protestant University of Rwanda (PIASS)

Implemented Activities by EAR[36] in Rwanda

Implemented activities by churches in Rwanda include community mobilization on environmental conservation, training and sensitization on energy saving stoves (EAR Diocese Shyogwe), training on soil management and soil erosion prevention, tree plantation and distribution of seedlings in local communities, and the distribution of ceramic water filters in local communities. Initiatives carried out by EAR include community improvement initiatives and are operated as a joint activity between the Butare, Cyangugu, Kigeme and Shyogwe Dioceses of the Anglican Church of Rwanda. The four dioceses agree that the church has a critical position to play inside the socio-economic development of the human beings. They advocate harmony and participation in the healing technique of human beings inside the four dioceses via social transformation, introduced through non-secular change and participation of the community in identifying and enforcing applicable tasks to overcoming every day issues. The church has a role as a restoration ministry in reconciliation, restoration, and rehabilitation. The church has also been concerned with rural improvement, vocational education, schooling, and in the war against HIV/AIDS. The agricultural improvement Inter-Diocesan carrier (RDIS) is a community development undertaking, operated as a joint movement via the Butare, Cyangugu, Kigeme and Shyogwe Dioceses of the Anglican Church in Rwanda. The enterprise has deep involvement in the groups it works with, no longer only because of the presence of the Anglican Church inside the vicinity, but additionally on the basis of the numerous initiatives and programmes that it is undertaking – these include threat reduction and environmental protection, tree nursery preparation, improved cooking stoves, land terracing, swamp control, savings and credit scores, mobilization of saving groups, promotion of profits-producing sports, nutrition safety interventions, Irish potato developing and rice developing, pineapple growing and processing, fish farming, animal herding (goats, pigs and hens), water and sanitation, water conservation, water tanks, Biogas (very few trials, mainly in schools), go-phase/ability building, own family making plans, financial savings and credit, and animal husbandry. Moreover, the dioceses run various colleges and fitness facilities.

With reference to climate change mitigation and adaptation, huge achievements of the church have been seen with the advanced cooking stoves undertaking: from 2007 to 2013, RDIS distributed approximately 3,000 improved stoves, constructed from locally available substances (bricks, clay, cement). Since 2012, RDIS has been implementing a carbon project for improved cooking stoves and water ceramic filters in Rwanda. The reason for this project (carbon emission reduction for self-sustainable environmental care) is particularly to lessen the use of firewood, which is extremely scarce in Rwanda. RDIS is likewise concerned with reforestation through the establishment of tree nurseries and capacity building activities. Therefore, RDIS participates in the distribution and mobilization of the use of power-saving stoves as a way to reduce the use of charcoal and firewood.[37] This project has facilitated beneficiaries in the cooking process, which seems to be easily compared with the use of firewood – the process which is very quick, reduced smokes in the kitchen, and improves kitchen cleanliness. Water ceramic filters have reduced the time spent on boiling drinking water and water-born diseases have been reduced. According to beneficiaries, the project generated employment in the local community.

Even though churches are committed to addressing some of the effects of climate change, they still face the challenge of low community awareness concerning the risks of climate change, which constitutes an obstacle to ownership of protection measures. There remains a lack of knowledge and skills among community and church members in relation to climate protection, the collaboration between environmental actors (churches, civil society, foreign agencies and government services) can be difficult, and there are insufficient resources to implement projects to address climate change.

---

36 Eglise Anglicane au Rwanda.

37 2nd Assessment of Environmental Protection Activities in UEM member churches in the African Region, 2011-2015.

Conclusion

What can be concluded based on the arguments above is that globalization has certainly brought us to an era where the stability of environment is at stake. The results of globalization have led us to another level of environmental deterioration and global warming. In his opening address at the opening ceremony of UN Climate Change Conference COP25 on 2 December 2019, UN Secretary General Antonio Gutierrez spoke of "global heating". For a fact, the environmental risks are not being distributed equally across the globe due to the ever-rising levels of consumption which are, in turn, affecting the level of GHG emissions on a global scale, as well as climate stability and the degradation of soil and the pollution of air and water. Regardless of its negative consequences, the nature of 'interconnectedness' in globalization could also be seen as a vector in efficiently overcoming the environmental challenges that the world is currently facing. Collaboration has opened doors for green policies through the involvement of other bodies like NGOs, social movement groups and churches, which helps to raise awareness across the globe. I argue that every individual has a duty of engaging in activities that are sustainable and cause less harm to the environment, committing to activities in the most sustainable manner possible. People will be able to respond to global environmental challenges if they are equipped with knowledge, skills and with the capabilities and rights needed to pursue their basic livelihoods. They need employment and incomes so that they do not rely on the use of natural resources for their survival. These are the essential conditions which empower them to participate fully as citizens in their local, national, and global communities. These goals can only be reached if national governments, community groups, and churches allocate adequate resources to education, basic infrastructure, and the environment, and create the institutional framework which ensures broad access and opportunity. Citizens all over the world should also associate themselves in environmental education groups at a very young age as agents of change. At the same time, governments, especially of the industrialized nations, must make urgent and realistic commitments to pass legislation and to support the protection of nature and climate in a way that reduces harmful levels of consumption and mobility, provides incentives for, and promotes development and use of, innovative technologies for energy production, mobility and agricultural, as well as industrial production, including waste management. Shaping partnership approaches, empowering local communities, and the provision of incentives, especially to local communities living around protected areas, will sustain natural resources.

In this globalised world we also need to question our understanding of growth and development: I believe it can only be sustainable if it is done in a manner that cares for the wellbeing of all equally; those who have more economic power right now need to let go of some of their privileges (using airplanes, having more than one car per family, consuming but not producing food etc.). In the end, our survival as human race is only possible if we share what is available in terms of resources and take responsibility for world consumption (of food, of land, of water, of minerals, of disposing of waste without causing harm, etc.). Integration of indigenous knowledge in environment conservation should be emphasized. Ecological justice should consider the context where culture, values and the dignity of each country and local community are reflected and respected.

In the Rwandan context, there is a sense of responsibility for creation care in the community. However, the church has never been, and should not be, an observer when it comes to her responsibility as an institution called by God to be steward of God's creation. Moreover, there is a change in the understanding of what the church should do within the local community. Furthermore, the church is called to give spiritual hope and Christian education, especially more education related to the environment. By having the church as an actor, Christians can bridge scientific arguments on climate change that can be translated into Christian understanding and culture. The church has an important role in translating climate data and climate change information into cultural practices and behaviours of the people in the community. Thus, it is easy for Christian to believe that respect for God can be connected to the respect of creation.

Suggestions for Further Reading

Baerlein, T., Kasymov, U., & Zikos, D. (2015), 'Self-governance and sustainable common pool resource management in Kyrgyzstan', *Sustainability* 7 (1), 496-521.

Rice, J. (2007), 'Ecological unequal exchange: Consumption, equity, and unsustainable structural relationships within the global economy', *International Journal of Comparative Sociology*, 48 (1), 43-72.

Schlosberg, D. *Justice to Nature 2: Incorporating Recognition, Capabilities, and Participation* (Oxford, New York: Oxford University Press, 2007).

Umuziranenge, G. (2019), 'Parks' Governance and Management in Rwanda: Opportunities and Challenges of the Community Participation for a Sustainable Conservation: Case Study of Nyungwe National Park', *International Journal of Environmental Protection and Policy*, 7 (2), 61-71; DOI: 10.11648/j.ijepp.20190702.132.

Umuziranenge, G. (2019), 'Environmental Justice and Women Empowerment in Nyungwe National Park (Rwanda): Case Study of Kitabi Women Handcrafts Cooperative', *International Journal of Environment and Climate Change*, 77-87; DOI: 10.9734/IJECC/2019/v9i230098.3.

Umuziranenge, G., Muhirwa, F. (2017), 'Ecotourism as potential conservation incentive and its impact on community development around Nyungwe National Park', *Imperial Journal of Interdisciplinary Research*, Vol-3, Issue-10. 447-4564.

Umuziranenge, G. (2019), 'Community Perceptions of Human-wildlife Conflicts and the Compensation Scheme around Nyungwe National Park (Rwanda)', International *Journal of Natural Resource Ecology and Management*, 4 (6); 185-217, DOI: 10.11648/j.ijnrem.20190406.15.

Umuziranenge, G., Ntiranyibagira, E. (2019), 'Nature conservation policies and practices in Africa: Critical analysis, ideological challenges, and strategic vision for protected areas sustainable management'. ASC-TUFS Working Papers 2019: Challenges of Development and Natural Resources Governance in Africa.

Umuziranenge, G. (2016), 'The role of churches in addressing climate change: case study of Rwanda', in: Dietrich Werner, Elizabeth Jeglitzka (eds), *Eco-Theology, Climate Justice, and Food Security Theological Education and Christian Leadership Development*, Globethics 2016.

Umuziranenge, G. (2019), 'Community empowerment and Environmental Justice in Rwanda', in Cornelia Füllkrug-Weitzel and Dietrich Werner (eds), *Ethics for Life – Voices from Ecumenical Partners on a New Paradigm of Life and Society* (Berlin: Bread for the World, 2019), 183ff, see: https://www.brot-fuer-die-welt.de/fileadmin/mediapool/2_Downloads/en/20_About_Us/Ethics-for-Life.pdf.

Umuziranenge, G., Muhirwa, F., Nshimiyimana, B., Majyambere, M. (2021), 'Peoples's perceptions on conservation opportunities and challenges for Nyungwe and Gishwati-MukuNationa Parks in Rwanda', ASC-TUFS working papers 2020.

74. Detached from the World and Attached to Nature: Contribution of Monasticism for Biodiversity in Ethiopia and Eritrea

Abate Gobena[1]

Introduction

Ethiopia and Eritrea share a similar history and tradition in relation to the advent and spread of Christianity. The Royal Court of Aksum, including current Ethiopia and Eritrea, embraced Christianity in the first half of the fourth century as a result of the work of St. Frumentius, who later became the first bishop of Aksum after he won the conversion of King Ezana.[2] The direct contact of Aksum with the Greco-Roman world, especially the tight economic and political relationship through the port of Adulis (Eritrea), helped in the growth of the church.

As Eritrea had been part of Ethiopia until its independence in 1993, the history and tradition of Christian Ethiopia also applies to Eritrea and its Orthodox Church. *Gi'iz*[3] language (classic Ethiopic), ተዋሕዶ *Tewahido*[4] *(miaphysite)* doctrine, the liturgical rite and monastic tradition can be considered as being identical to each other. Monasticism is one of the very important spiritual and historical heritages that Ethiopia and Eritrea possess. Monasteries became learning centres, both for clerics and royal officials, and hence contributed to the shaping of the religious and cultural as well as socio-political life of their communities.

Monasticism in Ethiopia and Eritrea

Although ancient Ethiopia was the first African nation to officially proclaim itself Christian, it was only after the arrival of ተሰዓቱ ቅዱሳን *Tes'attu Qiddusan* (the 'Nine Saints')[5] in the latter fifth century that the country was united as a Christian nation.[6] These monks brought a new impulse to the Christian kingdom as they established monasteries in Aksum and its surroundings. The other groups of monks responsible for the spread of monasticism in Ethiopia and Eritrea are named as ጻድቃን *Ṣadqan* ('righteous'),[7] particularly named and remembered in relation to the areas they had lived and served in. In addition to the groups of saints

---

[1] Lecturer at Sankt Ignatios College (Stockholm School of Theology); PhD candidate at University College Stockholm; serving priest at Ethiopian Orthodox Tewahido Church, London (UK) and Stockholm (Sweden); see also: https://www.sanktignatios.org/abate-gobena/; email: abate.gobena@ehs.se, abate.gobena@sanktignatios.org, gobena2004@hotmail.com.

[2] Amidon, P. *The Church History of Rufinus of Aquileia* (Books 10 and 11) (Oxford: Oxford University Press, 1997), 20; Lusini, G. (2020) 'The Ancient and Medieval History of Eritrean and Ethiopian Monasticism: An Outline' in Kelly, S. (ed), *A Companion to Medieval Ethiopia and Eritrea* (Leiden: Brill, 2020), 194.

[3] *Gi'iz* language had been the national tongue of ancient Abyssinia (Ethiopia and Eritrea) and remained as the official sacramental language for both the Ethiopian and Eritrean Orthodox Churches. Several *Gi'iz* terms are used in this chapter to better understand crucial terms and concepts. Transliteration of *Gi'iz* terms follows as it is in *Acta Aethiopica* (see Sven Rubenson, *The Survival of Ethiopian Independence* (London: Heinemann, in association with Esselte Stadium and Addis Ababa University Press, 1976), 413-414) for the purpose of simplicity.

[4] ተዋሕዶ *Tewahido* is a *Gi'iz* adjective literally meaning 'united', used to denote the Christological doctrine of Ethiopian and Eritrean Orthodox Churches in contrast to Chalcedon (451) and its Christological decisions.

[5] The 'Nine Saints' are a group of monks who came from the Byzantine Empire, fleeing persecution due to their *miaphysite* faith in the aftermath of the Council of Chalcedon (451).

[6] Lusini , 194.

[7] Who also came from the Byzantine Empire and identified as '*Ṣadqan*' of Bareknaha (Eritrea), of Kedih (near Hawzén, Tigray), of Qahen (near Wuqro, Tigray), and of Degwa (near Aksum).

named above, there were also individual saints. It is worth mentioning here two of the prominent figures named as St. 'Abune' ('our father') Libanos,[8] who founded the important monastery of 'Debre' ('mount') Libanos (Eritrea) and St. 'Abba' ('father') Yohani,[9] who established a monastery named after him in a remote high cliff near Temben (Tigray, Ethiopia).

From their beginning in the late fifth and early sixth centuries until the present-day, monasteries in Ethiopia and Eritrea served as repositories of religious, cultural and natural heritages. The monks and nuns lead their monastic life in a harmonious cohabitation with all creation, i.e. animals, waters, vegetation and the land. The ascetics are seen as models of spiritual life, and numerous edifying literary works pivoting around them (in the form of acts and homilies) are always read, listened and used as guidelines by the monastic community, as well as the wider members of the congregation. For example, Act of St. *Abune* Gebre Menfes Qiddus[10] encourages "the clergy and the laity (men, women, elderly and children) to gather in the church to read or listen to inspiring messages for their social and spiritual benefits."[11] Such a message is typical of almost all the hagiographies.

Ascetic Life for the Care of Creation

The prime purpose of monastic life is to devote oneself to God through some measure of separation from the busy world, physical and spiritual, and to go to remote places to be alone with God.[12] Monastics leave their community to distance themselves from the temporal world in a quest for sanctity.[13] Ascetics devote themselves to prayers in order to make an intentional choice to gradually imitate the apostles, who have imitated Christ.[14] In this sense they resent everything – i.e. every care, every relationship and every superfluity – that could distract them from the ceaseless worship of God. Detached from the social world, monks try to deter destructions and maintain strong attachment to their new spiritual world and cohabit with the natural world. Act of St. Abune Gebre Menfes Qiddus, in the following paragraph, shows that eremitic life with strict abstinence enabled the saint to harmoniously live with all the creations around him.

> Neither I drink water nor think of eating food even tree fruits. I sought not clothing for my body, but stayed unclothed. When I stayed in the lake I lived with fishes, sea dragons and crocodiles. When I stayed under trees, in the forest, I lived with birds and wandered like them from mountain to mountain. I also lived with lions and leopards, bears and serpents.[15]

Ethiopian and Eritrean Orthodox tradition regards church and monastery grounds as sacred spaces. Unlike most of the convents in the West, the monasteries of Ethiopia and Eritrea embrace a wider area beyond the walls, fences or building complexes. The sanctity of the church, therefore, reaches out beyond the walls and further extends to outer yards and compounds. The creatures, objects and grounds within these

[8] St. Abune Libanos lived between the end of the fifth and mid-sixth century. He is also named '*Abba Meṭa'I*' in relation to a place where he lived and served.

[9] St. Abba Yohani is one of the pioneers of monastic development in Ethiopia and Eritrea. It is believed that he lived during the reign of the Axumite King Kaléb and his son and successor Gebre Mesqel in the sixth century.

[10] St. Gebre Menfes Qiddus is one of the most celebrated saints in Ethiopia and Eritrea, known for his strict eremitic life in the wilderness, living with and taming of lions and leopards. Marrassini, P. 'Gabra Manfas Qeddus', in Uhlig, S. (ed), *Encyclopaedia Ethiopica* (V2) (Wiesbaden: Harrassowitz Verlag, 2005), 621.

[11] EOTC, *Gedle Gebre Menfes Qiddus: BeGi'iz'na Be'Amarigna* (Addis Ababa: Tinsa'e Publishers, 1999/2000), 8.

[12] Brown, J.M. 'The 'Greening' of Christian Monasticism and the Future of Monastic Landscapes in North America', *Religions* 10 (7) 2019, 432.

[13] Adubato, S. 'Toward a Monastic Notion of the Common Good', *Church Life Journal*, January 2017, 2.

[14] 1 Corinthians 11:1; Weickert, D.C. *The Virtue of Detachment in the Christian Tradition: A Study of St. John of the Cross and Thomas Merton,* unpublished master's thesis: (Ohio: University of Dayton, 2012), 7.

[15] EOTC, *Gedle Gebre Menfes Qiddus: BeGi'iz'na Be'Amarigna* (Addis Ababa: Tinsa'e Publishers, 1999/2000), 64.

extended areas share in the holiness of the church. The sanctity of a certain church and/or monastery starts from the altar at the centre of the sanctuary and extends out to the grounds and includes natural and monumental features in them. In the process of consecrating a new church or monastery the clerics use the term *ዳሩ እሳት መሐሉ ገነት ይሁን daru isat, mehalu genet yihun,* which literally means "let its exterior be a fire and its interior a Paradise".[16] With such blessings, forests, bodies of water, soil, wildlife and other creatures within the boundary of a monastery will be part of the sacred space and hence receive due regard and protection in association with the church.

Live in and Care for the Forest

Monasticism in Ethiopia and Eritrea traces its source back to the ascetic movements in the Syrian and Egyptian deserts. The monastic traditions related to the desert wilderness in Egypt and Syria later translated into forest and mountain wilderness in the Ethiopian and Eritrean context. Such wilderness, named as *ገዳም gedam* in Gi'iz, literally translated as forest before it gradually grew to define the monastic centre.[17] The forests in the monastery grounds serve as shelters and sacntuaries for the saints during their earthly life. After the saints' departure, these vegetations remain respected due to their link to the life and miracles of the saints. As they have been sanctified by the saints, they will no longer be regarded as ordinary forests, but rather will be promoted into being great monastic centres and places of sanctity. Sanctification of sacred spaces is praised with a famous phrase *ሰብእ ይቄድሶ ለመካን፣ ወመካን ይቄድሶ ለሰብእ seb'i yiqédso lemekan, wemekan yiqédso leseb'i* which means "human (saint) sactifies a place, and in turn (sacred) place sactifies human." These forested sacred places, therefore, are hubs for ascetic devotion and also pilgrim centres for the wider community.

From the earlier times monasteries were known for the rich forest biodiversity found within their compounds. Records of travellers such as Francesco Alvarez in the sixteenth century,[18] for instance, witnessed the travelling team "saw trees of all kinds and other sweet-smelling and medicinal herbs in the valleys belong to the Monastery of *Debre* Bizen."[19] Based on their observation at *Debre* Bizen and elsewhere in the country, Alvarez added, "the lands around the monasteries were covered with very great forests".[20] While the deforestation in the surrounding areas escalated, the forests in monastery grounds remain until the present-day. This happened due to the presence of the monks and their life style with abstinence and little interference to and harmonious cohabitation with the nature around them. The compound and environs of the Monastery of *Debre* Bizen, for example, is among very few pockets covered with evergreen forests in Eritrea.[21] The same is true in Ethiopia, that the sacred church and monastery grounds appeared to be islands of natural biodiversity with remnants of ancient natural flora, some of which are endemic to the country.[22] Generally, studies indicate that while there is a general trend of deforestation

---

[16] Kiflé, K.W. *Sewasiw wegiss wemezgebe qalat haddis* (Addis Ababa: Artistic Printers, 1956), 302.

[17] Gobena, A., 'Eco-practice of the Ethiopian Orthodox Tewahido Church', in Philip, M. et al (eds) *Religion, Sustainability and Education* (Norway: Embla Akademisk, 2020), 285.

[18] Francisco Alvarez was a priest accompanying the Portuguese diplomatic mission to Ethiopia between 1520-1527 BCE, and he wrote an account of this mission.

[19] *Debre* Bizen (ደብረ ቢዘን) is one of the best-known monasteries in Eritrea, founded in the 1350s by St. Abune Filipos, who was a student of St Abune Absadi and Abune Absadi himself was a student of Abune Éwostatéwos. The monastery is located at the top of Mount Bizen (2,460 meter above sea level) near the town of Nefasit (27km East of Asmara); Stanley, L. *Narrative of the Portuguese Embassy to Abyssinia During the Years 1520-1527* (Alvarez, F. 1540) (London: 2017), 53.

[20] Ibid.

[21] Bein, E. et al. 'Useful Trees and Shrubs in Eritrea: Identification, Propagation, and Management for Agricultural and Pastoral Communities', Vol. 12 from *Technical Handbook*, Regional Soil Conservation Unit, RSCU/SIDA, 1996, 332.

[22] Gobena, p.285.

and significant decrease in the vegetation, the forest biodiversity found in monastery grounds has shown resilience to the pressure of degradation and remained almost constant over the centuries.[23]

Live and Pray in Waters

In Ethiopia and Eritrea there are saints celebrated in connection to miracles on bodies of water such as seas, lakes, rivers and springs. Based on hagiographic sources, their attachment to the waters can generally fall under three major categories: saints who stayed in lakes for prayers and devotion like St. Kristos Semra;[24] those who crossed over rivers with miracles, such as St. Abune Éwosṭatéwos[25] and St. Abune Filipos;[26] and those who made springs out of rocks or grounds for healing, like St. Abba Libanos.

According to her hagiography, St. Kristos Semra dwelt in the waters of Lake Ṭana (Ethiopia) for twelve years, praying several hours a day and seeking forgiveness for sinners.[27] The spot where the saint prayed is consecrated as a monastery and is preserved for centuries. Great ascetics like St. Abune Éwosṭatéwos and St. Abune Filipos are linked to miraculous crossing of rivers without a boat or a ship, for which a Gi'iz term *ከፋሌ ባሕር kefalé bahr* (divider of the sea) is used as a suffix to their names.[28] The Act of St. Ewostatewos further states that the saint miraculously crossed the sea in his journey to Armenia.[29] St. Libanos, for example, is known for his miraculous act of blessing springing water from a rock with his *በትረ መስቀል betre mesqel* (crosshead rod). Generally, part or whole of the water bodies linked to the life and miracles of ascetic saints are regarded as sites of healing and blessing, and as such are protected for their connection to the saints.

Live with and Care for Animals

There is reciprocity of relations in the life of the ascetics, that while they isolated themselves from society, they in fact strengthened relations with wildlife in the forest wilderness and also with creatures in the waters. In this regard, there are several notable monastics who lived harmoniously with lions, leopards, serpents and other wildlife. The Acts of St. Abune Gebre Menfes Qiddus[30] and St. Abune Samuel of Waldibba[31] state that the saints are known for living with and taming of lions. The Act of St. Abune Bertelomewos[32] of Zemeda added that the saint "embraced the leopard in his arms," with the sense of tender and care,[33] and

[23] Cardelus, C. et al. 'Shadow conservation and the persistence of sacred church forests in northern Ethiopia', *BIOTROPICA* 0(0) 2017, 5; Gebremariam, T.M. & Ping, F. 'Assessment of Deforestation and Desertification Induced Impacts on Ecosystem Services in Eritrea', IJSRP, 11(3) 2021, 18.

[24] One of the prominent female ascetics celebrated in the *Tewahido* Churches of Ethiopia and Eritrea.

[25] St. Éwostatéwos (1273-1352) is one of the famous monastics of the medieval period to whom monasteries of *Debre* Mariam (Eritrea) and Tara Gedam (Ethiopia) are dedicated.

[26] St. Filipos is the founder of the Monastery of *Debre* Bizen. He was the disciple of St. Absadi, who is the most prominent disciples and successor of St. Éwostatéwos.

[27] Belcher, W.L. 'The Life and Visions of Krəstos Śämra, a Fifteenth-Century Ethiopian Woman Saint', in Robert, D. (ed), *African Christian Biography: Narratives, Beliefs, and Boundaries* (Pietermaritzburg, South Africa: Cluster Publications, 2018), 81, 85, 89.

[28] This is related to the Biblical stories of the journey of Israelites to the Promised Land, Moses' crossing of the Red Sea and Joshua's crossing of the River Jordan respectively.

[29] EOTC (2016) *Gedle Éwosṭatéwos*, 75.

[30] EOTC (1999/2000) *Gedle Gebre Menfe Qiddus*, 12, 14, 18, 21, 25, 29, 64.

[31] St. Samuel of Waldibba is a late fourteenth and early fifteenth century saint considered to be the founder of the Waldibba Monastery in northern Ethiopia.

[32] St Bertelomėwos is a thirteenth century monastic saint celebrated for his care of wildlife.

[33] Getatchew Haile, *Voices from Dabra Zamaddo : Acts of Abba Bartalomewos and Abba Yohannes. Miracles of Mary* (Wiesbaden: Harrassowitz, 2013), 142

the Act of St. Abune Aregawi states that the saint used the back of a serpent to access the top of sheer cliff, named as *Debre* Dammo (in Tigray, Ethiopia, near the border Eritrea).[34]

Conclusion

The effect of the monastic tradition in the social and natural environment of Ethiopia and Eritrea is related to, and inspired by, sacred scripturs of the Old and New Testaments, as well as later Christian monastic traditions. Monasteries preserve natural, cultural and historical heritages and pass them to generations more or less unchanged. The great reverence given to the monastic saints enabled the monasteries to easily preserve the natural biodiversity within their sacred grounds. As part of their monastic devotion, monks and nuns live harmoniously with, and duly care for, the creation around them. This in turn resulted in the preservation and continued conservation of nature. In summary, we can conclude that the monastic tradition in Ethiopia and Eritrea contributed to, and can still help with, the preservation of forest biodiversity, at least in church and monstery grounds.

Suggestions for Further Reading

Adubato, S. 'Toward a Monastic Notion of the Common Good', *Church Life Journal*, January 2017.

Amidon, P. *The Church History of Rufinus of Aquileia* (Books 10 and 11) (Oxford: Oxford University Press, 1997).

Bein, E. et al. 'Useful Trees and Shrubs in Eritrea: Identification, Propagation, and Management for Agricultural and Pastoral Communities', Vol. 12 from *Technical Handbook*, Regional Soil Conservation Unit, RSCU/SIDA, 1996

Belcher, W.L. 'The Life and Visions of Krəstos Śämra, a Fifteenth-Century Ethiopian Woman Saint', in Robert, D. (ed), *African Christian Biography: Narratives, Beliefs, and Boundaries* (Pietermaritzburg, South Africa: Cluster Publications, 2018).

Brown, J.M. 'The 'Greening' of Christian Monasticism and the Future of Monastic Landscapes in North America', *Religions* 10 (7) 2019, 432.

Cardelus, C. et al. 'Shadow conservation and the persistence of sacred church forests in northern Ethiopia', *BIOTROPICA* 0(0) 2017, 1-8.

EOTC, *Gedle Gebre Menfes Qiddus: BeGi'iz'na Be'Amarigna* (Addis Ababa: Tinsa'e Publishers, 1999/2000).

EOTC, *Gedle Abune Éwostatéwos: BeGi'iz'na Be'Amarigna* (Addis Ababa: The Holy Tara Monastery, 2016).

Gebremariam, T.M. & Ping, F. 'Assessment of Deforestation and Desertification Induced Impacts on Ecosystem Services in Eritrea', IJSRP, 11(3) 2021, 18-29.

Gobena, A., 'Eco-practice of the Ethiopian Orthodox Tewahido Church', in Philip, M. et al (eds) *Religion, Sustainability and Education* (Norway: Embla Akademisk, 2020).

Kiflé, K.W. *Sewasiw wegiss wemezgebe qalat haddis* (Addis Ababa: Artistic Printers, 1956).

Lusini, G. (2020) 'The Ancient and Medieval History of Eritrean and Ethiopian Monasticism: An Outline' in Kelly, S. (ed), *A Companion to Medieval Ethiopia and Eritrea* (Leiden: Brill, 2020), 194-216.

Marrassini, P. 'Gabra Manfas Qeddus', in Uhlig, S. (ed), *Encyclopaedia Ethiopica* (V2) (Wiesbaden: Harrassowitz Verlag, 2005), 619-22.

Stanley, L. *Narrative of the Portuguese Embassy to Abyssinia During the Years 1520-1527* (Alvarez, F. 1540) (London: 2017)

[34] St. Aregawi is one of the 'Nine Saints' celebrated by both Ethiopian and Eritrean traditions as founder of monasticism and established the first monastery at *Debre* Dammo.

Weickert, D.C. *The Virtue of Detachment in the Christian Tradition: A Study of St. John of the Cross and Thomas Merton,* unpublished master's thesis (Ohio: University of Dayton, 2012).

75. Creation Ethics and Family Planning in the Context of DRC Congo: Fruitfulness Blessing in Genesis 1:28 and the Imperative of Mothers' Health-care and Child Protection

Véronique K. Kahindo[1]

Be fruitful, multiply, and fill the earth, and subdue it (Genesis 1:28a)

Introduction

This article aims to address the paradox between God's blessing in Genesis 1:28a and the growing imperative for mothers' health-care and child protection in the context of the family in the Democratic Republic of the Congo (DRC). It is not an exegetical study, but a reflection from which faith leaders[2] are called to fully commit themselves in tackling this paradox. Knowing that faith leaders are amongst the most persuasive and exercise considerable influence over culture and behaviour of their congregations,[3] the article argues for the urgent need for church leaders to focus on a responsible and relevant use of Genesis 1:28a that engages humans (male and female) in mutual complementarity and responsibility, to fulfil God's mandate of providing the world with a responsible generation that will ensure the sustainable development and protection of the earth. Given that most faith leaders in DRC are not specifically equipped for such a mission, the present article suggests that there be organised for them a systematic empowerment in both mothers' health-care and child protection in relation to procreative blessing in Genesis 1:28a.

In the Old Testament, the creation account climaxes with the blessing in Genesis 1:28.[4] In this verse male and female are assigned a double mission. The first one is, "Be fruitful and multiply and fill the earth and subdue it" (Genesis 1:28a). The second is, "Rule over the fish in the sea and the birds in the sky and over every living creature that moves on the ground" (v. 28b). Considering the first mission (v. 28a), in the Congolese context there has been uncontrolled procreation combined with an excessive failure to respect the basic rights of children, who, in many cases, end up on the streets, or in armed groups, or in young girls' prostitution. Similarly, mothers' health is so neglected that they end up aging earlier than their spouses, or dying from severe obstetric complications[5] while leaving several children behind who are often not adequately cared for by their step-mothers or by foster families with exactly the same results as mentioned above.

---

[1] Professeure Dr Veronique Kavuo Kahindo is lecturer in Biblical Studies and Old Testament In ULPGL-GOMA and also Language Program Coordinator. She holds a Doctorate from the University of South Africa (UNISA). She teaches Old Testament and Hebrew with a focus on Contextual Exegesis. This article stems from trainers' trainings the author been part of through World Vision International on Channels of Hope for Child Protection; for COVID-19; for Gender, and for Maternal, Newborn, and Child Health, in different areas of the DRC provinces in DRC. The author is grateful to Rev Siyani Zimba, her CoH Mentor.

[2] In the present article, the term 'faith leader' refers to Christian religious leaders regardless of their denomination, because the suggested religious response includes society as a whole.

[3] World Vision International, *Channels of Hope, Transforming Lives Positively*, 2014, 2. Available on CoH Transforming Lives Positively.FINAL_.digital.pdf (wvi.org), visited on 12/08/2021.

[4] B.C. Collins, *Genesis 1:26-28: Significance and Challenges*, BJU Press, Seminary Symposium November 12, 2018, 14.

[5] Anki Yambare, 'Analyse des déterminants de la Mortalité maternelle pré partum en République du Congo 2013-2015', 1-21, 2017. Accessible à Microsoft Word – Déterminants de la mortalité maternelle au Congo (archives-ouvertes.fr), vu le 29/10/2021.

Given that Congolese mothers and their children need to enjoy life in fullness and in dignity in God's creation, formal and informal systems in both mothers' health-care and child protection need to interact in order to tackle the above scourge. Otherwise, mothers and children in DRC are being discriminated and deprived of enjoying their full rights as humans made in God's image.

Under these circumstances, this article argues that faith leaders and the faith-based community engage in a systematic empowerment in order to provide faith-based response to the paradox between God's blessing of fecundity, fruitfulness, and filling the earth, and mothers' health-care and child protection.

Problem and Purpose Statement

In DRC, God's procreative blessing (Genesis 1:28a) is so often connected to legal and religious monogamous couples that during the nuptial blessing, faith leaders bless brides with procreation based on the literal reading of this part of the verse. Therefore, married couples always consider themselves as the sole ones commissioned to fulfil God's blessings of being fruitful, multiplying and filling the earth. This feeling is so ardent, especially when they consider that through this divine mission they represent the first couple that received God's mandated blessing. As a result, in many married couples the trend towards a highly uncontrolled fruitfulness is generally observed, bearing a large number of children with an average rate of six or seven children per couple.[6] Yet the majority of parents with over five children are not able to provide, either for the mother's health-care or for the children's protection in accordance with their basic rights. In view of the foregoing, two questions draw our attention:

- Does Genesis 1:28 give a *carte blanche* to married couples to bear as many children as possible until they fill the earth and then exploit it unrestrainedly?
- What does this verse mean in relation to its literary context?

The answer to the first question can be given with either yes or no, each answer representing the two schools of thought in our context, resulting from misreadings of Genesis 1:28. In the Congolese society, it is obvious that the 'yes' school is dominant because couples have many children. Among these, there are those who say 'yes' out of ignorance of birth control, or simply because gender discrimination is widespread, and children's rights are violated.

The truth of the matter is that most faith leaders, who should have guided believers in understanding and positively responding to the interpretation of this verse (and so address the paradox between having many children and caring for mothers' health and protecting children), lack the necessary competences, skills and information to engage with the issue in a helpful way. Rather, among them are many who often drive the wrong interpretation of verse 28, creating barriers that prohibit couples from using either birth spacing or birth control methods, thereby contributing in an indirect way to severe impact on the reproductive well-being of mothers and on the protection of their children's rights. This paradox can be addressed by suggesting systematic trainings and empowerment of the faith-based community in general, and faith leaders in particular, regarding the issue detailed above.

It is important to note that issues for mothers and children should not be addressed in isolation from the family, which is one of the elements in the system that influences either mothers and children's vulnerabilities or well-being.

Congolese Family Facing Procreation Issues

It is worth noting that the Congolese family is a biological unit where reproduction and biological continuity take place. Accordingly, it is a basic vital structure providing survival and life improvement opportunities

[6] F. Ezambe, 'La place de l'enfant dans la famille en Afrique: Circulation et don', *Revue Recherches Psychologiques et Educatives*, No 03 (Afrique conseil, Paris), 2010, 27.

to all members at large, especially social welfare for women and children. Strangely enough, it is at the family level that Congolese society undergoes underdevelopment and faces challenges of social change. Among these are poor housing conditions, poor health, poor food rationing, lack of clean water, nutritional deficiency, unemployment, gender and age inequalities, pregnant girls and non-marital children rejection, consequences of recurrent armed conflicts, etc.

Despite the above-mentioned ghastly conditions, it is observed that Congolese families have many children. In most instances, these children lack adequate care. Some are subject to abuse, neglect, and exploitation in their own families, at school, in the host families, etc. On the other hand, living conditions of multiparous mothers are also miserable.[7] In addition to the burden of caring for many children and looking after their spouses, they also assume the family economy and in many cases their health gets worse. If their husbands are not involved in the struggle of looking after the survival of their many children, they will be overburdened with great responsibility, together with plentiful motherhood or multiple close pregnancies. In many instances, they grow older than their husband, although they are still young. In such situations, some men prefer marrying another wife instead (a younger one perhaps), or pestering young girls.[8] Paradoxically, all these nasty situations do not prevent women from having several children. How can this be explained? Is it culture? Religion? Is it the status of women? Ignorance? Or is it governmental ineptitude? All of these are probably combined as interrelated factors.

However, in the DRC context, there are many dimensions that may contribute to multiple child births. They include a survival reflex or an unconscious response to the fear of extinction of the descendants;[9] family planning ignorance; reduced contraceptive use or access; women's low level of education; family economic needs (as children are a labour force for a quick income); and polygamy.[10] There are several factors that push men into polygamy: a remedy for infertility, their wife's poor health, early aging of the wife, menopause, and seeking male children to ensure the survival of the lineage, levirate[11] marriage,[12] etc.

Nowadays, there is an increase in three new types of families where women and children are at high risk. They include first, non-official, if not secret, polygamous families. Here, a married man with an official residence can be shared over different non-official or secret residences. In this new form of polygamy, each wife has her own dwelling where the husband is partly present, but almost absent in the daily life of his children. Second, there are many cases of single parenthood without male parents, headed by women whose husbands have emigrated, died or simply deserted. Finally, there are child-headed families, resulting from early pregnancies, or the death of the parents in armed conflict or as a result of the scourge of AIDs or other pandemic diseases.[13]

While not overlooking all the above-described female vulnerabilities, we now turn to women and children's vulnerabilities due to the misreading of Genesis 1:28a.

---

[7] Multiparous mothers refer to women who (1) have given birth two or more times; (2) have given birth to more than one offspring at a time. See: https://medical-dictionary.thefreedictionary.com/multiparous/

[8] G. Lawrence-Hart, 'The Socio-Cultural Significance of Polygamy in Africa', *International Journal of Social Sciences and Humanities,* vol 5, No 1 2019, 6.

[9] F. Ezambe, 29.

[10] M.E Baloyi, 'Critical reflections on polygamy in the African Christian context', *Missonalia*, vol. 41, No 02, 2013. 168–173.

[11] Levirate marriage is a type of marriage in which the brother of a deceased man is obliged to marry his brother's widow. In biblical tradition it is mentioned in Deuteronomy 25:5–10.

[12] G. Lawrence-Hart, 1.

[13] F. Ezambe, 28.

Mothers' Health-Care and Child Protection Issues and Genesis 1:28a

Be fruitful and multiply, fill the earth, and subdue it.

This phrase is frequently used by most Christian mothers in DRC when they are advised on birth planning. Among them, married women claim that they would not contradict their pastors' exhortations on the day of their wedding, and many also claim to fulfil the divine will by bearing children until they reach the menopause. Answering the question of being able to afford the basic requirements of their own children in the current challenging environment in which our country finds itself, they are convinced that God is blessing them with children, and that he will ensure their very survival in spite of any disasters (war, natural disasters, famine, etc.).

In contrast to this strong conviction, and despite their total commitment to God and to their faith leaders' prayers, the reality is that for a high proportion of mothers in DRC, maternity continues to be a life-threatening endeavour.[14] Pregnancies continue to be high risk, despite the limited support from medical facilities and the private sectors including NGOs, hospitals and individual physicians, Community Health Workers (CHWs), traditional birth attendants, village healers and many other formal and informal entities.[15] The paradox is that faith leaders in whom women have placed all their trust and whose instructions on childbearing cannot be contradicted, passively witness the maternal mortality that would be eradicated if some salutary measures were taken in time.

It appears that there are several factors which are associated with a higher risk of maternal death. These include hospital maternal death factors, victims' health history, multiparty (multiple pregnancies or births), age factors (younger or older ages), matrimonial situations (married women, single or rejected by their husbands), female poverty, the level of education (of either the wife, the husband, or both), employment status,16 moving on to the clinical aspects (mode of admission, delay, prenatal consultation and high blood pressure), direct obstetric causes (eclampsia, uterine rupture and complications related to abortion), gender inequalities and marginalisation.[17]

Furthermore, the maternal risk factors described above do not spare children from danger. In families with many children and very close pregnancies, infants face a higher risk of malnutrition and of dying before the following birth. In addition, when a child is born less than two years after the previous birth, that child is 60% more likely to die as an infant than a child who is born three to five years later.[18] If they survive, they are more likely to be vulnerable if the miserable socio-economic conditions of families deprive parents from becoming worthy parents. Combining both the high number of children with the poor socio-economic status of parents, the result is that mothers of many children have not enough time to interact with all of them and children therefore will lack parenting with more attention and love.[19]

In many cases, because of having many children and poverty, children are handed over to new families to take care of them. In some instances, they will receive less care, which they will then seek in the street or by joining armed groups. Moreover, the transfer of children can turn into the exploitation of children.

---

[14] Idem, p. 28

[15] K. Hanson, P. Berman, 'Private health care provision in developing countries: a preliminary analysis of levels and composition', *Health Policy and Planning*, 1998. No 13, 195–211.

[16] J-B Kahindo Mbeva, H. Karemere, P. Mitangala Ndeba, at. Al., 'Maternal Deaths Factors in Hospital Area: A Survey at six Health Districts in the East of the Republic Democratic of Congo', *International Journal of Innovation and Applied Studies*, Vol. 23, No. 4, 2018, 559-568.

[17] Anki Yambare, 1.

[18] World Vision International, *Channels of Hope for Maternal, Newborn and Child Health*, 2020, 1. Available on CoH MNCH_2020_FINAL.pdf (wvi.org). Visited on 12/08/2021.

[19] Provost, M. A. & Piché, C., 'L'enfant et sa famille: quelques nouveaux thèmes de recherche', *Santé mentale au Québec*, Vol. 8, No 2,1983, 68.

For young girls, in some cases they are involved in prostitution or are sexually abused by the adoptive parents.

In the same way, lacking sex education, many teenagers become pregnant. Facing rejection of the pregnancy's perpetrators, and realising their parents' reaction, school repudiation and rejection from the church they sometimes perform abortions with all the possible risks surrounding it. Others are encouraged to become involve in early marriage. Note that earlier pregnancies can affect health with a high risk of experiencing depression, birth complications, toxemia, anemia and even death.20 Such conditions lock women into vulnerability and poverty.

A responsible and relevant reading of Genesis 1:28, however, can help tackle these issues more responsively.

A Responsible and Relevant Use of Genesis 1.28a

With regard to the above-mentioned challenges of abundant reproduction in the Congolese family, with negative impacts to mothers and child well-being, the faith community appears to not be fully involved in awareness-raising to combat these vulnerabilities. Instead, the family conception of abundant childbearing is sometimes strengthened by the misreading of Gen 1:28a. Moreover, there are not many differences between the family's cultural behaviour and that of faith leaders regarding the reproductive handling. As the family members bless the bride during the customary marriage with abundant motherhood, so do faith leaders during the nuptial blessing based on Genesis 1:28a. To fight the above-mentioned misreading, faith leaders need to be empowered with responsible and relevant use of Scriptures. This leads us to answer the two questions that are in the problem statement.

First of all, Genesis 1:28a is not a pericope by itself.[21] It is rather part of the pericope of Genesis 1:11-30[22] (minus 14-19) in the literary context of fecundity. The main theme of this pericope is, "dominion over the earth and a seed that will fill the earth as the great blessings that God gives to mankind at creation."[23] Following this literary context, the purpose of Genesis 1:11-30 is that plants, trees, fish, bird, animals and human beings are required to overcome extinction through procreation. The earth is the indispensable place for their life and procreation.[24]

Next, in the set of literature (Genesis 1:11-30), verse 28 is a continuation of verse 27. That is to say, the phrase "and God blessed them; and God said to them" refers to the male (*zakhar*) and female (*neqebhâ*), and both form the human being or the whole humanity. The text does not refer to the man (*îsh*) and woman (*ishshâ*) (Genesis 2:22). In the latter case, there is a husband-wife relationship (the couple), whereas in Genesis 1:28 it is not.[25] Human beings, therefore, need to better understand their mandate on and over the earth, which is rather a responsibility to provide the world with a responsible generation that will ensure the sustainable development and protection of the earth assigned to them as a gift.

---

[20] A.F. Ogori & A.R. Yunusa, 'The Cause and Effect of Teenage Pregnancy: Case of Kontagora local government area in Niger state, Northern part of Nigeria', *International Open Journal of Educational Research,* Vol. 1, No. 7, 2013, 10.

[21] A pericope is a set of verses that forms one coherent unit or thought, thus forming a short passage suitable for public reading from a text, that usually refers to sacred scripture.

[22] R. Dupont, 'Les deux récits de la création, Gn 1-3:24', Thèse présentée à la Faculté des Arts de l'Université d'Ottawa en vue de l'obtention de la maîtrise ès arts en Sciences religieuses, 1968, 26.

[23] B.C. Collins, 14.

[24] A.S. Nnamdi & V. Ogbozor, 100.

[25] J.K. Kivatsi, 'Genre et Gestion des Ecosystèmes en Genèse 1 :26-28: Une Lecture Ecologique et Théologique', *Bulletin de Recherches Théologiques et Sociologiques*, No 8, 2017, 153-170.

Faith-based Responses to Mother's Health-care and Child Protection Issues

As we have stated, faith leaders need to be aware of the most vulnerable mothers and children from their community, including what makes them vulnerable and learning how to build their resilience. Their training program may focus on why they have been called to ministry by God.

Some issues that may be developed into modules include the following. Firstly, to serve all people with acts of love and compassion because all humans (male and female, adult and child) are created in God's image, called to be united in love with God and one another. Secondly, to seek the wisdom of the Holy Spirit as we search for answers and solutions to mothers and child vulnerability. Thirdly, to accept mothers and children with the same grace as Christ accepted us. Fourthly, to recognize and protect the equal worth and dignity of every human being (especially mothers and children). Fifthly, to promote peace and overcome violence in our community. Sixthly, to break the silence by speaking the truth in love. This a work of advocacy and reporting of mothers and child protection incidents. Seventhly, to strive for justice that brings fullness of life, healing, restoration, and reconciliation. Each subject would be supported by Bible verses used responsibly and relevantly. The interaction should take place both with the formal system (government services) and the informal system (parents, village chief, faith community, community members), especially during the work of advocacy.[26]

Conclusion

The present article is based on the assertion that faith leaders, who are amongst the most influential people, need to receive proper information and awareness to become powerful agents of change in the DRC social community regarding the protection of children and support and improvement of mothers' health. Their beliefs, values, role modelling and everyday messages can inspire entire communities to care for and love one another, and to deconstruct barriers to mothers' health and child protection.[27] Training modules suggested here can be extended to other issues such as gender and pandemic disease control.

Suggestions for Further Reading

Ampofowaa Twumasi B., 'Analyse des conditions des femmes africaines et la polygamie', in Ahmadou Kourouma, *Les Soleils des Indépendances, Monnè, outrages et défis, En entendant les bêtes sauvages, Allah n'est pas oblige, Quand on refuse on dit non, Le diseur de vérité*, Paris, Seuil, 2010.

Baloyi, M.E., 'Critical reflections on polygamy in the African Christian context', *Missonalia*, vol. 41, No 02, 2013. 164–181.

Collins B. C., *Genesis 1:26-28: Significance and Challenges*, BJU Press, BJU Seminary Symposium November 12, 2018.

Dupont R., 'Les deux récits de la création, Gn 1-3:24', Thèse présentée à la Faculté des Arts de l'Université d'Ottawa en vue de l'obtention de la maîtrise ès arts en Sciences religieuses, 1968, 26.

Ezambe F., 'La place de l'enfant dans la famille en Afrique: Circulation et don', *Revue Recherches Psychologiques et Educatives*, No 03 (Afrique conseil, Paris), 2010, 27 -35.

Hanson K., Berman P., 'Private health care provision in developing countries: a preliminary analysis of levels and composition', *Health Policy and Planning*, 1998. No 13, 195–211.

Kahindo Mbeva J-B, Karemere H., Mitangala Ndeba P., et al., 'Maternal Deaths Factors in Hospital Area: A Survey at six Health Districts in the East of the Republic Democratic of Congo', *International Journal of Innovation and Applied Studies*, Vol. 23, No. 4, 2018, 559-568.

[26] World Vision International, *Channels of Hope, Transforming Lives Positively*, p.2.

[27] World Vision International, *Channels of Hope for Maternal, Newborn and Child Health,* 1.

Kivatsi, J.K., 'Genre et Gestion des Ecosystèmes en Genèse 1,26-28: Une Lecture Ecologique et Théologique', *Bulletin de Recherches Théologiques et Sociologiques*, No 8, 2017, 153-170.

Lawrence-Hart G., 'The Socio-Cultural Significance of Polygamy in Africa', *International Journal of Social Sciences and Humanities,* vol 5, No 1 2019, 1- 6.

Main, M., Weston, D.R., 'The quality of the toddler's relationship to mother and to father: related to conflict behaviour and the readiness to establish new relationship', *Child Development*, 1981, No. 52, 932-940.

Nnamdi A.S. & Ogbozor V., 'The Hermeneutics of Genesis 1:28 and Environmental Ethics: A Socio-Ethical Evaluation', *Sapientia Global Journal of Arts, Humanities and Development Studies (SGOJAHDS),* Vol.3 No.2, 2020; 100 – 113.

Ogori A.F. & Yunusa A.R., 'The Cause and Effect of Teenage Pregnancy: Case of Kontagora local government area in Niger state, Northern part of Nigeria', *International Open Journal of Educational Research,* Vol. 1, No. 7, 2013, 1-15.

Provost M.A. & Piché C., 'L'enfant et sa famille: quelques nouveaux thèmes de recherche', *Santé mentale au Québec*, Vol. 8, No 2, 1983, 68–78.

Sikder S.S., Labrique A.B., Ullah B., et al., 'Accounts of severe acute obstetric complications in Rural Bangladesh', BMC Pregnancy and Childbirth, 2011, 1-13.

World Vision International, *Channels of Hope, Transforming Lives Positively*, 2014, 1-19, available on CoH Transforming Lives Positively.FINAL_.digital.pdf (wvi.org), visited on 12/08/2021.

World Vision International, *Channels of Hope for Maternal, Newborn and Child Health*, 2020, 1-3, available on CoH MNCH_2020_FINAL.pdf (wvi.org) visited on 12/08/2021.

Yambare A., 'Analyse des déterminants de la Mortalité maternelle pré partum en République du Congo 2013-2015, 1-21. Visited on Microsoft Word – Déterminants de la mortalité maternelle au Congo (archives-ouvertes.fr), vu le 29/10/2021.

76. Hope for the Forest – Atewa Forest in Ghana and Its Relevance for Church and Society

Seth Appiah-Kubi,[1] Emmanuel D Turkson[2] and Daryl E. Bosu[3]

Introduction

Since the earliest history of humanity, be it the biblical account in Genesis or the archaeological records of different civilizations, the relationship of humanity with nature has been a recurring journey of harmony and discord, with the latter mostly bearing the brunt of the excesses of humanity.[4] As a result, centuries of resource exploitation by humans have resulted in the gradual deterioration of the earth's ecosystem, leading to a nature-people imbalance threatening the very existence of humans, in essence working against the divine commission to care and till the earth, as in Genesis 2:15.

In most political economies around the world, and particularly in Ghana, dependence on extractive industries to drive a national development agenda without recourse to respecting the community of life and the balance of creation has led to destruction of many critical natural hotspots invaluable to the intergenerational wellbeing of the people.

The Atewa Forest Range is one such amazing habitat supporting a wide diversity of plants and animals and providing water for over 5 millions Ghanaians. However, it is now the Garden of Eden that the government of Ghana seeks to mow down to exploit the pittance of bauxite ore lying under this forest, amid a strong resistance from the communities, environmental groups and the international community.

This paper shares insights on the invaluable ecosystem services provided and supported by Atewa, while also shedding some light on political interests to exploit this forest for the bauxite resources that lie beneath this magnificent forest. We also share the journey of advocacy and lobbying with broad national collaborative engagement by A Rocha Ghana, a non-profit environmental conservation organisation in Ghana that has a vision to work together to care for God's creation always.

The Atewa Range Forest Reserve – A Crown of Jewel of Biodiversity in Ghana

The Atewa Forest Range falls within the eastern end of the Guinean Forest eco-region and was designated as one of the country's Globally Significant Biodiversity Areas (GSBA) in 1999, due to its exceptional

---

[1] The National Director of A Rocha Ghana, Seth holds a PhD in finance and is a Chartered Management Accountant, a member of Chartered Institute of Management Accountant (CIMA), UK. He has been involved in conservation and the security of natural resources for the past 12 years and has been a key part in formulating the conservation models used by A Rocha Ghana, involving community-based conservation, conservation education and conservation research. seth.appiah-kubi@arocha.org

[2] Emmanuel is Creation Care Officer at A Rocha Ghana with a B.Sc. in Entomology and Wildlife from the University of Cape Coast, a Bachelor's Degree in Biblical Studies from the American Bible University (Ghana Campus). He facilitates interfaith dialogues to promote environmental action, climate change and biodiversity conservation. emmanuel.turkson@arocha.org

[3] Daryl is Deputy National Director of A Rocha Ghana and holds a postgraduate certificate in LLB Law, advanced degrees in Conservation Finance and Green Business Modelling and Finance, an advanced certificate in Terrestrial Carbon Accounting and a first degree in Natural Resource Management. He is an Environmental Sustainability and Natural Resource Management Professional and an activist with diverse experience with extensive experience across the country and outside Ghana. daryl.bosu@arocha.org

[4] Reginal M. Harrell, *An Ecologist's Perspective of Creation Care and Restoration* (2012); see https://www.researchgate.net/publication/260907739_An_Ecologist's_Perspective_of_Creation_Care_and_Restoration.

biological value. It is one of only two reserves with upland evergreen forest in Ghana. This unique forest type is home to about 656 species of vascular plants, around 63 species of mammals, and 227 species of birds.[5]

The Forest Reserve area was declared a National Forest Reserve in 1925; later it was classified as a Special Biological Protection Area in 1994, and then as a Hill Sanctuary in 1995.

> The Atewa Forest is of exceptional biological importance being the finest example of Upland Evergreen Forest in the Upper Guinean Forest region (from Ghana west to Sierra Leone). Only about 5% of the Upper Guinean forest now remains, so sites like Atewa Forest are of global importance.[6]

Similarly, the forest has recently made it onto the list of the world's Alliance for Zero Extinction (AZE) sites. AZE is a joint initiative of biodiversity organizations from around the world working to prevent extinctions by ensuring the safeguard and effective conservation of key sites that are more endangered or are home to critically endangered species. AZE works closely with International Union for Conservation of Nature (IUCN) as the listing authority for defining species. It is interesting to note that to be on the AZE list, the area must contain more than 95% of the entire population of one or more species listed as endangered or critically endangered on the IUCN list of threatened species. The Atewa Forest has four or five species believed to be entirely endemic (being found in no other forest in the world) to the forest.[7]

The recent discovery of the endemic Afia Birago (*Phrynobatrachus afiabirago*) puddle frog in swampy habitats within the forest by a Ghanaian Scientist further deepened the justification for AZE designation. The Atewa slippery frog, which is a critically endangered species, was also recently discovered and named after a local community within the landscape called Sagyimase – *Conraua sagyimase.*[8]

This is a critical new development as Atewa Forest now becomes a 'no-go area' for project financing and development for the World Bank's International Finance Corporation (IFC), including over a hundred other finance institutions that sign up to the IFC's principles. The IFC Performance Standard 6: Biodiversity Conservation and Sustainable Management of Living Natural Resources recognizes that protecting and conserving biodiversity, maintaining ecosystem services, and sustainably managing living natural resources are fundamental to sustainable development. IFC places considerable emphasis on the avoidance of impact on biodiversity and ecosystem services in critical habitats such as the Atewa Forest Range.[9]

According to the star rating system,[10] a national equivalent of the IUCN red list system for the forest species in Ghana, the total list of plant species within the Forest Reserve includes five Black Star species, which are species of global significance with the highest conservation priority in Ghana.[11] From these five species, three have been assessed and classified on the IUCN red list, namely: *Sapium aubrevillei* (vulnerable), *Neolemonniera clitandrifolia* (endangered) and *Lecaniodiscus punctatus* (endangered).

---

[5] CERSGIS, ''Land-cover raster data for Ghana,'' (1990, 2000, 2010), see: https://cersgis.org/; and: https://cersgis.org/staticmaps/.

[6] *E. O Wilson, 2018*, see: Letter to the President of Ghana 26 March 2018, in: https://eowilsonfoundation.org/ghana-atewa-forest/.

[7] Lindsell, J., Agyei, R., Bosu, D., Decher, J., Hawthorne, W., Marshall, C., & Ofori-Boateng, C., ''The Biodiversity of Atewa Forest,'' (2019), see: The Biodiversity of the Atewa Forest January 2019 Research Report, in: https://ghana.arocha.org/wp-content/uploads/sites/15/2015/07/Biodiversity-of-Atewa-A-Rocha.pdf.

[8] See The Campaign Save Atewa Forest, in: https://www.atewa.org/index.php/news-and-updates/.

[9] IFC, World Bank, 'Biodiversity Conservation and Sustainable Management of Living Natural Resources', 2012, updated in 2019, see: https://documents1.worldbank.org/curated/en/898321491456820716/pdf/113846-WP-ENGLISH-PS6-Biodiversity-conservation-2012-PUBLIC.pdf.

[10] Hawthorne, W. A.-J, 'Forest Protection in Ghana with particular reference to vegetation and plant species', 1995, *see: https://www.iucn.org/es/content/forest-protection-ghana-particular-reference-vegetation-and-plant-species.*

[11] Abu-Juam, Obiaw, E., Kaawkye, Y., Ninnoni, R., Owusu, E., & Asamoah, A. *Biodiversity Management Plan for the Atewa Range Forest Reserves* (Accra: 2003).

In addition to these, 33 plant species from the Forest Reserve are classified within the Gold Star category, which means that these are fairly rare at an international and or local level.[12]

The scientific name of nine species are named after Atewa Forest and two are named after the alternate name for the range of hills, Kibi. These are four plants *Aframomumatewae*, *Monanthotaxis atewensis*, *Rinorea kibbiensis* and *Ochna kibbiensis*, two butterflies, *Anthene atewa* and *Mylothris atewa*, two arachnids, *Anansus atewa* and *Ricinoides atewa*, and a caddisfly (trichoptera), *Pseudoneureclipsis atewa*.[13]

Cooling Our Warming Homes

In addressing global risk of climate change, research on climate change resilience of ecosystems by Price et al[14] indicates that there is no ecosystem in Ghana that is more important in combating the effects of climate change than the Atewa Upland Evergreen Forest in Ghana. As our world warms and our communities and towns feel the impact of the increasing temperatures and erratic rainfall patterns, Ghana's remaining forests such as Atewa are crucial safety nets to help build resilience and support local and national adaptation.

Living Water for Millions of Ghanaians

The forest is in the Eastern Region of Ghana and about 90km north of Accra, the capital of Ghana. The forest functions as the source of three important rivers – Densu (1,873 km^2), Birim (3,922 km^2) and the Ayensu (1,238 km^2) rivers. It is a source of water for many businesses and for the households of over one million people in Accra.[15] Further analysis of all dependents on the water services from over 99 streams and rivers coming out of the forest prove that, in all, over five million Ghanaians benefit immensely from the hydrological services this forest provides.

The Ayensu and Densu flow south into the Atlantic, and the Birim River makes a long detour north and southwest around the Atewa Range before joining the Pra River, which flows through agricultural and forest areas in the Akan lowlands into the Gulf of Guinea at Shama in the Western region of Ghana. Of the three river basins that the Atewa Forest feeds, the Densu River Basin is the most densely populated one. This basin also has the highest dependency on, and share of, extracted water resources.[16] The Densu River belongs to the coastal river system of Ghana and is one of the two main sources of water supply for the Accra urban area. This same river also flows from its upstream section eastwards to the Akwadum-Koforidua area with a population density over 120,000, from where it gradually changes its course and flows in a southern direction past the town of Nsawam, into the Weija Reservoir (created for water provision and irrigation). When the Weija reservoir is full, excess flow discharges into the Densu Delta (Sakumo), a lagoon and salt pans complex which constitutes one of Ghana's internationally recognized protected areas (i.e. Ramsar sites). The Densu Delta is an important area for over 57 water bird species, including several migratory bird species, and also serves as a sediment trapping platform and a shoreline stabilizer for local

[12] Ibid.

[13] Gibbs, D., 'The Trichoptera of Ghana', *Deutsche Entomologische Zeitschrif*, (1973) (N.F.), 20, 2008, 363-424.

[14] Price, J., N. Forstenhaeusler, E. Graham, R. Warren, J. VanDerWal, I. Atkinson, D. Baird, and P. Lawry. 'Report on observed climate, projected climate, and projected biodiversity changes for Atewa Range Forest Reserve under differing levels of warming', https://www.wallaceinitiative.org.

[15] Schep, S., Guzmán, A., van Beukering, P., de Moel, H., Eiselin, M., Ayesu, S., Bekoe Ansah, K. *The Economics of the Atewa Forest Range, Ghana* (Accra: IUCN NL, 2016).

[16] Water Resources Commission, 'Integrated Water Resources Management Plan Densu river Basin', www.wrc-gh.org/ dmsdocument/16.

communities. Beyond the delta, the Densu River ultimately discharges into the Bay of Guinea (in the Atlantic Ocean) some 10 km west of Accra.[17]

The Cultural Value of the Atewa Forest

The Atewa Range has great cultural significance and interesting historical stories. The culture of the inhabitants of communities in this area is inextricably linked with the existence of the forest. The forest is locally referred to as *Kwaebibirem* (dark forest, due to its thick and dense canopy), which is traditionally regarded as the home of ancestral spirits who provide protection, success, and progress to the Abuakwa Stool and the people of the Akyem Abuakwa Traditional Area.

Historically, the forest has been conceived as a haven for the people in the traditional area, a belief that is rooted in the wars with the Asante and other tribal groups. It is taboo to fetch water from the river with any other utensil than a calabash. Also, the water from the river must not be heated or boiled.

Other myths around the Atewa Forest also give rise to particular traditions among locals. On the eastern side of the reserve, for example, it is traditionally taboo to enter the forest or fetch water from the river on a Thursday. Historical and cultural resources with a spiritual significance in the area include the Palace of the Okyenhene (*Ofori Panyin Fie*) and the royal mausoleums. These sites, together with other areas of the forest, provide a meaningful space for folktales (e.g., Okomfo Anokye's ram foot and the legend previously described in this section) and numerous manifestations of the local culture and spiritual values, such as festivals, rites, funerals, and music and dance performances.

The Woes of Atewa Forest: Local Pressures

Like many vulnerable rainforests across the world, the Atewa forest is under serious threat. There is the threat of land conversion within the forest reserve and surrounding areas. The main economic activities in the communities in the Atewa Range are farming and artisanal and small-scale gold, referred to as '*galamsey*'. As a visitor, you may walk through the forest and be greeted with the sound of chainsaws already feasting on the stems of high towering trees. To add to these threats, in September 2018 the government of Ghana signed a barter agreement with the government of China targeting the forest for bauxite under a two billion-dollar Sinohydro deal (Sinohydro Corporation Limited, a Chinese state-owned hydropower engineering and construction company). This deal is to finance and execute the construction of infrastructural projects in Ghana in exchange for access to sites to mine bauxite.

The Atewa Forest Range, which remains the last hope of survival for its endemic species and priceless water-provisioning, also hosts the third largest bauxite deposit in Ghana (but less than 20% of national bauxite reserves). The bauxite deposits are covered by the tropical forest in the forest reserve and 1.5 to 3.0 metres of thick overburdened soil.[18] The idea of developing a bauxite mining site has been around for a long time, since the first study by Patterson in the late 1960s.[19]

Mining bauxite in the Atewa Forest would mean that the forest would be razed down completely, in line with the current open pit mining technology deployed for bauxite extraction across the world. Runoff from the operations would likely contaminate the three major rivers and streams, and dangerous red dust would

---

[17] Ibid.

[18] Minerals Commission. *An Overview of Bauxite Deposits in Ghana Presentation to Members of the Ghana Technical Negotiating Committee (GTNC) on Bauxite* (2015).

[19] Patterson, 'World Bauxite Resources', Professional Paper 1076-B, by S.H. Patterson, H.F. Kurtz, J.C. Olson, and C.L. Neeley. United States Geological Survey (USGS), BiblioGov (27. März 2013), in: https://pubs.er.usgs.gov/publication/pp1076B.

pollute surrounding areas. Eventually, the forest, its water services, and the rare species it is home to may be lost forever.

The Atewa Forest range is gazetted as an area protected by the laws of the land; thus, mining it would be illegal and a blatant disregard for the forest's protected status.

Advocacy and Campaign against Mining the Forest

For the past ten years A Rocha Ghana has been on the forefront working with several state and non-state actors advocating against mining in all forms within the Forest Range. This has been done through a series of research work, community mobilisation and awareness, as well as stakeholder engagement. A Rocha Ghana has successfully rallied other environmental NGOs and international organizations to back the campaign through a series of stakeholder engagements and community groups, urging urge the government of Ghana to designate Atewa Forest Reserve as a National Park. This is motivated by the valuable services the forest provides, especially in the area of water provision for businesses and households.

The Concerned Citizens of the Atewa Landscape (CCAL), a community-based organization, NGOs, youth groups, interfaith groups, farmer-based associations, opinion leaders, and community leaders within the targeted forest landscape, organized a six-day walk covering an estimated distance of 95km from the forest area to the capital city, Accra, to protest against the government's intention of mining the forest reserve for bauxite. The group, numbering about 150 during the walk, presented petitions to several influential dignitaries, including the King of the Akyem Abuakwa Traditional Area, Osagyefo Amoatia Ofori Panyin, who expressed and shared in the position of the group to save Atewa Forest for water.[20]

The increasing advocacy made on behalf of and for the Atewa Forest cannot be over-emphasized. The voices of reason asking for the landscape to be excluded from a rather 'contemptible' agenda of bauxite mining keeps growing, echoing the same message of thousands of advocates spread across the globe.

Notable among them is the late Edward O. Wilson, a University Professor Emeritus and Honorary Curator in Entomology, who wrote a letter to the President, H.E Nana Addo Dankwa Akuffo Addo, to draw his attention to global concerns for the future of the Atewa Forest in Ghana, prompted by news that the hills on which the forest is located are to be mined for bauxite.[21]

It is worth mentioning that Oscar award-winning actor Leonardo DiCaprio added his voice to the call for the protection of the Atewa Forest. DiCaprio, who is a staunch environmentalist, believes that mining in the forest would put the millions of people and hundreds of wildlife species who depend on it at risk of extinction.

The chairman of the Council of Chiefs of the Ghanaian community in the Netherlands has signed a petition to the President of Ghana not to authorise mining in the Atewa Forest.

Atewa Forest and the Christian Community

> Some people in order to discover God, read books. But there is a great book: the very appearance of the created things. Look above you! Read it. God, whom you want to discover, never wrote that book with ink. Instead, He set before your eyes the things that he had made. Can you ask for a louder voice than that?[22]

---

[20] A Rocha Ghana, 'Atewa Heroes Walk 95km for Water: No Bauxite Mining!', 23. March 2018, in: https://ghana.arocha.org/news/atewa-heroes-walk-95km-for-water-no-bauxite-mining/.

[21] Wilson, E. O. (2018) 'Letter to Ghana President', in: https://ghana.arocha.org/news/read-edward-o-wilsons-letter-to-ghanas-president-to-save-atewa-forest/.

[22] St. Augustine of Hippo, *The City of God*, Kindle Edition, Veritatis Splendor Publications 2012.

The Atewa Range Forest, which is endowed with flourishing flora and fauna created by God, reveals the manifold wisdom of God. The forest is not just for the provision of ecosystem services, but also to reflect God's glory and a mastery art of creation.

The Atewa Forest is also typified as a cloud forest, where the highest parts are often shrouded in mist and clouds.[23] It is seen as a connection of the 'heavens' to the earth. From a theological point of view, one could say that Atewa is or has been a heritage of evangelism (Romans 1:20). And this is what is so crucial for the Christian community at the local and national level.

It wasn't surprising when the Christian Council of Ghana and its 18 umbrella church organizations, after participating in an Atewa Forest Exhibition program, wrote a letter to the president appealing to him to protect the forest and to upgrade its status to a National Park.

Through an interfaith network, the churches within the communities mobilized themselves to educate their members and other community members on the need to protect the forest and desist from the temptation of the seemingly benevolent promises of bauxite mining, where some members of the communities had been told of potential employment benefits from mining the forest.

For the Christian community, the protection of the Atewa Forest is a fulfilment of the many biblical mandates given to mankind: "God put man into the garden to dress and to keep it" (Genesis 2:15). There has not been a lot of support action from the Christian community at the national level. However, there is growing faith-based support for environmental action. In 2021, the Christian community participated in a national tree planting exercise and was able to plant over 3.5 million trees out of the 5 million target. This highlights the important role faith-based institutions have to play in joining global and local action to secure the environment for today and tomorrow. Faith-based organizations have the largest social following in Ghana, and if harnessed for a united and concerted goal, significant achievements can be made.

The Atewa Forest Range is indeed a memorial that reveals God as the provider and the one who sustains all life forms on earth. The forest has been providing 'living' water through successive generations and has never ceased. This is a symbol of God's providence and must be protected.

Atewa for a National Park

In the fight to save Atewa from further depletion, there has been a clarion call to raise the status of the forest from a Forest Reserve to a National Park, to once and for all safeguard this globally important forest from any potential future threats. Increasing the status of the Atewa Range Forest Reserve to a National Park is a key intervention to achieve a more optimal and sustainable flow of ecosystem services to both upstream and downstream beneficiaries.[24]

The International Union for Conversation of Nature (IUCN) has passed a global resolution asking for international urgent measures to safeguard the globally important Atewa Forest in Ghana.

Local and international business entities have also responded, where global manufacturing companies like BMW Group, Tetra Pak, and Schüco International KG have stated categorically that they will not be purchasing aluminium sourced from the Atewa Forest unless it meets stringent sustainability criteria.

These companies are all members of the Aluminium Stewardship Initiative (ASI), established to certify that members and their products in the bauxite-aluminium supply chain meet its sustainability standards.

While the companies recognize the government's desire to develop the aluminium sector for economic development and poverty reduction, they have firmly stated that their commitments to sustainability will not be compromised.

---

[23] Schep et al.

[24] Ibid.

Our Glimmer of Hope

After years of delays, one may be inclined to believe that the government finally started listening to the voices of reason asking them not to mine the forest. As it stands, it is not certain if plans to mine the Atewa Forest will go ahead, as the government has not given a definite decision to mine or not. The signs on the wall declare God's continuous glory as he keeps disclosing what the eyes have not yet seen, every time the forest has come under threat. God is using his own creations to demonstrate his manifold presence, holding at bay any forces that come close to destroying this magnificent Eden here in Ghana.

Suggested for Further Reading

Schep, S., Guzmán, A., van Beukering, P., de Moel, H., Eiselin, M., Ayesu, S., Bekoe Ansah, K. *The Economics of the Atewa Forest Range, Ghana* (Accra: IUCN NL, 2016).

A Rocha Ghana. (2018, March 23). *News*, retrieved from A Rocha Ghana: https://ghana.arocha.org/news/atewa-heroes-walk-95km-for-water-no-bauxite-mining/.

Abu-Juam, Obiaw, E., Kaawkye, Y., Ninnoni, R., Owusu, E., & Asamoah, A. *Biodiversity Management Plan for the Atewa Range Forest Reserves* (Accra: 2003).

IFC, World Bank Group. (1 January 2012). 'Performance Standard 6', *Biodiversity Conservation and Sustainable Management of Living.*

Minerals Commission. *An Overview of Bauxite Deposits in Ghana Presentation to Members of the Ghana Technical Negotiating Committee (GTNC) on Bauxite* (2015).

AZE. *https://zeroextinction.org/the-alliance/about-the-alliance/*. Retrieved from Alliance for Zero Extinction: https://zeroextinction.org/ (2005).

77. Water as a Sign of Reconciliation in the Christian Faith in Middle East Contexts[1]

Caleb Hutcherson and Wilbert van Saane[2]

Introduction

Water is a potential source of division and conflict in the Middle East. The increasing threats to water security and the existence of several transboundary water resources have caused conflict in the past and may do so again.[3] In the case of Lebanon, there have been tensions with Israel over the Hasbani-Wazzani water system and with Syria over the Orontes River, as the Lebanese scholar Nadim Farajalla demonstrates.[4] He also shows that water has been a chief victim of violence and war, such as the 2006 war, which caused damage to the Lebanese water infrastructure and pollution of ground and marine water.

Religious groups may offer resources that help prevent and resolve conflicts and promote creation care. The majority of citizens of Middle Eastern countries, including Lebanon, identify themselves as members of religious groups. Religious leaders are opinion-leaders and wield considerable political influence. In light of the water stress in many parts of the Middle East it is, therefore, vital to revisit the sources of the different religious traditions, and to read the sacred texts with an ecological hermeneutic.

In this paper we explore the reconciliatory aspects of water symbolism in the Bible and in Christian traditions. In doing so, we argue that water imagery in the Bible has conciliatory and redemptive significance that has often been deemphasized by our respective Protestant traditions' hermeneutical tendencies and church practices. That being the case, we contend that a re-centered, holistic understanding of water ought to be recovered in evangelical theology and practice. To do so, we draw from a variety of Protestant and Baptist (and Orthodox) sources, in reflection of the multi-denominational context of ecclesial life in Lebanon. Finally, based on this renewed evangelical Christian perspective of the reconciliatory power and material value of water, we will point to some implications of a more robust theology and practice concerning water that could support creation care and reconciliation in Lebanon and the Middle East.

Our contribution to the expanding field of eco-theology is specific and contextual. We will focus on water in Protestant theology and baptismal practice. We are concerned about water and conflict in the Middle East and especially in Lebanon, where we work in the service of evangelical churches. Our angle on this subject is historical-theological and missiological. Our theological position owes much to *missio Dei* theology, which was revived in the theology of Karl Barth and which, in recent years, has been adopted and developed by a number of evangelical theologians. We understand *missio Dei* as an essentially Trinitarian concept, which describes God as a relational being and conceives the world – human and non-human – essentially in terms of relations. Water is part of that network of creational relations, which God

---

[1] This text was first published in Wilbert van Saane, ed., *The Symbolism of Water in Religion: Proceedings of an interreligious conference on water and religion held at Haigazian University on March 2, 2018* (Beirut: Haigazian University Press, 2019), 77-98. It has been included in this volume with permission by Haigazian University Press.

[2] Caleb Hutcherson is Lecturer in Historical Theology at the Arab Baptist Theological Seminary. chutcherson@abtslebanon.org. Wilbert van Saane is Assistant Professor of Systematic Theology and Mission at the Near East School of Theology and Lecturer in Religion at Haigazian University. wilbert.vansaane@haigazian.edu.lb.

[3] Jacob D. Petersen-Perlman, Jennifer C. Veilleux and Aaron T. Wolf, "International water conflict and cooperation: challenges and opportunities," *Water International* 42 (2017): 105-120.

[4] Nadim S. Farajalla, "Water Resources and Conflict in Lebanon," in *Losing Paradise: The Water Crisis in the Mediterranean*, ed. Gail Holst-Warhaft and Tammo Steenhuis (London and New York: Routledge, 2010), 107-124.

is at work reconciling.[5] As we reflect from and on our evangelical tradition, we aim to treat this subject in an ecumenical spirit, aware of the importance of water symbolism in other religious traditions.

Water Symbolism in Christian History

In the Bible, water takes on multiple meanings. At times, water is a power of chaos and destruction that threatens life, as in the story of the flood (Genesis 7). At other times, water enhances life and signifies fertility, salvation or peace. A few examples of these latter uses of water imagery are the rivers that irrigate the Garden of Eden (Genesis 2), the crossing of the sea (Exodus 14) and the 23rd Psalm, whose poet famously wrote: "He leads me beside still waters. He restores my soul."

The key moment in the New Testament that involves water is the baptism of Jesus at the hands of John the Baptist. The gospels describe this as a joyful, very physical event. It occurred in a liminal place, in international waters – the Jordan River – and amidst creation. It brought together "all the people" (Luke 3:21). It was a moment of reconciliation between God, human beings and the non-human creation.

In its 2,000 years of history, the Christian tradition has dwelt heavily on the biblical water imagery in its songs, rituals, prayers, sermons and theologies. But nowhere is the symbolism of water as pervasively present as in Christian baptism. Baptist theologian Paul Fiddes has brought the different biblical connotations of water into focus by pointing to five Christian motifs: birth, cleansing, conflict, refreshment and journey.[6] He argues that, in the historical practice and theology of baptism, all these motifs are present. Fiddes goes on to explain that baptism does not merely *picture* these experiences of being in the world, but *enables* and interprets them as participation in God's creative-redemptive work.

The baptismal theology of the early church emphasized the motif of birth and rebirth. In a sermon on baptism, preached on 6 January 380 CE, Gregory of Nazianzus explains that the Scripture recognizes three births: natural birth, baptism, and the resurrection.[7] The ancient traditions often compare the waters of baptism to the womb of the church, out of which the believers enter into a new life. Bridal imagery also plays a role here, as in the Hymn of the Baptized of Ephrem the Syrian.

> Your garments glisten, my brethren, as snow;
> and fair is your shining in the likeness of angels.
> In the likeness of angels you have come up, beloved,
> from Jordan's river, in the armor of the Holy Ghost.
> The bridal chamber that fails not, my brethren, ye have received:
> and the glory of Adam's house today ye have put on.
> (…)
> Glory to them that are robed, glory to Adam's house!
> In the birth that is from the water, let them rejoice and be blessed![8]

Although the motif of birth and rebirth has not been absent in the later Western theological tradition regarding baptism – Augustine was fond of the metaphor of the church as mother and baptism as her womb – it has laid more stress on the motif of conflict, especially the conflict of death and resurrection. The focus in baptism moved from the Incarnation of Jesus and his identification with the whole cosmos to the atoning

[5] Christopher J.H. Wright, *The Mission of God: Unlocking the Bible's Grand Narrative* (Downers Grove: InterVarsity Press, 2006), 419-420.

[6] Paul S. Fiddes, "Baptism and Creation," in *Reflections on the Water: Understanding God and the World through the Baptism of Believers*, ed. Paul S. Fiddes (Oxford: Regent's Park College, 1996), 47-67.

[7] André Hamman, ed., *Baptism: Ancient Liturgies and Patristic Texts* (Staten Island, NY: Alba House, 1967), 89.

[8] Philip Schaff and Henry Wallace, eds., *Nicene and Post-Nicene Fathers, second series, volume XII: Gregory the Great, Ephraim Syrus, Aphrahat* (New York: Cosimo, 2007), 283.

death and resurrection, which were the ground for the justification of the believer. Baptism was increasingly viewed through the lens of Easter rather than Epiphany. In the fifth century, Pope Leo the Great advised that baptisms should no longer take place during the Feast of Epiphany, but rather at Easter and Pentecost: "It is appropriate that the power of baptism should change the old into the new creature on the day of the death of the Crucified and the Resurrection-day of the Dead."[9]

The Protestant tradition cemented this preference for the imagery of conflict and struggle between the powers of death and life. Protestant baptismal theologies included little reflection on Epiphany and the baptism of the Lord, so cherished in the Eastern traditions. The Epistles of Paul to the Galatians and the Romans became favored texts to explain the meaning of baptism. Martin Luther consciously foregrounded the conflict motif:

> Baptism, then, signifies two things – death and resurrection, that is, full and complete justification. (…) It is therefore indeed correct to say that baptism is a washing away of sins, but the expression is too mild and weak to bring out the full significance of baptism, which is rather a symbol of death and resurrection.[10]

Likewise, in his *Institutes* (IV.15) John Calvin argued that baptism not only attested the forgiveness of sins – the motif of cleansing and purification – but also showed "our mortification in Christ and new life in him."

The Reformers vehemently resisted the idea that the water of baptism had any divine power in itself. They argued that the water of baptism, like the elements of the Eucharist, did not infuse grace and could not be characterized as *ex opera operato*, that is, effective when performed in a valid way. The Heidelberg Catechism, for example, raised the question whether the "outward washing with water itself washes away sins." The answer was an emphatic no, for "only the blood of Jesus Christ and the Holy Spirit cleanse us from all sins". In Reformed thinking, baptism did not alter the fact that humans were sinners: justified sinners maybe, but still sinners. The water only *signified* washing. The conflict between death and new life was a life-time reality for Christians. In this conflict, baptism had a lasting significance. In Luther's famous words: "The only way to drive away the devil is through faith in Christ, by saying: 'I have been baptized, I am a Christian.'"[11]

Desacramentalization and Dualism

This brief survey of water symbolism in Christian history shows two problematic tendencies in the portrayal of water (and nature along with it) in Western Protestant theology: desacramentalization and dualism.

First, water was desacramentalized – that is, the spiritual effect of the physical substance of water was devalued. This tendency was already present in scholastic theology, which emphasized the exalted, rather than the incarnate, Christ and rationalized Christ's sacramental presence with the help of Aristotelian philosophical categories. The Reformation launched a trajectory that radically revised sacramental theology, denying any sacramental value to the elements of water, bread and wine in themselves. These desacramentalizing tendencies contrasted starkly with the theology of the Eastern churches, which continued to emphasize the incarnation, while retaining a more sacramental, poetic and flexible approach.

---

[9] Hamman, *Baptism*, 232.

[10] Quoted in Peter C. Hodgson and Robert H. King, eds., *Readings in Christian Theology* (London: SPCK, 1985), 277.

[11] Heiko A. Oberman, *Luther: Man between God and the Devil*, trans. Eileen Walliser-Schwarzbart (New York: Doubleday, 1989), 105.

Conversations within the ecumenical and liturgical movements of the twentieth century helped Protestants to recover a more sacramental understanding of baptism.[12]

Second, and as a result of such desacramentalizing tendencies, Protestant baptismal theology became more vulnerable to a cosmological dualism. Dualism has been present in both Western and Eastern theologies throughout Christian history, but in the predominantly Protestant nations in Europe it arguably had more devastating effects, especially since the Industrial Revolution. In Protestant theology and praxis, dualism was perhaps also more concealed than in Eastern baptismal rites, which included an explicit renunciation of the devil. In the following section, we will try to identify some aspects of Protestant baptismal theology that carry this dualistic tendency and are in need of revision.

Divisive Dualism

Having traced historical motifs for the symbolism of water in the Christian tradition and having identified two major problematic tendencies in Western Protestant theology, we now focus on the specific problem of cosmological dualism in Protestant evangelical theology. Simply stated, holding to a cosmological dualism leads to a separation between creation and redemption. Redemption becomes primarily concerned with the human soul; the rest of creation remains outside the economy of salvation. This tendency is not exclusive to Western Protestant theology, a point that ecotheologian Michael Northcott helpfully makes when he traces its roots back to the presence of Platonic dualism in Augustine's writings.[13] Then as now, dualism tempts us to neglect life-affirming water imagery in baptismal praxis and leads to destructive perspectives on the relationship between humans and the world.[14] In this section, we highlight the presence of this destructive dualism in various Protestant evangelical traditions.

To begin, it is helpful to point out that the Reformed tradition never had a negative view of creation itself. It presented 'the book of nature' as a source of revelation. However, this notion did not penetrate the Reformed understanding of baptism. Even for the nature-loving Calvin, the world was merely a theater for the glory of God: it displayed the glory of the creator, but salvation primarily lay beyond it. Consequently, Reformed baptismal texts and sermons articulated the washing of 'our impure souls' and the incorporation into the death and resurrection of Christ in mildly dualistic ways. Northcott observes that, while "Calvin still held to the divine intention to restore creation as well as the souls of the elect in the future time of salvation, this view is eclipsed in the strengthening individualism and anthropocentrism of other and subsequent Reformation theologians."[15]

In a similar way, the Lutheran tradition demonstrates dualistic tendencies. A good illustration is Luther's flood prayer, which has been used in Lutheran and Reformed churches ever since Luther – who was of course an Augustinian monk – penned it in the 1520s. While emphasizing the potentially holistic motif of the journey through water, this prayer has strongly dualistic overtones. It highlights the destructive nature of water and interprets the baptism of Jesus in terms of the flood. The prayer explicitly states that, in the flood, God destroyed "the unbelieving world" and petitions that "all waters be a blessed flood". It is worth quoting this prayer in full:

---

[12] Stanley K. Fowler, *More than a Symbol: The British Baptist Recovery of Baptismal Sacramentalism* (Waynesboro, GA: Paternoster, 2002). Anthony R. Cross and Philip E. Thompson, eds., *Baptist Sacramentalism*, vol. 1, 2 and 3 (Eugene, OR: Wipf & Stock, 2007, 2009 and 2020).

[13] Michael S. Northcott, *The Environment and Christian Ethics* (Cambridge: Cambridge University Press, 1996), 215.

[14] Graham W. Ashworth, "Creation Care and the Church: the call to a sustainable lifestyle," in *The Place of Environmental Theology: a guide for seminaries, colleges and universities*, eds. John H. Weaver and Margot R. Hodson (Prague: International Baptist Theological Seminary, 2007), 9-13.

[15] Northcott, *The Environment and Christian Ethics,* 219.

> Almighty and eternal God, according to your strict judgement you condemned the unbelieving world through the flood, yet according to your great mercy you preserved believing Noah and his family, eight souls in all. You drowned hard-hearted Pharaoh and all his host in the Red Sea, yet led your people Israel through the water on dry ground, prefiguring this washing of your holy baptism. Through the baptism in the Jordan of your beloved Son, our Lord Jesus Christ, you sanctified and instituted all waters to be a blessed flood, and a lavish washing away of sin. We pray that you would behold (name of candidate for baptism) according to your boundless mercy and bless him/her with true faith by the Holy Spirit that through this saving flood all sin in him/her which has been inherited from Adam and which he/she himself/herself has committed since would be drowned and die. Grant that he/she be kept safe and secure in the holy ark of the Christian Church, being separated from the multitude of unbelievers and serving your name at all times with a fervent spirit and a joyful hope, so that, with all believers in your promise, he/she would be declared worthy of eternal life, through Jesus Christ, our Lord.

It is notable that Luther's prayer makes no reference to the covenant that God established with Noah after the flood. "I establish my covenant with you that never again shall all flesh be cut off by the waters of a flood, and never again shall there be a flood to destroy the earth" (Genesis 9:11). The ecological implications of the post-flood covenant are evident and have been noticed by many theologians. In addition to that, although Luther's prayer mentions the sanctification of "all waters," it is a sanctification to serve as purification only. There is no reference to the quenching and refreshing qualities of water.

Likewise, the Baptist tradition has been vulnerable to a cosmological dualism. Baptist baptismal theology emphasizes the conflict motif, especially highlighting baptism as dying and rising with Christ through faith. The Baptist tradition of full immersion upon the confession of faith is a powerful enactment of this. In practice, baptism typically takes place in a deep bath of water inside church meeting rooms specially designed for this purpose. But it also can be done outdoors in 'living water', a practice often found among smaller Baptist congregations with more modest meeting facilities. From an ecological perspective, the practice of immersion in rivers, lakes and seas is promising. Yet Baptists too have fallen prey to a one-sided emphasis on the individual soul, overlooking the communal aspects of the conflict motif as well as its more universal dimensions of confrontation with cosmic, systemic, political and economic powers.[16]

We conclude this section with the observation that these dualistic theological tendencies are interwoven with evangelicals' practices of baptism. Like the theologies, these practices emphasize the conflict and purification motifs related to water in ways that often foster cosmological dualism and individualism. This emphasis on conflict and purification motifs comes at the expense of other motifs such as birth and rebirth, the journey, and refreshment that might help construct a more holistic and relational understanding of baptism and the water that is so central to its practice.

Reconciliation begins with repentance. Therefore, we acknowledge how our own traditions have engaged and sometimes perpetuated divisions among humans and between humans and non-human creation.

Reconciling Baptismal Water

Having outlined the dualistic tendencies, we now turn to the question of how Protestant evangelical baptismal theologies can recover a more conciliatory and holistic use of water imagery, one that promotes care for all of God's creation. In our view, the answer does not lie in exclusively foregrounding one particular motif or group of metaphors. That would mean an exchange of one lopsided baptismal theology for another. We advocate, rather, a renewed unlocking of the full range of biblical and historical water metaphors.

---

[16] Fiddes, "Baptism and Creation," 48. Ashworth, "Creation Care and the Church," 19.

Holding the various motifs from the Christian tradition together, Paul Fiddes argues that water might be understood as, "a place in the material world of 'rendezvous' with the crucified and resurrected Lord."[17] It is at and in the water where reconciliation takes place so that, in baptism, the whole person is inaugurated into a "new web of relationships that God weaves with His whole creation."[18]

What are the characteristics of this "new web of relationships" that baptism signals and inaugurates? First, the ritual of *baptism knows no class or hierarchy*, but puts all on the same level. This becomes very clear in the baptism of Christ, which subversively and confrontationally took place in the wild, away from the centers of power.[19] The evangelist Luke placed the baptism of Jesus and Jesus' followers in a decidedly universal context. All needed baptism. And all were baptized in the same water. For Luke, there was no distinction between women and men, Jews and Gentiles, ministers and house slaves.

The Apostle Paul also presented baptism as a levelling ritual. In a context of divisions and quarrels, he asked the rhetorical question: "Were you baptized into the name of Paul?" (1 Corinthians 1:13). The assumption here was that all members of the Christian community of Corinth were equal because all were baptized, not in the name of any apostle or teacher, but in the name of Jesus. No one could elevate themselves over others. Equality in baptism cleared the ground for reconciliation and unity. In order for equality to be established, the self needs to find its appropriate center. In the words of Miroslav Volf, "[t]he self is both 'de-centered' and 're-centered' by one and the same process, by participating in the death and resurrection of Christ through faith and baptism."[20]

The second characteristic is that *baptism signifies reconciliation and inaugurates reconciled life.* Without equality there can be no reconciliation. Because all are fundamentally equal in humbleness and in their need of God's grace, they can be reconciled. The water ritual is an appropriation of the reconciliation that Christ effected. It is a turning-point that marks the beginning of a common journey characterized by reconciliation with God, others, and indeed all creation. This is vividly illustrated in the ancient practice of stripping candidates for baptism prior to their immersion and clothing them in white afterwards.[21]

This understanding of baptism as reconciliation with God, others and creation is also found in the writings of Paul, which have often been read in a dualistic way. According to Paul, baptism signifies that the old life – characterized by strife, power abuse, and conflict – has been left behind. Baptized followers of Jesus live a life that is, instead, characterized by reconciliation (*katallage*). For Paul, reconciliation is not only a vertical, but also a horizontal affair; it has both individual and communal dimensions. All creation waits for and shares in Christ's reconciliation (Romans 8:19-25).[22] Paul's famous words on baptism in the Epistle to the Romans, which have often been taken to imply a cosmological dualism, are upon closer inspection intensely life-affirming and community-building.

> We died to sin; how can we live in it any longer? Or don't you know that all of us who were baptized into Christ Jesus were baptized into his death? We were therefore buried with him through baptism into death in order that, just as Christ was raised from the dead through the glory of the Father, we too may live a new life. (Romans 6:2-4)

---

[17] Fiddes, "Baptism and Creation," 57.

[18] Fiddes, "Baptism and Creation," 59.

[19] James W. Perkinson, "Protecting Water in the Anthropocene: River Spirits and Political Struggles in Detroit, Standing Rock, and the Bible," *CrossCurrents* 66/4 (2016): 460-484; see especially 470-473.

[20] Miroslav Volf, *Exclusion and Embrace: A Theological Exploration of Identity, Otherness, and Reconciliation* (Nashville: Abingdon Press, 1996), 70.

[21] George R. Beasley-Murray, "Baptism," in *Dictionary of Paul and His Letters*, eds. Gerald F. Hawthorne and Ralph P. Martin (Downers Grove and Leicester: InterVarsity Press, 1993), 61.

[22] Ralph P. Martin, *Reconciliation: A Study of Paul's Theology* (Atlanta: John Knox Press, 1981), 119-120. Corneliu Constantineanu, *The Social Significance of Reconciliation in Paul's Theology: Narrative Readings in Romans* (London and New York: T&T Clark International, 2010), 99-140.

Third, *baptism unifies*. This idea builds on the previous two. Since all are fundamentally equal and, by baptism, enter a life characterized by reconciliation, all are fundamentally one in Christ. The river of baptism is no longer a boundary, but a nexus.[23] The Epistle to the Ephesians states this unequivocally. "There is one body and one Spirit, just as you were called to the one hope of your calling; one faith, one baptism, one God and Father of all, who is above all and through all and in all." (4:4-6) Even though Christian communities may have domesticated baptism, baptism is not an esoteric privilege for a few, but a hospitable ritual that extends to all nations and expresses the fundamental unity that Christ embodied. The Gospel of Matthew concludes with this universal vision: "All authority in heaven and on earth has been given to me. Go therefore and make disciples of all nations, baptizing them in the name of the Father, and of the Son and of the Holy Spirit" (28:18-19).

Thus, rather than a source of division and conflict, the water of baptism is a symbol of the fundamental equality of all human beings; of their reconciliation with each other and with all nature through Christ; and of the essential unity that Christ gives. Baptismal theology finds its biblical center not in a cosmological dualism that disregards matter, but in a vision of one creation being reconciled to God and to itself through Christ. Fiddes' five water motifs – birth, purification, conflict, journey and refreshment – make much more sense when they are viewed against this background of reconciliation and unity rather than a soul-matter dualism.

It is the humble, tangible, material substance of water that reveals these truths. Staying on the shores is no good; we need to go "down in the river to pray" to learn these lessons. Through the centuries, Orthodox and Oriental theologies have far better preserved an understanding of God's revelation in and through the material world. Evangelical churches need to renew their appreciation of the physical, material aspect of baptism. This includes embracing that God has seen it fit to ordain the use of water (material creation) for baptism (physical/spiritual regeneration). By reemphasizing the material aspect of water, a new joy may be found in the rebirthing, washing and refreshing aspects of the physical experience of encountering God by faith in the water of baptism.

Implications for Creation Care

In this final section, we contend that this re-centered Protestant baptismal theology, which we described above, has important implications for how we protect water, and the broader ecosystem, in our case in Lebanon. In what follows, we trace these implications and offer some practical recommendations for renewing liturgical, ecumenical and missional practices. Evangelical churches in Lebanon, although small in number, may thereby contribute to addressing and resolving conflicts and crises related to water and the environment.

Before outlining some of these implications, we reiterate that renewal starts with repentance. It is essential that evangelical leaders lead their communities in confessing that God's good creation has been and continues to be destroyed and that Christian communities are complicit. Our confession includes the acknowledgement that our one-sided theologies and Christian praxes have contributed to environmental degradation – or have at least not voiced enough protest against it. This cannot remain a mere theory.

Liturgical Implications

A re-centered baptismal theology will touch churches on a deep level in their weekly worship. In most evangelical churches, water only has a place in worship when baptism is celebrated. This may take place quarterly or even less frequently, as opposed to Catholic and Orthodox worship, in which water is actively used on various occasions and ever-present at the entrance of many sanctuaries. A re-centered theology of

[23] Perkinson, "Protecting Water in the Anthropocene," 472.

water guides us towards incorporating water symbolism more frequently in our weekly services. Recovering symbolic practices such as foot-washing, anointing, blessings involving water, when accompanied by even a simple explanation of the full significance of water, can lead to transformed understanding and practice in the congregation.

Over the past decades, eco-theology has already led to the revision of Protestant baptismal texts and hymns. A good example of this is the following prayer found in *Common Worship*, published for the Church of England. In contrast to Luther's flood prayer, it celebrates water as God's good gift and is remarkably comprehensive in its use of biblical water motifs, including birth/rebirth, purification, refreshment, journey and conflict.

> We thank you, almighty God, for the gift of water to sustain, refresh and cleanse all life. Over the water the Holy Spirit moved in the beginning of creation. Through water you led the children of Israel from slavery in Egypt to freedom in the Promised Land. In water your Son Jesus received the baptism of John and was anointed by the Holy Spirit as the Messiah, the Christ, to lead us from the death of sin to newness of life. We thank you, Father, for the water of baptism. In it we are buried with Christ in his death. By it we share in his resurrection. Through it we are reborn by the Holy Spirit. Therefore, in joyful obedience to your Son, we baptize into his fellowship those who come to him in faith. Now sanctify this water that, by the power of your Holy Spirit, they may be cleansed from sin and born again.[24]

Furthermore, by giving attention to how we perform baptism itself, we can enact a re-centered evangelical theology of creation. Some local Protestant communities have already redesigned their baptismal spaces so as to reflect more accurately the various symbolic aspects of water. Liturgical scholar Benjamin Stewart describes how Lutheran churches in the United States have shaped baptismal fonts so as to evoke the image of an oasis, of water flowing on dry land and of deep, pooled water.[25] In Stewart's view, there is a need to make the rich water symbolism from our theological traditions visible and audible in worship. Throughout, the performative practices of the church – whether speaking, praying, or singing – are understood to actualize our theology of creation. By imbuing these practices with a more holistic theology related to water, we guide our communities to value all of God's physical creation.

Ecumenical/Interfaith Implications

The equalizing, reconciling and unifying nature of baptismal water, as described above, has unmistakable ecumenical and interfaith implications. As the story of the baptism of Christ in the River Jordan suggests, our participation in baptism may lead us to renew our relationship with others, even if they are inhabitants of the land across the river or across the sea. It is vital that we begin to view water bodies – rivers and seas – as God-given nexus rather than boundaries. This awareness of sharing in water may lead to a new perception of ownership of water resources. It may also give us new perspectives on trans-Mediterranean migration.

Here in Lebanon, it should inspire evangelical communities to consider acting in common with 'others'— other Christian and Muslim communities – to respond to our environmental crisis with a view to the common good. Churches and mosques may find that they have much common ground in their view

---

[24] *Common Worship: Christian Initiation* (London: Church House Publishing, 2006), 69.

[25] Benjamin M. Stewart, "Water in Worship: The Ecology of Baptism," *The Christian Century* 128/3 (2011), 22-25. See also Stewart's *A Watered Garden: Christian Worship and Earth's Ecology* (Minneapolis: Augsburg Fortress, 2011).

of water as a gift from God for life and renewal. Too often, we act in self-interest rather than with a holistic view to the inter-related interests of all who share God's world.[26]

Following on from this, we argue that this holistic view of water should shape how we think about and pursue public policy related to water and the environment. In recent history, privatized, small-scale solutions to the environmental crisis in Lebanon seem to have been more effective than large-scale public projects. The danger in these privatized solutions is that we all carry with us our own 'inward bent', the twisting of our interests that looks to our own material needs, protecting our 'own' family and religious group at the expense of 'others'. In turn, this lack of a sense of duty to the common good puts pressure on water systems and perpetuates the water and ecological crisis. So, purely privatized solutions cannot be the only solution. On the other hand, centralized public projects have been problematic. Any centralized solution must involve transparency and accountability so that those at the margins of social, political, and religious power are not penalized or excluded. An interfaith coalition of people of faith might advocate and hold accountable our various 'religious' politicians to consider and look after the needs of the people in Hermél, Akkar, or Chatilla, as carefully as they do the people in downtown Beirut or the Baabda palace. It also means that no country or people in the Middle East may be excluded from negotiations about water and other natural resources. The resources are so scarce that we simply cannot afford to compete – we must cooperate.

Missional Implications

Finally, this re-centered understanding of water has implications for how we evangelicals envision and practice mission. By drawing on a fuller symbolism in baptism, we proclaim that baptism is not merely a public confession or blessing that we receive; it is also a commissioning into participation with the creator's limitless love for and reconciliation of the whole of creation.[27] The reconciling dimension of baptismal water is a reminder that non-human creation is equally part of that commissioning. In baptism, Christians envisage the reconciliation of "all things, whether on earth or in heaven" (Colossians 1:20). Historically, evangelicals in Lebanon have understood their mission in terms of witness, education, social and medical work. By renewing our understanding and practices related to baptism, we are also reminded that our mission of reconciliation includes the threatened, scarce, and polluted waters and environment of Lebanon. Borrowing a term from an ecumenical conference, baptismal water makes us envisage and work for an ecological healing or 'eco-ciliation.[28]

Practically speaking, this renewed perspective should transform our practice of mission. Our mission of reconciliation should seek to preserve and enhance the environment, as well as coming up with strategies that reduce our impact on and destruction of the environment. Such reconciling work might begin with, though should not be limited to, conducting environmental audits of our practices and physical presence in our local communities. This allows us to become aware of and then turn away from the destructive ways in which we relate to our environment. Following on from this, we might continue by annually reviewing our performance, and also invite external accountability and constructive criticism from others. At both an institutional and individual level, we may well incur higher short-term costs for caring for the environment. Recycling takes more effort than throwing away everything in the general vicinity of a green or grey bin on the street. Long-term water solutions are costlier in time, money, and effort, than the short-term 'grey

---

[26] John Weaver, "Teaching environmental theology," in *The Place of Environmental Theology*, eds. Weaver and Hodson, 50.

[27] Wright, *The Mission of God*, 419.

[28] Jacques Matthey, ed., *Come Holy Spirit, Heal and Reconcile! Called in Christ to Be Reconciling and Healing Communities: Report of the WCC Conference on World Mission and Evangelism, Athens, Greece, May 9-16, 2005* (Geneva: WCC Publications, 2008), 83.

market' solutions. However, if we take seriously our mission of reconciliation, then we must act in ways that reconcile humans with our environment, protecting and restoring it, and ending our selfish destruction of it.

In addition, as we practice eco-ciliation, we must be motivated by the interests of others, rather than self-interest. This will require us to practice self-limitation, considering the needs of our 'other' along with our own. In our system of governance, religious communities ought to hold our political leaders accountable if and when their policies serve to preserve personal or confessional power and benefit at the expense of the environment and other confessional groups. In all these ways, practicing eco-ciliation in Lebanon depends on people of faith and hope working together.

Conclusion

In this paper we have explored some ways in which renewed understanding and practices related to water by evangelicals might contribute to protecting and caring for water and related ecosystems in Lebanon and the Middle East at large. We have done this in a spirit of contrition, since we are convinced that reconciliation begins with confession. Christians cannot claim any moral high ground when it comes to creation care and reconciliation. Evangelical theologies and practices related to water have at times perpetuated carelessness towards the environment and a devaluation of water.

We have argued that the quest for life-affirming theologies requires a thorough rereading of the Scriptures and Christian history in the hope of overcoming dualism and recovering water imagery that serves more sustainable and reconciliatory Christian practices. By renewing a holistic, robust understanding of the symbolism of water, we might open up ecumenical and interfaith avenues of reconciliation. A renewed understanding of water imagery carries profound implications for our liturgical practices, for our interactions with other confessional groups, and for how we think about and practice God's mission of reconciliation in the world.

The underlying question we have explored is whether religion, for us that is our evangelical faith tradition, has anything to contribute to protecting the environment and resolving conflict over key resources like water. We have argued that, indeed, theology and religious practice can answer this question positively—but with a complex 'yes'. To answer this question positively requires both a confession of the ways that evangelical theologies and practices have contributed to conflict and the degradation of the environment, as well as the ways that, in renewing our theologies and practices related to water, we might contribute to eco-ciliation – ecological healing and care based on who we understand God to be. By expanding and enriching our theologies and liturgical practices related to water, especially baptismal water, we can and should promote reconciliation in relationship to the environment for the benefit of all of God's creation.

Suggestions for Further Reading

Anthony R. Cross and Philip E. Thompson, eds. *Baptist Sacramentalism*, vol. 1, 2 and 3. Eugene, OR: Wipf & Stock, 2007, 2009 and 2020.

Paul S. Fiddes, ed. *Reflections on the Water: Understanding God and the World through the Baptism of Believers*. Oxford: Regent's Park College, 1996.

Stanely K. Fowler. *More than a Symbol: The British Baptist Recovery of Baptismal Sacramentalism*. Waynesboro, GA: Paternoster, 2002.

Gail Holst-Warhaft and Tammo Steenhuis, eds. *Losing Paradise: The Water Crisis in the Mediterranean*. London and New York: Routledge, 2010.

Michael S. Northcott. *The Environment and Christian Ethics*. Cambridge: Cambridge University Press, 1992.

Benjamin M. Stewart. *A Watered Garden: Christian Worship and Earth's Ecology*. Minneapolis: Augsburg Fortress, 2011.

John H. Weaver and Margot R. Hodson, eds. *The Place of Environmental Theology: a guide for seminaries, colleges and universities*. Prague: International Baptist Theological Seminary, 2007.

Part II: Asia and Pacific

78. The Biblical Foundation for Life-Giving Agriculture and Practical Dimensions of Eco-Diakonia in South Korea

Kyeong Ho Han[1]

Biblical Foundations

Now no shrub had yet appeared on the earth and no plant had yet sprung up, for the Lord God had not sent rain on the earth and there was no one to work the ground. (Gen. 2:5, NIV)

The Lord God took the man and put him in the Garden of Eden to work it and take care of it. (Gen. 2:15, NIV)

God Created Humankind as Homo Colens (農人)[2]

In the above phrases, we can notice that God created humankind as a being to work the ground. The original writing oh "work the ground" is *abad adama* in Hebrew. *Abad* means to serve or work, *adama* means the ground or soil. After creating Adam, God have him the role of taking care of eden. The "taking care of" is *shamar* in Hebrew whereas Eden is the Garden of life.[3] God created humankind for a particular tole in His creation.

We can understand here that the aim of human life is to work on the ground and to take care of others' lives. "Work the ground" here means that humankind can live by producing crops. We call this first human Adam "*Homo Colens*" (a being working the ground, a tiller, *Nong In* in Korean, 農人 in Chinese). A farmer is often called "Nong Min" (農民) or "Nong Bu" (農夫) in Korea.[4] The meaning of those words, "Nong Min" or "Nong Bu", limit the understanding of the work of farmers as an economic activity and do not fully contain and express their God-given task of mission through their farming and tilling the ground. God created the first humankind as Nong-In (農人), as a farming-being or a life-giving being. As a human-being is formed from the dust of the ground, it is so natural that a human-being cultivates the ground and produces life.

The primary mission given to the "Nong In" are two mandates, to work the ground and to take care of it. We can understand at this point that the relationship between humankind and ground is very close and cannot be separated. We also see already here that the role of humankind is to take care of others' lives, that is to say that eco-diakonia which is the keyword of this handbook is a given mandate from God rooted already in creation.

In South Korea, the Life-giving agriculture movement spread over the country in the 1990s. The main activity of the movement was producing and supplying life-giving agricultural products, and to practice

---

[1] Rev. Kyeong Ho Han is an ordained pastor of the Presbyterian Church of Korea; Th. M in Missiology at Presbyterian University and Theological Seminary. Currently, he is the Chair of Korean Christian Life-Giving Agriculture Forum and the Chair of the Asia Christian Life-Giving Agriculture Forum; President of Asian Rural Mission Society; Chief-editor of *Rural Community and Christian Ministry*, a quarterly journal on life-giving theology and rural ministry.

[2] Besides *Homo Colens,* there is *Homo Agricola* [*Ager* (a field or a farm) + *colere* (till)]. *Colens* and *cola* are derived from *colere* to till (work the ground). So *Homo Colens* is a tiller and *Homo Agricola* is a farmer.

[3] *Shamar* means take care of, protect and preserve etc. I understand Eden is not a confined place specially but is symbol of globe (earth) that God created.

[4] *Nong Min* means farmers including social class consciousness, *Nong Bu* means also farmers as a individual being. Min is peoples, Bu is husband. In(人) is humankind.

aspects of eco-justice. This is in accordance with the spirit of creation. "Nong"[5] (農, not as a job) is the beginning and foundation of a life-giving movement and the eco-justice movement.

We assumed for many years that the Ark of Noah was built only for human salvation. But as the contamination and destruction of the ecosystem becomes greater and greater, we gradually also taught ourselves to see all the other creatures in the Ark. We realised that God saved not only Noah's family but also all other living creatures. Thus, God created humankind as a being working the ground, *Nong In* (農人). This is not a new insight, merely one we lost sight of. Therefore, we need to see the real image of humankind under the huge shadow of urban civilisation. The changing historical contexts opens our eyes open and reawakens us.

The term "*Nong In*" does not refer simply to any farmer, but to the first of humankind who was created by God to work the ground and to care for others right at beginning of creation. *Nong In* is the self-identity of humankind. But this first image has been lost and is now often hidden deep in our minds because of Adam and Eve's sin. Therefore, we need the new movement for life-giving agriculture for recovering the first image of what it means to be a human being. We believe this movement of rediscovery is a real event of salvation.

The Murder by Cain and the Beginning of City Life

When did city life began? The bible tells us that this is related to the event of Cain killing Abel. After the killing, Cain was separated from the ground, isolated from other peoples and ran away from God (Gen. 4:11-14). Nobody protected him anymore. "So Cain went out from the Lord's presence and lived in the land of Nod, east of Eden. Cain made love to his wife, and she became pregnant and gave birth to Enoch. Cain was then building a city, and he named it after his son Enoch" (Gen. 4:16-17, NIV). The city Enoch is the first city according to biblical tradition. The Bible therefore says that city life is closely related the sin of killing one's neighbour. This is a very meaningful insight. Because of greed and arrogance, humankind was expelled from Eden; the anger of Cain made him kill his brother Abel and to construct a city just for himself.

Who were the descendants of Cain? "Lamech married two women, one named Adah and the other Zillah. Adah gave birth to Jabal; he was the father of those who live in tents and raise livestock. His brother's name was Jubal; he was the father of all who play stringed instruments and pipes. Zillah also had a son, Tubal-Cain, who forged all kinds of tools out of bronze and iron. Tubal-Cain's sister was Naamah" (Gen. 4:19-22, NIV). Lamech is sixth descendant of Cain. Raising livestock was done outside of the city to provide for the ruling class and soldiers. Playing stringed instruments was for their enjoyment. Bronze and iron were used for weapons. We can discover, in this passage, the inequality, enjoyment, violence and war by the dominant class and the rich which are all predominant characteristics of city life. How has this come to be?

City life spread over the globe rapidly (Gen. 6:11-13). Eventually, it was purged by floodwater because of sinful life. After that, humankind built another city symbolised now by the tower of Babel. Humankind was punished by confusing the one language of the human family.[6] City life can make humankind arrogant, the collectivisation of greed leads to imperial power and finally disobedience to God.

The History of Salvation Began with the Leaving of City Life

Terah, the father of Abraham, set out from Ur of the Chaldeans to go to Canaan. But when they came to Haran, they settled there (Gen. 11:31). Abraham set out from Haran to Canaan. It was God's command. The cities Ur and Haran were prosperous big cities of Mesopotamian civilisation. But God guided Terah and

---

[5] *Nong* (農) in Korean is a prefix with a meaning similar to agri in English. *Nong Min* (農民) means farmers, *Nong Up* (農業) means agriculture as a job or economical meaning, *Nong Chon* (農村) means rural village. But the word *Nong* (農) above not only contains these three meanings but also transcends them in this paper.

[6] It was recovered by the Holy Spirit at Pentecost (Acts 2:1-13).

Abraham to move from city life to Canaan life (nomadic and agricultural life). We should pay attention to this providence of God. On the other hand, Lot, the nephew of Abraham, liked to live in the city Sodom and Gomorrah (Gen. 13:10-13, NIV). Lot therefore is the symbol of humankind's desire for city life.

Jesus and the Roman Empire

Jesus was born at a time when Israel was governed by the Roman Empire. The Roman Empire built a great civilisation of cities. But Jesus grew up in Galilee, a rural region based on fishing. 80% of the land at that time was possessed by the rich living in Jerusalem. The people of Galilee were poor. Compare Galilee to the Roman Empire! Roman civilisation symbolises the strong, ruling power, the great city, the rich. On the other hand, Galilee symbolises the weak, the people below, those colonised and oppressed by Rome, small rural and fishing villages, all of them poor. However, the Gospel was proclaimed in Galilee. Jesus was crucified by the Roman Empire. The Roman Empire has perished but the Gospel still is alive until now. We realise that salvation power comes out from the weak Galilee, not from the strong great city.

Christians as Actors of Eco-diakonia

What does it mean in this world to live as a disciple of Christ? I argue that we should recover the identity of being a *Nong In* in the original image of creation and to live our lives as actors of eco-diakonia. Can the civilisation of today save humankind? Can neo-liberalism? Can scientific technology? We should think deeply and seriously. But it is impossible for us to escape from city life. The more serious the problem is the more urgent it becomes that we all must return to its root and origin. We do not all need to become rural farmers. We do not all need to return to rural village lifestyles. But we should think deeply of the nature of humankind and modern civilisation and change our thoughts and our daily practices in revolutionary ways to become actors of eco-diakonia.

The Example of Practice in South Korea

The Ho Jeo Church in Rural Village

In 1990s Korea, environmental organisations and consumer life co-operatives, *Hansalim,* were organised and spread over the country as the life-giving spirit took hold of the country. In accordance with this stream of renewal, a small rural church named Ho Jeo took part in the life-giving agriculture (LGA in below) movement. The church established Ho Jeo Consumers' life Co-operative in April 1989. Ho Jeo church is located at Wonju city in Gangwon province and belongs to PCK in Korea.

The main task of all consumers' life co-operatives is to supply life-giving agricultural products. This was because of consumer demand in cities. So Ho Jeo Co-operative produced and supplied their products to co-operatives and churches in the city. For this, Ho Jeo Co-op educated members in various areas: why do we need to change the agricultural method from conventional methods to life-giving methods; what are the methods of life-giving agriculture; to whom should we supply the products; what is the co-operative movement all about; how do we get profits through co-op activity amongst others. At first, only a few farmers decided to change their conventional methods. However, year by year, many farmers joined the emerging LGA movement.

In the early stages, many obstacles hindered the co-op's development. A rural society is often marked by mentalities linking blood and village. Thus, farmers often forget to discriminate between the public or private. Farmers may also not want to change their thoughts from experience – most of them are rather conservative. Many problems therefore occurred. Conflicts occurred within families too between generations on whether or not to use chemicals. This also happened between members within the co-op.

However, they realised in the long run that they had to change their habits and the activities. Firstly, a democratic training programme was introduced where they discussed many issues through meetings, then concluded and practiced new ways together. The board meeting was held every month. Through these meetings, members gradually became themselves the host(master) of co-op instead of remaining just guests. The Host-spirit which was enhanced by exercising joint democratic activities gave them power to manage the Ho Jeo Co-op on their own. We made efforts to improve three innovative spirits at the same time: a democracy-sprit, a co-operation-spirit, and a life-giving spirit.

The budget of the co-op is supported by members' shareholding (investments). Members invested money individually and continuously. At the start, the amounts were really small. Most of the farmers were still poor and did not have enough money. When we did a project, we collected the money by ourselves until we had collected over the half of the total amount needed. Members brought their own portions. The church supported the remaining financial needs. Participation-consciousness could be strengthened through money-participation, as members themselves became the hosts of the co-op. The co-op thus could develop under the host-consciousness of its members.

At first, the coop supplied life-giving products to church members directly in Seoul, South Korea's capital city. But we knew that this would be unfeasible long-term. The church is essentially a worship community in grace. The activity of selling the products seems to fit more with economic trade. Thus, there occurred conflicts or struggles due to issues relating to trade, for instance, the price and the quality of products. If the church members of city churches complained to their pastors, they would not continue the trade with the co-op system. Church members acted more as regular consumers rather than Christians orientated by alternative values. Most of them did not understand the actual situation of farmers and of agriculture. They had not developed a sufficient life-giving-consciousness but instead were looked at the rationality of the products given their price. It became so difficult that the trade could not be maintained.

Then a special church appeared before us. The church, named Go Deung located in Suwon city in Kyunggi province, became our friend. It was a small church with about hundred members. They well understood the situation of farmers and difficulties of life-giving agriculture (LGA). Year by year, the relationship between Ho Jeo Co-op and Go Deung church developed. Both used to have an annual meeting for planning in December. During this meeting, they looked back at the activities of the past year and looked forward to those of the next. The trade was systemised between the two groups. Products also were produced according to the plan. The relationship continued for over twelve years. This relationship became known to Korean churches as an excellent example of co-operation in the movement.

The activities of Ho Jeo Co-op brought changes both to church members in cities and village peoples. Firstly, changes in the relationships between church members appeared. Before, relationships were very simple and mainly faith-based. However, the co-op provided work relationships. Common work helped the relationships mature. Secondly, church members took pride in their dedication to the villagers. The virtuous position of church rose in the mind of the villagers too. Thirdly, church numbers increased and members became more independent economically in result.

Similar changes also occurred amongst the villagers. Several leaders appeared through the education and activities of the co-op. Improving host-consciousness, the chief director borrowed much money from the bank to fund the purchasing of rice from co-op members in the autumn. He took out a mortgage to do so. In Korea, the government has bought rice from farmers after harvesting. But the price was very low. So, the co-op bought rice from co-op members and sold it to consumers. At this time, much money was needed. A young member decided to receive his rice selling money only after other members had received theirs. His good deed concession-spirit became carved into the minds of the other co-op members. Democratic processes became practiced in their daily life. The development of co-op helped their own improvements.

Ho Jeo Co-op has developed year by year gradually. Now the area of business has widened from Ho Jeo Myon to Gangwon province.[7] The name also changed from Ho Jeo (name of the Myon which is smaller than a city) to Wonju (name of city). After changing the name, citizens in Wonju city participated in the co-op. Farmers and consumers became members in one co-op. However, the leaders of the co-op soon also realised that this system is ineffective with regard to good management. Therefore, for more effective activities, farmers created a new organisation named Wonju Life-Giving Agriculture and consumers belong to the Wonju Consumers' Life Co-operative. Farmers are also members of the co-op. In recent years, they opened a shop in Wonju city to sell local food. Farmers and consumers work together. Ho Jeo has become a famous LGA area in Korea.

Ho Jeo Co-op has turned 32 this year. Last April, the chief directors of past had a meeting at the office of Wonju Life-Giving Agriculture in Ho Jeo Myon. It was very joyful day.

Ecumenical Movement: "Korea Christian Life-Giving Agriculture Forum"

A new ecumenical movement in Korea began in 2000. Pastor Sung Won Park staff at the World Alliance of Reformed Churches (WARC) invited Pastor Kyeong Ho Han to Geneva. He accepted the invitation and went to explain the biblical foundations of the LGA movement. He presented the situation of the Korean LGA movement and discussed this with attendants. At that time, staff from several international organisations who also had their headquarters in Geneva (WCC, WARC, World Alliance of YMCAs, World YWCA, Pax Romana, Lutheran World Federation, Frontier Internship in Mission) hosted a workshop named *Ecumenical Coalition for Alternatives to Globalization* (ECAG). The workshop was for preparing countermeasures against globalisation by neoliberalism. They perceived the importance of LGA for the future life of humankind. In 2002, Pastor Han was invited for a second time by ECAG and again went to Geneva. Attendants proposed to hold a global forum on LGA at Wonju city in Korea. Pastor Han accepted the proposal and it was agreed to hold this forum in 2005. On his return to Korea, Pastor Han organised the Korean Preparing Committee for a global forum. The first global forum on LGA was held 8th-14th April in the year 2005. We published a book including the presentations and the contents of all the processes from the forum.[8] This meaningful event helped open the eyes of churches globally to the importance of LGA.

After this first global forum, the Korean Preparing Committee did not disorganise, but converted to the Korea Christian LGA Forum (Korea Forum below). It was important to sustain the LGA movement in Korea. NCCK, YMCA, YWCA, associations of rural church pastors belong to PROK, Methodist, PCK, Right Farming Association by Christian farmers all took part in the Korea Forum. After that, Dr Hongjung Lee who was staff of CCA (Christian Conference of Asia), proposed the idea the Korea Forum of holding the first Asia forum in Korea. So CCA and Korea Forum together held the Asia Forum in Korea 25th-29th August 2006. Participators decided to establish the Asia Christian LGA Forum and to organise a steering committee. One person in each country takes part in the steering committee and discusses issues by SMS or online.

After the first forum, the Asia forum has been held every 3 years (the second in Kandy, Sri Lanka in 2010, the third in Sanchung near Busan city, Korea in 2013, alongside the 10th WCC general assembly in Busan, the fourth in Chiang Mai, Thailand in 2016, the fifth in Manado, Indonesia in 2019). The sixth forum will be held in Philippines in 2022 if the covidCOVID-19 pandemic allows. After each forum, a book of the proceeding is published.

We found out through these five Asia Forum meetings that the Asian agricultural field generally is characterised by similar conditions despite some regional differences. The controlling power of transnational corporations has become stronger gradually under the WTO regime. They have promoted a monopoly of

[7] The administrative units in Korea are Myon< Gun< City< Province.

[8] "Life-Giving Agriculture Is Possible! Report of the Life-Giving Agriculture Global Forum", 9th-13th April 2005, Wonju, Korea. Ecumenical Coalition for Alternatives to Globalization.

seeds. They have produced many GMOs and sold them to farmers globally along with chemicals. They have also spread monocultures over the world. The diversity of crop species decreased rapidly by their actions. Traditional agricultural knowledge which were handed down from ancestors have been disgraced. They have robbed Asia of excellent seeds in order to do research on them and claimed Intellectual Property Rights. Their motives only seem to be profit. Asian agriculture is controlled under their capital power. We do believe that agriculture which depends upon fossil energy will be met with a time limit soon. The climate crisis results in increasing food bankruptcy. The LGA movement therefore becomes more and more important to maintain a healthy and sustainable life.

Conclusion

The LGA movement in Korea was begun by Christian farmers in 1976. They organised the Right Farming Association (RFA). The base of their activity is faithful confession of God's Creation order. They are the pioneers of the LGA movement. RFA is active still now. In 1985, a new LGA movement was started by consumers. They organised Hansalim. Rural pastors of Methodist, PROK, PCK churches organised their associations respectively. They have begun their own LGA movement with their church members from 1989 onwards. Many Korean peoples and Christians have become concerned about food practices thanks to the LGA movement and their thinking of agriculture has been changed gradually.

The Korea Forum has formed domestic LGA Christian networks of related organisations and farmers by holding domestic forums intermittently. It has also held a forum for young and middle-aged farmers once a year for the succession of LGA. Most of Korean farmers are now old which is a serious problem. We need to allow future generations to grow well. In recent years, young Christians have returned to rural villages and have become farmers.

The Korea Forum also has held bilateral forums between Korea and other countries. Some of these bilateral forums were held with Philippines, Indonesia, India respectively. These allowed us to understand the situation of other countries in much more detail and help establish a very friendly relationship. We encouraged them participate in the Asia Forum. We also prepared a bilateral forum with Myanmar which unfortunately had to be postponed because of the COVID-19 pandemic.

The Korea Forum invited Indonesian and Malaysian pastors to visit to Korea to communicate and observe the LGA field and visit related churches for a week. Christian farmers from Indonesia and Malaysia came to Korea to learn and train in LGA farming for three months. The Elder Hankyu Jo (representative of Natural Farming Association in Korea) and Pastor Kyeong Ho Han (representative of Korea Forum) went to Malaysia SIB denominations to educate them (leaders and farmers of SIB) about LGA and the Korean co-operative movement for one week in 2015. After this, the two men used to visit Malaysia twice a year to observe their fields and progress and continue to teach them.

In 2019, the Korea Forum changed its cloth again and is now named Asia Rural Mission Association (ARMA) with the mandate to develop rural mission in Asia effectively and systematically. We need to strengthen the power of the organisation by equipping a regular directors' meeting which consists of urban and rural churches. They co-operate with ARMA by supporting finances. Professors in agricultural college and in the theological seminary also participated in the directors' meeting to support the theory behind the practice.

In addition, the Nong(農) Theology Study Meeting was established by pastors and scholars in 2019 under ARMA. The members of the meeting used to come together every month for presentations and discussion. They held an open seminar on 3rd November 2020. They published a book which gathered the papers presented in meetings across one year. The name of book is *Nong Theology* which is the way of life-giving and peace. It covers how Christians look into and interpret the Bible, the history and nature through the lenses of the Nong-concept and is maybe the first publication in the history of Christianity on this particular topic. We do believe that the history of humankind was dominated with building huge civilisations focused on city life. This civilisation however is confronted with a deep crisis. Now we must change the direction of life for our survival. Therefore, we reverse-turn from city life to Nong life.

The Korea Forum now prepares to publish an Asia journal of LGA. We already gathered writings and are currently editing it. Nine writers from eight countries sent their manuscripts to us. The first was scheduled to be published in October 2021. The plan is to publish two issues a year. We are to communicate with one another and improve relationships through the journal.

The Korea Forum has plans to visit six or seven Asian countries in two or three years. We want to meet leaders of denominations, ecumenical leaders, organisations and farmers related to LGA, and organisations of farmers' movement. We hope to meet them as they get involved in the training programme of LGA and the other programmes we run. We will discuss with them about the possibility of establishing an Asia LGA centre. According to the result of these discussions, our future direction will be determined. We will widen the network of the LGA movement in Asia and strengthen its power. As the LGA movement questions the consequences and impacts of highly advanced industrialised science and agricultural technology on God's creation, we need to continue re-reading the Bible through the eyes of the Nong-In (a farmer) whose life is rooted in a life-giving culture and in justice and peace.

Suggestions for Further Reading

Berry, Wendell. *What I Stand On: The Collected Essays of Wendell Berry 1969-2017*. New York: Library of America, 2019.

Davis, Ellen F. *Scripture, Culture, and Agriculture: An Agrarian Reading of the Bible*. Cambridge: Cambridge University Press, 2009.

79. COVID-19 and The Tree of The Garden in Modern Human Civilisation

Park Seong-Won[1]

Twenty years ago, when the world shifted from the 1900s to the 2000s, we were excited that human history was entering the 21st century, the new millennium. At that time, there was optimism that the infinite development of technology would make enormous improvement in human life during the 21st century, and scepticism that although technology might develop, without caution in consumerism and ecological destruction, we might be in danger of more diseases and ecological threats.

But what has happened? Unfortunately, as soon as we entered the 2000s, the world fell into a war spiral – with the Gulf War, 9/11 terrorist attacks, Afghanistan war, Iraq war etc. – and the economy was polarised by neoliberal economic globalisation and continued ecological destruction, resulting in serious ecological crises such as climate change and dust pollution. In addition, it was foreseen that new life-threatening diseases which we have never experienced before might arise, and that is now becoming a reality.

Dilemma of the Modern Human Civilisation

Twenty years ago, I was working at the World Communion of Reformed Churches, headquartered in Geneva, Switzerland, and whenever I had an opportunity to preach at either European or Korean congregation, I preached a sermon entitled "The Fruit of the Tree of Garden of the 21st Century" based on Genesis 3.

At that time, in this sermon, I mentioned the disease Ebola and warned that if we would not change the path of current human civilisation, we would face far more serious diseases than Ebola. Ebola is a terrifying disease with a fatality rate of 50 to 90 per cent that first appeared in the central African Congo in 1976. It swept Africa in 1998, putting the world in a state of panic. Ebola did not come under the spotlight this year as the world was engulfed with COVID-19, but it actually reappeared in Congo on 1st August 2018, setting a record of 3,470 confirmed cases, 2,287 dead, 1,171 survivors. A record of 1/3 of confirmed cases ended in death and this particular wave was declared terminated in 25th June 2020.

Twenty years ago, a warning was issued about future diseases; unfortunately, this was followed by a series of new, scary diseases: SARS in 2002, MERS in 2013, the Zika virus in 2015, Ebola again in 2014, and COVID-19 in late 2019, just a few days before 2020, resulting in an indefinite stop to all systems around the world.[2]

Is this image of us wearing masks during our daily lives the new normal? Is social distancing, for humans who are social animals, the new normal? This situation is clearly abnormal – an absolutely abnormal reality.

---

[1] Seong Won Park Park Seong-won is a professor of Youngnam Theological College and Seminary in Gyeongsan, Korea, also since 2017 is president of Gyeongan Graduate University in Andong, which is the capital of Korean Spiritual Culture and Neo-Confuzian tradition. He also was a Central Committee member of World Council of Churches. He is a prominent theologian and ecumenical activist and pioneer for ecumenical formation for theology of life and social transformation. Park also serves at the Ecumenical Committee of the Presbyterian Church of Korea and regularly is also involved as speaker in conferences on ecumenism, mission, economic justice, ecology, life-giving civilisation, and worship and spirituality in CCA. The article is re-published with the kind permission of the author.

[2] See on the history of past pandemics: Bhadoria, Pooja; Gupta, Gaurisha; Agarwal, Anubha, 'Viral Pandemics in the Past Two Decades: An Overview', in *Journal of Family Medicine and Primary Care*, August 27, 2021, Vol 10 (Issue 8), 2745-2750. doi: 10.4103/jfmpc.jfmpc_2071_20; also: Robin Marantz Henig: Experts warned of a pandemic decades ago. Why weren't we ready?; published April 8, 2020 July 2020 issue; in National Geographic, https://www.national geographic.com/science/article/experts-warned-pandemic-decades-ago-why-not-ready-for-coronavirus

Many people say "this too will pass!" and hope that the situation will soon end and we will be able to go back to living as we used to. But it won't. Some say human history should now be divided into BC and AC – before corona and after corona. This unparalleled reality is unlikely to change easily, with the world's nations sealed off by a virus which was never seen before. Even the world wars could not shut down all systems for so long and close national borders. Are we going to live like this? Or do we wish to change something?

These days, there is much analysis predicting post-COVID life. However, after seeing most of these analyses, I am doubtful whether we actually understand the core of the crisis. A leading Korean broadcast programme, "Programme on the Way of the Republic of Korea After Corona", focuses on how to adapt to the corona era rather than look for alternatives. The whole world is focusing on vaccine development in response to COVID-19. Of course, vaccine development is important to prevent the spread of the virus and treatment development of course should be a priority. Nonetheless, this is a defensive strategy, not a pro-active strategy to overcome COVID-19. What is more important is not to adapt to the Corona crisis, but to thoroughly find out the root cause of such diseases and find alternative ways to deal with it.

Many different theories abound in relation to the origin of the coronavirus – from the Wuhan Market in China, leaked from Wuhan Virus Research Institute near Wuhan Market, that the world's dominant forces intentionally spread the virus for population control or digital control and so on. Current information cannot pinpoint the real cause the ecological crisis is likely to be the root cause. To be more precise, the fact that humans have invaded the realm of nature too deeply is an important cause that has led to COVID-19.

These modern diseases, such as SARS, MERS and COVID-19, are all caused by viruses which originally existed only in animals but crossed species boundaries from animals to humans. The question is how did it happen?

Twenty years ago, a lab in Canada examined how the animal virus, Ebola, came to humans. When humans damaged the deep jungles of Africa for resource development, the virus that lived there moved from the monkeys to the humans in contact with these monkeys. The new diseases that humans are experiencing now are the cost of humans exploiting nature for development and material growth.[3]

Humans are meant to coexist with nature. However, modern civilisation has gone beyond co-existence. For development and economic greed, humans have ruthlessly damaged nature and disturbed ecological principles through genetic manipulation, which then forces nature to invade human territory. In addition to the human metastasis problem of animal viruses, today farmers are really struggling with animals when farming. In other words, humans are desperately fighting for food with animals, and animals are fighting for food with humans.

Animal counterattack began because humans encroached upon their habitats. The violation of human animal habitats is the first cause of SARS or MERS, or the outbreak of COVID-19, and the uncontrolled violation of nature by human beings has brought about this situation.

Another potential cause is the development of human technology, especially convergence technology. The Wuhan Virus Research Institute is suspected as the source of the COVID-19 virus leak. Ralph S. Baric, professor of mechanics at North Carolina University, and Zhengli-Li Shi, researcher at the Institute for Special Pathogens and Biological Safety in Wuhan Virus Research, announced that strains of the coronavirus in Chinese bats can infect people and cause pneumonia and lung damage in 2015 in *Nature Medicine*, a renowned international journal of medicine. The new virus might not be a naturally occurring virus but a virus combined by human technology.

[3] The role of the Canadian Science Center for Human and Animal Health in the discovery of the transmission of the Ebola virus is referred to in: Hana M. Weingartl, Carissa Embury-Hyatt, Charles Nfon, Anders Leung, Greg Smith & Gary Kobinger: 'Transmission of Ebola virus from pigs to non-human primates', in *Scientific Reports* volume 2, Article number: 811 (2012), in: https://www.nature.com/articles/srep00811

According to another source, there was a theory that COVID-19 is a combination of AIDS and other viruses, and unfortunately, the treatment drug given to the first COVID-19 patient in Korea was a cure for HIV and AIDS; news reports stated this patient was completely cured. It is also worth noting that Remdesivir, an Ebola treatment, is constantly being mentioned in relation to COVID-19 treatments.

In conclusion, regardless of the specific cause whether for economic or technical reasons or military purposes, COVID-19 is a clear reminder of human greed and the arrogance of technology as we destroy the ecosystems which support us.

A Theological Reflection on Dilemma of the Modern Human Civilisation

First, consider Genesis 1:6-7:

> And God said, Let there be a firmament in the midst of the waters, and let it divide the waters from the waters. And God made the firmament, and divided the waters which were under the firmament from the waters which were above the firmament: and it was so.

The keyword of Genesis 1:6-7 is "divide". The waters above the firmament have been divided from the water under the firmament. This division of the realm of sharing appears steadily if you look at the process of creation. Not only here but all throughout Genesis, we can see that God divides all creation into appropriate places, saying, "God shares light and darkness, shares the day and the night, shares the sun and the moon, divides the seasons."

As we can see from our current unprecedented rainy season, things in the universe should not be in one place at a time. Everything should be spatially distributed properly. The ecology of the universe created by God is designed this way.

Here, we have an important point to make clear. We clearly note here that literal meaning of the term "divide" has been highly problematic in connection with all sorts of unjust political systems like dictatorship, totalitarianism, imperialism, colonialism and etc. There is a clear satanic character in Apartheid systems. Therefore, the biblical term "divide" should not be understood in this way. It needs to be understood as "shared" or "allocated" based on God's given grace and justice.

According to Genesis 1:11-12, all living things in the universe, such as grass, vegetables, and trees, were created according to their kind.

> And God said, "Let the earth bring forth grass, the herb yielding seed, and the fruit tree yielding fruit after his kind, whose seed is in itself, upon the earth"; and it was so. And the earth brought forth grass, and herb yielding seed after his kind, and the tree yielding fruit, whose seed was in itself, after his kind; and God saw that it was good. God said, "Give the land the plants that sow, the plants that sow, and the trees that bear the fruit of the seed according to their kind." The earth gave the grass, the vegetables that bear the seeds according to their kind, and the trees that bear the seeds according to their end, which was good for God to see. Let the waters of the earth gather in one place, and the land be revealed, so that it will be as it will be.

If we look at Genesis 1:20-21, God not only created plants but also all kinds of animals – birds living in the sky, animals living on land and all kinds of fish living in the sea – and chose distinct habitats for each group. When the people of Israel came out of Egypt and entered the land of Canaan, God again divided the land for each of the twelve tribes to live in.

This sharing is God's detailed plan, which gave all beings their own place to carry out the meaning and mission of their existence and arranged it so that it would not cause chaos.

In light of this principle of dividing the realm of life, today's COVID-19 problem is the result of human invasions of habitats where animal viruses should exist. This is the consequence of breaking the fundamental principle of God's creation.

Examples of one organism intruding into another's territory have appeared repeatedly in human history. This is the case with colonial history, world wars and the racial conflicts around the world that are still taking place. Isn't all human conflict and injustice – colonial history, war, trade conflict, racial conflict, gender conflict, economic injustice – a phenomenon that occurs when one being dominates or seizes the unique position or rights God has given to another?

The norms God has given us are not just the norms of faith and theology. The term ecology is a combination of *oikos*, meaning household, and *logos*, which means the principle of knowledge in ancient Greek. Theologically, the universe is the *oikos*, or house made by God, and ecology is the logic in which the universe operates. What disturbs this order, this logic, is the ecological crisis. Today's climate change and outbreak of diseases such as COVID-19 came from the ecological crisis that disrupted the logic of the house made by God.

The term economy also originated from the same *oikos* root. Economy is a combination of *oikos*, meaning household, and *nomos*, meaning rule. Therefore, the economy is the rule and order of God's house. Economy is not about capital, production, consumption, finance, money-making or investment, but rather a rule that enables the lives of all family members making up the house. The real intention of this economy is distorted by modern capitalism and human greed; the skyrocketing housing prices, which are now shaking the foundations of Korean society, is also a phenomenon of this distortion. The house is a place to live, not a means of property accumulation, and breaking this rule of economics is leading to confusion.

Let's go back to COVID-19. Many things stopped with the advent of COVID-19. A keyword came up in my mind as I faced this unheard-of situation: repentance. *Shuv* is a Hebrew word meaning return; this is the root of *teshuvah* which means repentance or return to God.

The famous story of the fruit of the tree of knowledge of good and evil appears in Genesis III, and the way I see it, to desire and eat from the tree of knowledge of good and evil is to destruct the logic of God in reference to the ecological crisis. In Genesis I and II, after creation, God said all the fruits in the garden were free to be enjoyed by human beings ("We may eat of the fruit of the trees in the garden") except one He said not to touch the tree in the middle of the garden or there will be death: "You shall not eat of the fruit of the tree that is in the middle of the garden, nor shall you touch it, or you shall die." This means that human beings can develop nature considerably, but if they break the laws of ecology that God has planted in this universe, life will become impossible.

The COVID-19 incident is the outcome of human greed and arrogance that eventually broke the ecological order by crossing the boundaries of life given by God. Hence, repentance, return! If human beings do not turn away from colonialism, domination, and hegemonism that infringes on the existence and rights of nature, there will be no way to stop this cycle of tragedy. There were theories that if human beings don't stop destroying the ecosystem now, they will suffer from more natural disasters and serious diseases, and since then, the world really has suffered from numerous crises resulting from ecological destruction and diseases such as SARS, MERS, ZIKA, and now the all-stopping COVID-19 in the 21st century.

In the last year or so, a scientist working in Antarctica shocked us by warning that glaciers, even those which had never melted under any climate change, had begun to melt and would melt completely by 2030.[4] He stated that this would lead to a rapid rising of global temperatures and sea levels, putting survival on Earth in considerable risk. Ecologists believe that climate change has already crossed the Rubicon and is completely irreversible. Nonetheless, this world that is experiencing COVID-19 has no intention of stopping this ecological wreck and is still talking about economic activity.

My concern is that COVID-19 will not end easily and that if human beings do not immediately stop the ecological destruction, there could emerge a much stronger virus that could lead to an even more serious situation. There was a report that Bill Gates, who has donated enormous amount of money and is eager to

[4] See for instance in the Korean blog greenstart: https://blog.naver.com/greenstartkr/221998121817; also see: https://www.space.com/agu-antarctica-thwaites-glacier-future.

develop a vaccine for COVID-19, reportedly predicted that the disease that will follow COVID-19 will not be a type of coronavirus but a never before heard of disease that will lead to 30 million deaths within six months. Although I look into this phenomenon with a theological perspective and not complete accuracy, it seems that Bill Gates speaks with information. What is clear is that if we don't stop here, if we don't follow God's creation order here, there will be more serious diseases than COVID-19. We need to stop and turn around.

Humankind turning around from the current direction of civilisation and converting into a new life civilisation that aligns with God's creation principle has to be the New Normal. With the temporary suspension of church ceremonies, churches are questioning if online worship can count as true worship and offline worship services should be resumed at the risk of danger since offerings are decreasing. However, this is not what is important. What really matters is the prophetic mission of proclaiming to the world an urgent message of repentance: that we must restore the history of humankind, the economic activities of humankind, the science of humankind, and the whole life of humankind to God's creative order.

A Grand Direction for the Transformation of Future Human Civilisation

I believe humans should now shift their civilisation paradigm. Details should be viewed more deeply and systematically than there is room for here but, from broad perspective, I believe there are three points in terms of a shift in civilisation.

The first is that humans now have to live a life that is closer to the soil. Gyeongan Graduate University has been continuing to host a symposium since 2017 to study how humans should live in the fourth industrial revolution and the age of artificial intelligence. This is to find the meaning and place for human beings in this current age. In the first year of this symposium, I suggested that in the age of artificial intelligence, humans need to become much closer to the soil than to machines.

To divide world history largely into three equal parts, human beings concentrated on God until the Middle Ages. Since the Middle Ages, post humanism and reformation, we have so far focused on human beings. However, in the 21st century and beyond, humans must focus on soil or natural ecology. Artificial intelligence developers predict that artificial intelligence will achieve a singularity beyond humans in 2040 while ecologists see 2030 as a turning point in the ecological crisis. Nevertheless, Hollywood movies have already covered the prospect of a civilisation crisis beginning in 2020. The period between 2020 and 2040 is a time of divergence in which human civilisation must revolutionise the paradigm shift into entering life civilisation. The nucleus of this transition is centred on land, earth, and ecology.

The concentration on this land, earth and ecology, however, should be a new approach, repenting from the humanism of the past in which man reigned and ruled over nature. It must consider how nature and human beings will live in harmony with the right of life given by God. This is not to say that we should go back to more primitive times. Until now, modern civilisation had been running on industrialisation, but its limitations are finally being revealed, and it is necessary to emphasise getting closer to soil and the structure of life civilisation.

Secondly, humans must de-urbanise and restore small-scale village communities. The catastrophic impacts COVID-19 had in such a short period of time was due to globalisation and urbanisation because allowed the virus to spread and then flourish in each region. Although this has been the path to develop that humankind has walked thus far, industrialisation, urbanisation, and modernisation are the dilemmas of modern civilisation, in my opinion. Moreover, globalisation has created a "Development Pandemic" from this dilemma, which is now leading to an ecological crisis and the outbreak of diseases.

Sociologists have observed that the race to urbanise humankind will not stop until 2050. They estimate that more than half of the world's population will be centralised in cities by the middle of this century.[5] This would be a disaster. COVID-19 could be a small signal of what might occur.

We need to restructure society in a way as to spread out population and industries into rural areas and create small village communities. Gyeongan Graduate University created a village studies major in the Department of Social Welfare to study the academic basis for creating a village community in anticipation of this. However, perhaps people do not yet understand the importance of this as not many students are showing an interest. What is clear is that, in the future, the government should pursue a new social structure in which life on a small scale and life on a village unit are woven together. The Swaraj movement, which Gandhi advocated to lead an independent life against the British Empire, is needed.

I am not calling for the abandonment of cities. That would be unrealistic. The important point is that cities and villages must be developed in balance. There is a political capital relocation issue currently, but this does not end with a political capital relocation. The development of local villages determines the future.

Thirdly, it is necessary to compose an industrial structure map for the position of agriculture to return to an important position even if it is not the centre of the economy. According to ecologists, 70% of the area where humans live becomes a more ecologically healthy space when farming or pasture is secured. Of course, science must develop and various industries such as heavy industry, electronics et cetera must develop as well.

In the age of artificial intelligence, only 1% of humans who understand and deal with artificial intelligence are said to be needed. What will the other 99% do? 99 percent of human qualities and abilities will be simply redundant for the performance of most modern jobs.[6] In the age of artificial intelligence, those who understand and deal with artificial intelligence fully would be tiny minority and the majority of human beings will become a "useless class" as stated by Yuval Harari.[7] Instead of just saying that basic income should be given because human jobs are lost in the artificial intelligence era, society should allocate 1% of the population who handle artificial intelligence to take care of the industry and have the rest 99% lead a much more relaxed style of living.

Nevertheless, the core of the future depends on the food industry that guarantees healthy lives. There will come a day when the accessibility of healthy food will become a very important issue globally. In order to protect the future, we must design a future that centres life around agriculture. There are endless factors to think about creatively, not just regarding artificial intelligence, but to make life possible in the future of life civilisation. We really must think creatively from now on.

A Concluding Remark

The story ends by quoting a poem that has been widely mentioned on the internet written by a poet named Vivienne R. Reich.[8]

♤ Coronavirus' "Letter to Humanity" ♤
The earth whispered but you did not hear.
The earth spoke but you did not listen.

---

[5] See for instance: 'Two-thirds of global population will live in cities by 2050', UN states; in: https://www.cnbc.com/2018/05/17/two-thirds-of-global-population-will-live-in-cities-by-2050-un-says.html

[6] See: https://ideas.ted.com/the-rise-of-the-useless-class/

[7] See: https://post.naver.com/viewer/postView.nhn?volumeNo=7673204&memberNo=2367855; see also Yuval Noah Harari:,*Homo Deus: A Brief History of Tomorrow*. New York, Harper Collins, 2017.

[8] The following poem can be found in English and Korean language on her public blog: https://loveneverending.com/tag/vivienne-r-reich/ and: https://loveneverending.com/coronavirus-letter-to-humanity/; see also: https://www.youtube.com/watch?v=3Eqou1srkCc

The earth screamed but you turned her off.
And so, I was born…
I was not born to punish you…
I was born to awaken you…
The earth cried out for help…
Massive flooding. But you didn't listen.
Burning fires. But you didn't listen.
Strong hurricanes. But you didn't listen.
Terrifying Tornadoes. But you didn't listen.
You still don't listen to the earth when
Ocean animals are dying due to pollutants in the waters.
Glaciers melting at an alarming rate.
Severe drought.
You didn't listen to how much negativity the earth is receiving.
(…)
It was more important to get that latest iPhone than worry about what the earth was trying to tell you…
But now I am here
And I've made the world stop on its tracks.
(…)
I give you fever … as the fires burn on earth.
I give you respiratory issues … as pollution fills the earth air.
I give you weakness as the earth weakens every day.
I took away your comforts…
Your outings.
The things you would use to forget about the planet and its pain
And I made the world stop…
And now…
China has better air quality … Skies are clear blue because factories are not spewing pollution unto the earth's air.
The water in Venice is clean and dolphins are being seen. Because the gondola boats that pollute the water are not being used.
YOU are having to take time to reflect on what is important in your life.
Again, I am not here to punish you … I am here to Awaken you…
When all this is over and I am gone… Please remember these moments…
Listen to the earth. Listen to your soul.
Stop Polluting the Earth.
Stop fighting among each other.
Stop caring about materialistic things.
And start loving your neighbours.
Start caring about the earth and all its creatures.
Start believing in a Creator.
Because next time I may come back even stronger…

Suggestions for Further Reading

Park, Seong Won. "Towards Life-Enhancing Civilization". In Hope Antone, Wati Longchar, Hyunju Bae, Huang Po Ho and Dietrich Werner, Eds. *Asian Handbook for Theological Education and Ecumenism.* Eugene, OR: Wipf & Stock, 2013: Chapter 25, 218-225.

Oikotree Movement Website: Available at: https://oikotree.net/joint-struggle-movements-in-solidarity/

80. The Climate Justice Work of Casa in India: Perspectives, Challenges and Practice

Sushant Agrawal and Joycia Thorat[1]

> Soil is not our prison, it is our liberator. The soil is our meaning, and disengaging from the oil economy in a post-peak oil world means re-engaging with the soil and all of its life. All of its life include the ability of the soil to renew itself, the ability of the soil to provide for the needs we have, the ability of the soil to give us back the meaning of being human.
>
> Vandana Shiva

Introduction: Casa as a Pioneer of Climate Justice Work

The Church's Auxiliary for Social Action (CASA) is the key instrument and umbrella organisation for the social work of the Indian protestant and orthodox churches whose many unique characteristics make it exceptional. CASA evolved from the relief work committee of NCCI (National Council of Churches India), formerly known as CORAGS (Committee on Relief and Gift Supplies) in 1955. At the Triennial Assembly of the NCCI in October 1967, held in Shillong, CORAGS was reconstituted as Christian Agency for Relief and Social Action (CARSA), then to be changed into the Christian Agency for Relief and Social Action and Development (CASARD) in 1970 and ultimately the Church's Auxiliary for Social Action (CASA) in 1972. A conglomerate of 30 diverse denominations within the National Council of Churches in India today, CASA has cared for creation since its inception in 1947. As an ever-evolving and dynamic organisation, CASA is a pioneer in addressing climate justice work and environmental action, operating through its diverse bodies of many church denominations and ecumenical organisations in India.[2]

The first natural disaster addressed by CASA was the Bihar famine in 1966. NCCI organised a consultation to plan and execute relief work with the help of SCMI (Student Christian Movement of India) volunteers when J.P (Jayaprakash Narayan) set up the Bihar Relief Committee. Working with refugees and famine-affected people exposed CASA to ground realities. Therefore, by the end of the 1960s, CASA was actively involved in digging a variety of wells in villages, developing farmlands, assisting in agriculture and mobilising communities to work together. CASA is a pioneer in Disaster Mitigation and management; hence, recognising that India is prone to emergencies due to natural calamities like droughts, earthquakes, cyclones, and tsunamis, CASA set up an Emergency Department in the 1970s which focused on Disaster Management and Disaster preparedness.

In a national consultation in February 1977 held in Bangalore, the then Chairperson Paulose Mar Gregarious referred to CASA as a key player building up an extensive network of trained youth who can be catalysts in their societies for mobilising and organising laypeople for socially creative work. The WCC (World Council of Churches) Mission Team Visit who were sent to CASA in December 1977 stated that "CASA staff members, their 300 volunteers, and church leaders were operating cheerfully and efficiently in difficult circumstances." This also reflects the local churches that were active amid the floods and cyclones. Members of the church and many others readily responded with relief and the rehabilitation of those affected by severe calamities. In the 80s, the drought, the scarcity of drinking water, the increased use of irrigation

---

[1] Dr Sushant Agrawal is the Director of CASA and Former Moderator of Act Alliance.
Dr Joycia Thorat is Project Officer and National Gender Focal Point of CASA in India.

[2] The publication "'Mission Redefined' (CASA at 60 – Striving Towards Life in Fullness)" by Rev. Dr Soman Das has accurately documented CASA's efforts from the partition of India in 1947 to the Tsunami response work up until 2007

due to the loss of moisture in the soil, and groundwater evaporation led to CASA engaging in the *Water for Tomorrow Program*. CASA set up programs to train locals to assemble, manage and repair hand pumps and to strengthen capacities to mitigate. The priority was capacity building and mobilisation of communities. The *Integrated Rural Development Program* (IRDP) was a comprehensive program built to address development, capacity building and advocacy to be executed together with the local governance system. Between 1990 and 2005, CASA tackled numerous large disasters like the Maharashtra earthquake, Odisha super-cyclone, Gujarat earthquake, and tsunami. This was coupled with many minor calamities in which CASA has played a key assistance role having become an expert in adaptation, mitigation, disaster risk reduction and humanitarian assistance support (Preparedness, Mitigation, and Response).

CASA organised a consultation in July 2005 immediately after the Indian Ocean tsunami. The consultation participants affirmed and summed up: "the spectacle of the churches and CASA working together in a genuine spirit of partnership was a firm affirmation and clear manifestation of CASA as the specialised most effective instrument of churches in India with a mandate from church to pursue and fulfil the ongoing mission of Jesus in bringing life in full abundance to all." The 2006 Church leaders' consultation on the MDGs (Millennium Development Goals) was to reflect and evaluate the 8 MDGs. It is important to note that goal number 7 of the MDG Agenda was to *Ensure Environmental Sustainability*, which is set as a part of its intention to integrate the principles of sustainable development into country policies and programs and reverse the loss of environmental resources. The proportion of people without sustainable access to safe drinking water halved by 2015. A significant improvement in the lives of at least 100 million slum dwellers also was achieved by 2020. However, in the context of the plight of the poor, sufficient progress has not been made for those whose daily subsistence is often directly linked to the natural resources around them and affected by changing climate conditions. There is ample evidence to prove that CASA emerged as a pioneer in India, keeping this social organisation alive by paying attention to the needs of the community, especially with issues related to climate change.

Over the last 15 years, around the globe and the country, CASA's working environment has changed tremendously. From relief and rehabilitation (1947-67), need-based approaches (1967-87), issue-based approaches (87-97), rights-based organisation (1997-07), and finally moving into an orientation towards life in fullness (2003 to 2013) CASA is an organisation which continually adapts. The *fullness of life approach* has taken forward a holistic approach and transformational model integrating all creation. With the Paris Agreement of 1.5 degree Celsius (UNFCCC) limits to global warming pushing global communities on the urgency of care for creation, the launch of UN SDG Agenda (Sustainable Development Goals), the Sendai Framework and others have strengthened CASA's extensive experience of and focus on localised interventions which has fast-paced its engagement in its Climate Justice work. CASA's hallmark is its comprehensive and diverse approach to addressing climate justice. One of the immediate efforts by CASA at the national level was planting 10 lakh (1.000.000) of trees between August 2021 and August 2022 across India. This is done to increase the green cover and is part of CASA's Platinum Jubilee celebration. CASA West Zone has a green paper related to the ambitious plan of creating green jobs for rural youth, along with different faith groups, ecumenical organisations and churches with all green players and stakeholders in the country. CASA has several Climate Justice models already in existence in various parts of the country. In the following, we share a few models from the last decade:

Climate Smart Models of Casa

Model 1: Farmers schools in Himachal Pradesh (Uttarakhand)

Disaster statistics for mountain regions in Himachal Pradesh reveal a concerning trend of increasing occurrence of events. Agriculture has been affected the most by climate change. This has affected not only the crop patterns but also techniques and crop species due to weather changes, lack of correct information about the temperature, moisture, humidity of the land. The income of the farmers is being greatly affected in recent years as there are periods of low production. Therefore, it has become important for the farmers to know all about the factors of climate change, moisture, temperature, humidity of the land, changes in the weather and to carry out their farming activities accordingly.

Himachal Pradesh is prone to multiple natural and human-made disasters. Owing to its hilly terrain and fragile ecological systems, it is highly vulnerable to the impacts of climate change and climatic variability. There is strong evidence of an increase in the observed frequency and intensity of weather and climate-related hazards. Although the State has been undertaking several measures to set up the institutional framework for Disaster Mitigation (DM) as mandated by the DM Act 2005 as well as to strengthen the preparedness and risk reduction capacities, challenges still persist. The institutional framework and policy instruments to deal with climate change are still in its nascent stage and would require significant investment in the form of skilled personnel, empowered communities and financial resources. Given the huge capacity gaps of systems, processes and various stakeholder groups, exacerbated by climate change-related impacts and recurring disasters, a systemic approach towards long-term capacity building across governance levels and stakeholder groups is required. There is a significant increase in air temperature by about 1.6°C with winter warming at a faster pace. Further, at different altitudinal zones in Himachal Pradesh, the rate of increase in maximum temperature is found to be higher at higher altitudes compared to lower altitudes. An increasing trend of rainfall has been observed at higher altitudes and a decreasing trend in lower latitudes as a consequence.

To tackle the above situation an automatic weather recording station has been set up by the CASA at Diyar in Kullu Block of district Kullu, Himachal Pradesh. This centre was established on 22nd October 2020 under the Climate Farmers School Program. Under this weather centre, 700 farmer families of about 20 villages have been connected: They are being made aware about climate-sensitive farming and are being motivated towards this new approach. The weather recording station is being operated by Chetna Samiti Kullu in association with CASA, Local Van Samridhi, Jan Samridhi Community Users Group, while Agriculture Department and Krishi Vigyan Kendra, Bajaura are providing technical support. Meteorological data sharing is done automatically and every hour data is recorded in the weather recording station. After every fifteen days, the above data is shared to the farmers associated with the station online and by other means. Guidance is also being taken from time to time by sharing the above data with Agriculture Department and Kisan Vikas Kendra.

There is also Climate Sensitive Agriculture and Income Augmentation, as 270 farmers have been made aware about the importance of the said weather station and the data received from it. On the basis of this data, local farmers have been motivated to take up various farming activities.

To make the public more aware, representatives and farmers familiar with the operation of the weather centre (Members of the Legislative Assembly of Banjar, Mr. Surendra Shourie, Vice-Chairman of Panchayat Samiti Kullu, Mr. Yashpal Dadwal, Zilla Parishad member Jyeshtha Mrs. Rukmani Devi, local public representatives and farmers of two panchayats Diyar and Manjhli) have visited the weather station and appreciated the campaign. During these visits, they have been made aware of the operation and techniques of the weather station.

The key stakeholders are farmers of the surrounding villages, Chetna Samiti Kullu, CASA, Agriculture Department, KVK, Bajaura, GV Pant Himalayan Environment and Sustainable Development Institute, Mohal, Forest Department and Panchayat Raj Departments. After setting up the station, farmers are getting information about humidity and temperature along with weather information from the relevant area. This helps the farmers to better gauge the proper timing for crops to be planted and results in better crop Management Practices.

The weather station has helped the farmers to plan measures against frost, to decide time of transport and the storage of grains. It has also helped in planning the farming activities like land preparation and sowing etc. It also helped in forecasting the onset of disease and insect attack through insect and disease models and to take appropriate measures to protect livestock against rains and hailing.

Model 2: Capacity-Building and Strengthening Disaster Risk Reduction in West Bengal

India is one of the signatory states (2nd October 2016) towards the implementation of the Sendai Framework. The concept of Disaster Risk Reduction is focused on the approach of "understanding the risk", taking appropriate "risk reduction measures" where "capacity building of the vulnerable section" is core component of action.

Understanding the risks of the vulnerable is essential for any development planning. With this thinking, UNICEF – Department of Disaster Management, Government of West Bengal, CASA, State Inter Agency Group (IAG) and its district level lead organisation took the initiative to start a discussion on "*Child Centred Disaster Risk Reduction*" for Government Officials of Department of Disaster Management as well as for the District IAG Members.

The purpose of the capacity building program was to enhance the capacity of and empower the grassroot organisations for promoting Child Centric Disaster Risk Reduction (CCDRR) and Climate Change Adaptation (CCA) strategies to reduce the adverse effects of climate change and other disasters.

The process followed training and capacity building which remains an all-time need in Disaster Risk Reduction (DRR). Especially, considering the multi-hazard profile of the state, the level of interventions required at various stages to minimise the risk and engagement of different stake holders addressing the varieties of underlying causes are among of the other objectives of continuous efforts in capacity building. The State Disaster Management and Civil Defence Department from the Government of West Bengal are accountable to ensure that all key stakeholders engaged in the field of disaster management, directly or indirectly, are putting their efforts together to build the capacity of the community on DRR, those are treated as the first responders in any disaster situation. In this context, a state level meeting was called up at the Principal Secretary level on 17th February 2017 to review, co-ordinate and consolidate the capacity building efforts by different stakeholders. Representatives of UNICEF and State IAG (Secretariat-ship is shouldered by CASA), Defence, National Disaster Response Force (NDRF), Police, Fire and Disaster Management Department, State Disaster Response Force (SDRF), Administrative Training Institute (ATI) and key line departments were among the stakeholders. Taking this opportunity, UNICEF committed to support CASA in organising the training on a "Child Centred Disaster Risk Reduction" at the regional level in partnership with the State Inter Agency Group (IAG)-West Bengal.

The project benefited 29 Blocks in 4 districts with 400 schools and adjacent 400 villages (in Malda, Murshidabad, Purulia & South 24 Parganas) of West Bengal in 2020. Putting together the goals, objectives and experiences of UNICEF and CASA, the project was developed to strengthen the Disaster Risk Reduction (DRR) with a child-centred approach in the state. This project also technically supports the State and selects District Disaster Management Departments/ Authorities to take necessary action for reducing disaster risk to the children and their supporting systems. The facilitation was also taken by CASA staff members capacitated on Disaster Risk Reduction.

During the implementation of the program, CASA established working relationships with Government Departments in the State of West Bengal as well as in the districts.

The achievements of the project were quite notable in that the government departments, school teachers, line departments and gram panchayats all came forward and really understood the need of the disaster risk reduction and co-ordinated with CASA to give a new shape to the risk reduction and preparedness aspects. The community and students at school learnt about life-saving skills and prepared disaster risk reduction plans. CASA team members and volunteers gave special attention to Child Protection in Emergencies (Pandemic) during this period. A multi-hazard training module developed which incorporated COVID-19 protocols and was shared with the Department of Disaster Management and Civil Defence and IAG members.

CASA conducted a Rapid Visual Survey of 100 Amphan (cyclone Amphan) affected government schools in South 24 Parganas and the study report was shared with the Department of School Education, Government of West Bengal along with 262 model school disaster management plans to the "Chairman School Education Department of West Bengal".

CASA's findings and recommendations on the status of school safety and the status of students during the pandemic is highly appreciated by the State Disaster Management and Civil Defence Department and, at a high-level decision of State Government Authorities, CASA and UNICEF have been given the responsibility to take the process forward from April 2021 onwards. A decision taken by the State Government, it will institutionalise "Comprehensive School Safety and Security Program" in 63,700 government schools (sponsored and affiliated) across the state of West Bengal. As an implementing partner, CASA's role will be to train all the teachers and stakeholders on Comprehensive School Safety and Security Program (CSSSP) in the State to the concerned institutions and officials.

Model 3: Conserving Forest Through Seed Balls in Chhattisgarh

It's important to conserve forests which are part and parcel of the forest people's lives and livelihoods. CASA has initiated steps to conserve the forests in Chhattisgarh in order to meet the crisis and increase awareness regarding the same. The seed ball vegetation program in Chhattisgarh acts as a protector of the environment. It aims to conserve forests and the indigenous communities in the area. Active engagement in forestry activities by the people is a constructive approach to protect the earth. Seed bombing or seed ball vegetation is an activity which has been initiated in 16 villages of Chhattisgarh. The motive behind this is to increase forest cover which also benefits forest animals. The seed balls are made of a variety of seeds mixed with cow dung, cow urine and clay, which are then dried for 15 to 20 days. Through increasing forest cover, this project will help to combat the ill-effects of global warming. This way of growing the forests is gaining popularity and momentum in tribal areas and rural India. This activity helps safeguard villages and preserve the native forest communities. It has strengthened the relationship between nature and humans. Chhattisgarh – being a state with a large number of forest dwellers and whose sustenance is directly connected to the forest and its produce – provided CASA with the chance to offer some intervention on sustainable livelihood models. Lac cultivation and marketing is one of the other interesting business model CASA Chhattisgarh has developed which is providing income as well as protecting the forest, as the following quote from tribal tradition argues: "we are not defending nature, we are nature defending itself."

Model 4: Green Jobs, Sanitary Pads and Organic Farming in Maharashtra and Gujarat

The CASA West Zone is spearheading the green initiative through its various interventions. A Green Paper is being prepared there to address a localised just transition from non-renewable energy sources to renewable green jobs which will provide an income for the rural community in Maharashtra and Gujarat where CASA is operational (2021 to 2030).

Another part of this green initiative relates to sanitary pads, a monthly requirement to maintain menstrual hygiene, are often sold in markets which are not very healthy and are also made from non-biodegradable materials They are often unaffordable for rural poor adolescent girls. These girls then mostly stop schooling, unable to cope with this added requirement. Special efforts are made to train adolescent girls on menstrual hygiene with special support to prepare and use sanitary pads made of comfort cotton which is healthier, bio-degradable and cost effective.

In disasters including COVID-19, most relief organisations include sanitary pads purchased from the market as part of the relief kit. In the Mumbai floods in 2007, a large amount of plastic and sanitary pads led to choking the drainage which, in turn, exacerbated the urban flood disaster. Keeping this in mind, CASA West zone has initiated a project of training, manufacturing, promoting and supplying cloth sanitary pads to support clean environment and livelihood support for young village women. In Maharashtra, the state with the highest number of farmer suicides, CASA initiated two programs (Farmer's Suicide and Mitigation Program in Beed District and Comprehensive Food Security Program in Yavatmal District) in the last decade to address farmers' distress. Training on organic farming by introducing organic pesticides and organic manure with low-cost agriculture techniques, organic seed supply, tree plantations, are all parts of the capacity building and are key interventions under this project. Using nine different locally available leaves and organic material pesticides. which are prepared locally and supplied to farmers in an affordable price, has reduced the debt of farmers significantly and reduced the pressure to buy chemical pesticides which are bad for health and high on cost. Similarly, natural composts are prepared, marketed and trained for local levels which has been a huge benefit to the community. This learning has spread to different districts and other long-term program areas of CASA. CASA also promoted Gramin Vikas Karyakartha Prathisthan, a self-help group which undertakes local agro business ventures to support farmers and farm-dependent marginalised Dalit communities to earn more. The movement of organic farming is growing in CASA's program areas as the farmers understand the reliability and sustainability, its cost effectiveness and related health factors. Organic farming is also providing a steadier income for the local communities. Mini forest creation and tree plantations to increase the green cover are undertaken locally along with communities supporting local care for creation.

Conclusion

Lynn White once stated that our present science and technology are so tinctured with traditional Christian arrogance towards nature that it would be hard for the ecological and economic crisis to be resolved in that way. In the current economic system, the benefit often goes to a small minority in power while the majority is left with residual harm. Ecological devastation and global warming are injustices arising from misuse of God's creation. This invites us to a comprehensive ecological conversion. Indeed, we need a new holistic reformation – leading to repentance on all levels of our life and a critical reviewing of our ways, how we have acted towards the earth. We need a true metanoia, a reversal and renewal of our minds and inner attitudes to see creation with new eyes and to become motivated to transform our lifestyles to achieve ecological justice and social justice for all. The WCC in its General Assembly in Busan 2013 said " victims of climate change are the new face of the poor […] when creation is threatened in this way". Churches are called to speak and act as an expression of their faith commitment to life, justice and peace. A creation whose fragile balance has been upset calls on all of us to speak out and act for life, justice and peace and help restore its integrity.

We find this thought endorsing Vandana Shiva's argument in her classic work, *Soil Not Oil*.[3] "In a time of changing climates and millions going hungry, what is important is sustainable, biologically diverse farms that are most resistant to disease, drought and flood".[4] Therefore, it is noted by Shiva, "the solution to climate change and the solution to poverty are the same."

Eco-feminist theologians identify the roots of climate change as the hierarchical structures of domination and the dualistic thinking on the human relationship and earth. Re-thinking theology that facilitates ecological healing and liberation is the eco-feminist contribution. A Christian eco-feminist theology of creation demands a radical re-thinking of all our cosmic and cultural expressions which calls for a conversion. Liberation Theology expresses faith in a God who hears the cry and the anguish of the poor. Today, nature is the new poor and the climate victims sustaining life in these conditions need more focus.

The urgency of caring for our home has been highlighted by activists, theologians and UN bodies. Caring has been conventionally gendered as a women's task but care has to inform every aspect of public life – be it in the sphere of politics, in economy, in religion and the like. Women need to be included in the decision-making. This ethics of care will help forge new forms of affective and life-sustaining relations with the nonhuman world. To conclude, let us quote Kochurani Abraham, a feminist theologian: "Climate change, in spite of all its disastrous consequences can still be a *kairos*, a decisive and grace-filled moment in our evolutionary story of human becoming. It is a crucial phase that invites us to a core conversion experience, which could liberate us from hierarchical and dualistic thinking patterns and make us grow with other life forms on this planet. It is a decisive and critical moment that calls us humans to evolve with the rest of

[3] Vandana Shiva, *Soil Not Oil: Environmental Justice in an Age of Climate Crisis*. Boston, MA: South End Press, 2008.
[4] Shiva, *Soil Not Oil.*

creation, not as masters or mere stewards but as Eucharistic inter-beings, who break themselves to feed one another, who is willing to die that the other may live. Perhaps, this holy impatience is the challenge posed before us by climate change".[5] CASA is doing exactly the same.

CASA is calling the church and the larger community to engage with nature to restore life in all its fullness and for all.

Suggestions for Further Reading

Abraham, Kochurani. "Women and Climate Change: Beyond Gendered Prescriptions". Unpublished Paper presented at a conference on Climate Change organised by the Federation of Asian Bishop's Conference (FABC), Hua Hin, November 2019.

CASA. "The Green Guardians: Climate adaptation in the far-flung villages of Rajasthan". *CASA in Action Newsletter*, 131(3), (July-September, 2019). [Available at: https://casa-india.org/upload/Newsletter-sep.pdf], [Last accessed: 21st February 2022].

Das, Somen. "Mission Redefined: CASA at 60". New Delhi: CASA, 2007.

Shiva, Vandana. *Soil Not Oil: Environmental Justice in an Age of Climate Crisis*. Boston, MA: South End Press, 2008.

Van Voorhis, Bruce, Ed. *Light to our Path: A Compilation of Biblical Reflections.* Kowloon, Hong Kong: Asia Pacific Alliance of YMCAs, 2018.

——. *Revisiting the Reformation*, Kowloon, Hong Kong: Asia Pacific Alliance of YMCAs, 2017.

[5] Kochurani Abraham, "Women and Climate Change: Beyond Gendered Prescription", Unpublished Paper Presented at conference on Climate Change organised by Federation of Asian Bishops Conference (FARC), Hua Hin, Nov 2019.

81. Ecological Crisis in Myanmar: Churches' Involvement in Creation Care

Ciin Sian Khai and Suang Khen Pau[1]

Introduction

The ecological crisis is affecting all nations and ecosystems. Human beings are interrelated with nature and yet our current trajectory acts like we are not. World leaders are failing to protect our fragile earth.[2] Myanmar, sandwiched between India and China, is a beautiful country in Southeast Asia with diverse landscapes and is endowed with rich biodiversity and plenty of natural resources, especially mineral deposits. Despite being relatively untouched until recently, Myanmar is also facing environmental crises as a result of ecological exploitation.

This crisis directly affects all living and non-living things. Therefore, all people regardless of nation, faith, gender, and class have to take part in protecting our common habitat. As Christians are called to protect, preserve and develop nature for their survival as well as for the survival of plants and animals, the question is "how can the churches better take part in responding environmental crises in Myanmar?" This paper attempts to highlight some of ecological crises Myanmar faces while also looking at recent responses by Christians to those problems. Better stewardship of nature is a prerogative.

Dimensions of the Ecological Crisis Commonly Found in Myanmar

The environmental problems facing people in Myanmar today will be pointed out as follows.

Deforestation

Myanmar, particularly in the hills, still practices the traditional agricultural system known as *taungya*.[3] Trees were slashed in one forest area, burnt and then people plant crops.[4] Moreover, a shifting cultivation system is still practiced in many regions in the country. Thus, most of the cultivators who do not receive subsidies from the centralised government destroy their natural resources, cut down trees in the forest and overuse marginal lands for their own survival.[5] Since shifting cultivators tend to have no money to buy food sold in the villages, "they cut trees, burn, encroach and grow crops in forested areas."[6] Therefore, it is claimed here that the main reason for deforestation in Myanmar is the pattern and system of shifting cultivation.[7]

---

[1] Ciin Sian Khai, Dr theol. is Academic Dean, Zomi Theological Seminary, Kalaymyo, Myanmar; Pastor Suang Khen Pau is the Assistant Pastor of Emmanuel Baptist Church in Kalaymyo. He earned a Master of Sacred Theology from Dallas Theological Seminary.

[2] Italy's climate minister, Robert Cingolani accepted the criticism of Greta Thunberg and said, "Ms. Thunberg raised a serious problem, we were not credible in the past." BBC News, "Italy climate minister accepts Thunberg's 'blah, blah, blah' criticism" 29th September 2021 [Available at: https://www.bbc.com/news/world-europe-58743515], [Last accessed: 20th February 2022].

[3] Taungya is shifting cultivation or slash and burn farming. When the soil fertility depleted after two to three years, farmers shifted to another place and repeated this cycle, coming back to the same plot 20 to 30 years later. See Khin Maung Kyi, Ronald Findley *et al.*, *Economic Development of Myanmar, A Vision and A Strategy* (Singapore: Singapore University Press, 2000): 83.

[4] Kyi *et al.*, *Economic Development of Myanmar*, 83.

[5] San Thwin, *Deforestation Analysis in Eastern and Western Myanmar* (Göttingen: Cuvillier Verlag, 2003), 3.

[6] Thwin, *Deforestation Analysis*, 3.

[7] Thwin, *Deforestation Analysis,* 36.

Moreover, due to the decade-long military rule in the country, the Forest Department played no protective role to counter this deforestation.[8] In 1988, the Myanmar army took power in a coup, neglecting "forest protection in the different regions. Therefore forest administration became a very difficult task" because the army did not control the forestlands properly.[9] As a result, not only Myanmar's rich forests, including its tropical rainforests have degraded but coastal areas and wetlands have also ecologically deteriorated over the last decade. It is estimated that the annual rate of deforestation is 2.1 per cent of the total forested areas of the country.[10] Samuel Ngun Ling, a Myanmar theologian, says that it is the "cutting down of trees for legal or illegal exports to foreign countries, and devastating the forest by the wide-scale burning through the practice of the slash-and-burn agricultural system in rural areas, (which) has led to the change of climate."[11]

Karen Zau Nan, a lecturer at the Myanmar Institute of Theology, takes Kachin Land of Myanmar as an example. He says that over the last decade all forests and jungles in the land have been destroyed because of development, road and hydroelectric power projects.[12] Furthermore, Jangmaw Naw Hpung says that "the local authorities misused the natural resources for their survival. Because of lack of income, the local authorities were forced to sell this resource to China [...] dozens of big Chinese trucks are loaded with piles of pine logs and rough-hewn lumber from Myanmar."[13] In addition, there are mining projects, hydroelectric power projects, dam and road construction which result in even greater deforestation.[14] With regard to the main reasons for deforestation in Myanmar, Samuel Ngun Ling remarks:

1. Myanmar relies more heavily on wood fuel than on electricity or gas energy. Wood fuel accounts for 80% of the total energy needs of the country and the growing demand for wood fuel is at a rate of 1.1% annually.
2. Teak products or logging by commercial timber companies for national commercial purposes, whether in legal or in illegal frameworks, have caused serious damage to the sustainable capacities of Myanmar forests. The annual rate of only teak logs (not including hardwood logs) is estimated to be about 230,000 cubic tons per year so that logging becomes one of the major causes of forest degradation. It is often carried out exploitatively by politically elite groups in the name of the country's economic development.
3. Large-scale construction projects, such as the building of bridges, highways, dams, and irrigation systems, cause depletion of forest capacity and damages the natural environment.
4. The slash-and-burn method of cultivation practiced by tribal/ethnic rural communities is another cause of deforestation [...] It is generally believed that about 23% of the forested area is affected by this practice of shifting cultivation.
5. [...] The conversion of the forestland into commercial cash cropland, conversion of opium fields into crop fields, and the mining of rubies and gold have also caused deforestation.[15]

---

[8] Kyi *et al.*, *Economic Development of Myanmar,* 83.
[9] Thwin, *Deforestation Analysis*, 31.
[10] Kyi *et al.*, *Economic Development of Myanmar,* 80-81.
[11] Samuel Ngun Ling, "Towards the Integrity of God's Creation", *RAYS MIT Journal of Theology* 3 (February 2002): 3.
[12] Karen Zau Nan, "Mission as Multidimensional: A Mission Paradigm for Christian Churches in Myanmar", *RAYS MIT Journal of Theology* 7, (January 2006): 117.
[13] Jangmaw Naw Hpung, "Environmental Issues in Kachin Region", *Engagement,* Judson Research Center Bulletin, Myanmar Institute of Theology, 4 (June 2005): 103.
[14] Thwin, *Deforestation Analysis*, 1.
[15] Samuel Ngun Ling, "Environmental Challenges and Earthkeeping Activities in Myanmar", *Missio Dei: Journal of Evangelism and Mission* 2, (February 2008): 27-28.

Soil / Land Pollution

Myanmar is an agricultural country, where 70% of the total population depends on the agriculture sector, living from paddy cultivation and some other crops.[16] In Myanmar, one can easily find agricultural shops, markets, and even street-side mini-shops selling toxic chemicals, pesticides, insecticides, and chemical fertilisers. For the growth of their rice, maize, beans, and other vegetables, farmers – especially those in the rural areas in Myanmar – used these chemical fertilisers, pesticides, and insecticides without knowing their side effects.[17] Seeing only the growth of the product, cultivators used pesticides that destroy organisms and "kill earthworms which play an important role in fertilising and aerating the soil."[18] In the past forty years, especially nature all over the world has been poisoned and Myanmar is no exception.[19] Moreover, as the name of the national development project continued, ecological crises arise associated with the "degradation of land, pollution of soil and water, displacement of local people, the disintegration of land gravity power, and destruction of various ecosystems of the natural soil and land."[20]

Furthermore, fishing and mining are also the factors that cause ecological suffering in the country. In Myanmar, some fishermen used electric shock techniques to catch fish and other species living in the river which endangered and damaged the ecosystem of the river.[21] Gold hunters use mercury in gold mining some of which flow into the river or are released as particles in the air. Mercury damages human memory and causes sickness by damaging the nervous system destruction. The problem is that people just took gold from the water and left the mercury in the water. Since mercury is a very strong poison and lasts for a long time, it can pass from one living thing to another as it moves up the food chain.[22] Moreover, large scale construction, irrigation, hydroelectric power projects, mining projects in the name of national development cause soil erosion which is then offset by utilising toxic chemicals, pesticides, insecticides, and chemical fertilisers to maintain short-term yields. This all is destroying the soil of Myanmar.

Water Pollution

Myanmar is a fertile land with alluvial and meadow soils. As an agrarian land, she uses water resources for paddy cultivation, poultry, fish farming, and mining as well. Nowadays, people are facing water pollution as a serious life threat as a result of the exploitation of nature. In the hilly regions and uplands of the country, the water supply from small fountains, streams, and rivers is contaminated with toxic chemical substances due to the excessive use of pesticides, and fertilisers by the farmers in their slope farms.[23] Some local people practice a kind of poisonous fishing by Dichloro Diphenyl Trichloroethane (DDT) or poisonous leaves/roots in the rivers and streams.[24] Fishing by poisonous techniques, electrical shock, and an explosive bomb is a major threat to the extinction of aquatic animals in Chin State.

In the mining areas, especially in Kachin State and Shan State, where valuable minerals such as gold, silver, jade, ruby, and sapphire, et cetera are produced largely, a substantial amount of mercury and water is used for refinement daily. As a result, all the nearby rivers and streams are polluted with mercury, and eventually even the clean blue colours of the rivers have become dirty and red. At the same time, the farmers

---

[16] *Data Collection Survey on Agriculture Sector in the Republic of the Union of Myanmar*, Final Report, December 2013, Japan International Cooperation Agency (JICA), Sanyu Consultants Inc, RD Jr. 13-109, 122.
[17] Samuel Ngun Ling, "Environmental Challenges and Earthkeeping Activities in Myanmar", 30.
[18] Simon Pau Khan En, "Building An Eco-Just Society", *Engagement*, Judson Research Center Bulletin, Myanmar Institute of Theology 4 (June 2005): 56.
[19] Simon Pau Khan En, "Building An Eco-Just Society", 57.
[20] Samuel Ngun Ling, "Environmental Challenges and Earthkeeping Activities in Myanmar", 30.
[21] Jangmaw Naw Hpung, "Environmental Issues in Kachin Region", 101.
[22] Jangmaw Naw Hpung, "Environmental Issues in Kachin Region", 102-105.
[23] Samuel Ngun Ling, "Environmental Challenges and Earthkeeping Activities in Myanmar", 32.
[24] Iang Khen, "Environmental Education: A Myanmar Context", *KOINONIA: Journal of Christian Studies* 1 (2011): 24.

use tis same contaminated water for their paddy and vegetable cultivation. Subsequently, the chemical substances are unknowingly in daily food. "When people drink contaminated water and eat chemical substance-contained foods, they suffer a lot from high blood pressure, premature births, cancers, diabetes, brain damages, and other kidney and lung-related diseases."[25]

There were reports that "chemical substances are excessively contained in the ready-made foods, cookies, potato chips, snacks, and other playing toys for kids imported from China." "Dyed mushrooms, adulterated chili powder, and even fake eggs were imported from China."[26] The problem is that the Myanmar government does not have any monitoring system or refinery system for those foods and toys imported via the borders. Moreover, the overuse of monosodium glutamate, chemical preservatives, dyeing colours, and other flavour additives in every soup and meal is a serious problem for health in Myanmar today.[27]

Unfortunately, neither a monitoring nor a controlling system for food has yet been effectively implemented in the country. Indeed, water pollution in Myanmar leads to the danger of the extinction of rare water species, especially Irrawaddy dolphins. Except for municipal wastes, wastes of mining, mills, and factories, Myanmar does not have many industrial hazardous, radioactive and nuclear waste. However, these existing wastes still make the water so polluted and filthy resulting in the widespread of malaria, dysentery, and poor quality of drinking water. According to Samuel Ngun Ling, the problem facing the city dwellers in Yangon and Mandalay is both lack of systematic sewage disposal systems and the lack of recycling factories to clean up the waste.[28]

Air Pollution

In Myanmar, the reasons causing air pollution include smoke from slash and burn agriculture in the hilly regions, the use of firewood for cooking, wanton setting of fire in the jungle, plastic and other garbage (especially its incineration), and also carbon dioxide from vehicles and industries. As 70 per cent of the whole population of Myanmar live in rural areas, they are using huge amounts of firewood for cooking, which adds to air pollution. Because of air pollution, the people of Myanmar suffer from rhinitis, coughing, asthma, pneumonia, and other lung-related diseases. This also causes the extinction of wildlife and species, the migration of birds and animals into safe zones and multiple worsening effects on the ecosystems. It is observed that rare animals like pangolins and hornbills are in danger of extinction in Chin State. Since 2011, Myanmar has been experiencing a rise in air pollution in urban cities such as Mandalay and Yangon. Thus, the World Bank reported in 2017 that "air pollution in Myanmar causes more than 45,000 deaths, which is higher than in any other countries in the region; almost twice the average as for South-East Asia."[29]

Environmental Impacts of International Industries and Foreign Investments

No one can deny the fact that the natural resources of Myanmar have been exploited in the name of national development. Since a system of market-oriented economy was introduced by the military regime in 1990, natural resources like teak, pine, and hardwoods, and mineral resources like gold, ruby, natural gas, and crude oil have become the victims of that newly implemented economic system. Foreign investments, especially the Chinese companies and western companies like TOTAL and Chevron, have heavily invested in Myanmar

---

[25] Samuel Ngun Ling, "Environmental Challenges and Earthkeeping Activities in Myanmar", 32.
[26] Nyein Nyein, "Use of Chemicals in Food a Growing Worry for Burmese Consumers" 23rd August 2013, *The Irrawaddy* [Available at: https://www.irrawaddy.com/news/burma/use-of-chemicals-in-food-a-growing-worry-for-burmese-consumers.html] [Last accessed:20th February 2022].
[27] Nyein, "Use of Chemicals in Food".
[28] Samuel Ngun Ling, "Environmental Challenges and Earthkeeping Activities in Myanmar", 33.
[29] World Bank, "Myanmar Country Environmental Analysis", 11th June 2019. *World Bank Website*. [Available at: https://www.worldbank.org/en/country/myanmar/publication/myanmar-country-environmental-analysis], [Last accessed: 20th February 2022].

which does benefit multiple economic sectors; This is being done mainly in mining, the construction of dams and irrigation systems, logging, natural gas, and crude oil, and hydroelectricity. For instance, the 3.6 billion dollars of the Chinese-led dam project called the Mytsone Hydroelectric project, located at the confluence of the Mali Hka and Nmai Kha rivers of the Irrawaddy River in Kachin State, was suspended by the Thein Sein government in 2011 due to the protests and boycott of the people of Myanmar, as it will flood an area the size of Singapore.[30] If constructed, no doubt the dam will cause huge environmental problems, displacement of the local people, loss of thousands acres of farmland, wildlife, and species and their habitats, and it will also advance "the geopolitical interests of the Chinese government." It will also pollute the Irrawaddy River, the life artery of the region, and cause a problem for water transportation as it is a major waterway of the country. As has been pointed out, China still is the biggest foreign investor in Myanmar with more than 15 billion dollars direct investment in 126 businesses in 2018.[31]

Letpadaung Copper Mine owned by a Chinese company, Wanbao Copper Mining along with Myanmar's military-linked Myanmar Economic Holdings, created a serious social problem for the local people in the Sagaing region as it caused "confiscation of land, the disappearance of farmlands, and suppression against social activists and environmentalists, and air pollution." In February 2017, Amnesty International reported that "the project was plagued by human rights abuses citing the laws to harass activists, environmental damages, the use of repressive laws to harass activists and villagers opposed to the mine, and called on the Myanmar government to suspend operation."[32]

The 40-mile long Yadana natural gas pipeline owned by TOTAL and Chevron, in co-operation with Myanmar Oil and Gas Enterprise, destroyed rainforests and displaced several villages but the product still was sold to Thailand. The people of Myanmar do not benefit from this huge project but rather become the victims of these foreign-led economic development projects. Thus, there is an ironic joke among the people that "Myanmar is rich for its neighbouring countries." Benefitting only the foreign investors, Anna May Say Pa pointed out the negative aspects of such development programmes as follows:

> Five dams are planned on the Salween River which would lead to flooding and displacement of villagers and loss of livelihood. Rare species like the Irrawaddy dolphin face extinction. The floodplain of the planned Weigyi Dam would inundate the lands of the indigenous groups, the Yintalai. Widespread logging and mining in indigenous areas have devastated natural resources. Logging has led to substantial deforestation, destroying fauna and flora and the biodiversity of these areas.[33]

The Rainforest Action Network reported that "8,000 or 10,000 square kilometres are destroyed so Myanmar has one of the highest national rates of deforestation. Rampant jade and gold mining using mechanical methods have led to pollution and environmental degradation."[34] Myanmar is one of the world's biggest producers of jade but its mines have faced several accidents; especially of landslide, which killed 162 mineworkers in Hpakant in a single day on 2nd July 2020.[35] The excessive excavation of jade and other mineral

---

30 Reuters, "Factbox: Myanmar suspends controversial Myitsone Dam", 20th September 2011, *Reuters Environment.* [Available at: https://www.reuters.com/article/us-myanmar-dam-factbox-idUKTRE78T15S20110930?edition], [Last accessed: 20th February 2022].

31 Tom Fawthrop, "Myanmar's Myitsone Dam Dilemma", 11th March 2019, *The Diplomat*, [Available at: https://thediplomat.com/2019/03/myanmars-myitsone-dam-dilemma/], [Last accessed: 20th February 2022].

32 Oliver Slow, Win Zar Ni Aung and Ei Ei Mon, "Left Behind by the Letpadaung Copper Mine", 5th June 2019, Frontier [Available at: https://www.frontiermyanmar.net/en/left-behind-by-the-letpadaung-copper-mine/], [Last accessed: 20th February 2022].

33 Anna May Say Pa, "Women in Prophetic Ministry," *Engagement: Bulletin of the Judson Research Center for Interfaith Studies, Dialogue and Current Issues,* 13 (August 2021), 36.

34 Anna May Say Pa, "Women in Prophetic Ministry," 36.

35 BBC News, "Myanmar jade mine landslide kills 160", 2nd July 2020, *BBC News Website* [Available at: https://www.bbc.com/news/world-asia-53260834], Last accessed: 20th February 2022].

resources caused soil degradation, water pollution, and landslides. To solve the pollution, the following big questions need to be acted upon:

1. How can the slash and burn cultivation in the hilly regions be replaced with a better agricultural system?
2. How can a responsible government provide the need for electricity or gas to the rural areas instead of using firewood for cooking?
3. How can the church give self-awareness to those who are setting fires recklessly and trashing plastics at will?
4. How can carbon dioxide be reduced in urban areas?

The Myanmar Churches' Involvement in Creation Care

As Christians are stewards of the environment (Gen. 2:15), the churches and Christian organisations in Myanmar are doing environmental care within their capacities. The active projects and involvement of Christian organisations and institutions in earth-keeping movements in Myanmar will be described as follows:

Myanmar Baptist Convention

Christians in Myanmar accept that "Nature and environment are symbols of God's grace, love and mercy."[36] Thus, they regard our mother earth as "God's gift, our life, and our common shared home."[37] Thus, loving and caring for our mother earth is essential for everyone and it is, they believe, God-given responsibility, realising that integrating "ourselves into the complex web of eco-life" is of great significance. In view of the desperate need to preserve, protect and develop nature and its resources in Myanmar, churches have each taken steps in different directions, all working to contribute to fighting the ecological crisis.[38]

Churches and regional conventions under the umbrella of the Myanmar Baptist Convention have taken steps on ecological concerns as part of their ministry, but with limited programmes and activities. In 2000, for instance, the Myanmar Baptist Convention started on the "Advanced Leadership Seminar" yearly. As the MBC's initial step was seen as part of the leadership development programmes, many Baptist leaders from different rural areas came together at its Holistic Leadership Training Institute. In this Institute, courses on ecology, development, and leadership skills were taught as continuing theological education, aiming at increased awareness in the Churches for the stewardship of God's creation. Further, Church members are given environmental awareness for "sustainable development, reforestation, soil conservation, and new methods of agricultural technology and farming."[39]

Chin (Zomi) Baptist Convention

On 5th April 1994, the 68th Executive Committee meeting of the Chin (Zomi) Baptist Convention took place in the village of Zaungnak, Chin State, Myanmar.[40] In this meeting, a historic declaration on environmental protection was passed known as the Zaungnak Declaration,[41] to help change rural people's cultivation system from shifting cultivation to SALT (Sloping Agricultural Land Technology) Farming system.[42] This Declaration reads as follows:

---

[36] Samuel Ngun Ling, "Environmental Challenges and Earthkeeping Activities in Myanmar", 39.
[37] Samuel Ngun Ling, "Environmental Challenges and Earthkeeping Activities in Myanmar", 39.
[38] Samuel Ngun Ling, "Environmental Challenges and Earthkeeping Activities in Myanmar", 39.
[39] Samuel Ngun Ling, "Environmental Challenges and Earthkeeping Activities in Myanmar", 39.
[40] Zomi Theological College, *Chin Church History* (Falam: Zomi Theological College, 2007), 369.
[41] See Samuel Ngun Ling, "Environmental Challenges and Earthkeeping Activities in Myanmar", 45-46.
[42] Samuel Ngun Ling explains the three steps in SALT FARMING, it goes: "There are three steps in SALT FARMING: SALT- I, SALT-II, AND SALT-III. SALT-I represents Sloping Agricultural Land Technology; SALT-II as Simple Agro-livestock Technology; and SALT-III as Sustainable Agro-forest Land Technology. This farming system, already experienced with success in the Philippines, is said to have protected farmlands and forests from the hazards of climate

Statement of Confessions

1. We confess that the eternal God who created and holds sovereign power over everything has given human beings the authority to act as custodians over all other creations (Gen. 1:28). In the same way, we the Chin people confess that we are entrusted by God with a great task of looking after and protecting all things of nature that lie on the western mountain range of the Union of Myanmar.
2. We acknowledge, however, that ever since the days of our forefathers, trees have been set on fire for the slash and burn method of farming. As the result at present, forests have been destroyed; natural water is drying up gradually, soil is becoming less fertile, agricultural production is falling, the weather is becoming inclement, and animals and fish are becoming scarce in the mountainous area of the Chin state.
3. We therefore see the need to do away with the destructive method of slash and burn farming and change to the systematic method of terrace farming known as "SALT=I" (Sloping Agricultural Land Technology). We believe this method provides for the growing of small plants within the contour lines, which makes the soil fertile. This method also prevents soil erosion, conserves topsoil, supplies natural fertiliser, prevents the growing of weeds, protects moisture and therefore protects the environment and increases agricultural production. Besides, this method is cheaper, demanding less labour and is sustainable with one's own labour.
4. We discover that instead of turning domestic animals loose to graze, we should apply the simple Agro-livestock technology (SALT-II). If we put fences around our garden and grow plants for animal feed, we will be able to take care of our household needs and even do commercial livestock breeding, thereby promoting and sustaining the livelihood of the Chin peoples. This will not only prevent trees from being cut down and forests burnt, resulting in more barren mountains and unpredictable weather but also in the application of such methods as Agro-Forest Land Technology (SALT-III). Replacing trees makes the whole Chin region green and beautiful.
5. We find, soon after the above-mentioned methods of changes are undertaken, that we should give priority to the growing of trees and plants that are suitable to our environment and also learn to consume more of those home-grown products. Instead of trying to grow plants which are not suitable to our climate, we should concentrate on growing plants systematically that produce better yield in our region. According to the Chin people with the view to promoting their living standard and liberating themselves from the threat of social problems and upholding the great responsibility entrusted to human beings by God to care for His creation.[43]

But the Chin (Zomi) Baptist Convention does not only have a statement of confessions, but also has a *One Hundred Year Plan* as a response to *deforestation* as well as for eradicating poverty, based on the vision that in one hundred years Chin Land will be an admirable and abundant land. This *One Hundred Year Plan* has six steps:

1. Educating the Masses, 2001 to 2010;
2. Practical On-site Investigation and Research, 2011-2020;
3. Transition from Shifting Cultivation to Permanent Cultivation, 2021-2050;
4. Accumulating Income for Productions and Sales, 2051-2080;
5. On to Progress and Wealth, 2081-2099;
6. Completion of One Hundred Year Plan and Thanksgiving, 2100.[44]

change, water shortage, soil erosion, deforestation, and devastation. This system has been practiced in Hakha, Falam and Tedim townships of Chin State and in the Kale Valley of Sagaing Division with good success." See Samuel Ngun Ling, "Environmental Challenges and Earthkeeping Activities in Myanmar", 40.

[43] Samuel Ngun Ling, "Environmental Challenges and Earthkeeping Activities in Myanmar", 45-46.

[44] Zomi Theological College, *Chin Church History* (Falam: Zomi Theological College, 2007), 369.

Zomi Theological College (ZTC)

The Zomi Theological College (ZTC) was founded in 1953 as the theological department of the Zomi Baptist Convention.[45] ZTC (Now Chin Christian Institute of Theology or CCIT) has the Lailun Project[46] in line with the One Hundred Year Plan of Chin (Zomi) Baptist Convention, aiming at a theological focus from redemption to creation. On 20th February 2008, the ZTC founded "Post Eden Drive" and its motto is "Our People Our Land". With this project, the day-dream of ZTS is "from redemption to creation." It goes:

- To magnify God through use of created land (earth);
- To safeguard forests and animal lives with conservation in mind;
- To use contemporary method of cultivation and selection of seeds so that there may be 3 or 4 crops (harvest) per year;
- To use nearby flowing rivers and streams in various manner for development;
- To preserve and refurbish the places from which the Chins originated.[47]

The Post Eden Drive has five organic parts namely, development, education, health, environment, and network. Of these, the environment has six factors for implementation, namely, Forest Conservation, Wildlife Conservation, Nature Reserve, Smokeless Tourism, Tissue Culture, and Mini-hydro Electricity.[48] As the ZTC dedicated to Post Eden Drive, the ZTS students have been trained for church ministry and Christian Service. When the ZTC's students finish their course works and celebrate Graduation Service, they have self-dedication and service commitment to the ZTC's Applied Theological Education:

- I firmly state this vision, Post Eden Drive, PED for the becoming of our God-given land and our being of God-assigned people, on theological ground and practical necessity;
- I will work with my community for implementation to the practice of the diet menu, and for demonstration of the threefold sin and the threefold salvation;
- Hence, this self-dedication and service commitment, for our People Our Land, OPOL; God, help me.[49]

Other Christian Organisations

Other Christian organisations like the Myanmar YMCA and YWCA have become actively engaged in environmental-related activities, such as environmental care and awareness training.[50] Myanmar's YMCA is actively engaged with training related to environmental awareness and also "runs projects supporting sustainable livelihoods and community empowerment."[51] In addition, the YWCA of Myanmar has environmental awareness programs about plastic pollution. Their main concern and questions are: "Do you care about the earth? Do you care about the environment where you are living? Do you know that the enormous usage of plastic bags causes harmful pollution to our environment?"[52] There are also some organisations like Global *Zomi* Alliance, which awaken the people to protect nature and to be seriously concerned about the environmental crisis.[53] Some churches also observe Environment Day in their worship

[45] Zomi Theological College, *Chin Church History,* 107.

[46] "This place is in the Falam area (of Chin State, Myanmar) near Sunthla Village where Lailun Lungpuk was situated and farther due north to it." See Zomi Theological College, *Chin Church History*, 239.

[47] Zomi Theological College, *Chin Church History*, 239.

[48] Do Sian Thang, *Do Sian Thang A Nuntakna leh A Nasepna* (Yangon: Grace Printing House, 2015), 231.

[49] Do Sian Thang, *Do Sian Thang A Nuntakna le A Nasepna*, 139.

[50] Samuel Ngun Ling, "Environmental Challenges and Earthkeeping Activities in Myanmar", 39.

[51] World YMCA, "Inside YMCA Myanmar – three beacons of resilience, service, and hope", 24th September 2021, *World* YMCA, [Available at: https://www.ymca.int/inside-ymca-myanmar/], [Last accessed: 20th February 2022].

[52] YWCA of Myanmar Facebook Event: "Environmental awareness about plastic pollution" Saturday 18th May 2019 *Facebook* [Available at: https://www.facebook.com/events/2025937514195643/?active_tab=discussion], [ast accessed: 20th February 2022].

[53] There was a conference organised by Global Zomi Alliance 11th-14th December 2011 in Kalaymyo, where Do Sian Thang presented a paper titled "Ecology and Environment Concern", by which he urged the people to have a heart of loving nature by protecting, preserving and developing as true Christians. He raised a question, "Will there be a more

service in which special items and activities take place for congregations to engage in environment care. Some theological institutions include ecology as an elective subject in their academic curriculum.[54] Furthermore, although the 98% of Kachin population who belong to Christianity were influenced by the traditional teaching of Christian doctrine, which is about human dominion over nature, and therefore cut down almost all sacred forests in Kachin State, it has changed nowadays, and many Christian villagers "have re-established the so-called 'safety forest' fringing the entire habitation". "[T]his safety forest receives community protection, including the traditional punishment of any offender."[55]

Conclusion

Solving the ecological crisis is a big challenge for the churches in Myanmar as it demands co-operation among different religions, churches, government, and all people regardless of age, class, and gender.[56] In Myanmar, ecological problems should not only be seen as a matter only of non-human creature issues but rather as the comprehensive social-political agenda of the people,[57] as "it combines economics, politics, ethnicity, identity, and spirituality."[58] According to the National Sustainable Development Strategy of Myanmar, "deforestation, loss of biodiversity, urban air pollution, soil erosion, water contamination, and water-borne disease are the shared environmental issues which are caused by land clearance, excessive mineral extraction, vehicular congestion, and emissions, deficiencies in urban infrastructure, unmanaged industrial and municipal effluents."[59] As the ecological suffering of Myanmar leads to the suffering of all peoples living in the country, the following points are advised to be taken into action for building an eco-just society: reconstructing a new theology from an ecological perspective, formulating a relevant spirituality in coping with nature, promoting inter-religious co-operation for facing the environmental problems, and co-ordinating with the State collectively.[60]

Moreover, it is necessary for Christians in Myanmar to express "ecological concern in their practical way of living or spirituality" as spirituality in the Burmese context must be focused on the ecological issues of the country.[61] Christians in Myanmar need to rethink the ecological crisis as a challenge to their very Christian mission and to the theological formulation of their traditional understanding of theology and mission.[62] Only then can the churches in Myanmar be the nucleus and catalysts for taking initiatives in building an eco-just society in Myanmar.

---

serious sin than emitting Chlorofluorocarbon (CFCs)?"

[54] Myanmar Institute of Theology is one of the first theological schools which includes ecology as an elective subject in their teaching curriculum, where the authors have earned their advanced theological education. Chin Christian Institute of Theology and Chin Christian College have also included ecology as an elective subject in their school's curriculums.

[55] Jangmaw Naw Hpung, "Environmental Issues in Kachin Region," 104.

[56] Simon Pau Khan En, "Building An Eco-Just Society", 64.

[57] Joel Za Hlei Kap, "Introducing Ecological Theology in Myanmar", in *Ecotheology: A Theological Resource Book* (Yangon: Cherry Yeik, 2017), 3.

[58] Anna May Say Pa, Christopher Day, "The Karens: Claiming the Rights of Identity and Self-Determination", *Engagement: Judson Research Center* 3 (December 2004), 33.

[59] UN, "Natural Resources Aspect of Sustainable Development in Myanmar", http://www.un.org/esa/agenda21/natlinfo/countr/myanmar/natur.htm#mountains. [Last accessed: 10th September 2015].

[60] Simon Pau Khan En, "Building An Eco-just Society", 61-63.

[61] Simon Pau Khan En, *Nat Worship: A Paradigm for Doing Contextual Theology in Myanmar* (Yangon: Judson Research Center, 2012), 118-119.

Suggestions for Further Reading

Data Collection Survey on Agriculture Sector in the Republic of the Union of Myanmar. Final Report, December 2013, Japan International Cooperation Agency (JICA), Sanyu Consultants Inc, RD Jr. 13-109.
En, Simon Pau Khan. "Building An Eco-just Society". *Engagement*. Judson Research Center Bulletin, Myanmar Institute of Theology, 4 (June 2005): 54-65.
___. *Nat Worship: A Paradigm for Doing Contextual Theology in Myanmar*. Yangon: Judson Research Center, 2012.
Hpung, Jangmaw Naw. "Environmental Issues in Kachin Region". *Engagement*, Judson Research Center Bulletin, Myanmar Institute of Theology, 4 (June 2005): 99-106.
Kap, Joel Za Hlei. "Introducing Ecological Theology in Myanmar". In *Ecotheology: A Theological Resource Book*. Yangon: Cherry Yeik Publication, 2017: 1-40.
Khen, Iang. "Environmental Education: A Myanmar Context". *KOINONIA: Journal of Christian Studies* 1 (2011): 24-36.
Kyi, Khin Maung, Ronald Findley, R.M. Sundrum, Mya Maung, Myo Nyunt, Zaw Oo. *Economic Development of Myanmar, A Vision and A Strategy*. Singapore: Singapore University Press, 2000.
Ling, Samuel Ngun. "Environmental Challenges and Earthkeeping Activities in Myanmar". *Missio Dei: Journal of Evangelism and Mission* 2 (February, 2008): 27-50.
___. "Towards the Integrity of God's Creation." *RAYS MIT Journal of Theology* 3 (February 2002): 1-12.
Nan, Karen Zau. "Mission as Multidimensional: A Mission Paradigm for Christian Churches in Myanmar". *RAYS MIT Journal of Theology* 7 (January 2006): 106-123.
Say Pa, Anna May. "Women in Prophetic Ministry". *Engagement: Bulletin of the Judson Research Center for Interfaith Studies, Dialogue and Current Issues* 13 (August 2021): 34-40.
Say Pa, Anna May and Christopher Day. "The Karens: Claiming the Rights of Identity and Self-Determination". *Engagement: Judson Research Center* 3 (December 2004): 33-42.
Thang, Do Sian. *Do Sian Thang A Nuntakna le A Nasepna*. Yangon: Grace Printing House, 2015.
Thwin, San. *Deforestation Analysis in Eastern and Western Myanmar*. Göttingen: Cuvillier Verlag, 2003.
Zomi Theological College. *Chin Church History*. Falam: Zomi Theological College, 2007.

82. The Campaign for the Rights to Access Clean Water in Bangladesh

David Anirudha Das[1]

Introduction

Bangladesh is a country with a population of 166 million people, which has made significant progress with tremendous achievements in various socio-economic indicators. Bangladesh is recognised as a Least Developed Country (LDC), while governance and services to public sectors are still facing big questions as they have been for the last two decades. Some basic infrastructure providing water supply and sanitation have been improved. However, according to the WHO and UNICEF in 2019, only 65% of the people have access to safe water and only 57% people have access to minimum hygienic sanitation facilities. Still, there are many huge challenges in the country, which are inseparably linked with many other problems, and which all need to be addressed. Almost all of the causes of the lack of safe and clean water are questions of human rights, which essentially are addressed by the campaign to establish and protect the proper rights for access to clean water.

Identifying Key Challenges

a. Effects of Climate Change: Bangladesh is vulnerable to frequent environmental disasters due to combined effects of climate change, which is creating countless negative effects on all kinds of water bodies in the country. The quality of sources for drinking water is greatly diminished due to contamination and pollution and by frequent natural and human-made disasters as well.

b. Salinity: Salinity in Bangladesh's coastal areas has caused a grave lack of fresh water, as salinity in the water of those areas has now reached over 20 parts per thousand, but the human body can only tolerate five parts per thousand. Women in coastal areas need to go miles to collect a pitcher of safe drinking water every day. Worsening weather extremes that bring floods, storm surges and cyclones are contributing to increases of salinity, salt-water intrusion.

c. Arsenic Contamination: Many areas have no reliable access to safe drinking water due to arsenic contamination. More than 40% of children under five years die annually from preventable diseases related to unsafe water. People need to dig much deeper to get arsenic-free water. Close to many big rivers and the Bay of Bengal, the amount of arsenic material in the groundwater is also very high.

d. Excessive Extractions of Groundwater: Groundwater levels in all big cities and in 70% of the irrigation lands areas are falling down drastically as a result of excessive extraction to meet the growing demands of irrigation, urbanisation and industrialisation. As a consequence, much longer pipes are needed to go deep down for drinking water while the levels of surface water are also reduced.[2]

e. Unplanned Urbanisation and Industrialisation: Because of the haphazard and unplanned processes of urbanisation and industrialisation, the pollution of water and also of the air is increasing, specifically in city areas.

f. Riverbank Erosion and Landslide: Every year during the rainy season, riverbank erosion of big rivers and landslides in hilly areas are widespread phenomena. Because of this every year, hundreds of people

---

[1] Reverend David Anirudha Das is General Secretary of the National Council of Churches in Bangladesh, Dhaka, Bangladesh. Email: nccb.gs@gmail.com; www.ncc-b.org.

[2] Water politics, Article from Wikipedia, the free encyclopaedia, [Available at: https://en.wikipedia.org/wiki/Water_politics], [Last accessed: 2nd November 2021].

become highly distressed, often are internally displaced to the big cities as they search for livelihoods in a place where many have no access to safe drinking water.

g. Decreasing Ground Water Levels Due to Drought: During summer, people in comparatively dry areas, especially the north face major challenges in finding potable water because of increased cases of drought and decreasing ground water levels, which endangers both agricultural and domestic and industrial purposes.

h. Uncontrolled Population: The uncontrollable growth and increasing density of the population is causing additional needs for irrigation thereby adding to excessive extraction of groundwater causing additional lack of drinking water in urban slums and in coastal areas.

i. Geo-Political Effects: There are eight big rivers in the country which are trans-boundary or inter-state rivers shared by neighbouring countries. The sad thing is that these rivers and their water have become issues of intense political conflicts. Access to them is being "weaponised" by dams and barrages, which has a heavy impact on access to drinking water and ecosystems in the drought-prone area in Northern Bangladesh. Vice President Dr Ismail Serageldin has stated: "Many of the wars of the 20th century were about oil, but wars of the 21st century will be over water unless we change the way we manage water".[3] Once the surface water sources have dried up, there is an acceleration of droughts and during summer there is no water in the river, while during rainy seasons there are many floods every year.

j. Unfair Water Trade: For last few decades, there is a new trend, as in other commodities in the country, where water become a profitable and commercial trading business in the country and many have difficulties in paying the prices for bottled water, although access to safe water is critical to the health of many families in Bangladesh.

The Campaign for the Basic Right to Clean Water

Like other essential elements of life available from nature, water is a fundamental means of life for everybody. God created the earth, offering water for all, thereby providing water as both a loving gift but also a basic right for all human beings and for the whole of creation. In the following, some basic aspects of the Right to Access to Water are mentioned, which guide our combined efforts and interventions in the national water campaigns.

Ecotheological Aspects

Water means Life, given as an abounded natural resource from God. Therefore, water issues are an unavoidable part of our faith in God. Spirituality and ethical questions are interrelated and there is much to share between Christians and people of other faiths. As church and faith-based organisations, it is our imperative to ensure that "water for life" and "water for all" should have a clear priority in human rights work. Like all other human rights, the biblical principles on water affirm the need for equal access to this essential resource and the principles of non-discrimination, affordability, transparency and accountability of water usage.

As Christians, we are called to serve and stand with vulnerable people in regard to water as their right to life, health, and livelihood in situations marked by scarcity, conflicts, occupation and discrimination (Is. 1:17; Amos 5:24). We must remember that water is a blessing to be treasured, to be shared with all people and creation, to be protected from generation to generation, as it is a fundamental right which has a deep spiritual meaning. As Benjamin says, "If you know the water is safe, drink deeply and give thanks. Pray for the health

[3] This statement made by Ismail Serageldin, the Vice President of the World Bank, was quoted often, also in: Dr. Daniel Connell (Crawford School of Public Policy, Australian National University), 'Water wars, maybe, but who is the enemy?', April 2013, in: https://globalwaterforum.org/2013/04/10/water-wars-maybe-but-who-is-the-enemy/.

of this and all springs. And let the spring remind you: the task of reformation calls us to remember and clear out the life-giving springs where God's mercy and goodness have been promised to us".[4]

The Bible is also aware of human conflicts over water in ancient times. In Genesis 26:12-35, the first account of such a conflict over water does not only reflect the grave concern of water for their life as human beings, but also for all domestic animals and for planting. When Isaac planted his crops that year, he harvested a hundred times more grain than he planted, for the Lord blessed him. He became a very rich man, and his wealth continued to grow. He acquired so many flocks of sheep and goats, herds of cattle, and servants that the Philistines became jealous of him. So, the Philistines filled up all of Isaac's wells with dirt. These were the wells that had been dug by the servants of his father, Abraham. Finally, Abimelech ordered Isaac to leave the country. "Go somewhere else," he said, "for you have become too powerful for us."

The whole Bible thus expresses the significance of water not only as a deep spiritual truth, but also as an ethical and practical issue as Amos 5:24 states: 'But let justice roll on like a river, righteousness like a never-failing stream!" Thus, we are called to contextualise the biblical demands in our contemporary campaign for water justice.

Legal Aspects

Article 18(A) of the Bangladesh Constitution says: "The state shall endeavour to protect and improve the environment and to preserve and safeguard the natural resources, biodiversity, wetlands, forests, and wildlife for the present and future citizens". It clearly denotes that we have a legal basis for water to be regarded as a public right. On this basis, there are several policies by the government of Bangladesh related to water. But our present legal frameworks and policies in favour of water are still quite limited. We still lack various legal and policy-related safeguards that could eliminate the existing barriers to water accessibility.

The Water Policy and Public Rights policy of the government of Bangladesh constitutes access to safe water for the public and it is a collective right. The Sustainable Development Goals (SDG 6), which Bangladesh has ratified, states that we must ensure the availability and sustainable management of water and sanitation for all. In 2002, the UN recognised that the right to water itself is an independent right since it is one of the most fundamental conditions for survival. In accordance with resolution 64/292, the United Nations General Assembly explicitly recognises the human right to water and sanitation and acknowledges that clean drinking water and sanitation are essential to the realisation of all human rights, which are still in a weak or low profile in terms of implementation in Bangladesh.

In November 2010, the UN Committee on Economic, Social and Cultural rights adopted its general comment number 15 on the rights to water (R2W) stating that the human right to water entitles everyone to sufficient, safe, acceptable, physically accessible and affordable water for personal and domestic use. That means that the right to water denotes not only the availability of sufficient water but also availability of quality water. Only the combination of the quantity and quality dimension comprises the complete right to water.

The Bangladesh Water Act 2013 (BWA) is a framework law to integrate and co-ordinate the water resources management in the country. The Water Act aims at a new integrated approach to the protection, improvement and sustainable use of countries, rivers, lakes, estuaries, coastal waters and groundwater. This comprehensive legal framework needs to be properly implemented to face the growing challenges regarding the rights to access to water and the sufficient protection of water bodies and other resources in Bangladesh.

Aspects of Climate Change

According to the National Adaptation Program of Action in Bangladesh, it is a common conviction that water-related impacts of climate change are increasingly the most critical change factors for Bangladesh – largely

[4] Benjamin M. Stewart, "Stream, Flood and Spring: Water Renewing the Earth and the Church." 1st April 2016, *Living Lutheran* [Available at: https://www.livinglutheran.org/2016/04/stream-flood-spring/], [Last accessed: 22nd February 2022]..

related to coastal and riverine flooding, but also related to the enhanced possibility of winter (dry season) droughts in certain areas.

Some of the key issues related to climate change are inland and coastal flooding, low flows and droughts, changes of the riverbed level due to sedimentation and changes in morphological processes due to seasonal variation of water levels and flows as well as effects on groundwater. Most of the expected impacts on water resources will be aggravated due to infrastructure developments, such as extensions of the road communication networks and the construction of flood protection works.

Scarcity of freshwater is one of the major impacts of climate change in coastal Bangladesh. While contributing very little to global warming, Bangladesh is suffering a lot from its consequences. This is a mirror to the existing injustices and it is unethical for people to be denied their rights to water. Therefore. there is a strong commitment for an advocacy campaign for rights to water (R2W).

Economic Aspects

One of the problems in Bangladesh is that water and sanitation are not the subject of a separate budget line, but spread over the budgets of different institutions, which makes it difficult to assess how much of the government funding is actually spent on water and sanitation, and for what purposes. In the Annual Development Program (ADP) of the Bangladesh Planning Commission, the government's development investment in water supply and sanitation ranges between US$50 million and US$101 million from fiscal years 1994-1995 to 2000-2001, which needs to be increased with sector basis allocation for proper implementation.

From 1994-1995 to 2000-2001, the water resources subsector, including flood control and irrigation received much more funding than the water supply and sanitation sector. On average, US$74 million or US$0.55 per capita have been spent per year. In 1996-1997, the investment for water resources was more than four times as high as the amount provided for water supply and sanitation. As BWA 2013 confesses: "The National Water Policy of 1999 addresses some of the crucial challenges faced in relation to water management. Some of the topics covered by this policy include accessibility of water, users' responsibility, siltation and erosion, deterioration of water quality, decentralisation, and privatisation. Apart from the NWP, we have various other policies for water management".[5] So, from an economic point of view, there is much to do in terms of the advocacy for the campaign on water

Spelling Out the Rights to Water Campaign

The experience on the ground has shown that transformational interventions by marginalised people's participation on the ground are the most effective means for a Rights to Water Campaign. In the following, there are some relevant voices and actions from the ground on the Water Campaign (R2W).

NCC Bangladesh: Inter-Faith Peacemaker Teams

Since her inception, the NCC Bangladesh was closely involved with interfaith peace building activities to bring communal harmony and to ensure combined efforts for addressing contemporary socio-religious, ecological and economic issues. Thus, people co-operating between faiths on the ground have become the main actors to bring changes from the bottom level up.

For last five years, local inter-faith people have organised themselves as Interfaith Peacemaker Teams (IPTs) to raise questions. At present, 35 organised IPTs are bringing the whole community together with a focused mission on water and crosscutting issues.

[5] Bangladesh Water Act 2013, is a framework Law to integrate and co-ordinate the water resources management in the country. Resources Planning Organization, ExCo of National Water Resource Council.

Church members are playing an effective role in the campaign by hosting different church activities based on contemporary theological thoughts in line with the SDGs and policies of the government of Bangladesh. Some specific initiatives like pulpit preaching, Bible Studies, publications and workshop/seminars on the issue are used to change the mindset of the congregation and of other people of faith.

Christian Commission for Development in Bangladesh

This Commission is a Christian development organisation partnering with Brot für die Welt and other ecumenical bodies actively engaged with different faith communities in the country for holistic development. They launched a project in 2012 called Lighthouse in three coastal locations aiming at "improving resilience of the most vulnerable peoples". This project has achieved some major successes for the communities by providing improved infrastructure for clean water supply. The Lighthouse had an component which was called "Technical Solution and Community Centric Management: An Effective Solution to Fight the Water Crisis". It relates to the campaign for clean water by the following:

Household-based Rain Water Harvesting: Rainwater harvesting systems have been introduced widely along the south western coast of Bangladesh, especially after cyclones Sidr (2007) and Aila (2009). Although different types of water storage systems are available, the large plastic tanks are the most popular. So far, 200 household-based and two community-based rain water harvesting plants have been established in the project areas on cost-sharing basis with their beneficiaries. Here, household-based tanks are provided to families, who live far away from surface water sources. For instance, Halima, a mother of two schoolgirls, lives outside the embankment, at least five to six kilometres away from the nearest fresh water source. The Lighthouse provided her a household-based rainwater harvesting plant of 1000l capacity. Availability of safe drinking water thus has improved the health of the family, so that the daughters attend school more regularly.

Community-based Rain Water Harvesting: The community-based water harvesting plant at the Char Lathimara Union ensures water security for 36 families. These families were severely affected and displaced by Cyclone Sidr. Before establishing this water harvesting plant, the families relied on pond water, and the women very often used saline water. Now, the plant, with 6 tanks of 30 000l capacity, secures access to fresh water. The beneficiary families formed a committee with eleven members and balanced representation of men and women to discuss and decide on user-fees, maintenance, tank cleaning etc.

Pond-Sand Filter Technology for Clean Water: Pond-sand filter (PSF) technologies have been introduced in the Lighthouse project areas to clean the pond water. Usually, a 70-square-feet (7ft high x 10ft deep) sand-gravel layer is placed in a cemented tank next to a fresh water pond. Water from the pond is pumped by a hand tube-well and filtered through the sand gravel column. The filtered water at the bottom of the layer is fit for consumption. If someone wants to take a pitcher of filtered water, they first have to pump the same amount of pond water into the PSF. A community-based beneficiary committee looks after the smooth operation of PSF, which includes tidiness of ponds and their management, cleaning of PSF and maintenance of the hand pump tube-well. So far, the Lighthouse Project installed six new PSFs and repaired 49 non-functional PSFs in the project areas. The Lighthouse Project also helped re-excavate sixteen community ponds for PSF installation. Currently, the PSFs provide drinking water to more than 70% of the families and 100s of neighbours in the project areas.

De-Salinisation Plant for Saline-Free Fresh Water: The Lighthouse Project installed a desalinisation plant with a capacity of 1000 litres per hour in remote coastal villages. This plant uses a reverse osmosis process to de-salinise the water. This kind of treatment is required when the salinity is too high to drink the water. The plant has ended the drinking water scarcity of at least 3000 people living in Vamia area. In months of acute water crisis, other people living in a radius of ten to twelve-12 kilometres come to collect water from this plant. Quite often, local water vendors also collect water from this plant, and sell it to families living far away for an affordable price, managed by 11 members of the Community Team.

Water Safety Plans for Urban Slum: Several innovative teachers and students of Rajshahi University, with the help of the Government of Bangladesh and NGOs, organised the Water Safety Plan (WSP), which was carried out for safe drinking water supply to the urban slum community in Rajshahi City Corporation keeping their health hazards in mind. The population of this area is 2384 lakhs where 82% have very poor economic status and face recurring health hazards from waterborne diseases. Measures have been taken such maintaining proper distance between pit latrine and HTWs, constructing platforms in safety tanks of latrines, washing water supply pipelines and HTWs after water logging in the rainy period, chlorinating supply water from different sources to protect and free it from possible contamination by pathogens.

BMDA Rainwater Harvesting: The Barind Multipurpose Development Authority (BMDA) under the Ministry of Agriculture (MoA), Government of Bangladesh (GoB) has played an important role in the area for water resource management for domestic and agricultural use of clean water. There is a proverb for the drought-prone water stressed Barind area, "Barind is the land where life is written in water." Integrated Water Resource Management (IWRM) following the Bangladesh Water Act (BWA) 2013 and implementing its pilot model through the Rain Water Harvesting (RWH) technique is an effective scientific outcome. The total harvested amount of rainfall and runoff water can fulfil 71% of the total clean water demand from household use and agriculture. Moreover, the implemented RWH schemes reduce pressures on groundwater withdrawal and provide benefits to farmers, particularly women in their domestic uses, for pisciculture, duck rearing et cetera, through 4R (Reduce, Reuse, Recycle and Restore) principles of IWRM. Beneficiaries are happy about having fresh water.

KOINONIA is a Christian Organisation which has initiated an effective program on access to clean drinking water in the Hill Tracks areas entitled "Improvement of Health Condition of Ethnic Minorities in Chittagong Hill Tracts" (WSECD) since November 2015. The outcomes, amongst others, include people having access to clean drinking water in their immediate surroundings and also to different technological options for collecting water for drinking purposes.

The Ecumenical Water Network is a unique initiative to work effectively on water issues advocacy in the World Council of Churches. It is comprised of churches and church-related organisations who promote the preservation, responsible management and equitable distribution of water for all, based on the understanding that water is a gift from God, a common good and a fundamental human right. The Ecumenical Water Network is committed to the human right to water and to the goal of no longer ignoring the disastrous impact of bottled water on the environment and the well-being of many women, men and children worldwide. There are several campaign initiates taken by EWN to promote the human rights issue of water, which greatly encouraged churches and many faith-based organisations in Bangladesh to work towards the solutions of the water crisis and establish water justice.

Conclusion

As a Church, we are called to stand with the people on the ground who are struggling for their right to water. We must advocate for the most vulnerable as they defend their rights to life, health, and livelihood. We must remember that water is a blessing to be treasured, to be shared with all people and creation, to be protected for future generations and the creation itself. Jesus asked for water from the Samaritan woman, not only for a spiritual symbolic significance of eternal life, but also his request had a material dimension. Thus, we see that fresh water sources are essential for human life (Jn. 4:1-26).

The problems with water both in our country as well as globally are so giant, that sometimes one might feel that our struggles are like that of David and Goliath. In the struggle, we may feel small like David. But just as David knew that God was with him, the interdependence with God and with friends globally give us confidence that we can win like David in the attempts to restore the access and quality of water as it designed by God and should be pursued for His glorification in the years to come.

Suggestions for Further Reading

Allison, M.A., S.R. Khan, S.I. Goodbred Jr, S.A. Kuehl. "Stratigraphic evolution of the late Holocene Ganges-Brahmaputra lower delta plain". *Sedimentary Geology* 155 (2003): 317-342.

International Water Management Institute. *Banking on Groundwater in Times of Change.* Colombo, Sri Lanka: International Water Management Institute, 2010. [Available at: https://doi.org/10.5337/2010.240], [Last accessed: 23rd February 2022].

Bangladesh Water Pollution Control Board. *Bangladesh Drinking Water Standards*. Dhaka: BWPCB, 1976.

Institute of Water Modelling. "Project Brief on Groundwater Model Study for Deep Tube Well Installation Project in Barind Area". Draft Final Report. Dhaka: Institute of Water Modelling, 2006.

Rasul, M.T. and M.S. Jahan. "Quality of Ground and Surface Water of Rajshahi City Area for Sustainable Drinking Water Source". *J. Sci. Res.* 2(3) (2010): 577-584.

Richards, L.A. *Diagnosis and Improvement of Saline and Alkali Soils*. USDA Agricultural Handbook No. 60. Washington DC: US Department of Agriculture, 1954.

Stewart, Benjamin M. "Stream, Flood and Spring: Water Renewing the Earth and the Church". 1st April 2016. *Living Lutheran.* [Available at: https://www.livinglutheran.org/2016/04/stream-flood-spring/], [Last accessed: 23rd February 2022].

WCC Ecumenical Water Network. *Together for Water.* Newsletter. Le Grand-Saconnex, Switzerland: WCC, January 2021. [Available at: https://www.oikoumene.org/resources/documents/wcc-ecumenical-water-network-newsletter-january-2021], [Last accessed: 23rd February 2022].

World Health Organization. *Guidelines to Drinking Water Quality.* 1st Ed. Geneva: World Health Organization, 1983.

83. The Eco-Diakonia Movement in Sulawesi Culture and Religion: Moving Together to Strengthen Our Diverse Communities in Contexts of Disaster

Junita Gereja Toraja, Ade Nuriadin, Irna Satigi[1]

Our families live side by side with nature. We grew up as a family of farmers and we were raised with a strong knowledge of nature, about harmonization of human relations and the interaction with the environment. Our life with nature has become a bridge to communicate with people of different cultures and faiths around us. Various activities carried out in relation to environmental preservation are not only influenced by farming traditions according to the culture that we are currently living in, but are shaped by our interest in learning from the culture where we came from. Thus, there is a communication process between the local community and us as immigrants where we currently live.

What is transmitted are good and helpful perspectives related to land management styles which are of relevance both for personal life and also for the wider community. When the Covid-19 pandemic arrived in our Indonesian context in March 2020, all activities were supposed to be limited, especially those that involved large numbers of people. This situation led to the majority of people in our community becoming aware for the first time that in a disaster situation (natural or non-natural), food needs to remain the most important priority. Based on this awareness, more and more people have turned to farming, even though they only use narrow spots of land in their yards. Thus, individual and small-scale farming practices recognized that all people had to provide their groceries independently and reduce gatherings in markets and shopping places.

We are realizing that activities related to being environmental stewards have emerged in various places in Indonesia. Whether it is in Poso, Central Sulawesi, or in the city of Palu, it applies also to the Toraja people. To understand this properly, it is important to realise that the Toraja people in Poso are not only workers in the government, but many also have land to be managed. The second largest employment in this area is farming. Toraja is an area that relies on its natural resources and for Toraja people the environment is close to their daily life.

Therefore the environment is also an important issue in the life of the Toraja Church. In the 25th assembly of this year (2021), several issues regarding the environment have become major decisions for the church. There was a general affirmation that environmental conservation is a key calling of the Toraja Church. There was a recommendation that all congregations should be assigned to program environmental conservation activities in their respective contexts, because many saw a crisis unfolding among the Toraja Christian community regarding environmental issues.

When 'One Hundred Years of the Gospel Entering Toraja'[2] was celebrated in 1998, one of the key themes for reflection was the environmental crisis. A call was made to return to solidarity with and to be friendly with nature (the 'back to nature' movement). Since then this call has been carried out by the Toraja Church

[1] Junita is a young ordained pastor in the Toraja Church, South Sulawesi, Indonesia. The focus of her work is on the ecumenical movement and on collaborating with young people from different backgrounds on interfaith issues. Ade Nuriadin is an independent filmmaker and founder of the Tana Sanggamu Institute, focusing on economic, social, cultural, and environmental issues after the disasters that occurred in Palu, Sigi and Donggala in 2018. Currently, Ade Nuriadin is collaborating with groups of young people, farmers, and women in a transformative movement to achieve sustainable community welfare. Irna Satigi is an ordained pastor in the Central Sulawesi Church (GKST), a lecturer, and currently registered as a postgraduate doctoral student at UKDW writing a dissertation on post-conflict theology in Poso.

[2] Charles Perry Lange, 'The Indigenous as Orthodox: Religious Evolution in Tana Toraja' (2020), in: SIT Digital Collections: https://digitalcollections.sit.edu/cgi/viewcontent.cgi?article=4371&context=isp_collection.

for the maintenance of creation and the emphasis on integrity of creation by exploring and actualizing the understanding of the Toraja people about the concept of the 'brotherhood of all creation'.[3] As a church institution, we have promoted campaigns for the use of yards, sorting waste and avoiding bottled drinks. Protecting the environment is also always a priority, considering that the land routes on the mainland of Central Sulawesi and even South Sulawesi are often affected by natural disasters. Central Sulawesi, where Poso is located, and areas in Central Sulawesi are highly prone to earthquakes. Thus, it is very important for all people to learn about the circumstances of and needs for resilience and protection. This is especially appropriate for us as immigrants and also the younger generation in this region. Learning from the experiences of natural disasters, as well as social disasters, we have to reflect in order to determine what steps need to be taken together as a community in the area.

Eco-Diakonia in Poso Culture and the Existence of the Toraja Church Community in Poso

For understanding the mission history of our region, we need to look at the work of Albert Christian Kruyt and Dr. Nicolaas Adriani, two missionaries from the Nederlandsch Zendeling Genootschap (NZG), one of the Dutch mission agencies.[4] Both were sent to Poso at different times. Kruyt was the first to enter the area as a missionary in 1892, followed by Adriani in 1895 as a linguist to accompany Kruyt. In the process of becoming acquainted with the culture of the Pamona people in the Poso area, they discovered that the Pamona people did not have a special language for religion. There are no words or concepts about religion or belief in the language of the Pamona people, but they understood religion as self-actualization.[5] Being successful in the work of the field is a witness to personal piety.

In the past, the understanding of the Pamona was that everyone who worked and wanted to achieve maximum results had to work seriously according to the prescribed stages in the farming tradition. Their farming tradition is called *ada mpo jamaa to Pamona* (the Pamona people's working tradition), which starts with the selecting of proper land to be worked on until it is ready to be planted. There are a series of stages, all of which begin with a prayer asking for permission from a *tumpu ntana* (earth guardian spirit) from a *Tadu* (leader). There are two main elements that need to be considered in the land selection process: first, the land must be fertile and must not have been cultivated before by anyone else, and secondly it should only be cultivated for a maximum of two harvest periods or approximately two years. The selected areas of land should only be as large as can be successfully worked on.

The next stage is the process of planting rice in the fields. This is carried out in several stages, namely *mompaho* (ploughing the soil to sow rice seeds) and *mompeewosi* (weeding), both of which are carried out at a certain plant age, waiting for the rice plants to bear fruit and the fruit to ripen. Then the rice plants are ready to be harvested, ending with *mompariala* (arranging the yields) and regular harvest in the barn. Each stage begins with a prayer ritual from the *Tadu*, but is also followed by obedience to the rules and prohibitions that have been determined from each member of the community. Thus, the success of this farming work is dependent on the surrender and obedience of each individual involved.

---

[3] See also Rannu Sanderan, 'TOSANGSEREKAN, A Theological Reflection on the Integrity of Creation in the Torajan Context' (2003), in: https://www.google.de/url?sa=t&rct=j&q=&esrc=s&source=web&cd=&ved=2ahUKEwi5oI7w--_1AhXYhf0HHVxNA6gQFnoECAUQAQ&url=https%3A%2F%2Fosf.io%2Fv5u8e%2Fdownload&usg=AOvVaw0zcp123E-aW3lfvHfmCQp5.

[4] See https://id.wikipedia.org/wiki/Albertus_Christiaan_Kruyt; see also Joost Cote, 'Missionary Albert Kruyt and Colonial Modernity in the Dutch East Indies' (2010) in: https://www.researchgate.net/publication/231995196_Missionary_Albert_Kruyt_and_Colonial_Modernity_in_the_Dutch_East_Indies.

[5] Albert Schrauwers, *Colonial 'Reformation' in the Highlands of Central Sulawesi, Indonesia, 1892-1995* (Canada: University of Toronto Press Incorporated, 2000), 32.

It is interesting that the Pamona people will not eat rice that has just been harvested before being prayed for by the *Tadu Mburake* (female priest). The new tradition of eating rice is known as *Mangore* (done within the family scope). After the work has been completed by each family in the fields of the community, there will always be a *Padungku* event (harvest thanksgiving), the time of which is mutually agreed upon by the whole community. In the past *Padungku* was done with each family preparing a meal dominated by freshly harvested rice. There then followed a gathering at the village hall, leading to a *molimbu* event (a meal together in a circular sitting formation). On this occasion, friends from neighbouring villages were invited to attend and enjoy a meal together with mutual hospitality.

However, the development of the Pamona people's lives was later been modernized, especially when the Dutch government introduced the wet rice field system. With this, the Pamona people increasingly left the farming system of their own tradition, together with an increased variety of types of plants. However, some elements of the Pamona farming tradition have been preserved until this day, such as the *Mangore* and *Padungku* traditions. The *Mangore* is somewhat less exposed, because it is personal and carried out within the scope of the main family; the *Padungku* tradition will be discussed below.

The Padungku Common Thanksgiving Cultural Tradition in Poso

Conversion to Christianity brought a significant change. The introduction of the farming system in wet rice fields automatically invalidated the local wisdom of the community, but only to the extent to which the tilling of the land could be done for only two harvest periods. On the other hand, people are nowadays competing to claim ownership of the widest possible territories of fertile land. The direct impact can be felt to this day, where land ownership claims are a major symbol of prestige, even though this may not be followed by the responsibility of cultivating it.

Padungku has been inculturated into the Christian tradition in Poso, becoming one of the annual common thanksgiving occasions and rituals. The essence of *Padungku* is not only gratitude for the rice harvest, but also extends to a moment of annual thanksgiving for success in all forms of work. Thus *Padungku* remains synonymous with eating together, entertaining friends and relatives, and sharing joy and blessings for others. In general, in addition to entertaining guests for meals, the host will also prepare a small menu for the guests to take home. *Padungku* is now synonymous with two elements, namely *mangkoni* (eating) and *mongkeni* (carrying).

Padungku is a form of proving one's own success at work. *Padungku* therefore does not belong to a particular religion, but should be a tradition belonging to all people who live on the land of Poso. An interesting development happened in one of the villages that I visited during the Padungku celebration in 2020. When Christians were holding a thanksgiving service for *Padungku* in the church, at one stage I simultaneously heard an announcement from the loudspeaker of the mosque calling people to come and pray together for *Padungku*. This was amazing, as until now in my understanding *Padungku* had only been a one-sided claim. *Padungku* as a common culture for thanksgiving in Poso should be a reminder that life is about working hard, about taking responsibility for the creation, and being reminded not to be greedy by taking everything just for oneself, but also sharing them with others. *Padungku* leads us to live a balance with both nature and also with others (humans and all creation).

Apart from being a personal reminder, *Padungku* also is a reminder that nature actually supports itself and the integrity of the people around it. Everyone can come to be grateful in *Padungku* without encountering any barriers. Thus, *Padungku* illustrates the theme of the 2022 Eleventh Assembly of WCC, 'Christ's love moves the world to reconciliation and unity'.

The Lumbung Diakonia Service

Matters regarding the preservation of resilience and the integrity of creation are reflected in the spirit of the Diakonia Barn (*Lumbung Diakonia*), initiated by the Toraja Church. *Lumbung Diakonia*[6] aims to support the diaconal service in the church with a wide scope, not only for the Toraja Church or the Toraja people, but for all. This was proven during the earthquake, tsunami and also subsequent liquefaction disasters of 2018.[7] It is not only the Toraja Church that is engaged with the *Lumbung Diakonia* program. There are several activities that others are attempting, one of which is shelter for disaster victims.

Nevertheless, there are priorities that churches still need to develop regarding eco-diakonia, as it is not just about giving for the needy today, but also for the balance of life in the future. It is obvious that this is lacking in some current church programs, but we can see good examples from some other organizations, such as the Tana Sanggamu Institute, inspiring an environmental awareness movement amongst young people after the disaster.

Tana Sanggamu Institute as a Concrete Example of an Eco-Diakonia Movement in A Disaster Context

The most frequent diaconal movement carried out by the Toraja Church is charitable diakonia. Transformative diaconal movements have also started to emerge, but when we talk about a transformative diaconal movement for environmental issues around Central Sulawesi, we need to be honest and admit that it does not really exist yet. The assistance provided is often for one-time use, even though Central Sulawesi is one of the areas that is most prone to natural disasters.

There are many other places in various regions of Indonesia where the Toraja Church is located. Reflecting on the natural disaster of 2018, broader movements that raise awareness of environmentalism and eco-diakonia do not yet exist. However, we also need to look outside the church and realize that there are several movements, examples of what we need to do or collaborate together with. Through a good friend in the Toaya area (a province of Central Sulawesi) who mobilizes young people and carries out real eco-diakonia, we have learned about their activities which started after the earthquake that hit Central Sulawesi in 2018.

During and after the earthquake, tsunami and liquefaction disasters of September 28, 2018,[8] groups of young people were encouraged to take action in disaster management. The young people involved came from several villages in Donggala Regency. Back then, the situation was very unpredictable, not to mention the emergence of great panic in the community due to lack of knowledge about disasters. We saw how houses fell, roads were torn apart, trees fell, and people panicked. Many people lost their property. What was even more sad was seeing the victims injured and even lose their lives, which was not handled properly. We also heard from survivors of the tsunami and liquefaction about what they experienced. That was the night we saw our own towns, villages and homes being destroyed.

The situation was complicated further by the fact that communication was completely cut off and all power lost – we were in a completely dark situation, which was not going to be solved overnight! Thus, we realized that something really substantial had to be done. One of the main priorities at that time was to connect with outside friends, so we agreed to leave home and join our fellow volunteers in Palu. From there, we began to gather strength, and on 4 October, six days after the disaster, we succeeded in establishing a volunteer post in Toaya Village.

---

[6] See for instance: https://pgi.or.id/lumbung-diakonia-gereja-toraja-menjangkau-yang-belum-terjangkau/.

[7] See https://en.wikipedia.org/wiki/Soil_liquefaction.

[8] See 'World Vision: Central Sulawesi Earthquake and Tsunami Emergency Response' (September 2018 – March 2019), in: https://reliefweb.int/report/indonesia/central-sulawesi-earthquake-and-tsunami-emergency-response-september-2018-march.

Little by little, we started to register the survivors who had evacuated themselves and their families to refugee camps, both in locations in the middle of the forest that were easily accessible and also areas with more difficult access. With this registration data, various logistical aids arrived, including volunteers from outside the region who relocated for a month during the emergency response period.

After the emergency response period was over, we realized that Donggala Regency had complex problems. In reality, Donggala Regency is an area with a fairly large number of people who work as farmers, laborers, and breeders – namely 52.33% of the total number of working people, which is 121,033 people (BPS data in 2017). Unfortunately, the majority of these people were from a group of professions with low wages, so it was not surprising that after three days of the disaster, many were already short of and even ran out of food. This was in a stark contrast to the potential of the fertile land and the large amount of land that could be cultivated as a source of livelihood for the community.

These problems prompted a group of young people to agree to form a grassroots organization, called the 'Tana Sanggamu Institute'. *Tana Sanggamu* means 'a handful of land', and is also related to the people's belief that this life comes from a handful of land where life is re-created in the world. For us, *Tana Sanggamu* also means protecting the land, which also means preserving the life and culture that has coexisted with it. Through the Tana Sanggamu Institute, we have carried out a learning process to find out about the challenges faced by the community after the disaster, equipping young people to re-build a prosperous life.

We found that farmers, laborers and fishermen had complex problems which were also connected with environmental and cultural issues. As a society that still adheres to cultural principles and values, we hear messages from our ancestors that the suffering we are enduring today is caused by our behaviour as humans in treating other humans, animals, plants and the universe badly. We interpret this in a spiritual context. When the situation reached a saturation point, that was when a disaster came as a warning in order to restore the entire social, cultural, economic, and even political order that had been damaged.

From the information and reflections that we have gathered, the Tana Sanggamu Institute has built an important environmental awareness movement for young people. This movement started from Toaya Village, where organic farming classes were initiated and regularly offered. The first class, which was held for eight subsequent meetings, was simply carried out on a terrace. Since then, we have had regular weekly meetings, and the participants were not only young people, but also female and male farmer groups. From these organic farming classes we then managed an organic garden, and at that time we planted peanuts on half a hectare. It took us about three months to manage the land, and as novice farmers with minimal experience, at harvest time we were quite satisfied with what we had produced, even though there were still many things that needed to be improved.

We are aware that as a community living with disasters that food availability is our main strength. The community must be independent with the strength of its own food. The community needs to have a family barn as a precaution against disasters or famines. In addition to building food strength, agriculture must be carried out with an ecological approach, which means not injuring other creatures and nature with harmful chemicals or exploiting land until there is no space to breathe. This is our interpretation of the message of keeping in touch with the universe from the ancestors.

We have created learning classes and discussions that we package in the Dialog Kampung program, with the goal of bringing together different elements and groups of society. The Village Dialogue seeks to gather knowledge from both the village and outside the village, all of which can be a contributing force to building environmental awareness. A reforestation action movement was later initiated by young people from different villages in areas that have a risk of flooding, landslides and tsunamis.

We also realized that in order to bring prosperity, it is also necessary to take an economic approach. We tried to build a social business based on ecological principles, producing organic fertilizer under the brand name 'Tana Organic' as an effort to meet the fertilizer needs of farmers and produce quality and healthy harvests. Rather than cutting down trees, we work with forest honey-bee farmers to obtain additional economic value from the forest – we have labelled this '#CekMaduPedia'. Then we also produced eco-print products to encourage other forms of economy that can be developed in the village environment with the brand name 'Gumbaldea'. This social business is certainly a learning process that is still growing and needs refinement.

Conclusion

Whatever the spirit of our sisters and brothers elsewhere, it must be the spirit of the youth in the church to look far ahead with a concern about nature as God's gift. Some of the community members still view the environment only as a tool to meet their needs. This paradigm, however, must be changed in order to properly place humans as biological and ecological beings. The results of the Toraja Church's activities in relation to the environment have shown significant impacts, such as reduced tree cutting, increased tree planting, and increased production of pigs and chickens. Environmental damage has also been addressed little by little – organic farming has become a widely discussed topic, the habit of making compost is widespread, growing organic vegetables has been widely practiced in yards, and so the health of mothers and children has been improved. From the local government side, regulations related to organic farming have been produced, and guidance for the promotion of organic agriculture is intensively carried out with the hope that the community will 'go organic' and 'go green'.

If there is commitment and action from all parties within the Toraja Church, local churches in Central Sulawesi and even adherents of other religions, everyone can then contribute to an integrated, comprehensive and sustainable environment. However, we need a concept that can unite all elements in a comprehensive working system for God, in order to build awareness on the importance of environmental management so that it remains sustainable – as it was created by God at the beginning.

One of the vocations of the Toraja Church is to build awareness amongst local congregations and the community that environmental integrity and natural sustainability do not happen automatically. Therefore, the church must remind its members that nature is a creation of God which must be respected by nurturing and preserving it in order to give life to all. Church leaders must mainstream creation care programs into the strategic plan of Toraja Church institutions at all levels. This must be done on the basis of living out the faith that all creation was mandated to create a harmonious life (Psalms 104:13-18), and that all creatures are something that are valuable and reflect the majesty of God: "When you send your spirit, they are created and you renew the earth" (Ps 104, 30).

This is in line with the ancient Toraja philosophy of *sangserekan bane*, meaning that Tallu Lolona are brothers who live together and take care of each other. This reminds us of Colossians 1:15-23, that all creation is saved because human life and the whole of creation are part a cosmic unity that has a value rooted in and fulfilled in Christ. While the world is God's creation, humans are the guardians of the environment, and therefore humans must harmonize themselves with their environment and develop an ethical attitude to save the environment. Destroying natural resources means death, because without nature we cannot live. We need to eat, we need to drink, we need a place to live, all of which are obtained from and nurtured by nature while working with its resources. Therefore, we as young people need to exercise a climate-friendly lifestyle, living in ways which save energy by avoiding fast food and restoring the integrity of life in its fullness for all.

Suggestions for Further Reading

Hasan dkk, Budaya dan Adat Istiadat Poso (*Culture and tradition of Poso*) (Yokyakarta, pustaka Timur: 2015)

Nuriadin, Ade dkk. Ngapa Nu Ranga-Ranga (Sejarah dan dinamika Masyarakat Desa Toaya Menghadapi Bencana – *History and Dynamics of Toaya Village Community Facing Disaster*). Institut Tana Sanggamu, Institut Mosintuwu dan Johanniter. 2019.

Schrauwers, Albert. *Collonial Reformation in the Highlands of Central Sulawesi, Indonesia, 1892-1995* (Toronto: University of Toronto: 2000)

84. *KEUGAHARIAN*: RESPONDING TO THE ECOLOGICAL CRISIS THROUGH A CHRISTIAN SPIRITUALITY

Junita Gereja Toraja, Ade Nuriadin, Irna Satigi [1]

Introduction

Since its general assembly in 2009, Communion of Churches in Indonesia (CCI) decided to prioritise the issue of the ecological crisis as one of its main concerns. It developed theological and missiological discourses of Indonesian churches. It also stimulated new activism within churches; there has been a trend for churches to organise "go-green" programmes at local and national levels. Subsequently, in the general assembly of CCI in 2014, CCI has been strengthening their commitment and promoting a new spirituality – after reflecting on the root of all crises in the world, including ecological crises: that is human greed. To overcome the crisis and/or to reduce the greed, we need to practice spirituality of *keugaharian* (sufficiency, moderation, temperance, sobriety, modesty, discretion), in which we, as human beings, should to be able to say "enough" to what we consume and what we receive in our life. Simultaneously, it should be ensured that the other beings or creatures exist in adequacy and sustainability.

The following reflections aim to elaborate the comprehensive understanding on spirituality of *keugaharian,* in the way the church incorporates its practice and its significance for people from other faith in Indonesia. Discussing the shift of theological and missiological frameworks – regarding discourse of ecology and the dynamic of eco-activism within CCI and its members – this paper also covers CCI's interfaith activities in responding to the ecological issue over the last decade (2009-2019) after their two last general assemblies.

The Meaning of *Keugaharian*

According to the Indonesian Dictionary, the term *keugaharian*[2] is derived from *ugahari* which means moderate, in the middle, simple, unpretentious. The term *keugaharian* itself has not been popular in Indonesian society, because it is rarely used. The discourse of *keugaharian* started from a dialogue by Plato when he was at the *palaistra* or *gymnasion* (place of education and physical training).[3] The dialogue is entitled "Xarmides". Through the dialogue, the concept of *sophrosune* (a Greek term which is understood as *keugaharian*) developed. The *sophrosune* term was derived from a Greek word *sun-phronesis* which generally means "by-wisdom". Someone who has the *sophrosune* is a person with "practical wisdom" or *prudentia* (Greek). With *sophrosune,* someone has their own control on desire to get anything just for personal satisfaction.

Louis-André Dorion translated *sophrosune* as *moderatio, temperantia,* which emphasises one's ability to do moderate to soften and mediate, to get at the midst. This is a combination practical wisdom and of intellectuality.[4] W.R.M. Lamb proposed some alternative translations of *sophrosune*, such as "temperance", "sobriety", "moderation", "discretion". Lamb also explained that "sophrosune, indeed, though it came to

---

[1] Jimmy Marcos Immanuel is a pastor of The Protestant Church in Western Indonesia. He currently works as an Executive Secretary of Communion of Churches in Indonesia (CCI) responsible for Witness and Integrity of Creation desk. He is active in interfaith dialogues and as co-founder of some interfaith and ecological platforms in Indonesia.

[2] See: https://learnindonesianhub.com/translate/indonesian/keugaharian/

[3] A. Setyo Wibowo, *Platon: Xarmides (Tentang Keugaharian)* (Yogyakarta: Kanisius, 2015), p.3.

[4] A. Setyo Wibowo, *Platon: Xarmides,* 9-10.

mean something like our 'temperance,' originally meant 'soundness of mind,' 'wholeness or health of the faculty of thought (*phronein*)'."[5]

In the Indonesian context, A. Setyo Wibowo, who translated and interpreted Xarmides, sees *sophrosune* or *keugaharian* as encompassing elements of morality, in which someone has to be aware about their own "framework to act", attitude, and element of intellectuality.[6] With this understanding, Indonesian people are more familiar with the term of *mawas diri* (self-correction through introspection). People who have *keugaharian* will always have self-correction and will be very critical in observing themselves and their surroundings. They become a very wise and careful person in considering and responding to ways of life through self-reflection when deciding their actions and choices. Wibowo cited examples of people with *keugaharian* such as well-behaved or polite (but not cowardly), modest, humble, with moderate attitude, understanding and listening to others, being proper and genuine, and always being aware like a referee.

Keugaharian in Indonesian Churches

The practice of the principles of *keugaharian* can be found in some local cultures in Indonesia. Traditional society may see it as one's own virtue like the concept of *ngerti isin*, from Javanese society with its literal meaning as "aware of shame." People who have *ngerti isin* must be careful in the presence of others as they become aware of their vulnerability in interaction with others.[7] In wider meanings, *ngerti isin* makes people behave well, be more polite, become aware about their personal attitude and their surroundings and gives people the ability to understand and decide whether something is good or bad.

CCI sees the already existing virtues in Indonesian traditions that are similar to Christian virtues and understands the need to revitalise them to the present context. The term *keugaharian* which is of typical Indonesian value interested CCI enough to put it on the formal discourse of Indonesian churches through its General Assembly (GA) XVI in Nias, North Sumatra, 2014. The theme of the GA was "God Brings Us Up Again from the Depths of the Earth" (Psalm 71:20b), with its sub-theme "*In Solidarity as Indonesian Citizens We Implement Principles of Pancasila to Overcome Poverty, Injustice, Radicalism and Ecological Crisis*."

The theme and sub-theme were based on CCI's reflections on the actual issues that existed in Indonesia and would become the struggle of the churches over five years (2014-2019), poverty, injustice, radicalism and ecological crises. CCI observes that the root of all four is human greed. This is also in parallel with international discussions through the World Council of Churches (WCC) in 2005, which raised the issue of economic injustice as a consequence of global capitalism. Economic injustice is caused by human greed where some people aim to have unlimited wealth and power. It was later proved that assets/wealth of the 1% richest people in the world is equal to the total assets of the other 99%.[8] As a response to this injustice, WCC proposed the concept of Alternative Globalisation Addressing Peoples and Earth (AGAPE).[9] After reflecting

[5] W.R.M. Lamb, in A. Setyo Wibowo, *Platon: Xarmides,* 11-12.

[6] A. Setyo Wibowo, *Platon: Xarmides,* 10-15.

[7] Ward Keeler, *Javanese Shadows Plays, Javanese Selves* (USA: Princeton University Press, 2017), 66.

[8] *See* "Oxfam Briefing Paper: An Economy for the 99%". Oxfam, January 2017.

9 The aim of this concept is "to inspire the churches and the wider ecumenical movement to continue to address current global problems so as to respond resolutely to the intolerable levels of poverty in our world." World Council of Churches, "Alternative Globalization Addressing Peoples and Earth (AGAPE): A Background Document" (Geneva: WCC, 2005). In line with this concept, on 27th March 2009, World Council of Churches (WCC) sent a letter to the G20. They had their concerns about the global financial crisis which had increased the number of unemployment, indebtedness and poverty. In the introductory paragraphs, the letter said: "...At the outset, the WCC considers this crisis as not merely a financial and economic one but as a crisis that has moral and ethical dimensions that have slowly been eroding our societies over a period of time. We are witnessing an era when greed has become the basis for economic growth. It is therefore necessary, in the understanding of the churches, to go beyond short-term financial bailout actions and to seek long term transformation based on sound ethical and moral principles which will govern a new financial architecture. The WCC has been expressing its concern on this since 1984, when it had issued a call for a new

more on greed as the source of global injustice, WCC launched a concept to reduce greed – the "greed line". The purpose is to make people understand their limits in fulfilling their desires. Konrad Raiser perceives the *greed line* as an effort to lift up the degree or quality of human life (the ideal standard), especially for those who have fought (worked hard) for their rights to live better life and yet experience poverty due to the impact of rich people's greed.[10] To counter this injustice, a greed line is needed to ensure that the structures of greed degrade gradually.

CCI perceives that the banality of humans' spirituality is the main cause of this globalisation of greed. Many have lost their spiritual life and tend to seek material satisfaction and a life of individualism.[11] After reflecting on this problem, CCI sought an alternative idea/concept of ethics and spirituality that would be distinctive of Indonesian values. The decision of CCI to use the concept of *keugaharian*[12] is not merely to promote its general notions, but also to develop Christian spirituality and ethics through this concept. CCI sees that *keugaharian* is also cross-denominational of churches, cultures and religion. By emphasising spiritual aspects of *keugaharian*, it is not just a matter of personal pietism, but rather becomes spirituality of people (community) who practice ethics against greed and work to overcome its consequences (injustice, poverty, radicalism and environmental damage). *Keugaharian* is expected to become ethos, attitude, identity, lifestyle, way of thinking, habitus, and even a movement of people to empower vulnerable or marginalised ones to fight for justice and a better world.

CCI emphasises sufficiency regarding the essence of *keugaharian*. This is based on the prayer taught by Jesus, about the sufficiency of blessings given by God (Mt. 6:11, cf. Prov. 30:8).[13] In this prayer, Christians should ask God to provide sufficient daily food/meal. The word "sufficient" is seen as their portion; one should not ask for something excessive beyond this portion. A Christian has to differentiate what they really need from what they want to consume to avoid being greedy. Theologically, this prayer is seen as God's wish for humans not to live lavishly, not in shortage, but to live an adequate life. This is not only a matter of eating

---

international financial order based on ethical principles and social justice. We believe it is time, once again, for such a transformation of the financial and economic systems based on values of honesty, social justice and dignity for all. While I appreciate the prompt actions taken by the G20 beginning with its meeting in Washington D.C. in November 2008 to salvage the system and prevent it from collapse, we would like to raise issues that need to be taken into account in transforming the current system…" See full letter at: WCC, *Letter to G20 countries on the current crisis,* [Available at: https://www.oikoumene.org/en/resources/documents/general-secretary/messages-and-letters/27-03-09-letter-to-g20], [Last accessed: 23rd February 2022].

[10] Marthin L. Sinaga and Olivia M. Payung Allo, "Hidup Berkecukupan dalam Etos Keugaharian: Aternatif Ekonomi Gerakan Ekumenis Indonesia?" in *Jurnal Teologi dan Gereja,* 16(27) (2015) (Jawa Barat: KPT GKI Sinode Jawa Barat, 2015): 37-38; Cf. Athena Peralta, *The Greed Line: Tool for A Just Economy* (Geneva: World Council of Churches, 2016).

[11] Persekutuan Gereja-gereja di Indonesia, *Himpunan Keputusan dan Notulen Sidang Raya PGI XVI* (Jakarta: PGI, 2015): 204.

[12] *Keugaharian* is often seen very close to the concept of 'frugality.' James A. Nash elaborated the concept: "Frugality is the subversive virtue, because it revolts against an economic system that depends upon intensive production and consumption to keep the system going and growing. Frugality is an encounter with an economic ethos that cannot afford frugality if that ethos is to thrive, and resists, even undermines, the central assumptions of that ethos." For Nash, frugality is not a popular term compared to the term "adequacy" which more refers to a situation of not being rich or poor. James A. Nash, "Toward the Revival and Reform of the Subversive Virtue: Frugality," *The Annual of the Society of Christian Ethics,* 59(1) (January 2005), 138.

[13] The Indonesian Bible Society translated this verse "*berilah kami pada hari ini makanan kami yang secukupnya*" which means asking God to provide sufficient or portioned food for people. Some English translations translate it "give us this day our daily bread." Both translations seem the same but, in the Indonesian translation, there is a stressed word "*secukupnya*" (sufficient) which facilitates some theological understandings. The word "bread" in its original language (Greek) is *artos* which has various meanings: 1) the bread or food itself, 2) symbolic of all of basic necessities. William D. Mounce, *Mounce's Complete Expository Dictionary of Old and New Testament Words* (Michigan: Zondervan Academic, 2009), 80; Lembaga Alkitab Indonesia, *Alkitab* (Jakarta: LAI, 1974).

and drinking, but also related to other blessings from God, such as income, assets or property, power, recreation, health, and others. However, it does not mean that people should not reach the highest position in their job or achieve an excellent economic level. The most important thing is that the position and economic level are obtained with wisdom (self-control/introspection, temperance, moderation) and the right way (truth and justice), not just for self-satisfaction or demands from others. The sufficiency or portion in this case can also be seen as spiritual worthiness, that someone reach certain position or better economic life because they are worthy of that blessing.

Someone who lives with spirituality of *keugaharian* is able to say "enough" for what they consume or receive, and they even dedicate their achievements (position, wealth, knowledge, etc.) to help other beings also live in sufficiency (better life) for integrity of creation, for the glory of God.[14] Our mission is to make sure that all beings live in sufficiency and discard injustice. It also encourages Christians to make those who are greedy become more aware and practice *keugaharian.* By doing this mission, Christians preach the Gospel to promote and manifest the sufficiency that God wants to happen in all beings. Christians with this mission exercise and discipline[15] are encouraged to develop their own spirituality, to be transformed, and to create transformation (sharing spirituality) in their community or society.

CCI believes that the root of the global crisis (greed) and its problems (poverty, injustice, radicalism, and ecological crisis) that we witness and experience can be overcome through the discipline and practice of the spirituality of *keugaharian.* In its General Assembly XVI, CCI formally discussed the issue of human greed and the spirituality of *keugaharian.* It is also elaborated in a very important document (a theological and missiological foundation for Indonesian churches to manifest the oneness and unity of churches through a five-year leadership programme and/or policy) of CCI which is called "*Pokok-Pokok Tugas Panggilan Bersama*" (Points of Common Calling of CCI), as follows:[16]

> In the spirit of building the independency and economic resilience of churches, and in order to strive for alternatives of good management of economy in the society, creativity and innovation from churches should be implemented in presenting alternative economy for social justice. Ecumenical movement, in global and national scope, has always been aware about the ethos and structure of greed which exist in our culture and society. On the other side, churches keep emphasising that our common house (*oikos*), which in Indonesia, has to be worth living, with justice, peace and prosperity for all people. Our support and hard work to present the civilised society would never happen without social and economic justice. [In the challenge of facing the globalisation of greed, spirituality of *keugaharian* needs to be maintained and developed, in which our behaviour and/or lifestyle shows modesty, autonomous/independent and eco-friendly. This can be "common calling" of all religions or cultural communities which have been practicing the principles of *keugaharian*]
>
> a. In the light of this understanding, churches have to consistently build ethos of living in sufficiency, nourish spirituality of *keugaharian* to counter the spirit of consumerism and ethos of greed, and to present the eco-friendly life style. Spirituality of *keugaharian* is needed as our spiritual reflection and our gratitude to God that every day we receive "sufficient food" (Mt. 6:11, cf. Prov. 30:8). This spirituality can be developed with other religious or cultural communities, as partners of churches. *Keugaharian* is also separated from "discipleship" which has been crucially needed by Indonesian churches to develop. Our spiritual and pious life, which is the inheritance of Indonesian churches, should be developed and enlarged as part of our witness and social participation. In this context, the activism and theology from "lay Christians" are very relevant to the purpose of the spirituality and

---

[14] Persekutuan Gereja-gereja di Indonesia, *Himpunan Keputusan dan Notulen Sidang Raya PGI XVI*, 201.
[15] Mary Frohlich emphasised "A spiritual discipline, in this sense, is a structured, committed approach to learning how to live spiritually. Even though such spiritual disciplines necessarily employ constructed forms, the original underlying emphasis is on the transformation of life rather than on mastery of the forms." Mary Frohlich, "Spiritual discipline, discipline of spirituality: Revisiting Questions of Definition and Method", *Spiritus: A Journal of Christian Spirituality*, Spiritus 1.1 (Maryland: John Hopkins University Press, 2001), 76.
[16] Persekutuan Gereja-gereja di Indonesia, *Himpunan Keputusan dan Notulen Sidang Raya PGI XVI*, 222-224.

discipleship, so the existence of churches can also be a space for spiritual growth which creates social impacts – a necessity in this era of globalisation and cultural transition. [To nourish and develop the spirituality of *keugaharian,* churches should become a "moral community" wherein our piety and spiritual life has social impacts. It is associated with the process of discipleship that we need at the hour.]

b. The growth or development of this spirituality, however, needs supporting structures for it. This can be started by activism in churches, as much as we can, to present "the commons" in any areas where churches exist (*presentia*). Therefore, churches with other communities should collaborate to strive for crucial and substantial things as basis for common good, such as water, energy (electricity), education infrastructure for the common. In our society, which tends to be market oriented and more individualistic, concept of the commons should be stimulated and implemented by churches. [To counter the globalisation of greed, which is more individualistic, our activism to improve the discourse of "the commons" in the society should be the main concern of Indonesian churches]

Keugaharian **and the Ecological Crisis**

As explained above, the concept of spirituality of *keugaharian* was formulated and decided by CCI to be the relevant response of Indonesian churches to global greed. The ecological crisis has become chronic in our current time and is a global problem, that almost all the countries are concerned with. Some international organisations have highlighted that ecological issues in Indonesia are at the worst level. It is the second biggest contributor of plastic trash in the world[17] and is among the worst countries for deforestation.[18] Irresponsible farming, mining and fishing have worsened the soil, water and air quality. It endangers and damages the biodiversity. This causes natural disasters that killed a lot of beings, humans and nonhumans alike, such as landslides, fires, droughts and floods. These also contribute to our global climate crisis.

People acting on greed have exploited the nature without considering its sustainability and the future of all beings. They try to receive as many benefits as they can for their satisfaction. This ethos of greed has been internalised and structuralised not only in the life of business actors (capitalists) but also in many other sectors. Our government at local and national level, in many cases, gave legal permits for corporates to exploit nature without doing comprehensive studies or analysis in advance, yet there is a lack of participation of indigenous and other local people who live in the exploited areas (a lot of cases of land grabbing, agrarian conflict and human violation happened in Indonesia).[19] A culture of corruption lies behind the legal permits. When the negative impacts occur during and after the exploitation, they wash their hands of it, whereby the vulnerable are left ignorant. The ideal concept of good governance and law enforcement is just so difficult to implement if greed still masters the leaders, politicians, judges, bureaucrats, policy-makers, armies, etc. The greed even reaches religious communities. Many churches, for example, received benefits from the exploitation through proposals of certain events (building or renovating church, celebrating Christmas or Easter, improving assets

---

[17] Ocean Conservancy, "Stemming the Tide: Land-based strategies for a plastic-free ocean," *Ocean Conservancy Report 2015* (Ocean Conservancy and McKinsey Center for Business and Development, 2015), 7, 11; Also see Jason Gooljar, "Top 20 Countries Ranked By Mass Of Mismanaged Plastic Waste", 6th April 2018 *Earth Day*, [Available at: https://www.earthday.org/2018/04/06/top-20-countries-ranked-by-mass-of-mismanaged-plastic-waste/], [Last accessed: 24th February 2022].

[18] "Forests also play a critical role in mitigating climate change because they act as a carbon sink – soaking up carbon dioxide that would otherwise be free in the atmosphere and contribute to ongoing changes in climate patterns." WWF, "Deforestation and Forest Degradation", World Wildlife Website, [Available at: https://www.worldwildlife.org/threats/deforestation-and-forest-degradation], [Last accessed: 24th February 2022].

19 See Human Rights Watch, "The Dark Side of Green Growth Human Rights Impacts of Weak Governance in Indonesia's Forestry Sector", Human Rights 2013 Report; Nigel D. White, *et al.*, "Blurring Public and Private Security in Indonesia: Corporate Interests and Human Rights in a Fragile Environment", *Netherlands International Law Review*, 65(2) (July 2018), 217-252.

of church, etc.) which were sent to corporates or capitalists who clearly exploited their environment. Many church leaders could not say "enough" or "stop" doing such things because they get used to it or dependent upon the exploiters. We can see the ethos of greed has created such structures in our society by causing individualism and simultaneously preserving a circle of interdependency amongst the greedy.[20]

Since its GA XV – 2009, in Mamasa, West Sulawesi, CCI has seen environmental issues as being a common concern. In the GA, Indonesian churches were encouraged to give their attention to this issue, as part of theological and missiological reflections within the churches. The churches should also respond to the issue by organising eco-friendly activities/programmes, such as conserving the environment and promoting perspectives of sustaining our natural resources for the prosperity of all people and the future generations.[21] The discussion about environmental issues was not actually a new one for Indonesian churches. In the midst of 20th century, Christian theology had criticised environmental problems in the West coming from the emergence of social movements (anti-establishment) and narrations written by some Christians who were sensitive about the problems, and developed the area of ecotheology.[22] Some well-known ecotheologians started the discourse, such as John B. Cobb, Joseph Sittler and Thomas Berry. The Western ecotheology influenced theological studies in Indonesia especially in seminaries and Christian colleges. It also became a discussion within Indonesian churches. Some churches even realised that they need to rethink their theology of creation which, at that time, positioned humans as the centre of all God's creation; the image of God *(imago Dei)*, the perfect creature who has dominion over all creatures. The churches transformed this anthropocentric theology to be eco-centric theology where all creatures, including human, live in interdependency.

With a formal discussion and decision on the issue of the environment in the GA XV – 2009, the member churches of CCI became more motivated to positively respond to the activism of environmental conservation. It became a common calling (theology and missiology) for Indonesian churches. After the GA XV – 2009, the *Marturia* (Witness) department of CCI started developing ecological programmes. One of the programmes is "Gereja Sahabat Alam" (*eco-friendly church*), in collaboration with the Ministry of Environment of Indonesia. As one of the outputs of this programme, it has produced ecological narratives for Indonesian churches to care more about their environment. Books were published as ecological handbooks for churches. Since 2012, CCI has also promoted not using plastics (especially for eating and drinking) in any church events. Besides, some interfaith platforms (co-initiated by CCI, such as SIAGA BUMI, Faith for Forest) on this global problem (as its common ground) have improved programmes and networks of CCI toward this issue. Meanwhile, member churches also started organising eco-friendly programmes such as planting trees or recycling activities such as creating Christmas trees and other handicrafts from trash or used plastic.

CCI realises that these eco-friendly programmes or the activism were not massively and continuously organised by churches and/or Christians. That is why in the GA XVI – 2014, CCI emphasised the ecological crisis as one of its central issues (2014-2019 period) so that Indonesian churches have to take it into account with more serious promotion and implementation. What CCI considered as a substantial aspect to respond the global crisis, and also the missing thing in the programmes and activism within churches, is spirituality. Spirituality of *keugaharian* is seen as being our critical need so the term "eco-friendly" would not merely be related to certain programmes of the churches, but a lifestyle or attitude, a way of thinking and identity of

[20] So, does the ethos of greed exist in us as consumers of products of the exploitation? We can do self-reflection/correction on how we participate in 1) The culture of consumerism, 2.) Plastic, water and energy waste, 3) Production of greenhouse gases, 4) And other activities which may cause the absence of self-control or just for self-satisfaction. The ethos of greed limits a person's capacity to think and decide whether something is good or bad for them and others; moral degradation.

[21] Persekutuan Gereja-Gereja di Indonesia, *Dokumen Keesaan Gereja 2009-2014* (Jakarta: PGI, 2009), 77-79.

[22] Al. Purwa Hadiwardoyo, *Teologi Ramah Lingkungan: Sekilas Tentang Ekoteologi Kristiani* (Yogyakarta: Kanisius, 2015), 74-75.

Christians. With this spirituality, Christians will not only talk about eco-friendly activism but also advocate for the vulnerable stakeholders who experience ecological and social injustice caused by the greedy.

In almost one decade, since the GA XV – 2009, the activism and/or responses of churches to overcome ecological crisis are not yet radically spirited by *keugaharian*. What churches have done, mostly, are still in the matter of programmes (organisationally) or an impact of what the other institutions (especially government and environmental defenders) have organised for this issue. A Christian who has *keugaharian,* with or without the programmes of churches or the other institutions, will immediately control themself to live an eco-friendly lifestyle (emphasising modesty and sufficiency for themselves and other beings), become sensitive or critical on the ecological issue, and collaborate with others to counter the ecological injustices that happen in their environment – for the integrity of creation.

Keugaharian may have been sporadically practiced by some Christians in Indonesia, and has not yet successfully been transformed to be identity of community and/or movement.[23] The concept of *keugaharian* can be strongly seen at the level of theological discourse in theological seminaries but not is even known among lay Christians. Together with its member churches, CCI still needs more time and effort to socialise, implement and develop *keugaharian*. Indonesian churches might have forgotten one thing, once we propose spirituality as an answer/response to the crisis so it requires strong commitment and must be practiced (exercised) with discipline (action and reflection) until it becomes internalised (personally and communally) and transformed to be habitus. Regarding to this situation, there are at least three tasks of CCI for the current 5-year plan (2019-2024). First, to further elaborate the concept of *keugaharian* and its details on how it is practiced in Christians' day-to-day life. Second, to make principles of *keugaharian* consistently enlightening and embedded in all actions and programs of CCI. Third, to create and promote best practices within churches (as the real model and motivation for other communities); hence, it should be pioneered by leadership of CCI and the other church leaders.

Conclusion

Keugaharian is a fluid concept which was concocted from intellectual dialogues and some virtues in many traditions, which stresses practical wisdom and the appropriate attitude of humans to live in this world. This concept may actually be commensurable with other religious concepts like *wasatiyyah* in Islam (which emphasises moderation in the way of thinking and behaving; being proportional, balancing extreme and fanatical acts in every aspect of human life).[24] The principles in *keugaharian* are suitable for any religions and culture as it bridges diverse identities and facilitates inclusive dialogues.

CCI had added another virtue from Christianity to the concept of *keugaharian*, which is the spirit of living in sufficiency. *Keugaharian* has become not only an ideal concept, but also Christian spirituality that should be practiced in daily life. Christians are expected to have self-control over their desire to receive anything beyond their portion and worth – which may cause crisis and/or injustice to other beings. We have learned that the excessively individualistic ethos which emphasises greed and damages the environment has taught us that we need to redefine our religious life and/or spirituality. K*eugaharian* can be one of the best alternatives. In the light of this spirit, if many people (Christians and other religious believers) in Indonesia consistently practice the spirituality of *keugaharian*, the ecological crisis, including the other detrimental impacts of the globalisation of greed, will optimistically be overcome.

However, as a spiritual discipline for a person, and to become a common movement in the society, it takes time for religious institutions like CCI to conscientise and implement this spiritual concept, sharing it with

[23] In some projects of CCI that I co-ordinated recently, I asked some church leaders about the concept of *keugaharian.* Most of them were not sure about what they understood from the readings and the seminars that they attended.

[24] Cf. Mohd Shukri Hanapi, "The Wasatiyyah (Moderation) Concept in Islamic Epistemology: A Case Study of its Implementation in Malaysia", *International Journal of Humanities and Social Science*, 4, (9) (July 2014): 51-62.

the most Christians in Indonesia. It really depends on the effort and commitment (discipline, evaluation) of member churches of CCI to actualise the concept of spirituality that they decided in GA.

Suggestions for Further Reading

Earth Day Network. "Top 20 Countries Ranked by Mass of Mismanaged Plastic Waste". 6th April 2018 *Earth Day Website* [Available at: https://www.earthday.org/2018/04/06/top-20-countries-ranked-by-mass-of-mismanaged-plastic-waste], [Last accessed: 24th February 2022].

Frohlich, Mary. "Spiritual discipline, discipline of spirituality: Revisiting Questions of Definition and Method". *Spiritus: A Journal of Christian Spirituality* 1(1) (2001): 65-78.

Hadiwardoyo, Al. Purwa. *Teologi Ramah Lingkungan: Sekilas Tentang Ekoteologi Kristiani*. Yogyakarta: Kanisius, 2015.

Hanapi, Mohd Shukri. "The Wasatiyyah (Moderation) Concept in Islamic Epistemology: A Case Study of its Implementation in Malaysia". *International Journal of Humanities and Social Science* 4(9) (2014): 51-62.

Hardoon, Deborah. "Oxfam Briefing Paper: An Economy for the 99%". 16th January 2017. *Oxfam*. [Available at: https://www.oxfam.org/en/research/economy-99], [Last accessed: 26th February 2022].

Human Rights Watch. "The Dark Side of Green Growth Human Rights Impacts of Weak Governance in Indonesia's Forestry Sector", *Human Rights 2013 Report*, 2013. [Available at: https://www.hrw.org/report/2013/07/15/dark-side-green-growth/human-rights-impacts-weak-governance-indonesias-forestry], [Last accessed: 26th February 2022].

Keeler, Ward. *Javanese Shadows Plays, Javanese Selves*. USA: Princeton University Press, 2017.

Lembaga Alkitab Indonesia. *Alkitab*. Jakarta: LAI, 1974.

Mounce, William D. *Mounce's Complete Expository Dictionary of Old and New Testament Words*. Grand Rapids, MI: Zondervan Academic, 2009.

Nash, James A. "Toward the Revival and Reform of the Subversive Virtue: Frugality". *The Annual of the Society of Christian Ethics* 59(1) (2005): 138.

Peralta, Athena. *The Greed Line: Tool for a Just Economy*, Geneva: World Council of Churches, 2016.

Persekutuan Gereja-Gereja di Indonesia. *Dokumen Keesaan Gereja 2009-2014*. Jakarta: PGI, 2009.

Persekutuan Gereja-gereja di Indonesia. *Himpunan Keputusan dan Notulen Sidang Raya PGI XVI*. Jakarta: PGI, 2015.

Sinaga, Marthin L., and Olivia M. Payung Allo. "Hidup Berkecukupan dalam Etos Keugaharian: Aternatif Ekonomi Gerakan Ekumenis Indonesia?" *Jurnal Teologi dan Gereja* 16(27) (2015): 37-38.

White, Nigel D. *et al.* "Blurring Public and Private Security in Indonesia: Corporate Interests and Human Rights in a Fragile Environment". *Netherlands International Law Review* 65(2), (July 2018): 217-252.

World Council of Churches. "Alternative Globalization Addressing Peoples and Earth (AGAPE)." *Justice, Peace and Creation Team, World Council of Churches*. Geneva: World Council of Churches, 2005. [Available at: https://www.oikoumene.org/en/folder/documents-pdf/agape-new.pdf], [Last accessed: 26th February 2022].

World Council of Churches. "Letter to G20 Countries on the Current Crisis". 27th March 2009. *WCC*. [Available at: https://www.oikoumene.org/en/resources/documents/general-secretary/messages-and-letters/27-03-09-letter-to-g20], [23rd February 2022].

World Wild Life. "Deforestation and Forest Degradation". *WWF Website* [Available at: https://www.worldwildlife.org/threats/deforestation-and-forest-degradation], [Last accessed: 23rd February 2022].

85. The Ecological and Ethical Significance of the Afforestation Program in Inner Mongolia

Wu Jianrong[1] and Qian Tiezheng[2]

As professional social service organisations with a Christian background, YMCA and YWCA of Shanghai are aware that no one's survival, health and happiness can be separated from the planet. Only a good natural environment and ecology can keep the human beings developing healthily for quite a long time. In Genesis, God gives human beings the important mission of looking after the world: "till it and keep it" (Gen. 2:15).

After the resumption of activities in the 1980s, especially after 1995, YMCA and YWCA of Shanghai took the lead regarding environmental protection in China, and carried out many advocacies and practical projects and activities related to environmental protection and sustainable development. Combining the concept of publicity with on-the spot participation, they raised the concept of environmental protection in the hearts of the public. Among these projects, the afforestation and anti-desertification projects in Dalad Banner and Alxa League of Inner Mongolia have the longest duration, the largest number of participants and the greatest influence.

This paper will sort through these two projects respectively and extract the ideas, practices and experiences of YMCA and YWCA of Shanghai.

Anti-Desertification and Afforestation Projects in Dalad Banner

YMCA and YWCA of Shanghai started the environmental protection and sand-fixation project in Inner Mongolia in 2001. At that time, YMCA and YWCA of Shanghai had the privilege of getting to know a local afforestation model figure in Inner Mongolia at a national meeting of NGOs. With her help, the groups have carried out in-depth exchanges and co-operation with the Anti-Desertification Association of Ordos, Inner Mongolia, for nearly a decade. This is the first step for YMCA and YWCA of Shanghai to participate in afforestation and desertification control.

At the beginning of the Dalad Banner project, YMCA and YWCA of Shanghai mainly focused their concerns on understanding the local situation, including the natural environment, desertification, current control methods and countermeasures, and the social living standards of local people. At the same time, the groups also publicised the concept of environmental protection to local people through professional methods and the way people lived, so as to let them understand that desertification was not a normal natural phenomenon, but an ecological problem. If this problem was not be taken seriously and reversed, it would have a further huge negative impact on their lives.

Meanwhile, Shanghai YMCA and YMCA also organised staff, volunteers, and college students to come to the desert of Dalad Banner in Inner Mongolia to make practical contributions to the prevention and control of desertification by planting poplar and other sand-fixing plants.

There was one thing that impressed almost all the participants. In the existing image, the focus of planting trees to combat desertification was on "planting", with that idea that the work was done after trees had been

---

[1] Dr Wu Jianrong is Director-General of YMCA of Shanghai, Director-General of National Councils of YMCAs of China. His main research fields include theology, sociology, and he has published or organised the compilation of more than ten academic works related to the social participation of religious groups, social work practice, community governance and so on. jianrw@hotmail.com.

[2] Qian Tiezheng is a staff member of the Research Department of YMCA and YWCA of Shanghai. His main research interests include religious sociology, religious policy and social participation of religious groups. bridgestoneq@hotmail.com.

planted. However, in practice, people have found that planting trees is only the first step, or the simplest step in the fight against desertification. After the saplings planted, they need to be watered regularly to stay alive. However, due to the lack of driveways in the desert, the nearest place a water tanker could reach was still quite a long distance from the planting area. Even though a water pipe was used for extension, the water cannot be pumped to the saplings. Therefore, this last section of the chain needs to be completed entirely by manpower in the way of delivering water buckets through a human chain. When they had completed the mission of delivering water and watering, many volunteers said, "when I heard about afforestation and prevention of desertification, I always felt that it was simply to plant trees. Unexpectedly, watering those trees is such a hard task. My concept of environmental protection and desertification control has been refreshed again."

In addition to carrying out environmental protection in Inner Mongolia, Shanghai YMCA and YMCA also held an environmental protection charity concert entitled "Desert is far, Love is here" in 2005 at the Shanghai Grand Theatre to raise money for the tree planting project in Dalad Banner in Inner Mongolia and some students in poor rural areas. Nearly 300 people attended, including government officials such as the then Secretary-General of the Shanghai CPPCC National Committee and the Director of the Civil Affairs Bureau, as well as church leaders including Luo Guanzong[3] and Cao Shengjie.[4] As the main performers, YMCA and YWCA Shanghai's fellowship teams, volunteers and staff presented a wonderful concert. It was worth mentioning that this concert did not sell tickets at a fixed price, however, a donation box was placed at the exit after the performance. Everyone could donate according toc their wishes. Many in the audience were deeply moved by the performance, and recognised the efforts made by the YMCA and YWCA of Shanghai in promoting desert prevention and poverty alleviation. They gave generously and offered love, one after another. In particular, officials from some competent government departments were impressed not only by the level of the performance and the dedication of the performers but also by the original ambition of YMCA and YWCA of Shanghai to devote themselves to environmental protection, as well as the achievements so far. This concert offered more people an "environmental protection feast", which was of great advocacy significance in the social context at that time.

Take thought for what is noble in the sight of all. (Romans 12:17)

Holding Advanced Ideas and Be Keenly Aware of Needs

As time goes by, especially this century, the public has a better understanding of environmental protection. However, YMCA and YWCA of Shanghai found out that for many people, environmental protection is only a concept, and their vision is relatively limited to how it is directly related to their lives. Take Shanghai as an example – citizens are often concerned about intuitive phenomena such as poor air quality in the city, garbage on roads and streets, and so on. When it comes to desertification, marine environmental pollution, global warming and other topics, there is only a very vague concept; that is, they know that these are environmental problems, and they also know that they should be treated and changed. But they do not know what such environmental disasters are, nor do they know how the problems thousands of miles away could affect them, let alone how to change and control them.

After discovering this problem, YMCA and YWCA of Shanghai put forward a new proposition for their own environmental protection services under self-pressure: how to make environmental protection publicity which would not only stay in oral and written forms but also be reflected in practice so that the concept of environmental protection for the public is not only a rational knowledge and concept but also a perceptual

[3] Luo Guanzong (1920-2011): Former Chairman of National Committee of Three-Self Patriotic Movement of the Protestant Churches in China, Former member of the Standing Committee of the CPPCC National Committee.

[4] Cao Shengjie(1931-): Former President of China Christian Council.

and emotional identity. Therefore, in the daily service, YMCA and YWCA of Shanghai pay keen attention to looking for environmental protection-related projects and co-operation opportunities, and to "take thought for what is noble in the sight of all." It is also an important premise and basis for YMCA and YWCA of Shanghai to always stand at the forefront of the times and take the lead in carrying out environmental protection projects.

> What good is it, if you say you have faith but do not have works? (James 2:14)

Be on the Scene and Participate in Person

The Bible asks us "What good is it if you say you have faith but do not have works?" When carrying out environmental protection projects, YMCA and YWCA of Shanghai also realise that environmental protection is not only in mind and in words. Instead, it should substantially improve the environment, and let people who are personally involved in environmental protection projects have more real and intuitive experiences and feelings. Therefore, based on the traditional environmental protection publicity, YMCA and YWCA of Shanghai have organised more participatory projects, inviting members, staff, young volunteers, young children, overseas friends to come to Inner Mongolia, which has not only made a substantial contribution to the local ecological improvement but also played a role in raising people's awareness of environmental protection. The combination of tree planting and educating people is also a critical way to influence others' lives.

Specifically, after participants devoted themselves to this project, especially after experiencing human chain watering, everyone realised that they then had a more intuitive and comprehensive understanding of environmental protection, and got rid of solidified thinking and romantic imagination. They rationally realised that the efforts and investment needed for tree planting, environmental protection and sand control were continuous and it would be a long-term process to change the situation of desertification. These projects gave them true awareness of the importance, arduousness and long-term nature of the cause of environmental protection.

> Go into all the world. (Mark 16:15)

Multiple Ways to Enhance the Influence

YMCA and YWCA of Shanghai realise that environmental protection is an overall cause. It is necessary to start with individuals, establish their awareness and guide their behaviours. Meanwhile, it also needs to arouse such awareness at the whole social level, i.e. the whole of society to form the awareness of ecological environment protection in order to make substantial efforts to improve the ecological environment at the macro level.

Therefore, on the basis of community guidance, YMCA and YWCA of Shanghai also face the public and carry out different forms of activities to enhance society's awareness and attention to environmental protection, so that sustainable development has become the consensus of the whole society. It also makes government departments pay attention to the attention and efforts of various social forces, including YMCA and YWCA of Shanghai, to environmental protection and sustainable development.

The charity concert mentioned above is of great significance in many ways. First of all, there is no doubt that the concert has raised a large amount of money for the Shanghai YMCA and the YWCA to be used for environmental protection and poverty alleviation. It was very important to bring real help to the improvement of the local environment and the improvement of learning and living conditions of the clients. Second, as mentioned above, through this event, the government has also seen the efforts and influence of the groups in this regard and has more recognised the contributions made by the Shanghai YMCA and the YWCA in the field of social services, which also helps the government to pay more attention to the issues of environmental protection and sustainable development. Third, the performance also provided a stage for fellowship members, volunteers and staff to show themselves, especially in such a famous place of the Shanghai Grand Theatre. It not only helped them gain a greater sense of achievement and pride after participating in daily activities, but more importantly, it made all participants feel that environmental protection and public welfare were not issues far removed from them. Their talents and services can also contribute to public welfare.

A Native Plant Against Desertification – Projects in Alxa League

In 2016, with the further popularisation and improvement of the concept of environmental protection and the knowledge of desertification prevention and sand fixation, YMCA and YWCA of Shanghai were concerned that Alxa League in Inner Mongolia was currently one of the largest sources of sandstorms in China and decided to carry out a new round of environmental protection sand fixation projects in this area. This time, they selected a native plant called *Haloxylon Ammodendron*, which is more likely to survive in the local environment.

This project was originally initiated by the Shanghai YMCA and the YWCA. However, in order to expand social influence and obtain more resources, they looked for partners and attracted like-minded organisations to join, including a foundation initiated by a well-known Buddhist group in Shanghai.

In the early days, YMCA and YWCA of Shanghai hired local farmers and herders to plant trees and water, which gave them extra income. Moreover, YMCA and YWCA of Shanghai instructed them to graft spores on the roots of *Haloxylon Ammodendron* to produce *Cistanche deserticola*, a crop with economic value, to help them further raise their income.

YMCA and YWCA of Shanghai also co-operated with local primary schools in Inner Mongolia to deliver environmental protection courses and youth moral development programmes. Although these children are living close to the desertification area, they actually have no more environmental knowledge than their peers in metropolises. Therefore, YMCA and YWCA of Shanghai passed on the correct environmental protection knowledge to them through lessons and games, and encouraged them to influence more local people around them. Meanwhile, through these activities, YMCA and YWCA of Shanghai also guided children to reflect on the moral character and values contained in the game, in order to help them to understand these ideas more intuitively, and improve their comprehensive moral quality, including the awareness of environmental protection.

In addition, YMCA and YWCA of Shanghai invited pastoralists and students from the Christian Church and Theological Seminary in Shanghai, as well as young staff and volunteers from Singapore, Japan, South Korea, Hong Kong SAR, to Inner Mongolia to jointly carry out environmental protection projects. The international co-operation not only helps YMCA and YWCA of Shanghai to learn advanced ideas and practices but also establishes friendship in the great cause of environmental protection.

Have it abundantly. (John 10:10)

Benefit the Local Area, There is More Than Environment

According to many people, environmental protection is a “loss-making business”, which means investing a lot of money, manpower and other resources, but unable to get any substantial economic benefits. Moreover, many people regard environmental protection as a “game for the rich” or “icing on the cake” after the economy has developed to a very high level. Therefore, it is not easy to make the wider public willing to accept environmental protection, participate in environmental protection and take the initiative to protect the environment. Given this situation, while promoting the cause of environmental protection, YMCA and YWCA of Shanghai also convey the concept of “Environmental Protection Plus” – that is, environmental protection does not contradict social progress and development. Instead, environmental protection has more and deeper positive significance besides itself including increased income, sound rules and regulations, and a better life.

The project in Alxa League has brought more long-term and stable benefits to local farmers and herders, that is, they no longer rely on the annual input of YMCA and YWCA of Shanghai as a source of income, but on their own work. Second, as the survival of *Cistanche deserticola* depends on the healthy survival of sand-fixing plants, it also urges local people to take better care of these plants in the long-term. More importantly, through this process, local people have a more comprehensive and positive understanding of sand fixation and environmental protection. They begin to understand that environmental protection is positively related to their economic income and that investment in environmental protection can be of direct benefit.

In addition to the economic benefits, YMCA and YWCA of Shanghai promote environmental protection together with their partners, and also make progress in other aspects. At the beginning of the co-operation, the local co-operative social organisations' understanding of their participation in environmental protection projects was "you give me money and I do what you want". However, they had no clear understanding of some financial requirements and evaluation systems that needed to be followed in the implementation of the project. Through co-operation, the local authorities gradually developed more understanding of these standardisation requirements and are more able to co-operate actively in the way required by the contract in the project implementation. Their overall standardisation has been significantly improved. Therefore, although this does not seem to be directly related to environmental goals, YMCA and YWCA of Shanghai help their partners and clients grow healthily in other areas through their environmental projects.

Inviting churches and seminaries to join the environmental protection programme broadens the minds and horizons of pastoralists, especially young seminarians. At the same time, it also makes the churches witness that promoting the cause of environmental protection is also working for God. It is "honouring God and benefiting people."

Neither Jews nor Greeks. (Gal 3:28)

Engaging in Co-operation and Establishing Interfaith Friendships

In the process of carrying out environmental protection, YMCA and YWCA of Shanghai also pay attention to co-operation and gather a wider range of forces to participate in this cause. From cross-faith to cross-country, YMCA and YWCA of Shanghai believe that ecology is related to the survival and fate of all mankind, so any differences in faith, race, skin colour and nationality cannot become an obstacle to everyone's common contribution to the cause of environmental protection.

The Buddhist foundation, which co-operates with YMCA and YWCA of Shanghai in the Project of Alxa, has tried to carry out various activities with the theme of "environmental protection" for a long time. However, due to the influence of their ideas and religious customs, their activities are mainly focused on freeing captive animals. In their view, freeing animals is protecting the environment. Unfortunately, although a lot of money has been invested, it cannot truly improve the ecological system. However, by participating in the anti-desertification project led by Shanghai YMCA and YWCA, they developed a deeper understanding of environmental protection. That is to say, freeing animals is not only to put the fish back into the river or release the rabbits back to the woods but also to restore and rebuild the whole ecological chain. When there is grass in the desert, grass will attract rabbits, and rabbits will bring foxes and eagles. As a result, the ecosystem of a region is restored and established. This is a higher level of "freeing animals" as well as the real sense of environmental protection. YMCA and YWCA of Shanghai strive to promote co-operation and their projects with words that their partners can understand and accept.

At the same time, YMCA and YWCA of Shanghai help their partners continue to grow. Such co-operation has improved the efficiency of funding, manpower and other resources of the project. At the same time, with the help of the wider mass base of Buddhism in contemporary Chinese society, it has not only allowed more people get to know Shanghai YMCA and YMCA, but also greatly enhanced the exposure and recognition of this project, and even the entire cause of environmental protection and sand control in the society. Moreover, such cooperation has also become a good example of cross-faith co-operation between groups of different religious backgrounds, sharing social responsibility for the benefit of people, and witnessing the whole process of changing lives with lives.

Moreover, as international social service organisations with extensive links around the world, YMCA and YWCA of Shanghai also make full use of various resources at home and abroad to learn and share their own experiences, jointly contributing to the cause of environmental protection and sustainable development.

Shanghai YMCA and YWCA also invite young people from Hong Kong SAR, together with young people from all over the country, including Shanghai, to participate in various activities. In this way, youth in Hong Kong not only have a more objective and intuitive understanding of the development of mainland China but also take advantage of this opportunity to deepen mutual understanding and friendship between young people from mainland China and Hong Kong. In addition, the participation of international friends has also enabled YMCA and YWCA of Shanghai to gain friendlier international relations and assume greater international responsibilities, which makes it possible to achieve sustainable development goals across a longer period of time and in a wider range of fields.

Therefore, when implementing the goal of sustainable development and carrying out environmental protection projects, YMCA and YWCA of Shanghai do not engage by working behind closed doors or fighting alone. Instead, they co-operate with all friendly parties at home and abroad with an open mind and a co-operative attitude, and work hard to promote the building of a community with a shared future for mankind.

> "forgetting what lies behind and straining forward to what lies ahead." (Ph. 13:13)

YMCA and YWCA of Shanghai believe that the road towards environmental protection sustainable development is endless which means that we need to constantly move forward and pursue the next stage. At the same time, we must not "forget behind" as well. We must not forget the great damage that we have done to the earth's ecology because of our ignorance and pride, nor can we forget the great efforts made by our predecessors to restore the environment. Only when we all join hands can we finally achieve the goal of sustainable development, so that our future generations can live in peace and joy in this beautiful home created by God.

Suggestions for Further Reading

Yiliang Qian (ed.), *The Letters to the Social Workers of YMCA in Shanghai*, Shanghai: Fudan University, 2018.

Zhiwei Zhang, *Struggle between Christianity and Secularity*. A Study of YMCA in Shanghai 1900-1922, Taipei: National Taiwan University, 2010.

Jianrong Wu (ed.), *Quarterly* (of MCA and YWCA in Shanghai, 1995-2020), Shanghai: Shanghai YMCA and YWCA.

86. The Construction and Practical Exploration of the Ecological Concept of Harmonious Co-existence: Fujian Christianity as an Example to Promote the Development of an Ecological Civilisation

Qiying Du[1] and Rebecca Yue[2]

Introduction

The severe destruction of the ecological environment leads to a serious threat to human life and development, a crisis of nature, and an ecological problem that brings about a broader humanitarian crisis. Ecology not only indicates the civilised development of nature but also often points to the harmonious relationship between human beings, society, and nature. The construction of a healthy, harmonious, and sustainable "ecological civilisation" is significant. It is the key to solving the ecological crisis and an essential factor in developing human civilisation and the well-being of people. Christian ecological theology aims to sort out and maintain the ecological balance between God, human beings and nature, replacing one-sided anthropocentric moral values with a harmonious concept of "community of life". It is the value of nature as a carrier of human interests, thus affirming the value of nature and calling on human beings to respect the integrity of nature itself.

As a concept that has been upheld by Chinese civilisation for thousands of years, the concept of "harmonious coexistence" or complementing each other is very consistent with the ecological ethics of Christianity and provides a platform for dialogue and convergence in the construction of a paradigm of "people and things – their harmony and symbiosis"[3] in China. This concept can provide a reference for contemporary ecological issues and promote a harmonious development and co-prosperity of human beings, society, country, and the environment. In recent years, the Church of Christ in Fujian Province has applied relevant ecological knowledge, upheld the value of community of life, and strived to construct the concept of ecological civilisation by exploring a path of harmonious co-existence with nature, people and society through practical actions. The students will apply and transform their ecological knowledge and skills into transformed voluntary lifestyle changes and behavioural habits conducive to ecological conservation and sustainable development.

Ecological Crisis: Alienated Homes

Scientific and technological progress increases day by day, and has promoted industrial and economic development. Along with the improvement of production technology, humankind's knowledge of nature has also grown; although man's desire to control the natural world and unbridled plunder and destruction have also grown. First, there is the well-known air pollution. The process of industrialisation has brought about severe atmospheric pollution, an increase in the greenhouse effect, and the gradual thinning of the ozone layer, which has caused global climate anomalies. In the last 20 years, the ozone layer is decreasing at a rate of 2-3% every ten years, and giant holes have appeared at the North and South Poles. Global warming poses a

---

[1] Qiying Du is Vice Provost of the Academic Affairs Office of Fujian Theological Seminary. He is now studying for a doctorate in the school of philosophy of Renmin University of China.

[2] Rebecca Yue is Director of Student Affairs in Fujian Theological Seminary. She is now studying for a master's degree at the Hong Kong Lutheran Theological Seminary.

[3] 'Tien-rén-hé-yi' (天人合一) ('the harmony between humanity and nature') is a core idea in Chinese traditional culture. See: Ruyu Hun, 'Chinese ecological pedagogy: humanity, nature, and education in the modern world', in *Educational Philosophy and Theory*, Vol. 51, 2019, in: https://www.tandfonline.com/doi/full/10.1080/00131857.2019.1572443

grave threat to all life on earth. Second, there is the degradation of vegetation. Vegetation is the main body of the terrestrial ecosystem and plays an inestimable role in maintaining the terrestrial ecological balance. In the past hundred years, the destruction of the vegetation by human beings has reached alarming levels. *The United Nations Global Ecological Environment Outlook* in 2000[4] points out that global forests have been reduced by half, 9% of tree species are on the verge of extinction, and 80% of the original forests covering the earth's surface have been destroyed. These are disastrous facts that have led to severe soil erosion as well as the threat of desertification. Once again, there is the emission of harmful chemicals. Industrial pollution from chemicals poses a significant threat to human life directly. Large industrial production leads to increasing sulfur oxides and nitrogen oxide, free in the atmosphere, which causes acidic precipitation. Acid rain pollutes water sources and soil, endangers the growth of crops, and directly endangers human life and health. Finally, the rapid global movement of money, technology, images, and ideology rapidly integrates the world into a global capitalist economic system. In this process of globalisation, the disparity between the rich and the poor has increased, and developing countries lacking bargaining power have become the victims of globalisation. However, even the ecological problems have become more and more serious.[5] Less economically developed countries unable to be self-sufficient. To survive, they destroy nature to obtain the only resources they can live on, which will lead to severe consequences of self-destruction. In short, ecological destruction has reached the point of no return.

In terms of theory, the so-called ecological equilibrium refers to a state of relative balance in an ecosystem. In this state, organisms within the ecosystem highly adapt to each other. Between organisms and the environment, the population structure and numerical ratio remain relatively stable over time. Ecology and consumption and decomposition are co-ordinated with each other, and the input and output of energy and materials to the system are close to a balance. However, the increased imbalance between the regenerating capacities of the earth and the extraction of the earth's resources by human civilisation today directly threatens the survival of human beings. The German theologian Jürgen Moltmann said about today's ecological crisis: "It is not only a crisis of humankind itself. It is also a crisis of life on this planet. A crisis so widespread and so irreversible that it is not too much to call it a cataclysm."[6] He believes that humans will not be spared from this unfolding ecological catastrophe and that the weakest organisms in the entire ecosphere will suffer first, followed by higher organisms. Therefore, the ecological crisis is not just a natural disaster in the general sense but a phenomenon that jeopardises human interests as well and threatens the survival and development of human beings as a whole. It decreases the environment's quality, disrupts the ecological order, and disintegrates the life-support systems – phenomena which are largely caused by human activities.

What is worse, the ecological crisis of modern industrialisation has led to the alienation of humanity from its own homeland, the soil and the natural environment, which is mainly reflected in the contradiction between humankind and nature. It makes our homeland no longer a dwelling place for a harmonious co-existence between human beings and nature. It thus reduces our homeland to a theatre for human deprivation and abuse. Jürgen Moltmann points out that "the ecological crisis in modern civilisation encompasses the crisis of the whole system, from the disappearance of forests to the epidemic of panic attacks, from the pollution of rivers and lakes to the nihilistic feeling about life that pervades many people in our big cities."[7]

In this sense, the ecological crisis is serious and widespread. On the one hand, human beings have destroyed the natural environment on which they depend. On the other hand, they have not only lost their homes in nature, but their spirits have also been unable to find a home in their physical bodies. Due to the

---

[4] See: UN Environment Programme, "GEO-6 Process", UNEP Website [Available at: https://www.unep.org/global-environment-outlook], [Last accessed 27th February 2022].

[5] G. K. Yang, "The Impact of Globalization and the Christian Response", in L. K. Lo (ed), *Love Your Neighbor – Theory and Practice of Social District Work in the Church* (Taipei: Campus Press, 2003): 126-127.

[6] Jürgen Moltmann, *God in Creation – A Theory of the Creation of Life,* translated by Kui Renlian et al. (Beijing: Sanlian Bookstore, 2002): 1.

[7] Moltmann, *God in Creation*, 35.

severity of the crisis, their home has been alienated into a place for "human power and domination," a site for "conquest and domination", and a "raw material" to be squandered and trampled at will.[8] Such an alienated home appears to be the garden at the disposal of human beings, but it is no longer the home of human beings where they really feel at home. There is only the maximisation of value and profit which counts in this garden, the expansion of the "mass production method", and no longer the existence of the "community of life". In Moltmann's view, the ecological crisis is not only a problem of the destruction of nature. It is also a crisis of fundamental human values and beliefs. John Cobb also clearly points out that, with the advent of the industrial revolution, the land was gradually understood as a commodity to be bought and sold or as a matter to be used by man.[9] The plundering and seizure of nature caused by the intensification of economic activities has far exceeded the internal growth rate of nature itself. This has led directly to a global ecological disaster. Cobb further emphasises the need for ecology to focus on the whole and interdependent relationships in and with the earth, rather than a modern mode of thinking that emphasises just subdivision and uni-directional thinking between humanity and nature.

Therefore, in the face of an increasingly severe ecological crisis, people realise that the ecological and environmental problems caused by human behaviour will eventually bring great disasters to human beings themselves. Thus, people today increasingly call for ecological protection and advocate for maintaining the living home of human beings together. This is a global crisis that cannot be solved by advanced science and technology alone. We need to treat the natural environment more reasonably under the guidance of a new ideology directed to seek harmony and development between human beings and nature.

Brotherhood and Sisterhood: A Christian Ecological Ethic

From the perspective of the Christian faith, both nature and human beings are God's creation, and both are cared for. According to the *Book of Genesis,* "God saw that everything made was good," and the world was in order. Humankind and nature maintained a harmonious, balanced and beautiful relationship. However, through greed, humankind broke all the harmonious relationships, including the relationships between humankind and God, men and women, and humankind and nature. The prophetic movement in ancient Israel emerged around the 8th century B.C., and people-to-people harmony became a major tenet of its belief. At that time, Israel was divided into the northern kingdom of Israel and the southern kingdom of Judah and both the northern and southern kingdoms reached unprecedented prosperity. However, the prosperity of both nations was based on the exploitation of the poor by the rich and the bullying of the weak by the strong, and the idolatry associated with wealth and corruption prevailed everywhere. It was a prosperous, seemingly wealthy, society, but full of sin, which had led to its downfall, and God's judgment was about to come through the invasion of powerful enemies.

When prophet Isaiah faced the world of Judah with internal troubles and external aggression, he turned his vision to the terminal landscape: the predator with the prey, beast and livestock living in peace with each other, the beast drawn by a child, the lion eating grass without harming life (Is. 65:25). Breastfed babies and weaned children are close to vipers and other snakes without coming to harm, and "in all the places of my holy mountain, all these do not harm people and do not harm things" (Is. 65:25b). This is a picture of the absolute beauty of the people's relationship and solidarity. "No man is an island of total isolation, but every man is a part of the earth, a part of the whole."[10] This is a picture of the absolute beauty of the people's

[8] Moltmann, God in Creation (Minneapolis: Fortress Press, 1993), 2-4 and 23ff.

[9] John Cobb and Herman E. Daly, *For the Common Good: Redirecting the economy toward community the environment, and a sustainable future* (Boston: Beacon Press, 1994), 100-117.

[10] John Donne, *For Whom the Bell Tolls: Meditations on the Edge of Life and Death*, translated by Lin Hesheng (Beijing: New Star Press, 2009): 5. John Donne (1572-1631) was a famous English poet and pastor, learned but poor and unmotivated, who experienced much suffering.

relationships and solidarity. There is no doubt that, from the perspective of Christian ecological ethics, the life of all things comes from the same author. Every birth, aging, illness and death is God's interpretation of life.

In the face of today's ecological crisis, Moltmann focuses on the relationship between creationism and ecology through his *God in Creation: an ecological doctrine of creation*, aiming to raise ecological awareness. He argues that creation is an open system and that created beings are a symbiotic fellowship. On this basis, Moltmann uses the concept of home to present this symbiotic fellowship as a spatial relationship that is both internally and mutually compatible. This symbiotic fellowship expresses the ecological ethics of people and things, solidarity. In a certain sense, the term "home" can refer to the land, the house, the hometown in the material aspect, as well as the family and life to which emotions are attached.

On the one hand, home represents affection, tranquillity, and security and is the place where people belong physically and spiritually. On the other hand, a home also embodies the relationship between people and geographic space, including the interdependence between people and people and people and society. For the planning of the home, God not only created but also emphasised rest. The word "rest" appears more than 200 times in the Bible. In the creation account, God rested on the seventh day from all His works. The Sabbath, the Sabbatical Year, and the Jubilee Year were prescribed in Israel's ordinances, and no work or interference with the outside world was permitted on the Sabbath or in the Sabbatical Year. Moltmann believes that the Sabbath was given a particular meaning when God made it a holy day. The Sabbath is a day of rest and recuperation for all things and an indication of the completion of the relationship between the Creator and creation so that all things created are sanctified and sacrosanct. Thus, Moltmann emphasises, "The Sabbath is the true sign of all Biblical – Jewish and Christian – creationism. Creation is completed through the peace of the Sabbath, a phrase that distinguishes two worldviews: one that sees the worldview as creation, and another that sees the worldview as nature; for, nature is constantly producing, and despite its seasons and rhythms, it knows no rest. It is the Sabbath that allows the world to be blessed, sanctified, and revealed as God's creation."[11] Therefore, all things should be properly nurtured. People should live and work in peace to better protect their homes, which is the spiritual meaning of the reconciliation between God and man, and between humankind and nature, people and things.

In God's creation, in this cosmic community of destiny, every being is an equal citizen, and all things should be in harmony, peace, integration, and co-operation with each other. "All things are of God" (Rom. 11:36), and Christ is all, and all is in Him. "There is only one whole Earth community, which includes all of its constituent members: human and nonhuman. In this community, each being has its role in fulfilling its dignity and inner spontaneity; each being has its voice; each being declares itself to the whole universe; each being enters into interaction with other beings. This capacity for an association, for manifestation to other existences, for spontaneous action, is possessed by every form of existence in the entire universe."[12] Therefore, all life is sacrosanct, and humanity, as a member of the cosmic community, should respect all creation and live in harmony with it.

In this way, the essence of harmonious co-existence lies in a harmony between humankind and nature, in the unity of heaven and man. Lin Hongxin points out that the book of Genesis depicts a picture of the relationship between human beings and all things under the guidance of the Creator, and that "God has both the transcendence of being all and the immanence of being in all, and the belief in the unity of all is the foundation and transcendence of the Creator in the immanence of all creation."[13] From this, it can be seen that through understanding the relationship between God, human beings, and nature, human beings can

[11] Moltmann, *God in Creation*, 13.

[12] John Cobb and David Griffin, *Process Theology – A Guiding Note*, translated by Qu Yuehou (Beijing: Central Compilation Press, 1999): 5.

[13] Lin Hongxin, *The People's Republic and the Community,* Journal of Christian Culture, Beijing: Institute of Christian Culture, Renmin University of China, Vol. 2, 2019, 81-82.

reacquaint themselves with their mission and calling. Then through the pull of God's love, the rift between human beings and nature can be bridged, awakening the consciousness of human beings to participate in maintaining and managing the benign development of nature and ultimately actively participating in the process of overcoming the ecological crisis.

Harmonious Co-existence: Fujian Christianity Promotes Ecological Civilisation Practice

Human beings are products of nature and depend on nature for their existence, and nature is the mother that nurtures us and the home where we live. Both Christian theologians and traditional Chinese culture's concept of harmonious co-existence agree that, in the era of human ecology, human beings should live on the common earth home, on which human beings and nature enhance each other and build each other. They co-exist, co-prosper, and are related to each other. We all cannot be good alone but should help the whole world. Happiness should not be the enjoyment of an independent unit but should be a familiar feeling of all human beings. We cannot ignore the differences between the North and the South, and we cannot break our commitments to combating climate change. All countries should take up their responsibilities, look at global development, further expand the pattern of co-operation, and promote a community of human destiny. Therefore, both the Christian ecological concept and the traditional Chinese concept of harmonious co-existence can provide some reference value for contemporary ecological issues and promote the harmonious development and co-prosperity of people, society, the state, and the environment.

Basic Situation of the Church in Fujian

Fujian is one of the provinces where the Christian Church in China was introduced early, established firmly, developed well, and had great influence. In 1842, Christianity was introduced to Fujian, and after a century of twists and turns, the Gospel took root, sprouted, grew, and blossomed. In 1949, after the founding of New China, the Church in Fujian followed the principles of autonomy, self-support, and self-evangelisation, and forged ahead along the path of patriotism and love for the Church. In the 1950s and 1980s, the Fujian Provincial Christian Three-Self Patriotic Movement Committee and the Fujian Provincial Christian Association were established to lead and co-ordinate the steady development of the churches in the province. Currently, there are nine working committees: Church Governance, Theological Education, Rural Churches, Writing and Publishing, Foreign Affairs, Women's Ministry, Church Self-support and Social Service, Anti-heresy and Sacred Music Ministry, as well as the Theological Thought Building Promotion Group, which work together with the two churches in the 10 prefectures and 61 counties (cities and districts) in the province to build up the church.

After the reform and opening up, the church in Fujian has carried out a rich and varied ministry in accordance with the teachings of biblical truth, doctrine, liturgy and tradition, and has formulated a series of rules and regulations to guide and regulate church building and management to ensure the healthy growth of the church. Under the Lord's favour, the church in Fujian is flourishing and the number of saved people increases daily. By 2017, there were approximately 900,000 believers, 375 pastors, over 3,000 preachers, 1,850 churches, and more than 2,510 congregations in the province. Nowadays, co-workers and co-workers in the province are working together with one mind and in partnership with each other, continuing to fight a good battle for the gospel ministry in all parts of the province along the direction of "healing, nurturing, and preaching well", and bearing a good testimony for the Lord in this age.

In order to meet the needs of pastoral staff for church development, the Church in Fujian has strengthened its theological education work. In 1983, the Church in Fujian established Fujian Theological Seminary, and in 2015, the State Administration for Religious Affairs officially approved its upgrading to an undergraduate Christian institution. Currently, there are 170 students enrolled, 44 full-time and part-time teachers, and the library has a collection of 80,000 titles and more than 110,000 volumes. Since its founding, the college has provided 2,179 faculty members for churches in the province, the vast majority of whom have become the backbone of grassroots patriotic religious groups and Christian activity sites. In order to supply believers with spiritual pursuits, help them take root in the truth, and stimulate their life pursuits and testimonies, the Church in Fujian attaches great importance to text publishing and distribution.

As a member of the universal church, the Fujian Church values and cherishes friendly relations with churches in other countries and regions. Since its reform and opening up, it has received visits from church groups and individuals from more than 20 countries and regions, including Europe, the United States, Australia and Southeast Asia, as well as Hong Kong, Macao and Taiwan. We have also organised delegations or participated in national delegations to visit churches and institutions in many countries and regions. Through these friendly exchanges, mutual understanding with the universal church has been enhanced and friendship has been established. In order to increase the ecological awareness of the grassroots churches, the Fujian churches regularly organise pastoral staff to hold training and other ministries related to ecological theology in the grassroots churches. At the same time, the two churches in Fujian lead the churches in the province to participate in various church ministries and social welfare projects, especially to strengthen services in environmental protection and public health, in recognition of Christ's love that glorifies God and benefits people throughout Fujian.

In recent years, the Church of Christ in Fujian Province has applied relevant ecological knowledge, upheld the value of community of life, strived to construct the concept of ecological civilisation, explored a path of harmonious co-existence with nature, human beings and society through practical actions, applied global awareness and open-mindedness, and paid attention to the needs of the people. The students will apply their ecological knowledge and skills and transform them into conscious and voluntary lifestyles and behavioural habits conducive to ecological conservation and sustainable development by applying global awareness and open-mindedness, paying attention to the global challenges facing humanity, and understanding the community of human destiny.

Some Practices of the Church of Fujian on Ecological Civilisation Construction

First, the ecological concept is actively cultivated and promoted. The Church in Fujian uses the creation of fruit farms to protect ecological homes. Sister You Muhua of Luoyuan County, Fuzhou City, established the Unity fruit farm. This fruit farm has developed with significant momentum with her skilful cultivation of longan and effective management and administration. Putian City, located in the Puxian Plain, is famous for its abundance of Xinghua Guiyuan (longan). As Fujian Province is a subtropical humid monsoon climate, 30% of the province's more than 20 million mu arable land area is in the plains along the river. Due to Putian's unique geographical location and conditions, in recent years, with the development of the rural economy, the city has been included in the State Council's national longan production base.

A good example is the Lilong Fruit Farm in Putian City, founded by the local church and the Bureau of Agriculture. The fruit farm was established not only for the church, but more importantly, for the ecological protection of Putian City. In Putian City, people store drinking water, in order to have year-round water supply by the Dongsheng Reservoir. This reservoir provides drinking water for 3 million people in Putian City, and water pollution seriously affected people's health. Therefore, the Putian government strongly advocates the community to plant longan fruit trees on the hills next to the reservoir, which effectively maintains the natural ecological environment of water sources and forests in the mountains. In order to respond to the government's call, in recent years, the Amity Foundation and the two local Christian churches have jointly agreed to invest certain funds to plant 100 mu[14] of various forest trees in Lilong Fruit Farm. The annual output of fruit trees is up to 200 kg per mu. If accumulated every five years, the yield can reach 1 ton per mu. The total yield can

[14] Mu is the unit of area that is often used in south Asia. 1 Mu corresponds to 1/15 ha1, about ⅔ × 1000 (or 666.7) m^2.

reach 100 tons. In addition to such a high yield of fruit, it also promotes adequate protection of the local natural environment. Therefore, through the development of Lilong Fruit Farm, the Christian Church of Fujian Province has achieved the healthy development of actively co-operating with society, applying modern ecological technology, and pioneering ecological civilisation.

Second, the concept of ecological civilisation has been incorporated into the teaching materials and classrooms so that teachers and students can absorb these ideas into their heads and hearts. Fujian Theological Seminary[15] has made full use of its classrooms and teaching to set up an environmental, ecological theology course to teach students to become advocates, defenders, and practitioners of ecological civilisation. We are guiding and pastoring more Christians to pay attention to ecological issues and to participate in protecting the ecological environment. In response to the global campaign to turn off lights for one hour, Fujian Theological Seminary conducts an annual Earth Hour event. The purpose of Earth Hour is not to save electricity but to make the public aware of the importance of protecting the earth and environment to develop good habits in their daily lives. Fujian Theological Seminary builds the students' ecological view of a "community home" in the classroom and teaching materials and conveys the concept of environmental protection through concrete practices and speaking up for the earth together.

On this basis, Fujian Christianity starts from the church itself and acts physically. In church construction, Fujian Christianity has always focused on conserving and making rational use of land resources and resources of light efficiency and stifling the phenomenon of disorder and comparison in building churches from a theological and pastoral practice perspective. In the design process of the church, various means are used to create an environment that is conducive to the comfort of worship while conforming to the concept of worship theology. In the construction and decoration of the church, people try to preserve the local environment as much as possible to ensure the integrity of the ecological system. The principle of energy conservation is followed, namely by saving energy and resources. The concept of environmental protection is harmless, pollution-free, and recyclable; the building materials are made of biodegradable resources, and the construction materials are strictly harmless (pollution-free and radiation-free). The concept of building a church under the ecological value of "harmony and progress" has been promoted to churches across the province and has received the expected results.

Third, there also have been efforts out of the campus to serve the community and beautify the living environment around the seminary. Fujian Theological Seminary organises teachers and students to protect the Min River, the mother river, actively, and the city's famous scenic spots – Gushan scenic area and Guling mountainous area. They hope to do a good job in pollution prevention and control according to the deployment requirements of the Fujian Provincial Government to systematically promote environmental protection and restoration of mountains, water, forests, fields, lakes, and grasses. This involves making the Min River a safe, healthy, beautiful, and prosperous river and contributing more to the construction of a modernisation in which people and nature live in harmony. To this end, Fujian Christian Council and Fujian Theological Seminary actively echo the government's call to beautify their living environment by organising believers, students, and teachers to pick up trash from the Min River scenic spots and local communities on a regular and irregular basis. Students who came out of school carried garbage cans, picked up white garbage, and cleaned up weeds, not afraid of being tired and dirty, and the scene was a scene of feverish labour. They cleaned up wall advertisements in the community, picked up street garbage and bagged it for centralised cleaning and placed shared bicycles for the community.

Students and teachers of Fujian Theological Seminary also use the Sunday services to guide the nearby villagers, encouraging them to consciously abandon unhealthy customs and behaviours. Through the environmental protection activities, awareness of teachers and students was further enhanced, and a beautiful

---

[15] National Committee of Three-Self Patriotic Movement of the Protestant Churches in China/ China Christian Council, "Fujian Theological Seminary Has an Opening Ceremony", 21st October 2020 [Available at: http://en.ccctspm.org/newsinfo/13781], [Last accessed: 28th February 2022].

and clean living environment was created for everyone. The Fujian Christian Council will establish an effective environmental hygiene management system and incorporate the daily maintenance of environmental hygiene into the management system of the grassroots churches in Fujian so that believers may be aware of the need to protect environmental hygiene. To do so, the following steps will be followed:

1. We will encourage believers to plant flowers and plants and allow them to share their experiences.
2. We will encourage believers to live a simple and green life.
3. We will remind believers to remember to turn off the air conditioners and lights after using the church premises.
4. We will collect things that believers no longer use, and those who need them can pick them up from the church, including books, toys, baby carriages, clothes, electrical appliances, etc.
5. We will formulate an environmental protection code for the church.
6. We should establish this code and make a joint commitment to implement it strictly.

In short, we will use the unique ecological concept of Christianity and environmental protection practices to reduce, reuse, and recycle to make the church a green church and become a pioneer in environmental protection for the benefit of society.

Conclusion

The Bible tells us that, when we should love God and love people, we should also love the world that God has created. Only when a person loves God the creator can they genuinely love nature as God created it, and only when a person loves nature as God created it can they truly love God the creator. In Christian eco-ethics, the relationship between humankind and nature is not a simple partnership, management or domination model. However, as God's co-creators, humankind should establish a harmonious fellowship with nature, an entirely harmonious living community between humankind and nature. In this sense, traditional Chinese ecological culture and Christian ecological ethics are very compatible, and both advocate the sustainable ecological development concept of "people and things – harmonious co-existence."

It is thus clear that in the home created by God, all things should live in harmony together. In this community of life in the universe, every existence has its role and value, and every life should be respected. Although human beings have been given the mission of "guardianship" and "management" in this home, they are the same as others and are not self-ruling subjects. It is time for human beings to awaken to their mission and their responsibility. In this cosmic community of life, we should take up our responsibilities, live in harmony with nature, and restore the glory of God's creation. Therefore, this ecological concept can provide some meaningful reference value for the current theoretical construction and practical exploration of Chinese Christian eco-theology. Fujian Christianity continues to promote the development of ecological civilisation based on it.

Suggestions for Further Reading

Cobb, John. "Out of the Deep Valley of the Dichotomy between Economics and Ecology". In Wang Zhihe, Ed. *Globalization and Postmodernity*. Guilin: Guangxi Normal University Press, 2003.

Cobb, John and David Griffin. *Process Theology: A Guiding Note*. Translated by Qu Yuehou. Beijing: Central Compilation Press, 1999.

Cobb, John and Herman E. Daly. *For the Common Good: Redirecting the economy toward community the environment, and a sustainable future.* Boston: Beacon Press, 1994.

Donne, John. *For Whom the Death Bell Tolls.* Translated by Lin Hesheng. Beijing: New Star Press, 2009.

Moltmann, Jürgen. *God in Creation: The Ecological Theory of Creation.* Translated by Kui Renlian et al. Beijing: Life, Reading, and Xinqi Sanlian, 2002.

Hongxin, Lin. "The People's Solidarity with the People, and the Solidarity with the Solidarity". *Journal for the Study of Christian Culture*. Beijing: Institute of Christian Culture, Renmin University of China, No. 2, 2019.

Yang, K. K. "The Impact of Globalization and Christian Response". In L. K. Lo, Ed. *Love Your Neighbor: Theory and Practice of Social District Work in the Church*. Taipei: Campus Press, 2003.

87. Rethinking Development: Conceptual Presuppositions for the Pacific We Want

Emele Duituturaga[1]

Introduction

Climate Change presents the single greatest threat to the livelihood, security and wellbeing of Pacific peoples.[2] The fact is the pacific island nations are on the frontline of the impacts of climate change and suffering from what is a climate crisis. Already, low lying coastal and riverbank communities are having to be relocated due to rising sea levels, landslides due to unprecedented torrential rain, disastrous and extreme storms and weather patterns, volcanic eruption, unprecedented torrential rain, damaging floods, destructive tropical cyclones have become our new norm. While the world is still negotiating scientific predictions and commitments to reduce carbon emissions, Pacific people are bearing the daily brunt of this climate crisis. We ask – where, just where, is the justice that those of us who are least responsible, suffer the greatest? What has become of the pristine beauty and peaceful Pacific we once knew? Why is this happening?

Leading the Pacific region's largest umbrella NGO has been undergirded by the quest for answers to these questions. Personally and professionally, it became a journey of rethinking, a praxis of action and reflection, debunking the myth that modernisation and westernisation is progress for all. Realising that development has become synonymous with neoliberal capitalism, we started to search, not for an alternative development paradigm, but for an alternative paradigm of life.

The peoples of the Pacific are the custodians of the largest, relatively peaceful and abundant oceans, with pristine beauty and rich and diverse cultures for thousands of years. However, colonial legacy has shaped what we have become. Portuguese navigator Ferdinand Magellan named the Pacific Ocean in the sixteenth Century. After braving perilous seas, his small fleet entered an unfamiliar ocean in November 1520 and he called this body of water *Pacific*, due to the calmness of the water at the time ('*pacific*' means peaceful). Renowned Pacific scholar Epeli Hauofa coined the term 'sea of islands'. He argued that there is a gulf of difference between viewing the Pacific as 'islands in a far sea' and 'a sea of islands'. The first emphasises dry surfaces in a vast ocean, whereas the second is a more holistic perspective in which things are seen in the totality of their relationships. It was continental men, Europeans and Americans, who drew imaginary lines across the sea, making the colonial boundaries that, for the first time, confined ocean peoples to tiny spaces. These are the boundaries that today define the island states and territories of the Pacific.[3]

Modernisation and globalisation have brought 'development' and opportunities to our shores, but they have also exposed our vulnerability as small island developing states. Development, as we have known it, has threatened our family and community bonds and values, weakened our ability to live off the land and sea, and upset our harmony with the natural environment. With fast pace changing times, the somewhat peaceful Pacific has emerged as a battleground for competing values strung with contested development paradigms. This has also sounded a war cry that Pacific Islanders must stand strong, now more than ever before, to

---

[1] Mrs. Emele Duituturaga is a development specialist who has served throughout the Pacific region in senior roles including CEO of the Fiji Ministry for Women, Social Welfare and Poverty Alleviation and Head of the Pacific Women's Resource Bureau for the Secretariat of the Pacific Community. She also served as Executive Director of PIANGO Secretariat. This article is the amended version of an article published originally in Cornelia Füllkrug-Weitzel and Dietrich Werner (eds), *Ethics for Life. Voices from Ecumenical Partners on a New Paradigm of Life and Society. Jubilee Volume 60 years of Bread for the World* (Berlin: Bread for the World, 2019), 236-246.

[2] 49th Pacific Islands Leaders Meeting Communique, https://www.forumsec.org/forty-ninth-pacific-islands-forum-nauru-3rd-6th-september-2018.

[3] Epeli Hau'ofa, *Our Sea of Islands* (University of South Pacific, 1993).

preserve our region, our heritage and the best aspects of our traditions, to enhance them for the benefit of future generations. It is time to rethink again what development should be about, and to envision and reshape the Pacific that we want.

This chapter recollects various efforts by Pacific scholars and civil society in 'rethinking development', coupled with a 'reshaping' agenda, to re-assert a renewed Pacific identify and strengthen solidarity in contesting the neoliberal development paradigm focused on insatiable growth at the expense of people and planet. The paper is based on our lived experiences as Pacific peoples and points to the eminent threat of climate change as sounding the alarm to urgently critique the development pathway being followed by Pacific island nations. In the search of an alternative paradigm, we have rediscovered the fundamental values of family, life, relationships, environment, spirituality and a traditional economy as key pillars of an emerging paradigm.

Rethinking Approaches

Pacific scholars of the 1970s and 1980s, such as Rusiate Nayacakalou,[4] Epeli Hau'ofa,[5] and Unaisi Nabobo-Baba, have written and articulated various rethinking approaches and paradigms that frame current thinking. In 2001, the *Re-thinking Pacific Education Initiative for and by Pacific Peoples* (RPEIPP) was initiated and led by a group of Pacific educational leaders, namely Professor Konai Helu Thaman from USP, Tonga's Minister for Education, Women and Culture, Honourable Dr. Ana MauTaufe'ulungkai and Associate Professor Kabini Sanga from the University of Victoria in New Zealand. The influences of RPEIPP have continued as Pacific educational leaders, scholars and emerging leaders took up the mantle of contextualizing their thinking, scholarship and leadership.

At the 2011 Pacific regional symposium,[6] Pacific educational leaders, scholars, leaders and emerging leaders reflected on the past decade of re-thinking as well as envision the future of Pacific education and leadership. They highlighted the need for Pacific people to critically rethink various developments in Pacific education, specifically formal education. The RPEIPP initiative contributed to embedding indigenous graduate attributes into teacher education courses, in the leadership training of young and emerging young Pacific leaders, and in communities – this was research that took into account indigenous knowledge systems.[7]

In 2010, the Pacific Conference of Churches (PCC) paper titled *Rethinking Oceania* urged Pacific leaders to envisage a new form of regionalism, giving legitimacy to the notion of self-determination that the course of our Pacific history will be one chartered by our people and their descendants.[8] The paper expressed the concerns of the Churches in Oceania with regard to how the people of Oceania ought to live and develop, as envisaged by those living outside the region.

It proposed a developmental model premised on sufficiency and solidarity, inclusiveness and participation – one that is no longer fuelled by the 'race to the bottom' and the 'endless growth' rationale for development. The neo-liberal ethic is challenged as being directly opposite to the ideal value of sufficiency, driving the consumerist idea of 'more and more' with the question posed, 'When is enough, enough?' Concern is expressed about addressing poverty and inequality, which is seen as more than the lack of basic needs, but essentially the lack of social and political relationships. Investment into building social and political

---

[4] https://en.wikipedia.org/wiki/Rusiate_Nayacakalou.

[5] https://en.wikipedia.org/wiki/Epeli_Hau%CA%BBofa.

[6] http://www.usp.ac.fj/news/story.php?id=927#.WX1SNVUjHIU.

[7] Unaisi Nabobo-Baba, 'Transformations from within: Rethinking Pacific Education Iniative. The development of a movement for social justice and equity', see https://openjournals.library.sydney.edu.au/index.php/IEJ/article/viewFile/7439/7795

[8] PCC (2010), *Rethinking Oceania – Towards Sufficiency and Solidarity, Inclusiveness and Participation.* See https://actnowpng.org/sites/default/files/Re-thinking%20Oceania%20pc.pdf.

relationships in the interest of peace and security is abandoned; instead, the peace and security of the region is vested in the protection of property and an individual's personal security, not so much in relationships. Climate change and its impacts, fuelled by a view of development that pays no regard to the health and wellbeing of both the Pacific human economy and natural ecology, demonstrates the unsustainable neo-liberal economic model adopted. The paper proposes culture and social development as key components of a new form of regionalism, with the key pillars of family, life, relationships, environment, spirituality and traditional economy.

In 2012,[9] Pacific civil society leaders met and reaffirmed the need to rethink development in the Pacific Islands, faced with a changing regional context and emergent challenges: climate change being a trigger for rethinking; reviewing what is considered the *Pacific Way*;[10] rethinking the role and contribution of civil society as development actors in their own right;[11] rethinking regionalism in light of the Pacific Plan Review commissioned by Pacific Islands Forum Leaders;[12] and the establishment of a new regional organisation – the Pacific Islands Development Forum,[13] spearheaded by Fiji following its suspension from the Pacific Islands Forum after the 2006 coup. Pacific civil society leaders assessed that the Pacific region had become highly contested for its abundance of natural resources and strategic military positioning, and so there was a need to think critically about the regionalism being promoted by super powers who were now key players in the geopolitics of the Pacific.

At the same time, other Pacific civil society actors were demanding a 'future we want'. In May 2012, leading up to the June Rio +20 United Nations Conference on Sustainable Development, Pacific CSOs issued a statement titled 'The Future We Demand'[14] which called upon UN member states for strong political leadership to avert the imminent disaster to our planet by urgently changing dominant development and political mind-sets and instead provide real and transformative solutions to the threat of climate change.

The second regional consultation for Bread for the World Partners in the Pacific in November 2013 involved 31 Pacific CSO representatives who met in Papua New Guinea to further develop an analysis of the root causes of problems faced in the Pacific. In the conference report titled 'A New Voyage: Pacific People Explore the Future They Want', Pacific CSOs deepened the critique of the dominant model of development with a call to rethink the model based on their experiences.[15]

In September 2014, Pacific CSOs met in Madang, Papua New Guinea, at what was known as the 'Wansolwara Dance Gathering' and the launch of the '*Wansolwara*' movement, for a week-long celebration of solidarity, a shared commitment of a movement to protect our *Wansolwara*, our *Mona Nui*, our *Oceania*, for the liquid continent to be free and self-determining.[16] Participants shared their stories and pledged support by creating art, music, poetry, dance, conducting discussions, and expressing support for the West Papua struggle for human rights and self-determination. This was the culmination of an earlier gathering in Nadave, Fiji, to plan for the Madang gathering. A direct quote from Arnie Saiki's report reads:

[9] A project meeting convened by PIANGO.

[10] The Pacific Way derived its name from a word coined by Fiji's former statesman and Paramount Chief, Ratu Sir Kamisese Mara, to describe the region's ceremonial and revered form of negotiations and dialogue.

[11] The Accra Agenda for Action, 2008, recognised that civil society organisations are "independent development actors in their own right." See Accra Agenda for Action (AAA) of OECD,2008, in: https://www.oecd.org/dac/effectiveness/45827311.pdf.

[12] The Pacific Plan underwent a major review in 2013 – see www.forumsec.org/.../pacific-plan-review-2013-message-from-sir-mekere-morauta.html? Following the review, forum leaders agreed to recast the plan as the Framework for Pacific Regionalism. See 'The Framework for Pacific Regionalism', in: https://www.forumsec.org/wp-content/uploads/2017/09/Framework-for-Pacific-Regionalism.pdf.

[13] http://pacificidf.org/.

[14] www.dawnnet.org/feminist-resources/content/future-we-demand.

[15] Bread for the World (2011). *A New Voyage: Pacific People Explore the Future They Want*. See https://www.brot-fuer-die-welt.de/fileadmin/mediapool/2_Downloads/Fachinformationen/Dialog/Dialog_11_a_new_voyage.pdf.

[16] Quoted from the report of the First Landing Meeting prepared by Arnie Saiki.

> In Nadave we spoke about how the (Alter)native is the empire in its many faces and forms. The (Alter)native is faceless yet seen in the sorrowful eyes and scars of struggles of our people for freedom, for honour and dignity, and for legitimacy; it smiles yet without warmth; it embraces yet without compassion; it sings yet without harmony of voices. It suppresses, at times by brute force as had happened in the days of our grandparents and still today to some of us, but most times by softly killing our people through charming, enchanting and charismatic words and by its crafty and uncompromising logical and judicial frameworks. It uses our mother's womb, our language, our symbols and traditions to give birth and reproduce itself. It forces us to re-dream our dreams in its way.[17]

Defining the Pacific We Want

For the Pacific Island Association of NGOs (PIANGO), a partner of Bread for the World, we considered that the Pacific Islands region is facing a multitude of pressing challenges, ranging from large-scale exploitation of resources, to environmental damage and the effects of climate change; from growing poverty, to increasing violence and conflicts; from neglect of rural development, to issues of governance such as corruption and mismanagement. It was clear that the pursuit of the 'The World We Want' as a theme for the post-2015 development agenda has made us think specifically of 'The Pacific We Want'.[18] We convinced ourselves that the Pacific we want will not be decided in New York, Washington or even Beijing, for that matter. It will be decided here in the Pacific by Pacific peoples. This began the quest for the Pacific we want and sparked PIANGO's internal rethinking of its own *raison d'être*, structures and *modus operandi*, and looking to secure genuine and durable partnerships within the architecture of a renewed Pacific regionalism. The issues of identity, unity and solidarity pursued by the PIANGO network in its own journey of re-emergence had catapulted us to rethink what we are driven by as a civil society organisation. We realised that the CSO sector in the Pacific Islands is very diverse and characterised by an increasing demand for effective leadership and impactive programming. We began to ask, 'What was our particular contribution to development in the Pacific region and in our own nations?' We wanted to determine how current CSO leaders could share and pass on their knowledge, experience and wisdom to nurture the next generation of CSO leaders, ensuring that there is transition between leadership changes and no leadership deficit. Our hope was that civil society would grow from strength to strength until the vision of the Pacific we want is fulfilled.

PIANGO's rethinking and reshaping initiative has focussed on: (a) creating space for a structured process of rethinking;(b) reflecting and reasserting *the Pacific we want;* (c) linking conversations and listening to what people are saying, and feeling the pulse and heartbeat of Pacific people; (d) framing and reshaping through civil society advocacy, next generation leadership development, regional architecture, think tanks, and media, and convening multi-stakeholder roundtable discussions with church, government, CSOs, including tradition, women, and youth leaders; and (d) taking stock of Pacific expertise, local culture, local epistemology and local passion, and bringing together practitioners and academics (p*racademia).*

An Alternative Paradigm

CSOs in the Pacific and across the globe are critical of the prevailing development paradigm which is focussed on growth-led economic development, leading to increasing poverty, alienation of resource owners, high unemployment and underemployment and many social ills. The neoliberalism and the promotion of free market capitalism being promoted by institutions such as the World Bank and IMF are viewed as the source of the problem. Even with their more recent emphasis on 'equitable growth', this thinking is still fundamentally flawed. However, the IMF and World Bank are also critical of these outcomes, and are seeking ways of gaining both growth and equity. Questions are continually asked about development pathways which

---

[17] Wansolwara Nadave Statement, in: https://de.scribd.com/document/250696367/Wansolwara-Nadave-Statement.

[18] 'The World We Want 2015' was launched as a campaign – see http://www.beyond2015.org/world-we-want-2015-web-platform.

require critical rethinking of development: What do we mean by development? What affects development? Where does development come from? Who benefits from development? Are we in control of our development? Why do we do what we do? If we could have the time again, what would we do differently? Is climate change a symptom of good or bad development? What are the signs? How can we take control of our own development?

For civil society, we are coming to associate the term 'development' as a synonym with capitalism, which leads us not to find an alternative development paradigm, but an alternative paradigm that has as its cornerstone what the PCC paper proposes: family, life, relationships, environment, spirituality and traditional economy.

To pursue this quest for an alternative paradigm, PIANGO proposes to continue and pursue the discussions of this conference and convene pracademic solutions, bringing academics and practioners to discuss theoretical approaches and evidenced based practice. Recognising the significant role that religion and faith plays in the life of Pacific peoples, contextual theology is very important. The aim is to develop effective community engagement and public policy solutions and programmes that are rooted in a solid understanding of contextual theology, academic theory, evidenced based research and years of practical experience in these fields. To this end, initial discussions are taking place between PIANGO, PTC and USP to establish a pracademia initiative.

While this may sound an impossible challenge, there are already global initiatives with similar objectives. PIANGO's Executive Director is a member of the Bread for the World Global Reference Group[19] which in 2014 identified the need for an alternative paradigm as one of the key challenges facing civil society. Discussing global changes in context, the group agreed unanimously that the current, predominant paradigm which is shaping development efforts is redundant. This paradigm's foundation is based on neo-liberal thinking and belief in continuous economic growth. Since the ecological limits of the world have already been reached a long time ago, it appears necessary to reassess the validity of such a paradigm. This is evidenced by the fact that, while poverty may decrease in some parts of the world, inequalities are rising. The group has encouraged Bread for the World to engage in conversations about a new paradigm to eventually replace the growth-driven paradigm, to instead focus on life itself, with its foundations to be highly ethical and built around four ethical elements: (1) ethics of nature (seeing nature as an equal partner); (2) ethics of caring (for people) and sharing; (3) ethics of commons (resources); (4) ethics of human rights beyond legal frameworks.[20]

The Pacific Way

Embracing an alternative paradigm should enable Pacific communities to safeguard the pristine beauty and rich cultural heritage of our Pacific which is under threat and further compounded by challenges such as climate change. We are continuously challenged to do everything within our power, individually and collectively, to develop and protect our communities and nations and the region, to be a beacon of hope and strength for our children and for our planet – mother earth. We need to look within ourselves, our cultures, and our societies for our own sovereign solutions to our problems, while at the same time we must keep an open mind to lessons from other parts of the world and those from other cultures who have come to live with us and call the Pacific home. Together, we must work to ensure that in our communities, people matter more than anything else, and where every person feels loved, needed and able to enjoy a free, responsible and worthwhile life. It is the Pacific way.

---

[19] An appointed group of partner representatives that meet annually as a think tank with the Executives of Bread for the World on strategic positioning and partnerships. See https://www.brot-fuer-die-welt.de/fileadmin/mediapool/2_Downloads/Ueber-uns/BfdW_JB_2014_E.pdf.

[20] Bread for the World Global Reference Group discussions.

This powerful notion of the 'Pacific way' must embrace new ways of thinking and acting, and appeal to the young generation who are mesmerised by social media and the age of information. The Pacific way must denote a style of leadership that is respected for its inclusiveness, effectiveness and freedom from corruption, that is people-centred and democratic in spirit. It needs to reach into communities and address the issues that are important to them. The Pacific way should deal openly, honestly and yet respectfully with problems, including failures of governance and corruption.

There is some agreement that however much it evolves to meet the demands of a changing world, the Pacific way will have at its core one unchanging truth: regional interconnectedness, the idea that there is a Pacific way of doing things that is open to, but different from, the way Americans, or Europeans or Asians do things.[21] It is the idea of a unifying regional consciousness that should inspire us as Pacific peoples.

Conclusion

The chapter has elaborated on how neoliberal capitalism has framed 'development' as we know it and that through modernisation and globalisation there has been systematic erosion of Pacific values, cultural identity, weakening of family and community bonds and disharmony with nature. Based on this, there is a call to rethink prevailing development models and to search for an alternative paradigm that recognises that in the Pacific, relationality – relationships, family, spirituality and community – are the bedrock of our societies, putting life at the centre and preserving the best aspects of our Pacific traditional heritage. Pacific civil society organisations like Pacific Conference of Churches and PIANGO have continued the rethinking momentum previously initiated by academics, but this chapter calls for a pracademia approach involving both practioners and academics to frame the necessary paradigm shift required. It also requires reflection on how to translate the new thinking into practical actions to equip Pacific peoples in adapting to quickly changing times and the changing climate, while embracing a new Pacific consciousness and an updated unique Pacific way.

Suggestions for Further Reading

Hau'ofa, Epeli: *Our Sea of Islands,* University of the South Pacific. 1993
Pacific Conference of Churches: *Rethinking Oceania*, PCC 2010
Wendt, Albert: *Towards a new Oceania*, Readings in Pacific Literature, University of Wollongong, 1993
Upolu Luma Vaai and Aisake Casimira *(eds): Relational Hermeneutics: Decolonising the Mindset and the Pacific Itulagi*. Suva: University of the South Pacific & Pacific Theological College, 2017.
World Council of Churches*: The Island of Hope – An Alternative to Economic Globalisation*, Dossier No.7, WCC, 2006

[21] EPG, 2004.press-files.anu.edu.au/downloads/press/p55871/pdf/ch0314.pdf.

PART III: LATIN AMERICA AND CARIBBEAN

88. BRAZILIAN TRAGEDY: RISKS FOR THE "COMMON HOME"?

Romi Márcia Bencke[1]

> What we are experiencing may be the work of a loving mother who decided to make her child be quiet, at least for a moment. Not because she doesn't love them, but because she wants to teach them something: "Child, be quiet." Earth is saying this to humanity. And she's so wonderful that she doesn't give an order. She is simply asking: "Silence." This is also the meaning of retreat.[2]

"The Brazilian tragedy: risks for the 'common home'?" was the theme of an international seminar held by the Brazilian ecumenical movement in 2021. The seminar analysed the Brazilian context based on the process of the deconstruction of democracy, which led the country to multiple emergencies: in the religious sphere, with the rise of fundamentalisms; in the economic sphere, with the dismantling of what still remained of the welfare state and the consequent deepening of inequalities; in the field of human rights, with the growing violence and murder of vulnerable people due to their ethnic, racial, social, territorial and gender characteristics; in the field of ecology, with the destruction of forests, biomes, native and traditional peoples; in the field of health, with the health crisis, caused by the numerous practices of administrative irresponsibility during the COVID-19 pandemic.

The federal authorities' attitude of denial, especially the President of the Republic and his ministers and supporters, contributed to a high rate of contamination and deaths. The seminar was conceived when several people who lived in the Amazon region died of suffocation due to the lack of medicinal oxygen. The most emblematic case was that of the city of Manaus. This fact revealed the lack of co-ordination and the erroneous decisions made by government authorities to contain the advance of the pandemic. In this period, new variants of COVID-19 appeared in the Brazilian territory. It should be noted that the deaths in Manaus were preceded by the most intense and aggressive forest fires in recent years, according to data from the National Aeronautics and Space Administration (NASA).[3] Between the months of January and November 2020, the state of Mato Grosso lost 8,500,000 hectares of its biome, affected by fire. The destruction meant the loss of approximately 40% of the Pantanal biome, that is, 2,150,000 hectares. It is important to establish the connection between deaths from lack of medical oxygen and fires. Both events were intrinsically related to the debates on the consequences of climate change in Brazil. The lack of medicinal oxygen in the Amazon was emblematic, precisely at a time when the Amazon biomes were being destroyed. In both the fire and health cases, there was indifference on the part of federal authorities, accompanied by an increase in false news that attributed the fires to native communities. At no time were there in-depth discussions about the responsibility of large landowners in these fires, which transform areas of native vegetation into pastures for intensive cattle ranching and the production of soybeans, corn and other agricultural commodities.

For at least five years, Brazil has experienced a sense of self-destruction and a collective feeling that the ability to react has been exhausted. In 2020, this sentiment deepened. The impacts of the pandemic and the

---

[1] Romi Márcia Bencke is a pastor of the Evangelical Church of the Lutheran Confession in Brazil (IECLB), general secretary of the National Council of Christian Churches of Brazil and a member of the co-ordination of the Ecumenical Forum ACT Brazil. romibencke@gmail.com

[2] Ailton Krenak, *O amanhã não está à venda* (San Pablo: Companhia das Letras, 2020) Kindle edition, 6.

[3] "Incêndio no Pantanal em 2020 incomoda pela sensação de impunidade, diz ambientalista", *Jornal da USP*, 17th February 2021, [Available at: https://jornal.usp.br/atualidades/incendio-no-pantanal-em-2020-incomoda-pela-sensacao-de-impunidade-diz-ambientalista/], [Last accessed: 30th April 2022].

fires were only partially minimised thanks to the actions of civil society organised in social movements and environmental organisations. The feeling is that we have no state. It is we who must act in favour of ourselves. In this scenario of abandonment, organised civil society has undertaken solidarity actions to supply, at least, for the hunger of part of the 116,800,000 people in a situation of food insecurity. Similarly, volunteers have helped the fire brigades to fight the fires and to care for injured animals.

Perhaps understanding this feeling of self-destruction and inability to react is difficult for those who do not know Brazil. It is necessary to relate the impact of the COVID-19 pandemic, the progressive environmental destruction,[4] which is also reflected in the indigenous genocide,[5] and the territorial insecurity of the *quilombola*[6] communities with the current anti-political movement, represented by the Bolsonaro government. The anti-politics has played out in the destruction of important public policies that were developed by the Ministries of Education, Environment and Women, Family and Human Rights.[7]

For Avritzer, the anti-politics of the government of President Jair Bolsonaro is verified in three combined actions.[8] The first is the destruction of the structures of the Brazilian state, based on the argument that it is necessary to combat the progressive policies of the left. The second is the destructuring of public health policies and the third action is the intimidation of other powers so that the anti-politics is not interrupted by legislative or judicial decisions. Avritzer draws attention to the fact that the Bolsonarist movement represents a new form of ideological and anti-institutional conservatism.

An important element that organises this new type of conservatism are the religious fundamentalisms of Christian origin. Fundamentalisms are understood as concrete ways of interpreting reality. This interpretation guides the social action of the subjects based on their religious and political ties. The interpretation of reality, recurrent in the new conservatism, is the need to destroy the social structures of the State and the public policies of the left. The fundamentalist movements reinforce the myth of a hegemonically Christian and conservative Brazil, defend the Christianisation of the original peoples and, as a way of making invisible the slave-owning past of the Brazilian elites, make the granting of property titles to the *quilombola* communities unfeasible.

The description of the current Brazilian scenario is important for establishing some criticisms of the ecotheology elaborated in Brazil. In the first place, it highlights the significant contribution of this theology to a hermeneutical turn, which establishes the interdependence of the human being with the other living

---

[4] In the Brazilian case, the destruction of the environment can be classified as ecocide, that is, a crime against the planet, according to the new classification of the crime prepared by an international commission made up of 12 jurists, based on the initiative of civil society. The intention is that the concept of "ecocide" be incorporated as a fifth crime in the Rome Statute, which guides the operation of the International Criminal Court in The Hague. Ecocide is understood as any illicit or arbitrary act carried out even with the knowledge that it may cause serious and lasting damage to the environment.

[5] Based on the precedents of the International Criminal Court, the "Articulation of the Indigenous Peoples of Brazil" [Articulação dos Povos Indígenas do Brasil] (APIB) requested an investigation for crimes against humanity, based on Art. 7. b, h and k of the Rome Statute – extermination, persecution and other inhumane acts, and genocide – and in Art. 6. b and c of the Rome Statute – causing serious physical and mental harm, and deliberately violating conditions with a view to destroying the indigenous peoples. See: Corte Penal Internacional, "Estatuto de Roma de la Corte Penal Internacional", 1st July 2002, [Available at: https://www.un.org/spanish/law/icc/statute/spanish/rome_statute(s).pdf], [Last accessed: 30th April 2022].

[6] *Quilombola* communities are made up of descendants of black slaves who resisted the slave regime that ruled Brazil for more than 300 years. Data from the Brazilian government indicates that there are 3,475 *quilombola* communities present throughout the Brazilian territory. See "Quadro Geral de Comunidades Remanescentes de Quilombos", Palmares Fundaçao Cultural, 16th June 2021, [Available at: https://www.palmares.gov.br/wp-content/uploads/2015/07/quadro-geral-por-estados-e-regioes-15-06-2021.pdf], [Last accessed: 30th April 2022].

[7] Leonardo Avritzer, "Política e antipolítica nos dois anos de governo Bolsonaro", in Fábio Kerche and Marjorie Marona (eds), *Governo Bolsonaro: retrocesso democrático e degradação política* (Belo Horizonte: Ed. Autêntica, 2021): 11.

[8] Avritzer, "Política."

beings on the planet, questioning the anthropocentric understanding. Undoubtedly, the most important Brazilian voice linked to the ecotheology elaborated in Brazil is that of Leonardo Boff, who defines ecology as:

> a knowledge about the relationships, interconnections, interdependencies and exchanges of everything with everything, at all points and at all times. [...] It is not a knowledge that concerns objects of knowledge, but the relationships between objects of knowledge. It is a knowledge of knowledge, related to each other.[9]

From this premise, spiritualities based on the ecological paradigm and planetary consciousness are developed, which understand the human being as the result of a long process of evolution of the cosmos, as a Child of the Earth.[10] It is important for theology to establish a dialogue with environmental sciences, to articulate the social dimension of the Christian faith and planetary consciousness, to include elements of the theologies of gender, Afro-American peoples, indigenous peoples, decolonisation, ecumenical and religious pluralism.[11] The limit of this approach is that it does not deeply problematise the system that structures inequalities, such as those established by racism, gender, the gap between the very rich and the very poor, and colonialism, which is constantly updated with mining and commodity agriculture. The tendency is to elaborate abstract theological understandings that tend almost towards an idealisation of the interdependencies and the sacredness of life.

Ecofeminist theology manages to go beyond the abstract need for paradigm shifts and planetary consciousness. By pointing out the various dimensions of patriarchal theological epistemology that permeate the understanding of the experience of the sacred, ecofeminist theology problematises the structures that hierarchically organise the relationships between human beings and other living beings. It deconstructs the essentialist and monotheistic dimensions of the Christian tradition, criticising the imposition of the truth of a unique and creator God, whose image will be associated with a God who is Lord and dominator, reinforcing patriarchal structures and annulling the dimension of mystery and other experiences of God. It also criticises the epistemology of eternal truths to present other epistemologies, which start from questions about human experiences that correspond to talking about God, the incarnation, the trinity, the resurrection and communion.[12] Based on these questions, other epistemologies are required, which are holistic, contextual, affective, inclusive.

In the current Brazilian context, it goes without saying that eco-diakonic theologies and practices are seen as a threat to an economic and productive system that has large areas of monoculture and livestock as a reference for food production, and that makes intensive use of poisons. In two years, 967 new pesticides were approved.

However, despite the resistance, there are eco-diakonic experiences that can serve as transforming examples. One of these good practices was developed by the Lutheran Diakonia Foundation – FLD-COMIN-CAPA. This organisation, located in the south of Brazil and created in 2000 by decision of the Council of the Evangelical Church of the Lutheran Confession in Brazil (IECLB), elaborated the Pampa project between 2013 and 2018. The pampa is a shared biome that extends through southern Brazil, Argentina and Uruguay, occupying a total area of 700,000km^2. The temperate climate guarantees the unique characteristics of the biome. One of them is the presence of 450 different species of herbs. It is also home to forests on the banks of rivers, shrubs, 150 species of legumes, 70 varieties of bromeliads and cacti, and

---

9 Leonardo Boff, *Ecología: Grito de la Tierra, Grito de los Pobres* (Madrid: Trotta, 1996): 16.

10 Afonso Murad, "Ecologia, ciência da fé e espiritualidade", *Revista Pistis y Praxis. Teología e Pastoral* 12(3) (2020): 519-540.

11 Murad, "Ecologia", 527.

12 Ivone Gebara, *Teologia ecofeminista – Ensaio para repensar o conhecimento e a religião* (San Pablo: Olho d'água, 1997): 59.

hundreds of animal species. The pampa, like much of Brazil's biomes, is threatened by monoculture and large-scale mining.

One of the actions of the FLD for the preservation of this biome was the implementation and dissemination of Social Technologies to value traditional knowledge and good practices for the management of ecosystems, essential for mitigation and adaptation to climate change. This project involved the Paulo Freire State School of Basic Education, located in the Santa Maria do Ibicuí settlement, in Manoel Viana, State of Rio Grande do Sul. Together with the school community, study plans were developed based on some social technologies implemented by the school and others that would be developed throughout 2018, such as the construction of a cistern, an ecological tank, an orchard and a garden. To build the lesson plans, four reflection and exchange meetings were held about the scholastic reality, contexts and motivations. Social technologies located in the schoolyard were identified and given a new meaning so that they could become elements of pedagogical practice. A lesson plan was developed for each of the social technologies. This collective experience was systematised in the publication "Learning Agro-Ecology in the School Yard: Pedagogical Practices with Social Technologies."[13] The initiative also received a Social Technology Certificate from the Banco do Brasil Foundation (FBB) in July 2019, with the title "Social Technologies as Pedagogical Spaces in the Schoolyard."[14]

Another example of good practice was the "Ecumenical Mission for the Waters of the Cerrado da Bahia." The objective of the mission was to denounce the predatory model with which the waters of the Cerrado are used by agribusiness and large companies, to demand that the State fulfils its role in the resolution of socio-environmental, territorial and water conflicts, and finally to announce another model of co-existence with the Cerrado, based on the defence of water as a human right and common good, on agro-ecology and on respect for the ways of life of native and traditional communities.

The Cerrado is the second largest biome in Brazil, with 2,000,000km^2. The Cerrado is designated as the richest "tropical savannah" in the world. It comprises about 5% of all diversity on the planet. The Cerrado is home to 30% of the different living beings identified in Brazil. The Cerrado biome can be considered the "water cradle" in Brazil, given that its sources feed 8 of the 12 hydrographic regions, among which three stand out: the basins of the Araguaia/Tocantins River, the San Francisco River and the Paraná River. Several indigenous ethnic groups and *quilombola* communities live in the Cerrado. However, the Cerrado is a threatened biome. The campaign "In defense of the Cerrado – without Cerrado, there is no life" denounces how more than half of its vegetal cover has been destroyed to make way for monocultures and pastures for agribusiness. One of the consequences of this destruction is the reduction of the water surface. A recent study carried out by MapBiomas indicates that Brazil has lost 15.7% of its water surface in the last 30 years, which is equivalent to 3.1 million hectares of water surface. The São Francisco River region alone has lost 10% of its surface in the last fifteen years. The main cause is the expansion of the agricultural frontier.

The Ecumenical Mission lasted three days. A public hearing was held at the Town Hall of the Municipality of Barreiras to denounce the violations of rights against five traditional communities. A visit also took place to the traditional communities and territories to listen to the main complaints of rights violations derived from conflicts over water resources. At the end, an ecumenical celebration was officiated with the presence of representatives of different faith traditions: Catholics, Protestants and religious leaders of Candomblé and traditional populations.[15]

---

[13] Julia Rovena Witt, *et al.* (eds), *Aprendendo agroecologia no pátio da escola: práticas pedagógicas com tecnologias implementadas na Escola Estadual de Ensino Fundamental Paulo Freire* (Porto Alegre: Fundação Luterana de Diaconia, 2019). [Available at: https://docplayer.com.br/136655744-Aprendendo-agroecologia-no-patio-da-escola.html], [Last accessed: 30th April 2022].

[14] See "Escola de assentamento vem se consolidando como escola agroecológica do campo", *FLD projetos de vida*, 12th August 2019, [Available at: https://fld.com.br/projeto-pampa/2019/escola-de-assentamento-vem-se-consolidando-como-escola-agroecologica-do-campo/], [Last accessed: 30th April 2022].

[15] See Sônia Gomes Mota *et al* (eds), *Relatorio de Atividades 2019* (Salvador, Bahia: CESE, 2020).

It is not possible to finish this article without sharing our attempts to answer the question posed by the International Seminar: does the Brazilian tragedy represent a risk for our "common home", or not? Taking into account the immense biodiversity of Brazil and its importance in guaranteeing life on the planet; taking into account that Brazil is home to 12% of the planet's drinking water; taking into account the importance of the Amazon and the other tropical forests that are in Brazilian territory, we could say yes, that the fact that Brazil has opted for a destructive anti-ecological-policy indicates that the country may represent a potential risk for the "common home." This is because the destruction of ecosystems directly contributes to climate change. The fragile planetary consciousness prevents us from understanding that our decisions and lifestyles can generate negative consequences for the entire planet. However, it is impossible not to blame the colonialist project that has structured Brazilian society and is still active through the action of the large international mining companies, the financialisation of the land, agrochemicals and the exploitation of fossil energy.

The seminar's question should perhaps have been about those responsible for the current Brazilian tragedy. There is an economic elite – not only a national one – that does not care about the future of humanity, but only about being able to extract everything that generates wealth and profit from this immense territory. An eco-diakonia has to raise the question of the ethical responsibility intrinsic to the destruction of life on earth. This question and its answers are essential in order not to fall into the risk of carrying out diakonia aimed solely at minimising the impacts of climate change through humanitarian aid. In this sense, it is necessary to promote a profound transition from a theology that lives in peace with the capitalist system towards an eco-diakonia that recognises and welcomes an economic policy oriented to social needs and ecological balance. An eco-diakonia needs to criticise and directly influence the system that feeds on the destruction of the planet and, in turn, to support and to reinforce initiatives inspired by non-monetary and extra-economic criteria. The firm option for eco-diakonia will be a necessary condition if we do not want to risk having to decide between compassion and profit. A decision for profit would lead us to be only agents that minimise the consequences of the unbridled exploitation of large companies in poor and emerging countries.

Suggestions for Further Reading

Avritzer, Leonardo. "Política e antipolítica nos dois anos de governo Bolsonaro", in Fábio Kerche and Marjorie Marona, Eds. *Governo Bolsonaro: retrocesso democrático e degradação política*. Belo Horizonte: Ed. Autêntica, 2021: 13-20.

Boff, Leonardo. *Ecología: Grito de la Tierra, Grito de los Pobres*. Madrid: Trotta, 1996.

FLD Projetos de Vida. "Escola de assentamento vem se consolidando como escola agroecológica do campo". 12th August 2019. [Available at: https://fld.com.br/projeto-pampa/2019/escola-de-assentamento-vem-se-consolidando-como-escola-agroecologica-do-campo/], [Last accessed: 30th April 2022].

Gebara, Ivone, *Teologia Ecofeminista: Ensaio para repensar o conhecimento e a religião*. San Pablo: Olho d`água, 1997.

Gomes Mota, Sônia, Antônio Dimas Galvão, Daniel Musse and Patrícia Gordano, Eds. *Relatorio de Atividades 2019.* Salvador, Bahia: CESE-Coordenadoria Ecumênica de Serviço, 2020.

Universidade de São Paulo. "Incêndio no Pantanal em 2020 incomoda pela sensação de impunidade, diz ambientalista." *Jornal da USP*, 17th February 2021. [Available at: https://jornal.usp.br/atualidades/incendio-no-pantanal-em-2020-incomoda-pela-sensacao-de-impunidade-diz-ambientalista/], [Last accessed: 30th April 2022].

International Criminal Court. "Rome Statute of the International Criminal Court." 1st July 2002. [Available at: https://www.icc-cpi.int/resource-library/documents/rs-eng.pdf], [Last accessed: 30th April 2022].

Krenak, Ailton. *O amanhã não está à venda*. San Pablo: Companhia das Letras, 2020. Kindle edition.

Murad, Afonso. "Ecologia, ciência da fé e espiritualidade." *Revista Pistis y Praxis. Teología e Pastoral* 12(3) (2020): 519-540.

Palmares Fundaçao Cultural. "Quadro Geral de Comunidades Remanescentes de Quilombos." 16th June 2021. [Available at: https://www.palmares.gov.br/wp-content/uploads/2015/07/quadro-geral-por-estados-e-regioes-15-06-2021.pdf], [Last accessed: 30th April 2022].

Witt, Julia Rovena, Juliana Mazurana, Letícia Paranhos M. de Oliveira, Eds. *Aprendendo agroecologia no pátio da escola: práticas pedagógicas com tecnologias implementadas na Escola Estadual de Ensino Fundamental Paulo Freire*. Porto Alegre: Fundação Luterana de Diaconia, 2019.

89. Christian Activism in Socio-Environmental Assemblies of the Argentine Patagonia

María Esther Norval[1]

I have set my bow in the clouds, and it shall be a sign of the covenant between me and the earth. (Gen. 9:13)

Introduction

If, as Christians, we recognise that God made a covenant with God's people from the beginning of creation, then, from that very moment, we have responsibility for the gift of life and the planet we inhabit. Humanity has been appropriating the planet for its own benefit, using resources excessively, forgetting the covenant with God and the responsibility that it entails.

The new covenant of God through God's son Jesus Christ, who gave his life to deliver us from evil, is a new inescapable commitment. This covenant seals God's commitment to humanity – expressed in the mandate "you shall love your neighbour as yourself" – and supposes our responsibility towards our current neighbour, but also towards future generations. Caring for our common home helps to ensure life in the future, and that vocation and challenge cannot be indifferent to us.

Context

For millennia, human beings have been changing their customs and ways of life; in this process, they not only used, but also abused environmental resources. Thus, at present, there are scientific studies that show that climate change is affecting us globally and negatively, that time is shortening and action must be taken drastically and quickly.

The international agreements signed decades ago are not made effective and governments do not put them into practice. The economic interests and the "political costs" for these leaders are the greatest impediment to creating and applying laws to protect life. For despite the fact that parliaments sometimes enact such laws, governments often either ignore them or do not make sure that the necessary controls for their compliance are carried out.

In this context, activism becomes essential. For information and awareness can no longer be left only in the hands of a few. It is time to act from citizenship; the indifference of the peoples gives many unscrupulous rulers the backing to do nothing or make grandiloquent announcements that never fully materialise.

This reality, at present, affects us Argentines in general, and in particular those of us who live in the south of the country, in Patagonian territory – a territory that was looted and its culture and indigenous peoples decimated since the beginning of colonisation. Since then, these people have never been consulted to express themselves on what they consider necessary for the promotion of a region highly coveted for its vast natural resources. In fact, the production of Patagonia has been mutating to the rhythm of the interests imposed by the international order: meat, wool, oil, minerals, fruits, water and tourism. Looting was almost always present, with little or almost no participation by the Patagonian people.

---

[1] María Esther Norval retired from the National Highway Administration of the Argentine Republic, Río Negro Regional, where she served for 33 years as Executive Secretary of the Presidency. She has a degree in Social Work, and is a member of the Evangelical Church of the Río de la Plata. Secretary of the Board of Directors of the Protestant Diakonia Foundation *Hora de Obrar*. maria_norval@hotmail.com

The first strong historical milestone in opposition to this subjugation was marked 18 years ago by a strong popular mobilisation in the Province of Chubut, which prevented the installation of an international nuclear dump. Shortly after, another strong action of resistance by the population began in opposition to the installation of metalliferous mega-mines, which continues to this day.

Production under the capitalist regime favours the large scale and the maximisation of rent. The international companies and large producers that dominate it leave the vast majority of small regional producers out of the system, taking away their livelihood base. Its production method, implemented through the use of highly polluting chemical products and genetically modified seeds, is falsely presented as an economic salvation and a factor in the development of the peoples, without considering the environmental liabilities that they leave in their wake.

In all the Patagonian provinces, there are abandoned mining ventures, which have caused irreparable environmental damage. In this sense, the poor management of water resources, which caused irrecoverable damage to rivers and lakes, was particularly negative.

In the Province of Río Negro, in 2017, based on intense awareness-raising work, which led to a confrontation with the provincial and national political power and affected local and international interests, the socio-environmental activism managed to stop the installation of a high-power nuclear power plant on the coast of the Atlantic Sea.

Through actions like this, the people show that when life is put at risk they react. At this time, the defence of water and territories represent the greatest challenge for the Patagonian environmental assemblies. For the constant disqualification of the struggle of the assemblies, added to the buying of consciences (of scientists, politicians, advisors and even university officials) by governments and international companies, makes the action of resistance and awareness difficult, and it is associated with a high cost for those of us who are committed to it in the field. Scientists and professors who get involved in activism do so out of their own conviction and often putting their professional careers at risk.

The popular initiatives to present bills endorsed by the signatures of thousands of citizens authorised to cast votes in provincial elections, have to overcome many problems to reach the legislatures, and when they arrive, even more problems are to be considered, dealt with and approved – frequently for reasons that respond to merely partisan interests.

The lack of promotion policies for sustainable and profitable regional production development has led to a deterioration of socio-environmental conditions. Among other negative consequences, this is manifested in the sustained migration of peasants to the cities, leaving fields – where families once lived and food was produced sustainably – in the hands of large landowners and transnational companies that are now destroying regional economies.

Activism

As the daughter and granddaughter of a peasant family, my life was always related to nature and the care that should be provided to the land, water, air, and the animals with which the family cohabitated. This interrelation of our lives and the environment that we inhabited was also marked by our Protestant Christian confession, from which my own commitment and activism derives. Identifying myself as a member of a Protestant Church, the Evangelical Church of Río de La Plata, is part of my letter of introduction in assemblies and movements.

Activism is carried out day by day, being attentive, with hours of work and thanks to economic resources from each person involved. It implies being permanently alert, based on painstaking efforts that are carried out in the territory, often through the organisation of "expeditions", that is, visits to places where conflicts are taking place, in order to gather on-site information by qualified professionals. Such people make available their expertise and resources in order to obtain data on various environmental issues in a scientific and reliable manner. This information is then shared through networks of environmental groups to other interest groups, such as citizen assemblies, where each member makes it their own and defends it as their own, individually and collectively.

Access to public information on projects promoted by governments (regarding mining concessions, forests, public works and real estate developments, and other private projects that affect the common good) is difficult. Even when there are laws in the country that guarantee citizens that access to information, it is often denied or the information is presented in a biased manner.[2] On the other hand, the legal resources in support of them – such as the requests for judicial protection actions – must be signed personally, which adds a great stumbling block to civil action in favour of environmental protection. Experience shows that magistrates frequently delay rulings or rule directly in favour of the projects being questioned, while those who dared to defend the territory and regional environments have to bear the monetary costs of legal expenses.

Two Concrete Examples

History of a Mobilised People: Opposition to the installation of a high-power nuclear power plant in the Province of Río Negro, Argentine Republic

In May 2017, during a visit to the People's Republic of China, the Governor of Río Negro, Alberto Weretilneck, jointly signed with the President of the Nation, Mauricio Macri, and the Chinese National Nuclear Corporation (CNNC) an agreement for the construction of a fifth nuclear power plant for the Argentine Republic, to be installed in the Province of Río Negro. That act meant the consolidation of a previous binational agreement, signed in November 2015 by the then President, Cristina Fernández de Kirchner.

From that moment on, some of the provincial citizens began to request information from the government regarding the aforementioned agreement, without success. Faced with government reluctance and rumours that a town on the Atlantic coast, located 80 km from the capital of the Province of Río Negro, would be the place where the nuclear power plant would be located, residents of Viedma and Patagones met in assembly to analyse the situation and discuss a possible course of action, in a space made available by the local Catholic bishopric.[3]

The assembly motivated many participating people, with different concerns and knowledge of the subject, to organise themselves into commissions, which began to study, to train, to look for specialists who could provide the information that the government did not want to give or considered inappropriate to make accessible to "common" citizens.[4]

The self-convened citizens began the membership meeting by requesting signatures in order to present a document before the provincial legislature. In this way, a massive popular assembly gathered in the cathedral of the city of Viedma publicly expressed its rejection of the installation of a high-power nuclear power plant on the Atlantic coast of Rio Negro and called for a citizen protest march on 9th August 2017, the date on which humanity commemorates the crimes caused by the launch of a nuclear bomb in the city of Nagasaki, during World War II. Social networks provided important support to convene the great march

[2] The Argentine Republic recently signed the significant "Acuerdo Regional sobre el Acceso a la Información, la Participación Pública y el Acceso a la Justicia en Asuntos Ambientales en América Latina y el Caribe," better known as "Acuerdo de Escazú." Nevertheless, an effective impact of it on public policies has not yet been perceived.

[3] See "Rechazan nuevo intento a una planta nuclear en Río Negro," *Agencia Digital de Noticias*, 10th October 2019, [Available at: https://www.adnrionegro.com.ar/2019/10/rechazan-nuevo-intento-a-una-planta-nuclear-en-rio-negro/], [Last accessed: 23rd April 2022].

[4] See Redacción Diario Río Negro, "Más de 5.000 firmas contra la planta nuclear en Río Negro," *Río Negro*, 4th July 2017, [Available at: https://www.rionegro.com.ar/movida-artistica-contra-la-central-nuclear-en-rio-negro-MK3084482/], [Last accessed: 23rd April 2022].

that took place in the streets of Viedma. The demonstrations of repudiation were replicated simultaneously in other places inside and outside the province, at the national level.[5]

Within the framework of such mobilisations, artistic expressions – musical, graphic and pictorial (murals), theatrical – were a significant way of revealing a tragic and worrying reality. However, those of us who participated in them were clear that we did not want to raise awareness through fear. Thus, the people who joined the assembly did so convinced of what we fought for together, based on the motto: "*no to nuclear energy, yes to life*." This is referring to a life represented by the threatened maritime and coastal ecosystems, made up of unique flora and fauna.

The experience of the assembly showed that the strength of citizen organisation was able to show that there were many people who did not want nuclear energy, forcing the provincial government to recognise that the project did not have social consensus. Since then, its members have continued to work without interruption, informing the public in different ways, given the well-founded suspicion that the latest legislation enacted on the matter still does not offer the guarantees that the citizens of the region need in order to see our desire to reject polluting nuclear projects materialised.

This activism led to the consolidation of our relationship with other assemblies that were formed throughout the province through the creation of the Movimiento Antinuclear Rionegrino and the formation of the Movimiento Antinuclear República Argentina (MARA), which took place in the face of new attempts to install a new nuclear power plant in other locations in the country.

Mobilised Present

Throughout the recent history of the Province of Río Negro, Patagonia and our country, the Argentine Republic, a type of mining that is highly polluting and of a predatory nature has attempted to advance, driven by large multinational groups with the consent of the alternating governments in power: metalliferous mega-mining.

The Argentine Patagonia has important aquifer basin reserves. However, fresh water is such a scarce commodity that it cannot be neglected in the slightest, because the Patagonian region is also characterised by its extensive desert plateaus, which lack this precious asset.

The Province of Río Negro also has a long history of resistance to successive attempts at establishing contaminating metal mines. Assemblies scattered throughout the geography of our territory resisted and continue to resist projects that seek to carry out various mega-mining ventures. A significant milestone in this fight was the sanction of Law 3981/05, which prohibited the use of cyanide and mercury in metal mining. It was a valuable conquest by the mobilised people, although the law was later repealed based on the wishes of an unscrupulous provincial government, lacking social consensus.

Faced with new mega-mining attempts, in February 2020, we met more than a hundred assembly members and native communities in Huahel Niyeu, Jacobacci, Río Negro Province, to organise resistance. In this framework, the need arose to generate new tools that would allow us to fight in the midst of the pandemic. In this sense, a multiplicity of virtual meetings made it possible for us to organise ourselves throughout the province.

This was the case in the (also Patagonian) Province of Chubut, where despite the limitations of the pandemic, during 2020 and 2021, the Unión de Asambleas Chubutenses managed to promote a popular initiative to ban metal mining activity based on the use of cyanide, sodium cyanide, sodium bromide, sodium iodide and mercury.

[5] To access audio-visual recordings of the event, see "9A No nuclear," 9th August 2017, video, 11:10, [Available at: https://www.youtube.com/watch?v=Yj5cq_wiu60], [Last accessed: 23rd April 2022]; and "No a la planta nuclear. Marcha en Viedma. Reseña de la movilización," 9th August 2017, video, 4:14, [Available at: https://www.youtube.com/watch?v=FdtoZdkAyao], [Last accessed: 23rd April 2022].

Such experiences unified us in the struggle. This is how the Rio Negro environmental activism began to work on a broader bill for the prohibition of metal mega-mining, which was presented at the end of 2020 in the province's legislature under the legal figure of a "Popular Initiative".

To strengthen legislative action, the assembly members prepared illustrative materials, with the aim of informing public opinion and the people. Thus, for example, the Curru Leufu Assemblies presented a very complete and up-to-date document, which explains in detail the reasons why mega-mining in the Province of Río Negro has neither acceptance nor social license.[6] At the time of writing this document, the activism is in the process of collecting signatures, linked to carrying out cultural activities aimed at informing and promoting the defence of life.[7]

Commitment to the Future

The destruction of the environment and climate change are problems that we face globally. Christians are part of humanity and we cannot disengage ourselves in the face of such a challenge. Rather, we must translate our faith into attitudes of protection and care for God's creation.

Related to the triad of society, environment and economy, we have an immense responsibility. After years of depredation, the great moment has come to change our lifestyles and the way we relate to each other. Faced with the pressing reality of today's world, we receive the call to manifest a prophetic attitude, gambling on sustainability.

Seen in this way, faith in a Christian key, which supposes a free, personal and existential adherence to God, should lead us to act in search of the historical experience of the Reign of God in our world of life. This is linked to the commitment to live the message of Jesus, the Christ, in our daily lives. A message marked by freedom, service, love, the dignity of the human person and the defence of life.

Such values are not limited exclusively to the human world, but also extend to the intimate relationship in which we find ourselves with the environment, which is nothing more than a macro-system, which covers us, welcomes us and brings us together with other living beings.

Hence, the Church reminds us at all times that Creation is a gift of God, in which we are offered living symbols of divine grace, which moves us to the ethical responsibility to protect it.

Sustainable development is then a lifestyle through which Christians manifest their experience of faith in Christ, which is authentically revealed as such to the extent that it includes a healthy relationship with other living beings: if you understand that human beings are not in a position of dominance or above other beings; if their lifestyle acts in favour of a social justice that dignifies the human person; if their lifestyle responds to the challenges of relativising the ideals of capitalism and if it generates inclusive human relations, in favour of the less favoured. Only in this way will the Christian testimony of faith in God be prophetic, real and valid to bear witness to that message for which Jesus gave his life, the Reign of God. That message moves us to affirm as Christians that this world, which is becoming unsustainable, is our greatest challenge as citizens and children of God.

Active individual and community involvement, in spaces that can affect an effective change in the current reality of human suffering and environmental destruction, is our challenge, which will make a difference right there, from our pact and commitment to our Lord Jesus Christ.

---

[6] Asambleas del Curruleufu, "Megaminería metalífera: Por qué en Río Negro le decimos no," *Asambleas del Curruleufu,* April 2021 [Available at: https://asambleasdelcurruleufu.files.wordpress.com/2021/04/asambleas-del-kurru-leufu.pdf], [Last accessed: 23rd April 2022].

[7] "¡Sumate a la Iniciativa Popular contra la megaminería contaminante en la provincia de Río Negro!," *Asambleas del Curruleufu*, 4th February 2021, [Available at: https://asambleasdelcurruleufu.wordpress.com/2021/02/04/sumate-a-la-iniciativa-popular-contra-la-megamineria-contaminante-en-la-provincia-de-rio-negro-informate-aqui-de-los-lugares-y-requisitos-para-firmar/], [Last accessed: 23rd April 2022].

Suggestions for Further Reading

Andrés, Roberto. "Dossier Patagonia No Nuclear: ¿Por qué rechazar el plan nuclear que acordó Macri con China? Hablan referentes y especialistas." *La Izquierda Diario*, 30th September 2017. [Available at: https://www.laizquierdadiario.com/Por-que-rechazar-el-plan-nuclear-que-acordo-Macri-con-China-Hablan-referentes-y-especialistas], [Last accessed: 23rd April 2022].

Concerned Health Professionals of New York, & Physicians for Social Responsibility. *Compendium of scientific, medical, and media findings demonstrating risks and harms of fracking (unconventional gas and oil extraction)*. 7th edn. December 2020. [Available at: http://concernedhealthny.org/compendium/], [Last accessed: 23rd April 2022].

Saiz, Agustín. "La Crisis Nuclear en el Escenario del Cambio Climático." *Antimafia dos mil*, 2nd July 2021. [Available at: https://www.antimafiadosmil.com/index.php/medio-ambiente/6599-la-crisis-nuclear-en-el-escenario-del-cambio-climatico], [Last accessed: 23rd April 2022].

Svampa, Maristella and Enrique Viale. *El colapso ecológico ya llegó. Una brújula para salir del (mal) desarrollo*. Buenos Aires: Siglo XXI, 2020.

90. Ancestral Spiritualities and the Mutual Nurturing of Life

Sofía Chipana Quispe[1]

Intentioning the Word: *Pachamama* Is Going to Heal Us

The words that I weave intertwine in August,[2] a full time for the high Andean peoples who live their bond with the telluric forces of Pachamama, Lady of the Cosmos and Time, designated in the local language as Mother Earth. Such designation is due to the interrelationships that are established with her as a vital source that makes life possible and protects it; so, in reciprocity, she needs to be fed, protected and loved. Thus, at this time, we approach her with great respect, asking permission so that she will welcome our seed sisters and they will reach maturity. But in our proximity, the pain of feeling how her cycles and rhythms are being altered and her body continually overwhelmed is also expressed. This occurs in the territorialities of deep respect of those worlds that we do not see, but that do inhabit, nurturing the beautiful biodiversity, in which the cosmic ancestral forces are present, as spirit guides, protectors, guardians.

From the various shared paths, this tapestry is not presented as an experience that derives merely from a project, but rather from the connection with the ancestral principles still present in the cosmogonies and cosmo-experiences of our beautiful Andean pluriverse. From there, it seeks to delve into Andean ancestral knowledge, wisdom and spiritualities, which were interrupted in their processes by the colonial policies of extermination and assimilation and the extensions of the same in the nation-states, and were relegated by the dominant knowledge.

Despite the thankless memory of the exterminations and submissions, which lives in the peoples of *Abya Yala*,[3] the ancestral spiritualities are interwoven with the broken and burned threads. For it is the force that sustains the community of life, which seeks to restore balance and harmony from the vital principles. That is why I will share the principle of the *uywaña*, the mutual nurturing of life, which enables reciprocal relationships in the community of life – the *ayllu* – in which the awareness of being nurtured and of nurturing in reciprocity amongst the various beings develops.

Resistances and Creativities of the Ancestral Wisdoms

We are located in a context in which the predominance of one dominant culture is established, which is presented from the hegemony of its epistemology. Aura Cumes calls this “the world of the one”, which reaches the various so-called indigenous peoples from educational centres in exclusive ways. Such ways, which are assumed as a kind of civilisation, were presented to them as a means that enables inclusion in the state system, which is based on the colonial heritage and modern thinking of absolute truths, invalidating the various understandings, wisdoms and spiritualities in indigenous cultures. However, these understandings were sustained in creative and dynamic ways, which made it possible, for example, for

---

[1] Sofía Chipana Quispe mailto:is Aymara from Bolivia. She is a member of the Community of Wise Women and Indigenous Theologians of Abya Yala, and of the Andean Theology and Pastoral Community of Peru, Bolivia and Argentina. warmi_pacha@hotmail.com

[2] This is the time of passage from winter to spring, in which the territorialities awaken and need to feed themselves through the ritual tables.

[3] Name that the Kuna peoples of Panama gave to the American continent, which would literally mean land in full maturity or land of vital blood.

4,000 potato varieties to be registered in the Andean region (Colombia, Ecuador, Peru, Bolivia, North Chile, Northwest Argentina), from the breeding and exchange of seeds.[4]

Although the culture of writing and Western technologies were imposed, the wisdom of the peoples found its refuge in other expressions, forms and modes that sustain life through the exchange of knowledge. This wisdom, in which we place the principle of the mutual nurturing of life, is presented as a proposal against uniformed thought. However, the task of weaving wisdom places us on paths that are not easy. On the one hand, not even the processes of intercultural education manage to get out of the "hidden curriculum" in which the individual prevails to the detriment of community processes. On the other hand, the repetition and memorisation of concepts move away from the senti-thinking processes, which start from life and its dynamic cycles intertwined in the exchange of relationships offered by the vital community.

In the face of invisible colonialism, the living word of Quechua is evoked, *kachkaniraqmi*, which is pronounced when a person wants to express that, despite everything, they still are; they still exist. From that evocation many peoples live intertwining with each other, forming a living tapestry through the impulse of memory. For the link with ancestry is assumed as the source of the understanding of life, from which one learns to read and narrate the stories and wisdom recreated, where spirituality, as Grimaldo Rengifo would say, is part of "a multiple process, in which the ritual tables have been great opportunities to converse and decide in a holistic way what is convenient for the circumstance."[5] That is why this same author maintains that:

> Recovery – seen in this way – is part of a return, of a ritual revolt towards a healthy life, of affection between human beings and nature. Here the result has not been the consolidation of the values of the individual, nor of competitive attitudes. The result has led to more community life, more affection and respect for the *wacas*[6] and, with it, the return to the diversity of seeds and nurturing that the circumstances demand.[7]

The Tapestry of Relational Spiritualities in *Abya Yala*

The encounter with the ancient roots of our peoples stems from the dynamic force of spiritualities, which returns us to our constitution as relational beings, following the cosmic principle that everything has its time and place. From there, necessary links are generated, even with some symbols of the imposed religion, which are interpreted from their own world experiences, generating a significant divergence with the dogmas and doctrines of Christianity. For it is not about syncretism, since from the reestablishment of balance and harmony, everything must be integrated through the *yanantin*, which is the dual force of correspondences, not limited to the human plane of the masculine and feminine, but of the forces that seek to complement each other to continue creating life.

The resurgence of ancestral spiritualities from the underground exceeds the comparison with the religiosities of popular Catholicism, leaving behind the tutelage of the churches in the process of their recovery, as Sylvia Marcos rightly puts it:

---

[4] CIP Centro Internacional de la Papa, "Datos y cifras de la papa," *CIP Website* [Available at: https://cipotato.org/es/potato/potato-facts-and-figures/], [Last accessed: 24th April 2022].

[5] Grimaldo Rengifo Vásquez, "Presentación," in Jorge Apaza Ticona, Valeriano Gordillo Condori and Sabino Orlando Cutipa Flores (eds), *La Crianza Mutua en las Comunidades Aymaras. Conversación con el agua. Crianza de la Llama. Crianza de Oca, Olluco e Izaño*. (Lima: PRATEC, 1998), viii.

[6] Ancestral presences, assumed as protectors, found in the local mountains and glaciers, also in the rocks or stelae with which there is a relationship of deep respect.

[7] Rengifo Vásquez, *La Crianza*, viii.

> "Indigenous spirituality" is not a matter of church, personal devotion or individual beliefs. It is that which unifies and identifies collectivities; which gives them cohesion. It is what is recovered from the ancestors, what gives meaning to their political and social struggles. It is definitely not an institutional religion.[8]

And, as the philosopher Josef Estermann points out:

> It is not limited to a certain field or to certain institutions and specialists, but is present in all aspects of life, from birth to death, from sowing to harvest, and of course in everything that has to do with the improvement of living conditions.[9]

For it is interwoven in the integrality of life, based on the principles of relationality, complementarity, correspondence and reciprocity, since life is not assumed in isolation, but in and through the relationships that seek balance; spirituality as the driving and sustaining force, which is why it could be called the *K'ạmasa*, the vital force.

The Wisdom of the Loving Nurturing of Life

The mutual nurturing of life is linked to the daily practices of the Andean populations linked to the land, the study of which gave rise, in the field of anthropology, to the "ontological turn". From this perspective, Tim Ingold described the relational ontology, which offers a significant contribution to the understanding of being and presence of the Andean *jaq'e*, noting that it is "the social condition of being a person, with all its ramifications of sociality in terms of the obligations and reciprocal duties between persons, whether human or nonhuman."[10]

From the academic spaces, based on the proposed conceptual categorisations, there is an effort to access the current experiences of the mutual nurturing of life, which are manifest as a form of relationship that the local community establishes with the various beings. As an example, I mention the experience of the water breeders, who together with the *Quispicanchi* community in Ayacucho, Peru, sow and harvest water, in a territory that has been affected in the 1980s by the armed conflict between the Shining Path communist party and the armed forces of Peru. This conflict meant the displacement of entire people groups to the capital cities, who after their return not only have to face depopulation, but also the phenomena of climate change, which manifests itself in the absence of rain or its irregular flow. This situation led Magdalena and Marcela Machaca to recover the ancestral practices of the community, as Magdalena comments:

> To found a lagoon, first there are the prayer rituals, which, they say locally, is like a request for permission from the deities of the place, so that it is not human will, but rather that it be the result of a conversation and empathy between humanity, our deities, and of nature itself [...] The lagoon does not exist because it exists; it is possible to make it develop, but on our own terms. Because many times we have been told it sounds romantic, those things they do sound nice, but that doesn't give you money, it doesn't feed you; yes it feeds you, now we are proving it.[11]

The experience of the nurturings is possible from the principle that everything has life and is interrelated as in a great tapestry, in which the vital force that criss-crosses all forms of life flows. From thence arises

[8] Sylvia Marcos, *Mujeres, indígenas, rebeldes, zapatistas* (México DF: Eón, 2013): 122.
[9] Josef Estermann, "El mercado religioso y la Religión del Mercado", in *Religión y desarrollo en los Andes: Deconstrucción intercultural de una relación difícil* (La Paz: ISEAT, 2008): 59.
[10] Denisse Arnold, "Hacia una antropología de la vida en los Andes", in Heydi Galarza (ed), *El desarrollo y lo sagrado en los Andes* (La Paz: ISEAT, 2017): 29.
[11] Magdalena Machaca, interviewed by the Ministerio del Medio Ambiente de Perú, video, 03:10, [Available at: https://www.youtube.com/watch?v=oRu2t0H0NbY], [Last accessed: 24th April 2022].

the awareness of mutual nurturing, which occurs in the community of life and requires attitudes of care, respect, love, tenderness, protection – even from those forces that can generate death, illness, or pose a certain threat, since the important thing is to enter into balance with those beings, so that they co-exist harmoniously.[12]

The nurturing of life and territories, as an ancestral heritage, implies certain ethical codes of cohabitation that are guided by rituals that have a pedagogical function. For they seek certain ways of interacting between the various communities and their protectors, who are offered food and drink as a sign of gratitude for providing the life of those beings and protecting them. In this relationship, it is possible to establish responsible and necessary care and consumption. That is why the indiscriminate hunting or mistreatment of any of these beings is censored, because "each being lives its own development, acquiring the vitality of other beings, and then dies. For no form of life is permanent, but extremely changeable."[13]

The Reciprocal Forces in the Nurturing of Life

In these times, the walking words of the peoples, connected to their ancestry, resurface from the common demand for the care and defence of Mother Earth. Such words are not located outside of her, as can be seen in the cosmopraxis[14] of the Andean peoples. For humanity is part of the great tapestry of interrelationships that flow reciprocally and in a complementary way to create life. We see this wisdom expressed when the various beings are equated with the category of *jaq'e*, in order to establish a symmetrical and loving relationship:

> All of us who live in this pacha are people; the stone, the earth, the plants, the fruits, the water, the hail, the wind, illnesses, the sun, the moon, the stars, we are all a family; in order to live together, we mutually help each other, we are always in continuous conversation and concord.[15]

Considering that symmetrical relationships have to do with affection, which is not an exclusive quality of people, but also of other beings: "We say to the fox: you are going to tell us how the agricultural season is going to be. You don't have to eat the sheep either, because you have your big guinea pigs, that's what you're going to be eating and that way nobody is going to bother you."[16]

In this way, it is possible to grow in the awareness of being nurtured by other beings, from dignified conversations with the person-animal, person-seed, person-river et cetera, so that the relationships with the protective spirits and the sources of life follow that same route, in which it is worth considering the times and spaces proper for carrying out such dialogues. Therefore, the wisdom of nurturing life is given in an integral way, seeking to overcome the dualistic or binary notion that separates the good from the bad, the sacred and the profane. From the perspective of said wisdom, based on the reciprocity that the interrelationships of all beings seek, the harmonisation of the various forces is fundamental, since the absence or discomfort of one affects the relationships in the living community.

In this way, the reciprocal nurturing of life guides Good Living as a cosmic-political proposal, which implies, according to the *Mayan-Xinca* sage, Lorena Cabnal, the *Ixina*, "the awakening to cosmic

[12] In general, these are places and presences that recall the earliest times, springs of water, forests, glaciers, ancient funerary remains, or places of fossils of ancient animals, ancient stones and rocks that are considered vital forces.
[13] Arnold, "Hacia una antropología", 114.
[14] Concerning the relational practices of co-partnership in the world.
[15] Jorge Apaza Ticona, "Cosmovisión andina en la crianza de la papa", in Juan van Kessel and Horacio Larrain (eds), *Manos sabias para criar la vida, tecnología* (Quito: Hombre y Ambiente, 1997): 103.
[16] Apaza Ticona, "Cosmovisión andina", 106.

consciousness to embrace a new era for bodies and territories."[17] Likewise, the recognition that the human community is one more thread in the great tapestry of life and not the protagonist. That is why Fernando Huanacuni pertinently maintains: "returning to our wisdom is not going backwards, but rather reconstituting ourselves in the principles and values."[18]

We Remain on the Path

We find ourselves in times in which the life of the Andean peoples and of the other kindred peoples in *Abya Yala* recovers affirmations from multiculturalism. But in which the peoples also live disagreements in their own communal organisations. It is about disagreements and imbalances due to the influence of ontological dualism, in which framework the care of the cosmos is in function of humanity. This means that the struggle for territory and land is mediated by functional legislative categories, as occurred in the process of agrarian reforms, which emptied the sense of the link with the land, territory and with all its interrelationships, which in turn led many peoples to assume the land as property, instrumentalising it as such.

Although there are a series of international treaties concerning the free self-determination of peoples, in the paths of self-affirmation or intracultural processes, ancestral vital principles are rescued as an ancient heritage that is nourished through the encounter of expressions of knowledge amongst the peoples. Said rescue is woven little by little and with a lot of effort, since it means swimming against the tide in order to maintain the vitality of the ancient wisdoms versus the dominion of the appropriation of life.

That is why, in communities seeking knowledge, wisdom and spiritualities, we are ready to follow the paths of *Suma Jakaña*, Good Living. This goes far beyond adhering to a partisan political discourse, since even in many peoples it is directed through ancestral principles. Such is the case of the profound strength of the mutual nurturing of life, which offers the possibility of generating relationships of mutuality with all communities of life, where spirituality is fully linked with and on the earth, and all the worlds that inhabit it. This implies walking a path that aims to get out of the structure of the globalising world system and the epistemic prejudices and racisms of its sciences and religions, which classify the pluriverse of the peoples as polytheistic, animistic, pantheistic, syncretic, superstitious, demonic and idolatrous.

We remain on the path, hand in hand with the sacred cosmic ancestry, as an encounter of nurturings that seeks to gestate sons and daughters of the earth, healers, who follow the routes of the cosmic conspiracies of the *Pachakutis*, necessary harmonisations in the web of life.

Suggestions for Further Reading

Arnold, Denise, Domingo Jiménez and Juan de Dios Yapita. *Hacia un orden andino de las cosas: Tres pistas de los Andes Meridionales*. La Paz: ILCA; Fundación Xavier Albó, 2014.

Escobar La Cruz, Remiro. "La técnica ancestral para recolectar agua". *El País*, 2nd May 2020, [Available at: https://elpais.com/elpais/2020/04/19/planeta_futuro/1587291656_149305.html], [Last accessed: 24th April 2022].

Estermann, Josef. "El mercado religioso y la Religión del Mercado", in *Religión y desarrollo en los Andes. Deconstrucción intercultural de una relación difícil.* La Paz: ISEAT, 2008: 53-65.

[17] Lorena Cabnal, "Documento en construcción para aportar a las reflexiones continentales desde el feminismo comunitario al paradigma ancestral originario del 'Sumak Kawsay', Buen Vivir", AMISMAXAJ Asociación de mujeres indígenas de Santa María Jalapa, 15, [Available at: https://amismaxaj.files.wordpress.com/2012/09/buen-vivir-desde-el-feminismo-comunitario.pdf], [Last accessed: 24th April 2022].

[18] Fernando Huanacuni, "El Buen Vivir, tradición indígena," in José María Vigil and Pedro Casaldáliga (eds), *Agenda Latinoamericana 2012 Mundial. Buen Vivir / Buen Convivir – Sumak Kawsay* (Panamá: Servicios Koinonia, 2012): 24.

Huanacuni, Fernando. "El Buen Vivir, tradición indígena", in José María Vigil and Pedro Casaldáliga, Eds. *Agenda Latinoamericana 2012 Mundial. Buen Vivir / Buen Convivir – Sumak Kawsay*. Panamá: Servicios Koinonia, 2012: 24-25.

Marcos, Sylvia. *Mujeres, indígenas, rebeldes, zapatistas*. México, DF: Eón, 2013.

Rengifo Vásquez, Grimaldo. *A mí me gusta hacer chacra*. Lima: Pratec; Ministerio de Educación, 2013.

Van den Berg, Hans. *La tierra no da así nomás. Los ritos agrícolas en la religión de los aymara-cristianos*. Cochabamba: Hisbol-UCB; ISET, 1990.

Van Kessel, Juan and Horacio Larrain, Eds. *Manos sabias para criar la vida. Tecnología andina*. Quito: Hombre y Ambiente, 1997.

91. Caregivers of the Common Home: A Popular Movement of Eco-Diakonia

Martha María Arriola[1]

Introduction

The Movement "*Cuidadores de la Casa Común*" (Caregivers of the Common Home) was born in Argentina six years ago, inspired in the Encyclical Letter *Laudato si'*.[2] In 2015, we came to know it through Monsignor Jorge Lugones and we knew that we wanted to respond, with a project, to the letter that Francis had written to us.[3]

We decided to popularise the encyclical letter, transform it into a training manual through popular education to reach out with it to the young people who suffer educational, economic, social, employment exclusion; the discarded persons of *Laudato si'*. Those whom we systematically stigmatise, because of their neighbourhood of origin and for "carrying a face."

"Caregivers" embrace them because they are victims of the system and allows them to discuss these myths from their own practice. They are sons and daughters of the people and the primary relationship with them is that of "body to body." Literally broken bodies, which often fall apart, until they no longer resemble human bodies. Ivone Gevara maintains that the body is the new starting point for theology, because it is the first reality that we are and know; it is impossible to say a word without counting on it.[4] The epistemological categories that Ana María Tepedino mentions for overcoming patriarchal theology are: the body, the relational and the everyday, illuminate the practice of the Movement.[5]

Relationships enter through the body, which is why they are felt and provoke different reactions. A theology made from the passionate and compassionate relationship with everything that exists takes us to the dimension of the reason of the heart, which again challenges dualism and maintains that everything is connected.[6] A knowing as old as it is new. In "Caregivers", everything is relationship.

The everyday, as a hermeneutic category joins the critique of rationality. There is an Argentine song that says "firewood, flour and clay burn, the everyday becomes magical," echoing that everything is possible there.[7] It is the space that we claim for naming God anew. We are listening: God does not abandon us; God is more than our words.

The proposal embodied by the Movement is carried out in "Territorial Nuclei" of "Caregivers of the Common Home," assumed by community organisations inserted in popular neighbourhoods, whose

---

[1] Martha M. Arriola is Argentinian, a popular educator, with a degree in Natural Sciences. She is a social psychologist, studying for a Master's Degree in Latin American Theology at the Central American University José Simeón Cañas, she has experience in public policies for community participation in the prevention of violence and youth, is a referent of the National Movement of Caregivers of the Common Home and a member of the National Justice and Peace Commission of the Argentine Episcopal Conference. mmarriola@yahoo.com.ar

[2] Francis, Encyclical Letter *Laudato Si'* On Care for Our Common Home (Vatican City: Vatican Press, 2015).

[3] Catholic bishop of Lomas de Zamora, Buenos Aires, Argentina. President of the Pastoral Commission of the Argentine Episcopal Conference. Referent pastor of the Movement *Cuidadores de la Casa Común*.

[4] Ivone Gebara, "A Mulher, a Teología. Contribuição Moral na América Latina", in M. Fabri (ed), *Temas Latinoamericanos de Ética* (Santuario Aparecida, 1988): 195-210.

[5] Ana María Tepedino, "¿Quiénes dicen las mujeres que soy yo?", in J.J. Tamayo Acosta (ed), *Diez palabras sobre Jesús de Nazaret* (Navarra: Verbo Divino, 1999): 442-448.

[6] See Ana María Tepedino. "¿Quiénes…?", 445. The concept of "heart" understood as the ability to tune in with other people and with the world.

[7] Peteco Carabajal, "Como pájaros en el aire," Side B, 5 in *Como pájaros en el aire*, Philips, 1985, vinyl. [TN: The lyrics in Spanish are: "arde la leña, harina y barro, lo cotidiano se vuelve mágico."]

referents have made their lives a commitment in the fight for justice and kinship. They live diakonia, whether they know it or not.

From *Laudato Si'* to the Training Manual for Caregivers of the Common Home

With a small founding group,[8] we gave ourselves a methodology: read the Encyclical Letter *Laudato Si'* slowly, pointing out the entry points for giving birth to the project. Among the first sparks that lit the fire is the quote that brought "Caregivers" to life: "Today, however, we have to realise that a true ecological approach always becomes a social approach; it must integrate questions of justice in debates on the environment, so as to hear *both the cry of the earth and the cry of the poor*".[9]

If *Laudato Si'* were a body, Chapter IV would be the heart: "Integral Ecology". In this neoliberal context of consumption, saturated with superfluous and ephemeral products, a new transition, revolutionary and structural, is gestated and matures. A paradigm shift where "good living" emerges, inherited from the original cultures, which practices new ways of producing, of relating to each other and to the little sister mother earth, being a sober, fair and responsible existence.

Integral ecology is a new vision of the world, of convergence of knowledge: scientific, popular, the wisdom of native religions and peoples. From that convergence, it makes a qualitative leap: the call is to transform ourselves into another species. *Homo sapiens* did not know how to take care of the only house we have, nor their brothers and sisters. It is time for the *homines curant* (human beings who care). "Caregivers" was born with this inspiration, nourished in its spirituality with contributions from teachers who are also part of the Movement.[10]

Sibling-like socio-ecological spirituality is the force that will resist the technocratic paradigm. With the discarded people, and with our sister mother earth, we gestate experiences of community salvation[11] – in the theological sense of it – an "already yes" of an eschatological "not yet." They are the experiences of "Caregivers of the Common Home," of "Boys and Girls of the People",[12] of the "Homes of Christ",[13] who live the mystique of making fraternity, sorority.

From that spirituality, "Caregivers" chooses to build their identity as workers in the care of the common home.

The Practice of Caregivers: Work + Spirituality = Revolution

In the encyclical letter *Laudato Si'*, work, the engine of transformation of the world, is very relevant.[14] That is why we set out to generate new working conditions, from the paradigm of caring, with young people in a situation of psychosocial vulnerability in the leading role. This process of community and popular

---

[8] We especially recognise Prof. Marcelo Vernet, co-founder of this movement, with whom we dreamed about it and gave birth to it. Marcelo left us on 28th August 2017 in the City of La Plata, Argentina.

[9] Francis, *LS*, 49.

[10] Francisco Bosch, Diego Sánchez (young theologians from the liberation theology tradition, with whom we travelled their *Via evolutionis*, the path on which to water the birth of the new species), Monsignor Jorge Lugones (shepherd "with the smell of sheep", as Pope Francis says), Josué Trujillo (land worker, Bolivian, teacher and catechist), Humberto Podetti (Professor specialising in Latin American History, current president of the National Justice and Peace Commission of the Argentine Episcopal Commission), Emilce Cuda (Argentine theologian, recently chosen by Pope Francis as head of the office of the Vatican's Pontifical Commission for Latin America), among others.

[11] Francis, *LS*, 149; 125; 127-128.

[12] Red Nacional de Organizaciones Comunitarias that work in the care of children and adolescents in Argentina.

[13] Red Argentina de Hogares that work in the recovery of adolescents and young people with problematic substance use, led by slum priests.

[14] The challenge of employment is located in Chapter III: "The human roots of the ecological crisis."

experience is a spiral of continuity and rupture, where each new level is related and interconnected to the previous one in a total cognitive, affective, spiritual and political overflow. Its starting point, like the explosion of the "Big Bang," is the figure of Saint Francis of Assisi – who contemplates in admiration and cares for each creature – and that of Blessed Charles de Foucauld with his little brothers of Jesus, who gestate the new civilisation of work.

From below and from outside, in Caregivers of the Common Home, we set out to create decent work, rising up and disputing the logic of the market.

The Movement has a presence in 18 provinces, in 108 "Territorial Nuclei,"[15] made up of 5,000 young people in popular neighbqurhoods from the urban or rural outskirts. From the end of 2015 through 2018, the foundations of the project were built through pre-existing links with grassroots organisations.[16] Initially, an awareness process was generated through the "Training Manual for Caregivers of the Common Home."[17] From the implementation of different strategies, the identity of the Movement and the commitment to decent work were forged,[18] a true utopia in times of the neoliberal government of *Cambiemos* in Argentina.[19] "Caregivers" positioned itself as a pioneer actor in the realisation of transforming social plans into work. The Province of Entre Ríos, from the Social Economy Secretariat of the Ministry of Social Development, transformed it into a provincial policy: Entre Ríos Caregivers of the Common Home Program, generating a substantive boost in the development of the project, with presence today in 15 locations.[20] At the national level, seven lines of work emerged: Care for the Earth, for Water, Recycling, Clean Energies, Community Tourism, Cultural Industries and Products, and Healthy Food. All of them have been progressively articulated in five regions: Northwest, Northeast, Patagonia-South, Centre and Province of Buenos Aires.

---

[15] Georeferencing of the Territorial Nuclei of the Carergivers of the Common Home Movement, [Available at: https://www.google.com/maps/d/u/0/viewer?hl=es&mid=1_Q3VW4tKRthJSP0CpvdVWexb7RPxHtW0&ll=-32.81497376944431%2C-64.90842428505002&z=5].

[16] Red Nacional del Banco Popular de la Buena Fe; Bishoprics of Lomas de Zamora, of Jujuy and recently Diocese of Añatuya, Santiago del Estero; Cooperatives; Civil associations and foundations.

[17] With activities such as the course "Formarnos Educadores Populares para el Cuidado de la Casa Común" National Meetings, on 28th-29th September and 19th-20th October 2018 at the Headquarters of the National University of Lanus, with 600 participants; the presentation of the Procodas Contest of the Ministerio de Ciencia y Tecnología de la Nación of the year 2017 [TN: Prodocas – Projects of technologies for social inclusion]; the presentation of productive projects to the Fundación del Banco de la Nación Argentina and the arrangement of the complementary social salary, see Boletín Oficial de Presidencia de la República Argentina, Ministerio de Trabajo, Empleo y Seguridad Social de la Argentina, Programa de Transición al Salario Social Complementario, Resolution 201-E/2017, Ciudad de Buenos Aires, 5th April 2017, [Available at: https://www.boletinoficial.gob.ar/detalleAviso/primera/162292/20170417], [Last accessed: 24th April 2022].

[18] An agreement was made with the Ministerio de Trabajo de la Nación to be able to integrate the training proposal in the Job Initiation Course [TN: CIT for the initials in Spanish] of the Youth with More and Better Work Plan. These three-month CIT courses did not have and do not have as their main objective the generation of associative youth work projects, but rather the training of young people in the world of work with initial formation, so that they recognise their skills and achieve the building of their CVs. In the Caregivers strategy, this was the initial track for the birthing, during those three months, of the associative work project ideas. Of the 30 enrolled in each of the courses developed, 30% managed to organise themselves to take on the next stage: the path to the initial consolidation of the project that was organised at the national level by the Regional Studies Foundation for all existing Territorial Nuclei. See Ministerio de Trabajo, Empleo y Seguridad Social, "Jóvenes: Formación, capacitación e inserción laboral para jóvenes de entre 18 y 24 años", [Available at: https://www.argentina.gob.ar/trabajo/jovenes], [Last accessed: 24th April 2022].

[19] *Coalición Cívica Cambiemos*. 2015-2019. Presidency of the Engineer Mauricio Macri.

[20] Ministerio de Desarrollo Social Gobierno Entre Ríos, Economía Social, Desarrollo Territorial de la Economía Social, Programa Cuidadores de la Casa Común, [Available at; https://www.entrerios.gov.ar/desarrollosocial/index.php?codigo=125&codsubmenu=94&modulo=&codppal=3], [Last accessed: 24th April 2022].

In 2019, the Movement visited Pope Francis and participated through Monsignor Jorge Lugones in the ILO Symposium on the future of work in the ecological transition.[21]

Caregivers and Their Incidence in the Public Policies of Argentina: The Fight for the Land

Creating work means going for the land. Until now, our orchards and crops have been grown on land granted on loan, which we were able to occupy or which belong to the organisations of the Movement.

Francis' plan for rising from the COVID-19 pandemic encourages us to a new imagination of the possible, with the realism that only the gospel can provide us.

Caregivers have a dream that is equal to that challenge: the "Marcha al Campo" ("March to the Fields"). We walk together with a group of very tenacious activists, who since the 1970s have struggled to put into practice this true process of territorial planning in Argentina, led by comrade Guillermo Gallo Mendoza, who launched it between 1973 and 1976 in the Buenos Aires province.[22] The dictatorship disappeared 30,000 companions and with them a project for the country.

The Marcha al Campo proposes to use the natural resource fiscal land with native forest, in an estimated 20 million hectares with a dual purpose: to generate work and food sovereignty. These are state lands that are idle or usurped by landowners.

This project already has a bill in Congress, presented by the national deputy María Rosa Martínez, a member of the Caregivers of the Common Home Movement.[23] In Argentina there are 4,145 neighbourhoods and popular settlements, where approximately 3.5 million people live in just over 40 thousand hectares.[24] The "owners of the land" – both vernacular and foreigners, who do not add up to more than 1,200 families and live in the main urban centres or outside the country – concentrate a total of 65 million hectares, which is equivalent to 40% of the Argentine territory. With more than 20 million hectares available, this is a real contradiction, an unforgivable social sin.

Together with this impulse, "Caregivers" has consolidated "Solidarity and Sustainable Productive Communities" (CPSyS) in lands that have been leased, transferred or occupied; and that make up regional networks – in the Provinces of Buenos Aires, Entre Ríos and Córdoba, with 19 CSyS. It is about the continuity of a history of more than 20 years: the land seizures in the Buenos Aires suburbs, accompanied by the first bishop of the Diocese of Quilmes, Monsignor Jorge Novak,[25] resignified in the Marcha al Campo, with organisations that gave it continuity since then.[26]

---

[21] "Monseñor Lugones presentó en UNESCO, París, a Cuidadores de la Casa Común," Cuidadores de la Casa Común, [Available at: https://cuidadoresdelacasacomun.org/sitio/mons-lugones-presento-en-unesco-paris-a-cuidadores-de-la-casa-comun/], [Last accessed: 24th April 2022].

[22] "Entrevista al Ing. Agrónomo Guillermo Gallo Mendoza. La hora de la Marcha al campo," *Grandes Alamedas*, 18th December 2020, [Available at: https://grandesalamedasblog.wordpress.com/2020/12/18/entrevista-con-el-ing-guillermo-gallo-mendoza-la-hora-de-la-marcha-al-campo/], [Last accessed: 24th April 2022].

[23] Honorable Cámara de Diputados de la Nación, "Proyecto de Ley Programa Nacional Marcha al Campo," 3905-D-2020, [Available at:https://www4.hcdn.gob.ar/dependencias/dsecretaria/Periodo2020/PDF2020/TP2020/3905-D-2020.pdf], [Last accessed: 24th April 2022].

[24] See Ministerio de Desarrollo Social, Secretaría de Integración Socio urbana, RENABAP, Registro Nacional de Barrios y Asentamientos Populares de Argentina, [Available at: https://www.argentina.gob.ar/desarrollosocial/renabap/tabla], [Last accessed: 24th April 2022].

[25] First Bishop of the Diocese of Quilmes. Co-founder of the Ecumenical Movement for Human Rights (MEDH), he was part of the group of bishops who most strongly denounced human rights violations in Argentina during the Argentine military dictatorship. He is today in process of beatification.

[26] Organisations such as: Organización Jaime de Nevares. Comunidad Productiva Solidaria y Sustentable "La Argentina." Ruta Provincial 74, Km 70. Las Armas, Maipú, Buenos Aires, Argentina. Comunidad Productiva, Solidaria y Sustentable FAIDI, Miramar, Buenos Aires, Argentina.

Universalising the Social Salary: Towards a Draft Law for the Protection and Encouragement of Decent Human Work

During the summer months of 2019, "Caregivers of the Common Home" together with the "UCA Social Debt Observatory"[27] formulated two initiatives: a draft bill to create the "Generalised Minimum Wage"[28] and the project "Neighbourhood Boards for Socio-Labour Integration" from which to bring together the social actors of each slum neighbourhood and settlement to plan the work, taking the seven axes identified in the Movement's practice. Both projects were delivered to the team of the Secretariat for Strategic Affairs of the Nation.

Key Imperatives for a Public Policy that Identifies New Signifiers for Decent Work for Young People in Situations of Psycho-Social Vulnerability

In addition to the work with the land and the consolidation of the "Solidarity and Sustainable Productive Communities" (CPSyS), two working processes emerge that are consolidated: community tourism,[29] and textile and plastic recycling for the manufacture of clothing and accessories.[30] At the same time, the Popular Grocery Stores for Caregivers of the Common House concentrate on the regional and/or national offer.[31]

Each process constitutes a concrete testimony of the abundance of work that we can and must generate. In almost all of them, we fight in a very unequal way against the drug trafficking networks and in all of them against the culture of the social plan without considerations. We are systematising the practice to extract significant lessons from it for influencing public policies.

Towards Eco-Diakonía

Caregivers of the Common Home is among the smallest social movements in Argentina. One of the challenges ahead is to position itself in the context of the continent's social movements to share learning, mysticism and journey, disputing and recreating the concept and practice of exercising power in a patriarchal civilisation. It will only be able to rise to the challenge if its practices are questioned by the old/new social ordering of the Jesus movement: "I have not come to be served, but to serve," a counter-cultural ordering that implies "the revolution of power."[32]

Suggestions for Further Reading

Boff, Leonardo. *Conversaciones*. Brasil: Foro Social Mundial, 2009.

Boff, Leonardo. *¿La Tierra como baúl de recursos infinitos o como Casa Común viva?* Amerindia, 13th June 2019. [Available at: https://amerindiaenlared.org/contenido/14900/la-tierra-como-baul-de-recursos-infinitos-o-como-casa-comun-viva/], [Last accessed: 24th April 2022].

---

[27] Observatorio de la Deuda Social Argentina, Pontifical Catholic University of Argentina, [Available at: http://uca.edu.ar/es/observatorio-de-la-deuda-social-argentina], [Last accessed: 24th April 2022].

[28] "Anteproyecto de Ley de Protección y Estímulo del Trabajo Humano Digno," Draft, [Available at: https://docs.google.com/document/d/1a0oSnaGT2Sms9U0H4GKQAacHrll4X553/edit], [Last accessed: 24th April 2022].

[29] Process consolidated in the *Red de Turismo Comunitario del Litoral y Noreste Argentino – Ruta del Agua* in the Provinces of Entre Ríos, Santa Fe, Corrientes, Misiones, Chaco and Formosa.

[30] Triple impact textile project: Dream big, start small.

[31] Cuidadores de la Casa Común, "Primer Almacén de Cuidadores de la Casa Común," *Facebook*, 10th June 2021, video, 00:33, [Available at: https://www.facebook.com/1743001232601403/videos/2933466383554876], [Last accessed: 24th April 2022].

[32] Clodovis Boff, *El Evangelio Del Poder-Servicio* (Bogotá: CLAR, 1985): 51-52.

Francis, *Letter to the Popular Movements.* 12th April 2020. [Available at: https://www.vatican.va/content/francesco/en/letters/2020/documents/papa-francesco_20200412_lettera-movimentipopolari.html], [Last accessed: 24th April 2022].

Pioli, Javier Juan. "Diaconía y desarrollo sostenible." *Website of the Centro Emmanuel.* Colonia Valdense, República Oriental del Uruguay. [Available at: https://centroemmanuel.org/diaconia-y-desarrollo-sostenible/], [Last accessed: 24th April 2022].

Nordstokke, Kjell, Ed. *Diakonia in Context: Transformation, Reconciliation, Empowerment. An LWF Contribution to the Understanding and Practice of Diakonia.* Geneva, Switzerland: Lutheran World Federation, 2009. [Available at: https://www.lutheranworld.org/sites/default/files/DMD-Diakonia-EN-low.pdf], [Last accessed: 24th April 2022].

92. "Caring for the Forests to Take Care of Life"

Laura Vargas[1]

Introduction

We live in complex, harsh and suffering times, largely due to human action or inaction. The economic model in which we are immersed has pushed the planet to its limits, and the survival of a large proportion of life is at risk. All human life, as well as that of animals and plants, is threatened.

> The pace of consumption, waste and environmental change has so stretched the planet's capacity that our contemporary lifestyle, unsustainable as it is, can only precipitate catastrophes, such as those which even now periodically occur in different areas of the world.[2]

At the International Conference "Saving our Common Home, and the Future of Life on the Planet", in July 2018 to celebrate the third anniversary of the Encyclical *Laudato Si'*, the President of the NGO 350.org and one of the key note speakers, William McKibben asked us to be aware that this world was governed by the three A's: Avarice, Arrogance and Apathy. The first two, he said, were located in the arena of the powerful of this world, while the third was our responsibility, because we had internalised the idea that nothing could be done in the face of such big problems. However, we know from history that, many times, great changes come from below and that organised and conscientious people have the ability to generate and fight for important and necessary changes to take place, and that is what it is about, generating a growing movement, with the active participation of many. Christians, cannot fall into apathy, but must follow the path of the Risen One, who has explicitly asked us to be able to read the *signs of the times*. The peoples and the earth cry out for a change; we cannot turn a deaf ear to these cries, which are a single cry of anguish to stop the suicidal destruction in which we are immersed. Faced with this reality, our faith proposes to us the key word *change (metanoia)*: changes in lifestyles, changes in our ways of thinking, changes in the ways in which we organise ourselves and relate to each other. We cannot continue to act and live in the same way as if nothing were happening, we need radical changes at all levels so that the future is possible for everyone. As believers in the God of Life, we know that the final word of history is life and not death. In the care of life, there is the germ of a new paradigm, the *paradigm of care*.

Three Interconnected Crises Put Humanity in Check

Environmental Crisis: As we write these lines, we are deeply moved by the information from the 6th report of the Intergovernmental Panel on Climate Change (IPCC).[3] There is no longer any doubt that the unprecedented climate crisis that we are living is generated by ourselves, and by the economic model that we have developed in the last 200 years together with the industrial revolution, whose exacerbation in the last five decades has led us to the abyss. The planet no longer supports the development model that, as it

---

[1] Laura Vargas is Executive Secretary of the Interreligious Council of Peru-Religions for Peace and Co-ordinator of the Interfaith Rainforest Initiative, IRI-Peru. laura.vargas@interfaithrainforest.org; laurav1948@gmail.com.

[2] Francis, *Encyclical Letter: Laudato Si' on Care for our Common Home* (Vatican City: Vatican Press, 2015): 161.

[3] See: IPCC, Climate Change 2022: Impacts, Adaptation and Vulnerability, Contribution of Working Group II to the Sixth Assessment Report of the Intergovernmental Panel on Climate Change [H.-O. Pörtner, D.C. Roberts, M. Tignor, E.S. Poloczanska, K. Mintenbeck, A. Alegría, M. Craig, S. Langsdorf, S. Löschke, V. Möller, A. Okem, B. Rama (eds.)]. Cambridge University Press. In Press. [Available at: https://www.ipcc.ch/report/ar6/wg2/], [Last accessed: 27th April 2022].

becomes general practice, causes increases in temperature that are already uncontrollable. And they are already affecting us dramatically. Every year, we have hotter summers that are generating tragic phenomena, such as forest fires in Greece, in addition to those in California, Brazil, Australia, and in our own country accompanied by the destruction of the habitats of animals and microorganisms. Temperatures bordering 50ºC in Canada, floods not seen before with a sequel of destruction and death in Germany, Belgium and China, among others. Hence, the urgency to work so that the global temperature increase does not exceed 1.5°C and that all countries commit at COP26 to increase their climate ambitions and the commitment to implement energy transition processes towards low emission energy sources, as the United Nations is asking us with the Decade for Restoration of Terrestrial and Maritime Ecosystems.[4]

Crisis due to the very serious loss of biodiversity: The chain of life is one of the most beautiful mysteries in the universe. We have been freely given the conditions for life to emerge and develop in all its complexity, from the primitive cyanobacteria that open up to the sunlight, and "that 3.6 billion years ago, they invented photosynthesis and drastically changed the evolution of life [...] they generated and currently maintain the entire existence of the planet,"[5] even the complexity of human beings. This chain is seriously affected by the extinction of species that are breaking the chain of life with very serious consequences for the survival of the rest, including ours. The saddest thing about this is that we are not aware of how serious the extinction of species is. Specialists are already talking about the sixth mass extinction and we contemplate the misfortune, or we live in total indifference, which is already sin in religious terms by omission. This is why the words of Pope Francis seem very lucid when, in the Apostolic Exhortation *Evangelii gaudium,* he tells us: "Thanks to our bodies, God has joined us so closely to the world around us that we can feel the desertification of the soil almost as a physical ailment, and the extinction of a species as a painful disfigurement."[6]

COVID-19 and the health crisis: This pandemic that has put the entire planet in check is a zoonotic disease with an incredible capacity for contagion, reinvention and reproduction, which has even deprived us of the right to grieve our deceased family and friends. This pandemic has stolen our remaining securities and confronts us with an urgent scenario that cannot wait. In fact, now that the figures of the fatalities in Peru have been revealed, we know that in the 17 months that we have been suffering, it has already taken the lives of around 200 000 brothers and sisters, and now with the third wave underway, the outlook is bleak.[7] No conflict in Peru, including the war with Chile and the internal armed conflict of the last twenty years of the last century was so deadly. The lethality of the pandemic surpasses all that has been experienced, and has generated serious consequences and mental health problems in many who have suffered the virus, in their families and relatives.

Today It Is COVID-19, What Will It Be Tomorrow?

More than 60% of all diseases that humanity suffers today have a zoonotic origin, and more than 85% of the most recent come from wild animals. These infectious diseases are produced by pathogens that inhabit wild animals and, when their ecosystems are destroyed, that pass to humans: ebola, sars, avian flu and now

---

[4] UN, "Preventing, Halting and Reversing the Degradation of Ecosystems Worldwide", *UN Decade on Ecosystem Restoration Website,* [Available at: https://www.decadeonrestoration.org/], [Last accessed: 27th April 2022].

[5] Jiri Komárek and Jarka Kómarkova, "Cianobacterias esenciales en la historia y en el futuro del planeta," *El País*, 3rd April 2010.

[6] Francis, *Apostolic Exhortation: Evangelii Gaudium, on the proclamation of the Gospel in today's world* (Vatican City: Vatican Press, 2013): 215.

[7] Editorial Note: According to the Coronavirus Resource Center at John Hopkins University, Peru is the country that has suffered the highest death rate per 100K population, at 648.01/100K, as reported on 1st March 2022. See John Hopkins University and Medicine, "Mortality Analyses," *Coronavirus Resource Center,* [Available at: https://coronavirus.jhu.edu/data/mortality], [Last accessed: 27th April 2022].

COVID-19. These are zoonotic diseases that are telling us that we human beings have developed a sick relationship with nature, we have broken the principle of reciprocity, *I give to you and you give to me:* "Our global economy, consumption patterns and production systems not only endanger nature, but also our own well-being."[8] We have turned nature into a resource that turns to money and the ownership and exploitation of which, one can profit; it has ceased to be a living being with whom to relate. Hence the need to heal the relationship we have with nature – she does not need us and through millennia will recover, but we will not be able to survive with a diseased nature. This moment is an urgent invitation to rethink and redo the relationship we have with Mother Earth, learning from our indigenous brothers and sisters, who over the centuries have developed a harmonious relationship with nature, which we call *good living*. A friend from the indigenous people *Ese Ejja,* César Augusto Yohahe used to tell us, "There are no forests without indigenous people, and there are no indigenous people without a forest, we are a unit." It is proven that Amazonian forests and ecosystems are better cared for when indigenous peoples take care of them. When Pope Francis visited us in Puerto Maldonado in January 2018, he told the indigenous peoples that:

> Those of us who do not live in these lands need your wisdom and knowledge to enable us to enter into, without destroying, the treasures that this region holds. And to hear an echo of the words that the Lord spoke to Moses: "Remove the sandals from your feet, for the place on which you are standing is holy ground" (Ex. 3:5).[9]

Later at the end of the Synod of Pan Amazonia and with the publication of the Apostolic Exhortation *Querida Amazonia,* he tells us:

> If the care of people and the care of ecosystems are inseparable, this becomes especially important in places where "the forest is not a resource to be exploited; it is a being, or various beings, with which we have to relate." The wisdom of the original peoples of the Amazon region "inspires care and respect for creation, with a clear consciousness of its limits, and prohibits its abuse. To abuse nature is to abuse our ancestors, our brothers and sisters, creation and the Creator, and to mortgage the future". When the indigenous peoples "remain on their land, they themselves care for it best", provided, that they do not let themselves be taken in by the siren songs and the self-serving proposals of power groups. The harm done to nature affects those peoples in a very direct and verifiable way, since, in their words, "we are water, air, earth and life of the environment created by God. For this reason, we demand an end to the mistreatment and destruction of mother Earth. The land has blood, and it is bleeding; the multinationals have cut the veins of our mother Earth".[10]

The Pope gathers in this long quotation the cry of the earth, and of its forests that are being destroyed by deforestation, by forest fires, by monocultures and intensive cattle ranching and by illegal activities (logging, mining, drug trafficking and land trafficking) that only seek profit, at any cost.

---

[8] Interfaith Rainforest Initiative, *Forests and Pandemics: How protecting tropical forests can prevent coronaviruses and other emerging diseases. An issue primer for religious leaders and faith communities,* [Available at: https://www.interfaithrainforest.org/s/Interfaith_ForestsPandemics_Primer_ENG.pdf], [Last accessed: 27th April 2022].

[9] Francis, "Address of the Holy Father at his meeting with indigenous peoples of Amazonia" (Coliseo Regional Madre de Dios, Puerto Maldonado, Peru, 19th January 2018), [Available at: https://www.vatican.va/content/francesco/en/speeches/2018/january/documents/papa-francesco_20180119_peru-puertomaldonado-popoliamazzonia.html], [Last accessed: 27th April 2022].

[10] Francis, Apostolic Exhortation *Querida Amazonia* to all the people of God and to all persons of good will (Vatican City: Vatican Press, 2020): 42.

Tropical Forests at the Centre of Life

Tropical forests are the most important terrestrial ecosystems on the planet, with more than 7 million square kilometres, and about one sixth of the fresh water in its rivers and lagoons. Tropical forests offer us food, medicine and fundamental eco-systemic services, such as being "a buffer against climate change; which regulates climate variability and stores around 130 billion metric tons of carbon, almost a decade of global CO_2 emissions."[11]

Destroying forests is not only an environmental problem, it is a serious public health problem, an ethical problem and, at its root, a spiritual problem. Values have been disrupted, hence the importance of having a holistic vision of nature and human beings, because everything is interconnected.

Peru has the fourth largest forest area in the world and the second in South America after Brazil. The Peruvian Amazon represents almost two-thirds of the entire national territory. In our country, for decades our Amazon has been deforested and degraded by one way of understanding development that has "its back turned to the indigenous cultures and to what is the main asset of this Region: its forests and healthy ecosystems. Rather, it seems that forests are presumed to be a hindrance, so many policies and decisions have had the objective of changing their use, replacing biodiversity with crops that, by not finding land suitable for agriculture, fail and at the same time expand in a vicious circle that continues to impoverish the Amazon and its inhabitants, despite this, a good part of them still remain healthy."[12]

If COVID is the result of the destruction of nature, we need to protect forests, peatlands, wetlands and change agricultural practices. According to the international scientific working group on pandemic prevention, organised by the Institute of Global Health at Harvard University,[13] the risks of producing these kinds of health catastrophes have increased in the last five decades due to alteration of ecosystems, climate change, deforestation, the trafficking of wild animals, and intensive agriculture. In fact, health is one, since the health of nature and that of human beings are mutually dependent, which also invites us to implement a multi-disciplinary approach. If, prior to this present time, we have developed segmented views of reality, today – in the face of the multiple crises that we are living – it has become necessary to have holistic views, with multidisciplinary approaches.

Amazon a Place to Hear God

In nature, everything is interconnected. This idea is one of the pillars of the Encyclical of Pope Francis, *Laudato Si', on Care for our Common Home*[14] and of the Special Synod of the Amazon,[15] which reminds

---

[11] Panel Científico por la Amazonia, "Resultados preliminares del Panel Científico del Amazonas (SPA)," 14th July 2021.

[12] Interfaith Rainforest Initiative-Perú, "Pacto por la Amazonía y sus Bosques Saludables, Documento base," February 2021.

[13] See: "New Report from Harvard and Global Experts Shows Investments in Nature Needed to Stop the Next Pandemic", 17th August 2021, *Harvard Global Health Institute*, [Available at: https://globalhealth.harvard.edu/new-report-from-harvard-and-global-experts-shows-investments-in-nature-needed-to-stop-the-next-pandemic/], [Last accessed: 27th April 2022].

[14] Francis, *Encyclical Letter: Laudato Si' on Care for our Common Home* (Vatican City: Vatican Press, 2015). [Available at: https://www.vatican.va/content/francesco/en/encyclicals/documents/papa-francesco_20150524_enciclica-laudato-si.html], [Last accessed: 27th April 2022].

[15] Pan-Amazon Synod – The Synod of Bishops for the Pan-Amazon, *Final Document: The Amazon: New Paths For The Church And For An Integral Ecology,* Special Assembly of the Synod of Bishops for the Pan-Amazon Region, 6th-27th October 2017 [Available at: http://secretariat.synod.va/content/sinodoamazonico/en/documents/final-document-of-the-amazon-synod.html], [Last accessed: 27th April 2022].

us that we have already destroyed too much. It is precisely because of this dramatic reality that we are living that the Interfaith Rainforest Initiative (IRI)[16] was born.

IRI is an international alliance of the world's leading Religious Consortia that aims to bring moral urgency and spiritual resources to global efforts to end tropical deforestation. It is also a platform for religious leaders and communities of faith to work hand-in-hand with indigenous peoples, governments, civil society and the private sector in actions that protect tropical forests and safeguard those who are their original owners.[17]

We are present in Brazil, Colombia, Peru, the Democratic Republic of the Congo, and Indonesia, which together are home to more than 70% of the world's Tropical Forests. Part of our working strategy is to influence governments and companies together with NGOs to stop or drastically reduce deforestation in our countries. The IRI has local chapters located in jungle areas with high deforestation and situations that seriously affect the lives of indigenous peoples.

In Peru, IRI has launched the Pact for the Amazon and Healthy Forests[18] understanding that the health of society and the health of nature are one; by taking care of one we take care of and protect the other. In this way, we seek to generate and make visible commitments and actions for a healthy Amazon, from both public and private interest groups. We have a declaration under the name of *Pacto por la Amazonia y los bosques saludables* (Covenant for Amazonia and healthy forests),[19] open to signatures and commitments from other organisations and persons, with the aim of generating a positive feeling of belonging, good-will and action for a healthy Amazon.

The IRI has positioned itself as a social and political actor to influence many other groups, especially indigenous peoples, in the rights of the peoples and of the ecosystems that sustain our life.

For believers, the Amazon is a space of life, and to speak of life is to speak of the fundamental principle that allows us to be and share this gift with all other living creatures on the planet. The life we share is a gift from God, which we have the task of caring for, protecting and giving to future generations in the same conditions as it was gifted to us. This wonderful gift is at serious risk from the triple global crisis that we are going through. The situation has never been so serious – "our Sister, Mother Earth,"[20] as Francis of Assisi called her, cannot give more, and cries out for a change in the relationship we have established with her. From the II General Conference of the Latin American Episcopate (CELAM II), taken place in Medellín (1968), we learned that in Latin America, the social, political, economic and – today we would add environmental – reality of the peoples is a space from which God is speaking. I think this voice is already a tumultuous roar, as it was so well expressed at CELAM III (Puebla, 1979); and the sad thing is that no one wants to listen to what God is asking of us.

As communities of faith, we believe that this crisis in which we find ourselves invites us to develop the paradigm of care and compassion for and with all living beings, and especially with our human brothers and sisters. Because "it is in caring that we find the fundamental ethos of the human being. This means that

---

[16] See Interfaith Rainforest Initiative Website at: https://www.interfaithrainforest.org/, [Last accessed: 27th April 2022].

[17] The organisation was launched in June 2017, in Oslo, Norway, through an initiative of the United Nations Environment Program, in partnership with Religions for Peace, the World Council of Churches, the World Parliament of Religions, the Faith and Forests Program of Yale University and the Pan-Amazonian Ecclesial Network (REPAM), with the support of the Government of Norway. The initiative is grounded in recognition of the fact that spiritual resources, guidance and moral authority, as well as the unparalleled influence of the world's religious leaders and faith communities, are urgently needed to protect the planet's tropical forests.

[18] "Healthy Amazon Pact Establishes Agenda for Debates Over Sustainable Development", 20th February 2021, *Peru Support Group Website*. [Available at: https://perusupportgroup.org.uk/2021/02/healthy-amazon-pact-establishes-agenda-for-debates-over-sustainable-development/], [Last accessed: 29th April 2022].

[19] Se Pacto Por La Amazonia website at: https://pactoporlaamazonia.org/

[20] Francis, *Laudato Si'*, 1.

in care we identify the principles, values and attitudes that makes of life a good life, and of actions, a challenge to accept."[21]

The human impact on nature urges us to restore, to heal, to regenerate what we have damaged, and / or mortally wounded. Not all is yet lost, because we have the ability to transform our impact on the planet through care and compassion. A sustainable economy powered by nature-based solutions and renewable energy will create new jobs, cleaner infrastructure and greater resilience in the future. An inclusive world in which we live in peace with nature will allow people to enjoy better health, fully exercise their human rights and, therefore, lead a dignified life on a healthy planet. Not all is yet lost, if, as the Argentine singer Fito Páez would say, *we come to offer our heart*.

Suggestions for Further Reading

Interfaith Rainforest Initiative. *A Catholic Toolkit on Forest Protection: Resources for religious leaders and faith communities*. [Available at https://www.interfaithrainforest.org/faith-toolkits/], [Last accessed: 29th April 2022].

Iniciativa Interreligiosa para los Bosques Tropicales. *Restauración de Bosques: Sanar los bosques tropicales para la renovación espiritual*. IRI, 2021. [Available at: https://bit.ly/ReforestacionIRI], [Last accessed: 29th April 2022].

Iniciativa Interreligiosa para los Bosques Tropicales – Perú. "IRI en el Perú: un bosque de fe y esperanza." June 2021, IRI Perú. YouTube Video, 04:40. [Available at: https://www.youtube.com/watch?v=FcLQhjpvr_U], [Last accessed 29th April 2022].

Ráez, Ernesto. *Verde y Fraterno: El Perú del tercer siglo y la crisis ecológica global*. Lima: IRI Perú, 2021. [Available at: https://bit.ly/LibroVyF], [Last accessed 29th April 2022].

[21] Leonardo Boff, *Saber Cuidar* (edición digital), 4. [Available at: https://www.rumbosostenible.com/wp-content/uploads/Saber-Cuidar-Libro-de-Leonardo-Boff.pdf], [Last accessed: 29th April 2022].

93. The Pastoral Ministry for the Promotion of Creation Care: Dialogues towards a Sustainable Production Model

Romario Dohmann[1]

Introduction

We know that, although the planet is inhabited by different and diverse species, without a doubt, the one that generates the greatest amount of environmental degradation is the human species. The capitalist mode of production, eager for raw materials, pollutes rivers and water tables, desertifies lands, and changes the climate, among other consequences.

Based on the conviction that the design, encouragement and accompaniment of initiatives that promote sustainability and climate justice is a fundamental part of our mission, in recent years the Evangelical Church of the Río de la Plata (IERP), through the Protestant Diakonia Foundation *Hora de Obra* has launched the Pastoral for the Promotion of Creation Care (PPCC).[2]

A primary objective of the PPCC lies in identifying and articulating action spaces aimed at raising awareness, advocacy and project planning that promote sustainable production, healthy consumption and, in general, environmental justice, both within the church and their congregations, as well as for society as a whole, in collaboration with other allied organisations.

In this article, I am going to consider, from a youth perspective, the proposal of systematisation of the origins and development of the pastoral for the care of creation elaborated by the pastor and professor Dr Daniel Beros.[3] I will integrate the experience of the youth of the ecclesial districts of the IERP in its appropriation and dissemination of the PPCC in its missionary task. In the last three years, this ministry has been one of the most debated topics and one that has most called on young people to organise themselves in the development of their activities.

A Fundamental Pastoral for Youth Work in the IERP

The PPCC began to develop in 2016, in a historical context in which in Argentina, Paraguay and Uruguay – the three countries throughout which the communities that make up the IERP are spread as part of the hegemonic system at the world level, governed by the forces of transnational financial capitalism, continued to deepen a profoundly asymmetrical insertion in the relations of production and exchange. Beros highlights the context in which the church begins to develop this ministry and says:

> The conditions of this "exchange" have been and continue to be imposed by the actors who control the (falsely) so-called "free market". They fundamentally benefit a few circles of global concentrated capital [...][4]

[1] Romario Dohmann is a member of the co-ordination team of the Pastoral for the Promotion of Creation Care of the Evangelical Church of River Plate (IERP) and is responsible for the *Crece Selva Misionera* programme, developed by the Protestant Diaconia Foundation *Hora de Obrar*. He also performs the function of general co-ordinator of the youth of the IERP. He is currently finishing his studies in Forestry Engineering at the National University of Misiones, Argentine Republic. romario.dohmann@horadeobrar.org.ar

[2] In some languages like Spanish, the term "pastoral" works in the absolute sense; in some other languages like English, one would speak of "the pastoral ministry" [editor's comment].

[3] Daniel Beros, "Pastoral de Promoción del Cuidado de la Creación de la Iglesia Evangélica del Río de la Plata. Orígenes, concepto, desarrollo, proyección", *Vida y Pensamiento* 39(1) (January-June 2019): 107-134.

[4] Beros, "Pastoral", 117.

This affects young people in their way of seeing reality, assuming the dominant form of production as the only prevailing one. This reality not only limits the economy of the countries, but also the conditions and expectations of the majority of the young men and women of the IERP, as they are children of workers and small rural producers. The impoverishment of working families and rural producers encourages youth migration from the countryside to the city, where young people are forced to study and work. This "free market," far from giving them freedom to choose, forces them to go to the city in search of better training and job prospects.

In the following table, we can see the exponential increase in migration from the countryside to the city from the decade of the sixties, which coincides with the beginning of the implementation of the so-called "green revolution."[5]

Figura 1. Evolución de la población urbana y rural en Argentina

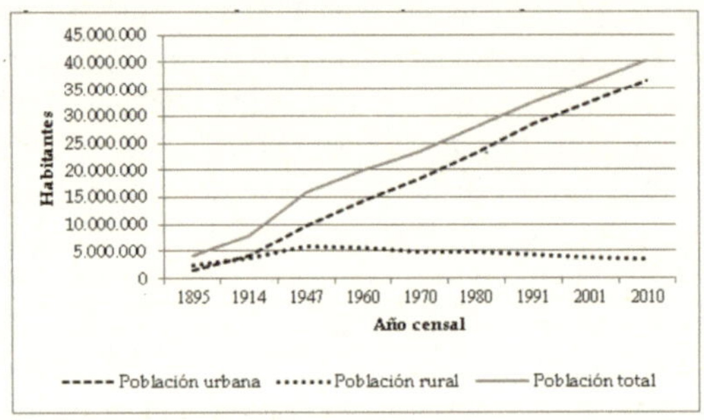

Fuente: Censos nacionales de población de los años 1895, 1914, 1947, 1969, 1970, 1980, 1991, 2001 y 2010. Instituto Nacional de Estadísticas y Censos (INDEC).

At the same time, it is not a minor fact that the aforementioned conditions continue also to affect negatively – although in a perhaps less brutal way – the inhabitants of the north, at the centre of hegemonic power. Deforestation and dependence on oil for agricultural progress increase greenhouse gas emissions.

Regarding production conditions in the Global South, Beros states:

> These crops, under prevailing economic rationality conditions, are carried out on the basis of "technological packages" that include, among other factors, the use of genetically modified seeds and the intensive application of agrochemicals.[6]

In this regard, we must remember that the region has historically been an exporter of the classic commodities demanded by the world food market: meat, wheat, corn and tobacco. Most of the young men and women of the IERP are linked to these types of products. This production model requires high doses of polluting chemicals that are harmful to the environment and human health. The consequences of their manipulation are public knowledge, generating debates and intergenerational conflicts in their own homes. This instils in the new generations a constant concern for the health and future of their families.

A general assessment of the significance of the situation described for the life of our peoples and societies should certainly not ignore the fact that, in most cases, monocultures represent the main or one of the main sources of income for state coffers (along with other intensive extractivist practices, such as "open pit" mining). The financing of certain policies that (despite contradictions and strong limitations) have sought to reverse some of the most drastic effects of the neoliberal policies applied in the region in recent decades

[5] Marcelo Sili, "La migración de la ciudad a las zonas rurales en Argentina. Una caracterización basada en estudios de caso", *Población y Sociedad* 26(1) (2019): 90-119, [Available at: https://cerac.unlpam.edu.ar/index.php/pys/article/view/3352/3867], [Last accessed: 8th April 2022].
[6] Beros, "Pastoral", 118.

depend to a great extent on this income. For through it, the relations of economic, political, scientific-technical and cultural domination that are imposed on our societies within the framework of the current capitalist global hegemony are decisively carried out.

Considering that the accumulation of capital is obtained to the detriment of ecosystems and the future of young people, for whom public policies for the benefit of their integral development are not created or implemented, the impact of this productive model has an enormous social cost for the continuity of the population in the region, since it forces not only migration from the countryside to the city, but also from the peripheral countries of the south to the central countries of the north. An aspect that is not minor is the existential anguish and the lack of perspective that torments young people, making it difficult for them to enter the labour market, as well as the definition of their vocation and cultural identification with their country of origin.

Responsibility and Advocacy of the Church in the Care of Creation

The 2017 Lutheran World Federation (LWF) assembly, emphatically highlighting that "salvation, human rights and creation are not for sale," marked a milestone in the region in terms of the position of the churches in the face of the extractivist model that compromises these three aspects of Christian witness.[7]

In the current situation, both in the field of theology and in the pastoral praxis of the churches, a critical assessment has not yet taken place, which is sufficiently acute, sustained and consistent, of the problem of monocultures in the light of the Word of God. If one considers the fact that a significant portion of the membership of several of the churches of the ecumenical community in the region is directly involved with monocultural production in their capacity as small and medium-sized rural producers – who in their situation and their dilemmas often debate within and among themselves "between fascination, guilt, fears, contained rage and resignation"[8] – the deficit might seem surprising. If one takes into account, however, "the very interweaving of ecclesial institutions and their ministers in relationships of economic and labour dependency,"[9] which ultimately refer to monoculture as a base of support, one becomes aware of the complexity within which the question arises.

The reflection of the young people leads them to recognise that the model is overwhelming and that it is extremely difficult to get out of the scheme that sustains "agribusiness" in which families live indebted to the seed companies, to the banks, to the concessionaire and to the very businesses that deliver merchandise to them on credit until they can gain from their crops. This model demands so much from the family that girls and boys are forced to work from childhood, depriving them of the possibility of recreation, their proper socialisation, with all the limitations that this implies in their social integration. In many cases, youth camps or gatherings in the church are the only spaces in which young people can meet, fraternise and even form couples among young people belonging to the same cultural context. In some cases, they are also unable to participate in summer camps because they are working in the fields with their parents.

The PPCC tries to respond from an ecumenical pastoral to a problem that affects many of the members of the churches that are conflicted by the effects of monocultures, especially derived from the intensive use of agrochemicals; and/or are captives of the imposed model; and/or have benefited from the high prices that – beyond certain variations – products such as soybeans have been having in the international market in recent years.

---

[7] See Urbina, Zoraya, "¡La Salvación, los derechos humanos y la creación no están en venta! Testimonio del Pastor José Pilar Álvarez, de Guatemala, en voz de Geraldina Álvarez Rocha", Twelfth Assembly-Lutheran World Federation, 14th May 2017, [Available at: https://2017.lwfassembly.org/es/news/regional-stories/la-salvacion-los-derechos-humanos-y-la-creacion-no-estan-en-venta], [Last accessed: 8th April 2022].

[8] Beros, "Pastoral", 121.

[9] Beros, "Pastoral", 121.

Working with young people in meetings and camps allows for a personalised and group approach, in which young people from different contexts share their visions, expressing their ideas and thoughts in their own words, learning that reality is not singular, but it is lived in many ways by everyone. The possibility of being able to see how the prevailing model affects their health, their personal development, their eating habits, their educational opportunities and their living conditions, allows them to return to the countryside – or even to the city – seeking to articulate a more critical environmental co-existence. Such a co-existence will be guided by the Gospel and the testimonies shared in the talks, the songs, the prayer and the communion in the games, the diaconic actions and the celebrations.

When dealing with an extremely complex issue, one cannot start from a place of guilt or from the assumption of abstract absolute positions. Rather, it is about beginning to offer spaces for dialogue, with a place for listening, critical analysis of the situation, biblical-theological and ethical reflection, and serious research in a search for viable alternatives.[10]

In this sense, the PPCC has proposed to address the problem from a broad ecumenism, which not only takes into account the ecclesial sphere but also attends, invites and involves (and gets involved) with popular organisations, with academia, political forces, et cetera. The opening of spaces for dialogue and community reflection on socio-economic, health and ecological issues derived from modes of production based on monocultures and the intensive use of agrochemicals in our region has taken place arising from the various catechetical and celebratory spaces, workshops and consultations that the pastoral program has accompanied and organised.[11]

The LWF has summoned young people from the IERP to the spaces of global representation in which environmental problems are discussed. In this way, the climate agenda is incorporated into the youth work of the church, allowing for the discussion of the global reality at the local level based on first-hand knowledge of the ongoing discussions (COP 24, COP 25, COP 26, in addition to other regional meetings and global online activities).

Young people share the same ideas dominant among adults regarding agro-ecology: that this type of agricultural production would not be profitable or marketable because it would not have a large-scale market, it would not be possible to implement price differentiation, while it considers assuming greater risks of losses without the support of the state. The young people propose to demystify this type of vision through visits and direct knowledge, in the field, of experiences of agro-ecological production in operation, in which a group effort of analysis takes place that proposes to contemplate in an integral way the social, the environmental and the economic dimensions, without prioritising one aspect over the other.

From the beginning, the PPCC recognised the need to promote a process of critical reflection on the issue of "care of creation" in the specific horizon in which the issue arises in our region, including those responsible for the catechetical task in the church. In relation to this, PPCC set ourselves an objective to elaborate teaching materials that make it possible to include creation care in the catechetical curriculum of our communities, both children's education and that of young people and adults, with particular emphasis on women's groups. As a result of the initiatives developed in this sense, we have advanced in the elaboration of a pedagogical and didactic proposal that will be made available to the entire church, particularly catechists and group leaders, in order to deepen the bonding process between evangelical spirituality and socio-environmental responsibility.[12]

Many of the catechists in the communities are active participants in youth groups. These reflections allow them to update and put into practice the catechetical material in their pedagogical work. This also allows them information which equips them to debate and challenge prejudices and myths in their

[10] Beros, "Pastoral", 112; 114.

[11] Beros, "Pastoral", 114-116.

[12] See Déborah Cirigliano Heffel, "¿Qué implica una pastoral de promoción? Educar para el cuidado promoviendo la reflexión."

communities, and propose a more informed way of thinking, based on developing experiences and scientific work. The catechetical task is highly valued in the communities of the church and this work proposal allows this kind of debate to take shape in different types of community activities.

In turn, the various initiatives proposed by the programme highlighted the need to offer systematic instances of theoretical-practical reflection, capable of addressing the field of intersection between productive, commercialisation and consumption practices together with their social, health and ecological impact. The objective is to contribute to the formation of an ecological consciousness in professionals and technicians, as well as of an interested public in general.[13]

These kinds of broad, scientific and pastoral perspectives allow families to be reached in rural and urban areas. In the case of cities, young people have felt particularly challenged by the problem of consumption and its effects on the environment. This has led various groups of young people to articulate with municipalities and environmental organisations their needs for training in recycling, reforestation, composting and healthy eating, in addition to cleaning rivers, streams, streets and routes for the separation of waste and the demand the municipalities act for its due treatment.

Crece Selva Misionera (Grow the Misiones Jungle)

The same extractivist model mentioned above affects one of the last jungle reserves in the region, the Misiones jungle. Deforestation and major droughts, consequences of the advance of the agricultural frontier and climate change, have generated serious health and environmental problems. In this sense, reforestation, whose laudable objective is to ensure that there is sufficient oxygen on the planet for the survival of life, constitutes an essential operation for the survival of living beings. The decrease in the green mass of our planet has the consequence that the carbon dioxide that we expel when we breathe increasingly loses the opportunity to be transformed into oxygen; since without trees or plants, photosynthesis is completely impossible.

Without reforestation, the well-known greenhouse effect will increase even more, since the heat of the earth is retained in the atmosphere because the levels of CO_2 and other gases do not allow that heat to be released. Thus, the trees are responsible for drawing down and filtering this CO_2, not only removing it from the earth, but also converting it into oxygen. Trees are also essential agents for conserving water and reducing soil erosion and river sedimentation. Large reforestations can even modify the local climate by lowering the high temperatures a little, created by the storage of thermal energy in a specific point and intensified by the steel and asphalt of the big cities.

It is precisely in this context that the "*Crece Selva Misionera*" (CSM) programme originates, within the Pastoral for the Promotion of Creation Care, with the aim of promoting reforestation based on the planting of native species on the banks of watercourses and fields. This programme makes it possible to relink generations and reflect from practice, both in rural and urban family spheres, about the environmental impact of the mode of production in which families are trapped. In this way, for these families, it is possible to imagine new production scenarios and reverse the effects on the soil, watercourses and, ultimately, progressively on the entire ecosystem, generating new conditions and possibilities for life in the countryside. It is noteworthy that in this programme the active participation in the planting and dissemination of activities is represented by 80% of young people, both from the church and from civil society in general.

In the current complex context, projects such as the Pastoral for the Promotion of Creation Care and *Crece Selva Misionera* become a seed of hope and a clear sign that, with planning, co-operation and joint work, it is possible to contribute to the reversal of the situation, in the search for a healthy and sustainable world, recognised and respected as God's good creation.

[13] Beros, "Pastoral", 126-129; 136.

Suggestions for Further Reading

Beros, Daniel. "Pastoral de Promoción del Cuidado de la Creación de la Iglesia Evangélica del Río de la Plata. Orígenes, concepto, desarrollo, proyección." *Vida y Pensamiento* 39(1) (January-June 2019): 107-134.

Fundación Protestante de Diaconía Hora de Obrar. *Fundación Hora de Obrar*. YouTube Channel. [Available at: https://www.youtube.com/channel/UC94XUq8rdabTuyyCYUE1GwQ], [Last accessed: 23rd April 2022].

PNUD. "Informe sobre Desarrollo Humano 2020. La próxima frontera. El desarrollo humano y el Antropoceno." [Human Development Report 2020 The Next Frontier: Human Development and the Anthropocene] United Nations 2020. [Available at: https://report.hdr.undp.org/es/index.html], [Last accessed: 23rd April 2022].

Sili, Marcelo. "La migración de la ciudad a las zonas rurales en Argentina. Una caracterización basada en estudios de caso." *Población y Sociedad* 26(1) (2019): 90-119. [Available at: https://cerac.unlpam.edu.ar/index.php/pys/article/view/3352/3867], [Last accessed: 23rd April 2022].

Urbina, Zoraya. "¡La Salvación, los derechos humanos y la creación no están en venta! Testimonio del Pastor José Pilar Álvarez, de Guatemala, en voz de Geraldina Álvarez Rocha." Twelfth Assembly, Lutheran World Federation. 14th May 2017. [Available at: https://2017.lwfassembly.org/es/news/regional-stories/la-salvacion-los-derechos-humanos-y-la-creacion-no-estan-en-venta], [Last accessed: 23rd April 2022].

94. ECUMENICAL AND PROPHETIC ADVOCACY IN ENVIRONMENTAL DEFENCE

Rolando Pérez-Vela[1]

Introduction

This paper seeks to highlight the role of faith agents in the processes of mobilisation and social protest in favour of climate justice. The approaches that we will share gather the results of a study on the participation of religious agents, linked to Catholicism and evangelical Protestantism, around two citizen initiatives of public advocacy in the context of socio-environmental conflicts in Peru. The first initiative is related to the conflict generated around a mining exploitation project located in the Cajamarca region, in the north of Peru. The second is related to the conflict that occurred in La Oroya, a city located in the central mountain range of Peru, in the department of Junín.[2]

Together with the study of these two cases, we add an analysis of Catholic and Evangelical activists' participation in other spaces and networks of political advocacy for the communities that suffer the violation of their environmental rights, as is the case of the Network Churches and Mining, the National Platform of People Affected by Toxic Metals and the Network Joining Hands against Poverty.

Religious Activism in the Mobilisation for Environmental Rights

A first reading in relation to the importance of religious capital in these cases of mobilisation and protest in favour of environmental rights is associated with the ways in which agents of faith can become not only mobilisers of the fight in favour of the rights of the affected population, but also a key support for the sustainability of protest strategies.

In the cases analysed, we observed an active participation of leaders and members of Catholic and Evangelical communities in the advocacy actions organised by civil society groups in each area. For example, in Cajamarca, the parishes of the rural towns of Celendín and Bambamarca housed the demonstrators who came from different rural towns to participate in the protest actions. Likewise, some of the parish priests and Catholic nuns accompanied the leadership of the local civic committee and the peasant patrols[3] in the organisation of advocacy actions. In the case of the community of La Oroya, the local parish became the most important reference of the organisations who demanded that the government adopt urgent measures to stop the environmental contamination generated by the mining company that operated in this settlement.

Activists linked to Christian communities have influenced social mobilisation in various ways. We mention six below:

---

[1] Rolando Pérez-Vela is a sociologist and social communicator, researcher in the field of media and religion, associate professor at the Pontifical Catholic University of Peru (PUCP) and director of the Peace and Hope Institute. rperez@pucp.edu.pe

[2] The city was built and grew around a metallurgical complex established in 1922. The Doe Run Company, a subsidiary of the United States of American Renco Group, is the company that operated there for more than 10 years. At the time of intense protests by civil society organisations, several studies revealed that in this city, 97% of children between 6 months and 6 years old had elevated levels of lead in their blood, as did the 98% of infants between 7 and 12 years of age. The percentage reached 100% of infants in La Oroya Antigua, the area of the city closest to the metallurgical complex.

[3] Ronda campesina [peasant patrol] was the name given to a type of communal defence organisation that emerged in rural areas of Peru in the mid-1970s.

In the first place, the agents of the faith communities who became inserted in the mobilisation initiatives in the field of climate justice have been key to sustaining the anti-establishment protest and the prophetic resistance. The groups we investigated provided "micro" resources, which were key to mobilisation.[4] This has been a task that local churches have developed at different times to care for people in need but, in the context described, it takes on significant political value, given its repercussions in the fight for community health and the construction of an alternative development model, which is based, among other things, on the affirmation of the common good and the protection of rights. But also due to the fact that it constitutes an act of visibility of the persons and communities affected, and of protest against the actions of those who caused the outrage and violation of human rights.

Secondly, another contribution has to do with the implementation of a creative communication strategy through the recreation and re-signification of traditional religious rituals. This takes place through their use as spaces for communicational mediation, developed in order to raise awareness and to make visible the problem of the violation of environmental rights in those communities affected by the operation of extractive industries. Our study shows the pedagogical value that religious rituals have, both for those affected and for the activists who work in defence of environmental rights. In many environmental advocacy campaigns, liturgical acts and "public prayer days" in favour of communities were fundamental, not only to highlight the collective invocation of divinity in the face of a situation of injustice, but also to generate awareness, both at the level of the non-religious community and of judicial and political operators. Such civic liturgies or religious rituals, from the perspective of rights, have a crucial value at a time when other rituals are constructed from the official bodies of the churches, supported by fundamentalist discourses that try to stop the processes in favour of a society based on equal rights and on the vindication of excluded minorities. The religious rite built within the framework of social conflict, in which the "common home" is run over, recreates and re-signifies social protest in such a way that it ends up becoming an act of "citizen spirituality." In the cases studied, it is interesting to observe that not only religious actors participate in these rituals, but also those who, in other circumstances, conceive religious or ecclesiastical acts as foreign to political and social contingencies. These types of practices, which take place in the public space around the protest, generate a re-enchantment in the lives of those faithful who distanced themselves from the institutional church because they perceive it as distanced from daily life and oblivious to social problems. It is here where the religious groups and leaders involved in social activism acquire new public legitimacy and build new bridges of trust with the people. In this way, they contribute to affirming the image of a church less engrossed in its internal world and open to society; that is, a more humane and compassionate church, close to those people and communities that are on the margins of life.

Thirdly, the action of religious groups in the context of protest against environmental injustices becomes a communicational mediation factor. This makes possible, on the one hand, the public representation of a particular rebellious and prophetic pastoral expression from which these religious sectors impregnate their theological-political stamp when entering the public arena. On the other hand, the religious rite and the participation of agents of faith in these public spaces update a certain collective memory. This shows a trajectory that is connected with speeches, actors and movements that, in previous times, inspired or encouraged a logic of pastoral action and a public profile of the churches, consistent with what is being built today. It is interesting, for example, to listen to the stories of the Catholic priests and lay people interviewed, remembering that their struggles are linked to the legacy of Christians who in the past committed themselves from their faith to the struggles against the injustices and abuses of their time. This perspective can be seen in the speech of the main Catholic leader of the campaign for the community of La Oroya, the Archbishop of the region, Monsignor Pedro Barreto. It can be appreciated in this journalistic note: "nobody will silence the voice of the Church in defence of the interests of the people, even though

[4] This happened, for example, by raising awareness, creating bridges of solidarity, activating support networks and taking in those affected.

there are some sectors interested in doing so." Barreto recalls that the Church, during the Second Vatican Council, expressed that it is the servant of the world and concludes:

> There are interest groups that want to silence the voice of the Church in defence of life, the dignity of the person and the environment. But never, nothing, and no one, is going to silence in us that prophetic voice that Jesus wants us to make today, because it is without a doubt the best way to seek the happiness of all, especially those who accuse us, as a Church, of getting into a matter that does not correspond to us [...] Therefore, we will continue fighting, but always with our heads held high because we know that we are defending life and that is the orientation that the Church wants us to carry out.[5]

The activation of this religious and political memory, for the Catholic case, updates the founding theological sources of the struggle of pastoral agents who decided to make a preferential option for the poor. The religious rite built from the ethical and prophetic resistance, as Renée de la Torre points out, accounts for the way in which, in the midst of the memories of colonisation, the memories of cultural resistance of the peoples are also reactivated.[6]

Fourthly, the action of religious groups are making an enormous contribution through pastoral accompaniment to environmental protest activists, reviving them and legitimising their cause. Its importance is enhanced if one takes into account that this type of struggle develops over the long term and confronts other actors and strategies that seek to weaken and counteract the protest initiative. Scholars maintain that in this context religious groups constitute a kind of community of challengers.[7] This lies in the fact that they can play the role of those who have the capacity and the spirit to challenge, encourage or (re)encourage the promoters of social mobilisations and citizen activists, in order to achieve those social changes that are not necessarily achieved in short-term perspectives.

Fifthly, religious groups and institutions provide a series of "mobilisation repertoires," which correspond to "macro" resources.[8] In the case of La Oroya, the Presbyterian and Jesuit groups mobilised religious actors towards the North American headquarters of the company that managed the metallurgical complex in that locality. As in other cases, such mobilisation contributed to diversifying the "mobilisation and advocacy repertoires."[9] The connection with networks of ecclesial actors strengthened the coalition of environmental organisations that led the advocacy campaign in favour of La Oroya.

Sixthly, the agents of the faith communities provide an ethical perspective of political action that comes from the prophetic religious worldview, making political protest humanised. What is observed is that religious groups participated in the initiative of civil society based on the assumption and understanding of a type of spirituality that is connected – as Boaventura de Sousa Santos maintains – with the defence of rights. And it assumes that the God who sustains said spirituality is indignant at the oppressions that prevent citizens from becoming subjects and experiencing the world as their own.[10] Fortunato Mallimaci qualifies this type of religious action as "militant sacrifice for the common good," since it generates the representation

---

[5] *Revista IDEELE*, 19th July 2010.

[6] See Renée de la Torre, "Una agenda epistemológica para replantear las maneras de entender la secularización en América Latina", in Verónica Giménez Béliveau and Emerson Giumbelli (eds), *Religión, cultura y política en las sociedades del siglo XXI* (Buenos Aires: Biblos, 2013).

[7] See Michael Young, "Confessional Protest: The Religious Birth of U.S. National Social Movements", *American Sociological Review* 67(5) (2002): 660-668.

[8] Among which are, for example, the provision of premises for meetings of activists, political lobbies for advocacy, the creation of bridges with influential actors (decision makers) and international activists, as well as the activation of transnational communication networks. See Daniel Levine, "Pluralidad, pluralismo y la creación de un vocabulario de derechos", *América Latina Hoy* 41 (2005): 17-34.

[9] See Maritza Paredes, "La glocalización de las protestas mineras y las elecciones de Tambogrande", in Narda Enríquez (ed), *Conflicto social en los Andes. Protestas en el Perú y Bolivia* (Lima: Fondo Editorial, 2014).

[10] See Boaventura de Sousa Santos, *Si Dios fuese un activista de los derechos humanos* (Madrid: Trotta, 2014).

of a type of laicity in the midst of the multiple laicities staged by public religion. This laicity contrasts with the separatist, authoritarian and anticlerical ones and manifests itself from civic faith, recognition and collaboration.[11]

These groups, inspired by Catholic liberation theologies or holistic evangelical theologies, fall under what Boaventura de Souza calls "pluralistic theologies."[12] Such theological options enable the experience of indignation to break with those instrumentalist conceptions and practices of ethics. They promote what Juan José Tamayo calls an "ethics of otherness," which fundamentally aims at creating conditions by which the Other is incorporated into the community, recovers their place in political life and actively participates in public life.[13]

Precisely, the appropriation of this theological logic allows not only the generation of advocacy initiatives aimed at changing a situation of injustice, but also the creation of new strategies of solidarity from the population and from other sectors, beyond the local sphere, generating new networks of articulation and the visibility of new faces in the public sphere.

Towards a Prophetic Public Pastoral as the Key of Ecological Diakonia

The case of Catholic and Evangelical activists involved in citizen initiatives in the context of extractivism in Peru presents us with a model that allows us to rethink a public pastoral proposal. In relation to their diaconal action, it is possible to identify at least three factors that are characteristic of them.

The first lies in the rereading and resignification of the sacred text, which is an important source of faith and spirituality, both for Catholics and Evangelicals. It is interesting to observe that the rereadings of the sacred text took place in the context of interaction with others, not only among the devout themselves, and through approaching the reality of the affected people.

Secondly, it is worth underlining the connection of their protest experience with that of those emblematic Catholic or Evangelical agents, who in the past were involved in citizen, anti-establishment or protest initiatives. This connection feeds the awareness of being part of a type of religious lineage that allows them, in this context, to feel capable and authoritative to enter the political contest in this area.[14] Additionally, it contributes to the updating of the theological foundational sources of a diaconal action in the holistic and liberationist perspective.

The third factor has to do with the role of the religious community to which they are attached, which gives them the support for getting involved, as religious agents, in social activism and political struggle. These referents or religious frameworks of reference constitute key sources that support the social and political activism of these believers, because they allow them to find dialogue regarding the new articulations between their faith and political action.

Another important aspect of this process of redefining the discourse and practice of these religious actors is related to what is known in progressive ecclesiastical circles as "the prophetic action of the church." This allusion to the prophetic perspective of religious activism has a particular relevance in this case because, for several of the investigated actors, the public space in which the mobilisation and protest takes place became the place of learning and appropriation of those forms and practices that correspond to a modality of political theology.

---

[11] Fortunato Mallimaci, "Hermenéutica y ciencias sociales: religión y secularización en debate", presented at the I Jornadas Internacionales de Hermenéutica, UBA/CONICET, Buenos Aires, May 2009.

[12] See Santos, *Si Dios fuese.*

[13] See Juan José Tamayo, *Otra teología es posible: Pluralismo religioso, interculturalidad y feminismo* (Barcelona: Herder, 2011).

[14] See Danielle Hervieu-Leger, *Religión, hilo de memoria* (Barcelona: Herder, 2005).

Alberto Melucci coined the category of "prophetic function," precisely to describe the rebellious role of certain sectors that participate in collective political action.[15] By taking his approach, we can corroborate that, indeed, the religious actors studied fulfil the function of revealing the problems and announcing to society the existence of situations of injustice. In addition, as the author himself maintains, these actors counteract the dominant cultural codes, and reveal that the rationality of the power apparatus is not the only possible one.

In this sense, an important component that accompanies the activists linked to these social collectivities, in our opinion, has to do with what Melucci calls a *moral utopianism*.[16] This is precisely one of the aspects through which religious actors make an important contribution to the social movement. The cases addressed in this writing reflect what Gonzalo Gamio suggests when he points out:

> the concern for the practice of justice and compassion acquires a basically ethical resonance in a surrounding world that is not confessional. The commitment to remembrance is an expression of this concern, and prophetic language takes on a new ethical-spiritual form in the context of modern culture.[17]

Final Reflections

The experience of these agents of faith places us in front of the configuration of a type of religious actors who constitute themselves as prophetic guardians of the "common home." For they enter the public sphere from the logic of solidarity with those affected by the violation of ecological rights and from citizen responsibility that moves them to raise their voices in the face of environmental injustices. Their case challenges us to think that it is not possible to build diaconal initiatives from ecotheology if it is managed from platforms and networks distant from the world and from the daily reality of the people and communities affected.

In this sense, the initiatives analysed present us with the challenge of developing strategies not only for making visible, but also for legitimising the narratives and proposals of the communities affected by ecological abuses. Along these lines, together with inter-institutional efforts, we need to rethink strategies for generating currents of opinion and public advocacy from the insertion in networks and movements of civil society, in order to generate significant and transcendent impacts among political decision makers.

In this way, the visibility of the faces of the faith communities from a citizen logic can have a pedagogical impact, not only at the level of the broader political community, but also within the ecclesial societies themselves, where we still find certain resistance to building a church sensitive to the clamour of the earth and the cry of the poor.

Suggestions for Further Reading

Fraser, Nancy. "Rethinking the Public Sphere: A Contribution to the Critique of Actually Existing Democracy." *Social Text* 25/26 (1990): 56-80.

Gutiérrez, Gustavo. "¿Dónde dormirán los pobres?", in Gustavo Gutiérrez, Javier lguiñiz, Felipe Zegarra, Manuel Díaz Mateos, Jorge Alvarez Calderón, Francisco Chamberlain, Yolanda Díaz, Amparo Huamán, Rolando Ames and Luis Fernando Crespo. *El Rostro de Dios en la Historia*. Lima: Instituto Bartolomé de Las Casas, 1996: 9-69.

Nugent, Guillermo. *El Orden Tutelar*. Lima: FLACSO-DESCO, 2010.

---

[15] Alberto Melucci, *Acción colectiva, vida cotidiana y democracia* (México: Colegio de México, 1999).

[16] "... the great collective processes offer a channel to express this moral utopianism, which would otherwise survive in marginal enclaves," Melucci, *Acción colectiva*, 96.

[17] Gonzalo Gamio, "Sentido profético y memoria. Elementos para pensar la injusticia," in *La verdad nos hace libres*, ed. Miguel Giusti, Gustavo Gutiérrez and Elizabeth Salmón (Lima: PUCP, 2015), 9.

Perez-Vela, Rolando. "Evangelical Representations in the Public Sphere: The Peruvian Case", in Jonathan D. James, Ed. *A Moving Faith: Mega Churches Go South*. New Delhi: SAGE, 2015.

Perez-Vela, Rolando. "La protesta religiosa contestataria. Apropiaciones de lo público desde el (neo) progresismo religioso", in Pablo Seman and Renée de La Torre, Eds. *Religiones y espacios públicos en América Latina*. Buenos Aires: CALAS- CLACSO, 2021.

Romero, Catalina. "Religión y espacio público: Catolicismo y sociedad civil en el Perú", in Catalina Romero, Ed. *Religión y espacio público*. Lima: CISEPA-PUCP, 2008.

Section IV

Models and Methods for Training and Competency Building in Creation Care and Eco-Diakonia

Part I: Africa and the Middle-East

96. Christian Formation for Climate Change Resilience in the Nigerian Context

Helen Ishola-Esan[1]

Introduction

The Bible depicts a close relation between God, mankind and the rest of creation, thus when men sin it affects not only our relationship with God, but also our relationship with other creatures, with the earth and its systems, including the climate system. In Genesis 3:17-19, when Adam and Eve sinned, it resulted not only in their separation from God but the field started producing thorns and thistles and farming became difficult for them. Similarly, Hosea 4: 1-3, Jeremiah 12:14 and Leviticus 18: 25-28 all depict that the lands suffer, weep and are defiled because of the sins of Israelites. Biblically speaking, anthropogenic activities affect the entire earth, which has always included the climate. These activities result in climate change which has been widely considered as "the most complex and serious environmental issue that human societies have ever faced."[2]

The industrialised and wealthy countries unwittingly contributed to the disruption of the atmosphere due to their activities causing man-made climate change. In the past decades, many researchers have reported about the alarming degree of soil deterioration due to erosion, urbanisation, industrialisation, climate abnormalities, poor soil fertility management practices, pollutants, excessive flooding, Al toxicity, nutrient depletion, salinisation and loss of soil carbon.[3] Thus, humans have woefully failed in their responsibility to care for the environment (Gen. 2:15).

The failure of human beings in their responsibility as care takers or stewards of the environment has led to the current climate change and ecological crisis and all the resulting challenges. Therefore, it behoves on the church, as the centre for the care of creation and environment,[4] to embark on Christian formation as a model and method of training others towards an eco-diaconal transformation of their environment. Eco-

---

[1] Helen Ishola-Esan, PhD is an Associate Professor in the Department of Christian Education and had served as the Head of Department as well as the Dean of the Faculty of Education in the Nigerian Baptist Theological Seminary, Ogbomoso, Nigeria. She is currently the President of Baptist Theological Seminary, Eku, Nigeria. She is a member of Council for Association of Christian Theological Education in Africa (ACTEA). She is also a member of some professional bodies such as African Association for the Study of Religions (AASR); Society Professors in Christian Education (SPCE); International Professional Managers Association (IPMA) and a Certified International Professional Manager (CIPM). She has published widely in the areas of Christian Education, Disability and Leadership/Administration. helenisholaesan@gmail.com.

[2] K.L. O' Brien, A.L. St. Clair and B. Kristoffersen, "The Framing of Climate Change: Why it Matters", in K.L. O'Brien, A.L. St. Clair and B. Kristoffersen (eds.), *Climate Change, Ethics and Human Security* (New York: Cambridge University Press, 2010), 3-22: 3.

[3] A.D. Mcbratney, J. Field and A. Koch, "The Dimensions of Soil Security". *Geoderma* (2014), 203-213: 213; Z.P. Stewart, G.M. Pierzynski, B.J. Middendorf and P.V.V. Prasad, "Approaches to Improve Soil Fertility in Sub-Saharan Africa", *Journal of Experimental Botany*, 71(2) (2020): 632-641.

[4] Helen O. Ishola-Esan, "The Role of The Church in Enhancing Environmental Stewardship", *Journal of Creation and Science (JCEC)* 1 (2014): 137-146.

diakonia transformation is part of the Christian ministry and calling. This corroborates the assertion that "to be like Christ, is to know the word of God, and to do the work of ministry."[5]

This paper intends to achieve four objectives. These are to:

1. elucidate the concept of Christian formation and its methods for climate change resilience;
2. discuss the current challenges of climate change;
3. document via empirical survey reports on the perceptions of the Church in Nigeria on the effects of climate change;
4. and itemise some Christian formation strategies and interventions.

The strategic measures and Christian formation interventions are core models for eco-diakonia transformation.

The Concept and Methods of Christian Formation

Christian formation and spiritual formation are used interchangeably in literature to describe the process of becoming Christ-like. The concept of Christian formation connotes the idea of conforming to the image of Christ (Rom. 8:29). James C. Wilhoit refers to the process of Christian formation as an intentional community involvement process of developing our intimacy with Almighty God and beginning to be like Jesus via the presence of the Holy Spirit power.[6] The process of formation being intentional implies that it is deliberate. This includes what is taught and sought. The content of such teachings shape people's spiritual lives. The experiences of their spiritual formation materialises outwardly through their activities. When Christians are taught intentionally about God's expectation for the physical environment and the role of Christians in being good stewards of creation, this sets the bar for climate change resilience.

Spiritual formation being communal in nature describes the fact that the Christian life is best lived in the context of a community. Africans are known as communal people and easily make their contribution towards the common good. Proper education (in Christian/spiritual formation) helps in achieving sufficient participation that the common good prevails. This substantiates the assertion that "religious beliefs significantly influence a community's understanding and experience of climate change adaptation indicating the need for an inclusion of such information in climate change adaptation education."[7] Adaptation and mitigation are crucial to manage the impacts of climate change. However, with regard to climate change adaptation, a greater focus on the human dimension of climate change than on mitigation strategies is required. This human dimension could be achieved more through a sound Christian formation experience and practice. Formation in Christ in us (Gal. 4:19), being transformed (Rom. 12:2) and being conformed to the image of Christ (Rom. 8:29) are core in the experiences and practice of Christian formation.

From my personal experience of teaching Christian spiritual formation as a theological educator for the past fifteen years, spiritual formation encompasses a wide range of experiences and characters such as change of mind and heart, nurturing integrative thinking, character formation and promoting a lifestyle of authentic discipleship and deep devotion/spirituality/piety. Being stewards of the environment is part of spirituality.

Christian formation processes, broadly speaking, refer to all efforts, resources, methods, tutoring, and disciplines intended to develop faith and spirituality.

---

[5] W.W. Chow, "An Integrated Approach to Theological Education", *Theological Education Today* 1(3) (September 1981): 1-7.

[6] J.C. Wilhoit, *Spiritual Formation as if the Church Mattered* (Grand Rapids, MI: Baker Academic, 2008).

[7] Simone Schuman, Jon-Vegard Dokken, Dewald van Niekerk and Ruth A Loubser, "Religious Beliefs and Climate Change Adaptation: A study of three rural South African communities", *Jamba* 10(1) (2018): 509.

The process of Christian formation is holistic in nature. It cuts across the three domains of learning. It involves cognitive dimensions through the acquisition of biblical/spiritual/moral knowledge. It includes display of psychomotoric/behavioural skills; this is seen in the practice of Christianity or simply practical obedience in living out the Christ-like life. And it comprises of affective intentions out of the experience of divine encounter with Jesus Christ through the power of the Holy Spirit that brings about a change in heart and character.

Climate Change in Context: Definition, Causes and Effects

Climate change is a long-term modification of weather conditions. Various indicators bear witness to this, "especially in the form of changes in temperature and rainfall."[8] Climate change can include both an alteration in average weather conditions and a change in variability, such as extreme events.

The causes of causes of climate change include the following:

- The combustion of coal, oil and gas releasing carbon dioxide and nitrous oxide in the atmosphere;
- Deforestation as trees help to regulate the climate by up-taking carbon dioxide (CO^2) from the atmosphere. When they are felled, this positive effect is lost and the carbon stored in the trees is released into the atmosphere, worsening the greenhouse effect;
- The increase in animal husbandry, because cattle and sheep produce large amounts of methane when they digest their food;
- Application of fertilisers containing nitrogen which produce emissions of nitrous oxide. Moreover, clearing of bushes, bush fires, overexploitation of lands, overgrazing, deforestation, and the harmful effects of biological control are at the origin of the destruction of the forests causing the rise in atmospheric gases.

Climate change constitutes a significant menace to the socio-economic development of developing countries and risks compromising the chances of meeting the challenges of poverty reduction.[9] For instance, in Nigeria, the 2012 flooding affected 30 States out of the 36 States, and killed more than 360 people (over 363) and ousted millions of people (over 2.1 million) and was considered as the worst extreme event in 40 years.[10]

Deforestation is increasing; for example, according to the World Rainforest Movement report of 1999 about 70-80% of Nigeria's original forest have been destroyed and the available forest is about 20%.[11] It has been estimated that Nigeria has lost a further 14% of forest between 2002 and 2020,[12] but between 2000 to 2005, Nigeria lost 55.7% of the original forest,[13] which contributed to the increase in the atmospheric CO^2 due to the absence of trees to absorb greenhouse gases. Forests, globally, have been the framework of life and subsistence for more than one billion human beings, of which 350 million depend directly on the

---

[8] IPCC. *Climate Change 2007: Impacts, adaptation and vulnerability. Contribution of Working Group II to the Fourth Assessment Report of the Intergovernmental Panel on Climate Change.* (Cambridge, UK and New York, USA, Cambridge University Press, 2007).

[9] M. Parry, C. Rosenzweig and M. Livermore, "Climate Change, Global Food Supply and Risk of Hunger", *Phil. Trans. Roy. Soc. B*, 360 (2005): 2125-2138.

[10] National Emergency Management Agency, *Report on the 2012 floods* (Abuja: NEMA, 2013).

[11] Larry Lohmann, "What Kind of Future for the World Rainforest Movement? 20 Years after 'Addressing the Underlying Causes of Deforestation'", *World Rainforest Movement* (September 2020) [Available at: https://www.researchgate.net/publication/349380032_What_Kind_of_Future_for_the_World_Rainforest_Movement_20_Years_after_Addressing_the_Underlying_Causes_of_Deforestation], [Last accessed: 3rd March 2022].

[12] Global Forest Watch, "Nigeria Deforestation Rates & Statistics", *Global Forest Watch* [Available at: https://www.globalforestwatch.org/dashboards/country/NGA/],[Last accessed: 3rd March 2022].

[13] UNFAO, *Global Forest Resources Assessment 2005: Progress towards Sustainable Forest Management.* (New York: Food and Agriculture Organization of the United Nations, 2006).

use of forests for their income, among which are the poorest people.[14] But faced with desertification, which is a process of qualitative degradation of the ecological balance and quantitative deterioration of biological resources which support life, the survival of the poorest is in the process of being increasingly compromised.

In this regard, the potential impacts of climate change must be systematically taken into account in social and economic policies, Christian education, development projects and international aid efforts in order to establish resilient key developments However, for developing countries, integrating climate change into the development planning process is still a major challenge due to many factors.

The main driver of climate change is the greenhouse effect. Some gases such as CO^2, chlorofluorocarbons, methane and nitrous oxide in Earth's atmosphere allow solar energy to enter the atmosphere but prevent it from escaping, causing global warming. These greenhouse gases are ubiquitously present in the air, but human activity increases their concentrations. Toward the end of the 21st century, global warming is expected to be between 0.3 and 5ºC.[15] And if global temperatures were to augment by 2ºC, coastal flooding could affect an additional 10 million people each year. If the temperature rises by 4ºC, East Africa and the Middle East could see the reduction of their water resources by half.[16] For 1˚C increase in temperature, it is estimated that diarrhoea will rise by around 5%.[17] It has been recorded that a sum of $2.5 trillion has been lost from disasters caused by climate change, and 70% of that is related to floods and droughts since the turn of the century.[18]

Resilience to Climate Change

Resilience to climate change, vulnerability and adaptation have been intensively employed as responses to extreme weather events. The effects of climate change are unavoidable and it is imperative to set up strategies of adaptation and mitigation to cope with and avoid the worst.

Resilience refers to the ability to "come back" or "bounce back" after a shock (it could be floods, drought, heat and so on). It is determined by its own means to the extent that the community is able to organise itself during a period of need. It does not translate a final state but the restoration of essential structures and its basic functions must be carried out as quickly and efficiently as possible.[19] In other words, resilience connotes the capability of a community, an organisation, group or structure to adapt to a changing environment. A population is resilient if it knows and can find the necessary capacities for its adaptation in the course of extreme weather events.

Adaptation is simply managing the avoidable. Adaptation entails forecasting the negative impacts of change climate and limiting the destruction each might cause by taking adequate measures in advance.

---

[14] 'Forests for People, the Planet and Climate'. Feature Story March 19, 2020 of the World Bank at the occasion of the International Day of Forests, in: https://www.worldbank.org/en/news/feature/2020/03/19/forests-for-people-the-planet-and-climate.

[15] IPCC. *Summary For Policymakers In Climate Change 2014: Impacts, Adaptation, And Vulnerability. Part A: Global and Sectoral Aspects. Contribution of Working Group II to The Fifth Assessment Report of The Intergovernmental Panel on Climate Change*. (Bremen: IPCC WGII, 2014): 1-32.

[16] N. Stern, *The Economics of Climate Change: The Stern Review* (Cambridge and New York: Cambridge University Press, 2007).

[17] D. Campbell-Lendrum and R. Woodruff, "Climate Change: Quantifying the Health Impact at National and Local Levels", In A. Prüss-Üstun, and C. Corvalan (eds), *WHO Environmental Burden of Disease Series* No.14 (Geneva: WHO, 2007).

[18] UNISDR, *Impacts of Disasters Since The 1992 Rio De Janeiro Earth Summit*. Disponible À L'adresse Suivante, [Available at: http://www.Preventionweb.Net/Fles/27162_Infographic.Pdf], [Last accessed: 13th August 2021].

[19] UNISDR, *Terminology on disaster risk reduction*, 2009. [Available at: https://www.undrr.org/publication/2009-unisdr-terminology-disaster-risk-reduction], [Last accessed: 13th September 2021].

Empirical Findings on the Church's Perceptions of the Effects of Climate Change

Methodology

A descriptive research design was adopted for this study. This method helped to find out how church pastors and leaders viewed the effects of climate change and some strategic measures and Christian formation interventions. Primary data was collected through semi-structured questionnaires administered online. A three-point Likert scale (levels of agreement: agree, disagree and I don't know) was used for respondents to have options. The instrument was validated by giving it to experts to check the contents. The reliability was determined in a test-retest method. A reliability coefficient value of 0.87 was obtained. This confirms the internal consistency of the instrument to achieve the set objectives of the study.

Study Areas and Sampling Procedure

This study was conducted in seven states of the Federal Republic of Nigeria, namely Adamawa, Lagos, Delta, Edo, Ogun, Oyo and Rivers (Figure 1). The questionnaire was sent to many pastors across the 36 states in Nigeria, although only these seven states responded.

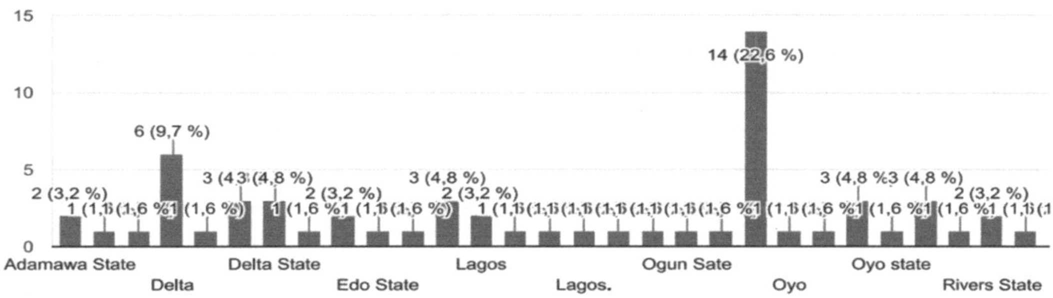

Figure 1: States of Residence of Respondents

Data Collection and Analysis

Data was collected from a total of 100 church pastors. Data collected included church's name, state of residence, Local Government Area, perceptions on climate change, strategic measures and Christian formation interventions. Both general perceptions on climate change as well as specific perceptions concerning their impact on different aspects of life was asked for as an option.

Different strategic measures were also proposed to collect opinions about each, such as reduced deforestation, increased afforestation (planting of trees), increased protected forest area during dry season, decreased forest fire or bush burning during dry season.

The data collected from questionnaires was coded, entered in spreadsheets, and analysed using descriptive statistics.

Findings and Discussions

Designations	Agreed	Disagreed	I didn't know
I am aware of climate change	99%	1%	0%
Climate change affects the quality of life of my members on food security	92%	6%	2%
Climate change affects the quality of life of my members with respect to quality of drinking water	76%	13%	11%

Climate change affects the quality of life of my members with respect to clean air	89%	4%	7%
Climate change affects the quality of life of my members with respect to life span	78%	6%	16%
Climate change causes an increase in annual rainfall (changing precipitation level)	57%	32%	11%
Climate change causes a decrease in annual rainfall (changing in rain pattern)	81	8%	11%
Climate change accounts for the beginning of rainfall earlier than before	56%	28%	16%
Climate change accounts for the raining season starting late	83%	9%	8%
Climate change accounts for the rainfall stopping earlier than before	83%	7%	10%
Climate change accounts for rainfall stopping after the normal period	79%	14%	7%
Climate change accounts for rainfall stopping in the course of rain season (drought)	83%	13%	4%
Climate change accounts for rainfall becoming unpredictable	98%	2%	0%
Climate change accounts for flooding (abundance of rains)	75%	12%	13%
Climate change accounts for decrease in flood frequency	40%	38%	22%
Climate change accounts for temperatures nowadays are getting hotter than those of the previous years	91%	3%	6%
Climate change accounts for long and sharp harmattan season	59%	28%	13%
Climate change accounts for short and less vigorous harmattan season	68%	14%	18%
Climate change accounts for more environmental pollution	79%	13%	8%
Climate change accounts for environmental degradation	87%	5%	8%

Table 1: Perceptions of respondents about climate change

Table 1 presents the perceptions of church leaders on climate change. The results indicate that perceptions were generally almost unanimous on the awareness of the climate change (99%), rainfall becoming unpredictable (98%), decease in the quality of life of church members on food security (92%), increase in temperatures nowadays (91%), decrease in the quality of life of church members with respect to clean air (89%), increase in environmental degradation (87%) and other parameters.[20] The 2017 hurricane

[20] O. Hoegh-Guldberg, D. Jacob, M. Taylor, M. Bindi, S. Brown, I. Camilloni, A. Diedhiou, R. Djalante, K.L. Ebi, F. Engelbrecht, J. Guiot, Y. Hijioka, S. Mehrotra, A. Payne, S.I. Seneviratne, A. Thomas, R. Warren, And G. Zhou, "Impacts of 1.5ºC Global Warming on Natural and Human Systems". In Global Warming of 1.5°C." 2018 An IPCC Special Report on The Impacts of Global Warming of 1.5°C Above Pre-Industrial Levels and Related Global Greenhouse Gas Emission Pathways. In Masson-Delmotte, V., P. Zhai, H.-O. Pörtner, D. Roberts, J. Skea, P.R. Shukla, A. Pirani, W. Moufouma-Okia, C. Péan, R. Pidcock, S. Connors, J.B.R. Matthews, Y. Chen, X. Zhou, M.I. Gomis, E. Lonnoy, T. Maycock, M. Tignor, and T. Waterfield (eds), *The Context of Strengthening the Global Response to The Threat of Climate Change, Sustainable Development, And Efforts to Eradicate Poverty*. In Press; M.A. Taylor, *Climate and Faith: Perspectives from The Margin*. (Baptist World Alliance Networking the Baptist Family to Impact the World for Christ. 22nd Baptist World Congress, 2021); O.D. Bello, A. Saïdou, E.L. Ahoton, A.V. Ezin, J.F.Y. Avaligbé, P.B.I. Akponikpè and N. Aho Assessment of organic carbon stock in cashew plantations (Anacardium occidentale L.) in Benin (West Africa). International Journal of Agriculture and Environmental Research, 3(4) (2017): 3601-3625.

was the worst ever recorded hurricane with its three Category 5 hurricanes across the Caribbean.[21] Many other extreme events such as rise in wildfires, superstorms, strong heat waves are among the manifestation of climate change across the globe. IPCC observed that the effects of climate change are unevenly distributed with developing countries being the most affected and suffering from the greatest impacts.[22] M.A. Taylor in his paper presentation during the 22nd Baptist World Congress highlighted that, on his small island in the Caribbean, a developing country, they are among the most vulnerable to the consequences and risks of climate change due to constant exposure to hurricanes, decline in quality of life, absence of rainfall causing failure of livelihoods, and vulnerability from extended hotter periods.[23]

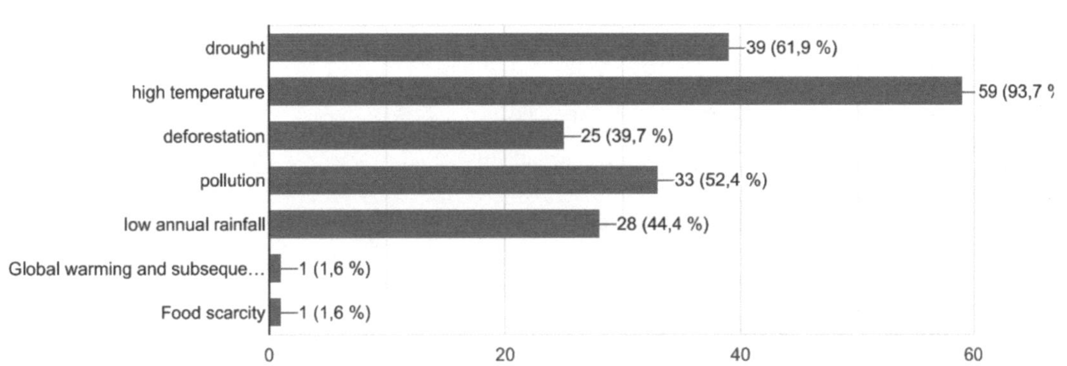

Figure 2: The most striking factors in climate change highlighted by respondents

Figure 2 above shows the most striking factors in climate change according to respondents. 94% of respondents considered high temperature to be the most striking factor of climate change, followed by drought according to 62% of respondents, then pollution (52% of respondents), then low annual rainfall (44%) and deforestation (39.7%). Food security and global warming and subsequent diseases are viewed by the respondents as the least striking factors of climate change in terms of risks associated with the change in climate. It has been indicated that Nigeria is already facing the effects of climate change including strong storms and flood especially in the South, inconsistent and erratic rainfall, rise in ambient heat, drought spells, and these risks lead to increases in pests and crop diseases, loss of biodiversity, high risks to health and the increase in infectious diseases.[24] As M.A. Taylor understated, it is unfortunate that the least contributing to climate change are the most negatively impacted as they are suffering from unaffordable health care, food insecurity, hotter weather, limited access to quality shelter and life.[25]

---

[21] Climate Studies Group Mona, "The State of the Caribbean Climate", Produced for the Caribbean Development Bank, 2020.

[22] IPCC. *Climate Change 2007: Impacts, adaptation and vulnerability. Contribution of Working Group II to the Fourth Assessment Report of the Intergovernmental Panel on Climate Change*. (Cambridge, UK and New York, USA, Cambridge University Press, 2007).

[23] Taylor, *Climate and Faith*.

[24] J.S. Babatolu and R.T. Akinnubi, "Smallholder Farmers' Perception of Climate Change and Variability Impact and Their Adaptation Strategies in the Upper and Lower Niger River Basin Development Authority Areas, Nigeria", *Journal of Petroleum & Environmental Biotechnology* 7(3) (2016): 1-7.

[25] Taylor, *Climate and Faith*.

Some Strategic Measures and Christian Formation Interventions

Designations	Agreed	Disagreed	I didn't know
Training of church members	97%	1%	2%
Christian discipleship for members	95%	3%	2%
Organise and observe Bible study to promote awareness on environmental care and climate change	92%	8%	0%
Develop theological education curriculum on eco-diakonia transformation for theologians	87%	5%	8%
Organise seminars to promote awareness on environmental care and climate change	100%	0%	0%
Observe periodic sensitisation on climate change challenges through workshops and other special events	98%	0%	2%
Preach structured sermons on environmental care and climate change from the pulpit	91%	9%	0%
Creation of environmental care and climate change communities in the church	99%	1%	0%
Organise conferences and workshops on eco-diaconal transformation	95%	3%	2%
Organise prayer opportunities to pray for divine intervention in climate change effects	89%		
Landscaping of church environment	87%	3%	10%
Reduce emission of poisonous gases from churches and theological institutions engines	95%	3%	2%
Sensitise Christian communities on climate change control strategies	97%	1%	2%

Table 2: Responses on Christian training interventions

The Christian training interventions are presented in Table 2. The results showed that 97% of respondents agreed on training of church members, 95% on Christian discipleship for members, 92% on organise and observe Bible study to promote awareness on environmental care and climate change, 87% on develop theological education curriculum on eco-diakonia transformation for theologians, 100% on organise seminars to promote awareness on environmental care and climate change, 98% on observe periodic sensitisation on climate change challenges through workshops and other special events, 91% on preaching structured sermons on environmental care and climate change from the pulpit, 99% on creation of environmental care and climate change communities in the church, 95% on organise conferences and workshops on eco-diakonia transformation, 89% on organise prayer opportunities to pray for divine intervention in climate change effects, 87% on landscaping of church environment, 95% on reduce emission of poisonous gases from churches and theological institutions engines, 97% on sensitise Christian communities on climate change control strategies.

There seems to be a general consensus that there should be a shift in paradigm as we cannot afford to do business as usual but need to see ourselves as stewards of God's creation. Therefore, churches must be at the forefront for the care of the creation and environment.[26]

Designations	Agreed	Disagreed	I didn't know
Reduce deforestation (felling of trees)	81%	11%	8%
Increase afforestation (planting of trees)	94%	2%	4%

[26] Helen Ishola-Esan and Oluwafemi Amoran, "The Role of Christian Educators in Environmental Sustainability in Nigeria", *Journal of Creation and Science (JCEC)* 3 (2016): 87-99.

Increase protected forest area during dry season	87%	5%	8%
Decrease in forest fire or bush burning during dry season	91%	1%	8%
Creation of green zones/areas in various communities	92%	3%	5%
Promote the use of renewable energy	92%	0%	8%

Table 3: Strategic measures for climate change mitigation

As Table 3 shows, the investigations revealed that among the churches questioned, the following actions were suggested to mitigate and adapt to the avoidable change in climate: reduction of deforestation by avoiding felling of trees (81%), increase in planting of trees (94%), increase in protected forest area during dry season (87%), decrease in forest fire or bush burning during dry season (91%), creation of green zones/areas in various communities (92%), and promote the use of renewable energy (92%).

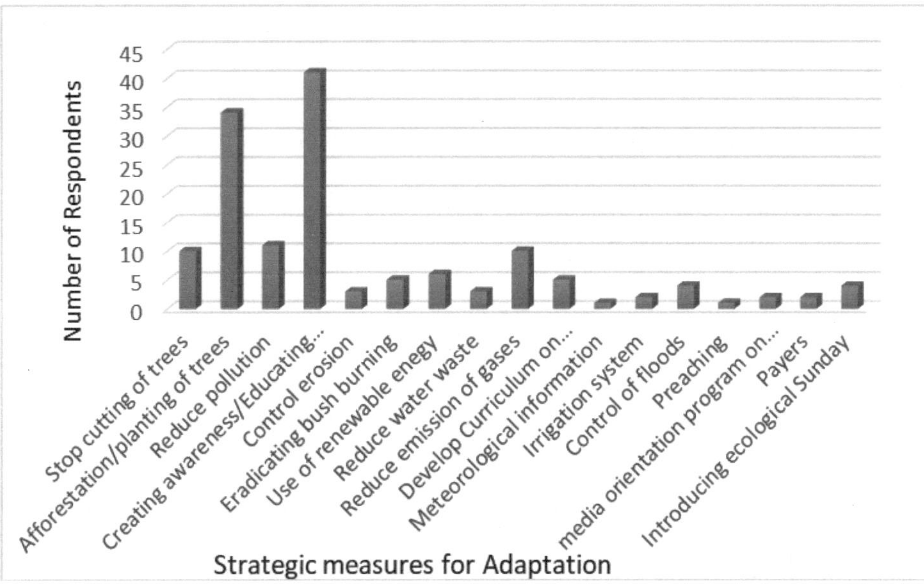

Figure 3: Strategic measures for climate change mitigation suggested by respondents.

Other strategic plans suggested by respondents include creating awareness and educating people, formation of environment protection groups, regular environmental sanitation, personal environment protection commitment programmes, eradication of bush burning, continuous environmental education. The suggestion was also made that a review of the methodology and evaluation of performance should be carried out every two years and to develop a curriculum for theological seminary on ecological issues, to curb pollution, introducing an ecological Sunday; engaging environmental services agencies for care of the environment, engaging in intentional sensitisation of people in the surroundings on environmental care.

Conclusion

The consequences and risks of climate change are evidenced to pastors and churches in the study areas. Among other disruptions of normal weather conditions are irregular rainfall, heatwaves, flooding in cities, drought spells in rural areas affecting the income and food security of poor farmers, increase in deforestation, environmental degradation. It is also clearly observed that there should be an increase in Christian training interventions for mitigation of climate change and the reinforcement of people's resilience to climate change. Many strategic measures are being suggested and, if implemented, will assure us of a better tomorrow in terms of reducing the effects of climate change, and increasing adaptation and resilience. Churches, therefore, need to be more proactive and on the frontline as the light and salt of the world by showing others good example in caring for the environment. Governments, industries and trades, organisations, communities and individuals need to take timely actions to mitigate or adapt to the effects of climate change, along with churches and other faith communities.

Suggestions for Further Reading

Ayre. C.W. "Christian Faith and the Earth: A Regional Response to a Global Issue". *Australian Journal of Mission Studies* 6 (2012): 20-27.

Babatolu, J.S. and R.T. Akinnubi. "Smallholder Farmers' Perception of Climate Change and Variability Impact and Their Adaptation Strategies in the Upper and Lower Niger River Basin Development Authority Areas, Nigeria". *Journal Of Petroleum & Environmental Biotechnology* 7(3) (2016): 1-7.

Bello O.D., A. Saïdou, E.L. Ahoton, A.V. Ezin, J.F.Y. Avaligbé, P.B.I. Akponikpè, and N. Aho. "Assessment of organic carbon stock in cashew plantations (Anacardium occidentale L.) in Benin (West Africa)". *International Journal of Agriculture and Environmental Research* 3(4) (2017): 3601-3625.

Boyer, J. S. "Plant Productivity and Environment." *Science* 218 (1982): 443-448.

Campbell-Lendrum, D. and R. Woodruff. *Climate Change: Quantifying the Health Impact at National and Local Levels.* WHO Environmental Burden of Disease Series No.14, 2007.

Chow, W.W. "An Integrated Approach to Theological Education". *Theological Education Today* 1(3) (September 1981): 1-7.

Climate Studies Group Mona, Eds. "The State of the Caribbean Climate". Produced for the Caribbean Development Bank, 2020.

Esan, V.I., M.B. Lawi and I. Okedigba. "Analysis of Cashew Farmers Adaptation in Climate Change in South-Western Nigeria". *Asian Journal of Agricultural Extension, Economics & Sociology* 23(4) (2018): 1-12.

Gurian-Sherman, D. *High and Dry, Why Genetic Engineering Is Not Solving Agriculture's Drought Problem in a Thirsty World.* Cambridge: Union of Concerned Scientists, 2012.

IPCC. *Climate Change 2007: Impacts, adaptation and vulnerability.* Contribution of Working Group II to the Fourth Assessment Report of the Intergovernmental Panel on Climate Change. Cambridge and New York: Cambridge University Press, 2007.

IPCC. *Summary for Policymakers. In Climate Change 2014: Impacts, Adaptation, And Vulnerability. Part A: Global and Sectoral Aspects.* Contribution of Working Group II to The Fifth Assessment Report of the Intergovernmental Panel on Climate Change. (2014): 1-32.

Ishola-Esan, Helen O. "The Role of The Church in Enhancing Environmental Stewardship". *Journal of Creation and Science (JCEC)* 1 (2014): 137-146.

Ishola-Esan, Helen and Oluwafemi Amoran. "The Role of Christian Educators in Environmental Sustainability in Nigeria". *Journal of Creation and Science (JCEC)* 3 (2016): 87-99.

Lohmann, Larry. "What Kind of Future for the World Rainforest Movement? 20 Years after 'Addressing the Underlying Causes of Deforestation'". *World Rainforest Movement* (September 2020) [Available at: https://www.researchgate.net/publication/349380032_What_Kind_of_Future_for_the_World_Rainforest_Movement_20_Years_after_Addressing_the_Underlying_Causes_of_Deforestation], [Last accessed: 3rd March 2022]

Masson-Delmotte, V., P. Zhai, H.-O. Pörtner, D. Roberts, J. Skea, P.R. Shukla, A. Pirani, W. Moufouma-Okia, C. Péan, R. Pidcock, S. Connors, J.B.R. Matthews, Y. Chen, X. Zhou, M.I. Gomis, E. Lonnoy,

T. Maycock, M. Tignor, and T. Waterfield, Eds. *The Context of Strengthening the Global Response to The Threat of Climate Change, Sustainable Development, And Efforts to Eradicate Poverty*. In Press.
Mcbratney, A., D.J. Field and A. Koch. "The Dimensions of Soil Security". *Geoderma* (2014): 203-213.
National Emergency Management Agency. "Report on the 2012 floods". Abuja: NEMA, 2013.
O'Brien, K.L., A.L. St. Clair and B. Kristoffersen. "The Framing of Climate Change: Why it Matters", in K.L. O'Brien, A.L. St. Clair and B. Kristoffersen, Eds. *Climate Change, Ethics and Human Security*. New York: Cambridge University Press, 2010: 3-22.
Parry, Martin. *Contribution of Working Group II to The Fourth Assessment Report of The Intergovernmental Panel on Climate Change*. New York: Cambridge University Press, 2007.
Parry, M., C. Rosenzweig and M. Livermore. "Climate Change, Global Food Supply and Risk of Hunger". *Phil. Trans. Roy. Soc. B* 360 (2005): 2125-2138.
Pennisi, E. "The Blue Revolution, Drop by Drop, Gene by Gene". *Science* 320 (2008): 320: 171-173.
Schuman, Simone, Jon-Vegard Dokken, Dewald van Niekerk and Ruth A, Loubser. "Religious Beliefs and Climate Change Adaptation: A study of three rural South African communities". *Jamba* 10(1) (2018): 509.Stern, N. *The Economics of Climate Change: The Stern Review*. Cambridge and New York: Cambridge University Press, 2007.
Stewart, Z. P., G.M. Pierzynski, B.J. Middendorf and P.V.V. Prasad. "Approaches to Improve Soil Fertility in Sub-Saharan Africa". *Journal of Experimental Botany* 71(2) (2020): 632-641.
Taylor, M.A. *Climate and Faith: Perspectives from The Margin. Baptist World Alliance Networking the Baptist Family to Impact the World for Christ*. Fall's Church, VA: 22nd Baptist World Congress, 2021.
UNFAO. *The State of Food and Agriculture 2016: Climate Change, Agriculture and Food Security*. Rome: Food and Agriculture Organization of the United Nations, 2017.
UNFAO. *Global Forest Resources Assessment 2005: Progress towards Sustainable Forest Management*. Rome: Food and Agriculture Organization of the United Nations, 2006.
Wilhoit, J.C. *Spiritual Formation as if the Church Mattered*. Grand Rapids, MI: Baker Academic, 2008.

97. Practical Models of Eco-Diaconia in Southern Africa: The Case of Community-Based Natural Resource Management (CBNRM) Model in Botswana

Senzokuhle Doreen Setume[1]

Introduction

We cannot overemphasise concerns over environmental problems due to human abuse of resources. Eco-diaconia is a humble call to humanity to take care of the environment. This chapter purports to demonstrate how communities can serve the environment through understanding the sanctity with which God has created the universe, including nonhuman beings. As we perceive in our minds, we shall live. Human beings cannot continue behaving the same way and expect different results. Global warming and other life-threatening situations have resulted due to humanistic attitudes, in particular, anthropocentrism. Kopnina, Washington, Taylor and Piccolo[2] define anthropocentrism as "the belief that value is human-centred and that all other beings are means to human ends". They further explain that the problem with such a mentality towards the conservation of natural resources is that it is "ethically wrong and at the root of ecological crises."[3] Anthropocentrism, in our capitalist times, inevitably breeds the commodification of natural resources in order to make profit. In order to conserve the environment, it is important not to take away the sacrality with which God has created His universe and everything in it. Eliade[4] has explained that the understanding of creation as sacred will impact on how humanity relates to their environment. According to Eliade, it is only through sacralisation that the world becomes the world, otherwise it is only chaos, the profane world. Failure to acknowledge creation as sacred leads to selfish and anthropocentric behaviours that have resulted in the current environmental crisis made up of global warming, deforestation and the general misuse of resources to meet the desires and wants of human beings.

This chapter discusses how the government of Botswana has incorporated the sacredness of creation into its conservation strategies through the use of the Community Based Natural Resource Management (CBNRM) model to preserve the environment in different communities. African local communities have long devised management strategies aimed at conserving the environment through psycho-social behaviour and indigenous knowledge that is embedded in the concept of sacredness.[5] From a theological perspective, sacredness is central as a conservationist strategy. This psycho-social behaviour and indigenous knowledge systems manifest through the environmental proverbs, sayings, rituals and taboos, health and healing practices observed by local communities. A political will is central in enabling communities to pursue some

---

[1] Dr Senzokuhle Doreen Setume is a lecturer in the Department of Theology and Religious Studies at the University of Botswana. She teaches courses such as African Indigenous Religions, Religions of Botswana, Religion and Science, Research Methodology and supervises students doing research. Dr Setume has presented papers at local, regional and international conferences. She has published journal articles and book chapters. Dr Setume is currently carrying out research in which she explores how twin burial rituals impacts on the process of grief for the surviving twin and their families. okuhlessd@gmail.com, setumesd@ub.ac.bw.

[2] Helen Kopnina, Haydn Washington, Bron Taylor and John J Piccolo, "Anthropocentrism: More Than Just a Misunderstood Problem", *Journal of Agriculture and Environmental Ethics* 31 (2018): 109-127.

[3] Kopnina et al., "Anthropocentrism", 110.

4 Mercia Eliade, *The Sacred and the Profane: The Nature of Religion* trans. Willard R. Trask (New York: HarpeTorchbooks, 1961).

[5] Senzokuhle Setume and Abednico Phili, "African Indigenous Knowledge systems and the conservation of the environment and cultural heritage in Botswana", in M. Christian Green and Muhammed Haron (eds) *Law, Religion and the Environment in Africa* (Stellenbosch: African Sun Media, 2020): 315-331.

of the activities with national/international implications such as ecological conservations, hence the significance of the Community Based Natural Resource Management models.

African Indigenous Religion and Conservation Strategies

Tarusarira,[6] consistent with other scholars that came before him (Mbiti,[7] Amanze[8]), conceptualise African Indigenous Religion (AIR) as a religion that is "expressed in the way Africans have always regulated their relationship with nature and with fellow human beings."[9] This attitude towards nature will further subject certain animals, hills, trees and intangible culture as sacred to followers and hence be treated with respect. Where animals and trees are needed for human needs, people will take from their environment only as much as was needed to meet their basic needs.

From an African perspective, a healthy life requires a state of equilibrium between all forms of life – human, animal and plant. It then becomes imperative that human beings become good stewards of the environment in order to ensure that this equilibrium is maintained. Poor environmental care will result in catastrophic situations where scarcity will threaten all forms of life and natural disasters such as drought and illness will occur. Tarusarira explains that for most African societies the "entire relationship between humans and nature, including activities such as land use, has deep religious and spiritual underpinnings. In general religion is central to many of the decisions people make about their own community developments".[10] Mbiti explains that Africans believe that God exists in nature. This mindset encourages positive relations towards the environment. Ikuenobe explains that "Traditional Africans had conservationist values, moral attitudes, practices and ways of life [...] which were destroyed by the exploitative ethos of European colonisation and modernisation".[11] The European ethos with its focus on profit leads to humanity demanding from Mother Nature more than what is necessary to meet their basic needs, hence the destruction of the environment.

African views and thoughts on ontology, cosmology, medicine and healing and religious practices supported their moral attitudes towards conservations and preservation of nature.[12] Nature is seen as holistic and an interconnected continuum of humans and all natural objects. Reality is seen as a composite unity and harmony of natural forces such as human communities, spirits, mountains, plants, rivers etc. Burnett and Kang'ethe explain that nature is interconnected with power inherent in all objects of nature in the following hierarchy: God, ancestors, humans, animals, plants and non-biological things.[13] When all things in nature are viewed as having some elements of divine power within them, it then becomes a divine responsibility that human beings should take care of nature, conserve and preserve it. To sum up the African worldview in relation to the environment, Ikuenobe explains that, for most Africans, the natural environment is divine for "it is in such things in which gods, deity, sprits and ancestors are made manifest [...] hence religious rites are performed with various natural objects."[14] Mbiti expresses the same sentiments

[6] Joram Tarusarira, "African Religion, Climate Change and Knowledge Systems", *The Ecumenical Review* 69(3) (2017): 398-410.

[7] John Mbiti, *African Religions and Philosophy. African Writers Series.* (London: Heinemann, 1969).

[8] James Amanze, *African Traditional Religions and Culture in Botswana: A Comprehensive Textbook.* (Gaborone: Pula Press, 2002).

[9] Tarusarira, "African Religion, Climate Change and Knowledge Systems", 401.

[10] Tarusarira, "African Religion, Climate Change and Knowledge Systems", 398.

[11] P.A. Ikuenobe, "Traditional African Environmental Ethics and Colonial Legacy", *International Journal of Philosophy and Theology* 2(4) (2014): 1.

[12] Ikuenobe, "Traditional African Environmental Ethics", 2.

[13] Burnett and Kamuyu wa Kang'ethe, "Wilderness and the Bantu Mind", *Environmental Ethics* 16 (2) (1994): 145-160.

[14] Ikuenobe, "Traditional African Environmental Ethics", 5.

when he explains that due to this African worldview, natural objects have religious significance and are treated by humans with reverence.[15]

This chapter will now demonstrate how communities can serve their interest through the understanding that God's other creation is sacred and therefore needs to be protected and accessed with respect through the Natural Resource Management (CBNRM) model that has been adopted by different communities in Botswana, Zimbabwe, Namibia and South Africa.[16]

The Community-Based Natural Resource Management (CBNRM) Model

In an effort to conserve natural resources, the government of Botswana has adopted the Community-Based Natural Resource Management (CBNRM) Model. This model aims at improving conservation through involving local communities while respecting the cultures and religions of these communities. The CBNRM model was meant to shift the management of natural resources to the community level. It was noted that "the management of the environment and the control of natural resources must be shifted to the level of the community, so that local people simultaneously benefit from the environment and take care of it". This principle was initially applied to the preservation of wildlife[17] but has been extended to other resources as well. Mbaiwa and Stonza explains the model in the following manner: CBNRM is used to explain "the way in which communities organise themselves to sustainably manage their natural resources".[18] CBNRM is, therefore, an incentive-based conservation philosophy that links conservation of natural resources with rural development.[19] The basic assumption of CBNRM is that for a community to manage its natural resource base sustainably, they must receive direct benefits arising from its use. These benefits must exceed the perceived costs of managing the resources. The assumption is that when community livelihoods are improved, community members would be incentivised to address conservation ideals.[20] These assumptions are based on three conceptual foundations, namely economic value, devolution and collective ownership. Economic value refers to the value given to wildlife resources that can be realised by the community or land owner. Second, emphasis is put on the need to devolve management decisions from government to the community or local land users in order to create positive conditions for sustainable wildlife management. Third, collective proprietorship refers to collective use-rights over resources by groups of people, which then are able to manage according to their own roles and strategies."[21]

Effectively used, the CBRNM has the potential to contribute meaningfully to the conservation of the environment. Botswana is one of the countries in Africa that is a popular tourist destination because she

---

[15] Mbiti, *African Religions and Philosophy*.

[16] J.E. Mbaiwa and A.L. Stronza, "The effects of tourism development on rural livelihoods in the Okavango Delta, Botswana", *Journal of Sustainable Tourism* 18(5) (2010): 635-656.

[17] Tsholofelo Dichaba and Phenyo Churchill Thebe, "In Search of Identity and Ownership of the MmaMotshwane Gorge: Heritage Tourism and Management of Mogonye Cultural Landscape", *Botswana Notes and Records*, 47 (2015): 56-68.

[18] Department of Wildlife and National Parks (DWNP), *Joint venture guidelines*. (Gaborone: Department of Wildlife and National Parks, 1999), cited in J.E. Mbaiwa, "Community-Based Natural Resource Management in Botswana", in R. van der Duim, M. Lamers and J. van Wijk (eds) *Institutional Arrangements for Conservation, Development and Tourism in Eastern and Southern Africa* (Dordrecht: Springer, 2015): 59-80: 60.

[19] O.T. Thakadu, "Success factors in community-based natural resource management projects mobilization in northern Botswana: Lessons from practice". *Natural Resource Forum* 29(3) (2005): 199-212; P. Blaikie, "Is small really beautiful? Community-based natural resource management in Malawi and Botswana", *World Development* 34(11) (2006): 1942-1957; J.E. Mbaiwa and A.L. Stronza, "The effects of tourism development on rural livelihoods in the Okavango Delta, Botswana", *Journal of Sustainable Tourism* 18(5) (2010): 635-656.

[20] M. Leach, R. Mearns and I. Scoone, "Environmental entitlements: Dynamics and institutions in community-based natural resource management". *World Development* 27(2) (1999): 225-247.

[21] Mbaiwa and Stronza, "The effects of tourism development", 59.

has managed to preserve her natural resources, in particular, wildlife. The country has over "45 community-based organisations (CBOs) with CBNRM projects."[22] One CBNRM Trust will be used to demonstrate the effectiveness of the model, Kgetsi ya Tsie (KyT) Trust in the Tswapong Hills.

Kgetsi ya Tsie (KyT) Trust in the Tswapong Hills

Kgetsi ya Tsie Trust is a CBNRM project that derives its name from a Setswana proverb *Kgetsi ya Tsie e kgonwa ke go tswaraganelwa* which literally means "a bag of locusts is better carried by many people"[23] that translates to a rich concept of "together we can". The group started in 1997 with the formation of small natural resource user groups in nine villages situated in the Tswapong Hills. The main objective of the KyT is to strengthen the local economy, based on traditional livelihood activities, by processing and marketing plant-based natural resource products (veld products). The Tswapong Hills are of great religious and spiritual importance to the communities as they are believed to have supernatural powers and ancestral spirits which are believed to dwell in the hills. Therefore, gathering of veld products in the area is done with such a revered attitude towards the environment. The KyT Trust differs from most CBNRM projects in Botswana because it is not dependent on wildlife resources as it specialises in the collection and processing of veld products. KyT's constitution stipulates that women should constitute at least 80% of the membership, making it the only CBO in Botswana that specifically targets women. According to Buzwani, Setlhogile, Arntzen and Potts, KyT seeks to assist rural women in the Tswapong Hills area to empower themselves, both socially and economically through the effective organisation of entrepreneurial activities centred on the sustainable management and utilisation of veld products.[24] KyT specialises in food products (jam, *phane* and *dicheru* for cattle); cosmetic products (*morula* oil and soap); herbal products (e.g. *monepenepe*); pottery; and the provision of micro loans for members. KyT has taken several steps to avoid resource degradation. Firstly, it issued 1,500 morula and monepenepe seedlings among its members for planting in yards and fields. The reported survival rate is around 60%. Secondly, members are trained in sustainable harvesting techniques, such as digging up only a few roots and recovering the remaining roots afterwards to avoid damage to the trees. Finally, cases of unsustainable harvesting practices are reported to the Chief, who takes the required action. While KyT does not have a resource monitoring system in place, some monitoring is done through members when they collect veld products.[25]

Other than the monetary benefits that accrue to members, KyT has yielded a number of vital non-material benefits. First and foremost is the empowerment of women as those involved have become more independent and self-reliant. Another non-material benefit is that membership of KyT is prestigious, and often leads to election into other positions such as positions on the Village Development Committees. Of equal importance is that members have learnt about the use and value of new veld products, new production techniques (e.g. jam production) and have become more business-minded. This may generate significant benefits outside the KyT sphere. KyT has embarked on other economic activities that are not directly linked to the harvesting of veld products. Examples in this category are catering services, the rental of houses, and cell phone and battery charging. The empowerment of women and prestige are the most important non-material results of KyT. The CBNRM Review found that nonmaterial benefits accrue to households as well as to the region at large. Knowledge about the uses and values of natural resources has improved, leading

---

[22] Mbaiwa and Stronza, "The effects of tourism development", 63.

[23] Rosaleen OB Nhlekisana, "A Reflection on Setswana Proverbs in Botswana's National Psyche and Nationhood", *Botswana Notes and Records: A Special Issue on Humanities at UB and Botswana's 50 Years of Independence* 48 (2016): 150-159.

[24] B. Buzwani, T. Setlhogile, J. Arntzen and F. Potts, "Best Practices in Botswana for the Management of Natural Resources by Communities", *CBNRM Support Programme Occasional Paper No. 17.*

[25] Buzwani et al., "Best Practices in Botswana", 24.

to environmental and livelihood benefits. Gaining business experience can also be viewed as an important outcome.

KyT as an organisation has faced come challenges as discussed by Buzwani, Setlhogile, Arntzen and Potts[26] and they have put measures in place to mitigate the challenges.

Conclusion

With the right attitude, societies can turn away from the negative impact that is caused by an anthropocentric world view that has caused ecological crises. The community-based model that the government of Botswana has adopted to conserve natural resources allows local communities to express their culture and religion as they interact with nature. The *Kgetsi ya Tsie* Cultural Trust has sought alternative ways of ensuring that nature is not completely destroyed through the way they harvested the veld products and started planting their own trees in order to avoid deforestation. Eco-diaconia has a symbiotic effect: as humanity takes care of the environment, the environment will continuously take care of humanity.

Suggestions for Further Reading

Arntzen, J., B. Buzwani, T. Setlhogile, D.L. Kgathi and M.K. Motsolapheko. *Community Based Resource Management, Rural Livelihoods and Environmental Sustainability*. Gaborone, Botswana: Centre for Applied Research, 2007.

Eneji C.V.O., G.U. Ntamu, C.C. Unwanade, A.B. Godwin, J.E. Bassey, J.J. Willaims and Joseph Ignatius. "Traditional African Religion in Natural Resources Conservation and Management in Cross River State, Nigeria". *Environment and Natural Resources Research* 2(4) (2012): 44-53.

Gibson, C.C., and S.A. Marks. "Transforming rural hunters into conservationists: An assessment of community-based wildlife management programs in Africa". *World Development* 23(6) (1995): 340-350.

Macdonald, D.W., D.D.P. Johnson, and H. Whitehouse. "Towards a More Natural Governance of Earth's Biodiversity and Resources". *Conservation and Society* 17(1) (2019): 108-113.

Manzoor, Javed. "Role of Socio-Religious Beliefs in the Conservation of Natural Resources Viz a Viz Modern Education and Technology: A Consideration from Poonch District of Jammu and Kashmir". *International Journal of Current Trends in Science and Technology* 8(1) (2017): 20532-20536.

Shereni, Ngoni Courage, and Jarkko Saarinen. "Community Perceptions on the Benefits and Challenges of Community-Based Natural Resources Management in Zimbabwe". *Development Southern Africa* 38(6) (2021): 879-895.

Stone, Moren T. and Lesego S. Stone. "Challenges of Community-Based Tourism in Botswana: a Review of Literature". *Transactions of the Royal Society of South Africa* 75(2) (2020): 181-193.

Stone, Moren Tibabo and Lesego Senyana Stone. "Community-Based Ecotourism and Bushmeat Consumption Dynamics: Implications for Conservation and Community Development". *Journal of Sustainable Tourism* (2020): 1-25.

[26] Buzwani *et al.*, "Best Practices in Botswana", 25-27.

98. THE CHILDREN OF AFRICA RETOOLING TO SAVE THE ENVIRONMENT: REIMAGINING ECO-DIAKONIA

Hauwa Madi[1]

Introduction

The church's concern for the suffering of the world is not a new development. However, the need for consistency and a deliberate effort to provide the necessary education, care and services has been sometimes neglected. The church has a ministry of service to the world.

As such, the church needs to create an "Eco-Diakonian Tradition". By this, we understand a "tradition" of Christian service and witness that will be a set of customs, beliefs and practices, that gives a deep sense of who we are in relation to the whole of creation. It should teach the child to locate their place in relation to creation and knowing that tradition well enough to be able to explain to another. Lack of such a tradition and a consciousness of it will continue to result in creation abuse and an incoherent attitude toward the environment.

Forming a tradition like this will thus fashion a model by which we live and relate to the rest of creation.[2] The Christian faith asserts the authority of God who has revealed Himself in both Scripture and nature.

God's words of command referring to the task "be fruitful and increase in number; fill the earth and subdue it" (Gen. 1:28), leaves no doubt that humanity has a task to perform. The words to "subdue" and "have dominion" attest to the fact that we are expected to exercise our God-given talents to enjoy and ensure the well-being of creation. Human dignity leaves no room for irresponsibility. To subdue implies control and authority over the earth. We can only have dominion and exercise proper control with a full understanding of what is under control.[3]

The intention of this paper is to put forth a vision to the church in Africa; to suggest, and show the need for, a tradition that maintains a learning environment to facilitate eco-diakonia as a deliberate Christian witness and service to contribute to environmental stewardship and the healing of creation. Thus, eco-diakonia can guide the church and religious educators when teaching children and expound the need for learning through models.

The learning process of the child is mobile, not static. Whether or not we are aware of it, the child learns from peers, community, neighbours, extended family, school, parents, siblings and everything or everyone around them. How we live confirms to the child what we believe individually and as a community. Teaching and learning "takes place in formal and informal settings by designated and undesignated teachers who relate to and embody the beliefs, values, and practices of the community".[4] Everyone around the child is already a teacher or a potential teacher. The child's learning cannot be limited to just one or two dimensions of their life (e.g., school and Sunday school). Many parents and Church leaders think it is the responsibility of teachers (academic and/or spiritual) to teach the child because they have the needed curriculum. However, Everist, quoting Maria Harris, notes that "curriculum is about the mobilising of creative, educative powers in such a way as to 'fashion a people'."[5] Knowledge is "shared meanings"; the one who is considered educated is the one who is able to discover, accumulate and distribute these shared meanings.

---

[1] Hauwa Eve Mari is a lecturer in the Department of Biblical Studies, Theological College of Northern Nigeria (TCNN); Email: evehauwa4bornagain@yahoo.com.

[2] Enno Wolthuis, *Science, God, and You* (Grand Rapids, MI: Baker Book House, 1965): 61.

[3] Wolthuis, *Science, God, and You,* 110.

[4] Norma Cook Everist, *The Church as Learning Community* (Nashville, TN: Abingdon, 2002): 21.

[5] Everist, *The Church as Learning Community,* 45.

Education also involves the transmission of culture – it is "the process by which a culture transmits itself across generations".[6] By culture, we mean the "shared values, attitudes and beliefs" a people have. It is necessary for the church in Africa to discern what aspects of the wider culture can be preserved, redeemed, or transformed.

The Inquiry

Many communities in Africa today are vulnerable; they are affected by climate and other ecological changes, which in turn are causing sand storms, food and clean water shortages. Sorley sums this up:

> As Africa enters the 21st century, we face a set of environmental concerns that are unprecedented in history. These include deforestation, the loss of biodiversity, land degradation and declines in per acre agricultural output, overgrazing, pollution, a warming and drying climate, and diminishing water supplies. All of these issues work together to perpetuate poverty, hunger, disease and death. What used to be occasional and infrequent difficulties have become chronic problems which affect millions of people each year.[7]

Many of the things that have led to major changes in the climate today have been common practices since long ago; cutting down trees for wood and fuel, bush burning, land clearing, overgrazing, continuous cropping, improper disposal of waste etc. In the past, these may not have had visible consequences but with chemicals taking the place of the organic, artificial items replacing the natural, growing populations and the depletion of most of our natural resources, many of our communities are in danger.

There is a need to identify the problem before it can be fixed; we need to identify what has been done so far and how it should be done instead. We need to understand the situation clearly before we can come up with solutions. I realise that I also am part of the problem. Admitting this will require humility for some people (James 4:10: "Humble yourself before the Lord and he will lift you up"). It is difficult to change unless we accept that there is a problem, that we are part of the problem and can also be part of the solution. Growing up as a little girl in my village of Shelleng Local Government Area of Adamawa State, in the North Eastern parts of Nigeria, I "unconsciously" learned that it was not wrong for me to eat peanuts while walking and throwing away the shells as I walked along as that was what everyone else was doing. I could eat mango or any other fruit, and throw away the seed wherever and whenever I was finished. No one ever considered such an attitude and practice harmful to the community and, to some extent, rightly so. These things we disposed of casually as they were organic. They easily decomposed or eventually grew into plants. The attitude of not disposing waste properly in Africa is common practice. The attitude has hardly changed, but the composition and quality of the "waste" has changed. It is no longer harmless organic waste but is now mostly synthetic material. This is causing drastic changes in the local environment.

Defecating, Improper Waste Disposal and Other Hazardous Lifestyles

Many homes in Nigeria do not have toilets and proper means of disposing of waste. Either a house is built without a toilet or has a modern toilet that uses the water system but the constant availability of water to maintain the system becomes a challenge. Walking around uncompleted buildings or in the bush you get "welcomed" by a strong stench and sounds of buzzing flies because people have defecated there. While growing up in the village, there were no toilets. People simply used to go out with a hoe, dig a hole and bury their excretion when they were done. This unorganised defecation was also the practice at some point in the Old Testament among the Jews (Deut. 23:12-14). There were hardly any toilets but excretions were not laying in the open with a strong stench or flies because everything was covered up. But today this is

---

6 Robert W. Pazmino, *Foundational Issues in Christian Education* (Grand Rapids, MI: Baker Books, 1997): 186.
7 Craig Sorley, *Honoring Christ in Caring for His Creation* (Doorlight Publications, 2016): 16.

not the practice in many communities. Everywhere is a "toilet" but no-one seems to cover their excrement. It then, unfortunately, gets washed away by the rain and comes into the water sources of many communities – thus explaining the cause of the many cholera outbreaks and persistent typhoid fever.

Disposal of other types of waste also cause a problem; when I look around, almost everyone is dropping plastic wrappers or other forms of litter. These don't decay easily, and they are blown away by the wind; thus they can transmit germs and make the environment look messy. You clean your own compound but the wind blows rubbish in from your neighbour's. Sometimes animals eat these plastics and can die when they do. I have also seen how plastic and other waste blocks ditches. There are communities where everyone collects their rubbish and dumps it in ditches or in the water drainage, waiting for the rain to wash it all away. Boys collect rubbish from shops for an insignificant amount and dump it in ditches so "the rain can wash it away". This blocks ditches, causing flooding which in turn can cause erosion as water has to find ways to pass and this, in turn, destroys farms and homes. Floods also carry germs which can lead to outbreaks of cholera. We want to use new things, to behave and act like people in the West; we are buying "modern" flashy things without considering the consequences of them or how we will dispose of the waste. The problem is our attitudes and lack of awareness of the issues. We just throw waste without thinking of the consequences.

Trees are being cut down without considering the long list of things that we gain from them. When I went to my village this April, I was shocked to experience sandstorms. My first experience was while I was in church but the worst sandstorm happened the next day when I was at home. While growing up, this was not an experience I had. It is true that before the rains become consistent, the wind often blows dust about, however, before it would stop as soon as it began raining. This experience of a sandstorm was quite different. When the wind started to blow, everywhere became dark and we couldn't even see the house next door. All the doors and windows were shut but we still had to use a face mask inside. After the storm, we had to wash and clean the whole house. I asked my mother how this came to be. She explained that it was due to the cutting down of trees which had recently become excessive due to people coming to cut trees secretly in the night. Many who do this do so for personal gain, not minding the effects it will have on the communities and environment. We have done more harm than good by cutting down trees. Apart from the sandstorms, there was the excessive heat, hardly any shade, and the air pollution made one feel suffocated. It was distressing to see the flat, treeless view across the village where once there had been a forest of trees.

A Generation in Limbo

My grandmother used to carefully select which wood she would cut for burning. She knew that some trees have smoky, smelly wood which is not healthy to burn due to gaseous emissions. But these days, every species of tree is cut for firewood. Why? Is it likely due to ignorance, greed, suffering or need? It is most likely because many do not know any better. How did this knowledge not get passed on? This is most likely due to "modernisation". People tried to be modern so in exchange for the knowledge and use of wood they opted for gas and kerosene. Some people tried to migrate to cities for a "better life" – they gained things there that they felt were better. Thus, our local language which was the medium of communicating and describing these trees, their properties and uses, was lost to the language of the city. Often, we fail to see the connection between language and environmental information; people know wisdom and trees in their local language – when they lose the language in most cases, they lose also the culture and its wisdom too.

Early Christianity brought by the missionaries to Africa did not connect solidly with the form of life that was already in existence. As Hopkins notes,

> The damning criticism of early twentieth century mission-Christianity this leads into is that it failed to bring a worldview. It merely brought a religion centred on an eschatological hope, accompanied by certain rituals and practices, but which did not connect solidly with a vision for life here. This form of Christianity succeeded in

> deconstructing elements of a traditional worldview, thereby clearing the path for the entry of a secularised successor. It is unfortunate that the evangelisation of northern Nigeria coincided with the heyday of fundamentalism in Western Evangelicalism, content in its circumscribed vision with lopping off offensive protuberances of late Romantic Western culture without challenging its secularising worldview. Not having a full-orbed Christian worldview themselves, the missionaries had no chance of passing one on – and the African Church has scarcely started to recover from this serious deficiency in its birthing […] So Christianity sacrificed rather than reinterpreting the spirituality of nature; it also fatally weakened the communal structures of society which had held the key to sustainable living.[8]

Retooling to Save the Environment

I have tried to teach my son to dispose of his rubbish properly. If we are out and about, for example in church, my son will not just throw plastic wrappers on the ground, he will come to me and put it in my bag so we can dispose of it later. This is unlike the other children who just throw them on the ground. And this example encourages me that it is possible to make a change and to make a difference!

The explicit curriculum in most, if not all, schools in Africa teaches about the environmental impact of common agricultural practices in Africa. For example, Iwena[9] and Are *et al*[10] discuss some of the major farming practices in Africa today, and their effects on the soil. It is said, "action speaks louder than words". Many times, knowledge acquired through the explicit curriculum is not transmitted into the existing reality in many African communities. Personally speaking, I cannot remember most of what I was taught in my Agricultural Science classes in both my Primary and Secondary Schools, but I do know how to work on our rice farm because I did it in practice with my mother. Ideas that do not form part of the explicit curriculum and yet have been accepted and transmitted as effective, can be termed as the "hidden curriculum". These are "non-academic and systematic side effects of education that are sensed, but which cannot be adequately accounted for by reference to the explicit curriculum."[11] What has been practiced traditionally is passed on from generation to generation and, for many traditional societies, the "hidden" curriculum is more effective than the "explicit".

The Educational Task of the Church

The educational task of the Church involves education for "proclamation" (*kerygma*), education for "community" (*koinonia*), education for "service" (*diakonia*), education for "advocacy" (*propheteia*), and the emphasis that centres and integrates these educational tasks of the church is worship (*leitourgia*).[12] For education to be effective, both knowing and doing must be emphasised. This brings honour, praise and glory to God.

Learning takes place beyond the classroom; it takes place everywhere humans interact. Going with Everist's claims, in many regards, "every learning environment is a classroom".[13]

> At the denominational level churches should set in place structures to ensure that creation care is mainstreamed right down to the congregational level. There should be two main aspects to this: on the one hand communicating

[8] Mark Hopkins, *Transforming Christian Attitudes to Creation Care: A Perspective from Public Theology* (Presented 30 November 2018, revised 2 December 2018), 3.
[9] O. A. Iwena, *Essential Agricultural Science for Senior Secondary Schools* (Ibafo, Nigeria: TONAD, 2018): 447-450.
[10] L. A. Are *et al.*, *Comprehensive Certificate Agricultural Science* (Ibadan, Nigeria: University Press, 2018): 125-128.
[11] Robert W. Pazmino, *Foundational Issues In Christian Education* (Grand Rapids, MI: Baker, 1997): 236.
[12] Pazmino, *Foundational Issues*, 44-53.
[13] Everist, *The Church as Learning Community*, 47.

creation care as an integral feature of the Gospel through all available means to all sectors within churches; and on the other hand mobilising congregations to engage together in creation care projects that will have impact within their communities.[14]

Models for an "Eco-Diakonian Tradition"

- **Learning By Doing:** everyday living of the gospel by individuals must include an eco-diakonal consciousness. This is to be reflected in the family, community and church interactions. Whatever model each church chooses or designs, it must ensure that it aims at helping students take responsibility for learning and supporting their efforts and that it helps students reach toward new knowledge, skills, and self-understanding.[15] Bruce Joyce, Marsha Weil and Emily Calhoun suggests four groups of models[16] that I think would be relevant to churches when it comes to developing an "eco-diakonian tradition" that would be useful in retooling the children of Africa to reimagine how best to relate and interact with the environment.
- **The Information-Processing Family:** The information-processing models are models that emphasise ways of enhancing the learner's innate drive to "make sense of the world by acquiring and organising data, sensing problems and generating solutions to them, and developing concepts and language for conveying them."[17] The church in Africa needs to come up with ways to encourage the younger generation to see for themselves the need and necessity to care for the environment. There should be processes for acquiring information, processing, testing and application.
- **The Social Family:** This model emphasises the importance of community as a learning environment; that is co-operative learning. As noted by Joyce *et al.*, when we work together, we generate a collective energy called a "synergy".[18] The church should become a community of learners, encourage the inclusion of ways to best practice and concretise the best ways to care for the environment in its doctrine and practice. The utilisation of local language(s) within the faith community can also aid in understanding how the environment was cared for in the past and how best to improve on these methods if need be. This is best accomplished through collective academic study and logical reasoning.
- **The Personal Family:** "The personal models of learning begin from the perspective of the selfhood of the individual. They attempt to shape education so that we come to understand ourselves better, take responsibility for our education, and learn to reach beyond our current development to become stronger, more sensitive, and more creative in our search for high-quality lives."[19] Children are to be given opportunities to be actively involved in the learning process. The church and community can create practical ways to encourage every child to explore their personal skills, self-understanding and responsibility to themselves, their environment and others
- **The Behavioural Systems Family:** (also known as behaviour modification, behaviour therapy, and cybernetics). Based on this model, human beings are self-correcting and can modify their behaviour patterns in response to information about how successfully tasks are navigated. The church needs to come up with ways that will encourage learning new patterns of behaviour, reducing phobic and other dysfunctional patterns of behaviour towards the environment, and learning self-control in relation to old harmful habits.

---

[14] Hopkins, *Transforming Christian Attitudes*, 6.
[15] Bruce Joyce, Marsha Weil and Emily Calhoun, *Models of Teaching: A Working Professional Repertoire* (London: Pearson Higher Education, 2015): 7.
[16] Joyce *et al.*, *Models of Teaching*, 9-20.
[17] Joyce *et al.*, *Models of Teaching*, 9-20.
[18] Joyce *et al.*, *Models of Teaching*, 13.
[19] Joyce *et al.*, *Models of Teaching*, 15.

Conclusion

Like the SIL Nigeria Faith and Farming programme, the church in Africa can come up with a model that best fits its context to ensure that it comes up with resources designed for the church as a community, the children and the environment through the use of local language(s) and already existing life patterns.

Suggestions for Further Reading

Are, L. A. *et al*. *Comprehensive Certificate Agricultural Science.* Ibadan, Nigeria: University Press, 2018.
Everist, Norma Cook. *The Church as Learning Community.* Nashville, TN: Abingdon Press; 2002.
Bruce Joyce, Marsha Weil and Emily Calhoun. *Models of Teaching: A Working Professional Repertoire*. London: Pearson Higher Education, 2015.
Iwena, O. A. *Essential Agricultural Science for Senior Secondary Schools.* Ibafo, Nigeria: TONAD, 2018.
Pazmino, Robert W. *Foundational Issues in Christian Education*. Grand Rapids, MI: Baker, 1997.
Sorley, Craig. *Honoring Christ in Caring for His Creation.* Doorlight Publications, 2016.
Wolthuis, Enno. *Science, God, and You.* Grand Rapids, MI: Baker, 1965.

99. Interreligious Eco-Diapraxis Toward Climate Change Mitigation

Salli Ndombo Effungani[1]

Introduction

The threat of global warming and the crucial search for environmental ethics and justice have traversed all fields of study, articulating its relevance and urgency. Most importantly, conversations on interreligious environmentalism or greening of religions is an inescapable signal which has evoked a new consciousness and has accentuated the significance of religion in addressing the ecological crisis. Religion has a moral authority to positively change attitudes and influence good practices. It is incumbent of religion to harness its loud voice and precedence, to advocate for public policies. Expatiating on the nexus between religion and ecological issues, Tucker and Grim intimate that there is no religion with a privileged ecological perspective, but multiple religious perspectives bring on board valuable contributions of religion to search for ecological solutions.[2] This is my point of departure in prompting the conversation beyond theory to interreligious eco-diapraxis towards climate change.

Climate change is a global crisis with devastating consequences. The continuous undertakings of humanity over centuries have been detrimental to the ecosystem, leading to extreme natural disasters. The rise of temperature levels has led to life-threatening conditions: extreme droughts, food and water shortages, deforestation, soil degradation, violent conflicts to name a few. The emissions of greenhouse gases, especially carbon pollution, is one of the major causes of global warming. This issue was discussed in depth during the 2015 Paris Peace Agreement on climate change. Delegates noted that, if humanity fails to slow global emissions, temperatures may rise beyond three degrees Celsius by 2100.[3]

The quest to limit global warming to 1.5 degrees continues to inform various conversations, and this was well articulated in 2019 by Patricia Espinosa, Executive Secretary of UN Climate Change. She opines that:

> Once a distant concern, climate change is now an existential threat and the greatest challenge facing this generation [...] We must limit global temperature rise to 1.5 degrees and, on the road to doing so, achieve climate neutrality by 2050. This must be done urgently and co-operatively; a global project requiring the best efforts from all nations, all businesses, and all people.[4]

I am congruent with Patricia for a united effort, especially where the unique role of religion is vociferous. This aligns with Posas' analysis of the role of religion in inspiring followers to action towards climate

---

[1] Salli Ndombo Effungani, PhD in religious studies (Christian-Muslim relations). She is the Programme officer for the programme for Christian-Muslim relations in Africa (PROCMURA) and Adjunct lecturer St Paul University, Limuru Kenya. Ordained minister of the Presbyterian Church in Cameroon (PCC). Member of the Circle of Concerned African Women Theologians. Emails: ndombosalli@yahoo.com; programmeofficer@procmura.org.

[2] Mary Evelyn Tucker and John Grim, "Introduction: The Emerging Alliance of World Religions and Ecology", *Journal of American Academy of Art and Sciences* 130(4) (2001): 1-20.

[3] NRDC, "The Paris Agreement on Climate Change", Issue Brief, Natural Resources Defense Council, November 2017. [Available at: https://assets.nrdc.org/sites/default/files/paris-agreement-climate-change-2017-ib.pdf], [Last accessed: 8th March 2022].

[4] United Nations Climate Change, *Climate action and support trends* (Bonn, Germany: UN Climate Change Secretariat, 2019). [Available at: https://unfccc.int/sites/default/files/resource/Climate_Action_Support_Trends_2019.pdf], [Last accessed: 8th March 2022].

mitigation.[5] The power of religion in shaping views, and instilling values among people and societies throughout history cannot be overemphasised. This resonates well with the context of the Global South; the African person is religious in all aspects. Before I present my case study, I will like to direct my discussion around one of the major concepts shaping conversations on interreligious global ethics towards ecology.

Conceptualising Interreligious Environmentalism: A Call for a Global Ethics

The concept, formulated by Hans Kung and adopted and declared by the Parliament of the World's Religions of 1993, calls for all people and religions to move towards a global responsibility in solving the crisis plaguing the planet and humanity. Most importantly, congress argued that ethical values held by each religion can be used to resolve many of the crises which the world and humanity are facing and added that religions should have a dialogue around the challenges facing the world and humanity at large. The parliament stated, "No better global order without a global ethic".[6]

I am alive to the fact that this concept has been critiqued, and has been found both limiting and promising in various aspects. There is an observation that an inter-religious conceptualisation of ethics may result in divergent understandings, with consequences such as undermining other religious groupings. Moreover, incorporating various interpretations may lead to generalisation. Knitter, discussing the pitfalls and promises of the concept, brings to light the issue of class inequality, where the privileged political elites will dominate any interreligious dialogue.[7] In my analysis of Knitter's critique of this concept, I see him projecting a trait of "*politicalisation*" of interreligious dialogue toward care for the environment as a pitfall. I investigate this argument, looking at examples of practical grass-rooted interreligious models towards climate change, to ascertain the existing gaps that may jeopardise interreligious eco-dialogue.

Knitter further suggests an ecological interreligious dialogue that begins with environmental ethics and leads to environmental mysticism. I am interested in Knitters' connection of creation and ecological interreligious dialogue, and the five steps recommended for such a dialogue: *Compassion*; *Conversion*; *Collaboration*; *Communication*; and *Communion*.[8] An overview of the aforementioned analysis raises my concern on how the concept of global ethics can inform interreligious initiatives toward climate change mitigation. This concern is only addressed by investigating a practical model.

The Case of Women "Njangi farming"[9] Groups in Muyuka, Cameroon

This study was conducted in April and May 2021. Muyuka is a town in Fako Division of the South West Region of Cameroon, known for its agricultural prowess, although now devastated by the Anglophone crisis. The study sampled three interreligious women farmer's groups: Muyuka Town (unity sisters), Ikata (women of the soil), and Muyenge (struggling women). The groups are composed of Christian and Muslim women farmers. Unity Sisters has 30 members (10 Muslim, 20 Christians); Women of the Soil, 40 women (15 Muslim, 25 Christians); Struggling Women, 35 (10 Muslims, 25 Christians). Therefore, a total of 105

---

5 Paula Posas, "Roles of religion and ethics in addressing Climate Change", *Ethics in Science and Environmental Politics* 8(1) (2007): 31-49.

6 Parliament of the World's Religions, *Toward a Global Ethic: An Initial Declaration of the Parliament of the World's Religions* (Chicago, IL: Council for a Parliament of the World's Religions, 1993). [Available at: https://parliamentofreligions.org/towards-global-ethic-initial-declaration], [Last accessed: 8th March 2022].

7 Paul Knitter, "Pitfalls and Promises for a Global Ethics", *Buddhist-Christian Studies* 15 (1995): 221-229.

8 Paul Knitter, "A common creation story? Interreligious dialogue and ecology", *Journal of Ecumenical Studies* 37(4) (2000): 285-300.

9 Njangi farming is a group farming system where the group comes together and decide to work on a particular woman's farm, and this keeps rotating until they complete all the farms.

women farmers; 35 Muslims and 70 Christians make up the three groups. Only 70 women participated in the study (45 Christians and 25 Muslims), due to the displacement caused by the Anglophone crisis. Fifteen women were sought out for qualitative data, using interviews as a tool, 55 women for quantitative data, using questionnaires as an instrument. 50 out of the 55 questionnaires were returned giving a responsive rate of 95%.

The case study employed a mixed-method approach, where both qualitative and quantitative data were collected. The non-probability sampling technique was employed since the study targeted the specific members of these interreligious women farmers groups. The triangulation method of data collection ensured that qualitative data was collected from a particular group of 15 key informants, and quantitative data was collected from the remaining 55 women. The embedding model of data analysis where quantitative data was supported by qualitative data was employed, using descriptive and inferential statistics, and generating themes that were categorised in domains. The study set out to find out:

1. Farmer's knowledge of climate change, and manifestations of climate change;
2. Reasons for constituting interreligious women farmers groups;
3. The group's model in mitigating climate change.

The role of women in agriculture is phenomenal, as stated by the UN Food and Agricultural Organization (UNFAO): "women comprise an average of 43 percent of the agricultural labour force of developing countries [...] Women in sub-Saharan Africa have relatively high overall labour-force participation rates and the highest average agricultural labour-force participation rates in the world."[10] Cameroon, like most countries in sub-Saharan Africa, agriculture is truly important, and women especially in the Muyuka area are predominantly farmers of cocoyam, cassava, yam, plantain, watermelon, egusi, groundnut, and cocoa. Molua notes that about 80% of Cameroon's poor people live in rural areas, and are primarily engaged in agriculture. Agriculture contributes to about 35% of Cameroon's GDP, with agriculture accounting for 70% of the national labour force.[11]

Climate Change and its Manifestation

	Women from the 3 groups (50)	
Options	**Frequency**	**Percentage (%)**
Climate Change		
Prolong dry seasons	50	100
Heavy rainfall	50	100
Strong winds	32	62
Dry water sources	40	90
New pests	38	76
Floods	48	96
Landslides	41	82

Table 1: Climate Change Manifestations, Source: Field Data, April 2021

There is 100% agreement on a change of weather pattern, with prolonged dry seasons and heavier rainfall. This is followed by floods, dry water sources, and pests as indicated by the Christian and Muslim

[10] UNFAO, "The State of Food and Agriculture: Women in Agriculture Closing the Gender Gap for Development," 2010-2011 United Nations Report (Rome: Food and Agriculture Organization of the United Nations, 2011). [Available at: http://www.fao.org/3/i2050e/i2050e.pdf], [Last accessed: 8th March 2022].

[11] Ernest Molua, "Farm income, gender differentials and climate risk in Cameroon: Typology of male and female adaptation options across agroecologies", *Sustainability Science* 6(1) (2011): 21-35.

women from each of the 3 groups. The interviews with the 15 key informants validate the above findings with reoccurring themes:

- Climate change is a bad thing;
- Human beings have not taken good care of the environment given to them by God;
- Climate change is responsible for poor harvest;
- God is not happy with what people have done to the environment;
- People have to change their behaviours toward the environment.

One of the women noted, "The climate has changed, we have been told even in church and by some NGOs that our farming practices, and other things that some people do, have made the climate to change [*sic*] and God is not happy with humanity."[12]

The interviews establish that the women have an understanding of climate change. Most importantly, the concepts of stewardship and ethical responsibility toward the environment have been highlighted and linked to religiosity. God is not happy, and therefore people have to change their behaviours towards the environment. This, in my opinion, justifies the indispensability of religion in addressing climate change.

Why Interreligious Women Farmer's Groups

15 women: 5 from each group were interviewed to understand the reasons for establishing the groups. Frequent themes are:

- Christian and Muslim women have been meeting in community meetings, school meetings, and markets;
- The majority of farmers are women;
- A majority of the population in the three communities are women;
- The challenge of poor agricultural harvest require concerted efforts;
- Activities to prevent climate change require the effort of everyone;
- When Christians and Muslims are involved in any activity in the community, they influence others to join.

The majority of women are farmers with knowledge about climate change and environmental care from non-governmental organisations and religious institutions. Although a majority of the women are Christian, they acknowledge the significance of bringing Muslim women on board, to influence a bigger population, and have everyone involved. Most importantly, the formation of the group was possible first because the women had a relationship, where they met in community meetings and markets.

There was first an informal relationship between the women. This is vital as it underpins my thesis on the interreligious approach to climate change mitigation. Here, I will make a proposition to Knitter's first step to ecological interreligious dialogue, where he argues that "dialogue begins with a shared feeling and suffering with those who are suffering."[13] In my opinion, "A man cannot cover a snake with an umbrella simply because they are both being rained on."[14]

For sustainable interreligious climate change mitigation, there must be an informal relationship existing among religious people. This will help identify the common need, which will then bring them together to dialogue, and finally put dialogue into eco-diapraxis. If there is no informal relationship and religious people live in scepticism and fear of the other, a dialogue will be initiated by other people, and even if they

---

[12] Interview with one of the women, 2nd April 2021.

[13] Paul Knitter, "Pitfalls and Promises for a Global Ethics", 221-229.

[14] A man and a snake have no formal or informal relationships. The barriers and fright that exist between the man and the snake, make it difficult for them to acknowledge a common problem. They will prefer to resolve the crisis individually, even when it requires united efforts.

are invited to dialogue, the dialogue will end as a theoretical concept and maybe "*politicalisation*" as Knitter noted.

Mitigating Climate Change

Options	Yes	
	Frequency	**Percentage (%)**
Mitigation		
Cleaning of water catchments and streams	50	100
Planting of trees	50	100
Use more compost manure	50	100

Table 2: mitigating climate change. Source: Field Data, May 2021

Options	Yes	
	Frequency	**Percentage (%)**
Adaptation		
Replace planting	50	100
Pesticides	50	100
Fertilisers	50	100

Table 3: climate change adaptation. Source: Field Data, May 2021

Quantitative data collected on mitigation strategies indicates both mitigation and adaptation interventions. This implies that women are involved in practical activities such as cleaning water catchments, planting trees, and using more manure and, according to them, this approach has been copied by other farmers in the community. As much as the women put in place mitigation strategies, they still have to include adaptation mechanisms such as using fertilisers and pesticides which sometimes, if overused, can also affect the ecosystem. These findings find credence in Nangia's report that women farmers in Muyuka, although with little education and resource, are on the front-line mitigating climate change, using local techniques.[15]

Contextual Analysis: Interreligious Women Farmer's Model

The old method of felling trees and burning weeds with fire to prepare the farm for planting continued to destroy the fertility of the soil, and also affected the water sources. This made the farmers employ shifting cultivation, which continued to exploit the forest. Over seven to eight years before the Muyuka area was engulfed by the Anglophone crisis, the model of the interreligious women farmers groups has changed this practice.

Instead of using fire to burn trees and weeds, weeds are put together to discompose and used as manure, which has also reduced the use of chemical fertilisers. Trees are being planted around the periphery of the farms and used as boundary demarcations. This model has been copied by other farmers and has yielded positive results. The water catchments are live again, and the Muyuka forest is gradually returning to its

[15] Ethel Nangia, "Gender Dynamics in Climate Change Mitigating Mechanisms and Outcome: Evidence from Women Farmers in Muyuka, Cameroon", *Greener Journal of Sciences* 8(4) (2018): 56-65.

lost glory. This was possible not because they are women, but more of the interreligious composition of the groups and activities.

Looking at this model takes me back to Hans Kung's view that a global ethic towards the environment should consider religion. More so, the fear of segregation, generalisation, and politicisation of interreligious dialogue projected by Knitter, in my opinion, requires some level of contextualisation as far as the concept of global ethics is concerned. Although the women were influenced by their religious convictions to care for the environment, their practical activities were not prescribed by any particular religious tradition. They planted trees together, not necessarily using a particular Christian or Muslim approach to tree planting.

Interestingly, the model strengthens interreligious relations. The women, through their "Njangi farming", eat, work and have fun together. Sometimes, other family members, children, and spouses join in this activity, thereby building a huge interreligious farmer's community. The women, alongside their families and communities, have moved from informal inter-religious relations to formal inter-religious relations. This model is a complete circle.

- Without an informal relationship between people of different religious groups, there will be no identification of a common problem;
- Without a common identification of the problem by the people, interreligious eco-dialogue will be politicised;
- A common identification of the problem by the people will lead to substantive interreligious eco-dialogue initiated by the people;
- With an effective eco-interreligious dialogue, there will be interreligious eco-diapraxis leading to a comprehensive approach to climate change mitigation;
- With sustainable interreligious climate change mitigation initiatives, interreligious relations are strengthened.

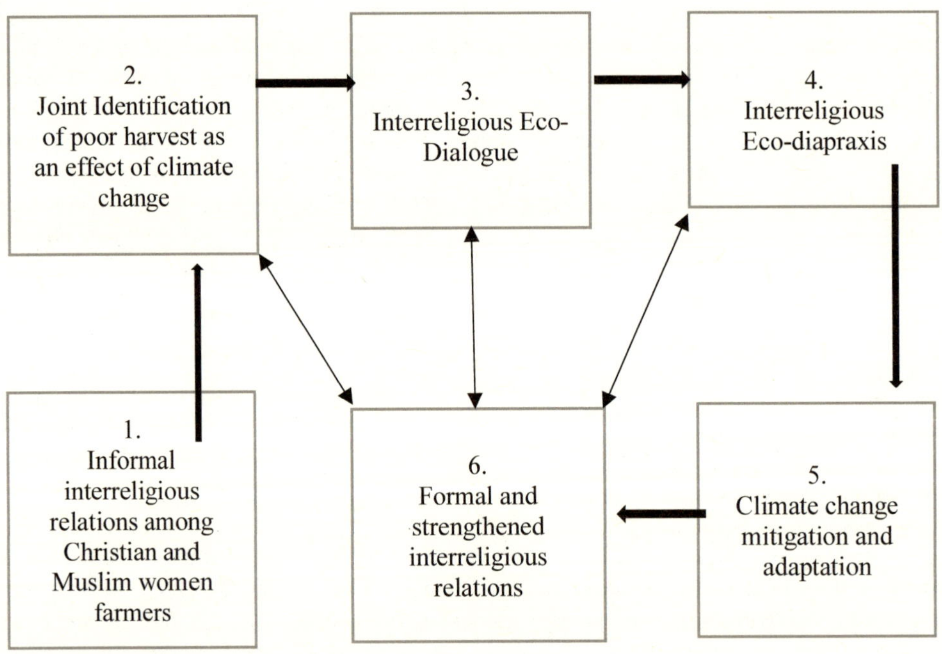

Figure 1: Diagrammatical Presentation of the Model. Source: Field Data, May 2021.

Conclusion

Interreligious eco-diapraxis has proven to be very effective. The practical initiatives are not in any way considered to be Christian- or Muslim-only efforts and, as such, are appealing and influence people around to join and practice the same farming methods. The actions of the women have been influenced by their knowledge of climate change, but most importantly, by their religious convictions of being stewards of the environment, with ethical responsibility. Interreligious eco-diapraxis should not begin with any dialogue. Building informal interreligious relationships, coupled with knowledge about climate change and the religious ethical responsibility towards the environment, will lead to the identification of climate change as a common concern, after which dialogue and diapraxis will follow. We need a conscious collaboration with the religious other in the Global South for effective and sustainable interreligious eco-diapraxis towards climate change mitigation.

Suggestions for Further Reading

Knitter, Paul. "A Common Creation Story? Interreligious Dialogue and Ecology". *Journal of Ecumenical Studies* 37(4) (2000): 285-300.

—. "Pitfalls and Promises for a Global Ethics". *Buddhist-Christian Studies* 15 (1995): 221-29.

Molua, Ernest. "Farm Income, Gender Differentials and Climate Risk in Cameroon: Typology of Male and Female Adaptation Options Across Agroecologies". *Sustainability Science* 6(1) (2011): 21-35.

Nangia, Ethel. "Gender Dynamics in Climate Change Mitigating Mechanisms and Outcome: Evidence from Women Farmers in Muyuka, Cameroon". *Greener Journal of Sciences* 8(4) (2018): 56-65.

NRDC, "The Paris Agreement on Climate Change" Issue Brief, Natural Resources Defense Council, November 2017. [Available at: https://assets.nrdc.org/sites/default/files/paris-agreement-climate-change-2017-ib.pdf], [Last accessed: 8th March 2022].

Parliament of the World's Religions. *Toward a Global Ethic: An Initial Declaration of the Parliament of the World's Religions.* Chicago, IL: Council for a Parliament of the World's Religions, 1993. [Available at: https://parliamentofreligions.org/towards-global-ethic-initial-declaration], [Last accessed: 8th March 2022].

Posas, Paula. "Roles of religion and ethics in addressing Climate Change". *Ethics in Science and Environmental Politics* 8 (2007): 31-49.

Ssebunya, Margaret and Beatrice Okyere-Manu. "Moral Responsibility and Environmental Conservation in Karamoja Mining Area: Towards a Religious Engagement". *Journal for the Study of Religion* 30(2) (2017): 90-104.

Tucker, Mary Evelyn and John Grim. "Introduction: The Emerging Alliance of World Religions and Ecology". *Journal of American Academy of Art and Sciences* 130(4) (Fall 2001): 1-22.

United Nations Climate Change. *Climate action and support trends.* Bonn, Germany: UN Climate Change Secretariat, 2019. [Available at: https://unfccc.int/sites/default/files/resource/Climate_Action_Support_Trends_2019.pdf], [Last accessed: 8th March 2022].

UNFAO. "The State of Food and Agriculture: Women in Agriculture Closing the Gender Gap for Development". 2010-2011 United Nations Report. Rome: Food and Agriculture Organization of the United Nations, 2011. [Available at: http://www.fao.org/3/i2050e/i2050e.pdf], [Last accessed: 8th March 2022].

100. LEARNINGS OF UEM-CHURCHES IN ECO-DIAKONIA COMMITMENT IN CENTRAL AND EASTERN AFRICA

Kambale Jean-Bosco Kahongya Bwiruka[1]

Introduction

In a recent article on youth environmental consciousness in Central Africa,[2] I highlighted that Africa as a continent is very diverse both in climate change experience and in the church initiatives to protect the environment. Countries in direct contact with well-known desert zones (Sahara in the middle north and Kalahari in the middle south) may have different experiences and actions as compared to countries (especially in Central Africa), where for a long time people were believed to be quite far from the danger of drought. When our geography teacher told us in 1984 that the Sahara Desert was progressing 3-4 centimetres towards the South every day, I was only 17 years old. I then said to myself "it will take centuries to reach our country, the Democratic Republic of Congo". But only 37 years later, things have changed a lot. We are now facing the huge impact of the climate change, and desertification is progressing significantly, if nothing very serious is done to prevent it.

In this regard, it is very important to look at what different actors, especially faith-based organisations like the churches, are doing to decelerate the rapid progress of global warming. It is relevant to understand whether the commitment of churches in environmental protection is regarded as an integral part of Christian identity or more or less just seen as part of general development work, and to see what the challenges might be faced.

More specifically, this article is based on the region of Central and Eastern Africa, where the United Evangelical Mission (UEM) has member churches in Rwanda, Democratic Republic of Congo, Tanzania and Cameroon. Being members of the same international organisation, these churches take part in joint environmental programmes that make them share the same realities although in different contexts.

Environmental Protection as Development Activity

Here the question is to understand the reference framework to which Christians are related when engaging in environmental activities. Is it their faith of serving God in protecting His creation or just economic reasons or is the commitment simply motivated by a more ecological consciousness?

In the abovementioned article, I stated that the youth environmental involvement in central Africa cannot be directly and primarily connected to their Christian conviction, even if some biblical and theological references may be given for their actions. Rather, environmental commitments of the youth are driven by various forces including the local or national environmental policies or the daily challenges in their lives. However, church leaders play a distinct and crucial role in mentoring the youth and empowering them in the environmental sector.[3] This reality may be observed by other Christian churches as well.

---

[1] Professor Rev. Dr Kambale J.-B. Kahongya Bwiruka (Democratic Republic of Congo) is an ordained pastor in the Baptist Church in Central Africa (CBCA), PhD in Intercultural Theology and Missiology at the Kirchliche Hochschule Wuppertal/Bethel in Germany, professor and UEM-Advocacy Officer for Africa Region.

[2] Kambale J.-B. Kahongya Bwiruka, "Environmental Commitment of Youth in Central Africa: Fact of faith or desire to participate in development program?" March 2021.

[3] Kahongya Bwiruka, "Environmental Commitment of Youth".

In fact, for many Christians in the region, protecting the environment has been regarded as being part of development programmes and projects. These activities are mostly inspired by governments, although sometimes motivated and rooted in the local practices and traditions like the protection of particular areas and species or farming principles according to seasons et cetera. Perceived in this way, Christians have not deeply integrated environmental protection as a spiritual task and responsibility towards divine creation. The consciousness that this task is "service to God" in a way which also worshipping him is part of the spiritual task for Christians, and is not yet internalised by many. Only a few Christians engage in such activities so as to contribute to carbon emission reduction and to mitigate the high trend of global warming with a spiritual and deeply Christian awareness.

For these reasons, the UEM has integrated the protection of the integrity of the creation in its corporate ecclesial and spiritual identity. It is stated as follows:

> "We believe that human beings are created in the image of God and therefore have inalienable dignity and rights. Therefore, we promote and defend human rights; we support initiatives to solve conflict peacefully; we join efforts to achieve just economic conditions and good governance; and we strive for the protection of the environment."[4]

In this regard, UEM member churches are invited through the pillar of advocacy to develop Eco-Diakonia by mainstreaming it in a way so that all kinds of programmes are promoting environmental protection. These programmes aim to restore and maintain the good quality of the creation (earth, water, air, animals, climate cycle, etc.) so that all inhabitants – human as well as nonhumans – live in a state of welfare and integral health of creation. Such programmes, which have a very high ecological impact, are also theologically motivated. Engaging in environmental protection is "serving God" in His task of taking care of His creation, maintaining it and to assume the human privilege of being created in God's likeness (Gen. 1).

In this regard, churches engage and raise awareness in focusing on various aspects of environmental protection like reduction of carbon emission, climate justice, renewable energy promotion, climate spirituality and ecotheology.

The Nature of Environmental Programmes within African UEM-Churches

The question at stake here is about the different kinds of challenges churches are facing to develop their own Eco-Diakonia concept. Are the concepts similar even in their differing contexts? What contributes to the regional choices of one or the other approach? In observing the UEM-member churches in their environmental commitment, it is obvious that the priorities are not the same in all churches, however it is possible to identify major actions in the four different sectors: reduction of carbon emissions, promotion of renewable energy, climate justice, and development of ecotheology.

1. Reduction of Carbon Dioxide Emissions:

a. Production and use of improved cooking stoves

This programme aims to reduce the pressure on the existing forests which are constantly harvested for firewood. The Anglican Church in Rwanda (EAR) has developed a professional model of stoves in

[4] UEM, "UEM Statement on Corporate Identity", *United Evangelical Mission Community of Churches in three continents* [Available at: https://www.vemission.org/fileadmin/redakteure/Dokumente/Corporate%20Identity.pdf], [Last accessed: 28th February 2022].

Shyogwe and has even integrated the programme of carbon credits. Based on this experience, the Baptist Church in DR Congo (CBCA) has also developed, with women, an alternative format of improved cooking stoves for local use, and the Evangelical Lutheran Church in Tanzania, Diocese of Karagwe is working towards similar projects. The main common characteristics of these improved stoves is to use much less wood in the cooking process.

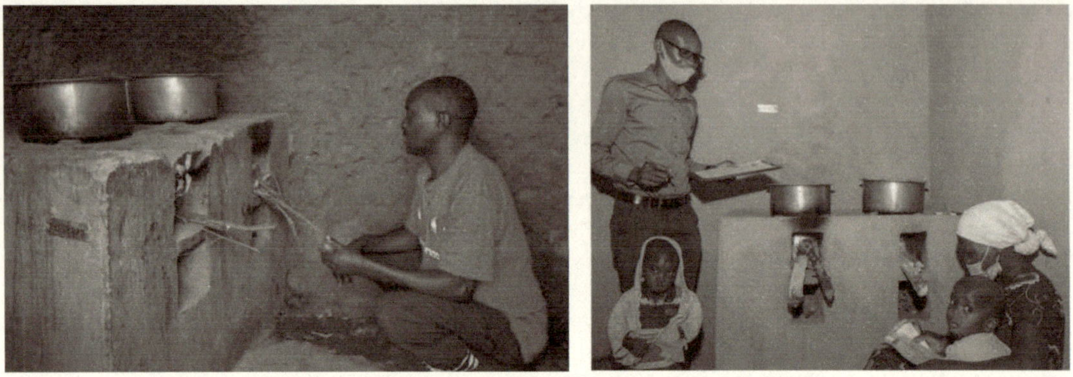

Figure 1: Photos from IRDIS Shyogwe Rwanda 2021

b. Planting Trees and Promoting Agroforestry

All UEM member churches are deeply involved in this programme, sometimes with amazing and creative concepts. For example, the ELCT-Eastern Coastal Diocese has developed an initiative called *"My tree, my mark, let's take care of environmental change"*. In this concept, Bishop Alex Malasusa has already planted a multitude of trees in the Kibiti region, and he intends to engage youth to learn to plant more. Therefore, he has given 800 acres of land to the youth desk. The land is located in the Southern part of Tanzania, in Ruvuma Region-Madaba. The aim is to set strategies to involve more youth and other congregants to renew the forest ecosystem.

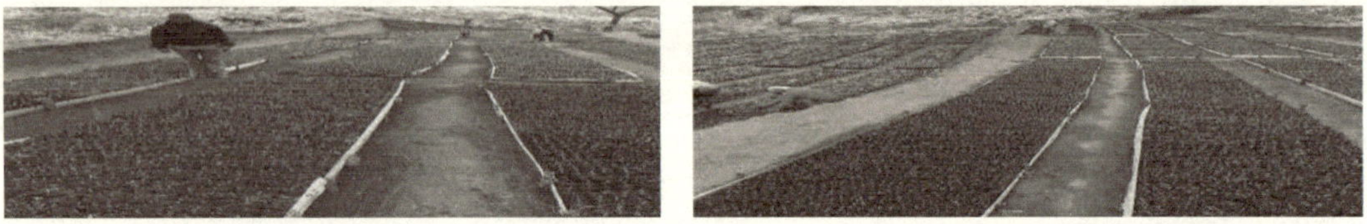

Figure 2: Photos from Onesmo Mdende ELCT-ECD Dar es Salaam-Tanzania

When visiting churches like ELCT-Karagwe, North Western Diocese, the Baptist church in Congo (CBCA), the Disciples Church in Mbandaka (CDCC) and the CADELU in Basankusu DR Congo, it becomes obvious that several churches have become highly engaged in planting many trees on the church grounds. If the first reason might be to protect church grounds from imminent land grabbing, at the same time it contributes to reduce the carbon emissions and encourages other people to invest in planting trees even if only for economic reasons.

2. Climate Justice

The UEM is very concerned with the working conditions in the processes of textile production in Africa as well as Asia. In this regard, churches are encouraged to promote organic cotton farming. A pilot project has been initiated since 2018 in the district of Busega-Tanzania, now extended to the District of Missenyi on the border with Uganda by the ELCT-North Western Diocese. Today, 500 farmers are benefiting from the advantages of organic cotton farming and more others are expected to join in the near future. The product doesn't use dangerous chemicals, neither in fertilising the soil nor in protecting the crops as pesticides. All products are made by the farmers themselves. Therefore, the soil is no longer poisoned and the health of the farmers is protected. On top of this, economic advantages of organic cotton are high comparing to the conventional cotton.

Figure 3: Photos from ELCT-NWD 2020

3. Renewable Energy

a. Biogas system in Tanzania and Democratic Republic of Congo

African Churches are developing different strategies to mitigate against the negative impacts of global warming. In Tanzania, the ELCT-North and Western Diocese has facilitated the installation of biogas systems for the organic cotton farmers in Busega to avoid the use of remaining cotton trees as firewood, which may contribute to the mutation of some pests when moving from one field to another. Also, biogas enables farmers to produce organic manure for their farms and reduce human pressure on the remaining forest in the region.

Similar systems have been installed by the Baptist Church (CBCA) in North-Kivu province, the church district of Kitsimba and Vayana in the Democratic Republic of Congo. Until the 1980s, that region was very fertile and produced vegetables, corn, maize, et cetera. But today, due to the demographic growth, the soil has become very poor, consequently leading to permanent socio-conflicts. Biogas is a way the church nourishes the soil, increases local food production and, at the same time, builds peace among communities.

Figure 4: Inauguration of the Biogas Systems in CBCA Vayana District and ELCT-NWD Busega 2021

b. Solar panel system

Solar panel systems are another model being developed in the region. Churches in Rwanda, Tanzania and DR Congo facilitate families to get suitable solar panel systems for domestic use, through different local and international solidarity initiatives.

4. Awareness Raising on Climate Issues

The biggest responsibility of the church on climate issues is to raise proper awareness among people about the quick global warming processes and the ways every person can contribute individually and collectively to mitigate the trend. One of the reasons for awareness-building is that sometimes the natural disasters caused by climate change are culturally interpreted as attributed to the power of evil spirits. Despite Christianity and modernity, some people still refer to traditional perceptions whenever they cannot find a direct explanation to a particular phenomenon.

In a recent article in the "*Westfalen Welt Weit*" Journal 2020,[5] I wrote about the cultural shock due to climate change in Central Africa, describing how people's lifestyles are changing. I also mentioned some beliefs associating natural calamities (floods, earthquakes, landslides, vast erosion, drying of rivers, etc.) with mysterious forces. I illustrated this with an experience I had in 2013 when I travelled with my three children from the city of Kampala in Uganda to the city of Beni in the Democratic Republic of Congo.

I hired a taxi from the Congolese border of Kasindi to Beni city for 77km. It was very hot. When we arrived at a place called Bulongo, the driver warned me to be very careful because the road could be suddenly cut by a mysterious river, which only appears under the blazing sun and makes cars sink. I then asked the driver where the Ruwenzori Mountain[6] was. He told me that it is on the right side of the road. I quickly realised that the so-called mysterious river was the water created by melting ice on the Mountain. When I explained this to him, he was amazed and understood that there were no mysterious invisible forces behind the river. Such misinterpretations are many in the region whenever a natural disaster occurs, which in reality is caused by climate change. That is why the church has a huge role for interpreting and explaining not only the causes and the impact of climate change on the entire planet, but also the human responsibility to protect and to restore creation.

For this reason, UEM church members are carrying out climate change awareness programmes to children, youth and adults in different ways and through various concepts:

1. The first concept is called "growing with my tree". This is a programme developed in Sunday schools and primary schools. It consists of initiating children and pupils to plant trees on the church compound or school ground and taking care of them the whole time of their schooling. The aim is to develop an environmental sense of responsibility in the children's mind.
2. The second concept is "my anniversary – my tree". Through this initiative, young people in the Evangelical Lutheran Church in Tanzania, Diocese of Karagwe have committed themselves to plant at least five trees each celebrating their anniversary. In the long run, Karagwe and the whole Kagera region will recover the green vegetation it once had.
3. The third concept is "the campaign against plastic". This campaign consists of transforming plastic waste. Old plastic items are used in netting baskets, producing artworks, flowerpots, and bricks for pavements. These activities are carried out mostly by youth and women groups.
4. The fourth concept is the "Youth Climate Action Day" which is celebrated every year. Under this concept, the UEM church members take part in the international celebration of the environmental day, especially through youth and children's activities. Different environmental initiatives are carried out like seminars, conferences, games, tree-planting, collecting and managing waste, etc. The programme receives small financial support from the UEM-Advocacy desk.

---

[5] Kambale Jean-Bosco Kahongya Bwiruka, "Kulturschock durch Klimawandel: Afrikanische Kirchen und der neue Lebensstil", *Westfalen Welt Weit. Nachrichten aus Mission, Ökumene und kirchlicher Weltverantwortung*, Jahrung 10 (2020), Evangelische Kirche von Westfalen, 14-15.

[6] In central and southern Africa, there are two high mountains, Kilimanjaro in Tanzania (5895m) and Mount Ruwenzori in DR Congo (5109 m). At the top of each of these mountains is a glacier which makes them a touristic attraction. Today, this ice is melting at breakneck speed.

These different environmental initiatives would be even more effective if they were integrated within the individuals as well as the collective spiritual life of the church as part of their Christian identity, which would amount to a deeper theological internalisation of eco-diakonia. But it seems that the journey towards ecotheology as well as eco-diakonia is still long for some churches in general and for Christians in particular.

Figure 5: Youth CBCA-Growing with my tree; Afforestation in ELCT-NED; Youth Climate Action Day ELCT-ECD 2020-2021.

Eco-Diakonia Understanding and Christian Belief

Thinking about Christian considerations for the care for creation in Central and Eastern Africa requires a clarification in the understanding of the concepts eco-diakonia and ecotheology.

In short, ecotheology is a form of constructive theology that focuses on the interrelationships of religion and nature, particularly in the light of environmental concerns. It starts from the acknowledgment that there is an intimate connection between Christian's faith in God as Creator, and how Christians treat the rest of the Creation.

Eco-diakonia on the other hand considers the commitment to care for the creation as "service" to God, in the sense of a spiritual responsibility. Therefore, "serving God" in the sense of worshiping him is not far away from "serving the creation or taking care of God's creation". In other words, caring for the creation is also worshiping God the creator. In this regard, eco-diakonia can be consider as part of ecotheology.

In my contribution on the book *Kairos for the Creation*, I focused on the reasons why ecotheology has been delayed, to a certain extent, in being embodied in African Christianity. The reasons for this delay are also valid to explain why many Christians do not associate eco-diakonia or caring for the creation immediately with their spiritual responsibility. My observation is that ecotheology was negatively affected or delayed by some theological interpretations, methodological choices and lack of cultural integration processes in the earlier history of Christianity in this region.[7]

The Dominance of Individualistic Soteriological and Eschatological Interpretations of Christian Faith in the Earlier Kerygmatic Communication of the Gospel

This traditional way of communicating the Gospel sets a kind of separation between humans and the rest of the creation, whereby human beings were presented to be the most important creature involved in salvation and in the Parousia. The individual human salvation used to be proclaimed without much interlinkage to the salvation of the entire creation. Ecotheology traditionally was therefore not prioritised and was even sometimes contradicted by the frequent references to eschatology. The widened theological understanding of "global salvation" (which involves *each person, the whole person and the whole creation*) is a very late theological development in African Christianity. It is still not yet well elaborated. The creation was often presented as only useful and designed for human welfare, not as a divine project of which the creator was proud in itself.[8] In such a world conception, humanity tends to consider nature as its property only and can harvest its products for their own consumption, own good, and own salvation without end. Some Christians today believe that considering the care for the creation as service to God appears like idolatry, which is not the reality, because the honour and glory is given to the creator and not to the creation.

This notion of human salvation has often been associated or narrowed down by a certain *eschatological orientation* of the Gospel, which led to a negative impact on the perception of nature. It is often stated that the present world, which is corrupt, will perish. Some believe then that Christians will live forever in the world to come, and will be rescued into an eternal and paradisiac world. As a consequence, an attitude spreads which is mirrored in the question: why should believers care too much for a homeland that does not belong to them? They are just foreigners and travellers on earth,[9] just passing through, with eyes fixed on the eternal city that God has prepared for them.[10] With such an attitude, some Christians think that

---

[7] Kambale J.-B. Kahongya Bwiruka, "Eco-Theology in an African Perspective: Why the Delay to Embody Eco-Theology in African Christianity?" In Louk Andrianos, Michael Biel *et al.* (eds) *Kairos for the Creation: Confessing Hope for the Earth* (Solingen: Foedus-verlag, 2019): 121-131.

[8] Genesis 1:29-30.

[9] 1 Peter 2:11; Hebrew 11:13-15.

[10] Andrew R. Mukaria, "Theological Ambiguity: A Challenge to a Constructive Ecotheology in Africa", *International Journal of Current Research* 5(5) (May 2013): 1255-1261. [Available at:

"human beings have no responsibility in what is happening today in their environment". Even the degradation of the environment may be attributed to the "will of God" or in Kiswahili language, "*Mapenzi ya Mungu*", to a divine order, where only God is in control and human beings have nothing to do.[11]

Discourses of Ecotheology Being Kept to Higher Spheres of Society and Church Leadership Instead of Relating to Grass Roots

One of the weaknesses is that methodologically some approaches used to advocate for environmental protection kept the discourse of ecotheology only in the higher sphere of the society and church organisations. Ecotheology has for a long time been a discourse in high leadership spheres of the church, but not sufficient energy was invested to reach African Christianity at the grassroots level. Likewise, many initiatives are on academic levels, even by governments. Most of these important projects and working processes are not sufficiently transmitted to the rest of society nor have the capacity to meet people in their daily lives and activities. All these initiatives and related knowledge systems will bear fruits only when they are fully and organically integrated into the daily church liturgy, through the hymn book, the songs of choirs, the daily prayers, and the preaching of the church.

Cultural Integration of African Wisdom

Early Missionary Christianity has traditionally rejected African wisdom, traditions and practices and labelled them as "paganism". This swift and general judgement has led to an avoidance of referring to African wisdom traditions even when they could enrich the understanding of the interconnectivity between humanity and nature.

There is a need of new reading of the biblical texts in association of better valorisation of some African cultural values related to the traditional strategies of keeping harmony on earth.[12] This connectivity can speed up the collective awareness on environmental protection. In African Wisdom, the concept of *bondedness of life* is crucial. It is based on the consciousness that all creatures are part of all others, that humans share a common destiny with nature.[13] The human and nonhuman beings, visible and non-visible world are connected. God, who is invisible, becomes visible in and behind objects and phenomena which symbolise or are the manifestation of the invisible world.[14] That's why African religion has erected the system of totem and taboos. A totem is any species of animal (in most of the cases), which is perceived to

---

https://www.academia.edu/3462529/Theological_ambiguities_A_challenge_to_a_constructive_ecotheology_in_Africa], [Last accessed: 1st March 2022].

[11] Mukaria, "Theological Ambiguity".

[12] The apostle Paul links the fall of human beings with the suffering of the whole creation. Therefore, the creation itself is waiting for salvation (Rom. 8:19-23). For the apostle, there is not individual human salvation without general salvation of the nature, since the human fall has dragged the whole creation into the fall. A second text which can be mentioned is the salvation of the biblical city of Nineveh motivated not only by the big number of people unable to distinguish their right hand from their left, but also because of the multitude of animals in the city (Jonas 4:11).

[13] Harvey Sindima, "Community of Life: Ecological Theology in African Perspective", *Religion Online.* 1990 [Available at: https://www.religion-online.org/article/community-of-life-ecological-theology-in-african-perspective], [Last accessed: 1st March 2022]. See also Charles Birch, William Eaken and Jay B. McDaniel (eds) *Liberating Life: Contemporary Approaches in Ecological Theology* (Maryknoll, NY: Orbis, 1990): 137-147.

[14] John S. Mbiti, *African Religions & Philosophy* (Nairobi: East African Educational Publishers, 2015): 55-56.

have a special relationship with a given clan. A totem is believed to have the responsibility of protecting the clan. But the obligation is mutual: as the totem cannot harm its tutelaries, the members of the clan must also not kill or harm it in any way.[15] In ecotheological perception, I would consider and interpret this in a way that the system of totem connects the human and the nonhuman in a mutual respect, acceptance and protection. This contributes to protect biodiversity. For example, in my village, I have to protect the wagtail (Bergeronnette), sparrows (Moineaux), dogs and gorillas, which belong directly to the totems of my two parents. But also, I have to respect the totems of other families in the village. Therefore, a variety of birds and mammals can live safely through mutual protection. The African Christianity still can refer to such systems, not as a totem, but as wisdom traditions which have the function of setting limits to human consumption and developing a new connection to nature which unfortunately is otherwise disappearing.

Ecological Challenges of the Church to the Economic Paradigm

Most of the time, local initiatives of environmental protection are challenged by capitalist international companies.

It is important to understand that when the vast majority of local people in Africa think of protecting the environment, their first concern is to save their village, their harvest, the river where they fetch water, their livestock, and all that relates directly to their well-being. The immense challenge they face, however, is that the whole damage of global warming goes much beyond their regional limited concerns and therefore also beyond their local contribution and impact. In this way, the local efforts for environmental protection seems not to be effective alone to change the warming trends.

In fact, what discourages people on the local levels is to see how big companies, especially from America, Canada, European and Asian countries, use their political power and financial influences to get large spaces and resources for exploitation from the African poor and easily corruptible governments. They destroy the remaining forests that the local people have been protecting. Thus, many local people do not see the point in trying to reverse the trend of climate change by planting just one or some hundred trees a year, while large areas of the forests they have been protecting are being devastated by much more powerful and sophisticated machinery.

I therefore believe that considering care for the creation as part of Christian life needs to move beyond individual or corporate actions of environmental protection. Churches also need to move beyond and to challenge the very economic paradigm which is at work in order to move from an overexploitation model to an ecological economy, which can protect local people and also their efforts for protecting the environment.

Conclusion

Christian organisations, especially churches in Central and East Africa, are genuinely committed to environmental protection. They have taken various initiatives, often responding to immediate economic, ecological or structural challenges. These initiatives can focus for example on protecting of land or fertilising arid spaces, on transforming plastic items and developing proper garbage systems. Other initiatives are geared towards the development of basic energy infrastructure such as the installation of solar panels and biogas systems. All these initiatives taken together provide a valid contribution to the goal of reducing the effects of global warming.

However, the spiritual component of this commitment is not yet sufficiently developed for many believers. We are convinced, however, that there are sufficient both biblical and theological reasons to

---

[15] Laurenti Magesa, *African Religion. The Moral Traditions of Abundant Life.* (Nairobi: Pauline Publications Africa, 2011): 74-75.

serve as a foundation for this Christian activity. In fact, the conviction needs to be widely circulated that the protection of creation is a service rendered to God. This service is not different from worshiping or praising God. Therefore, there is also an ecotheological and ecoliturgical work which needs to be intensified by pastors and theologians, to explain to Christians the close link between worshipping God in the church and serving God by working the fields, cleaning the waters, protecting natural reserves, reducing toxic waste, in short, by practicing eco-diakonia.

For these reasons, the church should help society to abandon the economy based on the overexploitation of resources, and to integrate the new paradigm of an ecological economics which gives space and sets certain limits in order to protect our earth. Human beings were not created to exhaust the earth, but to collect from it what they need to live, and leave the rest for other creatures, even for the earth to nourish and renew itself.

Suggestions for Further Reading

Kahongya Bwiruka, Kambale J.-B. "Environmental Commitment of Youth in Central Africa: Fact of faith or desire to participate in development program?" March 2021.

—. "Kulturschock durch Klimawandel: Afrikanische Kirchen und der neue Lebensstil". *Westfalen Welt Weit. Nachrichten aus Mission, Ökumene und kirchlicher Weltverantwortung* Jahrung 10 (2020), Evangelische Kirche von Westfalen, 14-15.

—. "Eco-Theology in an African Perspective: Why the Delay to Embody Eco-Theology in African Christianity?" In Louk Andrianos, Michael Biel *et al.* Eds. *Kairos for the Creation: Confessing Hope for the Earth.* Solingen: Foedus-verlag, 2019. 121-131.

Magesa, Laurenti. *African Religion. The Moral Traditions of Abundant Life.* Nairobi: Pauline Publications Africa, 2011. 74-75.

Mbiti, John S. *African Religions & Philosophy.* Nairobi: East African Educational Publishers, 2015. 55-56.

Mukaria, Andrew R. "Theological Ambiguity: A Challenge to a Constructive Ecotheology in Africa". *International Journal of Current Research* 5(5) (May 2013): 1255-1261. [Available at: https://www.academia.edu/3462529/Theological_ambiguities_A_challenge_to_a_constructive_ecotheology_in_Africa], [Last accessed: 1st March 2022].

Sindima, Harvey. "Community of Life: Ecological Theology in African Perspective", *Religion Online.* 1990 [Available at: https://www.religion-online.org/article/community-of-life-ecological-theology-in-african-perspective], [Last accessed: 1st March 2022].

UEM. "UEM Statement on Corporate Identity". *United Evangelical Mission Community of Churches in three continents* [Available at: https://www.vemission.org/fileadmin/redakteure/Dokumente/Corporate%20Identity.pdf], [Last accessed: 28th February 2022].

101. Envisioning an African Life-Sustaining Eco-Ethics for Earth Keeping in the Context of Climate Change

Gabriel Ezekia Nduye[1]

Introduction

This contribution presents ways in which a life-sustaining eco-ethics can enhance earth keeping. In African contexts, such eco-ethics have to be based on notions of responsibility and care as it is a divine given vocation for entire humanity. Therefore, the first part of this paper will give a brief description of climate change before exploring principles for earth keeping as a way to protect life. Perspectives for an African life-sustaining eco-ethics and a proposed framework for eco-ethics then will be outlined. This will be followed by some case study examples.

Climate Change: An Anthropogenic Phenomenon with Moral Implications

Since the Intergovernmental Panel for Climate Change (IPCC) was formed in the 1980s, the gravity of the global climate crisis has continued to increase.[2] After studying climate trends, it became clear that climate change is the direct result of the production and consumption of fossil fuels as this produces carbon dioxide, methane and nitrous oxide which are all greenhouse gases. It is leading to diverse impacts on various areas of life. Ethical and moral aspects are embedded in the climate change phenomenon and challenge how humankind relates to nonhuman beings.[3]

Earth Keeping: The Protection of Life

The doctrine of creation is about the network of life on which both humans and nonhumans depend for their continued survival.[4] It is for this reason that Genesis 1:26 records the goodness of creation entrusted into the care of humans.[5] Therefore, keeping the integrity of creation is a precondition for life-sustaining elements to remain intact. In the context of climate change, the church has no option but to turn into an earth-keeping ministry. However, for many years, theologians have kept environmental concerns outside or at the margin of the process of doing theology.[6] This calls for a new evangelical environmental ethics that will contribute to enhancing African life-sustaining attitudes in the context of climate change. There is

---

[1] Rev Gabriel Ezekia Nduye (PhD) works with the Evangelical Lutheran Church in Tanzania (ELCT) Southern Diocese (SD) in different capacities such as an ordained Minister; Director for the Centre for Agricultural Development (CAD) and Lecturer at Amani College of Management and Technology (ACMT) in Njombe region of Tanzania. His research interest and publications focus on the intersect between Theology and Development especially African Christian Ethics and public manifestations of the church in Africa that enhances life of all forms for common good. gabriel.nduye2@gmail.com.

[2] Denis G. Arnold, "Introduction: Climate Change and Ethics", in Denis G. Arnold (ed) *The Ethics of Global Climate Change*. (Cambridge: Cambridge University Press, 2011), 4-5.

[3] Dale Jamieson, "Energy, Ethics and transformation of Nature", in Denis G. Arnold (ed) *The Ethics of Global Climate Change*. (Cambridge: Cambridge University Press, 2011), 30.

[4] Clive Pearson, "On Being Public About Ecotheology", *Ecotheology* 43(6) (2001): 42-59.

[5] Anne Burghardt, "Introduction", in Anne Burghardt (ed) *Creation Not For Sale* (Geneva: Lutheran World Federation, 2015): 5-7.

[6] Davis John Jefferson, "Ecological Blind Spots in the Structure and Context of Recent Evangelical Systematic Theologies", *JETS* 43(2) (2000): 273-286.

a need for a renewed ecological commitment guided by the honour and reverence to life that belongs to God the creator.[7]

African Life Sustaining Eco-Ethics For Earth Keeping

Eco-ethics refers to the category of moral principles that guide human attitudes towards the environment and motivates what humankind ought to value, to be and to do in relation to the environment – their position in the web of life. Ecological ethics involves evaluating, justifying and prescribing values, norms and standards of character that contribute to the well-being of the earth.[8] This suggests that human beings need to live a well-balanced life, a life that is guided towards maintaining a healthy relationship with the rest of the world. The following dimensions are the prerequisites for a strong African life-sustaining eco-ethics.

African Indigenous Knowledge: A Fertile Soil for Life-sustaining Eco-ethics

African indigenous knowledge, also known as traditional or local knowledge traditions, entail the knowledge and skills, gathered across African generations, which guide indigenous communities in their interaction with their surrounding natural environment.[9] Although many consider such knowledge to be simple, as compared to modern scientific knowledge, it is argued that "African indigenous knowledge is a complex array of knowledge, skills, practices, and representation that guides and shapes human societies."[10] This knowledge results from the numerous relationships with natural systems that confront people in their general dealings in life. It is opposed to western scientific knowledge which is abstract in nature and relatively independent from practices and lived experience. For Kiplang'at and Rotich,[11] African indigenous knowledge has four key characteristics namely it is: holistic in nature, communally owned, community based and oriented towards the potential for life-sustenance.[12]

Reverence for Life: An Impetus for an African Eco-Ethics Approach

Life is the property that belongs to God, but gifted to the world out of his love. It marks the beginning and foundation of all ethical principles. Life has two sides, good and evil. The goodness of life involves preserving life, promoting life and helping life to achieve its highest quality and abundance. On the contrary, the essence of evil is to destroy life, harm life and hamper the development of life. The aim of any ethics should be to respect, protect, promote, preserve, help and re-flourish all forms of life. It is the reverence for life that motivates a behaviour of compassion for the life of all creatures. It is important to note that tracing the link between created order and the reverence of life constitutes a key thrust of life eco-ethics. Reliable African life-sustaining eco-ethics must primarily focus on uncovering the link that exists

---

[7] S. Gotliebe, "Liberating Faith: Religious Voices for Justice, Peace and Ecological Wisdom" (New York: Rawman and Littlefield, 2003): 895.

[8] Paul Haffner, *Towards a Theology of the Environment* (Herefordshire: Gracewing, 2008): 246.

[9] Douglas Nakashima, Kirsty G. Mclean, Hans Thulstrup, Ameyal R. Castillo and Jennifer T. Rubis, *Weathering Uncertainty: Traditional Knowledge for Climate Change Assessment and Adaptation.* (Paris: UNESCO and Darwin: United Nations University, 2012): 32.

[10] Douglas Nakashima and Marie Rove, "Indigenous Knowledge, Peoples and Sustainable Practices", in Peter Timmerman and Ted Mum (eds) *Encyclopedia of Global Environmental Change Vol 5.* (Chichester: John Wisley and Sons, 2003): 314-324.

[11] Joseph Kiplang'at and Daniel Rotich, "Mapping and Auditing Agricultural Indigenous Knowledge in Uasin Gishu and Keujo District in Rift Valley Province", *Innovation* 44 (June 2012): 81-100.

[12] Ashley Cobb, *Incorporating Indigenous Knowledge Systems into Climate Change Discourse: Linking Social and Natural Science, Local Knowledge, Development and Natural Resources.* Colorado: Conference on Earth System Governance (2011): 4.

between God's creation and the reverence for life.[13] This is important because the entire life and economic production depends completely on the health of the created order. Climate change signifies that the created order is ill, thus human life is in danger. Therefore, Christian stewardship becomes the key principle that commits Christian faith communities into the responsible custodianship for the household of God, i.e., earth-keeping responsibilities.[14]

A Proposed Framework for African Life-Sustaining Eco-Ethics

Climate change calls for an alternative system that is based on the protection of environmental resources as a common good. This is necessary because any sustainable life on earth needs a vibrant healthy life-support system, as Cavanagh and Mander have argued.[15] Steve de Gruchy points out that Christian faith communities have the duty to make the entire world a place closer to God's vision of Shalom that suggests the abundant life described in John 10:10.[16] A promising framework towards African life sustaining eco-ethics needs to undergo the following steps.

Un-Trapping the Notion of *Oikos*: A Paradigm Shift

Human economic activities stand at the base of the climatic crisis, of an extent the world has never seen. The Greek word *oikos* appears to be the root-base for the English words economy and ecology. Both words, economy (*oikos-nomos)* and ecology (*oikos-logos*), are concerned with the earth (web of life). While the former is about the rules of home or the rules of the household (Earth), the latter has to do with studying the home or household. This means that both terms are concerned with studying the way things relate to nature and are integrated within the web of life. From the classic point of view, economics is known to be a study only of how people make decisions in the case of scarce resources. Scarce resources are emphasised in the world of economics because it is believed that human want for goods, services and resources always exceeds what is available.

However, from the biblical point of view, economics should be understood as being intimately concerned with the earth and the way human beings live, relate and make use of earth services while respecting its integrity. Therefore, un-trapping the notion of *oikos* from the classical economic and ecological studies will create a new way of viewing and relating to the earth. In addition, Nurnberger[17] asserts that the earth has lost its sanity. Regaining the sanity of the earth requires the sanity of human minds, hence we need to gain a broader understanding of the earth as our common and only home.

---

[13] John O'Neill, Allan Holland and Andrew Light, *Environmental Values* (New York: Routledge Taylor and Francis, 2008): 1.

[14] Gabriel Nduye, *Sustainable Agriculture in the Context of Climate Change in Tanzania? On Cultivating an African Christian Ethic of Care* (Beau Basin: Lambert Academic, 2018): 160-161.

[15] John Cavanagh and Jerry Mander, *Alternatives to Economic Globalization: A Better World is Possible* (San Francisco: BK, 2004): 85.

[16] Beverly Haddad, *Keeping the Soul and Body Together: Reflections by Steve de Gruchy on Theology and Development*. (Pietermaritzburg: Cluster, 2015): 88.

[17] Klaus Nurnberger, *Why Science Needs Best Faith to be Responsible and Why Faith needs Best Science to be credible: Regaining Sanity for the Earth.* (Pietermaritzburg: Cluster, 2011): 7.

Embracing the African Concept of Ubuntu: Another Contribution to Eco-Ethics

Ubuntu is an ancient philosophy and way of life that has sustained African communities for centuries. According to Mkhize,[18] Ubuntu (in Swahili *utu*) is an African concept that describes the process of becoming human beings through wider relationships. For Msafiri,[19] Ubuntu connotes not only human aspects but goes beyond humankind to cover the entire universe. It engraves a broader understanding of God's created order and proper relationships to nature.

Ubuntu is the concept expressing the most important quality of being human. It concerns values that contribute to the well-being of an individual and community at large. The concept of ubuntu carries a strong sense of interdependence of life or interconnectedness. No life is possible when one stands alone; rather, a life only becomes viable in relation and in connection with others. This means that the best way to express a quality life in the community is by deeds of kindness, compassion, caring, sharing, solidarity, responsibility and sacrifice for common good.[20] Bujo points out that in the African context the notion of Ubuntu and community provides a solid foundation for life sustaining eco-ethics.[21] In the context where western individualistic ethics have been insufficient, an ethic based on a sense of community has the potential of adding responsible attitudes towards one another and towards the earth.[22] According to Ramose, the notion of wholeness speaks of continued relationships between humans and physical nature.[23] Similarly, the notion of care extends from caring for human neighbours towards the physical nature in fulfilment of the God-given duty.[24]

Reclaiming an Ecological-Economic Model

McFague contends that the current neoclassical economic model views human beings on the planet as a collection of individuals drawn together to gain a maximum benefit by exploiting the natural environment.[25] In the process of such exploitation, the ability of the earth to replenish and continue to support such economy is diminished. The climate change phenomenon is a clear manifestation of the dysfunction of the neoclassical economic system in managing the earth resources. This suggests that an economic model whose priority is not sustainability of the planet earth cannot be good for the survival of human and earth at large.[26]

An ecological-economic model has to be sought in order to reverse the current situation where the sustainability of life is uncertain due to conditions of climate change. An ecological-economic system focuses more on maximising the optimal functioning of the planet's gifts and services. It is about an economic system which encourages human beings to have a particular vision on how to live on planet earth

---

[18] Nhlanhla Mkhize, "Ubuntu and Harmony: An African Approach to Morality and Ethics", in Ronald Nicolson (ed) *Persons in Community: African Ethics in a Global Culture*. (Scottsville: University of KwaZulu Natal Press, 2008): 35.

[19] Aidan G. Msafiri, *Towards a Credible Environmental Ethics for Africa: A Tanzania Perspective*. (Nairobi: CUEA, 2007): 185.

[20] Mluleki Munyaka and Mokgethi Motlhabi, "Ubuntu and its Socio-Moral Significance", in Munyaradzi Felix Murove, *African Ethics: An Anthropology of Comparative and Applied Ethics* (Scottsville: University of KwaZulu Natal Press, 2009): 74-75.

[21] Benezet Bujo, *The Ethical Dimension of Community: The African Model and Dialogue Between North and South*. (Nairobi: Pauline Publications, 1998): 65.

[22] Ken Gnanakan, *God's Work: A Theology of Environment*. (London: SPCK, 1999): 168.

[23] Mogobe B. Ramose, "Ecology through Ubuntu", in Munyaradzi Felix Murove (ed), *African Ethics: An Anthropology of Comparative and Applied Ethics* (Scottsville: University of KwaZulu Natal Press, 2009): 309.

[24] Ramose, "Ecology through Ubuntu", 312.

[25] Sallie McFague, *A New Climate for Theology: God, the World and Global Warming*. (Minneapolis, MI: Fortress, 2008): 86.

[26] McFague, *A New Climate for Theology*, 87-88.

while respecting God's creation to sustain life.[27] The ecological-economic model functions under three guiding rules, as pointed out by McFague, which are to "take only your share, clean up after yourself and to keep the house in good repair for future occupants" [future generations].[28] The rules remind us that this home (earth) does not belong to anyone of us, rather it is loaned to us for free for our lifetime with the condition that we obey those rules so that it continues to feed, shelter, nurture and delight others in the future.[29] Steve de Gruchy argues "when we think of the earth as our home, as home for humanity, and when we think about economy, as rules for the home, then we are able to talk about God's economy, a system that balances what the earth does to human life and what human life does to the earth."[30]

Re-Learning Divinely Bestowed Services Engraved in Creation

There is a strong correlation between human well-being and the health of ecosystems. What science calls ecosystems, natural resources, environment or physical world, the Bible calls creation. God created everything, and all that He created is deemed perfect, giving inherent value to nonhuman entities independently from what the creation provides for human beings. It means the created order has an inbuilt capacity to produce services necessary for the sustainability of life on earth. These services are **providence services,**[31] **regulatory services,**[32] **support services**[33] and **cultural services.**[34] It is only God's created order that can grant these services to ensure all forms of life continue to flourish.

Some Practice Models of an African Life-Sustaining Eco-Ethics

The Ngoro[35] *Practice in the World of Agriculture*

The *Ngoro* practice refers to the process of pitting, crop rotation as well as fallowing in farming practices. These all safeguard the environment's ability to sustain all forms of life. It is largely practiced by the Matengo people located in the Mbinga highlands of Tanzania. In this practice, farmers are trained and guided to preserve soil fertility and the ecosystem at large for the sustainability of life, as they engage in their faming activities.[36]

---

27 McFague, *A New Climate for Theology*, 89.
28 McFague, *A New Climate for Theology,* 91.
29 McFague, *A New Climate for Theology*, 92.
30 Haddad, *Keeping Together Body and Soul*, 220.
31 **Providence Services**: This is a natural God-given capacity engraved in the natural environment to provide services such as quality food (fertile soil, fresh water, good weather, natural medicine, fibre, minerals as well woods).
32 **Regulatory Services**: This refers to the God-given capacity of the natural environment to regulate various conditions and prevent extremes. Such regulatory services are through ecosystem processes. For example; regulating waterflows, weather, soil quality, pollination etc are all done naturally.
33 **Support Services**: These include services such as nutrient cycling and soil formation as well as production of small elements that make environment healthier to support more forms of life.
34 **Cultural Services**: These are non-material aspects for spiritual enrichment and emotional relaxation such as recreational services, tourism services, sports, education, heritage as well as aesthetic enjoyment; from MEA, *Ecosystem and Human Well-Being: Current State and Trends*. (Washington DC: Island Press, 2005): 6.
35 ***Ngoro*** is a local name (Matengo tribe in Tanzania) for a kind of farming practice carried out in areas that are steeply sloped. It is an indigenous way of preparing land that does keep the soil fertility and productivity. This model of farming is ecologically sound in that it prevents soil erosion, conserves ecosystems and observes the integrity of soil organic.
36 Zacharia J.U. Malley, "The Ngoro System Cultivation System: Soil Productivity on Steep Slopes in Southwestern Tanzania", In J.F. Delvin and T. Zettel (eds), *Ecoagriculture: Initiative in Eastern and Southern Africa* (Harare: Weaver Press, 1999): 15-28.

Ecological Taboos Wisdom

These are avoidance rules that prevent people from not carrying out certain actions in order to preserve the ecosystem. Such avoidance and restrictions may include not entering certain parts of the forest or to not cut down trees that are termed as sacred. The ecological taboos are very common among Shona People in Zimbabwe and are capable of triggering a life-sustaining eco-ethics. Ecological taboos are used to prohibit and restrict people on the unsustainable use of the natural environment, thus shaping Shona's eco-ethics to ensure life is sustained as they believe that violation of those taboos will encourage anger to befall them from a supernatural Being. The taboos are also used to teach the younger generation of the society that human survival is intertwined with the surrounding environment and therefore keeps the integrity of creation and enhances the protection of life.[37]

Obligatory Anthropoholism

The term anthropoholism describes an emerging practice that can potentially enhance a life-sustaining echo-ethics. It is opposed to anthropocentrism, which has for many years tended to elevate the human being above all other beings thus leading to the mistreatment of nature. It argues that the human being is part of nature since he/she/they cannot exist independently from the environment or be understood without reference to the environment.[38] This approach is capable of transforming the human mindset by putting much emphasis on interdependence and interconnectedness between humans and nature. It is in line with the biblical creation story where the two first human beings were placed in the Garden of Eden and lived in harmony with nature. Also, an anthropoholistic approach is in line with African ontology (ubuntu), characterised by a holism that forges sustainable relationships with the environment and human responsibility rather than arrogance over or against nature.[39]

Conclusion

Adopting and exploring theories of responsibility and care, this contribution sought to explore ways in which an African life-sustaining eco-ethics can enhance earth-keeping attitudes which need to be envisioned in the context of climate change. The pre-requisite for enhanced human responsibility in honouring the integrity of creation includes viewing African indigenous knowledge as a fertile soil for an effective life-sustaining eco-ethics – understanding the link between the created order and an attitude of reverence of life. It also includes un-trapping the notion of *oikos*, embracing the notion of *ubuntu*, replacing the neo-classic economic model with an ecological-economic model and re-learning about the inbuilt earth services which constitute key elements for African life-sustaining eco-ethics. Finally, without being exhaustive, three practices were highlighted which can trigger and enhance life-sustaining eco-ethics in African contexts.

Suggestions for Further Reading

Arnold, Denis G., Ed. *The Ethics of Global Climate Change*. Cambridge: Cambridge University Press, 2011.

---

[37] Munamato Chemhuru and Dennis Masaka, "Taboos as source of Shona people's environmental ethics", *Journal of Sustainable Development in Africa* 12(7) (2010): 121-133.

[38] Samuel Akpan Bassey, "Anthropoholism as an authentic tool for environmental management", *International Journal of Environmental Pollution and Environmental Modelling* 2(3) (2019): 160-168.

[39] Chinedu Stephen Ifeakor and Andrew Ottech, "African Environmental Ethics: A Non-Anthropocentric African Environmentalism. The Journey So Far", *Igwebuike: An African Journal of Arts and Humanities* 3(6) (2017): 67-97.

Bassey, Samuel Akpan. "Anthropoholism: As an Authentic Tool for Environmental Management". *International Journal of Environmental Pollution and Environmental Modelling* 2(3) (2019): 160-168.

Bujo, Benezet. *The Ethical Dimension of Community: The African Model and Dialogue Between North and South*. Nairobi: Pauline Publications, 1998.

Burghardt, Anne, Ed. *Creation Not For Sale*. Geneva: Lutheran World Federation, 2015.

Cavanagh, John and Jerry Mander. *Alternatives To Economic Globalization: A Better World is Possible*. San Francisco, CA: BK Publishers, 2004.

Chemhuru, Munamato and Dennis Masaka. "Taboos as Source of Shona People's Environmental Ethics". *Journal of Sustainable Development in Africa* 12(7) (2010): 121-133.

Cobb, Ashley, *Incorporating Indigenous Knowledge Systems into Climate Change Discourse: Linking Social and Natural Science, Local Knowledge, Development and Natural Resources*. Colorado: Conference on Earth System Governance, 2011.

Conradie, Ernst. *Christianity and Earth-Keeping: In Search for Inspiring Vision*. Western Cape: SUN Press, 2011.

Erhard, Nancie. *Moral Habitat: Ethos and Agency for the Sake of Agency*. New York: New York State University Press, 2007.

Garvey, James. *Ethics of Climate Change: Right or Wrong in a Warming World*. New York: Continuum, 2008.

Gnanakan, Ken. *God's Work: A Theology of Environment*. London: SPCK, 1999.

Gotliebe, S. *Liberating Faith: Religious Voices for Justice, Peace and Ecological Wisdom*. New York: Rawman and Littlefield, 2003.

Haddad, Beverly. *Keeping the Soul and Body Together: Reflection by Steve de Gruchy on Theology and Development*. Pietermaritzburg: Cluster, 2015.

Haffner, Paul. *Towards a Theology of the Environment*. Herefordshire: Gracewing, 2008.

Ifiekor, Chinedu Stephen and Andrew Ottech. "African Environmental Ethics: A Non-Anthropocentric African Environmentalism: The Journey So Far". *Igwebuike: An African Journal of Arts and Humanities* 3(6) (2017): 67-97.

Jefferson, Davis John. "Ecological Blind Spots in the Structure and Context of Recent Evangelical Systematic Theologies" *JETS* 43(2) (2000): 273-286.

Kiplang'at, Joseph and Daniel Rotich. "Mapping and Auditing Agricultural Indigenous Knowledge in Uasin Gishu and Keujo District in Rift Valley Province". *Innovation* 44 (June 2012): 81-100.

Malley, Zacharia J.U. "The Ngoro Cultivation System: Soil Productivity on Steep Slopesin Southwestern Tanzania", in J.F. Delvin and T. Zettel, Eds. *Ecoagriculture: Initiatives in Eastern and Southern Africa*: Harare: Weaver Press, 1999: 15-28.

McFague, Sallie. *A New Climate for Theology: God, the World and Global Warming*. Minneapolis, MI: Fortress, 2008.

MEA. *Ecosystem and Human Well-Being: Current State and Trends*. Washington DC: Island Press, 2005.

Mkhize, Nhlanhla. "Ubuntu and Harmony: An African Approach to Morality and Ethics", in Ronald Nicolson, Ed. *Persons in Community: African Ethics in a Global Culture*. Scottsville: University of KwaZulu Natal Press, 2008: 35-44.

Msafiri, Aidan G. *Towards a Credible Environmental Ethics for Africa: A Tanzania Perspective*. Nairobi: CUEA, 2007.

Munyaka, Mluleki and Mokgethi Motlhabi. "Ubuntu and its Socio-Moral Significance", in Munyaradzi Felix Murove. *African Ethics: An Anthropology of Comparative and Applied Ethics*. Scottsville: University of KwaZulu Natal Press, 2009: 63-84.

Munyaradzi, Felix Murove, "An African Environmental Ethic Based on the Concept of Ukama and Ubuntu", in Munyaradzi F. Murove, Ed. *African Ethics: An Anthropology of Comparative and Applied Ethics*. Scottsville: University of KwaZulu Natal Press, 2009: 315-332.

Nakashima, Douglas and Marie Rove. "Indigenous Knowledge, Peoples and Sustainable Practices", in Peter Timmerman and Ted Munn, Eds. *Encyclopedia of Global Environmental Change Vol 5*. Chichester: John Wisley and Sons, 2003: 314-324.

Nakashima, Douglas, Kirsty G. McLean, Hans Thulstrup, Ameyal R. Castillo and Jennifer T. Rubis. *Weathering Uncertainty: Traditional Knowledge for Climate Change Assessment and Adaptation*. Paris: UNESCO and Darwin UNU, 2012.

Nduye, Gabriel. *Sustainable Agriculture in the Context of Climate Change in Tanzania? On Cultivating an African Christian Ethic of Care.* Beau Basin: Lambert Academic Publishing, 2018.

Nurnberger, Klaus. *Why Science Needs Best Faith to be Responsible and Why Faith Needs Best Science to be Credible: Regaining Sanity for the Earth.* Pietermaritzburg: Cluster, 2011.

O'Neill, John, Allan Holland and Andrew Light. *Environmental Values.* New York: Routledge Taylor and Francis Group, 2008.

Pearson, Clive. "On Being Public About Ecotheology". *Ecotheology* 43(6) (2001): 42-59.

Ramose, Mogobe B. "Ecology through Ubuntu", in Munyaradzi Felix Murove, Ed. *African Ethics: An Anthropology of Comparative and Applied Ethics.* Scottsville: University of KwaZulu Natal Press, 2009: 308-314.

Ross, Anne, Cathleen Sherman, Jeffrey D. Snodgrass, Henry D. Nalkore and Richard Sherman. *Indigenous People and Collaborative Stewardship of Nature: Knowledge Binds and Institutions Conflict*. Walnut Creek, CA: Left Cost, 2011.

UNESCO. "The Ethical Implication of Global Climate Change: World Commission of the Ethos of Scientific Knowledge and Technology", UNESCO Website, 2010. [Available at: https://unesdoc.unesco.org/ark:/48223/pf0000188198], [Last accessed: 11th March 2022].

102. Christian Formation for Climate Change Resilience: Case Studies of the Way a Christian NGO Facilitates Climate Change Resilience in Africa

Josias (Sas) Conradie[1]

Introduction

According to the World Economic Forum,[2] climate change is one of the five greatest risks facing Africa. Nine out of the ten countries most vulnerable to climate change are African countries. They include Sierra Leone, Central African Republic, South Sudan, Liberia, Guinea, Madagascar, Democratic Republic of Congo, Congo and Burundi.[3] African countries can expect an increase in extreme weather that threatens the health and livelihoods of people. Higher temperatures and the increasing severity and frequency of extreme events such as storms, droughts and flooding will change the quality of living for many. African cities will be especially affected as they are most exposed to climate extremes and least able to mitigate their impact.[4] Mass-migration as a result of flooding or droughts could put resources such as food, water and housing under pressure in areas less directly affected by climate change.[5]

Adapting to climate change and becoming more climate change resilient is therefore essential for the survival of many people in Africa. Measures to make farming practices more climate change resilient and ensure food security could include planting more adapted crops, crop diversification and rotation, agroforestry, the use of cover crops that manage nutrient levels and farming practices which are low in greenhouse gas emissions.[6] With African countries being so vulnerable to climate change, actions like these that will help Africa's 599 million Christians in Africa[7] (49% of the population in Africa in 2020)[8] becoming more resilient to climate change is essential. With Christians in Africa taking their faith seriously,[9] equipping African Christians to deal with climate change through Christian formation could be an important way to build resilience in Africa for climate change.

---

[1] Rev Dr Sas Conradie is the Tearfund Theology and Networking Manager (Africa). A minister in the Dutch Reformed Church in South Africa, his academic work focuses on church and community development in Africa, church based economic development, ecology and theological education. He can be contacted at sas.conradie@tearfund.org.

[2] World Economic Forum, "The Sub-Saharan Africa Risks Landscape," http://www3.weforum.org/docs/WEF_The_Sub-Saharan_Africa_Risks_Landscape_report.pdf.

[3] Ciara Nugent, "The 10 Countries Most Vulnerable to Climate Change Will Experience Population Booms in the Coming Decades," *Time*, July 11 2019 https://time.com/5621885/climate-change-population-growth/.

[4] Verisk Maplecroft, "Environmental Risk Outlook 2021," https://www.maplecroft.com/insights/analysis/environmental-risk-outlook-2021/#report_form_container.

[5] World Economic Forum, "These are the 5 biggest risks facing sub-Saharan Africa this year," https://www.weforum.org/agenda/2019/09/economic-growth-sub-saharan-africa-challenges-risks/.

[6] David Eckstein, Vera Künzel, Laura Schäfer, Maik Winges, *Global Climate Risk Index 2020: Who Suffers Most from Extreme Weather Events? Weather-Related Loss Events in 2018 and 1999 to 2018.*," Bonn: German Watch e.V. (December 2019), 20.

[7] Todd M. Johnson, Gina A. Zurlo, Albert W. Hickman and Peter F., "Crossing Christianity 2018: More African Christians and Counting Martyrs," *International Bulletin of Mission Research* 42.1 (January 2018): 20-28.

[8] Gina A. Zurlo, "African Christianity," *Gordon Conwell Theological Seminary*. March 18, 2020. Accessed August, 9, 2021. https://www.gordonconwell.edu/blog/african-christianity-101

[9] Joey Marshall, "The world's most committed Christians live in Africa, Latin America – and the U.S.," *Pew Research Centre*. August 22, 2018. Accessed August 9, 2021. https://www.pewresearch.org/fact-tank/2018/08/22/the-worlds-most-committed-christians-live-in-africa-latin-america-and-the-u-s/

However, because of extreme poverty in Africa, people in Africa might be less concerned about environmental issues, including climate change, even though they are directly affected by climate change. As Gitau writes:

> To the African farmer who is in poverty, there is no consideration for environmental care and protection. This is a matter of survival. The family has to be fed and cash crops have to be grown to enable the farmer to meet other essentials of life.[10]

That means that Christian formation should include measures to address poverty.

In this chapter I will reflect on various perspectives on Christian formation for climate change resilience, resources that Tearfund are using to facilitate Christian formation for climate change resilience in Africa and use examples from the organisation's work in Africa to show the impact of those resources.

Perspectives on Christian Formation

Christian formation is a change of understanding, a change of emotion resulting in a change in actions rooted in a biblical worldview based on the foundation of Jesus Christ that shapes and moulds a Christian's life. From this perspective, Christian formation is similar to discipleship. To be a disciple is to be called to a life of learning and formation in the likeness of Christ. Jesus draws his disciples apart and teaches them the deep patterns, ethics and actions of the Kingdom of Heaven (Matthew 5.1-12), the ways of prayer and worship (Luke 11.1-4), the principles of life together (John 13.1-20) as well as living a distinctive life of witness and service.[11]

Hollinger's view that Christian formation should include an understanding of the head, experienced by the heart and lived by hands, could be helpful when we consider Christian formation for climate change resilience.[12] Thought (head), passion (heart) and action (hands) are dimensions of faith that should be encouraged in Christians. Hollinger calls it a "whole faith for the whole person".[13] Theology (the head), spirituality (the heart) and mission (the hands) are dimensions of Christian formation. Helping Christians understand God and the various aspects of their faith, love of God and living for God should be integrated into Christian formation. This perspective on Christian formation can also be seen in the sending of the disciples to make disciples in Matthew 28:19-20:

1. Baptising them (Matthew 28:19) – commitment with the heart.
2. Teaching them (Matthew 28:20) – understanding with the head.
3. Teaching should result in obedience (Matthew 28:20) – obedience with action through hands and life-style.

This could be explained in the following graph:

[10] Simon K. Gitau, *The Environmental Crisis: A challenge for African Christianity*. Nairobi: Acton Publishers (2000), 1

[11] General Synod of the Church of England, "Developing Discipleship", *The Archbishops' Council 2015* (2015), 1. Accessed August 12, 2021. https://www.churchofengland.org/sites/default/files/2017-12/gs%201977%20-%20developing%20discipleship.pdf.

[12] Dennis P. Hollinger, *Head, Heart, Hands: Bringing together Christian thought, passion and action.* Downers Grove, Illinois: Intervarsity Press (2005), 16.

[13] Hollinger (2005), 32.

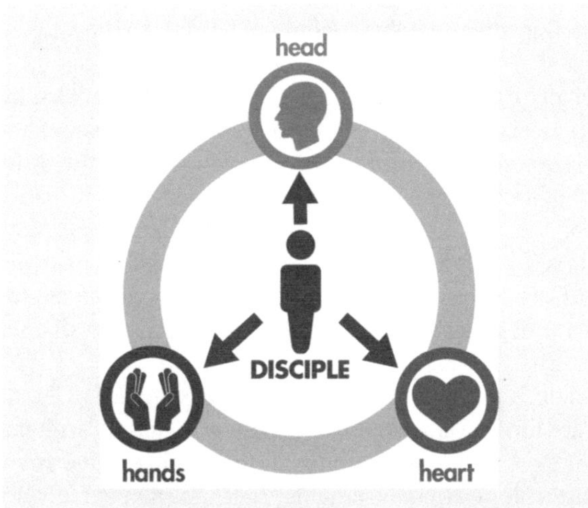

People learn in a connected way with their heads, hearts and hands all engaged. Such an integration ensures fuller assimilation into the understanding and experience of the learner, thus enabling a process of personal and group transformation. This is also the case with Christian formation. Our minds cannot be brought into harmony with God's designs and truth without our hearts being near to God and actions that reflect God's ways. Our hearts cannot experience the presence of and power of the Holy Spirit without knowledge of God to guide us and without actions that reflect the fruit of the Holy Spirit. And our actions of both proclamation and social action will wither without a theology to guide them and a heart to drive and sustain them.[14] We become more like Christ when we understand him, love him and live for him.

Christian formation is therefore the work of God's Holy Spirit in the lives of his people, growing them into the image, character and ministry of Jesus. God does this work by renewing the minds of people, reordering their loves, and redirecting their lives toward the end of glorifying God.[15] Followers of Jesus become rooted in the love of God, established in a community of faith, and empowered by the Holy Spirit to love God, and serve his purposes in every context of life and work, including as they respond to the challenges of climate change.

Christian Formation and Care for Creation

Christian formation as theological, spiritual and life-style formation has implications for the way Christians care for creation and respond to climate change. This would mean equipping Christians:

1. To acquire an understanding of both the theological reasons and climatological reasons for climate change. In other words, building theological resilience by understanding the changes in the natural world. Ruth Valerio argues that Christians should be informed and gain knowledge about climate change.[16] That would include helping people understand climate change and the biblical perspectives on caring for creation within their increasing fragile environment.[17] A core principle is to restore the relationship with creation as part of the restoration of the relationship with God and then to live in

[14] Hollinger (2005), 158.
[15] Cornerstone Presbyterian Church, "Christian Formation at Cornerstone Presbyterian Church," https://www.cornerstonepresfranklin.org/christian-formation
[16] Ruth Valerio, *Saying Yes to Life.* London: SPCK (2020), 20.
[17] Nick Spencer and Robert White, *Christianity, Climate Change and Sustainable Living.* London: SPCK (2007).

harmony with creation. It is important that traditional wisdom on how to relate with nature, including the sanctity of creation, should be incorporated into Christian formation.[18]

2. To be touched emotionally by climate change in their hearts and build spiritual resilience as a result. As part of our worship as our expression of our love for God, we should be touched by the needs of creation as well.[19] This emotional attachment to creation is not difficult for Africans to understand, as the relation with the natural environment is central to African spirituality.[20] Christians should also be given hope, based on their relationship with God to face an increasingly uncertain future.
3. To take action to live in ways that reduce carbon emissions[21] and adapt their lives to changing patterns of the environment. That means protecting vulnerable ecosystems while securing sustainable livelihoods.[22] In other words, helping Christians to build practical resilience as part of their Christian formation.

The Arusha Call to Discipleship[23] calls for discipleship that includes Christian formation for climate change: "We are called to care for God's creation, and to be in solidarity with nations severely affected by climate change in the face of a ruthless human-centered exploitation of the environment for consumerism and greed." This calls for a theological understanding that impacts people spiritually but then results in action and changed living. As Archbishop Thabo Makgoba explains, "Words, words and more words will not reverse environmental degradation or carbon emissions, but our actions together can. So act now for climate justice. Change begins with us!"[24]

Unfortunately, churches in Africa in general do not include care for creation in Christian formation.[25] For example, in Kenya there are few churches who have training programmes in environmental education.[26] Practical steps should be taken to put the 'Green Gospel' into practice by teaching the 'Green Gospel', expressing the 'Green Gospel' in worship and then living out the 'Green Gospel'.[27] The understanding of caring for creation and climate change results in an emotional change of heart to care for creation and climate change and a practical response to do something about climate change.[28] That would include modifying daily activities, such as rain water harvesting, tree planting and energy-saving stoves.[29]

---

[18] Gitau (2000), 54.
[19] Ruth Valerio, *Saying Yes to Life.* London: SPCK (2020), 20.
[20] Randee Ijatuyi-Morphé, *Africa's Social and Religious Quest: A comprehensive survey and analysis of the African situation.* Jos: Hokma House (2011), 49.
[21] Valerio, *Saying Yes to Life*, 20
[22] Ellen F. Davis, "Just food: A Biblical perspective on culture and agriculture," in *Creation in Crisis: Christian perspectives on sustainability*, ed. Robert S. White (London: SPCK, 2009), 136.
[23] The World Council of Churches, "The Arusha Call to Discipleship," https://www.oikoumene.org/resources/documents/the-arusha-call-to-discipleship
[24] Isabel Carter, "An interview with the Eco-Bishops," in *Climate change – Footsteps 99,* ed. Isabel Carter (London: Tearfund, 2016), 14.
[25] Gitau (2000), 106.
[26] Gitau (2000), 136.
[27] Gitau (2000), 103.
[28] George Fihavango, "Quest for Ecotheology in a Situation of Ecological Disaster" in *Christian Theology and Environmental Responsibility*, eds. J.N.K. Mugambi, and Mika Vahakangas (Nairobi: Acton Publishers, 2001), 108-109.
[29] Alice Kabugumila, "Tanzanian Women's Response to the Environmental Crisis" in *Christian Theology and Environmental Responsibility*, eds. J.N.K. Mugambi, and Mika Vahakangas (Nairobi: Acton Publishers, 2001), 70-71.

Tearfund Initiatives to Equip Christians for Climate Change Resilience

Tearfund is an international Christian relief and development organisation with a strong focus on advocacy for the environment and creation.[30] Tearfund developed and had been using a number of resources to facilitate Christian formation to deal with climate change and facilitate climate change resilience.[31] These resources focus on head, heart and hand formation.

a. Reveal

Reveal is a collection of tools for people working directly in different thematic areas with local communities or churches.[32] The tools include information sheets, activities, Bible studies and good practice guides that engage both the head, heart and hands in facilitating Christian formation in that specific area. One of the thematic areas is around climate and the environment.[33] These tools explain climate change and environmental degradation from a biblical perspective and help Christians to protect and care for their environment and adapt to a changing climate.

b. Footsteps

Footsteps Magazine has become a very popular publication with practical information on community development from a Christian perspective.[34] As such it has become an important resource for Christian formation in a number of areas. Footsteps 99 focused on helping Christians respond better to climate change, including understanding the biblical message of caring for the environment, climate change resilient farming, coping with heat exhaustion and heatstroke, the use of renewable energy in communities, advocacy and spiritual practices around climate change.[35]

c. Live Justly Global[36]

Live Justly Global helps young Christians live a life-style of justice in six key areas of life – advocacy, prayer, consumption, generosity, relationships and creation care.[37] Each of the ten sessions includes a biblical reflection and practical information on the theme, a story and prayer that touch the reader's heart, and action steps for groups and individuals to change behaviour. One of the sessions deals with justice and creation care with a vision for all creation to flourish.[38] The action step aims at examining the impact of life-style on the environment.

---

[30] Nigel Harris, "Foreword" in *Inspiring Change: Impact and Learning Report 2017*, Tearfund Impact and Effectiveness Team (London: Tearfund, 2017), 1

[31] Tearfund Learn, "Environment and climate," https://learn.tearfund.org/en/how-we-work/what-we-do/environment-and-climate

[32] Tearfund Learn, "Reveal toolkit," https://learn.tearfund.org/en/resources/series/reveal-toolkit

[33] Tearfund Learn, "Reveal toolkit: Climate and the environment," https://learn.tearfund.org/en/resources/series/reveal-toolkit/reveal-toolkit-climate-and-environment

[34] Tearfund Learn, "Footsteps magazine," https://learn.tearfund.org/en/footsteps-magazine/about-footsteps-magazine

[35] Isabel Carter (ed), *Climate change – Footsteps 99.* London: Tearfund (2016). https://learn.tearfund.org/en/resources/footsteps/footsteps-91-100/footsteps-99

[36] Tearfund Learn, "Live justly: Global edition," https://learn.tearfund.org/en/resources/tools-and-guides/live-justly-global-edition

[37] Jason Fileta (ed), *Live Justly Global.* Portland: Micah Challenge USA (2017).

[38] Jason Felita, "Justice and Creation Care: A Vision for All Creation to Flourish!" in *Live Justly Global*, ed. Jason Fileta (Portland: Micah Challenge USA, 2017), 110-123.

d. Self-help groups[39]

Tearfund has been using the concept of self-help groups (SHGs) in various contexts to help Christians in building climate change resilience.[40] The SHG approach embraces the principle that individuals can transform their own lives. Personal formation in general, and Christian formation in particular, through self-organised learning is at the heart of SHGs. 'Systems thinking' is being used to look at problems, such as a damaged environment, not as individual issues, but as just one interrelated part of a much wider overall system.[41] Information is provided that results in changed perspectives as well as a commitment to change followed up by practical action.

e. Church and community mobilisation process (CCMP)

The church and community mobilisation process is being used across Africa to empower people to transform their situation using their own God-given resources in a sustainable and holistic way.[42] Based on the understanding that poverty is caused by a broken relationship with God, self, others and the environment, CCMP enables people to describe their reality and transform it themselves by designing their own strategies to address their own issues.[43] These strategies include responding to climate change and building climate change resilience. The process helps Christians restore broken relationships, including with the environment, and to adapt their living as a result.

f. ROOTS 13[44]

ROOTS 13 is a booklet that helps churches and organisations to consider the impact of the environment on their work and the impact of their work on the environment. Sections on biblical perspectives on environmental issues and climate change, as well as on personal lifestyle, are included in the resource to help Christians understand climate change, become passionate about climate change and then take practical action and build climate change resilience.

Examples of Building Climate Change Resilience through Christian Formation

The various approaches and resources Tearfund is using to facilitate climate change resilience through Christian formation are having an impact on communities across Africa. Here are a few examples:

a. Malawi

The Assemblies of God Care and Synod of Livingstonia Development Department in Malawi are using CCMP to help communities respond to climate change.[45] That resulted in better environmental protection through use of community by-laws and afforestation, as well as improved food security among participating households as a result of improved yields due to the adoption of conservation agriculture and the use of

[39] Isabel Carter, *Releasing Potential: A facilitator's learning resource for self-help groups.* Addis Ababa: Tearfund Ethiopia (2013) https://learn.tearfund.org/en/resources/tools-and-guides/releasing-potential
[40] Carter, *Releasing Potential*, 79.
[41] Carter, *Releasing Potential*, 80.
[42] Helen Gaw, *Church and Community Mobilisation in Africa*. London: Tearfund (2018), 3.
[43] Francis W. Njoroge, *Church and Community Mobilisation Process Facilitator's Manual*. London: Tearfund (2019), 19, see in: https://learn.tearfund.org/en/resources/series/church-and-community-mobilisation-process-ccmp/ccmp-facilitators-manual.
[44] Rachel Blackman and Isabel Carter, *Environmental sustainability: Responding to changes in the environment and climate*. London: Tearfund (2009). See Roots 13 publication on Environmental sustainability in: https://learn.tearfund.org/-/media/learn/resources/series/roots/roots-13-e.pdf.
[45] Aaron Lewani, *Improving Peoples' Livelihoods through Enhanced Environmental and Economic Sustainability.* Unpublished Tearfund presentation on 21 July 2021

local fertilizer. Self-help groups that developed out of CCMP are especially effective in transforming knowledge about climate change and how to respond to climate change. Bible studies on stewardship of the environment enhance community members' change of mindset towards environment management.

b. Ethiopia

Christian formation through self-help groups also built climate change resilience among smallholder farmers of the Wolaita area in Ethiopia.[46] Climate change altered the rainfall season from two cropping seasons to one. As a result, these farmers have been facing critical food shortages due to the delayed rainfall. Climate change resilient farming practices as a result of the Christian formation process improved soil fertility and health, increased crop production 100-150%, increased household income, improved climate change resilience and facilitated more efficient resource utilization. Members of SHGs are therefore more resilient to drought than other households and are in a stronger position to cope with prolonged drought as a result of training on climate change adaptation.[47]

c. Nigeria

Tearfund in Nigeria looked at ways of turning waste into jobs as part of their response to climate change.[48] The result was that a group of young people between the ages of 18-35 gathered in Jos to discuss their response to climate change. The group did not have any knowledge of creation care and how they could respond to the climate change that is affecting communities in Nigeria.[49] At the suggestion of Tearfund's Ben Osawe, they decided to work through 'Live Justly Global'. That gave them a good understanding of biblical perspectives on climate change. Their hearts changed as the resource and interactive discussions brought them from a place of despair about environmental and economic challenges in general and climate change in particular, to a place of hope and action.[50]

The group decided to establish the Jos Green Centre in Jos, Nigeria,[51] as a youth-led hub of activists who respond to climate change and other environmental and economic challenges in the country while developing eco-friendly businesses.[52] They are using 'Live Justly Global' as a resource to equip young people in Plateau State in Nigeria. The group is especially involved in dealing with waste through policy work with the municipality, developing recycling and eco-friendly businesses, as well as training young people in making solar panels out of electronic waste.[53] The projects run by the centre support low income families by providing solar electricity created from electric waste that would otherwise become a hazard to the area.[54] These initiatives help to build climate change resilience as people move away from charcoal and kerosene, becoming less reliant on fossil fuels. Young people are trained in making charcoal briquettes from woody waste, tree planting, clearing of drainage channels to prevent flooding, recycling plastics,

---

[46] Desalegn Demissie, *The Role of Conservation Agriculture (CA) in mitigating the impacts of climate change on the lives of Smallholder farmers*. Unpublished Tearfund presentation on 21 July 2021

[47] Sarah La Trobe, *Saving for a Very Dry Day: The contribution of self-help groups to building resilience in East Africa*. London: Tearfund (2017).

[48] Ben Osawe, "Jos Green Centre, Nigeria" in *Entrepreneurship – Footsteps 103,* ed. Zoe Murton (London: Tearfund, 2017), 15.

[49] Naomi Foxwood, *The Amazing story of 'Jos Green Centre,' Nigeria*. Unpublished Tearfund presentation, May 2017.

[50] Fwangmun Oscar Danladi, *Teaching Elephants to dance: How theology is driving youth movement/initiative in Nigeria*. Unpublished presentation, 2016.

[51] Jos Green Centre, "Who We Are," https://josgreencentre.wixsite.com/mysite/about

[52] Osawe, "Jos Green Centre, Nigeria", 15.

[53] Ulan Garba Matta, "Nothing Goes to Waste" June 2019 https://renewourworld.net/2019/06/nothing-goes-to-waste/

[54] The Climate Coalition, "Jos Green Centre — the youth-led centre in Nigeria working for the environment and their local communities," 10 March 2021, https://theccoalition.medium.com/jos-green-centre-the-youth-led-centre-in-nigeria-working-for-the-environment-and-their-local-7c93c1c4beb1

starting innovative green businesses and changing mindsets about climate change. At the same time, the young people integrate prayers for the climate and environment into their spiritual life. In this process, their understanding of climate change changes, they respond spiritually and emotionally with their hearts, but they also adapt their lives as a result.

Conclusion

The Intergovernmental Panel on Climate Change concluded in their Climate Change 2021 report that the rate of surface temperature increase has generally been more rapid in Africa than the global average, with human-induced climate change being the dominant driver.[55] Extreme hot weather will continue while marine heatwaves will increase. It is therefore essential that churches in Africa include climate change resilience as part of Christian formation as they prepare Christians for living in extreme climate conditions. This formation has to include theological resilience, spiritual resilience and practical resilience.

The good news is that there are already excellent resources that Tearfund and others have developed to help churches in building climate change resilience as part of their Christian formation processes. There are also already excellent examples emerging in Africa where people have been equipped to be more resilient in the face of changing weather patterns. The challenge is to scale up and expand these initiatives to equip more people to face the challenges of climate change in future.

Suggestions for Further Reading

Blackman, Rachel and Isabel Carter. *ROOTS 13: Environmental sustainability*. London: Tearfund, 2009.

Carter, Isabel. *Releasing Potential: A facilitator's learning resource for self-help groups*. Addis Ababa: Tearfund Ethiopia, 2013.

Collins, Jude. 'Interview: From e-waste to electricity', in 'Sustainable Energy." *Footsteps* 114 (2021): 20.

Cornerstone Presbyterian Church. 'Christian Formation at Cornerstone Presbyterian Church' see https://www.cornerstonepresfranklin.org/christian-formation (accessed 14 August, 2021).

Danladi, Fwangmun Oscar. *Teaching Elephants to dance: How theology is driving youth movement/initiative in Nigeria*. Unpublished presentation, 2016.

Danladi, Fwangmun Oscar. *The 7-stage process of seeding a culture of movements for change: Case study of Jos Green Centre*. Unpublished paper, 2016.

Davis, Ellen F. 'Just food: A Biblical perspective on culture and agriculture', in *Creation in Crisis: Christian perspectives on sustainability*, edited by Robert S. White, 122-136. London: SPCK, 2009.

Demissie, Desalegn. *The role of Conservation Agriculture (CA) in mitigating the impacts of climate change on the lives of Smallholder farmers*. Unpublished Tearfund presentation given on 21 July 2021.

Eckstein, David, Vera Künzel, Laura Schäfer and Maik Winges. *Global Climate Risk Index 2020: Who Suffers Most from Extreme Weather Events? Weather-Related Loss Events in 2018 and 1999 to 2018.* Bonn: German Watch e.V., December 2019.

Fihavango, George. 'Quest for Ecotheology in a Situation of Ecological Disaster', in *Christian Theology and Environmental Responsibility*, edited by J.N.K. Mugambi and Mika Vahakangas, 96-111. Nairobi, Acton Publishers, 2001.

Felita, Jason. 'Justice and Creation Care: A Vision for All Creation to Flourish!', in *Live Justly Global*, edited by Jason Fileta, 110-123 (Portland: Micah Challenge USA, 2017).

Fileta, Jason. *Live Justly Global*. Portland: Micah Challenge USA, 2017.

[55] Intergovernmental Panel on Climate Change, "Climate Change 2021: The Physical Science Basis; Regional fact sheet – Africa," https://www.ipcc.ch/report/ar6/wg1/downloads/factsheets/IPCC_AR6_WGI_Regional_Fact_Sheet_Africa.pdf

Foxwood, N. *The Amazing Story of 'Jos Green Centre,' Nigeria*. Unpublished Tearfund presentation, May 2017.

Gaw, Helen. *Church and Community Mobilisation in Africa*. London: Tearfund, 2018.

General Synod of the Church of England, 'Developing Discipleship', *The Archbishops' Council 2015* (2015), https://www.churchofengland.org/sites/default/files/2017-12/gs%201977%20-%20developing%20discipleship.pdf (accessed August 12, 2021).

Gitau, Simon K. *The Environmental Crisis: A challenge for African Christianity*. Nairobi: Acton Publishers, 2000.

Harris, N. 'Foreword', in *INSPIRING CHANGE: Impact and Learning Report 2017*, edited by Tearfund Impact and Effectiveness Team, 1. London: Tearfund, 2017.

Hollinger, Dennis P. *Head, Heart, Hands: Bringing together Christian thought, passion and action.* Downers Grove, Illinois: Intervarsity Press, 2005.

Ijatuyi-Morphé, R. *Africa's Social and Religious Quest: A comprehensive survey and analysis of the African situation*. Jos, Nigeria: Hokma House, 2011.

Intergovernmental Panel on Climate Change. 'Climate Change 2021: The Physical Science Basis; Regional fact sheet – Africa', see https://www.ipcc.ch/report/ar6/wg1/downloads/factsheets/IPCC_AR6_WGI_Regional_Fact_Sheet_Africa.pdf (accessed August 12, 2021).

Jos Green Centre, 'Who We Are', see https://josgreencentre.wixsite.com/mysite (accessed 11 August 2021).

Johnson, Todd M., Gina A. Zurlo, Albert W. Hickman and Peter F., 'Crossing Christianity 2018: More African Christians and Counting Martyrs', *International Bulletin of Mission Research,* 42.1 (January 2018): 20-28. DOI: 10.1177/2396939317739833 (accessed 11 August 2021).

Kabugumila, Alice. 'Tanzanian Women's Response to the Environmental Crisis', in *Christian Theology and Environmental Responsibility*, edited by J.N.K. Mugambi and Mika Vahakangas, 64-73. Nairobi, Acton Publishers, 2001.

Kyomo, Andrew A. 'The Environmental Crisis as a Pastoral Challenge in Africa', in *Christian Theology and Environmental Responsibility*, edited by J.N.K. Mugambi and Mika Vahakangas, 57-63. Nairobi, Acton Publishers, 2001.

La Trobe, Sarah. *Saving for a Very Dry Day: The contribution of self-help groups to building resilience in East Africa*. London: Tearfund, 2017.

Lewani, Aaron. *Improving Peoples' Livelihoods through Enhanced Environmental and Economic Sustainability*. Unpublished Tearfund presentation on 21 July 2021.

Marshall, Joey. 'The world's most committed Christians live in Africa, Latin America – and the U.S', *Pew Research Centre*, August, 22, 2018. https://www.pewresearch.org/fact-tank/2018/08/22/the-worlds-most-committed-christians-live-in-africa-latin-america-and-the-u-s/ (accessed August 9, 2021).

Matta, Ulan Garba. Renew Our World Campaign: 'Nothing Goes to Waste', see https://renewourworld.net/2019/06/nothing-goes-to-waste/ (accessed 11 August 2021).

Murton, Zoe., ed. *Footsteps 103: Entrepreneurship.* London: Tearfund, 2017.

Njoroge, Francis W. *Church and Community Mobilisation Process Facilitator's Manual*. London: Tearfund, 2019.

Nugent, Ciara. 'The 10 Countries Most Vulnerable to Climate Change Will Experience Population Booms in the Coming Decades', *Time*, July 11 2019; see https://time.com/5621885/climate-change-population-growth/ (accessed 11 August 2021).

Osawe, B. 'Jos Green Centre, Nigeria', in 'Entrepreneurship' Murton, Zoe (ed) 2017, *Footsteps* 103, London, Tearfund, 15

Spencer, Nick and White, Robert. *Christianity, Climate Change and Sustainable Living*. London: SPCK, 2007.

Tearfund Learn, 'Environment and climate', https://learn.tearfund.org/en/how-we-work/what-we-do/environment-and-climate (accessed 11 August 2021).

Tearfund Learn, 'Footsteps magazine', https://learn.tearfund.org/en/footsteps-magazine/about-footsteps-magazine (accessed 11 August 2021).
Tearfund Learn, 'Reveal toolkit', https://learn.tearfund.org/en/resources/series/reveal-toolkit (accessed 11 August 2021).
The Climate Coalition, 'Jos Green Centre — the youth-led centre in Nigeria working for the environment and their local communities 2021'; see https://theccoalition.medium.com/jos-green-centre-the-youth-led-centre-in-nigeria-working-for-the-environment-and-their-local-7c93c1c4beb1 (accessed 11 August 2021).
The World Council of Churches, 'The Arusha Call to Discipleship', https://www.oikoumene.org/resources/documents/the-arusha-call-to-discipleship (accessed 11 August 2021).
Valerio, Ruth. *Saying Yes to Life.* London: SPCK, 2020.
Verisk Maplecroft, 'Environmental Risk Outlook 2021', https://www.maplecroft.com/insights/analysis/environmental-risk-outlook-2021/#report_form_container (accessed 11 August 2021).
World Economic Forum, 'The Sub-Saharan Africa Risks Landscape', http://www3.weforum.org/docs/WEF_The_Sub-Saharan_Africa_Risks_Landscape_report.pdf (accessed 11 August 2021).
World Economic Forum, 'These are the 5 biggest risks facing sub-Saharan Africa this year', https://www.weforum.org/agenda/2019/09/economic-growth-sub-saharan-africa-challenges-risks/ (accessed 11 August 2021).
Zurlo, Gina A. 'African Christianity', *Gordon Conwell Theological Seminary,* https://www.gordonconwell.edu/blog/african-christianity-101 (accessed 11 August 2021).

103. The South African-German Research Hub on Religion and Sustainability (SAGRaS): An Inter-contextual Initiative for Transdisciplinary Research on the Role of Religion for Ecological Sustainability[1]

Juliane Stork,[2] Jacques Beukes,[3] Philipp Öhlmann,[4] Ignatius Swart,[5] Tanya van Wyk[6]

Introduction

Fundamental socio-ecological transformations are needed to develop pathways into a sustainable future. This process requires not only appropriate policies, but necessitates radical paradigm shifts and changed mindsets.[7] Religious communities are crucial stakeholders for achieving these paradigm shifts because of their ability to act as agents of social change and to function as sources of knowledge. They bear a significant transformative potential, i.e. the "capacity to legitimise, in religious or ideological terms, the development of new motivations, activities, and institutions"[8] and strongly shape social and cultural values and worldviews. While ecological teachings and ecological engagement have substantially increased in religious communities during recent decades in what has been called a "greening of religions",[9] the impact of these teachings on religious communities' collective actions and their adherents' individual behaviours

[1] Parts of this text have been previously published in other works by the authors.

[2] Juliane Stork is John S. Mbiti Research Fellow at the Research Programme on Religious Communities and Sustainable Development at Humboldt-Universität zu Berlin. She is a research affiliate at the Faculty of Theology and Religion at University of Pretoria and currently works on her PhD thesis in intercultural theology.

[3] Jacques Beukes is currently a senior lecturer in the Department of Practical Theology and Mission Studies at University of Pretoria's Faculty of Theology and Religion. His research foci are youth and children's ministry, diaconal studies, theology and development, congregational studies, and community development. He has published various articles, book chapters, and a book in these fields. He serves on the editorial board of the journal, *Religion & Development*.

[4] Philipp Öhlmann is postdoctoral researcher in the International Research Training Group "Transformative Religion" at Humboldt-Universität zu Berlin and visiting scholar in the Department of Theology and Religious Studies at University of Botswana. Moreover, he is one of the leaders of the Research Programme on Religious Communities and Sustainable Development at Humboldt-Universität zu Berlin, research associate at University of Pretoria and executive editor of the journal *Religion & Development*. His research focuses on religion and economics, religion and ecology, as well as African Christianity and sustainable development. Dr Öhlmann obtained his PhD in Diaconal Studies from Heidelberg University and holds a Master of Science in Agricultural Economics.

[5] Ignatius Swart is professor in the Department of Religion and Theology at the University of the Western Cape, South Africa. He has an extensive research and publication record in the related fields of theology and development, religion and development, religion and welfare, and diaconal studies. He serves as an academic editor of the journal *Religion & Development*.

[6] Tanya van Wyk is associate professor of Systematic Theology and Christian Ethics in the Faculty of Theology and Religion at University of Pretoria. Her research foci include feminist theology, ethics and political theology. Van Wyk is one of the academic editors of the journal *Religion & Development*.

[7] Martin L. Parry (ed), *Climate Change 2007 – Impacts, Adaptation and Vulnerability: Contribution of Working Group II to the Fourth Assessment Report of the Intergovernmental Panel on Climate Change* (Cambridge: Cambridge University Press, 2007).

[8] Shmuel N. Eisenstadt, "The Protestant Ethic Thesis in an Analytical and Comparative Framework", in Shmuel N. Eisenstadt (ed), *The Protestant Ethic and Modernization: A Comparative View* (New York, London: Basic, 1968).

[9] Jonathan Chaplin, "The Global Greening of Religion", *Palgrave Communications* 2(16047) (2016). [Available at: https://doi.org/10.1057/palcomms.2016.47], [Last accessed: 11th March 2022].

in the realms of ecology and sustainability remains largely unknown. The question of how religious communities contribute to socio-ecological transition and sustainability is the core theme being investigated by the newly established international and transdisciplinary research consortium, the *South African-German Research Hub on Religion and Sustainability* (SAGRaS).

SAGRaS approaches this question in five case studies in Buddhist, Muslim, mainline Protestant, new Christian and African traditional religious communities. As a collaborative initiative, SAGRaS scrutinises ecological theologies to determine what types of ecological values are represented in each of the respective religious communities and what their impact is. Core points of analysis address the following questions: What forms of environmental commitment exist in these religious communities and what does their specific commitment depend on? What theological considerations lead to ecological action? Under what circumstances does ecological theological preaching or interpretation of scripture translate into action by the communities' adherents?

SAGRaS was founded by scholars from University of Pretoria, University of the Western Cape and Humboldt-Universität zu Berlin and is funded by the National Research Foundation in South Africa and the German Federal Ministry of Education and Research. The inter-contextual research hub operates from 2022-2025 in South Africa and Germany. It relies on the perspectives of various different stakeholder groups, including religious leaders, academic researchers, development practitioners and policymakers, who are actively involved in the consortium. The research will be conducted by transdisciplinary collaborative research teams from both countries made up of academic experts on the respective religious communities and of development policy and practice partners who are implementing measures to reach the UN's Sustainable Development Goals (SDGs). Furthermore, the research will also be conducted in close collaboration with representatives of the religious communities to ensure a research design that produces relevant results for all stakeholders involved.

Background: Religion, Culture and Socio-Ecological Transformation

SAGRaS explores the potential of religion and religious communities to promote socio-ecological transformation and the global transition towards sustainable societies. This undertaking is based on the assumption that the kinds of innovation required by socio-ecological transformations towards achieving sustainability need to be seen in the first instance as a process of change at the cultural level – the level of values, mindsets and attitudes. Religion is operative at precisely this level and the desirable notions of the quality of life, of wellbeing, of cultural and social values (and of sustainability) are fundamentally influenced by religion, as captured by concepts such as *buen vivir*, *ubuntu* and human flourishing. The consortium therefore seeks to engage with the cultural and value-based foundations of sustainability and the underlying prerequisites for the socio-ecological transformation of societies.

Religious communities, as important societal actors, are among the largest social service providers in many parts of the world today. Eighty-four per cent of the world's population is affiliated with a religious community.[10] Religious communities reach believers across social strata and age groups, while also influencing politics and the media. Most importantly, religion shapes social imaginaries and people's values.[11] The UN Environmental Programme's report on "The Role of Environmental and Spiritual Ethics

---

[10] Conrad Hackett and David McClendon, "Christians Remain World's Largest Religious Group, But They Are Declining in Europe," 5th April 2017, *Pew Research Center News Release*, [Available at: https://www.pewresearch.org/fact-tank/2017/04/05/christians-remain-worlds-largest-religious-group-but-they-are-declining-in-europe/], [Last accessed: 11th March 2022].

[11] Roger S. Gottlieb, "Introduction: Religion and Ecology – What Is the Connection and Why Does It Matter?", in Roger S. Gottlieb (ed), *The Oxford Handbook of Religion and Ecology* (Oxford: Oxford University Press, 2006).

in Galvanizing Nature Based Solutions"[12] further elaborates on the essential role of religious values in shaping the behaviour of people towards achieving sustainability. Religious communities are important sources of relief and psychosocial support in times of global crises and contribute substantially to the resilience of individuals and communities – this might also be true for ecological crises and the necessary adaptations to the changing climatic conditions. By fundamentally shaping people's worldviews, religion can be an important source for the promotion of sustainable development and behavioural change. But it can also hinder these processes and constitute a source of exclusion, marginalisation or opposition to transformations in the striving for sustainability. It becomes vital, therefore, to deepen our understanding of how religious communities use their value-shaping role in the light of the great global challenges of our time and in what directions their influence will shape societies facing the challenges of climate change and global environmental degradation.

Recognising the necessity to engage with religious actors in the promotion and implementation of the SDGs, governments and international development initiatives around the globe have started collaborations with religious communities. Leading examples of such engagement with religion are the World Faiths Development Dialogue initiated by the World Bank in 1998[13] the Religions and Development initiative at the University of Birmingham funded by the UK Department for International Development (DFID),[14] and the initiative on religion and development started by the German Federal Ministry of Economic Cooperation and Development in 2014.[15] Recently, the United States Agency for International Development also embarked on a process of strategic religious engagement, while the United Nations established an Inter-Agency Task Force on Religion and Development.[16] Specifically focused on ecological sustainability, the United Nations Environment Programme (UNEP) has established the Faith for Earth Initiative that engages with faith-based organisations for achieving the SDGs.

In a "turn to religion"[17] in academia, there has been a steeply increasing interest in religion in the sustainable development debate, leading to the emergence of a new research field.[18] Where more than 20

---

[12] UNEP, "The Role of Environmental and Spiritual Ethics in Galvanizing Nature Based Solutions" (Nairobi: UNEP, 2020). [Available at: https://faithfornature.org/wp-content/uploads/2020/10/The-role-of-Environmental-and-Spiritual-Ethics-in-Galvanizing-Nature-Based-Solutions-Final-Version-002.pdf], [Last accessed: 11th March 2022].

[13] Deryke Belshaw, Robert Calderisi and Chris Sugden (eds), *Faith in Development: Partnership Between the World Bank and the Churches of Africa* (Oxford: Regnum Books International, 2001); Paul M. Bisca and Rebekka Grun, "Higher Power to Deliver: The Overlooked Nexus Between Religion and Development," *Brookings, Future Development Blog* [Available at: https://www.brookings.edu/blog/future-development/2020/02/25/higher-power-to-deliver-the-overlooked-nexus-between-religion-and-development/], [Last accessed: 11th March 2022].

[14] Séverine Deneulin and Carole Rakodi, "Revisiting Religion: Development Studies Thirty Years on," *World Development* 39(1) (2011), [Available at: https://doi.org/10.1016/j.worlddev.2010.05.007], [Last accessed: 11th March 2022]; Gerrie Ter Haar, "Religion and Development. Introducing a New Debate," in Gerrie Ter Haar (ed), *Religion and Development: Ways of Transforming the World*(New York: Oxford University Press, 2011); Emma Tomalin (ed), *The Routledge Handbook of Religions and Global Development* (Hoboken: Taylor and Francis, 2015).

[15] BMZ, *Religionen als Partner in der Entwicklungszusammenarbeit* (Berlin: Bundesministerium für wirtschaftliche Zusammenarbeit und Entwicklung, 2016).

[16] United Nations, *2018 Annual Report of the United Nations Inter-Agency Task Force on Engaging Faith-Based Actors for Sustainable Development: Engaging with Religion and Faith-Based Actors on Agenda 2030/the SDGs* (New York: United Nations Inter-Agency Task Force on Engaging Faith-Based Actors for Sustainable Development, 2019), [Available at: https://wedocs.unep.org/bitstream/handle/20.500.11822/27504/UNIATF2018.pdf], [Last accessed: 11th March 2022].

[17] Emma Tomalin, "Global Aid and Faith Actors: The Case for an Actor-Orientated Approach to the 'Turn to Religion'", *International Affairs* 96(2) (2020): 323-342. [Available at: https://doi.org/10.1093/ia/iiaa006], [Last accessed: 11th March 2022].

[18] Ignatius Swart and Elsabé Nell, "Religion and Development. The Rise of a Bibliography", *HTS Teologiese Studies/Theological Studies* 72(4) (2016). [Available at: https://doi.org/10.4102/hts.v72i4.3862], [Last accessed: 11th March 2022]; Barbara Bompani, "Religion and Development: Tracing the Trajectories of an Evolving Sub-

years ago, the sociologist Kurt Ver Beek famously stated that "spirituality [was] a development taboo",[19] numerous research projects have now approached this field from different thematic, methodological and disciplinary angles. A multitude of books, articles and reports have begun to explore the manifold relationships and interactions of religious beliefs, religious practices and religious communities with the economic, social, ecological, political and cultural dimensions of sustainable development.[20] This field is highly inter- and trans-disciplinary,[21] ranging from religious studies and theology[22] to anthropology,[23] sociology,[24] political science,[25] development studies[26] and economics.[27] In the wake of this emergent field, several studies have also focused on ecological sustainability, highlighting the role of religion in this respect.[28] In a survey on Religious Leaders' Perspectives on Corona conducted by the Research Programme

---

Discipline", *Progress in Development Studies* 19(3) (2019). [Available at: https://doi.org/10.1177/1464993419829598], [Last accesssed: 11th March 2022].

[19] Kurt A. Ver Beek, "Spirituality: A Development Taboo," *Development in Practice* 10(1) (2000): 31-43. [Available at: https://doi.org/10.1080/09614520052484], [Last accessed: 11th March 2022].

[20] For overviews, see Ben Jones and Marie J. Petersen, "Instrumental, Narrow, Normative? Reviewing Recent Work on Religion and Development", *Third World Quarterly* 32(7) (2011): 1291-1306. [Available at: https://doi.org/10.1080/01436597.2011.596747], [Last accessed: 11th March 2022]; Swart and Nell, "Religion and Development. The Rise of a Bibliography"; Bompani, "Religion and Development: Tracing the Trajectories of an Evolving Sub-Discipline"; Jens Köhrsen and Andreas Heuser, eds., *Faith-Based Organizations in Development Discourses and Practice* (Abingdon and New York: Routledge, 2020); Tomalin, *The Routledge Handbook of Religions and Global Development*; Tomalin, "Global aid and faith actors".

[21] See Swart and Nell, "Religion and Development. The Rise of a Bibliography."

[22] Andreas Heuser, "Refuse to Die in Poverty!: Armutsüberwindung und Varianten des Wohlstandsevangeliums in Afrika", *Theologische Zeitschrift* 69, 1/2 (2013); Andreas Heuser, "Religio-Scapes of Prosperity Gospel: An Introduction", in Andreas Heuser (ed), *Pastures of Plenty: Tracing Religio-Scapes of Prosperity Gospel in Africa and Beyond* (Frankfurt am Main: Peter Lang, 2015); Paul Gifford, *Christianity, Development and Modernity in Africa* (London: Hurst, 2015).

[23] Erica Bornstein, *The Spirit of Development: Protestant NGOs, Morality, and Economics in Zimbabwe* (Stanford: Stanford University Press, 2005); Dena Freeman (ed), *Pentecostalism and Development: Churches, NGOs and Social Change in Africa* (Basingstoke: Palgrave Macmillan, 2012); Dena Freeman, *Tearfund and the Quest for Faith-Based Development,* Routledge Research in Religion and Development (Abingdon: Routledge, 2019).

[24] Peter L. Berger, "Max Weber Is Alive and Well, and Living in Guatemala: The Protestant Ethic Today", *The Review of Faith & International Affairs* 8(4) (2010): 3-9. [Available at: https://doi.org/10.1080/15570274.2010.528964], [Last accessed: 11th March 2022].

[25] Gerard Clarke and Michael Jennings (eds), *Development, Civil Society and Faith-Based Organizations: Bridging the Sacred and the Secular* (Basingstoke: Palgrave Macmillan, 2008); Barbara Bompani, "Religion and Development in Sub-Saharan Africa: An Overview", in Emma Tomalin (ed), *The Routledge Handbook of Religions and Global Development* (Hoboken: Taylor and Francis, 2015).

[26] Séverine Deneulin and Masooda Bano (eds), *Religion in Development: Rewriting the Secular Script* (London: Zed, 2009); Bompani, "Religion and Development: Tracing the Trajectories of an Evolving Sub-Discipline."

[27] Daniel L. Chen and Daniel M. Hungerman, "Economics, Religion, and Culture: A Brief Introduction", *Journal of Economic Behavior & Organization* 104 (2014): 1-3. [Available at: https://doi.org/10.1016/j.jebo.2014.04.008], [Last accessed: 11th March 2022]; Sedefka V. Beck and Sara J. Gundersen, "A Gospel of Prosperity? An Analysis of the Relationship Between Religion and Earned Income in Ghana, the Most Religious Country in the World", *Journal for the Scientific Study of Religion* 55(1) (2016): 105-129. [Available at: https://doi.org/10.1111/jssr.12247], [Last accessed: 11th March 2022]; Gharad Bryan, James Choi, and Dean Karlan, "Randomizing Religion: The Impact of Protestant Evangelism on Economic Outcomes", *The Quarterly Journal of Economics* 136(1) (2021): 293-380. [Available at: https://doi.org/10.1093/qje/qjaa023], [Last accessed: 11th March 2022].

[28] See Gottlieb, "Introduction: Religion and Ecology – What Is the Connection and Why Does It Matter?"; Mary E. Tucker, "Religion and Ecology," in Peter B. Clarke (ed), *The Oxford Handbook of the Sociology of Religion* (Oxford: Oxford University Press, 2011); Teddy C. Sakupapa, "Spirit and Ecology in the Context of African African Theology," *Scriptura* 111(1) (2013): 422-430. [Available at: https://doi.org/10.7833/111-1-12], [Last accessed: 11th March 2022]; Elisabeth Gräb-Schmidt, "Umweltethik", in Wolfgang Huber, Torsten Meireis and Hans-Richard Reuter (eds), *Handbuch Der Evangelischen Ethik* 1st ed. (München: C.H. Beck, 2015); Jens Koehrsen, "Eco-

on Religious Communities and Sustainable Development at Humboldt-Universität zu Berlin, 75 per cent of responding religious leaders worldwide considered the obligation to strengthen "environmental protection" as highly important in the post-COVID-19 future – environmental concerns thereby constituting the highest priority overall. Still, the specific role of religious communities for ecological sustainability in the contexts of Germany and South Africa remains unclear. SAGRaS seeks to address this lacuna through a comparative, empirical approach.

SAGRaS's Comparative Approach in a Nutshell

SAGRaS explores specifically the roles of religious leaders, youths and women in the striving for ecological sustainability to arrive at nuanced results from triangulated perspectives. Religious leaders are the key decision-makers. Youths represent the group most active in advocating for climate justice in social movements such as Fridays for Future. Women represent the group most affected by climate change and environmental degradation.[29]

The aim of the multi-religious approach reflected in the five case studies is to provide comprehensive findings on the role of religion for sustainability in a way that transcends the boundaries of existing approaches focusing on single religious communities. The case studies were chosen because they represent communities with well-developed eco-theological teachings, which differ vastly in terms of the collective and individual ecological actions produced by them.

1. Engaged Buddhism

This case study focuses on the international Buddhist organisation Fo Guang Shan, which has branches around the world, including in South Africa and Germany. From a comparative research perspective, Fo Guang Shan thus represents a notable example that can be studied to develop a deeper understanding of the overarching global dynamics within the context of intentional religious networks working on ecological sustainability. In the SAGRaS research, more specifically, the focus falls on the German and South African branches of this movement of engaged Buddhism[30] to explore the range of engagements and ecological initiatives developed within this movement in response to specific environmental challenges.

2. Islamic Eco-Jihad and Islamic Eco-Theology: Activism and Theology

Focusing on different Muslim ecological initiatives like "nourEnergy" or "green iftar" and on particular eco-theological concepts, this case study examines the entanglement of religious practices and normative ethics concerning environmental protection from an Islamic perspective.[31] The scope of this case study is,

---

Spirituality in Environmental Action: Studying Dark Green Religion in the German Energy Transition", *Journal for the Study of Religion, Nature and Culture* 12(1) (2018): 34-54. [Available at: https://doi.org/10.1558/jsrnc.33915], [Last accessed: 11th March 2022]; Emmanuel Anim, "Environmental Sustainability and Eco-Justice: Reflections from an African Pentecostal", in Louk Andrianos et al. (eds), *Kairos for Creation: Confessing Hope for the Earth: The "Wuppertal Call" – Contributions and Recommendations from an International Conference on Eco-Theology and Ethics of Sustainability* (Solingen: Foedus Verlag, 2019); Dietrich Werner, "The Challenge of Environment and Climate Justice: Imperatives of an Eco-Theological Reformation of Christianity in African Contexts", in Philipp Öhlmann, Wilhelm Gräb and Marie-Luise Frost (eds), *African Initiated Christianity and the Decolonisation of Development: Sustainable Development in Pentecostal and Independent Churches* (London: Routledge, 2020).

[29] Cf. Monika Barthwal-Datta and Soumita Basu, "Land, Water and Food," in *Gender Matters in Global Politics: A Feminist Introduction to International Relations*, Second edition (New York: Routledge, 2015).

[30] Cf. David E. Cooper and Simon P. James, *Buddhism, Virtue and Environment,* Ashgate World Philosophies Series (Florence: Routledge, 2005).

[31] Cf. Moegamad R. Gallant, "Sustainable Development: a Challenge to Muslim Countries" (Doctoral dissertation, University of KwaZulu-Natal, 2009), [Available at: https://researchspace.ukzn.ac.za/xmlui/handle/10413/399], [Last accessed: 13th March 2022].

therefore, to investigate Muslim contributions to environmental transitions in terms of (1) the kind of normative knowledge developed by an eco-theology,[32] (2) the intentions, motivations and objectives in Muslims' environmental actions,[33] (3) the performance of Muslim environmental practices,[34] and (4) relations to other Islamic, other religious and non-religious ecological activism.

3. Mainline Protestant Christianity

Since Lynn White's widely discussed article on the role of religion in environmental destruction,[35] mainline Protestant Christianity has come a long way in its development of sophisticated ecotheologies.[36] Ecotheologies in this movement are mostly based on new interpretations of the biblical creation stories (Gen. 1:2), which also have a substantial influence on the perceived role, responsibilities and contributions of women with regard to ecology and "nature".[37] Successful ecological networks have been established in these churches (e.g. The Green Anglicans who are active in South Africa or the German movement Umkehr zum Leben). This case study explores how well-established churches with long-standing traditions emphasise ecological theologies that influence whether congregations and individuals do or do not join collective ecological actions.

4. New Christian Movements

In South Africa, new Christian movements include churches founded independently of mainline Christian churches. Empirical research shows that an ecological movement is evolving in these churches.[38] The case study consists of an in-depth study of the largest church in South Africa, the Zion Christian Church (ZCC). Its members primarily belong to the group most vulnerable to climate change and ecological destruction.[39] On the German side, the case study focuses on independent Pentecostal and Evangelical churches in Germany. Only a few explicit ecotheologies can be detected in this movement in Germany,[40] as Pentecostal

---

[32] Cf. Sara Binay and Mouhanad Khorchide (eds), *Islamische Umwelttheologie: Ethik, Norm und Praxis,* Die islamische Theologie im Aufbruch Band 1 (Freiburg, Basel, Wien: Herder, 2019).

[33] Cf. Ursula Kowanda-Yassin, *Öko-Dschihad: Der grüne Islam – Beginn einer globalen Umweltbewegung* (Salzburg, Wien: Residenz Verlag, 2018).

[34] Cf. Rosemary Hancock, *Islamic Environmentalism: Activism in the United States and Great Britain* (Abingdon: Routledge, 2018).

[35] Lynn White, "The Historical Roots of Our Ecologic Crisis," *Science* 155(3767) (1967): 1203-1207. [Available at: https://doi.org/10.1126/science.155.3767.1203], [Last accessed: 13th March 2022].

[36] Pope Francis, "Laudato Si': On Care for Our Common Home," Encyclical letter (Vatican City, 2015), [Available at: http://w2.vatican.va/content/francesco/en/encyclicals/documents/papa-francesco_20150524_enciclica-laudato-si.html], [Last accessed: 13th March 2022]; Torsten Meireis, "Avatar: Nachhaltigkeitsethik, Kultur und Theologie," in Brigitte Bertelmann and Klaus Heidel (eds), *Leben im Anthropozän: Christliche Perspektiven für eine Kultur der Nachhaltigkeit* (München: oekom verlag, 2018).

[37] Tanya van Wyk, "Reproductive Health, Deconstructed: A Nonbinary Understanding of the Womb," in Jakobus M. Vorster et al. (eds), *Reconceiving Reproductive Health: Theological and Christian Ethical Reflections* (Cape Town: AOSIS, 2019): 1.

[38] Juliane Stork and Philipp Öhlmann, "Ökologische Nachhaltigkeit in African Initiated Churches," Kurzstellungnahmen des Forschungsbereichs Religiöse Gemeinschaften und nachhaltige Entwicklung 6/2019 (Humboldt-Universität zu Berlin, 2019), [Available at: https://www.rcsd.hu-berlin.de/de/publikationen/pdf-dateien/kurzstellungnahme-04-2019-oekologie-in-aics.pdf], [Last accessed: 13th March 2022]; Anim, "Environmental Sustainability and Eco-Justice"; Benjamin A. Ntreh, Mark S. Aidoo and Daniel N. A. Aryeh (eds), *Essays on the Land, Ecothology and Traditions in Africa* (Eugene, OR: Resource Publications, 2019).

[39] David Chidester, *Religions of South Africa,* The Library of Religious Beliefs and Practices (London: Routledge, 1992); Stork and Öhlmann, "Ökologische Nachhaltigkeit in African Initiated Churches".

[40] Thomas Kröck, "Klimawandel: Eine Frage Der (Un-)Gerechtigkeit," in Tobias Faix, Thomas Kröck and Dietmar Roller (eds), *Ein Schrei Nach Gerechtigkeit* (Marburg: Francke-Buchhandlung, 2016); Johannes Reimer, *Missio Politica: The Mission of Church and Politics* (Carlisle: Langham Creative Projects, 2017); Bernhard Olpen, "Jetzt wächst Neues: Schöpfungsverantwortung aus Sicht eines Vertreters der Pfingstbewegung", in Elisabeth Dieckmann,

sanctification theologies tend to reinforce traditional distinctions between inward renewal and engagement in worldly affairs, thus impeding ecological theologies and actions from gaining influence. The case study explores how ecological theologies develop within the framework of an other-worldly theological orientation and how inner and outer ecological impulses shape new ecological actions.

5. African Traditional Religions in South Africa

Religious environmental actions in African Traditional Religions (ATRs) have received little attention in the literature because of their heterogeneity across the continent.[41] ATRs have been described in recent literature as featuring an epistemological conception of the connectedness between humans and nature.[42] This literature calls for an "African" approach to environmental protection in opposition to the exploitative ways of the Global North. This case study aims to produce new insights into the environmental actions of this influential religious movement in South Africa.

An Innovative Approach to Researching Religion and Ecological Sustainability

Based on the five case studies, SAGRaS generates knowledge about the impact of religious concepts and notions of sustainability on the transformation of societies in the Global South and North. Drawing on the collaboration in this transdisciplinary consortium including investigators from various academic disciplines, civil society actors, policymakers and closely involving the religious communities themselves in the research process, SAGRaS intends to generate new insights into how religious communities can contribute to the transformation necessary for achieving sustainability and how other societal actors can draw on the resources inherent in such communities to foster this transformation.

SAGRaS has been conceptualised as a highly transdisciplinary initiative. Non-academic actors were involved in the planning stages and have therefore been involved in the research process from the start. While the main research activities will be carried out by university scholars, all the practitioners, policymakers and representatives of religious communities will jointly, and on an equal footing, contribute to the overall knowledge production. This includes participation in research workshops, joint work on publications, co-hosting of events and feeding knowledge into academic, practice, policy-making and religious discourse. SAGRaS thereby seeks to create common ground between the worlds of academia and practice, which provides the basis for implementation of the research results. This innovative form of cooperation will ensure direct use of the research results for all partners involved – ranging from policy implications for practitioners and policymakers to approaches to ecological actions for religious leaders and in-depth insights for researchers.

Several activities are planned to facilitate the implementation of the research results. A key activity will be the planned annual hybrid meetings where the case study designs, methodologies and results will be discussed by all the partners. A second activity envisaged will be the Religious Leaders' Forum on Ecological Sustainability to which religious leaders (research project partners and beyond) will be invited annually to meet in a hybrid format to exchange insights on different approaches to ecological theologies and on best practices to meet the challenges of ecological action and building sustainable communities. A third activity will involve the development of online postgraduate and practitioner courses, which will draw

---

Verena Hammes and Jochen Wagner (eds), *Verantwortung für die Schöpfung: 10 Jahre ökumenischer Tag der Schöpfung* (München: Herder Verlag, 2020).

[41] John S. Mbiti, *African Religions and Philosophy* (London: Heinemann, 1990).

[42] James N. Amanze, "From 'Dominion' to 'In Communion': Ecotheology from an African Perspective," *Anglican EcoCare Journal of Ecotheology* 2 (2016); Emmanuel Anim, "Environmental Sustainability and Eco-Justice" in Louk Andrianos, Michael Biehl, Ruth Gütter et al. (eds), *Kairos for Creation* (Solingen: foedus-Verlag, 2019); Jacob K. Olúpọ̀nà, "Religion and Ecology in African Culture and Society," in Gottlieb, *The Oxford Handbook of Religion and Ecology* (Oxford: Oxford University Press, 2006).

from the knowledge gained from the research with a view to creating a platform for advanced knowledge exchange and learning on religion and ecological sustainability. A fourth activity will involve the presentation of annual half-day policy and practice webinars, which will be co-hosted by policy and practice partners and serve as a platform for critically engaging with global policy events for ecological sustainability, such as COP 28. A fifth activity will take on the form of policy briefs, produced with the aim of informing development practitioners and policy makers on the results of the research. Finally, academic conferences, edited volumes, journal special issues and academic articles will form an indispensable part of the dissemination of the new academic knowledge. All results and knowledge products will be shared in an open-access format on the SAGRaS Digital Knowledge Platform.

Conclusion

SAGRaS explores and elucidates the nexus between religion and ecological development, between religious teachings and ecological actions. It does so by comparing different religious communities in two different countries across the South-North spectrum, that offer very different climatic and societal circumstances for climate change mitigation and adaptation. By providing the opportunity for inter-contextual and transdisciplinary exchange on the highly important issue of climate change, the research hub generates vital knowledge about the crucial religious stakeholders in the fight against climate change. Moreover, it provides an innovative space of knowledge production between various partners from different religious, geographic and professional backgrounds. It is therefore evident that SAGRaS explores new formats and research products to implement inter-contextual knowledge production processes between partners on an equal footing.

Suggestions for Further Reading

Golo, B.-W. K. "Religious Environmental Stewardship, the Sabbath and sustainable futures in Africa: Implications for Sustainability Discourse". *Consensus* 41(1) (2020): 1-14.

Haynes, J. "Environmental Sustainability", in J. Haynes, Ed. *Religion and Development: Conflict or Cooperation?* Basingstoke: Palgrave Macmillan, 2007: 124-149.

Moe-Lobeda C. and F. Helmiere. "Moral Power at the Religion-Development-Environment Nexus", in M. Clarke, Ed. *Handbook of Research on Development and Religion*. Cheltenham: Edward Elgar, 2013: 201-219.

Narayanan, Y. "Where are the Animals in Sustainable Development? Religion and the Case for Ethical Stewardship in Animal Husbandry". *Sustainable Development* 24 (2016): 172-180.

—. Religion and Sustainable Development: Analysing the Connections. *Sustainable Development* 21 (2013): 131-139.

Orellano, A., C. Valor and Emilio Chuvieco. "The Influence of Religion on Sustainable Consumption: A Systematic Review and Future Research Agenda". *Sustainability* 12 (2020): 1-21.

Tsimpo, C. and Q. Wodon. "Faith Affiliation, Religiosity, and Attitudes Towards the Environment and Climate Change". *The Review of Faith & International Affairs* 14(3) (2016): 51-64.

Van Wensveen, L. M. "Religion and Sustainable Development: A Typological Analysis", in G. Ter Haar, Ed. *Religion and Development: Ways of Transforming the World.* New York: Columbia University Press, New York, 2011: 81-108.

104. Educational Trends in Eco-Diaconia in the Context of Zimbabwe

Lovemore Togarasei[1]

Introduction

The Bible, right from its beginnings, highlights human beings' involvement with the environment. Thus, while nations are grappling with the effects of global warming due to human activities that have affected the earth, Christians are, as a group, grappling with theological readings of the environment. Many theologians have joined this call.[2] The Church in Zimbabwe cannot afford to ignore climate change and environmental issues. Of late, Zimbabwe has not been spared the effects of global warming. The country has experienced frequent floods and droughts that have generally affected people's quality of life. Taking a global overview of churches and the environment, Lluis Oviedo observes that a number of churches have, of late, been engaged in matters of the environment often through issuing statements and encyclicals.[3] He gives examples of the Swedish Lutheran Church, the Catholic Church, the Anglican Communion, the Methodist Church, etc. Even Evangelicals who, traditionally, have not been involved in these matters, are also taking keen interests.[4] In Zimbabwe, Marthinus Daneel gives an appraisal of how churches joined in the "war" for environmental conservation through tree planting.[5] But, although Daneel gives this appraisal, his observation is limited to southern Zimbabwe African Independent Churches (AICs) in the early 1980s. This trend has not continued, rather, with the increase of AICs that are numbering almost above 50% of the Christian population in the country, these churches are posing more danger to the environment than solutions unlike the churches of the early 1980s.

The mushrooming of AICs in the country, especially those meeting in open areas poses various dangers to the environment. Most meet where there are no ablution facilities and also cut wood for fire during their night vigils. In light of the above, this article looks at educational trends in eco-diakonia. Are there educational programmes available within church settings on climate change and the environment in general? To answer this question, the article considers both formal and informal education. I consider education very broadly to include the impartation of skills and the provision of knowledge on causes of climate change and global warming and the measures that individuals and communities can take to ameliorate the problem. To address the objectives of this article, I divide the article into four sections. In the first section, I consider environmental education in general before focusing on environmental education within churches. Under churches, I discuss some of the environmental programmes engaged in by some churches. In the third section, I consider formal eco-diakonia educational programmes within formal

---

[1] Lovemore Togarasei (PhD) is a Professor and Programme Leader at Zimbabwe Open University in the Department of Religious Studies and Philosophy. He teaches courses in Biblical Studies and has published widely in the area of the Bible and social transformation in Africa. He is the co-editor (together with Ezra Chitando) of *Lobola (Bride price) in Contemporary Southern Africa* (London: Palgrave Macmillan, 2021). E-mail: ltogarasei@gmail.com.

[2] See, for example, calls by Ernst Conradie, "Sustainability in African Theological Education", in I. A. Phiri, and D. Werner (eds), *Handbook of Theological Education in Africa* (Pietermartizburg: Cluster Publications, 2013): 707-713; Clemence Makamure, "Environmental Issues in African Theological Education", in Phiri and Werner, Handbook of Theological Education in Africa, 715-721.

[3] Lluis Oviedo, "Churches Concern for Environmental Issues: Making Sense of a New Christian Diakonia", *Forum Teologiczne* XVIII (2017): 1641-1196.

[4] K. K. Wilkinson, *Between God and Green: How Evangelicals are Cultivating a Middle Ground on Climate Change* (Oxford: Oxford University Press, 2012).

[5] Marthinus Daneel, "African Initiated Churches as Vehicles of Earth-Care in Africa", in Roger S. Gottlieb (ed), *The Oxford Handbook of Religion and Ecology* (Oxford: Oxford University Press, 2006).

theological programmes before ending with an evaluation and providing suggestions for strengthening eco-diakonia education in Zimbabwe. The article is based on review of literature and informal discussions I had with colleagues and students in some theological education institutions in Zimbabwe.

Environmental Education in Zimbabwe: A General Overview

Zimbabwe's learning institutions provide environmental education right from the primary school to university. At primary school level, environmental education is provided in subjects such as Agriculture while at secondary school it is provided in such subjects as Geography, Science and Agriculture. Indeed, the new Zimbabwe Curriculum Framework for Primary and Secondary Education (2015-2022) highlights environmental issues among the key curriculum areas for teaching and learning.

At a tertiary education level, such as teachers' colleges and universities, environmental education becomes much more specialised. Students study Geography as an area of specialisation while some institutions have Geography and Environmental Science programmes. The Midlands State University, for example, has a full faculty specialising in teaching and learning of Agriculture and Natural Resources Management.

Besides the education provided in formal teaching and learning institutions, the government of Zimbabwe has also instituted the Environmental Management Agency (EMA). Established by an act of parliament in 2002, EMA is responsible for "ensuring the sustainable management of natural resources and protection of the environment, the prevention of pollution and environmental degradation, the preparation of Environmental Plans for the management and protection of the environment".[6] EMA provides general environmental education through radio and other media outlets. Their website provides a lot of information on the environment including international conventions and manuals of some causes of environmental degradation and measures to be undertaken to protect the environment. The body also enforces environmental laws and policies.

Environmental Education in Churches

The Church wields tremendous influence in Zimbabwe by virtue of its long history and the number of its adherents. Education, health, politics and other departments of life have been directed by the Church in the greater part of colonial and postcolonial history of the country. Unfortunately, the same cannot be said of the Church's role in the area of the environment, especially with respect to AICs and Pentecostal churches. A number of these churches do not have formalised theological training for their ministers. The ministerial training is done in-house and sometimes just through experience. Therefore, theological positions, for example on the environment, are not well-reflected or articulated. The ministers then do not provide any environmental education to their members. Overemphasis of other-worldly spirituality (e.g., in some AICs) and health and economic prosperity (e.g., in Pentecostal churches), leave the environmental discourse unattended. Thus, cognisant of this gap, some environmental lobby groups, such as Isandhla Esihle, are now engaging the AICs to protect the environment.[7] They use both education and law enforcement to make sure the churches protect the environment. Isandhla Esihle encourages churches to register with them for an Environmental Impact Compliance. The organisation then assesses the churches for compliance and, if they find them wanting, they educate them on how to protect the environment and even gives them trees

---

[6] Zimbabwe's Environmental Management Agency Website [Available at: www.ema.co.zw], [Last accessed: 20th November 2021].

[7] Kubatana, "Open Air Churches Urged to Comply with Environmental Laws", 28th September 2020. [Available at: https://kubatana.net/2020/09/28/open-air-churches-urged-to-comply-with-environmental-laws/], [Last accessed: 13th March 2022].

for planting. Churches that fail to comply are reported to the ministry responsible for the environment and, if need be, are deregistered.

There are, however, some specific denominations that are undertaking projects for sustainable environmental management. One such Christian organisation is the Catholic Church of Zimbabwe. Steven Jerie has looked at an environmental project undertaken by the Roman Catholic Church Archdiocese of Bulawayo.[8] The project focused on restoration of degraded lands in Matobo through integrated catchment management. The project scored major successes in the areas of improved livelihoods and incomes as well as policy formulations for reduced loss of biodiversity through human actions. Having analysed the successes of the Roman Catholic Church project in Matobo, Jerie concludes that the church, "has thus lived up to the church doctrine of keeping the Lord's earth habitable today and for future generations."[9] Influenced by Pope Francis' Encyclical, Laudato Si', the Catholic Professionals Network of Zimbabwe is also engaging in environmental conservation in every business that the members find themselves engaged.[10] This initiative shows the influence that church leaders have in eco-diakonia since it is influenced by the Pope's teaching that, "We need a conversation which includes everyone, since the environmental challenge we are undergoing, and its human roots, concern and affect us all."[11]

While the general teaching of the Church is important for eco-diakonia, it is my opinion that the Church could be more impactful in its approach to environmental education if eco-diakonia is mainstreamed into theological education. This is because it is in theological education institutions that future church leaders are moulded. Below, I offer a bird's eye view of the place of environmental education in a few theological institutions in Zimbabwe.

Environmental Education in Some Theological Institutions

Three kinds of institutions that provide theological education can be identified in Zimbabwe. First, there are institutions that are church/denomination-affiliated and award certificates and diplomas. Second, there are institutions still affiliated with a church(es) but award degrees. Third, there are state institutions that offer certificate and degree programmes in theology and/or religious studies. As I write, the number of church-related theological institutions number no less than 20 with state institutions offering religion/theology programmes numbering more than 5. These numbers present a huge opportunity for addressing environmental issues through the church. Graduates from these institutions go on to minister to more than 80% of the country's population who profess to be Christians.

A look at the programme courses offered by most of the abovementioned institutions shows that they turn a blind eye on the environment. The Diploma in Religious Studies offered by a number of theological institutions affiliated with the University of Zimbabwe, for example, does not even have one course on ecotheology. The same applies to the programmes offered by Zimbabwe Open University, Theological College of Zimbabwe, Zimbabwe Christian College, Domboshawa Theological College, just to mention a few. Only a few institutions such as Africa University and Great Zimbabwe University offer a course(s) on environmental ethics but mainly from a philosophical perspective and not from biblical and theological perspectives.

---

[8] Steven Jerie, "The Role of the Church in Sustainable Environmental Management in Zimbabwe: a case study of the Bulawayo Archdiocese of the Roman Catholic Church", *Journal of Sustainable Development in Africa* 12(8) (2010): 217-226.
[9] Jerie, "The Role of the Church", 217.
[10] A. Kugwa, "Zimbabwe: Laudato Si' Campaign for a clear environment", *Vatican News,* June 2021. [Available at: https://www.vaticannews.va/en/church/news/2021-06/laudato-si-environment-zimbabwe-laity-commission.html], [Last accessed: 20th November 2021]; see also: https://www.youtube.com/watch?v=F8oU9Xqi1A4.
[11] Kugwa, "Zimbabwe: Laudato Si'".

Evaluation and Suggestions for Strengthening Eco-Diakonia Education in Zimbabwe

Our review of eco-diakonial education in Zimbabwe shows that a lot needs to be done for an effective response to the environmental crisis. From the history of the role of the church in social and economic transformation in Zimbabwe, it is my conviction that the church needs to play a very active role and this begins with a strong and well-articulated eco-diakonial education. Although environmental education is offered in schools, no tangible results have been realised especially in the activities of such churches as AICs. This is a conclusion also reached by Mukoni.[12] Mukoni's study targeted teachers in secondary schools around Gweru peri-urban and fully urban in Zimbabwe. This study assessed the transformative impact of environmental education in secondary schools using the systems thinking theory and social critical theory to analyse the role of learners and teachers in the development and maintenance of school grounds, bringing about awareness to other members of the school community as well as the role of pupils and teachers in the community as indicators of transformative social change. The idea was to gauge the pupils and teachers' actions to find out whether they have developed pro-environmental behaviour as a result of environmental education practice in the schools. The results showed that what is going on in the schools under the guise of environmental education is what Mukoni called "mere greening" of the curriculum which takes more of a factual stance of environmental education at the expense of action competence. He noticed that the education does not lead to transformation of communities, pupils and teachers as shown by their limited action in solving practical environmental problems in the context of their community. Environmental education practice in schools must be applied in solving the community's problems and it must promote the understanding amongst students on how to solve practical environmental problems. Following this observation, Mukoni made a recommendation that underlines the need for strengthening eco-diakonia in churches so that the Church complements the general environmental education being provided in schools.[13] He recommended that teachers need to model pro-environmental behaviour and forge partnerships with other environmental stewards such as community members and other organisations concerned with environmental issues. It is my argument here that one such organisation to complement the work of the schools is the church.

Oviedo, however, observes that ideologically, social and natural scientists have not taken theologians seriously when it comes to scientific issues.[14] He says this is because of theologians' lack of scientific knowledge. Whilst his observation may or may not be true of most trained theologians, it is true of most church leaders in Zimbabwe who have not received any eco-diakonia or general theological education. If Christians and theologians are to meaningfully engage in eco-diakonia, scientific knowledge is, in our opinion, indispensable. It is when they have enough education that Christians can meaningfully engage in addressing environmental issues.

In addition to equipping themselves with scientific knowledge, our other suggestion is that churches should be united and speak with one voice in their teaching on the environment. The world can only respect the teaching of the Church if the Church itself stands in unison with the moral authority that should characterise it. As stated by Oviedo, "The view is that churches that do not manage their problems well, will hardly be able to address greater, world level issues like those linked to climate change."[15] He goes further to observe that, "Christian churches can deliver their diaconate in the social field and environmental awareness if they do a good job of keeping the flame of faith in a transcendent and loving God burning, not when they neglect their own duties in order to better promote social and environmental causes or engage in ethical causes because religious activities are no longer appreciated or valued by the dominant secular

[12] Manuku Mukoni, "Environmental Education in Zimbabwean Secondary Schools: Greening or Transformative Social Change?" *International Journal of Asian Social Science* 3(4) (2013): 971-991.
[13] Mukoni, "Environmental Education".
[14] Oviedo, "Churches Concern for Environmental Issues", 175.
[15] Oviedo, "Churches Concern for Environmental Issues", 176.

culture."[16] It is in this light that I highlight strong theological eco-diakonia in order that the church does not take the role of secular environmental organisations but rather bases their environmental activism on the Word of God. Eco-diakonia should therefore be closely linked to the Christian gospel. As Oviedo concludes, "Church engagement to stop the wave of secularisation is their best contribution to environmental awareness."[17]

The Church must use its strengths to also address the causes of the current environmental crisis. One of the causes of the current global environmental crisis is greed and the understanding of development quantitatively. To address this, in its eco-diakonial education, the Church must address issues of development and sustainability where development is measured qualitatively in relation to equity and concern for future generations. As noted by I. K. Toroitich and G. Kerber, "Economies where the main criteria for success are the increase of gross national product (GNP) and gross domestic product (GNP) should shift towards 'economies of enough' that would support sustainable livelihoods, confronting greed and financial profits as main components of the prevailing development pattern."[18] To achieve this, the Church needs a theology of environment developed and offered at theological institutions and taken to the grassroots by the church's foot soldiers: the graduates of the theological institutions.

Conclusion

The current global ecological crisis calls for a multi-sectoral approach in addressing it. This article is based on the importance of theological education to the discourse of the environmental crisis. It opened with a review of trends in eco-diakonia in Zimbabwe. Having observed the shortcomings in the current offering of environmental education in general and eco-diakonia in particular, the article concludes that the church should become an active but well-informed partner in responses to the contemporary global environmental crisis. To do so, there is need to strengthen eco-diakonial education in theological institutions.

Suggestions for Further Reading

Conradie, Ernst. "Sustainability in African Theological Education". In I. A. Phiri and D. Werner, Eds. *Handbook of Theological Education in Africa*. Pietermaritzburg: Cluster, 2013: 707-713.

Daneel, Marthinus. "African Initiated Churches as Vehicles of Earth-Care in Africa", in Roger S. Gottlieb, Ed. *The Oxford Handbook of Religion and Ecology*. Oxford: Oxford University Press, 2006.

Jerie, Steven. "The Role of the Church in Sustainable Environmental Management in Zimbabwe: A Case Study of the Bulawayo Archdiocese of the Roman Catholic Church". *Journal of Sustainable Development in Africa* 12(8) (2010): 217-226.

Kugwa, A. "Zimbabwe: Laudato Si' Campaign for a Clear Environment". 22nd June 2021, *Vatican News* [Available at: https://www.vaticannews.va/en/church/news/2021-06/laudato-si-environment-zimbabwe-laity-commission.html], [Last accessed: 13th March 2022].

Makamure, Clemence. "Environmental Issues in African Theological Education", in I.A. Phiri and D. Werner, Eds. *Handbook of Theological Education in Africa*. Pietermaritzburg: Cluster, 2013: 715-721.

Ministry of Primary and Secondary Education. *Curriculum Framework for Primary and Secondary Education 2015-2022*. Harare: Zimbabwe Ministry of Primary and Secondary Education, 2015.

Mukoni, Manuku. "Environmental Education in Zimbabwean Secondary Schools: Greening or Transformative Social Change?" *International Journal of Asian Social Science* 3(4) (2013): 971-991.

---

[16] Oviedo, "Churches Concern for Environmental Issues".

[17] Oviedo, "Churches Concern for Environmental Issues", 178.

[18] I. K. Toroitich and G. Kerber, "Diakonia, Sustainability and Climate Change", *The Ecumenical Review* 66(3) (2014), 288-301: 290.

Oviedo, Lluis. "Churches Concern for Environmental Issues: Making Sense of a New Christian diakonia". *Forum Teologiczne* XVIII (2017): 1641-1196.

Toroitich, I. K. and G. Kerber. "Diakonia, Sustainability and Climate Change". *The Ecumenical Review* 66(3) (2017): 288-301.

Wilkinson, K. K. *Between God and Green: How Evangelicals are Cultivating a Middle Ground on Climate Change*. New York and Oxford: Oxford University Press, 2012.

105. INCREASING GLOBAL AND LOCAL RELIGIOUS ENGAGEMENT IN LEBANON: A RESILIENCE-BUILDING APPROACH ON ENVIRONMENTAL ACTION

Lara Hanna-Wakim[1] and Desiree El Azzi[2]

Introduction

Religion is quite an important driving force that continues to shape and influence the development of all aspects of life. The root cause of our environmental issues is our attitude towards natural resources. As a result, whilst regulations and agreements will aid it, consumption patterns are influenced by our daily environmental behaviour. Around the world, there are an estimated 37 million churches, 3.6 million mosques, 20,000 synagogues, and numerous other temples and houses of worship. These organisations control vast sums of money that, if used wisely, may make a significant difference in our current environmental crisis. They also serve as guiding lights for those seeking spiritual restoration and inspired action. Faith-Based Organisations (FBOs) should be brought closer to the ongoing talks on the environment, given the importance of religions in the globe.

Therefore, there is a growing recognition in the international community of the fact that religious organisations and faith leaders are critical moral and social agents for the protection of the environment and achieving sustainable development. Thus, FBOs are considered as essential players in eradicating poverty, improving people's health, protecting the environment, and thus achieving sustainable development.

With this context, the United Nations Environment Program (UNEP) in collaboration with the Holy See – Vatican City – established, in 2017, the Faith for Earth Initiative as an interfaith programme with the aim to strategically engage with faith-based organisations to collectively contribute towards the achievement of the Sustainable Development Goals (SDGs) and Agenda 2030.

The Faith for Earth Initiative falls within the framework of the "*Encyclical Letter Laudato Si'*" of the Holy Father Francis who explains the linkages between injustice, exclusion and environmental degradation.

The strategy of this initiative is based on three overarching and interlinked goals that mobilise faith actors and resources to employ innovative approaches to live in harmony with nature:

1. Strengthen Partnership with FBOs' Leadership for Policy Impact;
2. Increase Green FBOs' Investments, Operations and Assets; and
3. Establish an Accessible Knowledge-Based Support System using faith scripts and scientific evidence.

Having this in mind, we must acknowledge that we are in the midst of a climate emergency. Climate refugees, drought, deforestation, wildlife extinction, and the global COVID-19 epidemic demonstrate that humanity is facing an unspeakable disaster – social collapse is not an exaggeration. The climate catastrophe is evidently human made, as evidenced by massive, polluting industries, repressive activities of multinational businesses, and the hollow appeal of consumerism. Fortunately, scientists from all over the

---

[1] Lara Hanna-Wakim is the national co-ordinator of the "Faith for Earth Initiative" at the United Nations for Environment Program (UNEP) and professor of Sustainable Food Systems and Global Food Security at the Holy Spirit University of Kaslik, Ph.D. in Food Process Engineering, Diploma in Agricultural Engineering, Master's Degree in Food Quality Assurance and Management. Email: larahanna@usek.edu.lb.

[2] Desiree El Azzi is an Associate Professor at the Holy Spirit University of Kaslik, with a Ph.D. in Hydrology, Hydrochemistry, Soil and Environment. She is an agricultural engineer with a specialisation in Environmental Quality and Resource Management and a Master's degree in Ecosystem Functioning and Anthropisation. Email: desireeelazzi@usek.edu.lb.

world agree that there may be a tiny window of opportunity to reverse it via massive changes in infrastructure, economy, and human behaviour in the coming years.

For example, the Lebanese Maronite Order (LMO), a FBO that was founded in 1695, has been serving Lebanon and the environment with educational, pastoral, health, and economic development services. The personal, financial, and spiritual resources that FBOs bring to the table demand more recognition from the worldwide community striving to serve the same people. In fact, without any change now, nothing will be changed for the future. Change is never something that comes with ease, so we must be aware of not allowing our past to continuously repeat itself.

It has been often said that a value-based and ethical development system is required to create an equitable and sustainable future for people living on a healthy planet. Changes in mind-sets, behaviours, and consumption patterns are required to achieve the SDGs, and spiritual leaders are uniquely positioned to push these changes in an accessible and trustworthy manner.

The expected work in Lebanon will be the driving forces of the Faith for Earth Initiative in engaging with faith actors in response to the three interconnected planetary crises of climate change, pollution and ecosystem destruction.

Context and Objectives

Lebanon has long been known for its religious pluralism, which makes it unique in the region and beyond. To date, 18 confessions have been officially recognised by the State, among which are various Christian and Muslim communities.

Having a strong belief that these communities can have a significant impact on society through their behaviours, Faith for Earth project will bring together faith-based organisations, universities, schools, hospitals, NGOs and religious leaders to discuss potential actions for the protection of the environment. However, faiths tend to rely on their own teachings without creating an interfaith dialogue or exchange of knowledge to strengthen their global outreach; therefore, there is little interfaith partnership and lack of interfaith communication, collaboration, and interaction.

What Has the Power of Faith to Do with Environmental Action?

As we are all aware, actions have consequences, and because more than 80% of the people living on Earth are sensitive to spiritual beliefs and religion, an environmental message from their faith leaders is more likely to bring about change.

As a result of the enormous number of their followers in every corner of the globe – even in remote locations where environmental deterioration will be won or lost – FBOs have an unprecedented reach. They have enormous power to sway legislation and tilt the scales in the large worldwide movement required to address the planet's environmental problems.

Consequently, Lebanon can serve as model/hub for the MENA region, given the pivotal role that Lebanon can play in terms of religious, cultural and political diversity. Furthermore, to be affective, these Lebanese organisations need to be present at global environmental conventions and conferences to engage in dialogue with policy makers on the moral, ethical and religious obligations to protect the environment and implementing the SDGs.

Shifting the Needle on Environmental Protection in Higher Education: The Case of the Holy Spirit University of Kaslik

The Holy Spirit University of Kaslik (USEK) is a private Catholic Higher Education Institution founded by the LMO in 1938. For the past 7 years, USEK has been involved in several environmental activities at national and international levels in alignment with the SDGs. These achievements allowed USEK to be considered as the top green university in Lebanon. Some of the relevant activities are summarised below:

Greening the Curriculum. Extensive work was done since 2014 to integrate sustainability and environmental protection in the curriculum of all courses in all faculties. The Faculty of Agricultural and Food Sciences (FAFS) of USEK was a pioneer in creating the first and unique course related to Forestry which was honoured by the Ministries of Environment and Agriculture. Additionally, FAFS has established a unique collaboration with BTU, Cottbus (Germany) in terms of students and faculty exchange, including environmental topics in the curriculum along with grassroots activities to impact the local community and raise awareness on environmental challenges, water scarcity, food security among others. Furthermore, the Department of Religious and Oriental Sciences of USEK introduces students to the realities of living faith, the transmission of religious traditions, and the maturing of religions at all stages of life. The programme offered enables students to exercise a role of responsibility or intervention in relation to the transmission of religious traditions and maturation of faith. It provides spiritual accompaniment and vocations as well. It is worth mentioning that, presently, the total number of courses offered, at USEK, in fall 2020 included 2819 sections for 1407 unique subjects/courses. General requirement courses now also include Ecology, Environmental Sciences and Civic Engagement and citizenship. This way, the university is preparing environmentally conscious individuals who will work in different areas and domains, with a sustainability awareness.

Waterfull Initiative (SDG6 – Clean water and sanitation). USEK teamed up with a private water industry to ensure the right to clean drinking water to all USEK community. Every member currently has access to fresh drinking water all year round and fewer plastic bottles are being used.

ZeroWaste Campus. As holder of the title of first green university in Lebanon and 3rd most sustainable and green university in the MENA, USEK has set the example of environmental protection at the local and regional levels. Today, all campus waste is placed in a Materials Recovery Facility (MRF) where employees sort and dispatch all waste to local industries that recycle it or use it as raw material.

Carpooling. Since transportation is a major source of greenhouse gas emissions and other pollutants and with the increasing economic crises and Lebanese Lira devaluation, USEK decided to move towards a more sustainable transportation system. The aim is for a car-free campus coupled with a university-wide private shuttle system. Single-occupancy vehicle transportation is discouraged and instead carpoolers receive many benefits. In addition, a system relying on electrical shuttle for students and employees was developed on campus using electrical cars.

'Faith for Earth' Project in Lebanon: Goals and Pro-active Activities

Faith for Earth Lebanon project has three main goals:

- to inspire and empower faith organisations and their leaders to advocate for protecting the environment;
- to green faith-based organisations' investments and assets to support the implementation of SDGs; and
- to provide scientific knowledge/evidence and networks to enable faith leaders to effectively communicate with decision-makers and the public.

Faith for Earth Lebanon Team with the support of the United Religious Initiative (URI) for Lebanon is committed to building a common understanding between institutions and organisations to use their faith-based inspirations, knowledge, teachings, wisdom, and scripture for the benefit of the people of Lebanon and the planet. Hence, taking the lead in encouraging religious leaders to adopt a sustainable approach to development can have a strong impact on both public opinion and policy.

A primary goal of the project is to institutionalise its work and embed the need for faith engagement at high levels of environmental governance. A safe, clean and healthy environment is integral to the enjoyment of a wide range of human rights.

A series of activities were launched at the national level in partnership with different stakeholders and faith-based organisations, higher education institutions, NGOs, public and governmental entities, and young environmental activists:

1. Establish a diverse group of 18 faith leaders who, along with government officials, NGOs and young activists, form a national coalition for the protection of the environment by signing the Faith4Earth Pledge;
2. Conduct a series of trainings organised by USEK and other local universities, in collaboration with URI, for participants from schools, universities, hospitals staff, ministries staff and FBOs on environmental sustainability that includes:
3. Discuss the 2030 Agenda for Sustainable Development; assess understanding of related SDGs;
4. Explore environmental protection issues, such as hazardous waste management, ground water contamination, emissions et cetera;
5. Consider in what ways religious values address social issues;
6. Introduce green building certification and the development of a sustainability-themed magazine.
7. Produce an action guide on raising environmental awareness;
8. Appoint the members of this project as Faith 4 Earth Councillors (FECs) whose role is to convey the Faith4Earth Pledge.

Conclusion: What Can Faith-Based Organisations Do that Others Can't?

Because of the vast number of their followers in every corner of the globe, faith-based groups have unrivalled reach and mobilising power, including locations most at risk from environmental degradation. They have great power to influence policy and tip the scales in favour of the big global movement that we all recognise is required to address the planet's environmental problems.

Faith-based groups also have a distinct edge when it comes to tackling the cultural dimension of sustainable development by appealing to people's spiritual side and emphasising how faith and science can work together to address environmental challenges.

In conclusion, we admit that Faith for Earth Initiative is a pivotal project in Lebanon and the Middle Eastern Region. It will bring together faith-based leaders and representatives of indigenous peoples to inspire action among policymakers and faith followers by providing a forum for faith leaders to discuss the relationship between science and faith teachings as they relate to environmental sustainability.

Suggestions for Further Reading

Abumoghli, I. *Faith for Earth: Shifting the Needle on Environmental Action*. Nairobi: United Nations Environment Program, 2020.

Abumoghli, I. *Engaging with Faith-Based Organizations to Achieve the SDGs*. Nairobi: UN Strategic capacity building in collaboration with the UN Task Force on Religion and Development, 2019.

Clarke, M., and V.A. Ware. "Understanding Faith-Based Organizations: How FBOs are Contrasted with NGOs in International Development Literature". *Progress in Development Studies* 15(1) (2015): 37-48.

Faith for Earth. *Faith for Earth: Achievement Report 2020*. Online version: 10th February 2021. [Available at: https://www.unep.org/resources/annual-report/faith-earth-achievement-report-2020], [Last accessed: 14th March 2022].

Gemmill, B. and A. Bamidele-Izu. "The Role of NGOs and Civil Society in global environmental governance", in Daniel C. Esty and Maria H. Ivanova, Eds. *Global Environmental Governance: Options & Opportunities*. New Haven, CT: Yale Center for Environmental Law and Policy, 2002: 1-24.

KAICIID Dialogue Centre. *G20 Interfaith Forum* in collaboration with United Nations Alliance Of Civilisations and National Committee for Interreligious and Intercultural Dialogue in the Kingdom of Saudi Arabia, 13th-16th October 2022. Riyadh: KSA, 2020.

UNEP. *Environment, Religion and Culture in the Context of the 2030 Agenda for Sustainable Development*. Nairobi: United Nations for Environment Program, 2016.

PART II: ASIA AND THE PACIFIC

106. NURTURING RURAL LEADERS WHO SERVE THEIR PEOPLE AND CARE FOR THE SOIL: THE CASE OF THE ASIAN RURAL INSTITUTE IN JAPAN

Tomoko Arakawa,[1] Osamu Arakawa[2]

> Living together means sharing life together. Not only sharing our daily life with friends and neighbours of the present generation but also with people of future generations. Not only human beings but also the entire creation and the future.[3]
>
> Rev. Dr Toshiniro Takami (founder of ARI)[4]

It's early morning. Warm sunlight passes through the trees. The chickens are fed and the young seedlings are watered. It's time to return to work.

As you walk by lush vegetable gardens busy with bees, children greet you on their way to school. You will meet some of their parents later to discuss ideas for a new project to improve the life of the community that will benefit all.

The road is getting crowded. People are carrying their goods to the market – fish, fruit, vegetables. Many farmers are trying new organic methods that are free from chemicals. They have also begun co-operating so that their produce gets better prices at market.

You know it will be a busy day and you feel hopeful. The people are eager to make their village a good place for all.

At the Asian Rural Institute (ARI), we believe that rural communities can become such places, where children grow up healthy; where farmers have enough to eat and share; where people know their strengths and live in harmony with each other and with nature, being good stewards of nature.

We believe that rural communities around the globe can create true prosperity and that they are the key to a sustainable and resilient future. And we believe that such communities can be shaped through local rural leaders who are equipped with the right knowledge, values, and skills; and who understand about caring for creation in its deepest sense.

The Asian Rural Institute (ARI)[5] is a training centre for rural leaders who care for and cherish God's creation. Set on a six-hectare farm in northern Japan, it was founded in 1973 by a team headed by Rev. Dr Toshihiro Takami (1926-2018). Each year approximately 30 grassroots community leaders from countries in Asia, Africa, South America, and the Pacific take part in its nine-month Rural Leaders Training Programme. To date, ARI has graduated over 1,300 women and men from more than 60 countries – leaders

---

[1] Tomoko Arakawa is Director of Asian Rural Institute. She has been working at ARI since 1995 and has served as Director since 2015. tomoko_arakawa@ari-edu.org.

[2] Osamu Arakawa is Associate Director of ARI cum Farm Manager. He has been working at ARI since 2001. osamu@ari-edu.org.

[3] Asian Rural Institute, *The Heartbeat of Takami: A book of Toshihiro Takami's words* (Japan, Asian Rural Institute, 2018): 58.

[4] Rev. Dr Toshihiro Takami was one of the core founding members of ARI; was Chair of the Board and Director of ARI from 1973-1993 and continued as the Honorary President at ARI; in 1996 received the Ramon Magsaysay Award for Peace and International Understanding; passed away in September 2018.

[5] For more information, see the Asian Rural Institute website at: https://ari-edu.org/en/home/. [Last accessed: 14th March 2022].

who are working to build environmentally healthy, just, and peaceful societies according to the institute's motto "That We May Live Together."[6]

The training programme is intense. Running from spring to early winter, it allows the Participants (trainees) to follow the farming cycle in Japan and experience a great variety of topics[7] that will enable them to transform their communities, making them more sustainable and resilient. The contents of the training programme are based on a number of important key concepts and core values, each of which helps us realise our motto, "That We May Live Together." This strong philosophical base of ARI's training deeply influences participants, providing them with motivation and guidance.

The practically oriented curriculum empowers participants, through a spirit of servant leadership, to better facilitate and nurture self-development in their people. The programme is community-based and resource-focused, with a strong emphasis on hands-on participation in sustainable food production.

Foodlife – A Guide to Understanding Ourselves as a Part of God's Creation

At ARI, we grow our own food on our farm. Keeping a high rate of food self-sufficiency (over 90%), we grow over 60 varieties of crops and vegetables, and raise livestock – pigs, chickens, goats and fish. We practice organic farming, not using chemical fertilisers, pesticides, or herbicides. In Japanese, organic farming is written as 有機農業, meaning farming where life exists (有機 means having vitality, a life function and 農業 means farming and agriculture). Making and using organic fertilisers, managing pests with local materials, and using appropriate technology with integrated farming are practiced to protect the ecological system of the living soil for future generations. Organic farming can sustain our lives through a healthy relationship with nature, which is a gift of creation from God.

We call all activities related to food production and consumption on campus, *Foodlife*. *Foodlife* is an ARI term which expresses that food and life are inseparable: each depends on the other. Members of the ARI community spend one hour of *Foodlife Work* (daily farm work) every morning and evening, dividing ourselves into several groups. This work is in addition to the farming activities carried out by our farm staff and volunteers throughout the day.

Daily, morning and evening, *Foodlife Work* is managed by all members of ARI including participants, staff, volunteers and even visitors on a rotational basis. We wake up at 6:30 every morning to do our assigned *Foodlife Work* for an hour before breakfast, facilitated by the leadership of the Participants. Some go to the farm to cultivate land, some harvest vegetables, some feed livestock, while some cook our breakfast. After one hour of *Foodlife Work,* we gather in our dining hall, *Koinonia*, to eat breakfast and share the fruits of our hard work. In the evening, we join *Foodlife Work* for an hour once again.

The Participants of ARI take responsibility for the management of the fields and livestock with the support of the staff and other community members. Field and livestock management is group-based, and leadership is taken in turns by all the Participants no matter how much experience they have in agriculture. Therefore, leading *Foodlife Work* helps to develop leadership quality, because a group has to manage a great amount of work in a limited time with a variety of members who have different backgrounds. Once a week, the Participants have a Field Management Activity session. During each session, there are practical lectures, workshops, discussions or sharing on farming skills and management of the fields and animals. All of this work is hard, but it is spiritually rewarding because it is all for the sake of the entire community to live healthily and peacefully.

The basic philosophy of integrated farming at ARI is the full utilisation of space and resources that each integrated area of farm has. It also involves a mutual thriving of all farm areas. For example, we utilise pig

[6] Much of the information in this article is based on "School Guide" (2018) Asian Rural Institute. The school guide is available at: https://ari-edu.org/wp-content/uploads/2020/07/School-Guide.pdf. [Last accessed: 14th March 2022].
[7] See Curriculum of 2020 ARI Rural Leaders Training Programme in the Appendix below.

manure as an energy source and fertiliser, dry leaves for nursery beds and leaf compost, kitchen garbage for animal feed and compost. We regard the forest as an important part of integrated farming as well. While the forest protects land from landslides, soil erosion, typhoons and earthquakes, it provides us with fuel, dry leaves, natural pesticides, microorganisms, wild vegetables, and timber as well as increasing the biodiversity in nature. This is essential to create a balanced ecosystem.

We put value on the ecocycle through effective use of organic materials that come from both inside and outside of ARI. For example, we collect and reuse animal waste (manure, urine, bones, eggshells), rice husks, rice bran, rice straw, leaves, wastewater, rainwater, kitchen garbage, wild grass, indigenous microorganisms, wood (charcoal, wood vinegar, ash). We collect *okara* (a biproduct of making tofu) from a local tofu shop and fish waste from a local fish market every morning as ingredients for fermented feed for animals. Vegetable waste from a local school lunch cooking centre and a local supermarket are also utilised as animal feed. Our pigs love the protein-rich whey provided by a local cheese factory. We have started intensifying the utilisation of natural energy as well. We installed solar heating systems in the new buildings that were rebuilt after the Great Eastern Earthquake in 2011. These systems help us dramatically to cut our use of fossil fuels during the winter. A crop dryer that consumes a huge amount of energy is operated by straight vegetable oil made from used cooking oil. High food self-sufficiency by organic farming contributes to minimum food milage.

Actively participating in *Foodlife*, the whole cycle of food production and consumption, helps us understand the philosophy, practical skills, and knowledge of organic farming, the importance of food and food self-sufficiency, and the dignity of labour. But moreover, it gives the community of ARI a sense of wholeness. The cycle of preparing soil, sowing seeds, saving seeds, caring for, harvesting, eating, sharing, and recycling clearly shows us where we are from, how we are sustained and where we will end. This gives us a sense of security and a meaningful existence on this earth. *Foodlife* also gives community members of ARI a spiritual experience of connecting and reconnecting to each other, even amidst the conflicts and misunderstandings of everyday life. The ARI Training Handbook states, "*Foodlife* is a vital activity for human beings to maintain their lives and it connects God, the earth, and human beings – working as a medium for reconciliation and peace building."

Servant Leaders Who Serve the People and Care for the Soil

On 11th March 2011, the Great East Japan Earthquake occurred. Buildings collapsed, the tsunami drowned people and caused untold damage, and the Fukushima nuclear power plant exploded, and radiation spread. Many lives were lost. ARI also went through an ordeal. From this experience, we reaffirmed what was essential for human life – clean air, water, and soil. It is only when people lose these that they understood their importance, and that was exactly the case after the earthquake. When air, water, and soil are contaminated with radioactivity, one loses one's way of life. We realised how much these were precious and indispensable and how much we had previously taken them for granted.

The undesirable aspects and outcomes of development and economic growth also teach us things every day – excessive competition, disparities between rich and poor, losing and winning, faster, more efficient, more profit, more mass, more convenience, more growth, longer life, etc. Development and economic growth, in the hope that they can bring happiness to human beings, are replaced by the bloat of greed that will never end. Nature becomes just a resource that humans exploit. Food becomes a commodity. Life is measured by money. Workers become victims. People develop diseases of the mind and body. In addition, the cycle of life, a natural ecosystem that was once in exquisite balance, is destroyed. Climate change, flooding, drought, extreme high temperatures, torrential rains, sea level rise, grasshopper outbreak and a virus outbreak. Aren't these all the result of unrestrained human ego?

Human beings are being asked now about the way of their existence and how they should cherish and nurture life; how to place themselves in the cycle of life, following the laws of nature. That is how to be free from one's ego and greed, to know what is really needed, and to be humble before the magnificent nature that is beyond man. There may not really be so much that is necessary for human beings to live. This earth has beautiful and clean water, air, and earth. What is truly necessary is to exist as a part of the natural cycle without polluting it, and to be nourished by nature. To be a member of nature and to live with all other living things. To be able to eat and share food that sustains life with those whom you love. The soul will be saved by being forever rooted in the depths of nature that changes every minute.

To realise and sustain what is really needed, the world demands *Servant Leaders* who serve the earth and care for creation so that the world will be wakened to the dignity of life and the providence of nature. ARI trains grass-roots community leaders so that they are transformed into Servant Leaders, not conventional leaders. This is because community leaders with servant leadership who live among and serve their people, can guide the community to a desirable future where the dignity of life and providence of nature are highly valued.

Servant leadership is sustainable leadership that anyone can practice at anytime, anywhere. Ordinary people can take this leadership approach, regardless of nationality, culture, race, or religion, because the important thing in servant leadership is simply serving others, making use of the best parts of yourself. This leadership is also enduring because servant leaders will nurture the next leader. Servant leadership prioritises that which benefits all, not oneself or a part of the group. At ARI, the Participants learn servant leadership daily through serving others by such actions as cleaning the campus, dish washing, and working on the farm to produce food for others and even for future generations. The Participants are also given a lot of opportunities to take on actual leadership, not only in farm management, but also in other community activities such as Morning Gathering chairperson, during observation trips, and events like the annual Harvest Thanksgiving Celebration. We help them reflect on and improve their leadership through class sessions, consultation, and groups discussions.

Servant Leadership will then become embedded into their home communities after they graduate from ARI and return home. This is an alternative idea to secure the future. Strengthening rural communities by empowering their leaders with servant leadership and strategies for sustainable development; to educate compassionate leaders who have the integrity, resources, and local connection to bring a healthy and enduring impact. This can be done by sending our graduates home as Servant Leaders. They farm their land and train other farmers and their communities.

ARI is a place where men and women of different cultures and life experiences live, share, and learn while working to achieve a high rate of food and energy self-sufficiency. It is always full of surprises and excitement, and our souls resonate to the whole of nature. Like the splash of a flowing river, when all these people come, they are splashed and blown by the wind of the new Holy Spirit, and they go out with a new life. We believe that Servant Leaders who constantly serve new soil are born from such an environment. And we believe that such Servant Rural Leaders are the key to creating more resilient and sustainable communities for the future and this is how they are caring for God's creation.

Appendix

Curriculum of 2020 ARI Rural Leaders Training Programme

Leadership

Leadership
Servant Leadership
ARI History and Mission
Participatory Learning and Action
Independent Learner

Time Management
Presentation Skills
Presentation Skills 2
Facilitation Skills
Religion and Rural Life
Report Guidance
Coaching
Peace, Justice and Reconciliation
Dignity Workshop

Development Issues

Environment and Development
Nutrition and Development
Home Economy
Credit Union
Localisation
Gender Issues
Ashio Copper Mine and Shôzô Tanaka
Climate Change Challenge
Nasu Canal and Rural Development
Japan's Organic Farming Movement and JA
Rural Development in Kawanishi
Community Development Strategy in Yufuin
Nagai Rainbow Plan and Yoshihide Kanno
SDGs and ARI curriculum
Homeless Issue in Japan

Sustainable Agriculture/Technology

Organic Farming
Crops and Vegetables
Rice Cultivation
Livestock
Disease Control of Crops and Vegetables
Disease Control of Livestock
Alternative Energy and Appropriate Technology
Dangers of Chemical Farming
Natural Farming in Tropical Areas
Alternative Marketing Systems
Biogas workshop
Agricultural technique
Livestock technique
Meat processing

Others

Graduate Seminar (Organisational Sustainability)
Japanese Language (Intensive Language Class, Japanese Culture)

Practical Field Study

Crops and Vegetables Emphasis Bokashi fertiliser making, compost making, collection and utilisation of indigenous microorganisms, fermented plant juice, fish amino acid, water-soluble calcium, charcoal and wood vinegar making, rice husk charcoal, seed collection, seedling nursing using soil blocks, mushroom cultivation.

Livestock Emphasis Pigs (artificial insemination, delivery, castration), chickens (brooding), fish farming, livestock disease control, feed formulation, fermented feed, animal raising with fermented floor.

Meat Processing Sausage and ham making

Total training time: 1,880 hours

Suggestions for Further Reading

Much of the information in this article is based on “School Guide” (2018) Asian Rural Institute. The school guide is available at: https://ari-edu.org/wp-content/uploads/2020/07/School-Guide.pdf.

Berry, Wendell. “Think Little”, in *A Continuous Harmony: Essays Cultural and Agricultural.* Reprinted in the Whole Earth Catalog 1969. Menlo Park, CA: Portola Institute, 1969.

Cutting, Steven and Beverly Abma. *Rural Leaders, The Work and Community Impact of Graduates of the Asian Rural Institute*. Japan: The Asian Rural Institute, 2016.

Fukuoka, Masanobu. *The One-Straw Revolution: An Introduction to Natural Farming*. New York: New York Review Books Classics, 2009.

International Commission on the Futures of Education. *Reimagining Our Futures Together: A New Social Contract for Education*. Paris: UNESCO, 2021.

Kumar, Satish. *Elegant Simplicity*. Gabriola Island, British Columbia: New Society Publishers, 2019.

Montgomery, David R. *Growing a Revolution: Bringing Our Soil Back to Life*. New York: W.W. Norton & Company, 2017.

107. Theological Education for Eco-Justice Ministries: Reflections on the Serampore Initiatives[1]

George Zachariah[2]

Introduction

This essay is an attempt to introduce the initiatives of the Senate of Serampore College (University) in India to develop ecotheological research and dissemination of ecotheological insights to inspire and equip the churches in South Asia to engage in ministries of eco-diakonia and ecological transformation. The essay begins with a brief history of theological education in India with special reference to the Senate of Serampore College (University). It provides an extensive account of the Serampore initiatives to build ecotheological awareness and ministries in the Indian context. The essay concludes with some critical and self-reflexive observations and visions for the future.

Senate of Serampore College (University)

Serampore College is the first Protestant theological college in Asia established in 1818 by Baptist missionaries with the objective to "give an education in arts and sciences to students of every *caste, colour or country*, and to train people for ministry in the growing church in India."[3] Today, Senate of Serampore College functions as a university, and around sixty theological colleges and institutions are affiliated to it. Serampore is an ecumenical institution which brings together the Orthodox, Protestant and Pentecostal churches in India in the ministry of theological education and ministerial formation. Theological colleges from Sri Lanka and Bangladesh are also affiliated to Serampore. Its academic programmes include BD, MTh, DMin and DTh in various theological disciplines.

Theology is always done in context. Contextual theological reflections and doctrinal reformulations have always been a significant characteristic of theological education in India. Each generation made conscious attempts to indigenise Christian faith and to practice it in response to their particular religio-cultural contexts and existential realities. However, in the stratified Indian society, the relationship of domination has determined the politics of theological re-imaginations, and the selection of interlocutors. Subaltern theologies, such as Dalit theology, tribal theology, Adivasi theology and feminist theology which all emerged in India during the last decades of the last century, raised foundational questions on Indian Christian theology, theological education and its curriculum and methodologies. This critical interrogation has resulted in the reformulation of the mission statement of the Senate of Serampore College.

> We believe that the Triune God has offered the possibility of renewal of life and hope for the entire creation in and through Jesus Christ, and that as an instrument of God, the Church is called to be involved in God's mission of liberation, reconciliation and community building among all peoples through varied forms of ministry. Set in the midst of people of other faiths and ideologies as well as situations of life-negating forces, we are called upon

---

[1] This essay is dedicated to the memory of the Rev. Dr. Santanu K. Patro, former registrar of the Senate of Serampore College (University).

[2] Dr George Zachariah serves the Trinity Methodist Theological College, Auckland, Aotearoa New Zealand as Wesley Lecturer in Theological Studies. He has also served the Gurukul Lutheran Theological College and Research Institute, Chennai, India and the United Theological College, Bengaluru, India.

[3] Dietrich Werner *et al.* "Challenges and Opportunities in Theological Education in the 21st Century: Pointers for a New International Debate on Theological Education," in *Theological Education in World Christianity* (November 2009): 13.

> to equip the whole people of God to respond to the contextual challenges critically and creatively by being faithful to the Gospel of Jesus Christ. In light of this faith and self-understanding, we seek to equip ministers, leaders, scholars and the whole people of God to be committed to creative discernment of and active participation in God's liberative mission in the world at large and in South Asia in particular by providing programmes of theological study and ministerial formation at various levels through affiliated colleges and institutions.[4]

This discernment has also helped the Senate of Serampore College to initiate regular processes of curriculum revision. The following statement categorically explains the theological rationale for the curriculum revision process undertaken in 2014. "Theological education has the broad goal of equipping the people of God and the congregations, in their respective contexts, to live out the doxological-liturgical, *koinonial*, reflective, *diaconal* and missional dimensions of their existence, with a strong commitment to the liberation of the down-trodden (Dalits, Adivasis, tribals, women, the disabled, persons infected and affected with HIV and AIDS etc)."[5] Over the years, Serampore has provided the academic platform for contextual theological researches and reflections in new areas such as interfaith dialogue, Dalit theology, tribal theology, Adivasi theology, women's studies, disability theology, human sexuality and the like. These initiatives have significant impacts on the public witness of the Indian churches and the ecumenical movements.

The Ecotheology Movement in India

The environmental history of India starts with the indigenous communities and their cosmogonies, theologies and community practices of creation-care. Land, for them, was sacred. Their panentheistic spirituality and the custom of totem and taboo inspired them to practice a relationship of mutual flourishing with the rest of creation. Colonialism and missionary theology, which imposed an anthropocentric world view and salvation project, condemned the indigenous practices of creation-care as animistic, paganistic and pantheistic, and cancelled the ecotheological visions and practices of the indigenous and subsistence communities. Colonial extractivism led to widespread destruction of the commons in the subcontinent. Neo-liberal capitalism continued the colonial spirit of conquest through the colonisation of the *jal, jungle* and *jamin* (water, forest and land). Life-giving commons became commodities with a price tag, available in the market for corporations to plunder. Accumulation through displacement was the mantra of this trajectory of development and progress. Subsistence communities who have been living in communion with the commons from time immemorial were uprooted from their abode and livelihood.

The environmental history of India is also the history of the environmental justice movements. The colonial, capitalist, and casteist conquest of the commons and the commoners were contested by local communities. The Bishnoi Movement (1700s), the Mahar Stayagraha (1927), the Chipko Movement (1973), the Silent Valley Movement (1978), the Jungle Bachao Andolan (1982), the Appiko Movement (1983), the Narmada Bachao Andolan (1985), the National Fishworkers Forum (1985), the Anti-Tehri Dam Movement (1995), the Plachimada Struggle against Coca-Cola (2002), and a host of other movements continue to inspire communities to contest the colonisation and commodification of the commons and the displacement of the commoners. Such movements are also engaged in the process of envisioning and practicing commoning, creating alternative ecological relationships.

Religious environmentalism and ecotheologies are attempts to transform religions into public-oriented religions, articulating the theological foundations for engaging in creation-care and initiating programmes

---

[4] Senate of Serampore College, "Vision and Mission of Theological Education in India", Senate of Serampore College Website. [Available at: http://www.senateofseramporecollege.edu.in/pages/index/vision-and-mission], [Last accessed: 15th March 2022].

[5] *Regulations and Syllabus 2014, Degree of Bachelor of Divinity*, Serampore: Senate of Serampore College (University), 2014, 11.

for the restoration of creation. India is the cradle of several world religions, and has a long history of religious environmentalism and ecotheologies of diverse strands. Hinduism, Jainism, Buddhism, Sikhism, and Islam are known for their ecological visions and practices of creation-care. However, there are also criticisms regarding the politics of these ecotheologies, exposing their social location and reluctance to recognise the correlation between ecological restoration and social justice.

The history of the Christian ecotheology movement in India can be traced back to the ecological visions and practices of the indigenous and subaltern communities who embraced Christianity in the eighteenth and nineteenth centuries. They resisted the Western missionary theologies that desacralised nature and privatised salvation to a single species claiming to be created in the image of God. One can identify the determination and creativity of these communities to practise a syncretised faith of creation-care. The Christian Ashram movement in the 20th century practised ecological living and creation-care. Gandhian environmentalism inspired many Indian Christians to embrace ecological living. J.C. Kumarappa, an Indian Christian economist and close associate of Gandhi, has done substantial work to articulate the Gandhian environmentalism as an economy of permanence.[6]

One of the distinctive characteristics of the Indian ecotheological movement is its consistent attempts to approach the ecological crisis as a justice issue. In the wake of the first UN Conference on the Human Environment (UNCHE), held in Stockholm in 1972, M.M. Thomas observed that, "the churches have also the concern to see that the debate on environment does not become a provincial concern of the affluent rich societies […] It is certainly irresponsible to talk about environment in isolation from the massive world problem of poverty, war and oppression […] We need to affirm the centrality of man [*sic*] with his [*sic*] sufferings and hope in the environment debate."[7] The Christian ecotheology movement in India still continues this legacy to develop ecotheological reflections at the interface of Indian realities. Most of the major works in ecotheology in India emerged from theologians associated with the Senate of Serampore College.[8]

---

[6] J.C. Kumarappa, *Economy of Permanence: A Quest for a Social Order Based on Non-Violence* (Varanasi: Sarva Seva Sangh Prakashan, 1945). Also see Solomon Victus, *Religion and Eco-economics of Dr J.C. Kumarappa: Gandhism Redefined* (Delhi: ISPCK, 2003).

[7] M.M. Thomas, "The Concern for Cleaner Environment", *The Guardian* 4(24) (15th June 1972): 1-2.

[8] Some publications on ecotheology by Indian theologians associated with the Senate of Serampore College include Paulos Mar Gregorios, *The Human Presence: An Orthodox View of Nature.* (Geneva: WCC, 1978); Sebastian Kappen, *Paristhithi, Samskrithi* (Malayalam) (Kottayam: Ascend Publications, 1988); K.C. Abraham, *Ecojustice – A New Agenda for Church's Mission* (Bombay: BUILD Publications, 1992); Bastiaan Wielenga, *Towards an Eco-Just Society* (Bangalore: CSA, 1999); George Mathew Nalunnakal, *Green Liberation: Towards an Integral Ecotheology* (Delhi: ISPCK, 1999); Gabriele Dietrich, *A New Thing on Earth: Hopes and Fears Facing Feminist Theology: Theological Ruminations of a Feminist Activist* (Delhi: ISPCK, 2001); V.J. John, *The Ecological Vision of Jesus: Nature in the Parables of Mark* (Thiruvalla: CSS, 2002); Rajula Annie Watson, *Development and Justice: A Christian Understanding of Land Ethics* (Delhi: ISPCK, 2004); Aruna Gnanadason, *Listen to the Women, Listen to the Earth* (Geneva: WCC Publications, 2005); Chilkuri Vasantha Rao, *Ecological and Theological Aspects of Some Animal Laws in the Pentateuch* (Delhi: ISPCK, 2005); Ivy Singh, *Voices from Narmada: Doing Ecofeminist Theology* (Delhi: ISPCK, 2009); George Zachariah, *Alternatives Unincorporated: Earth Ethics from the Grassroots* (New York: Routledge, 2011); Wati Longchar, *Returning to Mother Earth: Theology, Christian Witness and Theological Education: An Indigenous Perspective* (Kolkatta: PTCA/SCEPTRE, 2012); Solomon Victus, *Eco-Theology and the Scriptures: A Revisit of Christian Responses* (Delhi: Christian Word Imprints, 2014); John V. Mathew, *Advaita Vedanta Re-explored towards Ecological and Dalit Theology* (Delhi: Christian Word Imprints, 2014); Zulunungsang Lemtur, *Climate Refugees: Towards a Tribal Christian Theology of Restoration* (Mokokchung: Tribal Development and Communication Centre, 2015); T. Swami Raju, *Eco-Concerns in Indian Religious Traditions: Inter-Religious Cooperation Towards Healthy Environment* (Delhi: Christian Word Imprints, 2018); Eric J. Lott, *Embodied God in Indian Eco-Vision: Engaging with Sri Ramanuja's Theology* (Delhi: Christian Word Imprints, 2019); Vinod Wesley, *Church and Climate Justice* (Delhi: ISPCK, 2021); R.C. Lalramchhana, *Cosmic Christology in the Gospel of Matthew: Matthew's Utilization of Nature Miracles and Jewish Cosmology* (Delhi: Christian Word Imprints, 2021);

Serampore Initiatives to Mainstream Eco-theology and Eco-Justice Ministries

The crisis of the earth and the emergence of environmental justice movements in different parts of the country prompted theological educators within the Senate of Serampore College to incorporate ecological concerns and ecotheological reflections into academic and ministerial formation programmes. By the 1990s, these concerns began to appear in the syllabi, worship, sermons, and the field education programmes. Courses in Christian Ethics incorporated environmental crisis as an ethical issue. Introduction to Christian Doctrines began to discuss ecological issues along with the doctrine of creation. Courses in the Hebrew Bible attempted to retrieve and reflect upon the ecological themes and motifs in the first testament. Social Analysis and Women's Studies departments also incorporated ecological concerns into their syllabi. A fully-fledged course on ecotheology was first introduced in the Serampore family at the Gurukul Lutheran Theological College and Research Institute, Chennai in 2007, under the visionary leadership of Dr K. Rajarathnam.

When the Senate of Serampore initiated a curriculum review process for the BD programme in 2009, the major emphasis was to make theological education a theological engagement with the context. Several new courses were introduced addressing contextual concerns. One of the introductory courses in the new curriculum was "Discerning the Signs of the Times" with the objective to enable the students to understand their social context as the locus for theological and ethical reflections and praxis. In this course, there are several units pertaining to ecological crisis and ecotheological reflections: Development as destruction: Stories from the neighbourhood, Terminator Seeds: Science and technology as agents of death, Climate change as climate injustice, and Destruction of *jal, jungle* and *jamin*: ecological crisis in our neighbourhood. For the first time in the history of Serampore, Green Theology was introduced as a required course in this curriculum. Different clusters made conscious attempts to mainstream ecological concerns, ecotheologies, earth ethics and eco-diakonia in their courses.

This curriculum was revised again, and the Green Theology course was also revised during that time. The very title of the revised course – Eco-Justice Theologies – reveals the perspectival changes in the new course. Science and Religion and a few other new courses were also introduced to the curriculum. The field education programme was also revamped, and the affiliated colleges were encouraged to arrange exposure programmes with environmental justice movements and environmental agencies.

The MTh curriculum was also revised in 2015. The new curriculum introduced new courses and new sections on the distress of the earth and ecotheological reflections in almost all departments. For example, in Christian Ethics, a new course entitled "Ecological Crisis and Eco-Justice Movements in India" was introduced. During this period, a few DTh research scholars also wrote their dissertations on ecotheology and earth ethics.

Some of the affiliated colleges of the Senate of Serampore initiated new programmes on ecotheology and eco-diakonia. In 2015, the United Theological College, Bengaluru, in collaboration with the Council for World Mission, started a diploma programme called Diploma in Eco-Justice Ministries. This is an online academic programme with three courses and a research project. People from different parts of the world are enrolled in this diploma programme.

Ecological consciousness and ecotheological reflections inspired the ecumenical movements in India to establish new units on eco-diakonia. The Commission on Justice, Peace and Creation (CJPC) of the National Council of Churches in India initiated several programmes to develop ecological consciousness among the Indian churches. CJPC has collaborated with the Board of Theological Education of the Senate of Serampore College (BTESSC) and organised different programmes on ecotheology and eco-diakonia for theological educators, students and church leaders. In 2010, they organised a pedagogical workshop for theological educators to mainstream ecological concerns in theological and ministerial formation.

---

and T. Nzanthung Ngullie, *Eco-Homiletics and the Craft of Narrative Preaching* (Delhi: Christian Word Imprints, 2021).

Eco-diakonia has become one of the important ministries of many of the mainline churches in India today. Ecotheological concerns are reflected in the sermons and liturgies. Eco-diaconal initiatives are undertaken by the churches and church-related organisations. Ecotheological sermons and articles are published regularly in church magazines. Many of the churches have established ecological commissions to spearhead eco-diaconal programmes. The Department of Ecological Concerns of the Church of South India is an example for the eco-diaconal ministries of the Indian churches.

Ecotheologies and Eco-Diakonia in India: Where Do We Go from Here?

As we have seen, awareness about the distress of the earth and the importance of eco-justice ministries has inspired theological institutions in India to incorporate these concerns in theological education. The ecumenical movement and the churches are also inspired to engage in eco-diaconal ministries. Even though the Serampore initiatives and the eco-diakonia of the Indian churches and the ecumenical movements are committed to affirm the ecological crisis as a justice issue, it is important to become self-reflexive and evaluate the social location of the ecotheological and eco-diaconal movements in India.

The distress of the earth and the earth community is essentially a justice issue because those who are least responsible for the crisis are forced to bear its gravest consequences. The correlation between ecocide and genocide exposes the connection between colonialism, neo-liberal globalisation, casteism, patriarchy and the ecological crisis. While the Global North has contributed disproportionately to the destruction of life on earth, the Global South – particularly the indigenous and subaltern communities in the Global South – continues to suffer the worst environmental catastrophes. Global negotiations and covenants on climate change are always controlled by the wealthiest developed nations, and instead of changing their carbon-intensive economic orders, they use the climate crisis as an opportunity to continue their economic colonisation of the Global South through "disaster capitalism." It is the polluters and colonisers of the global commons who decide which communities are worth protecting and saving. It is in this context that our ecotheologies and eco-diakonia should strive to offer alternative discourses and diaconal models, privileging the voices of the commons and the commoners. It requires the ethical courage to interrogate the caste-blindness of the mainstream ecotheology movement in India. The caste-blindness of the mainstream ecotheologies is not an innocent deficiency or omission; rather it exposes the social location and the caste privilege of the ecotheology movement in India.

Alternative ecotheology and eco-diakonia movements should be intersectional and emerge from the subaltern and indigenous resolve to problematise the ecological crisis at the interface of caste, patriarchy and neo-liberal capitalism. It offers us a radically different vision of the redeemed earth. Ecological justice, social justice, economic justice and gender justice are integrally connected. Informed by this discernment, let us engage in alternative ecotheological reflections and eco-justice diaconal initiatives.

Suggestions for Further Reading

Abraham, K.C. *Ecojustice – A New Agenda for Church's Mission*. Bombay: BUILD Publications, 1992.

Dietrich, Gabriele. *A New Thing on Earth: Hopes and Fears Facing Feminist Theology: Theological Ruminations of a Feminist Activist.* Delhi: ISPCK, 2001.

Gregorios, Paulos Mar. *The Human Presence: An Orthodox View of Nature.* Geneva: WCC, 1978.

John, V.J. *The Ecological Vision of Jesus: Nature in the Parables of Mark*. Thiruvalla: CSS, 2002.

Longchar, Wati. *Returning to Mother Earth: Theology, Christian Witness and Theological Education: An Indigenous Perspective*. Kolkatta: PTCA/SCEPTRE, 2012.

Nalunnakal, George Mathew. *Green Liberation: Towards an Integral Ecotheology*. Delhi: ISPCK, 1999.

Ngullie, T. Nzanthung. *Eco-Homiletics and the Craft of Narrative Preaching*. Delhi: Christian Word Imprints, 2021.

Raju, Swami T. *Eco-Concerns in Indian Religious Traditions: Inter-Religious Cooperation Towards Healthy Environment*. Delhi: Christian Word Imprints, 2018.
Singh, Ivy. *Voices from Narmada: Doing Ecofeminist Theology*. Delhi: ISPCK, 2009.
Victus, Solomon. *Eco-Theology and the Scriptures: A Revisit of Christian Responses*. Delhi: Christian Word Imprints, 2014.
Wesley, Vinod. *Church and Climate Justice*. Delhi: ISPCK, 2021.
Wielenga, Bastiaan. *Towards an Eco-Just Society*. Bangalore: CSA, 1999.
Zachariah, George. *Alternatives Unincorporated: Earth Ethics from the Grassroots*. New York: Routledge, 2011.

Appendix I: Senate of Serampore BD Curriculum Eco-Justice Theologies

Course Objectives

1. To enable the students to understand critically the distress of earth from the vantage points of the subsistence communities who are disproportionately affected by the crisis and to become involved in the civil society interventions to resist the abuse of nature.
2. To invite the students to critically look at our traditions of theology and biblical interpretations which have legitimised the plunder of earth, and to engage in deconstructing the doctrines and scriptures and traditions, using the hermeneutical key of the lived experiences of the Dalits, tribals, Adivasis, women, poor and other marginalised communities.
3. To inspire the students to form concerned groups in their respective theological colleges, faith communities and civil society, and to engage in vocations of eco-justice ministries both in church and society in solidarity with the social movements of our times.
4. To equip the students to transform the churches – local congregations – into intentional communities of creation-care and healing through their informed, committed, and creative involvement and leadership.

Course Outline

Unit 1: From Ecology to Eco-Justice

- Ecological Crisis as a Crisis of Faith and Justice
- Modern Science and Technology and its Violence against Earth
- Colonialism, Globalisation, and Development and the Colonisation of the *Jal, Jungle* and *Jameen* (Water, Forest and Land)

Unit 2: Analytical Mediation

- Deep Ecology
- Social Ecology
- Gandhian Philosophy
- Dalit/Tribal/Adivasi Perspectives on Eco-Justice

Unit 3: Subaltern Eco-Justice Movements

- Case studies of select subaltern eco-justice movements

Unit 4: Eco-Justice Theologies and Ethics

- Ecological Sins of Christian Theology and Biblical Interpretation
- Eco-Justice Hermeneutics
- Eco-Justice Theologies
- Earth Ethics

Unit 5: Towards Eco-Justice Ministries and Congregations

- Eco-Justice Spirituality

- Eco-Justice Liturgy and Proclamation
- Eco-Justice Congregations
- Eco-Justice Interfaith Engagements

Appendix II: Senate of Serampore MTh Christian Ethics: Ecological Crisis and Eco-Justice Movements in India

Course Objectives

1. To enable the students to understand and address the complex connections between the distress of the earth community and the wider socio-economic structures such as class, race, and patriarchy.
2. To help the students to understand critically the distress of the earth community from the vantage points of the subaltern social and eco-justice movements, and to become involved in their struggles to resist the abuse of nature and to create viable alternatives.
3. To invite the students to critically look at our traditions of theology and biblical interpretations which have legitimised the plunder of earth, and to engage in deconstructing the doctrines and scriptures and traditions, to create a redeemed earth.
4. To inspire the students to form concerned groups in their faith communities, and to engage in vocations of eco-justice ministries both in Church and society in solidarity with the social movements of our times.
5. To equip the students to transform the churches – local congregations – into intentional communities of creation-care and healing through their informed, committed, and creative involvement and leadership.

Course Requirements

- Seminar Presentation 40%
- Research Paper 60%

Course Outline

Unit I: Introduction to the Course
Unit II: Ecological Crises in India: A Contextual Scan
Unit III: Social Analytical Mediation: Environmental Philosophies
Unit IV: Critical Review of Dominant Environmentalism
Unit V: Narmada Bachao Andolan: A Case Study for Eco-justice Movements
Unit VI: Theological and Ethical Reflections on the Ecological Crises
Unit VII: Ethical Reflections on Climate Change
Unit VIII: Theological and Ethical Reflections on the Ecological Crises: Perspectives from India

108. The Role of Environmental Training and Building Awareness in Indonesian Churches

Jhon Kristo Naibaho[1]

The World in Peril: Confession

We confess that the whole creation bears the mark of God and belongs to Him. However, other than that, one confession that is currently no less important is that God's creation, this world, is presently not doing well. Our world is continuously moving towards destruction. Large-scale exploitation of natural resources are ongoing. People's consumptive behaviour in developed nations has not yet changed. Deforestation, particularly in developing countries, seems unstoppable. Climate-related disasters such as droughts, bushfires, and floods have become more and more frequent. Those who contribute the least to greenhouse emissions are suffering the most in this climate crisis. Simultaneously, the socio-economical disparity between the wealthy and the poor nations has grown even wider.

Indonesia, as one of the developing nations and rich in natural resources, has its unique environmental problems:

- Rapid and massive deforestation for the mining industries and palm oil plantations;
- Destruction of the ecosystem and the threat of extinct species;
- Agricultural conflicts between large corporations and local communities, where the corporation most likely comes out as the winner;
- Rain and dry seasons have become more irregular;
- Densely populated cities produce a massive amount of plastic waste;
- Economical policies that do not consider environmental rights, where the economy is placed well above ecological sustainability;
- The extreme disparity between the rich and the poor;
- Lack of environmental awareness in the community.

These environmental problems become one of the Christian contexts in Indonesia – the context of the theological church. The question is: what can be done by the Indonesian churches to make her relevant to this context?

Lack of Environmental Awareness as the Main Issue

Churches in Indonesia have seriously discussed environmental issues since the mid-1980s. During the XI General Assembly of Council of Churches in Indonesia (CCI) in 1989 in Surabaya, for example, the call for evangelism was not merely coined just for the people. The good news was also for all of creation. It was defined there as:

> Evangelism for all beings has the meaning of being responsible for the wholeness of God's creation. God gave the mandate to tend and to look after all of His creation (Gen. 2:15). After the fall, the earth was also cursed (Gen. 3:17-18) and was subjected to vanity and enslaved by mortality. All creation is in labour pangs as it awaits liberation and the glorification of God's children (Rom. 8:20-22). God desires the complete and total restoration

[1] Jhon Kristo Naibaho is a pastor of HKBP (Protestant Christian Batak Church). Email Address jhonkristo@gmail.com. He completed his doctoral studies at STFT Jakarta (Jakarta Theological Seminary) in the field of Ethics. Currently, he serves as Head of Research and Development Agency of the HKBP.

of relationship for all of His creation (Is. 11:1-10). Christ came to restore all things (Rev. 21:15) and in Christ, we are a new creation (2 Cor. 5:17).[2]

This formula became one of the important pillars in Indonesian churches to begin discussing environmental issues or the wholeness of creation in its context. However, although environmental issues have been discussed for a few decades, in all honesty, environmental awareness in the community is still very low among believers. This environmental awareness has not yet been incorporated into daily lifestyle.

Why is environmental awareness still very low? I suggest that it is because believers do not have proper understanding of the ecological paradigm. The way we treat other creations depends on how we view those creations. As long as people still consider that the created world is just an object, then destruction would also continue. Leonardo Boff discussed it this way: "The state of the world is connected to our state of mind. If the world is ill, that is the sign that our psyche is also ill."[3] Similarly but in a stronger tone, Sallie McFague affirmed, "The environmental crisis is a theological problem, a problem coming from views of God and ourselves that encourages or permits our destructive, unjust actions."[4]

The fact that many church members do not yet have the right ecological paradigm is understandable. Environmental discussions have so far been considered elitist in nature. The relationship between environmental issues and the Christian faith is usually discussed during church's general meetings, general assemblies, extra-ordinary meetings, or in theological campuses. In other words, it has not become a part of the congregational discussions. Therefore, it is not surprising that church members do not see the relationship between environmental destruction with their Christian faith.

Eco-Liturgy as a Proposal

Wherever a church is present, it does not exist in seclusion. The church exists in a particular context within its world. Churches are influenced by and are influencing that context. Currently, one of these contexts for world churches, including in Indonesia, is environmental destruction and climate-related disasters. In the last few decades, the level of environmental disasters has increased significantly, and it is all related to economical activities as well as people's lifestyles. Jürgen Moltmann stated, "The destruction of the environment that we are causing through our present global economic system will undoubtedly seriously jeopardise the survival of humanity in the 21st century."[5] We are certainly moving towards our deadly abyss. We are in the process of destroying ourselves and not only that, but we are also killing future generations before they even exist. Therefore, one very pressing need right now is to change and repent.

Paradigm and lifestyle changes must go hand in hand. We cannot expect someone to suddenly have an environmentally friendly lifestyle without having adequately understood the relationship between human beings and other creations. On the other hand, good ecological knowledge is not going to change anything if it is not followed by ethical conduct that supports the well-being of the whole creation. "Effective change," according to Larry Rasmussen, "is the result of the dialectical play of both elements: attitude and behaviour. A strategy that relies on only one will be ineffective."[6]

So, what can the Indonesian churches do to change that paradigm and increase environmental awareness among members? One of the ways is for churches to understand their liturgical purpose. Mainstream

---

[2] Robert P. Borrong, *Etika Bumi Baru* (Jakarta: BPK Gunung Mulia, 2003): 267.

[3] Leonardo Boff, *Cry of the Earth, Cry of the Poor* (Maryknoll, NY: Orbis Books, 1997): 6.

[4] Sallie McFague, *A New Climate for Theology: God, the World, and Global Warming* (Minneapolis, MN: Fortress, 2008): 31.

[5] Jürgen Moltmann, *The Spirit of Hope: Theology for a World in Peril* (Louisville, KY: Westminster John Knox Press, 2019): 7.

[6] Larry L. Rasmussen, *Earth-Honoring Faith: Religious Ethics in a New Key* (New York: Oxford University Press, 2013): 121.

churches in Indonesia, particularly the HKBP where I come from, is liturgical church. The meaning of liturgy here is how the worship service is governed by strict rituals and guided by a liturgical book and the church calendar. In HKBP, the liturgical book is called the *Agenda*. Those who serve as the liturgos (worship leaders) are called *Paragenda*.

Every Sunday, the Christians are gathered at church. From the beginning until the end of the service, they are guided by the liturgos who use the *Agenda*. Many of the HKBP's members have already understood fully the order of their church's liturgy. They know when to stand, to respond, to sing, to pray, to hear the sermons, and so on. We will not find any surprises in these liturgical routines.

It can be said that the liturgy in HKBP is understood as the order of worship that guides the congregation in doing worship services so it follows the HKBP's traditions. In addition, HKBP emphasises worship services as the fellowship of believers, who gather at a particular place and time to worship. The liturgy is formal in nature and church members are encouraged to diligently attend worship activities conducted at the church.[7] This liturgical understanding is not wrong. However, within the context of current environmental destruction, this liturgical understanding must be expanded because liturgy, in its basic form, does not only function to invite the congregations to gather and have fellowship in the church. Liturgy, in the end, sends out God's people to go into the world to bring good news. Liturgy should equip and move church members to enter the world.

Liturgy itself has a wide range of meanings. Liturgy is the public work of God's people – it is the expression of believers. On the root of the word liturgy, Frank C. Senn stated:

> in the ancient Greek city-states *leitourgia* was a form of public service – public works that citizens undertook for their community. This might have included building a bridge or sewer or erecting an image of the patron deity. When the apostle Paul gathered funds from the congregations in Macedonia and Greece for the relief of the poor in Jerusalem (see 2 Corinthians 8-9), he was doing a liturgy. He referred to himself as a "liturgist" (*leitourgos*). In some ancient Greek city-states, the work of the citizen assemblies (*ekklesiae*) was a liturgical work, a form of communal public service. In this way *leitourgia* was also associated with *ekklesia*, the assembly called out of the world to do work of the world in a more disinterested way.[8]

Based on the definition above, we could see that liturgy relates to day-to-day living, and it becomes a part of life as well as the profession of church members. Liturgy is not merely about worshipping inside the church building on a particular day and time. Christian liturgy helps to orientate God's people into the world. This kind of liturgy emphasises the relationship between worship and ethics, between liturgy and the Christian daily life.

If that is the case, then liturgy is supposed to make God's people more sensitive towards a social reality that is happening around them. Worship cannot be separated from social issues. Church buildings that are always packed during worship service are not going to change anything if God's people are not equipped and sent out to the world to make improvements. The Bible shows us that God was very angry towards His people who only cared about rituals but were blind towards evil, injustice, corruption, and so on.

In the liturgy, we are surrendering ourselves to be changed to become like Him. "To become like Him" here is to have the same mindset as to how God would see the world and to act according to how God would want to show His love to the world. Mark Labberton stated it well, "Worship sets us free from ourselves to be free for God and God's purposes in the world. The dangerous act of worshipping God in Jesus Christ necessarily draws us into the heart of God and sends us out to embody it, especially towards the poor, the forgotten ones, and the oppressed. All of this is what matters most and is most at stake in worship."[9]

[7] Jhon Kristo Naibaho, "Menuju Ekoliturgi Indonesia", D.Th. dissertation (STFT Jakarta, 2017): 84-85.

[8] Frank C. Senn, *Embodied Liturgy: Lessons in Christian Ritual* (Minneapolis, MN: Fortress, 2016): 18.

[9] Mark Labberton, *The Dangerous Act of Christian Worship* (Downer's Grove, IL: InterVarsity, 2007): 14.

The problem is, church liturgy has put too much emphasis on, and has directed believers' attention towards, heaven. Liturgy is over-emphasising God's transcendence. The congregants do not sufficiently have the inspiration nor the encouragement to worship simply in the day-to-day living, including on how to view and respond to environmental issues. In the context of environmental crisis, according to Sallie McFague, there are at least three callings that need to be answered by the church. First, the church must be environmentally friendly. Environmental friendliness has to become an additional characteristic of the church to complete the existing characteristics, such as to become one, holy, universal, and apostolic. Second, if the church is environmentally friendly, then it should become actively involved in taking a stand against issues which compromise the well-being of all creation, such as climate change and exploitation. Churches must get involved in economical studies and public policies. Churches must not allow human beings and the world to suffer because of investors' financial greed, or unfair political policies from governments. Third, through sermons, the preacher could actively and regularly mention and remind church members about God's love towards other creatures and how God allows the human being to become His partner to work for the goodness of all creation.[10]

According to Borrong, the church is an institution that that is a source of moral and ethical strength for the congregations. The environment could be well taken care of if moral responsibility to protect its life can be instilled into congregations. This is an urgent duty of the church in the current context of environmental destruction. The church must continually conduct training and teachings to build morals and spirituality that increase awareness for ecological care. Therefore, the duty to protect and care for the environment should become a part of worship (liturgy) and mission of the church – as a part of worship and mission of Christians themselves.[11]

Liturgy that can encourage environmental sensitivity and awareness such as this is called eco-liturgy. Liturgy is the believers' communal response towards God's work. In the liturgy, people have fellowship with one another as well as with God, and through liturgy, believers are sent out into the world to become a blessing. In the liturgy, God who is transcendent also becomes immanent. From the environmental perspective, we realise that Christian worship does not exist in a void but also in the universe, on earth, under the heavens. Even the church calendars themselves are a part of the natural world's cycle.

The church building, which we call God's house, from its foundation to its roof, is a combination of human creativity and creation's gift. It can stand because of the ground, water, sand, wood, air, the sun, and so forth. The sacrament, as an important part of our liturgy and theology, could not be celebrated and would be difficult to conceptualise without the presence of bread, wine, and water.[12] Therefore, liturgy is not only a spiritual but also an eco-spiritual experience. Liturgy should have sharpened and increased our environmental sensitivity.

From this environmental sensitivity standpoint, in due course, it will become eco-spirituality. Eco-spirituality is a daily lifestyle that places us as an inseparable part of this universal network of life. Eco-spirituality is an awareness that human beings are not lords over creation, but parts of creation itself. In other words, eco-spirituality is a lifestyle conversion from a life that only concerns itself with the well-being of humanity into a life that is concerned about the whole creation. Denis Edwards explained it as follows:

> Ecological conversion involves not only particular actions but also the action that is one's whole life. It involves me living the vocation that is my own, with a loving eye for the natural world around me, committing myself to be an Earth-loving and ecologically acting parent, homemaker, farmer, teacher, builder, business person, church leader, or student. It is a matter of being called to a lifelong commitment to the good of the Earth community, in

---

[10] McFague, *A New Climate*, 33.
[11] Borrong, *Etika Bumi*, 269, 274.
[12] Naibaho, *Menuju Ekoliturgi*, 4.

and through all that makes up the reality of my daily life, and seeing this as the way of following Jesus the Wisdom of God in this time.[13]

A Way of Praying, A Way of Living

In eco-liturgy, things that we consider basic and have taken for granted such as water, the air, the ground, sunshine, food, would be seen and considered differently. Those simple things have sacramental values in them. The Holy Communion, for example, could open our eyes to the problem of food shortages. When we come to God's communion table, we are also reminded that there are billions of others who do not have access to adequate food supplies. In this situation, the prayer that Jesus taught becomes even more relevant: "Give us today our daily bread."

Eating is no longer just an issue of the stomach. Eating becomes something spiritual, or specifically, something eco-spiritual. Every piece of food on our dinner table has stories to tell, that it was produced by farmers by tilling the land; they water it, sunshine makes it grow and the right climate produces the harvest. It is very important to instill this kind of environmental awareness among HKBP church members, who are mostly agricultural communities. This kind of liturgy reminds us that the ground needs to be loved and appreciated, the water needs to be protected and used sparingly, and climate stability needs to be maintained.

Prayer life should also determine the way we act. Liturgy and ethics must not be separated. Therefore, eco-liturgy and ecological ethics should go hand in hand. Liturgical church should become ecological church, and liturgical Christians should become ecological Christians. Environmental awareness and concern towards the well-being of all creation are the callings of Christianity. Christian commitment to the community of life on our planet will involve a commitment to the liberation of human beings from poverty and oppression and commitment to the well-being of all the other species of Earth.[14]

This is the Christian calling in Indonesia. Theologically and traditionally speaking, Christianity has ample resources to become an ecological religion and for the church members to become environmentally friendly. To quote again from Sallie McFague, "It has enormous worship and liturgical potential. [...] We must change how we think about ourselves and we must act on that new knowledge. We must see ourselves as both radically dependent on nature and as supremely responsible for it."[15] This is our urgent call. We should respond to it immediately.

Suggestions for Further Reading

Boff, Leonardo. *Cry of the Earth, Cry of the Poor*. Maryknoll, NY: Orbis, 1997.

Borrong, Robert P. *Etika Bumi Baru*. Jakarta: BPK Gung Mulia, 2003.

Edwards, Denis. *Partaking of God: Trinity, Evolution, and Ecology*. Collegeville, MN: Liturgical Press, 2014.

Labberton, Mark. *The Dangerous Act of Christian Worship*. Downer's Grove, IL: InterVarsity Press, 2007.

McFague, Sallie. *Life Abundant: Rethinking Theology and Economy for a Planet in Peril*. Minneapolis, MN: Fortress, 2001.

——. *A New Climate for Theology: God, the World, and Global Warming*. Minneapolis, MN: Fortress, 2008.

Moltmann, Jürgen. *The Spirit of Hope: Theology for a World in Peril*. Louisville, KY: Westminster John Knox Press, 2019.

---

[13] Denis Edwards, *Partaking of God: Trinity, Evolution, and Ecology* (Collegeville, MI: Liturgical Press, 2014), 179.

[14] Edwards, *Partaking of God*, 178.

[15] Sallie McFague, *Life Abundant: Rethinking Theology and Economy for a Planet in Peril* (Minneapolis, MN: Fortress, 2001), 209-210.

Naibaho, Jhon Kristo. "Menuju Ekoliturgi Indonesia." D.Th. diss., Sekolah Tinggi Filsafat Teologi Jakarta, 2017.

Rasmussen, Larry. *Earth-Honoring Faith: Religious Ethics in a New Key*. New York: Oxford University Press, 2013.

Senn, Frank C. *Embodied Liturgy: Lessons in Christian Ritual*. Minneapolis, MN: Fortress, 2016.

109. WALK THE TALK: LESSONS FROM THE LIVING WATER CAMPAIGN FROM AMITY FOUNDATION IN HONG KONG

Tong Su[1]

Save a Drop, Change a Life – the Amity Living Water Campaign

Amity Foundation Hong Kong[2] started the Living Water Campaign (henceforth "the Campaign") in 2011 to raise public awareness of the global water crisis and to raise funds to build water and sanitation facilities for needy communities in China and across the globe.

Innovative advocacy and fundraising activities and events, with complimenting effects and benefits, have been strategically "woven" into the Campaign to both maintain momentum and maximise impact. The Campaign is recognised as one of the leading forces to champion responsible lifestyles and to bring about positive social changes. The many participants and collaborating partners of the Campaign come to regard themselves as an indispensable part of a joint effort to reach Sustainable Development Goal 6: water and sanitation for all.

An average of HK$500,000 has been raised by the Campaign each year since 2011. Over 30 water and sanitation facilities, ranging from village drinking water systems, primary school shower rooms, to tube wells and toilets in impoverished areas, have been built with funds raised from the Campaign. Hundreds of thousands of people's lives have been changed for the better in many "forgotten corners" of the world.

Beginning as a humble attempt in the field of eco-diakonia, the Living Water Campaign is continue to grow stronger in its efforts to integrate advocacy, fundraising and sustainable development work in relation to water and sanitation issues at local, regional and global levels. By introducing approaches and methods adopted and sharing the lessons gained so far, we hope more people can draw hope and inspiration and start to make positive changes to the world by walking the talk.

The Formation

Since its establishment in 1985, The Amity Foundation, an NGO initiated by Chinese Christians, has been carrying out development projects in relation to water and sanitation. The work has greatly contributed to poverty alleviation and social development in mainland China and is now being extended to under-developed areas in some countries in Southeast Asia and Africa.

A 2010 research study, sponsored by EED and conducted in Amity's water project villages in Guizhou and Guangxi on mainland China revealed convincing evidences of how improved access to clean potable water helped in the growth of economy, health of the people, social coherence and gender equality.[3]

---

[1] Ms. Tong Su is the Project Co-ordinator of Amity Foundation Hong Kong. She began to work for Amity in 1992 and has accumulated extensive knowledge, skills and network in the field of social development work.

[2] The Amity Foundation [see: www.amityfoundation.org] is an independent Chinese social organisation, founded in 1985 on the initiative of Chinese Christians. It works to promote education, public health, social welfare, community development, environmental protection, disaster relief and other philanthropic undertakings in China and other parts of the world. Amity Foundation Hong Kong, with identical vision and mission of its mainland headquarters, focuses more of its work in advocacy, fundraising and overseas liaison.

[3] Theresa Carino, *Research Project on Sustainability of Water Projects in China.*

Amity Foundation Hong Kong (Amity HK) was initially a liaison office based in Hong Kong. It started to lay more emphasis in public awareness building and fundraising work in 2005. The advocacy and fundraising for water and sanitation became the centre stage of Amity HK's work around five years later.

In 2008, a devastating earthquake took place in Wenchuan, Sichuan Province, in mainland China. Amity HK was heavily involved in fundraising and on-site relief operations and rehabilitation work for affected rural communities. The irreplaceable role of water and sanitation in emergency relief and recovery from disasters repeatedly presented itself to us. Ultimately, a key feature in the full recovery of normal village life was the rebuilding of many water towers funded by Christian churches and organisations, like the Hong Kong Council of the Church of Christ in China and ACT Alliance.

To harness sympathy and support for Amity's wide range of social development work, Amity HK used to organise exposure trips for the overseas supporters to visit Amity's development "project areas", which, at that time, were mostly in mainland China. These trips did not only enhance participants' understanding of the contexts in which Amity worked but also challenged them to think about possible causes of and solutions to the development issues they encountered. In 2010, Amity HK organised such an exposure trip to Guizhou, one of the most impoverished provinces in China, for Hong Kong Sheng Kung Hui Women's League. A donation was made to Amity HK after the trip with the designation for "water projects". The group said of their experience: "we saw many different needs in the poor villages. We reckon the best place to start helping them is the provision of safe drinking water for people. Without water, nothing can go far."

In Hong Kong, the water prices are among the lowest in the world. There is very little incentive for people to respond to callings from research organisations, academic institutions and the government to save water even though most of them understand the importance of water in personal lives and social development. There were some theological reflections on water being part of the creation, on the duties to preserve natural resources and on the duty to provide "a glass of water" (Mt. 10:42) to all as Christians. But these reflections were seldom heard by the majority of Christians across the city.

Meanwhile, environmental issues and the climate crisis were given increasingly more limelight globally. The Hong Kong education authority saw the trend and made the content on water and sanitation an important part of the curriculum for primary and secondary school students. Students were also required to have relevant Other Learning Experiences (or "OLE") activities as a supplement to what they study in school.

The local Christian churches and schools in Hong Kong have been the two major blocks of support in terms of people and donations for Amity HK. For an Amity campaign in Hong Kong, it seemed right to start there.

The Formula

A carefully designed sustainable campaign incorporating advocacy, fundraising and sustainable development started in 2011. The name of "Living Water" was given to the Campaign as it carries both deep Biblical and straightforward practical meanings.

Advocacy – Let the Stories be Heard, Let the Needs be Seen

The essence of advocacy is inspiration. And inspiration needs knowledge. Amity HK arranges with churches, schools, and even kindergartens in Hong Kong to have lectures and presentations delivered to the congregations and younger generation in the public. They are told about the pressing global water crisis and the difficult situations in which a part of the world population are still living. They are also told about actions already taken to address the problems. They are always asked what they can do to help at the end.

Amity HK continues to organise exposure trips for its supporters, now with a greater focus on water and sanitation issues. Journeys for Living Water, as these trips are called, prove to be the most powerful way of advocacy for the Campaign. They allow unique immersion experiences during which the participants actually can "stand in the shoes" of the people and communities they visit. The participants meet, talk and sometime eat meals with the locals, hearing them talk about the difficulties and dreams. They are introduced to local government officials and NGO personnel and learn what has been done and what kind of gap there still is. The trips always make participants think. became the most active promoters of the Campaign on their return. A grade four girl, a student of SKH Ma On Shan Holy Spirit Primary School in Shatin District of Hong Kong, did a touching presentation during the school's Christmas Tree Lighting Ceremony in 2012. She shared the unforgettable experience of taking the Journey for Living Water with Amity HK to the remote hilly areas of Guangxi in the summer. She ended her sharing with a passionate call to all her school mates for actions in the spirit of love and service. The elementary school has been one of the "pillar" partners of Amity HK for the Campaign since then.

Fundraising – Harness Generosity, Walk with Partners

Now that a solid foundation has been laid with people who sympathise and support the cause because of advocacy activities like lectures, presentation and Journeys for Living Water, the Campaign aims further to find ways to engage the public and solicit useful resources for Amity's sustainable development work.

Walk for Living Water (or "WLW") is a fundraising walkathon organised by Amity HK each spring since 2011 around 22nd March (the UN Water Day). It has become the signature event of the Living Water Campaign. Participants are required to make a donation and take up the challenge of walking for one to two hours while carrying water using the traditional bamboo pole-and-bucket sets.

An average of 500-1,000 participants expressed their willingness to support the Campaign by showing up at the fundraising walkathon each year. While church congregations and schools form the biggest groups of the participants, quite a few corporations also help by providing sponsorships and sending staff and their family members to attend the event.

Organizing Walks for Living Water (WLWs) is no easy job, especially for a small organisation like Amity HK which currently only has 5 staff members. However, thanks to help from loyal partners and many volunteers, the WLWs engage people from all walks of life in Hong Kong. Because of the engagement, young people get valuable opportunities to learn about the plight of people living in deprived areas regarding their access to water and sanitation facilities, and they also witness that small efforts made together can lead to great changes. Because of the engagement, government authorities like the Water Supplies Department can reinforce its message to persuade citizens to save water which is crucial to the survival of all humankind. Many of these people and agencies eventually keep coming back and join WLW every year and become the important power that keeps the Living Water campaign rolling forward.

Ms Lam Yi Ning has been taking part since the first WLW in 2011 when she was still in elementary school. She was diagnosed with a brain tumour and suffers a lot of difficulties in her life and study. She not only actively takes part in all kind of activities of the Campaign, including the very challenging Journeys for Living Water to remote areas, but also helps to champion the cause of saving water and helping others. She is by far the longest serving Ambassador of the Living Water Campaign. "If someone like me can do something to make a difference, you can too," wrote Yi Ning, in her appeal letters to her teachers, doctors and friends.

Sustainable Development – Goal of Service, Witness of Love

How can people believe that even their smallest action in the spirit of love and service can make a difference?

The Amity Living Water Campaign chooses to answer the question by translating the goodwill and resources contributed by participants of all the advocacy and fundraising activities into new water and sanitation facilities in needy communities in mainland China and other places around the world. These needy communities are identified with help from Amity HK's mainland China headquarters and many NGO partner organisations. Detailed work plans and budgets of the water and sanitation constructions form as a result of discussions participated by all stakeholders. The Campaign has helped to build over 30 water and sanitation facilities for needy communities in mainland China, Nepal, Sri Lanka, the Philippines and Myanmar, mostly by working with local churches and Christian faith-based organisations and institutions, with funds raised from the Campaign.

While setting high standards of project management to hold the implementing partners' work accountable, we respect their local wisdom and understand their limitations. They are willing to provide regular updates of construction projects and share touching stories from the beneficiary communities. This timely and genuine information become valuable inspiration and encouragement for supporters of the Living Water Campaign when stories are publicised and shared via websites and social media platforms.

With help from the local implementing partner organisations, Amity HK is able to bring more groups of people to go on Journeys for Living Water and to also visit communities where new water and sanitation facilities were built with resources raised. In each place, the participants refresh their understanding of the complex issues of human societies and come back to Hong Kong with even more powerful stories. They told people around them that changes are taking place because of their participation in the Amity Living Water Campaign and are encouraged more to actively join this "chain of love in action".

Ms Ma Mei Nor, an evangelist who serves at HK SKH Good Shepherd Church has dedicated a lot of her time and efforts to promote and raise funds for the Campaign among her congregation, the schools and kindergarten affiliated to the church, and her family since 2012 when she returned from her first Journey for Living Water. When reflecting on that trip to the mountainous He Zhang County in western of Guizhou with her son, Ms Ma once said with emotion, "after visiting the new water facility built uphill and on our way back downhill, a lady smiled at me from her road-side cottage and wanted to offer a cup of water to me. How foolish I was then not taking it – I did not realise then that the lady was trying to show gratitude to the people who helped her village by presenting me with the most precious thing in her life."

Thus, the solid and positive impact on people's lives, in the form of newly built water and sanitation facilities, becomes the testimony that greatly encourages both Amity HK and the supporters to reignite the fire for a new round of the Living Water Campaign.

New Initiatives under COVID-19

Due to COVID-19 and related social distancing requirements, WLW2020 and WLW2021 were held via online platforms. While donations still go to Amity, participants could take the walk by choosing their own time and route.

With the CCOVID-19 pandemic still rampant, travelling will not be possible for a long while. The opportunity however arises as people are now more experienced in communicating through technology. Therefore, Amity HK began the exploration in 2021 for a new method to bring together people serving and being served in the Campaign.

Riding on the annual cycle of the WLW, Amity HK held the first online Living Water Townhall with the theme on "Water and Human Needs" via Zoom on 22nd February 2021 to enable hundreds of students in SKH Tsang Shiu Tim Secondary School to join a virtual experience interacting with the beneficiaries and local partners of Living Water facility construction projects in Nepal and Myanmar. We were thrilled to learn that the results from the exit survey after the online exchange were mostly positive. For instance, one in two students who had more direct dialogue with guest presenters would like to join the coming WLW.

Encouraged by the successful results of the first Living Water Townhall, Amity HK worked with Fanling Kau Yan College and NLSI Lui Kwok Pat Fong College, another two Christian secondary schools in Hong

Kong and organised the second and the third Living Water Townhalls on 22nd March and 12th July respectively. Overseas guests were invited by Amity HK from Sri Lanka, the Philippines, Indonesia, Norway and the UK and they shared a wide range of topics in relation to water and sanitation. Some showed videos depicting the daily hardships people are facing in water-deprived communities, others talked about the importance of engaging women in the planning and execution of water and sanitation projects. The guests from the Philippines and Sri Lanka shared how inter-faith co-operation was enhanced during the implementation of Amity's living water construction projects. Other topics included the importance of water and sanitation for people suffering from natural disasters and creative ways to raise funds for the Living Water Campaign. Students had good opportunities to talk with the guests and also shared information on water situations in Hong Kong. The enthusiastic students were organised by the teachers, both during the Townhalls and afterwards, to come up with action plans. "Shorten shower time to save water", "spread the Campaign messages to more people", "make a donation to help poor people" and "study hard" are among the many things the students have decided to do.

Reflecting on the Townhalls so far, we note that this means sharing appeals to a wide cross-section of young people. The deep-drive into the root cause of water deprivation provided excitement for learning and elicits natural empathy for others' sufferings. Moreover, it could reach audiences across time-zones and in large numbers. From the enthusiastic responses from our partners such as Transform Nepal, Toungoo Diocese of the Church of the Province of Myanmar, South Christian College of United Church of Christ in the Philippines, Board of Social Responsibility in Diocese of Colombo of Church of Ceylon etc., we believe scaling up such conversations across many territories is just a matter of will.

Join Hands and Unite Voices

There is no quick and easy solution to the environmental and climate issues the world is facing. And no campaign should stand alone if any impact is expected to be sustained.

We were very excited to learn in the spring of 2021 that the Norwegian Missionary Society was inspired by the Campaign and successfully organised their version of Walk for Living Water in Norway too.

Amity HK already started a pilot online youth exchange with member organisations of the Asia and Pacific Regional ACT Alliance Youth Community Practice, like the National Council of Churches in the Philippines and YAKKUM Emergency Unit in Indonesia, recently to set up a new model of co-operation under the COVID-19 new normal.

"Only when people change will we be able to solve the problems people create," said Mr Qiu Zhonghui, General Secretary of the Amity Foundation during the WCC seminar on "Food and Water for Life!" on 4th May 2019 which Amity HK helped to organise with Hong Kong Christian Council and Tao Fong Shan Christian Centre, where the event took place. To support the WCC's Food for Life Campaign, Amity translated into Chinese the Food Advocacy Tools for Congregations with the Ten Commandments of Food[4] with a wider circulation among Chinese readers.

The Living Water Campaign started out as just a humble attempt. But we see that the campaign gives people some hope, when hope seems out of reach. Through the past 10 years, some people's confidence in solving the global crisis grew, many people deepened their understanding and trust of others, more people learned to take steps to take actions and share what they have.

Circumstances are fast changing. China has declared its "complete victory" in poverty alleviation in 2020. However, the global environment is deteriorating. The wealth gap is widening between countries and regions. On top of this, the COVID pandemic has created barriers to fundraising, exchange and sustainable

[4] "WCC general secretary reflects on "Ten Commandments of Food", 4th May 2019, *WCC News* [Available at: https://www.oikoumene.org/news/wcc-general-secretary-reflects-on-ten-commandments-of-food], [Last accessed 16th March 2022].

development work. It is time for like-minded individuals and organisations to join hands and unite voices in order to solve the intractable water and sanitation issues facing all humankind.

Suggestions for Further Reading

Allan, Tony. *Virtual Water: Tackling the Threat to Our Planet's Most Precious Resource* London: I. B. Tauris, 2011.

Amity Foundation. "Living Water Campaign". *Amity Foundation Website* [Available at: https://amityfoundation.org/eng/index.php/cause/living-water-project/], [Last accessed: 16th March 2022].

Black, Maggie and Jannet King. *The Atlas of Water: Mapping the World's Most Critical Resource.* Oxford: Myriad, 2009.

China Water Risk, Website available at: www.chinawaterrisk.org, [Last accessed: 16th March 2022].

Gleick, Peter H. *Bottled and Sold: The Story Behind Our Obsession with Bottled Water.* Washington D.C: Island Press, 2010.

Schwartz, Judith D. *Water in Plain Sight: Hope for a Thirsty World.* New York, NY: St Martin's Press, 2016.

Sphere Standards. *The Sphere Handbook.* Geneva: Sphere, 2018. [Available at: https://spherestandards.org/handbook/editions/], [Last accessed: 16th March 2022].

United Nations. "World Water Day 22 March", *United Nations Website* [Available at: www.un.org/en/observances/water-day], [Last accessed: 16th March 2022].

Water Footprint Network. Website available at: www.waterfootprint.org, [Last accessed: 16th March 2022].

Water Conservation. Water Supplies Department, the Government of Hong Kong Special Administrative Region. Website available at: www.waterconservation.gov.hk/en/home/index.html, [Last accessed: 16th March 2022].

World Council of Churches. "WCC general secretary reflects on "Ten Commandments of Food", 4th May 2019, *WCC News* [Available at: https://www.oikoumene.org/news/wcc-general-secretary-reflects-on-ten-commandments-of-food], [Last accessed 16th March 2022].

Part III: Latin America and the Caribbean

110. Hope for All of Creation: Practical Guide for the Church in its Care for the Environment

Benita Simón Mendoza[1]

Introduction

The socio-environmental crises that are currently being unleashed in different parts of the planet do not represent new phenomena. Thanks to computer globalisation, these events become a permanent part of the news – to the point that their daily recurrence leads us to stop for just a few seconds to regret them, and then simply continue to go through other headlines. This shows our dehumanisation and hardening in the face of the suffering of an enormous number of people. However, our indifference is even greater in the face of the suffering of innumerable species of plants, animals, micro-organisms and even non-biotic elements of nature that suffer from abuse, indiscriminate exploitation and massive disappearances.

Faced with this panorama of death and destruction, we must remember that the God whom we say we love and serve is the Creator of the universe and loves everything which is created, both macro and microscopic. So the latent question is: what are we Christians doing towards the task that has been entrusted to us for responsible stewardship? Faced with this question and as a necessary resource for understanding why and how we can be such responsible stewards, the material *Hope for all Creation* (*Esperanza para toda la Creación*) is presented, which, in addition to articulating valuable content for self-training, is a practical guide to accompany groups of people in their development and support related to creation care.

Why Does Esperanza para toda la creación Come to Light?

In Latin America, environmental care does not appear as one of the most popular themes in the literature produced from the Christian faith. In fact, there is little known material and, in many contexts, there is not even access to material related to the topic. Given this situation, it is understandable that, when the issue of responsible stewardship of creation is raised in our faith communities, questions arise such as: Is care for creation part of our mission as sons and daughters of God? Is it something to teach/study or to put into practice? Is it more important than what we are already doing? Would there be strong biblical foundations in this regard? How to act in the face of such a wide-ranging problem that often seems *far away*?

And although at first glance such questions seem to have obvious answers, suffice it to remember that for a long time we have relegated the issue of care for creation to a lower level of importance on ecclesiastical agendas. We have observed that in most churches and faith communities, even when there is some knowledge about environmental problems, in practice there is no commitment to its care and restoration, so not only do we lack biblical foundations that move us to act, but we also lack interest in the technical aspects.

---

[1] Benita Simón Mendoza (benita@centroesdras.org) is an indigenous woman from the Maya Kaqchikel people of Guatemala, specialising in care, restoration and environmental education issues. She is currently the co-ordinator of the Environment Programme of the *Fundación Centro Esdras.* In addition, with the Rujotay organisation, she co-ordinates local advocacy projects in her hometown.

Faced with this situation, as a necessary "breather," a project arose that led to the preparation of the material *Esperanza para toda la creación*.[2] It is a comprehensive resource for the Christian Church, articulating biblical foundations, which support *why* Christian individuals and communities, as part of our mission, must be responsible stewards of creation. It provides a technical basis offering a general overview of the current reality of the environment. Finally, it presents practical ideas that support *how* we can be responsible stewards, *where to start*, and *how to move forward.*

On the Biblical Foundations

Some probing questions addressed to various Christian people show that the current creation theology in many churches is basically based on three biblical references. The first of these is in Genesis 1. From there, it is normally appreciated that God created everything visible, although without giving greater importance to the value and purpose that the Creator pursues with the creation of it. These points often remain as they are without further study and therefore only the notion that "God created" is extracted. As a consequence, there is a leap then in the reading of the biblical narrative, marked by disinterest in environmental issues, until the book of Psalms. Since nature is referred to poetically there, the corresponding passages are recognised as inspiring, but no relationship is established with the way in which we live. Thirdly, another great leap is often made to arrive at the book of Revelation, where the idea is finally internalised – perhaps unconsciously – that creation ends in *nothingness*. According to that kind of reading, in the end of time, matter will disappear and the people who are saved will be taken to a purely spiritual dimension.

It is evident that the first mandate given by God to the human being, namely to exercise responsible stewardship, which the Scriptures show us, has historically lacked importance in the preaching of the gospel in a large part of the churches of Latin America. The reasons for this are surely addressed in greater depth in other articles and sections of this *Handbook*. However, it is worth recognising here that many anthropocentric and biblically unfounded ideas that unfortunately predominate in the theology that is preached in the churches, greatly contribute to rendering invisible the urgent need that exists to embrace our identity as agents for the restoration of creation. Among others, it should be mentioned:

- A widespread *religious escapism*, which maintains that the focus of life lies in the afterlife, repeating that this world will end in destruction and only the human being will be taken to a spiritual world;
- A *scant study of the creation theme from the Scriptures*, simply because many of our presentations of the biblical message begin with sin and not with the affirmation of the goodness of God's entire creation, which remains throughout the Bible as the place or space in which God develops God's history with humanity;
- A *fragmented preaching and understanding of the gospel*, which has led us to use the Bible as a book of "recipes, answers and solutions" to justify what we need or want, without letting it show the truths with which we must be confronted in our faith, leaving the whole stage scenario aside.

These and other factors seriously limit the understanding and relevance that the issue of the responsibility of Christian stewardship towards creation should have in the agendas of the Christian faith communities.

[2] See also: Claudia Florentin, "'Esperanza para toda la creación': Guía práctica para la Iglesia en su cuidado del ambiente", 10th March 2021, *Agência Latino-Americana e Caribenha de Comunicação* [Available at: https://alc-noticias.net/es/2021/03/10/esperanza-para-toda-la-creacion-guia-practica-para-la-iglesia-en-su-cuidado-del-ambiente/], [Last accessed: 3rd May 2022]; Tearfund, "Esperanza para toda la Creación", *Tearfund Website*, 2021 [Available at: https://learn.tearfund.org/es-es/resources/tools-and-guides/hope-for-all-creation], [Last accessed: 3rd May 2022].

On the Technical and Practical Foundations

Today it is not a secret to most people that the planet is going through a variety of environmental crises due to climate change, change in land use, pollution of bodies of water, the greenhouse effect and other phenomena that threaten the state and diversity of the planet. However, in many contexts in Guatemala and Latin America, environmental education has generally been limited to promoting the reuse of materials in order to make decorative handicrafts (which, although it lengthens the time of use of a material, does not change the impact it generates in the medium and long term) or to reiterate slogans such as "put the garbage in its place"; but what is the place of garbage in countries where there is no waste management? In other words, we have reproduced a supposed environmental education that is completely decontextualised, both in relation to rural communities and large cities, in which there are supposed to be better conditions for the implementation of laws on the management of household and industrial waste.

Therefore, when thinking of a comprehensive resource that would properly address the care of creation, aimed at churches and communities of Christian faith, we sought to attend to the following needs:

- Delve into the *biblical foundations* of the subject;
- Guide people and groups, with *technical* bases that will help measure the deterioration that the planet is experiencing;
- Channel biblical foundations and technical bases into concrete initiatives, that is, *practical actions*, for individuals, families and communities, posing the following question: how do we use what we now know to change life habits and seek to influence environmental restoration?

What Does the Material Contain and How Is It Structured?

The material that we are presenting is structured in seven chapters or sessions, each of which, as we have seen, develops three main perspectives: 1. Biblical foundations; 2. Technical bases; 3. A practical guide to work on ideas of personal, family and community transformation.

The following table provides an overview of the content:

STRUCTURE OF THE MATERIAL	BASIS FOR BIBLICAL FORMATION	TECHNICAL AND PRACTICAL BASIS
SESSION 1	God and Creation: How does the Bible teach about the love that God has for God's creation? The Bible study goes deeper and reveals that God values all creation and sustains it despite the evil that is in it because of humanity.	The diversity created and the current state of the environment: The wonder of God's creation is measured by its diversity of ecosystems, its beauty and its different ways of functioning.
SESSION 2	Us and Creation – Stewardship: What does it mean to be stewards in the 21st century? How should the words "dominate" and "subjugate" be understood in a world that exploits and destroys the environment?	Climate change and the effects of pollution: The effects of climate change and pollution in different areas of the environment such as soil, air, infrastructure, water, health and biosphere. In addition, we begin to think about the different levels of viable action in favour of the environment.

SESSION 3	Jesus and Creation – Integral mission: Jesus in his teachings used examples from nature and animals to clearly convey his message. His teachings and examples of nature, in addition to being a pedagogical resource, are also a call to learn from nature and to understand that this was and is an important theme for the restorative Mission of Jesus. Jesus did not come only for human beings, but for all of creation, and so this must be part of the mission of those of us who follow him.	Problem of poor waste management and The 3 Rs ("reduce", "reuse", "recycle")[3] (Part 1): Emphasis is placed on issues that correspond to all people and populations, such as: the problem of poor waste management (effects and impacts) that we generate as individuals and the basic practices of the 3 Rs.
SESSION 4	The Future of Creation: Often, we rely on what the book of Revelation tells us so as to define literally what will happen to the Earth in the future, for which we tend to fill ourselves with fear and anguish. However, as mentioned before, God has a deep love for all of creation, so this part addresses what the Bible really teaches about what God will do with creation, that is, is God really going to destroy God's own creation if God loves it so much?	Circular Economy and The 3 Rs (Part 2): It is vital to reduce the amount of materials that are discarded, there is already a lot of garbage in the world and it will continue to be produced. So, how to reduce the impact generated? What if that which is thrown away is actually a wasted resource? This session addresses the differences between the linear and the circular economic system, and towards which we should aspire as individuals, populations and nations.
SESSION 5	Sufficiency in God: Throughout the Scriptures there are different ways in which God invites humanity to live with the full awareness that it is God who holds up and sustains all that is necessary. On the contrary, the world wants to make us feel that many material goods are needed to find satisfaction. This session delves into the ways in which the Christian faith invites us to live in different ways, inspired by the Reign of God.	Living more sustainably: Why does such an unfair and harmful economic system prevail in the world despite the effect it causes on life on the planet? Some examples of countercurrent life models are identified, alternatives that allow us to approach the economy of the Reign.
SESSION 6	Biblical-theological debate: After addressing, in the previous sessions, important theological bases that support the care of creation, this session has a guide to carry out a small apologetic debate among the group. Someone in the group (facilitator) assumes the role of a Christian person who does not consider the care of creation important; other participants articulate the biblical bases learned in the previous sessions to argue the importance of caring for creation.	Integration 1, A Healthy and Creation Friendly Community: There is a broader picture of various feasible actions for individuals, families, churches and communities. It has already been mentioned that there are different levels of action and in the face of the gigantic environmental problem, it is necessary to answer the question: Where to start to make significant changes? Work begins on the construction of an action plan.

[3] See for instance: https://www.epa.gov/recycle

SESSION 7	The role of the Church in advocacy for the environment: Through some biblical stories, it is discovered how the Bible invites us to act in strategic and objective ways to seek justice in all areas in which life is being destroyed. The vulnerability of people and natural ecosystems is an opportunity for the Church to raise her prophetic voice and advocate for the transformation of the realities of exploitation, indifference and abuse.	Integration 2, Developing our action plan: In this last Session in which the integral resource accompanies the group, the bases are laid for the project that is born as a consequence of what has been learned and grown throughout the 7 Sessions. The ideas and dreams that have been developed are clearly articulated.
Annex: Material for the participants in the group	There are the guides for developing the Bible Study of the 7 sessions, with pages in which annotations can be made.	Useful for recording learning and personal activities, some sessions contain outlines as a summary of the topics.

How Can this Material Be Used?

The material was envisioned from the beginning to be used in two ways: the first as a self-training book, since anyone can access the content through readings and accessing the audio-visual resources that are a part of it. The second usage is for both the biblical and technical-practical topics to be used when addressing directed groups. For this, there needs to be a person willing to facilitate the sessions. However, it is important to mention that it is not necessary for the facilitator to be an expert in socio-environmental issues. What is required of them is an interest and willingness to prepare themself with the content and guides prior to the group session, all of which facilitate the sharing of the topics. The group for its part must be willing to participate in the seven sessions guided by the material; which has been designed for a population of young people and adults; although this does not necessarily exclude children, adolescents and the elderly, since the adaptation of the dynamics for different groups depends to a great extent on the capacities of the facilitator.

To concretely imagine the use of the material, it begins with the facilitator. The facilitators need to take some time to read the basics, both biblical and technical, ideally visiting some additional resources to expand or deepen the topics. After having personally read the content of the biblical base, they review the Bible study guide to be clear on how to lead the first part (biblical) with the group. They also review the guide for the second part (technical-practical) and prepare the suggested materials for use with the group – presentations with audio-visual resources, dynamics, analysis, et cetera.

The resource, *Esperanza para toda la creación*, is offered in such a practical manner that even for worksheets or presentations on specific topics there are already digital files available to be used and adapted to each group.

How to Find It?

This resource has been prepared by the *Centro Esdras*, with the support of organisations such as Tearfund and Latin Link Switzerland. That is why some reference to this material in digital format can be found on the websites of these organisations. However, it is on the institutional page also of the *Centro*[4] itself where all the digital resources for each of the seven sessions are condensed, both those that are considered

[4] See Centro Esdras, http://centroesdras.org/.

complementary to learning (videos, songs, articles, books, websites, et cetera), as well as PowerPoint presentations for developing activities with the group, worksheets, and an important Annex designed so that the people of the group can record their learning and carry out personal activities.[5]

In Guatemala, one can also find this material in a physical version. *Centro Esdras* is helping more churches and Christian organisations have access to this material through work groups, Bible study groups, family groups, neighbourhoods, Bible schools and other places of faith.

Gratitude to God and Dreams for the Book

In recent years, more Christian people, churches and organisations have become aware of the need to and interested in taking better care of God's creation, seeking alternatives to live differently. The dream for this book is for more groups to have the essential tools to embrace their beautiful identity as sons and daughters of God, who assume their missionary role, seeking to give continuity to the ministry of reconciliation inherited by Jesus. This is a reconciliation that allows us to imagine and move towards new realities, where justice and dignity are realities for society and the environment.

Suggestions for Further Reading

Potter, Suzanne. *Estamos conectados. Una perspectiva cristiana sobre el medio ambiente*. Guatemala: Centro Esdras, 2012.

Simón, Benita and Angela Hochstrasser, Eds. *Esperanza para toda la creación. Guía práctica para la Iglesia en su cuidado del ambiente.* Guatemala: Fundación Centro Esdras, 2021. [Available at: http://centroesdras.org/medio_ambiente/#1607540361085-c49f177a-1913], [Last accessed: 4th May 2022].

Stam, Juan B. *Las Buenas Nuevas de la Creación*. San José, Costa Rica: Kairos, 1995.

Watson, Joana. *Advocacy Toolkit – A Roots Guide*. Teddington, Great Britain: Tearfund, 2015. [Available at: https://learn.tearfund.org/en/resources/series/roots-guides/advocacy-toolkit--a-roots-guide], [Last accessed: 4th May 2022].

[5] See Benita Simón and Angela Hochstrasser (eds), *Esperanza para toda la creación. Guía práctica para la Iglesia en su cuidado del ambiente* (Guatemala: Centro Esdras, 2021), http://centroesdras.org/medio_ambiente/#1607540361085-c49f177a-1913.

111. GIVE ME THAT WATER: REFLECTIONS FROM CHILDHOOD ON THE CARE OF WATER[1]

Elizabeth Salazar-Sanzana[2]

"Many small people, in many small places,
They will do small things that will transform the world."
(African proverb)

The water on the planet is one and it is running out. From that reality, we proposed action seeking to promote, through the biblical-theological pedagogical process, analysis, awareness, reflection and the initiative of daily actions on the environmental crisis. Understanding that neoliberalism pushes us towards a relationship with creation based on individualism and that there is a notorious apathy, we proposed a group reflection.

Contextual Experience

We focused on a specific context in southern Chile, in a city surrounded by native forests, wetlands, lagoons, a river and the ocean. This was a neighbourhood which was growing and had considerably increased its constructions; the hills of native trees giving way to a residential sector. The "modernisation" and added value was established to the detriment of natural wealth, clandestine garbage dumps and the privatisation of water, which has already been denounced by environmental organisations. Our children of reference are from a school, from the religion class, between 11 and 14 years of age, who reflected on the environment from a perspective of faith. The register of their reflections arose spontaneously after being questioned by their families, who observed changes in attitude in food, waste management and water care. There were 4 cycles of 5 encounters based on various biblical texts. For this systematisation, we chose relevant points from the sessions of John 4: the Samaritan woman and Jesus.

The first task was to define that the environment refers to the entire cosmos and we expanded the definition to include a holistic view, with an emphasis on the economy, politics, gender and culture. We recognised creation as a gift from God, with a Christian responsibility to protect it and change our relationship from regarding it as an object to recognising it as a subject with rights. Among the elements incorporated by the group was the bond of balance and harmony with creation, which the *Mapuche* people have. It is a relationship of connection with mother earth, of respect for her sustenance – that is why they take care of her and learn from her.

A "Denunciation Wall" was started, in which harmful actions toward the environment in the city were exposed. This listed polluting companies, bad habits of family consumption, garbage dumps, technological

[1] Editor's note: This paper is about a particular pedagogical experience and makes use of a special literary and very authentic narrative style and in the present tense for the reader to be present in the midst of the school class. The author's narrative fluidly follows the development of the pedagogical process around the biblical text of John 4. Her way of referring to this learning experience about water literally flows. Thus, when the readers meet a "she," they will know it is the Samaritan woman who is intended, and when they encounter a "he," they will know it is Jesus. In the same way, when the writer talks about "them," the readers will understand that she is talking about this lively group of school children making their discoveries around the biblical text.

[2] Elizabeth Salazar-Sanzana (draelizabethsalazar@gmail.com) is a Chilean theologian and pedagogue with a PhD from the Methodist University of Sao Paulo. She is a member of ASETT, FTL and the Christian Unity Commission of the Pentecostal World Fellowship, a Professor of Theology at the Evangelical Theological Community of Chile, and at other Latin American institutions.

waste and other topics of interest. Another step was to recognise good deeds and provide contributions for building the awareness of their peers. They made posters for classrooms, homes, neighbourhoods, and churches. The most sensitive issue was water; they worked it as a vital resource and symbol of good living, which God wants for everyone. The *metanoia* (change of direction) proposed by Jesus in the gospels occurs in this learning of faith, as a gift of grace and that helps us in this learning to learn.[3] It draws their attention.

"Give me water"

Thirst as a vital need from infancy helps participants to imagine what Jesus and his disciples might feel on their pilgrimage. They see examples of water as a blessing and drought as punishment. They also consider the contrast of Chile, with glaciers to the south and desert in the north, but much of the territory has a shortage of water. The reflection arises from the humanitarian crisis in the north of the country, by the displaced who migrate illegally from various precarious situations and, deceived by the unscrupulous, cross the desert and are abandoned, losing their lives.[4]

They know in detail about the drought in the region and the inadequate plantations that dry out the underground water tables. It was important to observe from the windows of the school a garden and a hand pump, since they are told that these items and their use is considered a crime of robbery. Groundwater in the region is privatised and owned by foreign investors. Water shortages, due to neoliberal policies, have drastically reduced the natural resource.[5]

Although sensitive to this reality, they reread Jesus' request and suspect something more than being thirsty. They think he is testing whether she believes she owns the well. There is also the fantasy that Jesus does not want to be alone and asks for water in order to start a conversation. Panotto will say that, through fantasies, children achieve their precious exploits.[6] For them, there is a sovereign and divine explanation for asking for water, although they do not know how to explain it. It is clear that Jesus teaches his followers to re-establish ties with the other, even with the enemy. The encounter through need reveals his face: "I was thirsty, and you gave me something to drink" (Mt. 25:35).

"How can you ask me for a drink?"

It is very significant for children, to make them discover their legitimate space in society. In this situation, they capture the inequality of gender and religion. For the group, she asks the logical thing, since she knows her marginality. We guide the attention to the indifference that exists for the other, their humanity and understanding them as God's creation. There is fear of incorporating the other as my neighbour. It is related to what happens with migrants and the difficulty of integrating and creating ties. It is selective xenophobia that does not affect the first world. What is considered different is identified: skin colour, religion, culture, sexual choice, disability, poverty and age. They like to ask questions, and to the sound of the group *Los Jaivas*, singing "All Together", they continue to question life: "Why live so far apart, if the earth wants to bring us together?"[7]

They believe that the woman is surprised because she is a Samaritan more than because she is a woman, since the men were used to being served. According to the group, she distrusts but she is not afraid of him and faces him. The asymmetry that the group points out is similar to that mentioned in studies of the

[3] Matthias Preswerk, *Educación Popular y Teología de la Liberación* (San Jose: Celadec, 1995): 225.

[4] See "Cifras Fundamentales de la Migración en Chile", *Migración en Chile*, [Available at: https://www.migracionenchile.cl/], [Last accessed: 4th May 2022].

[5] Since August 2021, it was declared a drought zone.

[6] Nicolás Panotto, *De juegos que hablan de Dios* (Quito: WorldVision, 2016).

[7] Los Jaivas, "Todos Juntos," Side B (single), in *Ayer Caché (*Santiago de Chile: IRT, 1972) vinyl. [Available at: https://youtu.be/hmq6QKqmIaw], [Last accessed: 5th May 2022].

intercultural reading of the Bible, which is a hermeneutical practice in which diversity, asymmetry and cultural differences between readers are thematised and used.[8]

In this dialogue, the family memory and the historical account of common situations of vulnerability emerge,[9] such as the 2010 earthquake, where the tragedy worsened with shortages of drinking water, looting and contamination of the lagoons. It became necessary to share water from hand pumps; traumatic experiences were lived, and recounted by their families and congregations. It is observed that in the face of need, people build solidarity bonds, asking from or giving to whomever, without concern. A collective sharing is achieved that breaks with social and religious separations. The social experience – that is, the co-operation and coordination of actions with those around us – is based on the primary activity of building bonds, relationships, and carrying out communication or dialogue, in the face of a reality or common need.[10] A similar experience was lived in 2010 in the north, outside the *San José* mine, when 33 miners were trapped. Their family members held vigils at the site for 69 days and shared their pain, hope and food. Also, the largest fire in the country, in 2017, summoned everyone to overcome the disaster. Family members of the group were among the victims of the fire. In that situation, there were no questions or answers, only the sharing that overcomes all separation.

There are diverse experiences that destroy walls, and build bonds and affections. The fragile threads of daily faith, spontaneous ecumenical practices without any pretence, make their way, sustaining life in crisis. Even incorporating the ancestral spiritualities that add up as forces that emerge from memory. Experiences are added, transforming into a great patchwork quilt of solidarity and friendship. They are friendships of earthquake, tsunami, fire, "friendships of" survival. There is a common need that unites and brings together those who gather around the well. The bonds through need unite in the faith, the everyday, the superfluous and the most antagonistic protagonists.

"The well is deep"

The group wonders, is she showing solidarity or is she being cheeky? Perhaps, for an adult-centred theology, this position might not attract attention, but it is more than curiosity. For some, this evens out their own asymmetries with a Jewish man, who discouraged any friendship. Apparently, Jesus does not perceive that he is at a disadvantage. He is thirsty and she has a way to draw water out and give it to him. In the group, they think that she has greater power and knows it, others think that she is a good person, empathetic and warns him with concern, in her servile habit.

The opinions of this intervention of the woman configures axiological questions for us that the group knows: solidarity, human rights, the perception of equality. Even if, for a moment in dialogue, she is empowered in a privileged position. From this advantage, she dares to question him, not as a teacher and messiah, but because he is there, having other options on the way. They think that Jesus was strategic, because he wanted to overcome this discrimination and they associate it with the episode when he uses childhood as an example, to change a system of abuse.

They are struck by "the Samaritan" and the nationalist discourse arises. They consider themselves privileged to be Chilean and mention that many yearn to live here. They empathise with those who suffer elsewhere, such as in the East, with droughts, famine and violence. We work on the harmfulness of nationalism, and this turns us to the social problems of the country. They are quickly self-critical, without giving reason, and some emphasising that God wants a world in peace and justice.

We promote a holistic vision, of living together in peace in diversity in this universe. From that holistic harmony in which, as children, they show their faith in God the Creator, this vision is raised from their daily

[8] Hans de Wit, *Por un solo gesto de amor* (BuenosAires: Isedet, 2010).

[9] Maurice Halbwachs, *La memoria colectiva* (Zaragoza: PUZ, 2004).

[10] Samuel Palma, *El quehacer nuestro de cada día* (España: Caligrama, 2021).

lives, clarifying that currently in a neoliberal society, this goes against the grain. They are very critical of people who take advantage of others and feel superior; they insist that global warming is a product of this mindset. The vision they have of the Realm of heaven arises, where everything will be harmony and there will be no war or violence. It is concluded that when the asymmetries caused by power relations are overcome and it is assumed that we are different, but without fear of that difference, there is acceptance and openness to dialogue and equity. They give examples of how well it is lived when differences are recognised, incorporated, accepted. They mention close examples: cousins with Down's Syndrome, a deaf mother, and a brother with cerebral palsy.

To love this creation in its diversity is to accept belonging to this larger family: humanity, which opens us to bonds of affection and respect. In this process of reflection and awareness, the children's sense of belonging has been fundamental for establishing a connection with creation. Belonging is based on perception, in relation to the entire universe. While working with a plastic activity, the issue of the importance of each one of them, for their family, for the church, for God, for the universe is presented. It is possible to make the connection with what they are and with the cosmos as a whole.

Children, at the level of a confession of faith, acknowledge being part of the body of Christ (the church). In this body, everyone is important, as the image and likeness of God, in equal condition, with privileges and responsibilities. They speak widely and with emotion of their communities of faith, of the love that unites them, they share their identity specificities. Each of them defines themselves based on their adherence to faith and two of them identify their ancestral *Mapuche* roots.

When we speak of identity in the religious field, it is necessary to establish the distinction between identity and a sense of belonging. Identity emerges in the singular as a result of the intersection of the subject's plural senses of belonging, through time.[11] Hence, identity is not equal to belonging. Identity has been conceived as "a quality or set of qualities with which a person or group is intimately connected."[12] Thus, identity refers to how individuals define themselves based on certain shared characteristics, namely: social categories such as ethnicity, religion, gender, nationality; "social stratum", as a group of which one is a part. Thus, the religious identity presuppositions are not static, they are in permanent transformation, either due to the mutations that operate in the immediate environment or the changes of the people themselves (adherence / conversion / religious experience).

We must take into account this dynamic of religious adherence as part of the sense of belonging. For children, this is crucial as they affirm their identity in these various belongings, which is why their connection with the communities of faith, along with their families, is so strong. This is crucial to reinforcing their perception of being active stewards of our "common home."

"If you knew… you would ask me and you would receive"

This conversation broke the aforementioned asymmetries, and brought her closer, still without understanding, to her interlocutor. Dialogue is openness to friendship and to the offering of a different water. The children insist that Jesus wanted to share and teach sharing. In bibliodramas,[13] the reactions are creative and close to contextual: "I don't have money", "no, I prefer what I already know", "what do you want in return?" The loving attitude, grace and justice of Jesus does not harmonise with current neoliberalism, in which all action is intended to gain, seeking the good for oneself, self-satisfaction.

When the topic of the husbands is brought up, it is irrelevant to them. They are given an explanation about the reasons for female rejection and they connect it to current situations: the contempt for poverty, disability and people living on the streets.

---

[11] María Toledo, *Sobre la construcción identitaria* (Santiago: Atenea, 2012): 43-56.

[12] Jorge Larraín, *La identidad chilena* (Santiago: Lom Ediciones, 2001): 23.

[13] Anete Roese, *Bibliodrama. A arte de interpretar textos sagrados* (São Leopoldo: Sinodal, 2007).

The group enjoys the bibliodramas which reveal a Jesus who is popular, strategic, sarcastic, and understanding. These experiences are significant, they question the text and its context; their value is in creativity and theological deconstruction, which they do with immediate practical implications. With art, seriousness and joy, they sent letters to churches, replicated the bibliodramas and raised awareness about water. The close, familiar faith moves them towards processes of simple change and to co-ordinate diakonal actions. They are a transformation of justice, of bond building, of hope, trust and respect, it is faith in action that modifies their reality.

"Is this not the Christ?"

The group is struck by the fact that she did not keep the news to herself; by the fact that she left the routine, the pitcher, and shared the news with her people. But why does she tell them that "it is possible" that he is the Christ, since she had believed him? Could it be that she is afraid of her neighbours and relatives, that they might not believe her and mistreat her? Could it be a strategy? Could it be a "right to doubt"? They think that what she did is positive, so everyone is free to decide whether to believe it or not. This point allows us to work on the freedom that the Spirit gives us to receive and accept the good news. She takes part in the invitation: "Let him who is thirsty come [...] take freely the water of life" (Rev. 22:17), water of healing and salvation in the story of Elijah and Naaman (2 Kings 5:9-14). Also, the text of the blind man healed in the pool of Siloam (Jn. 9:1-12). God's blessing, offered by grace to the Samaritan woman, reaches everyone, but it is accepted in freedom. What Ortega shares is enlightening:

> In Hebrew the sky is called "*shmain*", which means "the water below." Water is a little bit of heaven on earth, an image of the grace of God that comes from above, ensures life, and then returns to heaven, after bearing fruit. However, balance and harmony are necessary with every blessing we receive.[14]

The group points out the attitude of solidarity that does not harmonise with what they generally observe, where every action is intended towards gain and self-satisfaction.

Conclusion: A Drop in the Ocean

The gratuitousness and love of God in creation confronted us with the immensity of the problem. This group of children, united in faith, without pretence, writes a story of commitment and sensitivity. It is an attractive and playful process, reading the Bible and discovering the connection between human dignity and God's creation; the consideration of the common home that we have with animals and the whole universe. They show ethical responsibility that fills us with hope. Unfortunately, as Gebara says: "the little things, the possible things are most of the time undervalued and seem to be the most difficult."[15] The strength of God in the most fragile is underestimated, without considering that Jesus was a child and places childhood as an example to follow.

Like the aforementioned African proverb: it's the small things that will transform the world. Faith assumes the limits of our human condition and drives us to new horizons. It is everyone's responsibility to take care of what has been entrusted to us. Thus, ecological concern must go hand in hand with social integration and care for the lives of those who are most vulnerable. The group managed to identify irresponsibility at the macro and micro level, positioning themselves as agents of change.

---

[14] Ofelia Ortega, *Encuentro sobre Cambio Climático y Agua* (Matanzas: AIPRAL, 2014): 2 (translation by the author).

[15] Ivone Gebara, *Compartir los panes y los peces* (Montevideo: DobleClic, 2008): 140.

Knowing about conversion, metamorphosis, resurrection, helped the call for attitude change. It was the necessary slogan for the hope of transformation, from small gestures and practices, to great voices of announcement. Through childhood, we have learned that it is not helpful to constantly pose the question or the dilemma of conscience, "why do I do it?" or give a reason for each action, because a duty to do is assumed by being: Being part of this cosmos; Being part of this humanity; Being part of those who are failing, for not knowing; Being part of our common home.

Suggestions for Further Reading:

Comunicaciones ESSBIO. *El caso de ESSBIO y NuevoSur: Lecciones del* 27F. s.l.: ESSBIO, s.f., https://www.essbio.cl/pdf/inversionistas/Libro-essbio-FINAL.pdf.
Gebara, Ivone. *Compartir los panes y los peces.* Montevideo: Doble Clic, 2008.
Halbwachs, Maurice. *La memoria colectiva.* Zaragoza: PUZ, 2004.
Larraín, Jorge. *La identidad chilena.* Santiago de Chile: Lom Ediciones, 2001.
Ortega, Ofelia. *Encuentro sobre Cambio Climático y Agua.* Matanzas: AIPRAL, 2014.
Palma Manríquez, Samuel. *El quehacer nuestro de cada día.* Sevilla: Caligrama, 2021.
Panotto, Nicolás. *De juegos que hablan de Dios*. Quito: World Vision, 2016.
Roese, Anete. *Bibliodrama. A arte de interpretar textos sagrados*. San Leopoldo: Sinodal, 2007.
Toledo, María. *Sobre la construcción identitaria.* Santiago de Chile: Atenea, 2012.
Yus, Rafael. *Educación integral: una educación holística para el siglo XXI.* Bilbao: Desclée de Brouwer, 2001.
Wit, Hans de. *Por un solo gesto de amor.* Buenos Aires: ISEDET, 2010.

112. Mayan Peoples Epistemological Paradigm – For the Construction of Human Plenitude in Harmony with Nature and Cosmos

Vitalino Similox Salazar[1]

Introduction

We envision a plural epistemological scenario, permanently enriched with different perspectives, in terms of practices, knowledge, wisdom, and other knowledge traditions and spiritualities, which allows us to claim that there is more than one vision of the world and that there are other southern experiential epistemologies, involved in social, political and cultural struggles, especially those of indigenous peoples.

Ecclesial, theological and ecumenical institutions, in this context of otherness, are fundamental for an active and purposeful participation to support, from their nature, the overcoming of this epistemological racism. They are a strong option for recovering and legitimizing these other models of knowledge and views that are an alternative to the ecological destruction, to epistemological extractivism and epistemicide. In truth, it is up to them to propose and cooperate in the transition from a capitalist society of overproduction of material goods, to a bio-centred society that sustains all life with human-spiritual values. It is a difficult process that requires, in the words of Pope Francis, a "radical ecological conversion, which will lead us to incorporate care relationships, protection and cooperation: a development made *with* nature and not *against* nature."[2]

This paper describes the epistemological route of Mayan peoples, inspired by their paradigm as an expression of their constellation of beliefs, values and techniques, whose essential focus is the protection and promotion of natural life, the link between territorial life and nature, which gives support to their cultural identity practices, their principles and values, as well as an exercise in epistemic pluralism. It is a proposal to make human plenitude possible in respectful and harmonious relationships with mother earth and the cosmos.

Substantiation

Each culture possesses and develops its particular forms or methods to understand and interpret its reality according to its worldview, science, philosophy and technology, as well as its values and principles system. Mayan culture has a methodology for building and organizing the nature of its knowledge, science and philosophy. Their experience enables human fulfillment and success, which is reflected in a dignified life and in a good living. In the Mayan Kaqchikel language, it is said: "*Ruxe'el k'aslemal*" which means a happy life, a fulfilled and useful life, in freedom. A life that is attuned to the thinking of a pluralizing concept of knowledge, recognizing that humanity has the right to achieve knowledge in different ways, affirming that there is not a single form of science, but a plurality of scientific illustrations on planet earth. This points to an instinctive knowledge of the sacred uniqueness and the deep interconnectivity of the world with reason. Effectively, this is a knowledge that is substantiated on their own cosmo-scientific principles whose characteristics are:

---

[1] Vitalino Similox Sálazar (vsimilox@yahoo.com). Presbyterian pastor, Protestant theologian, with a Ph.D. in Sociology. Collaborator in the organization of the Mayan universities in Guatemala, First Rector of the Maya Ixil University and current Rector of the Maya Kaqchikel University, Chimaltenango, Guatemala.

[2] Francis, *Encyclical Letter Laudato Si' on Care for our Common Home* (Vatican City: Vatican Press, 2015).

Holistic: An integral vision of life, in which everything is in everything, related to the rationality of the whole. The development or plenitude of the human beings in the ability to relate harmoniously and respectfully to mother earth, nature, the cosmos and divinity for the happiness of all.

Systemic: The conjugation and interdependence of time (calendars), numbers (mathematics), social and political organization and spirituality, as the synthesis of the cosmos.

Circular: Time is one and at the same time repetitive. There is no beginning and end, time is continuous. Time is understood not as a progressive linear process, but an integral one.

Pyramidal: The process of evolution and perfection of the human being, the circular construction, the stages and the necessary changes in the process of balance.

Balanced: In different manifestations, nature and the cosmos are governed by the principle of balance, both at macro and micro levels. The equilibrium does not represent a static condition but it is a dynamic and cyclical state in which a concentration of energy occurs and not the cancellation of it. The balance in the daily life of the human being is a state of dynamic balance in thoughts, attitudes and relationships.

Multipolar: Everything has a duality and exists in contradictory pairs. Individual and community are two poles of the same unit; without community there is no individual.

Complementary: This is understood as the balance between opposites, it occurs in complementarity – the other is not annulled, it is complemented by the other one. The difference is a part of the whole. Complementarity seeks optimization through the combination of forces.

The practice of research, in the experience of the Mayan peoples, has been a "process of vindication and changes in perception, feeling, understanding and realization, as well as a transition towards the new signs of time."[3] It has meant, that there is the recognition of their rights as peoples who have a science, a philosophy and a technology. This research, "has been an action that has implied a movement of life, as a discovery of realities, that moves people to understand their life, organize it, experience it, and also understand the life of nature and the cosmos."[4] To be a researcher,

> …the person must be emotionally, spiritually and mentally balanced, to have the ability to listen and dialogue. In addition to these qualities, the current sages and timekeepers of Mayan peoples, know the language of the sacred fire, and dreams, and the messages from clouds, volcanoes, rivers, animals, trees, etc.[5]

This is, effectively, a learning process of life in its broadest plenitude, from the micro-organism to the largest galaxy.

Epistemological Route of Academic Training: Leading to Live in Harmony with Nature and the Cosmos

The essential focus of academic human formation is primarily its relationship with natural life and with cultural life. It prioritizes the protection and promotion of life with nature, the bond with territorial life, which gives sustenance to cultural identity practices. It is based on Mayan science, philosophy and technology, for which the present work develops the three main pillars for this time: philosophy, health and agriculture. The study program of the Maya Kaqchikel University, Guatemala, expresses this in its entire proposal. We consider here the development of their different areas of study.

---

[3] *Fundamentos de la investigación desde la visión de la cultura Maya* (Guatemala: Fundación Universidad Maya, 2008), 52.

[4] *Fundamentos de la investigación*, 65.

[5] Protocolo y metodología de investigación desde la experiencia de las universidades Mayas Ixil, Kaqchikel y Chorti (Guatemala, 2020).

Mayan Science, Philosophy and Technology[6]

The philosophy of Mayan peoples is based on their belief system, values, principles and norms, their moral judgment and their intelligence. It focuses on the plenitude of life for humanity, a fulfilled and healthy humanity. Its frame of reference is set in 13 braids:[7]

1. We are one expression more of life in the universe.
2. We all have the same right to exist.
3. Respect the sacred space of each of the living beings.
4. Maintain in harmony our three dimensionality (material, energetic and social).
5. Contemplate, appreciate and observe the beauty of mother nature and the cosmos.
6. Permanent connection and communication with all living beings.
7. Permanent gratitude.
8. Give back from what we have received.
9. Take only what we need to live.
10. Live in complementarity.
11. Value all expressions of life in all its dimensions.
12. Walk with time and space, according to own calendars.
13. Love at all levels.

The formation focuses on the interdisciplinary relationship between the natural sciences and the social sciences; the link between the natural context and cultural creation; the civilizing evolution of the Mayan peoples; the intercultural relationship of the Mayan peoples with other peoples of Mesoamerica and the world; the contrast between the Mayan civilization with the invasion and colonization. The main contents are divided into four areas.

The bio-socio-political area. This includes the history of the Mayan civilization and the Mayan peoples, Mesoamerica and the ancient cultures of the world; the political and social organization of the Mayan peoples, their political and commercial relationship with other peoples of the world; the invasion and colonization of *Abya Yala* and Mesoamerica; nation states and globalization.

The epistemological area. Includes the Mayan cosmovision, the ancestral paradigm, holism, the theory of complexity, systems and chaos; the Mayan oral tradition; the scientific principles and processes in the codices, the *Popol Wuj*, spirituality, the *nawales* and Mayan books.

The technological scientific area. Includes the study of agriculture, botany, livestock, zoology, food, nutrition, architecture, mathematics, astronomy, spirituality, medicine, politics, linguistics, education and psychology.

The arts and aesthetics area. Includes the study of Mayan music, dance, weaving, drawing, painting and culinary art.

Health Sciences[8]

This degree is understood and formulated as a *comprehensive health system.* A proposal that meets the fact that the current biomedical system is in crisis:

---

[6] See "Ciencia, Filosofía y Tecnología Maya," Carreras, Universidad Maya Kaqchikel, Chimaltenango, Guatemala, 2020 https://www.universidadmayakaqchikel.org.gt/ciencia-filosofia-y-tecnologia-maya/.

[7] See Donato Camey Huz, "Trece principios para una vida plena," in José Donato Camey Huz, et al., *Llegó aquí la palabra. La cosmovisión maya viva y difundida a través de los medios de comunicación comunitarios*, 11-21 (Guatemala: ICCO Cooperación, s.f.).

[8] See "Licenciatura en Ciencias de la Salud," Carreras, Universidad Maya Kaqchikel, Chimaltenango, Guatemala, 2019, https://www.universidadmayakaqchikel.org.gt/licenciatura-en-ciencias-de-la-salud/.

> it does not respond to the health needs of the population according to their cultural identity and their specific ways of life. Society and the environment are sick and with new health demands.[9]

Talking about health for the Mayan people is complex, as the word "health" itself does not exist in any of the Mayan languages. There are similar words, for example, *raxnakil kaslemal*, which means "fullness of life". Because they are integral, holistic cultures, where everything has to do with the balance of a person's life, it is difficult to categorize, make specific terms such as health, agriculture, education, etc. In reality, the Mayan people do not segment, they guide life in an integral way, where everything is related.

The comprehensive health system aims to have a career with comprehensive characteristics that responds to the real health needs of the population; that not only has a biomedical base, but also one of the confluences of human knowledge for the maintenance and restoration of existential balance.

The thematic axes of the degree with its main contents includes: epistemology of the Mayan people; population health, alternative health practice in harmony with mother nature; biomedicine and psychobiomedicine.

The program of the degree seeks not to base the competencies of graduates on a conception of health attached only to healing, but that their training is directed towards a full knowledge of the ancestral networks of health care, mainly based on the health practice of indigenous peoples; the use and promotion of alternative health practices in harmony with mother nature; a broad sense in the search for human dignity in the exercise of the right to health and lifestyle in harmony with mother nature; the maintenance of the inter-harmonic health of ecosystems.

Ancestral Mayan Agricultural Science[10]

In the face of the environmental crisis, the need arises to explore, recover and propose from the ancestral Mayan knowledge and wisdom, the agricultural science that prioritizes solving the needs of the population: food, economy, trade and processing of raw materials.

The ancestral Mayan agricultural science is based on organizational recognition, mathematics, astronomy and the relationships between the different populations – vegetables-animals-minerals – in addition to recognizing fundamentally that the earth itself is a living being and that it generates life. Thus, it presents an effective alternative for feeding the world population without putting the health of the planet at risk, preserving biodiversity and local ecosystems. It is a real contribution to the challenge of climate change and pandemics, including COVID-19.

This agricultural science is the evidence of extensive processes of observation, reflection and the continuous collection of knowledge to be able to reach practical conclusions for life, a technical response to the vindication of the rights that peoples have to land and territory.

The Mayan Ancestral Agricultural Science degree aims to prepare professionals in agricultural sciences with the ability to establish agricultural production processes and systems based on the life principles of the Mayan peoples and complemented with the knowledge and sciences of other peoples. Through the creation of technical, productive, economic and political conditions, it is possible to solve the food deficit in quantity and quality necessary for the well-being of humanity and that has a favorable impact on the protection and rescue of natural assets, land and territory. Likewise, it seeks to graduate professionals with technical, scientific and social skills for the establishment of agricultural production systems in harmony with the environment and mother earth, and with positive effects on people's nutrition, economy and health.

---

[9] Words of Donato Camey Huz, director of the degree in Health Sciences at the Maya Kaqchikel University, Chimaltenango, Guatemala.

[10] See "Ingeniería en ciencias agrícolas y ambientales," Universidad Maya Kaqchikel, Chimaltenango, Guatemala, 2020, https://www.universidadmayakaqchikel.org.gt/ingenieria-ciencias-agricolas-y-ambientales/.

The contents of the career are divided into ten full semesters of study that propose that the skills of graduates include:

1. To identify with the development of their community and to contribute to the structural changes of the country through the interaction of the principles of life of the Mayan peoples and their relationship with natural resources.
2. From the principle of Good Living, to be able to intervene and influence the cycle of community and public policies related to agricultural production, livestock and renewable natural resources.
3. Contribute to the process of generating knowledge in the field of agricultural and environmental sciences that is relevant to the realities of indigenous peoples.
4. Have training from the Mayan worldview to dialogue with the actors involved in the current economic transformation.

Conclusion

The epistemology of the Mayan peoples stands out for its remarkable concern for the human being. Their scientific knowledge converges with other ancestral cultures of humanity, in their desire to understand and improve the lives of all living beings in the cosmos. The life of the human being today, for its realization, needs to be located within mother earth, within the universe to perform its function of being guardian of the different ecosystems throughout the planet, to defend life against the ferocity of neo-liberal and, now, globalizing capitalism.

Today, the life project of humanity is nourished by the earth sciences, deep ecology, bioethics and the heart of indigenous peoples, including the Mayan culture, which in its historical evolution has been situated for centuries in life and for the life of nature, the cosmos and the human person. The challenge is not only to include indigenous people and other culturally differentiated people in higher education, it is also imperative to incorporate their knowledge, traditional wisdom, values, linguistic systems, worldviews, ways of learning, and modes of knowledge production, for ecological transformation, care of creation, and to decolonize knowledge from its epistemological proposal.

Suggestions for Further Reading

Camey Huz, José Donato. "Trece principios para una vida plena," in José Donato Camey Huz, et al., *Llegó aquí la palabra. La cosmovisión maya viva y difundida a través de los medios de comunicación* comunitarios, 11-21. Guatemala: ICCO Cooperación, s.f.

Francis. *Encyclical Letter Laudato Si' on Care for our Common Home.* Vatican City: Vatican Press, 2015.

Fundación Universidad Maya. *Fundamentos de la investigación desde la visión de la cultura Maya* (Guatemala: Fundación Universidad Maya, 2008), 52.

Protocolo y metodología de investigación desde la experiencia de las universidades Mayas Ixil, Kaqchikel y Chorti. Guatemala, 2020.

Universidad Maya Kaqchikel. "Ciencia, Filosofía y Tecnología Maya." Degrees. Universidad Maya Kaqchikel, Chimaltenango, Guatemala, 2020. https://www.universidadmayakaqchikel.org.gt/ciencia-filosofia-y-tecnologia-maya/.

Universidad Maya Kaqchikel. "Ingeniería en ciencias agrícolas y ambientales." Degrees. Universidad Maya Kaqchikel, Chimaltenango, Guatemala, 2020. https://www.universidadmayakaqchikel.org.gt/ingenieria-ciencias-agricolas-y-ambientales/.

Universidad Maya Kaqchikel. "Licenciatura en Ciencias de la Salud." Degrees. Universidad Maya Kaqchikel, Chimaltenango, Guatemala, 2019. https://www.universidadmayakaqchikel.org.gt/licenciatura-en-ciencias-de-la-salud/.

113. Care for Creation: What does a Promotional Pastoral Ministry Imply? Fostering Reflection and Educating to Care

Deborah Cirigliano Heffel[1]

Introduction

As churches, we have not always been able to recognise the mission to which we are called within our current production system. This capitalist and extractivist production model has been characterised by the exploitation and abuse of the resources that our Earth generously provides, deifying private property and the accumulation of resources, land, living beings, and even people. However, within our faith communities, which have been in constant dialogue with civil organisations, there have emerged deep reflections on our prophetic role in the midst of these realities that deepen injustice, exclusion, and violence.

The 23rd General Assembly of the World Alliance of Reformed Churches (Debrecen / Hungary, 1997), responding to the call of the Southern Africa region to recognise global economic injustice and the destruction of the environment, urged its member churches to enter into a process of recognition, education, and confession. After listening to this claim and acknowledging how threatened God's gift of creation is, member churches committed to a statement of faith which is known as The Accra Confession.[2]

As a result of a deep ecumenical theological reflection in the light of the Gospel, and considering the precedent of The Accra Confession, the World Council of Churches on 2nd September 2009 signed a declaration on eco-justice and ecological debt.[3] It is in this context that the Evangelical Church of the River Plate (IERP) and the NGO *Hora de Obrar* designed its Pastoral Ministry for the Promotion of Creation Care (PPCC). This programme aims to offer our church's districts, congregations, and community spaces for respectful dialogue and careful reflection on the consequences that our production practices have on our health and environment. The main goal is to promote an active awareness of our responsibility as Christians and as faith communities in the promotion of creation care.

The initiative focuses fundamentally on: 1) institutionalising a policy of care for creation in the entire IERP; 2) promoting eco-friendly production methods which respect both our environmental and human health, 3) fostering responsible, conscious consumption and healthy eating. The above-mentioned three axes seek to articulate interdisciplinary knowledge and experiences with theoretical and technical contributions from the fields of environmental and health sciences, agronomy, economics, among others.

Development: An Experience of Collaborative Training

The PPCC programme proposed, as one of its activities, the elaboration of catechetical materials on Creation Care to be used by various groups within the church (adults, women by themselves, youth, and children). This material was compiled as a result of workshops and training sessions carried out with church members responsible for catechesis.

---

[1] Deborah Cirigliano Heffel (deborahciriglianoheffel@hotmail.com) is a graduate in Psychology and co-coordinator of the Pastoral Ministry for the Promotion of Creation Care (PPCC), Hora de Obrar. She is a member of the IERP, living in Paraná, Entre Ríos, Argentina. With the collaboration of Ruth Schwittay (ruthsch@gmail.com), who is a secondary level teacher, former catechist, translator, retired, member of the IERP, living in CABA, Argentina.

[2] World Communion of Reformed Churches, "The Accra Confession", *WCRC Website*. [Available at: https://wcrc.ch/accra/the-accra-confession], [Last accessed: 3rd May 2022].

[3] World Council of Churches, "Statement on eco-justice and ecological debt", 2nd September 2009, *WCC Website,* [Available at: https://www.oikoumene.org/resources/documents/statement-on-eco-justice-and-ecological-debt], [Last accessed: 3rd May 2022].

Catechesis in the Evangelical Church of the River Plate plays an essential role in the training of our lay members. It is a place for learning and exchange. It varies according to the districts and communities: in some cases, it is called "Sunday school", being a space for children only, sometimes separated from worship services, and sometimes involving some activity carried out during the service. These spaces include teaching and learning biblical stories, articulating messages from the Bible applying our current contexts and challenges, and promoting dialogue and collaborative work. They are not considered as places where one arrives empty and leaves full of knowledge, but rather as spaces where we can collaboratively think of proposals for a harmonious co-existence based on the Gospel.

In this spirit, PPCC decided to organise training workshops with catechists to plan how to incorporate the topic of Creation Care in catechesis. We consider that Creation Care should be a transversal axis to be given since it implies caring for oneself, promoting healthy connections with others, with the environment that surrounds us, and with everything with which we relate.

During 2017 and 2018, a series of workshops were held with catechists from the different districts in our church (these being the Metropolitan District, Misiones, Paraguay, Uruguay, Entre Ríos, the Western District, and the Southern District). During the meetings, they were asked to work in groups, identifying the most significant issues to be dealt with in the diverse catechesis groups of children, youth, men, and women. Also, the meetings become a space to talk about troubling environmental problems, which are very difficult to express out loud mainly because of the contradictions they present. For example, agricultural producers find it difficult to produce sufficient yields without resorting to agrochemicals, although they intuit or know from their own experience the consequences that these products have on their own health. Because of the lack of public policies, the agronomists themselves (not all, but a great majority) tend to assume that they can only produce profitably by using agrochemicals, which creates a fake contradiction between economic development and care for creation.

The group of catechists organised themselves in three small groups which were to deal with a specific topic: land, water, and food. As there was no time to elaborate on them during the workshops, the participants promised to work on different proposals to approach each of the topics from their own perspectives. Later on, the proposals were combined, and a special booklet was designed compiling them all together.

At this point, it is important to highlight the pastoral and pedagogical work of Pedro Kalmbach, who played an essential part in the organisation of the workshops. He was one of the co-ordinators in PPCC for the first three years of the programme, working together with Daniel Beros, and Ruth Schwittay, a teacher and former catechist with extensive experience in training catechists with the IERP. All of them would agree that the material produced is the result of the work carried out during those years.

> In *El Cuidado de la Creación: Materiales para el trabajo en comunidades de fe*, we can discover proposals to implement in faith communities, through which we can reflect on Creation Care based on our reality, illuminated by biblical texts and with examples of its real-life application.[4]

The activities planned by the workshop participants were designed to be adapted to different realities and contexts. After the material was published, we began to distribute it in the different districts, so that it could be used, transformed, modified, and contextualised accordingly.

After having agreed on the need for permanent revision and dialogue, the PPCC co-ordination team decided to carry out a new series of workshops in 2020. This time, 25 participants attended the meetings, which, due to the pandemic, were held virtually. The attendees shared their concerns about different

[4] Ruth Schwittay and Pedro Kalmbach (eds), *El Cuidado de la Creación. Materiales para el trabajo en comunidades de fe* (Buenos Aires: Iglesia Evangélica del Río de la Plata, 2019): 5.

environmental problems and expressed a need to incorporate these problems in catechesis with children, youth, and their families.

During the preparation of the workshops, the PPCC co-ordination team acknowledged that, apart from needing appropriate materials for broaching the theme of creation care, the catechists needed to be trained on pedagogical and didactic approaches to children, youth, and adults to be able to successfully use the material provided. Thus, it was agreed to implement the workshops as a practical and concrete process of elaborating an encounter with children. In this way, five different training meetings were prepared to introduce five fundamental steps in the organisation of a workshop:

a. Introducing the topic, "breaking down" the biblical text;
b. Getting to know the people who participate in the meeting;
c. Defining an objective for the meeting taking into account what was previously analysed;
d. Preparing the activities for the meeting;
e. Evaluating the workshop.

The biblical texts to be worked on were proposed by the members of the organising group, who selected the ones best suited to catechetical work. Other aspects were also taken into account, such as whether it was possible to use them with children, whether they reflected various characters (boys, girls, women, young people, the elderly et cetera). We intended to select texts which presented challenges and were worth analysing.

This series of workshops not only provided attendees with useful material but participants were also presented with tools that they could use in their own meetings and workshops that would allow them, in turn, to continue reflecting on what the Bible has to tell us about our relationship with creation. We understand that a personal interpretation of the Bible, embracing God's Word, is a fundamental aspect of our protestant theology. In this sense, we are committed to the formation of critical, reflective, and creative leaders who can interpret biblical readings in the light of current challenges, and who can think about reality considering what the Bible tells us.

In this cycle of virtual training, working groups were set up around biblical texts that were chosen for thinking through the following topics: the importance of water, food distribution, legal rights, and our responsibility in Creation Care. It is worth mentioning that these topics arose through gathering the interests of the participants. In the formation of the groups, the interest of each participant was respected. The participants were mostly grouped by district or congregation of origin, although there were also mixed groups. The development of the activity and the exchange showed great richness from the diversity of problems present in the districts and communities, associated with the characteristics of each place. The proposal offered the possibility of "putting yourself in the other person's shoes" and of problematising the impact of production and consumption practices, land and water pollution in the context of an anti-evangelical extractivist system, contrary to the abundant life to which we are summoned.

As a result of these meetings, we came up with new pedagogical and didactic proposals that will be edited and published soon.[5] This new material will be shared to be read, used, and modified according to the different contexts, following our permanent reflective and dialogical position.

[5] See: Fundación Protestante Hora de Obrar [Ruth Schwittay (Comp.)]; *Planificación de clases para el cuidado de la creación. Materiales para catequistas*, Pastoral de Promoción del Cuidado de la Creación, Iglesia Evangélica del Río de la Plata, 1st Edition, Argentina, 2021, 84 pgs.; apart from the printed version of this publication, a digital version of the material is foreseen, which will be accessible through the web pages of the Iglesia Evangélica del Río de la Plata (http://ierp.org.ar/) and Fundación Protestante Hora de Obrar (https://www.horadeobrar.org.ar/).

What Does a Promotional Pastoral Ministry Entail?

We want to close this article with a statement that represents the spirit of the programme and its methodology: this programme is a pastoral ministry because it seeks to accompany processes of reflection on how to live better lives. An abundant life implies a harmonious relationship with everything that surrounds us, and this life is not possible when our practices imply the suffering of people being deprived of their lands, on a planet that suffers and cries out for its creator.

We promote a culture of care, respect, and awareness of the consequences of the prevailing production model. We educate to care by fostering reflection. We do not transmit already processed preconceptions (such as ultra-processed foods that have little to do with their origin), but rather we promote collective processes of dialogue, where convictions arise from experiences and challenges and, by being together, we strengthen each other.

Suggestions for Further Reading

Beros, Daniel C., and Pedro Kalmbach, Eds. *Riesgos y Desafíos del actual modelo de producción agrícola: Un abordaje interdisciplinario*. Buenos Aires: PPCC, 2018.

Duarte, Carlos A. *Soja y Monocultivos: Una mirada pastoral.* Buenos Aires: Iglesia Evangélica del Río de la Plata, 2013.

Pioli, Javier, Ed. *Por una cultura del cuidado de la vida: Memorias de un seminario sobre diaconía y desarrollo sostenible (ODS).* Colonia Suiza, Uruguay: Centro Emmanuel, 2018.

Schwittay, Ruth, and Pedro Kalmbach, Eds. *El Cuidado de la Creación: Materiales para el trabajo en comunidades de fe*. Buenos Aires: PPCC, 2019.

114. Theological Education in Latin America and the Caribbean: Pedagogical Road to Ecumenical Eco-Diakonia

Dan González-Ortega[1]

Introduction

The purpose of this article is to build a theological and social framework for the action of Latin American institutions for theological education and the eco-diakonic leaderships that they help to form. The intention is to motivate readers to build their own proposal, both in the field of diakonia, and in the concept of it, to further contribute to theological formation.

By virtue of this objective, I will rescue from biblical theology the concept of diakonia versus that of stewardship, given the imprint of domination and even abuse that its semantic rooting gives it in passages such as Genesis 1:28 (וְכִבְשֻׁהָ [*ve<u>k</u>i<u>b</u>shuhā*], "subdue") and 2 Samuel 13:14 (וַיְעַנֶּהָ וַיִּשְׁכַּב [*vayeanehā vayshekab*], "forced her to copulate"). This theoretical commitment is profoundly ecological, since the relationship between humanity and the *oikos* goes from being utilitarian and abusively violent (*ve<u>k</u>i<u>b</u>shuhā*) to a relationship of subjective equity (*diakonia*).

In this text I will present, in an introductory way, some biblical elements that support my concept of diakonia, always having as a horizon the pedagogical practice of the institutions of Latin America and the Caribbean, where there is a long history of formation in this sense. To systematize my proposal of the basic meaning of service (*diakonia*) I will refer to three important aspects:

- service as a vital attitude;
- service as animation;
- service as attention to needs.

The Bible and Its Interpretation as the Foundation of Service (Diakonia)

The Greek concepts, *διάκονος [ā], διήκονος, διάκων,* belong to a language imported mainly by early Christianity. Since, while the Greek version of the First Testament uses these words very sporadically to speak of service, incipient Christianity will be the "religion" that will build its entire "ministry" because of this diaconal political tradition.

The word diakonia is found in Greek texts such as those of Herodotus, Euripides and Aristophanes, to designate people who were dedicated to domestic tasks of various kinds. Those who served (*diakonia*) were considered helpers, executors of a task, assistants, ministers. The particle *ken* that traverses the word *dia-**ken**-ia* philologically imprints great vigor on the action or service that must be rendered: diligence, excellence, disposition, tenacity in the task.[2]

Seen from this philological-historical perspective, *diakonia* was not an exercise that was built from the upper echelons of society in a "polis" (city). Lofty people did not usually "serve", but rather "served"

---

[1] Dan González-Ortega (rectoria@comunidadteologica.org.mx) is a Doctor of Theology (PhD), Pastor of the Mexican Communion of Reformed and Presbyterian Churches (CMIRP) and Professor of Bible and Biblical Hermeneutics at the Latin American Faculty of Reformed Theology (FLATER). He is rector of the Theological Community of Mexico (CTdeM), Executive Secretary of the Community of Ecumenical Theological Education of Latin America and the Caribbean (CETELA).

[2] The Online Liddell-Scott-Jones Greek-English Lexicon, "διακόνιον," (Irvine, CA: University of California, 2011), http://stephanus.tlg.uci.edu/lsj/#eid=25871&context=lsj&action=hw-list-click.

themselves of the work of lower-ranking people. It is precisely this concept that Christianity adopts to describe its mission in the world.

In the Second Testament, it is common currency to link "service" with the identity of whoever considers themself a follower of Jesus, as an act of imitation of their own master: "the Son of Man came not to be served but to serve…" (Mk 10:45); "and whoever wishes to be first among you must be your slave" (Mt 20:27).

That said, we can now consider that the central value of the culture in which Jesus lived is "honor". A value that is understood as the esteem that a person has in the eyes of others and depends on their family origin and the social position they occupy. The attitude of Jesus and his person were hardly honorable according to the reckoning of that society: they accuse him for not being of a "noble" enough origin and he, in turn, is very critical of honor (Mk 12:38-39; Lk 9:9-14). He admonishes to look for the hidden places, and to become like the slaves, and not like the lords. And this becomes strongly countercultural.

In the narratives about Jesus in the gospels, this whole attitude is born from the understanding that he has of the Reign of God, since he proclaims service as the key to action (Mk 10:42-45).

Three Aspects of the Basic Meaning of Diakonia in Theological Formation Processes

Service (diakonia) as a vital attitude

In the gospels, the term diakonia and its lexical family appear to indicate a basic attitude in following Jesus and as the fundamental key to be able to put oneself in the perspective of the Reign of God (see Mk 9:35). In this attitude, a transforming and transformative experience is revealed, as shown by the model proposed in the healing of Peter's mother-in-law: "and she began to serve them" (Mk 1:31). Service is the commitment to a way of relating, of building community, of making possible the Reign of God in the style of Jesus of Nazareth (Mk 10:43-45).

In Nicaragua, the Interchurch Center for Theological and Social Studies, through its Evangelical Faculty of Theological Studies, has worked for several decades on its service proposal from a very concrete way of understanding the following of Jesus from a biblical perspective.[3] From this perspective, the diaconic gamble that Central American theological education claims is one that is based on the prioritization of human dignity, especially of the people most excluded by a dominant culture. Jesus, in the gospels, has a service agenda with deep commitments with the liberation, reconciliation, healing and uplifting of marginalized people.

In this sense, the testimony provided since the 1990s by the Evangelical Seminary of Theology (SET) in Matanzas, Cuba, is commendable. Since those years, the island has been experiencing an acute economic and values crisis which goes back to the so-called "special period", when the Soviet Union and the socialist countries of Eastern Europe were dissolved. This crisis has been getting worse throughout all these years, due to among other factors the aggressive policy of the governments of the United States of America against Cuba. Given this scenario, the SET has implemented comprehensive training programs in the production of food sovereignty processes and access to basic needs for the people of the city of Matanzas. The center of such initiatives is human dignity and the power that each Cuban person can develop in the face of adversity and lack of opportunities.

In that context, Dr Ofelia Ortega, former rector of the SET, designed a novel strategy to produce food at the seminary. People from the Matanzas community could attend the seminar and help make compost, plant vegetables and take care of the vegetation together with theology students. From this experience, theological

[3] See Benjamín Cortés-Marchena, *La diaconía cristiana en procesos de transformación social* (Managua: UENICMLKJr-CIEETS, 2014), 57.

reflection was carried out based on the relationship of each person with the earth and with the environment. Diakonia, the human person and ecology thus developed a fruitful synergy.

In this context, Dr Carlos E. Ham, current rector of the SET, has systematized this experience and that of other spaces of diaconic participation in Cuba based on his pastoral experience, proposing on this basis a model of empowering diakonia as a new method for service and transformation in the ecumenical movement and local congregations.[4]

Thus, the first important element that must be recognized from the contribution of theological education institutions in this region of the world is that diakonia is a service qualified by its Christian inspiration – it is a step of faith. On the other hand, diakonia emphasizes the "prophetic voice", asking the world about the origins of the evil that afflicts human dignity and creation as God's good. Diakonia, from this "vital attitude", becomes a prophetic witness to a world of oppression, marginalization, suffering and death.[5]

Service (diakonia) as a ministry of animation

The central value of the Eucharistic celebration (communion table) in the life of the first communities and the fact that it was carried out in houses made it possible for this concept to acquire a new definition.

The first meaning of the term was related to the service at the tables by the slaves (Jn 2:5; Lk 12:37), or the tasks that the women carried out attending to the guests (Lk 10:40). Together with the existential reconfiguration that Jesus had proposed for the service, it made it possible for the term diakonia to be applied to the responsibilities that were acquired when preparing everything necessary for the Eucharist.[6] This understanding was later expanded to designate the person who cared for the community, that is, its animator or missionary, "the one who is at the service of the saints" (1 Cor 16:15). This meaning will later define, in the pastoral letters, the instituted ministry of the diaconate (1 Tim 3:13).

From there arises a type of leadership that is expressed as diakonia, that is, as a service of community animation, called to promote apostolic dynamism, in the Pauline sense of apostle as missionary and preacher, who pushes and dynamizes the sap of the group as a whole. It is therefore a leadership that must spring from circular spaces,[7] assuming an egalitarian attitude in all its areas and promoting plurality and consensus, from the certainty that we are all animated by the same Spirit: that of Jesus (Jn 14:16-17).[8]

This development does not mean that the intra-ecclesial ministry of diakonia is a bureaucratic way of limiting or restricting the concept, as the EST Faculty (Escola Superior de Teologia) in southern Brazil shows in its theological training on diaconic work. The courses that this house of studies teaches today allow the leadership of the churches to access this important perspective,[9] which allows adding to the intra-ecclesial task the notion of service as a process of community animation where the liturgy, as the whole life of the church, results in a process of democratization of the service.

Assuming a ministry of community animation, where the symbol is the Eucharistic table, allows people to be included and empowered to exercise service after service, as Orthodox traditions tacitly call diakonia when they speak of "the liturgy after the liturgy." Returning to daily life from a diaconic perspective has a

---

[4] Carlos Emilio Ham Stanard, *Diaconía de empoderamiento: un modelo para el servicio y la trasformación en congregaciones locales* (La Habana: SET-Caminos, 2020).

[5] See Kjell Nordstokke, ed., *Diaconía en Contexto* (Geneva: LWF, 2009), 26.

[6] See Elisabeth Schüssler Fiorenza, *En memoria de ella: Reconstrucción teológico-feminista de los orígenes del cristianismo* (Bilbao: Desclée de Brouwer, 1989), 212.

[7] Gerd Theissen, *La redacción de los evangelios y la política eclesial. Un enfoque socio-retórico*. (Madrid: Verbo Divino, 2002), 50-52.

[8] See Cortés-Marchena, *La diaconía cristiana*, 84; 110.

[9] See "A Diaconia como prática social e saber acadêmico," Faculdades EST, Noticias, accessed November 12, 2021, http://www.est.edu.br/noticias/visualiza/a-diaconia-como-pratica-social-e-saber-academico.

deep spiritual dimension through the common table, where believers are nurtured and included regardless of their condition.[10]

The ministerial exercise of animation that diakonia has within the church, trains each believer in such important values of recognition and appreciation of other people, which allows the local church to become an agent of hospitality, reconciliation and transformation as fundamental contributions sustained in a theology of service, which is already the curriculum of our Latin American and Caribbean theological education institutions.

In Latin America and the Caribbean, theological education is praxis. To form people theologically is also to train community leaders (theology students) to encourage their communities of faith in liturgical action as a service. For example, since 2012, students from the Theological Community of Mexico and young people from the churches with which this institution is related, have made systematic trips to the Lacandona Jungle (Chiapas, Mexico) to hold workshops on climate justice, food sovereignty and Mayan spirituality of relationship with creation as a sister. All this is to dedicate significant time during these visits to the reforestation of the jungle so deforested in that part of the Mexican territory.

It can be concluded in this regard that the historical identification of worship or liturgy, remains that of "service". If the Eucharist continues to be the center of Christian worship and is the symbol of community life, then it is possible to rescue the process of democratizing hospitality as the foundation of life in Christ. When we speak of "liturgy" from the classrooms of theological education in Latin America and the Caribbean, we are constantly reminded that the origin of this term comes from the Greek words *laos* (λάος) – which literally means "vomit", but which by context translates as "people" (those who are not citizens) – in addition to the word *érgon* (έργον), which results in a synonym of *diakonia*, that is, service – that is, the service that the people (new citizenship) of Christ lavish on themselves. In some way we can say that *diakonia* as animation is a good and relevant part of the economic dimension of Christian service.

Service (diakonia) as attention to the needs of otherness and alterity

In the book of the Acts of the Apostles, through the description of a conflict in the community of Jerusalem (Acts 6:1-7), a direct mention is made with the term *diakonia* to care for the needs of the community, specifically to the needs of widows (Acts 6:1).

A final meaning of the term *diakonia*, gathered from the Second Testament, is that of offering, in the sense of providing for needs, explicitly gathered from Paul's authentic correspondence. The apostle initiates a collection among the communities that he had founded to be sent to the Jerusalem community. This collection has a double meaning for him: to help the local community there that is going through a difficult time and, at the same time, to symbolize the experience of communion and solidarity between the churches with the "mother" community in Jerusalem. This experience gives us two new clues for the experience of diakonia: that of sharing in solidarity and that of ecclesial communion. For this reason, it is more than appropriate to consider:

> [...] diakonia is not the practice of paternalism or subjugation of those who share or help their brother or sister who is in need or excluded; instead, it is integral solidarity that promotes the rediscovery of the spiritual and cultural strengths of those who suffer hardship, or the children excluded from their future by the policies of a given socio-economic system. Diakonia has, first of all, an ethical rather than a moral and functional meaning. It is about the defense and promotion of life in its entirety, totally and absolutely. Hence, Christian diakonia is not just any philanthropy; it has its own pastoral and social dynamics, ethics, theology and philosophy of human development, forms and content, and projects and programs for carrying out the ministry. In this spirit of love, liberation and prophetic vision, diakonia is placed at the heart of the evangelical mission that proclaims health and salvation, a ministry that is a witness to the faith of the Church of Christ, which announces the Reign of God

[10] See Nordstokke, *Diaconía en Contexto,* 32.

to the world, whose ministry and life is both a result of justification and sanctification in the grace that is in Jesus Christ.[11]

Attending to human needs, as a diakonic act, requires a deep spirituality based on the theology of the cross. This should convince us that only God can end evil. The cross is a resounding denial of God to human self-sufficiency and an evangelical proclamation of the triumph of God over suffering, violence and death. Therefore, a diakonic spirituality of this nature creates a frank opening to empathy with people who suffer, and results in the daring action of mobilization for solidarity through grace.[12]

Institutions of theological education in the Latin American region conceive the learning process as an academic task, but also as a *Missio Dei* (Divine Mission). A clear example is the service provided by the Theological Community of Mexico (CTdeM) through its Ecumenical Chaplaincy. This institution has an educational program called "Diploma in Pastoral Accompaniment and Chaplaincy" where it trains pastoral agents and leaders to serve society in its most severe circumstances, even in the most serious emergencies. Those who graduate from this program constantly join a broader project of the CTdeM called "Ecumenical Chaplaincy", developed by teams of chaplains oriented to specific tasks: students, hospitals, human rights, gender, interreligious accompaniment and migration.[13] The work of the chaplaincy has been highlighted in the face of catastrophe situations, with the caravans of Central American migrants and, in the present, providing pastoral support to people in the crisis caused by COVID-19.

In addition, the service in perspective of otherness (alterity) also considers the subjectivity of the environment (the neighbor-creation), giving expression to the reason why the human being is defined by the vocation of "caring for and tilling the earth," according to Genesis 2:15-17; 3:23.

Institutions of theological education, such as the Andean Ecumenical Institute of Theology (ISEAT) in Bolivia, have been insisting since 1994 on the rescue of the indigenous perspective of *sumak kawsay* (living well) as "unprecedentedly viable"; that is, a resource that projects the possible future from the critical deconstruction of the present. It is not about the dream as a banal escape, but as a possible thought, rooted, in this case, in material practices that have the capacity to resist from an ethics that conceives the planet as a great common home. The concept questions at least three of the foundations that gave rise to the current situation of environmental ruin: the economic, the philosophical and the religious-symbolic dimensions.[14] From this perspective, ISEAT designed an entire curricular program for the formation of lay leadership, which has been offered, since 2011, as a "Diploma in new visions of development and Living Well".

From a contextual theological education, our Latin American and Caribbean educational community "is interested in accompanying the process of the discursive construction of 'Living Well' to land it as a political reference: the society that we are going to build must give joy and generate coexistence between people and other beings, who share with us their passage through this world."[15]

After the weight with which ISEAT raised its prophetic voice, eco-justice theology has adopted a very strong, almost leading, diaconic role in institutions such as the Latin American Biblical University (UBL) in Costa Rica, the SET in Cuba, the CTdeM in Mexico, CEDEPCA and SEMILLA in Guatemala. Teachers such as Dr Karla Koll, Dr Neddy Astudillo or Dr Marilú Rojas have been a forceful presence, with a clear

---

[11] Cortés-Marchena, *La diaconía cristiana,* 111.

[12] See Nordstokke, *Diaconía en Contexto,* 37.

[13] For people in conflict with their own faith communities, a temporary liturgical space of refuge has been opened called the "Ecumenical Eucharistic Community."

[14] Alejandro Dausá, "El Vivir Bien como inédito viable," *Religión, espiritualidad y cambio climático*, ISEAT, February 15, 2013, http://www.iseatbolivia.org/iseat2013/index.php/documentos-en-linea/category/10-religion-espiritualidad-y-cambio-climatico.

[15] Abraham Colque, "Los diversos caminos del Vivir Bien," *Boletín informativo* 14, no. 27 (2011): 1-2.

and strong voice regarding what can already be called *eco-eros-sofía*,[16] which results in a very innovative contribution from a Latin American feminist theology of liberation of bodies, knowledge and paradigms of theological education in this region, which thus expresses the ecological commitment of *diakonia*.

Conclusion

As we have seen, *diakonia* gives meaning to the work of Christianity, what we call mission. And we can conceptualize this through a systematization that considers the three aspects developed here: vital attitude, ministry of animation and attention to needs.

However, the debate around *diakonia* is in full swing, as the *Missio Dei* is contextualized according to the times. In the present, then, it has been the ecumenical movement led by the World Council of Churches (WCC) that has tried to bring together the different voices that articulate theologically and practically the understanding and relevance of *diakonia* from the churches and the Christian world, helping to understand *diakonia* as an urgent mark of ecumenical life.

From its origin, the Jewish sect that followed in the footsteps of Jesus of Nazareth defined itself as an assembly (*Ekklesía*) that responded to a dynamic of unity, but paradoxically so: "catholic" as an expression of the "multiform" being of the different Christianities. "The Church" would be, thus, by definition: diverse and inclusive where its "catholicity" is precisely the possibility of respecting the different ways of being a believer and taking advantage of the gifts and capacities of each person and each community, which 1 Peter 4:10 calls "administration of the manifold grace of God."

Seen from this place, the being of an ecumenical *diakonia* and, following the clues provided by the position of the WCC,[17] I have tried to outline in this essay a proposal of the basic meaning of service traversed by three important aspects: its political dimension, its economic dimension and its ecological dimension. The telling of the invaluable contribution that ecumenical theological education institutions make to the construction of knowledge and learning, but above all of Christian testimony that is given on the ground – where life becomes flesh – has allowed us to concretize it.

Suggested For Further Reading

Colque, Abraham. "Los diversos caminos del Vivir Bien," *Boletín informativo,* Year 14 No. 27 (2011): 1-2.

Cortés-Marchena, Benjamín. *La diaconía cristiana en procesos de transformación social.* Managua: UENICMLKJr-CIEETS, 2014.

Dausá, Alejandro. "El Vivir Bien como inédito viable." *Religión, espiritualidad y cambio climático.* ISEAT. February 15, 2013. http://www.iseatbolivia.org/iseat2013/index.php/documentos-en-linea/category/10-religion-espiritualidad-y-cambio-climatico.

Faculdades EST. "A Diaconia como prática social e saber acadêmico." *Noticias*. Accessed November 12, 2021. http://www.est.edu.br/noticias/visualiza/a-diaconia-como-pratica-social-e-saber-academico

Ham Stanard, Carlos Emilio. *Diaconía de empoderamiento: un modelo para el servicio y la trasformación en congregaciones locales*. La Habana: SET-Caminos, 2020.

Nordstokke, Kjell, ed. *Diaconía en Contexto: Transformación, reconciliación, empoderamiento.* Geneva: LWF, 2009.

Ortega, Ofelia and Chris Ferguson. *La Diaconía Ecuménica: reconciliadora, compasiva, transformadora, profética, procuradora de justicia*. Quito: CLAI, 2006.

[16] Neologism coined theologically by Dr. Marilú Rojas, a Mexican, and about which she speaks abundantly in this book.

[17] Ofelia Ortega and Chris Ferguson, *La Diaconía Ecuménica: reconciliadora, compasiva, transformadora, profética, procuradora de justicia* (Ecuador: CLAI, 2006).

Schüssler Fiorenza, Elisabeth. *En memoria de ella: Reconstrucción teológico-feminista de los orígenes del cristianismo*. Bilbao: Desclée de Brouwer, 1989.

Theissen, Gerd. *La redacción de los evangelios y la política eclesial. Un enfoque socio-retórico.* Madrid: Verbo Divino, 2002.

115. Science and Religion in Schools: Their Importance for Building an Integral Ecology in the Future

Lorena V. Oviedo[1]

The Importance of the Integration of Science and Religion in Education

To reflect today on the urgency of certain topics, such as ecology in relation to theology, requires us to highlight the relation between sciences and religion and their significance for school education. Formal school education has gone through explicit and implicit debates to come close to some of the contents of ecology. These are topics that can be found in themes developed in different areas. These topics have not been controverted in the sense that they have to be taught or integrated as part of the culture currently. What seems to be under observation is that their approach or explanation is usually elaborated from a perspective that eliminates views from the respective other discipline, either natural sciences or religion. The need for an interdisciplinary approach to the environmental phenomenon is now a common conviction. We can perceive the limitations of purely specialised access. In this sense, some authors appeal for an "integral ecology," which refers back to the need to make connections between the knowledge developed by the different natural and human sciences and others coming from the philosophical and the religious fields. It is this context in which this interesting topic emerges: the relation between science and religion. This topic purports to approach not only the importance of complementing the views of science and religion on their own, but also the fact that a combination of both disciplines or fields of human knowledge sheds lights on a better comprehension of reality.

This study will attempt to describe the interactions between science and religion as they happen in schools.[2] The hypothesis is that the projection of a jointly articulated cosmovision by natural and human sciences, as well as the religious sciences or theology through the schools offers a pedagogical method, apt for an integral ecology in the future.

The Reality in Schools

Currently, the situation in Argentinian schools is one of unawareness of the possible links between the vision of the world provided by the natural and social sciences and that vision that originated from the field of the significance of religions, deeply rooted in the Argentinian and Latin-American cultures. This mutual unawareness is detrimental to education since it shows a supposed contradiction between the two, which hinders the need for a certain integral vision that education attempts to provide. This topic has been historically aggravated by an interpretation from a positivist and illuminist historiography which has elaborated a definition of the relation between modern science and the religious phenomenon as necessarily

---

[1] Lorena V. Oviedo (lvoviedo12@gmail.com) is a Professor of Theology and Pastoral Care with a lay orientation from the Catholic Institute of Teachers of Córdoba (Argentina). She has a degree in Religious Sciences and also in Educational Sciences from the Catholic University of Córdoba, from where she also has an advanced degree in Educational Sciences. She is studying a Master's degree in Epistemology and History of Sciences at UNTREF (National University of Tres de Febrero). She teaches at the General Paz Military Lyceum, and at the Ntra. Sra. Del Valle School. She is treasurer of the Dialogue between Science and Religion (DeCyR) Foundation and secretary of the magazine Quaerentibus-Theology and Sciences (www.quaerentibus.org). Member of the Permanent Seminary of Theology, Philosophy, Science and Technology of the Faculty of Theology of the UCA (Catholic University of Argentina), https://seminarioteologiafilosofiacienciaytecnologia.wordpress.com.

[2] This work is based on the Argentinian school reality, but many of the observations here seem to find parallels with the realities of the educational system of other Latin American countries.

conflictive. This has been reversed, in part, in the context of a post-modernity which has become open to different rationalities and aware of the methodological limits of the sciences.[3]

Argentinian schools removed the teaching of religion from its curriculum in 1884.[4] This took into account the denominational plurality of the population, but it did not replace the denominational teaching with an informative one. Thus, religion as a phenomenon disappeared from public schools.

In Catholic schools, for their part, an absolute separation between the views of the sciences, and catechesis or religious teaching was produced. In some points of contact, the difficulty to face them generated a certain harmony, but this harmony was based on mutual unawareness.

In this context, the topic "science and religion" appears as a possible bridge for deepening mutual understanding between the worldviews produced by sciences and religions as isolated ways of thinking. The interdisciplinary topic thus proposed would allow for diverging from the current antagonistic conception, and introducing students who think more flexibly to integral and complex thoughts than the previous generations. This proposal might be a path to overcome reductive perspectives and, furthermore, it might be a strong booster for anthropological and cosmological questions.

In addition, the absolute secularity of the public school system has led to a certain limbo in religious questions and the substitution of religious answers for those of the empirical sciences. Correlatively, in Catholic confessional schools, there is a fragility in the curricular answers to the articulation of the key themes about the cosmovision offered by the sciences (the origin and end of the universe, evolution, mind and brain, et cetera).

Finally, the topic acquires greater urgency due to the growing ecological complexity. The immense techno-scientific power is causing a radical modification of nature. This sets a new scenario for the education of people who will have to resort to diverse conceptual and hermeneutic systems in order to approach the world in which they will have to live.

The education of science and religion in schools might be a valuable contribution in order to obtain tools for analysing a complex, changing world that humans have to face.

Examples of Co-ordination between Scientific and Religious Subjects

The co-ordination between the human cultural universe and the religious universe is produced in the intellect and the conscience of the believing human being. These universes are not parallel lines where communication cannot occur. The contact points are in the human person. To find them is not an exclusive competence of religious subject-matter, catechesis, or theology. All teachers, from different subjects, must act in mutual agreement. The ideal is that all teachers develop their own programme with scientific competence, but which, in the appropriate points, helps students to look beyond the limited horizon of human knowledge. We can find several examples for specific topics. We will mention two: the historical crisis of heliocentrism and the evolutionist theory.[5]

---

[3] A relevant contribution to the topic of science and religion is the classification of the possible links between both fields of human knowledge: See Ian Barbour, *Religión y ciencia* (Madrid: Trotta, 2004); Lucio Florio, *Ciencia y religión: Perspectivas históricas, epistemológicas y teológicas* (Salta: Eucasa, 2020.) For the connection between typologies and pedagogy, see Lorena Oviedo and Lucio Florio, "Ciencia y religión: palabras que designan una frontera fecunda del conocimiento humano", in Dorando Juan Michelini *et al.* (eds), *Convivir en un mundo con fronteras* (Río Cuarto, Córdoba: ICALA, 2019).

[4] José María González Alonso, "Why did Argentina banish religion of public schools?", 25th January 2018, *Latin American Post*, translated by Marcela Peñaloza. [Available at: https://latinamericanpost.com/19288-why-did-argentina-banish-religion-of-public-schools], [Last accessed: 1st May 2022].

[5] There are now analytical histories about the topic of science and religion. See J.H. Brooke, *Ciencia y religión. Perspectivas históricas* (Madrid: Sal Terrae, 2016).

First, the crisis produced by heliocentrism among astronomers (Copernicus, Kepler, and Galilei) and the theologians and authority figures of the time, on the other hand, might be good material for reflecting upon. This crisis was overcome after several centuries by means of a biblical hermeneutics that made it possible to separate the revealed message from the visions of the world by the hagiographers. The overcoming of the opposition between religion and natural sciences happened after the establishment of certain criteria for biblical hermeneutics oriented by literary and historical principles.

Second, there is the matter of biological evolution that generated a new vision of life and of the human being. Today, we can develop a vision about creation that was not present at the time that the sacred texts were written: we have a comprehension of a creator God that is much richer than that which the static perception of life allowed us to glimpse.

The subject of biology develops the theory of the origin and evolution of life. Religion classes of the same year discuss the history of salvation, whose beginning is creation. Especially since the nineteenth century, evolutionary thought has supported the idea of a common evolutionary history of species and the biosphere. The human being is considered one more link in the chain of evolutionary interaction, as a small branch tip in the phylogenetic tree.[6] The theological vision about life in the Catholic Church is based on the biblical revelation, understood in the framework of tradition which leaves behind a fundamentalist reading of the Bible. Life is created, sustained, and animated by the spirit of God. The whole biblical vision is described with an intuitive idea of life. The evolutionary explanation of life makes it possible to find out God's creating and recreating action. The integration of the evolutionary vision with the theological allows students to approach the mystery of God's creation through the contemplation of life in evolution.[7]

Example of Curriculum Proposal: from Ecology to Ecotheology

The possible subjects or curricular units involved here are the following "Philosophy," "Culture and Society," "Earth Sciences," "Biology," and "Religion."[8]

Substantiation:

Shortly before the end of the high school formation process, it seems appropriate to plan an interdisciplinary work on one reference text,[9] such as Pope Francis' encyclical *Laudato Si'*,[10] or another text coming from a pastoral or theological setting, which addresses the ecological theme. The formation is urgent: in values of environmental care and the search for orientations for protecting our "common home," as well as reflecting upon the importance of the human being's commitment in the Anthropocene period for the care of all creation.

---

[6] See Lucio Florio and Lorena Oviedo, "Hermeneutic and Pedagogical Perspectives of the Relationships between Science and Religion", *European Journal of Science and Theology* 16(5) (October 2020): 1-11, [Available at: http://ejst.tuiasi.ro/Files/84/1_Florio%20&%20Oviedo.pdf], [Last accessed: 2nd May 2022].

[7] Among the varied bibliography on theology and evolution, the following can be consulted: Karl Schmitz-Moorman, *Teología de la creación en un mundo evolución* (Villatuerta: Verbo Divino, 2005.); Ludovico Galleni, *Darwin, Teilhard y los otros. Las tres teorías de la evolución* (Buenos Aires: Epifanía, 2010).

[8] The curriculum units mentioned are only examples, due to the existing variation in the curriculum of every country and region.

[9] Reference texts can be found in the ecclesial determinations of the confession to which they belong. As an example, in the Catholic sphere, the following can be consulted: Congregación para la Educación Católica, *Dimensión religiosa de la educación en la escuela católica. Orientaciones para la reflexión y revisión* (Vatican City: Editrice Vaticana, 1988).

[10] Francis, *Carta Encíclica Laudato Si' of the Holy Father Francis on Care for our Common Home* (*LS*) (Vatican City: Editrice Vaticana, 2015.)

Objectives:

- Run a diagnosis of the status of the biosphere's most important features: water, climate, biodiversity.
- Discover the scientific estimation about the planet's future.
- Identify the human causes of the environmental crisis.
- Read the biblical texts linked to the relation between the human being and nature.
- Interpret the central topics proposed by the encyclical *Laudato Si'* or other selected text regarding the care of the common home.

Activities:

Work integrally with students and teachers of the different subjects involved.

Beginning:

The teachers present to the students the general aim of the work that will be performed through interdisciplinary studies. Then, they explain the activities to be carried out.

Procedure:

The contents of the religion class in the last year of high school are organised around the respective Church's social thought. This Church must have a method, oriented toward illuminating the problematics of social questions. The method is centred in the Church's prophetic mission that *announces* (God's Word), *denounces* (that which contradicts it), and *co-operates* (transforms that reality which it denounces through the values it announces). This is signified in three dimensions: the historical (seeing), the theoretical (judging), and the practical (acting). This method, which sets a way of thinking about the social issues in an evangelical way, can be carried out in three moments: 1) Seeing: *to let oneself be impacted by the beauty of creation and listen to the Word about its vision of creation as salvation;* 2) Judging: *discerning through evangelical criteria;* 3) Acting: *converting to the sanctifying and creating action in God's work: the ecological conversion.*[11]

During the first week, students will work on the basic concepts of the environmental reality: nature's ecological issues, political and economic ideas explaining the reasons behind the environmental destruction, and the philosophical and religious conceptions that underlie the ways of using and dealing with the natural environment.

In the second and third weeks, students will attempt to relate the theological and philosophical criteria that might support the access and treatment of the biosphere, in line with sustainable development. To this effect, they will work on political, economic, and social models that might interlink with principles animated by theology. Particularly, they will attempt to analyse the extent and the limits of ecotheology.

Only by way of example, we will mention the following topics:

- In "Philosophy", ideologies and their environmental implications.
- In "Religion", the method of the corresponding Social Doctrine of the Church, with a particular emphasis on the encyclical *Laudato Si'* or on the document selected according to the denominational setting of the schools.
- In "Earth Sciences", students will deepen the diagnosis of the planet's greatest ecological issues, as well as the prognoses regarding them.
- In "Culture and Society", the cultural and political movements regarding the environmental issue in our times will be worked on.

---

[11] J. Bautista Duhau, "Conversión ecológica", Nociones clave para una ecología integral, SPTFCyT Seminario Permanente de Teología Filosofía Ciencia y Tecnología, 27th August 2017, [Available at: https://drive.google.com/file/d/1Z6N2lfjWvMBLNEvwxAcn2mDF1ok6zxgQ/view], [Last accessed: 3rd May 2022].

Evaluation:

The following should be taken into consideration:

- Class participation.
- Creativity in the presentations required by the teacher.
- New contributions and critique in the activities carried out.
- Integral classroom work.
- Participation in the different project areas.
- Final exposition of the work done.

The curriculum proposals aim to improve the dialogue between religion and the natural and human sciences. We insist on this dialogue, not only from the contents but also from the interaction between teachers, that is, from the conceptual and the interpersonal dimensions. These proposals are designed as an itinerary for high school, in which students and teachers accept responsibility for, review and deepen the contents.[12] By presenting interdisciplinary work in the different years and subjects of secondary school, it is possible to deepen similar matters from diverse perspectives, enabling a complete treatment of them.

This interaction in the search for dialogue suggests that the biblical vision certainly demands a rationality on the part of the hagiographer and of whoever interprets it centuries later. There exists a creator God. This pulls us closer to the logic of the cosmos, the universe, and life, which are part of the greater project of the economy of salvation. God's plan seems to be provident, fruitful, random and deterministic and, at the same time, it seems kind and merciful to us, in our community and personal history.

Conclusion

We finish this proposal by evidencing four main ideas:

After a period of conflict between science and religion, an era of dialogue between the two modes of approaching reality has opened. Although not generalised, there seems to be a cultural tendency toward a co-existence between science and religion.

The mission of the Christian denominational school is to build an integration between ways of knowing and, in particular, between faith and science. Therefore, it is appropriate to build spaces from the curriculum itself. Hence the importance of achieving a plan that aims at those points of contact between science and religion, such as the origin of the universe and of life, evolution, the end of the universe, mind, brain, et cetera. A curriculum that places in the centre the worries related to the ecological state of this world, in addition to the teaching of particular disciplines, the matter of dialogue between science and religion, will efficiently contribute in the configuration of people capable of understanding the world and relating the different access modes that the human experience offers.

It can be hypothesised that the students, after their passage through the school, will remember the experience of the rapprochement between science and religion. This should be done in the method and in the content because some of the problems addressed today will be modified by the advance of science or by future theological reflection. Nevertheless, the students will have had the experience of an interaction between the disciplines that will allow them to deal with the new problems or, at least, not see them as

[12] Regarding an experience at a non-denominational university level, cf. Lucio Florio and Lorena Oviedo, "Ciencia y Religión con aplicación sobre el problema medioambiental en un curso de Doctorandos en la Universidad Nacional de San Luis. Una experiencia novedosa", *KIMÜN. Revista interdisciplinaria de formación docente* 4(6) (January-June 2018): 78-91, [Available at: http://ppct.caicyt.gov.ar/kimun]. For a curricular project of "Science and Theology" see Ludovico Galleni, "Una proposta: il programma di un corso su Teologia e Scienza," *Quaerentibus: Teología y Ciencias* 6 (2016): 82-116, [Available at: http://quaerentibus.org/assets/q06_una-proposta---il-programma-di-un-corso....pdf], [Last accessed: 3rd May 2022].

contradictory to each other. For this reason, the curriculum should explicitly seek to bring together themes and methodologies through interdisciplinary work in forms and questions of study.

The relationship between science and theology offers a theoretical and a practical feature. On the one hand, it seeks to foster the relationship among sciences that, after some time of confrontation, are once again linked. On the other hand, due to the current crisis situation in the relation between humans and nature, the confluence of scientific, human, and religious interpretations is deemed very necessary. The purpose of the dialogue between science and religion is not only to answer ancient problems but also to open perspectives on the interaction of the biosphere, the manipulation of life, the protection of nature, the environmental issues, among others. All of these are challenges that the contemporary human community must think about in order to illuminate the task of conserving the biosphere, if only to protect the human family.

Suggestions for Further Reading

Barbour, Ian. *Religión y ciencia.* Barcelona: Trotta, 2004.

Brooke, John. *Ciencia y religión. Perspectivas históricas.* Madrid: Sal Terrae, 2016.

Congregación para la Educación Católica. *Dimensión religiosa de la educación en la escuela católica. Orientaciones para la reflexión y revisión.* Vatican City: Editrice Vaticana, 1988.

Duhau, J. Bautista. "Conversión ecológica". *Nociones clave para una ecología integral.* SPTFCyT Seminario Permanente de Teología Filosofía Ciencia y Tecnología. August 27, 2017. https://drive.google.com/file/d/1Z6N2lfjWvMBLNEvwxAcn2mDF1ok6zxgQ/view.

Florio, Lucio. *Ciencia y religión. Perspectivas históricas, epistemológicas y teológicas.* Salta: Eucasa, 2020.

Florio, Lucio and Lorena Oviedo. "Hermeneutic and Pedagogical Perspectives of the Relationships between Science and Religion". *European Journal of Science and Theology* 16(5) (October 2020): 1-11.

Florio, Lucio and Lorena Oviedo. "Ciencia y Religión con aplicación sobre el problema medioambiental en un curso de Doctorandos en la Universidad Nacional de San Luis. Una experiencia novedosa". *KIMÜN. Revista interdisciplinaria de formación docente* 4(6) (2018): 78-91.

Francis. *Encyclical Letter Laudato Si' of the Holy Father Francis on Care for our Common Home.* Vatican City: Editrice Vaticana, 2015. [Available at: https://www.vatican.va/content/francesco/en/encyclicals/documents/papa-francesco_20150524_enciclica-laudato-si.html], [Last accessed: 3rd May 2022].

Galleni, Ludovico. *Darwin, Teilhard y los otros. Las tres teorías de la evolución.* Buenos Aires: Epifanía, 2010.

Galleni, Ludovico. "Una proposta: il programma di un corso su Teologia e Scienza". *Quaerentibus. Teología y ciencias* 6 (2016): 82-116. [Available at: http://quaerentibus.org/assets/q06_una-proposta---il-programma-di-un-corso....pdf], [Last accessed: 3rd May 2022].

Oviedo, Lorena and Lucio Florio. "Ciencia y Religión: palabras que designan una frontera fecunda del conocimiento humano", in Juan Michelini *et al.*, Eds. *Convivir en un mundo con fronteras.* Río Cuarto, Córdoba: ICALA, 2019: 22-25.

Schmitz-Moorman, Karl. *Teología de la creación de un mundo en evolución.* Navarra: Verbo Divino, 2005.

OTHER VOLUMES IN THIS SERIES

The Handbook of Theological Education in World Christianity

Dietrich Werner, David Esterline and Namsoon Kang

2010 | 800pp | ISBN: 9781870345880

Theological Perspectives, Ecumenical Trends, Regional Surveys

Theological education is vital for the future of World Christianity – this conviction lies at the heart of this publication. Theological education has the potential to be the seedbed for the renewal of churches, their ministries, mission, and commitment to Christian unity.

If theological education is neglected by church leaders or in funding, the consequences are far reaching; they might not be visible immediately, but they will certainly become manifest over time in the theological competence of church leadership, the holistic nature of mission, and the capacities for ecumenical and interfaith dialogue and the interaction between church and society.

Handbook of Theological Education in Africa

Isabel Apawo Phiri and Dietrich Werner

2013 | 1110pp | ISBN: 9781908355195

"This Handbook of Theological Education in Africa is a fascinating witness to the explosive status quo of Theological Education. The historical and regional (inter alia) surveys open our eyes and ears to see and hear how fast it has taken root historically, geographically, and ecumenically. The landscape of African Theological Education has changed drastically during the final twenty to thirty years of the last century. There is very much to appreciate about it and what has been achieved. We have grounds to make us rejoice, and for which to thank the Lord."

John Mbiti, Theologian and Philosopher, former Director of Bossey Ecumenical Institute

Anthology of African Christianity

Isabel Apawo Phiri, Dietrich Werner, Chammah Kaunda & Kennedy Owino

2016 | 1240pp | ISBN: 9781911372103

By the beginning of the twenty first century, Christianity in Africa has taken shape and established roots in all areas of African reality. It has come to stay. Therefore we welcome Christianity afresh in Africa, where it has arrived to continue the ancient and vibrant Christianity in Egypt, Ethiopia and Eritrea. It is appropriate that the Anthology of African Christianity presents, in valuable detail, this new reality that describes its African landscape in totality.

Orthodox Handbook on Ecumenism

Pantelis Kalaitzidis, Thomas Fitzgerald, Cyril Hovorun, Aikaterini Pekridou, Nikolaos Asproulis, Dietrich Werner and Guy Liagre

2014 | 962pp | ISBN: 9781908355447

Resources for Theological Education

"Reading the articles in this Handbook about Orthodox theologians on ecumenism, one feels awe at the courage and decisiveness of these great figures who were able to overcome stereotypes and long established perceptions. With God's blessing these Orthodox theologians were able not only to lay foundational stones in the history of Orthodoxy, but also in the history of Ecumenism contributing to theological progress and a better mutual understanding between Churches inside and outside the Orthodox tradition. As a result of their theological work Orthodox theology has become a historic factor and transforming element in the ecumenical movement. This publication will support the ecumenical involvement of Orthodox students, scholars and theologians worldwide, but particularly in the Conference of European Churches, in order also to sustain the continuation of ecumenical collaboration in the work of Christian Advocacy in the European Institutions and beyond."

Guy Liagre, Conference of European Churches, General Secretary

Asian Handbook for Theological Education and Ecumenism

Dietrich Werner, Hope Antone, Wati Longchar and Hyunju Bae

2013 | 675pp | ISBN: 9781908355416

This impressive and comprehensive publication focuses on key resources for teaching on Christian unity and common witness in Asian contexts. It is a collection of articles that reflects the ongoing 'double wrestle', with the texts of biblical tradition as well as with contemporary contexts, as the churches in Asia reflect theologically on what it means to be the churches in Asia in each particular period of time, especially in expressing their unity in Christ and in witnessing together the love of Christ amidst the realities and challenges posed by the changing and pluralistic context of Asian communities. There is no doubt that this handbook will contribute significantly to the ongoing theological reflections and discussions in the area of theological education.

International Handbook on Ecumenical Diakonia

Godwin Ampony, Martin Büscher, Beate Hofmann, Félicité Ngnintedem, Dennis Solon, Dietrich Werner

2021 | 764pp | ISBN 978-1-913363-91-8

Contextual Theologies and Practices of Diakonia and Christian Social Services – Resources for Study and Intercultural Learning

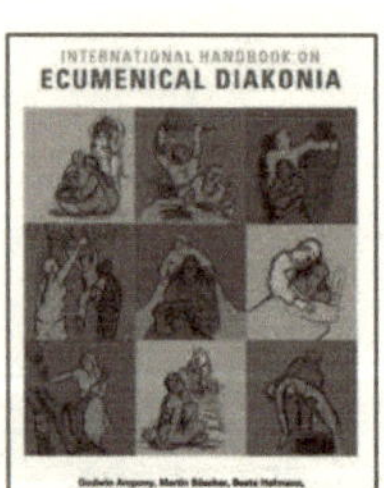

Training and education for Diakonia, for social care, support for the vulnerable, advocacy for those marginalized and suffering from injustices today needs high quality resources and intercultural, contextual as well as interdisciplinary approaches. This was the core conviction of major institutions of diaconal work and research in Germany and some of their international partners to come together in 2018 to plan for an International Handbook on Ecumenical Diakonia. Conceptualized together by the Institute for Diakonic Science and Management (IDM) in Bielefeld/Bethel, the United Evangelical Mission, an international communion of 38 churches in Africa, Asia and Europe, the v.Bodelschwingh Foundation, Bread for the World, Desk for Theology and Ecumenism, Diakonia Germany, the All African Conference of Churches (AACC), and also supported by the Desk for Ecumenical Diakonia in the World Council of Churches a project was developed to bring together key resources on biblical-theological foundations, regional and confessional expressions, new themes and trends and educational approaches and curriculum models for diakonia and Christian social services which can enrich current training courses for diakonia and widen the horizon by inter-contextual and inter-cultural perspectives.